The Reluctant Welfare State

Engaging History to Advance Social Work Practice in Contemporary Society

SIXTH EDITION

BRUCE S. JANSSON
University of Southern California

BROOKS/COLE
CENGAGE Learning

Australia • Brazil • Japan • Korea • Mexico • Singapore • Spain
• United Kingdom • United States

BROOKS/COLE
CENGAGE Learning

The Reluctant Welfare State: Engaging History to Advance Social Work Practice in Contemporary Society, **Sixth Edition**
Bruce S. Jansson

Assistant Editor: Stephanie Rue

Editorial Assistant: Caitlin Cox

Technology Project Manager: Andrew Keay

Marketing Manager: Karin Sandberg

Marketing Assistant: Ting Jian Yap

Marketing Communications Manager: Shemika Britt

Project Manager, Editorial Production: Christy Krueger

Creative Director: Rob Hugel

Art Director: Caryl Gorska

Print Buyer: Paula Vang

Permissions Editor: Robert Kauser

Production Service: Matrix Productions

Copy Editor: Janet Tilden

Cover Designer: Gia Giasullo

Cover Images: Large image, Culver Pictures, Inc./ SuperStock; small images, top to bottom, Paul Edmondson/Brand X/Corbis; Ted Spiegel/ Corbis; Geoffrey Gove/Corbis; Bob Rowan; Progressive Image/Corbis

Compositor: Newgen-Austin

For product information and technology assistance, contact us at:
Cengage Learning Academic Resource Center, 1-800-354-9706
For permission to use material from this text or product, submit all requests online at **www.cengage.com/permissions**
Further permissions questions can be e-mailed to
permissionrequest@cengage.com

Library of Congress Control Number: 2007940981
ISBN-13: 978-0-495-50714-7
ISBN-10: 0-495-50714-8

Brooks/Cole
10 Davis Drive
Belmont, CA 94002-3098
USA

Cengage Learning is a leading provider of customized learning solutions with office locations around the globe, including Singapore, the United Kingdom, Australia, Mexico, Brazil and Japan. Locate your local office at: **international.cengage.com/region**

Cengage Learning products are rerresented in Canada by Nelson Education Ltd.

For your course and learning solutions, visit **academic.cengage.com**

Purchase any of our products at your local college store or at our preferred online store **www.ichapters.com**

Printed in the United States of America
1 2 3 4 5 6 7 12 11 10 09 08

This book is dedicated to Betty Ann

Brief Contents

Contents

Preface

I have changed the title of this edition to underscore major revisions in it. This book exposes students to history not as an end in itself, but to improve their social work practice in contemporary society. Engaging history makes students more effective practitioners—and *uniquely* does so—in numerous ways, including the following:

- Helping students understand *why citizens and professionals need a welfare state in the first instance* when many students take it for granted. Social policy history uniquely poses this question by allowing us to examine long periods in American history when Americans had few rights, services, safety net programs, and regulations.

- *Sharpening ethical reasoning* of students who encounter in social policy history many instances of discrimination, prejudice, and harsh orientations of citizens and policy makers toward vulnerable populations. I've significantly amplified discussion of ethical reasoning in the second chapter of this book—and used it throughout the text to criticize the reluctance of the American welfare state. I devote considerable space to ethical issues associated with social justice.

- Helping students *develop analytic skills* by critically examining the American welfare state so that they can identify its strengths and weaknesses. I pose this question not only in the first chapter, but in many subsequent chapters that analyze hardships imposed on citizens by the relatively primitive welfare state of the United States throughout much of its history. I also analyze and summarize many positive reforms that have been enacted in the United States, particularly in the 20th century, while discussing many gaps, omissions, and errors in American social policy in historical eras as well as in contemporary America.

- Helping students evolve their own policy identities as they *grapple with contending ideologies* that profoundly shape how they relate to vulnerable populations and an array of policy issues.

- *Preparing students to work in a diverse American society* by highlighting the oppression of 13 vulnerable populations throughout American history and into contemporary society, as well as empowerment strategies used by them to better their condition. I discuss the oppression of these populations during each historical era and in the contemporary period—while also identifying notable reforms that they and their allies have achieved.

- *Exposing students to policy advocacy and motivating them to make it a part of their professional practice*. I make even clearer in this edition that policy reforms occur not magically, but through determined efforts of policy advocates. I have added profiles of specific policy advocates at the end of each chapter, including many social work reformers—and used a policy advocacy framework in Chapter 2 to analyze how they obtained policy reforms in specific historical periods.

- Helping students understand *the structure and policies of the contemporary welfare state* by showing them how the American welfare state evolved incrementally through time. In Chapter 13 I summarize those policies that survived the vicissitudes of history—and emphasize the fact that contemporary social workers must understand the history of these policies in order to make intelligent referrals.

- Helping students understand the policies of the contemporary welfare state *in specific policy sectors, including health, mental health, child welfare, income security, civil rights, and housing areas*. I summarize key reforms in each of these areas in a Policy Scorecard in Chapter 13.

- *Exposing cultural, economic, political, sequential, and institutional factors* that provide the context for policy advocacy not only in specific historical eras, but in contemporary society. I introduce these factors in Chapter 2, discuss them in each historical chapter, and summarize them in Chapter 13. Only by understanding the context of the American welfare state can we grasp how it evolved and develop effective strategies to reform it.

- Demonstrating how social workers can develop *Policy Advocacy Background Documents* to facilitate policy advocacy in contemporary society. In Chapter 14 I provide an example of such a document that is authored by colleague Ralph Fertig.

- Helping students develop *referral, case advocacy*, and *empowerment skills* as they learn about the structure and programs of the American welfare state, as well as the entitlements and rights that have been enacted. I argue that knowledge of the evolution of the American welfare state, as well as citizens' entitlements and rights, helps students develop referral and case advocacy skills.

- Analyzing *the nature of the social work* profession as it evolved through time, including its commitment to social justice, its structure, internal factions, and policy advocacy efforts.

When it is taught with these specific outcomes in mind, social policy history becomes a living and vital experience for social work students. It gives them substantive information about the contemporary welfare state, including its structure and policies. It sensitizes them to the oppression of vulnerable populations, as well as ways they have fought back and survived. It motivates them and instructs them in policy advocacy. It requires them to develop ethical reasoning skills. It facilitates their ability to critically analyze and evaluate specific policies. It helps them understand the societal context in which they will work. It familiarizes them with the social work profession. It facilitates their referral and case advocacy skills. It allows them to understand why professionals and consumers need a welfare state in the first instance.

I have incorporated in this edition some materials to facilitate students' learning of these specific perspectives, skills, and knowledge, including:

- more than 40 ethical reasoning and policy analysis exercises that are scattered throughout the text

- a policy advocacy framework in Chapter 2 that is used throughout the book to analyze the work of policy advocates and to highlight key challenges they confront

- profiles of specific policy advocates at the end of each historical chapter

- discussion of unmet needs and policy issues that persist in contemporary society at the end of each chapter as a means of linking historical eras to the present

- analysis of a policy failure or error that occurred in each policy era to help us avoid errors of the past as we move forward

- analysis of a policy initiative that was relatively successful in each policy era to identify policy reforms that should be considered in contemporary America

- discussion of how knowledge of the evolution of the American welfare state in different historical eras helps us to understand the structure and content of the contemporary American welfare state and to make intelligent referrals

Students often emerge from a course in social policy history motivated to become policy advocates in contemporary society. To facilitate this coupling of social policy history and policy advocacy, Brooks/Cole Cengage Learning is offering a discount to students in schools or departments of social work where the *Reluctant Welfare State* and my text on policy advocacy (*Becoming an Effective Policy Advocate*, 2008) are used in tandem.

I've made substantial revisions to this edition. The first, second, thirteenth, and fourteenth chapters have been substantially rewritten. I've combined Chapters 7 and 8 of the fifth edition into a single chapter (Chapter 7) on the

Great Depression and the New Deal. The new Chapter 14 shows students how to use history to facilitate social work practice in contemporary society in three areas: policy-sensitive practice, policy-related practice (which includes skills in making referrals and case advocacy), and policy advocacy. I've updated this edition to include the last four years of the administration of George W. Bush up to the eve of the pivotal 2008 national elections. I've added fresh websites to most chapters.

To help faculty teach social policy history so that it encourages creative thinking, I have enlarged and revised the Instructor's Manual with Test Bank: *Creative Ways to Teach Social Policy History and to Link It to Contemporary Society and the Profession* with co-author Professor Esther Gillies. This publication is provided free of charge to faculty who adopt this text and is available either in hard copy or via the publisher's website at academic.cengage.com/social_work/ jansson. (Professor Gillies has also developed PowerPoint slides that can also be accessed via the book companion website.)

I hope that this edition enhances social workers' practice in contemporary society. I hope that it motivates many students not just to learn about how the American welfare state has evolved, but to work to make it more humane in the future. If so, they will join force with tens of thousands of policy advocates in local, state, and national venues who have obtained needed policy reforms over a period of more than 200 years.

ACKNOWLEDGMENTS

I thank Clinical Associate Professor Ralph Fertig from the School of Social Work at the University of Southern California for giving me critical feedback on many chapters of this edition, as well as authoring the Policy Advocacy Background Document on homelessness in Chapter 14.

I also thank Clinical Associate Professor Esther Gillies, also from the USC School of Social Work, for adding end-of-chapter material that links issues in prior historical eras to ones in contemporary society. She has co-authored the teaching manual with me, as well as developed PowerPoint slides that can be used by faculty who adopt this text.

Many of the changes in this edition were stimulated by comments from the following reviewers:

William Donlan, Arizona State University

Frank Ridzi, Le Moyne College

Jessica Cabness, University of South Florida

Rhonda Vickery Impink, Indiana State University

Mary Montimny-Danna, Salve Regina University

Kay Ketzenberger, University of Texas of the Permian Basin

Cassandra J. Bowers, Wayne State University

Contributors to the Instructor's Manual with Test Bank: *Creative Ways to Teach Social Policy History and to Link It to Contemporary Society and the Profession* include Tony Bibus, Elizabeth Bussiere, Richard Cohen, Patrick Cunningham, Elizabeth Dane, Susan Einbinder, Ralph Fertig, Esther Gillies, Rebecca Irwin, Katherine Kranz, Sharon Lardieri, Edith Lewis, Claire Lipscomb, Emma T. Lucas-Darby, Robin Lugar, Edward McKinney, Margaret Mead, Munira Merchant, Terry Mizrahi, Brij Mohan, Mary Montminy-Danna, Barbara Pillsbury, Elizabeth Rogovsky, Tim Sampson, Susan Sarnoff, Robert Scheurell, Anneka Scranton, Susan Smith, Terry Smith, Katherine van Wormer, Jim Vanderwoerd, Ruta Wilk, Bonni Zetick, and Sharyn Zunz.

Marcus Boggs, the sponsoring editor for this edition, encouraged me to undertake this revision. Caitlin Cox expedited getting this book into production. Stephanie Rue helped with the production of ancillary materials. Not least, Betty Ann provided moral support for this revision.

1

The Symbiotic and Uneasy Relationship between Clients, Social Workers, and the Welfare State

Throughout this nation's history, those who must bear the brunt of social problems—individuals contending with poverty, discrimination, and disease—have depended in considerable measure not only on their personal and familial tenacity and on community supports but also on the policies of public and nonpublic agencies; federal, state, and local governments; and courts. At various times, these policies, singly and in combination, have provided assistance to some, have left others with no assistance, and have worsened the plight of many others.

This text shows how knowledge of the history of social welfare policy can help professionals provide more effective services in contemporary society through better referrals, case advocacy, and policy advocacy. By studying the evolution of the American welfare state, we learn about its structure and the myriad programs allowing us to assist consumers and clients through referrals. By learning how specific entitlements and rights have evolved through history, we can better help clients get access to them through case advocacy. By understanding how thousands of policy advocates have made the reluctant American welfare state more humane, we can stand on their shoulders by engaging in policy advocacy.

Our motivation to become policy advocates in contemporary society is increased by an understanding of the long road toward more equality endured in American history by at least 13 vulnerable populations or out-groups in historical eras as well as in contemporary society: women, African Americans, Asian Americans, older persons, Native Americans, Latinos, gay men and lesbians, children and adolescents, persons with chronic physical challenges, persons with mental and substance-abuse issues, the lesbian-gay-bisexual-transvestite-queer-questioning population, and persons accused of violating laws and residing in (or released from) correctional institutions. Moreover, we often discuss problems of persons in the lower economic strata of society to which members of many of the other vulnerable populations disproportionately belong. Rather than focusing exclusively on the hardships these groups have endured, we also acknowledge their resilience and strength in forging survival strategies.

WHY ANALYZE THE EVOLUTION OF THE AMERICAN WELFARE STATE?

Social welfare history is a laboratory where we analyze how Americans have responded to an array of social problems such as homelessness, poverty, malnutrition, mental and physical illness, disrupted families, orphaned or abused children, violence, and discrimination. During the colonial period, released indentured servants often experienced poverty as they tried to eke out an existence on the American frontier. Poor immigrants encountered poverty, discrimination, and disease in the rough American cities of the 19th and early 20th centuries. Native Americans, African Americans, and Latinos encountered hostility from the broader society as they endeavored to improve their economic conditions or merely to retain their traditional lands and customs. Homeless persons in the

20th century had counterparts in the 19th century who were commonly called vagabonds. The predicament of people with AIDS in the 1980s and 1990s, in which a desperate medical condition is compounded by unfavorable health and social policies, was foreshadowed by the treatment of those with malaria, typhoid fever, tuberculosis, cholera, and syphilis in earlier eras.

Americans have fashioned a reluctant welfare state during their history. Although they have made it more humane through thousands of social reforms and funding enhancements, they continue to provide uncertain or harsh remedies for many residents who experience specific social problems—and particularly for the 13 vulnerable populations that we discuss throughout this book.

WHY DO AMERICANS NEED A WELFARE STATE?

Imagine American society—or any society—with virtually no social programs, regulations, or civil rights. Let's make several assumptions about this imaginary society. Assume that its economy is organized in a capitalist fashion where its citizens work in corporate or other business settings—and where people are expected to meet their own needs through wages, investments, and savings. Also assume that all who live in this society are expected to purchase their medical care, their housing, their education, and their social services with personal assets. Assume, as well, that no civil rights laws exist to protect specific groups or persons that might be subject to violent acts or discrimination in places of work, schools, communities, health care facilities, commercial operations, or social service agencies. Assume, as well, that persons purchase their own means of transportation (principally cars). Assume that they fund their retirements exclusively from their savings. Also assume that this imaginary society possesses no regulations over businesses, landlords, drug companies, or medical providers. Nor does the society possess police, fire, and public health programs—or social service agencies.

To say the least, life in such an imaginary society would be uncertain and difficult. Minus a police force, citizens would be subject to violent acts and theft. Minus fire departments, their homes and businesses would be threatened with destruction as small fires became conflagrations. Minus public health departments that regulate restaurants and markets, sewage disposal, and refuse—as well as inoculate people against diseases—communities would encounter devastating epidemics.

If government did not build and maintain roads, bridges, and airports, people could not travel to work or other destinations. Minus any public transportation, the nation would experience gridlock on those roads that did exist. Individuals who lacked the resources to purchase cars would be mostly unable to work if no system of public transportation existed—or to get to health facilities, grocery stores, drugstores, and other destinations essential to their well-being.

Even if we gave government some minimal police, fire, and public health functions—and allowed it to construct highways, bridges, and other physical amenities—life would still be brutish and uncertain for many people. With no minimum wage requirements, employers could pay employees whatever the market would bear, regardless of the impact on workers. Indeed, it is likely that many workers' wages would be comparable to wages in developing nations, such as $2.50 per hour. If the United States currently possesses tens of millions of persons who subsist under or near official poverty lines because minimum-wage jobs pay them at such low levels, imagine how many more persons would face this economic crunch if the government had established *no* minimum wage.

The plight of workers would be made even more harsh, moreover, because government —under our minimalist assumption—would not require or help to fund some fringe benefits that many workers currently receive. Many American corporations currently fund their employees' health insurance partly because they receive huge tax incentives from the federal government to do so— incentives that would not exist in our imaginary society. Nor would employers provide workers' compensation to fund health care for people who are injured at work. Not required to heed work safety requirements currently established by the Occupational Safety and Health Administration (OSHA) or similar agencies in many states, many employers would *not* purchase machines with safety features, *not* reduce pollution at the work site, and *not* curtail workers' exposure to toxic chemicals— omissions that would endanger the lives of many employees through death or illness. With no regulations prohibiting the use of child labor, many employers would hire children even for physically taxing work. Not prohibited from making employees work long hours, some employers would fire workers who were unwilling to work as much as 14 hours per day.

Imagine, too, how uncertain life would be if no safety net programs existed such as those that currently provide food, health care, housing, preschool education, income, and other basic needs to tens of millions of Americans. Many Americans cannot currently purchase these necessities because they have lost their work due to downsizing or recessions, are disabled or in poor health, are unable to find work, or receive extraordinarily low wages. We can surmise that hordes of people would have to resort to begging or theft to survive in our imaginary society.

Residents of our imaginary society would be harmed, as well, if the United States lacked policies to address global issues. Absent any policies that dealt with such issues as immigration, the spread of diseases across national boundaries, global environmental issues such as carbon dioxide emissions that threaten global warming, and efforts to address an array of social problems in developing nations, residents would experience many uncertainties. They might be unprotected against a flu epidemic such as the one that killed 20 million persons worldwide in 1918. Lacking protections, immigrants might be attacked by xenophobic citizens without any legal protections. American workers would find their work safety and wages deteriorating if international trade treaties allowed American corporations to victimize workers in developing nations where they moved their operations. Such places as Florida and the Gulf Coast might be inundated by the ocean if international treaties failed to avert or slow global warming stemming from the emission of carbon dioxide and other pollutants.

Nor would many persons belonging to vulnerable populations fare well. Individuals harboring prejudice could prey on persons of color without any restrictions, whether by denying them jobs and promotions, forcing them to attend segregated schools, not allowing them to live in their neighborhoods, denying them access to public places like restaurants, and (even) physically harming or killing them. Persons with physical and mental challenges would receive few of the work, housing, and transportation accommodations currently required by federal legislation. With no civil rights legislation to protect them, women would suffer discrimination at work with no legal recourse available against their employers—and would lack legal protections against sexual harassment at work and in schools. The degradation of working conditions of American workers would markedly accelerate if international treaties failed to establish any work safety or wage policies that American corporations were required to honor in those developing nations where they moved their factories.

Life would be difficult, too, for tens of millions of retirees. Assume that roughly half of the persons who reach age 65 do not own their own homes and lack significant savings—and that a significant percentage of them are burdened with debt. With no government-funded pensions and no subsidized health programs, many older people would be in desperate straits when confronted with poor health caused by chronic health conditions. Unless physicians and hospitals agreed to serve them on a charitable basis, they would lack health care. They would be unable to purchase medications. Unable to afford rent, many of them would be forced to live on the streets unless relatives or charities came to their assistance.

Those middle- and upper-income persons who believe that *they* could live easily in our imaginary society should reconsider just how much they currently benefit from an array of social policies. They currently benefit from the nation's largest housing subsidy program that allows them to deduct much of their mortgage payments from their income when calculating their federal and state taxes. (These tax benefits are larger in their cumulative size than all of the nation's welfare programs.) We have already discussed how the federal government underwrites their medical insurance payments by giving their employers tax breaks for funding them. Private entrepreneurs are enriched by their ability to deduct a significant share of their business expenses from their income when computing their federal and state taxes.

Many American social policies favor affluent Americans. They greatly increase their resources, for example, as they pay relatively low federal taxes—and combined federal and state taxes—as compared to residents in European nations even if *they* often think they pay exorbitant taxes. Upper marginal tax rates are around 35% for affluent Americans, but they often exceed 50% for affluent Europeans. Affluent Americans pay only a 15% tax on capital gains when they sell stocks, bonds, houses, property, or other investments at a profit—and often pay few or no taxes on dividends or on payments they receive from many state-issued bonds that pay interest that is tax-exempt. It can be argued that Americans have *two* welfare states: one for relatively poor and the other for relatively affluent persons. Other tax loopholes greatly assist affluent persons.

Affluent Americans benefit in many other ways from the American welfare state. Many of them would contract diseases if the nation lacked public health programs that inoculated its residents and that screened for such diseases as tuberculosis. Many middle-income persons are helped, moreover, by social policies when they experience unexpected and costly illnesses and suffer bankruptcy due to unexpected economic setbacks. They benefit from parks, roads, bridges, and airports that often are constructed with public funds; subsidized secondary schools and public universities; and government-subsidized health programs.

WHY VULNERABLE POPULATIONS ESPECIALLY NEED A WELFARE STATE

If those who lived in our imaginary society would generally suffer uncertainty and ill effects if our imaginary society truly existed, the members of vulnerable populations would be placed in particular jeopardy by the absence of government programs, regulations, and civil rights. Such forms of prejudice as racism, homophobia, gender-based discrimination, ageism, classism, hostility to immigrants, xenophobia, and dislike of persons with mental and physical issues are deeply rooted in American society.

Prejudices often profoundly shape the political process and the kinds of policies that impact vulnerable populations. Since low-income persons vote in relatively small numbers and since many Americans do not understand or care about economic issues affecting people who are struggling financially, the Congress and state legislatures often enact policies that are relatively harsh toward them or that siphon scarce resources toward more affluent persons and interests. Since children cannot vote and often lack substantial support from the broader population, legislatures often give their programs relatively scant funding—while funding at far higher levels programs for elderly populations that are more powerful politically. Even older men and women, however, encounter remarkably harsh policies, such as ones that require them to "spend down" their assets when they experience catastrophic illnesses until they become personally bankrupted in order to qualify for assistance.

Vulnerable populations need a welfare state, moreover, because they are more likely to experience poverty, economic uncertainty, and victimization. Poverty exists disproportionately, for example, among single women with children, persons of color, and persons with mental and physical challenges. If no governmental safety net programs existed, many members of these groups would not even be able to meet their survival needs, such as food, medical care, income, and housing.

Vulnerable populations are also more likely than other persons to be victimized by landlords, employers, merchants, middle-income and affluent communities, credit card companies, and schools.

Absent protections and rights, immigrants to the United States would find themselves in particular jeopardy. They might be denied access even to emergency medical services, to schools, to work safety protections, and to a minimum wage—even as they filled jobs that most citizens did not want and even as they paid payroll and other taxes.

Our discussion should not suggest that members of vulnerable populations need or seek handouts. Indeed, their members have often displayed remarkable resilience and ingenuity in addressing their own needs during specific historical eras and in contemporary society. As we discuss at many points in this book, they have developed their own self-help strategies, community institutions such as churches and businesses, and power resources in local communities. Yet government can sometimes play a supportive role, such as by providing resources to help build communities, help small businesses emerge, enact zoning requirements that decrease the number of bars and liquor stores in low-income areas, fund affordable housing, promote quality schools, fund job training programs, and promote the development of healthy neighborhoods with recreational facilities, full-service grocery stores, and safe streets.

MOVING FROM OUR IMAGINARY SOCIETY TO A WELFARE STATE

Let's define a welfare state as *an organized and societal response to the needs and rights of residents*—something that our imaginary society does not possess. A vast array of social policies form the foundation of welfare states, and we can classify these policies by their *form, purpose*, and *the way they have been grouped or clustered*. We can also identify policies that shape *implementing and funding systems* that allow specific policies to be actualized.

The Form of Social Policies

In its broadest sense, social policy represents a collective strategy to address social problems. This collective strategy is fashioned by laws, rules, regulations, budgets, and personnel of government—that is, enactments that affect or bind the actions of residents, government officials, professionals, and the staff of social agencies. Let's consider these aspects of social policy in more detail.

Constitutions define the social policy powers of government at the federal and state levels. As we have already noted, the failure of the federal Constitution to enumerate social welfare functions for the federal government was interpreted to mean that such functions should be left to state and local governments and to the private sector. As a result, the development of social welfare policies in this country was seriously delayed. States, too, possess constitutions that establish important duties of state governments, as well as how they govern themselves.

Some social welfare strategies involve *public policies*—laws enacted in local, state, or federal legislatures. The Chinese Exclusion Act of 1882, the Social Security Act of 1935, the Adoption Assistance and Child Welfare Act of 1980, and the Americans with Disabilities Act of 1991 are examples of public laws, as are the state and local laws that established poorhouses and mental institutions in the 19th century.

Court decisions play important roles in American social policy. By overruling, upholding, and interpreting the federal and state constitutions, statutes of legislatures, ordinances of local government, and practices of public agencies such as mental health, police, and welfare departments, courts establish policies that significantly influence the American response to social needs. For example, in the 1980s, the courts required the Reagan administration to award disability benefits to many disabled persons even though many administration officials opposed this policy.

Budget and spending programs are also an expression of policy, as society cannot respond adequately to social problems if resources are not allocated to the relevant programs and institutions. For example,

Americans chose not to expend a major share of the gross national product on social programs prior to the 1930s but greatly increased levels of spending during the Great Depression and in succeeding decades. Despite the large increases in spending on social programs in the 1960s, the 1970s, and even the 1980s, the nation chose to devote a significant portion of its federal budget to military spending during the Cold War and also to make successive tax cuts—policies that greatly reduced the resources available for social programs.

International treaties, as well as policies of the United Nations, govern an array of economic, social, migration, environmental, and national security issues in an era of globalization. The lives of residents of the United States are profoundly influenced by this growing body of policies.

Stated or implied objectives also constitute a form of policy. For example, the preambles and titles of social legislation suggest broad purposes or goals. Thus, as its title suggests, the Personal Responsibility and Work Opportunity and Reconciliation Act that Bill Clinton signed in August of 1996 emphasized rules and procedures for getting welfare recipients off welfare rolls rather than focusing on the provision of training, education, or services.

Rules, procedures, and regulations define the way in which policies are to be implemented. Legislation often prescribes, for example, the rules or procedures to be used by agency staff in determining applicants' eligibility for specific programs. Courts often prescribe procedures that the staff of social agencies must employ to safeguard the rights of clients, patients, and consumers. An example of such procedures can be found in the protections afforded to people who are involuntarily committed to mental institutions. Government agencies issue administrative regulations to guide the implementation of policies—regulations that have the force of law.

Informal policies as compared to *written or official policies* are subjective views of persons and groups that influence whether and how they implement specific policies. If we want to know how the poorhouses of the 19th century worked—or how social agencies implemented welfare reform in 2003—we have to examine how their staff implemented formal policies that were given to them by legislatures and public officials. Informal and formal policies sometimes work in tandem, such as when the line staff of agencies fully understand and agree with official policies. They sometimes clash, however, when staff do not fully implement official policies—or even, in some cases, seek to sabotage them.

The Purpose of Social Policies

No matter their specific form, social policies can be classified by their ultimate purpose in the welfare state as they address specific social problems or issues, such as the following:

- *Needs-meeting policies*, including programs that give persons food, medical care, housing, and income (which would include such contemporary programs as Food Stamps, Medicare, Medicaid, rent subsidies and public housing, Supplementary Security Income (SSI), and Temporary Assistance to Needy Families (TANF)

- *Regulations* that restrict the ability of landlords, employers, corporations, manufacturers of drugs and food, providers of health and mental health services, and the police to victimize consumers or persons with whom they deal

- *Opportunity-enhancing policies* such as primary, secondary, and post secondary educational programs; preschools; job training; job-finding programs; subsidies to small businesses; tax incentives to help persons start businesses or to encourage corporations to train low-income persons; and programs that help persons become American citizens

- Policies that establish and fund *social and medical services* to help persons with a range of personal and familial problems as well as an array of medical problems

- *Civil rights policies* that specify the rights of specific groups, such as women, men, persons of color, persons of every national origin,

persons with mental and physical challenges, older persons, children and youth, persons of all faiths, and persons with specific sexual orientations

- *Referral and linkage policies* that establish case management, ombudsman, and outreach programs

- *Equality-enhancing policies* that target resources to low-income populations (such as the Earned Income Tax Credit and many means-tested programs) and that tax resources away from affluent persons, such as the progressive federal income tax

- *Asset accumulation policies* that help consumers to develop savings accounts and acquire real estate—as well as to develop small businesses

- *Infrastructure development policies* that promote development of transportation systems and parks

- *Economic development policies* that provide tax incentives and loans to citizens and businesses to stimulate job training for employees, or to facilitate the economic development of low-income areas

- *Protective policies* that help persons who are subject to abuse or violent actions of others, such as protective services for children and policies that protect women from battering—as well as policies that promote safe neighborhoods

- *Preventive policies* that aim to avert the emergence of specific social problems

- *Disaster relief policies* that not only shape the immediate response to such natural disasters as Hurricane Katrina in August 2005 in New Orleans and the Gulf Coast but also support efforts to reconstruct devastated areas in their aftermath

To these domestic policies, we need to add policies that are germane to globalization.[1] With the accelerating movement of capital, labor, pollution, and diseases across national boundaries, Americans have increasingly had to cope with an array of global issues—even if they have developed humane policies only reluctantly in recent decades. They have had to develop:

- *Immigration policies* to determine how to deal with legal and social issues associated with persons who cross international boundaries with or without specific kinds of visas or other legal documents

- *Policies shaping work conditions (wages, work safety, child labor, and hours of work) of workers* in the nations with whom the United States conducts trade under various trade agreements such as the North American Free Trade Agreement (NAFTA) and treaties of the World Trade Organization (WTO)

- American policies germane to festering *health, poverty, economic, and environmental conditions in developing nations,* such as the HIV/AIDS epidemic in many African, Asian, and Eastern European nations

- American policies that shape *global environmental problems* that powerfully influence the health and well-being of citizens in all nations

- *National and international security policies* that provide safety to nations around the globe from invasions and terrorism but that also discourage any nation, including the United States, from operating outside the orbit of the Geneva Agreements, the United Nations, and international law

The Grouping or Clustering of Social Policies and Social Problems

Social policies, as well as many social problems, are *grouped* or *clustered* in specific *policy sectors,* such as mental health, health, child welfare, safety net, welfare, education, gerontology, and civil rights. This grouping or clustering partly reflects historical traditions where specific policies were clustered in specialized programs and agencies that addressed specific social problems. "Problems of the mind" came to be addressed by specific organizations, such as "asylums" (later called hospitals for mentally ill persons), family counseling agencies, community

health centers, and private counseling services with social workers, psychologists, and psychiatrists. Problems of neglected or abused children were clustered in public child welfare agencies, child guidance clinics, and family counseling clinics. "Welfare" agencies came to subsume public cash assistance to an array of "needy persons" including single mothers and blind, disabled, and elderly persons.

This grouping or clustering of social policies into policy sectors had both positive and negative consequences. If people had problems of the mind, for example, they knew where to go for counseling and related services. If people believed that a child was abused or neglected, they knew that child welfare agencies addressed such problems. In similar fashion, persons with medical, housing, education, and familial problems knew where to go to get assistance with them. People who believed their civil rights had been infringed knew to approach specific enforcement agencies such as the Equal Economic Opportunity Commission (EEOC).

Grouping or clustering also facilitated the training of professionals and staff who came to be employed by organizations in these policy sectors. Counselors, teachers, physicians, nurses, and child welfare workers receive training geared toward the social problems commonly addressed by specific policy sectors.

Yet grouping and clustering also has had negative consequences. It creates relatively independent fiefdoms, or silos, in the American welfare state. Persons with mental health problems, for example, often need counseling, but they may also need help with specific medical and substance abuse problems. If their mental distress is caused or exacerbated by their economic condition or homelessness, they may need job training, employment, and housing assistance. Yet they often find it difficult to access these various services due to their separation from mental health services in separate bureaucracies or agencies.

Many social problems, moreover, defy simple remedies by a single set of agencies. Many homeless persons need, for example, a combination of housing, mental health, substance abuse, welfare, medical and economic assistance. Many persons who graduate from foster care at age 18 require a similar combination of services and benefits. Professionals and staff who are trained *only* to relate to consumers or clients from highly specialized vantage points are often incapable of orchestrating services and benefits that speak to their broader needs.

Policies That Shape Implementing and Funding Systems

No matter their form or purpose—or how they are clustered or grouped—specific social policies require two additional features if they are to be actualized rather than being only policies on paper:

- Policies that mandate and shape implementing systems to allow these various policies to be placed into action so that consumers can use and benefit from them—such as administrative regulations, policies that allow public agencies to contract with private agencies to deliver services, and civil service and other regulations shaping staffing patterns of public and private agencies

- Policies that establish how funds are raised and distributed to fund social programs, whether from budgets of local, state, or federal governments, federal and state income taxes, property taxes, earmarked taxes such as the payroll tax used to fund Social Security and a portion of Medicare, tax concessions that subsidize some of the costs of specific services or benefits, or consumer fees

THE GRADUAL EVOLUTION OF THE AMERICAN WELFARE STATE

If welfare states eventually come to possess all of the various policies we have described, they do not obtain all of them from inception. The early American welfare state, which existed during the colonial period and the 19th century, was relatively primitive in comparison with the contemporary American welfare state in terms of the number of social policies in place, as well as their implementing and funding systems. Only over a period of 220 years from the establishment of the Republic to 2009 has the American welfare state acquired tens of thousands of policies in local, state, and federal jurisdictions, as well as large and complex implementing systems and massive resources.

Indeed, as we shall see in many succeeding chapters, American society often resembled our imaginary society in important respects in some prior historical eras. Only relatively recently did American enact, for example, civil rights policies that protected many vulnerable populations including women and persons of color, the elderly, and disabled persons. Only relatively recently did the United States enact the Food Stamps Program, Head Start, rent subsidy programs, and hundreds of other social programs that we currently take for granted. As we discuss in succeeding chapters, persons who lacked even minimal resources had little recourse but to "do without" or to seek admittance to an institution known as a "poorhouse" or "almshouse" that often treated them harshly. Or they had to rely on their own support and survival systems and strategies, such as assistance from churches, family networks, and political machines—as well as personal resourcefulness.

This book chronicles and analyzes the emergence and evolution of the American welfare state. Only gradually did the elements of the contemporary American welfare state emerge over this time span. While many background cultural, economic, demographic, and other factors played a part, policy advocates were the key precipitators of the rise and development of the American welfare state. Singly and in tandem in specific time periods, they mobilized support and resources for additions to the American welfare state—often facing considerable opposition from other persons, groups, and interests. They also fought against efforts to downsize or eliminate specific policies in specific historical eras and in contemporary society.

The history of American social policy can be divided into a series of policy eras—specific periods that have an identifiable policy direction, substance, and intensity. The *policy direction* of an era describes the general nature of the policies enacted then. In relatively conservative periods, the emphasis of policy makers was and is on maintaining the status quo, eliminating reforms established in a preceding era, or making major amendments of prior enactments. As we discuss in succeeding chapters, many conservatives favor *devolution* (ceding federal policy roles to states and local governments) or *privatization* (ceding public policy roles to for-profit corporations and private markets). In relatively liberal eras, policy makers enact major new reforms that redistribute services and resources or that increase the role of government. The *substance* of policy refers to the general strategies favored by decision makers in a specific era. For example, between roughly 1905 and 1917, legislators enacted regulatory reforms that established minimum public health, housing, and work safety standards. Decision makers in the 1930s placed far more emphasis on legislation that redistributed resources and jobs to unemployed and poor persons. Reformers in the 1960s emphasized provision of social and

medical services, as well as the establishment of civil rights laws. Reformers in the early 1970s emphasized provision of cash benefits to people rather than social services, which received more attention in the 1960s. The *intensity* of reform describes the rate of policy activity. Relatively few policy changes occurred in the 1920s and 1950s, for example, but many changes were initiated in the 1930s, 1960s, and 1980s.

American social welfare policy has evolved in a series of phases (see Table 1.1). Some eras are sufficiently similar to others that they can be grouped together; in Table 1.1, various conservative eras are presented together because each is characterized by lack of interest in social reforms.

Let's briefly review the evolution of the American welfare state. During the 17th and 18th centuries, American colonists brought with them from Europe a cultural inheritance that powerfully influenced the early development of American social welfare policy. As we discuss in Chapter 3, these early Americans were children of sweeping

T A B L E 1.1   Social Welfare Policy Eras in U.S. History

Policy	Time Period
Initial policy inheritance	Medieval and colonial eras
Americanizing of the policy inheritance	1800–1902
First urban reform movement	1902–1917
Development of initial federal programs	1932–1941
Development of federal roles in services	1960–1968
Conflicting policy tendencies	1945–1952
	1961–1963
	1969–1980
	1992–2000
Conservative policies	1868–1902
	1917–1932
	1941–1944
	1952–1960
	1980–1992
	2000–2008

religious, political, and cultural movements in Europe, such as the Protestant Reformation and the Enlightenment. The ideas of these original settlers influenced the course of American social policy development in the 19th and 20th centuries, and many of their assumptions and beliefs persist in contemporary America.

The social welfare institutions developed during the first half of the 19th century were consonant with the realities of an agricultural, dispersed, and entrepreneurial nation. Social welfare policy was dominated by municipal and county programs and by local philanthropic efforts. (States began to assume significant welfare functions only in the latter part of the 19th century.) The inability of Americans to develop major social welfare programs in this period is illustrated by their failure to assist the freed slaves in the aftermath of the Civil War or to regulate the emerging industrial order.

Americans developed their first sustained urban reform movement during the progressive era between 1902 and 1917. Reformers emphasized a regulatory and local response to the many social problems in the burgeoning cities; they enacted regulations to improve working conditions, public health, and housing.

During the Great Depression of the 1930s, which occurred about 150 years after the founding of the republic, Americans developed their first set of major national social welfare programs, which assisted those who were poor or unemployed; these efforts culminated in the passage of the Social Security Act in 1935. Programs established during the 1930s represented a remarkable policy breakthrough for the United States, but reforms were still deeply conditioned by traditional American beliefs that limited the size and scope of federal social programs.

Many social programs were enacted during the administrations of John Kennedy and Lyndon Johnson in the 1960s, when the federal government assumed major roles in medical care, education, mental health, and job training for the first time. Programs were established for specific populations, such as children and elderly people, and civil rights laws and regulations were passed. Reformers emphasized the establishment of service-oriented and

medical programs rather than the redistribution of economic resources to people living in poverty.

The period encompassing the presidencies of Richard Nixon, Gerald Ford, and Jimmy Carter from 1969 to 1980 seems at first glance to be profoundly conservative, but this appearance is deceiving because many major reforms were enacted during this era. Democrat Bill Clinton pledged himself to a relatively liberal agenda in his campaign of 1992 but was unable to get most of it enacted, especially after 1994, when Congress was dominated by Republicans such as House Speaker Newt Gingrich.

Conservative eras often interrupted the evolution of social reforms. In the period between the Civil War and 1902, for example, national discourse was dominated by Social Darwinism, which emphasized individualism and deterrent policies. The decade of the 1920s was characterized by preoccupation with material success rather than with social reform to address the needs of women, factory workers, and African Americans in the South. President Dwight Eisenhower presided over the conservative decade of the 1950s, when Cold War rhetoric and suburbanization of the nation drew attention away from the social needs of many urban and rural residents. The administrations of Ronald Reagan and George Bush (1980–1992) were profoundly conservative. The presidency of George W. Bush, beginning in 2000, ushered in another conservative period of unknown duration.

At various points in American history, conflicting policy tendencies have existed. Although a Democrat (Harry Truman) led the nation following World War II and proposed some liberal reforms, he confronted a conservative Congress. Similarly, a Democratic president, John Kennedy, was unable to pass liberal legislation between 1961 and his death in late 1963 because of opposition in Congress. The presidencies of Richard Nixon and Bill Clinton, respectively from 1969 to 1974 and 1993 to 2000, were also periods when both conservative and relatively liberal policies were enacted.

This book analyzes policies in the different eras presented in Table 1.1, beginning with the colonial period and ending with the presidency of George

W. Bush (discussed in Chapter 12). Drawing on the discussion of preceding chapters, in Chapter 13 we examine why the American response to social needs has been reluctant, and we explore the many policies and programs of the American welfare state and the unfinished reform agenda in the United States. In Chapter 14 we provide a case example of the evolution of policies in the United States and the need for policy advocacy in contemporary society with respect to homelessness. We also discuss how social welfare history helps contemporary social workers to engage in referrals and case advocacy, as well as to develop policy background statements as a prelude to engaging in policy advocacy.

THE HIGH STAKES FOR CONSUMERS AND SOCIAL WORKERS

As professionals who wish to help vulnerable populations and others, social workers have been and are inextricably linked to the American welfare state. If they cannot call upon its resources, regulations, and rights in specific situations, they cannot fully help consumers of service. If they can't refer low-income persons to mental health or substance abuse services because these agencies require waiting times of weeks or months, they cannot help them in the fullest sense of the word. If they work with women who have been released from prison only to find that no halfway homes exist to help them make the transition to the community, they must silently watch as their clients engage in self-destructive acts, such as substance abuse, that land them back in prison.

A symbiotic relationship exists, then, between social workers and the American welfare state. Social workers need to know all they can about the structure and programs of the American welfare state to truly help their clientele in many situations. Often they need to work on three levels:

> Level 1: Referring their clients to programs and telling them how to take advantage of rights they possess under current regulations

> Level 2: Engaging in case advocacy with their clients to help them obtain services and rights when they are denied access to them or made to wait excessive periods

> Level 3: Participating in policy advocacy when they determine that existing policies of the American welfare state are defective

By analyzing the evolution of the American welfare state, social workers gain knowledge that is instrumental to each of these three levels. They can understand what programs and policies were added to—or deleted from—the American welfare state in specific eras so that they know what programs and policies exist in the contemporary welfare state that can benefit their clients (level 1). They can understand why their clients often cannot easily obtain key services and rights to which they are entitled when they learn about the underfunding of the American welfare state and its excessive complexity, harsh rules and regulations, and discriminatory views of some staff and officials (level 2). This knowledge, in turn, allows them to be informed case advocates for their clients. An understanding of the welfare state's evolution familiarizes social workers, as well, with its gaps and omissions, such as the lack of medical insurance for tens of millions of Americans because the nation failed to develop national health insurance, the paucity of funding for children's programs, the failure of many private insurance companies to cover mental health services, and the harsh treatment given to women who are incarcerated for substance abuse. This knowledge allows them, in turn, to become policy advocates (level 3).

DEVELOPING CRITICAL PERSPECTIVES ABOUT THE AMERICAN WELFARE STATE

As we analyze the evolution of the American welfare state, we also develop critical perspectives about its policies, implementing systems, and funding. We ask questions such as the following:

- Do specific policies, implementing systems, and funding advance important values, such as addressing the needs of specific populations, advancing social justice, preserving the self-determination of its beneficiaries, and preserving the confidentiality of consumer information?

- Do specific policies actually help their beneficiaries—or do they harm or have no effect on clients?

- Are specific policies and programs sufficiently cost-effective so that taxpayers are not paying exorbitant amounts for policies that have few or no positive effects on consumers?

We don't have the field to ourselves as we seek answers to these questions. Indeed, we frequently encounter *divergent* perspectives not only in specific historical periods but in contemporary society. As one example, Thomas Jefferson, an icon of American history, not only believed that the federal government should have very negligible powers in dealing with social issues, but actually owned slaves even as he crafted such documents as the Declaration of Independence in 1776 that espoused that "all men are created equal … (and) are endowed by their Creator with certain inalienable rights."

As we study the evolution of the American welfare state, we engage in a voyage of personal discovery in which we develop our personal *policy identity* as we encounter specific developments and perspectives. Throughout history, social policies have been associated with political controversy and conflict. Some people (we often label them *conservatives* today) opposed the development of policy initiatives to address the social needs of people—such as the use of federal funds to build mental institutions in the 1840s, the development of civil rights legislation in the 1960s, and the advancement of major initiatives to help homeless people in the 1990s.[2] Contemporary conservatives view themselves as ideological descendants of the founding fathers, 19th-century capitalism, and Presidents Coolidge, Hoover, Eisenhower, and Reagan. *Libertarians* have sought to curtail government control or regulation of individuals. Emphasizing the Bill of Rights, they oppose laws that outlaw the use of drugs like cocaine, that prohibit

abortion, or that censor publications. They want to enhance the freedom of individuals to the extent possible, in contrast to conservatives, who support the criminalization of specific drugs and abortion. Social reformers (today we often refer to those who seek incremental reforms as liberals), including Dorothea Dix, Jane Addams, Franklin Roosevelt, Lyndon Johnson, and Nancy Pelosi, obtained enactment of a range of policy reforms despite the concerted opposition of conservatives and many interest groups. Contemporary liberals perceive themselves as ideological descendants of Presidents Theodore and Franklin Roosevelt, Wilson, Kennedy, and Lyndon Johnson, professional leaders like social worker Jane Addams, and activists like Reverend Martin Luther King and Cesar Chavez. These individuals were in the vanguard of the movement to build an American welfare state, even if the political opposition that they encountered meant that it was a reluctant welfare state. American radicals, including union organizers, socialists, and communists, have periodically pressured liberals and conservatives to consider major expansions of the welfare state, just as various social movements have sought reforms for specific causes. American radicals trace their heritage to union organizers and legendary radical figures of the 19th and 20th centuries, such as Eugene Debs and Norman Thomas, as well as the socialists and communists of the 1930s. They often identify with grassroots social movements, including movements to abolish imprisonment for debt and to end slavery prior to the Civil War, the Industrial Workers of the World in the Progressive Era, the Southern Tenant Farmers Association, the unemployed workers movement, the industrial workers movement in the New Deal, the civil rights and welfare rights movements of the 1960s, and organizations representing homeless persons in the 1980s (Figure 1.1).

People in societies with conflicting policies and relatively harsh traditions must at some point shape their personal values. Do they share the values of contemporary American conservatives, libertarians, liberals, or radicals? Do they favor the expansion of the federal government's social welfare role, advocate the status quo, or want reductions in existing programs? People must decide what policies they

FIGURE 1.1 (*left*) An American conservative: President George W. Bush; (*center*) an American liberal: Franklin Delano Roosevelt; (*right*) an American radical: Jesse Jackson.

advocate with respect to contemporary social problems such as homelessness and the provision of medical care to those who cannot afford insurance.

While recognizing that they are not homogeneous groups, we can compare conservatives, libertarians, liberals, and radicals with respect to 10 dimensions, as illustrated in Table 1.2. They differ in their attitudes toward the federal government and state and local governments; in their beliefs about the causes of social problems; in their views of capitalism, human nature, the safety net, abortion, nongovernmental associations and agencies, and subgroups; and in the core values they consider most important.

For conservatives, freedom is fundamental; they value the freedom to retain personal wealth and to conduct enterprises with minimal public regulation. Conservatives are optimistic that unfettered capitalism will produce prosperity if government does not place excessive regulations upon it. Rather than favoring government programs or tax policies that redistribute wealth, they believe that economic growth will "trickle down" to persons in the lower economic strata. Many conservatives believe, as well, that communities, families, churches, and nongovernmental organizations can meet most needs of individuals and that these nongovernmental entities can even replace many public programs—for example, by encouraging individuals and communities to care for homeless persons. To the extent that social programs

are developed, many conservatives prefer to have them vested not with the federal government but with local and state governments, which would bear their full funding and implementation—or with the private sector, whether corporations or faith-based organizations. If local resources are unavailable to implement specific programs, conservatives often favor policies such as block grants, where state and local units of government receive fixed annual allowances from the federal authority in a particular realm (such as welfare or housing and community development) and are free within broad guidelines to decide precisely how to use them.

Conservatives are relatively pessimistic about the fundamental nature of human beings, particularly those of limited means. They tend to believe that people in need can be corrupted by social programs—that is, that those who receive benefits will rely on them *instead of* seeking gainful employment. To counter what they regard as the "perverse incentives" provided by welfare and other social programs, many conservatives want to make social benefits less munificent and to set time limits and other conditions to their receipt. To prevent large numbers in the population from using social programs, conservatives usually want to tighten eligibility requirements. In contrast to their pessimism about persons in the lower economic strata, conservatives tend to be relatively optimistic about persons

TABLE 1.2   Comparison of Different Ideologies

	Conservatives	Libertarians	Liberals	Radicals
Views of federal government	Negative, except in military and international policy and as source of subsidies for business	Negative	Relatively positive	Positive, unless it is under control of monied interests
Views of state and local government	Relatively positive	Negative	Divided, but federal government is often preferred	Less positive than views of federal government
Views of causes of social problems	Emphasis on personal and cultural factors	Unclear	More emphasis than conservatives on environmental factors	Environmental factors generated by monied interests
Views of capitalism	Positive	Positive	Positive, but regulations are favored	Negative, unless workers are empowered
Views of human nature	Relatively optimistic about affluent people, less optimistic about poor people	Favor policies that maximize the liberty of all people	Relatively optimistic about poor people but less optimistic about rich people	Pessimistic about monied interests, but optimistic about other people
Views of safety net	Want relatively meager safety net	Unclear	Want relatively generous safety net	Favor generous safety net
Attitudes to abortion and other moral issues	Divided, but a significant faction favors government controls	Dislike government regulation of social matters	Usually oppose restrictions on abortion but favor restrictions on drugs	Often oppose restriction of social matters
Core value	Liberty, though some government incentives and regulations are favored	Liberty	Liberty, but social justice is also important	Social justice
Views of nongovernmental and governmental programs	Favor nongovernmental initiatives	Favor nongovernmental initiatives	Favor a mixture of both	Favor governmental programs, but often recommend worker or citizen inclusion in government decisions
Views of subgroups who lag behind others in economic status or who experience discrimination	Tend to deny their existence or minimize discrimination	Unclear	Favor some redistribution and strong civil rights	Emphasize oppression of out-groups and seek major corrective action

in the upper economic strata. Far from contending that wealth or inheritances might corrupt those individuals, conservatives want them to retain much of their wealth, on the assumption that they will place it in job-creating investments that will ultimately spur economic growth. In seeking the causes of social problems, conservatives often implicate personal or cultural factors. They contend that many people use social programs because they do not want to work or because American culture fails to emphasize "personal responsibility."

Conservatives do not emphasize disparities in economic and social status among subgroups (such as African Americans or women) and the general population and often dispute data suggesting that these disparities are wide or growing. Conservatives such as Ronald Reagan opposed civil rights legislation in the 1960s. Conservatives tend to oppose affirmative action, as well as redistributive policies such as increasing the tax rates on affluent Americans. They often question whether widespread discrimination exists or discount its importance.

Conservatives are not a homogeneous group, as an examination of the contemporary Republican Party makes clear. Persons from the "religious right," who constitute a large proportion of the contemporary conservative movement, strongly believe the government should act to restrict abortion, censor pornographic literature, outlaw certain drugs, and allow prayer in the public schools. They have often clashed with other conservatives who oppose some of these policies. Some conservatives, such as Newt Gingrich, carry an antigovernmental ethos far further than do moderate Republicans such as Senator Olympia Snowe, who are more supportive of government programs, less inclined to cut domestic spending deeply, and more inclined to retain many government regulations. While often criticizing big government, conservatives support tax deductions for mortgage holders, tax reductions on dividends and capital gains, and other policies that advance their economic interests.

Nor do conservatives always act in a manner that is consistent with their stated principles. Even as they often oppose the expanding size of government, they also support specific social programs.

Farmers in relatively conservative areas often support the Food Stamps Program, partly because it expands markets for their products. Conservatives often support Medicare and Social Security Programs partly because their relatives, as well as many constituents of conservative legislators, use and like them.

Libertarians agree with conservatives about the primacy of freedom, but—unlike conservatives—they oppose policies that enforce a single standard of public morality. For example, they oppose laws that restrict abortions, criminalize drugs, or impose censorship of journalism or art. Like conservatives, libertarians favor relatively low taxes, since they regard them as infringing on the economic independence of individuals.

Whereas liberals want to keep government powers more limited than do radicals, they are less sanguine than conservatives about unfettered capitalism. Left to its own devices, they contend, capitalism often produces considerable inequality, as is apparent from the disparities between wages, salaries, and private wealth that exist in the United States today. Moreover, they point out, many capitalists victimize people; examples include avaricious landlords, entrepreneurs who pay low wages, and purveyors of tainted food and drugs. Believing that many people are subjected to discrimination in employment, education, use of public places, and accommodations, liberals have often favored the enactment of civil rights legislation. Placing somewhat more emphasis upon equality than do conservatives and wanting to restrict the victimization of people, liberals favor an array of government regulations and programs, such as minimum-wage legislation; regulation of working conditions; subsidies for persons of low income through welfare programs, Medicare, Medicaid, and Food Stamps; and job-training and Head Start programs to provide individuals with the skills and knowledge necessary to be productive members of society. Liberals are less inclined than are conservatives to believe that nongovernmental associations, not-for-profit agencies, churches, or civic groups can solve or address major social problems without government assistance; however, they often support partnerships between government and these entities.

FIGURE 1.2 Hybrid politicians.

Liberals are more optimistic about the government's ability to ameliorate major social problems such as poverty and homelessness. Whereas conservatives emphasize the negative qualities of government bureaucracy and regulations, liberals are more inclined to support them.

Liberals recognize disparities in economic and social status between vulnerable populations (such as women or African Americans) and the mainstream population. They favor redistributive policies, such as the progressive income tax, and redistributive programs such as Medicaid. Many liberals have supported civil rights laws for vulnerable populations. Just as conservatives are not a homogeneous group, varieties of liberals exist (Figure 1.2).

If some liberals favor a relatively expansive welfare state that attempts both to equalize opportunity and to decrease economic inequality (stalwart liberals), others are content to equalize opportunity through Head Start and similar programs and a minimal set of safety net programs such as Food Stamps (traditional liberals). Stalwart liberals favor relatively generous welfare programs, tax policies that redistribute resources to people in the lower economic strata, and affirmative action programs that provide special assistance to groups who lag behind the rest of the population. Nancy Pelosi, Hubert Humphrey, Claude Pepper, Robert Kennedy, and Martin Luther King, Jr. exemplify stalwart liberals. Traditional liberals, such as John Kennedy and Lyndon Johnson, emphasize educational, medical, and job-training

supports for individuals but do not favor tax or welfare policies that substantially redistribute resources to poor persons. Stalwart liberals seek to temper freedom with social justice by supporting a wide range of social programs and arranging for some redistribution of resources to low-income persons, whereas traditional liberals, who are more cautious in seeking reforms that address economic inequality, prefer to equalize opportunity through the expansion of educational, medical, and social services. In the 1980s, the Democratic Leadership Conference (DLC) was established by Democratic leaders such as Bill Clinton to develop a centrist position. Calling themselves "New Democrats," they favored social reforms that promoted personal responsibility and opportunity. When Bill Clinton became president from 1993 through 2000, he often followed a "moderately liberal" course—a course that makes him a "hybrid politician" with both conservative and liberal tendencies—much like Republican Richard Nixon (see Figure 1.2).

Nor do liberals always follow their stated principles. Although they tend to favor greater equality, they often support tax loopholes and other tax concessions for large corporations. Even when they seek increased funding of social policies, they sometimes favor large tax cuts that deplete the Treasury. They sometimes favor relatively harsh treatment of such groups as welfare recipients even when they realize that people on the bottom rung of the economic ladder need enhanced job training, child care, and subsidized medical care.

Many kinds of radical positions exist. Emphasizing equality, radicals are deeply pessimistic about the efficacy of unfettered capitalism in advancing social justice. Some radicals, such as socialists, want to transform capitalistic institutions into publicly run industries or favor worker ownership of corporations. Realizing that these policies are difficult to implement because of the sheer power of corporations, radicals favor the major redistribution of wealth through tax policies, as well as both far-reaching government programs that provide services and benefits to all people residing in America and programs that are targeted to less affluent residents. Whereas liberals favor government programs and progressive taxes but usually want to keep them within certain limits, radicals have fewer inhibitions about far-reaching government interventions. Although they also advocate broader reforms, some radicals emphasize far-reaching reforms to help specific groups, such as African Americans and women. Feminists favor far-reaching policies to equalize conditions between women and men—for example, affirmative action and tough regulations against sexual harassment and discrimination in the workplace, not to mention greatly increased funding of child care. Many of them favor, as well, a constitutional amendment to guarantee equal rights for women.

Radicals are often critical of existing social policies, which, they argue, reflect the interests of corporate and conservative groups, such as American free trade policies that often enrich corporations while ignoring working people in the United States and developing nations. Some radicals view government programs as a conspiracy to defuse pressure for social change by making relatively small concessions to working-class persons. They often advocate grassroots organizing to develop constituencies for radical policies, such as efforts to unionize workers in low-wage service industries.

More than some liberals, radicals link the oppression of vulnerable populations to the economic and political subjugation of the working class, which subsumes many persons in those populations. To upgrade the economic and political status of women and African Americans, for example, they would favor sweeping economic reforms such as curtailing the ability of corporations to move their operations to low-wage nations, seeking "living wage" policies, and decreasing high wages of corporate officials. (To view discussions of the way persons with different ideologies view social policy, visit the websites listed in Insert 1.1.)

In addition to ideology, we must recognize that religious beliefs often shape people's beliefs about specific social policies. Some persons oppose legalizing abortions, for example, on religious grounds. Some persons contend that specific biblical passages suggest positions in accord with contemporary conservatives on many social policy issues. Indeed, substantial numbers of Christian fundamentalists have aligned themselves with the Republican Party in the last four decades. By the same token, other people contend that their religious beliefs lead them in relatively liberal directions, such as many persons affiliated with Unitarian and Quaker religions, as well as some Methodist and Episcopal churches. Persons who attend church infrequently or not at all tended in the 2004 presidential election to vote for the Democratic Party, in contrast to persons who attended church at least once a week. We should realize, however, that connections between religion and social policy beliefs can change over time on both a personal and group basis—and that cleavages exist within many religious groups. As one example, some fundamentalist Christians question whether they should affiliate with *any* political party or even participate in politics—just as members of many churches, mosques, and synagogues differ in their political affiliations.

DEVELOPING PERSONAL AND PROFESSIONAL POLICY IDENTITIES

The "raw stuff" of social welfare history provides a powerful tool for a personal voyage of discovery that helps us to develop our own personal and professional policy identities. We don't have the luxury of being neutral or above the fray when we

---

INSERT 1.1 **Using the Web to Understand Policy in a Society with Conflicting Tendencies**

Visit **academic.cengage.com/social_work/jansson** to view these links and a variety of study tools.

Go to **http://www.loc.gov** I recommend going to this website in many succeeding chapters because the Library of Congress (loc) is a vast repository of historical materials, which are often digitalized. Click on "Memory" to locate current online exhibits and familiarize yourself with the kinds of digital materials you will use at this site while reading subsequent chapters.

Go to **http://www.archives.gov** I will recommend this website of the National Archives in many succeeding chapters because it, too, is a vast repository of historical materials in digital format. Click on "educators and students" and proceed to "online exhibits." Visit one of these online exhibits to familiarize yourself with the kinds of online materials that you can visit in subsequent chapters of this text.

Go to **http://www.pbs.org/thinktank/transcript305 .html** Read an interesting discussion about liberalism called "Does Liberalism Have a Future?" (Discussants are E.J. Dionne, Todd Gitlin, Ronald Waters, and Will Marshall in April 1996.) To what extent does the discussion support the assertion that different kinds of "liberalism" exist? Are observations made in 1996 still relevant today?

Go to **http://www.pbs.org/thinktank/show_252 .html** Read "The Heart and Soul of Conservatism," a discussion by Christopher DeMuth, John Judis, David Brooks, and Bill Kauffman in March 1996. Does this discussion support the contention that different kinds of conservatism exist? Are observations made in 1996 still relevant today?

---

examine an array of specific policies that were encountered by vulnerable populations from the colonial period onward and as we take a close look at major American catastrophes such as the Civil War, the depression of 1893, and the Great Depression of the 1930s when as many as 25 percent of Americans (and 75 percent of persons of color) became unemployed in a society that lacked safety net programs such as unemployment insurance. We view competition between military spending and domestic spending in eras such as the 1950s when roughly three-fourths of the entire federal budget was consumed by military spending. We see the widespread lynching (hangings) of African Americans in the South in the first half of the 20th century—with crowds often gathering in a festive atmosphere to witness these executions.

As we view these raw social needs and developments, we also observe how Americans responded to them. Once again, we don't have the luxury of neutrality. We ask, for example, if the work relief programs of the New Deal were meritorious (as many liberals contended) or manifestations of "big government" (as many conservatives contended). We ask if

the Civil Rights Acts of 1964 and 1965 were meritorious (as many Democrats and moderate Republicans contended) or ill-considered (as Republicans such as Ronald Reagan and George H. W. Bush contended).

We can use our perspectives from the past to inform our positions in contemporary society. For example, do we think contemporary policies are deficient when we learn the following facts?

- Roughly 90,000 people spend the night on the streets in a single urban county (Los Angeles).

- About one-half of American prisoners have substance abuse or mental problems but receive little or no treatment within prisons or after their release.

- The United States ranks 84th among nations in the world in inequality, behind China, Egypt, Indonesia, Pakistan, and Russia.

- About 40 percent of persons who "graduate" from foster care at age 18 become homeless within three years.

- About 45 million Americans lacked health insurance in 2008.

As we examine such complex social problems in American history as drug addiction, alcoholism, serious mental disorders, juvenile delinquency, and child abuse, we learn that easy answers or panaceas seldom exist. Since these problems are often caused by a variety of personal, familial, genetic, community, economic, cultural, and other factors, panaceas rarely work.

In making judgments about policies in prior historical eras, we also learn that we must make them with due recognition of realities that existed in them. Federal, state, and local governments had relatively few resources in many historical eras as compared to contemporary society—and they often possessed relatively primitive administrative or implementing capabilities. Americans in some historical eras had relatively low expectations about specific social problems—such as often not even favoring civil rights legislation prior to the 1960s. Scant knowledge existed about the causes and incidence of specific social problems. While we may rightly criticize the failure of public officials to address specific problems in prior eras, we often cannot expect them to exercise policy options that might be more feasible in contemporary society.

These provisos should not discourage us from developing our personal identities as we examine historical developments. We will discover that dissenting points of view often *did* exist in prior eras, such as opposition to slavery prior to 1860 and a desire for federal civil rights legislation prior to 1964. Courageous policy advocates often *did* emerge—sometimes even endangering their lives when they championed unpopular causes.

We can criticize policies in bygone eras, moreover, even when little or no dissent existed. For example, relatively few Americans opposed the public lynching of African Americans in the South in the 19th century and well into the 20th century, yet we can say that this practice violated the ethical principle of not killing. When we discover that most Americans agreed that women ought not go into professions mostly reserved for men in the same period, we can strongly disagree with this exclusionary policy on the grounds that it violated women's civil rights.

Social workers should *expect* to be outside mainstream opinion on some issues because of the nature of their work.[3] We see firsthand persons widely regarded with indifference or suspicion by other citizens who do not actually work with homeless persons, persons with substance abuse, ex-offenders, persons on welfare, and persons accused of using physical violence against children. As we examine the life stories of members of vulnerable populations, we often discover that many factors shaped their lives in ways that make it difficult to blame or condemn them for their problems —such as being abused as children or as adults, living in extreme poverty, lacking education, and suffering from other traumas. We also discover that people who do not know these life stories and who have not interacted with such persons often jump to simplistic conclusions.

Social policy history provides us, then, with an ideal means of evolving our personal and professional *policy identities*, which consist of a set of explicit values and positions that shape our selection or rejection of policy choices. In our personal lives, we decide what causes and what public officials we will support or reject. We decide what personal commitments we will make to policy advocacy outside of our employment. In our professional lives, we decide what policies to question as an employee of an agency, when to participate with other social workers to seek to change specific policies, when to use agency resources to register voters, and when to support specific political candidates by contributing to the political action arm of the National Association of Social Workers.

The reading of social welfare history serves, then, as a steppingstone into the contemporary era. We discuss in the next chapter how it improves our ability to engage in referrals, case advocacy, and policy advocacy.

WHAT YOU CAN DO NOW

You are now equipped with an orienting perspective about the evolution of the American welfare state. You can do the following:

- State why Americans need a welfare state by describing the negative consequences of living in a society with *no* welfare state.

- Understand why societies need welfare states.

- Analyze why the American welfare state also possesses a global dimension.

- Define the term "welfare state."

- Identify an array of vulnerable populations—and state why the members of these groups particularly need a welfare state.

- Identify different kinds of policies that exist within the American welfare state and are enacted in its relationships with other nations.

- Identify specific policy eras associated with the evolution of the American welfare state from colonial times to the present.

- Identify and discuss divergent ideologies that have shaped the response of Americans to the American welfare state and many of its policies, including conservative, libertarian, liberal, and radical ones.

- Discuss the symbiotic, yet uneasy, relationship between social workers and the American welfare state, and explain why social workers must make referrals, engage in case advocacy, and participate in policy practice and policy advocacy to be effective professionals.

- Define "policy identity" and explain why social workers need to develop policy identities at both personal and professional levels.

ENDNOTES

1. Bruce Jansson, *Becoming an Effective Policy Advocate: From Policy Practice to Social Justice* (Belmont, CA: Brooks/Cole, 2008), Chapter 5.

2. For a discussion of varieties of liberals and conservatives, see James Riechley, *Conservatives in an Age of Change: The Nixon and Ford Administrations* (Washington, DC: Brookings Institution, 1981), pp. 22–41.

3. See the debate between Mimi Abramovitz (who favors a social reform perspective) and D. Ray Bardill (who opposes a social reform perspective) in the *Journal of Social Work Education,* 29 (Winter 1993), pp. 6–18.

2

Making the American Welfare State More Humane—Past, Present, and Future

Learning about social welfare history helps us to understand the basic structure of the contemporary American welfare state, thereby allowing us to be more effective in providing referrals and case advocacy for clients. It also helps us understand and appreciate the tradition of policy advocacy that emerged in the United States through the efforts of legions of change agents, including many social workers.

In this chapter, we will:

- Provide a policy advocacy framework that illuminates how policy advocates gradually made the American welfare state more humane over time, even though it remains deeply inadequate in the contemporary period;

- Discuss how policy advocates of the past and present engage in ethical reasoning to decide whether existing policies are flawed and need to be reformed;

- Discuss the ethical principle of social justice in the context of 13 vulnerable populations, and explore how policy advocates have often sought to secure policy reforms that would increase social justice in the United States and abroad;

- Discuss how specific cultural, economic, political, and other factors have alternately facilitated and hindered the work of policy advocates in specific eras and in the contemporary period;

- Urge contemporary social workers to stand on the shoulders of policy advocates of prior eras;

- Argue that contemporary social workers who understand the evolution of the American welfare state are better equipped to interact with the welfare state on three levels: referrals, case-based advocacy, and policy advocacy.

UNDERSTANDING THE ROLE OF POLICY ADVOCATES IN MAKING THE AMERICAN WELFARE STATE MORE HUMANE

We provide a policy advocacy framework that illustrates how policy advocates have obtained many social reforms from the colonial era to the present (see Figure 2.1). This framework allows us to identify and understand a set of activities and strategies that reformers have used throughout history, no matter what the era. Whether the reformers were Dorothea Dix in the 1840s, Jane Addams near the turn of the 20th century, Frances Perkins during the New Deal, Martin Luther King in the 1960s, or someone trying to make American immigration policies more humane in the contemporary period, they had to *decide what is right and what is wrong* and *navigate the American welfare state* (see circles 1 and 2 in Figure 2.1); *diagnose opportunities* as well as *constraints* in context (see the bottom and top of Figure 2.1); *place issues on agendas* of decision makers (circle 3); *analyze social problems* (circle 4); *develop proposals* (circle 5); *get proposals enacted* (circle 6); *implement policy reform* (circle 7); and *assess policy reforms* (circle 8).

The policy advocacy framework makes clear that policy advocates have *never* worked in a

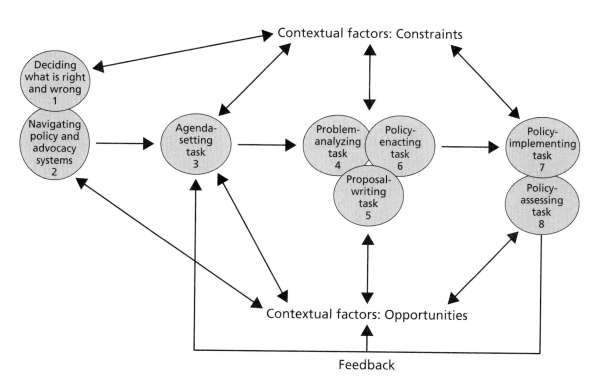

FIGURE 2.1 A dynamic model of policy practice and policy advocacy. Each task shown here involves participants' skills and competencies.

vacuum. They have had to diagnose the context to identify constraints and opportunities affecting their efforts to change existing policies. Sometimes they have been overpowered by the context, such as when powerful forces and factors exist that are unfavorable to a proposed policy reform. When feminists such as Susan B. Anthony and Elizabeth Cady Stanton proposed even before 1860 that women should be given the right to vote, for example, the sexism of the nation, as well as the influence of powerful interest groups, proved to be too strong for them to surmount. Despite the best efforts and remarkable courage and persistence of these policy advocates, women were not given the right to vote at the same time that freed male slaves were given this right. The Fifteenth Amendment, enacted in 1870, gave all adult *males* the right to vote. Similarly, Presidents Harry Truman, Richard Nixon, Jimmy Carter, and Bill Clinton *all* failed to secure passage of National Health Insurance due to organized opposition from medical providers and insurance companies.

In many other cases, however, contextual factors have included a combination of opposing and supportive elements so that policy advocates *were* successful. With respect to women's suffrage, for example, feminists changed the context by using nonviolent forms of protest prior to World War I and then getting President Woodrow Wilson to support women's suffrage by hinging their support for the war effort on his solemn promise to support their cause. With this more favorable context, they secured enactment of the Nineteenth Amendment to the Constitution in 1920.

Policy advocates throughout American history have had to engage in these policy advocacy tasks to get policy reforms in place. By observing how policy advocates in prior eras engaged in them, we can better understand how contemporary policy advocates get social reforms enacted—and how we, too, might undertake them to get social reforms enacted when we determine that existing policies are ethically flawed.

WHO ENGAGED—AND ENGAGES—IN POLICY PRACTICE AND POLICY ADVOCACY?

Many kinds of persons have engaged in policy practice and policy advocacy in prior historical eras as well as the contemporary period. *Elected public officials* create public policies in local, state, and federal governments. They include heads of government such as mayors, governors, and presidents, who often assume a leadership role in developing social policies because they are expected to propose specific policies as well as budgets to fund them. Elected officials often resort to use of the media in the modern period to increase public support for their policy proposals. *Legislators* enact statutes or laws that establish social programs, regulations, and civil rights laws—and must approve the budgets that are submitted to them by heads of government, usually after making many modifications in them. High-level members of government agencies in local, state, and federal governments are not only charged with the implementation of many policies, but often develop policy proposals that are considered by legislatures as well as heads of government. These high-level members include *political appointees* (persons at the highest levels of government agencies appointed by the head of government) and *civil servants* who receive their positions through competitive exams and interviews. Because elected public officials appoint civil servants to top government posts and oversee the agencies in the executive branch of government, they have considerable power over policies that shape the implementation of public programs, such as administrative guidelines that spell out operational policies not contained in legislation.

Executives and staff associated with the operations of public programs can also influence social policy. Assume, for example, that a child welfare worker in a public agency observes a flaw in her program, such as failure to address mental health needs of some children in foster care. She could bring this flaw to the attention of her supervisor in hopes that this would lead to changes in high-level policies of the child welfare agency itself. If this strategy did not work, she would have other options, such as reaching another high-level official in the agency. She might contact an advocacy group for children, asking them to analyze the issue. If no other strategy worked or was feasible, she could become a whistleblower by informing a higher-level government agency or funder of the problem.

Not-for-profit agencies have been a prominent feature of the American welfare state. Partly because many Americans did not like government, they often turned to not-for-profit agencies to provide health, children's, counseling, and many other kinds of services. Their *boards, directors, and staff* have often been policy advocates. They can support or oppose specific propositions on the ballot, register voters, and make policy proposals to heads of state and to legislators. Staff members at not-for-profit agencies can lobby public officials to enact specific policies. They can educate voters about a specific issue. Just like government agencies, they establish many policies to determine how a specific program is implemented. (When a government agency contracts with them to implement a publicly funded program, they must heed those public policies that have been established for that program.) The boards, directors and staff of for-profit agencies—which must pay property and income taxes, unlike not-for-profit agencies—have also participated in policy deliberations in the United States even though they are sometimes accused of seeking policies that advance their financial interests.

Many persons wrongly assume that *only* high-level government and agency officials can engage in policy practice and policy advocacy. In fact, *line staff and their supervisors* assume critical policy roles in both public and private sectors. Within their agencies, they can identify flaws such as gaps, omissions, or errors in the way particular programs are implemented—and use this information to change agency policies. They can identify unmet needs in their communities—and use this information to broaden existing agency programs to address them

or to propose new programs. They can identify *informal* policies in their organizations that impede their programs, such as a disinclination among staff to serve a specific kind of client or a tendency to omit important services when helping clients. They can advocate information exchanges within and among agency staff to help them better implement specific policies.

Leaders and staff of *advocacy groups*, as well as volunteers that help advocacy groups, have frequently engaged in policy practice and policy advocacy in historical eras and the contemporary period—such as groups formed to end slavery, to end the use of child labor, to foster civil rights in the 1950s, and to bring more humane treatment of female prisoners (and their children) in the contemporary period. Examples in the contemporary period include the National Coalition Against Homelessness, Mental Health America, and the Children's Defense Fund.

Unions have often engaged in policy advocacy, including the United Automobile Workers (UAW), the Congress of Industrial Organizations (CIO) before it joined the American Federation of Labor (AFL) to become the AFL-CIO, and the Service Employees International Union (SEIU) that currently represents many workers in public social service agencies as well as some not-for-profit and for-profit ones.

Many organizations have been established at local, state, and federal levels to represent *specific kinds of providers*, such as not-for-profit providers of day care services, subsidized housing programs, and child welfare agencies such as the Child Welfare League of America.

Consumers engage in policy advocacy when they seek improvements in policies and services. They may complain, for example, to elected officials about the services they received in a publicly funded hospital or mental health program—and their complaints may lead to policy changes in these organizations. Or they may seek changes by talking with staff and administrators. Or they may testify at legislative hearings about the inadequacy of specific programs.

Clergy and members of churches, synagogues, and temples, as well as organizations that represent them, have often been policy advocates. As one example, the American Friends Service Committee (AFSC), a Quaker organization, has often championed the rights of prisoners and immigrants.

Coalitions, formed to pool efforts of organizations and individuals, have often succeeded in mobilizing resources behind a specific reform cause.

Professionals often engage in policy advocacy, as illustrated by American social workers such as Jane Addams, Bertha Reynolds, Whitney Young, and (in the contemporary period) U.S. Senator Debbie Stabenow. Indeed, the Code of Ethics of the National Association of Social Workers *requires* social workers to engage in policy advocacy to advance the ethical principle of social justice.

DECIDING WHAT IS WRONG AND WHAT IS RIGHT

Policy advocates in each historical era, as well as contemporary society, have engaged in ethical reasoning as they decided what policy reforms were needed—because this determination was the starting point for their work (see circle 1 in Figure 2.1). Examples abound in each historical era, such as the following:

- Quakers who sought to end slavery in the colonial period;

- Dorothea Dix, who wanted to take mentally ill persons out of poorhouses;

- abolitionists who also wanted to end slavery in the 1850s;

- reformers who established the Freedman's Bureau during the Civil War to assist freed slaves and who got the Congress to enact a series of civil rights bills;

- persons who fought for such regulations in the progressive era as requiring factories to conform to just-enacted fire codes;

- advocates who established work relief programs for millions of unemployed Americans in the Great Depression;

- civil rights activists who sought civil rights statutes in state and federal legislators in the 1950s and 1960s;

- women who fought for parity in wages with men in the 1970s;

- reformers who fought budget cuts proposed by the Reagan administration in the 1980s;

- children's reformers who sought subsidized child care in the 1990s;

- activists who work to strengthen provisions in treaties that protect workers in developing nations from insufficient wages, unsafe working conditions, and use of child labor today.

Policy advocates not only have decided what was *wrong*—they also have decided what was *right* so that they could determine what social policies to defend if they are attacked. In conservative periods such as World War II, the 1950s, the 1980s, and the presidency of George W. Bush, many existing social policies were attacked by conservatives. Policy advocates in these periods have fought:

- proposed funding cuts in many domestic programs;

- proposals to convert entitlements such as Medicaid—which are automatically funded to the level of claimed benefits each year—into programs funded by the general government budget, making them more susceptible to cuts;

- proposals to privatize government programs such as Medicare and Social Security by asking people to develop their own medical and pension accounts;

- proposals to cut taxes so markedly that funding of the American welfare state would be jeopardized;

- proposals to rescind specific civil rights statutes or to dilute them.

Much like policy advocates of past eras, *we* engage in *ethical reasoning* as we read about the American welfare state's evolution—and we can then use our ethical reasoning skills for policy advocacy in the years to come.

USING ETHICAL REASONING TO DECIDE WHAT IS WRONG AND WHAT IS RIGHT

When confronting specific policies, social workers must answer the elemental question, "What is wrong and what is right?" since they can decide whether and when to engage in policy advocacy only after they have answered this question. They can answer it, in turn, only by engaging in ethical reasoning since it is the only way to reach moral conclusions. Possibly the most important reason for studying social welfare history is to enhance our ability to engage in ethical reasoning as we examine specific social needs and problems in historical eras and then decide whether ordinary people and public officials addressed them in ethical—or unethical—ways. We ask questions such as the following:

- Should private individuals, agencies, or public officials have chosen alternative policies?

- Did practical resources and technical realities preclude a different policy response?

- Did private individuals, agencies, or public officials wrongly rescind a meritorious social policy?

When we engage in ethical reasoning, we often use words such as *right, wrong, duty*, and *obligation*. We commonly approach ethical reasoning in three ways:

- Using an *outcomes approach* in which we try to determine whether a specific policy (or the lack of a policy) actually harmed a specific group of people by not addressing or by aggravating their social needs;

- Using a *first ethical principles* approach in which we try to determine whether a specific policy (or the lack of a policy) violated an ethical principle that most of us hold in common, such as "not killing," "honesty," "confidentiality," or "preserving self-determination";

- Using a *relativist approach* in which we try to determine whether a specific policy (or the lack

of a policy) is consonant with the norms or culture of the nation during a specific period or the political interests of ourselves or a group that we favor.

DETERMINING THE ETHICAL MERIT OF SPECIFIC POLICIES WITH RESPECT TO OUTCOMES

When using the first of our three approaches to ethical reasoning, we examine the relative ethical merit of a specific policy—or the absence of a policy—with respect to *outcomes*.[1] (The branch of philosophy that uses this approach to ethical reasoning is called *utilitarianism*.) When evaluating the ethical merit of a specific social policy, for example, we ask if it:

- improves the well-being of its beneficiaries— often called client- or consumer-positive outcomes;

- not only improves the well-being of its beneficiaries, but does so at a reasonable cost—often called cost-effectiveness outcomes;

- provides other benefits to the nation, such as helping people avoid having to join welfare rolls, making people more likely to join the labor force, and improving the educational performance of children by ensuring that they are not hungry while at school. We sometimes ask if the overall benefits to society of this social policy exceed its overall costs to the nation— often called cost-benefit outcomes.

We sometimes possess data that help us to decide when specific policies improve people's well-being or provide other benefits to the nation —whether we are evaluating policies in specific historical eras or in the contemporary period. The absence or insufficiency of data ought not suggest, however, that we cannot engage in ethical reasoning when examining social policies in historical eras or in contemporary society. We can make informed judgments about outcomes of programs in many cases. We can use the best theory that exists to reach plausible conclusions. We can decide when certain policies violate specific ethical principles.

Using the Food Stamps Program to Illustrate Ethical Reasoning with Respect to Outcomes

The Food Stamps Program is currently a significant part of America's safety net, but does it improve the well-being of its beneficiaries, do so at a reasonable cost, and provide other benefits to the nation?

To see if it improves the well-being of its beneficiaries, we would search existing research on the program to answer questions such as the following:

- Does it decrease the incidence of malnutrition in children and adults who use it?

- Does it improve the *quality* of the food that they consume?

- Does it improve the economic well-being of its beneficiaries by "freeing up" income they would otherwise have to use to purchase food?

- Does the program also produce less tangible but important outcomes such as reducing stress among low-income families who do not have to worry about meeting their basic nutritional needs—and does this yield better family and personal functioning and mental health outcomes?

To see if the Food Stamps Program achieves its benefits at a reasonable cost, we would examine how much it costs, per person per year, to provide free or subsidized food to its beneficiaries. If the program cost $20,000 per recipient per year to provide its benefits, for example, we would readily conclude that it was *not* cost-effective because the cost per recipient would exceed the value of its positive outcomes per person. (In actuality, Food Stamps cost taxpayers roughly $5,000 per recipient per year.)

To determine whether the Food Stamps Program also provides other benefits to society

that more than offset its cost to taxpayers, we could examine existing research to see if any data exist with respect to such benefits. If working poor persons can obtain free or low-cost food through the program, for example, will they be less likely to resort to welfare? Does the program improve the health of its beneficiaries sufficiently that they are less likely to use publicly subsidized medical programs such as Medicaid or use emergency rooms? Does the program increase the economic well-being of farmers by enlarging domestic markets for their products—and does it support the financial success of grocery store owners?

If we obtained affirmative evidence with respect to the outcomes, cost-effectiveness, and cost-benefit outcomes of Food Stamps, we would conclude that it is an ethically meritorious program. We might reach this conclusion if we found affirmative evidence with respect to at least one or two of these outcome measures. If we could not find data that measured these kinds of outcomes, we could still declare it to be ethically meritorious based upon our best guesses about its effects— even if, in the best of worlds, we would prefer definitive evidence.

When we *have* definitive evidence, we call a social policy an "evidence-based policy." When we lack definitive evidence but can make a strong theoretical case for *likely* positive outcomes for a policy, we can use the term *"likely"* evidence-based policy—hoping that researchers will soon accumulate data that will demonstrate that the policy is evidence-based.

When evaluating social policies in past historical eras, we must often make informed guesses about outcomes associated with a specific social policy because we lack definitive data. Take the example of so-called poorhouses or workhouses in which destitute persons were commonly placed during the 19th century and well into the 20th century. We don't know with certainty what effect residency in a workhouse had upon its recipients, because data were not systematically collected, but we can guess that these harsh and demeaning places conferred many negative effects on residents. While residents received bare sustenance as well as lodging, they were provided with no job training to equip them to locate jobs. They received no assistance with personal problems, such as alcoholism or depression, that might have led them to have trouble finding work. They were treated as *guilty* persons whose presumed defects of character (such as laziness) had led them to seek assistance even when their unemployment was due to labor market realities such as recessions or depressions. We can speculate that workhouses might have caused some persons to revert to homelessness rather than suffer the indignity of entering a workhouse—possibly leading to health problems from exposure to the elements, not to mention personal injury if they were assaulted while residing on the streets.

When using an outcomes approach, then, we determine the relative ethical merit of specific social programs or policies by ascertaining whether they lead to:

- positive program outcomes as shown by evaluative research based on client-positive, cost-effectiveness, or cost-benefit approaches;

- probable positive outcomes, as judged by our knowledge of human behavior and economics;

- probable negative outcomes, as judged by our knowledge of human behavior and economics;

- negative outcomes, as shown by evaluative research based on client-positive, cost-effectiveness, or cost-benefit approaches.

DETERMINING THE ETHICAL MERIT OF SPECIFIC SOCIAL POLICIES BY USING FIRST ETHICAL PRINCIPLES

Although it is useful to examine the outcomes of policies to determine their ethical merits, this approach can lead to flawed conclusions in certain situations.[2] Assume that the Tuskegee experiment conducted from 1932 to 1972, in which African Americans with syphilis were deliberately not treated so that researchers could study the unchecked course of the disease, *had* enhanced medical knowledge about the disease and *had* increased medical knowledge sufficiently to allow physicians to treat other victims of the disease more effectively. From a pure outcomes perspective, we might have concluded it to be ethical. Yet *all* of us would agree that the Tuskegee experiment was ethically flawed even under these assumptions—and we reach this conclusion *not* with reference to outcomes, but by using first ethical principles in an approach to ethical reasoning called *deontology*. Deontologists contend that ethical principles should take precedence over outcomes even when the latter are positive.

But how do deontologists derive these ethical principles? Some consult the precepts of major religions or religious writings such as the Koran or the Bible. Still others contend, as did the philosopher Immanuel Kant, that society simply could not function unless its members adhered to ethical principles such as not killing and being honest. If people feared on a daily basis that someone would attack them or that physicians, pharmacists, professors, and family members would frequently give them false information, they would be forced to lead reclusive or defensive lives.

First-order ethical principles include the following values:

- honesty (the right to receive correct and accurate information)

- freedom (the right to hold and express personal opinions; the right to vote in free elections)

- self-determination (the right to make decisions about important choices of life, such as whether to use specific kinds of medical and social services, where to live, and where to go to school)

- confidence-keeping or confidentiality (the right to divulge personal and important information only to designated persons)

- not killing (the right to stay alive)

- due process (the right to procedural safeguards when accused of wrongdoing or denied benefits)

- fairness (the right to receive the same rights, basic necessities, and opportunities as other persons when one has followed specific societal norms such as working—unless prevented from doing so by circumstances beyond their control, such as mental and physical challenges)

- social justice (the right of members of vulnerable populations *not* to experience flagrant inequalities in civil rights, life conditions, and access to opportunities)

First-order ethical principles are highly useful in decision making. Based on these principles, we reject the Tuskegee experiment as unethical on the grounds that it violated the first principles of honesty, self-determination, and not killing. We reject public lynching of African Americans in the South with respect to the ethical principles of not killing, fairness, and due process. We criticize the failure to provide all citizens with health insurance as violating the ethical norms of fairness and social justice.

The ethical principles of "fairness" and "social justice" deserve additional explanation. I define "fairness" as requiring that persons who "play by the rules of the game" will receive rights, basic necessities, and opportunities that are not flagrantly discrepant from other persons. Working women should receive wages similar to those of working men when they perform the same level or kind of work—and they should be promoted when they perform their work at similar levels as men. Ex-prisoners who do not engage in criminal behavior and who work hard ought to be accorded rights, necessities, and opportunities equivalent to those of persons who do not possess criminal records. Persons with physical challenges ought not to be discriminated against in job or housing markets—and, indeed, should be given workplace and housing accommodations to allow them to surmount barriers imposed by their physical conditions. Persons who work in relatively unskilled positions should receive wages sufficient for them to lead a decent life. Yet extensive data suggests that the ethical principle of fairness is often breached in contemporary society with respect to working women,

ex-prisoners, and persons with physical challenges. In the case of single heads of households (usually women), their wages, health benefits, and access to child care are often so inadequate that they must work multiple jobs simply to survive. Ex-prisoners suffer extraordinary discrimination in job markets—often leading them to become homeless. An extraordinary percentage of persons with physical challenges live below poverty levels since they cannot find work or obtain workplace accommodations.

If the ethical principle of fairness requires society to treat all persons who play by the rules equitably, the ethical principle of social justice requires society to provide members of vulnerable populations with rights, life conditions, and opportunities that are not flagrantly discrepant from those of the mainstream population. (Social justice is discussed in more detail later in this chapter.)

Ethical reasoning by using first ethical principles allows us to be relatively certain that we do not reach ethical conclusions that diverge from widely accepted ethical norms. Yet reasoning from first principles also has its own shortcomings. We sometimes disagree about how to define specific ethical principles since they are relatively general in nature. Indeed, courts have often wrestled with how to define "due process," "fairness," "confidentiality," "social justice," and "self-determination." When ethical principles conflict with one another, moreover, we frequently find it difficult to make ethical choices. Consider, for example, the ethics of euthanasia, which is the taking of the life of persons by prescribing or giving them lethal drugs when they are diagnosed as terminally ill and when they request them. The ethical principle of self-determination suggests that physicians should prescribe or even administer legal doses of drugs when patients want them. Yet the ethical principle of not killing suggests that physicians should not honor such requests. When ethical principles conflict, as in the case of euthanasia, it sometimes is not clear what choice ethical persons *should* make, since they must somehow prioritize one principle or find a compromise solution that balances competing ethical principles.

HOW CULTURE, SELF-INTEREST, IDEOLOGY, RELIGION, AND POLITICS SHAPE ETHICAL REASONING

Some philosophers criticize *both* utilitarians and deontologists, arguing that most people make ethical choices *not* through an extended process of ethical reasoning but by resorting to norms that they derive from their particular culture. When people in the colonial period placed wrongdoers on public display, they accepted a widely held norm that such punishment was morally acceptable. When people in the 19th century placed destitute persons in workhouses rather than giving them welfare assistance in their homes, they believed they were acting ethically, whereas most contemporary Americans would cringe at this policy. Philosophical *relativists* emphasize how culture in specific historical eras powerfully shapes perceptions of what is "right" and what is "wrong."[3]

Some relativists also contend that ethical choices are often shaped by self-interest and by politics. Take the case of social workers who support expanded funding for mental health programs. While they take this position partly to advance the well-being of persons with mental conditions, they also realize that the enhanced funding provides employment to members of their profession. Feminists and persons of color sometimes support affirmative action because they realize that members of *their* groups will benefit from this social policy. Were we to contend that self-interested choices were immoral, we would wrongly call into question an array of meritorious policies.

Ideology also influences ethical choices. As we discussed in Chapter 1, conservatives, libertarians, liberals, and radicals place different emphases on first-order ethical principles such as individual liberty, fairness, and social justice. When judging the ethical merit of a specific social policy or trying to balance different first-order ethical principles, then, the ideologies of specific persons may lead them to divergent conclusions, as suggested by controversial issues such as abortion, gun control, and affirmative action. In the case of affirmative action, for example, some conservatives oppose it on the grounds that it restricts the liberty of those persons *not* given priority in hiring decisions (such as males and Caucasians), while some liberals support it to advance fairness and social justice for women and persons of color.

Relativism usefully advances our knowledge about the way people often make ethical choices, but it has its own shortcomings. Absent *any* first-order principles or *any* consideration of outcomes, ethical choices would have no parameters. We could even justify slavery in America prior to the Civil War on the grounds that it was consonant with the culture of the South—and would find it difficult to argue with Southerners who supported it because it helped the Southern economy.

We discussed in Chapter 1 how religious beliefs also influence some persons' ethical positions with respect to social policies such as abortion and sex education—and we discuss in Chapter 12 how they lead some persons to favor governmental subsidies for "faith-based charities." As with ideology, however, religious beliefs can lead to divergent positions with respect to specific social policies. Many persons support women's right to choose whether to give birth to a fetus or oppose public subsidies of faith-based charities on the basis of *their* religious beliefs. Persons who view themselves as "secularists" sometimes disagree with ethical positions of persons affiliated with specific religions.

PRACTICAL CONSIDERATIONS AND ETHICAL CHOICES

Our choices may also be shaped by *practical considerations*, such as the availability of resources, political feasibility, ease of implementation, and legal considerations. We may decide not to contest a social policy that we believe is unethical because we think

INSERT 2.1 Using the Web to Under-stand Different Approaches to Ethical Reasoning

Visit **academic.cengage.com/social_work/jansson** to view these links and a variety of study tools.

Go to **http://ethics.sandiego.edu** and view Lawrence Hinman's Web slides on utilitarianism in the section on ethical theories. Next, view his Web slides on "Immanuel Kant: The Ethics of Duty" for deontological ethical reasoning. Do these slides help you better understand the differences between utilitarian and deontological styles of ethical reasoning? Finally, proceed to his slides on "Ethical Relativism." What "extraneous factors" shape how people make ethical choices?

to the federal government as compared to state governments or private health plans and insurance companies. Inclined to be more favorably disposed to government, some liberals favor single-payer plans that give government the central role in implementing national health insurance.

Yet practical considerations ought not impede us from making ethical judgments about social policies in specific historical eras or in the contemporary period. Persons sometimes decide prematurely that a specific social policy is not feasible, only to be proven wrong when it is successfully enacted and implemented. Even when we decide that specific policy proposals are impractical, we can often revise them so that they *are* feasible. We risk becoming opportunists with no moral foundation if we focus excessively on practical considerations when making moral judgments about social policies.

that it is not politically feasible to change it. We must take account of these practical considerations when making moral judgments about policies that existed in specific historical periods. Persons in some eras lacked knowledge or resources to imagine or implement policy options we take for granted in contemporary society. In the colonial era and the 19th century, for example, local, state, and federal governments possessed scant resources since the United States was a developing nation, much like many developing nations in the contemporary world. Government agencies lacked the ability to implement large-scale social programs such as Medicare even if sufficient resources had been available to fund them. It was not even constitutionally certain that the federal government could implement large programs until well into the 1930s. We also need to recognize that American culture has markedly changed over time, so that people in some eras may not have been able even to imagine some of the ethical options that contemporary Americans favor.

Ideology can also shape perceptions of the practicality of a specific social policy. Often believing that the federal government is incapable of implementing social policies efficiently, some conservatives may oppose, for example, versions of national health insurance that grant significant roles

AN ECLECTIC APPROACH TO ETHICAL REASONING

Whether we are examining ethical issues in contemporary society or making ethical judgments about policy choices in historical eras, we should ask a variety of questions that reflect all of the philosophical schools considered here. (See Box 2.1.)

Our ethical reasoning should consider first-order principles that have obtained a wide following in Western societies. Even when we subscribe to first-order principles, however, we often cannot rigidly follow their dictates without examining some possible consequences of a specific course of action. Relativists usefully note that most people do not make ethical choices in an extended process of deliberations; rather, they tend to rely on the norms and traditions of their society or their specific community, as well as their personal interests. Practical considerations must be taken into account. Ethical reasoning, then, forces us to consider many kinds of information when making ethical choices. It requires us to integrate or synthesize the information during a *process of reasoning* in which we look for points of convergence and divergence. If

---

BOX 2.1   Some Sensitizing Approaches for Evaluating Social Policies

Some Considerations Drawn from Deontologists

- Identify first-order principles that are relevant to an ethical dilemma and decide, on balance, which choices or actions best satisfy them.
- When first-order principles conflict—that is, point to different choices—seek a compromise solution that satisfies each to some degree.

Some Considerations Drawn from Utilitarians

- Conduct research to identify the likely client-positive, cost-effectiveness, and cost-benefit outcomes of specific options or actions (or, when data are lacking, use knowledge and theory to infer the likely effects of specific policies).
- Select the option or choice that maximizes positive consequences for individuals, populations, and society.

Some Considerations Drawn from Relativists

- Analyze cultural factors that shape the ethical choices of people in specific historical periods, as well as other pertinent factors such as institutional and fiscal realities.
- Analyze how the interests of people—including ourselves—shape policy choices.

Practical Considerations

- Consider the practical implications of specific policies, such as their political and economic feasibility, as well as administrative aspects.

---

deontology and utilitarian perspectives *converge* to suggest that a specific course of action or a specific policy choice is more meritorious than others, we can be fairly certain about our resulting decision—if the policy is also feasible. If these different considerations lead us toward *diverging* paths—that is, suggest different actions or choices—we must devote time and thought to seeking some resolution. Perhaps we will decide to give priority to one of the perspectives, or perhaps we will seek a compromise solution that draws on a range of considerations. Whatever our ultimate choice, we engage in a process of *ethical analysis* as we use a variety of considerations to decide whether a policy is (or was) meritorious.

THE SPECIAL ETHICAL CASE OF "SOCIAL JUSTICE"

We have discussed both outcomes and first-principle approaches to assessing the ethical merit of specific social policies—as well as relativist ethical perspectives. Now we use these ethical perspectives to examine the principle of *social justice*, which lies at the heart of the Code of Ethics that governs social work practice.

When discussing social justice, we often begin with a specific vulnerable population or out-group as our point of departure. We have many choices. The lower echelons of society constitute an *economically* vulnerable population or out-group whose members are subject to class-based prejudice. African Americans, Latinos, Asian Americans, and Native Americans are examples of *racially* vulnerable populations or out-groups whose members have often been subject to racial prejudice. Certain groups, notably women and older people, have often been kept out of the economic and social mainstream by virtue of the specialized roles ascribed to them; we can call these groups *sociologically* vulnerable populations or out-groups. As one example, women were traditionally expected to limit themselves to child-rearing and homemaking functions; indeed, middle-class married women did not enter the labor force in large numbers until World War II. *Nonconformist* vulnerable populations or out-groups

---

INSERT 2.2   Ethical Analyis of Key Issues and Policies: The Case of Abortion

---

The Supreme Court's *Roe v. Wade* ruling (1973), which prohibits states from banning abortions prior to the third trimester of pregnancy, illustrates the joining of different ethical considerations. The Court found *first-order principles* of not killing (the fetus) and self-determination (for the pregnant woman) to be relevant to the case. It also considered the fact that many women, when denied abortions, obtained illegal ones under dubious medical circumstances and sometimes died or suffered serious injury as a result (a *utilitarian consideration*). The Court struck an *ethical balance* between the two first-order principles: it guaranteed that women's self-determination would be prioritized in the first and second trimesters, while granting states the right to prioritize the not killing of fetuses in the third trimester. And the justices paid attention to *practical considerations* when they acknowledged that it is not possible to prevent many women from seeking abortions, even if government wants to stop the practice. (Many women will seek illegal abortions.)

This ruling illustrates, as well, how *cultural norms* shape our policy choices. Whereas many Americans in 1973 continued to believe that abortions should not have been legalized, public opinion had shifted profoundly toward freedom of choice in the wake of the feminist movement of the late 1960s and early 1970s, which emphasized women's rights. Even a decade earlier than 1973, the Court would probably not have made this ruling. Of course, if we prioritize women's right to choose, we might criticize Supreme Court justices for not reaching a similar conclusion earlier, though our knowledge of the culture of the 1950s and early 1960s would help us to understand why this was so.

Whether or not we agree with the Court's decision, it reflects the *balancing process* that often occurs in ethical reasoning. In this case, several first-order principles were considered and balanced against one another. These principles, in turn, were balanced against utilitarian and practical considerations. Ethical

reasoning is often influenced by the political and cultural context, as reflected by the growing importance of women's rights in the early 1970s.

At numerous places in this text, ethical issues are posed. No single right solution exists, since alternative resolutions are often possible. In each case, however, a *deliberative process* should be undertaken to weigh alternative resolutions and to work toward a preferred solution.

The role of ideology in ethical reasoning about abortion became clear in April 2007 when the Supreme Court ruled on the constitutionality of federal legislation banning during the second trimester so-called partial-birth abortions in which the fetus is removed intact from the mother's uterus. Most states had already banned this procedure as compared to abortions in the first trimester (which represent the vast majority of abortions), but they had mostly made an exception if the health of the mother would have been endangered were she to give birth. Most pro-life advocates favored banning the procedure with no exception for the mother's health, to the anger of pro-choice advocates who favored giving the mother the right to choose whether or not to have an abortion—and particularly if physicians believed her life to be in danger. In a 5 to 4 majority, the Supreme Court sided with pro-life advocates by arguing that states could ban partial-birth abortions even if a woman's life was at risk. In his opinion for the majority, Justice Anthony Kennedy appeared to be establishing a legal argument for *never* removing a fetus from a woman's uterus—possibly setting the stage for revocation of *Roe v. Wade*. This ruling appears to support ethical relativists' contention that ideology often shapes ethical reasoning, since the appointment of conservative jurists to the Supreme Court by President George W. Bush in 2007 gave conservatives a narrow majority on the Court shortly before the Supreme Court made this ruling.

---

include persons widely *perceived* to have different sexual orientations (for example, gay men and lesbians), to have violated social norms (for example, criminal offenders and juvenile delinquents), to possess stigmatizing social problems (for example, persons diagnosed with mental illness or persons with physical challenges), or people who are homeless for extended periods. (That certain populations are often *perceived* to be "nonconformist" by the broader society should not suggest that, in fact, they do not possess legitimate lifestyles, sexual orientations, and abilities.) Widely perceived to be outside prevailing norms, members of these groups have often experienced discrimination. Some groups, such as Asian

© Kris Timken/Blend Images/Photolibrary

© Alison Wright/Corbis

FIGURE 2.2

Americans, Jewish Americans, and certain white ethnic groups, have found it difficult to obtain assistance from policy makers because they are widely perceived to be problem-free, *model* vulnerable populations or out-groups. Although many members of these groups have made remarkable progress in entering the economic mainstream, this progress has tended to impede awareness of the major social problems that many of their members still experience. Many members of white ethnic groups lack health insurance, for example, just as many Asian Americans are poor, including many Vietnamese and Cambodian immigrants. We can identify *dependent* vulnerable populations or out-groups, such as children, who occupy an unusual status. Generally lacking political clout, children depend on the goodwill of adults for requisite services, housing, and resources. *Nonresident or migrating* vulnerable populations or out-groups include persons who have recently come to the United States on a documented or legal basis and ones who are undocumented or have uncertain immigrant status.

When discussing social justice, we usually compare a vulnerable population or out-group with a "mainstream population"—that is, persons *other* than members of this specific vulnerable population or out-group. (See Figure 2.2.) The mainstream

group becomes a comparison group: Caucasian males or all males (in the case of women), Caucasians (in the case of specific racial groups), relatively affluent Caucasians or relatively affluent persons in general (in the case of low-income persons), persons who do not have physical or mental challenges (in the case of persons who possess these challenges), heterosexual persons (in the case of the lesbian, gay, bisexual, and transsexual, or LGBT, population) and persons who have not been incarcerated (in the case of persons who are in jail or who have spent time in jail). If we call each of these comparison groups a "mainstream population," it becomes clear that *multiple* mainstream populations exist—and we select which one will be the comparison group when we examine the status of specific vulnerable populations.

When we select a mainstream or comparison group that we compare with a specific vulnerable population, we want to know to what extent the two groups differ from one another along one or several dimensions. We often compare them with respect to income, educational attainment, and other factors commonly associated with social class; relative access to health care, mental health services, and other services; relative access to educational enrichment programs; relative participation in the political process such as by voting; relative upward or downward mobility over long periods or during specific periods such as in recessions; relative health outcomes such as life expectancy and relative illness or morbidity; and relative mental health outcomes. We also compare a specific vulnerable population or outgroup with a comparison group to determine whether they possess equal rights with respect to the right to vote, access to legal representation, filing of grievances, access to public facilities, obtaining jobs, and gaining admittance or ownership of housing, as well as access to tax and legal protections.

When we compare a specific vulnerable population with the mainstream population, we ask whether the specific vulnerable population or outgroup differs from others in important ways. When we discover differences, we often engage in ethical reasoning to see if the differences are ethically acceptable or unacceptable. If we find them to be ethically questionable or unacceptable, we often label the differences as a violation of *social justice*. We often find three specific kinds of differences between members of vulnerable populations and a mainstream or comparison group to be unethical, whether we are using an outcomes or first ethical principles method of ethical reasoning: *violations of civil rights, violations of life conditions*, and *violations of access to opportunities*.

Social Injustice through the Violation of Civil Rights of Vulnerable Populations

Let's begin with violation of civil rights, which was a common practice until relatively recently in American history—and continues to exist today. To a degree that contemporary Americans can hardly comprehend, vast numbers of persons in the United States were not allowed to vote, use public accommodations, obtain jury trials, receive treatment from courts on a nondiscriminatory basis, obtain fair treatment from police, receive nondiscriminatory treatment at places of work (when seeking jobs, promotions, and equal pay), obtain access to housing on a nondiscriminatory basis, and gain access to hospitals and other health care providers on a nondiscriminatory basis.

Violations of civil rights can be declared unethical from an *outcomes* perspective. When vulnerable populations do not possess fundamental rights enjoyed by others, they are less likely to be productive, confident persons because they fear reprisals or unfair treatment from others—and these behaviors are harmful to the broader society and to themselves. Fearful persons are less likely to succeed in school, to apply for promising job openings, or to move into integrated neighborhoods. Nor are violations of civil rights helpful to the broader interests of American society, which needs contributions from all of its members in the economy, the arts, science, academics, and the professions. If significant groups of persons are systematically excluded from these areas, the entire nation's economy suffers from this exclusion.

Nor is flagrant violation of civil rights ethically acceptable from a first ethical principle perspective since it violates ethical norms of due process, fairness, honesty, confidentiality, and, in some cases, not killing. When persons of color disproportionately receive death sentences as compared to Caucasians who committed similar crimes—and are executed in greater numbers—we can reject this policy as violating the first principles of not killing and fairness, not to mention due process.

Philosophers with a relativist perspective correctly note that our views of what constitutes *unacceptable* violations of civil rights are powerfully shaped by culture and politics. Prior to the Civil War, for example, relatively few Americans believed that African Americans or women should vote—much less that they should be protected from discrimination in places of employment. Powerful political interests opposed the granting of civil rights to African Americans or women in this period, such as cotton-processing corporations in the North, plantation owners in the South, and sellers of liquor who feared that women would seek laws prohibiting the sale of their products if they could vote. Yet women obtained the vote by 1920—and the Civil Rights Acts of 1964 and 1965 gave persons of color the right to vote in the South and forbade discrimination against them or women. Political interests that had opposed the extension of these rights had been eclipsed by economic and cultural changes in the nation.

It is interesting to speculate what cultural or political factors in the early part of the 21st century will be viewed by Americans as similarly promoting flagrant violations of civil rights in another 50 or 100 years. (We will examine some contemporary violations of civil rights in Chapters 13 and 14.)

Social Injustice through the Violation of Life Conditions of Vulnerable Populations

Violations of life conditions exist when members of vulnerable populations receive wages, pensions, health care, nutrition, housing, or other life amenities that are vastly inferior to those granted to a mainstream population. Such inequalities are most marked when members of vulnerable populations lack resources or services even to meet their *basic survival needs.* They are also most marked when members of vulnerable populations are far more subject to uncertainties over these life conditions during recessions, sickness, unemployment, or other life vicissitudes—such as when women and persons of color are disproportionately laid off from their jobs when a recession occurs as compared with white males or when they lack sufficient resources upon retirement to meet their basic needs.

Even when members of specific vulnerable populations can meet their basic survival needs, however, they can still experience social injustice *whenever* large discrepancies exist in life conditions of their members as compared to a mainstream population. While such programs as Food Stamps, unemployment insurance, the Earned Income Tax Credit, and Medicaid have usefully expanded the resources of low-income persons in the United States and probably reduced the gap in resources between low-income and affluent persons, they have not fundamentally changed the huge gap in income between affluent and nonaffluent populations. In 2006, for example, the income share of the wealthiest 1 percent of American households was the same as it was in 1917; it increased sharply

from 1981 to the present after declining from 1913 to 1980. (See Figure 2.3.)

After-tax income for the top 1 percent of the population and the top 20 percent of the population has *also* markedly increased from 1979 to 2004, as documented in Table 2.1. If the top 1 percent and the top 20 percent have respectively added $553,800 and $63,100 to their incomes during this period, the lowest fifth has added only $800, the second fifth merely $4,700, and the middle fifth only $8,500.

When examining inequalities in life conditions, we must also compare communities where vulnerable populations reside with those of mainstream populations. Many persons of color reside, for example, in crime-infested areas that make life hazardous on a daily basis. Due to discrimination in real estate as well as the inability of many persons of color to afford houses or apartments in more affluent communities, they are often subject to involuntary segregation in areas distant from many places of employment, lacking good transportation systems, lacking adequate grocery stores, and lacking recreational facilities.

The children of low-income persons of color receive their education mostly in segregated schools. These schools are often burdened with poor facilities and teachers as compared with schools in more affluent areas. When children are segregated by both race *and* class because many middle-income persons of color have migrated to housing outside low-income areas, they do not see models of success in their communities or receive mentoring from persons who have attended college.

When making these observations, we need to beware of suggesting that low-income persons of color in segregated communities are necessarily victims of dire circumstances. Many strengths exist in these communities, including churches, small businesses, neighborhood associations, and advocacy groups. Many persons surmount their environments. Some schools provide outstanding educational services in low-income and segregated communities. Yet persons of color who live in segregated low-income areas must surmount barriers not encountered in more affluent areas.

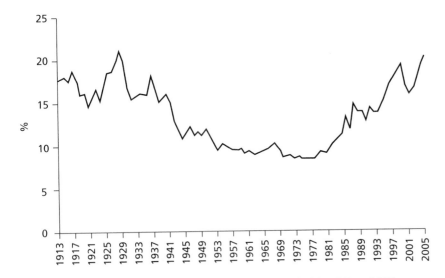

F I G U R E 2.3 Income Share of Highest-Income Households, 1913 to 2005.

SOURCE: Thomas Piketty and Emmanel Saez, "Income Inequality in the United States," *Quarterly Journal of Economics,*
February 2003 as updated at http://elsa.berkeley.edu/~saes/TabFig2005pre1.xls.

T A B L E 2.1   Average After-Tax Income by Income Group (in 2004 Dollars)

Income Category	1979	2004	Percentage Change 1979–2004	Dollar Change 1979–2004
Lowest fifth	$13,900	$14,700	6%	$800
Second fifth	28,000	32,700	17%	4,700
Middle fifth	39,900	48,400	21%	8,500
Fourth fifth	52,300	67,600	29%	15,300
Top fifth	92,100	155,200	69%	63,100
Top 1 Percent	314,000	867,800	176%	553,800

SOURCE: Congressional Budget Office, Effective Federal Tax Rates: 1979–2004, December 2006.

Discrepancies in life conditions are unethical when members of vulnerable populations experience negative *outcomes* as compared with members of specific mainstream populations. Persons who suffer flagrant inequalities in life conditions, such as insufficient resources to meet their survival needs, suffer adverse consequences with regard to health, mental health, education, unemployment, and other areas. Persons who live in racially segregated, low-income communities often encounter problems related to substance abuse, juvenile delinquency, and poor educational outcomes.

Huge inequalities in income between different social classes also yield negative societal outcomes. Societies with large populations that are dependent on welfare and other public programs may experience lower rates of economic growth than other nations. Persons in vulnerable populations who experience markedly lower rights, life conditions, or opportunities than mainstream populations are likely to feel alienated—*particularly* as they follow widely supported societal norms such as seeking employment and working hard. When alienation reaches a threshold, it inhibits proactive decision making, confidence, and formation of a positive self-image—and increases the likelihood of self-destructive behaviors.

We have focused on persons of color in our discussion of inequalities in life conditions, but members of other vulnerable populations also suffer extreme inequalities in comparison with a specific mainstream population. Persons with serious mental and physical challenges suffer disproportionate poverty—which, in turn, contributes to their disabilities. Female, single heads of households are among the poorest members of our society—to the point that an academic coined the term *feminization of poverty*. Such women often work multiple jobs in a desperate effort to meet their children's basic needs—wreaking a toll on their mental and physical health, not to mention their ability to obtain further schooling that might allow them to obtain a higher-wage job. Persons who are released from prison often become homeless or soon return to prison because they are shunned by employers and receive scant help for their substance abuse and mental health problems. When LGBT persons observe that they are denied health and retirement benefits because they cannot marry—unlike heterosexual persons—they are understandably resentful about this unequal treatment, which could even undermine their relationships.

Social Injustice as Illustrated by Denial of Opportunities to Vulnerable Populations

Violations of access to opportunities exist when members of specific vulnerable populations or out-groups receive substantially inferior educational, health, job training, transportation, child care, and preschool services in comparison with a mainstream population. If members of specific vulnerable populations lack access to these services beneath an acceptable threshold, many of them are condemned to unacceptable conditions as they move through different stages of life. A low-income child from a racial minority group will find it difficult to better her condition if she cannot obtain quality education and health services, not to mention preschool services and child care. A person with physical challenges cannot expect to meet his survival needs if he lacks access to job training and technology—and if he is not mainstreamed into public schools. A woman who is denied access to science and math programs because of her gender finds her career choices circumscribed as compared to men who are more likely to gain access to these programs.

Lack of provision of opportunities to vulnerable groups can be ethically criticized through an outcomes or utilitarian approach. Low-income persons of color, persons with mental and physical challenges, and ex-offenders who do not receive exemplary education and job training will likely earn lower incomes than persons who have access to these amenities. Their lower income from relatively unskilled jobs will be compounded over the course of their lives by inability to get promotions and to upgrade their career trajectories. They will be less likely to find jobs in which employers fund health insurance policies and pensions, making them more likely to join the ranks of the medically uninsured and to be relatively poor when they retire.

Society, too, bears substantial and unnecessary costs by not investing in opportunities for members of vulnerable populations. Such costs include unnecessary welfare costs for members of vulnerable populations who would have *avoided* welfare had they received better education, job training, medical care, and transportation. Some persons who serve time in prisons impose unnecessary *additional* prison costs on society when they are not given job training, substance abuse, medical, and other services when they are released from prison or when they are in prison. Persons with mental and physical challenges impose welfare, health, and other *additional* costs on society when they are not helped to enter and remain in the workforce or when they do not receive adequate assistance in their communities and homes. Persons who fail to enter the workforce or to upgrade their careers due to lack of education, job training, and other services pay far lower taxes than they otherwise would have if their incomes were higher—thereby depriving society of revenues it could use to fund other programs that invest in people and infrastructure.

Social policies that create inequalities of access to opportunities are unethical because they contradict the first ethical principle of fairness. Persons who work hard but who earn such low wages that they cannot afford preschool education, child care, education in junior colleges or colleges, vocational training, and transportation ought to receive subsidies from society to help them defray these costs that are self-funded by persons with greater resources but *who often work no harder* than low-wage earners—who often work multiple jobs just to make ends meet. These policies also violate the ethical principle of self-determination because persons who lack opportunities have fewer choices in life than a mainstream population. Consider the bleak prospects of an inner-city youth who not only has not proceeded beyond high school, but who has received such poor education in high school and prior levels of education that he remains illiterate; and compare his future with that of a college-bound youth who has graduated from an excellent suburban secondary school system. If an inner-city youth is far more likely to be limited to relatively unskilled and low-paying jobs, a suburban Caucasian youth has more options that will almost certainly begin with a college education that will lead to higher-paying jobs. High levels of self-determination are possible *only for those who have real choices in life*—but the job, education, career, and other choices of many inner-city youths who are members of racial minority groups are relatively circumscribed as compared with the choices available to many suburban Caucasian youths.

The Challenge of Reducing Social Injustice over Time

Gains in rights, life conditions, and opportunities for vulnerable populations should be celebrated, but they don't diminish social injustices if *discrepancies* between vulnerable populations and mainstream populations do not diminish over time. If, for example, educational attainment of relatively affluent persons improves at an equal, or even a greater, rate than low-income persons of color over a specific time span, discrepancies not only remain but may have increased over time.

The problem of constant or increasing discrepancies between vulnerable and mainstream populations is one of the most vexing ethical problems in the United States, as we discussed earlier in this chapter. Widening discrepancies may partly reflect the truth of the adage, "The rich get richer and the poor get poorer." Affluent persons are able to improve their condition relative to poor persons because their affluence itself, independent of social policies, helps them obtain better educational attainment, jobs, housing, and other amenities and opportunities over time. To offset this discrepancy between rich and poor, Americans need to invest resources at an escalating rate over time—rather than at a stagnant or constant level. Unfortunately, the United States has *not* invested increasing amounts of resources in many of its domestic child care, job training, substance abuse, and mental health services, as illustrated by Figure 2.4, which demonstrates that federal investments in domestic (non-entitlement) programs have stagnated since 1977. (These are called "social investments" in Figure 2.4.)

Nor should we forget that the United States expends vast resources on affluent persons even as it funds safety net and other programs for members of vulnerable populations—expenditures that help affluent persons improve their well-being at an even faster rate than low-income, racial minority, and other vulnerable populations. These benefits and programs include tax deductions for mortgages, low taxes on stock dividends, low taxes on capital gains from investments, tax deferrals on funds placed in private pension accounts, and low taxes

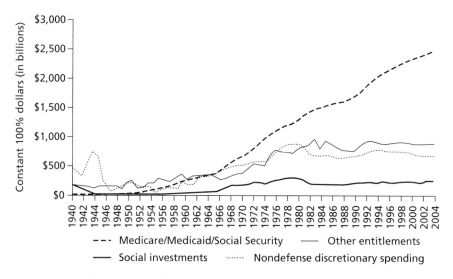

FIGURE 2.4 Four Kinds of Federal Expenditures, per Capita, 1940–2004.

SOURCE: Office of Management and Budget, *Budget of the U.S. Government, FY 2000, Historical Tables.* (Washington, D.C.: GPO, 1999), table 3.I, pp. 48–49.

on estates. When coupled with resources that affluent persons *already* possess, these additional resources allow them to increase their wealth and amenities at a far greater level than would otherwise be possible.

THE CLASH BETWEEN LIBERALS AND CONSERVATIVES OVER SOCIAL JUSTICE

Relatively liberal persons dislike discrepancies between vulnerable and mainstream populations for the reasons we have discussed, whether using an outcomes or firsts principles perspective. Many conservatives begin with the belief that members of some vulnerable populations often *create* their relatively low income by not prizing hard work to the same extent as affluent persons. They believe that this tendency toward laziness is promoted, moreover, by social polices that create "perverse incentives." If low-income persons receive, for example, relatively generous benefits from such safety net programs as Temporary Assistance for Needy Families (TANF) and Food Stamps, some conservatives predict that these persons are more likely to believe they do not have to earn greater resources so they will not need to use benefits from these programs.

In turn, conservatives often believe that inequalities between social classes increase the work incentives of relatively poor persons by making them realize that they *have* to work hard (or harder) to gain equivalent resources. Were society to be relatively egalitarian in its income distribution, these work incentives would be greatly reduced, they believe.

Conservatives, too, doubt that outcomes research demonstrates that inequalities in rights, life conditions, and opportunities yield negative outcomes for members of vulnerable populations or for the general society. Some of them believe that such research is flawed—and often conducted by relatively liberal persons who twist data to promote their agenda of reducing inequalities.

Conservatives tend to be unwilling to increase taxes to fund social policies that might reduce inequality among vulnerable populations. Keeping taxes low, they often contend, puts greater resources in the hands of relatively affluent persons who then use them to make investments that produce more jobs for Americans—including members of vulnerable populations.

From the perspective of first ethical principles, conservatives often prioritize the ethical principle of freedom over fairness. Better not to encumber citizens with government programs or taxes, they contend, than to engage in "social engineering."

Many liberals, in turn, question each of the conservatives' assertions. They assert that the members of many vulnerable populations have relatively low incomes and other life conditions not because they do not wish to work, but because many jobs, such as relatively unskilled jobs, pay low wages. They point out that the vast majority of low-income persons, whatever their ethnicity or race or disability, work hard—often with multiple jobs. Far from increasing their desire to emulate relatively affluent persons, extreme inequality merely increases the alienation, anger, and stress experienced by low-income persons.

Existing welfare and safety net programs, liberals contend, do not create perverse incentives. With payments and benefits already pitched at relatively spartan levels, such programs do not induce persons to want to rely on them if they can find work that reimburses them sufficiently to meet their survival needs.

Rather than assuming that members of vulnerable populations are intrinsically lazy, liberals contend, it would be more accurate to view them as mostly adhering to American values of working hard and seeking upward mobility. Why not use affirmative strategies to better help them navigate education and job markets by giving them positive assistance rather than lowering their resources in hopes that this will induce them to work harder?

Rather than viewing government and taxes as intrinsically evil, liberals view them as positive instruments for advancing important outcomes and first principles. People *have* to rely upon government and taxes, liberals contend, to decrease inequalities, advance other ethical principles, and improve outcomes.

Debates between conservatives and liberals have frequently taken place in American social welfare history, as we will see in many succeeding chapters. Nor are these debates likely to dissipate in coming decades as our society has become (or remains) polarized by ideology and partisan politics. We can look upon social welfare history as a laboratory for deciding who is right and who is wrong at specific points in time and in the contemporary period.

A RELATIVIST VIEW OF SOCIAL JUSTICE

We have used an outcomes and first ethical principles approach to social justice from both liberal and conservative perspectives, but cultural and political factors have powerfully shaped how Americans have responded to inequalities throughout their history. In some eras, such as the Gilded Age near the end of the 19th century and the contemporary era, Americans have been inclined to tolerate, or even to favor, wide gaps in income between relatively affluent and poor Americans. In the New Deal and Great Society, by contrast, greater emphasis was placed upon diminishing large inequalities in income—or at least not favoring them. Even in the colonial era, titans of American history such as Thomas Jefferson favored a relatively egalitarian society of small landowners. In those periods when marked inequalities were tolerated or favored, efforts to develop social policies to avert them faced greater opposition than in other eras. In evaluating the policies of the past, we need to ask what kinds and thresholds of inequality were disliked, tolerated, or even favored in specific historical eras, by whom, and with what impacts on the selection of social policies.

Political factors have powerfully shaped national responses to inequality during specific historical eras. In some periods when persons of color and women were disenfranchised, for example, political pressure to reduce inequality was markedly reduced. In periods when conservatives were in the political ascendancy, such as the Gilded Age, the 1920s, the 1980s, and the period from 2001 through 2006, efforts to reduce inequality were often relegated to the political back burner.

We should realize, too, that our perspectives about specific kinds of inequalities can be influenced by our religious beliefs, social status, and personal values—although generalizations are hazardous. Even though many affluent persons are disinclined to attack inequalities because they benefit from existing social and economic arrangements, some affluent persons *do* support policies to redress specific kinds of inequality—such as when the wealthy father of Bill Gates, the founder of Microsoft, recently objected to the demand of many conservative politicians that estate taxes be rescinded even on persons like himself. If some persons with fundamentalist Christian perspectives are relatively conservative in their ideology, many religious persons possess liberal or radical perspectives, including the evangelical governor of Georgia who recently bucked the will of his fellow conservatives to seek higher state taxes to better fund his state's educational system, which had been widely viewed as among the worst in the nation.

When studying the evolution of the American welfare state, we need to identify political and cultural factors that influenced whether Americans in specific historical eras were troubled by specific inequalities. Curiously, leaders such as Thomas Jefferson in the colonial era were, for example, possibly *more* concerned about economic inequalities than many contemporary American leaders because they wanted to create a republic dominated by relatively small landowners who would (they hoped) possess relatively similar economic resources. In contemporary America where wage disparities are vast and where a relatively small number of Americans own a large share of the nation's assets and wealth, many leaders are relatively oblivious to economic inequality in the United States—even favoring specific tax policies that further widen the gap between rich and poor.

SOME COMPLEXITIES IN THINKING ABOUT SOCIAL JUSTICE

Our discussion up to this point suggests that inequality is a multidimensional concept, since it involves rights, life conditions, and opportunities—and many vulnerable populations as well as many mainstream populations against whom we compare specific vulnerable populations. So we have to select which dimension, which vulnerable population, and which mainstream population we are discussing rather than discussing equality or inequality in general.

No matter which dimension or populations we select, reasonable people can differ about "how much inequality" represents a violation of social justice. Since it is seldom possible to achieve *complete* equality in life conditions or opportunities, we have to decide what constitutes "undesirable" levels of inequality—the inequality threshold that makes us believe that social injustice exists. No simple solution exists—indeed, our choice about how low or how high to set the bar is, itself, an ethical one. If we condone economic inequality that consigns a vast portion of the American population to bare existence in a nation with unprecedented wealth, we risk setting the bar too low. (We can aspire to complete equality with respect to formal civil rights, but even rights guaranteed by law are only imperfectly implemented and enforced by government authorities—as illustrated in contemporary America by the continuing sentencing of more persons of color than Caucasian persons who commit similar crimes.)

Magic bullets rarely exist when we wish to diminish inequalities. Take, for example, the gap in school performance between low-income persons and relatively affluent persons. Even were we to give low-income students educational services equal in every respect to ones received by more affluent persons, the gap in educational achievement between these populations would not suddenly disappear since many factors *outside* schools shape educational achievement. Researchers have discovered, for example, that low-income children often hear fewer words in their homes—and a smaller variety of words—than children of affluent parents in the years prior to the first grade. They have discovered, in turn, that this paucity of words powerfully shapes the educational achievement of low-income children as compared to more affluent children. This sociological and linguistic factor could possibly be offset by emphasizing reading and language in preschool and child care programs used by low-income children, but even this remedy might not completely eradicate differences in educational performance based on social class. Affluent students bring other advantages to education as compared with low-income students. They *expect* to go to college from an early age—and these expectations are repeatedly reinforced by teachers, parents, and friends, whereas many low-income students do not receive this reinforcement or even believe they will complete high school.

Yet many policy options *do* exist for redressing specific kinds of inequalities, such as the following:

- civil rights laws and regulations
- progressive taxation that makes relatively affluent persons pay higher taxes than less affluent persons
- increasing benefits of safety net programs such as TANF, Food Stamps, Supplemental Security Income (SSI), and Earned Income Tax Credit (EITC) programs
- affirmative action programs in college admissions and employment
- opportunity-enhancing policies in schools, such as targeted enrichment programs
- policies that allow low-income families to move to areas that are integrated by social class and race
- programs that link low-income individuals with technology

NAVIGATING THE SOCIAL WELFARE STATE TO SEEK REFORMS

When we determine that existing social policies are morally flawed, we then must decide whether to engage in policy advocacy, and, if so, we must then decide where to focus our energies in the multifaceted welfare state (circle 2 in Figure 2.1).

When we navigate the American welfare state, we are working on three levels:

- making referrals
- engaging in case advocacy
- engaging in policy advocacy

When making *referrals*, we try to link clients or consumers to specific services and benefits in the American welfare state. We can only make referrals intelligently and skillfully, however, if we understand the basic structure of the American welfare state. This understanding is enhanced by studying the evolution of the American welfare state when we learn which policy reforms were enacted in which time period and at what level of government. Our knowledge of social welfare history also allows us to understand what gaps and omissions exist in the American welfare state—allowing us to better understand predicaments encountered by consumers and clients.

When engaging in *case advocacy*, we aim to help consumers and clients obtain benefits, rights, and services to which they are entitled—and to which they believe they have been denied access. Denials occur for several reasons. Sometimes persons are denied timely provision of services and benefits because of overburdened staff. Or staff may wrongly conclude someone is not entitled to benefits or services due to their income or diagnoses. In yet other cases, persons may receive prejudicial treatment due to their membership in a specific vulnerable population, such as by gender, race, or sexual orientation. Social workers who engage in case advocacy need to be well versed in regulations and laws that specify consumers' or clients' rights. While personal intervention by social workers often suffices, they must sometimes help consumers or clients get legal counsel.

In the case of *policy advocacy*, we must decide whether to work on changing policies in local, state, or federal jurisdictions. Do we focus on the private or the public sector? Do we focus on policies in a specific policy sector, such as health, mental health, child and family, civil rights, or safety net areas? Do we want to enact new legislation, change regulations that govern how a specific program is implemented, or find a public interest attorney to initiate litigation against an organization or official? Do we focus on policy changes in a specific organization, agency, or network of agencies?

Social workers also have to decide what kinds of policies to change—such as constitutions, public policies, court decisions, budget and spending programs, rules, procedures, regulations, official policies, informal policies, and policies shaping implementing systems.

They also have to decide what kinds of persons to include in their policy advocacy efforts, whether by enlisting them on their side or approaching them to make specific policy changes—persons such as board members, directors, and staff of social agencies; leaders and members of advocacy groups; elected public officials; civil servants; members of organizations representing the providers of social services or benefits; and leaders or member of coalitions.

Social welfare history enhances our ability to navigate the American welfare state by introducing us to its programs and policies in different levels of government and policy sectors.

DIAGNOSING THE CONTEXT

An array of contextual factors influences ordinary people and legislators as they consider and select social policies in specific eras. When we decide to engage in policy advocacy, we need skills in *diagnosing the context* as it facilitates and impedes specific policy reforms. (Diagnosing the context is shown at the top and bottom of the policy advocacy framework

in Figure 2.1.) The context includes cultural, economic, institutional, social, and legal factors, as well as the sequencing or timing of key events. In succeeding chapters, we will discuss these factors as they have shaped policy selection in various eras—and as they continue to shape the selection of policies in the contemporary period and in coming decades.

THE TWO-SIDED CONTEXT: OPPORTUNITIES AND CONSTRAINTS

Policy practitioners and advocates in the United States have often confronted a two-sided context. On the one hand, the United States has often provided a difficult environment for achieving many policy reforms. On the other hand, policy advocates have often found that many contextual factors facilitated the enactment of reforms in specific eras and in contemporary society. As shown in the following list, contextual factors have provided both opportunities and constraints for policy advocates who wished to reform social policies in the United States in specific historical eras. These factors will be discussed in succeeding chapters. We will discuss at greater length the ways in which many of them continue to shape the evolution of the American welfare state.

1. *Cultural factors* include the way Americans have perceived the importance and causes of specific social problems, the extent to which they have believed that those in need were responsible for these problems, and the extent to which they thought that society has been obligated to assist those in need with ameliorative programs. We discuss how perceptions of various subgroups within the population, such as women and racial groups, have shaped social policies.

   With respect to cultural factors that have often created *constraints* for policy reformers, we shall ask to what extent Americans developed a multifaceted mythology to justify their failure to develop a relatively generous welfare state, including the following:

- Believing that many social problems derive from defects of character rather than from environmental conditions;

- Believing that charitable acts mostly bring adverse consequences such as encouraging recipients to be lazy, encouraging fraudulent use of social programs, encouraging large numbers of persons to rely on public welfare rather than working, and slowing economic growth by diverting resources from economic investment to charity;

- Believing that specific problems can be "solved" through panaceas, thus impeding deeper analysis of the causes and persistence of many social problems—and the need for innovative and far-reaching solutions;

- Falsely believing that a generous welfare state is not needed because ample opportunities exist for all people in America to become relatively affluent;

- Believing that private markets, left to themselves, can solve most social problems —and that social programs and regulations wrongly upset or disrupt private markets;

- Viewing government and government institutions as intrinsically flawed so that they can seldom assume constructive, effective roles in averting or addressing social problems;

- Believing that economic and social inequality is inevitable and that it is required to motivate low-income persons to work harder so they can become substantially more affluent.

We shall also ask what cultural factors have created *opportunities* for policy advocates, including the following:

- Sympathizing with persons who are perceived to be victims of circumstance—and

therefore to be "deserving" of assistance from the welfare state, such as children and older adults;

- Resenting persons and interests that unfairly victimize specific populations—therefore creating support for regulations and civil rights;

- Favoring provision of policies and programs that enhance opportunities for specific populations, such as preschool education and job training programs;

- Favoring programs and policies that reflect rights conferred by the Constitution and statutes such as due process, civil rights, the ability of the federal government to regulate interstate commerce, and the right of the federal government to advance the "general welfare";

- Believing that all who live among us should have their minimal survival needs met so that persons do not starve, go entirely without medical care, or have no shelter.

2. *Economic factors* include the extent to which the government has possessed resources, such as tax revenues, to fund social programs; the extent to which corporations have provided social benefits to employees; and the budgetary priorities of governments.

Economic *constraints* include the following factors:

- Believing that taxation is intrinsically evil —leading to taxes that are too low to provide sufficient revenues to support specific social policies;

- Believing that affluent persons should pay relatively low taxes since higher ones will jeopardize their willingness and ability to make job-creating investments;

- Believing that it is better to run substantial annual budget deficits than to raise taxes— thus enhancing antispending sentiment on the grounds that providing funds for social programs will raise deficits;

- Diminishing resources for domestic spending because of excessive commitments to military expenditures;

- Favoring relatively harsh treatment of immigrants in specific policy eras, such as depriving them of legal rights and the ability to benefit from social programs—particularly when they are perceived as taking jobs away from citizens;

- Structuring the tax code to confer huge tax concessions upon affluent Americans in the form of deductions, tax credits, and tax loopholes.

Economic factors that provide *opportunities* for policy advocates include the following:

- The sheer size of national economic resources in the United States, creating a large reservoir of national income that can fund social programs;

- The existence of *entitlements* that are less susceptible to cuts because they are automatically funded each year to the level of claimed benefits rather than having to compete for funding with other programs in the general budget—such as Medicare, Medicaid, Social Security, SSI, and unemployment insurance;

- The relatively high rate of economic growth in the United States in specific eras that created opportunities for many people;

- The American proclivity to use the tax code to help persons obtain assets and gain income, such as tax deductions for interest payments on mortgages—and the EITC for low-income families;

- The existence of a vast frontier in the colonial period and the 19th century that created opportunities for many people, including European immigrants, to acquire land;

- The willingness of Americans to allow many immigrants to come to the United States.

3. *Institutional factors* include the extent to which governments have possessed administrative capabilities to develop and implement social programs and the balance between federal, state, and local jurisdictions in administering social policy.

Institutional factors that provide *constraints* to policy advocates include the following:

- Believing that the federal government ought not to assume major roles in funding, administering, or monitoring the American welfare state—while overestimating the capacity of state and local governments to assume these roles;

- Buck-passing by federal authorities to the states—or state authorities to the federal government—so that *no* level of government addresses important issues or problems;

- Simplistically believing that the private sector can address or solve social problems;

- Channeling public resources through private entities and faith-based organizations without sufficient governmental monitoring.

Institutional factors that have provided *opportunities* to policy advocates include the following:

- The sheer number of entities that can contribute to policy solutions, including federal, state, and local governments as well as the private sector—providing policy advocates with many points of access;

- The diminishing influence of corruption, patronage, and nepotism in American government institutions in the 20th and 21st centuries as compared with the 19th and early 20th centuries.

4. *Social factors* include wars, migrations of populations, demographic changes, industrialization, global economic competition, and urbanization —that is, changes in the social environment that shape the selection of policies.

Social factors that have provided *constraints* to policy advocates include the following:

- Considerable prejudice, such as sexism, racism, classism, xenophonia, anti-immigrant sentiment, and homophobia;

- Competition between vulnerable populations for scarce resources, such as between African Americans and Latinos.

Social factors that have provided *opportunities* include the following:

- Empowerment strategies of advocacy groups representing vulnerable populations, as well as self-help and other survival strategies of these populations;

- Some diminishing in overt prejudice in the United States since the advent of civil rights legislation for specific vulnerable populations;

- The powerful influence of the Great Depression and the civil rights movements in fostering social and political pressure for enactment of an array of social reforms.

5. *Sequencing of events* describes the effects of the *timing* of important developments in the evolution of the U.S. welfare state.

Sequencing events that have provided *constraints* to policy advocates include the following:

- Postponement of the development of American *federal* social programs, aside from veterans' programs, until relatively late in our national history—that is, during the 1930s and succeeding decades. This late development of a substantial American welfare state contributed to American reluctance to fund a generous welfare state because many people in America did not experience its positive benefits until relatively late in their national history as compared to citizens in many European nations;

- The emergence of the Cold War in the late 1940s, which led to military spending that constricted resources for domestic spending in succeeding decades—with high military spending continuing even after the end of the Cold War in 1991. Military expenditures in the Vietnam and Iraq wars also depleted resources that could have been used to address domestic needs.

Sequencing events that provided *opportunities* to policy advocates include the following:

- Policy reforms during specific eras (such as the Progressive, New Deal, and Great Society eras) that have facilitated reforms in succeeding eras by setting precedents that expanded the horizons of many Americans to include social reforms they often considered to be not feasible prior to that era.

6. *Legal factors* have assumed major significance in the development of the American welfare state because of the importance of federal and state constitutions, as well as court decisions, in shaping public policies.

Legal factors that have provided *constraints* for policy advocates include the following:

- The assumption by many public officials and courts until well into the 1930s that the federal government lacked a constitutional basis for developing social policies because the U.S. Constitution did not explicitly mention social policy as an enumerated power for the federal government —thus implying that state and local governments should assume this role;

- Adverse rulings by lower courts, as well as the Supreme Court, that undermined the ability of state and federal governments to issue regulations and enforce civil rights policies in various areas.

Legal factors that have provided *opportunities* for policy advocates include the following:

- Court rulings that have supported the ability of state and federal governments to develop regulations, civil rights legislation, and social programs, particularly from the late 1930s onward;

- The emergence of public interest legal advocacy groups that have brought many successful class action suits on behalf of vulnerable populations.

7. *Political factors* include power resources and tactics of specific interest groups, legislators, presidents and other chief executives, and professional groups. Political factors that have provided *constraints* to policy advocates include the following:

- Relatively weak trade unions in the United States as compared to many European nations, making it difficult to rally support for reforms that assist working-class populations;

- Nonvoting by significant numbers of low-income persons in the United States, detracting from support for many social reforms;

- The sheer power of American conservatives throughout American history;

- Diversion of liberals' efforts to fighting against moral crusades by conservatives advancing temperance, antidrug, antiobscenity, antigay, anticrime, and antiabortion projects.

- The role of powerful interest groups in opposing social reforms in the decades following 1980, including fundamentalist religious groups, groups representing corporate interests such as the American Chamber of Commerce,

and affluent contributors to political campaigns;

- The relatively conservative nature of leadership in the Republican Party, particularly from 1930 to 1960 and from 1980 to 2008.

Political factors that have provided *opportunities* for policy advocates include the following:

- Development of large unions in the late 1930s and succeeding decades that have financed relatively liberal political candidates and supported relatively liberal legislation;

- The influence of relatively liberal presidents such as Franklin Roosevelt, Lyndon Johnson, and Bill Clinton;

- The relatively liberal nature of the modern Democratic Party, particularly its northern wing, from the 1930s onward;

- The ability of social programs to attract additional support from their beneficiaries, such as elderly persons supporting Medicare and Social Security—and their ability to generate support from providers, such as support for Medicare from hospitals and physicians after its enactment.

As we examine the impact of contextual factors on social policy, we will discover that, in every era, some contextual factors have inhibited the development of ameliorating policies while others have promoted such policies. We will return to many of these factors in specific chapters and also review their cumulative effects in contributing to the reluctance of the American welfare state in Chapter 13.

ENGAGING IN POLICY ADVOCACY

As we discuss in succeeding chapters, policy advocates have often decided in prior historical eras and in the contemporary period that specific social policies *are* ethically defective—whether by their presence (an ill-considered policy) or by their absence (the failure of *any* policy to address an important issue). When they have made this decision, they can choose to be bystanders or policy advocates. Tens of thousands of persons have made the latter choice in the course of American history and in the contemporary period, resulting in myriad social reforms at many levels of government and in both the public and private sectors.

Once they have decided to take action, policy advocates engage in six tasks, as illustrated by circles 3 through 8 in Figure 2.1.

Placing Issues on Policy Agendas

Policy advocates had to gain the attention of key decision makers in the arena where they chose to be active (circle 3 in Figure 2.1). Confronting decision makers in community, organizational, and legislative settings with "full plates" of issues with which to contend, policy advocates have had to convince them to prioritize *their* issues. We shall discuss how policy advocates have often succeeded in this goal in different historical eras, such as by deciding *which* decision makers would be most amenable to their issues, *when* to introduce their issues, *how* to build support for their issues, and *how* to gather evidence and data supporting policy change.

Analyzing Problems

Policy advocates have also had to analyze those social problems or issues that concerned them in order to develop policy proposals to address them (circle 4 in Figure 2.1). They have needed to ask questions such as the following:

- What political, fiscal, cultural, economic, and other factors have led to this specific, festering problem or issue?

- How serious or widespread is this problem or issue?

- What remedies currently exist for it—and why are they insufficient?

- What adverse consequences does the problem or issue pose for specific persons, communities, and society?

Policy advocates have enhanced the trust of decision makers by developing and displaying their knowledge about a specific problem or issue.

Reformers, legislators, and presidents have developed proposals to address social problems from the inception of the republic to the present. When constructing legislation to address problems of unemployed persons, for example, legislators have had to *analyze* the problem, such as determining its causes and prevalence. As we shall see, they often decided that unemployment was caused by character "defects" of individuals, such as laziness—a perception that led, in turn, to punitive responses such as poorhouses or harsh welfare programs. Yet other reformers, such as the ones who secured the enactment of unemployment insurance in the 1930s, contended that unemployment was caused by economic factors beyond the control of individuals, such as recessions or depressions—a perception that led, in turn, to proposals to provide economic assistance to millions of Americans who lost their employment. It should be no surprise that Americans are more likely to implicate character defects when they are prejudiced against specific groups that they associate with specific problems. Equating poverty with Irish immigrants in the 1850s—a group that was greatly stigmatized by the dominant white Protestant population—many Americans favored punitive policies such as housing unemployed people of Irish extraction in poorhouses. Equating poverty with the mainstream population in the 1930s, when as many as 40 percent of the population was unemployed because of the Great Depression, Americans enacted nonpunitive policies such as work relief programs and unemployment insurance.

When people analyze problems, they also gauge their prevalence. In some cases, they underestimate the actual prevalence of specific social problems, such as when a legislator opposed federal funding for shelters for battered women in the 1980s on the grounds that the problem had been invented by do-good social workers. In other cases, they may overstate the prevalence of a problem, such as when temperance crusaders exaggerated the prevalence of alcoholism in the decades before the Civil War and in the 1920s.

How persons frame social problems influences the kinds of proposals that they develop to address them. To understand why Americans emphasized poorhouses in the 19th century, then, we must understand how they perceived poverty, as well as how they perceived specific victims of poverty such as Irish Americans or African Americans. To understand why federal legislators enacted the War on Poverty in the 1960s, we need to understand how they perceived poverty. To understand why Republicans and Bill Clinton approved welfare reform legislation in 1996, we need to understand how they perceived persons on welfare and why they believed specific policies would reduce welfare rolls. To understand why House Republicans opposed giving a tax credit to poor people while granting it to middle-class people in 2003, we need to understand why they opposed augmenting the income of working but poor Americans.

Developing Proposals

Policy advocates have needed to develop policy proposals to address the problem or issue that they have identified (circle 5 in Figure 2.1). They have had to identify what benefits, services, or regulations their proposal will contain. They have had to identify who would administer their proposed policies, such as which level of government, private or public sector, or some combination of these. They have had to discuss who would be eligible for benefits or services and which ones to provide. Policy advocates have also had to determine the cost of their social reform, as well as identifying ways to fund it. Would it be funded from *annual general operating funds* of local, state, or federal governments or by some combination of these governments? Would it be funded by *earmarked taxes*, such as payroll taxes or so-called sin taxes (on cigarettes

or alcohol)? Would it be funded wholly or in part by *consumer fees*—and, if so, would all consumers pay the same fees or would they be paid on a sliding fee scale? Would it be funded entirely or in part by the *private sector*? Or would it be funded through so-called *tax entitlements* that give providers or individuals tax incentives to fund specific social benefits, such as letting corporations write off their contributions to employees' health insurance from their corporate taxes or letting many homeowners write off their mortgage interest payments from their personal income? Or would it be funded through the use of *tax credits*, such as allowing low-income households to receive a tax rebate from the Internal Revenue Service? Or would it be funded through some combination of these various strategies for funding specific social benefits?

Policy advocates have had to wrestle, as well, with sharing of responsibility across the public and private sectors. Perhaps they wished public agencies to receive the funds for a specific initiative, but to have the power to contract with nongovernment agencies in implementing it. Or perhaps they wanted to give the private sector the primary implementing role, such as by giving corporations federal tax incentives to provide job-training services to welfare recipients. Or perhaps they wanted federal or state governments to carry exclusive responsibility for administering specific policies.

In many instances, of course, *different* proposals were advanced to address specific social problems. If some reformers in the 1990s favored welfare reforms that emphasized the provision of remedial education, training, child care, and health care for impoverished single women and their families, other persons favored relatively punitive legislation that sought to force welfare recipients from the rolls by establishing two-year limits on assistance while providing relatively negligible job training and child care assistance. Indeed, controversy often exists when policy reforms are considered.

Getting Proposals Enacted

Policy advocates have rarely been able to take for granted that their policy proposals would be enacted by those decision makers that they had approached. They have needed to develop and use power resources to persuade decision makers to take their proposals seriously, such as by mobilizing pressure on the decision makers, finding key decision makers to endorse the policy, and testifying before legislative hearings (circle 6 in Figure 2.1). They have sometimes developed coalitions to pool resources of different organizations and people to develop and implement political strategy. Policy advocates sometimes did not initiate new proposals, but focused instead upon preventing cuts in, or termination of, existing social policies—or *blocking* ill-considered proposals.

Conservatives—sometimes with support from some liberals—have often been able to block social reforms by cutting taxes so as to deplete the funds available for social programs; by supporting costly ventures, such as military programs, that divert resources from the domestic agenda; and by seeking cuts in social programs in the annual appropriations process.

At the same time, however, social reformers have often met with considerable success, as a large proportion of the federal budget is devoted to domestic programs. Drawing on broad support from the public, reformers helped elect liberal presidents such as Theodore Roosevelt, Woodrow Wilson, Franklin Roosevelt, Harry Truman, John Kennedy, and Lyndon Johnson, each of whom used the powers of office to enact hundreds of social reforms. Reformers have often built broad coalitions to support reforms. For example, during the Great Depression, Franklin Roosevelt drew together a coalition of persons of color, intellectuals, ethnic minorities, working-class persons, and trade unions. Civil rights and liberal religious groups obtained broad public support for civil rights legislation in the 1960s. By linking liberal groups and agricultural interests, reformers secured the passage of the Food Stamps Program as well as numerous expansions of it.

Democrats, too, have often sought the allegiance of centrist or moderate voters. Witness Bill Clinton's desire to co-opt many conservative themes, such as welfare reform, crime, and ending federal deficits, as a means of expanding the constituency of the Democratic Party.

Just as conservatives have blocked reforms by appealing to popular beliefs—for example, the widespread belief that most welfare recipients cheat—liberals have often obtained public support for reforms by appealing to widely held values. Although many Americans do not want to help those they regard as undeserving—for example, those whose ill fortune can be linked to immoral behavior—they are often sympathetic to the needs of those whom they see as innocent victims of adversity, such as unemployed people, persons with medical conditions, retirees who need pensions, widows, and children. Americans sometimes support programs that equip people to find opportunities, such as educational and preschool programs. They have shown their unwillingness to allow persons in poverty to starve by supporting a "safety net" that provides for individuals' basic needs, even if the safety net programs often provide meager resources. Americans have also supported laws that protect people from capricious discrimination in areas such as employment, housing, voting, access to courts and public facilities, and nursing homes.

Liberals have had some surprising successes not just in passing laws but in securing funding for them in subsequent years. Interest groups such as the Child Welfare League of America, the American Association of Retired Persons, the National Association of Social Workers, and advocacy groups for special populations such as persons with disabilities have lobbied legislators to fund social programs. In many cases, lobbyists have persuaded conservatives to support these policies by pointing out that many of their constituents would benefit from such programs.

Getting Enacted Proposals Implemented

Policy advocates have often discovered that they also could not take for granted that enacted policies would be implemented successfully (circle 7 in Figure 2.1). Meritorious policies sometimes come to naught, or are seriously compromised, by inept implementation. Perhaps agencies that implemented them failed to heed key provisions or even the overall goals of a policy reform. Perhaps insufficient funding existed for them. Perhaps resources were fraudulently siphoned off. Perhaps implementing staff lacked important skills. Perhaps agencies failed to collaborate with other agencies.

As one example of poor implementation, Dorothea Dix, the social reformer who persuaded many state legislators to fund the construction of mental institutions so that persons with mental problems could be removed from inhospitable poorhouses, discovered that many states funded them at such low levels that they became understaffed and overcrowded—particularly when poorhouses and hospitals *also* placed growing numbers of elderly people in them. More recently, the nation observed the poor implementation of policies developed to respond to natural disasters in the wake of Hurricane Katrina in New Orleans in the fall of 2005.

As they observed these implementation deficiencies, policy advocates engaged in *troubleshooting* as they diagnosed and then sought to address problems. They sought to persuade or pressure implementers to do better work, to secure greater resources for the program, or to seek new leadership.

Starting Over Again, If Necessary

Policy advocates should assess the effectiveness of implemented social policies (circle 8 in Figure 2.1). If they prove *not* to accomplish goals established for them by policy advocates, they should be improved or terminated, and policy advocates should propose policy alternatives. If they are successful, they should be continued and even expanded. We determine their success by analyzing their ethical merit using both the outcomes and first ethical principle approaches that we discussed earlier in this chapter.

Social welfare history demonstrates the need for policy assessment, because we see both policy successes and failures. Many mental institutions became places to warehouse persons with mental problems from roughly 1880 to 1955. Yet safety net programs such as Food Stamps and EITC have given necessary nutritional and economic assistance

to tens of millions of low-income persons and families during the past 35 years.

LINKING SOCIAL WELFARE HISTORY TO CONTEMPORARY SOCIETY

When we study social welfare history, we can make important connections to contemporary society. I develop some of these connections in the concluding sections of chapters 3 through 12. To illustrate the importance of policy advocacy in creating a more humane welfare state, I discuss the work of one or more policy advocates so that we can not only be inspired by them, but learn from their tactics. I discuss how some social problems that festered in prior eras still exist in contemporary America. So that we can learn from some of the failed policies of prior eras, I discuss one or several of them in specific chapters in the hope that we can avoid making similar errors in contemporary society. I also discuss some promising social policies of prior eras that could be considered in contemporary society.

I link history to contemporary society in chapters 13 and 14 in several ways. I discuss how the contextual factors listed in this chapter both promoted and constrained policy reforms in prior eras and in contemporary society. I identify many policies enacted in prior eras that remain in place in contemporary society. I argue that contemporary social workers need to stand on the shoulders of policy advocates of prior eras.

LOOKING TO THE FUTURE

While Americans have made considerable progress on some fronts, the American welfare state continues to be riddled with gaps, omissions, and errors. Social welfare history allows us to understand why Americans constructed a welfare state with these deficiencies. It teaches us how we, too, can use ethical reasoning to identify gaps, omissions, and errors—and embark on policy advocacy to reform it.

Viewed in this way, then, our knowledge of the evolution of the American welfare state is our prologue to the present and the future, as we will discuss in Chapters 13 and 14.

WHAT YOU CAN DO NOW

You are now equipped to do the following:

- Use the policy advocacy framework in Figure 2.1 to gain an overview of the way policies are developed in American society.

- Define *policy practice* and *policy advocacy*.

- Identify an array of persons who engaged in policy advocacy in prior eras, as well as in the contemporary period.

- Engage in ethical reasoning using first ethical principles.

- Engage in ethical reasoning using an outcomes approach.

- Engage in ethical reasoning using a relativist approach.

- Use an eclectic approach to ethical reasoning.

- Use the ethical principle of social justice to critique existing social policies and evolve new ones.

- State why social workers need navigational skills to make referrals, engage in case advocacy, and engage in policy advocacy.

- Identify constraining and facilitating contextual factors that have shaped the size and nature of the American welfare state, including cultural, economic, institutional, social, sequential, and political factors.

- Identify six policy advocacy challenges as identified by circles 3 through 8 in Figure 2.1.

- Describe how social welfare history contributes to social workers' skills in the contemporary era.

ENDNOTES

1. The classic statement of utilitarianism is found in Jeremy Bentham, *An Introduction to the Principles of Morals and Legislation* (London: Athlone Press, 1970). For a critique of this approach, see J. L. Mackie, *Ethics: Inventing Right from Wrong* (London: Penguin Books, 1977), pp. 126–134.

2. For an excellent discussion of various moral rules, see Tom Beauchamp and James Childress, *Principles of Biomedical Ethics*, 4th ed. (New York: Oxford University Press, 1994).

3. A sophisticated advocacy of relativism (he calls it "intuitivism") is made by Mackie, *Ethics*.

3

Fashioning a New Society in the Wilderness

T A B L E 3.1   Selected Orienting Events

1100s–1400s	Peak of feudal society
1492	Columbus's first voyage to the New World
1500s–1700s	Policy of mercantilism developed
1517	Reformation begins when Luther posts his 95 theses
1534	Henry VIII separates Church of England from Roman Catholicism
1600s	English Enlightenment (see John Locke's publication of *Two Treatises of Government* in 1689)
1601	Passage of English Poor Law Act
1607–1733	England establishes 13 permanent colonies on the Atlantic Coast
1676	Bacon's Rebellion in colonial Virginia
Late 1600s	Establishment of laws in southern colonies reducing blacks to chattel
1680	House of Burgesses in Virginia recommends that every county build a workhouse
1700s	Scottish and Continental Enlightenment (see Adam Smith's publication of *The Wealth of Nations* in 1776)
1763	Proclamation Line established to separate settlers' lands from Native American lands
1775–1783	American Revolution
1787	Constitutional Convention held in Philadelphia
1788	Constitution ratified by the states
1789	George Washington elected to first of two presidential terms
1791	Bill of Rights ratified as first 10 amendments to the Constitution
1800	Thomas Jefferson elected to first of two presidential terms

Distant as the colonial era is from contemporary society chronologically, it placed in motion many cultural, legal, social welfare, and political traditions that are still present today. At the end of this chapter, we will discuss what we can learn from the colonial period about policy advocacy, social policy, and the contemporary American welfare state.

It was a diverse group of white settlers that came to the New World in the 17th and 18th centuries, predominantly from England but also in surprising numbers from Germany, the Netherlands, and Africa. In New England, Puritans and Protestants who were fleeing religious persecution in Europe wanted to establish spiritual communities based on their brand of Protestantism. Many Catholics came to Maryland to seek freedom from persecution in England. Large numbers of settlers hoped to better their economic condition in the New World, particularly as population growth in Europe limited access to land acquisition and other economic opportunities. A large percentage of white immigrants became indentured servants in the hope that they could better their lot once their term of service was completed. Many slaves were brought forcibly to the New World from Africa, primarily to work on tobacco and cotton farms and plantations. Because these groups of people were so disparate and had such different motives for coming to the New World, it was unclear what ideas and institutions, much less what kinds of social policies, they would fashion—and how they would interact with the First American population.

Deeply influenced by European institutions and ideas, the colonists rapidly created a new society in the wilderness. By 1800, they had fashioned institutions and a political culture that differed dramatically from those in the European nations from which they had come.

As we shall see, many constructive accomplishments, such as forming a new nation in the wilderness, were counterbalanced by oppression of women, First Americans, and Africans who were forced to migrate to America by slave traders. The colonists, moreover, often adopted a harshly moralistic attitude toward persons who genuinely needed economic help.

THE FEUDAL INHERITANCE

During the decline of the Roman Empire after the fourth century, marauding bands of outlaws pillaged local villages and took land from local farmers in England and other European countries. Local populations gradually ceded title of their lands to powerful noblemen and monarchs, who allowed them to remain on the land but required them to render services in return for protection. By the 12th century, most of Europe had become splintered into a series of fiefdoms that had developed localistic, hierarchical, communalistic, and traditional social institutions.[1]

Medieval society was hierarchical. Land was held by monarchs, noblemen, and the Catholic Church. Noblemen paid taxes to monarchs and helped obtain recruits for their armies. In return for protection, rights, and assistance, serfs worked the land for noblemen, monarchs, and the Church, paid taxes to them, and gave them a share of the produce from the land. Citizens also paid mandatory taxes to the Church in return for its religious, social, and legal assistance.

Medieval society was not capitalistic. Commodities were bartered in markets and in private transactions. Land was not bought and sold in the modern sense but was transferred through inheritance to successive generations of noblemen so that it remained within specific families for centuries. (Noblemen were forbidden to sell their property outside their families by prohibitions known as *entail*, which reflected the prominence of tradition and family.) Serfs were bound to the land; that is, they were required to work it. Although bound to the land, they also possessed rights to work specific amounts of land, which prevented noblemen from summarily evicting them; their children often inherited those rights. The serfs received no money for farming the land but could sometimes sell surplus goods in local farmers' markets after coinage appeared. Some pastures and woodlands were reserved for the common use of a village so that peasants could graze cattle in them and gather fuel.[2]

Serfs did not live in dispersed housing but within small villages. Villagers elected members who negotiated with the nobleman's representative (the bailiff) to decide which fields would lie fallow, who would tend animals in common pastures, and which members of the villages would serve in the king's armies to meet the monarch's manpower levy.

The work ethic in the modern sense did not exist in this subsistence-oriented society. Serfs worked to meet basic obligations and subsistence needs—and no more. Numerous religious, seasonal, and traditional holidays were observed each year. Noblemen did not expect more than this minimal labor from serfs because they, too, were oriented to a subsistence and bartering economy. Little work was performed in the fall and winter owing to inclement weather.

Though noblemen, crusaders, and traders accumulated vast wealth, the acquisition of wealth by exploiting market mechanisms—for example, charging interest on loaned money or raising the prices of food or commodities—was regarded with considerable suspicion. Early merchants who sought to accumulate money, or who tried to increase prices—and profits—by withholding grain from the market, were often persecuted. Some medieval theorists even developed the notion that wealth should be shared, as it belonged to the society in which it was developed; however, this idea was not carried to the logical conclusion that society should take lands or resources from noblemen, the Church, or kings and redistribute them to serfs.

Medieval society emphasized conformity with tradition. People were born into a position or status in society and usually remained within it. Rarely did people move their places of residence. Rights to the use of land as well as attendant obligations to noblemen were inherited. Persons who violated traditions—for example, those who failed to honor obligations or to maintain deference to social superiors—were subject not only to peer pressure but to various courts. Noblemen who tried to evict serfs from the land and serfs who refused to provide required service to noblemen were subject to sanctions.

The Catholic Church was the only recognized church in the medieval period and was intimately associated with governmental institutions. It was, in effect, a government paralleling secular jurisdictions, with its own taxes, laws, and courts. In addition, many ecclesiastical officials served in secular government and in the monarch's inner circle of counselors. Those who wished to establish a separate church—or to urge reforms in the existing one—met with strenuous persecution from Church or governmental officials and were sometimes sentenced to death. Just as noblemen did, the Catholic Church used serfs to farm its vast amounts of land. (In England, King Henry VIII declared the English branch of the Catholic Church to be a state church in 1534 and succeeded in wresting control of it from the Vatican.)

SOCIAL POLICY IN MEDIEVAL SOCIETY

In this localistic, traditional, and hierarchical society, social problems were usually addressed through family and peer relationships and by mutual obligation. Noblemen provided food to serfs in return for labor and maintained stocks of food as reserves for famine. Villagers shared oxen and helped one another plant and harvest crops as they moved together from field to field. Families and villagers were expected to assist elderly persons, children, and those who were mentally ill.[3]

The medieval Church assumed social welfare functions by providing food and lodging to people who were hungry, sick, or transient. Such

---

INSERT 3.1   Using the Web to Understand How Americans Fashioned a New Society in the Wilderness

---

Visit **academic.cengage.com/social_work/jansson** to view these links and a variety of study tools.

Go to **http://www.pbs.org/wgbh/aia/part1/title .html** Click on "Part I: Narrative" as well as the other links: "Map of the British Colonies"; "Europeans Come to Western Africa"; "New World Exploration and English Ambition"; "From Indentured Servitude to Racial Slavery"; "The African Slave Trade and the Middle Passage"; "The Growth of Slavery in North America." What do these links tell you about the economic and racial causes of slavery in the colonies?

Go to **http://www.earlyamerica.com/earlyamer ica/index.html** Click on "Milestone Events" and then choose the "Whiskey Rebellion" link to review materials that illustrate how tenuous the power of the federal government was in the early Republic. Click on "Constitution" to find in its text those provisions that became relevant to enactment of

social policies in the United States. Does the text support the contention that the Constitution *indirectly* allowed the federal government to support social policy rather than directly? Click on "The Declaration of Independence" to ascertain whether this seminal document suggests that the United States revolution was primarily a war for independence rather than a true "revolution."

Go to **http://www.pbs.org/ktca/liberty/** Click on the "Perspectives on Liberty" link and then the "Daily Life in the Colonies" link to gain an understanding of the extent to which the colonies were primarily agricultural in nature.

Go to **http://www.usconstitution.net/articles. html#Preamble** to learn about the Articles of Confederation. Click on the link that compares the Articles with our current constitution. Compare the documents. Was George Washington really the first president of the United States?

---

individuals approached monasteries and requested food or lodging, which was given without any inquiry as to the reasons for their destitution. It was the Church's canon law that established principles about vagrancy and poverty during the Middle Ages, long before secular governments had developed such policies. Viewing involuntary poverty as its own deterrent because few people *want* to live in poverty, Church leaders saw no need for punitive policies. As Tierney notes, Church officials "no more thought of punishing a man for being afflicted with poverty than we would think of punishing a man for being afflicted with tuberculosis."[4] Even by the 12th century, the Church supervised the care of the poor through the use of tithes, which local parishes collected and used to help fund poor relief. This positive belief about the rights of people who were poor, and the duty of society to afford relief to them, was eventually transferred from the Church to government, as we will discuss in due course, but the initial and primary impetus for poor relief came from the Church. Monasteries' welfare functions

were usually limited in extent, however, so that only a small proportion of their resources was expended on aid and services.[5] Unemployment hardly existed because most persons worked the land or engaged in hunting. Massive problems, such as plagues and famines that often overwhelmed local helping institutions, were viewed fatalistically as problems that society could not avoid.

The relatively small size of formal social programs should not obscure the fact that medieval society was organized to provide economic and social security. Most people had rights and obligations to farm land, use common pastures and woods, and occupy housing in local villages; these rights and obligations were protected and enforced by tradition, courts, and the Church. Entry into trades was strictly regulated to prevent excessive enrollments and to guarantee life membership to incumbents.[6]

Feudal society should not be glamorized, however. Extraordinary social and economic disparities existed between noblemen and serfs. Serfs were bound to the land, could not hunt without scrutiny of gamekeepers, had no chance for upward mobility, often could not own land, could not migrate, and could be conscripted into armies to fight battles that were often based on monarchs' petty territorial and religious objectives. One legacy of feudal society, then, was a social and economic conservatism that discouraged basic changes in land ownership and participation in political affairs by ordinary people.[7]

THE GRADUAL UNRAVELING OF FEUDALISM

The early American settlers immigrated from European societies that were in the throes of transition from feudal institutions to individualistic, democratic, and capitalist societies. To understand the perspectives of the early settlers, we need to examine how the roles, sanctions, and controls that existed in feudal society gradually weakened during the 16th, 17th, and 18th centuries, as manifested by the emergence of capitalism, the displacement of serfs from the land, the development of new social classes, the rise of restrictive notions of the proper roles of government, the Protestant Reformation, changing conceptions of the meaning of human existence, and the Enlightenment. Historians do not understand the precise relationships among these developments—for example, whether capitalism, religion, or cultural changes assumed the primary role in unraveling feudalism. Despite its complex origins, the unraveling was vitally important to the origins of American society, whose early immigrants came from societies in which older ideas were widely criticized as new ideas and institutions emerged.

The barter and subsistence economy of medieval society was gradually replaced by a capitalistic economy; this development had profound social and political consequences throughout Europe. (Our examples below are drawn from the experiences of England.) Paper money, coins, and precious metals were increasingly used as mediums of exchange as bartering diminished. Buyers and sellers of commodities and land, instead of charging or paying a traditional fee, increasingly made economic decisions according to dictates of the market. A merchant might successively raise the price of bread, for example, until demand for it diminished, just as noblemen who wanted to raise cash would sell their land at the highest possible price. People became commodities themselves in labor markets; they worked for wages. Whereas some employers paid a fair wage, others successively lowered wages to levels that labor markets would bear, regardless of their laborers' survival needs. This use of money and markets was complemented by the concepts of saving, investment, and profit. Where they had once merely sought subsistence, people began to hoard money, which they invested in land or other goods to increase their net worth. Indeed, some persons loaned their assets to others at the highest possible rate of interest.[8]

This gradual conversion to capitalism had many consequences. Capitalism fostered widespread economic and social uncertainty among agricultural laborers, who could no longer assume a relatively secure position on the land of their ancestors. Many of them had succeeded in converting their status from serfs to peasants; rather than being bound to the land, they became tenant farmers who rented their land. However, they soon discovered that noblemen, freed from ancient obligations, could now force them off the land. They found themselves buffeted by the uncertainties of inflation, depressions, unemployment, and displacement. Increasingly, they had to seek available work even if it paid a meager wage. Many of those who had once occupied a secure niche within villages that were affixed to feudal estates now roamed the countryside or sought uncertain lodging in London and other growing cities. Urban dwellers could not raise subsistence crops, collect fuel from forests, or raise animals on common pastures. Thus, unemployment and hunger became major social problems; they brought a good deal of hardship to many persons and increased social tension within England. Peasants resented their loss of economic security, and many middle- and upper-class persons resented and feared dispossessed persons.[9]

The simplicity of feudal society, which facilitated the perpetuation of social power by noblemen, was fractured by the rise of new social classes. Small urban areas began to develop by the 14th century, as domestic commerce and foreign trade expanded. Merchants increasingly resented efforts by the royal court and by noblemen to tax and regulate them. By the end of the 17th century, a virulent animosity had developed between upper and lower strata in English society. The upper strata feared the increasing numbers of vagabonds and persons without employment. Some gentry and merchants referred to the poor as "savages," "beasts," and "incorrigibles." Many believed that peasants and the urban poor were intrinsically lazy and could learn habits of productivity only when subjected to harsh discipline.[10] Landless persons at the bottom of the social order were less likely to respond with deference to social elites and often rioted to protest enclosures of fields, the raising of rents charged to tenant farmers, and the lack of food during famines. In the 17th and 18th centuries, many people feared that "unruly mobs" would be aroused by demagogues to seek major changes in society. These fears reached fever pitch at the end of the 18th century with the French Revolution. Riots, mobs, and incidents of violence, though sporadic, were a decided feature of English life in the long transition from feudal to modern institutions and contributed to the decline of feudal patterns of deference and authority.[11]

Many persons in England sought to establish limits on the powers of central government. Many merchants hoped to reduce taxes and regulations. Elected representatives in Parliament, who sought to share decision-making powers with the monarch, had achieved a balance of power by 1700. Parliament obtained the power to veto tax initiatives while ceding trade policy to the crown. Monarchs, who had previously been able to dominate national politics, increasingly had to exercise power by rewarding persons through appointments, granting trade and commercial privileges, and distributing other favors. Religious dissenters wanted the ability to worship without interference from the state church. Landowners wanted to be able to enclose or sell their fields without having to honor ancient rights of peasants. All of these cases reflect a notion of the self-directing and autonomous individual that was strikingly different from the collective notions of the feudal era. Complementing the notion of individual autonomy were economic concepts of personal initiative and risk taking. Many persons, including Protestants, Catholics, and Anglicans, believed that hard work, frugality, and saving resources were superior to traditional ideas about subsistence and seasonal labor.[12]

This emphasis on freedom, autonomy, and personal initiative in the secular world complemented the religious beliefs of many Protestants. Protestantism can be traced to 1517, when Martin Luther, a Catholic priest who had become disenchanted with the corruption and ritualism of the Church, posted 95 theses on the door of a church in Wittenberg. The theses stated his opposition to the use of "indulgences" (which allowed people to contribute money to a worthy cause so as to receive forgiveness for sins) and other Church practices. After he was excommunicated in 1521, he founded the Lutheran Church, which became merely one of many sects that were established during the Protestant Reformation. Protestants hoped to increase the personal involvement of parishioners in the church by requiring church members to read and study the scriptures, by placing more emphasis on sermons, and by giving congregations enhanced roles in church governance. In the several centuries after the Protestant Reformation, there emerged an array of sects that drew on some of the ideas developed by Luther, Calvin, and other Protestant leaders; these sects included Anabaptists, Congregationalists, Methodists, Presbyterians, and Quakers. Some Protestants did not object to the concept of an official state church; they hoped to persuade the king to make their faith the established orthodoxy. Others, however, moved inexorably to the notion that all religions should be tolerated in English society, a concept that fundamentally challenged the notion of a single state church. The major religious purpose in life, Protestants believed, was to control such evil passions as pride, greed, lust, laziness, and desire for power by cultivating reason and moral virtue, by working hard, and by avidly reading the scriptures. In this emerging religious perspective, each person was charged with developing a personal quest for a moral existence. The Protestants differed among themselves about whether the individual could actually earn salvation by working hard and suppressing the passions through devotion, but they all emphasized work as a means of controlling the passions. Whatever their precise beliefs, members of Protestant sects were persecuted extensively in England and other countries. When emigration to the New World became an option in the 17th and 18th centuries, many Protestants seized the opportunity.

The emerging emphasis on work and careers sometimes fostered suspicion of people living in poverty, on the premise that persons who were truly hard-working should have something to show for it; after all, God was likely to bestow good fortune on moral persons. This judgmental orientation, reinforced by a growing class consciousness, resulted in an extraordinarily harsh orientation toward persons in poverty, which contrasted markedly with the nonpunitive relief policies of the medieval monasteries.[13]

In the 17th century, a number of English political theorists, including John Locke, espoused limited government, free speech, secularism, optimism, science, and the use of reason to discover natural laws. Locke contended that government did not exist in the primeval "state of nature," but that citizens developed a "contract" for a limited government when they discovered that some people attacked others and took their property. Thus, the citizens constructed a government that would emphasize preserving law and order. To ensure that despots would not arise, the citizens established a multi-branched system of governance with checks and balances. We shall see that, although the American colonists drew on many sources when they constructed their constitution in the 1780s, ideas of Locke and other writers during this so-called English Enlightenment deeply influenced their work. These writers fervently questioned monarchical and religious authorities. The colonists were also influenced by writers such as Adam Smith (who questioned excessive governmental intrusion into private matters) and Voltaire (who opposed state religions) in the Scottish and Continental Enlightenment of the 18th century.

POLICY CHOICES IN THE PERIOD OF TRANSITION

Some English social welfare policies during this period of transition from feudal to postfeudal society advocated assistance to persons who were unemployed and poor, within the limits of a society that lacked resources and governmental agencies. Other policies, however, reflected a punitive orientation; these negative policies may be traced both to social elites' fear and anger and to the economic, political, and individualistic ideas that had contributed to the unraveling of feudalism.

Positive Policies

Officials in the small towns of feudal Europe had regulated virtually every facet of economic and social affairs during the 16th and 17th centuries. Entry into trades, decisions about who could set up businesses, the prices of commodities, wage rates, and locations of new construction were strictly regulated by the monarch and by local officials, partly to protect peasants from economic uncertainties. Local regulations were supplemented by a national policy of the English government to manage the economy so as to conserve food at home and to facilitate the development of foreign trade. A parliamentary act of 1548, for example, required citizens to eat fish on Fridays and Saturdays; the goal was to promote the building of ships and to conserve livestock. (This regulation was extended to include Wednesdays through the passage of legislation in 1563!) The English government encouraged immigration of Flemish experts in cotton and weaving to promote the development of a textile industry, provided government subsidies to various industries, and aggressively sought foreign markets.[14]

A policy called *mercantilism* had evolved by the 17th century; this policy envisioned the development of colonies in the New World to provide raw materials and new markets for England. Mercantilism is a system by which a government regulates its agriculture, industry, and commerce to create a favorable balance of trade. Mercantilism's proponents were convinced that external trade was needed to promote the prosperity of England. The monarch commissioned trading companies to settle lands in the New World, encouraged emigration to these settlements, and hoped that the settlers would both provide markets for English produce and supply England with gold and raw materials. To stimulate the growth of the merchant marine, the Parliament required that trade with these colonies be conducted in English ships.

Mercantilism can be viewed not only as an exercise in economic nationalism but also as a social policy to increase jobs and economic growth in England and thereby to help the large number of persons who had been cast off the land by enclosures and population growth. It was supplemented by other economic measures that were not narrowly constructed to encourage trade; for example, controls were placed on the prices of commodities and foodstuffs so that everyone could afford basic necessities such as bread and corn. Moreover, in an attempt to accommodate the many unemployed persons flooding the countryside, the English government tried to intervene in job markets so as to stimulate employment. Landed gentry were sometimes asked, for example, to hire servants even when they did not want them and to extend terms of indentured status for servants and of apprenticeship for workers.[15]

As we have seen, the Catholic Church had required its local parishes to collect taxes and to use part of these proceeds to care for those in need. The Church of England inherited this custom but did not faithfully put it into practice, largely because of the vast number of those who needed help in the wake of enclosures, population growth, and urbanization, but also partly on account of corruption within the church bureaucracy. Government authorities decided to supplant this local system of welfare by requiring the parishes to appoint unpaid overseers, who were charged with collecting taxes and distributing relief to those in need. In the landmark Elizabethan Poor Law Act of 1601 (see Box 3.1), the national government consolidated various laws that had assigned welfare roles to local parishes. When parishes could not meet their responsibilities, counties were required to assume relief-giving functions. In effect, then, government became the chief enforcer of poor relief by 1601, thus supplanting the Church of England.

Local parishes fulfilled their welfare responsibilities in several ways. They could provide "outdoor relief" to persons in their homes; provide "indoor relief" to persons in special institutions that came to be variously known as almshouses, poorhouses, or workhouses; or require persons to become indentured servants or apprentices. These latter two options were more punitive than outdoor relief, as they conditioned relief on residence within an institution or assumption of a specific labor status.

The Elizabethan Poor Law represented, on balance, a positive policy, even though it required that some able-bodied persons be made to work in poorhouses and urged relatives to care for their own impoverished relatives. (We shall see, however, that in many local jurisdictions the law was administered in a punitive fashion during the next several centuries.) Research on poor law institutions of southern England suggests that poor law officials undertook a range of welfare roles that sometimes approached those of modern welfare states. They provided unemployment relief; initiated public works; regulated local prices to help poor persons; gave in-kind assistance such as food, clothing, and wood; provided health care; removed children from abusive households; and gave legal protections to apprentices. More than 50 percent of the people in southern England used outdoor relief in specific years. Many local jurisdictions possessed "laws of settlement" that entitled people to receive local poor law relief after a year's residence. Often used in punitive fashion to force people to leave if they became destitute before a year's residence had elapsed, laws of settlement could also be viewed more positively, as guarantors of poor relief for new agricultural migrants once they had lived for a year in a new location.[16]

BOX 3.1   The Elizabethan Poor Law Act of 1601

Be it enacted ... that the Churchwardens of every Parish, and foure, three, or two substantial Householders there ... to bee nominated yeerely ... under the hande and seale of two or more Justices of the Peace in the same Countie ... shall be called Overseers of the poore of the same Parish, and they ... shall take order from time to time ... for setting to worke of the children of all such whose parents shall not ... bee thought able to keepe and maintaine their children; and also for setting to worke all such persons maried, or unmaried, having no meanes to maintaine them, use no ordinary and dayly trade of life to get their living by, and also to rayse weekely or otherwise (by taxation of every inhabitant ... in the said Parish) a convenient stocke of Flaxe, Hempe, Wool, Threed, Iron and other necessary ware to set the poore on worke,

and also competent summes of money for, and towards the necessary reliefe of the lame, impotent, old, blinde, and such other among them being poore, and not able to worke, and also for the putting out of such children to bee apprentices ... it shall and may be lawfull for the saide Churchwardens and Overseers ... to errect, build ... convenient houses of dwelling for the said impotent poor, and also to place Inmates or more families than one in one cottage, or house.

The Father and Grandfather, and the Mother and Grandmother, and the children of every poore, old, blinde, lame, and impotent person ... not able to worke, being of sufficient ability, shall at their owne charges relieve and maintaine every such poore person....

Because the poor law did not outline in detail how local overseers were to implement their local programs, considerable local variation ensued. Some overseers placed more emphasis on indoor relief than others. Controversy regarding the relative merits of indoor and outdoor relief developed in the nation. In certain periods, advocates of a harsh policy enacted national policies to promote construction of workhouses; however, this punitive policy also provoked widespread revulsion, which sometimes took the form of riots by poor people in periods of high unemployment. In southern England, a relatively benevolent interpretation of the poor laws was dominant until well into the 18th century.[17]

Whether motivated by the feudal Catholic tradition of sharing wealth or the Protestant emphasis on giving as a moral duty, affluent persons gave money to many charities, including 800 hospitals in England by the 16th century. These hospitals served persons of limited means; some specialized in providing care to specific groups such as orphans. Local governments often shared in the costs of construction and implementation of these institutions, but most charity in 17th-century England was provided by private philanthropy. Charitable trusts and bequests were so common that the 1601 Statute of Charitable Uses was enacted to regulate them.

Punitive Policies

Punitive policies of the time included restrictive interpretations of the Elizabethan Poor Law, denial of civil liberties to the poor, and harsh use of laws of settlement. The Elizabethan Poor Law assigned responsibility for the poor to local public officials. Those in poverty could be assisted in their homes, but some could be placed in poorhouses and set to work on a "stocke of Flaxe, Hempe, Wool, Threed, Iron, and other necessary ware." When those living in poverty were regarded as "undeserving," policies tended to be punitive; in 1723, for example, Parliament enacted a law that mandated the use of poorhouses by local parishes rather than the continuation of the less stigmatizing policy of outdoor relief.[18]

Some theorists were so critical of people in poverty that they proposed enslaving them to teach discipline and moral virtues—with heavy reliance on corporal punishment. Parliament at one point enacted a law requiring those who were indigent to wear a sign marked with a P! (It was later rescinded.) Those in need were exposed to harsh discipline, backbreaking work, and moral teaching in the many workhouses that were constructed in the 17th and 18th centuries. The harshness of the workhouse strategy was offset, however, by the fact that few counties constructed them until the 18th and 19th centuries—and by the leniency of some local officials, who chose to provide outdoor relief instead.[19]

Laws of settlement, which required persons to remain in their native counties, were enacted during the long transition from feudal to postfeudal society and remained in effect until the 1870s in parts of England. In the 16th and 17th centuries, laws of settlement were sometimes viewed as protections for transient persons, as they entitled them to local relief after a year of residence. By the late 18th century, however, local officials began to urge local landowners not to hire laborers for more than a year, so as to limit parish and county welfare costs.[20] Vast numbers of peasants found themselves carted home after brief stints of labor.

Children were often subjected to treatment that would be regarded as harsh by modern standards. A common belief was that the central task in child-rearing was to break the will of children so that they could become right-living persons. Regarded as little adults, children were often apprenticed or indentured at an early age and subjected to rigorous working conditions. Free education was not widely available until well into the 18th century, and then only at the primary school level.

European nations overwhelmingly consisted of white residents. As we discuss subsequently, however, many Europeans possessed racist views toward persons of color that would soon lead to oppression of First Americans, as well as citizens in Caribbean, Central America, and South American locations. Sexism, too, was rampant in Europe with women not even allowed to read in many places—which would soon foster oppressive laws and policies in the American colonies.

THE AMERICAN COLONISTS

Recent historical research—by Gordon Wood and Joyce Appleby, for example—emphasizes the extent to which the culture and institutions of the American colonists resembled those of European nations.[21] Indeed, American society in 1750 was similar in many respects to England. By 1800, however, the Americans had created a political culture and institutions that departed markedly from their counterparts in England; they had, indeed, founded a new society in the New World. To understand the evolution of American social policy in the colonial period, and to obtain clues about its likely direction in the 19th century, we need to understand this process of transformation at the inception of the Republic.

Patterns of Continuity

The earliest American settlers in the early part of the 17th century created communal, hierarchical, and regulated enclaves that conformed to older traditions. Settlers in the Massachusetts Bay Colony in the 17th century worked fields together, much as their feudal ancestors did, on land given to trading companies by the crown. (See Insert 3.2.)

The farmers were expected to give a large share of their produce to the company, in exchange for the right to work company lands. They lived in villages that were surrounded by company fields, rather than in the dispersed patterns characteristic of American agriculture in the 18th and 19th centuries. Similar patterns were observed in the settlements in Virginia in the early 17th century.[22]

The social structure in these earliest colonies was also hierarchical in the feudal sense. A few wealthy investors received rights to large tracts of land and were served by a landless class of indentured servants. A variety of artisans and craftsmen occupied an intermediary position in the social structure. As participation in the process of governance was conditioned on both holding land and meeting specific religious requirements, many persons were disenfranchised.

Early life was tightly regulated. In Virginia, for example, each settler was required to plant a certain amount of corn to ensure adequate food crops. The colonists decided who could and who could not trap certain kinds of animals, where common pasturage would be located, the maximum levels of wages that could be paid, and the maximum prices

---

INSERT 3.2   Critical Analysis: What Promoted the Mass Exodus from Europe?

The fraying of feudal society promoted the emigration of large numbers of citizens from Europe to the American colonies in the 17th and 18th centuries. To understand the causes of this mass exodus, ponder the following questions.

1. In 14th-century, medieval society, why would emigration have been difficult, even if citizens had access to ships? Consider how most people were bound to the land as serfs and unable to leave. Or how entrepreneurial activity was restricted to a relatively few merchants, so that incentive to colonize distant lands was limited. Or how, prior to the Protestant Reformation, relatively few people possessed a religious motive to flee European societies. Or how, absent strains of individualism that appeared during and after the Protestant Reformation, people lacked a worldview that promoted personal risk taking.

2. Consider how each of the factors associated with the fraying of feudalism contributed to emigration by providing motives, as well as people. More people now *wanted* to leave Europe, particularly the following groups:

   - descendents of serfs who became tenant farmers with uncertain economic futures
   - persons in growing towns who lacked steady work
   - persecuted members of Protestant sects

   In addition, population growth in Europe, as well as enclosures of land, limited people's access to the land and also their economic opportunities. Finally, with the rise of crime and the appearance of vagabonds and class tensions, members of the upper orders now possessed a motive to force less prosperous individuals to leave England.

3. Consider, as well, how a *demand* for immigrants in the New World helped to promote a mass exodus. (We will see that many American landowners needed labor, thus providing a vast market for indentured servants, and how the huge tracts of frontier land beckoned some immigrants even in the colonial era.)

---

that could be charged for specific products. Regulations were also promulgated that established apprenticeship requirements for entry into the various trades.[23] The individual colonies created official churches—Protestant churches in New England and a Church of England in Virginia. They also divided the countryside into parishes and imposed on all citizens, including those who worshiped in different churches, a tax to support the official church. Officials in these early churches, who were accorded extraordinary deference, often assumed roles in secular governance.

Wood contends that the politics and culture of Americans in the different colonies mirrored England even in 1750, long after the earliest settlements—and that both the colonies and England retained many ideas and institutions from medieval Europe. Most English-speaking Americans, for example, remained loyal to the English monarchy. State religions still existed in many colonies. While not as well established or affluent as its English counterpart, an American aristocracy existed; this aristocracy was deeply prejudiced against ordinary people, from whom it demanded considerable deference. Like the royal court in England, this aristocracy freely obtained favors from legislatures and royal governors in the various colonies. Many colonies required parents to pass their land on to their oldest son or their children, rather than selling it.[24]

Although people in England and America did not think in terms of social classes until well into the 19th century, they conceptualized society as a series of vertical ranks or titles, ascending from indentured servants and tenant farmers at the lowest ranks to a landed aristocracy at the top. Marked inequalities existed in England and America; at the lowest ranks, indentured servants, tenant farmers, and common laborers possessed scant resources and no land. Furthermore, between one-half and two-thirds of white immigrants in the 18th century entered indentured service before or after arriving in the colonies. (Evidence suggests that many who became indentured servants were driven from

England, Scotland, and Wales as unemployment increased markedly during the 17th century; but a considerable number were also felons who were deported to the colonies as indentured servants.[25]) Local courts provided protection for some indentured servants who were beaten or whose term of service, typically four to seven years, was not honored by their masters, but their legal rights were not as complete as in England. Servants were beholden to their masters, who had paid their transportation costs to this country. Owners could try to extend the period of indentured service by appealing to local courts if their servants ran away, swore at them, or committed other petty offenses. Female indentured servants were often denied permission to marry because their masters feared the women would leave their service.[26]

Indentured servants who had completed their terms often had difficulty finding an economic niche for themselves. Lacking funds to purchase land, many became tenant farmers and worked at low wages for landowners. Some became part of the relatively poor and landless population in the small cities of colonial America. Those who purchased land often had to go to relatively cheap land on the frontier, where they encountered danger from Native Americans. Those servants who chose to become apprentices in hopes of entering a trade had to serve an additional seven years as assistants to tradesmen and were often mistreated by their masters.[27]

Although the early cities were small, the sizable numbers of unskilled and semiskilled persons who came to reside in them were subject to the numerous recessions that bedeviled the fragile American economy. In a credit-hungry economy, many Americans became overextended, could not pay debts, and were imprisoned. Produce was often plentiful, but grain exports to Europe were sometimes so great that shortages occurred in American cities. Consumer goods were often scarce in a nation that imported most of its manufactured goods. Nash argues that these urban, white, and landless people often became increasingly aware of differences in wealth, and thus the likelihood of urban unrest in hard times increased.[28]

Riots were common in both England and the American colonies. Sometimes they were provoked by frustration at the slow workings of cumbersome bureaucracies. Periodic food shortages or rising prices of food prompted riots in local jurisdictions, even in the colonies. American squatters—people who inhabited land without having obtained legal title—often rioted to persuade local officials to give them titles or to allow them to purchase their land at reasonable fees. A series of nine major rebellions, each lasting a year or more, erupted in rural areas in the 17th and 18th centuries. These rebellions were waged by persons with a homestead ethic who believed that their land titles had been unfairly seized by trading companies or that their land was excessively taxed by legislatures. Thus, Bacon's Rebellion in 17th-century Virginia involved a number of landless freedmen and indentured servants who protested against the monopoly of land by large owners.[29]

American colonists in 1750, then, had not developed a distinctive culture or set of political institutions. They often thought of themselves as Europeans rather than as occupying an independent status in the New World. English émigrés primarily read literature from England, conversed about English politics, and often intended to return to England once they had obtained sufficient funds.

Patterns of Change

Between 1750 and 1800, a dramatically new society was created. To understand how this came about, we need to analyze the forces and events that powerfully transformed the American colonies. The first enclaves in the early 17th century were semifeudal in nature, with villages and state churches, but that pattern soon changed. Realizing that landless persons could settle freely on open land at the frontier, trading companies decided it was in their interests to sell land to immigrants, who eagerly bought what was offered. When governments were established in the different colonies, they also sold large amounts of land to individuals.

Access to land was the most powerful transforming factor in the New World. Whereas two-thirds of colonists owned land in 1750, only one-fifth of English citizens owned land. As they obtained property, many Americans came to perceive themselves not as common laborers, but as stakeholders in the emerging society. They increasingly demanded to participate in local and colonial politics; as landholders, they often were able to vote. They placed greater emphasis on work and initiative than landless people in England because they realized that their personal economic fate hinged on their ability to produce and sell crops and other commodities, such as candles or garments. The colonies lacked a large, landless, and destitute population, such as that existing in London and other English cities by 1750. This new society was a *landed* one, mostly composed of persons with holdings of between 90 and 160 acres.[30]

Nor did these colonists live in the localistic and static world that had existed in Europe for centuries. As indentured servants finished their terms of service, they often moved onto small plots of land at the frontier, where they were joined by new immigrants from Europe. As land became scarcer on the eastern seaboard, they moved to new areas. In a relatively brief period, huge areas of Pennsylvania, New York State, and the Carolinas became flooded with immigrants. The dynamic and changing nature of this new society was fostered not only by mobility but by population growth owing to the relatively high birthrate and to continuing immigration. The white population in the colonies practically doubled every 20 years, increasing from 1 to 2 million between 1750 and 1770 and from 2 to 4 million from 1770 to 1790.

In a society with such mobility, the semifeudal norms and traditions of the early colonies quickly eroded. Many observers noted that frontier people were a raucous lot; they were often violent, they lacked governmental institutions, and they possessed a fierce individualism.

Maintenance of an official church became increasingly problematic in the various colonies. America soon became a sanctuary for numerous Protestant sects who, despite various "toleration acts" in England, were still subject to widespread persecution; their children were excluded from English universities, their suffrage was subjected to numerous restrictions, and they were forced to tithe to the Church of England. As members of the various sects became representatives in local and colonial government, they urged separation of church and state and termination of the requirement in a number of colonies that citizens pay taxes to support the state church. Separation of church and state, which was made explicit in the Constitution, was inevitable in a country with so many religious sects.

Although England was the birthplace of capitalism and its attendant class of merchants, many English people, especially the landed aristocrats, still viewed capitalism with suspicion. Americans came to embrace it with a fervor and a completeness unknown to the English. In 1750, American society was still largely rural, with only 5 percent of the population living in cities. However, most Americans were small capitalists on their farms, where they labored to produce crops and commodities for export to Europe, which provided a vast market during a period of rapid population growth. Although factories had hardly emerged in the New World, many farmers supplemented their income by producing a wide array of goods—including hats, candles, clothing, and tools—in their homes and barns.[31]

The conflicts of colonial politics further eroded the communal and hierarchical nature of the early settlements. Settlers in the western sections of the colonies demanded funds for a militia to protect them from First Americans and for the construction of roads and other improvements. These demands were often resisted by easterners, and intense competition for the limited public funds ensued. Many colonists soon came to oppose the royal governors appointed by the crown who, they believed, sought to advance the trade and financial interests of the monarchy by exploiting them—for example, by taxing them excessively; by demanding excessive exportation of agricultural products even at the risk of food shortages; by forbidding them from establishing manufacturing that would compete with English goods; and by demanding that trade with England be transmitted in English ships.

Conflict also increased between ordinary people and the American aristocracy. Unlike the long-established and wealthy aristocracy of England, American aristocrats tended to be self-made men who lacked lineage to centuries of noblemen. They were poorer than their English counterparts; few had huge houses and manorial estates. Lacking the trappings of the English aristocracy and enveloped in a society where most people owned land, they commanded less respect from Americans than did the English aristocracy from the English.

The American settlers entered a New World where ancient rights to land, an entrenched aristocracy, and a monarchy did not exist. The absence of these practices, classes, and institutions contributed to an indigenous culture that was increasingly antithetical to them. Had these practices, classes, and institutions already existed in the New World, colonists would not only have been reminded of them, they would have encountered sanctions for not honoring them.

THE AMERICAN REVOLUTION AS CATALYST

An array of economic, social, and religious factors were antithetical to the hierarchy, social controls, and deference that the American colonists brought with them from Europe, but the colonists had not yet decisively overthrown the old order, even if they constantly squabbled with royal governors of the colonies, chafed at various taxes and regulations that the Crown imposed on them, and established legislatures or assemblies in the various colonies. According to historian Gordon Wood, the American Revolution was the catalyst that moved Americans to define their differences from the Old World and to forge a distinctive set of institutions.[32]

What were the events leading up to the Revolution? King George was worried about the costs incurred by the Crown in seeking to protect the colonies from Native Americans. Partly to offset these costs, the Crown exacted new taxes on a wide range of goods. Already resentful of the various controls and taxes that the Crown imposed on the colonies, many colonial leaders were outraged by this new burden.

Many colonists were familiar with the arguments of English parliamentary leaders who had sought to eclipse the power of the monarchy for decades and had obtained from it many concessions that increased the power of the Parliament. Some of these leaders even wanted to end the monarchy in favor of a republic. Drawing on the arguments of these parliamentary leaders, colonial leaders like Thomas Jefferson and James Madison developed a rationale for making the colonies independent from the Crown; these efforts culminated in the Declaration of Independence of 1776.

The demand for independence and the associated attack on the monarchy drew a wide and favorable response because large numbers of colonists, ensconced on their own plots of land and wanting to participate more fully in their own governance, had no wish to return to an old regime that might rescind their economic and political gains. The imposition of taxes on their goods by the Crown in the 1760s was a symbol of a different (and English) society that was not consonant with the New World. Were they to relent to the Crown, might they endanger not merely their political right to resist taxes imposed on them in London but their landholding, entrepreneurial, and individualistic culture? Might not those American aristocrats who still fancied themselves as possessing the prerogatives of English aristocrats try to repress the political freedom and power that ordinary people were obtaining in the New World? When viewed narrowly, the American Revolution was simply a rebellion against an overreaching Crown that insisted on its right to impose taxes without consulting the colonies' elected assemblies. When viewed more broadly, however, the Revolution was the catalyst for colonists to define their new society in terms markedly different from the customs of the Old World.[33]

When King George agreed to rescind only some of his new taxes and when he did not honor the Americans' insistence on independence, war ensued; it lasted seven years. By the time the

American Revolution had ended, about one-tenth of white males had joined the militia. The sheer length of the conflict dramatized the formal separation from England and encouraged widespread acceptance of a new ideology of republicanism that deemphasized hierarchy, lauded individualism, favored the toil of ordinary people, and sought democracy. The battle against the Crown was supplemented, moreover, by intensive conflict *within* the colonies. Many Loyalists (or Tories), often drawn from the ranks of the large landowners and the aristocratic class, did not participate in the Revolution; some resettled in Canada and elsewhere.

Although it fostered widespread acceptance of an ideology that extolled individualism, the leveling of distinctions between people, and freedom, the American Revolution may be contrasted to the French or Russian Revolutions, in which social classes were pitted against one another and revolutionaries sought to redistribute wealth. A host of research strongly suggests that the American Revolution, though accompanied by a surge in idealism and sacrifice, had relatively limited effects on social reform. It did not help to obtain legal parity for women, to provide just treatment to Native Americans, to end slavery, or to reduce the marked inequality between social classes.[34] Our purpose is not to question the legitimacy of the colonial grievances but merely to underscore their limited and focused nature, which did not include the grist of true revolutions: the questioning of social relations *within* a society and between its social classes. As most Americans possessed land, no large class of landless and urbanized people existed (as in the French Revolution), and no large class of landless peasants existed (as in the Russian Revolution). These American revolutionaries fought both for independence *and* to establish a society grounded on individualism and freedom, but not to effect dramatic changes in the nation's social structure.

The achievement of independence enhanced the self-image of the colonists, who had managed to outwit and outduel a major world power. They confidently believed they could create a utopia of yeoman farmers by embracing capitalism and democratic institutions. Europeans such as Locke, by contrast, knew that their ideas could be only partially realized in societies encumbered by centuries of tradition as well as by classes and institutions that resisted change. As Commager put it, the Europeans imagined the Enlightenment while the Americans created it.[35]

It is fitting that land ownership figured prominently in the ideology of colonial leaders like Thomas Jefferson. We have noted how the widespread ownership of land promoted individualism and a leveling of class distinctions. The importance that colonial leaders attached to land ownership is illustrated by a portion of a letter that Jefferson wrote to James Madison in 1785 during a visit to France. In the letter, Jefferson contrasted social conditions in France and in the colonies:

> The property of this country is absolutely co-centered in a very few hands, having revenues of from half a million of guineas a year downwards. These employ the flower of the country as servants, some of them having as many as 200 domestics, not labouring. They employ also a great number of manufacturers, and tradesmen, and lastly the class of labouring husbandmen. But after all these comes the most numerous of all the classes, that is, the poor who cannot find work. I asked myself what could be the reason that so many should be permitted to beg who are willing to work, in a country where there is very considerable proportion of uncultivated lands? ... The earth is given as common stock for man to labour and live on ... it is too soon yet in our country to say that every man who cannot find employment but who can find uncultivated land, shall be at liberty to cultivate it, paying a moderate rent. But it is not too soon to provide by every possible means that as few as possible shall be without a little portion of land. The small landowners are the most precious part of a state.[36]

FROM REVOLUTION TO
LIMITED GOVERNMENT

If the Revolution brought independence and the rejection of many ideas and institutions drawn from England, it also ushered in an era of limited government, in which the federal government's responsibility for social policy would be stifled.

When they finally achieved their independence in 1783, the Americans confronted a dilemma. If the 13 colonies became separate nations, they would confront many problems. Trade would be difficult with 13 separate currencies. They could not easily fashion treaties with foreign nations that had designs on frontier lands—especially Spain, France, and England—if they lacked a common foreign policy and navy. They could not easily fend off Native Americans on the frontier without a shared militia. Nor could they easily plan and build roads and canals across their boundaries if they remained independent. At the same time, each of the colonies jealously guarded its prerogatives; none wanted to yield excessive authority to a central government that might usurp its freedom in a manner akin to King George and the English Parliament.

They turned to the difficult task of constructing a Constitution in 1787. Meeting in Philadelphia, 55 delegates from all states except Rhode Island commenced their work in May 1787 and approved a document in September. It became the law of the land in June 1788 when the ninth colony, New Hampshire, ratified it.

Although they realized that they needed their government to have *some* powers, the framers of the Constitution were also obsessed with the dangers of an oppressive central government. To avoid this possibility, they created a complex system of checks and balances, including a popularly elected House of Representatives, senators elected by legislatures in their states, a president elected by an electoral college rather than by direct election, and an independent judiciary. To further circumscribe the federal government, the framers enumerated its specific powers; the list included the right to issue currency, to form a militia, and to make treaties. (Furthermore, as we

note subsequently, they specifically reserved to the states all powers not given to the federal government when they added the Tenth Amendment to the Constitution as part of the Bill of Rights.)[37]

The Constitution had momentous implications for the development of social policies in the new Republic. By not enumerating social policy as one of the federal government's powers, the framers intended that it fall entirely within the province of state and local government. Until well into the 20th century, many presidents and legislators, as well as justices, assumed that it was unconstitutional for the Congress to enact social policies.

Because the founders realized that the government would need to evolve to meet the changing needs of the nation, they inserted four provisions that *eventually* provided a legal rationale for the development of federal social policy:

1. They gave the federal government the power to regulate interstate commerce, which was used in the 20th century to regulate the working conditions of workers whose companies shipped goods to other states.

2. They included a clause that allowed the federal government to enact laws that furthered the nation's "general welfare." This ill-defined clause was later used by social reformers to justify a range of social interventions.

3. The founders stipulated that the federal government could "make all laws that shall be necessary and proper for carrying into execution the foregoing [enumerated] powers." Like the general welfare clause, this phrase was sufficiently vague to justify a broad range of legislation.

4. By allowing the Constitution to be amended, the founders provided a mechanism for change. Constitutional amendments protected the rights of African Americans and other groups in the wake of the Civil War.

As originally written, however, the Constitution must be viewed as retarding the development of federal social programs because it did not mention social welfare policies and appeared to restrict the federal government to specific and relatively limited powers. (See Insert 3.3.) By contrast, the French Constitution, which was written a few years later, outlawed slavery, guaranteed all citizens the right to work, urged humane care of the poor, and declared education to be a public obligation.[38] Moreover, as we discuss subsequently, the Constitution was both a sexist and a racist document severely limiting the rights of women and persons of color.

Although the Constitution ceded considerable power to them, local and colonial governments were extraordinarily weak in the colonial era. It is true that they imposed taxes and regulations on local citizens and businesses (for example, they often established prices and wages), required males to work certain numbers of days on roads and other public improvements, and constructed many roads and bridges (sometimes with tolls). But these local governments existed in an environment that was not conducive to the development of major powers, as Greene makes clear:

> With only a tiny bureaucracy and no police, a localized judiciary system that rarely met more than fifteen to thirty days in any given year, and legislators that in peacetime were rarely in session for more than a month in any given year, government was small, intermittent, and inexpensive. Except during wartime, taxes were low, and the only public activities that engaged most men were infrequent militia or jury service and some more frequent participation in vital public works such as building and repairing bridges and roads … [W]hile they wanted enough government to secure peace and to maintain … civil order, most Americans were … in favor of just so much government as will do justice, protect property, and defend the country.[39]

LEGITIMATING LIMITED GOVERNMENT

The framers wanted to put strict limits on the power of the federal government, but they did not agree

about *how* limited the new government would be. During the two terms of President George Washington, a heated battle developed between two factions led, respectively, by Thomas Jefferson, Washington's Secretary of State, and Alexander Hamilton, his Secretary of the Treasury. A self-made man with aristocratic inclinations, Hamilton wanted a relatively strong central government that would pursue mercantilist policies akin to the Crown. He wanted the federal government to invest resources in roads, canals, and bridges; to establish a national bank to oversee the economy; to fund promising new economic projects; to impose considerable taxes to fund these projects and pay off debts that remained from fighting the Revolutionary War; and to develop a strong navy and militia. Hamilton favored a relatively loose interpretation of the Constitution. While acknowledging that the Constitution mentioned only certain powers, Hamilton believed that it implied other powers, such as the power to establish a National Bank. By contrast, Jefferson favored a limited federal government; he supported "strict constructionism," according to which the government would be limited to the powers enumerated in the Constitution. He wanted the American economy to center upon agriculture; opposed a National Bank on the grounds that it was not mentioned in the Constitution; opposed mercantilist policies; wanted low federal taxes; and opposed a standing army.[40]

Jefferson's view of a limited government was shared not merely by many federal legislators but by many people in the various states. So-called anti-federalists had even sought to prevent ratification of the Constitution, which they believed conferred excessive powers on the federal government. Partly at their insistence, the first 10 amendments to the Constitution (the so-called Bill of Rights) were added in 1791 so as to protect citizens' rights from capricious actions of the federal government.

Often caught between the forces of Jefferson and Hamilton, President Washington tried to define the powers of the central government; usually he sided with Hamilton. His patience was tested on many occasions. One such incident was the so-called Whiskey Rebellion. Needing funds to retire

---

INSERT 3.3   Critical Analysis: The Omission of Social Policy from the Constitution

Speculate why the framers did *not* discuss social policy in the Constitution. Consider such factors as:

- the absence, in a rural society with small towns, of the social problems that exist in an urbanized society;

- the belief that the colonists were creating a society that would not have the major social problems that bedeviled Europe, such as poverty or other problems endemic to large cities like London;

- the legacy of local poor law traditions and private philanthropy, which led the framers to assume that local institutions would suffice;

- the widespread assumption that the federal government would possess relatively scant resources. While the Constitution empowered the federal government to "raise revenue," many framers opposed the imposition of large federal taxes.

---

the national debt and to fund the government, the Congress enacted an excise tax on distilled liquor at Hamilton's request. However, in western Pennsylvania, local insurgents questioned the federal government's right to impose these taxes. This tax revolt was quelled only after Washington personally accompanied troops into Pennsylvania.[41]

The battle between the Hamiltonians and the Jeffersonians persisted during Washington's tenure and during the presidency of John Adams. Then, in 1800, Jefferson narrowly defeated Adams in a tumultuous presidential contest. In his two terms, Jefferson implemented his limited-government vision; he sharply reduced expenditures and slashed taxes.

Defeated by Jefferson, the federalists soon disappeared as a viable force. With few exceptions, all of the presidents of the 19th century subscribed to Jefferson's views of limited government. As we shall see when discussing the Gilded Age in the decades after the Civil War, however, they frequently used federal resources and powers to help corporations and the railroads. Using Jefferson's doctrine of strict constructionism, none of them supported the use of federal resources to fund major social programs other than war pensions. The Jeffersonian influence was so pervasive and long-lasting that it is not possible to understand modern American conservatives without placing them in the context of Jefferson's ethos.

Some readers may wonder why a text on social policy devotes so much time to distant constitu-

tional developments and to these early disputes about federal power. However, this examination of the founders' philosophies clarifies an important aspect of social policy in the United States: that a strong defense of the central government's role in social welfare is relatively recent in American history. By contrast, in England and other European countries, extensive central government policy and regulatory roles existed even before the 18th century. Not until the 1930s, or almost 150 years after the founding of the republic, did Americans develop strong social policy roles for the federal government.

POSITIVE RESPONSES TO SOCIAL NEED

Americans inherited the same combination of positive and punitive social policies that existed in England in the 17th and 18th centuries, but they often did not enforce negative policies, on the assumption that pauperism and even poverty would not become widespread in their land-owning utopia. Furthermore, most early settlers brought with them the tradition of regulation of local economic affairs that had been so pervasive in Europe. Strange as it seems to contemporary Americans, cities, counties, and colonial assemblies limited wages and prices, granted business licenses to merchants, controlled the exportation of grain and other commodities, and regulated the rights and obligations of indentured servants and apprentices. These various regulations did not necessarily benefit poor persons, as they could be devised in a manner that assisted those with wealth or those masters who had indentured or apprenticed labor. Nonetheless, colonists believed that government should assume a wide range of functions to further economic development and to assist persons in the lower economic strata. From England, the colonists also brought with them the mercantile tradition, which gave government major roles in promoting job development and economic growth through the building of roads and bridges and other capital improvement projects. The development of regulatory policies at the local and state levels must be regarded as a positive social welfare response to social and economic needs.[42]

A tradition of private philanthropy developed with remarkable rapidity and often led to projects that were jointly funded by government and private donors. Benjamin Franklin participated in many partnerships between the public and private sectors—for example, the development of libraries, firefighting services, orphanages, and educational programs. The prevalence of Protestantism in the New World promoted the ethic of charitable giving. Wealth was often perceived by early Protestants as a mixed blessing; although it was the proper reward for a life of hard work, it could also promote laziness, pride, and greed—traits that were viewed by many colonists as sinful. Donating to charity became a way of easing this guilt about material possessions. Many of the earliest Puritan settlers believed that good works were morally correct but could not in themselves influence the Lord to grant salvation; however, by the middle of the 18th century, a growing number of clergy and citizens believed that moral living could increase the likelihood of achieving salvation. The sermons of preachers of the Great Awakening, a grassroots movement to revitalize and personalize Protestant religion during the 18th century, denied that good works could merit salvation but emphasized the importance of benevolence as a *sign* that one was saved.[43]

As in England, church parishes were a major source of charity. The Puritan churches of Massachusetts Bay, for example, elected officers whose major responsibility was to oversee sick and impoverished members of the congregation. Many American Protestants likened church organizations to extended families that cared for their members in times of adversity.[44]

Officials in colonial and local governments also continued the tradition of the English Poor Law by requiring the election or appointment of officials in local parishes who would collect taxes to pay for poor relief. Colonial assemblies were particularly generous in assisting persons who had been wounded or disabled in battles with Native Americans on the frontier. They often funded direct assistance to those individuals, without relying on local jurisdictions and without imposing the punitive policies that characterized other forms of assistance. Thomas Jefferson's portrayal of assistance to the poor in Virginia in the 18th century underscores generosity to those persons perceived to be incapable of working, even though he notes that vagabonds were sometimes placed in workhouses:

> The poor, unable to support themselves, are maintained by an assessment on the tytheable persons in their parish. This assessment is levied and administered by twelve persons in each parish, called vestrymen, originally chosen by the housekeepers of the parish, but afterwards filling vacancies in their own body by their own choice. These are usually the most discreet farmers, so distributed through their parish that every part of it may be under the immediate eye of some one of them. They are well acquainted with the details and economy of private life, and they find sufficient inducements to execute their charge well, in their philanthropy, in the approbation of their neighbours, and the distinction which that gives them. The poor who have neither property, friends, nor strength to labour, are boarded in the houses of good farmers, to whom a

stipulated sum is annually paid. To those who are able to help themselves a little, or have friends from whom they derive some succours, inadequate however to their full maintenance, supplementary aids are given, which enable them to live comfortably in their own houses, or in the houses of their friends. Vagabonds, without visible property or vocation, are placed in workhouses, where they are well cloathed, fed, lodged, and made to labour. Nearly the same method of providing for the poor prevails through all our states; and from Savannah to Portsmouth you will seldom meet a beggar.[45]

In some jurisdictions, such as Boston, widowed or divorced women with children successfully resisted the tendency to place all dependent persons in poorhouses and received outdoor relief.[46] Of course, these benign interpretations of the workings of poor law institutions were balanced by harsher interpretations, which we note later. Colonial courts also assumed a range of social welfare functions. Many children became orphans in colonial society because of their parents' early deaths from plagues, accidents, and childbirth. Local courts oversaw the economic affairs of these orphans to ensure that they received funds granted to them by their deceased parents' wills, which were often given in the form of proceeds over a period of years from the sale of livestock in the estate.[47]

Early Americans often supported the development of policies to equalize opportunity precisely because they favored self-improvement. Americans emphasized some opportunity-enhancing policies even before the American Revolution, which expanded options for many citizens. Some favored universal and public education, though universal education was not developed until the 19th century. Suffrage was generally tied to a property qualification, but it was already granted to more persons than in England. Perhaps the largest social welfare program of the colonial period and the early republic, however, was land distribution. Although wealthy people bought large amounts of land in early Virginia, many smaller farmers were able to acquire land from the Crown, trading companies chartered by the Crown, and colonial governments.[48] Americans also developed private philanthropic institutions, which tended to support opportunity-enhancing educational, health, and self-help projects that reflected the new society's preoccupation with self-improvement.

PUNITIVE POLICIES

Just as the English had done, many Americans viewed persons who were unemployed as undeserving and, hence, favored punitive treatment—in other words, indoor relief. In Massachusetts in 1780, vagabonds, paupers, and indentured servants were not granted the right to vote. The institution of the workhouse gained considerable popularity in colonial America. As early as 1688, for example, the House of Burgesses in Virginia recommended that every county build a workhouse. A frenzied period of construction occurred in New York State in the early and middle 18th century. Jurisdictions that lacked the funds to build workhouses adopted other punitive devices. A poor person or family could be auctioned to a low bidder who would take care of them in return for payments from local officials; a child could be placed as an indentured servant under a willing master; and persons without means could find themselves summarily escorted to the boundaries of a jurisdiction, as the American colonies had enacted laws of settlement similar to those in England.

Americans also took a dim view of "moral crimes." Many jurisdictions enacted laws prohibiting adultery and fornication, swearing, or even malicious gossiping. In colonial Virginia, persons found guilty of these crimes were generally made to devote a certain number of hours to public works—for example, the construction of a local bridge. Alcoholism was a major problem in the American colonies and sometimes led to imprisonment. Major crimes were similarly met with harsh treatment. Debtors were often imprisoned, even when they had no means of paying debts that were due to disability or health problems. As in England, capital punishment was extensively employed, sometimes even for petty theft, and executions were often public events attended by throngs of people.

Social welfare institutions did not extend assistance to African Americans, who were defined to be outside the social compact; this policy prevented slave owners from freeing their slaves when they could no longer work or were sick—actions that would have raised the poor law costs of local jurisdictions. Various colonies enacted laws that made slaves ineligible for assistance from poor law institutions and that forbade their owners from releasing them when they were ill or aged.[49]

The settlers lived in a violent world. Most of them possessed firearms to hunt, to fend off Native Americans, and to obviate the creation of standing armies. They waged several major wars, fought Native Americans, engaged in various sectarian and sectional battles, fought in taverns, participated in various rural and urban riots, and witnessed public executions and lashings.[50]

OPPRESSION OF VULNERABLE POPULATIONS OR OUT-GROUPS

If the colonists were sometimes punitive or harsh in their treatment of white citizens, such as indigent people, they were often brutal in their treatment of First Americans, African slaves, and women.

Oppression of Women

Contemporary historians have analyzed the lives of women in medieval society and concluded that, despite notable exceptions such as female royalty, they lived within relatively restrictive boundaries. Virtually without exception, people viewed both society and the family as hierarchies in medieval times—and the husband was seen as the superior member of the family, to which his wife and children were subordinate. Indeed, as Fraser notes, England was governed by feudal law "where a wife passed from the guardianship of her father to her husband [who] also stood in relation to her as a feudal lord." As the subordinate party, women were expected to be obedient, to confine themselves to household duties (or, in pastoral areas, to those farming duties that were most related to the household, such as milking cows, making cheese, and making clothing).[51]

It was widely assumed that women were "weaker vessels"—that is, inferior to males not just physically but also morally and intellectually. Prior to the 17th century in England, virtually no women were literate, and educational reformers in that century, who gave some women exposure to education, refrained from allowing them to learn subjects like Latin, a language essential in an era that emphasized classical studies.

The economic roles of women were circumscribed. The guilds and crafts that developed to regulate skilled work in the towns and cities were dominated by men; women were excluded or, at best, allowed to be second-class members. Much of the work that women undertook—as domestic servants, small retailers, spinsters, or midwives—was not organized into guilds or crafts, and thus women were deprived of the kinds of security that guilds and crafts afforded. Though husbands and wives often worked together in the fields in feudal settings, the husbands generally passed the rights to farm strips of land to their sons; consequently, daughters lacked land rights.[52]

Women had few legal protections in the medieval period. The Church of England provided wives some protections against cruelty, lack of support, and desertion. Divorce was not sanctioned, but women could petition the Church for separation; often, though, they made these petitions only after their husbands had left them.[53]

Accustomed to hierarchy in Europe, the colonists also assigned authority in families and in society to men. Men concerned themselves with farming, business, politics, and professions, whereas women were relegated to domestic matters and the raising of children. Although, on occasion, a woman whose husband died might assume management of a business, women generally refrained from seeking expanded economic and social roles.[54]

The Declaration of Independence and the American Constitution made no mention of "women" in their many passages. No one even thought to give women the right to vote. It was widely assumed that rights granted to persons in the Constitution applied only to males. It was no accident that the Declaration of Independence authored by Thomas Jefferson stated that "we hold these truths to be self-evident, that all *men* are created equal …" Feminism, in the modern sense of the word, did not exist in colonial America, even among such articulate women as Abigail Adams, the wife of John Adams. Virtually no one considered the possibility that women might vote. The colonists developed elaborate codes of etiquette that defined patterns of deference among the various members of the family, in a hierarchy extending from the husband to the wife to the children. Women could own property and sign contracts when they were unmarried or widowed, but they did not usually retain property or sign contracts when married. Children were the legal property of husbands after marriages had been officially dissolved, even when the husband had been unfaithful or abusive. Women were not allowed to serve on juries. Except for the Quakers, Protestant sects did not allow women to assume major roles in church governance. Married women were not expected to work outside the home, although women in lower-income groups most likely had to earn money to survive in many cases. Already in the colonial period, the wages of working women, married or unmarried, were far less than those of men who undertook comparable work. Furthermore, the segregation of working women into poorly paid work—as small retailers, seamstresses, laundresses, and domestic servants, for example—suggested that the feminization of poverty, a term used in the contemporary period, had relevance to many women in urban areas in the colonial era. Women were excluded altogether from the professions of law and medicine.[55]

Religious traditions encouraged colonists to believe that women were inferior to men. In medieval times, Catholic doctrine stressed that Eve had brought sin into the world by persuading Adam to eat the forbidden fruit in the Garden of Eden. Though a number of thinkers in the Renaissance criticized the notion that women were morally or intellectually inferior to men, the Protestantism of the 17th century retained strong misogynist (sexist) tendencies, including the portrayal of women as seducers. However, Protestant sects did support minimal literacy for women so that they could read the Bible.[56]

Although limited in their roles, women in the colonial period were probably not so restricted as women in the 19th century. The high mortality rate in colonial society meant that many women assumed responsibility for the trades or businesses of their deceased husbands. Because society desperately needed labor, women were able to enter some trades. Midwives delivered children. In agriculture, women not only helped their husbands run farms but also produced candles and cloth in a society that lacked manufacturing industries. Much like Gandhi in 20th-century India, women made homespun cloth during the American Revolution to reduce dependence on English imports. However, we should not exaggerate the economic roles of women in colonial times; as Harris notes, they often assumed economic roles only *after* their husbands had died, and they performed them in a larger context of subordination.[57]

The domestic burdens of women were also less onerous in the 18th century than in the 19th century because children generally entered trades at the age of 10 or 11. By the mid-19th century, however, children were increasingly seen as needing extended and intensive parenting, and women were required to devote a major portion of their lives to parenting and spousal responsibilities.

Some evidence exists that the economic conditions of women deteriorated toward the end of the 18th century. One contributing factor was that husbands, who often died before their wives, began to leave most of their estates to their children. In addition, although outdoor relief for women who were single heads of households had prevailed in earlier periods, women who could not fend for themselves were increasingly forced into newly constructed poorhouses. Some jurisdictions did allow women entering marriage to construct settlements that retained their rights to the property that was already theirs. However, few women availed themselves of these settlements; in consequence, they lost control of their property, both within the marriage and when their husbands died, divorced, or left them.[58]

Women suffered extraordinary hardship because no adequate method of birth control existed. Aside from abstinence and coitus interruptus, mostly herbal and other folk methods were used to prevent pregnancy; these were of dubious value. Moreover, because procreation was widely regarded as the ultimate purpose of marriage, few women used birth control at all, except to increase the interval between childbirths by means of abstinence. Women tended to marry in their early 20s and to have children every other year; a typical family might have seven children or more. It is estimated that as many as one in five women died during childbirth or from the toll of successive pregnancies. Moreover, many women were pregnant at the point of marriage—probably around 20 percent in some jurisdictions.[59]

Women in the colonial period gained some benefit from certain Protestant beliefs. In particular, American Protestants' strong belief that families should be "peaceable" and intact led them to support laws that granted divorces on grounds of desertion (the most common reason women sought divorce) and cruelty. (Most divorce petitions were initiated by men, but they were often rejected by local courts.) Laws existed in many colonies, as well, that forbade physical abuse of women and children and that punished rapists, although then (as now) many rapists escaped punishment by alleging that the woman had consented.[60]

Oppression of First Americans

In medieval Europe, most people lived in relatively homogeneous societies of white persons and had little or no contact with persons of other races. As Sanders suggests, the idea of race was only "dim and sporadic" for most Europeans during the Middle Ages.[61] But race assumed fateful dimensions in the minds of many Europeans by the late 15th century, as explorers like Columbus made contact with native peoples in the Caribbean and in Central and South America—and as Europeans, desperate for labor, sought to import African slaves into these regions.

Depicted in older history books as a heroic figure (Figure 3.1), Columbus has been portrayed less flatteringly by modern historians. After a first voyage in 1492 that was primarily a trip of discovery, Columbus set sail on a second voyage—complete with 17 ships and 1,200 men—intending to colonize the New World.[62] When he discovered that a small settlement called Navidad, left from the first voyage, had been burned and its inhabitants murdered, Columbus's dream of concord between the indigenous people and the Spanish ended. Dor-Ner suggests that

> the Navidad incident would set a pattern of violence and mistrust between Europeans and Native Americans that would be played out in blood as successive waves of Spanish, English, and French colonialists swept through the Americas … this poisonous attitude would in time … echo at the Little Big Horn, where Sitting Bull took no prisoners [and] would be brutally distilled in the infamous remark of General Philip Sheridan: "The only good Indians I ever saw were dead."[63]

Columbus and his Spanish successors quickly devised a method of controlling the indigenous people by placing them in a position akin to feudal serfs. Though indigenous people in their villages were allowed to keep their property, they were forced to give most of their produce to the conquerors in return for "protection." Moreover, tens of thousands of them were conscripted for forced labor in mining and other endeavors. The Pope and also Queen Isabella of Spain often tried to place moral constraints on Columbus and other conquistadors, but they had

© Bettmann/Corbis

FIGURE 3.1   The clash of cultures in the New World.

scant success in stopping the brutalization of the indigenous population, despite the protests of a handful of courageous priests.

The early forays into the Caribbean were soon followed by the pillaging of native settlements in Central and South America. Far more deadly to the indigenous people than the violence and servitude imposed on them by the conquerors were the diseases brought by the Europeans; they had no natural resistance to smallpox, measles, diphtheria, whooping cough, the bubonic plague, typhoid fever, cholera, scarlet fever, and influenza and died by the millions from these various diseases. In Central Mexico, the native population declined from 11 million in 1519 to 2.5 million in 1597—a staggering loss that was repeated throughout Central and South America and in the Caribbean.[64]

Medieval culture did not prepare the Europeans to resist exploitation of the native populations or to outlaw the use of slaves in the New World. As Christians, for example, the Europeans were prone to divide humankind into two groups: Christians and heathens. The Church had long held the notion that heathens could be placed in servitude once they had "rejected" Christianity; on this principle, the Crusades had sought to conquer Muslim peoples in the Middle East. Feudalism provided the notion that native villages could be controlled by recreating the feudal equivalent of serfdom; in the New World, far removed from the ancient protections that had provided some assistance to European serfs, the indigenous population and then the slaves could be exploited with little interference from European courts, the Church, or the Crown.

Nor should we forget racism. Placed in contact with people of different racial backgrounds, the Europeans were quick to interpret differences in skin color and costume as signs of primitive, heathen, savage, and lazy dispositions. As native peoples and slaves physically resisted exploitation, the Europeans could seize on this behavior as proof of their savagery. Nor did the Europeans develop racist ideas only during the conquest of the New World; they had long imagined that cannibalistic and savage people lived in undiscovered territories.[65]

Historians' early estimates placed the First American population of North America (excluding Mexico) at only 1 million persons, but recent research suggests that, in fact, this area was densely populated by Native Americans, who numbered some 10 million persons in 1490. Every portion of North America was occupied. This huge and dispersed population—including coastal tribes on the Pacific and Atlantic, tribes inhabiting the forests east of the Mississippi, the Plains tribes that hunted buffalo, tribes that occupied the Rocky Mountains, and tribes that lived in the deserts of the southwestern and western portions of the continent—represented a major barrier for the white settlers because these tribes occupied the land, the most valuable resource in the New World.[66]

The early colonists quickly encountered two groups of First Americans: a string of tribes that occupied coastal areas from New England to Florida and a group of tribes that inhabited inland areas like the Appalachian Mountains. Colonists in the earliest settlements in Virginia and Massachusetts took the view that First Americans in the coastal tribes could be converted to Christianity and, in the meantime, could help settlers by familiarizing them with native crops and hunting techniques. Early settlements in Massachusetts established "praying colonies," where converted First Americans lived as part of the community. The settlers were certain that the First Americans would choose Western culture not only so as to gain salvation but also to obtain its technological benefits; how could they, the colonists reasoned, retain their nomadic, un-Christian, and primitive existence when offered the benefits of civilization and Christianity?[67] This expectation was naive on many counts. First Americans valued their own culture, which differed markedly from the settlers'. The First Americans worshipped their own deities, did not collect or value property, led a nomadic life, and were content with a subsistence existence that required only as much work as was needed for survival.

As the numbers of white settlers increased, it became obvious that First American culture was endangered. Once they had given up feudal strip farming and communal property, many of the earliest settlers began to develop and enclose fields, much as the English landowners had done; this practice quickly depleted the First Americans' lands. If First Americans resisted, colonists cited their violence as evidence that they were savages beyond any hope of conversion to Christianity. If they did *not* resist, the relentless expansion of white settlements continued unabated. The settlers also conducted their share of unprovoked violence—for example, because some group within their settlement enjoyed slaughtering First Americans, because they were overcome with fear as they heard of other violence, or because they wished to retaliate for some earlier violence. Petty theft by a First American led in one case to the massacre of an entire tribe.[68]

As in the Caribbean, the spread of diseases, such as smallpox, cholera, and diphtheria, was even more devastating to First Americans than was warfare. As these diseases were wholly new to the First Americans, they lacked biological resistance to them. By roughly 1675, the coastal tribes extending from New England to the Carolinas had been virtually eliminated; the few survivors pushed westward to join with still-powerful inland tribes.

The inland tribes in and around the Appalachian Mountains proved able to resist the white settlers until the mid-18th century. Their remarkable resilience was made possible by their geographic remoteness from the coastal settlements and by their ingenuity in developing alliances with the French and adapting their hunting practices to provide furs to the white settlers' commercial markets.

The white settlers could have agreed to permanently cede large portions of lands on the frontier to the First Americans, but they did not do so for several reasons. England and the trading companies, which had established the white settlements in the first instance to provide raw materials and markets for the English mercantile system, supported continuing migration inland for furs and other commodities that could be used in England. Moreover, the colonists believed that land was created by God to be farmed and that forest and other unfarmed land occupied by nonfarming First Americans was wasted land that should be given to (or taken by) the white settlers.[69]

The settlers attempted to wrest the land from the First Americans in a manner that would make their exploitation appear to be compatible with moral codes. They successfully used the seemingly legal device of the treaty; by this means, they created the impression that First Americans had voluntarily and legally ceded land to the colonists. First Americans were made to sign under threat of coercion, while intoxicated, or in exchange for money or gifts. When the First Americans stopped teaching their children to use bows, they could no longer obtain food without guns, and so white settlers could entice them to sign treaties by offering them guns and other commodities. To decrease their dependence on the settlers, one tribe tried to revive ancient hunting skills in the mid-18th century, but few of them had the patience to undergo the years of practice required to use arrows when guns were available.[70]

However, the settlers were not so successful in obtaining lands from the inland tribes. Tribes in an area extending from New York State to the Ohio

Valley joined in a common negotiating alliance; their shrewd bargaining led the British Crown to draw a line, known as the Proclamation Line of 1763, that separated settlers' lands from First Americans' lands on the western frontier. (The Crown was willing to make this concession to thwart alliances between the First Americans and the French, who vigorously contested the English for possession of portions of the New World.) The Crown had difficulty enforcing this line, however, because individual settlers, trading companies, and colonies relentlessly sought lands beyond it. After the American Revolution, the Americans displayed far less resolve in enforcing the line than had the English.[71]

Inland tribes such as the Iroquois in the North and the Cherokees in the South were doomed, however. As the frequency of their contact with white settlers increased, they proved as vulnerable to the fatal diseases as their coastal counterparts had been. When they altered their hunting patterns to collect furs, as a means of purchasing guns and other products, they dispersed their tribal settlements and thus made them more vulnerable to attack. The white settlers soon employed treaties, as well as brute force, to displace them from their traditional lands. The ability of First Americans to resist the white settlers was further diminished by animosities between tribes, which were sometimes rooted in traditional rivalries and sometimes provoked by the increasing scarcity of land as the white settlers advanced. As the 19th century began, First Americans were in retreat from large areas immediately beyond the Appalachian Mountains and were being pushed into the inner and western recesses of the North American continent.

Even when some colonial leaders tried to develop positive solutions to help First Americans, they approached the problem simplistically, as is illustrated by George Washington's proposed "solution" (see Insert 3.4).

Oppression of African Slaves

Slavery had existed in Roman times, and Christians had long enslaved Muslims, but the numbers of slaves involved were relatively small, and slavery had ended in Europe by the end of the 14th century. To fill minor labor shortages, Portugal and Spain began using Africans as slaves in their domestic economies in the 15th century. Even this minor use of slaves might have ended had Columbus and numerous successors not established colonies in the New World, first in the Caribbean and then in Central and South America (Figure 3.2).[72]

The wholesale deaths of the indigenous populations from disease and overwork created an economic dilemma for the Europeans when they introduced the labor-intensive crops of sugar and then tobacco in the Caribbean and South America. To find laborers for these crops, the Europeans, drawing on their experience with slavery, decided to import vast numbers of Africans to the New World. By a quirk of biology, these African slaves proved to be relatively resistant to European diseases; thus, not only did they survive, they could be used as a self-replenishing source of labor. Moreover, the huge African population could be regularly raided for a seemingly endless supply of laborers. By 1670, Portuguese Brazil had at least 200,000 slaves, and the English had at least 20,000 slaves in Barbados.

The New World was a labor-hungry society because land had to be cleared, roads built, and crops raised in a harsh environment. Labor was particularly needed in Virginia and the Carolinas, where the settlers had decided to stake their economic existence on tobacco, a labor-intensive crop. Native Americans were a potential source of labor, but they were not willing to work in the settlers' fields and could not be easily enslaved because they could escape to the wilderness. White indentured servants became the major source of agricultural labor in the early Southern colonies, but they also proved unsuitable because many of them objected to the backbreaking work in the intolerable summer heat and had to be replaced when their prescribed term of indentured service was at an end. They posed a political problem as well, as the freed indentured servants roamed the American countryside and agitated against oppressive working conditions when they lacked funds to purchase their own land. When the English economy improved in the mid-17th century and the harsh working conditions

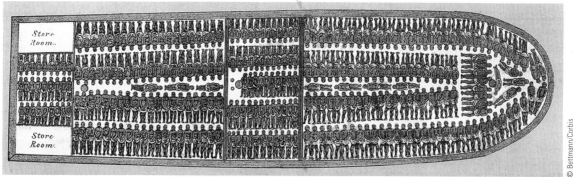

FIGURE 3.2 The slave trade.

of the tobacco colonies became well known, it was increasingly difficult to recruit the English as indentured servants.[73]

Massive importation of Africans was delayed, however, because the death rate from malaria and other epidemics was so high that planters would have lost most of their slaves. When the death rate declined, the advantages of slaves as a source of labor became obvious. Slaves were kept for life rather than for brief terms and provided a self-replenishing source of labor; the planters would be spared the task of continually recruiting and importing indentured servants. The political and social problems of accommodating freed servants were obviated because slaves were not released. Slaves could be brutally disciplined without the surveillance of local courts; by contrast, indentured ser-

vants could be whipped only with consultation from local courts and could request a hearing if they believed they had been mistreated.

For slavery to exist, however, the Southern plantation owners had to develop laws that circumscribed the rights of slaves and punished those whites who chose *not* to cooperate in maintaining slavery. In the tobacco colonies, that legal task had been accomplished by the beginning of the 18th century. Slaves were not allowed to own property; indeed, their property was confiscated in Virginia and given to local parishes for redistribution to poor whites. Whites were forbidden by law to have sexual relations with Africans, and persons who sheltered or assisted runaway slaves were subjected to harsh treatment. Slaves were thus reduced to the legal status of chattel.[74]

INSERT 3.4 **Ethical Analysis of Key Issues and Policies: George Washington's Solution for Native Americans**

When thinking about First Americans, George Washington toyed with a "solution": why not, he thought, give each First American a specific amount of land, say 60 acres, on condition that the individual settle on it and engage in agriculture.

1. Discuss this solution from the perspective of ethical principles, such as those discussed in Chapter 1.
2. Even *had* Washington obtained support from the Congress for this policy, how might it have worked in practice:

a. from the vantage point of First Americans?
b. from the vantage point of white settlers?

3. To the extent that Washington's solution would not have been ethical *or* practicable, what more ethical alternative approach might the U.S. government have used? In answering this question, discuss whether the Americans should have honored the Proclamation Line of 1763.

The new laws cemented the white population—including the poor whites—behind the oppression of the slaves. Although subject to punishment if they assisted runaways or engaged in sexual activity with them, all white people obtained the right to discipline slaves, even without permission from their owners. Some historians believe that by investing even the poor white population with superior legal rights, the large slave owners decreased the likelihood of alliances between low-income whites and slaves. (Before the enactment of these laws, indentured white servants had often worked in the fields alongside Africans and had even intermarried with them.) Indeed, by the 18th century, many white people in Southern jurisdictions, even those of modest means, saw owning slaves as a sign of respectability and upward mobility.

Although some slaves had reached the New World earlier, the torrent of importation began after 1676, when the Royal African Company's monopoly was shattered and many private companies entered the lucrative slave trade. Shipments from Africa rose from 10,000 individuals per year in the 1690s to 40,000 per year in the 1790s. Roughly 1 million slaves were imported to the colonies or born in the colonies *before* the American Revolution. So many slaves were imported that they constituted almost 20 percent of the population in the New World by the time of the American Revolution—and 40 to 60 percent of the population of many Southern jurisdictions. The slaves lived on plantations of differing sizes, ranging from huge plantations in rice-growing coastal regions of the deep South to far smaller holdings of fewer than five slaves in Virginia and Maryland, where masters typically were of relatively modest means.[75]

As with Native Americans, a vicious circle of violence developed. Slaves did not enjoy the harsh working conditions associated with tobacco farming and often refused to work as hard as their masters desired. Their resistance confirmed the white settlers' beliefs that they were uncivilized and beyond hope of conversion to English values or religion. Racism—the imputation of negative characteristics to entire groups of persons who share similar physiological characteristics—became pervasive in the white community.

The slaves' working and social conditions were often degrading in the extreme. In the rice-growing areas of the coastal Carolinas, slaves worked in gangs of 50 or more as they planted, cultivated, and harvested rice. Less prosperous farmers used smaller groups of slaves to plant corn and other crops. Available evidence suggests that owners made frequent use of whipping; vicious punishment of runaways; "intrusion, inspection, and harassment" of the minutest aspects of their personal lives; sales of "surplus" slaves in a pattern that disrupted familial relationships; imposition of a class system with preferential treatment given to those slaves who worked in the owners' houses; and a conscious pattern of disrupting families by taking children from them at an early age and often placing husbands and wives in separate sleeping quarters.[76]

By defining African Americans and Native Americans as nonpersons, Southern white settlers did not have to feel guilty about their actions or policies. Violence was often rationalized as serving the broader needs of society or even of the nonpersons themselves. In killing Native Americans, for example, many colonists believed they were promoting the advance of Christianity and civilization, just as many slaveholders believed that harsh treatment of slaves helped teach them discipline and good work habits.

But slavery was not only a Southern institution in the colonial period. Slaves were also held in the Northern colonies, until all but New York and New Jersey eradicated the practice during the period from 1776 to 1783. (New York and New Jersey enacted laws that ended the institution in 1799 and 1804, respectively.) Agitation by Quakers and other religious groups assumed a major role in ending slavery in the North.[77]

Although slavery was largely eliminated in the North, Northern representatives at the Constitutional Convention in the 1780s had to decide whether to accede to Southerners' wishes to retain the institution. Many of the framers of the Constitution eyed slavery uneasily because they feared that social turmoil from slave rebellions would allow England to conquer the South (for its cotton) or might require the federal government to commit troops to restore tranquility.

(These pragmatic fears were more prevalent than moral outrage.) Northerners also feared that Southerners would bolt the Constitutional Convention—and the new nation—if they mentioned abolition, but they did not want slavery transplanted to the frontier. They also did not want Southerners to capture control of the Congress by adding large numbers of slave-favoring congressmen as new states entered the union from frontier areas.

This conflict between Northerners and Southerners became the most contentious division during the Constitutional Convention and led to a series of compromises. The Northerners obtained exclusion of slavery from the frontier north of the Ohio River in the Northwest Ordinance of 1787 and were allowed to place a tax on imported slaves. But Southerners won most of the concessions: slavery was not limited to those states where it existed; slaves were counted as though they were three-fifths of a person for purposes of apportioning congressional representatives; and Congress was not permitted to interfere with the importation of slaves until 1807. (Legislation to prohibit importation was finally enacted in 1808.) Slavery was legitimized by the Constitution, which referred to it in five places.[78]

In retrospect, both Southerners and Northerners miscalculated during the Constitutional Convention. Southerners assumed that they would soon control the Congress as new slave states were added to the Union and as the population of Southern states increased; thus, they believed no additional interference with the institution would develop. Northerners assumed that slavery would disappear naturally, as the economy grew and as yeomen farmers populated the West. Neither side realized that both regions would obtain new states on the frontier, and a political stalemate would culminate in a civil war. Already, in 1787, the two regions disagreed on other issues as well. Southerners wanted a weak central government that could not impose tariffs or supervise interstate commerce, whereas many Northerners favored a stronger central government.

Appleby argues persuasively that the framers left war as the only means of abolishing slavery when they legitimated it in the Constitution. Once legitimated, slavery could not be abolished without passage of a constitutional amendment, but the necessary two-thirds vote of both houses of Congress or ratification by three-fourths of state legislatures would have been unattainable once the many Southern states were part of the Union. Had the framers *not* mentioned slavery in the Constitution, it could have been eliminated by a simple majority vote in Congress, in a manner akin to its abolition by a majority vote in the British Parliament.[79]

When considering African slaves and Native Americans, many colonists were afflicted by racism. Benjamin Franklin feared that African people would "darken" the people of America, who could, by excluding Africans and Native Americans, increase "the lovely White." And Jefferson advocated the removal of Africans from America so that the New World would be a "sanctuary" for European immigrants and their progeny. Moreover, the Congress in 1790 enacted legislation that restricted citizenship to Caucasians—legislation that was used to deny citizenship to Asian immigrants in the 19th century and later.[80]

OMINOUS SIGNS

From the earliest colonial era, ominous signs existed that American society would develop a particularly harsh set of policies toward women, persons living in poverty, as well as African Americans and First Americans.

The colonists lived in an agrarian society. They cannot be blamed if their policies and ideas, when inherited by subsequent generations, proved inadequate to the social problems of an urbanized and industrialized nation. Nevertheless, the pervasive influence of certain colonial ideas in the 19th century—and even in the 20th century—served to retard the development of national social programs.

Feudal society was replete with regulations and traditions that stifled upward mobility, changes in residence, sale of land, and changes in occupation, but it also offered many protections to its citizens precisely because it was so regulated. Courts protected the rights of serfs and their successors, whether tenant farmers, indentured servants, or apprentices. The early colonies inherited many of these feudal regulations but lacked England's rich history of enforcement.[81]

The English landed gentry were descendants of the noblemen of feudal times, if not by direct family lineage then by accepting the prescribed social roles when they purchased large estates. In the transition from feudal to postfeudal society, many of the landed gentry in England resorted to enclosure and other policies that harmed emancipated serfs. Others, however, imbued with a sense of obligation to persons in lower social and economic strata, supported policies of job creation and mercantilism. Conservative philosophers like Edmund Burke contended that English society was an "organic" entity bound together by ancient traditions.

The Americans in the upper social strata had weaker notions of their social obligations than did their English counterparts. Few aristocrats and noblemen came to America; most immigrants were from the lower and middle classes. These self-made individuals—the American version of an aristocracy—sometimes believed, by the 19th century, that *everyone* should be able to obtain economic success. An example of American elites' limited sense of social obligation is provided by colonial Virginia. Although Virginia's landholding aristocracy appeared similar to its English counterpart, available evidence suggests that many powerful landowners possessed scant interest in the needs of the lower strata of society; they expanded their holdings through ruthless exploitation of indentured servants, tenant farmers, and slaves.[82]

Governmental institutions were extraordinarily weak in the colonies and mostly devoted to protecting public order. In the 19th century, the functions of local, state, and federal jurisdictions were curtailed even further when an ideology of limited government became ascendant.

The early Americans hoped to create a utopia of land-owning, hard-working, moral citizens. Education would allow children to develop their reason and to learn good work habits. Widespread ownership of land, the colonists believed, would inspire settlers to work hard so as to improve their holdings and increase their personal wealth. Granted democratic institutions, Americans would inform themselves about policy issues so as to prevent the rise of despots who might try to concentrate property and power in the hands of social elites, appease landless and urban lower classes by taking private property from other citizens, or create an urbanized society. By maintaining an agricultural society, Americans would be able to avoid such social problems as unemployment, alienation, crime, and social disorder; colonists believed that these problems inevitably infested urban areas, where wage-earning and poor residents were more prone to social disorder and the appeals of despots. Moreover, the early Americans placed extraordinary faith in the family, where moral conduct and the work ethic would be taught and modeled.

To summarize, the colonists believed that virtuous conduct was systematically fostered in America by education, widespread land ownership, the absence of excessive economic and social inequality, a system of governance that prevented the emergence of despots, cohesive families, and an agricultural economy. They were convinced that major social problems could not arise in the New World, precisely because they had masterminded a set of political, educational, familial, and economic institutions that would avert them.[83] Thomas Jefferson waxed ecstatic in a letter to John Adams about the utopian nature of this new nation as compared with Europe:

> With respect to aristocracy, we should further consider, that before the establishment of the American States, nothing was known to history but the man of the old world, crowded within limits either small or overcharged, and steeped in the vices which that situation generates. A government adapted to such men would be one thing; but a very different one, that for the man of these States. Here every one may have land to labor for himself, if he chooses, or, preferring the exercise of any other industry, may exact for it such compensation, as not only to afford a comfortable subsistence, but wherewith to provide for a cessation from labor in old age. Every one, by his property, or by his satis-

factory situation, is interested in the support of law and order. And such men may safely and advantageously reserve to themselves a wholesome control over their public affairs, and a degree of freedom, which, in the hands of the *canaille* [the proletarians] of the cities of Europe, would be instantly perverted to the demolition and destruction of everything public and private. The history of the last twenty-five years of France, and of the last forty years in America, nay of its last two hundred years, proves the truth of both parts of this observation.[84]

This belief that Americans had created a utopian society served to retard the development of social programs by blinding the colonists and succeeding generations of Americans to the existence of social needs in their midst. If America is a utopia, few social programs or regulations are necessary. Even in the 19th century, when the nation began to develop an urban society and poverty and other social needs became relatively widespread, the persistent notion of the American utopia perpetuated a kind of collective denial.

Americans aimed to achieve freedom in their new society by developing state and federal constitutions, elaborating a Bill of Rights, ending taxation without representation, establishing freedom of religion, and expanding suffrage. Liberty is an important social objective, but Americans failed to grapple with another vital objective—that of equality, which would have required them to develop institutions capable of reducing economic and social discrepancies. Whereas the slogan of the French Revolution was liberty *and* equality, the American Revolution emphasized liberty. When the framers anxiously submitted the Constitution to state conventions for ratification, widespread protests erupted against their work on the grounds that they had not included a Bill of Rights to protect citizens' freedom against capricious acts of government. In response, the first 10 amendments were added to the Constitution by the First Congress in 1791.

Although the colonists wanted to limit the power of government, they often supported the regulation of prices, economic planning, and public improvements. With the American Revolution completed and the Constitution written, however, a remarkable political conflict took place in the 1790s between allies of Jefferson, who formed the Republican party (which later became the Democratic party), and allies of Washington, Adams, and Hamilton, who formed the Federalist party. The Federalists, who had favored economic planning and a somewhat stronger federal government, were routed in the election of 1800 by the Jeffersonians, whose beliefs formed an American consensus about drastic reductions in the economic role of government, reductions in various federal taxes, and a strict interpretation of the Constitution so that the government did not exceed its enumerated powers. The American consensus engineered by Jefferson meant that the federal government would remain exceedingly weak for generations.[85]

PRECURSORS TO A RELUCTANT WELFARE STATE

Although the term "welfare state" would not be coined until the 20th century, precursors to a limited American welfare state already existed in the colonial period.

American social policy in the colonial era cannot be easily characterized because, like English policy in this period, it reflected conflicting tendencies. On the one hand, mercantile policies, local regulation of prices and wages, and the development of poor law institutions represented positive responses to social problems. Indeed, these policies can be viewed as distant descendants of feudal notions of social obligation, even if they accorded to governments helping roles that, during the feudal era, had been implemented by the Church and noblemen. On the other hand, many American colonists possessed moralistic (and punitive) orientations toward unemployed persons, believed that government should assist only destitute persons, were extremely fearful of the national government, and believed that social problems like unemployment emanated from moral defects. With the victory of Jefferson in

1800, moreover, the nation tilted decisively toward a limited federal government that was not even granted explicit powers to develop and implement social policies by the Constitution.

An array of factors shaped American social welfare policies in the colonial era and led to a reliance on relatively modest local policies. Cultural factors included an emphasis on individualism and limited government. Among political factors, the lack of a large class of landless people and the subjugation of persons of color meant that little pressure was exerted on public officials to develop policies that would redistribute land or resources. Institutional factors included a weak central government as well as relatively weak local jurisdictions. Americans were already displaying an aversion to taxation as reflected by their dislike of British taxes and a Whiskey Rebellion that questioned the authority of the federal government to levy taxes.

Social welfare policy in the colonial period centered on the local poor law institutions, which included a mixture of indoor (institutional) relief and outdoor relief. Local courts assumed relatively minor social welfare functions with respect to orphans, divorce petitions, and prosecutions of persons accused of rape. Nongovernmental social welfare agencies made an appearance in the colonial period; the pattern of relatively weak governmental welfare institutions supplemented by nongovernmental programs was already emerging.

The policies of the Americans toward African slaves and First Americans, however, appear particularly onerous, even when we note that these white settlers had only the harsh precedent of the Spanish conquests of the Caribbean, Central America, and South America to guide them.

LINKING THE COLONIAL ERA TO CONTEMPORARY SOCIETY

An American tradition of policy advocacy began even before the American Republic was founded with the election of George Washington as the first president in 1789. Moreover, some social issues in the colonial period still resonate in contemporary American society.

What We Can Learn from Policy Advocates of the Colonial Era

A robust tradition of policy advocacy was much in evidence as Americans moved toward declaring independence from England in 1776, ratified their Constitution in 1788, and elected George Washington to the first of two terms of office in 1789. No one better exemplifies this tradition of policy advocacy than Dr. Benjamin Rush. (See Insert 3.5.) By observing his policy advocacy, we can better understand policy advocacy challenges we confront in contemporary society.

We can discern from Insert 3.5 that Rush applied moral reasoning to a remarkable array of issues. He was morally outraged by the lack of medical treatment for residents of poorhouses, the existence of slavery, the lack of a public system of education, women's lack of access to education, the widespread abuse of alcohol and tobacco, the poor treatment of prisoners, indeterminate prison sentences, and capital punishment. His persistence in addressing these issues is truly remarkable: his efforts included writing a tract against slavery in the early 1770s, helping to form the Pennsylvania Society for the Abolition of Slavery in 1774, and becoming president of the Pennsylvania Society for Promoting the Abolition of Slavery and the Relief of Free Negroes in 1803.

Rush's policy advocacy illustrates a tension in policy advocacy between "playing it safe" and "taking risks" when diagnosing the context. On the one hand, it is tempting to select only issues that have widespread support when engaging in policy advocacy. If *everyone* engaged in this practice, however, no one would seek important policy reforms that are associated with widespread opposition from the general public or public officials. Many people supported slavery even in the North in the colonial period, as suggested by our discussion of the disinclination of public officials to abolish it in the Constitution. Indeed, abolitionists were even physically attacked

---

INSERT 3.5 Profiles in Policy Advocacy: Benjamin Rush (1746–1813)

Benjamin Rush—physician, abolitionist, Revolutionary patriot, temperance advocate, humanitarian, and signer of the Declaration of Independence—was born in Byberry, Pennsylvania, on January 4, 1746, fourth of seven children born to John Rush and Susanna Hall (Harvey) Rush. Shortly after the death of his father, Benjamin's mother opened a country store, which provided a comfortable, but not luxurious, living for the Rush family.

In 1759, at 13 years of age, Rush was admitted as a junior to the College of New Jersey (now Princeton University). After receiving his bachelor's degree, Rush initially decided to pursue a career in law but was persuaded by his uncle, Reverend Samuel Finley, to study medicine instead. Between 1761 and 1766 he served as an apprentice to Dr. John Redman, a leading physician in Philadelphia. Meanwhile, Rush also attended medical courses given at the College of Philadelphia by medical professors Dr. William Shippen and Dr. John Morgan.

Rush's interest in politics began while he was a medical student; the British attempt to place a stamp tax on legal documents aroused his political consciousness. Rush, nevertheless, remained a medical student and, in 1765, decided to continue his studies abroad.

In 1766, Rush enrolled at the University of Edinburgh in Scotland. There he became a protégé and friend of Dr. William Cullen, one of the leading chemists of his day. In 1768, Rush received his M.D. and, after a brief stay in London and Paris, returned to the colonies in July of 1769.

Upon returning to the colonies, Rush began his medical practice, which quickly prospered. Some time later he was appointed professor of chemistry at the College of Philadelphia and held the first chair of chemistry established in the American colonies. When Rush was not engaged in his private practice or teaching, he was writing. In 1770 he published the first American textbook on chemistry. Two years later, he released *Sermons to Gentlemen upon Temperance and Exercise*, the first American work on personal hygiene. Also, in November of 1770, Rush became a charter member and curator of the American Philosophical Society.

In the period between 1770 and 1773, Benjamin Rush's reform interests led him to work outside of his private practice. He worked as a physician in almshouses, bringing medical care to the poor and participating in the Society for Inoculating the Poor. In that same period, Rush was asked to support a Philadelphia Assembly bill to double the importation tax on slaves, which would have made it prohibitively expensive to bring new slaves to the colony. The successful passage of that bill signaled the beginning of Rush's campaign against slavery. Despite the fact that his family owned slaves, Rush wrote "An Address to the Inhabitants of the British Settlements in America, upon Slave-Keeping, by a Pennsylvanian," attacking the institution of slavery and those who participated in it. Particularly controversial was Rush's claim that the black was in all ways equal to the white person. In 1774, he was instrumental in the formation of the Pennsylvania Society for the Abolition of Slavery.

Rush held the British responsible for bringing the institution of slavery to the American colonies and devoted much of his time to supporting America's political struggle against the Crown. He served as a propagandist, condemning the Tea Act, and wrote essays on patriotism, as well as on slavery in the colonies. The latter he usually wrote under pseudonyms. Rush was also an observer at sessions of the First Continental Congress, held in Philadelphia in 1774. There he met and befriended John and Samuel Adams, Thomas Jefferson, and George Washington and renewed his friendship with Benjamin Franklin, whom he met while in London.

In January of 1776, Rush wed Julia Stockton, who was 14 years his junior. In February of that same year, Rush formally entered politics when he was elected to Philadelphia's Committee of Inspection and Observation, which had as its main objective the implementation of the measures passed at the first Continental Congress, held in 1774. Several months later, Rush was elected to the Provincial Conference to draw up rules for Pennsylvania's constitutional convention. He was subsequently chosen as a member of the second Continental Congress, and, on July 4, 1776, he became one of the signers of the Declaration of Independence.

At the end of the Revolutionary War, Rush once again became a professor of chemistry at the College of Philadelphia, which by now had become the University of the State of Pennsylvania (1780). In the summer of that year, Rush founded the Philadelphia Humane Society and began promoting the idea of preventive medicine. In 1783, Benjamin Rush, who by then had earned the respect of those in the American medical profession, was offered a highly prestigious staff position at Pennsylvania Hospital, which he gladly accepted.

(Continued)

The end of the war and the emergence of a newly independent nation also brought to Rush's attention another set of social issues worthy of his reform efforts. He was particularly concerned with the need to develop a public educational system. For Rush, education was a key factor in reforming the character of the newly freed colonies, and he believed schools would serve to unite a diverse group of people. In 1786, Rush wrote the first American essay advocating the establishment of a government-supported educational system. He also believed, unlike many of his contemporaries, that women should have access to education, although he believed they should be trained differently from men.

Rush also advocated a need for temperance and prepared the way for what became known as the American temperance movement. Rush's medical experience led him to see the "evils of alcohol." In 1784, he published his *Inquiry into the Effects of Spiritous Liquors upon the Human Body, and Their Influence upon the Happiness of Society*. This was the first essay to detail the physiological effects of alcoholism. It included warnings not only about the physical effects of alcohol on the body but also the dire moral consequences one would face as a result of overconsumption. Rush also spoke out against the use of tobacco, which he believed was another cause of poor health in men.

Rush resumed his crusade for the abolition of slavery in the late 1780s. In March of 1787, he renewed his membership in the Pennsylvania Society for Promoting the Abolition of Slavery and the Relief of Free Negroes Unlawfully Held in Bondage. Shortly thereafter, he became the Society's secretary and, in 1803, became its president. During this same period, Rush was involved in the penal reform movement and was a founder of the Society for Promoting Political Inquiries. He believed prison terms should be adjusted to fit the crime and fixed by law. Rush opposed capital punishment. His penal reform efforts paved the way for the creation of the Philadelphia Society for Alleviating the Miseries of Public Prisons.

During the last two decades of his life, Benjamin Rush devoted most of his time to practicing medicine. He died on April 19, 1813, in Philadelphia.

in Northern cities in the 1840s and 1850s. Nor did widespread support for giving women access to education exist in a period when many colonists doubted that women possessed the intellectual capability to benefit from it. Not intimidated by adverse public sentiment, Rush plunged ahead even when prospects for immediate policy successes were bleak.

What We Can Learn from the Persistence of Unmet Needs and Policy Issues during the Colonial Era

Battles over the meaning and implications of specific provisions of the Constitution did not abate in the centuries following clashes between George Washington, Alexander Hamilton, and Thomas Jefferson over the relative power given to the federal government. While the terms "liberal" and "conservative" were not used in the colonial period, they came to suggest distinctly different approaches to interpreting the Constitution in the 20th and 21st centuries that were present even in the colonial period.

If liberals tended to believe the Constitution conferred relatively broad powers on the federal government (following in the footsteps of George Washington and Alexander Hamilton), conservatives tended to view it as conferring relatively narrow power to the federal government (sharing the outlook of Thomas Jefferson). If liberals believed that the Constitution provided relatively loose guidelines that could be adapted to changing issues and conditions in society, conservatives believed in "strict constructionism"—that is, adhering to the literal words and intentions of the framers of the Constitution. This conflict between liberals and conservatives over the Constitution emerged with extraordinary force in the second term of the presidency of George W. Bush when he appointed two conservative jurists to the Supreme Court—leading to conflict between conservative, moderate, and liberal jurists. These clashes would have huge implications for women's right to choose, affirmative action, regulations of corporations by the government, the right to free expression, the rights of criminal defendants and persons accused of crimes such as terrorism, and the separation of church and state.

These conflicts over interpretation of the Constitution have strong implications for persons who favor relatively broad powers for the federal government and who oppose strict construction of its provisions. If they do not want the U.S. Supreme Court to veer in a conservative direction, they must get involved in electoral politics so that a relatively liberal president is elected. Had George W. Bush *not* become president in 2000 or 2004, relatively liberal jurists would have been selected rather than justices John Roberts and Samuel Alioto—leading to markedly different court rulings on abortion, affirmative action, corporate powers, rights of employees, and rights of unions. (We discuss these issues in the administration of George W. Bush in Chapter 12.)

What We Can Learn from Failed Policy Strategies of the Colonial Era

Many Americans subscribed in the colonial era to sexism and racism, leading them to support policies in conflict with principles enunciated in the Declaration of Independence. Colonists therefore left to future American generations a legacy that would eventually lead to a bloody civil war, violent repression of suffragettes in the early part of the 20th century, a civil rights movement that brought many deaths and injuries in the middle of the 20th century, and ongoing oppression of many vulnerable populations in contemporary society.

Oppression of vulnerable populations is not a uniquely American phenomenon. Subjugated Muslim populations in France erupted in violence in 2005 and 2006 in response to segregated housing, poverty, and discrimination. Persons descended from Indian and Caribbean ancestors are often impoverished, segregated, and shunned in Great Britain. Tribal warfare in Africa has led to the deaths of hundreds of thousands of persons in such nations as Rwanda and Uganda. Women are often forcibly placed in prostitution in many nations of the world.

Yet oppression of the 13 vulnerable populations that we identified in Chapter 1 and Chapter 2 is particularly troublesome in a nation with enunciated principles of equality in the Declaration of Independence—and in a nation that came to be as affluent as the United States in the 20th and 21st centuries. It is fortunate that many Americans came to realize in succeeding generations that prejudice, discrimination, and hostility to women, persons of color, the disabled, low-income persons, First Americans, children, and many other vulnerable populations are discrepant with the first principles of equality enunciated in the colonies even before the American Republic was formally begun. Not only is oppression of vulnerable populations unethical; it is costly to the nation. Absent decent schools for all Americans, for example, some persons are prevented from becoming productive participants in a global economy. Women subject to harassment on the job are not only less productive, but suffer emotional trauma.

Many colonists, too, were imbued with a moralistic stance toward social problems such as poverty. We discuss in the next chapter how the equating of social problems with faults of character or even "sin" left the United States with another legacy that persists even in contemporary society. Moralistic approaches to myriad social problems continue to impede constructive efforts to help and empower persons to surmount them, as reflected by harsh welfare laws that fail to give single heads of households sufficient job training, child care, health care, transportation, and housing to allow them to better their (and their children's) condition.

What We Can Learn from Promising Strategies of the Colonial Era

The policy of selling federally owned land in the territories on the frontier to settlers had already commenced in the early years of the American Republic. Indentured servants who had finished their service, immigrants, and citizens purchased land on the frontier at federal auctions. The purchase of land proved to be a disaster for some persons due to the harsh environment and economy that they encountered. Not only did they have to clear the land and plant crops, but they had to barter or sell agricultural products in an uncertain economy—and face the uncertainties of weather. Nor were some persons of modest means able to afford land at federal auctions—leading some of them to squat on frontier land illegally.

Those persons of modest means who *did* obtain land and homes often benefited from such ownership. Assets can provide a buffer from economic uncertainties, since they can be used as collateral for loans, rented, or sold at a profit if they appreciate in value. Ownership of some assets may enhance the well-being of those persons who see themselves as having a stake in society—as Thomas Jefferson surmised. The colonial experience suggests that contemporary American public policy should try to help persons of modest means gain access to land and homes, but, as can be seen in Insert 3.6, existing policies often benefit *current* homeowners more than they help potential owners.

What We Can Learn from the Colonial Era about the Structure of the American Welfare State

Americans possessed a primitive welfare state in the colonial period—if we can even apply the relatively modern term "welfare state" to the modest collection of poorhouses, prisons, and local governments of that era. We must remember that the new Republic was mostly agricultural and that its citizens were—with notable exceptions—relatively poor. Aside from supervising the sale of land at the frontier, engaging in international diplomacy, waging war with First Americans, and building some canals and other public improvements, the just-formed federal government possessed virtually no resources and had virtually no social welfare functions—forcing local governments and states to assume these functions.

Since local and state governments themselves had few resources and negligible social welfare responsibilities, they, too, had only primitive social welfare roles or institutions. Most people believed that, with abundant land and the need for considerable labor to clear and farm it, most persons could and should find work—thus making it unnecessary to help them with government programs.

We can observe from the colonial experience that Americans would build their welfare state in the coming centuries "from the bottom upward," unlike many European nations that already had large regulatory, tax, and social welfare functions vested with central governments and monarchs. The vesting of poorhouses, jails, schools, and mental services with local and state governments at the outset of the Republic and through the 19th century would have some salutary benefits. By being closer to residents, these institutions would be more likely to reflect their wishes and needs.

At the same time, however, a bottom-up strategy would present problems for future generations of Americans. In relatively poor jurisdictions or in relatively conservative areas, local services would be short-changed and underfunded—as is currently reflected in states such as Georgia that severely underfund their educational and social welfare institutions. Some Americans would come to think, moreover, that the federal government ought to have virtually no role in social welfare policy—accurately noting that the Constitution failed even to mention social policy as a federal responsibility. Yet many social problems would subsequently *require* a federal response due to their complexity, their prevalence across the nation, or their cost.

With rare exceptions, we can view the 132 years following the year 1800 as the triumph of local and state roles in social welfare policy. When the federal government *did* develop social welfare roles in the decades following 1932, Americans fashioned a very complex welfare state in which local, state, and federal policies and programs existed side-by-side. Social workers need *navigational skills* (as we noted in Chapter 2 in Figure 2.1) partly because of this complexity that derives from the bottom-up approach that was followed by the addition of many federal programs after 1932. They have to decide where best to refer clients or consumers to services in this mosaic of programs and policies. They have to decide what entitlements clients or consumers possess with respect to which resources, services, and rights. To the extent that social workers wish to reform existing policies or propose new ones, they must decide what level of government and what policies to engage.

INSERT 3.6 Critical Analysis: Does the United States Favor Current Ho\[\] Renters?

Contrast the economic situation of persons with no assets and persons with assets that *do* appreciate in value. Then ask whether the United States helps persons of modest means sufficiently to get homes when it gives only *current* holders of mortgages the ability to write off their mortgage payments from their taxable income—a policy that adds to their economic resources. By contrast, renters, who are less affluent as a group than homeowners, are not allowed to write off any of their rent against their taxable income. To the extent that the existing tax code favors current owners of homes, what other policies does—and should—the United States pursue to enable renters to become homeowners?

The decision to help persons acquire property and homes is praiseworthy but hardly a panacea. Many Americans acquired land on the frontier only to become bankrupt when they could not get their land to be productive rapidly enough to repay the bank loans they used to acquire the property or when they encountered natural disasters such as drought or hail. We are currently witnessing huge numbers of foreclosures in contemporary society after banks and other lenders engaged in deceptive lending practices to lure persons of modest means to purchase homes. These misfortunes in the colonial era and in contemporary society suggest the need for strong governmental roles in regulating the lending industry and in providing constructive assistance to persons and families that experience economic misfortune soon after acquiring property and loans. Even today, insufficient social policies exist on either count with respect to families at risk of foreclosure due to deceptive lending practices.

We can see, too, from the colonial experience that Americans would likely develop many *means-tested* social programs that conditioned the receipt of benefits or services upon tests of character and income. To gain assistance from poorhouses or outdoor relief in the colonial period, for example, applicants had to *prove* they were "deserving" of such assistance—that is, were not "freeloaders" and were truly impoverished. It was already widely assumed by many colonists that such assistance would be offered only for brief periods of time and under sufficiently harsh conditions that recipients would never want to seek assistance again. Unfortunately, this harsh orientation toward the provision of assistance even in contemporary society focuses attention on deterrence rather than on providing constructive policies to help persons surmount problems and empower themselves.

WHAT YOU CAN DO NOW

You are now equipped to do the following:

- Analyze how the early colonists evolved a culture and institutions that diverged from ones in medieval society.

- Identify relatively punitive and positive policies in medieval society and in the colonies.

- Explain why the American revolution was not a true "revolution" but nonetheless greatly transformed American cultural and institutions.

- Trace how the American Constitution evolved —and why it failed to even mention social welfare policy—while nonetheless providing a basis for the future development of federal social welfare roles.

- Describe the harsh treatment of First Americans, women, free African Americans, and slaves in colonial America and by the framers of the Constitution.

- Discuss what we can learn from the colonial era and apply to contemporary society, including the successes and failures of policy advocates, social problems that persist today, failed policies, promising policies, and the structure of the American welfare state.

ENDNOTES

1. Gerald Handel, *Social Welfare in Western Society* (New York: Random House, 1982), p. 31.

2. K. D. M. Snell, *Annals of the Laboring Poor: Social Change and Agrarian England, 1660–1900* (Cambridge: Cambridge University Press, 1985), pp. 166–194. For a discussion of the social structure of feudal villages, see George Homans, *English Villagers of the Thirteenth Century* (New York: Russell and Russell, 1960).

3. Homans, *English Villagers*, pp. 353–381.

4. Brian Tierney, *Medieval Poor Law: A Sketch of Canonical Theory and Its Application in England* (Berkeley, CA: University of California Press, 1959), p. 12.

5. Gerald Handel, *Social Welfare in Western Society* (New York: Random House, 1982), p. 62.

6. Edmund Morgan, *American Slavery, American Freedom: The Ordeal of Colonial America* (New York: Norton, 1975), pp. 65–66.

7. Joyce Appleby, *Capitalism and a New Social Order: The Republican Vision of the 1790s* (New York: New York University Press, 1984), pp. 1–23.

8. Joyce Appleby, *Economic Thought and Ideology in Seventeenth-Century England* (Princeton, NJ: Princeton University Press, 1978), pp. 158–198.

9. Margaret James, *Social Problems and Policy during the Puritan Revolution* (London: George Routledge and Sons, 1930), pp. 78–130; Snell, *Annals*, pp. 228–269. Peasants' resentment at the loss of their ability to raise crops on common pastures and on strips of land is discussed by Snell, *Annals*, pp. 209–227; and by Louise Tilly, "Food Entitlement, Famine, and Conflict." In Robert Rotberg and Theodore Rabb, eds., *Hunger and History* (Cambridge: Cambridge University Press, 1983), pp. 135–151.

10. James, *Social Problems*, pp. 241–302; Morgan, *American Slavery*, p. 326.

11. Charles Tilly, "Collective Action in England and America." In Richard Brown and Don Fehrenbacher, eds., *Tradition, Conflict, and Modernization: Perspectives on the American Revolution* (New York: Academic Press, 1977), pp. 45–50.

12. For discussion of changing beliefs in the transition from feudalism, see Appleby, *Economic Thought*, pp. 183–184, 190–198, as well as Robert Webb, *Modern England: From the Eighteenth Century to the Present* (New York: Dodd, Mead, 1970), pp. 43–46.

13. James, *Social Problems*, pp. 271–283; Morgan, *American Slavery*, pp. 321–325.

14. Morgan, *American Slavery*, pp. 196–197.

15. Ibid., p. 67.

16. Snell, *Annals*, pp. 104–137.

17. Ibid., p. 105.

18. Daniel Baugh, "Poverty, Protestantism, and Political Economy: English Attitudes toward the Poor, 1600–1800." In Stephen Baxter, ed., *England's Rise to Greatness* (Berkeley, CA: University Press of California, 1983), pp. 84–94.

19. Snell, *Annals*, p. 107.

20. Ibid., pp. 110–114.

21. Gordon Wood, *The Radicalism of the American Revolution* (New York: Alfred A. Knopf, 1992); Joyce Appleby, *Liberalism and Republicanism in the Historical Imagination* (Cambridge, MA: Harvard University Press, 1992).

22. Francis Bremer, *The Puritan Experiment* (New York: St. Martin's Press, 1976), pp. 51–52.

23. Ibid., pp. 89–93; Morgan, *American Slavery, American Freedom*, pp. 133–149.

24. Wood, *The Radicalism of the American Revolution*, pp. 11–92.

25. Appleby, *Liberalism and Republicanism*, p. 153.

26. Morgan, *American Slavery*, pp. 126–128.

27. Ibid., pp. 238–239.

28. Gary Nash, "Social Change and the Growth of Pre-Revolutionary Urban Radicalism." In Arthur Young, ed., *The American Revolution: Explorations in the History of American Radicalism* (DeKalb, IL: Northern Illinois University Press, 1976), pp. 11–12. Also see Gary Nash, "Social Development." In Greene and Pole, eds., *Colonial British America*, (Baltimore: Johns Hopkins University Press, 1984), p. 247.

29. Richard Brown, "Backcountry Rebellions and the Homestead Ethic." In Richard Brown and Don Fehrenbacher, eds., *Tradition, Conflict, and Modernization: Perspectives on the American Revolution*, pp. 73–95; Edward Countryman, "Out of the

Bounds of Law: Northern Land Rioters in the Eighteenth Century." In Young, ed., *The American Revolution*, pp. 37–70.

30. Wood, *Radicalism of the American Revolution*, p. 123.

31. Ibid., pp. 325–347.

32. Ibid., pp. 169–197.

33. Ibid., p. 229.

34. Jack Greene, "The Limits of the American Revolution." In Jack Greene, ed., *The American Revolution: Its Character and Limits* (New York: New York University Press, 1987), p. 12.

35. Henry Commager, *The Empire of Reason: How Europe Imagined and America Realized the Enlightenment* (Garden City, NY: Anchor Press, 1977).

36. Merrill Peterson, ed., *Portable Thomas Jefferson* (New York: Viking Press, 1975), pp. 396–397.

37. Christopher Collier and James Collier, *Decision in Philadelphia: the Constitutional Convention of 1787* (New York: Random House, 1986), pp. 181–194.

38. Commager, *The Empire of Reason*, p. 226.

39. Greene, "Limits of the American Revolution," pp. 8–9.

40. Richard Smith, *Patriarch: George Washington and the New American Nation* (Boston: Houghton Mifflin, 1993), pp. 50–51.

41. Ibid., p. 145.

42. Louis Hartz, *Economic Policy and Democratic Thought in Pennsylvania* (Cambridge, MA: Harvard University Press, 1948), p. 4; Morgan, *American Slavery*, pp. 134–136.

43. Robert Bremner, *American Philanthropy* (Chicago: University of Chicago Press, 1970), pp. 5–42.

44. Ibid.

45. Peterson, *Portable Jefferson*, pp. 180–181.

46. Alfred Young, "The Women of Boston: 'Persons of Consequence' in the Making of the American Revolution, 1765–76." In Harriet Applewhite and Darline Levy, *Women and Politics in the Age of Democratic Revolution* (Ann Arbor, MI: University of Michigan Press, 1990), p. 186.

47. Morgan, *American Slavery*, pp. 165–170.

48. Jack Sosin, *The Revolutionary Frontier, 1763–1783* (New York: Holt, Rinehart & Winston, 1967), pp. 172–192.

49. Young, "The Women of Boston," p. 340.

50. Countryman, "Out of the Bounds of Law," p. 74.

51. Susan Amussen, *An Ordered Society: Gender and Class in Early Modern England* (Oxford: Basil Blackwell, 1988), p. 133; Antonia Fraser, *The Weaker Vessel* (New York: Knopf, 1984), p. 5.

52. Maryanne Kowaleski and Judith Bennett, "Crafts, Guilds, and Women in the Middle Ages: Fifty Years after Marian K. Dale." In Judith Bennett et al., eds., *Sisters and Workers in the Middle Ages* (Chicago: University of Chicago Press, 1989), pp. 11–38.

53. Amussen, *Ordered Society*, pp. 95–133

54. Joan Wilson, "The Illusion of Change: Women and the American Revolution." In Young, ed., *The American Revolution*, pp. 426–431.

55. Nancy Woloch, *Women and the American Experience* (New York: Knopf, 1984), pp. 76–80; Linda Kerber, " 'I have Donmuch to Carrey on the Warr': Women and the Shaping of Republican Ideology after the American Revolution." In Applewhite and Levy, *Women and Politics*, p. 233; and Elaine Crane, "Dependence in the Era of Independence: The Role of Women in a Republican Society." In Greene, *The American Revolution*, p. 262.

56. Barbara Harris, *Beyond Her Sphere: Women and the Professions in American History* (Westport, CT: Greenwood Press, 1978), pp. 20ff.

57. Ibid., p. 20.

58. Crane, "Dependence in the Era of Independence," pp. 260–266.

59. John D'Emilio and Estelle Freedman, *Intimate Matters: A History of Sexuality in America* (New York: Harper & Row, 1988), pp. 22–23.

60. Ibid., p. 31.

61. Ronald Sanders, *Lost Tribes and Promised Lands* (Boston: Little, Brown, 1978), p. 17.

62. For example, see Zvi Dor-Ner, *Columbus and the Age of Discovery* (New York: William Morrow, 1991), p. 201.

63. Ibid., p. 208.

64. Ibid., pp. 216–217.

65. Sanders, *Lost Tribes*, p. 7.

66. Jim Potter, "Demographic Development and Family Structure." In Greene and Pole, eds., *Colonial British America*, p. 133; Angie Debo, *History*

of the Indians of the United States (Norman, OK: University of Oklahoma Press, 1970), pp. 53ff.

67. Bremer, *The Puritan Experiment*, pp. 198–204; Morgan, *American Slavery*, pp. 22, 47.

68. Gary Nash, *Red, White, and Black: The Peoples of Early America* (Englewood Cliffs, NJ: Prentice Hall, 1974), pp. 69–87.

69. Morgan, *American Slavery*, pp. 22–24; John Yolton, *The Locke Reader* (Cambridge: Cambridge University Press, 1977), pp. 289–292.

70. Francis Jennings, "The Indian's Revolution." In Young, ed., *The American Revolution*, pp. 333–336.

71. Ibid.

72. Nash, *Red, White, and Black*, pp. 156, 160.

73. Morgan, *American Slavery*, pp. 295–297.

74. Ibid., pp. 330–337.

75. Ibid., p. 330; Nash, "Social Development," pp. 244, 254; Collier and Collier, *Decision*, p. 16; and Peter Kolchin, *American Slavery, 1619–1877* (New York: Hill and Wang, 1993), pp. 28–34.

76. Richard Dunn, "Servants and Slaves: The Recruitment and Employment of Labor." In Greene and Pole, eds., *Colonial British America*, pp. 179–180.

77. Sylvia Frey, "Liberty, Equality, and Slavery: The Paradox of the American Revolution." In Greene, ed., *The American Revolution*, pp. 235–236.

78. Collier and Collier, *Decision*, pp. 137–179; Harold Hyman, *Equal Justice under Law: Constitutional Development, 1835–1875* (New York: Harper & Row, 1982), p. 4; and Kenneth O'Reilly, *Nixon's Piano: Presidents and Racial Politics from Washington to Clinton* (New York: Force Press, 1995).

79. Appleby, *Liberalism and Republicanism*, pp. 223–225.

80. Ronald Takaki, *Strangers from a Different Shore* (Boston: Little, Brown, 1989), pp. 16, 207.

81. Stanley Elkins, *Slavery: A Problem in American Institutional and Intellectual Life* (New York: Grosset & Dunlap, 1963), pp. 27–37.

82. Morgan, *American Slavery*, p. 235.

83. Bernard Bailyn, *The Ideological Origins of the American Revolution* (Cambridge, MA: Harvard University Press, 1967), pp. 272–319.

84. Peterson, *Portable Jefferson*, p. 538.

85. Appleby, *Capitalism*, pp. 53–61.

4

Social Welfare Policy in the Early Republic: 1789–1860

T A B L E 4.1   Selected Orienting Events

1820s	Speenhamland System introduced in the South of England
1824	First House of Refuge founded in New York; Yates Report issued in New York State
1828	Andrew Jackson elected to first of two terms
1830s	Zenith of Sunday School movement
1830s–1840s	Chartist Movement in England; zenith of antebellum temperance movement
1830s–1850s	Movement to establish public schools
1834	Report of English Poor Law Commission issued
1843	New York Association for Improving the Condition of the Poor established in New York
1845	The term *manifest destiny* coined
1848	Seneca Falls Convention
1845–1849	Irish potato famine
1853	Charles Loring Brace founds Children's Aid Society of New York
1854	President Pierce vetoes a bill, initiated by Dorothea Dix, to fund construction of mental institutions by means of revenues from land sales

H aving established their independence from England and written their Constitution, Americans were free to shape their national destiny both geographically (how would they define the boundaries of a nation with seemingly endless expanses of land on their Western frontier?) and institutionally (what political and social institutions would evolve?). Between the inception of the republic in 1789 and the Civil War in 1861, Americans devoted vast energy to problems of poverty, street children and orphans, mental illness, crime, illiteracy, and alcoholism and developed policies concerning Native Americans, Spanish-speaking persons, and African Americans.

Most of the programs and policies were fashioned in local and state legislatures in this period; aside from the use of federal troops on the frontier, the involvement of federal authorities was relatively minor. In these local undertakings against social problems and in local skirmishes with native peoples on the frontier, an American policy identity began to evolve—a curious mixture of idealistic, simplistic, and punitive approaches to social policy.

At the end of the chapter, we discuss what we can learn from the early Republic about contemporary policy advocacy, social policy, and the structure of the American welfare state.

SOCIAL REALITIES IN THE NEW NATION

American society was regionalist in the early 19th century. The Northeast, the Northern frontier extending from Pennsylvania to Kansas and Nebraska, and the South were characterized by very different social and economic patterns. New Englanders, who had developed some factories and industries by 1860, were concerned with developing their shipping, fishing, and manufacturing industries in the face of efforts by England and other European nations to sabotage the emerging American industry. To make Americans dependent on them for manufactured items—such as steel, shoes, and textiles—the English dumped these items on the American market at artificially low prices, refused to allow the export of machines and technology to America, and discouraged the development of an American shipping industry.

The Northern frontier—the contemporary Midwest—produced agricultural staples such as corn, wheat, beef, and pork. Settlers on the Western frontier, who desperately sought cheap land and a ready supply of credit to purchase and develop it, pressured federal authorities and state and territorial legislatures to provide militia to fend off Native Americans. They also sought federal and local funds to build roads and canals so that they could send their agricultural commodities to the East.

Long before the outbreak of the Civil War, Southerners were intent on ensuring the growth and stability of slavery and their agricultural economy based on tobacco and cotton. They won federal policies that allowed them to expand slavery into frontier areas such as Texas, and they enacted in Southern legislatures, with scant dissent from whites, a series of measures that made it impossible for slaves to marry, to obtain property, or to be educated.

Politicians and political parties often sought to advance the particular economic goals of these regions in battles over tariffs, internal improvements such as canals and roads, and the price of land that was charged by federal authorities to settlers on the frontier. New England wanted relatively high tariffs to protect its growing industry. Frontier areas and the South wanted lower tariffs to minimize the cost of their goods. Frontier areas often wanted public improvements to allow transportation to and from their areas. Southern and frontier interests also wanted cheap land so that settlers could readily obtain land on the frontier, whereas many New Englanders opposed these policies because they feared loss of their population to Western lands. National politicians often catered to these regional issues in national elections, which were sometimes determined by patterns of regional support. For example, support from frontier and Southern regions was crucial to Thomas Jefferson's presidential victory in 1800 and to Andrew Jackson's election in 1828, whereas Abraham Lincoln became president in 1860 by obtaining support from New England and the Midwest.

The settlement of areas extending from Pennsylvania to Nebraska, from the Carolinas to Texas, and from the East Coast to the gold mines of California occurred with unprecedented speed. This speed and range of settlement was made possible by a

---

I N S E R T 4.1 **Using the Web to Understand How Americans Made Social Policy in the Early Republic**

Visit **academic.cengage.com/social_work/jansson** to view these links and a variety of study tools.

Go to **http://www.legacy98.org** Click on the "History of the Movement" and then click on "Declaration." How does this document demonstrate that early feminists were ahead of their times?

Go to **http://www.pbs.org/kera/usmexicanwar/** Click on various items related to the American conquest of Mexico. How do these items suggest that the American acquisition

of Texas and much of what became the American Southwest represented imperialist expansion that led to the subjugation of persons of Mexican descent in the American Southwest?

Go to **http://www.pbs.org/wgbh/amex/orphan/index.html** This site discusses so-called orphan trains, on which children were sent to homes in the West. Were the orphan trains meritorious or did they lead to exploitation of innocent children?

---

number of factors. Continued immigration from Europe and large families in non-frontier communities provided a plentiful supply of individuals willing to settle new territories; soil and weather conditions were favorable to settlement; and the settlers encountered ineffective resistance from the indigenous population of Native Americans and Spanish-speaking persons, who were outnumbered and technologically outgunned.[1] Settling the frontier may sound romantic to contemporary readers, but realities were often harsh. Much like Mexico or Brazil today, the United States was saddled with extraordinary debt as it tried to build its agriculture and industry from scratch. Enormous debts were amassed as Americans borrowed from banks and wealthy individuals in Europe who financed the speculative American economy. During much of the century, the American banking and currency system was in chaos; it was characterized by frequent and sharp recessions; fluctuations between inflation and deflation; unregulated banks that would frequently go bankrupt or charge excessive rates of interest; and the inability of authorities to develop a national bank that could, like today's Federal Reserve system, promote or discourage economic expansion to avert the twin perils of recession and inflation. Locally and nationally, considerable effort was expended in debates about banking and currency policies to foster economic growth and to avert recessions. (Americans were inclined to support a variety of economic

panaceas—for example, abolishing national banking institutions, using hard rather than paper currency, or issuing more paper currency.)

The debates about the economy were fueled by the economic difficulties of countless Americans. Subject to the vicissitudes of world markets and to frequent recessions, farmers, merchants, and bankers often could not repay loans from local or foreign creditors; many local laws allowed imprisonment of debtors even when small sums were involved. (Local courts often practiced leniency.) There was widespread agitation against imprisonment for debt, as well as against local banks and speculators who charged excessive rates of interest or profiteered in land speculation prior to the Civil War.[2]

The scant public resources of the debt-ridden nation were largely devoted to internal improvements that would allow transportation within and settlement of this frontier empire. Despite the initial appearance of industry in New England, American society was predominantly an agricultural nation prior to the Civil War. In 1830, 91 percent of Americans lived in towns of fewer than 2,500 persons. Eastern cities remained small by modern standards; Philadelphia contained only 120,000 persons in 1830, even though it had grown from 40,000 persons in 1785. Many rural Americans were only distantly aware that a growing population of poor persons lived in urban settings. Farmers, after all, were able to obtain a subsistence living even when they experienced hard times and could not understand that urban Americans lacked this security.[3]

This enormous frontier brought Jefferson's yeoman republic into existence, diverted attention from serious social problems in the nation, and blunted interest in reforms. Indeed, many Americans assumed that anyone could obtain land and fend for themselves; compassion for persons who lacked the physical and financial means to homestead successfully was limited. Preoccupied with personal economic issues, with settling the Western frontier, and with regional issues, relatively few persons were concerned about barbarous working conditions in the new industries of New England, the plight of tenant farmers on the frontier, or the accumulation of massive quantities of land by speculators and railroads in the West.[4]

IMMIGRATION AND URBANIZATION

Jefferson's dream of an agricultural utopia seemed partially realized in the early 19th century, when small landowners, who were often reasonably secure financially, were the dominant social group in the new nation. Together with growing numbers of small businessmen, local officials, and government officials, they formed the American middle class, whose average income was relatively high by English standards. A social and political elite of clergy, businessmen, and large landholders dominated local politics and commanded deference from other citizens.[5]

America had developed a network of cities even before 1860, particularly on the East Coast, and these cities grew at fantastic rates as the nation industrialized in the wake of the Civil War. Before and after the war, cities were plagued by many problems. They increasingly became repositories for immigrants from Ireland and Germany. Between 1814 and 1845, nearly 1 million impoverished Irish citizens—mostly Catholic peasants from southern Ireland, who replaced the predominant immigrant group of the 18th century, the so-called Scotch-Irish from Ulster, who were Protestant—entered the

United States. These were followed by another 1.2 million Irish immigrants in a scant seven years after the disastrous potato famine of 1845–1849, which decimated Ireland's population.[6]

Early American cities were rough places. Shantytowns and tenements were hurriedly constructed by speculators in the absence of housing codes. Abundant public health hazards—including open sewers and poor sanitation—gave rise to epidemics. Prostitution, gambling, street begging, and drinking were rampant. Widespread unemployment accompanied the major recessions in 1819, 1833, 1837, and 1857, when as many as one-fifth of the entire populations of New York and other large cities received welfare benefits in almshouses or from outdoor soup kitchens maintained by public and private agencies.[7] When discussing the hardships of the Panic of 1819, historian Charles Sellers notes:

> Distress was most acute in the cities … In Philadelphia, three out of four workers were reported idle … philanthropic groups distributed soup to the starving … the 8,000 public paupers who alarmed other New Yorkers in 1819 swelled in a year to nearly 13,000 … even the smaller towns faced the prospect of families naked—children freezing in the winter's storm … and everywhere the cities and towns lost population as the destitute fled back to kin in the countryside for subsistence.[8]

Those most susceptible to economic straits during recessions were unskilled laborers, such as cartmen, chimney sweeps, woodcutters, and stevedores, who constituted the largest group in the labor force.[9]

When American industry was still in its infancy, employees of shoe, textile, and other enterprises often worked in groups of as many as 12 employees or in larger groups in the nation's few factories. Working conditions were generally oppressive. A working week of six 12-hour days was typical; income was at subsistence levels; and rates of job-related injury were high. A wave of strikes occurred in the 1820s and 1830s in Eastern cities. Between 1833 and 1836, there were 172 strikes in New

England; strikers demanded a 10-hour day and mobilized a brief "general strike" of 20,000 workers in Philadelphia. Unions maintained a precarious existence, however, because of the newness of American industry, facing court rulings that were adverse to unions, frequent recessions, and company owners' strong-arm tactics against union organizers.[10]

Census and tax data suggest that, contrary to popular belief, extraordinary differentials in wealth existed in the United States. With the influx of immigrants and the emergence of agricultural, professional, industrial, merchant, and banking elites, economic inequality increased in the cities of New England between the 1820s, when 1 percent of the population held one-fourth of the wealth, and the 1850s, when 1 percent of the population held one-half the wealth. Both before and after the Civil War, mobility between social classes was limited. Residential segregation of social classes existed in all cities. Less information exists about the extent and nature of poverty in agricultural and frontier communities, but a large class of low-paid agricultural laborers helped landowners clear the land and prepare the soil for cultivation. Work on the frontier was often brutally hard; settlers used hand tools and oxen to clear wooded areas. Immigrants were often conscripted to work for labor-contract companies that skimmed profits from their subsistence wages and intimidated them from seeking private employment.[11]

The extraordinary migration of Americans across the landscape, both on the Western frontiers and to Eastern cities from the countryside, itself caused social problems. Prostitution arose to accommodate the imbalanced sex ratios on the frontier and the trend to delay marriage. As people tried to eke out an existence on the frontier or in the growing cities, some responded to economic uncertainty with suicide and alcoholism. In the absence of governmental institutions, churches, and local leaders, unlawful behavior was widespread in many frontier communities.[12]

A youth crisis developed in the 1840s, when many teenagers, finding themselves without work opportunities at the end of apprenticeship programs, roamed the streets and countryside. However, the crisis eased by the end of the century with the rise of high school education and increasing numbers of jobs in industry (Figure 4.1). As we shall see, Americans built large numbers of orphanages to house youth who left their homes before the age of 16 or those whose parents voluntarily committed them for lack of personal resources to care for them.[13]

Where social institutions existed to address economic and social needs, they were often poorly maintained. Touring America in the 1840s, Charles Dickens, the noted English author, found American prisons and almshouses to be scandalous, even when compared with the inhumane English institutions of that period. Almshouses, which represented the major social strategy to deal with social problems, were typically crowded, unsanitary, and poorly staffed. In these institutions, orphans mingled with those who had been categorized, rightly or wrongly, as mentally ill, delinquent, or senile.[14]

A MORAL CRUSADE

In the first half of the 19th century, a moral crusade was conducted to rid the land of a host of social problems. Most Americans were disturbed not by social and economic inequality but by "willful" violation of the social norms that had characterized village life in earlier periods. Troubled by high levels of drinking, vagrancy, begging, and unemployment, many citizens were determined to battle them by a variety of policy initiatives—for example, building institutions, converting people to evangelical Protestantism, conducting outreach projects to teach morality to poor people and immigrants, and prohibiting consumption of liquor.[15] (See Insert 4.2.)

Historians have advanced many explanations for the moral crusade in the first half of the 19th century. Some implicate the alarm felt by many citizens at the rapid growth of cities and the influence of the frontier; both were widely perceived as causing lawlessness, alcoholism, internal discord, prostitution, and gambling—in short, as ruining the morals of American sons and daughters who migrated to urban areas from the tranquility and social order of villages. Others note widespread popular animus toward the growing legions of Irish and German immigrants, many of whom were Catholic; members of the established Protestant population came to believe that they were being inundated by uncivilized people who would provide a breeding ground for alcoholism and crime. Still others implicate religious motivations; the 1820s and 1830s witnessed the eruption of a vast religious movement that sought to convert Americans to evangelical Protestantism, complete with fiery sermons, streamside baptisms, and tent revivals. Armed with religious fervor, many Americans sought to convert souls not just to religion but away from what they perceived as evil habits, such as drinking.

Nor were fears of social problems altogether unfounded. In fact, Americans consumed extraordinary amounts of liquor early in the 19th century as compared with later periods. Many social problems were highly visible; beggars and street children were seen in the growing cities and vagabonds in the countryside. Still, contemporary historians correctly note that many of these fears were exaggerated. Fears of immigrants were partly based on

FIGURE 4.1 Street children at about the time of the Civil War.

INSERT 4.2 **Critical Analysis: Comparing Moral Crusades in the 19th Century and the 1990s**

Many historians believe that Americans in the early portion of the 19th century exaggerated the moral ills that Americans possessed.

1. Discuss the various factors that, singly and in combination, led Americans to exaggerate moral ills in the early portion of the 19th century.
2. In the 1990s, broad concern developed about crime in the United States even though many kinds of crime were actually declining. Not only did Americans add to their police forces, but some states, such as California, went on a prison construction binge.

Moreover, Americans were reluctant to enact gun controls in many jurisdictions partly because they wanted to allow people to keep weapons to defend themselves. (Many of these weapons end up killing not criminals, but family members in accidental shootings.) Why have Americans been so fearful of crime in the contemporary period?

3. Can you think of other situations in which citizens have developed exaggerated fears that have led to specific policy enactments regarding issues such as drugs, homeless populations, or (even) terrorism?

---

prejudice against Catholics and foreigners. While possessing social problems, cities were hardly bastions of alcoholism and crime.

However, these fears arose in the context of explosive social and economic change. The scale of migration to the frontier is without parallel in world history (except perhaps for the movement of tens of millions of Russians from their western settlements to an eastern frontier to escape the Nazis during World War II). Although most of America remained predominantly agricultural, the large and rapidly expanding Eastern cities were new and strange phenomena. As villages expanded into larger towns and towns became cities with heterogeneous populations that included immigrants, local leaders were less able to use peer pressure to enforce social norms of deference and religious observation. The social reform policies of the early and middle 19th century cannot be understood without placing them in the context of these rapid social changes and the fears they engendered.[16]

In the first half of the 19th century, America had a potpourri of Protestant sects, some Catholic strongholds in Eastern cities, and a small number of Jewish settlers. Local clergy assumed major social and political roles in promulgating social norms, in inveighing against such sins as drinking and swearing, and in urging citizens to be industrious.

Partly because of this religious backdrop, social problems were generally seen in moral terms. Many

persons believed that bankruptcy was caused by profligate spending; crime by drinking or lack of deference to social superiors; and insanity by lust. Problems were commonly perceived to be interrelated; thus, persons who ceased to attend church might be expected to become alcoholics and then delinquent or insane.[17]

Social theorists, politicians, and citizens believed that alcoholism, crime, insanity, gambling, prostitution, and vagrancy were caused solely by individual and moral defects—or by immoral special interests such as the liquor industry. They stereotyped paupers as the progeny of families with intergenerational poverty, and they equated common social problems with immigrant populations, whose numbers expanded sharply in the last half of the century. This preoccupation with morality blinded Americans to alternative explanations of social problems, such as lack of employment, an undisciplined economy that led to frequent recessions, discrimination against immigrants, and lack of adequate social institutions for urban residents. Furthermore, these moral conceptions of social problems led Americans to embrace equally simplistic solutions, which tended to combine moral, religious, educational, disciplinary, and deterrent policies.[18]

To implement their moral crusade, 19th-century social reformers usually turned to local governments and nongovernmental organizations such as sectarian agencies and churches. The development of national solutions to social problems was impeded by the localistic nature of the new society. As we discussed in Chapter 3, the colonists harbored fears that the newly established federal government would interfere with the autonomy of the states, and a national grassroots movement nearly sabotaged approval of the American Constitution, in the belief that it gave the national government excessive authority. After the Republic was established, these fears did not diminish. In the early 19th century, John Calhoun, Henry Clay, and other successors to Hamilton wanted the federal government to subsidize canals, roads, bridges, and other public improvements, but their limited programs were constantly attacked by allies of Jefferson, who believed them to be unconstitutional. Thus, Madison refused in 1817 to fund internal improvements because the power to do so was not mentioned in the Constitution, and in 1830 Jackson vetoed federal assistance to a local turnpike on the grounds that it represented favoritism. Indeed, the Jacksonian era (1828–1836) represented a golden age of decentralization and of limited governmental institutions. Critics believed that this preoccupation with localism and limited government severely impeded the nation's ability to cope with pressing economic problems; for example, Jackson's dismantling of the national bank in 1832 meant that federal authorities could not soften the frequent violent swings in the economy. Nor did federal authorities possess sufficient resources from their minimal taxes to fund significant programs even had they desired them; the entire federal government numbered 153 people at the start of Jefferson's administration in 1800 and had increased to only 352 people by 1829.[19]

Localism led not only to attacks on powers of the national government but also to opposition to economic activity by state governments. In the early 19th century, many states provided major funds for internal improvements such as turnpikes and canals, but by mid-century these interventions were increasingly seen as ill-advised use of governmental power that helped certain sections of the population at the expense of others. Many Americans initially resisted assistance to local educational institutions by the states, on the grounds that it represented undesirable centralization of authority. The major exception to this trend to limit governmental powers was a series of Supreme Court rulings that gave state governments the right to use private land for public purposes (eminent domain) and the right to charter monopolies, as well as rulings that gave the federal government the right to interpret the interstate commerce clause in relatively broad fashion.[20]

Presidents continued to believe that social welfare programs belonged exclusively within the province of local government. Dorothea Dix successfully persuaded the Congress to enact a bill in 1854 to allow the federal government to give the proceeds of some federal land sales to states to help them construct mental institutions, but President Franklin Pierce vetoed it with a message that expressed the philosophy of virtually all of the presidents of the 19th century:

> I can not find any authority in the Constitution for making the Federal Government the great almoner of public charity throughout the United States. To do so would, in my judgment, be contrary to the letter and spirit of the Constitution and subversive of the whole theory upon which the Union of these States is founded ... And when the people of the several States had in their State conventions, and thus alone, given force to the Constitution, ... they ingrafted thereon the explicit declaration that "the powers not delegated to the United States by the Constitution ... are reserved to the States." ... Can it be controverted that the great mass of the business of Government—that involved in the social relations ... the mental and moral culture of men ... the relief of the needy or otherwise unfortunate members of society—did in practice remain with the States?[21]

SOCIAL REFORM POLICIES

Americans developed three kinds of social policies in the early and middle 19th century. First, many popular policies consisted of "moral treatment" for Americans who had fallen (or might fall) into sinful lifestyles, including crime, alcoholism, mental illness, or neglect of religion. Second, some social policies were initiated to give Americans political, economic, and social opportunities, such as voting rights, public education, land distribution, and abolition of imprisonment for indebtedness. Finally, policies were devised to control, regulate, and oppress people of color—notably, African Americans and Native Americans—and Spanish-speaking persons. (We will discuss the latter policies in Chapter 5 in connection with the frontier and the Civil War.)

Temperance

The temperance movement, which easily exceeded abolitionism in size and political influence, was the largest social reform movement in the several decades preceding the Civil War. In 1833, the American Temperance Society had 6,000 chapters, with a combined membership of 1 million persons.

The making and selling of alcoholic beverages had been a major business in America since colonial times, when many farmers had derived substantial income from grain sales to distilleries. Alcoholic beverages were sold in a national network of taverns that served local residents in towns and travelers along many stagecoach routes. The tavern was a central social institution in American villages, towns, and cities.

But many Americans perceived even social drinking as immoral behavior with ominous implications for individuals and the nation. Temperance reformers believed that someone who sipped alcohol socially moved inexorably toward heavier use, which eventually culminated in alcoholism, crime, insanity, and poverty. They feared that the nation's population would descend into debauchery and decline as large numbers of Americans followed this course. Alcoholism was widespread, and scores of inebriates could be found in cities and in many towns, but this catastrophic scenario mainly reflected the reformers' own fantasies and fears.

Temperance crusaders sought to restrict licenses for taverns, to tax alcohol heavily, and to limit retail sales of alcohol to consumers in various localities in the 1820s and 1830s. In some areas, they obtained legislation that allowed courts to impose fines or prison sentences on sellers and users of alcoholic beverages. Countless pamphlets were written and distributed to warn Americans of the dangers of alcohol, to link drinking with atheism and immoral living, and to warn that "the very first drink is a long step toward Hell."

When these various remedies still had not eradicated the problem, temperance reformers turned to state legislatures to obtain passage of laws modeled after legislation that had first been enacted in Maine. Local and state temperance societies circulated petitions and presented hundreds of signatures to local and state politicians; scrutinized the positions of candidates of both major parties as a prelude to supporting or opposing them in local elections; and solicited contributions for acceptable candidates. In the 1840s and 1850s, 13 states enacted prohibitions on the sale of alcohol that made it possible to seize and confiscate alcoholic beverages. Court cases involving illegal sales of alcohol were placed in preferred positions on court calendars to avoid customary delays in litigation.

Despite these ambitious efforts, the temperance movement had only limited success. Most states rescinded their prohibition laws by the 1870s because of adverse court rulings that declared that governmental interference with the making and selling of liquor was unconstitutional. Although many white Protestant citizens supported prohibition, Irish and German immigrants vehemently opposed it—as did substantial numbers of middle- and working-class Americans—on the grounds that drinking and socializing in taverns were integral to their culture. So divisive was the issue in some areas that politicians sought to avoid it by insisting that decisions be made by voters in popular referenda, where restrictive measures were defeated. Local police were often reluctant to enforce prohibition statutes or were so understaffed that enforcement was impractical.

Despite repeated defeats, efforts to limit consumption of alcohol continued, if ineffectually, in the latter part of the 19th century and resurfaced with the imposition of national prohibition by the Volstead Act of 1919, which was subsequently repealed during Franklin Roosevelt's administration in 1933.[22]

The temperance crusade illustrates analytic deficiencies that were common to reformers in the antebellum period. Alcoholism is caused by many factors, including culture, the presence of role models in families, genetic predisposition, poverty, psychological and physical factors, advertising, and peer pressure. When they contended that immorality was the primary cause of alcoholism and that prohibition would eradicate the problem, temperance reformers took a simplistic approach to a complex problem. In reality, neither the legal prohibition of alcohol consumption nor horror stories of ruined lives will suffice as deterrents, as our long history of temperance reform proves.

Antipauperism Strategies

Americans had always believed that individuals could be self-sufficient if they worked hard and adhered to moral principles. Armed with this moral perspective, most Americans were not overly fearful in the 17th and 18th centuries that lack of work would be a major social problem because they believed that virtually all Americans could own land. Although some Americans urged a deterrent approach to welfare, including incarceration in hostile and punitive workhouses, it was commonly assumed in the colonial era that local poor relief would be used mostly by persons who had a legitimate claim to it, such as those disabled as a result of accidents, wars, disease, or old age.

By the early 19th century, and certainly by the 1830s, many Americans feared pauperism as much as alcoholism. They saw numerous very poor people for the first time, not only within large cities in the East but even in smaller towns. As Americans became part of the world economy, periodic recessions led to massive unemployment, particularly in urban areas. Shortages of food and fuel became so acute during severe winters that large numbers of families

risked starvation and death. Disease and work-related accidents left many persons temporarily or permanently disabled; high rates of mortality and social dislocation increased the population of orphans, who sometimes became street beggars. Particularly from the 1840s onward, Eastern cities received waves of immigrants from Europe, who were penniless and without job skills; many vagabonds roamed the American countryside in search of employment. Children who had lost their parents or who had left their homes in their early teens in search of work were often on the streets; some shined shoes or sold newspapers for small change. With the demise of indentured service in the 19th century, new immigrants were cast into the job market and were free to migrate wherever they wished after their arrival. Technically, they could be returned to their first residence if they sought relief in a new location, but laws of settlement were difficult to enforce in a society with extensive migration.[23]

To address the problem of pauperism, American reformers devised three major strategies:

1. They sought to vastly increase the number of almshouses and to modify their internal operations to make them truly deterrent.

2. They tried to establish personal contact with millions of low-income youth to prevent pauperism.

3. They tried to establish systems of surveillance so that charity was not given indiscriminately to destitute persons.

The second and third strategies led to the development of various nongovernmental organizations, which we will discuss shortly.

Numerous Americans had advocated the construction of workhouses in the colonial era, but in many areas they had not been built because of indifference to the plight of the poor, the relatively small numbers of public wards, and the absence of economic resources to build and maintain them. Indeed, some localities resorted extensively to outdoor relief, and laws of settlement were often not vigorously implemented. The antipauperism reformers of the 1820s and 1830s sought to breathe new life into the older deterrent ideas and policies that had not been fully implemented. Before 1820, New York State had allowed localities to decide for themselves whether to use almshouses, apprenticing out, or outdoor relief. In 1824, the Yates Report, which was issued by the secretary of the state of New York, recommended the construction of poorhouses by every county in New York State; an ambitious construction program followed. Subsequent legislation in New York State strengthened laws of settlement and required their vigorous enforcement. New York City, which bore the brunt of the state's welfare costs, succeeded in obtaining state resources to assist it in enlarging its poorhouse and its house of correction.

The work component of the poorhouse and its internal programs were strengthened. Women and children were often put to work weaving garments and making other articles, whereas able-bodied men were made to engage in manual labor, such as working on public roads and chopping wood. Some antipauperism advocates even hoped that the poorhouse might actually cover its expenses through the sale of commodities and the labor of its residents. Residents were increasingly placed under a rigorous regimen that extended beyond work. They were required to follow a strict schedule, which included spartan meals, long hours, lectures on morality, and religious observation. Poorhouses truly became "total institutions" that sought the moral regeneration of residents through techniques that their supporters believed could be applied with scientific precision.[24]

As in the instance of temperance reformers, antipauperism advocates soon found that their ambitious plans were foiled by numerous factors. Most persons who sought public relief could not be "saved" because the reasons for their pauperism had nothing to do with their moral character. Poorhouses increasingly became places of residence for elderly persons who were sick or disabled and for persons with mental disabilities or disorders. Poorhouse officials had no recourse but to provide outdoor relief when recessions occurred because the number of nearly starving citizens far exceeded available spaces. Epidemics as well as occupational accidents filled workhouses

with persons with disabilities in an era that lacked medical science and work safety provisions. Many orphans needed assistance because their parents abandoned them or died in epidemics. Immigrants were often forced to seek assistance because they arrived penniless in the new nation. (See Figure 4.2.)

These crushing realities, which were more significant causes of pauperism than moral character, were generally ignored in an era that was fascinated with personal morality. Antipauperism crusaders joined other reformers who sought to form nongovernmental organizations that could establish personal contact with poor persons to elevate them to high moral standards. One of the major crusades to reach the poor was the Sunday School movement, an effort to bring hundreds of thousands of low-income children into Sunday schools. At its zenith around 1835, the American Sunday School Union, which possessed its own administrative staff, independent of existing denominations, had roughly 400,000 recruits. Thousands of middle-class teachers were recruited, trained, and supervised; they provided highly structured religious and moral instruction to low-income youth to help the children internalize such moral principles as honesty and industry. Teachers avoided physical punishment, relied on a system of rewards and punishments, provided structured lectures and exercises, and used extensive peer pressure to discipline recalcitrant children. (Children who did not take moral instruction seriously were given dunce status and, if necessary, expelled.) Leaders in the Sunday School movement were convinced that its success hinged on the instructional skills of the teachers, whose training and supervision was rigorous. Massive parades of the various schools were held in cities to increase community recognition of the movement and facilitate the recruitment of youth.[25]

As in the case of temperance and antipauperism, however, Sunday School leaders found their hopes dashed by the time of the Civil War. Immigrants were increasingly Catholic and resisted efforts by condescending Protestants to instruct them. Volunteer teachers willing to submit to high standards and intense supervision became more difficult to find. The zeal of reformers

© Library of Congress

FIGURE 4.2 A product of the era of institutions.

diminished as the reform momentum declined, and many of them turned to other causes. But as with the temperance crusade, it was the intrinsic weakness of the Sunday School reformers' ideology that led to the movement's demise. Poor immigrants often resisted reformers' outreach because they themselves realized that their poverty was caused by labor markets, poor health, and unemployment rather than by lack of moral character.

Some reformers believed that the rise in pauperism was the result of undisciplined and indiscriminate relief giving by charitable and public organizations. Many nongovernmental charitable groups had arisen in the early 19th century; these included organizations that helped specific ethnic groups or occupations, widows or single women, and individuals with specific problems, such as debtors. Local politicians also gave funds to applicants who came to their offices, whether the money came from personal coffers or from the city treasury. Reformers feared that devious applicants could seek aid from multiple sources, feign poverty, or use charity to avoid work. (See Insert 4.3.)

The remedy to prevent indiscriminate giving was to tighten the administration of charity institutions. For example, the nongovernmental Association for Improving the Condition of the Poor (AICP), which was active in New York City during the 1840s and 1850s, divided the city into many districts, where agencies were convened regularly to exchange information about recipients and to tighten their giving procedures. Procedures for carefully interrogating applicants were established so that false stories could be detected. A cadre of middle- and upper-income staff was trained to become skilled interviewers who would be in a position to deny assistance to undeserving persons and then to initiate an intensive personal relationship with them and teach them moral virtues through instruction and by personal example. The AICP also developed the first model tenement and helped to enact a pure milk law—projects that suggest its leaders also sought broader social reforms. (We will note in Chapter 5 how charity organization societies, which were similar to—but larger and more bureaucratic than—the antipauper organizations in the antebellum period, developed in a number of cities after the Civil War.)[26]

INSERT 4.3 Ethical Analysis of Key Issues and Policies: When Are People "Deserving" or "Undeserving" of Assistance?

1. Discuss under what circumstances, if any, people in need are undeserving of financial assistance. To ground your analysis in concrete cases, establish a typology of people who cannot support themselves, and analyze why persons in each group do not work:

   - persons who become unemployed during recessions

   - workers who cannot support themselves (or their families) because their wages are too low

   - people who do not work because of mental disorders or disabilities, physical disabilities, or substance abuse

   - people who lack the skills to obtain employment

   - people who do not want to work (list possible reasons for this choice).

2. If relatively few people become destitute because of "character defects," discuss the ethical dangers faced by policy makers who devise punitive policies for their relief-giving programs. Specifically, discuss the ethical dangers of poorhouses, by referring both to first ethical principles and program outcome (or utilitarian) considerations.

Character-Building Institutions

In the early and middle 19th century, reformers organized the construction of many public institutions, including prisons, mental institutions, houses of correction, orphanages, houses of refuge for youth, and institutions for people who had been diagnosed as deaf, blind, or "feebleminded." An institutional strategy was ideally suited to these reformers who wanted to change moral behavior by placing persons in an environment where they could be subjected to intensive moral treatment, undiluted by external distractions.

It is difficult for contemporary citizens to understand the mindset of the reformers who established institutions in the 19th century because we live in an *anti-institutional* era in which institutions are widely reviled. As Eric Monkkonen argues, reformers in the 19th century were proud of these institutions, which, they believed, rescued unfortunate individuals from unsavory lives and influences in the external world, from incarceration in poorhouses, or from lodging in police stations.[27] Citizens would boast of the institutions in their locale as local landmarks. Leaders of churches and ethnic groups avidly raised funds for these highly visible institutions, thousands of which dotted the American landscape by the latter part of the 19th century, and invested extraordinary effort

in keeping them running. As we shall see, the idealistic origins of these institutions were often subverted when reformers found that they could not secure operating funds sufficient to prevent overcrowding and warehousing of residents in a custodial environment.

In colonial societies, prisons had merely held lawbreakers without attempting to change their behavior. Prisoners comprised an indiscriminate mixture of people—youth, murderers, burglars, debtors, and others. Children younger than 7 could not be imprisoned, but some jurisdictions allowed children between the ages of 7 and 14 to be imprisoned and even subjected to the death penalty if courts believed they knew the difference between right and wrong. These prisons were often privately owned; the proprietors charged inmates a fee for their residence and would not discharge them until they, or their friends, had paid their bills.

Reformers in the 19th century sought to transform prisons from custodial institutions to ones that systematically instructed their residents. Daily regimens of labor, reflection, and instruction were planned as a method of changing the behavior of inmates. Physical punishment was avoided insofar as possible; reformers hoped to create an environment where inmates would voluntarily modify their behavior and adopt moral virtues.[28]

Many reformers became convinced that persons with mental problems should be removed from almshouses and placed in separate institutions for the insane. They, too, wanted to use moral treatment to rehabilitate persons with mental disorders. A cadre of reformers—including many physicians who subsequently became the superintendents of mental institutions—lobbied for the construction of these institutions, including Dorothea Dix. (We present a Profile in Policy Advocacy that discusses Dorothea Dix's remarkable work at the end of this chapter in Insert 4.6.)

These reformers, like many Americans in this era, viewed cities as unwholesome places that created, or at least exacerbated, mental problems. They wanted relatively small institutions to be located in rural areas, where staff could establish a personal and caring relationship with residents and supervise regimens that included meditation, moral and religious instruction, gardening, recreation, and hard work. Like prison reformers, they opposed the use of physical restraints whenever possible because they wanted residents to internalize new moral codes.

Many of these mental institutions probably realized the objectives of their founders and superintendents. Their records show that many residents were discharged after marked improvement. Apart from the moral and religious overlay, their approach to treatment of mental illness had much in common with contemporary efforts to create a supportive and low-stress environment for patients with psychiatric disorders. But these institutions, like prisons, were ultimately sabotaged by political and demographic realities. Funds were provided to construct many institutions but not to foster their maintenance or expansion. After the Civil War, their clientele increasingly consisted of low-income, non-English-speaking, Catholic immigrants who resisted the moral regimens that were established by middle-class Protestant reformers. The state mental institutions depended on local boards of overseers for referrals from local poorhouses, but they increasingly referred older persons and those with senile dementia who could not benefit from moral treatment. As low-income and elderly residents moved into the institutions, some middle-class persons began to use private institutions. Consequently, the state mental institutions, now perceived as repositories for destitute persons, were even less likely to receive adequate funding from state legislatures.[29]

New institutions for children were built. Convinced that they possessed scientific knowledge about the idiosyncratic needs of specific groups, reformers set about developing *specialized* services for each group, rather than mixing them together. The dizzying array of specialized institutions for children included houses of refuge, orphanages, homes for "wayward children," and institutions for the "feebleminded."

Houses of refuge were intended for delinquent and neglected children. Colonial laws gave authorities the right to sever parental custody when children were neglected or had become vagabonds, though some authorities only reluctantly removed children from their homes. Roughly one-half of the children admitted to the houses of refuge came from court orders, and the remainder were voluntarily placed by parents because they lacked the funds or capacity to care for them. Like prisons and mental institutions, houses of refuge combined lecture, study, and physical labor. Reformers believed that these houses were effective in helping many youths, but many residents fled from them, and considerable turmoil existed within them.[30]

Orphanages were established for poor children, usually of school age, whose parents (or parent) could no longer support them or would not support them. Some came from intact families, whereas others were wayward children who lived on the streets. (Most street children, variously called waifs, ragamuffins, and half-orphans, were poor urban working-class children without intact families.) To understand a common scenario by which children entered orphanages, consider a woman whose husband died and left her with five children to support. What was she to do? Unless her husband left her a business or farm, she often had to resort to taking in laundry or boarders or doing piecework at home—for example, sewing garments. (Other occupations were closed to most women in this period, and, with five children, she could hardly become a live-in domestic servant—a primary source of income for unmarried women.) Surveying her bleak economic prospects, the woman might voluntarily send three of her children to an orphanage, where they would remain until the age of 16. In other cases, local justices of the peace committed children to orphanages if they ruled that their parents could not properly meet their needs or if the children were living on the streets.

Large numbers of orphanages were constructed in the 19th century by churches, as well as by Irish, German, and other immigrant groups; indeed, Baltimore alone had 28 of them by 1910. Although all orphanages provided moral training, their programs varied widely. In some, children attended public schools, whereas others provided some of their education within the institution. Some emphasized vocational education; others provided general education. Some were built in cities, whereas others were in rural settings. In addition to orphanages, some specialized institutions for wayward children—that is, children who lived on the streets—arose in many cities.[31]

By 1840, "idiocy" was widely seen as a special problem; it was even included on questionnaires of that year's census. No consensus existed about its precise causes; some reformers believed it stemmed from lack of willpower, whereas medical theories implicated physiological factors. Like orphans and neglected children, "feebleminded" people were often housed in poorhouses and mental institutions until reformers determined to wrest them away. Once in a specialized institution, children and adults were placed under a rigorous regimen of training, both to increase their willpower and to impart skills that would make them productive laborers. Early reformers hoped that, with careful training, the inmates might eventually leave the institution; but, by the latter part of the 19th century, superintendents had lowered their goals merely to training the inmates to perform various duties *within* the institution, where most spent the remainder of their lives.[32]

These various institutional approaches, including prisons, mental institutions, orphanages, homes for wayward children, and houses of refuge, achieved considerable success at first—at least compared with what had preceded them. By placing children in houses of refuge, reformers kept them away from hardened criminals in the prison population; by placing children in orphanages, reformers separated them from destitute adults in poorhouses. Prisons became public institutions that possessed a rehabilitation strategy, and persons with mental disorders were rescued from workhouses. Initially blessed with relatively low staff-to-resident ratios, these institutions could provide individualized and intensive services. Because they existed in a society that was generally indifferent to the fate of criminals, persons with mental disorders, or delinquent youth, however, the institutions did not receive sufficient public funding to sustain these intensive and ameliorative services. Furthermore, politicians were unwilling to divert scarce public resources to institutions when funds were needed for road construction and other internal improvements in a growing society.

Various institutions—particularly workhouses and prisons—were continually engulfed in scandal; superintendents were variously charged with fraud, excessive leniency, or providing contracts to political cronies. Moral reform was often impeded by inadequate funding, which prevented the institutions from hiring enough trained staff. In some cases, superintendents came to see that it was in their professional interest if residents were institutionalized for the remainder of their lives because the superintendents could then petition for additional funds on the grounds that they lacked sufficient space for their inmate population. Public authorities, desperate for places to put older people who could not survive in independent living arrangements and who lacked relatives to care for them, often placed them in large numbers in mental institutions or even poorhouses; the result was to overwhelm the staffs of these organizations.[33]

An articulate if idiosyncratic dissenter from the institutional consensus emerged in the 1850s. Charles Loring Brace founded and then became director of the private Children's Aid Society of New York. Brace believed that street urchins and other vagabond children were intrinsically creative but that their natural virtues became stifled when they were placed in institutions. Contending that low-income and immigrant families were often as oppressive as institutions, he took the dramatic step of sending over 90,000 of these children to live with families on or near the frontier between 1853 and 1895. Brace remains a controversial figure; whereas some people believed he was rescuing the children from poverty and from oppressive families, critics argued that the children were placed with families who had been inadequately screened and who used them as unpaid farm labor. Few Americans in this era joined Brace in arguing against the use of institutions that sought to radically reform their residents through a prescribed and rigorous regimen.[34]

The reformers of the early and middle 19th century can be criticized for believing institutions to be a panacea, but they often responded with compassion to the plight of children begging on the streets, criminal offenders incarcerated in brutish settings, and persons with mental disorders who were bound in chains. In considering alternatives, we should not quickly conclude that deinstitutionalization is a panacea. We see its consequences in contemporary society, where persons with psychiatric disorders are released to the community without adequate housing, income, or medical and social services; children are placed in inferior foster homes; and homeless people are left to lead dangerous and degrading lives on public streets. Like the institutions

of the 19th century, community-based programs today are often sabotaged by poor funding and inadequate staffing. (See Insert 4.4.)

Opportunity-Enhancing Policies

In the early and middle 19th century, America extended suffrage to most white males, developed public schools, and distributed land to many settlers. Americans in the 20th century take these institutions and policies for granted, but they represented major—even unimaginable—reforms to Europeans. In Europe, during the first half of the 19th century, suffrage was extended only to persons with considerable property, education was restricted to affluent persons who could afford tuition, and land was not widely distributed. Cambridge University refused to fill a position in American studies with an American scholar in the 1840s because its officials feared he would discuss universal suffrage.[35]

No system of public education existed in the United States in 1800, but by 1860 the nation possessed a national network of primary and secondary schools. This massive growth in public education, which extended to girls as well, represented a major policy advance in the 19th century. Four systems of education existed prior to these reforms: private tutors, boarding schools, day schools that were run by various sects, and charity schools that gave free education to the urban poor. Thomas Jefferson and other colonial

---

INSERT 4.4   Critical Analysis: Why Didn't the 19th-Century Reformers Seek Community-Based Solutions?

1. In contemporary society, we take for granted such community-based programs as foster care for children, halfway houses for persons with psychiatric disorders, or independent living centers for persons with physical disabilities. We can hardly imagine a society where social services focused on placing people into institutions, whether through voluntary or involuntary commitments. Why didn't reformers in the 19th century seek community-based programs? In answering this question, consider such factors as:

- their views of pathology as compared with ours
- their views of civil rights or liberties as compared with ours
- the extent that their society possessed staff and program expertise to implement community-based programs.

2. Although no one would like to return to institutional domination of the human services, discuss what roles institutions can legitimately assume even in contemporary society. (Try to be specific, giving examples of kinds of persons who might benefit from institutional care for varying lengths of time.)

leaders who had espoused free public education had been staunchly resisted by those who did not want high taxes and who believed that education should be provided by the family or by religious sects. Several rationales for publicly funded education emerged by the 1820s and gathered momentum in succeeding decades. An uneducated citizenry, educational reformers argued, would not be able to participate in American democracy, which could lead to tyranny, mob rule, and other evils. In short, much like founders of other institutions in this period, they defined education as a moral enterprise that would teach youth moral rules and so allow them to avoid poverty, alcoholism, and crime. Many people viewed public education as a method of assimilating Irish immigrants into American culture. Some reformers, noting uneasily the strikes and protest of the period, favored public education as a means of controlling the populace; Ralph Waldo Emerson, the noted author, declared, "You must educate them to keep them from our throats." Some persons also realized that a literate workforce was needed if America was to develop an industrial economy. Thanks to the rise of public education in the 19th century, more than one-half of white children between the ages of 5 and 19 were enrolled in schools in 1850.[36]

Crusades to end imprisonment for debt represented one of the major social reform movements of the 19th century. Previously, many Americans who had incurred large debts to start farms and businesses had found themselves threatened with imprisonment when they fell behind in their payments. Agitation in various states led to gradual relaxing of these laws and finally to their abolition in most states by the time of the Civil War.

By 1830, all white males were granted the vote in most jurisdictions. Along with suffrage came greater political participation. In presidential contests, for example, opposing candidates were variously called "atheists," "criminals," and "agitators." Interest groups had already assumed prominence in American politics, as persons with similar interests found that they could obtain policy changes by joining with others, lobbying, assisting friendly legislators, and making campaign contributions (or bribes) to politicians.

Political appearances could be deceiving, however. American interest group democracy, which seemed to give the common people an unprecedented role in political life, often empowered corporations and privileged persons. Fearing that one faction could dominate American politics, Jefferson and many of the colonial leaders had constructed elaborate checks and balances to prevent this possibility, but these safeguards did not prevent specific interest groups from gaining enormous power. By the latter half of the 19th century, industrial tycoons dominated the politics of the nation, just as land speculators and agricultural interests possessed considerable power in the antebellum period.[37]

RADICAL MOVEMENTS: CONSPICUOUS BY THEIR ABSENCE

Although, as we have seen, Americans pioneered opportunity-enhancing policies, comparisons between England and the United States during the 1830s and 1840s suggest that the United States provided an environment hostile to social reform. England was hardly kind to poor people and those with mental disorders, but a relatively strong (by American standards) political mobilization of the lower class known as *chartism* developed in the late 1830s. In his classic work on the English working class, G. D. H. Cole contends that chartism arose partly from discontent when advocates of poorhouses insisted on building them even during a marked downturn in the economy, but its leaders quickly embraced universal male suffrage, equal electoral districts, annual Parliaments, payment of legislators, secret ballots, and removal of property qualifications for legislators. To support these working-class demands, 150 local groups were quickly organized. They sent huge petitions to Parliament urging their measures; one was over six miles long and was signed by more than 3 million people, at a time when the population of Britain numbered only 19 million. While often split by schisms over tactics and their precise program, many chartists broadened their demands in the 1840s to include the repeal of tariffs on corn, demands for a 10-hour day, more humane treatment of people in workhouses, development of free education, factory regulations, and legislation to strengthen unions.[38]

Poor persons and laborers were more organized in England than in the United States for several reasons. First, many American workers, such as Irish Americans, tended to identify with their ethnic groups and often did not identify with, or organize around, their social class. Second, prejudice often splintered workers; for example, white Protestant workers tended to be suspicious of Irish Catholic workers. Third, partly because the federal government was so weak, Americans focused on local issues such as securing city jobs, garbage collection, and other amenities rather than on national economic and social policies. Fourth, American workers probably regarded poor relief as primarily relevant to paupers (that is, to nonworkers), whereas English workers viewed poor law institutions as relevant to working-class interests.[39]

Finally, more dissent and argument existed in England about the causes and nature of poverty. Many English people subscribed to the moralistic and individualistic explanations that were widely accepted by Americans, but some English theorists and citizens emphasized economic and social factors that perpetuated pauperism and poverty. However, the former group, led by Edwin Chadwick, controlled an influential commission whose findings in 1834 recommended that indoor relief and punitive policies replace the relatively generous poor relief that existed in many parts of England. Convinced that nonpunitive administration of the poor laws harmed the economy and drained the public treasury by enticing many people not to work, Chadwick was determined to enforce a harsh workhouse regimen. (He found particularly abhorrent the Speenhamland system of relief in the 1820s, where local poor relief officials actually supplemented the wages of working people in the community whenever the price of bread rose above a certain amount—a policy that suggested that people ought to have a guaranteed income even if they worked in low-wage jobs.) Chadwick's harsh policies were sharply questioned by those who saw industrialization, recessions, low wages, and inflation as the primary causes of dependency. Some reformers even proposed health insurance and old-age pensions for the poor. Reformers found assistance from some aristocrats and the English Conservative party; Benjamin Disraeli and other conservative leaders assumed attitudes befitting the heirs to the feudal nobles, who had provided assistance to serfs during hard times.[40]

Given this contrast between the United States and England, with its more vital radical traditions, it remained to be seen whether Americans could couple their extraordinary interest in facilitating economic, educational, and political opportunity with compassion for persons who were less successful than others. Compassion existed, but it often took the form of relatively harsh, condescending, or moralistic assistance to poor persons who were incessantly accused of causing their own plight by insufficient application or virtue. Ominously, the working class in the United States was poorly organized, when contrasted to European nations, and so provided uncertain pressure for the development of social welfare programs.

OPPRESSION OF VULNERABLE POPULATIONS OR OUT-GROUPS IN THE EARLY REPUBLIC

In the 18th century, as we have seen, the American colonists lived in a triracial society that included white settlers, African Americans, and Native Americans. As the 19th century unfolded, Americans encountered other indigenous populations; in the Southwest portion of the continent, for example, they met Spanish-speaking people who lived in areas that became part of Mexico after its independence from Spain in 1821. Moreover, Americans imported significant numbers of Asians from China, Japan, Korea, and the Philippines to work in agriculture and construction projects in the latter part of the 19th century. We also need to discuss white ethnic minorities, particularly the Irish, whose Catholicism, as well as their sheer numbers and poverty, exposed them to the ire of the white Protestant population even before the Civil War. And we must extend our analysis of the policies, laws, and culture that affected women in the colonial period to the first seven decades of the new republic.

We discuss the oppression of Irish immigrants and women in this chapter, as well as some emerging policies toward sexual matters that had important implications for women and persons who deviated from commonly accepted sexual norms. (We save discussion of the oppression of African slaves, Native Americans, Asian immigrants, and Spanish-speaking persons for Chapter 5.)

Oppression of Women

The doctrine of separate spheres, which had emerged in the colonial period, grew stronger in the early 19th century and led to the cult of domesticity, which consigned women to household and familial functions while reserving the professions and business to males. The economic roles of women were further constrained by the increasing importance attached to child rearing. Whereas children in the colonial period had often been regarded as little adults who were to begin full-time work at the age of 11, they were increasingly viewed as requiring extended moral education and socialization within the family. Although this child rearing could have been shared equally by both parents, Americans in the early 19th century developed the notion that women were uniquely equipped to perform this function. Sometimes perceived as immoral temptresses in the colonial period, women came to be portrayed as morally superior to men— and consequently as best suited to inculcate moral character into the nation's youth. Married women were urged to devote themselves to raising children and to administering their households; they had few rights to own or manage property, except in those cases where their husbands predeceased them.

Almost no married women from the middle or upper classes worked outside their households, and even many working-class women sought to avoid external work. (Female slaves were given no choice.) Widowed women often encountered bleak realities. As in the colonial period, husbands often left the bulk of their estates to their children, so that widows were left to fend for themselves; to survive, they might rent out rooms in their homes, which were often occupied, as well, by one or more of their children, who now owned the house. High rates of male mortality meant that 32 percent of adult women and 61 percent of women over the age of 60 were widows in the 1850s.[41]

The prohibition against labor did not extend to single women, who often worked as domestic and live-in servants. Working conditions for servants were hard: low wages, only one day off each week, and often harsh treatment by employers. Partly because they wanted more independence, some single women found work in factories in New England, where they worked long hours at low pay, but factory jobs were not plentiful; the nation did not industrialize in a major way until after the Civil War. Women were virtually excluded from medicine, law, and the clergy, though growing numbers of them became schoolteachers (as public education became more common) and, after the Civil War, nurses.[42]

But seeds of discontent and protest were finally sown in 1848 at a convention in Seneca Falls, New York, which issued a Declaration of Sentiments modeled after the Declaration of Independence. The 68 women and 32 men who signed it declared, "We hold these truths to be self-evident: that all men and women are created equal" and "have the duty to throw off such government" that visits on them "a long train of abuses and usurpation." In this remarkable and prescient document, the signers attacked the cult of domesticity and the prevalent notion that women were intellectually and legally inferior to men; they demanded suffrage, access to the professions, and legal rights—such as the ability to hold property while married. The Seneca Falls Convention was followed by similar conferences, roughly one each year, between 1849 and the outbreak of the Civil War in 1861.

Historians have identified various reasons why feminism arose in this period. The cult of domesticity, which virtually imprisoned women in their homes, subjected them to so much boredom and so many restrictions that a vanguard of women protested. Moreover, many women became leaders in the budding abolitionist movement, which fostered women's rights in several ways. As they worked to end slavery, which represented an incongruity between the equal rights doctrines of the nation and its practices, women came to recognize a similar incongruity between these doctrines and their own limited legal and social roles. Furthermore, many women experienced discrimination in their work for abolition, both from male abolitionists (who sought to limit them to background roles) and from the public (who often objected to *any* woman speaking in public). Also, more women were receiving the rudiments of education in a growing number of high schools and academies for women—and Oberlin became the first college to admit women in 1837.

But we should not imply that the women who subscribed to feminism in this period, such as Susan B. Anthony and Elizabeth Cady Stanton, represented the mainstream of female (or male) thought at the time. (We provide a Profile in Policy Advocacy that draws on Elizabeth Cady Stanton's remarkable policy advocacy in Insert 4.5 at the end of this chapter.) Indeed, many avant-garde women were content to seek access to the professions and to positions in teaching *within* the old framework of separate spheres and the cult of domesticity and did not agree with "radical feminists" who sought an array of public and political reforms. (In Chapter 5, we note how male abolitionists mostly abandoned women in the wake of the Civil War by refusing to include women in constitutional amendments designed to give the freed slaves certain civil and legal rights.)[43]

Women's freedom was also constricted by the lack of effective birth control in the colonial period. In 1800, each married woman had an average of 6.4 children; with so many children, women could not easily pursue their independent interests. Moreover, many women died during childbirth or from the toll of successive pregnancies.

A remarkable decline in the number of children per family took place in the 19th century. Although it is common for birthrates to decline when nations industrialize, birthrates plummeted in the United States in unprecedented fashion for an agricultural society—to 4.9 children per married woman by 1850 and to 2.8 children by 1880. Historians do not fully understand why this came about. Various explanations have been suggested. One incentive for women to limit family size—particularly in the wake of the Civil War, when the nation rapidly industrialized—was that larger investments of effort were required to prepare children for the labor force in an urban society than when they were laborers on family farms. Another factor was that, by the end of the 19th century, many Americans viewed sex as a reflection of romantic love, in contrast to the predominant colonial attitude that sex was a utilitarian, procreative enterprise, a means of having children. In addition, Americans' extraordinary emphasis on moral qualities in the 19th century prompted interest in the control of sexual activity. The remarkable reductions in birthrates could not have occurred, however, without greater use of contraception. While women had long resorted to a small range of unreliable techniques—the use of sponges, douches, coitus interruptus, and abstinence during the most fertile portion of the menstrual cycle—they gained access to vulcanized rubber condoms and diaphragms after midcentury. Though available primarily by word of mouth and through vaguely worded advertisements, these techniques probably assumed larger roles in limiting families as the century progressed.[44]

Of course, women's (and men's) freedom to control procreation could be limited by public policies. Named after Anthony Comstock, its sponsor, the Comstock Law of 1873 outlawed the circulation of contraceptive information and devices through the U.S. mails because of fear that the use of contraceptives would excessively limit the growth of the American population. Comstock, who worked for the U.S. Postal Service, devoted the next four decades to prosecuting purveyors of "obscenity," including physicians who openly dispensed contraceptives. (In addition, many local jurisdictions enacted obscenity laws that were used by the early

20th century, along with the Comstock Law, to prosecute feminists who sought to openly discuss contraception or to distribute birth control devices.) Moreover, by the late 19th century, many physicians opposed abortion. Before the Civil War, abortion had been used without stigma to limit family size, even if it relied on herbs and other uncertain techniques, but physicians increasingly came to see it as an unnatural curtailing of women's reproductive function.[45]

Nor did public policies target only birth control devices. Homosexuality was not stigmatized in the 19th century, though various localities had laws against sodomy (sexual intercourse between men). But by the end of the century (when the term *homosexuality* was first coined), physicians had declared that same-gender sexual relations represented medical pathology; this development presaged the stigmatizing of such behavior in the 20th century.[46]

Oppression of Irish Immigrants

Some contemporary writers wrongly imply that white ethnic populations, such as the Irish immigrants, assimilated to their new land with ease and with minor discrimination from the dominant population. In fact, the Irish, whose numbers in America increased dramatically in the decade after the potato famine that lasted between 1845 and 1849, illustrate the nature and extent of problems that white, low-income, ethnic immigrants encountered in the new nation. (The problems of the Irish were later experienced by millions of Italian, Jewish, and Eastern European immigrants in the period from 1870 to 1924.)

With the advantage of hindsight, we can see that Ireland was a nation courting disaster in the decades before 1845. Its population consisted of millions of impoverished farmers, whose numbers had so greatly increased in the 70 years before the potato famine that Ireland was the most densely populated nation in Europe. Many Irish peasants lived in degrading poverty, often as tenants to absentee landowners or as owners of small plots of less than five acres. This agrarian and impoverished society depended for its survival on the potato—a crop that had been introduced to Europe from South America and that provided extraordinary

nourishment for its burgeoning population. Even a few acres of this easily grown crop sufficed to feed a family the bulk of its diet.

Although there had been periodic and small famines, no one was prepared for the widespread potato rot in 1845, which devastated the crop on which the nation depended. Imbued with the doctrines of laissez-faire economics, the British government responded to the catastrophe with sublime confidence that market mechanisms would suffice to improve Ireland's depleted food supply. The government's plan was simply to buy stocks of corn and, by periodically selling some of its reserve, to keep the market price of corn at a level that the Irish peasants could afford. Moreover, the government hoped that relatively modest increases in poor law relief would tide the peasants over until the ensuing year when, it was assumed, the potato harvest would return to normal.[47]

Tragically, the plant disease that devastated the harvest in 1845 continued to attack the crops during the next four years. About 750,000 persons, or nearly one-eighth of the population, died of starvation or disease. Cecil Woodham-Smith notes unimaginable horrors:

> At a farm in Caheragh, County Cork, a woman and her two children were found dead and half-eaten by dogs; in a neighboring cottage five more corpses … were lying … Father John O'Sullivan … found a room full of dead people; a man, still living, was lying in bed with a dead wife and two dead children, while a starving cat was eating another dead infant.[48]

People weakened by malnutrition succumbed to mass infections like typhoid fever and dysentery in a nation with only 28 hospitals. A number of factors—crop failures in other parts of Europe; British hatred of the Irish; prevailing notions of limited government; British insistence on financing poor relief from taxes levied on the already impoverished Irish citizens; and punitive responses to widespread riots in the Irish countryside—prevented the use of humane policies to address the emergency.

Roughly 1.5 million Irish peasants sought refuge in the United States from 1845 to 1854, in what was merely the start of a long-term migration from Ireland. Driven by poverty, hatred of landlords, and a desire to join relatives in America, another two and one-half million immigrants had reached the United States by 1900. Of course, this reprieve from starvation and hardship required funds for steamship passage, which were often obtained by selling family heirlooms. Moreover, many people died in passage from various diseases.

Once in the new land, the Irish soon encountered misfortune on a scale just short of the starvation that they had escaped. Ships were sometimes turned away by American authorities, on the grounds that passengers were too diseased. Anti-Catholic, anti-Irish, and anti-immigrant sentiments often sparked riots against the emigrés. As unskilled peasants with no capital and no knowledge of the agricultural techniques needed to develop larger farms on the frontier, most of the Irish immigrants moved to Eastern and Midwestern cities, where they lived in appalling poverty in low-income ghettos. They could perform only unskilled tasks such as cleaning stables, unloading boats, and pushing carts; women found work as domestics. In a land with few regulations, they occupied shantytowns built by speculators; as many as nine people lived in a single room, and many were crowded into cellars. Cholera epidemics swept through these low-income areas; indeed, one report suggests that, in some Irish communities, more than half of the children died and the average age of persons buried was less than 15. Other Irish became the labor force for companies and governments building railroads, roads, and canals. Still others became the labor force for coal mines.[49]

Soon, considerable numbers of the Irish occupied American poorhouses and jails. Irish immigrants commonly took to whiskey to forget their troubles, and alcoholism as well as poverty led to high rates of crime. Protestant Americans believed they were being overrun and often responded with hatred. (Indeed, in 1847 alone, 37,000 Irish immigrants arrived in Boston, a city that had only 115,000 residents in 1845.) In the 1850s, a potent Know-Nothing movement argued that Catholics represented a menace to American national and Protestant identity and that Catholics would dilute the pure "Anglo-Saxon" racial stock of America. Hatred of Catholics spawned the American Political party, which elected six governors in the 1850s. As Higham notes, nativism was an important ingredient in American public life between 1860 and 1925; always simmering, it boiled over again in the 1890s and in the period from 1905 to 1924.[50]

Subjected to discrimination and encountering dire poverty, the Irish immigrants developed remarkable strategies for coping with their environment. They quickly discovered that they could use politics to enhance their well-being, simply by exercising their massive voting power in local elections. In cities such as Boston in the latter part of the 19th century, they were able to elect a succession of Irish mayors, who helped them get jobs, protected them from discrimination and violence, and approved community improvements. The Catholic Church became a prime benefactor, as well, by underwriting charities and helping them form social, athletic, and community groups. Like succeeding waves of immigrants from other nations, the Irish formed tightly knit urban enclaves, both to protect themselves and to evolve community institutions to advance their collective fortunes.[51]

PRECURSORS OF THE
RELUCTANT WELFARE STATE

Many Americans viewed the social problems of the new nation as a pestilence that threatened its moral and social order. Social problems were generally viewed as emanating from the moral defects of citizens—and particularly immigrants in the burgeoning cities. Reformers, correspondingly, tried to develop institutions that could purge these defects from stigmatized groups—people with mental disorders, criminals, paupers, and delinquent youth—or sought preventive strategies, which included temperance and moral instruction through the Sunday School movement or the expanding network of public schools.

In short, the services available to citizens who needed assistance were harsh and controlling. Relatively few reformers acknowledged that structural factors—such as the nation's uncertain economy, the blighted conditions of its cities, or discrimination against its immigrants—assumed a major role in causing social problems. The lack of strong reform and political organizations that represented the policy needs of the lower class, such as were developing in England, deprived the nation of alternative perspectives. Nor did the nation develop expansive notions of social obligation; social programs, most reformers believed, should concentrate only on the provision of institutional and social services to individuals who were truly destitute and ill rather than to a broad range of its citizens. (Public education was an important exception, though even education was conceived primarily as moral instruction.) Most services were, moreover, to be provided by local governments and private philanthropic organizations; Americans accorded the federal government virtually no social welfare roles other than maintenance of some institutions for the deaf and a small program of pensions for veterans.

In Chapter 5, we discuss how these various beliefs about social policy made the nation ill equipped to cope with the social problems that accompanied industrialization in the wake of the Civil War. Furthermore, when coupled with widespread racism, these beliefs led to particularly oppression of Native or First Americans, Asian Americans, Spanish-speaking persons, and African Americans.

LINKING THE EARLY REPUBLIC TO CONTEMPORARY SOCIETY

What We Can Learn from Policy Advocates of the Early Republic

We have an embarrassment of riches when seeking policy advocates in the early Republic due to swirling currents of feminism, abolitionism, and mental health reforms. Let's start with Elizabeth Cady Stanton, who, along with fellow feminists, engaged in policy advocacy efforts that were 60 or more years ahead of her time. (See Insert 4.5.)

Elizabeth Cady Stanton's policy advocacy illustrates key tensions and challenges that are encountered by any policy advocate who engages in tasks identified in Figure 2.1 in Chapter 2. It was grounded in her *moral outrage* at the blatant contradiction between the affirmation of the rights of *men* in the Declaration of Independence and the outright ignoring of the rights of *women*. Are we not, she asked, all members of the human species, and do not we all deserve equal treatment under the law and in such pursuits as education, the professions, and business? Why, she asked, should women be deprived of the right to vote when their views should hold equal weight to those of men? Why should women be placed in separate classes from men in some educational institutions? Imagine, in turn, her moral outrage when women were betrayed by many male abolitionists and public officials who had promised to include female suffrage in Constitutional amendments in the wake of the Civil War—not just because this was a morally correct policy, but to repay the legions of women who had participated in abolitionism. Imagine, too, her outrage when even the Bible, widely viewed as sacrosanct by Christians, used blatantly sexist language—leading her to author *The Woman's Bible* as a nonsexist alternative.

Elizabeth Cady Stanton also had to develop sophisticated *navigational skills* as she and other feminists decided whether to focus on getting suffrage for women through the states or through a federal constitutional amendment. This navigational issue split the suffrage movement into two factions as the American Women's Suffrage Association approached state legislatures to change their constitutions to allow women to vote while the National Women's Suffrage Association sought a broader range of reforms for women including a federal constitutional amendment.

This split between the two suffrage associations illustrates a tension that all policy advocates encounter: whether to seek half a loaf or a full loaf—which, in turn, reflects one's ultimate goals. Feminist

INSERT 4.5   Profiles in Policy Advocacy: Elizabeth Cady Stanton (1815–1902)

Elizabeth Cady Stanton—suffragist, reformer, and the leading philosopher of the 19-century feminist movement—is best remembered for her leadership in the crusade to free women from the legal and social obstacles that prevented them from achieving equality with men. She was born in Johnstown, New York, on November 12, 1815, the seventh of ten children born to Daniel Cady, a farmer turned successful lawyer, and Margaret (Livingston) Cady, the daughter of one of the oldest and wealthiest families in New York.

Stanton's life and thought were most influenced by a tragedy that occurred when she was 11 years old. Her only brother, described by Stanton as "a young man of great talent and promise," died in 1826 due to an illness. The death of her brother devastated her father, who held his son very dear to his heart. Stanton, many years later, recalled that her father said to her, "Oh, my daughter, I wish you were a boy!" The young Stanton responded, "I will try to be all my brother was." Thus her brother's death and her desire to fill the emotional void left in her father's life became a powerful force in the creation of Stanton's identity.

Stanton immediately set out to prove that she could match her brother's abilities. She decided to do this by studying Greek and learning how to manage horses. She excelled in both equestrian skill and the classics. Stanton's only wish was that her father would recognize her achievements and allow her to assume the place formerly held by her brother. He never did. Instead, after showing her father an award she won in a Greek competition against a group of boys, her father kissed her and said with a sigh, "Ah, you should have been a boy!"

Stanton longed to attend Union College in Schenectady, New York, where her brother had studied. Instead, her parents enrolled her at Emma Willard's Seminary in Troy, New York, an exclusive school for women. Stanton was angry that she could not attend college with her male counterparts and argued that single-sex education was a mistake. Though she strongly disapproved of her situation, she remained at the seminary from 1830 to 1832.

Stanton's exposure to the reform movements of her era came through visits to the home of her cousin, abolitionist Gerrit Smith of Peterboro, New York. It was during one of these visits that the young Elizabeth Cady met and was attracted to Henry B. Stanton, an abolitionist 10 years her senior. In May of 1840, despite her father's objections, the couple was married in a ceremony from which the promise to obey was omit-

ted. While on their honeymoon, the newlyweds attended the World Anti-Slavery Convention in London. There, Stanton met Quaker abolitionist and women's rights advocate Lucretia Mott. The two shared their anger over the fact that women delegates were prohibited from speaking and voting at the convention. They left the convention determined to hold a women's rights convention and form a women's rights organization as soon as they returned to America.

Their plans were put on hold for eight years. Meanwhile, Stanton gave birth to her first three children (she gave birth to a total of seven) and moved to Seneca Falls, New York, with her husband. On July 19 and 20, 1848, the first women's rights convention was held in Seneca Falls. At the convention, Stanton presented a draft of a Declaration of Sentiments, which declared that women were equal to men. She also proposed a resolution asking for the American woman's right to vote. Her resolution was the first in a long crusade for women's suffrage. It was adopted by the convention.

Shortly thereafter, Stanton began writing articles on women's rights and the suffrage movement for Amelia Bloomer's temperance paper, the *Lily*. During this same period, she also took to wearing a short skirt over her trousers as publicized by Bloomer. It was through Bloomer that Stanton was introduced to Susan B. Anthony in 1851. Together, Stanton and Anthony worked on women's rights issues for nearly half a century. They worked well together. Stanton, who was a strong speaker and excellent writer, produced the correspondence and delivered speeches, and Anthony, who was a good organizer and campaigner, did her part to arrange conferences and establish networks throughout the women's rights movement. In 1860, Stanton became the first woman to formally address a joint session of the New York State legislature, where she advocated a stronger married women's property bill, which was subsequently approved. Later that year, she shook up the audience at the national women's rights convention by proposing a set of liberalized divorce laws.

With the onset of the Civil War, Stanton's attention was directed back to the abolition of slavery. Together with Susan B. Anthony, she organized the Women's Loyal National League in 1863. The league's purpose was to launch a massive petition campaign to abolish slavery by constitutional amendment. Following the end of the war, however, Stanton opposed both the Fourteenth and Fifteenth Amendments because they extended civil rights and franchise only to African American males while excluding women. Her determination to reform society's view of women and their role in U.S. politics drove her to run for Congress in 1866. Unfortunately, she was not elected.

In 1868, Stanton and Anthony began publishing *Revolution*, a women's rights weekly distributed in New York City. Stanton often contributed editorials in support of the right to vote, greater employment opportunities for women, and a woman's right to serve on juries. In 1869, the two also founded the National Woman Suffrage Association, which had as its main goal the passage of a federal women's suffrage amendment. Elizabeth Stanton served as president of this organization for the next 20 years.

Also in 1869, Stanton began touring the country, giving lectures on women's issues. She was quickly becoming a popular speaker and widely respected authority on the women's rights movement. In 1871, Stanton and Anthony campaigned for women's suffrage in California. Stanton was called on regularly to address Congressional committees on issues related to women's rights in general and the federal suffrage amendment in particular.

In 1895, Elizabeth Cady Stanton was honored when New York City officials declared her birthday "Stanton Day"; at least 6,000 people gathered at the Metropolitan Opera House in her honor. In that same year, remaining true to her controversial nature, Stanton released *The Woman's Bible*, in which she corrected what she believed was a degrading view of women in the standard *Holy Bible*. Attacks were launched at both her and the book by clergy, the press, and many of her colleagues in the suffrage movement.

Ever tenacious, Stanton continued to transmit her views on religion, divorce, and women's rights issues in newspaper and magazine articles. Several of her last efforts were aimed at securing the support of President Theodore Roosevelt. In 1898, she moved to New York City, where she lived until her death in August of 1902. A powerful and emotional epitaph was offered by Susan B. Anthony: "Well, it is an awful hush."

pragmatists in the wake of the Civil War *diagnosed the context* to indicate that rampant sexism in the United States precluded a federal constitutional amendment because most voting men simply would not abide universal suffrage. Other feminists were determined to go straight for a complete victory through a federal constitutional amendment *even if* this tactic would likely mean defeats in the short term. No easy solution exists to this tension between pragmatism (which *did* lead to 12 states enacting universal suffrage by 1917) and idealism (which eventually *did* bring the 19th Amendment to the federal Constitution in 1920, granting women the right to vote).

Another remarkable woman in the early Republic paved the way for policy advocacy in the contemporary period: Dorothea Lynde Dix. (See Insert 4.6.)

Like the work of Elizabeth Cady Stanton, Dorothea Dix's career illustrates that personal characteristics such as *persistence* are critical to policy advocacy —persistence that is fueled by *moral outrage*. Policy advocates are sometimes rewarded with quick successes, but they must often engage in policy advocacy for long periods of time to gain victory—particularly when they encounter a context that is relatively hostile

to their goals. Dorothea Dix *did* achieve a string of successes in different states, persuading state legislatures to establish at least 33 mental health facilities over a span of roughly 20 years, not counting her work after the Civil War. But she was denied her goal of having the federal government help fund mental health facilities in states by use of proceeds from federal land sales when the president vetoed federal legislation she had persuaded both Houses of Congress to approve. Undeterred by this setback, she continued to be an advocate for mentally ill persons after the Civil War.

Her modus operandi was to engage in a massive campaign to educate the public and elected officials about the maltreatment of mentally ill persons that would markedly change the *context* of the issue. Realizing that most persons had scant understanding of mental illness, much less the maltreatment of mentally ill people in poorhouses and prisons, Dix focused on tirelessly educating them through herculean efforts that included traveling 10,000 miles by carriage, interviewing more than 10,000 mentally ill persons, and visiting 300 county jails and 500 poorhouses.

She coupled this public education with assertive communications with members of state legislatures.

INSERT 4.6   Profiles in Policy Advocacy: Dorothea Lynde Dix (1802–1887)

Dorothea Lynde Dix, daughter of Joseph and Mary (Bigelow) Dix, was born in Hampden, Maine, on February 11, 1802. Dix is best remembered as a teacher and crusader for the humane treatment of the mentally ill. She is credited with having prepared the way for this country's mental health movement.

Dix's childhood, which was greatly influenced by her parents' relationship with her grandparents, was a combination of blessings and challenges. Her paternal grandfather, Elijah Dix, was a wealthy doctor and land speculator. When Joseph Dix married Mary Bigelow, a woman several years older than he was, Elijah reacted with great displeasure. Elijah also believed Bigelow was beneath his son's class. In addition, once married, Joseph would not be allowed to complete his studies at Harvard because Harvard refused to allow married individuals to matriculate. Thus, the relationship between Dorothea Dix's parents and her grandparents was already severely strained by the time she was born.

Shortly after their marriage, Joseph and Mary Dix moved to Hampden, Maine, where, despite their disagreements, Joseph was made land agent for one of Elijah's holdings. The couple soon discovered, however, that Elijah's kindness was still limited when it came to his son Joseph and his daughter-in-law Mary. They were provided with a one-room shack for a home. Life in Maine was fraught with hardships, least of which was the bitter cold of winter. It was during one of these cold winters that Dorothea Lynde Dix was born.

Joseph Dix, who left his job as a land agent to become a Methodist preacher, rarely spent time with his wife and daughter. As a result, Mary Dix became discouraged and suffered from depression and was unable to give Dorothea the love and attention all children need and deserve. At 12, Dix left her parent's home and moved to Boston to live with her grandmother. Once there, Dix's hopes for love and kindness were quickly dashed, as her grandmother meted out severe punishments, which she viewed as the only way to instill self-discipline, tidiness, and respect for adults.

There is very little record of Dix's formal education. Many believe that either she taught herself how to read and write while still living with her parents or she attended the Hampden Academy. What is certain is that her primary vocation was teaching, which she began to do at the age of 14, in Worcester, Massachusetts. At 19, Dix opened a school in Orange Court at her grandmother's home. Dorothea Dix taught, directed the school in Orange Court, and

published several literary works until 1836, when she experienced a severe physical and emotional collapse.

In 1837, while recovering from her health problems, Dorothea Dix visited England and learned about the York Retreat. The York Retreat was an asylum for those suffering from mental illness, where patients were clinically assessed and treated. This visit triggered Dix's interest in the treatment of mental health, but her crusade for reforming the entire mental health establishment would be triggered by things she saw closer to home.

Her grandmother had died by 1841, leaving a portion of her estate to Dix. Combined with her own monies, she had enough to live comfortably for the rest of her life. Instead, she returned to teaching, only this time she taught Sunday school at the East Cambridge women's jail.

Her first experience inside the East Cambridge jail would change the course of Dorothea Dix's career. Inside she spoke to poor women who were incarcerated for no reason other than mental illness. While walking around the jail, she also noticed that the area set aside for these women was cold and lacking even the slightest hint of humanity. She quickly learned that one of the major problems facing the mentally ill in jail was the ignorance of those in charge. Their reference to the mentally ill as "lunatics" unaware of their own feelings substantiated Dix's hypothesis. Deeply angered over the inhumane conditions that existed at East Cambridge jail, Dorothea Dix committed the rest of her life to crusading for the humanization of treatment for the thousands of mentally ill people living in America.

Her initial work began in Massachusetts, where she conducted surveys of all of the facilities housing the mentally ill. She soon realized that the conditions at other facilities were far worse than at East Cambridge. Together with Dr. Samuel Gridley Howe, Dix sent a "memorial" to the Massachusetts legislature, documenting the results of her surveys and requesting that the state legislature provide funds for the treatment of the indigent mentally ill. In 1843, after Dix's initial request had been denied, her second request was approved by the Massachusetts legislature.

Dix also began crusading in neighboring states, including New York, Rhode Island, Connecticut, and New Jersey. Her first major victory came in Trenton, New Jersey, where she fought for and won the establishment of the State Hospital in Trenton. At least 32 other mental health facilities were established in the following decades, after Dix had interviewed more than 10,000 mentally ill persons, traveled 10,000 miles by carriage, and visited 300 county jails and 500 poorhouses. By 1848, Dorothea Dix had taken her crusade for the humane treatment of the indigent mentally ill to the nation's capital. Aided by several congressmen, Dix produced a bill that would have provided federal land grants to states for erecting mental health facilities. Unfortunately, President Franklin Pierce vetoed the bill in 1854, claiming the bill was neither constitutional nor economically feasible.

During the Civil War, Dix served as Superintendent of United States Army Nurses, where she was responsible for recruiting nurses for the Union Army. As she did in her many other endeavors, Dix exceeded her mandate and began working on ways to improve the quality of army hospitals. By 1863, the Surgeon General had reclaimed authority over the recruitment of nurses, and in 1866 Dix left Washington, DC, returning to her advocacy for the mentally ill.

Even though her own health was quickly deteriorating, Dix continued her tireless activism within the mental health movement for several years after the war. In July of 1887, Dorothea Lynde Dix died at Trenton Hospital, which she had fought for and won for the wellness of others.

Placing her findings about the maltreatment of mentally ill persons in their state in a "memorial" that was circulated to them and to the mass media and that was filled with lurid details that she had collected directly from mentally ill persons and her own observations, she made it virtually impossible for them to do nothing. Her tactic of using a memorial not only succeeded in placing the topic on legislators' *agendas*, but was preceded by concrete *policy proposals* about where to locate and build one or more mental facilities in specific states and how to fund them.

Dorothea Dix's policy victories also illustrate an important reality in policy advocacy: the importance of *troubleshooting* or *implementation*. It was beneficial to move mentally ill persons from jails and poorhouses into mental institutions, but only if these institutions themselves delivered humane services. Unfortunately, once the aura of success had waned, many states ceased to provide sufficient funding for these mental institutions—and began *also* moving to them large numbers of older persons with dementia and chronic diseases who previously had been placed in poorhouses. By the beginning of the 20th century, then, mental institutions were often in disrepair and overcrowded—with their staff often chosen according to political connections rather than professional merit. They often became merely custodial institutions. Mental institutions began to be emptied with the development of psychotropic drugs in the wake of World War II that allowed many mentally ill persons to be deinstitutionalized into the community. (We discuss subsequently how this policy, too, has proved problematic in many states up to the present time.)

What We Can Learn from the Persistence of Unmet Needs and Policy Issues during the Early Republic[*]

More than 150 years ago, efforts of Dorothea Dix and subsequent pioneers in the field of mental health drew attention to the plight of the mentally ill who were subjected to inhumane treatment while confined to jails and prisons for lack of any other available resources. Her work was devoted to changing the response to the mentally ill to include humane treatment and removal from the prison system. She was successful. The activity of those early advocates resulted in the development of an extensive and comprehensive state system of mental health hospitals across the country providing care for the mentally ill that persisted for the better part of a century.

Fast-Forward 150 Years from the Mid-1800s to the Early 21st Century The issue is "treatment of the mentally ill." The question is, "How well treated are the mentally ill today?" What would Dix find if she were to reappear and visit the jails of today?

---

[*] This section is authored by Esther Gillies, MSW, Adjunct Professor at the School of Social Work at the University of Southern California.

According to Department of Justice statistics, the number of United States residents being held in federal and state correctional facilities and municipal jails had soared to 2.2 million by the end of 2005 (Bureau of Justice Press Release, 2006). Although this statistic in itself is alarming, of greater concern is the issue highlighted by Human Rights Watch, the largest human rights organization in the United States, which found that of those incarcerated in prisons today, about half the jail and prison population in the United States—1,254,800 men and women—has mental health problems (Fellner, 2007).

As a result of inadequate and inaccessible mental health treatment in the community, people with mental illness often engage in behavior deemed illegal, thus thrusting them into the criminal justice system, which is not designed to deal with mental health issues. Human Rights Watch reports that Bureau of Justice statistics indicate that "51% of state inmates with mental health problems were convicted of nonviolent offenses, primarily drug and property offenses. One in five had no prior criminal sentence. Another one in three were non-violent recidivists" (2007). Availability of adequate mental health services in the community prior to the criminal offense could have acted as a deterrent to behavior that resulted in incarceration.

Further, even though prisons are housing men and women suffering from serious mental health disorders, including schizophrenia, bipolar disorder, and major depression, Bureau of Justice records indicate that the federal prisons have provided treatment to only about 24 percent of the inmates identified with mental health problems (Fellner, 2007).[52]

How could this have happened? The problem appeared to be rooted in the mid-1800s. History tells us that over time, disillusionment with the established state mental hospital system emerged as incidents of physical neglect, physical abuse, and sexual exploitation of the patients crept into the system. Due to poor funding, moreover, these institutions often became severely overcrowded and understaffed. Many persons were "warehoused" for decades with little or no treatment. Additionally, attitudes within the society were changing as increased emphasis was placed on the civil rights of citizens. Involuntary commitment to long-term care was no longer seen as a viable option in our society. Segregation of the mentally ill in hospitals became a questionable practice.

With the advance of medical science and the emergence of psychotropic drugs in the mid-1900s, the attention paid to civil rights of all individuals in the society including the mentally ill, plus the rising costs of providing services for the mentally ill, policy makers fashioned a new response to treatment of mental illness that focused primarily on deinstitutionalization of the mentally ill by providing ongoing treatment in community-based mental health centers. Lawmakers quickly adopted the concept, and between the 1960s and the 1980s the large state-operated mental health hospitals were systematically dismantled. Problems were generated, however, when funding for the proposed community mental health centers was never fully implemented. A gap formed when the old system for treatment of the mentally ill was gone and the new proposed system never became available to the majority of those in need.

Some of today's prison systems have responded to the current problem by incorporating mental health services into the correctional system itself. In a 2006 PBS documentary, "The New Asylums," Reginal D. Wilkinson, the director of the Ohio Department of Corrections, a system touted for its forward-thinking approach to dealing with mental health issues of inmates, states that when he was appointed to his current position, "In addition to becoming the Director of the Ohio Department of Corrections, I became a de facto director of a major mental health system." Mental health services are provided within model programs like the corrections system in Ohio, but the primary purpose of the services is to improve the management of inmates within the prison system. Additionally, for inmates who are released, there is no community system of mental health services in place that can maintain the improved level of functioning achieved while in prison. This results in a high rate of readmission of the mentally ill to the prison system.

For the most part, the mentally ill have been left with no safety net and in many cases no services whatsoever. Jamie Fellner, director of the U.S. Program at Human Rights Watch, writes, "...the United States succeeded in shutting down the large, barren public mental health hospitals in which hundreds of thousands of people with mental illness were involuntarily confined and received little treatment. It now involuntarily confines hundreds of thousands of people with serious mental illness in large, barren prisons in which they receive little treatment. Prisons are today's mental health facilities" (2007).[54]

The plight of the mentally ill today is strikingly similar to that encountered by Dorothea Dix in the mid-1800s. The mentally ill were then and are now being confined to prisons and jails for lack of other options. Because the response to the problems of the mentally ill promoted by Dix and other mental health advocates of the time advanced the cause of the mentally ill, resulted in more humane treatment of the mentally ill, positively contributed to the development of the field of mental health as we know it today, and in general was a very positive step forward in the treatment of the mentally ill, one could suggest that there are lessons to be learned for advocates today from her approach to the problem. Analyzing the processes used by Dix that were successful in effecting change and understanding the key issues then and now could enable current advocates to build on past successes and create more effective strategies tailored to meet the challenges of mental health care in the 21st century.

The problem of abuse and discrimination against the mentally ill is not new. What is new is the need for solutions consistent with the times to address the problem in the context of modern society. A study of the work of Dorothea Dix and other advocates of her time provides us with a picture of a response that was appropriate and effective in the mid-19th century and for many years thereafter. The effective intervention and change strategies utilized then are foundational to the work of advocates addressing this ongoing and persistent social problem today.

What We Can Learn from Failed Policy Strategies of the Early Republic

We must remember when criticizing social service strategies in the early Republic that virtually no scientific data existed about the causes of specific social problems such as substance abuse, mental illness, child abuse, or child neglect. Partly because of this dearth of knowledge, as well as the tendency in this era to equate *any* social problem with moral lapses or sinfulness, the early Republic resorted to widespread construction of institutions where persons could be regulated and given moral instruction, as well as required to participate in religious ceremonies.

Morality has its uses but is a flawed strategy for dealing with social problems that stem from physiological, mental, familial, relationship, or other causes. Yet moral approaches to persons with social problems still strongly persist in contemporary society. Homeless persons are often viewed as morally defective, as are persons with sexual disorders or mental disorders, persons who are convicted of crimes, and those who are involved in substance abuse. We are gradually moving toward a best-practices approach in contemporary society even if many social problems still elude effective solutions. Moreover, a best-practices approach still competes with moral views of many social problems, making it difficult to surmount ancient prejudices.

What We Can Learn from Promising Policy Strategies of the Early Republic

Americans placed extraordinary emphasis in the early Republic upon creating opportunities for citizens through widespread distribution of land and the development of public education. We take the American emphasis on creation of opportunities for granted, not realizing how unusual it was when compared to European nations in the early part of the 19th century.

Americans in contemporary society risk, however, not realizing the promise of promoting opportunities for their citizens, particularly ones who would gain the most from subsidized childcare, job training, subsidized scholarships in community college, and universal preschool. Public expenditure in these social investments by the federal government actually decreased from 1978 and 2008 when measured in constant dollars.

What We Can Learn from the Early Republic about the Structure of the American Welfare State

A veritable explosion of nonpublic charities—usually connected with Christian churches in an era when relatively few Jewish, Muslim, or Buddhist Americans existed—took place in the early Republic. Many denominations sponsored orphanages; the Sunday School movement; houses of refuge for youth; institutions for the deaf, blind, and "feeble minded;" societies to prevent pauperism; secondary schools; and colleges. (Later in the century, many denominations built hospitals.) The Catholic Church became a key resource for Irish immigrants prior to and after the Civil War.

This explosion of nonpublic and usually church-sponsored charities created a useful supplementation of public agencies partly because public services were poorly funded. A wider range of options for social and educational services had become available in the American welfare state.

Yet the development of church-sponsored social welfare would invite controversy roughly 150 years later in contemporary society. With separation of church and state enshrined in the Constitution, would charities supported by specific religions proselytize their users even when individuals did not wish to be converted? Are "faith-based services" more or less effective than services provided by nondenominational charities? To what extent should social services provided by religious groups receive subsidies by governments?

WHAT YOU CAN DO NOW

After reading this chapter, you are now equipped to do the following:

- Analyze the role of morality in defining social problems and developing systems of intervention.

- Identify opportunity-creating policies that emerged in the early Republic.

- Analyze the emphasis upon institutions in the early Republic.

- Define "manifest destiny."

- Analyze how Americans oppressed women and Irish Americans in the early Republic.

- Analyze the policy advocacy of Elizabeth Cady Stanton and Dorothea Dix.

- Analyze how the emerging American welfare state was greatly expanded by charities sponsored by religious organizations—principally Christian ones in the early Republic.

- Analyze how we can learn lessons from the past, such as placing persons with mental problems in harsh settings—only now prisons rather than poorhouses.

ENDNOTES

1. James Davis, *Frontier America, 1800–1840: A Comparative Demographic Analysis of the Frontier Process* (Glendale, CA: Arthur H. Clark Co., 1977), pp. 19–21; Richard Slotkin, *The Fatal Environment: The Myth of the Frontier in the Age of Industrialization, 1800–1890* (New York: Atheneum, 1985), pp. 3–47.

2. Edward Pessen, *Jacksonian America: Society, Personality, and Politics* (Homewood, IL: Dorsey Press, 1978), p. 85; Malcolm Rohrbough, *The Land Office Business: The Settlement and Administration of American Public Lands, 1789–1837* (New York: Oxford University Press, 1968), pp. 137–156.

3. Paul Boyer, *Urban Masses and Moral Order in America, 1820–1920* (Cambridge, MA: Harvard University Press, 1978), pp. 3–4; Raymond Mohl, *Poverty in New York, 1783–1825* (New York: Oxford University Press, 1971), pp. 3–13; and Richard Bushman, "Family Security in the Transition from Farm to City, 1750–1850," *Journal of American History*, 6 (Fall 1980), 238–256.

4. Davis, *Frontier America*, pp. 16–17; Slotkin, *The Fatal Environment*, p. 47.

5. Stephan Thernstrom, *Poverty and Progress: Social Mobility in a 19th Century City* (Cambridge, MA: Harvard University Press, 1964), pp. 33–57.

6. Charles Sellers, *The Market Revolution: Jacksonian America, 1815–1846* (New York: Oxford University Press, 1991), p. 389.

7. Mohl, *Poverty*, pp. 14–34; Pessen, *Jacksonian America*, pp. 55–58.

8. Sellers, *The Market Revolution*, p. 137.

9. Eric Foner, *History of the Labor Movement in the United States*, Vol. 1 (New York: International Publishers, 1955), pp. 106–143; Mohl, *Poverty*, pp. 20–30.

10. Foner, *History of the Labor Movement*, Vol. 1, pp. 108–120.

11. Pessen, *Jacksonian America*, pp. 77–83.

12. Sellers, *The Market Revolution*, p. 261.

13. Michael Katz, Michael Doucet, and Mark Stern, *The Social Organization of Early Industrial Capitalism* (Cambridge, MA: Harvard University Press, 1982), pp. 242–284.

14. Rowland Berthoff, *An Unsettled People: Social Order and Disorder in American History* (New York: Harper & Row, 1971), pp. 148–161; Boyer, *Urban Masses*, p. 68.

15. Boyer, *Urban Masses*, pp. 12–21, 67–75; Thernstrom, *Poverty and Progress*, pp. 42–46, 50–56; and Nathan Huggins, *Protestants against Poverty* (Westport, CT: Greenwood Press, 1971), pp. 3–14.

16. Berthoff, *An Unsettled People*, pp. 288–292.

17. Boyer, *Urban Masses*, pp. 3–64; Mohl, *Poverty*, pp. 159–170.

18. Michael Katz, *Poverty and Policy in American History* (New York: Academic Press, 1983), pp. 134–156; Huggins, *Protestants against Poverty*, p. 177; and Mohl, *Poverty*, pp. 259–265.

19. Sellers, *The Market Revolution*, pp. 37, 114–124; Bray Hammond, *Banks and Politics in America from the Revolution to the Civil War* (Princeton, NJ: Princeton University Press, 1957), pp. 451–499; and Pessen, *Jacksonian America*, p. 147.

20. Louis Hartz, *Economic Policy and Democratic Thought in Pennsylvania* (Cambridge, MA: Harvard University Press, 1948), pp. 309–320; Carl Kaestle, *Pillars of the Republic: Common Schools and American Society, 1780–1860* (New York: Hill and Wang, 1983), pp. 136–181; Robert Steamer, *The Supreme Court in Crisis: A History of Conflict* (Amherst, MA: University of Massachusetts Press, 1971), pp. 41–44, 61–62; and Edward White, *The American Judicial Tradition: Profiles of Leading American Judges* (New York: Oxford University Press, 1976), pp. 49–61.

21. June Axinn and Herman Levin, *Social Welfare: A History of the American Response to Need* (New York: Harper & Row, 1982), pp. 80–84.

22. Ian Tyrrell, *Sobering Up: From Temperance to Prohibition in Antebellum America, 1800–1862* (Westport, CT: Greenwood Press, 1979), pp. 3–13, 63–67, 87–115, 235–245, 290–297.

23. Gerald Grob, *Mental Institutions in America: Social Policy to 1875* (New York: Free Press, 1973), p. 168;

Merrill Peterson, ed., *The Portable Thomas Jefferson* (New York: Viking Press, 1975), pp. 180–181; and Mohl, *Poverty*, pp. 14–34.

24. Katz, *Poverty and Policy*, pp. 90–98, 134–142, 157–165.

25. Boyer, *Urban Masses*, pp. 34–53.

26. Boyer, *Urban Masses*, pp. 86–94; Mohl, *Poverty*, pp. 47, 241–258; and Huggins, *Protestants against Poverty*, pp. 111–135.

27. Eric Monkkonen, "Nineteenth-Century Institutions, Dealing with the Urban 'Underclass.'" In Michael Katz, ed., *The "Underclass" Debate: Views from History* (Princeton, NJ: Princeton University Press, 1993), pp. 334–365.

28. Joseph Hawes, *Children in Urban Society: Juvenile Delinquency in Nineteenth-Century America* (New York: Oxford University Press, 1971), pp. 20–24, 45–51; Robert Mennel, *Thorns and Thistles: Juvenile Delinquents in the United States, 1825–1940* (Hanover, NH: University Press of New England, 1973), pp. 3–31.

29. Grob, *Mental Institutions*, pp. 103–110, 156–157, 174–220; David Rothman, *The Discovery of the Asylum: Social Order and Disorder in the New Republic* (Boston: Little, Brown, 1971), pp. 206–236.

30. Hawes, *Children*, pp. 45–51; Mennel, *Thorns*, pp. 12–31.

31. Peter Halloran, *Boston's Wayward Children: Social Services for Homeless Children, 1830–1930* (London: Associated University Presses, 1989); Nurith Zmora, *Orphanages Reconsidered: Child Care Institutions in Progressive Era Baltimore* (Philadelphia: Temple University Press, 1994).

32. James Trent, *Inventing the Feeble Mind: A History of Mental Retardation in the United States* (Berkeley: University of California Press, 1994).

33. Ibid., pp. 60–95; Walter Trattner, *Homer Folks: Pioneer in Social Welfare* (New York: Columbia University Press, 1968), pp. 76–81.

34. Mennel, *Thorns*, pp. 32–40.

35. Joyce Appleby, *Capitalism and a New Social Order: The Republican Vision of the 1790s* (New York: New York University Press, 1984), p. 2.

36. Sellers, *The Market Revolution*, pp. 368–369; Kaestle, *Pillars*, pp. 75–103; Michael Katz, *The Irony of Early School Reform: Educational Innovation in Mid-*

Nineteenth Century Massachusetts (Cambridge, MA: Harvard University Press, 1968), pp. 124–160.

37. Pessen, *Jacksonian America*, pp. 104–114.

38. G. D. H. Cole and Raymond Postgate, *The British Common People, 1746–1946* (New York: Barnes & Noble Books, 1961), pp. 279–327.

39. Ibid., pp. 279, 315; Ira Katznelson, "Working-Class Formation and the State: Nineteenth-Century England in American Perspective." In Peter Evans, Dietrich Rueschemeyer, and Theda Skocpol, eds., *Bringing the State Back In* (Cambridge: Cambridge University Press, 1985), pp. 270–278.

40. Cole and Postgate, pp. 278–280; Michael Barker, *Gladstone and Radicalism: The Reconstruction of Liberal Policy in Britain, 1885–1894* (New York: Harper & Row, 1975), pp. 37–40; and Norman Gash, *Reaction and Reconstruction in English Politics: 1832–1852* (Oxford: Clarendon Press, 1965), pp. 139–140, 149–150.

41. Barbara Harris, *Beyond Her Sphere: Women and the Professions in American History* (Westport, CT: Greenwood Press, 1978), pp. 40ff; Katz, Doucet, and Stern, *The Social Organization*, pp. 290–292.

42. Harris, *Beyond Her Sphere*, pp. 60ff.

43. Ibid., pp. 73ff.

44. John D'Emilio and Estelle Freedman, *Intimate Matters: A History of Sexuality in America* (New York: Harper & Row, 1988), pp. 58–60; Sellers, *The Market Revolution*, p. 258.

45. D'Emilio and Freedman, *Intimate Matters*, p. 85.

46. Ibid., pp. 121–130.

47. John Ibson, *Will the World Break Your Heart? A Historical Analysis of the Dimensions and Consequences of Irish-American Assimilation.* Doctoral dissertation. Brandeis University, 1976; Cecil Woodham-Smith, *The Great Hunger: Ireland 1845–1849* (New York: Signet Books, 1962), pp. 24–30, 86.

48. Woodham-Smith, *The Great Hunger*, p. 177.

49. Ibid., pp. 224, 248.

50. Ibid., pp. 243-265; John Higham, *Strangers in the Land: Patterns of American Nativism, 1860–1925* (New York: Atheneum, 1972), pp. 3–11.

51. Lawrence Fuchs, *The American Kaleidoscope: Race, Ethnicity, and the Civic Culture* (Hanover, NH: University Press of New England, 1990), pp. 35–53.

52. Bureau of Justice Statistics. (2006). Bureau of Justice statistics press release (online). Retrieved from http://www.ojp.usdoj.gov/bjs/pub/press/pripropr.htm on July 17, 2007.

53. Fellner, J. (2007). Prevalence and policy: New data on the prevalence of mental illness in U.S. prisons (online). Retrieved from http://hrw.org/English/docs/200701/10/usdom15040.htm on July 16, 2007.

5

Lost Opportunities: The Frontier, the Civil War, and Industrialization

TABLE 5.1   **Selected Orienting Events**

1803	Louisiana Purchase
1820	Missouri Compromise
1828	Andrew Jackson elected to first of two presidential terms
1836	Battle of the Alamo
1838–1839	Forced march of the Cherokees
1845	The term *manifest destiny* coined
1846–1848	Mexican–American War
1848	Treaty of Guadalupe Hidalgo; Seneca Falls Convention
1859	Charles Darwin publishes *On the Origin of Species by Means of Natural Selection*
1860	Abraham Lincoln elected to first of two presidential terms
1861–1865	Civil War
1863	Emancipation Proclamation
1865	Lincoln assassinated
1865–1868	Presidency of Andrew Johnson
1865–1872	Freedmen's Bureau in existence
1865–1900	The Gilded Age; rapid industrialization
1868	Ulysses Grant elected to first of two presidential terms
1873–1878	Extended period of recession
1877	President Hayes uses federal troops to end national railroad strike
1880–1914	Arrival of 21 million immigrants in the United States

T A B L E 5.1	**(Continued)**
1882	**Chinese Exclusion Act**
1887	**Dawes Act**
1890	**U.S. Census declares frontier to have officially ended; passage of Sherman Antitrust Act**
1902	**Reclamation Act**

In this chapter we focus on three epic developments that posed enormous challenges to the new nation during the 19th century: the rapid settlement of the frontier (over the first eight decades of the century), the Civil War (in the middle of the century), and the development of an industrial system (primarily during and after the Civil War). Americans' responses to these three events can be understood as a lost opportunity for social reform. Rampant sexism and racism continued to shape Americans' responses to these epic events as well as the myriad social problems that they spawned, as reflected by policies they developed regarding women, First Americans, Spanish-speaking Americans, African Americans, and Asian Americans.

At the end of the chapter, we discuss what we can learn in contemporary society about policy advocacy, social policy, and the structure of the American welfare state from frontier settlement, the Civil War, and industrialization.

SOCIAL POLICY AT THE FRONTIER

Life on the American frontier has been romanticized in countless films and books. In reality, while many white settlers—along with speculators and railroad companies—became rich, others could not obtain land or were bankrupted in the volatile swings of the frontier economy. The frontier was also the stage for the persecution of First Americans, Spanish-speaking persons, and other groups.

Land Policy

In the early and middle 19th century, most of the unsettled land in the United States was in territories owned by the federal government. Federal authorities had to decide on an appropriate policy: whether to give land to settlers, to allow persons to buy unlimited quantities of land, to sell or give the land to churches and other organizations, or (most radically) to distribute the land to former slaves, Native Americans, impoverished immigrants, urban dwellers, and squatters.

The basic strategy for distributing the land, which was developed by the 1780s, was to sell it in blocks at public auctions to the highest bidders, provided their bids exceeded a prescribed minimum price. The advantages of this strategy, from the government's point of view, were that public auction of vast quantities of unsettled land would most likely keep land prices relatively low, would avoid the large public bureaucracies required if the government were to distribute land directly to individuals, and would conform to the tenets of capitalism, which governed the distribution of American lands almost from the beginning of the national experience. Tens of millions of acres were sold at federal land offices between 1790 and 1890, when the frontier no longer existed.

Far from proving equitable, however, the auctions often enriched relatively affluent Americans, speculators, and railroad companies. Competitive bidding at auctions tended to favor already wealthy persons who had recently sold their farms in settled areas. Believing that railroad lines through the territories would stimulate economic growth, the federal government gave (or sold at minimum prices) vast tracts to the railroad companies, which then sold the land to settlers—at inflated prices. Speculators and land companies soon discovered how to manipulate the auction system. Using scouts and information leaked by officials at federal land offices, they located valuable farmland and other lands, made mutual agreements not to engage in competitive bidding, and secured large tracts at the minimum federal price, which they later sold at higher prices to settlers.[1]

It is a myth that the frontier was largely sold to farmhands, poor immigrants, or poor urban dwellers. A large class of squatters settled frontier lands without titles, as they lacked funds to purchase them; they grew several crops on the land before moving westward to renew the process. The federal government periodically tried to help squatters and persons of limited means. Many "preemption laws" allowed squatters to purchase their land at the federal auctions. Furthermore, to help poorer persons buy land, federal authorities successively lowered the minimum sizes of land blocks from 320 to

---

INSERT 5.1 **Using the Web to Understand How Americans Made Social Policy on the Frontier, during the Civil War, and during Industrialization**

Visit **academic.cengage.com/social_work/jansson** to view these links and a variety of study tools.

Go to **http://www.loc.gov** Click on "American Memory." Click on "African American History" and proceed to "Slave Narratives—Audio Interviews." Listen to an interview with a former slave.

Go to **http://www.loc.gov** Click on "American Memory." Click on "Government, Law" and proceed to "Haymarket Affair." Then click on "Dramas of Haymarket" and read the materials about labor strife in the late 19th century. You can also read from the transcripts of the trial against the protesters in "Trial of Illinois vs. August Spies" by selecting a specific volume.

Go to **http://www.loc.gov** Click on "American Memory." Click on "Immigration, American Experience."

- Proceed to "Chinese in California." Browse the subject index for specific materials and photos.
- Also proceed to Northern Great Plains photos as well as the subject index to better understand the settlement of the frontier.

Go to **http://www.loc.gov** Click on "American Memory."
Click on "Native-American History."

- Proceed to Edward S. Curtis's photographic images sorted by cultural area.

- Proceed to "American Indians of the Pacific Northwest" and browse the subject index.
- Proceed to "Western U.S. Photographs, 1860–1912" to better understand the settlement of the frontier.

Go to **http://www.archives.gov/education/lessons**
Go to "Era 1850–1877."

- Proceed to "Civil War as Photographed by Matthew Brady." View specific photographs.
- Proceed to "Fight for Equal Rights: Black Soldiers in the Civil War."
- Proceed to "Fugitive from Labor Cases: Henry Garnet (1850) and Moses Honner (1860s)."

Go to **http://www.archives.gov/education/lessons**
Go to "Era 1870–1890."

- Proceed to "Homestead Act of 1862."
- Proceed to "Maps of Indian Territory."
- Proceed to "Affidavits and Flyers from the Chinese Boycott Case."

Go to **http://cherokeehistory.com/index.html#links** and spend some time navigating the site—read the extensive and rich history of the Cherokee Tribe. Was the forced march of the Cherokees to Oklahoma merely one of a series of oppressive acts by white settlers that were visited on this tribe?

160 to 40 acres and decreased the required down payment. But these policies were insufficient to make land ownership possible for many squatters and other would-be settlers. Relatively little land was distributed to freed slaves in the wake of the Civil War, and land was not widely used for charitable institutions, aside from land grant colleges.[2]

Settlers' problems were compounded by inadequate regulation of the frontier banks that financed land purchases. In the absence of sufficient federal currency, notes of local banks were used as currency, but their value fluctuated wildly in periodic recessions or when the banks had to repay their foreign creditors. President Jackson's veto of the United States Bank in 1832 compounded the economic turmoil.

The frontier also provided rich opportunities for deception and fraud. Speculators, railroads, and steamship companies hired salesmen who, with promises of fertile American lands, would persuade European peasants to part with their life savings in exchange for a plot of barren land in a remote location. By hiring persons to falsely claim squatting rights, speculators were able to buy land at minimum prices. Federal land agents often gave information about choice lands to speculators for a fee—and themselves participated freely in land speculation.[3]

Conquest and Oppression of First Americans and Spanish-Speaking Persons

During the colonial period, prejudice against First Americans was softened by the condescending belief that the destructive influence of tribal customs made them lazy. In the 19th century, such environmental explanations of the differences between First Americans and whites were increasingly supplanted by unmitigated racism, which promoted vicious suppression of First Americans and Spanish-speaking persons on the frontier. American anthropologists became convinced that white persons from England and Germany, whom they called Anglo-Saxons, were biologically superior to other races in intelligence and industriousness. They

went on to argue that this supposed superiority had allowed Anglo-Saxons to conquer indigenous persons, develop new technology, and establish democratic and legal institutions. Unlike many colonial theorists, who assumed that First Americans shared common biological origins with whites, these anthropologists contended that Anglo-Saxons derived from a biological stock different from that of other races.[4]

Scientists have since disproved these theories of biological superiority. They have shown that all human races derived from ancestors in Africa or Asia—something that 19th-century anthropologists would have found disconcerting—and that there is no significant difference in brain size between races.[5] Racist ideas that placed Anglo-Saxons on a biological pedestal were nonetheless widely accepted in the 19th century and were linked to nationalism through the concept of *manifest destiny*, a term coined by Democratic politician John O'Sullivan in 1845. According to the doctrine of manifest destiny, God willed Anglo-Saxons to develop the North American continent as a laboratory to show the world that Americans could build a utopian society that fused capitalism, Protestantism, and democracy. Anthropologists and politicians argued that indigenous peoples who blocked the expansion of the frontier should be violently suppressed and that Anglo-Saxons should not dilute their stock by marrying members of other racial groups.[6]

In the colonial period, the frontier had been circumscribed by territorial claims of the Spanish and the French, by the determination of the English Crown to limit settlers' advance on some Native American lands (see the discussion of the Proclamation Line in Chapter 3), and by the tenacity of First American tribes, whose resistance to the advance of white settlers was often effective. By the early 19th century, with the departure of the European powers and with huge increases in the numbers of white settlers, the balance of power at the frontier shifted toward the settlers who, moreover, continued to make use of their advanced weapons, their ability to play tribes off against each other, and their willingness to entice or force tribal leaders to sign treaties. What's more, the unexpected acquisition of the Louisiana Territory from the French in 1803 opened up a frontier extending from the Mississippi to the Pacific, with the exception of huge Spanish territories on the Southwestern and Western parts of the continent. (Those territories became part of Mexico when it gained independence from Spain in 1821.)

When Jefferson negotiated the Louisiana Purchase, he had the notion that First Americans should live on small tracts of land in their existing territories (with the remaining lands to be sold to white settlers by federal land agents). However, he came to adopt a "removal policy," which would relocate most Native Americans who lived west of the Mississippi to lands far from the existing frontier. This relocation policy was anathema to many First American leaders, such as the legendary Tecumseh, who tried over some decades to organize an effective resistance by tribes in the Ohio Valley and the South. But the push of the white settlers was inexorable; often under force of arms, tribal leaders (or those cooperative individuals identified as leaders by white officials) ceded vast tracts to the American government. Those few federal officials who sought to protect land granted to First Americans by these treaties had little success in restraining settlers from occupying the land and brutalizing the Native Americans who lived there.[7]

Even those First Americans who chose to become farmers were displaced as the frontier moved westward. Consider the Cherokees, who farmed lands in Georgia. Many Cherokees signed treaties with federal authorities that guaranteed tribal jurisdiction over certain lands and declared their statehood independent of Georgia, so as to forestall efforts to take their land. Some politicians resisted their removal and cited treaty obligations, but the Georgia legislators declared the Cherokees to be merely tenants who could be evicted and removed to Western territories. (Georgia invited its citizens to plunder the Cherokees and enacted legislation that made it illegal for Cherokees to testify in court against white men who took their property!) In desperation, the Cherokees appealed to President Jackson, who promptly ruled that the issue was a state matter; Jackson strongly supported the congressional "removal legislation" that was enacted

in 1830. The Cherokees then appealed to the U.S. Supreme Court on the grounds that, as a foreign power, their land claims could not be violated by Georgia. Though showing some sympathy to them, the Supreme Court ruled the Cherokees to be merely a "domestic dependent nation" that could not claim to be a foreign power; as such, the Court argued, the Cherokees lacked jurisdiction. When a subsequent Supreme Court ruling was more favorable, President Andrew Jackson simply ignored it; Cherokees were rounded up into stockades and forcibly marched to territories in an area that later became the state of Oklahoma. It has been estimated that as many as 45 percent of the tribe died of starvation or disease during this forced exodus. Similar policies were used to evict other large Southern tribes such as the Chocktaws, the Chickasaws, and the Creeks; the Seminoles in Florida were pushed into swampy and undesirable lands that became their reservations. Tribes in the Ohio, Indiana, and Illinois areas were similarly removed to the West, often under treaties that promised that their Western lands would be kept intact for them for "perpetuity." By the end of the 1830s, then, many displaced tribes existed in territories west of the Mississippi, in areas that later became Kansas, Arkansas, Oklahoma, Nebraska, and Texas. Other tribes were confined to relatively small reservations in scattered locations in Florida, Minnesota, and elsewhere[8] (Figure 5.1).

Settlers also dealt brutally with Spanish-speaking people on the Western frontier. The Louisiana Purchase gave most lands west of the Mississippi to the Americans but *not* the lands held by Spain, which became part of Mexico in 1821. White settlers found the area that became Texas to be suitable for ranching and for cotton in the 1820s and 1830s. As they pushed west and were resisted by the indigenous population, episodes of violence escalated, but the region was easy to conquer because of the political instability and weakness of Mexico. When a particular battle at the Alamo in San Antonio in 1836 was publicized as the massacre of innocent white settlers by barbaric Mexicans, many Americans supported the efforts of the white settlers to gain independence from Mexico and

FIGURE 5.1 A 19th-century Native American.

establish a territorial government, which became an American state in 1845. When the Mexican government refused to recognize this new state constructed from Mexican territory, the United States declared war in 1846 and, in a one-sided affair, routed the Mexicans in a series of battles that culminated in the ransacking of Mexico City in 1847.

The Mexicans ceded territory that is now California, Nevada, New Mexico, Utah, parts of Colorado, Wyoming, and Arizona—and they recognized the independence of Texas. In an attempt to protect the stranded Spanish-speaking persons in the ceded territory, they insisted on a provision in the Treaty of Guadalupe Hidalgo that required Americans to honor the civil liberties and rights of the indigenous and Spanish-speaking population. But the provision had little effect. Spanish-speaking persons were told that their land titles, which existed under Mexican law, had to be converted to American titles; this policy led to the transfer of millions of acres of land to white settlers in Texas and then other areas that had been ceded by Mexico. (The indigenous persons lacked legal resources and access to impartial judges.) White squatters often claimed their land extralegally—and many indigenous Spanish-speaking persons were massacred by land-hungry settlers. Landless, lacking resources, and denied civil rights and civil liberties, the Spanish-speaking population proved a useful source of labor for American ranchers and eventually for growers of vegetable and cotton crops. Large farming operations were made possible by the passage of the Reclamation Act in 1902, which provided federal funds to build an irrigation system that brought water from the Colorado River to California. Isolated from urban populations in labor camps that were organized by large owners and companies, the Spanish-speaking farm workers were brutally suppressed when they complained about their subsistence wages and harsh working conditions.[9]

In effect, then, the settlers had engaged in three conquests by the mid 1840s: the initial development of the frontier in the colonial period, a massive relocation of First Americans from the formation of the republic to the late 1830s, and the acquisition from the Mexicans of much of the Western and Southwestern part of the continent in the 1830s and 1840s. These conquests led to the formation of various states east of the Mississippi, as well as Texas, and paved the way for the establishment of many Southwestern states, as well as California, which became a state in 1850.

But the white settlers had created a problem for themselves when they had forcibly relocated many tribes west of the Mississippi, for First Americans now occupied vast tracts of land that white settlers desired—and some of these lands also contained minerals. A fourth conquest was needed to obtain lands that First Americans held under treaties with the United States in areas that later became the states of Nebraska, Kansas, Arkansas, and Oklahoma, as well as the areas ceded to the United States by Mexico, such as Colorado and California. They also had to dispossess tribes from the Badlands in what later became North and South Dakota, from the areas that became Montana and Idaho, and from their territories in the Pacific Northwest.[10]

This fourth conquest used many of the techniques perfected earlier. Once again, tribes were induced to sign treaties by which they ceded land in exchange for minimal cash and more promises that their (now smaller) reservations would be guaranteed to them for perpetuity. First Americans' resistance was softened by running railroads through their lands (and thereby allowing both settlers and troops to penetrate their territory more rapidly), by mass killing of the buffalo on which they depended for sustenance, and by threats that Congress would rescind prior treaties if they failed to sign new treaties. The removal policy came to a climactic and tragic conclusion in the wake of the Civil War, when President Grant chose Civil War generals such as Sherman and Sheridan to evict First Americans from lands west of the Mississippi. They resorted to the usual mixture of unenforced treaties and brutal assaults, but they undertook this policy with a savagery that was unmistakable in its intent: to kill all First Americans who would not agree to settle on reservations. In 1868, thanks to the skilled tactics of Sitting Bull, Crazy Horse, and other First American chiefs and warriors, the American government signed a treaty that guaranteed a huge area of the Badlands to the Sioux and Cheyenne. White settlers' discovery of gold on those lands, however, placed enormous pressure on the government to evict the First Americans. George Custer, a flamboyant Civil War general, was given the task of killing the First Americans who still occupied this area. Confident that the First Americans lacked courage to fight, he marched a small contingent directly at First American forces numbering in the thousands—and he and his forces were killed in a battle popularly known as Custer's Last Stand. Instead of viewing Custer's demise as the result of the government's illegal abrogation of

its treaty with the Sioux, most white Americans sympathized with Custer, who was widely perceived as an innocent victim of savages. The First Americans had won a Pyrrhic victory because they soon encountered the entire army of the United States, which indiscriminately attacked them; the final massacre of women, children, and men took place at Wounded Knee in 1890.

In the 1870s, many public officials began a movement to break up reservations, on the grounds that tribal ownership of land represented an unnatural and communalistic experiment inconsistent with Anglo patterns of individualistic land ownership. The Dawes Act, which Congress enacted in 1887, conditioned First Americans' continued access to the land on their acceptance of individual plots; each head of family would be given 160 acres. Although some protections were initially established, the new policy meant that whites could take land from First Americans, one by one, by a variety of tricks—by coercing or enticing them to sell their land for minimal prices, by using devious legal techniques to obtain title to their plots, or by arguing that Native Americans had failed to claim some of their allotments. In this way, speculators and crooks were able to liquidate vast holdings. For example, five major tribes had held an area equivalent to half the size of Oklahoma, but their holdings were reduced from 19.5 million acres in the 1850s to slightly over 300,000 acres by 1956.[11]

Finding Laborers

Americans on the Western frontier often needed to obtain labor to grow crops, to build public improvements such as railroads, and to work in mines. Many white settlers in Texas imported slaves from other sections of the South to make it a major cotton-growing region. We have already noted that, once dispossessed from the land, the Spanish-speaking population provided the major source of labor for the cultivation of cotton, fruit, and vegetables in California.

Asian immigrants provided another source of labor. About 1 million Asians arrived between the gold rush of 1849 and the Immigration Act of 1924 in a complex pattern representing migrations from China, Japan, Korea, the Philippines, and India. (Chinese and Japanese constituted the bulk of the migration.) Like European immigrants, most of the Asians came voluntarily in search of a better life, but, like slaves and Native Americans, they possessed physiological characteristics that made it easy for the white population to identify them and often to stigmatize and segregate them.

The Asian influx began with Chinese immigrants, who came to America to find gold in the 1840s and to do manual labor for farmers, manufacturers, miners, and the railroads that were extending lines eastward from the Pacific. In 1870, California's 63,000 Chinese constituted almost 10 percent of the state's population. Chinese laborers were ideally suited to employers' needs: They could be paid minimal wages (coercive tactics were used when they threatened to strike for higher wages) and used to depress the wages of white workers, and they did not constitute a political threat because as "aliens" and persons of color, they were denied legal rights. (The California Supreme Court ruled in 1854 that Chinese people could not testify in court against whites, even if one of their number had been murdered by a white citizen.) They were disallowed from owning mines by tax levies, could not become citizens, were required to attend segregated schools, and could not vote.

Rampant racism and fears by white laborers that they would lose their jobs to Chinese workers led to the enactment of the Chinese Exclusion Act of 1882, which excluded further Chinese immigrants despite their usefulness to employers. Japanese labor soon provided a low-wage substitute, particularly for white landowners who sought to grow fruit and vegetables in California. By 1902, California's 139,000 Japanese residents vastly outnumbered the roughly 70,000 Chinese residents.

Like the Chinese, the Japanese immigrants were often greeted by racist epithets, such as "Jap," and realtors often refused to sell them houses. The Japanese were attacked by white laborers and were denied citizenship and the vote. A sizable

network of Japanese businesses developed; some (such as restaurants and boarding houses) catered to Japanese clients. When the use of refrigerated railroad cars created large national markets for fruits and vegetables, the Japanese quickly became major producers of these products; they ingeniously adapted Japanese irrigation techniques to American farms. By initially leasing or renting land, they obtained resources to purchase their own land.

But the growing Japanese population soon encountered white racism. Angered by their competition, white laborers demanded that the Chinese Exclusion Act, due for renewal in 1902, include a ban on Japanese immigration. President Theodore Roosevelt, anxious for diplomatic reasons not to antagonize Japan, opposed this policy and at one point used federal troops to protect the Japanese from race riots in San Francisco. However, in the Gentleman's Agreement of 1907, he persuaded Japan not to permit further emigration of laborers to the United States, except for family members of existing residents. (Once he had left office, Roosevelt favored exclusion of the Japanese.) Moreover, angered by the success of the Japanese in agriculture, California enacted legislation in 1913 to disallow Japanese immigrants from obtaining land and to restrict their leases to three years. On discovering that the Japanese were circumventing the law by registering their land in the names of their American-born children, the California legislature further tightened the legislation so as to disallow this practice and even leasing itself. (Similar legislation was enacted in 12 other states.) The Japanese suffered another rebuff in 1922, when the Supreme Court ruled that Japanese Americans could not become citizens because 1790 federal legislation specified that citizens must be Caucasians. To make matters worse, legislation enacted by Congress in 1924 restricted the number of foreign-born persons admitted each year to 2 percent of the number of that nationality residing in the United States in 1890—a measure clearly directed at the Japanese population, which had numbered only 2,039 persons in 1890. (The Chinese were still banned from any immigration.)[12]

INSERT 5.2 Critical Analysis: The Historical Roots of American Violence

---

In the early part of the 21st century, the United States has far higher homicide rates than other industrialized nations. Does the American historical experience cast any light on this phenomenon? In thinking about this issue, consider the American attachment to personal ownership of weapons, relatively unrestricted by government policy, and ask whether this attachment stems from the widespread ownership of weapons on the American frontier. Or did other cultural factors and economic factors lead Americans to purchase and use guns even in the 19th century, including a male-dominated society and culture as well as advertising by the gun-producing industry?

Why did Americans retain their widespread ownership and use of guns even when the nation urbanized in the late 19th and 20th centuries—and when relatively few Americans used their guns for hunting? Would restriction of gun ownership dramatically reduce homicides in contemporary America? Why does Canada possess far lower rates of homicides committed with firearms even though more Canadians possess them? Why has considerable public sentiment for stronger controls over gun ownership been ineffective in producing legislative action by state and federal legislatures, governors, and presidents?

Appraisal of Frontier Policy

Many persons benefited from the expansion of the frontier. Imagine the euphoria of the descendant of a serf who managed to survive the westward trek and the first penniless years on a small tract in the American Midwest. Despite abuses of the auction system of land disposal, a large class of yeoman farmers developed; they participated vigorously in local politics and helped one another with practical tasks. Civic participation in territorial governments was promoted by a desire to achieve admission to the Union as a state, which conferred tangible benefits—in particular, protection from First Americans and access to federal funds for internal improvements. A tradition of sectarian and private philanthropy developed in some frontier communities.

But speculation, greed, and violence were as much the legacy of the frontier as mutual aid. (See Insert 5.2.)

Americans came to the frontier as individualists and as persons who believed in limited government; accordingly, they fashioned local institutions that emphasized the protection of property rights rather than the development of programs and institutions that would help individuals who were disabled, sick, or poor or who were First Americans displaced by the white settlers. As with farm foreclosures of the 1920s and 1980s, the society demonstrated little compassion for persons who were bankrupted by economic forces beyond their control. Assessed in terms of the sheer speed at which the population was dispersed through the countryside and the rate at which the land was cleared and cultivated or ranched, the American frontier was an unqualified success. Measured in terms of the development of social institutions to meet common human needs or the distribution of lands to needy persons, however, the American frontier was a failure, particularly when the crushed lives of the indigenous peoples are entered into the balance.

The American frontier not only reflected American individualism but also perpetuated and intensified that individualism. As stories of settlement, conquest, and success reached Americans in other sections of the country, prevailing American individualism was reinforced: Frontier success seemed to confirm the idea that anyone could succeed by working hard and taking risks. If unlimited land is available, some Americans asked, why do Americans need to develop other social resources and programs to help the needy?[13]

Arguably, the frontier both reflected and intensified American racism as well. First Americans and Spanish-speaking residents who attacked white settlers as they moved across the land were portrayed as barbaric and uncivilized peoples. Asian Americans who helped construct railroads on the frontier were often vilified as subhuman. Some commentators viewed the frontier as a laboratory experiment that juxtaposed "advanced" with "lesser" peoples—an experiment that confirmed the racial and genetic superiority of Anglo-Saxons. The pangs of guilt felt by some white settlers were eased by their belief that their conquest would improve the general quality of the human race and the nation.

The development of farms, plantations, and mines in newly developed territories, as well as the construction of roads and railroads to reach these areas, required large amounts of labor. As Southerners had done, entrepreneurs on the frontier used slaves to grow cotton and tobacco and employed Latinos and Asians on farms, in the mines, on the railroads, and in emerging industries. These laborers were often treated brutally by their employers—and they resided in jurisdictions that enacted harsh legislation to deprive them of their basic rights. Nor were federal authorities helpful; indeed, immigration legislation and various court rulings served to buttress and supplement the discrimination and racism rampant in local jurisdictions.

THE CIVIL WAR AND THE OPPRESSION OF FREED SLAVES

As a percentage of the total population, more American lives were lost during the Civil War than during World War II. However, battlefield casualties reflect only one portion of the human toll. Millions of people were dislocated during and after the war, and freed slaves were cast into a society with few economic or social supports. Of course, slaves *were* freed, which was an enormous achievement.

Origins of the Civil War

Was the war fought to help the slaves or for other objectives? Controversy exists among historians about the war's precise causes, but research suggests that the war can be attributed to multiple factors, many of which had little to do with improving the condition of freed slaves.[14]

By 1830, the American nation included three societies that were profoundly different from one another. With poor soil and long winters, New England had relatively marginal agriculture, and many of its citizens had begun to envision their region as a center for commerce and industry. Its leading citizens demanded high tariffs to protect fledgling industries from foreign competitors and demanded federal subsidies for its small shipping industry.

The expanding Northern frontier, which extended into Ohio, Indiana, Illinois, and Missouri, became the breadbasket of the nation; its crops were increasingly transported to New England in exchange for commodities. This area sought federal funds to develop roads, canals, and railroads that were vital to trade with New England. New England and the frontier communities gradually became closely linked because each depended on the other for goods. During years when crop yields were poor on the frontier, New England had to import food, and so there were fewer resources to build industry; likewise, a recession in New England meant that prices for agricultural produce from the frontier plummeted.

The economy of the South, which included the Old South (states such as Virginia, the Carolinas, Alabama, and Georgia) and a Southern frontier (territories in states that are now Mississippi, Louisiana, and Texas), depended on tobacco and cotton, which were often cultivated by slaves. Like the agricultural produce of the Northern frontier, cotton and tobacco became part of the world economy thanks to New England shippers, who bought and exported Southern cotton to finance the expansion of New England industry. The conditions of the slaves varied, but many historians believe that the American version of slavery was even more repressive than slavery in South America and the West Indies. Reduced to chattel and lacking support from church, government, and legal institutions, slaves were wholly at the mercy of their masters.

Even this cursory discussion points to sectional rivalries that precipitated the Civil War. Most Northern families, who usually knew someone who had gone to the frontier to obtain land, wanted to preserve the frontier for white settlers. But the frontier also appealed to Southerners, who wanted new lands for cotton plantations. Slavery could not easily coexist with a paid labor force, as it required supportive laws, local police, courts, and public opinion to keep the slaves in their bondage and to ensure the return of runaways. Northern settlers were not likely to cooperate in the maintenance of slavery because they came from areas dominated by small farmers and paid workers, who feared the preemption of land by plantations. Whereas abolitionists in the North were widely reviled in the 1830s because of deep-seated racism, by the 1850s growing numbers of Northerners came to view the institution of slavery as morally flawed.[15]

This rivalry for land was exacerbated by political realities. A delicate balance existed in the Congress among New England, the Northern frontier, and the South. New England wanted high tariffs and subsidies for ships; the frontier areas wanted public money for internal improvements and cheap land; and the South wanted low tariffs and, at least until the 1830s, some internal improvements. In the decades following the 1830s, however, Southern views and institutions became markedly different from those of the North. Its leaders rallied behind an extreme view of limited government; they wanted virtually no taxes, no internal improvements, and low tariffs. Whereas the North already emphasized railroads and public education by the 1840s, the South remained a relatively backward agricultural area dominated by cotton and tobacco. Although many Southern leaders prior to the 1830s had not defended slavery but rather contended that its swift elimination would be impractical, they idealized it in succeeding decades as a means of avoiding the chasm between social classes that existed under "wage slavery" in New England's emerging industrial system.

As the cultural and policy views of the North and South diverged, each side came to view with alarm the possibility that the other might dominate the Congress by obtaining new representatives from frontier states. Both Northerners and Southerners realized that the region that controlled Congress could also write legislation to outlaw or condone slavery in the frontier areas.[16]

Because Northerners and Southerners had known since the early 19th century that cohabitation of specific territories was difficult, they had avoided armed conflict by partitioning the frontier into slaveholding and free territories. A series of ingenious compromises from 1787 to 1850 gave sections of the frontier to each side, as illustrated by the Missouri Compromise of 1820 and the Compromise of 1850.

When the Territory of Missouri applied for statehood in 1818, free states and slave states each had 22 senators in the U.S. Senate. To retain this balance, the Missouri Compromise proposed to admit Maine as a free state and Missouri as a slave state—and to avert future discord by prohibiting slavery to the north of a line extending westward from Missouri's southern boundary through the remainder of the Louisiana Purchase. This outcome seemed to be a draw between slave and free states. However, the Compromise ignored the fact that settlers from *both* the North and South would soon stream into frontier lands, with the hope of eventually claiming them for the North or the South regardless of the Compromise of 1820.

By 1850, an atmosphere of mutual paranoia had developed. Once again, there was a balance between slave and free states (15 of each) in 1848, but the American conquest of Mexico made available a huge territory that would eventually give rise to many new states. Utah and then California sought admission as free states, while Texas, already admitted as a slave state in 1845, claimed half of New Mexico. The Compromise of 1850, which was achieved with considerable difficulty in this tense atmosphere, sought to give both North and South concessions. California was admitted as a free state, whereas the remainder of the formerly Mexican land was divided into the territories of Utah and New Mexico, which had no federal restrictions on slavery. But the Compromise contained a fatal flaw: It did not specifically address the needs of two new territories that were rapidly filling with settlers from both the North and South—namely, Kansas and Nebraska.

Under the terms of the Missouri Compromise of 1820, these territories should have been free, but increasing numbers of Northerners and Southerners were not in a mood to compromise. Many Southerners were convinced that the Congress did not have the right to declare that they could not bring slaves into *any* territory or state; many Northerners believed slavery should be outlawed from the start in all territories. In this embattled atmosphere, the Congress decided to allow each territory to choose for itself whether to be free or slaveholding.

When Congress relinquished its role of partitioning the frontier, the battle between the North and South moved to the territories, where determined settlers from each region confronted one another. As battles were waged, dramatic stories of the other side's brutality spread through the North and South. In the 1850s, settlers from both the North and South poured into the Kansas and Nebraska territories. Rival territorial conventions and legislatures convened by slaveholding and Northern settlers declared opposite policies in the territories. Armed conflict between Southerners and Northerners became commonplace, as individuals took the law into their own hands.

Another provision of the Compromise of 1850 further embittered the atmosphere. To appease Southerners, the Compromise included a stronger fugitive slave law, which denied fugitives the right to trial by jury and permitted their return to slavery merely on the testimony of a claimant. Fugitives who escaped to the North—even those who had lived there in freedom for 30 years or more—were hunted down by Southern slave catchers. Previously, many Northerners had seen slavery as a distant institution, but this law made them realize the extent to which they had cooperated with the South in preserving slavery—and helped abolitionists to dramatize its inhumanity.

Regional polarization was soon reflected in a realignment of the nation's political parties. Two major political parties existed in 1850: the Whigs and the Democrats competed relatively evenly in the South and the states that now compose the Midwest. With the rapid emergence of the Republican Party after the presidential election of 1856, the Republican Party (to which Abraham Lincoln tied his fortunes) supplanted the Whig Party and quickly became the party of the North; its leaders demanded that slavery be outlawed from the outset in all territories. Leaders of the Democratic Party, which became the party of the South, argued that Congress lacked the constitutional authority to outlaw slavery in the territories or anywhere else. Many Southerners believed that they had no recourse but to secede from the Union when Lincoln was elected president in 1860. They were convinced that he would close the territories to slavery and, with Congress controlled by Northerners, eventually try to amend the Constitution so as to end slavery. The South fired the first shot by attacking a federal fort in South Carolina in 1861, but the seeds of the Civil War were sown in the conflict over the rich lands of the Western frontier.

If many Northerners fought the war primarily to secure land and political power for their region, a second cause of the war was nationalism. South Carolinians had threatened to secede from the Union in 1832, but they were intimidated by Andrew Jackson, who believed the Union should be preserved at all costs. Southerners' contemplation of secession in the 1850s exposed them to Northerners' nationalistic wrath. But nationalism did not foster humanitarian proposals to help slaves; indeed, nationalism was often linked to racism, as Americans envisioned the dominion of the Anglo-Saxon race from coast to coast.

The Northern desire to abolish slavery may be cited as a third cause of the war. If *any* group were to fight the war with the interests of slaves at heart, it should have been the abolitionists, who courageously endured the wrath of Northern white audiences when they promoted their cause in the decades preceding the war. However, even the abolitionists had limited notions of the social reforms that freed slaves would need in the wake of emancipation. Most abolitionists were imbued with the prevailing racism of their era. On the one hand, they were attracted by the gentleness commonly ascribed to African Americans in the 19th century and argued that the laziness attributed to African Americans was not an intrinsic characteristic but rather was due to environmental factors. On the other hand, many abolitionists were also convinced that African Americans had a savage side to their nature, could not be trusted, and were consumed by sexual urges. Some abolitionists even believed that African Americans should not be allowed to intermarry with whites and that they should not be given the right to vote.[17]

Another limitation of abolitionists was that, like their contemporaries, they applied a moral ideology to the social problems of poverty, alcoholism, and crime. Many abolitionists believed that slaves were morally flawed because the plantation environment had encouraged them to be shiftless and promiscuous. To rehabilitate slaves, they urged utilization of the same set of educational and poorhouse institutions that Northern reformers sought for immigrants living in poverty. Their ideology blinded them to the need to distribute land to freed slaves, to provide them with resources with which to purchase their own land, or to help them migrate to Northern cities, where the emerging industrial order offered vast economic opportunities. Furthermore, many abolitionists pointed to the relative poverty of African Americans in the North, where they were concentrated in urban areas such as New York City and Philadelphia, as evidence that African Americans needed a supervised moral regimen after they had obtained their freedom. Some abolitionists even ascribed the widespread discrimination by Northerners against African Americans—who were denied the vote in most Northern states, placed in segregated public schools, and denied access to public transportation and public accommodations—to the poor reputation that African Americans had brought on themselves by not sufficiently improving their economic status.[18]

Even those who supported the Civil War out of a genuine desire to help the slaves, then, rarely envisioned the need for reforms such as massive distribution of land or resources to them. The primary motivations for the war were sectional rivalries, nationalism, and the Northerners' moralistic ideology rather than a desire to help freed slaves by enacting sweeping economic and social reforms. It is ironic that the moral treatment ideology, which was a simplistic approach to the social needs of poor whites, was applied to the African American population, whose problems were so obviously linked to the oppression they had experienced in both the South and the North.

Once emancipated, Southern slaves were ill prepared to participate in the capitalist economy. They had been systematically denied education by white owners, who feared it might make them rebellious. Some slaves were allowed to attend white Protestant churches but had to sit in segregated galleries.

We should not portray slaves as docile victims, however. Slaves developed complex tactics for coping with their oppression. Couples married and had tightly knit families even within the confines of a plantation. While owners could sell their slaves at any time, many encouraged stable families to encourage their slaves to produce more babies. Slaves often embraced evangelical Protestantism, which they infused with their own rhythmic singing and turned to their own purposes. As Sellers notes, "A gospel subversive of slavery resonated through spirituals and resentment of oppressors through secular songs and tales." They learned to present themselves to whites as compliant and docile while maintaining "day-to-day resistance of malingering, stealing, tool breaking, and arson." Many ran away, whether singly or in small groups, despite the obvious danger to themselves; a few, like Nat Turner in 1831, even took the suicidal course of open rebellion.[19]

Social Policy during the War

The primary issue to be resolved during the war was the legal status of slaves. In its infamous Dred Scott decision of 1857, the Supreme Court had declared that slaves—and free descendants of slaves—were not persons and thus not entitled to constitutional protections or citizenship, even when they lived in free territories. Known as the Great Emancipator,

Lincoln was hardly a militant opponent of slavery; he often infuriated abolitionists, who wanted him to seek an immediate end to slavery. Prior to the war, he had not proposed to terminate slavery; instead, he wanted only to restrict it to existing slave states. Nor did he immediately declare the slaves to be free once the war began, because he hoped Southern states would negotiate an early end to the war if they were allowed to retain slaves in existing states. When he finally issued the Emancipation Proclamation in 1863, he declared only those slaves to be free who were in areas still in rebellion against the Union, in an obvious effort to get border states, such as Kentucky, to cease hostilities.[20]

In the turmoil of the Civil War, the social welfare issues of dislocated persons received only secondary attention and were addressed improvisationally. The Union (Northern) Army was the major instrument of social welfare, by virtue of its presence in the South. Vast numbers of African Americans had to be supported as they left plantations, either because the Union Army had conquered Southern territory or because slaves fled behind Union lines. The Union Army constructed and maintained many camps where former slaves were placed in barracks or tents and given food and health care. These camps provided harsh surroundings; roughly 25 percent of their occupants died of disease. Remember, though, that mortality rates were similar for Union troops because of the lack of modern medical technology to stem epidemics and infection. Some of the military administrators of the camps, like most citizens of the era, believed that the freed slaves were intrinsically lazy, and so they placed many of them on work details on camp fortifications or had them work under contract labor on plantations in conquered territories.

Many Northern philanthropic societies sent legions of volunteers to assist refugees behind Union lines; some were nonsectarian, whereas others drew assistance from churches. They provided clothing, food, and medical supplies and developed some schools. Various government departments developed programs in the South, though often in isolation from one another. The War Department operated the camps for the freed slaves, and the Treasury Department controlled lands that had been confiscated from Confederate landowners.

The first systematic inquiry into the condition of freed slaves, which was conducted in 1862 when President Lincoln appointed the American Freedmen's Inquiry Commission, recommended the establishment of a federal agency to coordinate the work of federal and private agencies and to develop new programs to meet the needs of freed slaves, which could not be sufficiently addressed by private philanthropy. After extended debate in the Congress, the Bureau of Refugees, Freedmen, and Abandoned Land was established. Though the bureau was informally known as the Freedmen's Bureau, its official name emphasized refugees because many legislators did not want to show favoritism to African Americans. President Johnson opposed the bureau on the grounds that it would do more for African Americans than had been done for whites. A debate about the proper location of the agency in the federal bureaucracy nearly stalemated the legislation; abolitionists wanted it to be placed in the Treasury Department—which controlled lands that had been abandoned by, or confiscated from, Confederate supporters—to facilitate transfer of formerly Confederate lands to freed slaves; but legislators placed the agency in the War Department.[21]

The Freedmen's Bureau was established in 1865 in a manner that virtually ensured that it would be unable to develop sweeping economic and social programs to help the freedmen. Its position in the War Department reflected its status as a wartime, rather than permanent, agency; indeed, it was terminated in 1872. Virtually no funding was given to the new agency; it was assumed that private philanthropy, largely from the North, could address most of the needs of freed slaves. The legislation was staunchly opposed by Southerners—and some Northerners—on the grounds that it represented unconstitutional delving by federal authorities into welfare matters, which were perceived by many persons to belong to the jurisdiction of state and local governments. The Freedmen's Bureau was given authority to establish courts in the South to help African Americans obtain their freedom, to make certain that terms of contract labor between freed slaves and landowners were clearly written and honored, and to distribute confiscated and abandoned land, but it lacked even a full-time director of legal affairs. Because it was located in the War Department, many army officials were appointed to its staff; some of them were sensitive to the economic and social needs of freed African Americans, but others favored punitive or racist remedies.[22]

Other policy setbacks during the Civil War had ominous implications for the freed slaves. In an agricultural society, freed slaves desperately needed land; without it, they had to work as tenant farmers or sharecroppers. Legislation that established the Freedmen's Bureau promised 40 acres of abandoned or confiscated land to every male refugee, but it could not be implemented unless governmental authorities identified abandoned land, took possession of it, and distributed it to the penniless former slaves. However, confiscation of land ran counter to American veneration of property owners' rights and the belief that government had no right to interfere with it; even many abolitionists did not support land confiscation during the war. Furthermore, Southern landowners were able to use elaborate legal strategies to prevent the confiscation of their property; one effective tactic was to use local or even federal courts to oppose the rulings of courts operated by the Freedmen's Bureau. Relatively few African Americans were resettled on farms; the Freedmen's Bureau was able to resettle roughly 40,000 freed slaves—out of a total of more than 3 million—on abandoned or confiscated land. The most successful efforts to redistribute land were undertaken by Generals Sherman and Grant, who unilaterally gave land to African Americans in conquered territories in Georgia and Alabama. These policies were foiled after the war, however, when President Andrew Johnson declared that African Americans occupied the lands illegally and required them to surrender their lands to the prior owners.[23]

Reconstruction

As the war neared its conclusion, Lincoln faced difficult choices. He could have supported a policy of guaranteeing freed slaves the right to vote, access to public accommodations, and access to federal courts when they were harassed by local citizens. He also could have excluded former Confederate officials from local, state, or federal government to prevent the restoration of racist policies. But he chose the more cautious approach of deferring to the Southern states and restoring their power as quickly as possible, partly because he did not want to stiffen the resolve of the South to fight to the bitter end. He appointed military governors in each state and promised a return to civilian and Southern rule, subject only to the requirement that 10 percent of the white population vote their loyalty to the Union and agree to end slavery. This passive federal role—which allowed Southern states to retain laws that prohibited African Americans from voting as well as other infringements of their civil liberties—was stoutly opposed by many abolitionists, who feared that the South would soon return to a system of quasi-slavery, where African Americans would be nominally free but would lack land, resources, and the vote. The abolitionists' arguments were not heeded by Lincoln, however, who seemed intent on restoring order in the South as soon as possible and on terms that were acceptable to established Southern leaders.[24]

Lincoln's failure to abolish slavery earlier in the War partly stemmed from his precarious political situation in a nation where many Northern Americans were not fully committed to ending it. Their commitment was markedly decreased because the Union Army had only 10 battlefield successes before the summer of 1864 and had been repeatedly outmaneuvered by such Southern generals as Robert E. Lee. Lincoln's popularity declined to such low levels that many experts believed that a pro-South former general in the Union Army would defeat Lincoln in the upcoming presidential election of 1864. Had this occurred, the Congress may have agreed to end the Civil War with slavery still intact in the old South and possibly elsewhere. Only dramatic victories by Union forces, such as the conquest of Atlanta, Georgia, in September 1864, allowed Lincoln to win a resounding victory in November. He immediately invested extraordinary energy in securing the enactment of the Thirteenth Amendment to the Constitution in 1865, which, unlike the Emancipation Proclamation, abolished slavery within the United States or any place under its jurisdiction.

With hindsight, we can see that the war, while emancipating slaves, did not change white racism in the North or the South. Even had Lincoln not been assassinated, it is unlikely that he could have imposed on Southerners enlightened policies toward the freed slaves because most of them—like most Northerners—were antagonistic to African Americans. Indeed, on the eve of his assassination, Lincoln was still uncertain about suffrage for African Americans and was contemplating the vote merely for "the very intelligent, and especially those who have fought gallantly in our ranks."[25] We shall never know what policies Lincoln would have sought, for he was assassinated and replaced by Vice President Andrew Johnson in 1865. Johnson was an unabashed Southerner who had always detested African Americans and whose dislike of the Southern aristocracy was transformed into a crusade to develop a political base among white monied interests in the postwar South. His term of office (1865–1868) was an unmitigated disaster for freed slaves. He proposed to allow Southern states back into the Union with virtually no requirement that they protect African Americans' civil or voting rights. He pardoned vast numbers of Confederate officials so that they could resume political careers in the South, and he even appointed some of them as officials of the Freedmen's Bureau. He declared the bureau's courts to be exempt from the requirement that their officials pledge loyalty to the Union. He sought to dissolve the Freedmen's Bureau when its officials advocated policies that he disliked. (See Insert 5.3.)

Southerners who had expected the worst from the North—confiscation of land, restrictions preventing Confederate officials from holding political office, and requirements that they protect the civil liberties of African Americans—were astounded to discover that they had a strong ally in the White House. Johnson's policies emboldened Southern white leaders to develop "Black codes" that limited African Americans' ability to move around the countryside, restricted their rights of assembly and free speech, and subjected them to whipping for discourteous or insubordinate behavior.[26]

Southern actions and President Johnson's open support of white Southern interests outraged many in the North, who wondered whether the Civil War had been worth the carnage if the South continued to oppress freed slaves. Indeed, Lincoln's assassination and Johnson's provocative policies radicalized the North. In quick succession, a number of Northern states rescinded legislation that deprived African Americans of the vote and other civil liberties. Johnson and the Democratic Party were resoundingly defeated in the congressional elections of 1866, in which Republicans successfully argued that Johnson was a captive of the South. Northerners demanded passage of a succession of civil rights acts. The Thirteenth Amendment to the Constitution, which abolished slavery, was ratified by Northern states in 1865. The Military Reconstruction Act of 1867 required Southern states to include universal suffrage in their constitutions before they could be readmitted to the Union and allowed the army to serve as protector of civil rights by bypassing local courts.

The Fourteenth Amendment, which was ratified in 1868, rescinded the provision in the Constitution that had counted each African American as only three-fifths a person, required that all citizens be given "equal protection" under the law, and stipulated that all persons be accorded the protection of due process. The Fifteenth Amendment, which was enacted in 1870, established universal suffrage of all adult males, though it did not exclude the use of poll taxes and literacy tests, which Southern jurisdictions eventually used to disenfranchise African Americans. Civil Rights Acts enacted in 1870 and 1875, respectively, limited the ability of states to enforce discriminatory legislation and outlawed segregation in public facilities and schools. The Ku Klux Klan Act of 1872 declared infringements of the civil rights of persons to be a federal offense.[27]

INSERT 5.3 Ethical Analysis of Key Issues and Policies: The Case of Governmental Help for Freed Slaves

---

Discuss the ethical merit of the government's policies toward freed slaves in the wake of the Civil War:

1. How had slavery ill prepared the slaves for survival in a competitive, capitalistic economy? (Identify an array of personal, economic, and social factors that enable people to compete in a capitalistic economy.)
2. How might the federal government have redressed the obstacles or impediments that the freed slaves encountered? (Identify specific, tangible steps the government might have taken to better help the freed slaves enter the economic mainstream.)
3. What ethical principles did the government violate by *not* helping the freed slaves more assertively in the wake of the war?

Southern behavior was constrained not only by this federal legislation but also by the ongoing presence of federal troops and area offices of the Freedmen's Bureau. Since the South remained an occupied society until 1877, Southern whites were impeded from violating the rights of freed slaves or from attacking Northern liberals who had settled in the South. The Freedmen's Bureau continued to hear cases in its courts, to build schools, and to provide rations to former slaves who were starving or penniless, although its programs reached only a small fraction of the intended recipients.[28]

The Southern states reeled before this onslaught of federal legislation. The Democratic Party, which had dominated the South for decades, was now supplanted by a Republican Party that consisted of a range of white and African American voters. The transformed Southern legislatures now contained significant numbers of African American legislators, as well as sympathetic whites who had migrated to the South during and after the war. These bodies enacted many reforms, including the development of schools and mental institutions and public improvements such as roads. Taxes were raised by the Republican legislatures to rebuild Southern institutions that had been devastated by war.[29]

The liberalizing of Southern politics had been accomplished, however, only by the North's imposition of laws and troops. Southern states twice refused to ratify the Fourteenth Amendment, even when the North had required this action as a precondition for the removal of military governors. By so doing, the Southern states indicated that they preferred living under military occupation to acceding to a constitutional amendment that extended equal protection of the laws to all citizens. What would happen, some wondered, if the North lost the desire to allocate resources or troops to the South?

Even before this question could be answered, ominous signs appeared. The Ku Klux Klan, in essence an arm of the Southern Democratic Party, began to intimidate African Americans and whites from the North. Northern troops, which numbered only 15,000 soldiers, could not curb the Klan's actions in dispersed rural areas of the South. Civil rights advocates were dismayed by the resurgence of the Democratic Party in the South in the 1860s and early 1870s. The Democrats achieved this dramatic comeback by playing on the racial fears of poor whites, with the claim that Republicans represented freed slaves and Northern settlers, popularly known as carpetbaggers. Democrats also argued that Republican governments in the Southern states, which had raised taxes to pay for schools and internal improvements, were imposing "big government"; why not return, they asked, to the laissez-faire government and low taxes that had marked the South before the Civil War?

The response of the Republican Party in the South to these Democratic attacks was hardly encouraging to freed slaves. Although one wing of the Southern Republican Party, which included many African American legislators, had strongly supported civil rights and social programs to help freed slaves and poor whites in the aftermath of the war, the party soon came under the domination of Southern Republicans, who softened their advocacy of civil rights legislation and displaced the freed slaves and their allies with moderate and conservative white Southerners.

Northerners' growing indifference to the South was also alarming to the freed slaves, who believed that institutionalized repression of African Americans would reemerge without unrelenting Northern pressure on the South. Many abolitionists, considering their work done, turned to other causes, and ceased to pressure the Republican Party to support civil rights measures. Other urgent concerns, including economic problems, the disastrous recession of 1873, policies governing the rates charged by railroads for transporting goods, labor disorders, currency policy, and tariffs, also distracted Northerners from issues in the South. Northern imposition of civil rights legislation had been partly motivated by anger at the South both for precipitating the war and for its defiant postwar passage of codes repressing African Americans, but the desire for revenge was dulled with the passing of years. The costs of maintaining the military occupation of the South made many Northerners disinclined to continue it.[30]

A symbolic event in 1877 illustrated the decline of Northern pressure on the South. In the 1876 presidential contest between Democrat Samuel Tilden and Republican Rutherford Hayes, the vote had been so close that the electoral college was stalemated. To break the stalemate, the Democrats finally agreed to support Hayes, but only if he agreed to withdraw troops from the South. That fateful deal dimmed the hopes of African Americans in the South, who were left to the mercy of Southern whites. The Republican Party, which had spearheaded federal civil rights legislation after the war, had viewed the Southern question as negotiable in the push and pull of the political process.

Reformers lost an opportunity to improve the lot of freed slaves after the Civil War. The major instrument of reform, the Freedmen's Bureau, was distressingly underfunded and had limited social welfare functions. More than 30 percent of its scant resources were devoted to educational programs for African Americans, but education could hardly suffice if African Americans had no land, resources,

homes, or civil and political rights. The education given by the Freedmen's Bureau focused on moral rules because it was widely assumed that African Americans, like low-income persons in the North, could succeed in life only if they were instructed in the tenets of honesty, religion, and thrift. Although initially enacted to last only one year after the end of the war, the Freedmen's Bureau did manage to survive until 1872.[31]

Approximately one-fifth of African American families owned land in 1870, but most of them were tenant farmers who became mired in debt as they borrowed money from white Southerners for seeds, fertilizer, machines, and food. Many African American landowners were forced into foreclosure by their inability to repay debts or to secure loans from white-controlled banks. African Americans who relocated to Southern cities were subject to unrelenting discrimination in job markets and to segregated housing and schools.[32]

There seemed room for optimism even as late as 1877, however. African Americans still voted in most Southern jurisdictions; around 10 percent of school-age African Americans attended schools that had been established by the Freedmen's Bureau; and a small group of African American landowners and small businessmen existed. These gains were offset by a continuing erosion of civil rights. Civil rights legislation and the Fourteenth Amendment were interpreted so restrictively by the Supreme Court that they afforded few protections for African Americans. The requirement that persons could not be deprived of their civil liberties without due process was ruled by the Supreme Court to apply only to discrimination against African Americans by individuals; states' discriminatory laws (such as those requiring poll taxes or literacy tests for voters) were thus legitimized.

In the late 19th century, a new generation of political leaders who hardly remembered the Civil War came to power in the North and South. They increasingly assumed that African Americans should not participate in political, social, or economic affairs. Southern states enacted a new wave of laws, so-called Jim Crow legislation, that deprived African Americans of their basic civil rights. These laws were not rescinded until nearly a century after the Civil War.[33]

It is instructive to compare the advantages enjoyed by European immigrants with the condition of freed slaves. White immigrants were given access to cheap land on the frontier—often 160 acres per person. Other white immigrants—or their children—developed small businesses in rural areas or in cities. Often literate even before they came to the United States, white immigrants sent their children to public schools in the North. As factories developed, immigrants obtained jobs in them, albeit at low wages. Enjoying free movement, immigrants and their descendants traveled between cities and regions to better their condition. They formed churches and associations to promote the interests of their groups; powerful political machines in major cities distributed jobs to the Irish, Italians, Germans, and others.

By contrast, freed slaves were mostly mired in isolated rural areas where they could not emulate the white immigrants' economic development. Lacking assets such as land and small businesses, they could not develop capital or borrow funds from banks. Mostly illiterate, they often lacked access to the public schools that could prepare them to compete in the capitalist order. Separated from the industrial centers that dominated the American economy by 1900, they could not find an economic niche in manufacturing that might bring a measure of security to them and their children. Trapped in a sharecropping system, African Americans could not save funds, and so they had no resources—much less land or businesses—to pass on to their children when they died. Dispersed in remote areas with poor communication, they could not easily organize associations akin to the self-help groups formed by the Irish and Italians. Once the repressive codes were in place and they had been denied suffrage, they could not develop political machines that would distribute jobs and resources to African Americans. Freed slaves, then, were subjected not just to personal discrimination but to a *structural* discrimination that made it likely that they would fall behind white immigrants in the North—not because African Americans lacked the work

ethic or supportive families but because they were denied access to the assets, economic opportunities, and associations enjoyed by their Northern white counterparts.[34]

The Betrayal of Women during and after the Civil War

Curiously, abolitionism and the Civil War were associated with policy issues affecting women. Many women entered the world of politics by participating in temperance, charity, and church movements in the antebellum period, though they often occupied decidedly subordinate positions, in separate women's auxiliaries. The women in the abolitionist movement were more daring. Many of them defied the widespread custom that women could not engage in public speaking to mixed audiences, despite jeers from skeptical audiences, and were so bold as to sign public petitions, despite Congress's consideration of legislation in 1834 to disallow petitions signed by women. Numerous women became leaders in the abolitionist crusade.

These abolitionist leaders, often with support from male abolitionists, applied the logic of emancipation to themselves and began to question traditional marriage vows that required women to pledge obedience, as well as sexist language in the Bible and hymns, discriminatory property laws, and the condescension of males. As we discussed in Chapter 4, a small number of women and men held the first convention devoted to women's rights in 1848 in Seneca Falls, New York, where they issued a declaration of principles that advocated changes in property laws to allow married women to inherit their husband's property and to keep earned wages. They also sought liberalization of divorce laws and universal suffrage. These women found their hopes dashed in the wake of the Civil War, however. Having expended enormous energy to emancipate slaves, many of them hoped that women would receive the vote when it was given to freed slaves with passage of the Fourteenth and Fifteenth Amendments. But male legislators, many women, and the Republican Party were not willing to accept this major policy change.[35]

The women's movement focused on suffrage in the Gilded Age but divided into two factions. The American Women's Suffrage Association circulated petitions that beseeched the state legislatures to change their constitutions so as to grant women the vote, whereas the National Women's Suffrage Association sought a range of reforms for women, including passage of a federal constitutional amendment to enact universal suffrage. Both groups were frustrated, despite some modest gains. Most states and the Congress resisted universal suffrage because of the sexism of the era as well as the determined lobbying of the liquor industry, which was certain that women would support prohibition. The two factions of the women's movement united in 1890 into the National American Women's Suffrage Association but had scant success in obtaining suffrage reforms during the remainder of the century, though some states liberalized property laws and women continued to increase their enrollments in secondary and college education.[36] However, by 1916, 12 states had granted suffrage to women due to incessant pressure from suffragettes on state legislatures.

THE OPPRESSION OF WORKERS DURING THE EARLY STAGES OF AMERICAN INDUSTRIALIZATION

The speed of the American transition from an agricultural to an industrial society was unprecedented in world history; it is rivaled only by the pace of Japanese and Russian industrialization in the mid-20th century. No more than 20 percent of Americans lived in cities in 1860, and the nation ranked fourth in the world in the value of its manufactured products; in 1920, however, more than 50 percent of Americans lived in cities, and the nation ranked first in industrial output. Indeed, the total population of urban areas grew from 5 million in 1860 to 25 million in 1900.

Industrialization before the Civil War

Industrialization began prior to the Civil War, when most nonagricultural workers were still employed in such skilled crafts as carpentry, blacksmithing, and shoemaking. Textile, food processing, and mining industries, as well as factory-based mass production of shoes, developed in New England in the 1830s and 1840s. Some textile plants were located in rural areas, where they employed middle-class women who boarded on the premises; others were located in urban areas, where they employed entire families. Even before the Civil War, factory owners used large numbers of children and women to minimize their labor costs, particularly in textile factories. Railroads were rapidly constructed in the North; indeed, by 1840, the United States had laid twice as much track as all of Europe.

In the absence of regulations, workers were subjected to brutal working conditions; they commonly worked for more than 12 hours per day (some worked as many as 15 hours) at abysmally low rates of pay and in unsanitary, dark, and dangerous conditions. Skilled workers who had made entire products in shops or homes before industrialization were often reduced to laboring as unskilled tenders of machines.

Industrialization was accompanied by a turbulent economic environment, marked by frequent recessions and cutthroat competition between domestic and foreign enterprises. England tried to sabotage the development of industry in America by imposing tariffs on American imports, by prohibiting the export of technology to America, and by dumping commodities on American markets at artificially low prices. American industrialists, in turn, were vulnerable to bankruptcy because they accumulated enormous debts to build factories and acquire machinery.[37]

Already considerable in the colonial period, economic hardship in Eastern cities became even more serious as cities grew in size and recessions threw many into unemployment. To make matters worse, factory workers in the growing cities of New England had no fallback strategies. Distressed farmers could try to maintain a subsistence living through simple bartering or by producing their own food, but urban dwellers often did not own land. Moreover, farmers could survive hard times by selling a portion of their lands or working for other farmers; city dwellers had no such opportunity. Finally, farm families could pool their resources in times of need, but that was not an option for many city dwellers, who were separated from their families. Industrialization spawned other problems, too. Unskilled factory work was repetitious and exhausting; and, because early equipment was often dangerous, work-related injuries were common.[38]

Why Industrialization Took Off and Rapidly Accelerated

For a number of reasons, a truly dramatic acceleration of industrialization occurred during the Gilded Age, which extended from the Civil War to the end of the 19th century. Further expansion of the railroads opened up new markets and supplied agricultural produce and raw materials to the growing urban areas. Funds to build factories and purchase machinery were obtained from foreign sources, as well as from a rapidly expanding American banking system.

Massive immigration provided a cheap and plentiful labor supply. From 1860 to 1890, nearly 10 million northern European immigrants came to American cities (including 3 million Germans, 2 million English, Scottish, and Welsh, and 1.5 million Irish) to join the 4 million who had immigrated in the 1840s and 1850s. A subsequent wave of immigrants from southern and eastern Europe dwarfed prior immigration; nearly 18 million people arrived between 1890 and 1920. Hungry for cheap labor, industrialists actively resisted any effort to stem this immigration. (We discuss immigrants more fully in Chapter 6.)

Americans obtained a competitive advantage over Europeans because their new plants were able to incorporate rapidly developing technology. Moreover, the American business environment— high tariffs, minimal safety regulations, and low taxes—was very favorable to entrepreneurs.

Finally, between 1885 and 1900, the Supreme Court restricted the right of government to regulate corporations by ruling, for example, that manufacturing did not fall under the jurisdiction of the federal government because it was not "commerce" and that government could only gingerly regulate corporations because their rights were protected by the due process clause of the Fourteenth Amendment, which had originally been enacted to safeguard the rights of freed slaves. The Sherman antitrust legislation, which was enacted in 1890 to restrict corporate monopolies, was applied by the courts to union monopolies! Even the power of the federal government to collect income taxes was declared unconstitutional in a Supreme Court ruling in 1895. It is small wonder, then, that industrialization proceeded rapidly.[39]

Along with industrialization came rapid population growth. Cities expanded at phenomenal rates. Frontier towns, such as Cleveland, Detroit, Pittsburgh, and Chicago, became major industrial centers, and with this growth came increasing social and economic problems. In some cities, packs of wild dogs roamed the streets and maimed or killed children. Typhoid, cholera, and malaria epidemics were common and sometimes decimated the populations of entire cities. Dangerous work conditions led to scores of injuries and deaths. Immigrants were particularly subject to wretched housing and industrial exploitation. The prewar pattern of periodic and devastating recessions continued unabated after the war. Major recessions caused unemployment rates that often exceeded 25 percent in major cities; indeed, 10 percent of the population of New York City was receiving welfare after the recession of 1873. Recessions sometimes lasted for many years; the devastating recession of 1873 (known as the long recession) lasted until 1878. Many people fell behind with their rent payments and were evicted. Unable to find work in the industrial order and lacking the security of family farms, large numbers of Americans became vagabonds and roamed the countryside. Indeed, 10 to 20 percent of Americans in the late 19th century lived in families where someone had "tramped." As they fell on hard times, citizens frequently came into contact with orphanages, workhouses, and police departments.[40]

Perhaps more than in any other period, American society was characterized by extreme economic inequality. Two classes predominated, the laboring and entrepreneurial classes. Because most people were poor, the middle class was small—no more than 16 percent of wage earners. Factory owners characteristically hired labor on a daily basis at factory gates and retained workers for only brief periods; in many plants, there was a complete turnover of labor each year. Americans of all social classes moved frequently, but transience was particularly marked among the working class, whose members had to remain mobile to find jobs in an uncertain economy.[41]

In contemporary cities, relatively affluent suburbs encircle low-income urban areas. In the Gilded Age, by contrast, American cities were not segregated by social class. Because industry was located in the centers of cities, most people lived nearby for easy access to work. The large ethnic enclaves—Irish, Italian, Jewish, and others—were overwhelmingly poor but contained an array of small businesses, churches, and voluntary associations.

Prior to the Civil War, industrialization had been marked by the development of small industries. In the latter part of the century, however, massive corporations were formed and systematically drove small competitors out of business. Not content to concentrate on making one product, many tycoons bought related companies. Andrew Carnegie coupled his steel empire with railroad and mining interests, and John D. Rockefeller extended his oil empire to include railroads and refineries. Massive cartels monopolized the production of certain products, charged exorbitant prices, and conspired to bankrupt competitors.

The Victimization of Workers

Reformers obtained some policy victories during the Gilded Age, including the establishment of limits on the working hours of federal employees, local housing regulations, some local regulations on the working conditions of women and children (see Figure 5.2), establishment of the Interstate Commerce Commission, and passage of the Sherman antitrust legislation. However, the scope of these policies did not begin to match the magnitude of social needs. Many jurisdictions did not enact regulations on industry, housing, public health, or employers' labor practices. Unemployment insurance, workmen's compensation, or pensions for the elderly were hardly discussed. The Interstate Commerce Commission was not able to regulate railroads because it was not given formal powers or sufficient resources to accomplish its task.[42] The ineffectiveness of the Sherman Antitrust Act, enacted in 1890, was illustrated by the acceleration of the development of cartels after its passage.

Intolerance of poor persons increased after the disastrous depression of 1873. As the frontier closed and cities swelled with poor immigrants, many Americans feared that this growing class of landless persons could disrupt existing institutions. They supported the repression of unions and strikes, as well as the suppression of "foreign radicals." At the same time, there was a surge in punitive policies toward Native Americans and freed slaves, whom many Americans believed to be unreceptive to educational and moral uplift projects.[43]

The nation seemed to be returning to the mercantile policies of the colonial period except that they now benefited corporations. Land subsidies to railroads, high tariffs to discourage imports, subsidies to shipping industries and telegraph lines, and public funding of improvements to rivers and harbors were motivated by a desire to build America's economy. Colonial mercantilism had been a top-down policy, in which top officials and royalty engineered tariffs and subsidies to help the national economy and unemployed citizens. The bottom-up mercantilism of the Gilded Age was prompted by political pressures from corporations, which made flagrant use of bribes and lobbying to advance their economic interests.

Although no nation had yet developed advanced policies to assist industrial workers, to upgrade cities, and to help persons who experienced unemployment, European societies were beginning to fashion social policies to mitigate the social and economic hardships that accompanied industrialization. The English Parliament, for example, enacted factory regulations in 1833, 1844, 1847, 1853, 1867, 1874, and 1878, as well as many public health measures. Germany enacted old age pensions and unemployment insurance in the 1880s. The United States, which had pioneered suffrage, land distribution, and public education, lagged behind other nations in enacting social reforms.[44]

Most historians have emphasized that the federal government adopted virtually no ameliorative policies during the Gilded Age, when the reluctance of the American response to social needs was particularly evident. Sociologist Theda Skocpol has recently argued that the federal government authorized generous social spending for veterans' pensions after the Civil War. She notes that "this was not merely a military program" and that the government continued to make substantial outlays on pensions—one-fourth (or more) of its expenditures—until well into the 20th century. Eventually, she contends, the pensions became virtually an old age pensions program; by 1910, 28 percent of all men aged 65 and over received federal benefits averaging $189 per year.[45]

Skocpol is wrong, however, when she argues that these pensions constituted major involvement in social policy by the federal government. Although the pensions may have absorbed one-fourth or more of the federal budget, the federal budget itself was so meager that the nation devoted only 5.5 percent of its GNP to public spending (at all levels of government) in 1920, as compared to 25.5 percent for France and 19.1 percent for Great Britain.[46] (Whereas some Civil War veterans had died by 1920, their numbers were augmented by large numbers of veterans of World War I.) One-fourth of such a small federal budget is not very much spending. Nor did the pensions breach the constitutional delegation of social programs to local governments because the benefits were linked to a national war, which clearly belonged within the purview of the federal government. It was not until the New Deal of the 1930s that the federal government took a major role in social policy—and

increased its social spending sufficiently to signal a sharp departure from its limited role in the previous 150 years.

Corporations and financiers took advantage of a power and policy vacuum after the Civil War. When the nation began to industrialize rapidly, agricultural interests were placed on the defensive and were fragmented. Unions would have been a logical countervailing force to business, but they were extraordinarily weak and focused on crafts and skilled trades rather than on unskilled workers in factories. Unions were organized by geographic locality and sought a basic wage for all skilled workers in that area. Their modest organizing successes in various cities in the 1830s were shattered by the recession of 1833, which allowed employers to violate agreements, to fire union members, and to hire nonunion members. There were a number of strikes and riots by factory workers in specific locations, but few unions larger than specific work sites developed. American courts, which began a pattern of rulings that severely limited the ability of unions to organize, often declared unions to represent unlawful conspiracies or to violate the rights of workers by coercing them to enlist. Many American economists believed as well that the "unnatural" wage increases obtained by unions decreased economic growth by absorbing funds from the pool of investment capital.[47]

Economists' theories hardly deterred workers from striking: Between 1881 and 1905, 7 million workers participated in 37,000 strikes. Some Americans began to fear that the nation was headed toward class war. After the Civil War, unions of unskilled workers were ruthlessly suppressed. Armed guards beat up strikers or intimidated union organizers. Owners of some Colorado mines forcibly placed strike leaders on a train to Arizona and told them not to come back. Industrialists found powerful allies in government and courts. Local politicians frequently used police and local militia to break strikes, and they were soon joined by federal officials, who used the National Guard and federal troops. In 1877, President Hayes mobilized federal troops to break a national strike against the railroads in which nearly 100 people died as rioters torched railroad facilities. Other sensational strikes punctuated the 1880s and 1890s. In the 1886 Haymarket Square riot in Chicago, for example, policemen and strikers were killed. In the Pullman Strike of 1894, federal troops quelled a strike against the railroads, but only after 700 freight cars were burned and 13 people died.

Recessions and immigration frustrated the work of union organizers by breaking their momentum. Waves of immigrants provided industrialists with an inexhaustible source of cheap labor, which they used to break strikes and to depress wages. The weakness of unions in the late 19th century is illustrated by the strange saga of the Knights of Labor, a national organization that organized district assemblies of skilled and unskilled workers from many trades. The Knights engaged in secret rituals, often opposed unions and strikes on the grounds that brotherhood would solve industrial problems, and supported the development of self-employment and cooperative schemes. Although the Knights often supported progressive social legislation, their ideology precluded the development of effective pressure on industrialists.[48]

Corporate interests became major contributors to the Democratic and Republican parties at local

© Bettmann/Corbis

F I G U R E 5.2 Victimization of women and children in industrial plants in the 19th century.

INSERT 5.4   Critical Analysis: The Conservatives' Contradiction

We have noted how, with the victory of Jefferson in 1800, a limited vision of American government triumphed over Hamilton's perspective that government should actively intervene in the economic order to promote trade and economic growth. By the Gilded Age, industrialists publicly favored limited government. Yet they often used the power of government to advance their own economic interests—by supporting some policies (such as tariff and tax policies) and opposing others (such as regulations to require safe working conditions,

to support union organizing, or to help unemployed workers). This contrast between word and deed has been called the conservatives' contradiction.

Discuss the causes of this contradiction. In light of industrialists' success in getting assistance from government, was the government truly limited in the Gilded Age?

Provide examples of conservatives' use of government to advance their economic and political interests in the United States today.

and national levels and used campaign contributions to obtain antiunion legislation, defeat adverse regulations, obtain tax concessions, and get government contracts. The weakness of governmental institutions and the lack of competing groups, such as unions and agriculture, allowed corporate and banking interests to dominate the political field and to secure favorable policies. Then, as now, American conservatives engaged in hypocritical behavior, simultaneously lambasting the role of government while getting huge concessions from it to advance the interests of affluent Americans and corporations. (See Insert 5.4.)

Social reform was also impeded by changes in popular culture. Prior to the Civil War, many Americans had believed that the primary purpose in life was to lead a virtuous existence, which might lead to social mobility; most persons, it was widely believed, were destined to remain in relatively humble positions. Americans continued to emphasize moral virtues after the Civil War, but they placed far more emphasis on social mobility. Although pauperism had always been reviled, many Americans came to believe after the Civil War that poverty was itself an indication of personal failing. Increasingly, affluent persons were honored as models of success who inspired Americans of humbler origins to redouble their efforts. The Calvinist ambivalence about wealth, which was both revered as a sign from God of His pleasure and feared as a corrupter of moral virtue, was increasingly transformed into unambiguous worship of wealth.[49]

This shift in culture was reflected in the stature of Herbert Spencer, an English writer who popularized and applied to society the theories of the English naturalist Charles Darwin. Darwin had fashioned a theory of the evolution of animal and plant forms to explain how different species emerged. He maintained that genetic mutations can provide some individuals within a species with a competitive edge, which allows them to survive—and breed—more effectively than other members of the species. As these new characteristics are perpetuated from generation to generation through natural selection, adaptive mutations thus lead to modification of the species. Spencer theorized that genes also influence how persons fare in society. He argued that persons who excel in business or other endeavors, much like animals or plants that survive in nature, possess superior genetic characteristics. His logic led him to conservative political conclusions: If affluent classes possess superior genes, he asked, should not society allow their numbers to increase, while adopting policies to bring reductions in the numbers of low-income persons? By propping up ne'er-do-wells, in Spencer's view, governments and social agencies were artificially and wrongly interfering with natural selection within the social order.[50]

Spencer's use of Darwinian theory represented a sloppy and misguided application of biological theories to society. Poverty and other social ills are caused by innumerable factors, including environmental and societal conditions, as is illustrated by the plight of people of color in the United

States in the 19th century. No evidence has been found by contemporary scientists to suggest that groups—whether social classes or ethnic groups—possess genetic characteristics that predispose them to inferior educational and economic performance. (In 1994, reviving some very old ideas, Richard Herrnstein and Charles Murray argued in their book *The Bell Curve* that genetic characteristics caused "lower intelligence" among African Americans. However, the book's poor methodology and flawed data drew extensive criticism from social scientists.[51])

The influence of Spencer in the Gilded Age should not be exaggerated, however. Many Americans did not read him, and others ignored those portions of his teachings that urged the elimination of social programs. But his deification of affluent persons struck a responsive chord with many Americans during a period of phenomenal economic growth. Where Americans had once romanticized yeomen farmers, they now glorified affluent industrialists and businessmen within urban settings. Industrialists could not have wished for a more receptive environment!

THE INADEQUACY OF A PRIMITIVE WELFARE STATE TO MEET EPIC SOCIAL NEEDS

The three central experiences of this era—the frontier, the Civil War, and industrialization—posed different social welfare challenges. Each benefited many persons, yet each created social casualties—in particular, displaced First Americans and Spanish-speaking persons, Asian immigrants, destitute farmers, and exploited laborers on the frontier; freed slaves and poor white refugees during and after the Civil War; and workers who were unemployed, underpaid, or disabled during the early stage of American industrialization.

Americans during the Gilded Age glamorized the successes, paid relatively little attention to the casualties, and chose not to construct policies to alleviate suffering. The nation virtually pursued a policy of

genocide toward First Americans and Spanish-speaking persons. Asian and Latino laborers were deprived of their fundamental rights and subjected to virulent racism in local communities. Freed slaves were left to wander in a racist society and were given scant assistance as they made the difficult transition from slavery to freedom. Industrialists had a free hand to exploit workers—including women and children—in dangerous working environments.

American interpretations of the frontier, the Civil War, and industrialization are striking in their similarity. Americans idealized the frontier as a place where Christian religion and values were defended against savages; they viewed industrialization as an American success story in which self-made men rose to prominence by dint of hard work; and they perceived the Northern victory in the Civil War as a triumph of morality over the greed of slaveholders and of nationalism over the renegade Southern secessionists. By idealizing positive outcomes of these experiences, Americans more easily rationalized or denied the suffering that accompanied them.

Many Americans interpreted the negative outcomes of these three experiences in a manner that blamed their victims rather than American social institutions and values. In this interpretation, First Americans caused their own demise by not farming land or by unleashing "unprovoked" attacks on white settlers. Their problems, settlers reasoned, surely arose because of their savage nature rather than because the settlers took their land. Asians and Latinos were perceived as the bearers of alien religious and cultural traditions that imperiled the culture of the white settlers; white laborers were apt to accuse them of stealing scarce jobs. Most Americans believed that the slaves, once freed, were given the same "fair shake" that had been extended to white immigrants; their lack of economic success was commonly attributed to personal shortcomings rather than to the racism of their society or the intrinsic difficulties in making a transition from slavery. Likewise, it was widely believed that any person in industrial society could achieve social mobility by working hard; consequently, union demands for fair pay were often viewed as the work of foreign agitators who wanted to introduce alien socialist institutions.

Moral treatment was an intervention based on the assumption that the moral character of individuals was the most potent factor in shaping their destinies, but this assumption was untenable when applied to landless, uneducated, and impoverished former slaves, who were released into a Southern society that detested them; to First Americans, whose land was taken by false treaties or violence; and to the urban poor, who were at the mercy of exploitative employers and an unstable economy.

Few Americans in this era could even envision a major and ongoing social policy role for the federal government. The federal civil rights legislation, the Freedmen's Bureau, and the stationing of troops in the South represented remarkable departures from the limited role of the federal government prior to the war, but these were ultimately regarded as temporary measures. Lacking a tradition of federal intervention, Americans were disinclined to regulate the emerging industrial order or to develop federal policies to distribute free lands to impoverished persons. Although the federal government did enact pensions for Civil War veterans, as we have seen, these expenditures were very limited and did not set a precedent for an expanded federal role in social welfare.

Nor did states and local governments evolve robust social programs to meet the needs created by the frontier, the Civil War, and industrialization. Governments were poorly funded. They were often corrupt, with corporate interests freely bribing public officials so they would not regulate them and would give them large subsidies. Even the Spartan set of mental institutions and poorhouses, respectively at state and local levels, were relatively inhumane places where the poor and mentally ill were warehoused.

Each of the three central experiences of this era also unleashed powerful political forces that prevented Americans from grappling with social problems. In the decades following the Civil War, the powerful and affluent agricultural interests who had instituted slavery regained their power in the South, established a strong Southern constituency for the Democratic Party, and successfully bargained in the Congress for withdrawal of Northern troops and lifting of federal pressure to honor the civil and voting rights of freed slaves. (They were aided by Northern entrepreneurs who bought, sold, and profited from Southern cotton and tobacco and favored the use of the former slaves as cheap labor.) American land policy at the frontier empowered speculators, white settlers, and railroads, who pressured public authorities to repress First Americans or to place them on reservations. A new and powerful class of entrepreneurs created by industrialization resisted unions and regulatory policies of the government.

By the end of the 19th century, Americans had developed a conservative consensus that embraced moralistic and punitive stances toward persons in poverty, embodied a restrictive concept of social obligation, portrayed social problems as temporary rather than endemic to the social fabric, and favored limited government. Especially striking, however, was the inability of most Americans to support compensatory strategies to help populations that needed special assistance. Most Americans believed that government risked favoritism if it singled out specific groups for assistance. No group in American history possessed such desperate needs as the freed slaves, whose economic problems stemmed so clearly from the horrors of slavery. The disinclination of Americans to use compensatory strategies in cases of obvious need during the 19th century represents a legacy of lost opportunity that has influenced social welfare policy to this day, as well as the well-being of African Americans who still have not received compensation for the misery that Americans caused by policies of slavery and failure to enact permanent civil rights legislation until 1964 and 1965. (Some Southern states finally apologized to African Americans for slavery, but not until 2007.)

Indeed, the major policy roles of the federal government in the Gilded Age involved concessions to corporations. The government repressed strikes on key occasions, issued rulings that chilled union organizing, gave huge land grants to railroads, raised tariffs to protect manufacturing (often at the expense of consumers), and failed to enact regulations—such as workplace safety standards—that curbed the greed of corporations.

LINKING THE PERIOD OF LOST OPPORTUNITIES TO CONTEMPORARY SOCIETY

We can learn about policy advocates from such notable individuals as Frederick Douglass and Eugene Debs, whose work testifies to the courage and audacity of persons who question the status quo. We can learn about how some unmet needs and policy issues in this era persist today. We can identify policy successes in this period that have utility in contemporary American society. We can learn about the structure of the American welfare state from policy developments in this era.

What We Can Learn from Policy Advocates of the Period of Lost Opportunities

Two policy advocates from this era provide remarkable examples of moral outrage and determined efforts to obtain social reforms: abolitionist Frederick Douglass and radical organizer Eugene Debs. Their work is even more impressive because they sought policy changes in a very inhospitable context where racism, sexism, and classism were dominant features of the American cultural and political landscape.

Douglass's commitment to policy advocacy spanned many decades. (See Insert 5.5.) His moral outrage stemmed from his personal exposure to prejudice as someone who had actually been a slave—not gaining his formal freedom until he was 30 years old.

If Frederick Douglass attacked racism in the United States, Eugene Debs attacked the rampant economic inequality of a nation in the early stages of industrialization. Just as Douglass had personally experienced racism in his life, Debs experienced animus toward working people in his stint with the Terre Haute and Indianapolis Railway, where workers experienced extraordinary rates of fatality and injury. (See Insert 5.6.)

Debs's career illustrates the pivotal role the trade unions have played in seeking social reforms in the United States even if they have had fewer members and less political clout than unions in many European nations in the 20th and 21st centuries. Debs was a pioneer in developing them at a time when they were often ruthlessly suppressed. (Workers did not achieve the right to organize through the use of secret ballots until 1936.)

Debs also realized that policy advocates *had* to intersect with electoral politics to be able to change social policies. After serving a term in the Indiana state legislature, he formed the Social Democratic Party of America to provide a third party alternative to the relatively conservative Democratic and Republican Parties—soon helping to merge it with the American Socialist Party. He then ran for president on successive occasions including 1899, 1904, 1908, and 1912—even running while in prison in 1920.

It is easy to dismiss Debs as ineffective even though he attracted almost 6 percent of the national vote in 1912—and almost that many votes in 1920. Yet his decision to position himself to the far left of the American political spectrum was an honorable choice in an era when corporate and affluent persons paid *no* federal income taxes prior to 1914 and virtually no local or state taxes and when inequality in the United States was more severe than at any other point in the nation's history.

Like many suffragettes and such notable reformers as Martin Luther King, moreover, Debs was willing to go to prison to make a moral case for unpopular causes—whether for supporting railroad strikes that were ruthlessly and violently repressed by President Grover Cleveland or by publicly speaking against American involvement in World War I. In contemporary society, the placing of Debs in jail by federal officials is regarded as an infringement of his constitutional right to freedom of speech. Today's freedom of speech is illustrated by the opposition to the Iraq War voiced by both Republican and Democratic presidential contenders in 2007 and 2008—who were *not* placed in jail!

What We Can Learn from the Persistence of Unmet Needs and Policy Issues during the Period of Lost Opportunities

Extreme economic inequality existed in the Gilded Age because there were no strong countervailing forces to balance the influence of corporations. With relatively weak unions and weak-kneed public officials often receiving bribes from corporate tycoons, no method of bolstering immigrants' wages existed, such as a minimum wage. Nor could unions force corporations to raise wages when strikes were often brutally suppressed by corporations and the government—and when corporations were free to fire workers who tried to organize unions. So the nation had many strikes (37,000 of them from 1881 to 1905), but they had little effect in raising workers' wages.

With millions of immigrants in the United States, moreover, corporations could easily fire workers because they knew that other immigrants, desperate for resources, would take their place. Many immigrants could be easily intimidated by employers because they had come from authoritarian nations where working-class persons had few rights—and because they feared deportation.

Inequality was fostered, moreover, by American tax policies. Believing that the Constitution did not enable the federal government to levy an income tax on persons and corporations, reformers did not get the Sixteenth Amendment to the Constitution enacted until 1913—meaning that the federal govern-

---

I N S E R T 5.5 Profiles in Leadership: Frederick Douglass (1817–1895)

Frederick Douglass—orator and abolitionist—is widely acknowledged as the most significant African American leader of the 19th century. Douglass, whose real name was Frederick Augustus Washington Bailey, was born a slave in Tuckahoe, Maryland, sometime in 1817. His mother, Harriet Bailey, was a slave; his father was an unknown white man, perhaps his owner. At a young age, Douglass was taken away from his mother and forced to live on a plantation some 12 miles away. His childhood was anything but stable; he never enjoyed the security of a family life. In his autobiography *Narrative of the Life of Frederick Douglass* (1845), Douglass wrote, "My mother and I were separated when I was but an infant—before I knew her as a mother. ... I never saw my mother, to know her as such, more than four or five times in my life; and each of these times was very short in duration, and at night." Though many later criticized him for losing sight of the cause for freedom and equality, most of Douglass's life was dedicated to the crusade to end slavery and the promotion of civil and human rights for all Americans.

Frederick Douglass quickly recognized that to be an effective leader in the abolitionist movement, he was going to have to be educated. Douglass's education began when he was eight years old and sent by his owner to Baltimore to work as a house servant. There, his mistress, over the objections of her husband, taught Douglass the fundamentals of reading. When his mistress's lessons ceased, Douglass continued his education by learning what he could from white children who shared their reading and writing skills with him. He soon concluded that it was through depriving slaves of an education that the white man was able to maintain control over them. Once he was able to read and write, Douglass began teaching other slaves, despite the risk of severe consequences.

By the time he was 16 years old, Douglass was once again working on the plantation as a field hand, but his desire to be free was much greater than before. In 1833, he was jailed for attempting, unsuccessfully, to escape from slavery. He was released to his owner, who in turn sent him back to Baltimore to begin training as a ship repairman. In 1838, Douglass tried to escape to freedom again. This time, he succeeded in escaping to New York by using a black sailor's affidavit, which certified that the bearer was a free person. Once in New York, Douglass sent for his soon-to-be wife, Anna

Murray. Shortly thereafter, the couple married and moved to New Bedford, Massachusetts, where Douglass sought work at the shipyards.

The year 1841 was a major turning point in the life of Frederick Douglass. A speech he gave on abolition, in Nantucket, Maryland, earned him the recognition of abolitionist leader William Lloyd Garrison. So impressed with Douglass's presentation was Garrison that he hired him to be a full-time lecturer for the Massachusetts Anti-Slavery Society. Within two years, Douglass was debating against some of the sharpest minds in America, including Henry Highland Garnet. At a Negro Convention Movement gathering in Buffalo, New York, Garnet, also a former slave, called on slaves to rise up against the American slave system. Douglass countered Garnet's proposal, arguing that if slaves were to rise up they would surely be crushed. The audience supported Douglass's call for a peaceful approach to ending slavery.

Douglass's skills as an orator were so impeccable that audiences sometimes questioned whether he could have been a slave. In 1845, he responded to their skepticism by writing *Narrative of the Life of Frederick Douglass*. Because this book contained much factual information, including the fact that he was a runaway slave, Douglass ran the risk of being recaptured by his former owner. To avoid this possibility, Douglass launched a two-year speechmaking tour of the British Isles from 1845 to 1847. When he left the United States, he was Garrison's protégé; when he returned, he was an emergent African American leader in the abolitionist movement.

In 1847, Douglass returned to the United States a free man. British friends and admirers had purchased his freedom for $750. They also gave him a $2,000 "testimonial," which he used to establish the *North Star* as a weekly journal in Rochester, New York. Together with Garrison's *Liberator*, the *North Star* became a leading publication of the abolitionist movement. Aside from abolition issues, Douglass's journal included articles promoting vocational education for African Americans and calls for those in the African American community to live righteously.

Douglass also became involved in supporting reform movements outside his own. In 1848, at the first major assemblage of women's rights advocates at Seneca Falls, New York, Douglass was the only man to take a firm position in support of the right of women to the franchise. He also supported the temperance movement, opposing the consumption of alcohol, which he believed was linked to crime and poverty.

In 1852, Douglass spoke on the issue of alcohol consumption at a meeting of the New York State Temperance Convention in Rochester.

Douglass viewed the onset of the Civil War as the beginning of the crusade for freedom. After the Emancipation Proclamation of 1863, he helped recruit African American troops for the Union Army, enrolling two of his sons. Although he was proud that African Americans were fighting against the secessionists, he was concerned that they were discriminated against in pay, promotions, and treatment when captured. When he took his concerns to Abraham Lincoln, he was told that the American public was not prepared to support equality of treatment for African American troops. Douglass found solace in knowing that the 200,000 armed African Americans were a major factor in the Union Army's eventual victory.

Throughout the Reconstruction period, Douglass continued to fight for African American equality and urged that the newly freed Americans be given civil rights and the vote. In the 1870s, he took the job of editor of the *New National Era*, a weekly paper aimed at providing moral support to freedmen. In 1877 Douglass, a loyal supporter of the Republican Party, was rewarded by President Rutherford B. Hayes with an appointment as marshal of the District of Columbia. This marked the first time in the history of the United States that an African American held public office other than in the post–Civil War South. Douglass considered the appointment a victory for the African American community. Another first for African Americans came in 1881, when President James A. Garfield appointed Douglass recorder of deeds for the District of Columbia.

During his tenure in public service, Douglass continued to speak out against segregation, disenfranchisement, and the lynching of African Americans. Ever optimistic, he continued to believe that African Americans would one day witness equality in the United States. In 1884, two years after the death of his first wife, Douglass married Helen Pitts, a white woman who had worked in the recorder's office as his secretary. Douglass came under intense criticism from the white and African American communities. Douglass responded, saying his first wife "was the color of my mother, and the second, the color of my father."

In 1889, Douglass was appointed minister-resident and consul general to the Republic of Haiti. On February 20, 1895, Frederick Douglass, then about 78 years old, died at his home in Washington, DC. Earlier that day, Douglass had attended a convention of woman suffragists.

I N S E R T 5.6   **Profiles in Leadership: Eugene Victor Debs (1855–1926)**

Eugene Victor Debs—labor union organizer, founder of the American Socialist Party, and several-time presidential candidate—is best remembered as one of the most popular crusaders of the labor and social movements in American history. He was born in Terre Haute, Indiana, on November 5, 1855, the third of six children born to Marguerite "Daisy" (Bettrich) Debs and Jean Daniel Debs. His parents were Alsatian immigrants who arrived in the United States in 1849. Turning his back on his father's substantial land holdings, Daniel Debs, a well-educated and intensely romantic man, became a manual laborer once in the United States. With the help of Marguerite, who was a millworker, he later was able to open a grocery and butcher shop that brought the Debs family into the prosperous middle class.

After dropping out of high school at the age of 14, Eugene Debs was employed by the Terre Haute and Indianapolis Railway, first as a locomotive cleaner and then as a fireman. He worked in railroading for five years before finally heeding his mother's warnings that the work was dangerous and likely to lead to his early death. Upon leaving his railroad job, Debs was hired as a billing clerk at a local business. Shortly thereafter, Debs became an elected city official, assuming the duties of city clerk of Terre Haute in 1879. In 1885, after two terms in the city clerk's office, he was voted to the state legislature. He refused to run for reelection because he felt he was ineffective.

After his term in the state legislature expired, Debs became involved with the Brotherhood of Locomotive Firemen (BLF). His ambition led him to take on the job of secretary of the local lodge and subsequently editor of the BLF national journal, *The Locomotive Fireman's Magazine*. So impressed with his hard work and dedication were the union's officials that they promoted him to secretary-treasurer and moved the BLF headquarters to Terre Haute.

By the time of his resignation as secretary-treasurer in 1892, Debs had been instrumental in increasing BLF membership from 2,000 to 20,000. His work at the BLF consumed most of his time and energy, leaving little for his wife, Katherine Metzel, who suffered much from loneliness and isolation.

Although he was initially opposed to strikes and a supporter of craft unionism, Debs later believed that the labor reform movement would be best served by an industrial union of all workers, skilled and unskilled. In 1893, shortly after leaving his position at the BLF, Debs formed the American Railway Union (ARU), which

had as its main objective the organization of all railway workers under one central leadership. Following the first major victory for ARU against James J. Hill's Great Northern Railroad in April of 1894, thousands of unskilled workers became members of the union. By its second national convention, the ARU membership had increased to 150,000.

In May of 1894, workers at the Chicago-based Pullman Sleeping Car Company, many of whom were members of the ARU, went on strike to protest drastic wage cuts and high rents at the company town. The Pullman management justified their actions by claiming that the wage reductions and high rents were necessary to survive the depression that began in 1893. The ARU members responded by boycotting trains to which Pullman cars were attached. As a result, rail traffic from Chicago to the West Coast ground to a halt. Initially, Debs was hesitant in promoting the idea of an all-out boycott of the railways. But once the rank-and-file took action, he had no choice but to support ARU members and lead the strike against the Pullman Company. The strike was quickly named the "Debs Rebellion" by Chicago newspapers. Debs, however, cautioned the strikers to refrain from violent confrontations with Pullman management or strikebreakers. Nevertheless, President Grover Cleveland ordered the military to the area, and over the course of the next few months at least 30 civilians were killed and 60 wounded in riots that broke out between ARU members and American soldiers.

When the military presence failed to end the strike, a federal court injunction was issued, setting a far-reaching legal precedent. The injunction ordered the officers of the ARU, among them Debs, to do nothing to further or sustain the boycott. In protest, Debs chose to ignore the injunction, and in July of 1894 he was indicted by a grand jury for conspiracy to interfere with interstate commerce. Debs was subsequently charged with civil contempt and, after losing his case in the Supreme Court, was ordered to serve six months in prison at Woodstock, Illinois. Moreover, the ruling in the Debs case sustained the government's right to enjoin strikes for the next half-century. While Debs was in prison, the ARU collapsed.

But Debs's time in prison would raise his political consciousness. After reading Marx's *Das Kapital* and the works of Laurence Gronlund and Edward Bellamy, Debs concluded that the American worker could never get economic justice under capitalism. He left prison determined to devote the rest of his life to crusading for workers' rights and advocating socialism.

In 1897, after supporting the Democratic and Populist candidate William Jennings Bryan, Debs founded the Social Democratic Party of America. In 1900, his party merged with a faction of the Socialist Labor Party to form what became known as the Socialist Party of America. And although he was not an effective party leader, when it came to spreading the socialist message and winning votes, Eugene Debs was unsurpassed. Using his strong oratorical skills, Debs attacked the capitalist structure and extolled the virtues of socialist democracy.

In his first presidential election in 1899, Debs amassed nearly 100,000 votes, despite the fact that his party was still in its infancy. He ran again in 1904 and 1908. During the 1908 campaign, he whistle-stopped across the United States on the "Red Special." In the presidential election of 1912, Eugene Debs attracted nearly a million votes, almost 6 percent of the national turnout.

In 1917, after the United States declared war on Germany and its allies, the Socialist Party convened in St. Louis and voted to oppose the war as a conflict be-tween competing imperialisms and a fight for capitalism rather than democracy. In the months following the vote in St. Louis, Debs refrained from speaking out against the war for fear of being arrested. But after witnessing many other Socialist leaders being jailed for their stand in opposition to the war, Debs spoke out in Canton, Ohio. In June of 1918, Debs was arrested by federal authorities and charged with violating the Espionage Act. For speaking out against a war he viewed as unjust and unjustified, Eugene Debs was given a sentence of 10 years in prison.

Even in prison, Debs remained true to his crusade for social reform. With the aid of a ghostwriter, he attempted to publish a number of articles dealing with the prison environment. Most newspapers, however, refused to run the pieces, and it wasn't until 1927, after his death, that they were published as *Walls and Bars*.

In 1920, Eugene Victor Debs, who ran a presidential campaign from behind bars, again won nearly 1 million votes. On Christmas Day in 1921, President Warren Harding ordered him to be released from prison due to his deteriorating health. Debs, whose character was such that he became a legend in his own lifetime, died on October 20, 1926.

ment lacked *any* method of curtailing the wealth of America's affluent class of tycoons or its corporations. Their wealth grew at remarkable rates as the nation industrialized—and they succeeded in enacting protective tariffs so that corporations in other nations could not compete with them.

The economic inequality in contemporary America is remarkably similar to that of the Gilded Age—with many experts arguing that the nation is increasingly divided into the haves and have-nots with a diminishing middle class.

What We Can Learn from Positive Strategies of the Period of Lost Opportunities

It is difficult to locate policy successes in an era with vast social needs and only a primitive welfare state. None of the safety net programs that we take for granted existed in this era—and only a minimal set of poorhouses and mental institutions, even if the

nation was well on its way toward creating universal public education through high school. Some private charities existed as well as a growing number of private hospitals that were usually organized by religious denominations.

We can learn much today from the empowerment strategies of immigrants in the Gilded Age. Often destitute and subject to virulent discrimination from employers and other residents, millions of immigrants managed to improve their lot by resorting to empowerment strategies. Irish Americans immigrants, vilified by many Americans, developed tight-knit communities in Eastern and Midwestern cities. The Catholic Church provided them with food, resources, and schools. They formed associations that organized social events. Jewish immigrants similarly banded together in New York City and elsewhere. Not only did they develop synagogues, but also formed after-school tutoring and cultural groups. Those Jews who formed businesses, such as small retail operations or larger factories, hired their fellow Jews in a mutual self-help strategy. Similar strategies were used by Polish, Russian, Hungarian, Italian, and other groups of ethnic immigrants.

Members of these ethnic groups sought citizenship at the earliest possible moment by helping one another learn sufficient English and American history to pass citizenship classes. Attaining citizenship, they realized, would give them the power to vote, which they could then use to advance the collective interests of their specific ethnic group. Those elected candidates who got into office because of their votes were then beholden to them, providing patronage jobs in sanitation, fire, police, and other departments. Elected officials provided contractors from their communities with jobs—and these contractors then hired persons from their own ethnic communities to provide the labor for projects such as building and repairing roads; constructing and maintaining sewage and electrical systems; and building local transportation systems. If elected officials failed to deliver these concessions, they were voted out of office by specific ethnic groups.

In effect, then, ethnic groups built their *own* welfare states in a nation that possessed only a primitive one. This survival strategy helped them to cope with recessions, illness, poor housing, and disability. Because virtually no federal programs and few state ones existed, local governments became a key part of the American welfare state in the middle and late 19th century and the beginning of the 20th century. They supplemented the existing network of city and political connections with mutual self-help projects within their own communities.

Cohesive ethnic communities carried with them, as well, some negative features. As the film *Gangs of New York* illustrated, ethnic communities often warred with one another through ethnic gangs, who sometimes attacked members of other ethnic communities who entered their communities. Members of specific ethnic groups sometimes dominated the workforce of specific factories and excluded members of other ethnic groups from joining them. Ethnic conflict often disrupted public schools. Considerable corruption existed in local political institutions, with widespread bribery used to get city jobs and contracts.

A key challenge facing designers of modern welfare states is to fashion links with informal neighborhood institutions to better help persons with specific social needs rather than *only* working through formal institutions such as welfare offices, public hospitals, and employment agencies.

What We Can Learn from the Period of Lost Opportunities about the Structure of the American Welfare State

Even though many ethnic communities have vanished in contemporary society as their members have left enclaves and assimilated into the broader society, many persons with specific social problems do not use formal services funded by the welfare state, but gravitate toward family, relatives, churches, employers, neighbors, and local institutions. We ought therefore to define some of these informal institutions as resources that are *adjuncts* to welfare states. Skilled social workers with knowledge of specific communities make referrals to, and work with, these informal systems as surely as they refer clients to formal programs.

As we discuss subsequently, the contemporary American welfare state has forged many links with nonpublic entities. It provides tax concessions to millions of Americans to enable them to get health insurance through employers and to encourage employees to establish private pension funds that in many cases provide retirement resources that exceed what persons get from their Social Security pensions. Federal departments such as the Department of Housing and Urban Development (HUD) provide grants and loans to community-based not-for-profit housing groups to construct affordable housing. State and federal authorities allow many religious charities to receive contracts and grants from public agencies if they form special entities that provide services to the public that do not proselytize or provide other religious information to clients. More controversially, the administration of George W. Bush has given grants to faith-based groups even when they provide religious materials to clients—a policy currently being challenged in the courts.

In short, then, we need to include links between government programs and resources with nongovernmental entities when we discuss the structure of the American welfare state—and when we discuss referral resources that are available to social workers. We must also realize that many citizens and oppressed populations develop informal mechanisms to address their collective and personal needs.

WHAT YOU CAN DO NOW

After reading Chapter 5, you are now equipped to do the following:

- Analyze how settlers conquered First Americans and Spanish-speaking persons on the frontier.

- Identify specific kinds of laborers that settlers imported for mining, ranching, railroad construction, and other tasks on the frontier—and how these groups encountered racism.

- Identify how the federal auction system helped many immigrants and others to obtain land, but also enriched many others.

- State the different causes of the Civil War.

- Analyze various efforts to prevent the Civil War—and why they failed.

- Describe the mind-set of abolitionists, as well as the hardships they endured from fellow citizens.

- Analyze social policies enacted during the Civil War and its immediate aftermath.

- Analyze why freed slaves often did not substantially improve their economic situation after the Civil War even though they had been emancipated.

- Describe specific changes in social policies that helped emancipated slaves after the war.

- Analyze how Southerners imposed Jim Crow laws on slaves in the decades following the Civil War—and why Northerners and the Supreme Court failed to help them retain their legal rights.

- Discuss the betrayal of women during and after the Civil War.

- Describe the sheer speed of industrialization in the United States in the wake of the Civil War—and analyze why it occurred so rapidly.

- Analyze how workers were often victimized in the early stage of American industrialization.

- Discuss why and how the federal government, as well as the states, failed to redress many of the social problems that accompanied industrialization.

- Analyze how Americans possessed only a primitive welfare state in the Gilded Age—and how it impeded a constructive remedy to social problems on the frontier, during and after the Civil War, and during the early stages of industrialization.

- Analyze models of leadership such as Frederick Douglass and Eugene Debs.

- Discuss what we can learn from the period of lost opportunities about persistent needs, failed strategies, promising strategies, and the structure of the American welfare state.

ENDNOTES

1. Jack Sosin, *The Revolutionary Frontier, 1763–1783* (New York: Holt, Rinehart & Winston, 1967); Malcolm Rohrbough, *The Land Office Business: The Settlement and Administration of American Public Lands, 1789–1837* (New York: Oxford University Press, 1968), pp. 200–220.

2. Rohrbough, *The Land Office Business*, pp. 200–220.

3. Ibid., pp. 190–199.

4. Reginald Horseman, *Race and Manifest Destiny* (Cambridge, MA: Harvard University Press, 1981), pp. 116–138.

5. Stephen Jay Gould, *The Mismeasure of Man* (New York: Norton, 1981), p. 74.

6. Horseman, *Race and Manifest Destiny*, pp. 154–155, 220.

7. Angie Debo, *History of the Indians of the United States* (Norman, OK: University of Oklahoma Press, 1970), pp. 90ff.

8. Ibid., pp. 102ff; Robert Berkhofer, *The White Man's Burden: Images of the American Indian from Columbus to the Present* (New York: Knopf, 1978), pp. 157–165.

9. Carey McWilliams, *North from Mexico: The Spanish-Speaking People of the United States* (New York: Greenwood Press, 1968), pp. 98–105, 169–183; Richard Slotkin, *The Fatal Environment: The Myth of the Frontier in the Age of Industrialization, 1800–1890* (New York: Atheneum, 1985), pp. 161–207; and Rodolpho Acuna, *Occupied America: The Chicano's Struggle toward Liberation* (San Francisco: Canfield Press, 1972), pp. 105–106.

10. Debo, *History of the Indians*, pp. 133ff.

11. Berkhofer, *White Man's Burden*, pp. 166–175; Debo, *History of the Indians*, pp. 276ff.

12. Ronald Takaki, *Strangers from a Different Shore* (Boston: Little, Brown, 1989), pp. 1–11, 79–131, 179–229.

13. James Davis, *Frontier America, 1800–1840: A Comparative Demographic Analysis of the Frontier Process* (Glendale, CA: Arthur H. Clark Co., 1977), pp. 15–17; Slotkin, *The Fatal Environment*, pp. 47, 281.

14. Kenneth Stampp, *The Imperiled Union: Essays on the Background of the Civil War* (New York: Oxford University Press, 1980), pp. 191–245.

15. James McPherson, *Ordeal by Fire: The Civil War and Reconstruction* (New York: Knopf, 1982), pp. 42, 72.

16. Stampp, *The Imperiled Union*, p. 192.

17. Lawrence J. Friedman, *Gregarious Saints: Self and Community in American Abolitionism, 1830–1870* (Cambridge: Cambridge University Press, 1982), pp. 168–169; James McPherson, *The Struggle for Equality* (Princeton, NJ: Princeton University Press, 1964), pp. 147–148.

18. Friedman, *Gregarious Saints*, pp. 169–178; McPherson, *The Struggle*, pp. 143–147.

19. Charles Sellers, *The Market Revolution: Jacksonian America, 1815–1846* (New York: Oxford University Press, 1991), pp. 399–400.

20. McPherson, *Ordeal by Fire*, pp. 278–279; John Hope Franklin, *From Slavery to Freedom* (New York: Knopf, 1974), pp. 275–280.

21. McPherson, *Ordeal by Fire*, pp. 394–396; McPherson, *The Struggle*, pp. 189–191.

22. McPherson, *Ordeal by Fire*, pp. 509–511.

23. Ibid., pp. 396–398, 506–509, 579–580; McPherson, *The Struggle*, pp. 407–416.

24. McPherson, *Ordeal by Fire*, pp. 391–392, 476; McPherson, *The Struggle*, pp. 308–314.

25. Mark Neely, *The Last Best Hope of Earth* (Cambridge, MA: Harvard University Press, 1993), pp. 178–181.

26. McPherson, *Ordeal by Fire*, pp. 497–503, 513–533.

27. Ibid., pp. 543–546, 566–567, 576–577.

28. C. Vann Woodward, *Reunion and Reaction: The Compromise of 1877 and the End of Reconstruction* (Boston: Little, Brown, 1951), pp. 12–13.

29. John Franklin, "Public Welfare in the South during the Reconstruction Era," *Social Service Review*, 44 (December 1970), pp. 379–392; Michael Perman, *The Road to Redemption: Southern Politics, 1869–1879* (Chapel Hill, NC: University of North Carolina Press, 1984), pp. 22–25.

30. Perman, *The Road to Redemption*, pp. 50–56, 1490–178; Friedman, *Gregarious Saints*, pp. 264–280.

31. McPherson, *The Struggle*, pp. 256–259, 386–397, 407–412.

32. Franklin, *From Slavery*, pp. 324–338.

33. C. Vann Woodward, *The Strange Career of Jim Crow* (New York: Oxford University Press, 1957).

34. J. Owens Smith, *The Politics of Racial Inequality: A Systematic Comparative Macro-Analysis from the Colonial Period to 1970* (New York: Greenwood Press, 1987), pp. 105–126.

35. Eleanor Flexner, *Century of Struggle: The Women's Rights Movement in the United States* (Cambridge, MA: Harvard University Press, 1975), pp. 44–45, 71–77, 145–154.

36. Nancy Woloch, *Women and the American Experience* (New York: Knopf, 1984), p. 195.

37. David Brody, *Workers in Industrial America: Essays on the Twentieth-Century Struggle* (New York: Oxford University Press, 1980), pp. 3–9; Eric Foner, *History of the Labor Movement in the United States*, Vol. 1 (New York: International Publishers, 1955), pp. 51–53.

38. Richard Bushman, "Family Security in the Transition from Farm to City, 1750–1850," *Journal of Family History*, 6 (Fall 1980), pp. 238–256.

39. Thomas Cochran, *The Age of Enterprise: A Social History of Industrial America* (New York: Harper & Row, 1961), pp. 129–153; Edward White, *The American Judicial Tradition: Profiles of Leading American Judges* (New York: Oxford University Press, 1976), pp. 86, 100–105; and Robert Steamer, *The Supreme Court in Crisis: A History of Conflict* (Amherst, MA: University of Massachusetts Press, 1971), pp. 143–149.

40. Paul Boyer, *Urban Masses and the Moral Order in America, 1820–1920* (Cambridge, MA: Harvard University Press, 1978), pp. 123–131; Foner, *History of the Labor Movement*, Vol. 1, pp. 439–474; Herbert Gutman, "The Failure of the Movement by the Unemployed for Public Works in 1873," *Political Science Quarterly*, 80 (June 1975), pp. 254–277; and Thomas Sugrue, "The Structures of Urban Poverty: The Reorganization of Space and Work in Three Periods of American History." In Michael Katz, ed., *The "Underclass" Debate: Views from History* (Princeton, NJ: Princeton University Press), pp. 91–92.

41. Michael Katz, Michael Doucet, and Mark Stern, *The Social Organization of Early Industrial Capitalism* (Cambridge, MA: Harvard University Press, 1982), pp. 14–63, 102–130.

42. Stephan Skowronek, *Building a New American State: The Expansion of National Administrative Capacities, 1877–1920* (Cambridge: Cambridge University Press, 1982), pp. 150–160.

43. Gutman, "The Failure"; Slotkin, *The Fatal Environment*, pp. 477–498.

44. Derek Fraser, *The Evolution of the British Welfare State: A History of Social Policy since the Industrial Revolution* (New York: Barnes & Noble, 1973), pp. 1–22; Deltev Zollner, "Germany." In Peter Kohler and Hans Zacher, eds., *The Evolution of Social Insurance, 1881–1981* (New York: St. Martin's Press, 1981), pp. 4–33.

45. Theda Skocpol, *Social Policy in the United States: Future Possibilities in Historical Perspective* (Princeton, NJ: Princeton University Press, 1995), pp. 37–71.

46. Carolyn Webber and Aaron Wildavsky, *A History of Taxation and Expenditure in the Western World* (New York: Simon and Schuster, 1986), p. 451.

47. Foner, *History of the Labor Movement*, Vol. 1, pp. 77–81, 101–113; Sidney Fine, *Laissez-Faire and the General Welfare State: A Study of Conflict in America, 1865–1901* (Ann Arbor, MI: University of Michigan Press, 1956), pp. 52–64.

48. Leon Fink, *Workingmen's Democracy: The Knights of Labor and American Politics* (Urbana, IL: University of Illinois Press, 1983), pp. 3–17; Foner, *History of the Labor Movement*, Vol. 2, pp. 47–92.

49. Carl Kaestle, *Pillars of the Republic: Common Schools and American Society, 1780–1860* (New York: Hill and Wang, 1983), pp. 36–39, 92.

50. Richard Hofstadter, *Social Darwinism in American Thought* (Boston: Beacon Press, 1955), pp. 41–50.

51. Richard Herrnstein and Charles Murray, *The Bell Curve: Intelligence and Class Structure in American Life* (New York: Free Press, 1994). For a critique of Murray's work, see the essay review by Leon Kamin, "Behind the Curve," *Scientific American* (February 1995), pp. 99–103.

6

Social Reform in the Progressive Era

T A B L E 6.1	Selected Orienting Events
1882	Chinese Exclusion Act passed by Congress
1886	Formation of the American Federation of Labor (AFL) with Samuel Gompers as president
1889	Jane Addams establishes Hull House
1890s	Populist movement in rural areas
1890	Establishment of the National American Women's Suffrage Association
1893–1896	Depression of 1893 causes severe unemployment
1896	The Supreme Court legitimizes separate facilities for African Americans in its *Plessy v. Ferguson* decision
1899	Legislation establishing juvenile courts enacted in Illinois and Colorado
1901–1908	Presidency of Theodore Roosevelt
1904	National Committee on Child Labor organized
1905	Formation of Industrial Workers of the World (IWW)
1909	Initiation of the Pittsburgh Survey by Paul Kellogg; White House Conference on Care of Dependent Children
1909–1912	Presidency of William Howard Taft
1911	Fire at the Triangle Shirtwaist Company in New York City
1911–1920	Most states enact mothers' pension legislation, and many states enact workmen's compensation
1912	Unsuccessful Bull Moose campaign by Theodore Roosevelt and the Progressive Party; Children's Bureau established
1913–1920	Presidency of Woodrow Wilson
1914–1918	World War I (entry of United States in 1917)
1916	Margaret Sanger opens first birth control clinic in New York City; passage of child labor legislation by Congress

T A B L E 6.1   **(continued)**

1918	Supreme Court overrules federal child labor legislation
1920	Nineteenth Amendment to the Constitution grants suffrage to women
1921	Enactment of Sheppard-Towner legislation
1924	Enactment of Immigration Act of 1924

Quiescence was shattered in the 1890s when a rural reform movement known as *populism* mobilized farmers of the Midwest and South to protest low agricultural prices, high interest rates, excessive charges by granaries and railroads, and profiteering by food processors. As the populists lashed out against bankers, Wall Street, and corporations, they obtained a variety of regulatory measures in local and state jurisdictions and developed cooperative storage facilities. Their reform momentum died as quickly as it had started, however, when farm prices improved, limits were placed on rates of railroads, and cooperatives were developed. Moreover, as populism was a rural movement, its impact on urban reform was negligible.

Urban reform had to await the turn of the century, when a reform movement known as *progressivism* developed. It was not a focused reform movement but embraced a variety of antimonopoly, city beautification, civil service, governmental, and social reforms. Progressives advocated prohibition, laws to outlaw prostitution, and efforts to limit immigration, along with policies to limit child labor, correct unsafe working conditions, and provide unemployment insurance.

The number of reform projects that were included within the progressive movement makes it difficult to establish a profile of the typical progressive reformer. Many were middle-class Americans bewildered by the emergence of massive corporations, big city bosses, and large urban immigrant populations; however, many affluent Americans, political machines, and trade unions also supported various progressive reforms. Progressivism was not dominated by members of the Democratic or Republican Party. Despite its amorphous nature, progressivism was the first sustained reform movement in the United States that addressed a variety of urban issues.

At the end of this chapter, we discuss what we can learn from the Progressive Era about policy advocacy, social policy, and the structure of the American welfare state in contemporary society.

REALITIES IN THE EARLY STAGES OF INDUSTRIAL SOCIETY

Immigrants bore the brunt of industrialization in Northern and Midwestern cities. Around 21 million of the total U.S. population of 92 million in 1914 were immigrants who had arrived since 1880. Major American cities consisted of separate ethnic settlements, each with its own churches, political machines, and newspapers. In the 12 largest cities, 40 percent of the population consisted of immigrants, and another 20 percent consisted of second-generation descendants; altogether, 60 percent of the U.S. industrial labor force was foreign-born.[1]

Whereas immigrants prior to 1885 had largely come from northern and western Europe, so-called new immigrants from 1885 to 1924 predominantly came from southern and eastern Europe, particularly Italy, eastern Europe, and Russia. Most Italian

---

INSERT 6.1 Using the Web to Understand How Americans Fashioned Reforms in the Progressive Era

Visit **academic.cengage.com/social_work/jansson** to view these links and a variety of study tools.

> Go to **http://www.loc.gov** Click on "American Memory." Click on "Women's History." Proceed to "Photos—1875–1938." Examine the time line, historical overview of the National Women's Party, and tactics and techniques of the suffragette campaign. Also examine photographs.

> Go to **http://www.archives.gov/education/ lessons** Go to "Era 1870–1990." Proceed to "Photographs of Lewis Hine: Documentation of Child Labor."

> Go to **http://www.archives.gov/education/ lessons** Go to "Era 1890–1930."

- Proceed to political cartoons illustrating progressivism and the election of 1912.
- Proceed to "Women's Suffrage and the 19th Amendment to the Constitution."
- Proceed to photographs of the 369th Infantry and African Americans during World War I.

> Go to **http://www.historyplace.com/unitedstates/ childlabor/index.html** Click on different industries where children worked during the Progressive Era, and examine pictures taken by photographer Lewis Hines. Does this site illustrate the pervasiveness of child labor during this period?

> Go to **http://www.ilr.cornell.edu/trianglefire/** Click on various sites that discuss the tragedy known as the Triangle Fire that killed 146 workers, mostly women, in 1911. Why did this fire become such a galvanizing event?

> Go to **http://archives.gov/education/lessons/ woman_suffrage/script.html** and read the script for "Failure Is Impossible" for a reenactment of the suffragettes' crusade to obtain the vote. Why did it take so long for suffragettes to obtain the vote?

> Go to **http://www.thirteen.org/tenement/** for a virtual tour of a tenement house in New York City on the Lower East Side. Did the immigrants view tenement houses as oppressive, or did they have a more positive view?

> Go to **http://en.wikipedia.org/wiki/Hull_House** and read about Hull House. Then click on the mission, teachings, and selected notable residents. How did the size and funding of settlements, as well as the dominant population, limit their impact in huge cities with massive immigrant populations? How did Hull House accomplish many reforms even with such limited resources?

> Go to **http://www.clpgh.org/exhibit/stell30.html** This site discusses the Pittsburgh Survey that was fashioned by Paul Kellogg and others. How did empirical data strengthen the hands of reformers in the Progressive Era?

> Go to **http://www.reuther.wayne.edu/exhibits/ iww.html** and read about the Industrial Workers of the World. Why were the leaders of this group persecuted during the Progressive Era?

---

immigrants were rural peasants who had been forced to leave villages by an agricultural depression, rising taxes and rents, and competition from factories that mass-produced products that the peasants formerly made in their homes and shops. Husbands or unmarried men often emigrated in hopes of returning to Italy with resources gained in the United States, but ultimately they often decided to pay the transportation costs of relatives, families, and brides. (In 1908, however, after a bad recession, as many Italians returned to Italy as entered the United States.) Russian

Jews, by contrast, were mostly artisans and small merchants whose earnings had been eroded by competition with industrial products and who had suffered appalling persecution. Entire Jewish families emigrated, usually with little desire to return. Both Italians and Jews were wooed by steamship companies, whose salesmen promised prosperity for the price of a ticket. But word of mouth was the primary recruiter, as preceding immigrants revealed that American life—though harsh in the industrial cities—was better than conditions in their homelands. As they streamed in torrents along roads to seaports, they were often robbed by bandits, only to then endure the epidemics of the steamship passage.[2]

Many immigrants were shocked to find themselves in dark and crowded tenements in Eastern and Midwestern cities, which differed from the outdoor living of their native villages. A typical apartment contained two or three rooms with no bathroom or inside toilet; people bathed in a large tub in the kitchen. They moved frequently to pursue better job opportunities, to find less exploitative landlords, or to escape eviction.

Traditionally, historians have viewed industrialization as ruining the homogeneous villages of agrarian society and replacing them with urban ethnic enclaves that were unpleasant places to live. To

be certain, different ethnic groups *did* establish their own enclaves; for example, Polish, Jewish, and Italian areas were remarkably separate from one another. Moreover, these enclaves possessed many social problems. In the absence of public health regulations and modern refrigeration, food poisoning was commonplace. Medications sold on street corners and in pharmacies were touted as cure-alls for many conditions but often contained toxic substances or had no medicinal value. Residents lived in fear of devastating fires. The hastily constructed wooden tenements, many of them home to hundreds of families, were potential incinerators in the absence of housing codes. In some cases, entire sections of cities burned, as in Chicago in 1871 and in San Francisco after the 1906 earthquake. The fire at the Triangle Shirtwaist Company in New York

© Hulton-Deutsch Collection/Corbis

F I G U R E 6.1 Overcrowded tenement housing in New York circa 1900.

INSERT 6.2 Critical Analysis: Nongovernmental Instruments

The term *social policy* usually connotes governmental policies, such as legislation and governmental budgets, but immigrants constructed and used an array of *nonpolicy* instruments to protect and advance their interests, such as political machines, self-help organizations, and charitable agencies. Moreover, people often fend off economic hardship by *personal strategies*—for example, by owning assets like homes, purchasing insurance policies, and hiring relatives as employees in family businesses.

Compare and contrast nonpolicy strategies used by persons of low income, such as immigrants in the early 20th century, with strategies used by more affluent people. Even with immigrants' ingenuity in using nonpolicy strategies, was there a level playing field? What kinds of policy enactments, in eras *after* the progressive period, provided low-income persons with survival resources and services that supplemented or supplanted their nonpolicy instruments?

City in 1911 killed 146 girls and women, many of whom were impaled on iron fences after they leaped from a 10-story building with no fire escapes. This catastrophe mobilized pressure for fire and occupational safety regulations. High levels of crime existed in American cities. Street gangs from different ethnic enclaves preyed on one another. Immigrants lived in dilapidated and crowded tenement buildings that often were fire hazards (see Figure 6.1).

Despite these problems, however, we should not overlook immigrants' ability to craft a range of institutions to help them cope with adversity. The immigrants brought with them their customs, which differed markedly from American practices. Children and adolescents were subject to strict discipline and generally remained with their families until they married. Daughters' marriages were often arranged by the family. Although fathers had ultimate authority, mothers collected the paychecks of all working members, purchased household goods, and parceled out sums to each family member. The immigrants shopped in crowded outdoor markets or from ever-present peddlers who sold produce on the streets. They paid substantial sums to companies selling health insurance, life insurance, and funeral benefits. Often with the aid of the Catholic Church, synagogues, or fundraising efforts in their communities, they constructed a range of self-help and benevolent organizations that helped them during adversity. Each of the immigrant groups organized itself, as well, within the political process; they often linked themselves

to political machines that provided members of their groups with jobs, protection, and community amenities. Fearing hospitals, which they associated with death, they generally relied on midwives drawn from their own communities, as well as purveyors of folk medicine. The institutions of these urban ethnic enclaves, as well as the jobs and protections they received from political machines, allowed them to cope with a hostile environment in the absence of the governmental social policies that we take for granted today.[3] (See Insert 6.2.)

Nor were these urban enclaves temporary. When ethnic groups moved to obtain better housing, they moved en masse to new locations. Although historians once thought that ethnic traditions eroded quickly as immigrants assimilated, it now appears that many ethnic enclaves persisted for generations, and their members retained considerable portions of their culture.[4] (Even in the contemporary period, ethic enclaves exist in all large Eastern and Midwestern cities.)

Social workers and schools tended to encourage immigrants to adopt American child-rearing practices, medical practices, diet, and clothing and viewed with distaste the immigrants' outdoor markets, which they believed to be unsanitary. When the children of immigrants quickly adopted American customs, conflict erupted within immigrant families, which often pressured children to accept arranged marriages, not to Americanize their names, to date only with chaperones present, and to speak their own dialect.

Unfortunately, social workers did not recognize the immigrants' values and customs as salutary alternatives to the American emphasis on individualism. An ethic of mutual assistance was deeply rooted in the immigrants' culture; they were extraordinarily generous to one another, exchanged job information, formed many ethnic associations, shared resources during hard times, and supported political leaders who pledged to help them with jobs and food. Social workers tended to believe that immigrant parents were excessively authoritarian, but each family constituted a small welfare state, in which children's earnings were joined with other family assets and family members cooperated during hard times. The American disdain of the immigrants' diet, which emphasized potatoes or pasta, was equally misdirected, for this diet allowed them to survive with minimal resources.[5]

While their ethnic enclaves helped them cope with adversity, the immigrants encountered an industrial system that oppressed them. By 1900, many jurisdictions placed curbs on the hours of labor, but poor enforcement meant that six-day weeks and 12-hour workdays were commonplace. To override these statutes, moreover, employers sought to persuade workers to sign "voluntary agreements" to work long hours. Immigrants received abysmal wages. Though $15 per week was needed for survival by families in Pittsburgh in 1909, two-thirds of immigrants earned less than $12.50, and half earned less than $10. Barely half the workers in American industry could survive on one paycheck.[6]

Many workers were even more concerned about the dangerous working conditions than about low pay. Industrialization required the use of labor-saving machinery, but these machines lacked safety devices. Roughly 35,000 Americans were killed and 536,000 injured each year during the Progressive Era. In other words, the number of Americans injured in workplace accidents each year was about the same as the total of those killed or injured during the entire Vietnam conflict of the 1960s. Specific industries were particularly hazardous; 328 railroad workers were killed each month in this era, and 46 deaths and 528 injuries occurred in just one steel plant in South Chicago in 1906. American rates of industrial accidents were far greater than rates that existed in European nations, where factory regulations had been enacted and enforced. American workers were not likely to collect funds from their employers when they sued them after industrial accidents because corporate attorneys were frequently able to delay litigation or to use a variety of legal tactics to place the blame for accidents on the workers. Workers collected in only 15 percent of disability lawsuits where employers were proven to be negligent.[7]

Employers were unsympathetic to union organizing. Many believed that their workforce, much like their equipment and plant, was their personal property, and they feared that wage increases could bankrupt them in the unpredictable economic climate of this period. Employers used a range of tactics to quell unions, such as lockouts, violence, spies, and private police forces. Local governments and courts frequently helped employers by issuing injunctions against strikes, denying permits for union demonstrations or picketing, threatening to deport aliens, and using police to intimidate or repress workers. Trade unions grew from 447,000 persons in 1897 to more than 2 million persons in 1904, but they were usually relatively weak because they focused on skilled crafts rather than the unskilled workers who dominated the steel, garment, meat packing, and other basic industries. Nor was it easy for immigrants to organize unions *across* ethnic groups because they spoke different languages and often harbored considerable prejudice against other nationalities.[8]

Periodic recessions were devastating to workers. In many jurisdictions, 30 percent of the labor force was unemployed in the depression of 1893, which lasted until 1897 and was a grim forerunner of the Great Depression of the 1930s. Unemployment was not buffered by insurance, Food Stamps, and other programs that contemporary Americans take for granted. Unemployed persons, who often had no savings, were frequently evicted from their homes and had to obtain meager benefits from breadlines or poorhouses. Social conditions can be summarized with the word *insecurity*, particularly for persons in the lower third of the economic ladder. Few policies or programs existed to protect persons from disease, poverty, discrimination, disability, crime, fires, and poor living conditions. It often seemed to citizens of humble means that social predators endangered them at every juncture, whether employers who overworked them, businesses who sold them dangerous foods or medicines, or slum landlords who exacted exorbitant rents.

Families were splintered by these adverse economic conditions. When destitute women with young children approached public authorities, they were sometimes told that they could receive assistance only if their children were placed in foster homes or with adoptive parents because officials assumed that their own households were unwholesome—or they voluntarily relinquished them because they could not support them. Many children were pressured by their parents to take jobs at an early age. Finally, families were often divided when their individual members went to different cities to seek work.[9]

THE GENESIS OF REFORM

Social Darwinism, the political power of corporations, and the national preoccupation with upward mobility made it seem unlikely, in 1900, that Americans would develop a major reform movement to address social problems. Political institutions seemed impervious to reform. Most state legislatures met for a few months in alternate years and devoted themselves to housekeeping matters. Government was dominated at all levels by the use of patronage to obtain nomination to political office, to secure electoral victories, and to obtain governmental employment. In many cities, political machines used ethnic loyalty and the lure of jobs in municipal services to secure the support of ward and precinct workers, who worked to ensure that incumbents were reelected. In local, congressional, and presidential elections, the Democratic and Republican Parties delivered nominations to persons who were connected to machines or who could bring corporate donations to the party. In an era dominated by parties and lobbyists, presidents and governors were relatively weak figures who tended not to initiate legislation but to acquiesce in decisions fashioned in smoke-filled rooms.[10]

It seemed that government could not implement social programs or enforce regulations, even if they could be developed. In the absence of a modern civil service, patronage rather than competitive exams was used to fill most positions. Many bureaucrats could be bribed or intimidated by party officials. Perhaps the most damaging weakness of government, however, was its paltry size; Americans were unwilling to levy sufficient taxes to fund government institutions at any level. In fact, progressive reformers in 1900 had to contend with a primitive welfare state that lacked virtually all of the social programs and policies we regard as essential in contemporary society. As Insert 6.3 and Figure 6.2 suggest, they had to start "from scratch" in their efforts to get even rudimentary reforms in place.

Patterns of party support frustrated efforts to develop social reform. Voting patterns were dictated by complicated sectional and ethnic traditions, so that neither Democrats nor Republicans focused on the needs of the working class. Democrats were the dominant party in the South, Republicans had considerable strength in New England, and the two parties divided the votes in the Midwest and West. Various ethnic groups supported one of the two major parties on the basis of local tradition rather than for the party's positions on social issues.

CATALYTIC EVENTS

The depression of 1893, which lingered through 1896, had a decisive effect on the nation. It triggered widespread discontent with the Democrats and President Grover Cleveland, who had the misfortune to be in office during the depression years. Believing that his inactivity and economic policies had caused and sustained the depression, many voters changed their allegiance to the Republican party. (With the exception of Woodrow Wilson, who held the presidency from 1913 to 1920, Republicans dominated national politics until the Great Depression of 1929, when the political balance swung back to the Democrats.)[11]

I N S E R T 6.3   Critical Analysis: Confronting the (Nearly) Blank Policy Slate

When analyzing the challenges confronted by reformers at the turn of the 20th century, we should remember that they lived in a society that possessed few of the policies that we take for granted today. Recall the discussion in Chapter 5 about the social problems that accompany industrialization and urbanization, such as unemployment, unsafe working conditions, poor housing, poverty, and victimization of workers. If we conceptualize ameliorative policies to address these problems as a puzzle, we realize that *all* of the pieces in Figure 6.2 were missing in 1900.

Imagine yourself working as a reformer in a society that lacked most of these policies, as well as government bureaucracies capable of administering them *or* sufficient taxes to fund them. (As a federal income tax did not yet exist, the primary governmental revenues consisted of local property taxes, which were absorbed by schools and local services such as police departments.) Where would you start? How would you obtain popular support in a nation whose leaders extolled limited government and in which there was no

strong, grassroots pressure for social reforms from groups such as organized labor?

Whichever reforms they chose to seek, progressive reformers knew that they would confront determined opposition. Conservatives would argue that many reforms were unconstitutional or too costly—or that they would expand government excessively. Corporate leaders would oppose many of these reforms on the grounds that they would diminish profits or force tax increases. Even charity workers and private charities would often oppose some reforms—for example, welfare programs—on the grounds that government ought to leave charity in their hands. Often desperate for the funds that their children earned, some immigrants themselves could be expected to oppose curtailment of child labor. Undeterred by these realities, progressive reformers pressed forward. We shall ask later in this chapter which pieces in Figure 6.2 they obtained—and which ones they did not obtain. Why did they win certain kinds of reforms but not others?

The depression of 1893 also brought widespread disenchantment with corporate tycoons; these heroes of virtue, hard work, and success had not been able to usher in unlimited prosperity, as the script of the Gilded Age had dictated. Their willingness to fire workers, to shut down plants, and to use violent means of suppressing labor strikes during the depression tarnished their reputations. Many Americans read in the newspapers about industrialists' blatant efforts to garner special treatment for themselves and their corporations by bribing public officials or by threatening to relocate to other jurisdictions that promised more favorable tax concessions. Outlandish efforts to bribe politicians and to finance their campaigns were publicized. The flamboyant lifestyles of corporate executives—once considered a just reward for hard work—came to be resented when more than 25 percent of adult males were unemployed in many areas.[12]

Some Americans began to wonder whether the fantastic growth of industry might be a mixed blessing. Industrialization had seemed at first to represent

a new economic frontier that, like the Western frontier, could lead to unlimited opportunities for millions of Americans. But small entrepreneurs were increasingly driven from business by the ruthless tactics of corporate entrepreneurs, who managed to aggregate vast economic empires. Many Americans grew alarmed at the size and power of corporations, which prompted doubts that they could be effectively regulated. Lurid stories about the victimization of hapless workers, women and children among them, tarnished the reputation of industrialists. Reports of adulterated food, unsafe medicines, and other defective products convinced many Americans that corporate executives needed to be restrained by enactment of regulations. Social reform thrives when culprits are identified; their perceived infamies inflame the passions of the public and inspire efforts to regulate them. As tycoons were forced from their pedestals, they were subjected increasingly to proposals to limit their power over labor, to curtail the size of their companies, and to limit their ability to bribe politicians.

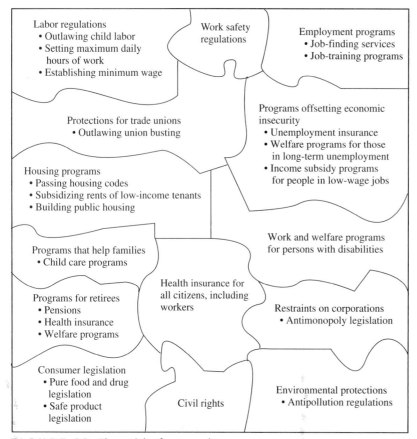

Labor regulations
- Outlawing child labor
- Setting maximum daily hours of work
- Establishing minimum wage

Work safety regulations

Employment programs
- Job-finding services
- Job-training programs

Protections for trade unions
- Outlawing union busting

Programs offsetting economic insecurity
- Unemployment insurance
- Welfare programs for those in long-term unemployment
- Income subsidy programs for people in low-wage jobs

Housing programs
- Passing housing codes
- Subsidizing rents of low-income tenants
- Building public housing

Programs that help families
- Child care programs

Work and welfare programs for persons with disabilities

Health insurance for all citizens, including workers

Programs for retirees
- Pensions
- Health insurance
- Welfare programs

Restraints on corporations
- Antimonopoly legislation

Consumer legislation
- Pure food and drug legislation
- Safe product legislation

Civil rights

Environmental protections
- Antipollution regulations

F I G U R E 6.2 The social reform puzzle.

INTELLECTUAL FERMENT AND AROUSED PUBLIC OPINION

The nation's major policy swings have been associated with shifts in emphasis between environmental and personal explanations of social problems. During conservative periods—such as the Gilded Age, the 1920s, the 1950s, and the 1980s—the focus is on personal and moral problems. In reform periods—such as the Progressive Era, the 1930s, and the 1960s—attention shifts to environmental factors. Historians do not know why these tidal swings in public opinion occur.

By the turn of the 20th century, many Americans believed that environmental factors, such as overcrowding, tenements, and poor working conditions, thwarted the healthy development of city dwellers. Many progressives also feared that political machines, large corporations, and widespread corruption threatened democratic institutions. An environmental focus was critical to the development of a reform movement. When the public's attention was drawn to various environmental conditions that were believed to cause social ills, support for social reform to modify those conditions increased.

In the Gilded Age, reform was deterred by the conventional wisdom that the American Constitution was sacrosanct and should be interpreted literally and that the meaning of life derived from work, competition, and upward mobility.[13] By the late 19th century, however, many Americans questioned these verities. They countered the

Social Darwinists' argument that life should be devoted to competition, for example, with the assertion that cooperation and creativity were higher values. Ministers known as social gospellers argued that the gospel required people to help the downtrodden. Social workers like Jane Addams and philosophers like John Dewey believed that people were intrinsically cooperative and became competitive only when they were exposed to environmental cues and models—including an American culture that emphasized winning at all costs. Addams extolled a "cooperative ideal" when she contended that government should try to instill a spirit of cooperation in its citizens, whether through example (by developing social programs, for instance) or through education. She argued that regulations and social programs represented expressions of altruism rather than unwarranted interference in the private affairs of industrialists and citizens.[14] (We will discuss Jane Addams near the end of this chapter.)

Addams and other reformers wondered how the competitive and materialistic values of Americans could be transformed. Unlike European radicals and socialists, who romanticized the working class and believed that its victory over bourgeois interests would transform society, Addams idealized different groups at different points in her career. She variously hoped that immigrants would infuse American society with their simple peasant and altruistic virtues; that the creativity and playful virtues of youth would be emulated by others; and that women would transform American society by asserting values of nurturance that stemmed from their family roles. Although each group proved unequal to her high expectations, she seemed never to become disillusioned.[15]

Many reformers also contended that unregulated economic activity would create unacceptable levels of social distress. Whereas economic theorists in the 19th century had commonly argued that the natural balance of supply and demand was disrupted when government exacted taxes or regulated hours and working conditions, writers like Richard Ely asserted that, unless regulated, business practices concentrated power in the hands of elites, who consigned workers to poverty and diverted their own wealth into nonproductive ventures such as speculation and corporate takeovers.[16]

A phalanx of theorists questioned provisions of the Constitution and the American legal system. Some argued that the Constitution constructed by the founding fathers adequately addressed the needs of an agricultural republic but was inadequate for an industrial society, which required government to assume an active role in economic and social affairs. Many progressives felt that the Supreme Court did not have the right to overrule progressive social legislation, and they proposed legislation to circumscribe its powers.[17]

Progressives also began to question whether America was a model society that should be emulated by the rest of the world. The nation *had* led the way in opening opportunities to citizens by enacting universal suffrage, land ownership, and education, but it had lagged in providing security to its citizens. On extensive trips to Europe, social workers Jane Addams and Grace Abbott, as well as other reformers, discovered various social programs and regulations that offered support for workers and families.[18]

Some reformers attained extraordinary popularity in the Progressive Era; in public opinion polls, for example, Jane Addams was voted the most exemplary American. Politicians of both parties who espoused various reforms were elected in large numbers to local, state, and national legislatures. As progressives opened up the political process by allowing voters to place issues (so-called initiatives) on the ballot, many reform measures were enacted even when legislators showed scant interest in them. The sheer number of progressive measures enacted in cities and states attests to the popularity of reform during this period.

Some historians have used concepts from social psychology to explain why middle-class Americans became more interested in reform in certain periods. Richard Hofstadter, for example, argued that middle-class Americans supported reform because they feared that corporations and political machines threatened their economic and social roles. It seems unlikely, however, that a single motivation explains this swing in public opinion. Different persons and groups probably supported reform for different reasons. Many Americans supported reform because of personal exposure to social ills; they read about the corruption of officials whom they had elected, trembled when epidemics struck their cities, read about or saw corporate executives' flaunting of power, or ate food or consumed drugs that made them unwell. Religion should not be ignored as a motivating force for reform in the Progressive Era. Many middle- and upper-class Americans felt guilty about the sorry condition of the bottom third of their society and the victimization of women and children by employers. Some realized, despite their prejudices, that the economic institutions from which they derived personal benefit were fueled by immigrants' labor.[19]

Furthermore, pragmatism propelled many Americans toward reform as they became convinced that conservative policies had not been effective. While conservatives in the Progressive Era continued to voice the laissez-faire homilies of the Gilded Age, they were on the defensive because reformers successfully argued that their policies had led to a disastrous depression, the victimization of women and children, and the rise of monopolies. The fruits of capitalism had failed to reach some of the desperately poor immigrants who crowded American cities.[20]

Although portrayed by conservatives as outside agitators or socialists, reformers were able to enlist popular support by employing a symbolism that seemed respectable and American. They spoke of saving the American family, saving children, opening up politics to the people, increasing economic opportunity, and preventing poverty and crime. Many Americans believed that the family was in a state of serious decline because children and women had to work, women were separated from their children when they applied for assistance, and children were placed in prisons because of the lack of juvenile facilities. Americans also feared that their political institutions were increasingly dominated by political machines or corrupt politicians. They favored proposals to save democracy itself, including placing policy proposals on the ballot (so voters could bypass elected officials) and instituting the

civil service so that many governmental positions would be filled through competitive exams rather than through patronage. Trust-busting was defended on the grounds that it would enhance economic opportunity for ordinary citizens. When it was perceived as addressing these noncontroversial goals, reform obtained widespread support.[21]

Many Americans in the Progressive Era also believed that they were rediscovering their own land. The rhetoric of the Gilded Age had suggested that the nation was free of problems and on a path of unlimited prosperity, democracy, and territorial expansion. By the turn of the century, however, reformers and journalists engaged in a frenzied search for factual evidence of social problems, such as the number of children and women exposed to dangerous working conditions, the number of children placed in adult prisons, the toxicity of many drugs, high rates of infant mortality among specific groups, and instances of political corruption. The appetite for facts and figures was insatiable; the social worker and reformer Paul Kellogg, for example, initiated an exhaustive six-volume survey of social conditions in Pittsburgh that described occupational hazards, housing, health, and other facets of residents' lives.[22]

As social facts were discovered, they were disseminated to the public through popular and professional journals and newspapers. Reforming journalists, popularly known as *muckrakers*, dramatized their findings by highlighting the evil nature of the wrongdoers and the innocence (and vast number) of the victims. Professionals and academics presented findings in more neutral terms. In either case, the general public was fascinated by the endless evidence of wrongdoing and suffering, which bolstered support for reform.

THE SPECTER OF SOCIAL UNREST

Progressive leaders were largely unconcerned with the possibility of social unrest by the millions of immigrant workers who provided cheap labor for American industry. With notable exceptions, most workers were relatively tranquil in this period despite their appalling working and living conditions. Immigrants who did not speak English, who lacked citizenship, who often hoped to return to Europe, and who feared unemployment were not likely to engage in militant protest. Most women were not amenable to strikes because they hoped to work only for a brief period before marrying.

Still, the emergence of fringe—but vocal and radical—organizations, such as the Socialist Party and the Industrial Workers of the World, represented a new phenomenon in the nation. Their leaders espoused ideas that departed from the conventional political beliefs of the nation; many advocated political organization of the working class, supported national strikes, favored the nationalization of some industries, and called for a national minimum wage. As we shall see later in this chapter, fringe parties had scant success in obtaining political offices, except at the mayoral level; nonetheless, they constituted a political threat to many Americans, particularly because the unskilled labor force that they sought to organize was so huge. In this climate, many progressives presented themselves as moderates whose sensible and pragmatic reforms would blunt protest and maintain tranquility.

As many scholars have recently analyzed, a dark side of progressivism existed. While often siding with underdogs, many progressives were prejudiced against immigrants, whom they regarded as uncivilized, ignorant, and immoral. Charity workers often wanted to imbue immigrants with middle-class values. Progressives who enacted a modest welfare program for women known as *mothers' pensions* wanted to withhold it from immigrant women until they had been investigated to determine whether they deserved assistance and would use it wisely. Furthermore, many progressives were deeply prejudiced against African Americans, as we shall discuss in more detail later.

REGULATORY REFORMS IN THE PROGRESSIVE ERA

The hallmark of progressives' reforms were myriad *regulations* that they got enacted mostly at local and state levels of government, along with some at the federal level of government. Regulations are governmental rules that establish what corporations, social agencies, public officials, professionals, restaurants, pharmaceutical companies, developers, landlords, employers, bars or taverns, banks, and others can and cannot do. Regulations also come with penalties if persons break them, including fines, revoking of business licenses, and even imprisonment.

We take regulations for granted in contemporary society. We assume that employers cannot hire 8-year-old children, that pharmaceutical companies cannot put unauthorized toxic chemicals in drugs, and that landlords must provide fire exits in apartment buildings. The primitive welfare state of the year 1900 lacked even these basic rules to guide people's actions. In their absence, corporations could make dangerous or shoddy products, establish inhumane working practices, and subject workers to hazardous conditions. In the absence of public scrutiny, politicians could accept bribes, hire relatives, and tamper with elections. Homer Folks, a progressive reformer in New York State, found that state institutions were rarely audited, that laundry and food concessions were awarded to politicians' friends, that no system of external monitoring existed, and that it was impossible to distinguish staff from residents in some institutions because they were similarly dressed. He conducted a tireless campaign to establish audit, licensing, and monitoring programs for public bureaucracies; to place staff positions under the civil service; to oust political appointees; to establish standards of sanitation; and to enforce existing laws that required children and insane persons to be removed from almshouses. Similar projects were undertaken by many other reformers in other states.[23]

Many of the regulations were obtained only after exhausting political battles. Thus, advocates of child labor laws, who formed reform organizations in each state as well as at the national level, fought those who argued that these laws violated parental rights, that immigrants needed the earnings of their children to survive, and that child labor prevented the overcrowding of schools. Reformers who sought federal labor laws, such as a minimum wage and maximum hours of work, were told that the Constitution did not give the federal government jurisdiction in social matters.

The regulatory reforms of the era were supplemented by efforts to rationalize the social services system and to develop a social work profession. The reformers viewed with horror the provision of services by amateurs and political appointees. The National Conference of Charities and Corrections sponsored conventions of administrators and staff of agencies to exchange information and provide training. The New York Charity Organization Society established an annual summer course for social workers in 1898, which was followed in 1903 by the formation of the Chicago School of Civics and Philanthropy and in 1904 by the New York School of Philanthropy and the Boston School for Social Workers. By 1919, the leaders of 15 schools of social work had formed the Association of Training Schools for Professional Social Work. These early social workers usually identified with private agencies; they tended to view public institutions as last-resort programs for people in extreme poverty, people with mental disorders, and criminals. However, they increasingly departed from the moralistic ethos of 19th-century social service staff (who had used such value-laden labels as deserving and undeserving) by providing services based on the analysis of familial, personal, and neighborhood factors that contributed to their clients' problems. Instead of dictating to clients and offering personal models of morality, many social workers sought to develop give-and-take exchanges with clients and local interventions. Social work pioneers hoped to professionalize social programs by credentialing their staff in training programs.[24]

Progressive Era reformers such as Jane Addams, who advocated coupling personal service with public sector reforms, came into conflict with social workers who believed private agencies should dominate in the provision of outdoor relief and opposed the development of public programs. But this conflict had diminished by 1909, when Addams was selected as president of the National Conference of Charities and Corrections.[25]

THE LIMITED SOCIAL PROGRAMS OF THE PROGRESSIVE ERA

Although many new regulations were passed into law, the few social programs that were enacted underscored the limited nature of social reform in the Progressive Era, as none of them required the expenditure of large sums of money or the distribution of resources or services to poor persons. The main programs of the day included workmen's compensation, mothers' pensions, juvenile courts, the Children's Bureau, and protections for female workers in various states.

Limited Policy Reforms for Women and Children

The mothers' pension movement swept the nation between 1911 and 1919, when most states developed such programs. Whereas today most single mothers have been deserted, are divorced, or have had children out of wedlock, in the Progressive Era most single mothers were widows. When they sought governmental assistance for single mothers, progressive reformers focused on the needs of women who had been widowed, in the belief that such women would be viewed more sympathetically than would women who had been divorced or deserted. Without governmental assistance, they contended, single mothers—whether widowed, divorced, or deserted—would have to work such long hours that they could not properly care for their children, and many of them would have to continue to divide their families by sending some of their children to orphanages.

Mothers' pensions can be viewed as a first breach in the American orthodoxy that the government should not provide outdoor relief to people in need. Indeed, many progressives hoped that it would be followed by other programs, such as unemployment insurance and old age pensions. But mothers' pensions were hardly the far-reaching reform that sociologist Theda Skocpol suggests when she contends that Americans constructed a "maternalist welfare state" in the Progressive Era. As Linda Gordon notes, these pensions were granted to relatively few women—only 46,000 women nationally by 1919. Residency and citizenship requirements excluded many immigrants. The programs operated with such low appropriations that long waiting lists often existed. Many applicants were screened out as unsuitable because of health problems or poor housing. Even in Los Angeles, with a reputedly generous program, only 24 percent of single mothers received public or private assistance. Pensions were so miserly, moreover, that large numbers of women who received them *had* to work. Although legislation rarely indicated that women with out-of-wedlock children or women who had left their husbands could not receive mothers' pensions, local administrators could and sometimes did exclude them from the program on the grounds that they were morally undeserving. Many states allowed women to receive assistance even when their husbands were still present, but it is likely that such assistance was given reluctantly, lest it reduce the husband's incentive to work.[26] (See Insert 6.4.)

Progressives succeeded in obtaining special courts, known as *juvenile courts*, in many jurisdictions. Prior to this reform, children were tried in adult courts, detained in jails for extended periods, and remanded to adult prisons, even though houses of refuge and legal precedents that exempted minor children from penalties established for adult offenders already existed in the 19th century. In many jurisdictions, children who were less than 14 years of age were exempted from capital punishment and from other penalties, but these exceptions could be waived in certain circumstances. Judge Ben Lindsey in Denver and many social reformers in Chicago and elsewhere believed that mixing children with adult criminals was harmful to children and that confinement did not address familial, school, and other causes of delinquency. Because probation hardly existed as an option, even children who had committed minor offenses were institutionalized.[27]

When children were tried in juvenile courts, judges and staff could explore their family situations, examine a range of options including probation, and, in principle, refer children to special juvenile institutions when they needed to be committed. In practice, however, judges still lacked innovative community programs to which they could refer juvenile offenders. Furthermore, funding was insufficient to hire the staff needed, the courts lacked bilingual staff able to converse with immigrant children and parents in their native tongues, and most judges lacked training in social matters.

The idea of establishing a national Children's Bureau originated in 1904 in the National Committee on Child Labor, was reaffirmed in a White House Conference on Care of Dependent Children in 1909, and was finally enacted in 1912; it received a meager budget of $25,640, as compared with the $1.4 million that funded the federal Board of Animal Husbandry. Conservatives hobbled the agency still further by limiting its authority to data gathering and advisory functions that precluded it from providing resources directly to

---

INSERT 6.4   Ethical Analysis of Key Issues and Policies: The Stigmatizing of Single Mothers

As our discussion of mothers' pensions suggests, single mothers in the early part of the 20th century were viewed as morally suspect by many people, even by many advocates of mothers' pensions.

1. Speculate why single mothers were widely distrusted in American society in the early part of this century. What policies did progressives institute that reflected this suspicion?

2. What policies might progressives have considered that would have had greater ethical merit than mothers' pensions?

3. What similarities exist with contemporary portrayals of mothers on Temporary Assistance to Needy Families (TANF)?

children or to local units of government. Its dedicated social work staff issued many seminal reports in the succeeding years, but the bureau did not provide a frontal attack on the poverty, malnutrition, or poor health of the nation's children; furthermore, the bureau tended to avoid controversial issues, such as passage of national child labor laws. Its greatest triumph was the enactment in 1921 of the Sheppard-Towner legislation, which provided federal matching funds for states to provide clinics for pregnant women and young children. However, the American Medical Association viewed the program as a competitor to private doctors and succeeded in precluding programs funded by the legislation from providing medical services; thus, the programs were limited to educational and social services. Even this small program was terminated in 1929 on the grounds that it violated states' rights and represented socialized medicine.[28]

Reformers believed that they had made a lasting breakthrough in 1916 when they finally obtained passage of national legislation to restrict the use of child labor. Specifically, the legislation prohibited interstate commerce of the products of firms that employed children who were less than 14 years of age and mines that employed children less than 16 years of age. However, reformers' hopes were dashed when the Supreme Court nullified the legislation in 1918 on the grounds that the law fell outside the province of interstate commerce, which had been widely regarded as the only way that child labor laws could be constitutionally legitimized. Although the ruling did not frontally challenge the right of the federal government to regulate child labor, and the staff of the Children's Bureau was able to obtain measures that prevented federal contractors from using child labor during World War I, the ruling had a chilling effect on social reform at the national level.[29] Moreover, in 1922, the Court declared unconstitutional a second anti–child labor law, enacted in 1919 and based on the national power of taxation.

Progressives did obtain minimum wage legislation for women in 15 states and the District of Columbia by 1923 and legislation that established maximum hours of daily labor in 41 states by 1921.

For reasons we shall discuss later, these measures applied only to women; it was not until 1938 that federal legislation that covered all workers was enacted.

Private Philanthropy

When discussing progressives' reforms, we should remember that they did not wish to supplant private philanthropy with publicly funded programs. Accustomed to the sectarian and privately run institutions that evolved in the 19th century, they strongly supported the continuation of these institutions, as well as the construction of hundreds of sectarian hospitals across the nation as physicians developed surgical and diagnostic techniques that shifted medical practice from their offices and patient homes to institutional settings. Indeed, some social workers opposed certain publicly funded programs, such as mothers' pensions, on the grounds that they would wrongly supplant private charity.

Nor did strict boundaries exist between public and private sectors. Mothers' pensions were sometimes administered by private agencies. Judges sometimes committed neglected children to sectarian orphanages. Settlement houses often received contracts from public authorities.

Middle-class progressive reformers who had not personally experienced social problems made determined efforts to live among immigrants by establishing settlement houses in Eastern and Midwestern cities. Hull House, the settlement house that Jane Addams established in Chicago in 1889, was modeled after Toynbee Hall in London, which had been founded by Arnold Toynbee, an English social reformer. Addams's Hull House was a remarkable institution. She carefully documented living conditions and the ethnicity of area residents, often as a prelude to seeking corrective legislation from local and state governments. She recruited large numbers of volunteers, who provided an array of services to immigrants. Hull House became a mecca for social reformers in the nation and the world and held numerous seminars on social problems. Addams sought to organize immigrants against the political machine on the grounds that it was corrupt and did not seek ameliorative reforms. More than 400 settlement houses had been established by 1910, many in white immigrant neighborhoods but some in African American neighborhoods in the North and the South. The settlement houses provided many services and programs, including arts and crafts, vocational training, cultural events, English language instruction, classes preparing immigrants for citizenship, assistance with unionization of workers, voter registration, and health services. Following Addams's example, the staff of some settlement houses developed surveys of housing and other social conditions in their neighborhoods as a prelude to seeking regulations.

We should not idealize the settlement house movement, however. Whereas Addams made social action an important part of Hull House's program, other settlements were relatively inactive. Many settlement leaders were condescending to immigrants, whom they regarded as ignorant of hygiene, proper diet, and morality. Some sought to convert immigrants to Protestantism. Imbued with the racism of the period, some leaders moved their settlements out of a neighborhood when African Americans moved in, refused to serve them, charged them fees to keep them from receiving services, or opened separate and segregated facilities for them. (Even Hull House had no African Americans on its board as late as the 1930s.) In an era when government funds were rarely used to provide contracts or grants to nonpublic agencies, the settlements' boards often consisted of affluent people with conservative ideology, which further constrained their social reform work.[30]

Even enlightened settlement staff worked under difficult circumstances. They had to raise funds to support their work, often from conservative people and institutions. The settlements existed in turbulent communities, where successive waves of immigrants moved in and out in complex patterns. The immigrants themselves tended to view the affluent white volunteers and staff as authority figures, and political officials were inclined to view them as competitors for the immigrants' allegiance.

These criticisms of settlement houses ought not to obscure some of their achievements. Unlike the settlement staff, most affluent white Americans avoided the immigrant enclaves of major cities. Those settlement workers who did engage in social reforms provided a style of work that contrasted with that of other private agencies, which often focused on a narrow casework approach, opposed even to such modest policies as mothers' pensions. The policy advocacy tradition of social work very much derives from the work of reformers such as Jane Addams and other settlement house leaders.

Limited Reforms for Workers and Persons with Mental Illness

Employers used a variety of legal defenses to place part or all of the responsibility for work-related injuries on employees. They argued that employees knew about dangers before they took employment; that employees were careless in their work; or that negligence of a fellow employee, rather than negligence of the employer, had caused work-related injuries. Litigation was so time-consuming that workers often died before awards were made to them. Its cost forced many workers into indebtedness and eventually into poor relief programs. Despite their legal successes, employers also found the costs of litigation to be prohibitive; ever-mounting awards to disabled workers and the costs of liability insurance increased their costs of doing business.

Workmen's compensation laws, which had been adopted by virtually all states by 1920, provided a partial remedy that was acceptable to many employers and to some unions. The laws established a state fund that received its revenues from a payroll tax levied on employers. Workers who were injured were entitled to obtain an award, the amount of which was determined on the basis of the specific type of injuries. Under the legislation, workers usually forfeited their right to sue employers.

Workers soon discovered that workmen's compensation was not a panacea. The payment schedules for specific injuries were appallingly low—indeed, far lower than jury awards that had preceded the enactment of workmen's compensation. Nevertheless, the legislation took the edge off discontent, and consequently eased public pressure to improve workplace safety. Unions were divided in their attitudes to workmen's compensation; some believed this legislation was an improvement, but others believed it helped employers more than workers. Moreover, workmen's compensation covered only bodily injuries; in Great Britain, by contrast, industrial diseases were also covered.[31]

The Progressive Era saw the introduction of an initial set of aftercare services for people who had been institutionalized in mental asylums. As late as 1905, virtually no aftercare services existed in the United States; released mental patients had to fend for themselves with no assistance from anyone. Beginning in New York State and expanding to other states, social workers were employed by mental institutions to follow their wards on release and to give them services. Moreover, the work of Clifford Beers, himself a former mental patient who had written about his ordeal in public institutions, led to the establishment of nongovernmental societies for mental hygiene in various states, as well as the National Committee for Mental Hygiene, which pressured public authorities to improve mental hospitals and to develop programs to prevent mental illness. Even these reforms failed to assist most persons with mental problems in community settings because they reached only a small fraction of persons due to the poor funding of outpatient clinics by local, state, and federal governments.

Health Reforms within a Flawed Capitalistic Model

Contemporary Americans cannot easily understand just how precarious the health of many Americans was at the start of the Progressive Era. As many as 20 percent of the populations of entire cities were killed by such epidemics as cholera, typhoid fever, and malaria. Children died in great numbers from influenza, whooping cough, measles, and scarlet fever.

These health problems partly derived from the poor state of scientific knowledge about health, but major scientific advances at the end of the 19th century meant that the United States could drastically curtail death and injury from these diseases if it found ways to get people inoculated for some of these diseases—and if sanitation was sufficiently improved to prevent the spread of cholera.

Notable public health reforms took place during the Progressive Era. Some local governments and private charities established public health centers in many American communities where residents received newly developed inoculations. Hired by local governments, public health inspectors enforced regulations that required sanitary conditions in housing, restaurants, and other businesses —and assumed key roles in upgrading sewer and sanitation systems to avert the epidemics that had devastated cities during the 19th century with malaria, typhoid fever, and cholera. The spread of diseases such as tuberculosis was markedly cut through quarantines of persons with them.

The education of physicians, too, was markedly improved with the establishment of licensed medical schools that replaced the odd assortment of unregulated places of training for physicians of the 19th century that sometimes did not even require completion of a high school degree. If medical care had largely taken place in physicians' offices and patients' homes in the 19th century, the construction of hundreds of hospitals by many religious denominations in the early years of the 20th century provided a medical care setting that took advantage of ongoing improvements in surgery and medication.

These improvements took place, however, within a flawed two-track model of medical care. Physicians and nongovernmental hospitals were funded by fees charged to patients—and patients would pay for these charges from their personal income. Unlike schoolteachers, nurses, and social workers, then, physicians would not be salaried persons, but private entrepreneurs operating in a capitalistic model.

This capitalistic model, however, placed many patients in jeopardy since many of them could not afford the fees, whether because they were poor or because they needed expensive care. Rather than using the mainstream model, then, they either went untreated or sought care from public hospitals and clinics funded by cities and counties across the nation. This publicly funded system was often far inferior to the mainstream system and required a demeaning means test. Its institutions were often poorly staffed—and patients were often put in large wards that were meagerly staffed. Many of these so-called medical institutions were part of poorhouses where destitute persons lived and where infirm elderly persons were warehoused.

Realizing how unethical a two-track model of health care was, some prescient leaders of the American Medical Association (AMA) decided during the Progressive Era to explore public systems of health care that would be financed not by patients' payments but by the government. They proposed that each state establish universal health care funded by tax revenues, but encountered angry resistance from other members of the AMA who contended that universal health care was "socialistic" and "un-American"—and would somehow destroy the patient-doctor relationship. These dissenters voted the reform-minded leaders of the AMA out of office—and their perspectives prevailed in the AMA for the next 50 years. Almost single-handedly, the AMA prevented public officials from enacting some form of national health insurance during the Franklin Roosevelt and Harry Truman administrations—and almost blocked the passage of Medicare and Medicaid in 1965.

The Limited Nature of Progressives' Social Reforms

When viewed from the perspective of the 19th century, progressives achieved extraordinary reforms in a brief period of time; they passed a variety of regulations, reforms for women and children, and workmen's compensation. These reforms required sustained effort over a period spanning 20 years. When viewed from a contemporary perspective, however, the progressives' reforms underscore the reluctance of the American welfare state. Most important, progressives' reforms did not require large government expenditures; they did not involve major benefit or service programs. As we have discussed, both mothers' pensions and Sheppard-Towner services were minuscule programs. As we

noted in Chapter 5, government spending in the United States in 1920 was only 5.5 percent of the GNP, as compared with 19.1 percent in Great Britain and 25.5 percent in France, and a considerable portion of these American expenditures went to veterans' payments—not only to the surviving veterans of the Civil War and the Spanish-American War but to recent veterans of World War I.[32]

In addition to the political and cultural barriers to reform, which we shall discuss shortly, another serious obstacle was that state, local, and federal governments lacked revenues to fund major social programs, even had the progressives desired them. We have noted that local property taxes were the primary source of governmental revenues in this period—and they were used primarily for schools and public services. The Congress had enacted a federal income tax in 1894, only to have the Supreme Court declare it unconstitutional. In 1913, to bypass the Court, progressives secured the Sixteenth Amendment to the Constitution, which empowered the Congress "to lay and collect taxes on incomes," but the rates were established at such low levels that most citizens paid no income taxes at all. When a substantial federal income tax *was* levied to help fund American military efforts in World War I, it was promptly cut drastically during the 1920s so that only about 5 percent of Americans paid any federal income tax by 1932.

CULTURAL AND POLICY REALITIES THAT LIMITED REFORM

Despite their skill in uncovering the devious actions of corporate tycoons and exploiters of powerless populations, progressives were often naive in their approach to social reform. They assumed that regulations would bring dramatic changes when, in fact, they often had negligible effect. The naivete of progressives took two forms. First, their *legalistic bias* made them assume that laws would lead to dramatic changes in the behavior of wrongdoers, though they soon learned that persons and institutions subject to regulations were resourceful in evading them—whether by co-opting or bribing government officials or by escaping detection because regulatory agencies lacked funds and staff to adequately monitor compliance.

Furthermore, their *procedural bias* led them to believe that changes in the procedures of government would make government dramatically more responsive to the needs of the people; thus, they fought for the passage of such laws as the initiative, the referendum, and the recall, which, respectively, allowed citizens to place legislation on the ballot, to hold popular votes on measures that had already been enacted by legislators, and to vote from office public officials who were believed to be corrupt or misdirected. These measures assumed that an aroused citizenry would vote for progressive legislation; as reformers soon learned, the same techniques could also be used to recall liberal legislators or to place conservative measures on the ballot. (It is an irony of history that conservative initiatives to cut government social spending, such as California's Proposition 13 in 1978, were one legacy of progressive procedural reforms.)

Few persons in the Progressive Era would have argued that regulations to control the actions of industrialists, politicians, and landlords were unnecessary. However, a law enforcement approach, which fostered the use of regulatory strategies, precluded the enactment of major social programs to deliver resources and services *directly* to these powerless groups. Some progressives sought unemployment insurance, health insurance, and other programs, but many emphasized regulations rather than an array of reforms. In fairness to them, the minimal resources of local, state, and federal governments, as well as the lack of a tradition of governmental social programs, provided a hostile context for broader reforms.

Progressive reformers also diminished their effectiveness by relying on local governments—whether cities, counties, or state legislatures—to take the lead in addressing the mounting social ills of the nation. Child labor laws, workmen's compensation, mothers' pensions, and many other reforms were enacted locally; tens of thousands of regulations and proposals were advanced at local levels of government. Local reforms were needed, of course, but national programs offered certain advantages. A strategy of policy localism required expenditure of vast amounts of energy in reinventing the wheel in each of the states and local jurisdictions. Moreover, resistance to reforms in specific localities was often heightened by opponents' argument that a specific local reform—such as prohibition of child labor—might make industry move to other localities where this restriction did not exist.

Because most Americans and some reformers believed that social welfare issues belonged to local governments under the Constitution and by the precedent of the poor laws, efforts to secure national reforms occurred belatedly during the Progressive Era and were limited to modest reforms such as the Children's Bureau. Other national initiatives included the 1916 child labor legislation and the 1910 Mann Act, which prohibited the transportation of women across state lines for immoral purposes. Efforts at the national level were further hampered by the Supreme Court, which continued to limit the power of the federal government—for example, in rulings that restricted the federal government to those functions specifically enumerated in the Constitution.[33]

Progressives' effectiveness was also diluted by the range of their interests. At least six overlapping reform agendas existed:

1. Some progressives, who emphasized procedural reforms in government, sought policies to reduce corruption, to give more power to experts in governments, and to foster greater participation by citizens in government.

2. Some progressives sought to regulate the economic system, to restrict the size of corporations, or to develop federal controls over banking and currency.

3. Members of professions such as medicine, nursing, law, teaching, and social work sought to develop licensing laws and accredited educational programs to upgrade the knowledge and skills of professionals.

4. Some progressives sought legislation to restore morality to American life by curbing immigration, restricting gambling, ending prostitution, or limiting alcohol consumption.

5. Some reformers focused on regulations to limit the ability of corporations, owners of rental housing, and others to victimize workers or the public.

6. Some progressives pursued programs to redistribute resources to impoverished workers, destitute women, and other groups.

Most progressives embraced more than one of these agendas.[34]

The range of the reform agendas limited progressives' impact in several ways. First, by devoting their energies to many causes and issues, reformers decreased the likelihood that they could significantly affect any one of them. Furthermore, the six agendas received unequal attention; reforms that assisted powerless and impoverished groups tended to attract less support than did other reforms. In particular, trust-busting, good-government reforms (such as the initiative, referendum, and recall), prohibition, and restrictions on immigration absorbed the attention of many reform leaders and the general public.[35]

These emphases reflected the middle-class perspectives of many reformers. Middle-class citizens did not monopolize progressivism; the six progressive agendas were supported variously by trade unions, political bosses, and immigrant groups. Nonetheless, the middle class shaped the direction and content of many reforms. Relatively affluent persons often had scant personal knowledge of the problems that immigrants and factory workers encountered in their daily lives. Trust-busting, city beautification, civil service, professional licensing, and other such reforms did not directly address the appalling social conditions of poor persons. The prominence of moral reforms during the Progressive Era also suggests the imprint of middle-class reformers, many of whom sought temperance, termination of gambling, elimination of prostitution, and anticrime measures. Some progressive reformers were biased against immigrant groups and sought legislation to limit immigration. Despite valiant attempts, reformers like Jane Addams were unable to prevent Congress from passing anti-immigration legislation, which would have become public law had it not been vetoed by Presidents Taft and Wilson. We have already noted the punitive administration of mothers' pensions to immigrant widows, who had to convince investigators that they were deserving before the pension would be granted.

This middle-class imprint on reform can usefully be contrasted with England and other European nations, where strong political parties dominated by factory workers and radicals were beginning to emerge. While the Labor Party was still in its infancy by 1910, its presence led to competition between the conservative and the liberal parties for workers' votes —a competition that partly led Lloyd George, the leader of the Liberal Party, to support a range of social legislation. (Ramsay MacDonald became the first Prime Minister from the Labor Party in 1924.) Even those progressives who most favored social reforms were often uncomfortable with class conflict and had little sympathy for groups that advocated sweeping reforms.[36]

POLITICAL REALITIES THAT LIMITED REFORM

Even had they focused on helping immigrants and workers, the reformers would have had minimal policy successes. The Supreme Court, as well as local and state courts, impeded social reforms by making a succession of adverse rulings—for example, a state law that sought to limit hours of bakers to 10 hours per day was ruled unconstitutional.

Neither the Republican Party nor the Democratic Party focused on the needs of workers, persons with low incomes, or oppressed groups such as African Americans because voters in the Progressive Era tended to vote not on the basis of social class but according to local and family traditions that stemmed from ethnicity and sectionalism. (To the extent that workers and persons of low income voted at all, they split their votes between the two major parties, though African Americans usually voted for the Republican Party because of its historic role in ending slavery.) Because party leaders lacked an incentive to concentrate on assistance to those in need, social reformers often found it difficult to get their attention.[37]

Reformers also had difficulty obtaining assistance from the groups that most needed social reforms—immigrants, workers, and African Americans. Political cooperation among immigrant groups was impeded by language barriers, ethnic rivalries, and residential segregation. Immigrants often distrusted middle-class reformers, who proposed civil service and other reforms that seemed irrelevant to their practical needs, and resented reforms to curb corruption in politics—including the political machines that represented the primary vehicle for distribution of jobs and food to immigrants.[38]

Unions, which largely represented skilled crafts, were uncertain allies for social reformers. Samuel Gompers, the leader of the American Federation of Labor (AFL), attributed the demise of the Knights of Labor in the 1880s to its diversion to extraneous political and social issues and resolved, in consequence, to concentrate exclusively on union members' wages and fringe benefits and on organizing skilled or semiskilled white, native, and male workers. His tactical defensiveness was increased, moreover, by repeated court injunctions that declared specific strikes to be illegal. Gompers's tactical decisions helped the AFL make gains in the early years of this century but at the price of indifference to social reforms and abandonment of workers who were unskilled, female, immigrants, or people of color. Furthermore, the trade union movement remained weak. Employers mounted a decisive counterattack by means of lawsuits, bloody repression, spies, scabs, and red-baiting. The fledgling labor movement was fraught with internal dissension and outmoded organizing techniques. In the 19th century, factories had been dominated by skilled craftsmen who possessed considerable autonomy and worked within highly defined trades. But in the 20th century, factories were dominated by machinery, which relegated workers to tedious and unskilled work under the scrutiny of central management. Instead of organizing the workers of entire factories, unionists still tried to rally those groups of skilled workers within factories who performed specific tasks; this approach left many workers unorganized and led to turf rivalry between competing craft unions within specific factories. Gompers's decision to avoid political partisanship also limited labor's ability to develop political power and to obtain support for minimum wage and collective bargaining legislation. Labor's noninvolvement in politics was illustrated in 1908, when the AFL raised only $8,000 for electoral campaigns![39]

Even had they tried, trade unionists would have found it difficult to organize and politically mobilize unskilled and semiskilled workers, who formed a massive constituency. Immigrants, who composed 60 percent of the industrial workforce in 1913, had extraordinary economic and social needs and were not likely to protest low wages, particularly when they knew that they could be easily replaced by other immigrants. African American workers, who constituted more than 10 percent of workers in Northern iron and steel plants, felt beholden to foremen who had hired them in an era of intense racial discrimination and were reluctant to make trouble. Female workers, who dominated the garment industry, often hoped to work only for a brief period before they married. The nation possessed, then, an enormous pool of relatively passive laborers who were susceptible to victimization and feared retribution from local courts and police forces if they supported strikes.[40]

Gompers did not provide much assistance to social reformers. The AFL often opposed health insurance to workers on the grounds that it would undermine union efforts to obtain fringe benefits from employers. Many union leaders opposed the development of workmen's compensation laws on the grounds that workers could obtain larger awards from court litigation. A powerful radical movement might have pressured politicians to redistribute resources to the working class, but its power was limited. The Socialist Party, which was established in 1901, managed to elect 56 socialist mayors, but its power resided mostly in local jurisdictions, and its elected officials were often indistinguishable from other progressive reformers. The Industrial Workers of the World (IWW) was organized in 1905 and had 100,000 members by 1916, but it had little power in large industries; it represented only extremely poor workers in mining, lumbering, and agricultural sectors. (Most of its members lived in western states.) As the Socialist candidate in the presidential election of 1912, Eugene Debs, a fiery labor leader, succeeded in obtaining nearly 1 million of the almost 15 million votes cast, but he was not a serious threat to the major political parties.[41]

Social reformers were themselves impeded by their lack of interest in partisan politics during much of the Progressive Era. Many of them were contemptuous of existing parties, which they believed were corrupt and not interested in promoting reforms. Because many believed that their strength derived from the morality of their positions buttressed by public exposure of wrongdoing and social ills in the mass media, they envisioned social reform as a nonpartisan activity to pressure leaders of both parties to support reforms. Nonpartisanship allowed the progressives to maintain their political purity, but it prevented them from developing a partisan reform constituency. Their efforts to obtain support from politicians in both political parties meant that they controlled neither of them. Relatively conservative persons remained in control of the caucuses and conventions of the two major parties and often dictated their policies—under the influence of corporate interests, who remained the major source of campaign contributions for many political candidates.[42]

In many cases, reformers' energies were depleted by the task of continually raising funds to maintain staff for their nonpartisan organizations. Thousands of reform groups and settlements were formed in local, state, and national settings; these organizations often vied with one another for philanthropic contributions, and their leaders sometimes found that they had to tame their activities to retain the support of affluent donors.[43]

WOMEN AND CHILDREN: SEIZING THE OPPORTUNITY

If these various cultural and political obstacles impeded the enactment of benefit and service programs, how *did* progressives enact considerable legislation that benefited women and children? Curiously, the Supreme Court, while overruling laws that limited hours of work and minimum wages for men, *allowed* similar legislation for women, as in *Muller v. Oregon* (1908), which upheld an Oregon statute. Were not women, after all, particularly vulnerable and weak, and did not the nation depend upon their health to produce progeny?

Given a legal loophole that did not extend to men, women were not timid in seizing the opportunity. Women's organizations were remarkably numerous and well organized in the Progressive Era. Unlike European nations, which hardly allowed women to obtain higher education, nearly one-third of U.S. college students were women in 1900; that figure rose to one-half by 1920. Not allowed to enter the professions or many occupations—and otherwise limited to nursing and secondary school teaching—many of these well-educated women invested themselves in social reform activity; in many cases, they even decided to forgo marriage. Starting from local literary clubs, the General Federation of Women's Clubs became a massive national organization, with local chapters that had over 1 million members in 1911. The U.S. Women's Trade Union League sought to organize trade unions among female workers. The National Consumers League, headed by Florence Kelley, sought child labor laws and protectionist legislation for women. A network of more than 400 settlement houses organized grassroots pressure for various reforms. While focusing on prohibition, the Women's Christian Temperance Union also supported a range of social legislation that would help women and children. The female leaders of these organizations, frequently in contact with one another, maintained pressure on politicians through petitions, lobbying, and publicity. They formed alliances with male-dominated interest groups in state capitols. They were remarkably adept, moreover, in using moral arguments with male legislators, by contending that reforms for women and children were needed to protect them from victimization by employers.[44]

Even the tactical ingenuity of these dedicated women, however, proved insufficient to obtain unemployment insurance, old age pensions, or major federal legislation. Indeed, the focus on women's and children's legislation merely underscores the reluctance of Americans to address a range of social needs that exist in any industrialized and urbanized society.

SOCIAL REFORMERS AND THE BULL MOOSE CAMPAIGN OF 1912

During the first decade of the 20th century, both the Republican and Democratic parties were often dominated on specific issues by conservative politicians who insisted that federal authorities ought not to assume social welfare roles; who believed that social activists were "demagogues," "socialists," and "sentimental idealists"; and who sought to focus party platforms on international, tariff, currency, national defense, and related issues. Various conservatives supported specific pieces of social legislation—many of them, for example, favored the establishment of the Children's Bureau—but they often opposed specific reforms. Each party contained an insurgent wing that favored social legislation and other reforms, but its members were often outmaneuvered by conservatives in party-nominating conventions and in legislative arenas. Corporate officials continued to assume a dominant role in American politics and often tried to persuade candidates from both parties to oppose reforms such as lower tariffs; it was not until 1914 that Woodrow Wilson was able to slash tariffs and thus reduce prices of many commodities for workers and immigrants.[45]

Social reformers such as Jane Addams and Paul Kellogg (we discuss both of them at the end of this chapter) experienced many policy successes in municipal and state arenas during the first decade of the 20th century as they secured passage of mothers' pension, workmen's compensation, and juvenile court legislation. They grew more confident as they became national celebrities. Many were frequently requested to give speeches, some authored popular books, and Jane Addams was called an American reform goddess—even voted as the most popular American in a number of polls.

However, frustration also made many of the reformers want larger policy victories. The prodigious effort to enact legislation in many states and municipalities took its toll. Why not, some asked, obtain sweeping national legislation to regulate the working conditions of women and children, establish upper limits on the hours of work, establish a progressive tax system, set a minimum wage, and extend the vote to women? A few avant-garde reformers even favored passage of national health insurance, unemployment insurance, and old age pensions.[46]

Many social reformers dreamed that a fundamental political realignment might occur so that voters could choose between a relatively liberal party (with a constituency of intellectuals, workers, immigrants, and social reformers) and a relatively conservative party (with a constituency of businesspeople and affluent persons). It seemed that this dream of realignment might come to pass in the election of 1912. Theodore Roosevelt, who became president in 1901 after the assassination of William McKinley, had gingerly broached various reforms in his first term but had refrained from supporting many controversial reforms so as not to alienate the conservative wing of the Republican Party, whose support he needed if he was to obtain the party's nomination in 1904. He became bolder during his second term, however; on the eve of leaving office, he left a lengthy reform agenda to Vice President William Taft, which he hoped Taft would support if elected in 1908.

Roosevelt's hopes in Taft were misplaced. Taft became a captive of the conservative wing of the Republican Party during his term in office from 1909 to 1912. A large, phlegmatic man, Taft believed that major social reforms were not needed. As Taft became more conservative, the charismatic and energetic Roosevelt became more liberal. Dashing to and from his wild game safaris in Africa, he added support of national child labor legislation, a progressive income tax, and workmen's compensation to his reform agenda. He proposed the creation of an industrial commission to conduct national economic planning, which would be charged with fostering economic growth and regulating trusts so that their power and job creation potential could be realized. Feminists persuaded him to support a constitutional amendment to give women the vote.

Taft feared that Roosevelt, backed by social reformers, would try to regain control of the Republican Party by seeking its presidential nomination in 1912. Many reformers had maintained a nonpartisan stance prior to 1912 and had supported neither of the two major parties, but a number of them, including Jane Addams and Paul Kellogg, openly advocated supporting Roosevelt for the nomination.

The stage was set for a confrontation at the Republican convention in Chicago in the summer of 1912. However, the hopes of social reformers were dashed when Taft and entrenched party leaders secured the nomination for Taft in a series of power moves. They were further disheartened when the Democratic Party nominated Woodrow Wilson, the governor of New Jersey and former college president, who favored states' rights and focused on trust-busting and lowering tariffs. Instead of realignment, *both* parties seemed to be following a conservative course.

Many social reformers believed that realignment might still occur if a new political party were established with Roosevelt as its leader. With lightning speed, reformers called a convention of the Progressive Party in Chicago and persuaded a reluctant Roosevelt to accept its presidential nomination. The new party and its nominee were hardly rabid social reformers—only 25 percent of its platform, as well as of his acceptance speech, was devoted to social reforms—but they were far more reformist than alternative parties and candidates. Their platform included support for social insurances, workmen's compensation, a minimum wage, women's suffrage, and a child labor law. Jane Addams became the first woman to address a major political convention when she seconded the nomination of Roosevelt. Party members entered the campaign in an atmosphere of religious and moral fervor, but many practical problems bedeviled them. They had to secure a place on the ballot in the various states, obtain campaign funds, and develop a massive constituency in a nation that was wedded to the Democratic and Republican parties. Roosevelt doubted that he could prevail in the election of 1912, but he and others hoped they could educate the public sufficiently that workers and liberals would support the Progressive Party and that it would replace the Republican Party.[47]

Wilson, who had supported some progressive reforms as governor of New Jersey, tried from the outset to portray Taft as an extremist on the right and Roosevelt as an extremist on the left. He persuaded Samuel Gompers and many other union leaders to support him, by promising them that he would seek legislation to improve the legal status of organized labor. When he was portrayed as a left-winger by both Wilson and Taft, Roosevelt counterattacked vigorously by arguing that Taft and Wilson held outmoded and conservative ideas. He succeeded in differentiating his positions from those of Wilson by questioning Wilson's assertions that a minimum wage would depress prices, by arguing that a welfare state was needed in an industrial society, and by insisting that states' rights had to be superseded by national planning. He drew enormous and enthusiastic crowds at his campaign appearances. When the results were tallied, Roosevelt made a respectable showing but lost the election because ethnic and regional loyalties, as well as the allegiance of many immigrants to political bosses, led many Democratic voters to support Wilson. Wilson won, not because he was overwhelmingly popular—he received less than 50 percent of the popular vote—but because the Republican vote was split between Taft and Roosevelt.[48]

Many persons who had voted for Roosevelt still believed that political realignment was possible if the Progressive Party could be kept intact and if it waged successful campaigns in the congressional elections of 1914 and the presidential election of 1916. The reformers hoped that Roosevelt would win in 1916, that the Republican Party would die, and that conservatives would gravitate to the Democratic Party. To ensure that the Progressive Party maintained its reforming mission, social reformers succeeded in creating a national department of the party, directed by Jane Addams, that focused on social research and the development of social policies. Promisingly, 20 members of Congress declared their allegiance to the party, as did a number of local officeholders.

Practical realities doomed the reformers' dreams of political realignment to failure, however. Political experts decided that party funds should be devoted to hiring political experts and financing campaigns, and so, to the dismay of reformers, the social service department of the party was terminated. The party was unable to raise the funds necessary to get on the ballot in some jurisdictions. Most damaging to the Progressive Party, however, was Woodrow Wilson's unexpected support for social legislation during his presidency. Although he had argued in the campaign of 1912 that federal authorities should not enact a minimum wage or place restrictions on child labor and had lambasted the idea of a welfare state as paternalistic, he realized in the aftermath of his victory that he could significantly add to the political base of the Democratic Party if he adopted some of the reforms proposed by the Progressive Party. He even cautiously wooed social reformers like Jane Addams. He enacted child labor legislation, banking legislation, tariff reductions, and eventually women's suffrage.[49]

The fate of the Progressive Party was virtually sealed by its poor showing in the congressional elections of 1914. Except in a few scattered locations, the party was defunct well before the presidential election of 1916. Roosevelt tried to secure the Republican nomination in 1916 but was again rebuffed by party conservatives, who nominated Charles Hughes. Wilson again ran successfully on the Democratic ticket, with the assistance of many progressive reformers.

The failure of the Progressive Party during and after 1912 demonstrated that social reform could not proceed beyond the limited policy successes of the Progressive Era unless reformers could obtain a power base by capturing a major party that had significant support from liberals, the working class, and people of color. The demise of the Progressive Party also illustrated the precarious position of social reform in America, despite growing social problems in the cities. It would take a catastrophic depression in the late 1920s to galvanize workers, the poor, and people of color behind social reforms—and it

would be a distant cousin of Theodore Roosevelt, Franklin Delano Roosevelt, who would finally accomplish the political realignment that the progressives had sought.

THE OPPRESSION OF VULNERABLE POPULATIONS OR OUT-GROUPS IN THE PROGRESSIVE ERA

It would be a mistake to view progressivism as a reform movement fought for, by, and on behalf of the immigrants who constituted such major portions of the nation's urban population. Americans of this era harbored very contradictory opinions about this huge population; though they freely used—and depended on—immigrants as cheap labor to fuel industrial growth, they resented, and sometimes even feared, this population for reasons of eugenics (would intermarriage dilute the Anglo-Saxon race?), social unrest (could America have a revolution if "agitators" awoke these immigrants, and did the big-city political machines constitute a threat to democracy?), public health (did the immigrants pass diseases, such as tuberculosis, to others?), and culture (did Catholicism, Judaism, and ethnic cultures threaten Protestant values and American culture?). Nor were the progressives, aside from many settlement workers and certain other reformers, free from racism; indeed, no significant civil rights legislation was enacted or seriously considered in this period, and some decided setbacks occurred. Although women were often in the vanguard of social reform in the Progressive Era and made some economic and other gains (for example, regulation of their working conditions and hours), they remained shackled by traditional notions of their role in society.

The Oppression of Women

As we discussed in Chapter 5, women's suffrage became the central reform issue of the women's movement with the formation of the National American Women's Suffrage Association in 1890. Between 1890 and 1905, women presented many petitions requesting state legislatures to modify their constitutions so as to grant women the vote, but they had scant success. Even many women regarded the issue as tangential to their economic and social needs. The male and female leaders of antisuffrage organizations contended that female voters would destroy the unity of households by voting for their own interests and would fall prey to demagogues because of their "hysterical" tendencies. Moreover, the liquor interests strongly opposed suffrage on the grounds that women would support temperance.

More progress was made after 1905 because feminist leaders had developed sophisticated organizing skills and because women's prominent roles in the Progressive Era made the issue seem less radical. Indeed, 12 states had granted women the vote by 1916. Instead of emphasizing feminist arguments, suffragettes argued that female voters would support progressive reforms on education and family issues— an argument that was received favorably by males imbued with the 19th-century belief that women's superior moral qualities and temperament made them best suited to attend to family matters and children. (See Figure 6.3.) Immigrant husbands increasingly supported suffrage for women, who were

© UPI/Time-Life Pictures/Getty Images

F I G U R E 6.3   Women representing three states at a march of 25,000 advocates for suffrage.

providing a major source of labor for the garment industry. Militant suffragists, who used disruptive organizing tactics, alienated some voters but dramatized the issue. A dramatic breakthrough occurred during World War I, when Woodrow Wilson finally agreed to support the issue, after such leaders as Carrie Chapman Catt threatened to target Democratic candidates for defeat and argued that suffrage was needed to maintain national unity during the war. The Nineteenth Amendment to the Constitution was finally enacted in 1920.[50]

Although suffrage got the most attention, other developments were of equal importance to women. There were major increases in female employment in industrial settings, as well as clerical, stenographic, and sales positions. (These occupations, as well as teaching, social work, and nursing, were gender-segregated and poorly paid, however.) Moreover, there was a sizable increase in the number of married women who worked; whereas only 14 percent of all women workers were married in 1900, more than 24 percent were married in 1910.

But economic gains ought not to be overstated. Protective labor laws were developed to "protect" women from exertion that could endanger their reproductive functions or expose them to excessive mixing with men, who might debase them morally and sexually. Abramovitz argues that these laws served to preserve "a sex-segregated labor market, the relative subordination of women to men, and the overall marginalization of women workers." Women were rarely unionized and represented a relatively docile labor force, although there were some dramatic strikes in the garment industry, such as the 1909 shirtwaist strike, in which tens of thousands of women in New York City and Philadelphia protested unsafe working conditions and low wages. Whereas 20 percent of men were union members according to a national survey of 15 occupations in 1905, only 3 percent of women belonged to unions. Mothers' pension laws, which might have been fashioned to provide major resources to single heads of households—or to help them obtain child care so that they could continue to work—were primarily developed with the needs of children in mind. As in prior eras, it was assumed that women with children ought not to work, and so the pensions were devised to provide just enough money so that mothers could stay at home. Little organized day care existed for working women in this period.[51]

Moreover, obstacles to women's sexual freedom persisted. The repertoire of birth control techniques had expanded to include condoms and diaphragms, but women learned of these techniques only by word of mouth and through vaguely worded advertisements, rather than at public family-planning clinics; even physicians often opposed their use on the grounds that they interfered with the natural reproductive functions of women or reduced the growth of the white population. Moreover, the obscenity laws of most states prohibited public discussion of these techniques or the distribution of birth control devices. As we noted in Chapter 4, the Comstock Law, enacted in 1873, outlawed the distribution of birth control information through the federal mails.

Margaret Sanger founded a birth control movement, but its leaders were frequently jailed under obscenity laws. Realizing the futility of trying to change obscenity laws, Sanger focused increasingly on persuading physicians to prescribe birth control, because they could legally do so when medical needs existed. Her efforts gradually gained support in the medical profession, which often prescribed birth control by the late 1920s. Most low-income persons lacked personal physicians, however, and did not have access to birth control because public birth control clinics were still outlawed in many jurisdictions.[52]

During this period, women were subjected to medical practices that contemporary Americans can scarcely fathom. Assuming that women's reproductive systems were the cause of many of their physical ailments, physicians performed large numbers of hysterectomies. Indeed, some physicians assumed that women's *normal* state was to be sick. Menstruation, menopause, and childbirth were viewed as essentially medical conditions that required endless medications and surgeries. As "delicate" people, women had to be shielded, moreover, from those occupations that required physical (or even mental) exertion. Women were also commonly believed to be subject to bouts of hysteria—a condition that required bed rest in darkened rooms for weeks or even months at a time, on the theory that the absence of stimuli would allow them to recover.[53]

By 1930, little progress had been made in dispelling the cult of domesticity for married women, which had originated a century earlier. It consigned women to childbearing and domestic duties, while precluding them from entering the professions or business. Women were endlessly exhorted to use materials from child psychology and home economics in perfecting the science of homemaking and to refrain from careers or other employment. Men objected if eminent women were nominated to serve on commissions or in administrative positions, even within the emerging social work profession. Moreover, women's access to law, medicine, and business, which had increased in the Progressive Era, eroded in subsequent decades. Many women were midwives at the turn of the century—a respected profession—but male physicians increasingly supplanted them by defining childbirth narrowly as a medical condition that required licensed (male) physicians. (By contrast, most babies were and are delivered by midwives in many European nations.)[54]

The Oppression of African Americans

The civil rights gains of freed slaves were nullified following the Civil War; Southern whites regained their political power when Northerners withdrew military and legislative pressure on the South and when the Supreme Court rendered federal civil rights laws useless. Republicans hoped to regain their Southern constituency, but Democrats had become the dominant party of the South by 1900 and staunchly resisted federal efforts to protect or help African Americans. Most African Americans lived in rural areas as tenant farmers; low wages and indebtedness to plantation owners enmeshed them in grinding poverty. Increasing numbers moved to Southern cities where, aside from a small elite group of affluent African Americans, they were unemployed or worked as domestic servants or in

other low-paying and unskilled jobs. Rich or poor, they all lived within a segregated society. Americans had developed, in effect, a social system that approached apartheid and was maintained by Jim Crow laws, police, courts, and white racism.[55]

The situation was more favorable for African Americans in the North, but only modestly so. Poverty and lack of jobs in the South led to a steady and growing migration of African Americans to Northern cities, where their presence was still relatively small in 1915. The enticement of jobs in burgeoning industries like meatpacking and steel drew African Americans to the North, where their wages, though low, were nonetheless considerably higher than what they could earn in the South. Neighborhoods occupied by African Americans were even more blighted than those occupied by other immigrant groups, were more likely to be the headquarters of organized crime and drug interests, and had virtually no health or other services. African Americans experienced extraordinary discrimination in job markets; they were excluded from skilled trades and unions, were often used as scabs to break unions, and were subject to race riots and mob violence when they competed with whites for jobs. Most African Americans in the North, like their urban counterparts in the South, worked in unskilled jobs.[56]

African Americans in both the North and the South evolved ingenious strategies for coping with adversity and for seeking social reforms. African American women assumed even more assertive roles than white women in promoting self-help and charitable projects. They developed mutual benefit societies that provided insurance for sickness and funerals. They participated in church groups such as the Women's Convention of the Black Baptist Church, which had 1.5 million members in 1907. They formed Women's Clubs to promote charities, such as the National Association of Colored Women. They formed their own settlement houses, and they established 200 hospitals and nurse-training schools. Unlike white women, African American women placed particular emphasis on education; they regarded schools—from kindergarten to college—as a kind of antipoverty program. In the South, educational needs were extreme. Because local jurisdictions underfunded public schools for African Americans, private support had to be found. Even as late as 1940, only 1 percent of African Americans, male and female, had four or more years of college; and many Southern colleges for African Americans were only the equivalent of secondary schools.[57]

In the broader African American community, a conflict between Booker T. Washington and W. E. B. Du Bois reflected the dilemma of oppressed people. Washington, the son of a slave woman and her white master, preached accommodation; he wanted African Americans to conquer racism through honesty, hard work, and the help of kindly patrons. But Du Bois wanted African Americans to develop political power so that they could obtain civil rights laws and get access to the same educational advantages as whites. Du Bois and other African American leaders formed the National Association for the Advancement of Colored People (NAACP) in 1909 and succeeded in getting 6,000 members by 1914, mostly from the African American middle class.

The Oppression of Asian Immigrants

Asian immigrants on the West Coast also suffered discrimination and poverty. As we noted in Chapter 5, hundreds of Chinese immigrants came to California in the late 19th century to work on the railroads and in the mines and were followed by Japanese immigrants over the next two decades. Many Americans viewed Asians as sinister and untrustworthy people and worried that they brought diseases to America; editorialists wrote hatefully of the "yellow peril." To survive, many Japanese Americans capitalized on their ability to farm hillside land, and both Chinese and Japanese immigrants developed specialized niches in urban America; they ran laundries and small businesses. However, both groups frequently encountered prejudice and adverse policies.

California enacted Alien Land Laws in 1913 and 1920 to prohibit land purchases and ownership by Japanese residents. Even in this period, long before World War II, many people feared that the Japanese would overrun the West Coast and even attack the United States. Many Americans urged extension of the provisions of the Chinese Exclusion Act of 1882 to the Japanese but had to content themselves with measures such as the Gentleman's Agreement of 1907, in which Japan agreed to stop the migration of laborers to the United States. (For diplomatic reasons, Roosevelt did not want to antagonize the Japanese government by legally prohibiting Japanese immigration.)[58]

In both Hawaii and California, the Japanese immigrants fashioned an ingenious survival strategy. Taking advantage of a shortage of craftspeople and artisans and also of entrepreneurs, the Japanese quickly filled these economic positions. In Hawaii, their access to supplies from Japan and the difficulty of obtaining supplies from the United States, because of the distances involved, allowed them to develop a monopoly of retail grocery and dry goods stores. In California, bringing skills in hillside and irrigated farming from Japan, they leased or owned substantial acreage and were able to monopolize the burgeoning fresh vegetable crops. As in Hawaii, Japanese Americans were adept at becoming entrepreneurs; by 1919, they owned 45 percent of the hotels and 25 percent of the grocery stores in Seattle. Both Chinese and Japanese Americans achieved these stunning successes by pooling funds in their own communities to allow one another to invest and thus sidestepping the restrictive lending policies of commercial banks. Far weaker on the West Coast, unions did not systematically prevent Asian Americans from entering the trades, unlike unions in the East and Midwest that denied entry to African Americans.[59]

The Oppression of Spanish-Speaking Persons

In the Southwest lived large numbers of Latinos whose land had been taken from them in the middle and late 19th century. Their numbers were swelled by Mexican immigrants, who were able to move freely across a relatively unrestricted border until 1924, when the U.S. Border Patrol was created. It is impossible to know precisely how many Latinos came across the 2,000-mile border, but some scholars estimate roughly 195,000 migrated between 1900 and 1920; their numbers grew dramatically in the wake of the economic dislocation accompanying the Mexican revolution of 1910. By 1930, the U.S. population included more than 2 million people who had been born in Mexico.

These immigrants, as well as the indigenous Latino population, became the labor force for the irrigated cotton, vegetable, and fruit enterprises of the Southwest. Along with ranching and meat processing, these enterprises expanded enormously after the Reclamation Act of 1902 provided large federal funding for irrigation projects. Latinos worked not only in the fields but in numerous canning and food-processing plants. They lived in barracks in remote rural areas and were subject to the punitive labor policies of large landowners, who paid low wages and brutally suppressed protest. Like many rural African Americans in the South, they were denied education and excluded from economic opportunities that developed in urban America.

Nor were conditions much better for those Latinos who settled in growing urban areas of the Southwest, where employers used them as a reserve labor force to break strikes and depress wages. Those few business ventures that were owned by Latinos were located in Spanish-speaking communities and were mostly small stores.[60] As a strictly regional population in the Southwest (only 15 percent lived outside the Southwest even as late as 1930), Latinos were isolated politically and subject to local and regional groups, such as growers, who wished to subjugate them. The Mexican government frequently protested the working conditions and suppression of the Latino population to the U.S. State Department, but to no avail.[61]

These Spanish-speaking persons in the Southwest differed markedly from European immigrants—and from African Americans. Like African Americans, they met the labor needs of white landowners, who could tap an inexhaustible supply of workers who migrated back and forth across the border. Indeed, in the wake of the Mexican Revolution, about 10 percent of the population of Mexico had emigrated to the United States; most were "unofficial immigrants," who evaded various fees, visas, and (after 1917) literacy tests. Also like African Americans, they could not easily enter the economic mainstream because they had limited access to schools, lived in areas where industrialization had hardly emerged, and lacked capital or the capital-raising techniques used by Asian immigrants.[62]

Unlike African Americans, however, these Spanish-speaking people had not been forcibly taken from their homeland or placed in bondage. Moving back and forth frequently between Mexico and the United States, they developed a "sojourner mentality"—a belief that they would soon return to Mexico. Whereas this mentality impeded their development of economic roots—for example, by preventing them from buying homes—it allowed them to retain their culture, with its emphasis on Catholicism, families, communities, and mutual assistance. Communities organized *mutualistas*, or mutual aid funds, to provide insurance, funeral, and limited welfare benefits. They observed Mexican holidays and traditions. This vibrant culture allowed Latinos to maintain their equilibrium even when they confronted oppressive conditions and grinding poverty.[63]

As a sojourner group that served the economic needs of white agricultural entrepreneurs, Spanish-speaking people of the Southwest would be linked in ensuing decades to immigration policy. Growers, who craved cheap labor, wanted no limits on immigration or else lax enforcement. They counted on ineffective border patrols and often sought exclusions for Latinos when restrictionist immigration policy was passed at the national level. For example, they had Western hemisphere people exempted from restrictive quotas in the National Origins Act of 1924 (though Asian immigration was eliminated altogether). Growers also sought to define a special class of immigrants, known as *braceros*, who would be allowed to enter the nation only for specific harvests or brief periods; this program was first initiated in 1917, when almost 80,000 workers were admitted. With a relatively open border in the 1920s, many Mexican immigrants came to the United States. Considerable prejudice against Latinos in the broader population, however, led to strident efforts to restrict the flow of migration in the 1930s and subsequent decades, as illustrated by the 1994 passage of California's Proposition 187—a measure that proposed to bolster border patrols *and* deny "illegal" Latinos educational, health, and other benefits.[64]

The Alliance of Progressivism and Racism

Many progressive reformers saw no contradiction between social reform and racism, as the actions of Theodore Roosevelt and Woodrow Wilson demonstrate. Roosevelt raised storms of protest when he invited Booker T. Washington, the African American leader, to the White House for lunch during his first term. Although Washington, unlike Marcus Garvey, was no militant and favored accommodation to existing policies, this luncheon led Roosevelt's foes to portray him as a radical on racial issues; even as late as 1912, the luncheon was cited as evidence that Roosevelt was a "nigger lover." Roosevelt was hardly a defender of civil rights, however. After the luncheon with Washington, he refrained from all public meetings with African Americans. He took no actions against Jim Crow legislation in the South, sided with white authorities in the infamous Brownsville incident in 1906 (in which African American soldiers were executed on undocumented charges that they had raped white women), and did not contest lily-white delegations to Republican conventions from Southern districts. Jane Addams vainly protested Roosevelt's acceptance of white Southern delegations to the convention of the ostensibly reformist Progressive Party in 1912.

Like most white Americans in this era, Roosevelt upheld a racial ideology that extolled the virtues of the Anglo-American race to the detriment of other races, including African Americans, Asians, Latinos, and Native Americans. The racial doctrines that had fueled manifest destiny, which we discussed in Chapter 5, lived on in many white Americans, who believed that the superiority of Anglo-Americans was proven by scientific evidence (later discredited) such as alleged differences in skull size and intelligence. Roosevelt's ideological orientation and his desire to obtain white Southerners' support for the Republican Party led him to neglect the problems of African Americans and other people of color.[65]

Woodrow Wilson was even less sympathetic than Roosevelt to the needs of African Americans. Raised in the South, he had adopted the racial orientations of affluent Southerners. Moreover, he was the presidential nominee of the Democratic Party, which had relied on race baiting throughout the late 19th century to secure the support of Southern whites. Whereas Roosevelt had given African Americans some token posts in government, Wilson refused even to give the ambassadorship to Liberia to an African American, openly supported segregated restroom facilities in federal departments, and condoned lynching in the South. So detestable were his policies to African Americans that most of them continued to vote Republican, even though many social reformers switched their allegiance from the defunct Progressive Party to Wilson in 1916.[66]

The courts reinforced prevailing attitudes. In the infamous ruling in *Plessy v. Ferguson* (1896), the U.S. Supreme Court condoned a Southern state's law that mandated that African Americans travel on separate railway cars from Caucasians—a ruling in marked contradiction to civil rights legislation passed by the Congress in the wake of the Civil War. Even before this ruling, the U.S. Supreme Court had upheld rulings of other courts that federal civil rights legislation of the Reconstruction era applied only to the discriminatory acts of *individuals* rather than to the laws of state and local governments.[67] These rulings dealt a death blow to civil rights in the United States because they upheld the legality of Jim Crow legislation (discussed in the preceding chapter) that required African Americans to use separate restrooms and rooms in restaurants and other public places, that consigned them to separate areas of trains and buses, and that imposed literacy tests and other devices to stop them from voting. Save for the actual institution of slavery that had been prohibited by the Thirteenth

Amendment to the Constitution, the South had virtually returned to the same policies that had brought the nation into the Civil War about 40 years earlier. Many progressive leaders, including Presidents Roosevelt and Wilson, failed to speak out against these unethical court rulings that would take about 60 years to be rescinded with the Civil Rights Acts of 1954 and 1965.

Jane Addams and a small band of social reformers were exceptions to the alliance of progressivism and racism. She supported the establishment of settlement houses in African American communities, sought to improve schools, and urged better protection of African Americans from lynching and race riots. She argued that African Americans possessed qualities of altruism and gentleness that made them superior in some respects to the dominant population. Her beliefs were not shared, however, by most policy makers in the North or South or by most Americans.[68]

The Imposition of a Racist Policy of Immigration

We have discussed the torrent of immigration to the United States from European nations in the period from 1880 to 1920. With the frontier closed, immigrants concentrated in major cities and became a low-paid labor force for the industrial system of the United States.

Deliberating in a nation already dominated by immigrants, the founding fathers finally decided to make no mention of immigration in the Constitution and to allow Congress to shape the relevant policy. In the succeeding years, Americans adopted an extraordinarily liberal policy for white immigrants; they applied no annual limits, required no literacy test, and allowed people to naturalize within five years. No one anticipated, however, that immigrants would arrive in such numbers in the 19th century and the early part of the 20th century—or that many of them would not be Protestants. As Higham suggests, Americans have oscillated between periods of confidence, when they believed the nation could absorb immigrants without threat to their culture or economy, and periods of fear, when they believed the

nation could be endangered by the immigrants' religions and culture; when they feared immigrants would take their jobs; and when they feared that immigrant anarchists or radicals would bring social unrest. We have already discussed nativism during the Irish immigration of the 19th century. However, confidence reigned supreme in the first decade of the 20th century, when many Americans believed that the nation could socialize and convert immigrants to American culture. Moreover, immigrant groups, such as the German-American Alliance, Irish groups, and Jewish groups, developed considerable political power; they fought efforts to limit immigration by threatening not to vote for candidates who supported restrictive immigration policies.[69]

Even during this period of confidence, however, groups such as the Immigration Restriction League devised ways of limiting immigration—for example, by imposing literacy tests. The racist ideas associated with the doctrine of manifest destiny in the 19th century—for example, the fierce concern to prevent the "dilution" of Anglo-Saxon stock through intermarriage—began to resurface with the continuing influx of immigrants, who averaged 650,000 per year between 1907 and 1917. (Immigrants of non-Caucasian races, such as Asians, were perceived as a particular threat.)[70] Anti-Catholicism, always present, began to reemerge. The rise of the Industrial Workers of the World (IWW), a radical labor group, was linked by many people to "foreign agitators." A sharp economic downturn during and after 1913 led to a growing sense that immigrants threatened local jobs. And the immigrants of this era, like the Irish before the Civil War, were widely believed to bring with them diseases; a popular book of the era stated:

> The new immigration contained a large and increasing number of the weak, the broken, and the mentally crippled of all races drawn from the lowest stratum of the Mediterranean basin and the Balkans, together with hordes of the wretched, submerged populations of the Polish ghettoes. Our jails, insane asylums, and almshouses are filled with human flotsam and the whole tone of American life, social, moral,

and political, has been lowered and vulgarized by them.[71]

Those seeking to restrict immigration found that their power increased steadily in the years preceding World War I. One victory was to enact a literacy test for immigrants who wished to become citizens in the Immigration Act of 1917. However, a curious combination of industrialists (who wanted immigrant labor) and friends of immigrants (such as the National Liberal Immigration League) held off restrictionist legislation; President Wilson vetoed legislation enacted by Congress in 1914. World War I and its aftermath vastly increased fear of foreigners; Americans were angered by various European powers and alarmed by the Russian Revolution. A "crusade for Americanization" developed during and after the war to make foreigners speak English and to identify and prosecute "bolsheviks" in a red scare that led to the imprisonment of many foreigners. After passage of a series of lesser measures, the Immigration Act of 1924 not only limited overall rates of immigration but also gave preference, within the diminished flow, to people from Northern Europe; it accomplished this by the ingenious device of limiting immigration to 2 percent of the population of the corresponding nationality in the United States in 1890, when relatively few Japanese, Italians, Eastern Europeans, or Russian Jews had arrived. Thus restricted, Italian immigration dropped from 42,000 to 4,000 persons per year and the Japanese immigration to 40 per year. Only Mexican immigrants escaped the restrictions, probably because their regional isolation in the Southwest made them less frightening to nativists and because agricultural, food-processing, and railroad interests in the region wanted to exploit them as cheap labor.[72]

THE RESILIENCE OF JANE ADDAMS AND HER ALLIES

Progressive reformers such as Jane Addams tried to develop social reforms in a society where individualism

and competitiveness blinded its citizens to social problems. Unlike European reformers, who received support from trade unions, American reformers had to raise funds from the wealthy to establish organizations for social reform. There were few social welfare precedents, aside from local poorhouses and charities. Reformers had to obtain statistics about the incidence of various social problems, educate the public, fashion legislative testimony, engage in lobbying, network with reformers in other jurisdictions, and build coalitions. Despite their national popularity, they encountered extraordinary hostility from corporations, political machines, affluent citizens, conservatives, and even groups they sought to help, such as trade unions and immigrants. When Addams courageously attacked U.S. involvement in World War I, she was reviled as a traitor, even by many of her fellow reformers.

The persistence of the reformers was striking. Many began their work in the 1890s and continued to seek reforms until the United States entered World War I in 1917. During and after the war, when the nation turned toward conservatism, many collapsed from exhaustion, left the country, converted to conservatism, or turned to psychotherapy, which was in vogue in the 1920s. Some reformers bucked the conservative trend even during the 1920s, however. Addams continued to reside in Hull House, sought many new reforms, and correctly predicted that the United States would need to address the needs of the expanding African American population in Northern cities.

THE EMERGENCE OF SOCIAL WORK

An important question had to be answered during the Progressive Era: Who was to staff those social agencies that helped immigrants, poor people, children who could not remain with their natural families, and so many other troubled individuals? By 1920, a new profession, called social work, had developed schools in which people were trained to give these kinds of services. The development of social work was marked by considerable tension between different factions, each of which left an imprint on the profession; these complex origins foreshadowed much controversy about the direction of social work during the remainder of the 20th century.

In particular, there was a striking difference in approach between those who came from settlement houses and those intent on developing a methodology for helping people in one-on-one transactions. Recall from Chapter 4 that, even as early as the 1840s, various agencies in Eastern cities undertook to systematize relief-giving to people in poverty by using volunteers to interview them, determine whether they were truly needy, and supervise them while they received assistance, with an eye to making them independent as soon as possible. In some cases, agencies compared their records so as to be certain that people were not receiving assistance from more than one source.

In the decades after the Civil War, these early attempts to turn relief giving into a disciplined process were enlarged in many jurisdictions. Local, nongovernmental agencies—called charity organization societies (COS)—developed in most cities to provide assistance to destitute people. Initially, these agencies did not actually give relief to individuals; instead, they sought to coordinate relief giving, with an eye to preventing people from seeking simultaneous assistance from two or more agencies. The agencies were administered by a paid male who recruited and supervised female volunteers—usually relatively affluent, white, English-speaking women; these women who came to be known as friendly visitors were supposed to provide moral uplift to impoverished people. Some COS agencies eventually came to give out relief themselves, thereby joining the various sectarian agencies that had long provided aid to destitute persons. To coordinate and systematize their growing operations, private relief-giving agencies began to hire staff, usually women who remained in nonadministrative posts.

Relief giving by private agencies in the latter part of the 19th century was a grim undertaking. Friendly visitors and paid staff were taught to engage in a careful diagnostic and supervising process, as they screened, aided, and finally discharged poor people who needed assistance. Above all, they were to avoid giving indiscriminately or letting their emotions dictate their actions. Indeed, it was their duty to turn away, or refer to poorhouses, those people who were not bent on achieving independence and moral improvement; these qualities were monitored both at point of intake and throughout the helping process. The friendly visitors did detailed research on the motivations, history, and living arrangements of families as they decided whether and how to help destitute people. Moreover, they were to provide instruction to their wards, both through teaching (such as how to keep a clean house and prepare decent meals) and through personal example. As models of hard work, thrift, and morality, they could, it was hoped, inculcate those virtues in their clients. These friendly visitors probably exhibited contradictory tendencies in their work—both punitive attitudes and a desire to help. In screening "undeserving" from "deserving" poor people, they were certainly punitive. As white, English-speaking people, they most likely were perceived as condescending and harsh by their immigrant wards. They were often unaware that the poverty of the immigrants stemmed not from faults of character, such as laziness, but from the lack of available work or discrimination in hiring. Yet they could be advocates for their wards with local police, educational, and other agencies and provided hands-on assistance by actually visiting the homes and neighborhoods of their clients.

Some leaders of the charity societies formed quasi-public organizations at the state level to inspect state mental institutions, to collect data about pauperism and other social problems, and to combat patronage and corruption in public institutions. A national organization, the National Conference of Charities, was established in 1879 after members of various state boards of charities, who had been meeting annually in the American Social Science Association, decided that they needed their own organization; it convened annual conferences of leaders in this emerging field. (In 1884, it changed its name to the National Conference of Charities and Corrections.) Admission was also open to people engaged in private, nongovernmental charity in local agencies, who soon dominated the organization.[73]

The paid staff who supplanted volunteers in the last decades of the 19th century were the forerunners of the social work profession; they articulated a helping methodology called casework, which explained the techniques charity workers should use when helping individual clients.

We can now contrast the charity organization societies with people who administered and worked in settlement houses. These two factions were quite different, even though they both attended the annual meetings of the National Conference of Charities and Corrections. Settlement staff tended to be somewhat more reform-oriented, more inclined to decrease the personal distance between paid staff and neighborhood residents, and less convinced that helping could be reduced to a science. These differences sparked frequent conflict between the two groups. For example, during the Progressive Era, many charity organization leaders opposed the development of mothers' pensions, which, they argued, represented an unwarranted intrusion into the work of nongovernmental agencies. By contrast, Jane Addams and many other social workers who were identified with social reform militantly supported mothers' pensions. (Even as late as 1932, some social workers believed that private agencies could manage the economic destitution that accompanied the Great Depression, which began in 1929.)[74]

How was a profession to be molded from these two disparate factions? Both charity workers and settlement staff realized that extended training was necessary if they were to develop a profession—and training had mostly taken the form of practical experience on the job, brief seminars, or courses in sociology, which had begun to be taught in universities in the 1890s.

Wenocur and Reisch contend that the charity organization movement seized the initiative, with the assistance of the Russell Sage Foundation.[75] Mary Richmond, who was a noteworthy theorist in the methodology of investigating and assisting individuals and had worked extensively with the Baltimore Charity Organization Society, had long espoused the development of a training school to be affiliated with a university. Her fledgling efforts, such as a six-week summer program of the New York Charity Organization Society in 1898, whetted appetites for more ambitious projects. The training period was extended to one year and then, with the establishment of the New York School of Philanthropy in 1910, to two years. (This program later became the Columbia University Graduate School of Social Work.) In quick succession, other schools were established in Boston and at institutions of higher education, including Bryn Mawr, Ohio State, Indiana University, and the University of Minnesota. Casework became the dominant curriculum focus of these various schools, although smatterings of other subject matter were included. In 1907, settlement leaders in Chicago founded the Chicago School of Civics and Philanthropy, which later became the School of Social Service Administration of the University of Chicago. However, its existence did not fundamentally challenge the dominance of those who saw the profession essentially as an extension of the charity societies' work. The emerging casework, as articulated by Richmond in her classic book *Social Diagnosis*, lacked the punitive qualities of much of the charity societies' work and was geared toward helping individuals with personal problems rather than toward determining whether they "deserved" monetary assistance, but it still focused on one-on-one transactions.[76] The founders of the Chicago School worried that the emphasis on casework, so entrenched in many of the early schools, would prove to be an excessively narrow focus for the new profession.

Wenocur and Reisch contend that the leaders in this early movement to develop a profession were constrained by economic realities. The budding profession depended, after all, on affluent philanthropists and university elites to provide resources and institutional support for the new training programs and agency services. From this vantage, the emphasis on personal casework was an ideal choice, for it was far less controversial than the social reform practiced by some settlements. Moreover, it seemed scientific in its emphasis on careful investigation and diagnosis, by comparison with the mix of social reform, recreational, and socialization services offered by settlements—and the leaders of the new profession could convincingly argue to universities, philanthropists, and the Russell Sage Foundation that this "core technology" required extended training in professional schools. (To obtain public support, professions needed to convince others that, without the training they provide, consumers would be endangered—an assertion the leaders of the new profession made unabashedly as they argued that good intentions and altruism, by themselves, were insufficient to provide assistance to destitute families, disrupted families, mental patients, and other people in need.) The emphasis of the new profession on training staff to work in nongovernmental agencies was also attuned to an era that had few governmental services, aside from poorhouses, mental institutions, and correctional facilities.[77]

If we place the emerging profession in the larger context of the Progressive Era, we can see that its leaders were captive to the intellectual currents and political assumptions of the period. Many of them were content to seek the regulation of child labor, women's working conditions, and other specific situations; they did not envision major social programs such as those in the New Deal. Many of them sought reforms of government, including the eradication of patronage and corruption from the administration of mental institutions and poorhouses. Many brought into the profession a preoccupation with the investigation and diagnosis of dispossessed and impoverished individuals that derived from charity projects in the 1840s and later decades. Just as social reformers often stood at the periphery of progressivism, which was mostly preoccupied with the establishment of "good government," trust-busting, and moral issues like temperance, they often were at the periphery, also, of the emerging profession; indeed, Mary Richmond believed that the settlements' mixture of social reform, recreation, and socialization work was an unsuitable methodology for the new profession—and even inimical to its survival. Like the leaders of the charity societies, most leaders of the new profession assumed that nongovernmental agencies would provide the focus of its work; indeed, they looked with considerable cynicism at patronage-ridden public agencies such as mental institutions and poorhouses.

It was too soon to tell, in 1920, precisely how the new profession would develop. Given that both the charity society and settlement movements shared an emphasis on helping people in poverty, that aspect of social work was likely to continue. A social reform impulse deriving from the influence of settlement workers and certain charity society people, such as Homer Folks, was likely to remain. But a clever prognosticator might have guessed that tensions in the profession at its inception would also persist. Might not casework, soon to be married to the just-emerging tenets of Freud (and later the tenets of so many other psychological theorists), lead some practitioners to want to serve neurotic individuals from the middle and even upper classes rather than poor people? Might not the descendants of Jane Addams within the profession—those who wished to emphasize macro matters such as policy, administration, organizing, and social reform—be marginalized in a profession whose organizing principles reflected the person-to-person transactions of the charity societies? Would not endless disputes emerge about the precise educational content of the professional schools—and even whether a master's degree in a graduate facility was necessary or whether certain tasks could be performed by people with only a bachelor's degree? (We will discuss in Chapter 7 and elsewhere how some of these tensions emerged over the next few decades.)

Lest we imply that social workers alone were subject to the limitations of their time, consider physicians and attorneys, who tightened the educational requirements of their disciplines in this era and made salutary advances but also made decisions that set back the course of social reform in the United States. Although the medical profession had existed for centuries, it did not possess a monopoly over health care in the mid-19th century. Prior to the discovery of bacteria and an understanding of their role in illness, herbalists and other folk practitioners seemed as credible as physicians. The revolutionary scientific discoveries in Europe in the last four decades of the 19th century, which led to the development of inoculations, safer surgical techniques, and effective medications, checked scourges such as cholera, syphilis, and typhoid fever—and lent to physicians, who claimed credit for these new findings, a credibility that rival professions lacked. Seizing the moment, physicians organized a grassroots campaign—conducted by chapters of the American Medical Association— to have state legislatures pass licensing laws that would require providers of surgical and pharmaceutical remedies to hold a medical degree. Like social workers, they linked their training facilities to universities and required a bachelor's degree for admission to them.

Who would dispute the fact that this profession made salutary contributions to society as it waged war on ancient epidemics? But the medical profession also retarded social reform and, in some cases, restricted human rights. As we have already noted, the profession medicalized many of women's health conditions, such as childbirth, and subjected women to strange remedies such as months of bed rest and an epidemic of hysterectomies. Many physicians opposed the use of birth control on the grounds that women should not interfere with natural processes of reproduction. Moreover, physicians were not reluctant to profess knowledge of sexual matters; their pronouncement that homosexual behavior was medical pathology was not reversed until the 1980s.

Leaders of the American Medical Association (AMA) had entertained the notion of government health insurance (by the various states) in the early 20th century, as they observed successful projects by the English and Germans, but swung against the notion in the years before and after World War I. Indeed, they launched a campaign of virulent invective against the proponents of health insurance, which included many progressive reformers and social workers; health reformers were called "bolsheviks," "communists," and a threat to "the doctor-patient relationship." When they coupled this invective with a well-financed lobbying campaign in all states that were entertaining the idea of health insurance, they established the AMA as the primary lobbying group in the health field. The AMA's campaign helped convince large segments of the public that health insurance was un-American; it was so effective that it sabotaged the enactment of health insurance in the 1930s, the late 1940s, and the 1970s—and nearly blocked passage of lesser measures such as Medicare in the 1960s. The AMA also retarded the development of a strong public health system in the United States by arguing on many occasions that even inoculations should be done only by private physicians.[78]

The AMA's reactionary tendencies were illustrated by its strident opposition to the Sheppard-Towner bill, a modest measure initiated by social workers in 1918 that sought to improve maternal and child health facilities and services in rural areas through federal grants to state health departments. Although the legislation was enacted in 1921, its proponents had to overcome charges that it represented "state medicine." Pathetically small, this program struggled to survive and finally succumbed in 1929, largely because the medical profession "sought (successfully) to wrest control of infant and maternal health from female-run public clinics and place it, instead, in the hands of private, male physicians."[79]

The legal profession also threw roadblocks in the path of reform. Recall that progressives were interested in regulatory reforms, mostly in state and local jurisdictions. As we have already noted, the Supreme Court struck down legislation to limit hours of work for men and to prohibit child labor. Moreover, many Supreme Court justices continued to believe that the Constitution did not sanction the federal government's intrusion into social matters, *except* under very limited conditions that involved a specified power of the federal government, such as its jurisdiction over interstate commerce. (Recall from Chapter 3 that the Constitution reserved to the states all powers not specified in it— and, aside from vague clauses like the general welfare clause, the Constitution was silent on social policy matters.) Social reformers thus had to ponder how to frame social legislation so that it would conform to the narrow and specific wording of the Constitution. Amending the Constitution, although possible in principle, was difficult in practice. Congress passed a constitutional amendment in

1924 to authorize federal laws regulating the labor of youth under the age of 18, but the amendment failed to gain ratification by three-fourths of the states, and thus did not pass into law.

The intransigency of the courts, and particularly the Supreme Court, enraged progressive reformers like Theodore Roosevelt. Because the Constitution gives Congress the power to organize and establish rules for the Supreme Court, progressive reformers proposed taking the powers of constitutional review from the Supreme Court by legislation—or increasing the size of the Court to dilute the power of its sitting justices. These projects were not successful. In 1916, however, reformers did succeed in securing the appointment to the Court of Louis Brandeis—an attorney who advocated "sociological jurisprudence," which would factor the effects of laws on the well-being of citizens into constitutional rulings—over an avalanche of protests by many jurists and conservatives who alleged that he would disregard the intentions of the framers of the Constitution.

These legal disputes in the Progressive Era gave the Supreme Court a central role in the unfolding of social reform. Until about 1938, as we will note in ensuing chapters, a succession of adverse rulings by the Supreme Court enormously delayed the federal government's assumption of responsibility for social policy. Even after the Court had acceded to the notion that the federal government could establish social programs and regulations, it remained a key player in shaping the content of those decisions. (We note in later chapters how relatively liberal rulings of the 1950s and 1960s assumed enormous importance in speeding social reforms and how a succession of more conservative rulings in the 1980s and 1990s aligned the Court against social reformers.)[80]

THE EVOLUTION OF THE RELUCTANT WELFARE STATE

Progressives dramatically expanded social obligation to include a host of regulations, as well as a limited set of social programs such as mothers' pensions and workmen's compensation. These accomplishments may not appear dramatic or far-reaching to contemporary citizens, but they constituted remarkable innovations in a society where social policy had previously been restricted to poorhouses, mental institutions, prisons, schools, and houses of refuge.

The progressives made a contribution to the development of the modern welfare state by championing the role of government in addressing social problems, although their emphasis was usually on regulation at state and local levels. Government, they believed, could serve as a force for the amelioration of social needs rather than as merely a passive umpire that preserved law and order. Further, many progressives believed that government need not merely provide funds and concessions to affluent persons and corporations but also ought to assist vulnerable populations such as women, children, immigrants, and factory workers. In a sense, then, progressives legitimized a vision of positive and compassionate government that had not hitherto been expressed as widely or as articulately in a nation preoccupied with laissez-faire doctrines and the deification of monied elites. The policies that they enacted, in turn, served to educate the nation's citizens to the possibilities of governmental action, as workers, renters, and consumers benefited from improvements in working conditions, housing, and public health.

Nonetheless, the progressive movement must be viewed as having made only modest social welfare innovations in a nation with extraordinary social needs. Regulations hardly constituted frontal assaults on poverty, low wages, or industrial accidents. Workmen's compensation and mothers' pensions were limited programs by any standards. The nation instituted notable public health reforms, but within a larger flawed model of medical care. When compared with European nations, the United States spent paltry sums on domestic programs—sums that were not markedly increased by the progressive reformers. Few Americans empathized with the social needs of African Americans, Latinos, and Asian Americans; indeed, many progressives were deeply suspicious of these groups and were also prejudiced against immigrants.

Many reformers realized that low-income and working-class Americans would need to rally behind a reform-minded president if the nation were to develop more far-reaching reforms. But it was unclear how such a reform constituency could develop; the failed campaign of the Progressive Party in 1912 illustrated how far there was still to go. As we will discuss in Chapter 7, it took the catastrophe of the Great Depression to push the nation to develop major federal social programs, and it took the leadership of President Franklin Roosevelt—a relative of President Theodore Roosevelt—to achieve the political realignment that the progressives had fantasized might be possible.

LINKING THE PROGRESSIVE ERA TO CONTEMPORARY SOCIETY

What We Can Learn from Policy Advocates of the Progressive Era

Moral outrage at such indignities as those suffered by children laboring in factories, immigrants toiling for virtually no pay, and tenants living in squalid conditions was the catalyst for the policy advocacy of Jane Addams, as well as Paul Kellogg. (See Inserts 6.5 and 6.6.)

Addams was deeply disappointed by the social and economic arrangements that existed in American society. She wanted, above all, to find a "higher ideal" of cooperativeness and collaboration to replace the competitiveness and self-seeking ambition that she saw around her in a society with extremes of inequality.

In each of her books, Addams wrote of her hope that a specific group might lead the nation to a higher moral ground, whether immigrants, youth, or women. Immigrants, she believed, were imbued with a culture of cooperation that they had obtained in the villages and peasant life of the European and Russian societies from which they had

emigrated. Youth possessed an innocence that might, if not ruined by acculturation to baser values around them, lead the nation in more altruistic directions. Women, she believed, were inculcated with a cooperative ethic in marked contrast to the values of men that were found in competitive corporate endeavors. She even hoped that most mothers would refuse to send their children to war due to their cooperative and life-sustaining ethic, only to find that most of them supported American involvement in World War I.

It is not surprising, then, that Addams sought to create in Hull House a microcosm of the nation she hoped to create. It operated on three planes. On the one hand, it provided personal services and assistance to immigrants from many nations who had settled in Chicago, including language skills, cultural activities, and case advocacy to help immigrants obtain necessary legal documents and citizenship. Addams realized that immigrants needed help simply to survive in their new, complex, and often hostile environment.

It also provided policy advocacy in the neighborhood and city surrounding Hull House, as well as in the state capital of Springfield. Addams sought regulations against child labor, regulation of factory conditions, housing codes, and myriad other specific reforms from a range of public officials. At one point, Hull House even backed a political candidate to run against the notorious Chicago machine, which was a corrupt group of politicians mostly interested in perpetuating their power through patronage and collection of bribes. She soon discovered, however, that electoral politics was a challenging arena as the machine candidate easily bested her favored candidate.

Hull House also served as a focal point for national reform. Many progressive reformers actually stayed in Hull House for varying lengths of time, with Addams presiding over many forums and discussions among them about political strategy for sustaining a national reform movement. She worked closely with a dizzying array of reformers including Alice Paul (who sought many public health reforms) and Theodore Roosevelt.

Addams's conviction that progressives had to be active in politics led her to become a key leader in the

I N S E R T 6.5 **Profiles in Policy Advocacy: Jane Addams (1860–1935)**

Jane Addams—recognized around the world as a pioneer in the field of social work—is best remembered as the founder of Chicago's Hull House project and the recipient of the 1931 Nobel Peace Prize. Born on September 6, 1860, in Cedarville, Illinois, Jane was the youngest of eight children born to Sarah (Weber) and John Huy Addams, a founding member of the Republican Party and an Illinois state senator from 1854 to 1870. Sarah Addams died before Jane's fourth birthday. Senator Addams, a Hicksite Quaker and an abolitionist, became a dominant force in Jane's life, influencing her ambitions and helping to shape her political views. He instilled in Jane an appreciation for the meaning and value of hard work and civic duty, which became evident once she launched her own career. Despite her physical ailment—tuberculosis of the spine—and the challenges presented by those who opposed her efforts to effect positive social policy, Jane Addams earned a place in history as a social reformer committed to peace and the improvement of the human condition.

Shortly after her illness forced her to drop out of the Women's Medical College in Philadelphia in 1881, Addams focused her career interests on mission work in general and the operation of settlement houses in particular. She discovered the need for this type of service in 1887 while visiting the Toynbee Hall project in London's East End. The Toynbee Hall project was a pioneer effort aimed at providing young members of the clergy with exposure to the lives of the area's urban poor. The project's purpose was to teach these individuals how to provide better services to those in need. Jane Addams was so inspired by the Toynbee Hall project that she returned to the United States with a vision of replicating what she had witnessed in Europe.

In September of 1889, Addams, accompanied by her friend and confidante, Ellen Gates Starr, left the safety and comfort of her home in Cedarville and moved into the Charles J. Hull mansion, which later became known as the Hull House. The Hull House was located in a blighted neighborhood on South Halsted Street in Chicago. Like the Toynbee Hall project, the Hull House had as its main objective introducing middle-class individuals to the life of the urban poor. Unlike the Toynbee Hall project, however, the majority of people who became involved in learning about and providing social services at the Hull House were young, middle-class American women. At its peak operating capacity, the Hull House had 13 buildings staffed by 65 persons, most of whom were college-educated professionals. Aside from providing much-needed community services, the Hull House served as a real-world training center for several well-known and respected social workers, including Edith and Grace Abbott, Alice Hamilton, Florence Kelly, Francis Hackett, Sophonisba Breckinridge, Jessie Binford, and Julia Lathrop. Due to the success of its programs and dedicated personnel, the Hull House project, under the supervision of Jane Addams, became widely recognized as a leader in the settlement house and social reform movement.

By 1895, Jane Addams had taken her leadership skills and reform-oriented thinking from the successful Hull House project to Chicago's City Hall. Her new objective: municipal reforms, aimed primarily at improving the working conditions faced by the city's workers. She gained insight into the problems faced by the municipal workers during her brief stint as the inspector of streets and alleys for the Hull House district. Addams became a labor rights activist and participated in the Pullman strike of 1894, the building trades strike of 1900, the anthracite strike of 1902, the Chicago Stockyards strike of 1904, and the textile workers strike of 1910.

With the advent of the Spanish-American War in 1898, Addams's interest in world peace and the promotion of social justice everywhere was broadened. To share her personal views on pacifism and social ethics with others, Addams began delivering public lectures, including several held at the University of Chicago in 1899. She subsequently published her first book, *Democracy and Social Ethics*, which was released in 1902. In it, Addams called for both the reform of municipal politics and an end to war.

By 1909, Jane Addams had achieved national recognition and was widely respected as a leader in the peace and social reform movement. That year, she became the first woman to head the National Conference of Charities and Correction. Three years later, she found herself campaigning for Theodore Roosevelt's Progressive Party. Addams would soon discover, however, that, with the coming of World War I, large segments of the American public, including Roosevelt himself, would lose their taste for her reform efforts and turn against her.

Addams's involvement with the Women's Peace Party, her protests while at the International Congress of Women at The Hague in 1915, and her affiliation with Henry Ford's Peace Ship placed her in the crosshairs of intense criticism and rebuke from

(Continued)

interventionists—those who saw war as the only solution to the European crisis. Addams's critics went so far as to charge her with being a communist revolutionary and German sympathizer, despite her unwavering commitment to improving the lives of her fellow Americans. Her membership in the Daughters of the American Revolution was revoked. Even her service in the Department of Food Administration during the Hoover years was not enough to calm the attacks that had been launched against her. Undoubtedly, for several years before, during, and after World War I, Jane Addams's faith and devotion to her ideals were challenged beyond the point at which most others would have conceded defeat.

Jane Addams, however, did not surrender in the face of adversity. She continued to work at Hull House for more than 15 years after World War I, seeking a variety of reforms. Her life serves as a testimony to what can be accomplished through hard work and attention to civic duty. To many of her critics, the life of Jane Addams was wasted chasing utopian ideals. What was true for many skeptics then is still true for many skeptics today: social reform and improving the human condition occur only in pipe dreams. Yet a close analysis of Jane Addams's accomplishments shows that her work produced very real results, as seen in the lives of many Americans. For her tireless devotion and commitment to advancing the social justice, Jane Addams received the Nobel Peace Prize in 1931, four years before her death in May of 1935.

Progressive Party when it selected Theodore Roosevelt to be its candidate in 1912 against what Addams believed were relatively conservative Democratic and Republican candidates. She was the first woman to give a keynote address at a national political convention—and she worked closely with Roosevelt to develop a political platform that envisioned expanding the progressive reform drive to the federal level to bring reforms such as unemployment insurance.

As a pioneer founder of the social work profession, Addams toiled endlessly to imbue it with a policy advocacy mission rather than only providing services to clients. She reasoned that persons such as immigrants, caught in a web of hostile institutions and lack of social programs, could collectively progress only if Americans created a humane welfare state.

Addams's political involvement extended to international affairs. As a pacifist, but also because she feared it would blunt the progressive reform movement, she strongly opposed American involvement in World War I, which she viewed as a conflict between corrupt and colonialist regimes. She was vilified by many Americans for this position, since the American public overwhelmingly supported American involvement.

Her conviction that the profession should make policy advocacy central to its work was her legacy to the profession—and it is the reason that I dedicated my book (*Becoming an Effective Policy Advocate*, now in its fifth edition) to her.

If Addams possessed organizing and leadership skills that are needed by policy advocates, Paul Kellogg—her close friend and ally—provided pivotal data that buttressed progressives' arguments that large numbers of Americans lived in abject poverty. Paul Kellogg made it clear that social science and policy advocacy go hand-in-hand. (See Insert 6.6.)

Progressive reformers often possessed relatively little empirical data about the social conditions they wanted to correct, such as the actual number of immigrants, their income levels, and their social conditions. We take for granted in contemporary society the collection of such statistics by an array of governmental authorities, such as the U.S. Census Bureau, and private research groups, such as the Center on Budget and Policy Priorities, the Urban Institute, and the Brookings Institution. As compared to modern policy advocates, progressive reformers had scant information—a condition that Kellogg hoped to partly correct through a survey of Pittsburgh, a prototypical industrial city that relied heavily on immigrant labor. The so-called Pittsburgh Survey exposed the sheer magnitude of harsh economic and social conditions that immigrants experienced.

A false dichotomy is sometimes evident among academics even in contemporary society between

---

I N S E R T 6.6   Profiles in Policy Advocacy: Paul Underwood Kellogg (1879–1958)

Paul Underwood Kellogg believed that, if citizens had access to the facts of social justice in America, they would take action to improve the human condition around them. As a journalist, he also believed that presenting facts to the citizenry was most effective when the facts were expressed in terms of real people and real situations. Paul Underwood Kellogg's contribution to the social reform movement of the early 1900s was his ability to keep the public well informed of labor conditions in America and social justice everywhere.

Kellogg was born on September 30, 1879, in Kalamazoo, Michigan. He was the youngest son born to Frank Israel and Mary Foster (Underwood) Kellogg. His father owned a lumber business until the early 1890s. Shortly after the company failed, Kellogg's father abandoned his family and moved to Texas.

Kellogg's interest in journalism began when he was a teenager. In high school, Kellogg was named class historian. After graduating in 1897, he was given a job on the editorial staff of the *Kalamazoo Daily Telegraph*. In 1901, Kellogg left Michigan to attend Columbia University in New York City. In the summer of 1902, he studied at the New York Charity Organization Society's Summer School of Philanthropy. In that same year, Kellogg was hired by Edward T. Devine as assistant editor of *Charities*, the Society's official publication. By 1903, Paul, who was now joined by his brother Arthur Piper Kellogg, worked on expanding the scope of *Charities*, which they accomplished by merging it with the *Commons*, the official publication of the settlement house movement.

In February of 1905, Kellogg married Helen Hall, administrator and head resident of New York City's Henry Street Settlement, a settlement house where the couple resided for many years.

Although Kellogg contributed many articles to the literature on social conditions in America, he is best remembered for his work on the Pittsburgh Survey. Together with a team of scholars and community leaders from Pittsburgh, Pennsylvania, Kellogg gathered information on nearly every aspect of life in the city. He subsequently published the group's findings in articles and later in a six-volume series. His methods of gathering information in general and the Pittsburgh Survey in particular served as a model for later sociological surveys. More important, the Survey was instrumental in keeping the citizenry informed of facts related to working conditions, housing conditions, and other areas in need of reform. (The Pittsburgh Survey led to reform efforts to shorten the industrial workweek, improve housing, and provide workers' compensation coverage.)

Between 1907 and 1908, prior to returning to his New York office, Kellogg headed the Pittsburgh Survey research team. Once back in New York, he began reshaping *Charities and the Commons* into the *Survey*, which later became social work's semi-official journal. The *Survey* was widely recognized as a stalwart reporter of the social decay in America and the policies and programs that sought to reverse it. In 1912, Paul Underwood Kellogg became editor-in-chief of the *Survey*, and his brother Arthur became managing editor.

In keeping with his conviction that a well-informed public would support social reform, Kellogg kept the *Survey*'s agenda broad enough to include coverage of issues that other publications stayed away from. The *Survey* dealt with major issues of urban and rural America during the first half of the 1900s, including housing, recreation, urban renewal, improvement of industrial conditions and workers' benefits, social insurance, regional planning, public health, and environmental conservation. The *Survey* also allowed the editorial staff to explore other issues in depth, including issues on the African American community, coal mining and labor conditions, Mexico, fascism, unemployment, juvenile delinquency, and many other subjects. The *Survey*'s small staff of writers was made up of many early 20th-century reformers, who often worked for little or no pay.

Between 1911 and 1913, Paul Kellogg was secretary to the Committee to Secure a Federal Commission on Industrial Relations and was founder and director of the Foreign Policy Association. Throughout his career, he was extremely supportive of and active in the National Federation of Settlements, the American Association of Social Workers, and the National Conference on Social Welfare. In 1934 and 1935, he served as vice chair of an advisory council to President Franklin D. Roosevelt's Committee on Economic Security, which helped create the framework for the Social Security Act.

Paul Underwood Kellogg's life and career were devoted to informing the American public about the social conditions many of his critics would have preferred to ignore. Kellogg, who was not a trained social worker, used his expertise in journalism to promote social reform by appealing to the American conscience.

those who seek policy reforms through "policy analysis" (which uses data extensively) and "policy activism" (which uses community and political organizing). *Both* data and organizing are needed to achieve policy reforms, as I discuss in my text on policy advocacy (*Becoming an Effective Policy Advocate*, 5th ed., 2008).

Kellogg also illustrated how policy advocates need to make extensive use of the mass media to heighten public awareness of social conditions that need to addressed through policy reforms. He edited a series of publications that disseminated information to the American public, including the influential magazine, *The Survey*, that was a kind of ongoing documentary of social conditions that needed to be reformed, as well as promising policy proposals.

What We Can Learn from the Persistence of Unmet Needs and Policy Issues during the Progressive Era

After the nation enacted restrictive and racist immigration legislation in 1924 that greatly reduced immigration from non-European nations, it was widely assumed that massive immigration to the United States had permanently ended. In fact, tens of millions of immigrants entered the United States from the mid-1960s to the present with a radical shift from European nations to Mexico, Central America, and Asia.

These immigrants came to the United States for many reasons and in many ways. Some of them were refugees from civil conflict and civil wars in such places as Bosnia, Kosovo, Guatemala, El Salvador, Vietnam, Cambodia, and Thailand. Large numbers came to the United States in the wake of the Vietnam War. Others were persons seeking asylum from dictatorial regimes in Russia and Eastern Europe. Some came through the established immigration procedures such as obtaining so-called green cards to perform specific work and get specific education in the United States. Others received amnesty from the Immigration Reform and Control Act of 1986, which granted amnesty to 3 million undocumented workers—mostly from Mexico and Central America—who could prove they had lived in the United States for at least four years. Still others were undocumented persons who came into the United States to find work or to join family members—an estimated 12 million persons in 2007.

While most of these immigrants voluntarily entered the United States to better their economic condition, just like immigrants of the late 19th and early 20th centuries, many encountered abysmal conditions. Take the example of New Orleans in the wake of Hurricane Katrina in August 2005. When low-income African Americans fled the city, corporations aggressively advertised in Mexican and Asian cities for workers who could legally enter the United States, but only if they worked for specific named corporations. Promised fair wages and good working conditions, they soon found themselves exploited by American corporations that often paid them less than the minimum wage or not at all, failed to provide them with work safety equipment even as they often demolished buildings containing asbestos and toxic chemicals, often required them to work for 12 hours per day, and stated or implied they would be sent to the Immigration and Naturalization Service (INS) for deportation if they complained about their pay or working conditions. They lived in motels with as many as 10 persons in a room.

The United States has engaged for decades, then, in a hypocritical game of exploiting immigrants' labor at low wage rates for jobs that many Americans will not accept, accepting their Social Security payments and other taxes, yet not granting them the right to safety net programs and protections that other working Americans receive. Afraid of deportation, immigrants rarely report theft or violence against themselves to the police. Some are even reluctant to send their children to public school for fear of exposure to the INS.

The plight of immigrants from Mexico is particularly appalling because, as we learned in Chapter 5, most of the American Southwest, parts of Colorado, and California *ought* to belong to Mexico. This land was ceded to the United States only because it invaded Mexico, conquered Mexico City, and forced the Mexican government at gunpoint to sign the Treaty of Guadalupe. Even Abraham Lincoln concluded that American conduct in the Mexican-American War was ethically reprehensible.

As this edition goes to press in 2008, the federal government has been unable to fashion immigration legislation that would grant amnesty to millions of immigrants currently in the nation, while establishing a humane system for providing work visas to others in coming decades.

What We Can Learn from Failed Policy Strategies of the Progressive Era

While progressive reformers are to be lauded for trying to create some social reforms in a society with only a primitive welfare state, they failed sufficiently to expand their horizons to the federal government. Social problems such as unemployment, poverty, and oppression of vulnerable populations require substantial federal direction and resources if they are to be addressed adequately. It took the Great Depression in the 1930s and the civil rights movement of the 1950s and 1960s to make clear that state and local governments, left to their own devices and resources, cannot address national problems adequately.

In their defense, progressives sought reforms in a context that was not hospitable to bolder reforms, so progressives' failure to develop more ambitious reforms reflected these realities. In some ways, progressive reformers can be viewed as showing that government *can* assume a proactive role in addressing social problems, even if their reforms represented only a small step toward the creation of a more humane American welfare state.

What We Can Learn from Promising Strategies of the Progressive Era

Most persons think about social programs when they discuss welfare states, such as the various safety net programs like Food Stamps, Medicaid,

Medicare, Social Security, anc Few persons realize that any 1 must also contain many regu regulations that progressives ir

Free-market conservatives often contend that government regulations are both unnecessary and ineffective. They correctly note that corporations often must expend considerable amounts of resources to achieve compliance. They correctly contend that government expenses must expand to monitor compliance with regulations. They often argue that free markets work best when regulations do not exist.

Conservatives fail to remember, however, the social conditions of the late 19th century when almost no regulations existed. Minus regulations, unethical businesses, professionals, developers, landlords, public officials, and others had free rein to exploit clients, workers, and the general public. Had not progressives and several succeeding generations of reformers developed myriad regulations to protect vulnerable populations—and Americans in general—from exploitation by corporations, landlords, owners of child care and nursing home institutions, and others, many Americans would be unnecessarily victimized. As our discussion of exploited immigrants in post-Katrina New Orleans suggests, yet additional reforms are needed to protect vulnerable populations such as immigrants.

What We Can Learn from the Progressive Era about the Structure of the American Welfare State

Social workers need to be familiar with the regulatory side of the American welfare state. For example, they need to be able to refer clients to local authorities when they reside in inadequate structures that violate local building codes and to refer clients to authorities that regulate work conditions when they are exposed to unsafe conditions. Progressives were the prime movers in developing these regulations, as indicated in Box 6.1, which lists the major progressive reforms that regulated

BOX 6.1   Selected Regulations Enacted in the Progressive Era

Regulations of Industrialists

- Curtailment of the size of trusts (federal)
- Limitation of working hours of women and children (local)
- Regulation of working conditions in plants (local)

Regulations of the Food and Drug Industry

- Restrictions placed on the content and labeling of food and drugs (federal and local)

Regulations of Developers and Owners of Rental Properties

- Housing codes (local) and development of zoning laws to govern construction

Regulations of Politicians

- Passage of initiative, referendum, and recall procedures (local)
- Restrictions on lobbying and campaign contributions (local)
- Limitation of patronage through passage of civil service legislation (local and federal)
- Curtailment of the power of machines and bosses through the establishment of nonpartisan elections and commissions (local)

Protections for Immigrants

- Controls on persons who hire immigrants (federal and local)

Protections for Women

- Curbs on interstate transportation of nonconsenting women to prevent kidnapping for prostitution (federal) and laws to restrict prostitution (local)

Development of Fire Codes

- Controls on construction of industrial facilities as well as housing (local)

Regulations of Taverns and Distilleries

- Enactment of prohibition (local)

Regulations of Immigration

- Many proposals advanced to restrict immigration (federal)

Regulations of Banks

- Laws regulating reserve requirements of banks (federal)

Regulations Governing Professional Activities

- Enactment of licensing laws for medical, dental, legal, and other professional activities (local)

Public Health Regulations

- Laws regulating disposal of sewage and garbage as well as food processing in restaurants (local)

Working Hours of Women and Children

- Laws regulating hours and working conditions of women and children (local and federal)

Working Hours of Federal Employees

- Federal legislation limiting the hours of work of federal employees

Many regulations have been enacted, of course, in the decades following the Progressive Era up to the present. As just one example, civil rights legislation from the mid-1960s to the present has greatly expanded regulations that diminish discriminatory actions against members of vulnerable populations. We will discuss many of these regulations in succeeding chapters.

the political process, banking and economic institutions, conditions of employment, food and drugs, employment of immigrants, and housing. Although most were enacted in local jurisdictions, they also gave state and federal governments new policy roles.

WHAT YOU CAN DO NOW

After reading Chapter 6, you are now equipped to:

- Analyze social and economic realities confronted by Americans in the early stages of industrial society.

- Discuss the sheer size of immigration in the period from the Civil War to 1924, as well as the social and economic conditions confronted by immigrants.

- Analyze coping and survival strategies of immigrants.

- Discuss how and why social reform took place in the Progressive Era, including catalytic events, intellectual ferment, aroused public opinion, and the specter of unrest.

- Analyze why progressives emphasized regulations—and the sheer number and kind that they enacted.

- Discuss some limits of social reform in the context of limited reforms obtained for women and children, persons of color, workers, and persons with mental illness.

- Analyze why progressives obtained relatively limited reforms in the context of cultural and political realities.

- Analyze why and how the United States evolved a flawed model of health services—and why universal health insurance was rejected.

- Discuss why the Bull Moose Campaign of 1912 took place and why it failed to realign American politics as some progressive reformers had hoped.

- Analyze the causes and nature of the oppression of women, African Americans, Asians, Spanish-speaking persons, and immigrants.

- Discuss why and how the social work profession emerged in this era, as well as some tensions within the profession—and discuss some commonalities between the social work, legal, and medical professions.

- Describe the contributions of policy advocates such as Jane Addams and Paul Kellogg.

- Discuss what we can learn from the Progressive Era about persistent unmet needs, failed strategies, promising strategies, and the structure of the American welfare state.

ENDNOTES

1. David Brody, *Workers in Industrial America: Essays on the Twentieth-Century Struggle* (New York: Oxford University Press, 1980), p. 15.

2. For comparisons of Russian and Italian immigrants, see Elizabeth Ewen, *Immigrant Women in the Land of Dollars: Life and Culture on the Lower East Side, 1890–1925* (New York: Monthly Review Press, 1985), pp. 30–57.

3. Ibid., pp. 112–113, 131; Timothy Walch, ed., *Immigrant America: European Ethnicity in the United States* (New York: Garland, 1993), pp. ix–xiv; and

Edward Kantowicz, "The Changing Face of Ethnic Politics: From Political Machine to Community Organization." In Walch, ed., *Immigrant America*, pp. 179–197.

4. John Bodnar, *Steeltown: Immigration and Industrialization, 1870–1940* (Pittsburgh: University of Pittsburgh Press, 1990), pp. 127–149; David Salvaterra, "Becoming American: Assimilation, Pluralism, and Ethnic Identity." In Walch, ed., *Immigrant America*, pp. 29–54.

5. Ewen, *Immigrant Women*, pp. 76–91.

6. Brody, *Workers*, p. 16.

7. James Weinstein, "It's Good for Business." In Arthur Mann, ed., *The Progressive Era: Major Issues of Interpretation* (Hinsdale, IL: Dryden Press, 1975), p. 112.

8. Brody, *Workers*, p. 24; Lizabeth Cohen, *Making a New Deal: Industrial Workers in Chicago, 1919–1939* (New York: Cambridge University Press, 1990), pp. 11–52.

9. Mark Leff, "Consensus for Reform: The Mothers' Pension Movement in the Progressive Era." In Frank Breul and Stephen Diner, eds., *Compassion and Responsibility: Readings in the History of Social Welfare Policy in the United States* (Chicago: University of Chicago Press, 1980), p. 245; Roy Lubove, *The Struggle for Social Security* (Cambridge, MA: Harvard University Press, 1968), pp. 98–99.

10. Stephan Skowronek, *Building a New American State: The Expansion of National Administrative Capacities, 1877–1920* (Cambridge: Cambridge University Press, 1982), pp. 39–42, 45–46, 165–176.

11. Arthur Link and Richard McCormick, *Progressivism* (Arlington Heights, IL: Harlan Davidson, 1983), pp. 18–20; David Thelen, "Not Classes but Issues." In Mann, ed., *The Progressive Era*, pp. 40–42.

12. Thelen, "Not Classes," pp. 42–45.

13. Sidney Fine, *Laissez-Faire and the General Welfare State: A Study of Conflict in America, 1865–1901* (Ann Arbor, MI: University of Michigan Press, 1956), pp. 126–168; Robert Steamer, *The Supreme Court in Crisis: A History of Conflict* (Amherst, MA: University of Massachusetts Press, 1971), pp. 149–171; and Edward White, *The American Judicial Tradition: Profiles of Leading American Judges* (New York: Oxford University Press, 1976), pp. 105–108.

14. Jane Addams, *Newer Ideals of Peace* (New York: Macmillan, 1907), p. 85.

15. She idealizes youth, immigrants, and women, respectively, in these books: *The Spirit of Youth and the City Streets* (New York: Macmillan, 1909); *Twenty Years at Hull House* (New York: Macmillan, 1961), pp. 169–185; *The Long Road of Women's Memory* (New York: Macmillan, 1917).

16. Fine, *Laissez-Faire*, pp. 198–251.

17. Charles Beard, *An Economic Interpretation of the Constitutional Convention* (New York: Free Press, 1965), pp. 152–188; Frederic Howe, *Confessions of a Reformer* (New York: Scribner's, 1925), p. 169; John Gable, *The Bull Moose Years: Theodore Roosevelt and the Progressive Party* (Port Woolington, NY: Kennicat Press, 1978), pp. 11–13.

18. Lela Costin, *Two Sisters for Social Justice* (Urbana, IL: University of Illinois Press, 1983), pp. 31–38; Allen Davis, *American Heroine: The Life and Legend of Jane Addams* (New York: Oxford University Press, 1973), pp. 24–52.

19. Link and McCormick, *Progressivism*, pp. 15, 19–20; Thelen, "Not Classes," pp. 40–45; William Allen White, *The Autobiography of William Allen White* (New York: Macmillan, 1946), p. 484.

20. Fine, *Laissez-Faire*, p. 168; Thelen, "Not Classes," pp. 40–41.

21. Joseph Castrovinci, "Prelude to Welfare Capitalism: The Role of Business in the Enactment of Workmen's Compensation Legislation in Illinois, 1905–1912," *Social Service Review*, 50 (March 1976), p. 277; Lynn Gordon, "Women and the Anti-Child Labor Movement in Illinois, 1890–1920," *Social Service Review*, 51 (June 1977), pp. 314, 319. For a discussion of the sheer power of the save-the-children ethos, see Michael Katz, *In the Shadow of the Poorhouse* (New York: Basic Books, 1986), pp. 113–115.

22. Richard Hofstadter, *Age of Reform: From Bryan to FDR* (New York: Knopf, 1955), pp. 185–195; Clarke Chambers, *Paul U. Kellogg and the Survey: Voices for Social Welfare and Social Justice* (Minneapolis, MN: University of Minnesota Press, 1971), pp. 33–40.

23. Walter Trattner, *Homer Folks: Pioneer in Social Welfare* (New York: Columbia University Press, 1968), pp. 76–84.

24. Roy Lubove, *The Professional Altruist* (Cambridge, MA: Harvard University Press, 1965), pp. 3–54.

25. Allen Davis, *Spearheads for Reform: The Social Settlements and the Progressive Movement, 1890–1914* (New York: Oxford University Press, 1967), p. 195.

26. Theda Skocpol, *Social Policy in the United States: Future Possibilities in Historical Perspective* (Princeton, NJ: Princeton University Press, 1995), p. 76; Linda Gordon, *Pitied but Not Entitled* (New York: Free Press, 1994), p. 49.

27. Charles Larsen, *The Good Fight: The Life and Times of Ben Lindsey* (Chicago: Quadrangle Books, 1972), pp. 27–32.

28. Trattner, *Homer Folks*, p. 107; Costin, *Two Sisters*, pp. 100–118; and Josephine Goldmark, *The Impatient Crusader* (Urbana, IL: University of Illinois Press, 1953), pp. 100–104.

29. Costin, *Two Sisters*, p. 52.

30. Many monographs on settlements have recently been written, including Mina Carson, *Settlement Folk* (Chicago: University of Chicago Press, 1990); Ruth Crocker, *Social Work and Social Order* (Urbana, IL: University of Illinois Press, 1992); Howard Karger, *The Sentinels of Order* (Lanham, MD: University Press of America, 1987); Elisabeth Lasch-Quinn, *Black Neighbors: Race and the Limits of Reform in the American Settlement House Movement, 1890–1945* (Chapel Hill, NC: University of North Carolina Press, 1993); Rivka Shpak Lissak, *Pluralism and Progressives* (Chicago: University of Chicago Press, 1989); Ralph Luker, *The Social Gospel in Black and White* (Chapel Hill: University of North Carolina Press, 1992); and Judith Ann Trolander, *Professionalism and Social Change* (New York: Columbia University Press, 1987). For an excellent overview of settlements, see Alfreda Iglehart and Rosina Becerra, *Social Services and the Ethnic Community* (Boston: Allyn and Bacon, 1995), pp. 107–148.

31. Lubove, *The Struggle*, pp. 52–57; Skocpol, *Social Policy*, pp. 73–74; and Weinstein, "It's Good for Business," pp. 113–114.

32. Carolyn Webber and Aaron Wildavsky, *A History of Taxation and Expenditure in the Western World* (New York: Simon and Schuster, 1986), p. 451.

33. Steamer, *The Supreme Court*, pp. 149–171.

34. Link and McCormick, *Progressivism*, pp. 69–70, 72; Paolo Coletta, *The Presidency of William Howard Taft* (Lawrence, KS: University Press of Kansas, 1973), p. 139; Davis, *American Heroine*, p. 189; Gable, *The Bull Moose Years*, pp. 90–91; and Link and McCormick, *Progressivism*, pp. 69–70.

35. John Buenker, *Urban Liberalism and Progressive Reform* (New York: Scribner's, 1973), p. 43; Michael Rogin and John Shover, "From Below." In Mann, ed., *The Progressive Era*, pp. 20–30; Davis, *American Heroine*, pp. 176–184, 189; Link and McCormick, *Progressivism*, pp. 69–70, 100–104; Paul Boyer, *Urban Masses and the Moral Order in America, 1820–1920* (Cambridge, MA: Harvard University Press, 1978), pp. 205–219; and Daniel Levine, *Jane Addams and the Liberal Tradition* (Madison, WI: State Historical Society of Wisconsin, 1971), pp. 144–159.

36. George Dangerfield, *The Strange Death of Liberal England* (New York: H. Smith and R. Haas, 1935), pp. 214–330; H. V. Emy, *Liberals, Radicals, and Social Politics, 1892–1914* (Cambridge: Cambridge University Press, 1973), pp. 235–280; and G. D. H. Cole and Raymond Postgate, *The British Common People* (New York: Barnes and Noble, 1961), pp. 481–496, 567–576.

37. Skowronek, *Building a New American State*, pp. 24–26.

38. Addams, *Twenty Years*, pp. 222–223; Hofstadter, *Age of Reform*, pp. 254–269; and Levine, *Jane Addams*, p. 75.

39. Brody, *Workers*, pp. 23–30, 82–88; Eric Foner, *History of the Labor Movement in the United States*, Vol. 2 (New York: International Publishers, 1955), pp. 184–188.

40. Brody, *Workers*, pp. 14–21.

41. Ibid., pp. 32–39.

42. Chambers, *Paul V. Kellogg*, p. 48; Davis, *American Heroine*, pp. 186, 193, 194; and Gable, *The Bull Moose Years*, pp. 6–7.

43. Davis, *American Heroine*, pp. 54–56, 125.

44. Gordon, *Pitied but Not Entitled*, pp. 67–87; and Skocpol, *Social Policy*, pp. 116–117.

45. Gable, *The Bull Moose Years*, pp. 6–7; Coletta, *The Presidency of William Howard Taft*, pp. 21–25.

46. Lee Kreader, "Isaac Max Rubinow: Pioneering Specialist in Social Insurance," *Social Service Review*, 50 (September 1976), pp. 293–298.

47. Ibid., pp. 16-20; Gable, *The Bull Moose Years*, pp. 6, 112–113.

48. Gable, *The Bull Moose Years*, pp. 131–133.

49. Davis, *American Heroine*, p. 197.

50. Eleanor Flexner, *Century of Struggle: The Women's Rights Movement in the United States* (Cambridge, MA: Harvard University Press, 1975), pp. 319–337.

51. Mimi Abramovitz, *Regulating the Lives of Women: Social Welfare Policy from Colonial Times to the Present* (Boston: South End Press, 1988), pp. 188, 190–193, 199, 248–255.

52. Nancy Woloch, *Women and the American Experience* (New York: Knopf, 1984), pp. 363–380.

53. Barbara Ehrenreich and Deirdre English, *For Her Own Good: 150 Years of the Experts' Advice to Women* (New York: Anchor Books, 1979), pp. 110, 131–133.

54. Ibid., pp. 93–98.

55. John Dittmer, *Black Georgia in the Progressive Era, 1900–1920* (Urbana, IL: University of Illinois Press, 1977), pp. 8–22.

56. Florette Henri, *Black Migration: Movement North, 1900–1920* (Garden City, NY: Doubleday, 1975), pp. 81–131.

57. Gordon, *Pitied but Not Entitled*, pp. 111–122.

58. Roger Daniels, *The Politics of Prejudice: The Anti-Japanese Movement in California and the Struggle for Japanese Exclusion* (Berkeley, CA: University of California Press, 1977), pp. 46–78; Jack Chen, *The Chinese of America: From the Beginnings to the Present* (San Francisco: Harper & Row, 1982), pp. 88–89, 99, 109–115.

59. J. Owens Smith, *The Politics of Racial Inequality: A Systematic Comparative Macro-Analysis from the Colonial Period to 1970* (New York: Greenwood Press, 1987), pp. 86–91.

60. Leobardo Estrada, F. Chris Garcia, Reynaldo Macias, and Lionel Maldonado, "Chicanos in the United States: A History of Exploitation and Resistance." In F. Chris Garcia, ed., *Latinos and the Political System* (Notre Dame, IN: University of Notre Dame Press, 1988), pp. 39, 41; Rodolfo Acuna, *Occupied America: The Chicano's Struggle toward Liberation* (San Francisco: Canfield Press, 1972), pp. 130–135; Ronald Takaki, *A Different Mirror: A History of Multicultural America* (Boston: Little, Brown, 1994), p. 317; and Paul Boyer et al., *The Enduring Vision: A History of the American People* (Lexington, MA: D. C. Heath, 1995), p. 532.

61. Estrada et al., "Chicanos in the United States," p. 40.

62. Lawrence Fuchs, *The American Kaleidoscope: Race, Ethnicity, and the Civic Culture* (Hanover, NH: Wesleyan University Press, 1990), pp. 118–122; Takaki, *A Different Mirror*, p. 317.

63. Ibid.; Alfreda Iglehart and Rosina Becerra, *Social Services and the Ethnic Community* (Boston: Allyn and Bacon, 1995), pp. 51–57, 159; Ronald Takaki, *A Different Mirror*, pp. 336–339.

64. Fuchs, *The American Kaleidoscope*, pp. 120–122; Takaki, *A Different Mirror*, pp. 331–334.

65. Thomas Dyer, *Theodore Roosevelt and the Idea of Race* (Baton Rouge, LA: Louisiana State University Press, 1980), pp. 21–44, 105; Gable, *The Bull Moose Years*, p. 74; Dittmer, *Black Georgia*, pp. 108–109.

66. Dittmer, *Black Georgia*, pp. 181, 186.

67. Steamer, *The Supreme Court*, pp. 125–126, 149–150.

68. Steven Diner, "Chicago Social Workers and Blacks in the Progressive Era," *Social Service Review*, 44 (December 1970), pp. 231–236; Levine, *Jane Addams*, pp. 192–194.

69. Fuchs, *The American Kaleidoscope*, p. 16; John Higham, *Strangers in the Land: Patterns of American Nativism, 1860–1925* (New York: Atheneum, 1972), pp. 106–130, 158–193.

70. Higham, *Strangers in the Land*, p. 108.

71. Ibid., p. 159.

72. Ibid., p. 110; Estrada et al., "Chicanos in the United States," p. 44.

73. Walter Trattner, *From Poor Law to Welfare State*, 4th ed. (New York: Free Press, 1991), pp. 213–214.

74. Stanley Wenocur and Michael Reisch, *From Charity to Enterprise: The Development of American Social Work in a Market Economy* (Urbana, IL: University of Illinois Press, 1989), pp. 50–52.

75. Ibid., pp. 47–60.

76. Mary Richmond, *Social Diagnosis* (New York: Russell Sage Foundation, 1917).

77. Wenocur and Reisch, *From Charity to Enterprise*, pp. 77–78.

78. James Burrow, *Organized Medicine in the Progressive Era* (Baltimore: Johns Hopkins University Press, 1977), pp. 32–66; Ronald Numbers, *Almost Persuaded: American Physicians and Compulsory Health Insurance* (Baltimore: Johns Hopkins University Press, 1979), pp. 4–5.

79. Trattner, *From Poor Law to Welfare State*, pp. 198–200.

80. Gable, *The Bull Moose Years*, pp. 82, 93.

7

Social Policy to Address the Worst Economic Catastrophe in U.S. History

TABLE 7.1   Selected Orienting Events

1921–1923	Presidency of Warren Harding
1925–1928	Presidency of Calvin Coolidge
1929	Stock market crashes; Great Depression begins
1929–1932	Presidency of Herbert Hoover
1932	Reconstruction Finance Corporation established; Emergency Relief and Construction Act passed
1933–1945	Presidency of Franklin Roosevelt
1933	Civilian Conservation Corps (CCC), Agricultural Adjustment Agency (AAA), Public Works Administration (PWA), and Federal Emergency Relief Administration (FERA) established; Civilian Works Administration (CWA) established by executive order; Tennessee Valley Authority (TVA) created; Emergency Farm Mortgage Act and Farm Relief Act enacted
1934	Securities and Exchange Commission (SEC) created; CWA terminated by Roosevelt
1934	Committee on Economic Security established by Roosevelt
1935	FERA terminated; Social Security Act passed, with its constituent programs of Aid to Dependent Children (ADC), Old-Age Assistance (OAA), Aid to the Blind (AB), unemployment insurance, Social Security, child welfare, and public health programs; Supreme Court declares the National Recovery Administration (NRA) to be unconstitutional; Senator Huey Long assassinated; Works Progress Administration (WPA) established

TABLE 7.1   (continued)

1936	Father Coughlin and Francis Townsend support the Union Party; Congress of Industrial Organizations (CIO) founded; passage of Wagner Act establishing the National Labor Relations Board; Supreme Court declares the AAA to be unconstitutional; Roosevelt wins landslide victory for his second term
1937	Deep recession ends nation's economic recovery; Wagner-Steagall Housing Act passed
1938	Fair Labor Standards Act enacted
1939	Federal Security Agency established
Early 1940s	CCC, WPA, and the National Youth Administration (NYA) terminated
1940	Roosevelt elected to third term
1941	America enters World War II; Executive Order 8802 prohibits discrimination in war industry
1942	Some 120,000 persons of Japanese ancestry evacuated to relocation centers
1945	Roosevelt dies and is succeeded by Harry Truman

The Great Depression of the 1930s was the worst economic catastrophe in American history. Could the still-primitive American welfare state find ways to address the social needs of a population devastated by this catastrophe—and at a time when knowledge about how to restore economic growth was scant?

Social policy was transformed during this decade as Americans finally fashioned a series of social reforms that far surpassed the local and regulatory reforms of the Progressive Era and brought the federal government into a position of policy prominence. Governmental institutions, the presidency, politics, and the courts were also transformed during this fateful decade.

Bold as its reforms were by the standards of preceding decades, the social reforms of the 1930s were far too timid to address the nation's social needs—or to end the Great Depression.

Reforms during and immediately after the Great Depression can best be understood by analyzing the unfolding of reform in five periods:

1.   During the *era of denial* (1929 to March 1933), Americans were so stunned by the economic catastrophe that they took little corrective action.

2.   During the *period of emergency reforms* (March 1933 to January 1935), Americans supported a bewildering number of reforms but tended to believe that prosperity would soon return and that these reforms were temporary.

3.   During the *era of institutionalized reform* (January 1935 to January 1937), Americans made a number of reforms permanent.

4.   During an *era of policy stalemate* (January 1937 to December 1941), the momentum of New Deal reform was decisively broken.

5.   During the *era of pullback* in World War II (December 1941 to August 1945), many of the New Deal programs were rescinded, but a core of New Deal reforms remained intact and became the foundation of the modern American welfare state.

At the end of this chapter, we discuss what we can learn in contemporary society about policy advocacy, social policy, and the structure of the American welfare state from the worst economic catastrophe in U.S. history.

THE 1920s

The progressive reform momentum was shattered when Americans focused on preparations for World

War I, the war effort, and postwar diplomacy, including an ill-fated League of Nations, although this period did yield a few reforms, such as federal directives requiring recipients of war contracts not to use child labor.[1] In the 1920s, as in the 1950s and the 1980s, many Americans believed that economic activity carried out by private enterprise, left unfettered by government, would bring unlimited prosperity. The nation was presided over by three Republican presidents, Warren Harding, Calvin Coolidge, and Herbert Hoover, who strenuously resisted efforts of a small cadre of social reformers.[2] Harding stated his philosophy succinctly when he said, "What we want in America is less government in business and more business in government."

A second American industrial revolution occurred during the 1920s. Steel, mining, and railroad industries had developed during the first revolution; the second focused on consumer products—such as cars, radios, and refrigerators—and on the electrification of homes and industries. Enormous consumer needs remained unmet in the United States; only one in 10 urban homes was electrified in 1920; only one in 100 households possessed radios; and only one in three families had cars. Consumer appetites for new products were whetted by the rise of a large advertising industry.[3]

A trickle-down economic philosophy was dominant. Officials believed that economic assistance to affluent persons and industry stimulated investments that could bring jobs to poor and working-class Americans. The low tariffs of the prewar era were supplanted by protective tariffs for American industry; federal taxes had been increased to pay off the national debt in the wake of World War I, but new tax laws reduced them to one-quarter of their previous level; and many regulations that had been enacted during the Progressive Era were relaxed, not implemented, or struck down by the courts.[4] Policies that empowered industry and affluent persons were supplemented by vigorous suppression of organized labor. Companies sought to obtain the goodwill of employees by developing stock-sharing schemes, providing fringe benefits, and starting company unions that ostensibly gave workers a mechanism for negotiating higher benefits and wages.

When unions tried to organize, their leaders were often intimidated or fired—and strikes led to unabashed use of scabs, local police, the National Guard, and injunctions from courts that were usually favorable to management.[5]

Social reformers were on the defensive during the 1920s; some were stigmatized as radicals, communists, or traitors. African Americans continued to live under oppressive Jim Crow laws in the South, encountered race riots and residential segregation in the North, and found it difficult to obtain jobs in the industries that were now producing consumer goods in the second industrial revolution. Although African Americans were a significant presence in many Northern cities, most continued to work for white planters in the South.[6] Latinos and Asian Americans continued to experience rampant prejudice and adverse policies in the West and Southwest.[7] Women experienced new sexual freedoms in the era of the flapper, but found that their voting privileges did not lead to major policy reforms that would give them access to more remunerative work or to the professions.[8]

Americans were intrigued by social change and often tended to glamorize technology and science, but they were also fearful of new ideas; in the famous Scopes trial in 1925, for example, a schoolteacher was successfully prosecuted for teaching the theory of evolution in a Tennessee school. (The verdict was later overturned on a technicality.) Prohibition, enacted in the form of the Eighteenth Amendment to the Constitution in 1919, was supported by many Protestants, who insisted that local and federal officials strictly enforce the legislation.[9] Many Americans supported stringent reductions of immigration, whether on racial grounds or because they believed the nation could no longer absorb immigrants. The Immigration Act of 1924 was blatantly racist; its goal was to maintain the "racial preponderance [of] the basic strain of our people." A limit of 150,000 people was placed on immigration each year, with quotas for each nationality in proportion to its size in the existing population. This policy was intended to reduce the proportion of immigrants from southern and eastern Europe. A complete prohibition was placed on Japanese immigration.[10]

In contrast to these conservative reforms, which sought to restore traditional American values, there was a new interest in exploring sexual liberation and the psyche. Sigmund Freud was not taken seriously in his native Europe, but his theories—though not immediately adopted by social work practitioners—swept America, much as those of Herbert Spencer had done in the Gilded Age.[11]

The profession of social work grew rapidly during the 1920s. By 1929, 25 graduate schools existed, several professional associations had developed, and three journals disseminated information. Casework emerged as the central skill during the decade; its practitioners outnumbered other kinds of social workers by a threefold margin. Mary Richmond's classic treatise during the Progressive Era had emphasized familial, neighborhood, and societal realities, but in the 1920s, some caseworkers became excited about the personality—so much so that they risked ignoring environmental realities as well as the need for social reforms. Caseworkers tended to be employed in not-for-profit agencies and were often relatively contemptuous of public agencies, which, they believed, should aid only paupers and persons with chronic and severe mental conditions.[12] Some still proposed more fundamental reforms, but they were decidedly on the fringes of American society.

Surface impressions of prosperity in the 1920s were misleading because unemployment ranged from 5 to 13 percent, and agriculture was in a state of depression throughout the decade. Although the upper third of the populace conspicuously consumed consumer products, the lower third were often unemployed or lived near or below the poverty level in a society that had few governmental income transfer programs.[13]

THE ECONOMIC
CATASTROPHE BEGINS

The Great Depression began with the collapse of the stock market in October 1929. A speculative frenzy during the 1920s had led to higher and higher stock prices, with many investors relying on credit for stock purchases. When stock prices plunged, panicked investors rushed to sell their stocks—leading to even greater declines in stock prices. The panic soon spread beyond the stock market to banks, which had also overextended themselves by making loans without retaining sufficient reserves. As the word spread about the banks' growing insolvency, people rushed to take their savings from them—adding to the banks' insolvency. With the collapse of the stock markets and banks, the rest of the economy was doomed. As consumers lacked resources to purchase goods and services, businesses slashed prices to encourage consumption of their products—a strategy that lowered their profits and forced them to lay off workers. As unemployment precipitously rose to encompass 25 percent of all workers, demand for products declined yet further and precipitated even more layoffs, creating a vicious circle.

Persons of all social classes were devastated by economic suffering and resorted to desperate and improvisational survival strategies. Some moved into tents in the countryside during the summer; three or more families shared apartments; groups of single women shared apartments and lived from the wages of a single worker; people tried to grow produce in gardens; and teenagers roamed the countryside when their families could not support them. Lorena Hickok, a reporter who was commissioned by Eleanor Roosevelt to tour the country in a car, documented the suffering of members of all social classes in daily letters to the First Lady.[14] White-collar Americans feared foreclosure or evictions, had to pawn family possessions, were ashamed that their neighbors might discover they were on relief, and shunned clothes made in the sewing rooms of relief programs. Malnutrition and starvation were widely reported; and thousands of children were placed in summer camps to give them adequate food. Medical care was lacking for members of all classes, as many physicians and hospitals refused service to persons with no money. Even on welfare, many individuals lacked funds to heat or light their homes or to purchase clothing. Foreclosures, evictions, layoffs, family disruption, and suicides were commonplace. When touring major American cities in 1932, Harry Hopkins observed that the hundreds of thousands of Americans who lined the streets to watch FDR's procession did not protest, yell, or applaud but stood in stunned silence.[15] This widespread suffering persisted throughout the decade, despite periodic upturns in the economy. (See Figure 7.1.) Even when the economy improved slightly, however, vast numbers of persons could not find employment. When Congress impatiently imposed a rule in 1939 that no one could receive more than 18 months of work relief, investigators found that more than two-thirds of recipients had to return to work relief because they could not find jobs.[16]

Controversy exists about the precise causes of the Great Depression in 1929.[17] Some theorists contend that the nation's economic expansion was halted because industry and affluent persons had insufficient capital at their disposal. However, the aforementioned trickle-down policies placed vast sums of money in the coffers of affluent persons

© Corbis

FIGURE 7.1 Malnutrition during the Great Depression.

and corporations. Other theorists argue convincingly that the Great Depression occurred because the majority of American consumers lacked sufficient resources to purchase consumer goods. Some economists implicate excessive speculation and protective tariffs. Whatever its precise causes, the Great Depression of 1929, like the depression of 1893, put an immediate and decisive halt to prosperity, suggested that trickle-down policies were not a panacea, and alerted Americans to the realities of poverty, unemployment, and economic injustice.

THE PERIOD OF DENIAL:
1929–1933

The immediate reality of massive unemployment, depressed stock prices, lost fortunes, bankrupt companies, and deflated prices was obvious to everyone in 1929, including Herbert Hoover, the incumbent president. Americans had experienced many economic downturns in their history; however, most persons assumed that economic growth would resume.

Herbert Hoover at first seemed ideally suited to solve the nation's problems. A civil engineer who had orchestrated a massive food relief program for starving Europeans after World War I, he prided himself on a problem-solving style in which political considerations were given little role. He believed, like most Americans, that modest tinkering with the economic system would bring the nation out of its economic doldrums. In accordance with trickle-down economics, he favored passage of the Reconstruction Finance Corporation (RFC), which processed $2 billion for loans to corporations and banks, as well as various projects to encourage economic activity by bankers and corporations. To appease critics, and because he did not believe in major governmental programs, however, Hoover implemented these policies in a restrictive manner; he insisted, for example, that corporations and banks prove that they were on the verge of bankruptcy before they would be eligible for loans under the RFC.[18]

Hoover also believed that private agencies, principally the Red Cross and family service agencies, could address the needs of unemployed and poverty-stricken Americans without governmental assistance. He shared Franklin Pierce's ideology—enunciated in the Pierce veto of nearly a century earlier—that welfare issues belonged to local government and to private philanthropy. Some historians have emphasized progressive elements of Hoover's ideology, but the preponderance of evidence suggests that he was an inflexible conservative who adhered to Social Darwinism and equated federal social programs with socialism.[19]

Hoover's measures did not address the mounting economic needs of local governments, which were moving toward bankruptcy as their welfare expenditures increased. Pressure from the Congress to help local governments finally led to passage of the Emergency Relief and Construction Act in 1932, which authorized federal loans to local governments that could prove they had become bankrupt. However, as the depression worsened, some Americans began to wonder whether more drastic measures were needed. A small group of liberal politicians in the House and the Senate proposed measures that seemed radical to many Americans, such as federal funding of major public works projects; the development of federally funded employment offices; federal funding of unemployment and old age insurance; the development of dams; and reforestation projects to create jobs and economic growth in rural areas.[20] Senators Robert Wagner of New York, Robert La Follette of Wisconsin, and Edward Costigan of Colorado led this small cadre of reformers. They drew from some proposals fashioned in the 1920s by the American Association of Old Age Security, a reform group headed by Isaac Rubinow, who introduced to the United States concepts of social insurance that had been pioneered in Europe.[21] Even relatively conservative big-city bosses, such as Mayor James Curley of Boston, urged job creation and public works programs that went beyond the timid measures of Hoover.[22]

Hoover became more conservative, however, as the nation gradually moved toward more liberal ideas. An inflexible man who was isolated from, and insensitive to, political realities, he resorted to budget balancing and various monetary solutions to

---

INSERT 7.1   Critical Analysis: Which Social Problems Are Recognized?

When Hoover failed to recognize the extent and duration of unemployment from 1929 onward, he illustrated a recurring tendency of policy makers to deny the existence of important problems.

1. Identify some major social problems in recent American history that policy makers failed to recognize or to take seriously.
2. Identify other social problems that policy makers *did* take seriously (for example, by proposing major legislation or allocating major funding to address them).

3. What political, cultural, economic, or other factors seem to make policy makers deny some problems while taking others seriously?
4. Can advocates for specific social problems speed up the clock? In other words, is there some way they can gain policy makers' attention more promptly? (See circle 3 in the Policy Advocacy Framework in Figure 2.1, which discusses the agenda-building task of policy advocates.)

---

complement his woefully inadequate programs. He bitterly attacked liberals for advocating policies that he viewed as socialistic measures that would compound the nation's economic problems.[23] (See Insert 7.1.)

The nation's confidence in business—and in Hoover—began to waver by 1930. Hoover had won a sweeping victory in 1928, but the Republican Party suffered such extensive losses in the congressional elections of 1930 that its majority was reduced to a narrow margin. Most Democrats were as confused by the situation as Hoover, however, as they, too, tended to favor budget cutting, tax reduction, and trickle-down economics to cope with the depression. Though many social workers supported Roosevelt, Jane Addams and some other reformers voted for Hoover in the pivotal election of 1932.[24]

THE EMERGENCE OF FRANKLIN ROOSEVELT AS A NATIONAL LEADER

Franklin Delano Roosevelt was an unlikely person to develop the most sweeping social reforms that the nation had yet seen. He was born into an affluent family in New York State. He seemed destined to have a distinguished political career when he became assistant secretary of the navy under President Woodrow Wilson, but it was cut short when he developed polio in 1921—a devastating disease that meant he could no longer walk without assistance from others and from heavy apparatus tied to his legs. Aware that public knowledge of his malady would jeopardize his political future, he and his family carefully concealed his disease even up to the last months of his presidency in early 1945. Above all, Roosevelt strove to give the *appearance* that he could walk—finally mastering this deception by relying on his arms to support himself on two men on each side of him as he approached a podium.

Although his illness was a personal tragedy, polio also transformed Roosevelt. His experience made him more sensitive to others whose lives were devastated by polio and other problems such as poverty.[25] He expended a considerable share of his personal wealth to develop a place where persons with polio could get physical therapy for the illness in Warm Springs, Georgia.

He was married, moreover, to a remarkable woman—Eleanor Roosevelt—who pushed and prodded him continually not only to continue his political career, but to use his power to help others, including women, African Americans, and unemployed persons. She maintained contact with political leaders in New York State as he recovered in the years after he developed polio, allowing him to successfully run for the governorship of New York State in 1928. His governorship was highly successful and positioned him to successfully seek the nomination of the Democratic Party for the presidency in 1932, running against incumbent Herbert Hoover.

Franklin Delano Roosevelt (FDR) was not intrinsically a radical, however, and he even disliked persons with strong ideologies on the left or the right. Rather, he was a liberal pragmatist who also had some reservations about large ongoing public programs. As a pragmatist, he was acutely aware of the political context in which he worked, so he took a relatively conservative posture in the presidential campaign of 1932. While he expressed more sympathy for the unemployed than did Hoover and talked vaguely of reforestation schemes, he advocated a balanced budget and conservative fiscal policies and even derided Hoover for spending too much federal money.

However, Roosevelt was different from Hoover even before he became president. He was an innovator, willing to experiment with new initiatives to deal with the massive suffering of unemployed persons until he found something that worked. He carefully slipped into his campaign speeches a proviso that he would have to spend sufficient federal money to avert "dire suffering and starvation" even if that meant running federal deficits. He had already spent large amounts of federal resources as a public official. He had participated in the mobilization of national resources by the federal government as assistant secretary of the navy in World War I. As governor of New York State between 1928 and 1932, he had initiated the Temporary Emergency Relief Administration (TERA) to provide state funds to local units of government for outdoor relief to the unemployed. He knew many social workers, including Frances Perkins, who headed the Labor Department, and Harry Hopkins, who had worked in private philanthropic agencies and directed the TERA.

Roosevelt and the Democrats won a sweeping victory in 1932 primarily because, after three ineffectual Republican presidents in the 1920s, Americans wanted to give the Democrats a chance to address the nation's problems. Roosevelt's infectious optimism was appealing to Americans during a time of trouble, presenting a sharp contrast to Hoover's dour demeanor.

THE ERA OF EMERGENCY REFORMS: 1933–1935

When Franklin Roosevelt won his decisive victory in November of 1932, policy drift was no longer possible because the banking system was threatened with collapse owing to insufficient funds to cover withdrawals of panic-stricken depositors. Local governments encountered staggering welfare burdens because 20 to 60 percent of Americans were unemployed in many cities and neighborhoods. Millions of Americans, many of them youths whose parents could no longer support them, roamed the nation, obtained beans, coffee, and floor space from local police, and were told to move on the next day. Economic inequality, which had always been severe, became even more obvious at a time when unskilled and uneducated persons and people of color were massively unemployed. Many farmers lost their farms as they suffered catastrophic losses in a worldwide depression of prices of agricultural produce. Still other farmers fled an extraordinary drought that had developed in Oklahoma and adjacent states, a region that became known as the Dust Bowl.[26]

American business was in disarray. Prices of products decreased as demand plummeted and as exports were slashed because of the depressed economies of European nations. Consumer demand decreased further when employers reduced their workforces. Businesses went bankrupt as they slashed their prices in a desperate effort to retain customers. The suicide rate of investors, bankers, and company executives rose sharply.[27] Unions, which had made slow but steady progress in the late 1920s, went into virtual collapse since most workers were too desperate for jobs to contest employers' wage-cutting policies.

Roosevelt knew that if he followed Hoover's course of timid reforms, the Great Depression would almost certainly continue. He also knew that people would actually die from starvation or be seriously harmed if he did not spend huge amounts of federal resources to get them money that they could use to meet their survival needs.

Caught between American dislike of federal deficits and big government and the human suffering

---

INSERT 7.2   Using the Web to Understand How Americans Fashioned Social Reforms During the Great Depression

---

Visit **academic.cengage.com/social_work/jansson** to view these links and a variety of study tools.

> Go to **http://www.loc.gov** Click on "American Memory." Click on "Government, Law" and proceed to "Depression Era to World War II." Click on "FSA/OWI Photographs" and examine photographs.

Go to **http://www.archives.gov/education/ lessons** Go to "Era 1929–1945."

- Proceed to FDR's first inaugural address declaring "War" on the Great Depression.

- Proceed to "FDR's Fireside Chat on the Purposes and Foundation of the Recovery Program."

- Proceed to "Photographs and Documents Related to the Japanese Relocation during World War II."

Go to **http://newdeal.feri.org/hopkins/hop26.htm** Click on a report to Harry Hopkins on conditions in Buffalo in November of 1934. What does this report tell us about the severity of human suffering during the Great Depression?

Go to **http://newdeal.feri.org/speeches/1934g .htm** Click on a speech by Franklin Roosevelt that discusses how he established the center for treating polio at Warm Springs, Georgia in the 1920s. How does the speech cast light on FDR's character and motivation when he became president during the Great Depression?

Go to **http://newdeal.feri.org/Texts** Click on subject and view documents from the New Deal for your state. (If you cannot find your state listed, select a nearby state.) What insights did you obtain about social, economic, and political developments from reading three or four documents?

Go to **http://www.uwm.edu/Dept/ETI/pages/ surveys/each/wlsf95.htm** to read about workers' relief in Milwaukee County.

---

caused by the Great Depression, Roosevelt displayed a side of his persona that became his lasting legacy: a proactive ability to put forward unprecedented federal initiatives in an improvisational manner. Yet his reforms were tempered by conservative forces in the context in which he worked. The actual reforms that were enacted in 1933 and 1934 can be understood only in the context of this set of contradictory forces.

The Conflicted Context: Forces That Promoted Major Reforms

Roosevelt's sweeping personal victory in 1932 was the largest plurality a president had received since 1864, and it provided him with a power base during the remainder of the decade. The progressives' dream of a relatively liberal political party, which failed in 1912, was partially realized when Roosevelt obtained the votes of an unprecedented proportion of working-class citizens who wanted government to take an active stance in addressing unemployment and poverty. (Republicans, by contrast, obtained most of their support from middle- and upper-class voters.) This substantial realignment of parties on the basis of social class, which continued throughout the 1930s and into succeeding decades, was crucial to the development of social reforms in the Roosevelt administration and beyond.[28]

Roosevelt had extraordinary power because he had gained support not only from the working class but also from a sizable portion of the middle class, to whom Roosevelt appealed because he exuded confidence, because they no longer believed that Republicans could solve the economic problems of the nation, and because many of them had been directly affected by the depression.[29] As the Progressive Era had demonstrated, major reform cannot take place until considerable support exists within the American middle class so as to offset opposition from corporations, affluent persons, conservatives, and middle-class persons who oppose reforms.

The strongest pressure for reform derived, however, from the magnitude of human suffering that existed during the 1930s. It is not possible for persons in contemporary society to grasp the extent of this economic catastrophe, which affected persons of all races and social classes, persons of all ages, and both rural and urban Americans. Used to relatively brief recessions, we also must struggle to comprehend an economic catastrophe that lasted more than a decade —finally lifting only in 1941. Anyone who attacked New Deal programs was countered by the harsh realities that Americans confronted—including the constituents of conservative legislators from both parties. Roosevelt's freedom of action was enhanced by the disarray of Republicans and conservatives following his overwhelming defeat of Hoover.[30] Business interests, which had traditionally provided considerable support for conservative politicians, were discredited by the economic collapse because their speculation and greed were widely perceived as one of its causes. The catastrophe of the Depression shook the nation to its foundations, making residents want bold leaders willing to contemplate policies that would have been unthinkable several years earlier.

Roosevelt and his aides were often in disarray themselves, but they came into office with relatively well-developed ideas and many areas of consensus.[31] They rejected Thomas Jefferson's belief that the federal government should mostly attend to international affairs, as well as Adam Smith's laissez-faire economics and John Locke's restricted definition of government—beliefs that had dominated American politics from 1800 to the Great Depression save for the interlude of the Progressive Era. Roosevelt and his inner circle of advisors—the so-called "brain trust"—did not know the precise solutions, but they reasoned that interventions could be devised in a trial-and-error fashion until something worked.

Nor should we forget the crucial role played by Roosevelt's wife, Eleanor. She pressured him, almost nonstop, to attend to an endless list of domestic needs. She placed notes in a box near his bed so that he could read her social reform suggestions as he retired in the evening—prompting him at one point to plead that she restrict her suggestions to a specific number per day so that he could respond to all of them!

The Conflicted Context: Forces That Limited Roosevelt's Initial Policy Initiatives

Roosevelt realized that conservatives were a potential threat to social reforms. The conservative National Economic League had fought even the limited reforms of the Hoover administration. Although many businessmen supported specific pieces of New Deal legislation, they tended to be suspicious of Roosevelt both for his rhetoric—he often singled out the wealthy, bankers, and speculators for criticism—and for his expansion of federal power. The U.S. Chamber of Commerce stoutly resisted reforms in local and national arenas.[32]

Roosevelt encountered formidable political opposition from both political parties throughout the decade. Co-opted by corporate interests during the 1920s, the leadership of the Democratic Party favored high tariffs, limited assistance to poor persons, and a small federal bureaucracy. Roosevelt's victory over Newton Baker in the Democratic convention in 1932 was a decisive blow to this traditional leadership, but it maintained a strong—and hostile—presence in the party and often opposed Roosevelt's initiatives.[33]

In the early 1930s, most churches were profoundly conservative; Boston clergy from most faiths, for example, opposed federal and state programs to help the poor.[34] Many leaders of the Catholic Church became staunch defenders of the New Deal, but its bishops nonetheless opposed passage of child labor regulations, which they believed interfered with the privacy of the family.[35] Even though more than half the American population lived in cities during the 1930s, local, state, and national legislatures were dominated by rural legislators, who were often insensitive to the needs of city dwellers.[36]

Labor leaders tended to take a lukewarm stance toward social reforms during the New Deal because they were preoccupied with securing the right to organize. At the start of the decade, fewer than 3 million American workers were organized (which was 2 million fewer than in 1920), and most were skilled workers in various American Federation of Labor (AFL) craft unions. In the early 1930s, considerable unrest developed among assembly-line workers and miners under the leadership of men such as John L. Lewis, who headed the United Mine Workers. But the AFL eyed these unskilled workers nervously because they were unlikely candidates for skilled electrical, carpentry, and other unions. Prompted by worker unrest, and sensing that the New Deal provided workers with a less hostile environment than they had encountered under prior administrations, Lewis impatiently prodded the AFL to allocate resources to unions of unskilled workers. In 1936, giving up on the AFL, he formed the Congress of Industrial Organizations (CIO), which finally provided a home for steel, auto, mining, and other unions.

But the bloody strikes and the sheer effort of organizing these unions meant that Lewis and others devoted limited effort to securing broader social reforms for American workers. Indeed, in roughly one-half of the strikes during the New Deal, the goal was to obtain the right to form a union rather than to secure higher wages.[37] By 1936, labor had become the major single contributor to the campaigns of Roosevelt, but labor was uncertain in its support for some New Deal legislation and was hampered by internal dissension.[38] The AFL maintained a relatively conservative posture throughout the decade, sometimes even arguing that government work programs represented forced labor even as it often fought opportunistically to obtain jobs in government programs for its own members. It rarely initiated policy ideas and even feared the development of governmental policies that might facilitate the organizing of unskilled workers by rival unions in automobile, steel, and other plants.[39]

The specter of adverse rulings by the Supreme Court hung over the New Deal from the outset. The Court had declared federal child labor legislation to be unconstitutional in 1918, on the grounds that the federal government's power to regulate interstate commerce was not applicable in that case. In the New Deal era, four of the justices, known as the four horsemen, consistently opposed federal social legislation on the grounds that it was not an enumerated power in the Constitution; when joined by two moderate justices, they were able to overrule social legislation. (Only three relatively liberal justices were on the Court.)[40]

The United States also lacked fiscal and governmental institutions to implement sweeping reforms. The federal income tax was initiated in 1913, but taxes had been drastically cut during the 1920s and only modestly increased by the Federal Revenue Act of 1932; less than 5 percent of Americans paid a federal income tax even after this legislation. The government financed social welfare programs by running deficits in its budget, but many Americans, including some of Roosevelt's advisors, believed that deficits exacerbated the economic problems of the nation.[41] A federal civil service system was in place, but federal bureaucracies were relatively small in 1932 and riddled with patronage and corruption. When Frances Perkins was appointed secretary of labor, for example, she found that many of its top officials were receiving payoffs in return for obtaining immigration papers and visas for political supporters; they were hoping she would stay away from her office so that they could continue to receive these payoffs.[42] Local governmental institutions were even more archaic. Many public welfare offices, for example, were staffed by cronies of local politicians; welfare funds often found their way into the pockets of politicians; and punitive policies, such as publicizing the names of recipients, were used in some jurisdictions.[43]

Legislatures at national and local levels and even the presidency itself were unpromising vehicles for social reform. Many state legislatures met only every two years and busied themselves primarily with pork barrel and patronage matters. The Congress was saddled with a seniority system that rewarded older, Southern, and conservative legislators who chaired key committees. Committees generally lacked staffs to help them analyze legislation and develop positions. Patronage was frequently entangled with policy; when legislators or presidents broached policy recommendations, it was often assumed that their major motivation was to secure patronage jobs for loyal supporters.[44] The institution of the presidency was unequipped to develop policy. The presidency had become a symbolic post during the 1920s, when presidents satisfied themselves with budget-balancing and patronage functions. Roosevelt dramatically changed the presidency from a symbolic institution to a policy-initiating institution in his first year, when he presented a full legislative package to the Congress.[45]

Another factor that slowed the pace of reform was the absence of a well-developed radical movement in the United States such as existed in the stronger union and socialist movements in Europe in the 1920s and 1930s. When a challenge from the left did develop in 1934 and 1935 (which we shall discuss later), it was poorly organized and focused primarily on the personal agendas of charismatic leaders.[46] Local organizations of unemployed persons sprang up spontaneously in many localities, but their national impact was limited because they were not nationally coordinated, and their emphasis was on obtaining higher benefits from existing work and relief programs.[47] Local agricultural protest movements flourished but also focused on improving the benefits provided by existing programs, as well as on the implementation of policies to stem the tide of foreclosures. No alliances formed between groups that represented urban workers and distressed persons in rural areas; indeed, many farmers turned against the New Deal in the late 1930s because they resented its emphasis on urban reforms.[48]

Reform momentum was also impeded by dissension among Roosevelt's advisors, some of whom favored conservative policies. The inner circle of advisors included budget-conscious persons, such as Henry Morgenthau (secretary of the Treasury) and Lewis Douglas (director of the Bureau of the Budget), who sought to reduce social spending and often contended with Harry Hopkins (Roosevelt's most powerful social welfare advisor), who favored increasing social spending, even when it required massive deficits. Some advisors, such as Frances Perkins, sought federal policies that ceded major policy roles to the states, in contrast to advisors like Harry Hopkins, who tended to favor federal policy roles. Louis Brandeis, the attorney general, believed that a trust-busting strategy should be used, whereas Senator Robert Wagner, a key ally of Roosevelt, believed trust-busting hurt economic growth. Roosevelt often received contradictory advice and was himself confused about various issues, such as the merits of deficit spending.[49]

We have mentioned, as well, that Roosevelt was not a radical. He did not favor the ongoing assumption of major welfare programs by the federal government; he liked social insurance programs that were funded by payroll deductions rather than from general revenues; and he often acceded to advisors who advocated cuts in social programs to decrease federal deficits.[50]

Finally, Southern Democrats chaired the major committees of Congress and constituted a substantial voting bloc in the Democratic Party. Throughout the decade, Roosevelt realized that his social reforms could be enacted only if he kept the support of these conservative legislators, who might otherwise form a majority of the chamber if they voted with Republicans.

Battling for Resources as a Prelude to Reform

Roosevelt's greatest challenge in developing social reforms to help millions of unemployed persons was to find resources to fund them. He knew that he could not easily raise taxes in a nation that disliked them. He knew that even the revenues from the small federal taxes had been halved to only $2 billion by the Great Depression as businesses went bankrupt and as taxable income of citizens dwindled. He knew that the federal government already faced a deficit from the Hoover presidency—and that many Americans opposed increasing this deficit even to help destitute people. And he knew that no precedent existed in the United States for large peacetime spending in a nation whose federal budget totaled only $4.2 billion in 1933 or merely 10.8 percent of the GNP as compared to more than 20 percent in contemporary America.

So Roosevelt developed a clever strategy to disguise his intention to increase federal spending and to diminish political opposition to vast new expenditures once he launched the New Deal. He only vaguely suggested he might have to increase spending to relieve "starvation and dire suffering" during his campaign in 1932. Drawing upon the advice of an advisor, he segregated "emergency spending" from the "regular" or ordinary budget of the government soon after he took office. (If the emergency budget would consist of spending to relieve the suffering of unemployed people, the regular budget funded the ongoing costs of government, such as the War Department and the Post Office.) If the emergency budget would be funded by government borrowing through the sale of bonds to investors, the regular budget would be funded by tax revenues.

This division of government finances into two budgets allowed Roosevelt to promise simultaneously to balance the (regular) budget while seeking billions of dollars of funds for federal relief and work relief programs throughout the 1930s in the second (emergency) budget. Roosevelt *did* balance the regular budget by periodically cutting the spending of programs funded by it—often boasting to conservatives who opposed his "big spending" that he *was* a fiscal conservative. At the same time, he more than doubled spending of the federal government by expanding his emergency budget that was funded by the sale of bonds outside the regular budget process.

It was a politically ingenious strategy. When conservatives complained that he was spending excessively, he would cut spending in the regular budget, usually balancing it by cutting spending on veterans' programs, slashing the number of federal employees, cutting the War Department, and achieving many additional economies—while simultaneously incurring huge deficits to fund the emergency budget. Yet he frequently obtained funds for the emergency budget that funded New Deal programs—an emergency budget that usually exceeded the size of the regular budget. The New Deal was, in short, financed by borrowing and deficits, more than doubling the size of the annual federal budget from $4 billion to roughly $8 billion. If only 20 percent of the federal budget had been devoted to social programs when Roosevelt took office, more than 50 percent was devoted to work relief and relief programs from 1934 through 1939.

Even as they complained about Roosevelt's unprecedented spending, conservatives were poorly positioned to attack it because huge numbers of *their* constituents were unemployed and needed assistance from New Deal programs. They often voted almost unanimously to approve the sale of bonds to finance the emergency budget.

Using the Funds to Finance Emergency Relief

Having solved the problem of resources, Roosevelt immediately created unprecedented social programs to address "dire suffering" as he had promised during his campaign of 1932. He began creating the Federal Emergency Relief Administration (FERA) in early 1933 to address the plight of many states and localities that verged on bankruptcy because of mounting welfare costs and diminished revenues. It provided funds to states for persons who needed financial assistance and was virtually a carbon copy, though on a larger scale, of the Temporary Emergency Relief Administration (TERA) that Roosevelt had developed in New York.[51]

The legislation did not give a carte blanche to state and local governments. Hopkins, who was placed in charge of the FERA by Roosevelt, was a man of strong convictions who realized that poor law traditions in states and localities were often punitive, particularly to persons capable of working—the very group that now comprised the bulk of the population that needed welfare. He was also incensed by the orientations of many private agencies, which insisted on intensive casework screening of applicants as a condition of relief at a time when tens of millions of Americans were unemployed through no fault of their own. Hopkins did not hold the widespread belief that the poor should receive in-kind relief or food vouchers to prevent them from spending welfare funds on alcohol, tobacco, and other luxuries. If wealthy persons can drink martinis, he asked, why not allow poor persons to drink beer? Hopkins also realized that firm federal administration of relief giving would be needed if corruption and patronage were to be avoided. He did not want intensive casework to be used with recipients, but he wanted trained social workers to be hired in supervisory positions, so as to enhance the professionalism of welfare services and provide services to those who needed them.[52]

The subsequent legislation, which evolved in the course of consultations between Hopkins, Perkins, Senator Robert Wagner, and Roosevelt, contained provisions to minimize these various dangers. It required each state to designate a state commission that was separate from the existing welfare apparatus, both to underscore the temporary nature of the federal assistance and to establish new agencies that would not be punitive. The state commissions were required to establish offices in the various counties and to establish uniform eligibility processes to be used throughout the state. Federal officials had veto power over high-level appointments, to guard against patronage appointments, and required the use of social workers in key supervisory positions. The legislation gave federal authorities the right to federalize FERA programs in states where irregularities such as corruption or excessive patronage were discovered. It authorized $500 million in federal aid to destitute persons, of which half was given to states in a one-to-three match; the other $250 million was used as grants to states that could prove they lacked funds. The FERA was technically supposed to provide welfare payments only for unemployed persons, but many states also gave funds to the working poor, many of whom were unable to survive on their low wages. Its major thrust was to help states and localities with the costs of sustaining unemployed persons, but the FERA also funded and ran camps for transients, helped college students with loans, funded cooperatives among farmers, and purchased more than 4 million acres of land for resale to tenant farmers.[53]

The FERA was a startling departure from prior American welfare traditions. It represented the first major federal welfare program in the nation's history. The country was divided into five regions, whose federal administrators worked closely with directors of state emergency relief organizations to ensure that federal guidelines were followed. They were often greeted with hostility by local and state officials, who resented federal intrusion and sought to maintain patronage systems and punitive practices. The regional and federal administrators were not afraid to persevere to correct local abuses; indeed, they federalized FERA operations in six states because of irregularities.[54]

Although the FERA was innovative, it also had conservative features. Convinced that public welfare rightly belonged to states and local jurisdictions and that the depression would quickly end, Roosevelt hoped to terminate the FERA. (Note how he placed the word *emergency* in its title.) The legislation did not require local units of government to give recipients a minimum level of benefits because this policy would have been widely interpreted as undue interference with local prerogatives. Although federal authorities expected local government to use FERA funds to supplement their existing welfare expenditures, many cut their local funding, so that welfare recipients scarcely benefited from the infusion of new federal money.[55] Some local governments continued to give in-kind benefits—and residents of some states refused to enact state bond issues needed to raise local matching funds so that federal funding was terminated for brief periods that were called "foodless holidays."

The federal government instituted a range of food programs during the Great Depression, even though Hopkins and others preferred cash assistance to in-kind assistance. These included a Food Stamp program for federal workers who could show evidence of need and a massive surplus commodities program that distributed agricultural produce to the nation's poor.[56]

Moving from Cash Assistance to Creating Work Programs

Critics pointed out that the FERA mostly provided funds instead of trying to find jobs for unemployed persons. Some observers even suspected that, by allowing states to provide FERA funds to people who were working but still poor, the program encouraged employers to reduce wages. Accepting those criticisms of the program, Hopkins himself argued in the summer of 1933 that the FERA dole was holding back large numbers of persons who were able and willing to work.[57] Moreover, Roosevelt and Hopkins realized that work relief would be far more politically popular in a nation with a poorhouse tradition that had always been averse to providing cash assistance to nonworking persons.

To create a work relief program, Aubrey Williams, an assistant to Hopkins, proposed the use of FERA funds to create public works to be administered through county offices of the FERA in the various states. Its work projects would be developed by local FERA staff in consultation with local governmental officials. Roosevelt, who also disliked the use of doles for the able-bodied poor, quickly concurred with Williams's scheme by creating, through executive order, the Civilian Works Administration (CWA) as part of the FERA in 1933.

CWA funds came from the FERA budget, as well as surplus funds commandeered from the PWA program. Between November of 1933 and January of 1934, the federal government initiated 190,000 work projects that employed 16 million Americans —a remarkable feat by any standard, even though the CWA still did not reach most unemployed persons. The program was funded by a federal-local matching formula, in which the federal government paid most of the direct costs.

Most work projects were proposed by local officials, who submitted tens of thousands of ideas, not only because they wanted to help the unemployed but also because an enormous backlog of road repair and other public needs existed in bankrupted local jurisdictions. The projects were approved by local officials and state FERA officials, except for those that were initiated by federal staff and approved in the Washington headquarters of the FERA. Road-related construction projects accounted for 8 percent of CWA funds; other local improvement projects under the program included recataloging books in public libraries, constructing retaining walls, digging drainage ditches, and cleaning local parks.[58]

Many practical eligibility and reimbursement details had to be quickly solved to allow these projects to be implemented in 1933 and 1934. Hopkins angered unemployed persons who were

not on FERA rolls when he decided to require that 50 percent of the enrollees come from FERA relief rolls, but he remained adamant because he felt welfare recipients should receive priority. (He also feared that unions, which saw the program as a chance to obtain employment for unemployed union workers, would dominate the recruitment process and insist that virtually all jobs go to their members, to the detriment of FERA recipients.) State employment offices certified that CWA workers were unemployed and had tried to find jobs in the private sector. Reimbursement levels were established in Washington that gave workers in jobs that were classified as unskilled far less pay than ones classed as skilled positions—and adjustments were made to reflect regional wage and cost-of-living levels. (Hopkins succeeded in allocating most of the job slots to unskilled persons so that the program would not be monopolized by skilled workers.) CWA wage levels were hardly munificent; indeed, workers with relatively large families often had to supplement their CWA paychecks with FERA assistance to survive.

Roosevelt also had to contend both with Republicans' fears that the CWA would be used for patronage purposes by his administration and with Democratic officials who wanted to reward party members with jobs. Determined not to appease those Democrats who desired patronage, Roosevelt insisted that the federal FERA staff carefully screen the thousands of applicants for project supervisor positions and reject persons who lacked requisite skills, even when they were nominees of Democrats. Given the size of the operation (it involved 190,000 separate projects) and the speed of its implementation, it is remarkable that only 240 charges of serious irregularity were ever proved.[59]

The CWA was a bold initiative that gave new social welfare roles to the federal government. It was a massive program, even by today's standards, but was nonetheless an emergency measure that gave minimal benefits to destitute persons and reimbursed unskilled labor at significantly lower levels than skilled labor.

Even before he was elected, Roosevelt had promised to enact a scheme that would address

© Herbert Gehr/Time-Life Pictures/Getty Images

F I G U R E 7.2 CCC workers in the Great Depression.

unemployment among the nation's youth by devising conservation projects in national and state parks. No reform measure was more popular during the New Deal than the Civilian Conservation Corps (CCC), which was enacted in 1933 and provided assistance to 2.5 million young men. (See Figure 7.2.) Its popularity stemmed from its assistance to youth; from its conservation projects, which were often located in the districts of conservative legislators who might normally have opposed the program; and from its reduction of welfare rolls.

Eligibility was restricted at first to males between the ages of 18 and 25 who were currently on welfare rolls, but by 1937, in response to widespread protest against this restrictive eligibility policy, officials allowed any unemployed youth to apply. To spread

CCC benefits to as many youths as possible, Roosevelt tried to limit enrollees to one year's residence but then allowed youths to extend their stay for another year because of their difficulty in finding jobs in the private economy. Recruits were paid as little as $1 a day and required to send half their wages to their parents. The army and the Department of Interior jointly administered the CCC, with the army administering the camps under a strict regimen supervised by sergeants, while the Department of Interior planned and oversaw the work projects in the national and state forests to which the youths were sent each day in small work groups.

It would be hard to overestimate the meaning of the CCC to unemployed youths. Because the unemployment rate among youths was often double the rate for adults, many young persons would have been consigned to welfare for years had the CCC not existed. Transported great distances from Midwestern and Eastern cities to parks in the West, the participants underwent an extraordinary and broadening experience. The program was implemented with remarkable speed; 300,000 youths were placed in camps by the summer of 1933 and 500,000 by 1934.

Nevertheless, the program was not perfect. Critics feared that the CCC was militarizing America's youth by placing them in regimented settings under the control of the army. Others noted that the CCC did not prepare the youths for jobs after they had left the CCC; did not provide technical skills; did not emphasize remedial education; and did not offer employment counseling. The program was not large enough to meet the needs of the vast numbers of youth who needed jobs during the Great Depression. It also placed African American youths in segregated camps and did not address the needs of young women.[60]

Developing a Work Relief Program for Complex Projects

The CWA and CCC focused on work projects that could be speedily implemented and that emphasized unskilled labor, so they could not construct relatively complex projects that were needed to make internal improvements in the United States— for example, to address such natural disasters as floods and droughts or to build airports, roads, bridges, and military installations. Work on these projects, Roosevelt contended, served both the public interest and the needs of unemployed Americans. Accordingly, he developed the Public Works Administration (PWA) in 1933. Because large-scale projects can easily become enmeshed in corruption and patronage, Roosevelt appointed Harold Ickes to be its director. Ickes was a stern perfectionist who insisted on the highest technical standards. His administrative style and philosophy contrasted with the free-wheeling Harry Hopkins. Ickes believed that the hurriedly arranged projects of the CWA did not provide lasting economic

benefit to the nation—and he was furious when Hopkins was able, repeatedly, to raid PWA funds for the CWA and its successor, the Works Progress Administration (WPA).[61]

Ickes subjected each project to an identical—and lengthy—review process that made extensive use of engineers and other experts to convince legislators that projects were funded on their merits. He took care to assemble a skilled workforce, project managers, and contractors who could build a project to precise specifications. Because he distrusted corporations, which he regarded as placing profits ahead of the public interest, he contracted projects to the private sector only with reluctance and monitored them carefully.

As the first massive peacetime involvement by the federal government in complex public projects, the PWA had constructed by 1937 astonishing numbers of bridges, airports, dams, and school buildings. It had to surmount politics and troublesome lawsuits, as political and community rivals developed alternative projects or even alternative versions of the same project. Because the PWA required local units of government to contribute a large share of the cost of specific projects, many projects had to be canceled when local funds were not forthcoming. The PWA also had to overcome opposition from conservatives who questioned whether the federal government was competing with private business and thus overstepping its proper role.[62]

Prior to 1933, only 23 states had developed employment offices to help unemployed workers find jobs. But with the passage of the Wagner-Peyser Act in 1933, federal funds were made available to the states for that purpose, creating a national network of state employment offices. As well as helping unemployed workers find jobs, these offices were used extensively to recruit and screen persons for work in the CWA, CCC, and PWA.[63]

Trying to End the Great Depression Itself

Increasing Federal Spending. The FERA, CWA, CCC, and PWA rescued persons for brief periods from economic misery, but they did not directly address the collapse of the economic system itself, which had created the economic misery in the first place. Because the trickle-down theories of Herbert Hoover had not worked, Roosevelt proposed a combination of fiscal, monetary, regulatory, and market support strategies. Indeed, Rosen argues that Roosevelt valued these economic policies even more than his welfare and jobs programs.[64]

Hoover had feared federal deficits, but Roosevelt drastically increased social spending and produced unprecedented peacetime deficits that were funded by selling tens of millions of dollars of federal bonds. Innovative as this policy was, Roosevelt and his aides did not understand that far more drastic increases in social spending would have been a potent economic weapon against the depression because of widespread revulsion against deficits.[65] (Aggregate federal spending in the New Deal amounted to only 10 percent of GDP as compared to federal spending of 20 percent of the GDP during the 1950s and subsequent decades. Federal spending on Medicare, Medicaid, and Social Security alone comprised almost 10 percent of GDP in 2008.) Roosevelt's deficits were modest, too, compared to those during World War II or those from 1981 onward, save for a brief interlude during the presidency of Bill Clinton. The theories of the English economist John Maynard Keynes, which provided a rationale for incurring large deficits during recessions and depressions, were not widely publicized or accepted in the United States until 1936.[66] Even *had* Roosevelt wanted to increase spending on his New Deal by two or three times, he would have met stiff bipartisan resistance from Congress, since the nation had resorted to truly big budgets only during World War 1.

Restoring Confidence in Banks. In another strategy to end the Great Depression, Roosevelt hoped to restore confidence in the nation's banks. During the 1920s, many banks had insufficient reserves to provide a margin of safety for large numbers of withdrawals by account holders or to cover bad loans and investments—as happened in 1929 when the Great Depression began. The Federal Deposit Insurance Corporation, established in 1933, provided federal insurance to cover deposits when banks became insolvent.

Attacking Speculation in Stocks. Roosevelt also tried to prevent another catastrophic depression by placing restrictions on stock trading so that investors could not rely excessively on credit when investing in stocks. He established the Securities and Exchange Commission (SEC) in 1934 to establish regulations to forestall undue speculation by investors and stockbrokers. [67]

Stopping the Vicious Circle of Job and Price Cuts in Industry. Roosevelt's most difficult problem, however, was to arrest the vicious circle of economic developments that kept the Great Depression going. As consumers lost their jobs and had their wages cut, the demand for products and goods declined—prompting businesses to cut prices. As they cut prices, however, they had to lay off more employees or curtail production—a strategy that led to even greater inability by consumers to purchase their products—which, in turn, led to further layoffs and wage cuts in an escalating cycle.

To interrupt this vicious circle, Roosevelt enacted the National Industrial Recovery Act of 1933, which established the National Recovery Administration (NRA). It convened business leaders in various economic sectors, such as the steel, coal, and mining industries, to agree on prices they would, together, charge for products in their sectors. By establishing a set price, Roosevelt hoped to stop the cuts in prices that had forced cuts in employment and slashes in wages. To further guarantee that employers would not slash wages, the NRA required business leaders to establish common wage levels for their workers, with regional variations to account for differences in the cost of living. To avert the production of surplus goods that stimulated cuts in prices, the NRA also asked business leaders to establish production quotas for each company.[68]

Critics feared that businesses would use this participatory process to make excessive profits by establishing self-serving policies—whether through excessively low wages, high prices, or low levels of production to drive up prices. Some persons claimed the NRA was unconstitutional because it allowed businesses to use monopolistic practices, such as price and wage fixing, that were forbidden by the Sherman Antitrust Act. To forestall these abuses, the NRA required business leaders to establish prices that were fair, to refrain from using child labor, to allow workers to join unions, to honor specified minimum working conditions, to exclude women from dangerous occupations, and to include union representatives in industrywide negotiations. Roosevelt tried, in effect, to use the NRA not only to establish a process to stabilize prices and wages but also to advance indirectly the cause of social reform by abolishing child labor and legitimizing unions.[69]

Its goals were ambitious, but the NRA was hampered by many problems. Liberals who argued that the NRA put foxes in charge of the henhouse found their fears realized when some NRA negotiations led to price increases and production cutbacks that decreased employment while adding to the burdens of consumers. Employers who honored the minimum wage requirements of the NRA often worked their employees to exhaustion to recoup wage increases, whereas others resorted to a policy of labor turnover to reduce their labor costs. Many employers ignored provisions of the NRA by 1934, when they became convinced that it was unconstitutional.[70]

Businesses also found ways of harming labor. Because the provisions that allowed workers to organize unions were exceedingly vague, many employers formed company unions to thwart the establishment of independent unions and then told the NRA that their workers were already organized. General Hugh Johnson, the director of the NRA, took an aggressive stance in opposing efforts to form longshoremen's unions in California and even urged the use of federal troops to repress some legitimate unions on the grounds that their organizers were communists. Southern firms often succeeded in keeping extremely low wage levels for jobs held by African Americans by contending that regional wages were lower than in the North.[71]

The NRA was terminated in 1935 when the Supreme Court declared that its delegation of power to business leaders was unconstitutional. However, its demise had been widely predicted because it had not been effective. An elaborate bureaucracy was required to arrange and oversee negotiations in thousands of industries; price and labor codes were established in virtually every industry—including, for example, firms that made fishhooks. Because federal administrators could not effectively monitor so many codes, companies' compliance was far from perfect. Finally, the National Labor Board, which was established to monitor the provisions protecting workers who sought unionization, had too few staff and too little power to help most workers.

Stopping the Vicious Circle of Price Cuts and Increased Production in Agriculture.   Roosevelt similarly tried to stop the vicious circle of prices and employment in the agricultural sector. As the demand for agricultural products declined as consumers were unable to purchase as many of them due to unemployment or slashed wages, farmers would cut prices of their goods—which drove millions of them toward bankruptcy. Moreover, many of them would try to grow more crops so they could sell more products that would offset the lower prices they received—but the greater acreage of production would further depress prices in a vicious circle. To address this agricultural depression, Roosevelt established the Agricultural Adjustment Agency (AAA), which was financed by levying a tax on food processors.[72] The AAA convened producers of each of the major crops, such as cotton and corn, to negotiate the amounts of acreage they would grow, and then reimbursed farmers for *not* planting some of their land to avert the drop in prices for agricultural goods—allowing more farmers to remain solvent.

The worst casualties of the agricultural depression were tenant farmers and sharecroppers. They were desperately poor—and were often evicted by farmers when their profits decreased. The AAA developed safeguards to forestall abuse of tenant farmers by landowners; but because it lacked the staff to monitor landowners, evictions continued. The AAA required landowners to pass on to tenants a specified percentage of the monies they obtained from the government for withdrawing acreage from production, but many landowners gave share-croppers a smaller percentage or nothing at all. In 1934, the Southern Tenant Farmers Association was formed to try to stop evictions, but grassroots advocacy was difficult because the tenant farmers and sharecroppers, many of them African Americans in the South, were geographically dispersed and impoverished.[73]

As with the NRA, however, large producers often used the AAA to advance their own financial interests. They established production policies that were favorable to themselves but harmful to small farmers and took their poorest land out of production to avoid having to reduce their overall output. Many of them pocketed their growing profits as the prices of agricultural goods stabilized—and evicted many tenant farmers and sharecroppers.

Averting Foreclosures.   Roosevelt tried to provide assistance to millions of farmers and homeowners threatened with foreclosure. Farm mortgages were directly purchased and refinanced by the government when the Emergency Farm Mortgage Act and the Farm Relief Act were enacted in 1933. In assisting homeowners, the Roosevelt administration decided to take an indirect role; rather than helping homeowners directly, the National Housing Act of 1934 established the Federal Home Administration (FHA) to insure mortgages and home improvement loans, so that banks could refinance them at lower rates of interest and so banks would not become insolvent if consumers could not make their mortgage payments.[74]

Reviving Economies in Vast Regions.   Why not, some persons asked, use the power of the federal government to orchestrate the economic development of entire regions? With federal assistance, vast river systems in the United States, including the Mississippi and Missouri rivers, could be made to yield power if dams, generators, and transmission lines were constructed. The most prominent legislative advocate of regional development schemes was George Norris, a progressive Republican senator from Nebraska, who had made river development his major interest and who worked closely with Roosevelt to secure its passage.

The first project, the Tennessee Valley Authority (TVA), was initiated in 1933 and governed by a commission that was established to oversee development of a network of dams and generating plants. The TVA sold electricity to power cooperatives and nearby towns, manufactured and sold fertilizer, reforested vast amounts of land, and built flood control projects. It was partially responsible for the economic rebirth of a vast region; and thanks to the proceeds from the sale of power and fertilizer, the cost to the government was minimal. Private power companies, which often charged excessive fees for their power, protested vigorously that the federal government was competing unfairly with them. Their many legal and political strategies to sabotage the TVA included attempts to place allies on the commission that established TVA policy. Defenders of the TVA were able to institutionalize the experiment, however, even if they were unable to extend their bold design to the Missouri and other large river systems.[75]

CONSERVATIVE PRESSURE ON ROOSEVELT BY SUMMER 1934

Events of early 1934 were not encouraging to social reformers. Roosevelt, under severe pressure to cut spending to reduce deficits, terminated the CWA in 1934, despite protests from reformers.[76] Slowing the momentum of social programs also had a political rationale. Although Roosevelt had won a sweeping victory in 1932, as well as control of both houses of Congress, he feared that widespread grumbling about welfare cheaters and loafers in the FERA, CWA, and PWA would fuel a conservative resurgence in the congressional elec-

---

INSERT 7.3 Critical Analysis: When Would National Reforms Have Emerged without the Great Depression?

Hypotheticals—that is, surmises about the course of history if certain historical incidents had *not* occurred—are sometimes useful, because they force us to analyze history and to place specific developments in a broader perspective. Speculate whether major social programs would have been enacted at the federal level had the Great Depression *not* occurred. If they would not have been enacted in the 1930s, would *other* pressures or forces have eventually forced Americans to develop major national social programs? How would we view Franklin Roosevelt had he *not* presided over the nation during the Great Depression?

---

enduring or whether they would be rescinded when the Great Depression finally ended. Because such strong forces existed in the 1930s that opposed sweeping social reforms even when the nation was devastated by the worst economic catastrophe in American history, it is interesting to speculate when major federal reforms would have emerged had the Great Depression *not* occurred. (See Insert 7.3.)

HOW LIBERAL FORCES PROMOTED A RESURGENCE OF NEW DEAL REFORMS IN 1934 THROUGH 1936

When Roosevelt won a smashing victory in the congressional elections in November of 1934, Harry Hopkins and other social reformers believed they could finally prevail over both Republicans and budget balancers within the Democratic Party. Hopkins said to fellow reformers:

> Boys, this is our hour. We've got to get everything we want—a works program, Social Security, wages and hours [regulation], everything—now or never. Put your minds to work in developing a complete ticket to provide security for all the folks of this country up and down and across the board.[78]

Hopkins proposed the End Poverty in America (EPIA) plan, which included an ongoing federal jobs program, a massive low-cost housing program, a set of insurance programs, establishment of large manufacturing centers, and new rural programs to help poor farmers acquire land and equipment.[79]

Liberals generally supported the New Deal programs; more radical groups and individuals, while endorsing the goals of Roosevelt's reforms, wanted him to go much further. Huey Long, the charismatic and demagogic senator from Louisiana, pressured Roosevelt to place heavy taxes on

tions in November of 1934. Many Americans were uneasy about the sudden assumption of major policy roles by the federal government in a nation that had been dominated by state and local governments. Business and conservative interests, which had been on the defensive and in disarray in 1933 and early 1934, had also begun to develop a political counteroffensive—accusing Roosevelt of seeking to build a political dynasty by using New Deal programs for Democrats. Moreover, Roosevelt had his own doubts about the advisability of a strong federal role in public welfare, as he had always favored giving local governments the responsibility for welfare problems. He had developed the FERA because states were verging on bankruptcy in 1932—not because he wanted to institutionalize it. He did not want the federal government to assume a permanent job creation role. He continued to hope that easing of the economic depression would permit a reduction in size of the federal programs, though advisors like Hopkins feared that the government would have to continue to fund public works indefinitely.[77]

It was unclear in the summer of 1934 whether most New Deal reforms would prove incomes and estates of millionaires, to greatly expand federal works programs, and to pay a higher wage to workers in public works projects. He believed that the NRA and the AAA did little more than protect the interests of large industrialists and landowners. He criticized the low wages paid by the CWA and attacked the budget-cutting inclinations of Roosevelt. As a militant defender of small farmers and small businessmen, he believed that their economic opportunities remained limited, he resented affluent elites, and he tended to dislike the large New Deal bureaucracies.[80]

Father Charles Coughlin, a Jesuit priest from Detroit, attracted a massive audience to his national radio show when he proposed a variety of federal regulations of the banking system and monetary reforms. His initial support for Roosevelt turned to opposition when FDR failed to support his economic measures.[81] (Coughlin later turned sharply to the right and became virulently anti-Semitic.) Other reformers concentrated on single issues. Francis Townsend, a dentist in Long Beach, California, proposed and popularized a scheme to pay a monthly pension of $200 per month to all American citizens over the age of 60 on the condition that they pledge to spend it within 30 days and agree to give up all other income. It was to be financed from a federal sales tax. He hoped the scheme would simultaneously relieve grinding poverty among the elderly and revive the economy by requiring them to spend their monthly pensions before the end of each month. He obtained 20 million signatures on a petition by 1936.[82]

Representative Ernest Lundeen of Minnesota proposed a scheme of unemployment insurance in 1934 to pay compensation from the general revenues of the nation to all persons who were unemployed through no fault of their own. (Unemployed workers were to receive benefits equal to prevailing wages, and persons with part-time work were to have their wages supplemented to bring them up to the prevailing standard.) The scheme was to be administered by workers' and farmers' organizations.[83]

A bipartisan cadre of liberals often voted together on public housing legislation, legislation

protecting the rights of unions, legislation to oppose lynching of African Americans, and fair labor standards. Indeed, Senator Robert F. Wagner, a leading figure in this liberal bloc, initiated reform measures without FDR's approval as a means of pressuring the administration to be more daring.[84]

Roosevelt experienced mounting pressure from reformers and social workers. An influential contingent of social workers from New York State had assumed a particularly important role in supporting reforms during the early years of the New Deal when they offered suggestions and assumed key positions within the administration. (Hopkins and Perkins were merely the most visible members of this community.)[85] Many of them had become disenchanted with the New Deal by 1934, however; they resented the termination of the CWA, the opportunistic exploitation of the NRA by many businessmen, and the low levels of relief provided by the FERA and the CWA. Their anger mounted during 1935, when they believed Roosevelt hoped to discontinue federal assistance to many unemployed persons and destitute families. A radical contingent of the profession, led by Mary Van Kleeck, urged social workers to become radical critics of the New Deal rather than be co-opted by Roosevelt.[86]

Pressure for reform also came from the burgeoning unions that represented unskilled workers. These workers and their organizers had been radicalized by the inhumane labor practices of the corporations, high rates of unemployment among unskilled workers, and the bloody suppression of strikes in automobile and steel plants and in coal mines. Union leaders such as Walter Reuther in the auto industry and John L. Lewis in mining developed growing constituencies and power. Although they had supported the establishment of the NRA because of its protections for unions, they wondered why the Roosevelt administration seemed content with the vague and poorly enforced provisions of the NRA to protect collective bargaining.[87]

In 1934, the Southern Tenant Farmers Association (STFA) was formed to protect millions of agricultural laborers who found their lot even worse after passage of the AAA. A few African

American sharecroppers were helped by the FERA and the Resettlement Administration to obtain their own land, but most remained enmeshed in poverty and heavily indebted to landowners who charged them excessive prices for seed, fertilizer, and food. To make matters worse, as landowners curbed production to reap payments from the AAA, they evicted their tenant farmers. The STFA asked the administration to stop this wave of evictions and to help landless persons obtain their own farms.[88]

Although workers, liberals, and African Americans were often critical of Roosevelt, they nonetheless regarded him as preferable to Republican leaders, who became even more conservative and opposed to reform after the 1934 election. This support from the left emboldened Roosevelt to initiate and support reforms, not only because he wanted to keep their support but also because he wanted to prevent the emergence of a more radical rival. A poll in 1935 suggested that Huey Long would receive 6 million votes if he were to run for president in 1936—possibly drawing enough votes from Roosevelt to give a Republican candidate a chance to beat Roosevelt.[89] Father Coughlin and Townsend supported the Union Party, which frontally attacked Roosevelt as too conservative and sought to defeat both the Democrats and Republicans in the elections of 1936. Rivalry among leaders and groups on the left, the assassination of Huey Long in 1935, and Roosevelt's sheer popularity and tactical brilliance doomed the political aspirations of many of these leaders, but they pushed Roosevelt to consider policies that he might otherwise have neglected.[90]

A determined group of social reformers, including Isaac Rubinow, pressured Roosevelt and his aides to enact old age pensions, unemployment insurance, and national health insurance. Some of them had sought such legislation in the Progressive Era—and had continued their work during the 1920s by advocating so-called social insurances in various states. Although they differed over program details, these reformers were convinced that economic security would never be realized in the United States if these reforms were not enacted.

PIVOTAL NEW DEAL VICTORIES IN 1934, 1935, AND 1936

Despite the conservative pressures on Roosevelt, the New Deal reached its zenith of success in 1935 and 1936 with enactment of the Social Security Act, the National Labor Relations Board (NLRB), the Works Progress Administration (WPA), and the National Youth Administration (NYA); but the form and size of these initiatives often reflected compromises with conservatives.

The Social Security Act

The Social Security Act, which is the foundation of the American welfare state, contained many programs to address a variety of social problems. Roosevelt wanted to decide, once and for all, which relief functions would be maintained by federal and local governments. He also wanted to prevent destitution by developing social insurances to address the economic needs of persons who were unemployed and elderly. Finally, he wanted to develop some permanent and ongoing programs to constitute his legacy to the nation. Roosevelt had many policy interests, but he wanted a single piece of legislation to encapsulate them, because he realized that some relatively controversial measures, such as unemployment insurance, would not pass unless they were part of a larger piece of legislation that also contained more popular programs such as old age pensions and welfare assistance for older persons. He reasoned as well that the Supreme Court would find it more difficult to attack specific programs if they were part of multifaceted legislation. (See Figure 7.3.)

To plan this legislation, Roosevelt appointed a Committee on Economic Security in June of 1934. The committee, chaired by Frances Perkins, included the secretary of the treasury, the attorney general, the secretary of agriculture, and the administrator of the FERA. A large advisory committee and a technical committee were also formed. The committee accomplished its complex task with

© Bettmann/Corbis

F I G U R E 7.3   Franklin Delano Roosevelt signing the Social Security Act.

remarkable speed and was able, after marathon sessions during the Christmas holidays, to issue its final
report on January 15, 1935. The legislation passed
overwhelmingly in the Congress and was signed
into law by Roosevelt in August 1935. The Social
Security Act contained two social insurance programs, three relief programs, and other smaller
programs.[91]

Social insurances, principally unemployment
insurance and old age pensions (Social Security),
were attractive to Roosevelt for several reasons.
They were self-funding programs; their benefits
were financed from payroll taxes levied on employers and employees. Roosevelt favored the payroll
tax so that future generations would not have to
fund these programs from general revenues. He
also believed that these insurance programs would
reduce the size of welfare rolls, as the benefits paid
to older persons and unemployed workers in these

programs lifted them above the threshold of
poverty. Moreover, he knew that insurances
were politically acceptable to many Americans because they represented earned benefits rather than
welfare payments.[92] Roosevelt initially showed little interest in Social Security because he was preoccupied with the needs of unemployed workers, but
he vigorously declared his support of it when critical stories appeared in the press in 1934.[93]

Despite the political popularity of these programs, Roosevelt believed he needed to make concessions to conservatives to ensure their passage.
Over the protests of some liberals, he supported a
regressive system of payroll taxes that levied stiffer
taxes of Social Security on low-income wage earners than on more affluent persons, and he refused to
contribute general revenues to Social Security.
(Liberals believed the use of general revenues
would have been more equitable and would have

allowed major increases in the size of benefits.) Some liberals also opposed his decision—supported by Southern agricultural interests—to exclude farm and domestic workers from both unemployment and Social Security benefits.[94]

Although Roosevelt made concessions to conservatives, he also made policy choices that defied them. Some persons believed that participation in Social Security should be voluntary, but FDR insisted on mandatory participation. Frances Perkins, a believer in states' rights, initially favored allowing each state to keep its own Social Security fund, but FDR rejected this policy on the grounds that movement of workers between states would make it unworkable.[95]

Originally conceived as a measure to provide pensions to retired workers, Social Security was broadened in 1939 to include family members of the worker. Arthur Altmeyer, chair of the Social Security Board, explained that "this system, formerly a plan to provide old-age annuities for individual wage earners, has become a broad system of family insurance, which protects not only the wage earner but his wife and children, and if they are dependent on him, his aged parents."[96] Social Security was amended to include benefits to the wives, widows, and children of retirees—a salutary step even if it was grounded in a patriarchal notion of the family, in which men were regarded as breadwinners and it was assumed that women would not work.[97]

Senator Wagner and other liberals had introduced various versions of a federal unemployment insurance program since 1933, but much controversy existed about how best to proceed. Should funds collected by a payroll tax on employers be kept in a central pool in Washington or in each of the states? Should a general fund be established, or should separate accounts be maintained for each industry? Should the federal government take the lead in administering the funds, devise the level and duration of unemployment benefits, and levy taxes? Should employers' participation in the scheme be mandatory or voluntary?

The unemployment insurance program embodied in the Social Security Act represented an ingenious compromise between these policy alternatives. A payroll tax was levied on employers by states; participation was technically voluntary, but participating employers were given generous federal tax credits to offset most of their payroll taxes. States collected the payroll taxes, but they gave the revenues to the federal government, which maintained a central fund for each state that was then used to pay unemployment benefits to workers. The federal government paid the states' costs of administering their programs. Although this plan sounds complicated, it was a rather simple scheme to allow the federal government to bear most of the costs of unemployment insurance, while lending the appearance that participation by employers was voluntary.[98] Each state enacted its own unemployment insurance law that specified benefit levels and duration. Many liberal critics contended that the legislation penalized states with high levels of unemployment, whose funds would be more severely burdened than states with low levels of unemployment. Others feared that conservative states might choose to pay low benefits to unemployed persons. Why, some liberal critics asked, should workers have to be unemployed for four weeks before obtaining benefits? Many liberals favored federal contributions to the program to enable it to pay higher benefits for longer periods. They feared that workers would be forced onto welfare rolls because they could not survive on the meager assistance, which was limited to around 14 weeks in many states. Liberals were also unhappy that Roosevelt had capitulated to special interests when he excluded domestics, cannery workers, and farm laborers from coverage. They were nonetheless delighted that FDR supported the concept of unemployment insurance and that he had withstood pressure from conservatives for each state to have its separate unemployment program.[99]

Most liberals supported the Federal Emergency Relief Administration because it gave relief to a broad range of needy Americans—including families, single persons, older persons, and nonworking and working poor persons—and they were furious when it became apparent that Roosevelt had decided to scuttle the FERA and replace it with federal relief programs to only three groups of persons in need—elderly persons (Old Age Assistance, or

OAA); children in families with one caretaker (Aid to Dependent Children, or ADC); and blind persons (Aid to the Blind, or AB).[100] All other destitute persons, including single nonelderly persons and families with two parents, were returned to local or general assistance welfare programs, which were entirely funded by state and local resources. Many of these poor relief agencies were punitive in orientation and racist in their practices.

These three programs followed a similar format. States received matching or formula funds from the federal government. Under OAA, for example, the federal government paid one-half of local grants for each eligible person, as long as local grants did not exceed $30 per month. (The federal government paid only one-third of ADC grants.) Federal authorities insisted that a state agency be designated to implement the programs, that uniform standards of eligibility be established within each state to preclude specific counties from developing relatively punitive policies, and that fair hearings be established so that aggrieved recipients could appeal eligibility decisions.[101]

Liberal critics were pleased that Roosevelt had developed some permanent programs, but they were displeased that many persons were shunted to local welfare programs. They contended that the legislation gave states undue power to establish eligibility standards and levels of benefits. Would not Southern and relatively conservative states, they asked, make their programs so restrictive that they would deny assistance to vast numbers of poor persons and people of color? As federal authorities were given no power over the states' personnel decisions and were not required to use social workers in supervisory positions, critics wondered if patronage would dominate local agencies.[102] Some liberals were also unhappy that the ADC program restricted assistance to families with a single parent or that the welfare grants to these families included funds only for the children and not for the parent. The policy limiting the grants to children was not amended until 1950, when the name of the program was changed to Aid to Families with Dependent Children (AFDC). Even this restrictive program was more

liberal than a version advocated by some social workers, who wanted relief to be given only to those children who were found, on casework investigation, to reside in "suitable homes," on the grounds that many destitute mothers provided improper care.[103] As liberals had predicted, eligibility standards and grant levels were far more restrictive in Southern and rural states than in industrial states, and Southerners kept benefits low, partly to force African American women and their children to labor for miserable wages in cotton and tobacco fields, and partly because Southern states lacked the tax revenues to fund more munificent programs.[104]

Roosevelt confronted important ethical issues when he gave so much power to the states in the ADC program. (See Insert 7.4.)

Limited as they were, OAA, ADC, and AB were the first permanent and major federal relief programs. Many persons believed in 1935 that these programs would be extremely small. Social Security benefits, it was thought, would allow elderly persons to escape the OAA program; ADC did not attract much attention as most people thought it would be a federal-state version of mothers' pension programs; and AB applied only to a relatively small population of persons with a specific disability.[105] Had they guessed the future size of OAA and ADC rolls or realized that Aid to the Blind would be expanded in the 1950s and subsequent decades to include persons with mental and physical disabilities, many conservatives—and possibly Roosevelt himself—might have thought twice about establishing these federal programs.

Reformers were able to obtain provisions in the Social Security Act that provided grants to localities for child welfare and maternal health programs (Title V) and public health programs (Title VI). The amounts of money involved were small; $1.5 million was authorized for the child welfare funds, but the money was allowed to be used only for the administrative costs of state agencies. These small grant programs nonetheless represented grudging acceptance of the notion that local governments needed federal assistance in providing a range of social welfare services. Not until the 1960s were

---

INSERT 7.4   Ethical Analysis of Key Issues and Policies: Federal Leadership versus Deferring to the States

---

The central innovation of the New Deal was its development of the federal government's social policy roles. States and localities were the prime movers in social policy before the New Deal, as our discussion in Chapters 3 to 6 suggests.

1. Using the New Deal as an example, analyze the ethics of FDR's decision to make assertive use of federal power. What ethical criticisms would he have encountered had he *not* developed national programs in the Great Depression such as the CWA, PWA, TVA, unemployment insurance, and Social Security pensions? Consider the fiscal resources of the federal government (for example, its tax and borrowing powers) when compared with state governments particularly during the Great Depression, when many states verged on

bankruptcy and lacked the ability to issue and sell bonds on the magnitude used by Roosevelt to fund his emergency budget. Consider, as well, some other reasons why states often cannot or will not develop social policies, such as state officials' fears that corporations will relocate if state taxes are raised to pay for social programs or the bias against urban areas in many state legislatures.

2. Discuss whether Roosevelt gave states too much power in ADC, OAA, and AB. Keep in mind that Southern Democrats, a key part of Roosevelt's coalition, adamantly insisted that states have considerable powers, partly because they did not want many African Americans to get welfare rather than to work for starvation wages on large Southern farms.

---

federal programs enacted to fund a range of mental health, health, and other services.

The Social Security Act created programs that would have been unthinkable five years earlier. (See Table 7.2 for a summary of its major provisions.) It committed the federal government to permanently fund an assortment of programs. However, many concessions were made to Southern Democrats and other conservatives in the specific programs, and many programs were missing from the legislation altogether. Roosevelt had contemplated including national health programs in the act, but he changed his mind because he feared that opposition from the American Medical Association and conservatives could imperil its passage. A public works program was not placed within the Social Security Act because of the controversy it would have generated.[106]

Protecting Workers' Right to Strike

The National Labor Board that was established under the NRA had mediated conflicts between thousands of employers and employees. Senator Wagner proposed legislation that more clearly defined specific procedures to be followed when employees wanted

to initiate a union and proposed establishment of an independent board to enforce the rights of union organizers. He fervently believed that such legislation would not only eliminate conflict but bring economic recovery by increasing consumer purchasing power through the wage increases that would follow the growth of unions.[107] He proposed that employees should be allowed to circulate petitions to their fellow workers if they wanted an election to choose a collective bargaining agent and that secret elections, to be monitored by a National Labor Relations Board (NLRB), should be required if more than 50 percent of employees requested it. Employers would have to officially recognize any collective bargaining agent that received support from a majority of employees in the secret ballot, could not fire or intimidate organizers, and could not claim that a company union sufficed when workers wanted to hold elections.

When Senator Wagner introduced his legislation in 1934, Roosevelt withheld his support because he wanted union organizing to proceed gradually, so as to avoid political backlash from business and the general public. He also wanted to place the NLRB within the Department of Labor rather than establishing it as an independent agency,

T A B L E 7.2   Summary of the Major Provisions of the Social Security Act

	TITLE I : GRANTS TO STATES FOR OLD AGE ASSISTANCE
Nature of grants	Secretary of treasury pays to each state 50 percent of the sums expended in a year for assistance to people over age 65 who are not inmates of public institutions, but not including that portion of payments that exceeds $30 per month—and 5 percent of the federal payments are used to administer the programs by the states.
Requirements that states must meet	Each state must: • have a state plan for old age assistance that is in effect in all political sub-divisions of the state and that is mandatory on them • pay for the nonfederal share of the costs of assistance • designate a single state agency to administer the plan (or supervise the plan if local jurisdictions administer part of it) • establish an opportunity for a fair hearing before the state agency for any-one who is denied assistance • provide for methods of selecting personnel and administering the grants that are found by the Social Security Board to be necessary for the efficient operation of the plan • provide to the Social Security Board any information and data that it requests • pay to the United States one-half of the net amount collected by any state (or its subdivisions) from the estate of any recipient of old age assistance
Requirements that the Social Security Board cannot impose on the states	An age requirement of more than 65 years; any residence requirement that excludes any resident of a state who has resided therein five years during the nine years immediately preceding the application and who has resided therein continuously for one year immediately preceding the application
	TITLE II : FEDERAL OLD AGE BENEFITS
Establishing the trust fund	An account is created in the U.S. Treasury, known as the Old Age Reserve Account, to which funds are appropriated for each fiscal year in an amount sufficient to provide for the payments under this title to retired persons.
Definition of eligibility	People who are at least 65 years of age who have received after December 31, 1936, and before reaching age 65 a total amount of wages not less than $2,000. Ineligible categories of work include: • agricultural labor • domestic service • casual labor not in the course of the employer's trade or business • service performed as an officer or member of the crew of a vessel docu-mented under the laws of the United States or of any foreign country • service performed in the employment of the United States government • service performed in the employment of state governments or political subdivisions thereof • service performed in the employment of not-for-profit agencies
Amounts of benefits	If total wages after December 31, 1936, and before the age of 65 are not more than $3,000, the old age benefit shall be at a monthly rate of one-half of 1 percent of such total wages. If these total wages are more than $3,000, the monthly rate will be one-half of 1 percent of the first $3,000 plus one-twelfth of 1 percent of total wages that exceed $3,000 and do not exceed $45,000.

T A B L E 7.2   **(continued)**

TITLE III: GRANTS TO STATES FOR UNEMPLOYMENT COMPENSATION ADMINISTRATION

But in no case shall the monthly rate exceed $85.

If someone dies before reaching 65, there shall be paid to his estate an amount equal to 3.5 percent of the total wages determined by the Board to have been paid to him with respect to employment after December 31, 1936.

The federal government authorized appropriated funds to help states administer their unemployment compensation laws (Title IX discusses the actual unemployment program) provided that the state provides fair and efficient methods of implementing the program, including fair hearings. (If a state agency denies benefits unfairly, the Board can stop making further payments to that state.)

The Social Security Board, on collecting funds in the unemployment fund of each state, will give it to the secretary of the treasury, who will place it in the Unemployment Trust Fund.

Each state agency administering the program pays its benefits from funds from the Unemployment Trust Fund that are forwarded to it by federal authorities.

TITLE IV: GRANTS TO STATES FOR AID TO DEPENDENT CHILDREN

Nature of grants

States make payments to needy dependent children with the federal government paying to each state an amount equal to one-third of the total of the sums expended in a given quarter, but not counting the amount of grants that exceed $18 per month with respect to one dependent child (in a family) and $12 per month with respect to each additional dependent child.

Eligibility

The term *dependent child* means a child under age 16 deprived of parental support by reason of death, continued absence from the home, or physical or mental incapacity of a parent—and the child must be living with his father, mother, grandfather, grandmother, brother, sister, stepfather, stepmother, stepbrother, stepsister, uncle, or aunt in a place of residence maintained by one or more of such relatives as his or their own home.

Requirements that states must meet

The requirements are similar to those for Title I, but states cannot deny aid to any child who has resided in the state for one year immediately preceding the application or who was born within the state within one year of the application if the child's mother has resided in the state for one year immediately preceding the birth.

TITLE V: GRANTS TO STATES FOR MATERNAL AND CHILD WELFARE

There are five parts to Title V:

Part 1

Provides funds to be paid to the states to enable them to extend and improve services for promoting the health of mothers and children, especially in rural areas and in areas suffering from severe economic distress. States must have plans for the services funded by the part approved by the chief of the Children's Bureau. (The state plan must include state contributions to the services and administration or supervision of the spending by the state's health agency.)

Part 2

Provides federal funds to help each state extend and improve services for locating children with disabilities and providing them with medical, surgical, corrective, and other services and care, particularly in rural areas and areas with severe economic distress. State plans must be approved by the chief of the Children's Bureau.

(*continued*)

T A B L E 7.2 **(continued)**

Part 3	Provides funds for the purpose of enabling the Children's Bureau to cooperate with state public welfare agencies to establish, extend, and strengthen public welfare services, called child welfare services, for the protection and care of homeless, dependent, and neglected children, and children in danger of becoming delinquent.
Part 4	Provides funds to the states to allow them to extend and strengthen their programs of vocational rehabilitation of people with physical disabilities—and to allow them to continue to carry out legislation enacted in 1920 to provide vocational rehabilitation to persons disabled in industry or otherwise to help them return to employment.
Part 5	Provides funds for the maintenance of the Children's Bureau.
	TITLE X : GRANTS TO STATES FOR AID TO THE BLIND
Nature of the grant	The federal government pays one-half of the funds expended by a state for aid to blind persons but not counting expenditures exceeding $30 a month—and 5 percent of the federal funds are to be used to administer the program. Inmates of public institutions cannot receive assistance under this title.
Requirements that states must meet	The requirements are similar to those for Title I.

so that Frances Perkins could administer it. When the NRA was declared unconstitutional by the Supreme Court in May of 1935, however, Roosevelt supported Wagner's legislation, which had already been enacted in the Senate.[108] Despite strong opposition from business, the Wagner Act was enacted in 1935. It was partly responsible for an upsurge of union membership, which increased from 3.3 million workers in 1935 to 14 million workers in 1945.

The growth of union membership had extraordinary political implications. Unions became the pillar of the Democratic Party from 1936 until the 1970s, providing it with the bulk of its campaign finances as well as tens of millions of voters.

The Works Progress Administration and the National Youth Administration

Soon after he terminated the CWA in early 1934, Roosevelt decided to develop a new work program to consolidate existing federal jobs programs into one piece of legislation. The legislation, entitled the Emergency Relief Appropriation Act, was enacted in 1935 and required most of its funds to go directly to wages rather than to administrative overhead and to be spent quickly rather than held back for long-term projects. He mandated socially useful projects to be allocated to areas in relation to the number of workers who were on welfare rolls.[109]

The intense rivalry that had existed between Ickes and Hopkins in 1933 continued following passage of the legislation. Both men wanted to head this new consolidated agency and sought Roosevelt's support. Roosevelt favored Hopkins, but he had to move gingerly so as not to alienate Ickes, congressional conservatives who disliked Hopkins, or congressmen who wanted to exercise patronage in the massive new jobs agency. (Congress insisted that appointments of all persons earning more than $5,000 be subject to the consent of the Senate.)

Roosevelt developed regulations that allowed the work programs to avoid undue patronage and placed them under Hopkins's control. He made himself the nominal head of the agency to curtail efforts by senators to place political friends in key jobs. He placed Ickes in charge of a large decision-making committee that had the official power to decide which work projects to fund, but he placed Hopkins in charge of a division that was empowered to recommend small work projects and to veto other project applications. As mayors, governors, and other local officials initiated thousands of modest street, library, and public improvement projects, Hopkins forwarded them to the decision-making committees, which *had* to fund them to meet Roosevelt's guideline that work funds be spent immediately—thus *not* diverting most of the funds to Ickes's PWA. Hopkins used his veto power to defeat many of Ickes's large and complex projects, on the grounds that they competed with the private sector or that insufficient skilled labor existed to implement them. When the frustrated Ickes obtained a ruling that all projects of more than $25,000 should be given to the PWA rather than to Hopkins's division, Hopkins merely divided the larger projects into bundles of smaller ones.[110]

The programs of Hopkins's division, named the Works Progress Administration (WPA), dominated Roosevelt's public works strategy from 1935 onward. Between 1935 and 1940, $14 billion was allocated to it, and 7.8 million persons received work relief. The WPA completed a remarkable array of projects and assumed a major role in disaster relief work, including the aftermath of floods, droughts, and hurricanes. Millions of Americans took on some semblance of dignity as they worked on these projects. The WPA inherited the local, state, and federal staff of the FERA, which was phased out following passage of the Social Security Act. Ultimate approval of projects came from Washington, but district or state branches of the WPA initiated and approved projects in consultation with local and state officials. Various administrative arrangements were established; some projects were completely supervised by local officials and others by WPA staff. Local units of government were usually required to contribute some 20 percent of a project's budget through provision of in-kind costs such as materials and wheelbarrows.[111]

The WPA was criticized from both the left and the right. Conservatives believed that it provided make-work jobs, that it enticed some people to become dependent on public jobs rather than seeking employment in the private sector, and that it competed with the private sector. Hopkins's tireless advocacy of the program and his troubleshooting to deal with periodic crises in the field proved enough, however, to offset conservative criticism. Organized labor demanded that the WPA pay prevailing wages, but Roosevelt preferred a so-called security wage that was pitched between relief benefits and prevailing wages. Critics questioned Roosevelt's decision to restrict the WPA to persons who were already on welfare rolls, as this policy penalized many destitute persons who had avoided welfare. (Roosevelt consented to a compromise policy in which roughly 85 percent of WPA enrollees came from welfare rolls.) Other critics objected to the discrepancy between the wages of unskilled and skilled workers; the former received half the wages of the latter. To distribute WPA jobs broadly, only one member of a family was allowed to participate; this policy often meant that women and adolescents could not receive work relief because administrators gave jobs to male heads of household. The WPA did not provide training to its workers or match workers to jobs so that they could increase their employment prospects while holding WPA jobs. It did not enjoy good working relationships with public welfare and employment offices, which lacked the staff to make sufficient referrals to it.[112] The WPA was never funded at levels that would allow it to help more than two-thirds of eligible persons, and Roosevelt declined to institutionalize it by placing it within the Social Security Act because some of his advisors did not want temporary programs included within the act.[113] Both Congress and the president seemed to fear that a declaration of a permanent works program implied an admission to voters that the administration had failed to correct the nation's economic problems, and so the program struggled along with an uncertain future.[114]

Despite its shortcomings, however, the WPA was remarkably successful and virtually free of fraud. Above all, it gave hope to millions of Americans who were unemployed.

At the insistence of Eleanor Roosevelt, who was a determined advocate for youth, the National Youth Administration (NYA) was established within the WPA, with Aubrey Williams as its director. A broad range of programs was established, including college aid for impoverished students, aid for high school students, public jobs in recreation centers and municipal services, and camps for rural youth to provide them with trade skills. In 1936 and 1937, 600,000 youths, many of them in extreme poverty, were aided by the NYA, even though NYA wages were only one-third of prevailing wages.[115]

Backsliding in the Supreme Court?

The Supreme Court gave legal sanction to the conservatives when it declared the NRA and AAA unconstitutional in 1935 and 1936, respectively; indeed, between January of 1935 and June of 1936, the Court issued 12 rulings against the New Deal that rested on an assortment of constitutional objections. Roosevelt wondered whether virtually all major New Deal programs might be rescinded by the Court.[116] He wondered, too, if the Supreme Court would even declare the Social Security Act to be unconstitutional.

ROOSEVELT'S SMASHING VICTORY OVER REPUBLICANS IN 1936

Roosevelt won a resounding victory in 1936, with the support of a liberal coalition of intellectuals, workers, Jews, and people of color. As much as 80 percent of the working class voted for him as compared with only 42 percent of affluent persons. He also retained the support of the conservative South, which had traditionally voted Democratic. After Roosevelt's smashing presidential victory in November of 1936, everyone was asking where the New Deal would go next. Hopkins, Senator Wagner, and others believed that Roosevelt had received a mandate to continue New Deal reforms—to obtain public housing programs, federal regulation of child labor and working conditions, an expansion of the WPA, and antilynching legislation.[117]

THE ERA OF STALEMATE: 1937–1941

Roosevelt's momentum seemed assured after his victory in 1936, yet he soon ran into a number of political barriers that, with the exception of several notable policy successes, ended his reform momentum. As we shall see, too, Roosevelt himself lost interest in domestic reforms as he grappled with aggression by Germany, Japan, and Italy against other nations.

The Disillusionment of the Middle Class

With the realignment of political parties by social class in the 1930s, many middle-class persons joined working-class voters to support Roosevelt and congressional Democrats in the elections of 1932, 1934, and 1936. However, as the decade wore on, some middle-class voters began to hedge their reform interests because the nation's economic ills continued, and the unprecedented expansion of government bureaucracy led them to wonder if Roosevelt was leading America toward socialism. However, anger at the New Deal often focused not on Roosevelt, who retained his personal popularity throughout the decade, but on some of his advisors and programs. Hopkins was widely believed to want unlimited personal power. Perkins was perceived as soft on militant labor unions and as a charity-minded social worker who blindly supported new programs. Many persons resented the intellectuals who formed Roosevelt's brain trust.[118] Some middle-class Americans also became alarmed by labor organizations, such as the Congress of Industrial Organizations (CIO), which they feared would gain inordinate power. The sitdown strikes of 1937, in which workers occupied automobile plants, were profoundly disturbing to many middle-class citizens, who believed that such disruptive techniques exceeded the bounds of fair play.[119] Thus, in the late 1930s and early 1940s, middle-class voters gradually shifted their support to the Republican Party; indeed, when he was reelected in 1944, Roosevelt received only 53 percent of the votes cast.

Fears That Roosevelt Sought Too Much Power

These growing doubts about New Deal reforms among the middle class were supplemented by widespread opposition to Roosevelt's attempts to pack the Supreme Court and to purge the Democratic Party in 1937. Many liberals had been furious at the Court for its adverse rulings and had developed various legislative proposals for neutralizing it—for example, a proposal requiring a two-thirds vote of the justices to declare legislation unconstitutional. (Congress has the constitutional power to determine the size and voting procedures of the Court.) Had Roosevelt not acted, Congress might have enacted legislation to limit the Court, because 150 such measures were introduced in Congress in 1937.[120]

Roosevelt remained silent on the issue until 1937, when he introduced a legislative proposal to allow the president to appoint a new justice every time a justice failed to retire within six months of his 70th birthday. Perkins advised him not to introduce this proposal because the Court not only appeared to be wavering in its attacks on New Deal programs but was widely regarded as sacrosanct.[121] When Roosevelt persisted, he ran into a storm of political protest; he was accused of upsetting the constitutional balance of powers, seeking unlimited personal power, and trying to establish a fascist dictatorship.[122]

Moreover, Roosevelt was unable to purge the Democratic Party of dissident Southern Democrats, whose conservative opposition was magnified by their fears that Roosevelt would support civil rights measures. Enraged by these defections, he targeted several Southern politicians for political attack by traveling to their districts to campaign for their rivals. However, he suffered a humiliating defeat when each of these politicians was reelected.[123]

Roosevelt's political effectiveness in the early and middle 1930s depended in part on his image of political invincibility. He had obtained so many legislative and electoral victories that many opponents believed it would be fruitless to oppose his policies and feared that he might deny them patronage or personal support in their campaigns. His Supreme Court and political defeats in 1936 and 1937 tarnished his image of invincibility, however, and emboldened members of the conservative coalition, as well as some moderate Democrats, to question his policies.[124]

Fatigue with Reform

Many middle-class Americans had become less enamored with Roosevelt's policies by late 1935. Convinced that individuals were personally responsible for their unemployment, they resented federal work and relief programs, which they believed sapped the initiative of recipients. They increasingly questioned Roosevelt's economic policies as the nation remained mired in depression. Considerable animus developed toward Harry Hopkins, who was perceived to be a welfare czar and was widely believed to reward Democrats with jobs in the federal bureaucracy. Many Americans resented the burgeoning of the federal bureaucracies, which had become highly visible during the implementation of hundreds of New Deal programs. They also disliked the brain trust, academicians, and theorists, whose ideas had not solved the nation's economic malaise.[125]

Several Surprising Policy Successes in 1937 and 1938

Roosevelt was able to obtain some major policy reforms after 1936, despite the loss of his reform momentum. Despite the failure of his attempt to pack the Supreme Court with new justices, Roosevelt achieved a notable victory. The Court in several rulings made clear that it would not overturn the bulk of New Deal legislation—and would not question the constitutional ability of the federal government to develop and fund major social programs.

Funding of New Deal Programs.   The funding of the WPA, CCC, and NYA, particularly after the recession of 1937, was increased.

Fair Labor Standards Act of 1938. Perhaps Roosevelt's signal accomplishment was passage of the Fair Labor Standards Act of 1938. Fair working conditions and minimum wages had been established for each industry under the NRA, but many industries returned to sweatshop conditions when the Supreme Court declared the NRA to be unconstitutional. With assistance from Perkins, Roosevelt supported legislation that established minimum wages and maximum hours, but he had to make concessions to conservatives to secure its passage. Farm labor was excluded from the legislation to appease Southern and Western agricultural interests. Wage and hour standards were phased in gradually so that the minimum wage rose from 25 cents per hour to 40 cents per hour over a period of seven years. The maximum length of a workweek diminished from 44 to 40 hours per week in three years.[126] Even this legislation aroused considerable controversy. Southern Democrats feared it would elevate the wages of poor African Americans, even though agricultural laborers were excluded from it. The AFL opposed it because they feared the minimum wage might establish a ceiling on wages and would decrease the motivation of workers to join unions. Some critics were unhappy that the Department of Labor would administer the legislation because they believed Perkins favored unions.[127]

The Wagner-Steagall Housing Act. In 1937, Roosevelt was able to obtain passage of the Wagner-Steagall Housing Act, which established the United States Housing Authority to provide low-interest loans to local authorities to build public housing.[128]

Attacking Administrative Abuses of Welfare Programs. The Roosevelt administration expended considerable energy in implementing the many programs of the Social Security Act. Federal regulations and policies to govern OAA, ADC, AB, and unemployment insurance programs were issued. States were monitored to be certain that uniform standards of eligibility were established and followed, that names of recipients were not published, and that political criteria were not used

in eligibility decisions. Federal officials pressured states to develop their ADC and OAA programs rapidly; nonetheless, some states had barely started their programs by 1940. Federal authorities occasionally threatened to cut off federal funds to states that were remiss in administering their programs.[129]

Reorganizing Federal Social Welfare Programs. Roosevelt realized by 1937 that he also needed to simplify the organization of federal programs; social welfare programs were scattered in the Departments of Interior, Treasury, Labor, and Agriculture, as well as in independent commissions and elsewhere. No department focused on social welfare issues, and no cabinet-level secretary coordinated the planning and implementation of social programs. He appointed a committee to examine this issue; the committee recommended the establishment of a Department of Public Works and a Department of Welfare, whose directors would sit in his cabinet. The plan was defeated in the Congress in 1938 because legislators feared that it had been masterminded by Hopkins to enhance his personal power, to increase Roosevelt's political patronage, and to increase the power of the federal government. The plan was also attacked by advocates of existing programs, such as the CCC, who feared that these programs would lose power if they were transferred to the new agency.[130]

Roosevelt reluctantly retreated to a more modest proposal to create a subcabinet agency known as the Federal Security Agency (FSA) and a Federal Works Agency under the Reorganization Act of 1939. The FSA contained the CCC, the NYA, the Public Health Service, the U.S. Employment Service, and the Social Security Board, whereas the WPA and the PWA were placed in the Federal Works Agency. This legislation was enacted, but not until 1953 was a department of the federal government finally created to house the nation's social programs—the Department of Health, Education, and Welfare, which became the Department of Health and Human Services in the mid-1970s.

That Roosevelt even *had* to create the FSA speaks volumes about the social welfare accomplishments of the New Deal. If virtually no federal social programs or policies existed before 1933, a national welfare state now existed whose programs needed to be housed in articulated federal agencies.

ASCENDANT CONSERVATIVES

Roosevelt's surprising social policy successes in 1937 and 1938 did not, however, portend a resurgent New Deal—whether because of ascendant conservatives or the diversion of Roosevelt's attention to looming international threats from Germany, Japan, and Italy.

Though conservatives never loved Roosevelt, they sometimes tolerated him because of the nation's economic straits. A conservative coalition consisting of Republicans, Southern Democrats, and some political moderates had developed considerable cohesion within the Congress by 1935, however, and rallied opposition to FDR's policies. Southern Democrats, who held many committee chairs in the House and Senate and had traditionally possessed a good deal of power in the Democratic Party, felt that their party had been taken over by liberal Northerners and by urban reformers such as Senator Wagner. Their anger mounted when they

were not consulted by Roosevelt on many policy issues. (See Insert 7.5.)

Business interests, which had often supported Democratic candidates, increasingly gave their allegiance and money to Republicans when confronted with legislation that would markedly increase the taxes of affluent persons and corporations. With Roosevelt's electoral successes, Republicans' opposition to the New Deal became increasingly militant; they realized that they might remain the minority party for decades if they could not arrest Roosevelt's political momentum.[131]

Roosevelt's political problems were compounded by the increasing opposition of a group of 13 Republican senators, called the insurgent progressives, who were ideological descendants of the Progressive Era. They had provided vital support to New Deal programs during Roosevelt's first term and had championed agricultural reforms, the TVA, antimonopoly policies, and higher taxes on the wealthy; but they disliked large federal bureaucracies, feared Roosevelt had too much power, wished to preserve strong policy roles for states, and feared the use of social programs for political patronage. They increasingly resented the deployment of a major portion of New Deal resources to urban areas and workers. Their distrust of Roosevelt and his policies reached paranoid proportions by 1936, when they were convinced that he sought

---

INSERT 7.5 Ethical Analysis of Key Issues and Policies: Roosevelt's Dilemma: What to Do about Southern Democrats?

Southern Democrats presented Roosevelt with an ethical dilemma. They were a large part of his Democratic Party and controlled virtually every congressional committee. When they voted with Republicans *against* New Deal legislation, they could defeat social reform measures.

Roosevelt's dilemma was this: When should he oppose the policy preferences of Southern Democrats and when should he defer to them? Should he have risked defeat of the Social Security Act by demanding more liberal provisions in it, such as national minimum standards for welfare grants? Or was he correct in acceding to many of the Southern Democrats' demands?

Discuss the ethical merits of *both* approaches and then decide, on balance, whether he made the ethically meritorious choice.

Roosevelt also confronted a related ethical dilemma. Northern liberals, like Senator Robert Wagner, wanted federal legislation to make the lynching of African Americans (a common occurrence in the South) a federal crime. Believing the Southern Democrats would oppose his New Deal if he supported antilynching legislation, Roosevelt maintained a discreet silence on the legislation until late in the decade; even then, his support was tepid. Did he err, ethically, when he made this choice?

to establish a dynasty beholden to urban interests. Their anger mounted in 1937, when Roosevelt attacked the Supreme Court and did not publicly rebuke the disruptive tactics of automobile workers. Furthermore, they had come to detest the size of the federal government. Their distrust of Roosevelt was expressed in negative votes on many pieces of legislation and in increasing cooperation with Southern Democrats and more conservative Republicans.[132]

After Woodrow Wilson's failure to rally the leaders of European nations behind a League of Nations that would work to avert future wars, the United States moved strongly in the direction of isolationism in the 1920s. It almost completely demobilized its army and navy—leaving it with military forces far smaller than many European nations. Separated by two oceans from Europe and Asia, Americans felt secure from military invasion, prompting the leaders of both parties to cut military spending further.

Even in the aftermath of World War I, however, Roosevelt feared that the United States would go to war with Germany one day. He even saw to it that some of the WPA's projects were geared toward preparedness, such as the construction of military airports. His fears escalated when fascist Adolf Hitler cemented his control over Germany, articulated aggressive intentions toward the rest of Europe, and developed a racist concept that specific white Europeans (which he called Aryans) were innately superior over other peoples—and as a militarist elite gained control of Japan and began a course of conquest against other Asian nations. Germany soon made an alliance with Italy and its dictator Benito Mussolini, further increasing Roosevelt's fears of looming war.

ROOSEVELT'S PRIORITIZING OF MILITARY PREPAREDNESS

Firmly believing in isolationism, most Americans were not perturbed even by Germany's invasion of Poland in 1939 or by Great Britain's subsequent

decision to declare war on Germany. As these developments took place, Roosevelt's attention no longer focused on domestic issues even though the Great Depression and widespread unemployment continued. Often secretly, he sent money and supplies to Great Britain. He gave speeches that eloquently pointed to military dangers that loomed from Germany, Japan, and Italy. He sought small increases in military spending—and then larger ones. He urged Congress, with limited success, to institute a military draft and to upgrade the nation's military preparedness, such as by manufacturing tanks, airplanes, and weapons. He placed Harry Hopkins in charge of the Department of Commerce in 1938 so that Hopkins could work with industry to develop plans to build military equipment.

THE ECLIPSE OF MUCH OF THE NEW DEAL WORK PROGRAMS BEFORE AND DURING WORLD WAR II

Roosevelt suffered many policy losses during the waning years of the New Deal. A program to provide a large revolving federal fund to finance public works was defeated. Knowing they would be rebuffed, Roosevelt declined to support health legislation and a redistributive tax act. As the nation rearmed, Congress periodically raised the national debt limit but, as the price of their compliance, conservatives demanded and often obtained major cuts in social spending. Roosevelt failed in his bids in 1937 and 1939 to have the CCC made a permanent program because conservatives did not want to establish the principle that ongoing federal programs were needed for the nation's youth. An ambitious proposal to develop programs like the TVA in seven other river basins was defeated.[133]

The fiscal survival of the New Deal became even more imperiled when Roosevelt decided to increase funding for the War Department and the navy to prepare for possible war with Germany and

Japan. Facing an isolationist Congress, he sought only small increases in military spending in 1938 and 1939—but he persuaded the Congress in 1940 to increase military spending massively after Hitler invaded Denmark, Luxembourg, Belgium, the Netherlands, and France. Wanting to increase aircraft production to 50,000 planes per year and to augment production of other armaments vastly, he obtained military appropriations of $17 billion— nearly two times the entire federal budget of the preceding year.

It was obvious by 1940, then, that the New Deal was fiscally imperiled. As the nation spent greater funds on its military, unemployment began to subside and had largely vanished by late 1941. Because Roosevelt had justified his New Deal primarily to deal with unemployment, his rationale for the New Deal also vanished as unemployment finally began to decline when jobs in rearmament industries increased. It is ironic that the nation finally discovered in 1941 that massive spending— far greater than the relatively meager spending devoted to New Deal programs—would end the Great Depression.

Moreover, rising military spending led conservatives to urge even further cuts in New Deal spending, calling it "nonessential" spending as compared with military spending. Even Roosevelt had reduced his support of the New Deal by 1940, increasingly referring to it in the past tense and using its work programs for projects with military significance such as airports and ships. (Roosevelt even put a military officer in charge of the WPA.) It was a difficult period for many New Deal reformers, as they increasingly feared that key New Deal programs would lose funds or even be eliminated.

The increases in military spending in 1940 and early 1941 were small, however, compared to the military spending that would take place in the wake of America's entry into World War II after the surprise attack by Japan on the Hawaiian Naval Base known as Pearl Harbor. Military planners soon received military expenditures totaling $120 billion to increase the army to 8.5 million men when it had consisted of 140,000 troops only two years earlier.

Liberals watched with dismay as many New Deal work programs were dismantled during World War II when unemployment ceased due to military production and conscription of millions of men and women into the armed forces. The WPA, CCC, PWA, and NYA were terminated by 1943. Franklin Roosevelt failed to make much of an effort to save the programs, but they were probably doomed because unemployment had vanished. Nor was Roosevelt inclined to involve himself in domestic controversy since he wanted bipartisan support of the war effort—giving conservatives more power than they had possessed before the war. The huge wartime deficit— unprecedented in American history--also made it difficult to justify spending that was not essential to the war effort.[134]

It is important to remember, however, that many New Deal policies remained intact, including the Social Security Act, the Fair Labor Standards Act, housing legislation, the TVA, and the Wagner Act. To these were added a huge policy initiative during World War II: the GI Bill, which would provide college and vocational training to millions of veterans in the wake of World War II.

THE OPPRESSION OF VULNERABLE POPULATIONS IN THE NEW DEAL

In the New Deal, attention focused on the problems of unemployment and relief, as millions of Americans were economically devastated by the Great Depression. But women, Latinos, African Americans, and Asian Americans bore a disproportionate share of the economic suffering and sometimes wondered whether the New Deal spoke to their broader needs as well as their economic deprivation. In some cases, the economic plight of whites heightened animosities between the dominant population and vulnerable groups, both during the Depression and during World War II.

The Oppression of Women

The achievement of suffrage did not lead to policy gains for women, who found themselves unable to vote as a bloc or to agree on policy issues. Some women, including Eleanor Roosevelt, favored passage of protective legislation that shielded women from dangerous or physically taxing occupations; other women, who believed that protective legislation would merely close certain jobs to women, supported an equal rights amendment to the Constitution to grant women legal equality with men.[135]

Eleanor Roosevelt became a determined advocate for women during the early years of the New Deal. Because the CCC camps were statutorily limited to males, she persuaded her husband to establish 45 camps for 8,500 women under the FERA. Working closely with Molly Dewson, director of the women's division of the Democratic Party, she secured the appointment of many women to high-level posts in the FERA, the WPA, and other agencies.[136] Almost no women obtained work relief in the CWA, but 15 percent of WPA recruits were women. The Wagner Act helped spur organizing of women; between 1930 and 1940, for example, the International Ladies Garment Workers Union tripled its membership to 800,000 persons.

Although many women—about 20 percent— lost their jobs during the Great Depression, others found their employment to be more secure than men's; they tended not to work in heavy industry but rather in gender-segregated occupations that were relatively unaffected by the economic downturn. With the expansion of government programs, vast numbers of clerks and secretaries were hired, and the percentage of women in the federal workforce rose from 14 percent in 1929 to 19 percent in 1939— twice the rate of increase of male employment.[137]

Women also made major strides in obtaining sexual freedom. The flapper of the 1920s partially escaped Victorian moral codes. A majority of middle-class married women used birth control during the 1930s; their physicians provided them with the information they needed. However, many poor women, who could not afford doctors, lacked access to birth control information because birth control clinics were still illegal in many areas under the obscenity laws that had hampered Margaret Sanger two decades earlier.[138]

The economic and social gains of women in the New Deal should not obscure the continuing discrimination against them. It was widely assumed that married women should relinquish their positions to allow the employment of unemployed men; indeed, some women lost federal jobs after federal legislation in 1932 (which was not rescinded until 1937) stipulated that husbands and wives could not both hold federal positions. Many administrators in the CWA and the PWA assumed that husbands should receive priority in work relief programs. NRA labor codes tended to establish lower wages for women than for men in identical positions. Widows were not entitled to receive Social Security benefits of their deceased husbands until 1939; even under the new policy, the woman was not entitled to the benefits unless she was living with her husband at the time of his death.[139] Social Security was also expanded in 1939 to give modest benefits to the wives of retired workers—so long, that is, as she had been his wife for at least five years and was living with him at the time of the application. (Divorced women and remarried women had to forfeit these benefits.) Because Social Security benefits were tied to wage levels, female retirees, who usually came from low-wage occupations, received lower benefits than did males. Women who worked as domestics or in agriculture were not included in Social Security at all.[140] Unemployment insurance also discriminated against women. Because applicants were required to have a recent and extended employment record, women who left the labor force to have a child—or for other family reasons—could not easily reestablish eligibility after they resumed work. Many women were also denied benefits because they refused a "suitable job" that was a distance away or that required they work hours that were incompatible with their family responsibilities.[141] Nor were benefits paid for pregnancy or maternal (or paternal) leave—an omission that remains in place today. Until 1950, the ADC program did not provide benefits to the heads of households but only to the children, and federal authorities provided a smaller share of the funding of ADC than of OAA. Because it provided grants only to children in families headed by a single mother, ADC offered no assistance to the children of married women, many of whom were in considerable need. Trade unions generally excluded women from leadership positions and often negotiated contracts that gave women lower pay than men. The AFL leadership even demanded that women who were married leave their jobs so as to make available more employment for males.[142]

The cult of domesticity, which had dominated American family life for a century, remained intact; many married women who worked outside the home encountered hostility from their husbands and peers, even when they limited their horizons to gender-segregated and low-paying jobs. Moreover, psychologists, psychoanalysts, and physicians, such as Dr. Gesell and Dr. Spock, defined the role of the mother (*not* the father) as an all-encompassing one that was dictated by the needs of their children. Love between mother and child was the magic and necessary ingredient to be provided in "a perfectly nourishing environment" with mothers avoiding "outside commitments so as not to 'miss' a fascinating stage of development," so that mother and child "could enjoy each other, fulfilling one another's needs perfectly, instinctively, as if Nature in her infinite wisdom has created them [to be] two happily matched consumers consuming each other."[143] Thus defined as Supermom, women were truly confined to their homes through much of their married lives.

The Oppression of Latinos

Spanish-speaking persons constituted the majority of field workers in the irrigated farms of the Southwest by 1930. Despite some successes, violent suppression of agricultural unions, as well as red-baiting, led to the demise of pioneering unions. As farmworkers were not covered under the Wagner Act of 1935, they did not have collective bargaining rights that were enforced by the federal

government; thus, employers could fire anyone they suspected of trying to organize the workers. In remote farming areas, the workers lacked access to lawyers and advocates. Even the few unions that had developed ended with the onset of World War II, when many organizers and workers were drafted or migrated to cities. As we have already noted, farmworkers did not receive Social Security benefits or unemployment insurance.

When thousands of unemployed Latinos sought welfare in the 1930s, local welfare officials demanded massive "repatriation" (forced evacuation) to Mexico. Around 400,000 Latinos were forced to leave the country between 1929 and 1934. Many of them, with $14.70 in their pockets from the U.S. government, were placed on trains to Mexico City; the impact on families and communities was devastating.

When faced with the need to produce huge quantities of food during World War II, the federal government initiated the Bracero program through a bilateral agreement with Mexico in 1942. The Mexican government, which wanted to alleviate domestic unemployment, allowed a specified number of Mexicans to enter the United States to meet labor shortages on farms; in return, the U.S. government pledged to ensure a minimum wage and to guarantee their just treatment. Extended annually until 1964, the program brought a total of 5 million Mexican laborers to the United States. In addition, many undocumented workers continued to flow into the United States during this period. But not bound by any agreements with the Mexican government regarding undocumented workers, employers that hired them—mainly agribusiness and mining companies—were able to treat them virtually as they wished.

Despite efforts by the Mexican government to secure their rights, braceros were subjected to countless abuses—in particular, poor wages, lack of housing, and lack of health care—and unions were no more successful during and after World War II than in the 1930s.

During World War II, sizable Latino populations had settled in urban areas; they worked in munitions factories, ship building, and other industries. Like African American workers of the period, they lived in segregated communities, in neighborhoods that had been abandoned by white populations fleeing to areas with better amenities. These urban Latinos encountered considerable racial animosity. In Los Angeles, for example, white sailors on shore leave frequently attacked Latino youth who wore zoot suits—flamboyant outfits featuring long jackets with padded shoulders. Resentment at these attacks led to the so-called zoot-suit riots. The Los Angeles police, well known for their brutality against Latinos, regularly conducted mass roundups and incarcerations.[144]

The Oppression of African Americans

As the New Deal began, discrimination against African Americans continued unabated in both the North and the South. Because Jim Crow laws remained in force throughout the South, African Americans were disenfranchised, forced to live in segregated neighborhoods, required to sit at the rear of buses, and enrolled in segregated schools. Bad as these violations of civil rights were, they were overshadowed by the many instances of violence against African Americans. The Ku Klux Klan, long a presence in the South, had a resurgence in the 1920s and struck terror in the hearts of African Americans with a sustained campaign of lynchings and beatings.

Hard times increased racism because many whites feared that African Americans would take employment from them. Faced with layoff decisions, many employers fired African Americans and retained white employees, sometimes in response to agitation by white citizens. As had been common before the 1930s, African American workers were denied membership in many unions and were used as scabs by employers to break strikes. Southern whites were furious, too, that African Americans received far higher wages under the WPA than they had received in the fields, and they feared that the New Deal programs would disrupt the political and economic structure of the South by dramatically improving the economic condition of African Americans.[145]

African Americans desperately needed federal civil rights legislation that would rescind Jim Crow laws and outlaw discrimination by unions and employers, as well as job and service programs to provide resources and employment. But Roosevelt, during most of the New Deal, refused even to support legislation that would make lynching a federal crime; he finally gave it no more than verbal support late in the 1930s. Nor did he support legislation to eliminate the poll tax, which was widely used in the South to disenfranchise African Americans, or legislation to counter segregation in housing markets, despite urging by African Americans and Senator Wagner.[146]

Why didn't Roosevelt throw his support behind civil rights legislation? He knew that Southern Democrats would become determined opponents of his domestic programs if he supported civil rights legislation, particularly if they voted with Republicans in the so-called conservative coalition. (As we have seen, Roosevelt's forebodings came true in 1937 and succeeding years, when the conservative coalition militantly attacked many New Deal initiatives.)[147] Indeed, even before 1937, Roosevelt had to make key concessions in unemployment, Social Security, public welfare, NRA, and fair labor and standards legislation to obtain the support of Southerners.[148]

Roosevelt and his aides also felt that African Americans were discriminated against because they were poor *rather than* because they were African American, and thus New Deal programs like the WPA, which gave jobs to African Americans, would end discrimination more effectively than would civil rights legislation. This perspective was tragically naïve. Racism exists as a force that is independent of social class; in contemporary society, for example, affluent and well-educated African Americans still experience discrimination in job and housing markets. In the New Deal era, as we have already noted, some whites became even more hostile to African Americans, whom they viewed as competitors for jobs and even WPA positions. And the disposition of some whites to lynch African Americans was hardly linked to their precise economic status, as the epidemic of lynchings throughout the 1930s illustrated.

If many New Dealers were disinclined to support federal civil rights legislation, they were also reluctant to develop programs that specifically provided African American populations with resources and jobs. The creation of special programs for African Americans or even a policy of requiring quotas for African Americans in specific New Deal programs was opposed because such programs and quotas were perceived to represent reverse discrimination.[149] Without such special treatment, however, it was doubtful that African Americans could overcome the economic and social chasm that existed between themselves and the white population.

African Americans nonetheless obtained notable policy concessions. Because it was obvious that many local officials and project review committees would exclude African Americans from eligibility in the FERA and CWA programs in 1933, Hopkins, Williams, Perkins, and Ickes appointed African American advisors to monitor implementation of programs and to work in tandem with investigators to detect flagrant cases of discrimination.[150] They also appointed African Americans to high positions in New Deal social programs. (See Insert 7.8 for a Profile in Leadership on Mary McLeod Bethune.) Considerable success was obtained in enrolling African Americans, who constituted 10 percent of CCC enrollees and more than 15 percent of WPA workers.[151] The PWA and NYA were particularly innovative; the PWA established a quota system that required its private contractors to reach specific goals in their hiring practices; and the NYA was the only major New Deal agency that established special programs restricted to African American enrollees.[152] The inclusion of millions of African Americans in New Deal programs represented a major policy feat in a nation that had often denied African Americans access to local relief programs.

Discrimination nonetheless existed within New Deal programs. Except for a few camps in New England, the CCC was segregated. Roosevelt feared racial conflict within integrated camps as well as political opposition from Southerners. (Ugly incidents occurred in a number of camps before they were segregated.) African American enrollees were not transported to CCC camps in other states because of opposition by whites and fear for their safety.[153] Housing built by the PWA was often segregated.[154] Many New Deal programs—in particular, programs to help farmers refinance their mortgages or obtain loans—were of no assistance to African Americans, most of whom were tenant farmers. The NRA often allowed Southern industrialists to establish wage codes that froze the existing inequitable wages for African American workers.[155] Moreover, as we have seen, payments made to landowners under the AAA for withdrawing acreage from production were often not passed on to African American tenant farmers and sharecroppers, despite legislation that required such transfers.

Curiously, African Americans gained a major victory during World War II when reformers asked why African Americans should sacrifice their lives in the war if units of the army were segregated, if African American workers in war industries had to live in segregated housing, and if African Americans encountered discrimination in wartime industries. Many whites, including some liberals, exhorted African Americans not to raise these issues during the war so as not to divide the nation; but A. Phillip Randolph, the fiery African American director of the Brotherhood of Sleeping Car Porters and Maids, was so incensed by the prevalence of job discrimination against African Americans, even in war industries desperate for labor, that he advocated a massive march on Washington to force Roosevelt to sign federal legislation that would ensure the fair employment of African Americans in the defense industry. So as not to disrupt the war effort, Roosevelt finally relented in 1941 by signing Executive Order 8802 to prohibit discrimination in employment in the defense industry on the basis of race, creed, or national origin—on the condition that plans for the march be abandoned. (Executive Order 8802 also established the Committee on Fair Employment Practices to monitor the private sector, though the committee was given such scant funding that it could not assertively investigate many complaints of discrimination.)

Because Randolph was unable to persuade Roosevelt to sign an order to desegregate the armed forces, the war was fought with segregated battalions until President Truman finally desegregated the armed forces at the war's end.[156] Hundreds of thousands of African Americans who returned from the military at the end of the war encountered extraordinary prejudice in both the North and the South. Moreover, the African Americans who had migrated to cities during the war constituted a growing underclass with limited economic prospects.

Thus, the civil rights accomplishments of the New Deal were very limited. A huge chasm existed between white and African American populations in this era, as suggested by public opinion polls. Poll data in 1939, for example, indicated that 69 percent of whites thought African Americans were less intelligent and that most whites endorsed segregated restaurants, neighborhoods, and schools (respectively, 99, 97, and 98 percent of Southerners and 62, 82, and 58 percent of Northerners).[157]

An African American social worker ominously predicted in the 1930s that provision of welfare benefits to African Americans without civil rights and jobs legislation risked perpetuating their inferior economic and social status. Three decades later, Jesse Jackson, a former aide to Martin Luther King, Jr., repeated that warning when he noted the existence of a massive population of African Americans who encountered bleak job prospects, poor educational programs, and minimal job-training programs and whose survival often hinged on the receipt of welfare benefits.[158]

Yet World War II set the stage for the civil rights movement of the 1950s and 1960s. Persons of color were asked to risk their lives in armed conflict but were *not* granted basic human rights in the military or in the United States when they returned home. Angered by this inequity, a generation of African Americans vowed, upon their return, to fight for civil rights on the home front. They were joined by returning Latino, Asian American, and First American soldiers who experienced similar indignities on their return to the United States.

The Oppression of Asian Americans

The migration of Asians to the United States was effectively curbed with the Immigration Act of 1924, which limited annual immigration from specific countries to the percentage of the population of the corresponding group in the United States in 1890, when few Asians had migrated. (Chinese migration was banned altogether by the Chinese Exclusion Act of 1882.) Even though Asian immigrants were not allowed to own land in many areas by state legislation, they had shown extraordinary ability to continue farming—by leasing land or by finding cooperative Americans who put their own names on the deed but allowed the Asians to work the land. Moreover, Chinese American and Japanese American communities channeled their energies into developing a thriving network of small businesses. The Nisei (second-generation Japanese Americans, the children of the Issei, or first generation), who were U.S. citizens by virtue of birth, placed extraordinary emphasis on education, which was seen as a way of overcoming the barriers imposed by discrimination. Caught between American and Japanese culture, the Nisei nonetheless sought, with their parents' blessing, to master English, to go to college, and to use their educational achievement to obtain jobs that had been denied their parents.[159]

But a strong undercurrent of racism existed toward this out-group. This racism could be shockingly intense, as Takaki points out. He cites the example of a young Japanese man from Hawaii who went to get his hair cut. On hearing that he was Japanese, the barber drove the young man out of his shop "as if he were driving away a cat or a dog."[160] People even spat on Japanese persons whom they encountered on the street. First-generation Asian Americans were denied citizenship on the grounds that they were non-Caucasian aliens—and then denied access to relief programs during the Great Depression on the grounds that they were not citizens! Nor were the Nisei able to escape discrimination, even with their college degrees. As the depression hit, most Nisei were unable to find jobs for which they had been trained; virtually no jobs were open to them in engineering, manufacturing, business, or even high school teaching. Trapped in family businesses, almost no Nisei worked for white employers even as late as 1940.[161] Chinese Americans worked largely in restaurants and laundries, and a pattern of systematic discrimination prevented them from working in other occupations.

Recall that many Americans on the West Coast had feared an invasion from Japan even at the start of the century and had demanded the immediate cessation of all immigration from Japan. The attack on Pearl Harbor in 1941 brought an immediate fear that Japanese Americans would conspire with Japanese agents to facilitate an invasion by the Japanese. As other Asian Americans tried frantically to show that they were not of Japanese ancestry, Japanese Americans found themselves isolated and subjected to hatred and violence. They waited fearfully to see what would happen next.

Roosevelt had received confidential reports before and soon after Pearl Harbor that the Japanese Americans did not constitute a threat to national security. The press, however, printed a chorus of rumors that Japanese Americans were conspiring with Japanese agents and reported widespread calls for their immediate internment. Unlike General Delos Emmons in Hawaii, General John DeWitt of the Western Defense Command became a zealous persecutor of Japanese Americans and conducted many search-and-seizure operations to find hidden transmitters. White farmers, who resented the success of Japanese American farmers, demanded their evacuation, partly out of a desire to obtain their land.

Roosevelt was urged by his attorney general not to evacuate the Japanese Americans, and it was obvious that rounding them up without due process would be an infringement of their civil rights. Nevertheless, Roosevelt and other advisors were determined to proceed—and often used blatantly racist language in their private conversations.[162] Executive Order 9066, although it did not mention Japanese Americans, empowered the secretary of war to develop "military areas" where he could confine whoever he thought was a secu-

rity risk. Rumors that Italian Americans and German Americans might be apprehended sparked widespread protests, but no protests emerged when about 120,000 Japanese Americans were rounded up and taken to internment camps located in remote rural areas, with no due process and no hearings. (See Figure 7.4.) Because they were able to take only what they could carry, they were forced to sell their houses and belongings within a matter of days; under these circumstances, they were often forced to accept nominal amounts for their possessions.

The Japanese Americans were given numbers and were required to wear them on tags from the point of evacuation onward. They were housed in assembly centers, shipped to remote internment camps with no idea where they were going, and greeted by barbed wire and guard towers in the camps. Curiously, the American authorities, who had incarcerated them as security risks, soon sought to persuade draft-age youth to volunteer for the armed services, but only after they agreed to sign loyalty oaths; partly to protest the internment, many of them did not volunteer—and draft protests broke out in 1944 when the military tried to conscript them. Nonetheless, 33,000 Nisei served in World War II, many with distinction.

Evacuation orders had been rescinded before the end of the war, and some of those internees who agreed to sign loyalty oaths were allowed to settle in cities not on the West Coast, such as Denver and Chicago. But the damage had been done to several generations of Japanese Americans. Those who were still alive finally received symbolic compensation in the 1990s.

This incident involved a unique situation, but is not trivial. It was (and is) widely perceived by Asian Americans as an illustration of the impact of racism on American social policy. Leaders who had implemented dozens of humane policies were nonetheless able to take extraordinary actions that were fueled by racism; indeed, those actions provoked scant protest even from liberals.

To critics, the episode was the tragic culmination of the New Deal's consistently poor record on civil rights, not just for Asian Americans but for

FIGURE 7.4 The forced confinement of Japanese Americans in World War II.

other people of color and women as well. The American government did, however, finally rescind its ban on Chinese immigration in 1943—more than 60 years after its original passage. In the end, the ban was lifted for utilitarian rather than moral reasons; the United States could not justify Chinese exclusion without endangering its alliance with the Chinese.[163]

SOCIAL WORKERS IN THE NEW DEAL

By the end of the 1920s, social work had consolidated its position, with the development of many schools, most of which were associated with universities. An explosion of demand for social workers occurred as, freed from the old preoccupations with relief giving, the profession attended to a host of problems, including family disruption, medical problems, child pathology, school problems, and outpatient services to persons released from mental institutions. The old charity organization society agencies, some 200 nationwide, developed the American Association for Organizing Charity, where they officially changed their mission from relief giving to family casework. In the 1920s, nongovernmental social agencies developed so-called federated fund raising, in which many agencies banded together to seek donations from corporations and their employees in a united drive; this later became known as the United Way. In 1921, the new profession developed a mass-membership professional organization, the American Association of Social Workers, even if most of its early members lacked professional training. The future looked promising for this new profession; it had developed a core technology (social casework) and network of social agencies, sources of funding (the federation), and many schools.[164]

Social casework, which emphasized diagnosis and "scientific work," still bore some resemblance to the older charity work because it focused on the person in the environment.[165] Both in diagnosis and interventions, caseworkers examined environmental factors that shaped the problems of their clients and used this information to help clients cope with situational realities. But in the 1920s, the primacy of social casework was challenged by the emergence of psychiatric social work, which drew heavily on the ideas of Freud and his disciples, as illustrated by the works of Virginia Robinson and others, which were markedly different from older works by Mary Richmond. Psychiatric social work did not dominate the profession in many schools and agencies, but it was a highly visible wing of social work and had a particularly strong hold on certain schools, such as Smith College and the University of Pennsylvania, and certain kinds of agencies, such as child guidance agencies and psychiatric hospitals. Some proponents of social casework feared that this new contender, which emphasized intrapsychic matters and family relationships, could sever social work from its person-in-the-environment emphasis as well as its work with relatively impoverished populations.

Social workers were not usually involved in social reform projects or in public agencies during the 1920s. Even many of the old settlement houses, though still existing, had lost their reformist qualities, as well as their visible leadership within the profession. Social workers were not highly active in partisan politics, although they supported specific candidates whom they believed were interested in certain social issues.

Many social work leaders took an intense interest in the national presidential campaign of 1928, however. They couldn't agree on which candidate to support; Al Smith had been receptive to social workers during his tenure as governor of New York State, and Herbert Hoover had pursued humanitarian work after World War I in Europe and shown interest in unemployment issues during the 1920s.[166] Nevertheless, a sizable number of social workers continued to believe that social work should remain separate from partisan politics altogether.

Thus divided, the profession was as unready for the political upheaval of the Great Depression as many other citizens were. Many leaders maintained, as did Hoover, that private agencies would suffice to manage the economic destitution that occurred in 1929 and 1930. They were in for a rude shock, however, when they found that private agencies, like the Red Cross, lacked the funds to help the throngs of destitute people. Indeed, vast numbers of social agencies, one-third of them in New York City alone, went bankrupt because of the rising caseloads and the drop-off in private philanthropy. Increasing numbers of social workers realized by 1930 that strong governmental action was needed, even if many of them still did not see the Democratic Party as the necessary instrument of reform. (As we have already seen, Jane Addams voted for Herbert Hoover, not Franklin Roosevelt, in 1932.)[167] By 1932, however, many social work leaders had come to dislike Hoover for his disinclination to take bold action to help unemployed people.

Curiously, the Great Depression and World War II actually benefited the social work profession. Whereas most social workers had been employed in private agencies in the 1920s, thousands of jobs opened up in New Deal agencies in the 1930s. The number of people in social work positions increased from 40,000 in 1930 to 70,000 in 1940.[168] During the 1920s, a cohesive community of leaders in New York City became acquainted with Eleanor Roosevelt and Harry Hopkins and assumed leadership and consultative roles to Franklin Roosevelt during his governorship of New York State. Many of these social workers assumed influential positions in the New Deal, supported the FERA, the NRA, and the CWA, and sought to professionalize New Deal programs by insisting on prominent roles for social workers.[169]

Indeed, Hopkins supported many training programs for social workers. When the Social Security Act mandated the creation of the Social Security Board, social workers received key appointments to it and also to its Bureau of Public Assistance, which supervised ADC and the other welfare programs.

Social casework proved to be adaptable to these new public agencies, which sought to screen, refer, and give brief assistance to the many destitute people who used the New Deal programs. At the same time, the psychiatric wing of the profession continued to ply its trade in various private agencies, which existed throughout the 1930s.

Many of the new social work positions were filled by untrained people. Paid relatively low salaries and acutely aware that the New Deal programs provided only meager benefits to desperately poor people, these staff members developed lively protest movements to seek both better pay for themselves and greater benefits for their clients.[170] Mary Van Kleeck and the publication *Social Work Today* issued fiery denunciations of the New Deal, which many believed was captive to corporate interests. The so-called rank-and-file movement of nonprofessional public employees of New Deal programs developed unions of public employees, supported sweeping social reforms, and often joined with or helped to organize poor persons as well as their own clients. By 1937, however, their protests had dissipated, perhaps because many of them had become part of the establishment and civil service protections had been extended to them.[171]

World War II brought more growth to the profession. Social workers were hired by the Red Cross and other agencies that helped soldiers. Private agencies worked with relocated workers, day care, and other social issues on the home front.[172]

At various points during the 1930s and 1940s, social workers wrestled with the question of how selectively the profession should define its boundaries. One faction wanted the profession to markedly increase its membership to include the legions of untrained people who worked in public programs—and, in the 1940s, to include people with only a bachelor's degree. They believed that the power of the profession would increase as it broadened its boundaries and that the quality and prestige of many social work positions could be increased by including their incumbents in the profession. Another faction wanted to restrict membership in the profession to individuals with a graduate degree to keep the caliber of professional work at a high level and maintain the prestige of the profession. The two factions often clashed, but for the moment, the selective faction was victorious.[173]

As in the Progressive Era, opinions within the social work profession reflected attitudes within the broader society. Most of the leadership was sympathetic to Roosevelt, even if they were sometimes embittered by, for example, his termination of the CWA and some of the conservative features of the Social Security Act. In the 1930s, virtually all social workers were convinced of the need for government to fund and deliver a host of services; thus, the curious hold of nongovernmental agencies on social welfare was ended forever. Perhaps we can say that social work became a part of the broad coalition that Roosevelt had fashioned in the New Deal, to the extent that the profession was viewed as liberal in succeeding decades as well. When Richard Nixon and other conservatives cast about for enemies some decades later, they unhesitatingly seized on social workers; some social workers took that as a sign that the reformist traditions of the profession remained at least somewhat intact.

Yet, some social workers supported relatively backward-looking policies during the New Deal —for example, restriction of ADC grants to those families whom caseworkers judged to provide "suitable homes"; that policy would have given social workers a strange veto over the intake process in public welfare.[174] And some social workers remained safely outside the turmoil of the New Deal, working in child guidance and other agencies with a psychiatric focus.

On the left, a small faction sided with decidedly radical protests in the late 1930s, including the Communist Party, the rank-and-file movement, and the Socialist Party. They often argued that social work had been co-opted by Roosevelt to participate in inadequate social programs and that, by doing so, it was blunting significant social change that could occur only by aligning the profession with grassroots dissent.

This discussion of social work in the 1920s and 1930s suggests that a lively controversy existed within the profession over a number of issues. For example, to what extent should the profession engage in social action rather than just counseling? Should the profession have relatively broad or narrow membership? And to what extent should the profession ally itself politically with liberal forces? We can see certain central tendencies in the developments of the 1920s and 1930s, such as the dominance of casework, the decision by most social workers to support relatively liberal social policies but not radical reforms, and the preferences for a relatively restrictive membership policy. But these central tendencies ought not to obscure conflict within a profession that, in some respects, was a microcosm of the society that enveloped it.

THE EVOLUTION OF THE RELUCTANT WELFARE STATE

When viewed from the perspective of the Progressive Era, the New Deal represents a striking departure from traditional American policies on two counts. First, unlike progressive reformers, who focused on state and local reforms, Roosevelt created a *national* welfare state that superseded local programs. Second, he created social programs rather than focusing on a regulatory strategy, as was illustrated by the first major social programs in the United States that distributed jobs (the CWA, WPA, CCC, and PWA) and resources (the FERA and the Social Security Act) to destitute and elderly Americans. By going beyond the legalistic approach of progressives, Roosevelt drastically altered the scope of the American welfare state.

It is easy to criticize the New Deal from the vantage point of contemporary society. New Deal reforms did not include the range of civil rights,

medical, housing, Food Stamp, and other programs that were developed in subsequent reform eras, and they often were diluted by compromises with conservatives. Roosevelt nonetheless accomplished his reforms in a society where virtually no national social programs had existed and in the face of profound social, legal, and political opposition. In venturing into new policy territory, he often stumbled and changed directions, but he developed precedent-shattering policies that helped millions of citizens survive an economic catastrophe. He opportunistically changed policies as political realities changed, but he was remarkably consistent in his basic policy goals. He was a firm believer in capitalism, but he sought regulatory, tax, and social welfare policies to mitigate economic uncertainty and the suffering that accompanied it. He opposed ideology, whether socialism or unfettered capitalism, and preferred instead to seek practical reform policies in the political context that he encountered. In 1932, Frances Perkins wrote on a piece of paper a series of six reforms that she favored; by 1940, only national health insurance had not been enacted.[175]

Roosevelt's social welfare innovations were matched by political accomplishments that prevented conservatives from dismantling all of his social reforms after World War II. He created the modern Democratic Party, which, for all its faults, embraced a relatively liberal constituency. Voting preferences in the nation were associated for the first time with social class and with political ideology; African Americans, workers, Jews, and intellectuals tended to support the Democratic Party, whereas affluent Americans tended to vote Republican. The numerical size of this liberal constituency made it difficult for Republicans to rescind the New Deal—unless they could persuade large numbers of working- and middle-class voters that social reform was not in their best interest. This did not happen to any significant degree until the administration of Ronald Reagan in the 1980s.

Still, viewed from the vantage point of today's society, New Deal reforms were timid. The social reform agenda of the 1960s and 1970s was largely fashioned to address social problems that were not included within New Deal reforms—federal medical programs, national civil rights legislation, federal assistance for persons with mental disorders, programs to help persons with disabilities, educational and nutritional programs for those with few resources, and job-training programs. The various New Deal programs often helped less affluent persons survive their immediate destitution, and Roosevelt did obtain some tax reforms, but the federal tax system was not so fundamentally reformed as to alter existing economic inequality or to provide sufficient revenues to support an ongoing and substantial welfare state. The realignment of the political parties was not accompanied by an economic or social revolution that redressed inequalities between classes or races.

As a consummate politician, Roosevelt was sometimes overcautious in supporting social reforms. He did not aggressively support union organizing; did not try to institutionalize a public works program; delegated many social welfare functions to states and localities when the Social Security Act was enacted; and often resorted to budget-cutting even when it led to widespread suffering. Moreover, he did not seize the opportunity to mobilize a liberal party as aggressively as he might have; he was too enamored with coalition politics, except when he ineffectually tried to purge Southern Democrats. Roosevelt did not grasp the political uses of the labor movement until late in the decade.[176]

Particularly when prodded by conservatives, Roosevelt and Perkins gave states considerable discretion in setting eligibility and program standards in many of the New Deal programs, even when this policy allowed conservative and Southern states to impose punitive and racist standards. Workers in America were more heavily burdened by the payroll taxes of the Social Security program than were affluent persons, and they received only short-term and relatively miserly unemployment benefits. Americans in poverty who did not fit the restrictive eligibility requirements of OAA, ADC, and AB were forced to receive welfare assistance from relatively punitive local programs.

Where do we place the blame for these various shortcomings in New Deal policy? To some extent, Roosevelt reflected the hesitations and biases of American society. Because the nation entered the decade with no tradition of federal leadership in social welfare, the first programs were greeted with suspicion and uncertain funding. So preoccupied were reformers with establishing the precedent of federal programs that they often could not seek their enlargement or had to make compromises to conservatives in both parties to establish them.[177] Many of Roosevelt's advisors, as well as a large contingent of liberals in the Congress, had their ideological roots in the Progressive Era, when emphasis was placed on local reforms, and were reluctant to develop a large federal bureaucracy or permanent federal programs.[178] There was widespread prejudice against programs that assisted urban dwellers and workers, even though most Americans lived in cities. Work relief programs were controversial in a society that assumed industrious persons could find work or that believed government should not interfere with the private sector. Deficit spending was also unpopular.

Roosevelt was able to enact the policies of the New Deal only because the Great Depression brought unprecedented suffering and thereby created a political climate in which social reform could be tolerated. Roosevelt lacked strong and certain allies on the left whom he could rely on for consistent support. Charismatic but eccentric leaders such as Father Coughlin and Huey Long were as adept at demagoguery as they were at supporting reforms. The CIO proved a more certain ally, but the AFL was lukewarm about the Fair Employment Practices Act and opportunistically used programs like the WPA to secure jobs for its own members.

It is ironic, in retrospect, that President Ronald Reagan attacked Roosevelt's New Deal in the 1980s as America's venture into socialism. It was hardly socialism; it was a tentative foundation for a welfare state that would provide minimal public benefits to some people in poverty and to older Americans. The nation's social and economic inequalities, as well as its racist and sexist policies, remained intact.

LINKING THE NEW DEAL TO CONTEMPORARY SOCIETY

What We Can Learn from Policy Advocates of the New Deal

We suffer from an embarrassment of riches when we seek policy advocates who have much to teach us in contemporary society. Let's discuss Eleanor Roosevelt and Mary Abby Van Kleeck because each in their own way, but very different ways, tried to push the New Deal to be even more liberal in its approach. (See Insert 7.6 and Insert 7.7.)

We can learn from Eleanor Roosevelt that a commitment to engage in policy advocacy often stems from identification with "underdogs" in society rather than with established elites, whether low-wage workers, women, tenant farmers, or persons with serious mental conditions. In view of the fact that she grew up in an affluent family—and married a distant relative who himself came from high society—it is remarkable how completely she dedicated her life to helping the disenfranchised at home and abroad.

Eleanor Roosevelt also teaches us how closely linked electoral politics and policy advocacy often must be. Genuine advances for vulnerable populations often come through advances in public policy that require the assent of elected officials in local, state, and federal legislatures, as well as in mayoral, gubernatorial, or presidential offices. No matter how skilled policy advocates may be, they are not likely to succeed if they cannot appeal to sufficient numbers of public officials who *also* side with underdogs.

The linkage between electoral politics and policy advocacy was nowhere more evident than during the 1930s. The Republican Party was highly conservative in this era. Even President Herbert Hoover's timid measures to deal with the Great Depression were viewed as too radical by many Republicans. Had Franklin Roosevelt not achieved landslide victories in 1932 and 1936, it is unlikely that he would have been able to get the Congress to enact many of his New Deal programs.

Eleanor Roosevelt worked incessantly to advance Democrats' electoral fortunes in the 1930s.

She spoke at numerous campaign rallies. She talked political strategy with her husband. She sought promising candidates for specific offices. With universal suffrage achieved only about a decade earlier, she encouraged women to vote—and to vote for the Democratic Party. She freely gave her husband political strategy.

Yet Eleanor Roosevelt cannot merely be labeled a political partisan because she viewed herself as a person who linked the needs of oppressed populations with political elites of both major parties. To use the parlance of our policy advocacy framework in Figure 2.1, she was an agenda builder seeking to place many issues on the agendas of public officials. To educate herself about the hardships encountered by oppressed persons, she personally visited settlement houses, mental institutions, factories, mines, and rural areas. She commissioned reporter Lorena Hickok to roam the nation during the Great Depression and to relay specific information about persons that she observed, such as the man who told her that he could not afford dental care for his wife's rotting teeth.

She relayed the information that she gathered about social needs to the nation through her weekly radio program, her syndicated newspaper column, and her lectures in a way that no other presidential wife has even attempted. She became a public figure almost as widely known as her husband in her non-stop quest to induce Americans toward moral outrage at the demeaning conditions that she discovered.

She provided this information to her husband on almost a daily basis. Sometimes, of course, her efforts as a policy advocate were unsuccessful, such as when she tried to convince her husband to admit young women to the CCC. Yet she succeeded in getting women into the WPA and NYA, as well as bringing about other changes.

Eleanor Roosevelt also illustrates the importance of personal connections in policy advocacy because she had inside access to the most powerful public official in the nation—Franklin Roosevelt. None of us can aspire to privileged access on this level—but we can seek personal connections with leaders of advocacy groups and some public officials as we relay to them specific information about

INSERT 7.6   Profiles in Leadership: Anna Eleanor Roosevelt (1884–1962)

Anna Eleanor Roosevelt, sometimes called the "First Lady of the World," was born on October 11, 1884, in New York City, to Elliot and Anna (Hall) Roosevelt. Though her family was both distinguished and wealthy, Roosevelt nonetheless was lonely and unhappy throughout her childhood. Before she was 10, her parents and younger brother had died. She and her brother Hall were the only survivors.

Eleanor Roosevelt, who remembered herself as a child without beauty or the joy of youth, had often felt rejected by her beautiful mother, who nicknamed her "granny." Shortly after her parents died, Eleanor went to live with her grandmother, who was also distant. Eleanor Roosevelt was closest to her father, a charming and loving man. But he was an alcoholic who only occasionally saw Eleanor and who left an emotional void in her life when he died.

Eleanor Roosevelt's life and political thought were greatly influenced during her time at Allenswood, an exclusive girls' school outside of London. There, she came under the guidance and influence of Marie Souvestre, a liberal-minded teacher with a passion for reform crusades. Through her close involvement with Souvestre, Roosevelt became aware of her political consciousness and returned to New York City uninterested in the self-centered and frivolous lifestyle characteristic of her class. She joined the National Consumers' League, which was headed by Florence Kelley, and began visiting sweatshops and factories. She developed an activist spirit and a commitment to the poor by witnessing the oppression of workers, who had few protections in this era. She believed that the gathering of information was half the battle of reform — hence her promotion of the idea that successful reformers—were, first, successful investigators and educators.

She married Franklin Roosevelt, a distant relative, in 1905. It seemed at first that her family would become her major focus as she gave birth to six children between 1906 and 1916. But family life never satisfied her broader interests. Moreover, she had to constantly battle her mother-in-law, a dominating woman. She learned about her husband's infidelity in 1918. Although she and her husband decided not to obtain a divorce, they never again had conjugal relations, focusing instead on their political and reform interests.

She became increasingly involved in her husband's political career after 1910. By 1917, with America's entry into World War I, she was presented with the opportunity to focus her reform efforts on issues of vital and immediate concern. She began working at

Washington's Union Station canteen for soldiers who were headed to training camps. She also took charge of Red Cross activities and the knitting rooms at the Navy Department. At patriotic rallies, she gave speeches and called on Americans to do the right thing concerning the European crisis. She also became actively involved in a reform campaign to improve conditions for the mentally ill at St. Elizabeth's Hospital.

In the 1920s, following the onset of her husband's crippling disease, her political involvement and reform crusades began to intensify. She learned the politics of legislation while a member of the Women's City Club of New York and the League of Women Voters. Working on the New York Women's Democratic Committee and the New York State and National Democratic Committees, she learned how to use political mechanisms to achieve successful reform. During this same period, Roosevelt became involved with several settlement house programs, which drew her attention to the complex problems faced by the urban poor and the connections between impoverished neighborhoods, poverty, crime, and disease.

In 1922, Roosevelt became a member of the Women's Trade Union League, or WTUL, where she worked for improved labor conditions for women. It was during her involvement with the WTUL that she became devoted to promoting the rights of laborers everywhere. She went so far as to develop the concept of a "living wage," which included the basic material necessities as well as educational, recreational, and emergency needs.

By 1928, Eleanor Roosevelt began using both her status as "First Lady" and the publicity that surrounded her to assert her own personality and goals. As the leader of the national women's campaign for the Democratic Party in 1928, she insisted that the party appeal to independent voters, minorities, and women. When her husband became governor of New York, she was instrumental in the appointment of Frances Perkins to the industrial commissioner's office. During the Great Depression, she served as a conduit between reform associations and the New Deal's programs and machinery.

Once in Washington, DC, Eleanor Roosevelt became involved in a women's political reform movement, which led her to bring an unprecedented number of dynamic female reformers to the nation's capital. She was also instrumental in providing the women's movement with a national forum. During press conferences, Eleanor Roosevelt often called on women leaders to discuss their work and transmit their views and concerns. These events highlighted the importance of women's issues and spawned a community of female reporters and government workers.

Throughout the 1930s, Roosevelt toured the country, visiting coal mines, relief projects, and acting as an advocate for millions of poor and disadvantaged Americans. She shared her deep compassion for the suffering through her syndicated newspaper column, "My Day," her weekly radio programs, and the lectures and speeches she gave while touring the country. At the White House, Eleanor Roosevelt pressed the case for African Americans and young people, and she was instrumental in the creation of the National Youth Administration. She constantly pestered her husband to support liberal legislation such as antilynching laws.

During World War II, Eleanor Roosevelt continued to work for the disadvantaged and fought to keep the New Deal operational. Most of her humanitarian efforts during this period were focused on improving the situation for African Americans, women, Jewish refugees, and wounded veterans. But in the immediate

postwar years, she took up a new cause: world peace and aid for the millions of victims of the war.

President Truman appointed Eleanor Roosevelt as a U.S. delegate to the United Nations. There, she focused her attention and lobbying efforts on the creation of international law for the protection and promotion of human rights. On December 10, 1948, the Universal Declaration of Human Rights, which she essentially wrote, was approved by the General Assembly.

Throughout the 1950s, she continued to press for the causes of civil rights, humanitarianism, and international cooperation. In 1961, she was appointed by President Kennedy to her last official position as chair of his Commission on the Status of Women. Her work with the commission reflected her personal commitment to advancing the cause of women's equality.

Anna Eleanor Roosevelt, who broke and remade the mold for the role of the modern presidential spouse, died at her home in New York City on November 7, 1962, and was buried next to her husband next to his ancestral home and presidential library in Hyde Park, New York.

---

social needs that we observe. If we feel intimidated about forging these relationships with leaders and public officials, we must realize that persons with power *want* information about social issues so that they can assume a leadership role.

If Eleanor Roosevelt influenced social policy from inside the administration with strategic links to her husband and other influential politicians such as Democratic Senator Robert Wagner from New York, Mary Abby Van Kleeck sought to influence social policy from the outside as an advocate for unions, industrial workers, and women. She correctly identified some key concessions that Roosevelt made to corporations when it formed the National Recovery Administration (NRA), including allowing them to set prices and wages with relatively minimal influence from consumers or unions. Why not, she asked, allow unions to organize by enacting collective bargaining at once? (Such legislation was belatedly enacted in 1935, but only after Roosevelt had rejected the legislation in 1934 to avoid political backlash from the general public and from corporations.)

Nor was Mary Van Kleeck happy about Roosevelt's decision to end the Federal Emergency

Relief Administration (FERA) and replace it with Aid to Dependent Families (ADC), Old Age Assistance (OAA), and Aid to the Blind (AB). This policy meant that all *other* persons who needed cash assistance had to go to relatively punitive local welfare programs (often called General Assistance or General Relief) that received no federal funds and that gave out starvation-level benefits. This policy also meant that intact families with need for cash assistance had to go to these local programs.

Van Kleeck was also angry that social workers who actually delivered services and benefits to the recipients of these and other New Deal programs were severely underpaid and often worked under demeaning conditions. She led the charge to unionize these workers in the so-called rank-and-file movement that she also hoped would become a major force for policy advocacy to bring clients higher benefits and more lenient standards of eligibility. It would take many decades for social workers in public and some nonpublic agencies to become unionized under the aegis of unions such as the Service Employees Industrial Union (SEIU)—a union that has also assertively sought many social reforms.

INSERT 7.7   Profiles in Leadership: Mary Abby van Kleeck (1883–1972)

Mary Abby van Kleeck, once described by the *Survey* as a "stormy petrel," was born in Glenham, New York, the daughter of Reverend Robert Boyd van Kleeck and Eliza (Mayer) van Kleeck, Episcopal minister and daughter of one of the founders of the Baltimore and Ohio Railroad, respectively. In 1892, following the death of her father, the van Kleeck family moved to Flushing, New York. In 1904, van Kleeck received her A.B. from Smith College.

Van Kleeck's interest in the industrial workers' situation began in 1905, when she launched her career in social research. After serving as a fellow in New York's College Settlement Association, she focused on researching the conditions faced by women workers in New York factories, and, subsequently, on child labor within New York's tenements. In 1907, the Alliance Employment Bureau created a department of industrial investigations and named van Kleeck its director. There, van Kleeck's research was focused on investigating the industrial situation in general and women's employment in particular, where she documented unsafe working conditions and low wages. Her pioneer investigative work, which involved noteworthy research methods and attention to the relationship between wages and the workers' standard of living, earned her the support of the Russell Sage Foundation in 1908. In 1916, the Russell Sage Foundation established the Department of Industrial Studies and appointed van Kleeck director.

Between 1914 and 1917, van Kleeck taught courses on industrial conditions and industrial research at the New York School of Philanthropy. In 1915, together with Edward T. Devine, van Kleeck completed an occupation study on positions in New York's private agencies. Meanwhile, van Kleeck became involved in Mayor John P. Mitchel's committees on unemployment and the National Social Workers' Exchange.

By 1918, van Kleeck's expertise in the area of women's employment had earned her the recognition of the federal government's Ordnance Department, which subsequently appointed her director of the women's branch of the industrial service section. In her capacity as director, van Kleeck was successful in getting the War Labor Policies Board to adopt her proposed standards for the employment of women in defense industries. In July of 1918, van Kleeck became the director of the Department of Labor's Women in Industry Service.

In 1921, van Kleeck, a member of the President's Conference on Unemployment, was chosen to sit on the Committee on Unemployment and Business Cycles. At the same time, she served as a trustee for Smith College, chaired the National Interracial Conference, and bolstered the social work profession by organizing the American Association of Social Workers.

Unlike many of the social reformers of the 1930s, van Kleeck became a staunch critic of the New Deal. She criticized the New Deal for failing to address the problems that stemmed from both the economic and political structure of the United States. She charged that the New Deal maintained the status quo by weakening the rights of labor unions and bolstering the rights of industrial monopolies. She therefore advocated for comprehensive social insurance and social welfare programs and fought for the right of labor to organize and to strike. Her opposition to the New Deal and the policies championed by the National Recovery Administration led to her resignation from the Federal Advisory Council of the United States Employment Service in 1933, one day after being appointed to it. In 1934, in *Miners and Management*, van Kleeck argued that the economic and political structure of the United States would have to be transformed if poverty was to be prevented and the standard of living for *all* Americans raised.

Thus, van Kleeck advanced the idea of a planned economy in which industry and all natural resources would be socialized. In her 1936 economic and political analysis of the United States, *Creative America*, she outlined an approach to implementing what she envisioned to be a collective economy built on the principles of scientific management and political democracy. Her support for an alignment of social work with organized labor led van Kleeck to become actively involved in the rank-and-file movement, a left-leaning movement within the social work profession that sought to unionize welfare workers and staff in New Deal programs, as well as local social service agencies.

By 1928, van Kleeck understood that any analysis of problems arising from economic structures must include an international perspective. With this in mind, she became involved as associate director of the International Industrial Relations Institute; she chaired the program committee for the World Social Economic Congress and was president of the Second

International Conference of Social Work, which was held in Germany in 1932.

By the late 1930s, far ahead of her time, van Kleeck began studying the effects of technological change on employment and wages. In 1944, together with May L. Fledderus, director of the International Industrial Relations Institute, van Kleeck published *Technology and Livelihood*, an analysis of modern technology and the resulting change in labor requirements. Their study found that changes in technology led to an increase in productivity without a corresponding increase in employment opportunities and job security.

Mary Abby van Kleeck continued to research and write throughout the remainder of her life. She continued to promote the transformation of the economic and political structure of the United States, which she firmly believed was the primary source of social injustice and poverty. Because of her beliefs and crusades for radical change, in 1953 she received a subpoena from the Senate Permanent Subcommittee on Investigations, chaired by Senator Joseph McCarthy, which sought to link her to the Communist Party. Van Kleeck died in Kingston, New York, on June 8, 1972.

The life of Mary Van Kleeck illustrates how policy advocacy can be conducted within the framework of social work organizations, whether unions or the local and state chapters of the National Association of Social Workers. She also illustrates how some policy advocates usefully enliven discussion of policy options by challenging existing public officials to consider more radical alternatives—including such notable liberals as Franklin Roosevelt.

Policy advocates can work within the power structures of society or "on the outside" as leaders of social movements or advocacy groups. As a prominent African American leader, Mary McLeod Bethune worked in both capacities (see Insert 7.8). She organized and led the National Council of Negro Women and was vice president of the National Urban League—groups that pressured the government from outside for federal programs to help African Americans secure job training and educational scholarships—and also served with distinction as the director of the NYA's Division of Negro Affairs, where she was an advocate from a government position. Social work advocates in contemporary society often move back and forth between advocacy groups and positions within government. As one of the first persons of color to obtain a high-level post in government in the

20th century, Bethune also illustrates just how recently they were excluded from positions of power.

What We Can Learn from the Persistence of Unmet Needs and Policy Issues during the New Deal[*]

In the 1930s America was thrust into the depths of the Great Depression. Millions of Americans were without work; millions more were hungry or starving; millions were homeless. Being poor and all of its attendant problems now affected a broad cross-section of the country, and the scope of economic instability and deprivation affected all levels of American society. The federal government's response to the problem was the New Deal.

Fast-Forward to the First Decade of the 21st Century.   Today millions of Americans lack sufficient food; millions of Americans are homeless and live on the streets. Many of those who are hungry and/or homeless are employed and are still unable to meet the cost of basic needs for themselves and their families.

America's Second Harvest, the nation's largest network of emergency food providers, defines food

---

[*] This section is authored by Esther Gillies, MSW, Adjunct Professor at the School of Social Work at the University of Southern California.

INSERT 7.8   Profiles in Leadership: Mary McLeod Bethune (1875–1955)

Mary McLeod Bethune—humanitarian, civil rights activist, teacher, organizer, and social reformer—was born on July 10, 1875, in Mayesville, South Carolina. She is best remembered for her work in promoting education within the African American community and encouraging the development of pride, self-respect, and self-control among African American women. McLeod was the 15th of 17 children born to Samuel McLeod and Patsy (McIntosh) McLeod, slaves who were freed following the end of the Civil War. Whereas many of her colleagues succeeded in the face of adversity, it was actually the adversity McLeod faced beginning in her early childhood that stimulated her desire for learning and led her to become successful in all her endeavors.

Briefly, the incident that triggered McLeod's interest in books and learning occurred when she was nine years old. One day, she accompanied her mother to work at the home of a white family. While her mother did her chores, McLeod was invited to join a couple of white children who were playing in their playhouse. Midway through their games, she picked up one of the girl's books and attempted to read it. The owner of the book verbally chastised McLeod, reminding her that she was not allowed to handle books for purposes other than handing them to white people. Condescendingly, the white girl offered to instead show McLeod pictures, as if to imply that she was not capable of comprehending the written language. This marked the first time the young McLeod experienced the pain of exclusion. Moreover, this incident provided the catalyst for the beginning of McLeod's intense desire to be formally educated, which she was determined to accomplish so that others might be spared the pain she had experienced.

McLeod was 11 before she entered her first classroom. In 1887, she began studying at the Scotia Seminary, located in Concord, North Carolina. Upon completing her work at Scotia Seminary, McLeod accepted a scholarship to attend the Moody Bible Institute in Chicago from 1894 to 1896, where she was trained to become a teacher. Before she established her own school, McLeod's compassion for people led her to teach and work with people who were in jail and with those who were underprivileged. In May 1898, Mary McLeod married Albertus Bethune, a student at Avery Institute in South Carolina and later a businessman in Georgia. Unfortunately, he would not live long enough to share in the success of Mary Bethune's labors.

By 1899, Mary Bethune had opened a parochial school, which she operated with the help of a

Presbyterian church in Palatka, Florida. Five years later, after saving a little money from a brief stint as an insurance salesperson, she moved to Daytona. Once there, Bethune quickly recognized the educational needs that existed within the African American community. Several months later, Bethune opened the Daytona Educational Institute and Training School, which, from 1911 to 1930, also housed the McLeod Hospital and nursing school. In 1923, she merged her school with a Methodist men's college, Cookman Institute, and formed what became known as the Daytona Collegiate Institute. (In 1928, the institute was renamed Bethune-Cookman College.)

By 1934, Bethune, a longtime friend of first lady Eleanor Roosevelt, was busy with several federal projects involving education in the African American community. She was a member of the National Advisory Committee to the NYA. In 1936, President Roosevelt appointed Bethune director of the NYA's Division of Negro Affairs, a program that sought to eliminate race differentials in the distribution of NYA benefits and vigorously promoted education and training within the African American community. Unfortunately, in 1944, Bethune's work with the federal government ended because the NYA program was abolished.

Despite the setback of losing the NYA, Bethune remained actively engaged in addressing the needs that existed in other areas throughout her community. In 1935, she organized and presided over the National Council of Negro Women, which had as its main objective the advancement of African American women and providing solutions to many of the problems they faced. She also served as vice president of the National Urban League and was an active member of the National Association for the Advancement of Colored People. From 1938 to 1948, she was a prominent figure in the Southern Conference for Human Welfare. In 1951, she was appointed to the Committee of Twelve for National Defense by President Truman. In 1953, Bethune established the Mary McLeod Bethune Foundation for research, interracial activity, and promoting broader educational opportunities for African Americans.

In May 1955, Mary McLeod Bethune, who succeeded not despite adversity but because of it, died in Daytona Beach. In the summer of 1974, Bethune was honored by the U.S. government with the unveiling of the Bethune Memorial in Washington, DC. In 1976, a portrait of Bethune was place on permanent display in the South Carolina Statehouse. Both instances marked the first time an African American had received such honors.

insecurity as "limited or uncertain availability of nutritionally adequate and safe foods or limited or uncertain ability to acquire acceptable foods in socially acceptable ways."[179] Current estimates are that approximately 7.2 million households are food insecure and that members of more than 3.4 million households are hungry.[180]

According to America's Second Harvest Hunger Study of 2006, approximately 4.5 million people per week were receiving assistance from Second Harvest's emergency food services across the country. Of those 4.5 million people, 70 percent were food insecure and 30 percent were hungry. Of those seeking assistance, more than one-third were households with children under the age of 18. Only 10 percent were elderly; one-third of the households had at least one employed adult. Nearly 70 percent of those seeking services had incomes below the official poverty level in the month preceding the request for help. More than a third of those receiving food support reported having to choose between buying food and paying for heat, rent, or medical care.[181] The Hunger Study 2006 further reported that 3 million households receiving Food Stamps continued to be food insecure.

By 2006, the number of homeless persons in this country was hovering around 3.5 million, over 40 percent of them children.[182] The magnitude of the problem bears a striking resemblance to the situation of the 1930s, when shantytowns emerged in many communities across the country and soup kitchens were overwhelmed as they attempted to feed the hungry. Unlike the 1930s, however, today's homeless situation affects not only the unemployed but a vast number of working poor. In an article in the *Christian Science Monitor*, Roll states, "There is no town, city, or state anywhere in America where an individual or family working full-time and earning the minimum wage can afford a one- or two- bedroom apartment at the fair market rental rate established by HUD."[183]

The New Deal was America's first venture into the development of a universal economic safety net to ensure access to the basic necessities of life for its citizens. It was a beginning in the development of broad social programs and was limited to widows and children, the unemployed, the elderly, and some disabled. It was designed to address the ravages of the Great Depression on American Society and the effects of economic breakdown and poverty. At the time, in the 1930s, the programs developed within the New Deal made the difference between life and death, eating and starvation, housing and homelessness for millions of Americans.

What happened? How is it that the kernel of a solution to the problem in the 1930s did not grow into programs that would have eliminated or greatly reduced the problems of homelessness and hunger in the United States today? Why is it that these problems persist today?

A study of the Great Depression and the New Deal provides us with an understanding of the limitations of the initial attempts to create an economic safety net for poor people, the aged, and the disabled. A study of the Great Society, the 1960s, will facilitate a better understanding of attempts to grow the programs developed in the 1930s. A study of the 1980s will give us a better sense of how that growth became stunted.

The problems are not new. Broad-scale hunger and homelessness have been with this nation for at least 70 years. The challenge to advocates for the poor, the hungry, and the homeless today is to learn from past efforts, to build on successes and avoid the failures of previous attempts to address these basic quality-of-life issues.

The failure of corporations to give their workers an adequate wage led to the enactment of the Fair Labor Standards Act of 1938 that empowered the federal government to establish a minimum wage. Many reformers assumed that Congress would raise the minimum wage sufficiently over time so that it would keep up with inflation and provide workers with sufficient resources to have an acceptable standard of living.

The promise of the minimum wage policy has not been realized, however, in most parts of the nation in recent decades. Due primarily to opposition from Republicans and business interests, the level of the minimum wage has substantially eroded over a period of decades as Congress has not increased it to keep up with inflation—much less required all employers to pay their employees a living wage sufficient to meet their needs.

Conservatives and businesses have repeatedly argued that higher wages will cause many small employers to go out of business—and will cause many employers, large and small, to lay off workers. Yet states such as California that have developed *statewide* minimum wages that are considerably higher than the federal minimum wage have had strong economies in the years since they passed them.

The failure of the federal government to enact a sufficient minimum wage has caused great hardship for many families. Single female heads of household, for example, must often work two or even more jobs just to meet survival needs—not only exhausting the parent, but leaving her with insufficient time to parent her children.

What We Can Learn from Failed Policy Strategies of the New Deal

While the New Deal provided work to millions of Americans during a period of high unemployment, as well as cash assistance through the FERA, it did not provide these Americans with job training aside from those skills that persons learned fortuitously in specific work projects. Nor did the ADC program provide work training.

It is understandable that President Roosevelt's first challenge was the humanitarian one of providing work and survival resources to unemployed people. To *also* include job training in the CWA and the WPA would have been costly. Moreover, New Dealers were hard-pressed just to address the magnitude of needs in the Great Depression without also adding a job-training provision.

Yet a national system of job training that was linked to the work and relief programs of the New Deal might have provided a model for Americans in future decades—and might have offset the widespread belief even in the 1930s that persons who engaged in work and relief programs were "freeloaders," a stigma that dogged ADC (and later AFDC when the word "families" was added to the program's title) in succeeding decades.

What We Can Learn from Promising Strategies of the New Deal

The New Deal demonstrated that a long-held assumption in the United States was incorrect—namely, the idea that the federal government constitutionally could not become a major force in social welfare. It also undermined another widespread belief: that the federal government lacked the ability to develop and oversee major social programs. The New Deal had faults, but it was not corrupt, used public resources efficiently, and developed an array of enlightened policies including the Social Security Act. It also moved quickly, developing huge programs in a remarkably short period of time.

Had the New Deal been widely viewed as a failure, it would have deterred policy advocates from seeking federal remedies to many social problems in succeeding decades. In fact, scores of such policies currently exist, as we will see in succeeding chapters.

The New Deal also demonstrated that the American welfare state can and should help citizens find employment. While it can be faulted for not providing workers with job training and not developing a national system of vocational training, it nonetheless placed millions of persons in jobs who would otherwise have been unemployed. It experimented with ways, too, of ending the Great Depression, even if it failed to increase government spending sufficiently to end the Great Depression until the nation began to rearm just before its entry into World War II.

What We Can Learn from the New Deal about the Structure of the American Welfare State

The New Deal represents a pivotal point in American social policy. If social policies in local and state jurisdictions had been the backbone of the American welfare state before 1933, the federal government became the major financer and initiator of social policy by 1938. It is true that many federal policies that were established in the New Deal were administered and funded jointly with states and employers, such as the work and relief programs, as well as Social Security and unemployment insurance. But had the federal government not financed the major portion of these joint federal-state programs, they would not have gotten off the ground, much less continued, because of the inability of states to finance programs such as ADC by themselves.

Even today, then, social workers who wish to intelligently refer their clients to resources and services have to be knowledgeable about programs such as Social Security and unemployment insurance, as well as distant descendents of ADC such as the Temporary Assistance to Needy Families (TANF) program, which was established when the AFDC program was radically revised in 1996. As we shall see in succeeding chapters, social workers also have to be knowledgeable about a host of other federal and federal-state programs that were enacted in succeeding decades.

As if this challenge were not enough, social workers must also know about many local and state programs. General assistance or general relief, for example, is a descendent of poorhouses, although it provides its punitive benefits outside of residential settings. Localities and states continued those mental health, child welfare, public health, and health programs after the New Deal that they had implemented before it—even if the federal government from the 1960s onward contributed substantial resources and policy guidelines to them.

WHAT YOU CAN DO NOW

After reading this chapter, you are now equipped to do the following:

- Analyze the condition of the American welfare state when the Great Depression began in 1929.

- Explain why the Great Depression was the worst economic catastrophe to hit the United States.

- Analyze the timid response of ? to the Great Depression.

- Describe the evolution of the New Deal through five stages.

- Analyze the conflicted context that Franklin Roosevelt confronted as he sought to enact social reforms.

- Discuss why Franklin Roosevelt was uniquely suited to address the dire suffering caused by the Great Depression—and why he was also captive to forces that impeded a full response.

- Explain how Roosevelt secured resources for the New Deal.

- List specific policy reforms obtained by Roosevelt during the era of emergency reforms from 1933 through 1934.

- List specific reforms Roosevelt obtained in 1935 and 1936 including the Social Security Act, the WPA, the NYA, and the Wagner Act.

- Analyze political forces that led to a political stalemate from 1937 to 1941.

- Discuss how international events—and Roosevelt's preoccupation with them—hastened the demise of work relief programs.

- Explain why work relief programs were terminated during World War II

- Discuss ways we can link the New Deal to contemporary society by examining the policy advocacy of Eleanor Roosevelt, Mary Abby Van Kleeck, and Mary McLeod Bethune; the persistence of some needs and policy issues; failed strategies; successful strategies; and the structure of the contemporary welfare state.

ENDNOTES

1. Lela Costin, *Two Sisters for Social Justice* (Urbana,IL: University of Illinois Press, 1984), pp. 110–116.

2. William Leuchtenberg, *Perils of Prosperity, 1914–1932* (Chicago: University of Chicago Press, 1958). Some reformers remained active, as discussed by Clarke Chambers, *Seedtime of Reform: American Social Service and Social Action, 1918–1933* (Minneapolis: University of Minnesota Press, 1963).

3. Leuchtenberg, *Perils*, pp. 179, 186.

4. Ibid., p. 98.

5. David Brody, *Workers in Industrial America: Essays on the Twentieth-Century Struggle* (New York: Oxford University Press, 1980), pp. 48–78.

6. John Kirby, *Black Americans in the Roosevelt Era: Liberalism and Race* (Knoxville,TN: University of Tennessee Press, 1980), p. 3; Raymond Wolters, *Negroes and the Great Depression: The Problem of Economic Recovery* (Westport, CT: Greenwood Press, 1970), p. 7.

7. Cary McWilliams, *North from Mexico: The Spanish-Speaking People of the United States* (New York: Greenwood Press, 1968), pp. 215–226.

8. Nancy Woloch, *Women and the American Experience* (New York: Knopf, 1984), pp. 382–388.

9. Leuchtenberg, *Perils*, pp. 204–224.

10. Maldwyn Jones, *American Immigration* (Chicago: University of Chicago Press, 1960), pp. 270–281.

11. Leuchtenberg, *Perils*, pp. 163–188; Roy Lubove, *The Professional Altruist* (Cambridge, MA: Harvard University Press, 1965), pp. 85–89.

12. Lubove, *The Professional Altruist*, pp. 124–156; John Ehrenreich, *The Altruistic Imagination: A History of Social Work and Social Policy in the United States* (Ithaca, NY: Cornell University Press, 1985), pp. 43–77.

13. John Galbraith, *The Great Crash, 1929* (Boston: Houghton Mifflin, 1957), pp. 180–183.

14. Richard Lowitt and Maurine Beasley, eds., *One Third of a Nation* (Urbana, IL: University of Illinois Press, 1981).

15. William Leuchtenberg, *Franklin Roosevelt and the New Deal: 1932–1940* (New York: Harper & Row, 1963), p. 1.

16. Arthur MacMahon, John Millett, and Gladys Ogden, *The Administration of Federal Work Relief* (Chicago: Public Administration Service, 1941), pp. 183–184, 334–341.

17. Robert McElvaine, *The Great Depression: America, 1929–1941* (New York: New York Times Book Co., 1984), pp. 25–50.

18. William Bremer, *Depression Winters: New York Social Workers and the New Deal* (Philadelphia: Temple University Press, 1984), pp. 88–100; Charles Trout, *Boston, the Great Depression, and the New Deal* (New York: Oxford University Press, 1977), pp. 90–92.

19. Eliot Rosen, *Hoover, Roosevelt, and the Brains Trust: From Depression to New Deal* (New York: Columbia University Press, 1977), pp. 39–65.

20. Chambers, *Seedtime of Reform*, pp. 185–207; Joseph Huthmacher, *Senator Robert F. Wagner and the Rise of Urban Liberalism* (New York: Atheneum, 1968), pp. 71–102.

21. Chambers, *Seedtime of Reform*, pp. 217–218; Lee Kraeder, "Isaac Max Rubinow: Pioneering Specialist in Social Insurance," *Social Service Review*, 50 (September 1976), pp. 293–298.

22. Trout, *Boston*, pp. 62–63, 97–100.

23. McElvaine, *The Great Depression*, pp. 69–71.

24. Allen Davis, *The Life and Legend of Jane Addams* (New York: Oxford University Press, 1973), pp. 287–288.

25. Bremer, *Depression Winters*, pp. 101–113.

26. Leuchtenberg, *Franklin Roosevelt*, pp. 1–3, 18–31; Trout, *Boston*, pp. 71–93.

27. Trout, *Boston*, pp. 56–72.

28. Eric Schattschneider, *The Semisovereign People* (New York: Holt, Rinehart & Winston, 1960), pp. 86–89.

29. McElvaine, *The Great Depression*, pp. 6–7.

30. James Patterson, *Congressional Conservatism and the New Deal* (Lexington, KY: University of Kentucky Press, 1967), pp. 4–7.

31. Rosen, *Hoover*, pp. 303–328.

32. Patterson, *Congressional Conservatism*, pp. 13–31.

33. Rosen, *Hoover*, pp. 308–314.

34. Trout, *Boston*, p. xi.

35. George Flynn, *American Catholics and the Roosevelt Presidency, 1932–1936* (Lexington, KY: University of Kentucky Press, 1968).

36. Ronald A. Mulder, *The Insurgent Progressives in the United States Senate and the New Deal* (New York: Garland, 1979), pp. 12–13; Patterson, *Congressional Conservatism*, pp. 154–155, 160–161.

37. Brody, *Workers*, pp. 82–105.

38. Ibid., pp. 107–116.

39. Lowitt and Beasley, *One Third of a Nation*, p. 213; Trout, *Boston*, pp. 208–209.

40. Edward White, *The American Judicial Tradition: Profiles of Leading American Judges* (New York: Oxford University Press, 1976), pp. 178–199.

41. Henry Adams, *Harry Hopkins* (New York: Putnam, 1977), pp. 60–62; Bremer, *Depression Winters*, pp. 135–136.

42. George Martin, *Madam Secretary: Frances Perkins* (Boston: Houghton Mifflin, 1976), pp. 245–247; Lillian Mohr, *Frances Perkins* (Croton-on-Hudson, NY: North River Press, 1979), pp. 131–133.

43. John Salmond, *A Southern Rebel: The Life and Times of Aubrey Willis Williams, 1890–1965* (Chapel Hill, NC: University of North Carolina Press, 1983), pp. 45–56.

44. Patterson, *Congressional Conservatism*, pp. 32–76.

45. Leuchtenberg, *Franklin Roosevelt*, pp. 326–328.

46. Brody, *Workers*, pp. 120–129.

47. Lowitt and Beasley, *One Third of a Nation*, pp. 5–6, 12–13, 31–32.

48. Margaret Weir and Theda Skocpol, "State Structures and the Possibility of 'Keynesian' Responses to the Great Depression in Sweden, Britain, and the United States." In Peter Evans, Dietrich Rueschemeyer, and Theda Skocpol, eds., *Bringing the State Back In* (Cambridge: Cambridge University Press, 1985), p. 145.

49. Leuchtenberg, *Franklin Roosevelt*, pp. 145–149, 256; Martin, *Madam Secretary*, pp. 258–260; and Salmond, *A Southern Rebel*, pp. 68–70.

50. Bremer, *Depression Winters*, pp. 134–141, 155–157, 165, 167–170; Martin, *Madam Secretary*, pp. 258–259; and McElvaine, *The Great Depression*, pp. 250–263.

51. Bremer, *Depression Winters*, p. 129.

52. Adams, *Harry Hopkins*, pp. 52–53, 71–72.

53. Josephine Brown, *Public Relief, 1929-1939* (New York: Holt, 1940), pp. 146–159, 171–190, 218–298.

54. Salmond, *A Southern Rebel*, pp. 45–56.

55. Trout, *Boston*, pp. 148–149.

56. Gilbert Steiner, *State of Welfare* (Washington, D. C.: Brookings Institution, 1971), pp. 198–199.

57. Harry Hopkins, *Spending to Save* (New York: Harper & Row, 1936), pp. 108–110.

58. Salmond, *A Southern Rebel*, pp. 57–63.

59. Ibid., p. 59.

60. John Salmond, *The Civilian Conservation Corps, 1933–1942* (Durham, NC: Duke University Press, 1967).

61. Adams, *Harry Hopkins*, pp. 57–58, 82–88.

62. Richard Lowitt, *George W. Norris: The Triumph of a Progressive, 1933–1944* (Urbana, IL: University of Illinois Press, 1981), pp. 95–109.

63. Martin, *Madam Secretary*, pp. 296–298; Mohr, *Frances Perkins*, p. 141.

64. Rosen, *Hoover*, p. 59.

65. Susan Lee and Peter Passell, *A New Economic View of American History* (New York: Norton, 1979), pp. 383–387.

66. Dean May, *From New Deal to New Economics: The American Liberal Response to the Recession of 1937* (New York: Garland, 1981), pp. 160–161.

67. Leuchtenberg, *Franklin Roosevelt*, pp. 38–39, 42–46.

68. Wolters, *Negroes*, pp. 83–90.

69. Ibid., pp. 83–90.

70. Lowitt and Beasley, *One Third of a Nation*, pp. 341–346, 356.

71. Mohr, *Frances Perkins*, pp. 163–170; Wolters, *Negroes*, pp. 169–192.

72. Wolters, *Negroes*, pp. 3–38.

73. Ibid., pp. 21–77.

74. Leuchtenberg, *Franklin Roosevelt*, p. 52.

75. Lowitt, *George W. Norris*, pp. 16–25, 110–125.

76. Bremer, *Depression Winters*, pp. 134–136.

77. Adams, *Harry Hopkins*, p. 61; Leuchtenberg, *Franklin Roosevelt*, pp. 91–94.

78. Henry Adams, *Harry Hopkins* (New York: Putnam, 1977), p. 71.

79. Ibid., pp. 71–72.

80. Alan Brinkley, *Voices of Protest: Huey Long, Father Coughlin, and the Great Depression* (New York: Random House, 1982), pp. 8–81.

81. Ibid., pp. 82–142.

82. Abraham Holtzman, *The Townsend Movement: A Political Study* (New York: Octagon Books, 1975).

83. Paul Douglas, *Social Security in the United States: An Analysis and Appraisal of the Federal Social Security Act* (New York: McGraw-Hill, 1939), pp. 74–83.

84. Ronald A. Mulder, *The Insurgent Progressives in the United States Senate and the New Deal, 1933–1939* (New York: Garland, 1979), p. 73.

85. William Bremer, *Depression Winters: New York Social Workers and the New Deal* (Philadelphia: Temple University Press, 1984), pp. 126–132.

86. Ibid., pp. 158–163; John Ehrenreich, *The Altruistic Imagination: A History of Social Work and Social Policy in the United States* (Ithaca, NY: Cornell University Press, 1985), pp. 102–108.

87. Melvin Dubofsky and Warren Van Tine, *John L. Lewis* (New York: New York Times Book Co., 1977), pp. 203–221.

88. Raymond Wolters, *Negroes and the Great Depression: The Problem of Economic Recovery* (Westport, CT: Greenwood, 1970), pp. 39–55.

89. Brinkley, *Voices of Protest*, pp. 207–208.

90. Ibid., p. 255.

91. George Martin, *Madam Secretary: Frances Perkins* (Boston: Houghton Mifflin, 1976), pp. 341–356; Lillian Mohr, *Frances Perkins* (Croton-on-Hudson, NY: North River Press, 1979), pp. 203–206; and Edwin Witte, *The Development of the Social Security Act* (Madison, WI: University of Wisconsin Press, 1962), pp. 1–111.

92. Bremer, *Depression Winters*, p. 151; Martin, *Madam Secretary*, p. 345.

93. Mohr, *Frances Perkins*, p. 205.

94. Douglas, *Social Security*, pp. 62–68; Martin, *Madam Secretary*, p. 351.

95. Martin, *Madam Secretary*, p. 348.

96. Quoted in Mimi Abramovitz, *Regulating the Lives of Women* (Boston: South End Press, 1988), p. 253.

97. Ibid., p. 254.

98. Douglas, *Social Security*, pp. 28–54, 129–150.

99. Bremer, *Depression Winters*, pp. 150–155; Clarke Chambers, *Paul U. Kellogg and the Survey: Voices for Social Welfare and Social Justice* (Minneapolis: University of Minnesota Press, 1971), pp. 156–157.

100. Josephine Brown, *Public Relief, 1929–1939* (New York: Holt, Rinehart & Winston, 1940), pp. 303–312; Bremer, *Depression Winters*, pp. 166–167.

101. Douglas, *Social Security*, pp. 151–157, 185–196, 203–205.

102. Brown, *Public Relief*, pp. 303–306, 308, 312.

103. Winifred Bell, *Aid to Dependent Children* (New York: Columbia University Press, 1965), pp. 29–30.

104. Frances Piven and Richard Cloward, *Regulating the Poor: The Functions of Public Welfare* (New York: Pantheon Books, 1971), pp. 123–145; Bell, *Aid to Dependent Children*, pp. 41–46, 76–110.

105. Gilbert Steiner, *Social Insecurity: The Politics of Welfare* (Chicago: Rand McNally, 1966), pp. 18–26.

106. Chambers, *Paul U. Kellogg*, p. 157; Douglas, *Social Security*, p. 68; and Martin, *Madam Secretary*, p. 347.

107. Joseph Huthmacher, *Senator Robert F. Wagner and the Rise of Urban Liberalism* (New York: Atheneum, 1968), pp. 190–191.

108. Martin, *Madam Secretary*, pp. 381–383.

109. Adams, *Harry Hopkins*, pp. 72–73.

110. Ibid., pp. 73–88.

111. Arthur MacMahon, John Millet, and Gladys Ogden, *The Administration of Federal Work Relief* (Chicago: Public Administration Service, 1941), pp. 313–314.

112. Bremer, *Depression Winters*, pp. 137–141.

113. MacMahon, Millett, and Ogden, *The Administration*, pp. 26–27.

114. Ibid., p. 390.

115. John Salmond, *A Southern Rebel*, pp. 121–140.

116. Robert Steamer, *The Supreme Court in Crisis: A History of Conflict* (Amherst: University of Massachusetts Press, 1971), p. 199.

117. McElvaine, *The Great Depression*, p. 281.

118. Martin, *Madam Secretary*, pp. 323–324, 399–419; Polenberg, *Reorganizing Roosevelt's Government*, pp. 55–78.

119. Martin, *Madam Secretary*, pp. 399–406.

120. Steamer, *The Supreme Court*, p. 209.

121. Martin, *Madam Secretary*, pp. 387–390.

122. Mulder, *The Insurgent Progressives*, pp. 165–213.

123. Ibid., pp. 272–274; Patterson, *Congressional Conservativism*, pp. 277–287.

124. Patterson, *Congressional Conservatism*, p. 127.

125. Robert McElvaine, *The Great Depression: America, 1929–1941* (New York: New York Times Book Co., 1984), pp. 281–282; Richard Polenberg, *Reorganizing Roosevelt's Government: Controversy over Executive Reorganization, 1936–1939* (Cambridge, MA: Harvard University Press, 1966); and Charles Trout, *Boston, the Great Depression, and the New Deal* (New York: Oxford University Press, 1977), pp. 310–312.

126. Martin, *Madam Secretary*, pp. 391–395.

127. Ibid.; Mulder, *The Insurgent Progressives*, pp. 224–227; Patterson, *Congressional Conservatism*, pp. 149–154.

128. Huthmacher, *Senator Robert F. Wagner*, pp. 224–228.

129. Charles McKinley and Robert Frase, *Launching Social Security: A Capture-and-Record Account* (Madison, WI: University of Wisconsin Press, 1970).

130. Barry Karl, *Executive Reorganization and Reform in the New Deal* (Cambridge, MA: Harvard University Press, 1963); Polenberg, *Reorganizing Roosevelt's Government*.

131. James Patterson, *Congressional Conservatism and the New Deal* (Lexington, KY: University of Kentucky Press, 1967), pp. 50–76.

132. Mulder, *The Insurgent Progressives*, pp. 292–308.

133. Chapman, *Contours*, pp. 1–80.

134. Eliot Rosen, *Hoover, Roosevelt, and the Brains-Trust: From Depression to New Deal* (New York: Columbia University Press, 1977), pp. 115–119.

135. Nancy Woloch, *Women and the American Experience* (New York: Knopf, 1984), p. 424.

136. Susan Ware, "Women and the New Deal." In Harvard Sitcoff, ed., *Fifty Years Later: The New Deal Evaluated* (Philadelphia: Temple University Press, 1985), p. 120.

137. Ibid.

138. Woloch, *Women*, p. 443.

139. Abramovitz, *Regulating the Lives of Women*, p. 261.

140. Ibid., pp. 254–255, 292.

141. Ibid., p. 293.

142. Ware, "Women and the New Deal," pp. 121, 124; Abramovitz, *Regulating the Lives of Women*, p. 224.

143. Barbara Ehrenreich and Deidre English, *For Her Own Good: 150 Years of Experts' Advice to Women* (New York: Doubleday, 1978), p. 221.

144. Leobardo Estrada, F. Chris Garcia, Reynaldo Macias, and Lionel Maldonado, "Chicanos in the United States: A History of Exploitation and Resistance." In F. Chris Garcia, ed., *Latinos and the Political System* (Notre Dame, IN: University of Notre Dame Press, 1988), pp. 50–51.

145. John Kirby, *Black Americans in the Roosevelt Era: Liberalism and Race* (Knoxville, TN: University of Tennessee Press, 1980), pp. 97, 101–102, 141–142.

146. Ibid., pp. 34–35; Huthmacher, *Senator Robert F. Wagner*, pp. 171–173, 242.

147. Patterson, *Congressional Conservatism*, pp. 98–99.

148. Kirby, *Black Americans*, pp. 30–34, 57–62, 82–83.

149. Ibid., pp. 32, 61, 73–74; Salmond, *A Southern Rebel*, pp. 126–127.

150. Kirby, *Black Americans*, pp. 19–26, 37–47, 51–53, 58–59, 106–151.

151. Ibid., p. 142; John Salmond, *The Civilian Conservation Corps, 1933–1942* (Durham, NC: Duke University Press, 1967), p. 101; Wolters, *Negroes*, pp. 203–209.

152. Salmond, *A Southern Rebel*, pp. 126–127; Wolters, *Negroes*, pp. 196–206.

153. Salmond, *The Civilian Conservation Corps*, pp. 91–94.

154. Kirby, *Black Americans*, p. 34.

155. Wolters, *Negroes*, pp. 98–102.

156. John Hope Franklin, *From Slavery to Freedom* (New York: Knopf, 1974), pp. 559–563.

157. Gerald Jaynes and Robin Williams, eds., *A Common Destiny: Blacks and American Society* (Washington, DC: National Academy Press, 1989), pp. 59–60.

158. Kirby, *Black Americans*, pp. 142–145.

159. Ronald Takaki, *Strangers from a Different Shore* (Boston: Little, Brown, 1989), pp. 217ff.

160. Ibid., p. 179.

161. Ibid., p. 219.

162. Ibid., pp. 390–391.

163. Ibid., p. 378.

164. Stanley Wenocur and Michael Reisch, *From Charity to Enterprise: The Development of American Social Work in a Market Economy* (Urbana, IL: University of Illinois Press, 1989), pp. 115–135.

165. Virginia Robinson, *A Changing Psychology in Social Case Work* (Chapel Hill, NC: University of North Carolina Press, 1930).

166. Bremer, *Depression Winters*, pp. 16–24.

167. Ibid., pp. 34–37, 46–53.

168. Wenocur and Reisch, *From Charity to Enterprise*, p. 213.

169. Bremer, *Depression Winters*, pp. 126–132.

170. Wenocur and Reisch, *From Charity to Enterprise*, pp. 182–207.

171. Bremer, *Depression Winters*, pp. 159–165.

172. Leslie Leighninger, *Social Work: Search for Identity* (New York: Greenwood Press, 1987), pp. 103–124.

173. Ibid., pp. 125–150.

174. Bell, *Aid to Dependent Children*, pp. 29–30.

175. Ware, "Women and the New Deal," p. 119.

176. Brody, *Workers*, pp. 138–146.

177. Margaret Weir and Theda Skocpol, "State Structures and the Possibilities for 'Keynesian' Responses to the Great Depression in Sweden, Britain, and the United States." In Peter Evans, Dietrich Rueschemeyer, and Theda Skocpol, eds., *Bringing the State Back In* (Cambridge: Cambridge University Press, 1985), pp. 132–137.

178. Mulder, *The Insurgent Progressives*, pp. 1–34.

179. Food Insecurity and Hunger (2006). *America's Second Harvest Hunger Study—2006*. (Online). Retrieved from http://www.hungerinamerica.org/who_we_serve/Food_Insecurity/ on July 18, 2007.

180. Household Food Insecurity by Number. (2006). *America's Second Harvest Hunger Study — 2006*. (Online). Retrieved from http://www.hungerinamerica.org/who_we_serve/Food_Insecurity/household_insecurity_number.html on July 20, 2007.

181. Key Findings. (2006). America's Second Harvest Hunger Study — 2006. (Online). Retrieved from http://www.hungerinamerica.org/key_findings/ on July 19, 2007.

182. HUD Annual Homeless Assessment Report to Congress (2007). (Online). Retrieved from http://www.huduser.org/publications/povsoc/annual_assess.html on July 18, 2007.

183. Roll, G. (2006). Understanding Poverty and Homelessness in America. *Christian Science Monitor*. (Online). Retrieved from http://www.csmonitor.com/2006/0522/p09s01-coop.html on June 22, 2007.

8

The Era of Federal Social Services: The New Frontier and the Great Society

TABLE 8.1   Selected Orienting Events

1945–1952	Presidency of Harry Truman
1946	Full Employment Act
1950–1953	Korean War
1950s–1960s	Massive migration of African Americans from the South to the North
1953	Department of Health, Education, and Welfare established
1953–1960	Presidency of Dwight Eisenhower
1955	Bus boycott in Montgomery, Alabama, initiates civil rights movement
1960	John Kennedy wins presidential election
1961	Passage of Manpower Development and Training Act (MDTA)
1961–1963	Escalating racial violence and protest in the South
1962	Michael Harrington publishes *The Other America*
1963	President Kennedy delivers nation's first presidential address on civil rights; Mental Retardation and Community Mental Health Centers Construction Act is passed
1963	John Kennedy assassinated; succeeded by Lyndon Johnson
1964	Economic Opportunity Act, Food Stamps Act, and Civil Rights Act enacted
1964	Johnson wins a landslide victory over Goldwater in presidential election
1965	Medicare, Medicaid, Elementary and Secondary Education Act, Civil Rights Act, and Older Americans Act enacted
Mid–late 1960s	César Chavez organizes farmworkers
1967	Welfare amendments establish work incentives and work programs for AFDC recipients
1968	Martin Luther King assassinated

TABLE 8.1   (continued)

1968	Johnson decides not to seek Democratic nomination for another term
1969	Stonewall Inn riot initiates gay rights movement

Before he died, President Franklin Roosevelt hoped that a new reform era would begin after the end of World War II, but many conservatives were determined that this would not be the case. In fact, relatively few social reforms were enacted during the presidency of Harry Truman (1945–1952), and American policy was profoundly conservative during the two terms of Dwight Eisenhower (1953–1960). It was not until the presidency of John Kennedy (1961–1963) that the United States tentatively embarked on social reforms. The so-called Great Society during the administration of Lyndon Johnson (1963–1968) vastly increased the scope of the American welfare state, even if it was rudely interrupted by the Vietnam War.

At the end of this chapter, we discuss what we can learn in contemporary society from policy advocates of the Great Society and how this era can help us better understand social policy and the structure of the American welfare state.

WORLD WAR II, THE POSTWAR ERA, AND THE 1950s

Why Few Social Reforms Were Enacted during the Presidency of Harry Truman from 1945 through 1952

Despite the urging of some liberals, President Franklin Roosevelt mostly avoided pursuing changes in domestic policy during World War II—both because all of his failing energy was needed to prosecute the largest war in world history and because he wanted to avoid partisan conflict to achieve bipartisan support of the war effort. Emboldened by this power vacuum, conservatives not only terminated all the work relief programs of the New Deal but strengthened their numbers in the Congress in the elections of 1942 and 1944. Only the GI bill was enacted during the war, which distributed billions of dollars of educational benefits to millions of veterans from World War II.

When Roosevelt died in the spring of 1945, Vice President Harry Truman ascended to the presidency. Harry Truman had some progressive instincts, but he lacked the national stature and the extent of liberalism that Franklin Roosevelt had possessed. The tilt in Congress toward conservatism became even more marked in the congressional elections of 1946—meaning Truman had to confront a Congress in which both houses had solid Republican majorities.

Some liberals sought to enlist Truman's support before the defeat of Japan in August of 1945 for a national policy that would prevent the recurrence of another Great Depression. As a recession (or worse) was widely expected when military spending decreased after the war, they reasoned, why not commit the federal government to obtaining full employment and mandate spending on an array of social programs—such as health insurance, housing, and expanded Social Security—as the economic means to this goal? Social spending would thus be *required* to keep the economy in full employment. And why not establish in the White House a planning council of economists who would orchestrate this liberal scenario and also help the incumbent president to issue an annual economic report? After many meetings among themselves, with cooperation from some liberal congressmen and support from

---

I N S E R T 8.1   Using the Web to Understand How Americans Reformed Policies during the Tumultuous 1960s

---

Visit **academic.cengage.com/social_work/jansson** to view these links and a variety of study tools.

> Go to **http://www.archives.gov/education/lessons**
> Go to "Era 1945 to 1970s."

- Proceed to documents related to *Brown v. Board of Education*.
- Proceed to "An Act of Courage: The Arrest Records of Rosa Parks."
- Proceed to "Jackie Robinson: Beyond the Playing Field."
- Proceed to "Court Documents Related to Martin Luther King, Jr. and Memphis Sanitation Workers."

> Go to **http://www.archives.gov/education/lessons**
> Go to "Era 1960 to the Present." Proceed to "Civil Rights Act of 1964 and the Equal Employment Opportunity Commission (EEOC)."

> Go to **http://en.wikipedia.org/wiki/Cesar_Chavez** to understand the extraordinarily adverse odds that Chavez encountered. Click on Timeline, Early Years, and external links to learn more about his policy advocacy.

> Go to **http://www.english.upenn.edu/~afilreis/50s/home.html** Click on "gays in government,

1951," an actual speech from the House of Representatives. What does this speech tell you about the depth of prejudice against gay men in this period?

> Go to **http://www.stanford.edu/group/King/about_king/** Read about the "Address at March on Washington for Jobs and Freedom." Click on the" I Have A Dream" speech (written on April 16, 1963) link to download the text of the speech. Also click on the "I've Been to the Mountaintop" speech (his last speech written on April 3, 1968) link to download the text of that speech. What similarities do you observe in these speeches? What characteristics of these speeches proved so effective in mobilizing civil rights activists?

> Go to **http://www.kn.pacbell.com/wired/BHM/bh_hotlist.html** Click on "African American Mosaic" and scroll through screens displaying patterns of African Americans' migration in the 19th and 20th centuries.

http://www.congresslink.org/civil/essay.html Go to this site to study the Civil Rights Act. If you have any questions, you can go "live" for the answers. You can also follow the links for more detail on a "player" in the civil rights movement.

Truman, the legislation eventually was enacted as the Full Employment Act of 1946, which established a national full employment goal and installed the Council of Economic Advisors in the White House.[1]

But the legislation hardly resulted in a renewal of social reforms. Conservatives were able to dilute its language so that the government was not *required* to increase social spending when unemployment became severe. The president was at liberty, moreover, to ignore the recommendations of the Council of Economic Advisors. In addition, to the surprise of many economists, there was no depression in the wake of World War II. For one thing, Americans had amassed enormous savings in the form of war bonds that they quickly used at war's end to buy the consumer goods denied them during the Great

Depression and the war. Fueled by such spending, and by huge exports to nations whose economies had been devastated by the war, a postwar economic boom occurred, and conservatives sought to *reduce* government spending to avert inflation—hardly the scenario that the framers of the Full Employment Act had envisioned![2]

Other factors also prevented a postwar era of reform. Recall that a conservative coalition of Republicans and Southern Democrats had become relatively cohesive in 1937 and had fought many of Roosevelt's initiatives (or at least sought to dilute or modify them). When the Republicans won control of both houses of Congress in the national elections of 1946, they decided to make huge cuts in federal taxes that had been raised to fund the war effort—leaving Truman with scant resources for domestic spending at a time when both parties disliked federal deficits. Those tax revenues that remained were needed by Truman to fund veterans' health and other benefits, the GI Bill, and the debt accumulated during the war. Truman tried to avert these tax cuts, but the Congress overrode his veto of them with many Democrats joining Republicans.[3]

Nor did Americans want major social reforms in this period, partly because they were preoccupied with enjoying the first extended period of relative affluence since the onset of the Great Depression in 1929. Imbued with savings from the war period and enticed by an array of appliances and cars available for purchase, many Americans were oblivious to the needs of impoverished people in urban and rural areas—or to the needs of African Americans who still lived under the tyrannies of poverty and Jim Crow laws.

Social reform was also impeded by international developments. Idealists hoped that the end of World War II would usher in a period of international stability, orchestrated by the newly created United Nations. Indeed, in the immediate postwar period, military spending declined almost to prewar levels.

But international stability soon began to unravel as the relationship between the United States and Russia became increasingly tense. Josef Stalin, the Russian dictator, was convinced that Roosevelt had ceded Eastern Europe to him in the wake of the war in return for the vast sacrifice of Russian soldiers and citizens on the eastern front. Thus emboldened and eager to build a buffer between his nation and the hated Germans, who had invaded Russia on several occasions, Stalin quickly asserted control over Poland, Czechoslovakia, East Germany, and other Eastern European nations. Moreover, civil conflict in Greece and Turkey led Americans to fear that these nations could be taken over by the Russians.

Just as Franklin Roosevelt had been distracted from domestic to international affairs in the late 1930s, Harry Truman increasingly focused on Russia in the late 1940s. Believing that Stalin might

even want to extend his empire to Western Europe, Truman developed the Marshall Plan, a program of U.S. economic assistance to Western Europe, to prevent the Russians from capitalizing on discontent and insurrections there. Although Truman refrained from increasing the military budget, the huge expenditures for the Marshall Plan ruled out any major increases in domestic social spending, particularly when, as already noted, conservatives had cut the level of American taxes. Moreover, like Roosevelt in World War II, Truman gave only symbolic, verbal support to social reform between 1947 and 1949 because he needed the support of the conservative coalition for his foreign policy objectives, such as the Marshall Plan.[4]

Social reform in the Truman era was also retarded by the white population's racial animosities toward African Americans. During World War II, the large influx of African Americans seeking work in the war industries angered white residents of Detroit and other urban centers; intermittent race riots broke out. Considerable racial tension remained in Northern cities after the war. Moreover, Southern legislators, with support from some Northern Republicans, secured the termination of the Fair Employment Practices Commission at the end of the war, resisted Truman's efforts to revive it, and blocked other civil rights legislation. Truman deserves credit for desegregating the armed services after the war was over, in the face of outright defiance by some generals.[5]

The Chilling Effect of the Cold War on Domestic Reforms

But the *real* diversion of resources and presidential effort from domestic issues to military spending and international affairs—indeed the Cold War itself—commenced in 1950. For several years, some top officials, including Dean Acheson and Paul Nitze of the State Department, had been advocating a dramatic increase in U.S. defense spending to counter a perceived communist threat around the world, but they were worried that a budget-conscious

Congress and president would refuse. Shortly after these officials sent Truman a secret report detailing the need for a larger military, North Korea attacked South Korea. Truman decided to use the invasion as a pretext for a massive, and ongoing, increase in American military spending.[6] American military spending rose from about $10 billion to $40 billion annually—and to considerably higher levels during the Korean and Vietnam Wars. In constant dollar terms, after correcting for inflation, the military budget remained at the same extraordinary level for the next 42 years; in 1991, military spending was roughly $300 billion—and it had increased to more than $500 billion by 2007.

Because the overall federal budget was far smaller in the early 1950s than it is today, this military spending in combination with veterans' programs dominated the federal budget—consuming about 68 percent of it during the 1950s as compared to less than 10 percent in 2007. When other large portions of the budget were devoted to funding the national debt and funding the regular costs of government, almost nothing was left for domestic spending. Aside from programs established by the Social Security Act, the Fair Labor Standards Act, the Wagner Act, TVA, and scattered smaller reforms, the United States had reverted to the primitive welfare state that had existed in 1932. The New Deal now seemed only a distant memory.

Why, you may wonder, discuss the *military* budget in a book about social welfare policy? To some extent, any budget represents a competition between spending priorities. When Americans chose to spend about 68 percent of their national budget in the 1950s on military and related spending, they could *not* spend these sums on alternative programs. Moreover, as high military spending was coupled with low federal tax rates (as compared with international standards), funds available for social spending were restricted even more. Military spending gradually declined as a percentage of the gross national product (GNP) over the next 40 years because the American economy (and the federal budget) grew so rapidly, but even at that lower level it absorbed much of the federal budget. Indeed, even as late as 1975, military spending and military-related

items (such as the Atomic Energy Commission, the National Aeronautics and Space Administration, and interest on the national debt, which largely derived from former wars) together constituted roughly one-half of the national budget.

Thus, when reading this and ensuing chapters, you should bear in mind that social spending was constrained by military (and military-related) spending. Moreover, the Cold War consumed a large portion of the energies of presidents and congressional leaders during its 40-odd years, probably to the detriment of attention to domestic matters. A good case can be made that Americans ought to have raised their levels of taxation considerably during the Cold War to allow them to fund both military and domestic policies. Many experts contend, moreover, that military spending during the Cold War was greatly excessive, such as maintaining nuclear weapons sufficient to destroy the Soviet Union 50 times over.

Truman *did* try to get two key pieces of legislation enacted, but both were defeated by conservatives. He sought federal aid to education since many local governments were hard-pressed to fund public schools. He sought national health insurance but was stymied not only by conservatives but by the massive lobbying of the American Medical Association, which argued as it had during the prior three decades that government financing of health care would ruin the doctor-patient relationship. By contrast, virtually all European nations enacted national health insurance in the wake of World War II.

Eisenhower and the Conservative 1950s

Elected as a World War II hero and as a candidate who promised to end the unpopular war in Korea, Eisenhower was a president who had had virtually no experience in nonmilitary domestic matters. He was no liberal, though he was frequently attacked by conservative Republicans for not cutting social spending even further. Eisenhower wanted to keep taxes to a minimum so that government did not interfere with the private economy. He had no interest in expanding social spending, aside from small programs here and there. He did make truly massive government commitments to infrastructure improvements through the establishment of the interstate highway system and the St. Lawrence Seaway, but he saw these measures in military terms; they would facilitate the transportation of troops and military hardware in the event of a world war. (He had marveled at Germany's sophisticated transportation system during World War II.)[7]

Perhaps even more than Truman, Eisenhower was obsessed with Cold War diplomatic and military maneuvering. Flanked by the Dulles brothers (John Foster Dulles at the State Department and Allen Dulles at the Central Intelligence Agency), Eisenhower presided over numerous international crises abroad and innumerable debates within his administration about the size and composition of the American military forces. Fearing that the Russians wanted to bankrupt the United States by tricking it into excessive military spending, Eisenhower constantly sought to cut the defense budget. However, the costly technological advances of the 1950s—such as the development of missiles and advanced aircraft—and a continuing commitment to the defense of Europe left intact the large military budgets that Truman had initiated at the outset of the Korean War. Moreover, both Republican and Democratic members of Congress came to see military contracts as important sources of revenue for their districts—and political support for themselves—and would balk whenever Eisenhower proposed cuts in military spending.

It was ironic that Eisenhower, a former war hero, made an eloquent speech against the "military-industrial complex" as he left the presidency in 1960; he noted that every dollar spent on guns is a dollar not spent on humanitarian programs.[8]

Radicals, and even moderate liberals, were on the defensive in the 1950s. Senator Joseph McCarthy (R., Wisc.) led a crusade against "communists," a term he applied to many people who were left of center. McCarthy gained national notoriety by accusing the Department of State of harboring communists in 1950—and then developed

an expanding list of intellectuals, screenwriters, trade unionists, and activists whom he interrogated in lengthy public hearings. Even accusing the conservative Eisenhower administration of treason, McCarthy soon elicited a backlash against him that eventually led to a public investigation that discredited him and led to his resignation from the Senate. Such persons as social worker Bertha Capen Reynolds, one of McCarthy's targets, refused to be intimidated and retained her radical viewpoints in the 1950s and beyond.

The Democrats controlled the Congress during much of Eisenhower's tenure. In those circumstances, he made a deal with the Democratic leadership, including Lyndon Johnson. In return for support for most of his foreign policy initiatives by Democrats, Eisenhower agreed not to make an assault on those social programs that had survived the New Deal. Eisenhower realized that the American people, many of whom still vividly remembered the hardships of the Great Depression, wanted to keep those New Deal programs.

Indeed, Social Security was expanded in the 1950s to make it a family program that provided benefits to people with disabilities and to wives, widows, dependent children, and survivors of the men who had been its initial beneficiaries. When the Russians launched Sputnik into orbit, Eisenhower supported the National Defense Education Act, which provided federal funds for science and math training in the schools. But Eisenhower can hardly be called a reformist president, even if, unlike Ronald Reagan in the 1980s, he did not seek to undo social programs that had already been enacted.

Eisenhower's record on race relations was ambivalent. Partly because of his numerous links with Southern governors and friends, he believed that the federal government should leave racial matters to the states. Accordingly, he did not assume leadership with respect to lynchings, Jim Crow laws, or the denial of suffrage to African Americans in the South. When the courts finally ordered the city of Little Rock, Arkansas, to allow African American children to attend its schools in 1957, he sent federal troops to enforce the order only when his hand was forced by escalating violence, including danger to the lives of the African American children.[9]

THE TURN TOWARD REFORM

Many persons wondered whether the policy quiescence of the 1950s would continue after the presidential election of 1960, which pitted Vice President Richard Nixon against Senator John Kennedy, a relatively unknown Democrat who had served in the House (1947–1952) and had been elected to the Senate in 1952. Neither man projected a reformist image; indeed, the campaign focused on the first televised presidential debates, in which the two men promised to pursue anticommunist policies. It was only when Kennedy was pitted against Hubert Humphrey, a liberal reformer, in a key primary in West Virginia that he made social reform a prominent part of his campaign; he promised to help elderly people with their medical bills, to develop programs to help Americans living in poverty in Appalachia and inner cities, and "to get the country moving again." But his belated support of social reform and indifference to reform as a U.S. Senator did not endear him to liberals, including Eleanor Roosevelt, who gave her support to him only late in the campaign.[10]

A strange combination of affluence and poverty coexisted as the nation entered the 1960s. Several factors contributed to the postwar prosperity during the 1950s. With the economies of Japan and Europe devastated by World War II, the United States was uniquely positioned to become the major economic power in the world and to dominate world trade. Lacking economic competitors, American industry could both export at will and dominate domestic markets.[11] Economic growth was buoyed by rising wages, as well as funds that circulated in the economy from burgeoning Social Security and other social programs. It was also fueled by a partnership fashioned between government, the housing industry, and the automobile industry. The federal government provided cheap housing loans to veterans and other homeowners and underwrote a large share of the costs of a massive expansion of the nation's roads, which in turn promoted a housing boom in the suburbs and the production of large numbers of automobiles. The federal government also contributed indirectly to economic growth through its tax policies by allowing Americans to deduct interest payments on home mortgages and loans.[12]

Serious social problems existed, however. They were most obvious in the South and Southwest, where millions of African Americans, Latinos, and First Americans experienced appalling poverty, as well as violation of their fundamental rights. Although they had traditionally resided in rural areas, increasing numbers settled in urban areas, where they encountered overt discrimination; they were prevented from voting, using public facilities and transportation, and living in white neighborhoods.

Even in the mid-1950s, there were signs that African Americans in the South would demand civil rights that had been denied them throughout most of American history save for a brief interlude after the Civil War when federal troops occupied the South. Leaders of African American churches, who had often been resigned to the oppression of their people, began to discuss strategies for attacking racist policies. The urbanization of African Americans in the South allowed them to organize more easily against rampant discrimination than had been possible when they mostly lived in remote rural areas.[13]

The seeds of African American discontent in the North were sown in the 1940s and the 1950s by a massive migration from the South. African Americans fled the South for many reasons—to join friends who had already migrated to the North, to obtain jobs, or to escape oppression. (The mechanization of cotton picking caused major unemployment of African Americans in the South.) Of the 4.5 million African Americans who migrated to the North and West between 1940 and 1970, 90 percent settled in the large cities of six states: California, New York, Pennsylvania, Ohio, Michigan, and Illinois.[14] They were segregated in densely populated urban ghettoes, denied housing in white areas, limited to unskilled jobs, denied membership in unions, placed within segregated and inferior school systems, disenfranchised, and subjected to police brutality.

Despite its prosperity, the nation was marked by extreme economic inequality in 1960. The average income of persons in the most affluent one-fifth of the population was roughly nine times the average income of those in the poorest one-fifth of the population.[15] Poverty existed in low-income urban areas and in rural areas such as Appalachia, where housing, infant mortality, health, and income standards were similar to those in many third-world nations. In 1960, Social Security, unemployment insurance, and AFDC provided a very inadequate safety net. (The ADC program had been renamed the Aid to Families with Dependent Children program, or AFDC, in 1950 when cash benefits were extended to mothers as well as children.) AFDC was administered arbitrarily in many jurisdictions, with flagrant violations of the rights of persons who sought assistance.[16] Southern states paid scandalously low benefits. Because no subsidized nutrition program existed, many individuals—including those who received miserly AFDC payments—suffered malnutrition; indeed, surveys suggested that many children in Mississippi were malnourished even as late as 1967.[17] Since the federal government had developed no major medical programs, poor persons had to rely on underfunded county and municipal hospitals. There were virtually no neighborhood clinics for pregnant women or infants, for family planning, or for other special needs.

As government health insurance programs did not exist, millions of elderly persons found that they could not afford to pay their medical bills when they lost the private medical insurance provided as a fringe benefit by many employers in the postwar era. Social Security pensions, which were received by millions of elderly persons, had helped ease their economic burdens, but about one-third of them lived below poverty levels even in 1967.[18]

Women first entered the labor force in large numbers during World War II when they served as replacements for male workers who had joined the military, but many of their jobs were terminated when the veterans returned. The millions of women remaining in the labor force—in clerical, check out, sales, nursing, and teaching occupations—were usually consigned to low-paying jobs and rarely given assistance with their day care needs.[19]

Blue-collar workers contended with hazardous working conditions in chemical, plastics, pesticide, and assembly-line plants that were not subject to adequate safety regulations. Despite major gains in unionizing workers, many blue-collar workers lacked private health insurance and were forced to rely on charity medicine in public hospitals when they became seriously ill. Workers were buffeted by three recessions in the 1950s.

Persons with mental illnesses, developmental disabilities, or physical disabilities encountered desperate problems. Because most jurisdictions lacked statutes that placed limits on the involuntary commitment of persons with mental disorders to institutions, many unjustified admissions were made. Persons with severe mental disorders had to be admitted to hospitals because few community programs existed for them. Their rights were rarely safeguarded within institutions, where many remained for decades with little or no treatment. Along with a growing number of poorly monitored nursing homes, mental institutions also served as repositories for older persons who had virtually no access to community-based services.[20] The plight of children with developmental disabilities and their families was equally desperate, because public schools often shunned this population, few community-based services existed, and parents often had no access to appropriate institutions for these children.[21] Persons with physical disabilities were provided with virtually no supportive assistance, other than disability assistance and inadequate health services in county and municipal hospitals.[22]

In the 1950s, homosexuality was widely perceived as a mental problem rather than a personal orientation. As most states had statutes that defined their sexual practices as crimes, gay men and lesbians usually tried to disguise their sexual orientation to escape criminal sanctions, insensitive treatment by mental health professionals, or discrimination by employers.[23] Some gay men and lesbians were involuntarily committed to mental institutions by relatives who believed them to be mentally ill because of their sexual orientation. Many were fired from the federal civil service, the State Department, and the armed forces in the 1950s. Quite apart from inadequate laws and social programs, widespread public discrimination existed against many vulnerable populations in 1960, including people of color, people with disabilities, and gay men and lesbians.[24]

DOMESTIC POLICY DURING THE KENNEDY ADMINISTRATION

The lethargy of the 1950s was broken by the election in 1960 of John Kennedy, the youngest president in American history. He remains a controversial figure. Some historians and biographers portray him as a socially minded leader whose legislation was defeated because he confronted a relatively conservative Congress and public. Had he not been assassinated in 1963, they argue, he would have been reelected in 1964, would have obtained a sweeping electoral victory, and would have secured the enactment of many social reforms.[25] His detractors present a less flattering portrait; they contend that he was relatively conservative, possessed a limited reform vision, adopted reform causes only under strong political pressure, and enmeshed the nation in the Vietnam conflict.[26] A true portrayal probably lies somewhere between these two poles.

Kennedy had a limited understanding of poverty and racism because he was raised in a wealthy Boston family and attended private schools. He rarely assumed leadership roles on domestic issues while he served as a congressman and senator in the postwar era, though he dutifully voted Democratic positions on many issues. His orientations toward social reform were reflected in his ambivalence about Franklin Roosevelt. His father, a wealthy businessman, had had a conflicted relationship with Roosevelt, which ended in his resignation from a high-level position in Roosevelt's

administration.[27] Kennedy regarded New Deal reforms, which provided economic resources and jobs to the poor, as outmoded in an affluent era when, he believed, problems of poverty involved intergenerational pockets of poverty in inner cities and rural areas. Kennedy was a problem-solving pragmatist, whose advisors were adept at using economics and management tools to analyze complex problems. But social reform requires moral outrage—and it was the absence of a gut response to social problems that alienated many liberals from Kennedy in the late 1950s and led some of them to support his presidential bid only belatedly in 1960.[28]

Like many of his contemporaries, Kennedy accepted both cultural and structural explanations of poverty. The economic improvement of poor persons was impeded, he believed, by a culture of poverty that made them oriented toward the present, unable to defer gratification, and unwilling to perceive the utility of education. Structuralists believed that automation and technology consigned persons with few skills and little education to unemployment or dead-end jobs. In either case, remedies focused on changing poor individuals themselves, whether by providing them with different orientations or by giving them training or education.[29]

These approaches to poverty were based on questionable assumptions. Research suggests that, though structural unemployment exists, most low-income workers are able to find work but are subject to brief periods of unemployment because they work in seasonal occupations or for firms that are particularly subject to economic cycles. Perhaps more important than structural factors are overt and covert forms of discrimination that relegate people of color and women to low-paying unskilled and semiskilled occupations and subject them to adverse hiring and promotion decisions, particularly during recessions.[30]

The belief that poor people possess a distinctive and dysfunctional culture has also been questioned by many critics. Perspectives of poor persons often change when they receive work, which suggests that their presumed basic orientations are often adaptations to immediate situational realities. Certain attributes, such as present-orientedn may be functional for populations that have little hope of saving money from low-paying jobs. Some critics have questioned the methodology of middle-class social scientists, whose conclusions about the different culture of poor people sometimes derived from biased research instruments. Others have noted that many of the characteristics attributed to the poor by social scientists in the 1960s were identical to 19th-century stereotypes of paupers—and also Irish Americans and other ethnic groups—as lazy and unmotivated. Both in the 19th century and in the 1960s, many Americans condescendingly believed that poor persons would be magically transformed if they were personally exposed to middle- or upper-class persons who could teach them to be industrious.[31]

The various explanations of poverty and unemployment that were commonly advanced in the early 1960s led to a preoccupation with policies to change people in poverty by providing them with services and training, to the neglect of policies to redistribute resources and jobs to them. Scant attention was given to public works, tax incentives to employers to hire certain kinds of workers, affirmative action, the development of a national welfare system, or redistributive tax reform.[32] Services, education, and job training may eventually help some persons escape poverty, but they do not help them with immediate economic needs or necessarily improve their economic condition relative to other citizens.

In Kennedy's defense, he encountered a difficult political situation in 1960. He did not receive a reform mandate from the voters when they narrowly chose him over Richard Nixon, and most Americans did not give priority, based on public opinion polls of the early 1960s, to addressing issues of poverty or racial discrimination. Kennedy's political problems were magnified by divisions within the Democratic Party: Southern conservatives, whose support he desperately needed to defeat Republican opposition, stoutly resisted domestic reforms, whereas a group of Northern liberals, including Senator Hubert Humphrey, insisted that Kennedy develop a range of social reforms, such as executive orders and legislation to protect the rights of African Americans

in the South. Caught in this political cross-fire, Kennedy tried, with marginal success, to walk a political tightrope between the two factions. Many Southern conservatives believed he was a liberal reformer who might even vigorously seek a second Reconstruction, whereas Northern liberals thought he was overconcerned with appeasing Southern Democrats.[33]

Kennedy's precarious political position was exacerbated by his political style. Unlike many politicians, who pride themselves on attention to legislative details, Kennedy was widely perceived by members of Congress to have been a relatively lazy legislator who missed key votes and was remiss in his legislative homework. Many powerful senior legislators also believed Kennedy had succeeded to the presidency before his rightful time and resented his disinclination to consult with them unless he absolutely needed their votes. Some politicians believed that he prematurely and fatalistically discounted his chances to win key votes. Witty, articulate, and adept at using television to advantage, Kennedy was an entertaining president who had limited ability to convince powerful politicians to support his legislation.[34]

Poverty and Civil Rights: Toward Reform

Kennedy can best be described in the late 1950s as a potential liberal, because his background made him receptive to social reform but reluctant to give it precedence over foreign affairs. He was pushed leftward during the Democratic presidential primaries in 1960 when he ran against Hubert Humphrey, who successfully invoked the reform tradition of Franklin Roosevelt and, in the process, portrayed Kennedy as indifferent to social issues. When Kennedy also appealed to the Roosevelt tradition to win support of miners and other working-class voters in a pivotal West Virginia primary, he won a crucial victory and, with it, momentum that carried him eventually to the presidential nomination of his party. He realized, too, that he would have to actively pursue social reform if he wanted to keep the allegiance of the liberal wing of the Democratic

Party, a group that finally, if reluctantly, supported his bid for the party's nomination.[35]

Slow but decided shifts in public opinion facilitated Kennedy's movement toward social reform. Poverty and other social issues were rarely discussed in the 1950s in public or private arenas; indeed, a bibliography of academic writings on the subject of poverty in 1960 totaled two pages![36] The federal government had not even attempted to define poverty before the early 1960s, when it finally created a standard that is still used. In 1962, when Michael Harrington published *The Other America*, a book that discussed problems of the "invisible poor" in rural and urban settings, he was surprised to discover that it became a bestseller.[37] Academics, too, discovered the poor, as reflected by a rapidly expanding literature on the subject in the early 1960s. As the progressive and New Deal eras had demonstrated, social reform is possible in America when sizable numbers of middle-class Americans empathize with disadvantaged persons.

It was the civil rights movement, however, that decisively pushed Kennedy and the nation toward social reform. It began quietly in the South in 1955, when a young African American minister, Martin Luther King, Jr., was chosen by its organizers to head a bus boycott in Montgomery, Alabama, to protest the policy that required African Americans to sit at the back of the bus. African Americans won a decisive victory when this policy was rescinded, but only after a lengthy period of tense confrontation that included sporadic acts of violence against African Americans. The bus boycott initiated a long sequence of protests that successively challenged segregation in interstate transportation, lunch counters, train stations, public swimming pools, public schools, and colleges. Involvement in these issues led, in turn, to protests against literacy tests and poll taxes that disqualified African Americans from voting in the South. Many Americans in the North began to realize that a tangled web of racist policies in the South trapped African Americans at virtually every step. The nation became further sensitized to Southern injustices as nonviolent protests of civil rights demonstrators were repeatedly countered by violence, unfair rulings by Southern courts, intimidation, and murder.[38]

A particular murder in the summer of 1955—the killing of Emmett Till, an African American child from Chicago who was visiting relatives in Mississippi—brought the civil rights struggle of the South to the attention of African Americans in the North, as well as the mass media.[39] (See Figure 8.1.) Till had been warned by his mother to be meek when dealing with Southern whites. She told him, "If you have to get on your knees and bow when a white person goes past, do it willingly."[40] But Till, who had been reared in the North, bragged to several boys outside a grocery store that he had a white girlfriend in Chicago. When one of them dared him to talk to the white female storekeeper, Till bought some candy and told her, "Bye, Baby," as he was leaving. A girl who had heard about the incident predicted, "When that lady's husband come back, there is going to be trouble." Three days later, after midnight on a Saturday, the white woman's husband and his brother-in-law came to get that "boy who has done the talkin'."[41] They dragged Till from the country cabin, tortured him, murdered him, and dumped his body in a river. Later, they said they *had* to kill him because he refused to repent or beg for mercy. When his mother saw the mutilated body, she insisted on an open-casket funeral. And, indeed, a picture of the body, published in an African American magazine, so shocked Chicagoans that thousands attended the funeral. The subsequent trial of the accused white slayers was equally sensational. An African American man testified against them in open court—something that rarely happened in the South because of its risks. When the all-white jury exonerated the defendants, mass rallies of African Americans occurred throughout the North. Although justice was never done in this case, Emmett Till became a martyr, and the civil rights struggle became a national movement. Ominously, however, white Southerners reacted with rage at the audacity of the African Americans who had testified against the men and at the Northern sympathy for Till. It was clear that the old South would not quickly relent.

F I G U R E 8.1 (left) Grief-stricken Mrs. Mamie Bradley watches her son, Emmett Till, lowered into his grave; (right) Emmett Till.

The civil rights movement, like widespread unemployment in the Great Depression and child labor in the progressive era, provided an obvious and ongoing symbol that sensitized Americans to the needs of a particular group of people and forced political leaders to propose policy remedies. As in the 1930s when the depression did not abate, the vicious cycle of protest and repression would not disappear or yield to superficial remedies. Public opinion finally forced Kennedy to propose civil rights legislation in 1963.

The escalating protest and violence in the South in the early 1960s presented Kennedy and his brother Robert, the attorney general, with a dilemma. Kennedy needed the votes of Southern Democrats if the rest of his domestic and foreign policies were to be enacted, but he also needed the support of liberal Democrats, who were urging

him to support federal civil rights legislation or, at the very least, to issue executive orders that prohibited job discrimination in federally funded projects.

Kennedy tried for several years to follow a middle course.[42] He gave African Americans and liberals a symbolic victory when he created a presidential task force headed by Vice President Lyndon Johnson, but it made little progress in addressing discrimination against African Americans in employment. Though Robert Kennedy used federal marshals and FBI agents to protect demonstrators in the South, he avoided the use of federal troops, even in the face of rapidly mounting violence, and insisted, moreover, that Southern jurisdictions were capable of protecting civil rights demonstrators, despite the obvious hostility of many Southern police chiefs. Kennedy refused to issue executive orders to outlaw discrimination or to develop federal civil rights legislation because both he and his brother were convinced that the failure of Reconstruction was due to the imposition of civil rights policies on the South by the North.[43] They also naively hoped that civil rights legislation could be enacted by Southern states as more African Americans became enfranchised. Kennedy's middle course was successful in 1961 and much of 1962. Southerners believed that Robert Kennedy had not used federal marshals except as a last resort, and most African Americans believed that the Kennedy brothers protected them from white extremists.

Some policy successes were obtained, even as violence escalated. Directives from the Interstate Commerce Commission to desegregate bus and train stations were met with compliance and the support of Southern police departments. But events soon made African Americans, liberals, and many Northerners realize that aggressive federal intervention was needed. Robert Kennedy had hoped that the civil rights protesters would focus on voting rights rather than on desegregation of public facilities and schools because he thought registering African Americans to vote would be less likely to arouse a violent response and would eventually liberalize Southern politics.[44] When the Student Nonviolent Coordinating Committee (SNCC) brought thousands of white students to work alongside African Americans in registering voters in 1962 and 1963, however, activists were greeted with threats, intimidation, and physical violence. Many other civil rights groups took prominent roles in the movement, including the Congress of Racial Equality, the National Association of Colored Persons, and the Council for United Civil Rights Leadership.

Many Southern authorities assumed a passive role, overlooked violence, or jailed activists. The mass media were filled with accounts of Southern atrocities, but Northern opinion was most aroused, African Americans ruefully noted, when white students or activists were murdered in voter registration drives.[45] Resistance by high-level Southern politicians to federal court orders to desegregate universities further angered Northerners.

As violence increased, liberals introduced a series of civil rights bills in the Congress and demanded support from Kennedy. Despite protests by some of his top advisors, Kennedy finally decided in 1963 to propose his own civil rights legislation, which prohibited job discrimination on the basis of race and gender as well as discrimination in voter registration.[46] To make the legislation acceptable to moderates in both parties, he diluted voting provisions. In June of 1963, he gave a televised address to endorse the legislation, which was, sadly, the first presidential address in the nation's history devoted to civil rights issues. When Senator Everett Dirksen and other Republicans decided to join Northern Democrats, the legislation appeared destined for passage, but the ill-fated Kennedy could not claim credit for it because of his tragic death in November 1963.

The Course of Reform: Failures and Successes

Kennedy promised in the 1960 campaign that he would support aid to education and medical insurance for older Americans, but both his medical and educational proposals became enmeshed in ideological controversy. Although European nations had developed national health insurance schemes, many Americans believed that governmental financing of medical care would threaten the doctor-patient relationship and was, moreover, un-American. The American Medical Association led the opposition to *any* major federal programs, including public funding of inoculations, and was aided by disputes among legislators about financing and program details. Some legislators wanted to fund medical assistance to older Americans from Social Security payroll deductions, but others wanted to use a separate payroll tax or general revenues. Some legislators favored voluntary participation, and others wanted to make participation mandatory. Various legislative proposals went nowhere, although some progress had been made in congressional deliberations by the summer of 1963.[47]

As the nation's first Catholic president, Kennedy did not want to appear to favor parochial schools. When he excluded religious and private schools from funding under his education bill, however, he incited the wrath of the Catholic Church, which insisted that parochial schools receive funds as well. Kennedy's subsequent concessions to them emboldened Catholic leaders, as well as leaders of other denominations, to demand even more funds for their schools, to the chagrin of legislators who wanted to preserve strict separation of church and state. Passage seemed hopeless.[48]

Some economists believed that periodic recessions, pockets of unemployment, and low rates of economic growth were caused by inadequate pools of investment capital. Guided by economist Walter Heller, Kennedy proposed to increase depreciation allowances for businesses and to allow a tax credit for investments. These policies, which were enacted in 1962, were overshadowed by another proposal to drastically reduce the rates of taxes paid by businesses and wealthy persons. The bill encountered substantial opposition from conservatives, who feared that the tax cut could lead to government deficits. When Kennedy died, the legislation had passed in the House, but not in the Senate.

Judged in purely economic terms, Kennedy's tax measures probably spurred investment and economic growth; but from the vantage point of the poor and the working class, the policies contributed to economic inequality in the nation and drew attention from the need to reform the tax code so as to eliminate deductions and loopholes that benefited affluent taxpayers.[49] Moreover, as we will later note, they reduced the funds available for social programs in the Johnson administration, when the Vietnam War absorbed increasing resources.

Believing that many unemployed persons could not find work because they lacked the necessary skills, Kennedy proposed and obtained passage of the Manpower Development and Training Act of 1962 (MDTA); 600,000 workers had completed technical training by 1968, but the program was plagued by problems.[50] The dropout rate was high, the skills taught were not always needed in local job markets, and relocation assistance was limited. Some critics contend that job-training programs allow one group of trained workers to displace non-trained workers if new jobs are not simultaneously created.[51] MDTA nonetheless represented the

nation's first major job-training program since the work relief programs of the New Deal had not focused on training.

Kennedy sought and obtained major increases in the minimum wage, partly at the behest of unions, which hoped that this measure would deter companies from moving to the nonunionized and low-wage South.[52] Its supporters contended that it provided a wage floor for those workers—in particular, unskilled African American workers—who were severely underpaid compared with other workers, but some economists believe that it fostered unemployment by spurring employers to decrease the size of their labor forces.[53]

Kennedy established the Area Redevelopment Agency in 1961 to increase employment in depressed rural areas such as Appalachia by providing loans and subsidies to local businesses and by improving transportation systems.[54] Critics contend that the program created few jobs because its subsidies were too low or were targeted to tourism and other businesses that employed relatively few persons. Marred by political favoritism and corruption, the program was terminated in 1965.[55]

The concerns of a number of mental health experts about the absence of community-based care for persons who had been released from mental hospitals led Congress to establish a commission in 1955. The commission's report, *Action for Mental Health*, which was issued in 1961, recommended federal funding of community-based mental health services. Kennedy secured the enactment of the Community Mental Health Centers Act of 1963, which provided federal funding for the construction of mental health centers that offered a range of outpatient and preventive services. The act was quickly amended to provide funds for staff as well. Because appropriations for the legislation never met the expectations of its framers, it did not address all the community needs of mental patients, who often lived in substandard board-and-care facilities and skid-row housing.[56] It nonetheless led to the establishment of a national network of centers that provided outpatient services to millions of people.

Many Americans were alarmed by the marked expansion of AFDC rolls in the early 1960s. In

---

INSERT 8.2 Critical Analysis: The Limits of Social Services

Social workers have often been asked to solve problems by working directly with populations most affected by social problems, whether women on AFDC (as in the case of the services strategy of 1962), children who have been abused, homeless people, or mental patients. Yet the dilemmas of these clients are often profoundly shaped by economic factors, community factors, and family dynamics that the social worker cannot control. Most children who are reported as abused, for example, come from low-income families, where unemployment (or underemployment) is a stressor that may cause or exacerbate the abuse.

Analyze options that exist for social workers in these circumstances in their direct work with these clients and in their social advocacy work.

---

response, a services strategy was formulated in 1962 to cut the rolls through interventions of social workers. In this strategy, the federal government provided a 75 percent match to the states to encourage local welfare departments to provide social services to AFDC recipients. It was, at best, a naive proposal. The growth in AFDC rolls was the result of many factors, including migration of poor African Americans to urban areas in the North and the South, the absence of jobs for unskilled female workers, and the absence of day care. Furthermore, since rates of desertion by fathers are associated with social class, they are unlikely to decline unless jobs and resources are provided to low-income families. The rapid rise of AFDC rolls provided conservatives with the opportunity to propose punitive policies later in the decade.[57] (See Insert 8.2.)

Kennedy missed an opportunity to develop a variety of tax, income, and nutritional programs to reduce poverty. Moreover, convinced that the nation needed the capability to fight the Soviet Union, China, and one guerilla war at the same time to counter communist insurgency, he launched the fastest peacetime buildup of the military in American history and introduced military advisors into South Vietnam in an expansion of the military budget that constrained social spending.[58]

Kennedy deserves praise, however, for shattering the conservative complacency that characterized the 1950s. He came to office with no mandate to enact major reforms and inherited a Congress in which Republicans and Southern Democrats possessed a majority. Although unable to secure passage of most of his major social legislation, he established a policy agenda for his successor, Lyndon Johnson: civil rights legislation, the War on Poverty, the Food Stamps Program, Medicare, federal aid to public schools, and tax reform.

KENNEDY AND JOHNSON: A STUDY IN CONTRASTS

A novelist could not have fashioned a more unusual plot. The articulate and well-educated Kennedy, fearing lack of support from pivotal Southern delegates at the 1960 Democratic convention, chose Lyndon Johnson, a crude and politically astute Southerner, as his vice president, over the strenuous objections of Robert Kennedy. Political pundits saw it as a brilliant move to obtain the support of Southern Democrats. Who could have predicted that most of Kennedy's social legislation would eventually be enacted by Johnson, or that Johnson would carry the Vietnam policy that Kennedy had begun to its tragic conclusion?

Johnson excelled in political maneuvering. His grandfather and father had been involved in a strange mixture of populist and conservative Texas politics. His mother, an aristocratic figure unfulfilled in her marriage to an alcoholic Texan, urged him to rise above his humble origins. As early as college, when he was active in campus politics, Johnson displayed an uncanny ability to decipher the existing balance of political forces and to develop issues that could propel him into leadership roles. After a brief stint as a teacher, he became an aide to a congressman, secured an appointment as regional director in Texas of a major New Deal program, and successfully ran for Congress.[59] On his second attempt, in 1948, Johnson was elected to the United States Senate, where he quickly became a protégé of Senator Richard Russell, a powerful legislator.

By helping Russell with laborious details and serving as his confidante, Johnson cleverly positioned himself to run for the position of Senate minority leader, to which he was elected in 1953. In January of 1955, when Democrats won control of the Senate, he became majority leader. He became an expert in the intricacies of parliamentary procedures, honed his interpersonal and persuasive skills, and augmented his power by vesting in the majority leader the power to make committee assignments.[60] He had presidential ambitions but was not well known outside Texas and the Senate. Realizing that he could not advance beyond his position as majority leader, he accepted Kennedy's invitation to be vice president in 1960. He was deeply frustrated by 1963, however, because he was seldom consulted by Kennedy or his Ivy League staff. We can scarcely imagine how he felt when he learned, in a Dallas hospital, that Kennedy was dead and that he would soon be the nation's next president.

The Johnson administration achieved legislative successes that were matched only by those of Franklin Roosevelt: major federal resources allocated to public schools for the first time in history, medical insurance for the elderly, subsidies for health care of the poor, legal aid for the poor, job training for impoverished teenagers, enforcement of civil rights for African Americans, nutritional programs, preschool programs, community development projects, health care for migrant labor, and medical services for pregnant women and children. Whereas Franklin Roosevelt had succeeded in developing federal income and insurance programs for economic security, Johnson extended federal programs into areas that had fallen outside the province of federal policy. His legislative successes can be explained by a combination of facilitating factors.

When Kennedy died, many of his policy proposals were making their way through the legislative process. Thus, Kennedy provided Johnson with an instant agenda, which facilitated his legislative tasks.[61]

Johnson was aided, moreover, by sustained pressure from civil rights groups. Violent reprisals against civil rights demonstrators, who continued to protest, inflamed public opinion in the North, which became more sympathetic not only to African Americans but to the plight of poor persons.

Nor should we ignore Johnson's genuine compassion for those in need. It is always difficult to determine motivation when examining the actions of politicians; this was particularly so with Johnson, who possessed much political ambition and was obsessed with personal failure. Did he pursue his policy agenda to obtain a high reputation, or did he genuinely seek to help people with problems? No doubt Johnson, like most politicians, had mixed motives, but one of his closest aides, Joseph Califano, argues persuasively that Johnson often had noble motives that derived from his populist origins.[62] In any event, Johnson was *driven* to seek social reforms, spent incalculable hours writing legislation, and repeatedly brought himself to the point of exhaustion in seeking its enactment.

Johnson used his political skills to advantage. He immediately wrapped himself in the mantle of Kennedy by promising to enact Kennedy's legislative measures and by keeping his top staff. By portraying himself as a humble successor to Kennedy who would devote himself tirelessly to the fulfillment of the slain leader's unfulfilled aspirations, he endeared himself to the American people as well as to legislators. He summoned to the White House virtually every legislator, lobbyist, interest group leader, and citizen who could advance the progress of Kennedy's pending legislation. He obtained detailed information about their policy opinions, specific legislative objectives that they desired, and their willingness to compromise on key points. He assembled, in effect, a massive team to develop a legislative program in support of his domestic measures.[63]

Johnson was a welcome change to congressional leadership because he discussed specific pieces of legislation with them before the legislation was introduced to Congress. He was adept, as well, at giving legislators credit for specific pieces of legislation during the legislative process and at signing ceremonies. He bridged the chasm between the

White House and Congress, which had sabotaged Kennedy's legislation.

Johnson maintained political support from a broad spectrum of legislators and interest groups.[64] Many liberals, including Robert Kennedy, feared that, as a Southerner, Johnson would develop conservative policies, but Johnson dashed these fears when he declared his allegiance to Kennedy's entire legislative package, including civil rights. Indeed, his decisive commitment to civil rights, which he made almost immediately on succeeding to the presidency, was a remarkably bold move that signaled to Southerners, as it did to Northern liberals, that he would be a reform-minded president. Yet he was also adept at giving concessions to Southerners, as reflected by provisions in many pieces of legislation that gave Southern states a disproportionate amount of program funds by weighting their distribution to poorer states. (Southern states had the lowest per capita incomes in the United States.) He carefully cultivated support from both unions and businesses; he supported increases in the minimum wage, favored by unions, and he vigorously sought passage of Kennedy's tax cuts for businesses and individuals. His ability to appeal to both conservative and liberal audiences was illustrated by his support for both budget cutting and social reform. He prided himself on fiscal conservatism; he sometimes proposed cuts in the federal budget that exceeded those desired by House Republicans, and he blocked efforts by liberals to drastically expand funding for the War on Poverty, the Food Stamps Program, or the AFDC program. Yet he supported passage of a staggering number of social reforms and would brag, much like a fisherman who has had a good day, about the sheer number of programs that he had enacted.[65]

Johnson was a master of timing, negotiation, and compromise. Since he knew that momentum was crucial, he carefully introduced his legislation each year in a planned sequence, beginning with the easiest and ending with the most difficult. He made skillful compromises in legislation to defuse opposition yet astutely avoided an image of softness by refusing to back down when he believed that vital principles were at stake or that compromises

would make him appear overtimid. When he rewarded politicians with patronage and resources for their districts, it was not for votes on specific issues, which would have led them to expect rewards every time they supported measures, but rather for a pattern of support over an extended period. He had an uncanny ability to make slight changes in the wording of legislation so as to mollify objections of legislators or interest groups—but his compromises would be limited only to those changes that were necessary for passage.[66]

Johnson knew that his political honeymoon with the public would end and feared that his legislative successes would also come to a halt. However, he received extraordinary assistance from the Republicans when they nominated Barry Goldwater in 1964 to be their presidential candidate. The conservative Goldwater presented an easy target for Johnson when he violated the unspoken rule in American politics that legacies of the New Deal, such as Social Security and the Tennessee Valley Authority, would be placed above partisan politics. Because Goldwater both espoused foreign intervention against communist regimes and hinted that he might consider use of tactical nuclear weapons in such struggles, Johnson portrayed himself as a man of peace—a claim that still seemed plausible because he had not yet committed thousands of troops to Vietnam.[67] Enough liberal and moderate Democrats were elected in the landslide victory of 1964 that Johnson's legislative program could not be scuttled by the conservative coalition of Republicans and Southern Democrats. He proceeded to use this mandate to enact Kennedy's pending legislation, as well as many proposals developed by his numerous task forces, under the rubric of the Great Society.

JOHNSON'S POLICY GLUTTONY

For all his political skills, Johnson had a fatal personal flaw: policy gluttony. He wanted to be the most successful domestic *and* international president in

American history—to exceed even Franklin Roosevelt's accomplishments at home and abroad. He also wanted to have bipartisan support from both liberals and conservatives. His presidency would be, he hoped, a Texas barbecue with everyone attending and thanking the host as they left.

Imbued with this mind-set, Johnson risked overreaching by selecting incompatible goals. Might an aggressive foreign policy undercut his domestic reforms? Might huge tax cuts at the inception of his presidency—certain to be popular with many liberals and conservatives—deplete resources for both his foreign and domestic policies—making both conservatives and liberals unhappy? Could he maintain a coalition of supporters with these different policies in play?

Johnson's Fateful First Choice

At the time of Kennedy's death, a huge tax cut was pending in the Congress that would have cut most taxpayers' taxes by more than 20 percent. Rather than slowing the tax cut's momentum as he pondered whether the United States could afford it, as well as his impending social and military initiatives, Johnson sought and got its immediate passage. He got its passage, however, only by promising Congressional conservatives that he would not increase the national budget until tax revenues returned to their former pre-cut levels. This decision

meant that his administration would be strapped for cash as it eventually sought to fund both its domestic and international policies, which came to include the Great Society and the Vietnam War. When he did increase spending even before tax revenues exceeded the pre-cut levels, conservatives became infuriated with him, accused him of breaking his promise, and demanded domestic spending cuts. In turn, liberals complained that his Great Society was poorly funded because too many resources went to the Vietnam War. When asked after he left the presidency what his biggest mistake had been, he answered, "The tax cut of 1964." (We shall see in subsequent chapters how huge tax cuts in 1981, 2001, and 2003 greatly depleted domestic resources, particularly when coupled with rapidly growing military expenditures; see Insert 8.3.)

Johnson's Fateful Second Choice

As early as 1964, Johnson met secretly with foreign policy advisors such as Robert McNamara, Dean Rusk, and McGeorge Bundy to consider what he should do with respect to Vietnam. While President Kennedy had committed a relatively small group of "advisors" to Vietnam to provide military consultation to the Vietnamese government, he had refrained from committing large numbers of American troops to a complex political struggle in Vietnam. In 1954 the Geneva Treaty had divided

---

INSERT 8.3   **Critical Analysis: Linkages between Taxes and Social Policy**

Few social policy theorists discuss taxes in their writings; they focus instead on policy enactments and social programs. But social programs are ultimately funded by tax revenues, whether from general taxes or from payroll taxes.

As a proportion of income, taxes in the United States are far lower than in European nations, where higher rates of taxation on personal incomes are supplemented by a value-added tax that far exceeds local sales taxes in the United States.

In the context of U.S. history, what cultural and political factors promote Americans' distaste for taxes?

What implications have low taxes had for social policy expenditures, particularly when the United States has also spent a far larger share (in comparison with European nations) of its domestic wealth on military programs?

Did multi-trillion-dollar tax cuts during the presidency of George W. Bush affect domestic policy, particularly when coupled—as in the Johnson administration—with sharp increases in military spending that accompanied the war against Iraq?

Vietnam into two nations: a Northern communist regime and a Southern noncommunist nation. A three-sided conflict soon emerged: North Vietnam versus South Vietnam, and insurgents in South Vietnam versus the entrenched government in South Vietnam. This conflict escalated into a civil war.

The battle between North and South Vietnam got most attention in the mass media. Ho Chi Minh, the diminutive leader of North Vietnam, was determined to reunite Vietnam under communist leadership—and began steady infiltration of South Vietnam with the goal of toppling the government in South Vietnam. But a civil war had also broken out in South Vietnam because many insurgents believed the South Vietnamese government was corrupt and uninterested in land reforms that could benefit impoverished peasants.

As a hawkish anticommunist president, John Kennedy feared that a victory by Ho Chi Minh would not only make Vietnam a united communist nation, but would catalyze similar communist victories in other Asian nations in a so-called domino effect. But he realized that Vietnam provided unfavorable jungle terrain for military action against communist forces—and he knew that the regime in South Vietnam was corrupt and insensitive to the needs of its citizens. Why, he sometimes wondered, get American troops into the middle of a civil war? So he hedged his bets by only committing military advisors to South Vietnam while waiting to decide whether to commit American troops to the conflict. It is unclear what he would have done had he not been assassinated.

Lyndon Johnson, by contrast, decided in his talks with advisors in the summer of 1964 to commit large numbers of American troops to Vietnam, but he chose not to tell the public about his decision until after the presidential elections of 1964 were completed. Ironically, he ran as a man of peace against Barry Goldwater, whom he portrayed as a man of war.

This decision to go to war—eventually committing more than 500,000 American troops to Vietnam—when combined with his tax cut and his expansive domestic agenda, would have catastrophic consequences for his presidency.

Johnson's Fateful Third Choice

As his third choice, Johnson decided to go all-out in enacting domestic reforms even in 1964—but even more ambitiously in 1965 were he to win the election of 1964 decisively and get large Democratic majorities in both houses of Congress. Even with the fiscal constraints that he faced, Johnson secured the enactment of a prodigious number of domestic measures that greatly expanded the role of the federal government in social policy.

Civil Rights Legislation in 1964 and 1965

Johnson refused to compromise with Southerners in 1964 when they tried to dilute civil rights legislation drafted by the Kennedy administration. The Civil Rights Act of 1964 was a historic measure; it marked the first time since Reconstruction that the federal government had assumed a major role in protecting the voting rights of African Americans in the South. The act required the desegregation of public facilities and prohibited discrimination in the hiring practices of firms and institutions that received federal contracts. The U.S. attorney general was also given the right to file suits to desegregate schools.

The immediate effects of this legislation were diminished because litigation was often required to bring compliance, but within six months it led to a civil rights revolution for African Americans in the South. Public accommodations and public transportation were desegregated by 1965. The attorney general initiated suits against local school districts that discriminated against African Americans and supported an ever-tightening series of guidelines that ultimately required them to use one set of facilities for all students. It was an extraordinary set of achievements by any standard. Southern whites found they were unable to persuade the Supreme Court to overrule federal civil rights powers, as had occurred during Reconstruction. The Department of Justice, often headed by officials who questioned various aspects of civil rights legislation, did not attack its central provisions.[68]

The Civil Rights Act of 1964 was flawed in several important respects, however. It outlawed the use of literacy tests, but the tedious case-by-case enforcement process allowed many jurisdictions to continue discriminatory practices. Johnson did not aggressively implement Title VII of the act, which outlawed discrimination in employment; for example, he failed to give the Department of Labor a significant role in monitoring federal contracts for discrimination. Title VII established an Equal Employment Opportunity Commission (EEOC) to monitor discrimination in employment, but the commission did not receive the power to initiate suits until 1972. Furthermore, Johnson decided for political reasons not to aggressively attack de facto segregation of Northern schools.[69]

Johnson had not planned to introduce additional civil rights legislation in 1965, but he changed his mind when confronted with massive civil rights protests directed at continuing and widespread denial of suffrage to African Americans in the South. To allow faster legal action than had been possible in case-by-case litigation, the Civil Rights Act of 1965 gave the federal government the right to presume discrimination in any state or its subdivisions where less than 50 percent of people of color voted in federal elections and in areas that used literacy or other screening tests. In such areas, federal authorities were allowed to directly administer elections. These policies were remarkably successful in diminishing overt discrimination in voter registration.[70]

Earl Warren and the Supreme Court Buttress Johnson's Domestic Agenda

The Supreme Court, under the leadership of Chief Justice Earl Warren between 1953 and 1969, provided its own impetus to the advancement of civil rights and civil liberties. Warren had been governor of California and an important Republican politician who had, moreover, taken a number of conservative positions in California; indeed, as the state's attorney general, he had even assumed a key role in incarcerating Japanese Americans in World War II.

Eisenhower, looking for a prominent Republican and owing a political debt to Warren, felt he would be an ideal conservative choice when he appointed him chief justice in 1953. But Eisenhower had misread his man; Warren believed, above all, in the doctrine of fairness. Guided by that doctrine, he presided over a Court that in 16 years made a series of liberal rulings that radically transformed American jurisprudence. (Years later, Eisenhower believed the appointment of Warren was his biggest political error; he was not on speaking terms with Warren in the closing years of his presidency.)[71]

The precedent-shaking nature of the Warren Court began almost at the outset, with the historic *Brown v. Board of Education* ruling in 1954. Reverend Oliver Brown of Topeka, Kansas, had brought suit against his city's board of education because his child had to take a bus to the other side of town when a school reserved for whites was much closer. Thurgood Marshall of the NAACP argued that segregation had such harmful psychological effects on people of color that the mere fact of segregation meant inferior education. He and other civil rights attorneys had been impressed by some experiments conducted by the African American social scientist Kenneth Clark. In tests with African American children in the North, Clark found that, when asked to identify a doll that most resembled themselves (by color), many African American children refused to answer or would cry and run out of the room. When the same test was given to African American children in the South, Clark found a different, but equally disturbing, result; the children would often point to the brown doll and say, matter-of-factly, "That's a nigger. I'm a nigger," thus accepting as given their subordinate status.[72] Although some of the civil rights lawyers did not want to use this "soft" evidence, Marshall and others prevailed; they felt that the Court would not hold segregated facilities to be a violation of the equal protection clause of the Fourteenth Amendment to the Constitution without it. By contrast, the attorney representing the board of education contended that no definitive proof had been shown that segregated students fare worse in life *because* of their segregation. Were the court to rule in Marshall's behalf, it would repudiate more than 50 years of tradition stemming from the *Plessy v. Ferguson* decision of 1896, which had upheld the separate-but-equal doctrine. What was at stake was the very structure of education in many Southern jurisdictions, which established so-called dual school systems, one for white students and the other for African American students—and possibly, further down the judicial road, the structure of Northern education, which had dual systems based not on law but on the combination of neighborhood schools and residential segregation. In the North, thanks to this system, vast numbers of children of color went to de facto segregated schools. Warren, who was appointed chief justice after the deliberations on the *Brown* case had been under way for many months, decided he wanted a unanimous ruling and finally got one that upheld the logic of the NAACP and gave due weight to the psychological testimony derived from Clark's work.[73]

Other rulings, some almost as controversial, followed in rapid succession—rulings that forced localities to reapportion voting districts to protect voting rights of minorities; to respect the rights of apprehended criminal suspects; to protect the rights of persons with radical beliefs; to give procedural protections to persons on death row; to enhance the power of the press; to strike down state laws that outlawed interracial sexual relations and marriage; to require the provision of public defenders to impoverished defendants; and to overturn laws that prohibited the sale of contraceptives. The cumulative effects of these and other rulings were enormous. Many conservatives, infuriated by these rulings, sought to develop a grassroots campaign to impeach Warren and hoped that, one day, conservative presidents would make appointments that would turn the Court into a conservative institution. (As we note later, they succeeded in this objective during the 1980s.) We can say, then, that the Supreme Court was an important part of the social reforms of the 1960s under the leadership of Earl Warren. Though the Court is not a legislative body, its decisions had profound effects on the policies of local institutions that, in turn, affected the lives of people of color and people in poverty.

Medicare, Medicaid, and the Older Americans Act in 1965

An ingenious compromise fashioned by the administration and Wilbur Mills, powerful chairman of the House Ways and Means Committee, facilitated the passage of Medicare and Medicaid programs in 1965 as Titles XVIII and XIX of the Social Security Act. Medicare received widespread attention because of the political clout of elderly persons and the extensive discussion of their needs in preceding years. Kennedy's desire to obtain health insurance had been frustrated by controversy about details of the program, but Mills and Johnson developed a strategy that incorporated facets of the proposals by members of both parties.[74] The program was divided into two parts. Participation in Part A, which funded selected hospital services of elderly persons, was mandatory and financed by a payroll tax on workers and employers. Participation in Part B was voluntary. Part B financed physicians' services and was funded by a combination of monthly premiums on elderly persons and funds from the general revenues of the federal government.

Medicare was a godsend to many elderly persons, who lacked funds to pay for their medical bills without selling their personal possessions. Because the legislation made eligibility automatic on payment of payroll taxes and premiums, elderly persons were able to receive assistance without the stigma of a means test. They did not have to visit local welfare departments but obtained eligibility through Social Security offices. It is difficult to evaluate the effect of Medicare on the health and health practices of elderly persons on account of conflicting findings and methodological issues. For example, because most elderly persons participate in Medicare, it is difficult to assess whether they would have been more or less healthy without it. However, the program appears to have increased the utilization of physicians and hospitals by poor persons, who had often refrained from seeking medical care except in emergencies. Had the Medicare program not existed, it is likely that much greater numbers of elderly people would have become insolvent and forced on welfare rolls.

Another factor is that, prior to Medicare, some medical care was donated to impoverished elderly persons by doctors and hospitals; with the passage of Medicare, such donations were reduced.[75]

Medicare can be criticized on several grounds. Since it subsidized acute health care services, it provided only a limited buffer against medical insolvency and did not help persons with chronic conditions. It reimbursed only a maximum of 60 days in the hospital, covered only 100 days of convalescent care, and did not reimburse out-of-hospital nursing home care. These restrictive policies meant that many elderly persons who exhausted their scanty Medicare benefits had to suffer the indignity of depleting their savings and assets to become eligible for Medicaid, which is a means-tested program.[76]

At the insistence of the American Medical Association, physicians were allowed to charge higher rates for Medicare than the maximum fees that authorities would reimburse, and so elderly persons had to contribute their own resources. Studies reveal that these costs, plus various other out-of-pocket costs for services covered and not covered by Medicare, meant that elderly persons in 1986 financed nearly the same percentage of their total medical costs as before its passage.[77] Elderly persons' out-of-pocket medical costs would have risen even more rapidly without the assistance of Medicare, however, because of the increasing use of expensive medical technologies and sharp increases in the real cost of medical services.

Medicare contributed to medical inflation by reimbursing providers at prevailing rates, so that they had no incentive to decrease their charges or to curtail unnecessary surgeries.[78] Because, in line with the disease model of medicine, it was confined to financing existing curative services, Medicare did not promote innovative alternatives to nursing home care, failed to foster preventive services for elderly persons, and did not provide outreach services to the frail elderly.[79] In short, Medicare funded conventional services for a population that needed innovative programs, and it covered only a small fraction of their medical needs.

We now turn to Medicaid. State, county, and municipal officials had funded medical services to poor persons for decades but with considerable assistance from physicians who donated their time. The costs of these programs had steadily increased, and many poor persons delayed treatment because they had no access to such services. The Medicaid program was enacted in 1965 to address the medical needs of welfare recipients, as well as so-called medically indigent persons, who, though not destitute, could not pay their medical bills.

Whereas Medicare vested financing, administration, and policy roles in the federal government, Medicaid was a matching grant program, like AFDC, in which federal authorities paid a substantial share of the medical services but ceded major administrative and policy roles to the states. States had to provide some basic services, such as outpatient and emergency care, had to enroll AFDC recipients, and were allowed to decide which, if any, additional services they wanted to provide and to devise eligibility criteria. As in the AFDC program, conservative and poor states covered fewer services and had more restrictive eligibility criteria than other states.[80]

Many legislators wrongly assumed that Medicaid would be a small program that would focus on the medical needs of AFDC recipients. Governors of New York and California, who had already been pressured to devise health insurance programs, believed that they could use the relatively generous federal match of the Medicaid program to develop free health services for their blue-collar citizens as well; indeed, at one point, 40 percent of the population in New York State was eligible for its Medicaid program. As congressional legislators observed the mounting federal costs of the Medicaid program and realized that a disproportionate share of federal funds went to a few liberal states, they enacted policies in 1967 that would restrict Medicaid coverage in all states by 1970 to persons who earned no more than 133 percent of a state's AFDC standard.[81]

It is difficult to gauge the precise effects of Medicaid on poor persons. Their use of outpatient services increased dramatically, and rural residents similarly increased their use of all medical services. Although Medicaid funding led many physicians and hospitals to discontinue free or low-cost services to poor persons, the total number of services available to the poor increased.[82] Nonetheless, Medicaid can be criticized in much the same way as Medicare. It encouraged inflation by infusing massive resources into the medical system with few cost controls. It did not encourage the development of innovative outreach and preventive services to poor persons, who often distrusted medical authorities or postponed treatment until illnesses had become severe. Few poor persons entered the medical system used by middle-class Americans, as regular medical providers, resenting the restrictive levels of reimbursement that most states established, refused to serve Medicaid recipients. (More than 70 percent of physicians refused to serve them even in 2000.) Many poor persons were served by Medicaid mills, where physicians reaped large profits from high-volume services. Two systems of care continued after the passage of Medicaid: middle-class Americans used nonprofit or for-profit hospitals, and low-income and medically indigent persons used public hospitals and inner-city clinics.[83]

Another program to aid elderly people, the Older Americans Act (OAA), passed Congress in 1965. Under Title III, it authorized the development of a national network of Area Agencies on Aging (AAAs) to coordinate services for elderly people.[84] Since its inception, OAA has subsidized many kinds of services, including nutritional programs, services for the homebound frail elderly, and training programs. Critics contend that AAAs, which were supposed to be vigorous advocates, have often been preoccupied with delivering services.[85]

Federal Aid to Education in 1965

Kennedy's proposals to extend federal aid to public schools had foundered on constitutional and political issues associated with the relationship between church and state, but Johnson fashioned a clever compromise that eventually led to passage of the Elementary and Secondary Education Act of 1965 (ESEA).[86] It provided federal assistance to public schools with relatively high concentrations of low-income children, and it allowed private schools to share books and other materials that had been purchased by public schools.

Sharp differentials in educational spending at the local level between affluent and poor neighborhoods persisted even after ESEA was enacted. Its provision of funds with relatively few restrictions led many schools to use the funds to underwrite their regular expenses rather than to upgrade the instruction of low-income students; indeed, some jurisdictions even reduced their level of educational spending after they received ESEA funds.[87] Gaps in educational achievement between middle- and upper-income students and low-income students continue to defy solution. Are the gaps due to poor facilities, poor instruction, or familial background? Do low-income children often discontinue school because they believe it will not lead to jobs? What combination of outreach, instructional, facility, and other changes is needed to help low-income students improve their educational performance?[88]

Johnson also developed a range of educational subsidies for low-income persons who sought junior college and college education.[89] Despite the shortcomings of ESEA and other legislation, striking educational gains were made by African Americans in the 1960s at both secondary and college levels.[90]

The War on Poverty in 1964 and Succeeding Years

When Kennedy realized in early 1963 that his domestic policy was stumbling, he commissioned top aides to develop an antipoverty program, but they had only begun assembling lists of job-training and youth employment schemes when he died. The so-called War on Poverty was developed after his death and consisted of a collection of job-training, youth employment, and medical services that various government departments had failed to enact during the Kennedy administration.[91] Specifically, the legislation included the Job Corps, to provide impoverished youth with job training in urban and rural residential centers; the Neighborhood Youth Corps, to provide teenagers with employment in local agencies; a legal aid program to provide free legal assistance to the poor; and medical clinics in low-income areas. The measure also included a community action program that established local community action agencies (CAAs) to coordinate local programs for the poor and to fund and operate various programs. (The popular Head Start program for preschool children was funded from community action funds.) To coordinate these programs, the legislation set up the Office of Economic Opportunity (OEO); Robert Sargent Shriver, Jr., was its energetic director.

The community action program soon became the most controversial part of OEO. One group of officials believed the CAAs would concentrate on planning and coordinating functions in poverty areas. Another group, which included Richard Boone and David Hackett, believed that existing programs and agencies were unresponsive to poor persons and wanted the CAAs to be forceful advocates. To increase this likelihood, they placed in the legislation the requirement that the CAAs promote the "maximum feasible participation of the poor" in their governing boards.[92] Virtually no legislators noticed this phrase, but it was widely used by community activists in succeeding years to insist that poor persons be allowed to elect community representatives to the CAA boards.

Johnson and Shriver wanted OEO programs implemented as rapidly as possible because they realized that demonstrable results were needed if the programs were to appeal to a wide spectrum of legislators. However, the speedy implementation of dozens of different programs, as well as the administratively complex CAAs, led to widespread charges of corruption, patronage, and inefficiency.[93] In the early planning of OEO, administration officials hoped to focus on demonstration programs in a limited number of cities, but Johnson insisted on broader coverage to enhance the visibility and impact of OEO. OEO was plagued, moreover, with incessant charges and countercharges as well as by local confusion about the objectives of the CAAs.

There have been many criticisms of OEO. It was not wise to suggest that a War on Poverty could be declared, waged, and won with a collection of small programs that were supplemented by an ill-defined advocacy program. It is impossible to wage even a limited action against poverty if no income or resources are given to the poor, but OEO provided only personal and community services. When Sargent Shriver sought to include public works within OEO, he received a chilly reception from Johnson, who believed that services, training, and coordination could somehow end poverty without income transfers or creation of new jobs.[94] Policy expectations were established that could not be fulfilled, and political opponents criticized the limited effectiveness of OEO in reducing poverty and demanded its curtailment or elimination.

Moreover, it is not politically feasible for governments to directly subsidize local protest organizations, even if the concept appears attractive at first glance. Governmental officials who are the targets of such protests will attack the advocacy program as unwarranted federal intrusion into local affairs; many of those officials will be powerful mayors who constitute a significant part of the political constituency of the Democratic Party. Republican members of Congress, who were desperately seeking issues to slow the momentum of the Johnson legislative avalanche, were delighted when local Democratic officials such as Mayor Richard Daley of Chicago attacked the CAAs.

OEO cannot be dismissed as a disaster, however. Many of its programs were highly innovative and, though transferred from OEO to other agencies in subsequent years, continue to exist. OEO initiated a large legal aid program that represented poor people against landlords, local merchants, and unresponsive government agencies.[95] Neighborhood health centers markedly improved the health of many low-income persons, and nutritional and health programs for youth were established.[96] OEO administrators' growing doubts about advocacy by CAAs led them to focus funding on such service programs as Head Start, a popular preschool program that combined recreational, educational, and health programs in summer as well as during the school year. The effectiveness of Head Start in raising the test scores of low-income children has been questioned, but some studies suggest that it has had long-term beneficial effects on the educational performance of its enrollees.[97]

Welfare Reform in 1967

Relatively muted in the 1950s, resentment against AFDC recipients mounted during the 1960s when the program grew dramatically. One reason for this increase was that uprooted persons who fled rural areas and found bleak job prospects in urban areas were emboldened by civil rights protests to claim their right to AFDC. By the late 1960s, AFDC rolls were swelled further by women who realized that receipt of AFDC entitled them to receive Medicaid, Food Stamps, day care, and work-related incentive payments.

The mounting resentment against women on AFDC was fueled not only by the program's growth but also by changing orientations toward work. Despite increases in the number of working women during the 1950s, many persons still believed that women should remain at home with their children. This sentiment decreased markedly during the 1960s, however, as more women of all social classes joined the labor force. With this change in attitude, conservatives began to demand that female welfare recipients obtain employment instead of welfare.[98]

In the face of conservative opposition to AFDC, the Johnson administration had a number of options. They could have capitulated to conservatives and accepted a variety of punitive strategies to force women off the AFDC rolls; they could have insisted that women on AFDC should not be compelled to work; or they could have devised programs to make it possible for women on AFDC to work. Most of the women wanted to work, but the last option would have required careful planning because adult AFDC recipients averaged only an eighth-grade education, often suffered discrimination in labor markets, required expensive day care programs, sometimes possessed physical or mental problems, and often could not find employment. But the Johnson administration never chose a consistent

strategy. Some conservatives wanted to force women on AFDC to work. Northern liberals, who had become supporters of welfare rights, opposed compulsory assignment to jobs for women with young children, insisted that jobs pay at least the minimum wage, and demanded that the level of AFDC grants be raised.[99] The administration did not believe it could oppose conservatives, as they had considerable strength in the Congress, and Johnson was unsympathetic to welfare recipients, whom he believed often sought benefits rather than employment.[100]

The administration's policy approach, which was reflected in the welfare amendments of 1967, was a confusing mixture of incompatible policies; ultimately, it satisfied no one. Some punitive policies were adopted; in particular, all women who did not have children younger than six years of age were required to work, at prevailing rather than minimum wages. A federal freeze on funds for AFDC was enacted but, for technical and political reasons, never implemented. Liberals were delighted to obtain a series of exemptions in the law that allowed welfare women to escape the work requirement if they were ill or if work was "inimical" to the welfare of the family. Liberals also obtained a work incentive provision that allowed women who obtained low-paying jobs to continue to augment their wages with welfare payments up to a certain cut-off point; thus, many low-wage working women were able to earn more than they would have received as nonworking welfare recipients. Although women who obtained relatively high-paying jobs lost their eligibility, this policy led, overall, to large increases in the welfare rolls. Some liberals also liked provisions that established the Work Incentive Program (WIN), which funded training programs and day care.

The 1967 amendments represented, then, a confused policy. Liberals were victorious, on balance, because exemptions meant that few women were forced to take jobs and the rolls increased rapidly in the wake of work incentive provisions. Their victory came at a high price, however. The insistence that women should not be forced work blinded them to the reality that most w on AFDC wanted to work, though for decent wages. Instead of scheming to outmaneuver conservatives and dilute the work requirement, they could have tried more diligently to develop millions of public service jobs or subsidized jobs in private industry, backed up by good day care programs and large job-training and educational programs. They would have encountered formidable opposition from conservatives because the costs of day care, training, and job creation would have far exceeded the cost of merely providing AFDC grants or the cost of the WIN programs, which provided superficial training and inadequate day care services. Still, had the administration developed an effective and humanistic work strategy that had actually reduced the size of AFDC rolls, they might have outflanked conservatives and taken the AFDC issue from them.

Food Stamps in 1964

The Food Stamps Program was enacted in 1964 in the wake of a series of pilot feeding programs during the Kennedy administration. Policy makers realized that distribution of surplus food to the poor was cumbersome and required recipients to travel to centralized storage sites. Instead, families were allowed to purchase Food Stamps—coupons—at a price considerably less than their retail value; a number of grocery stores across the country agreed to accept Food Stamps as payment. Families on welfare were automatically eligible, but many poor families not on welfare could also be certified by local welfare departments. Localities were given the option of participating in the program; the Department of Agriculture paid the entire cost. Successive amendments in 1968, 1971, 1973, and 1978 dramatically expanded funding for the program, established national eligibility standards, made the program mandatory in all states, and developed methods to allow recipients to receive coupons without having to make any cash payments. The Food Stamps Program was a landmark achievement because it gave millions of impoverished families the resources to purchase food in quantities not possible with meager welfare checks.

THE BELEAGUERED PRESIDENT IN A TRAP OF HIS OWN MAKING: 1967–1968

All the decisions that Johnson had made in the preceding three years came into play as he entered 1966 and 1967. He refused to diminish his commitment to all-out war in Vietnam, despite discouraging reports from the battlefields that the enemy was not likely to yield and that mounting numbers of Americans would lose their lives or be maimed. He refused to diminish his commitment to domestic reforms and obtained the passage of dozens of new social programs, though they were often meagerly funded. He refused to push Congress to raise taxes, for fear of igniting pressure by conservatives to reduce social spending.

Johnson's extraordinary legislative successes on the domestic front were unprecedented in American history when measured by their sheer numbers. His successes in 1964 carried into 1965, when he obtained passage of 84 of the 87 measures that he submitted to Congress, and into 1966, when 97 of 113 measures were enacted.[101] Nor did he obtain these successes by waving a magic wand; he invested enormous amounts of time in the legislative process.

But even in 1965, Johnson had decided to embark on a high-risk gamble. Kennedy had committed large numbers of military "advisors" to South Vietnam, where the Vietcong, a communist group, was waging guerrilla warfare against the corruption-ridden and conservative dictatorial government. In 1964 and early 1965, Johnson went through an extended period of discussion with his top aides to decide whether he should send large numbers of American troops to South Vietnam. The details of these talks fall beyond our purpose here, but the ultimate decision does not, because committing hundreds of thousands of troops to South Vietnam by the end of 1965 had profound consequences for Johnson's social policies.[102]

To understand the complex relations between Johnson's foreign policy and his domestic policy, we need to return to our discussion of the sheer size of American military spending *before* Johnson committed troops to Vietnam and a fateful decision in 1964 to drastically lower U.S. income taxes. Recall that Truman had committed the nation to extraordinary levels of ongoing military spending in 1950 and that, in consequence, most of the American federal budget went for military purposes. Kennedy increased military spending even further, because he believed that the United States needed the capability to fight two and one-half wars simultaneously—that is, a war against Russia (probably in Europe), a war against China, and a war in a third-world country such as Vietnam.[103]

As a true believer in the threat of communist insurrection around the world, Johnson accepted this large military commitment with alacrity. But Johnson *also* accepted another legacy from Kennedy and his economic advisors, who were convinced that American economic growth would suffer unless the nation pumped more money into the economy. To do so, they thought, the government had two options: either to raise the federal budget or to lower federal income taxes so as to stimulate consumer spending. As conservatives were unlikely to allow an expansion of the budget, Kennedy's aides recommended large tax cuts, which Johnson obtained from the Congress in 1964 during the first year of his presidency.[104]

Johnson committed himself to ambitious domestic reforms, then, in an environment of economic scarcity occasioned by military spending and tax cuts—and this budgetary scarcity was further increased by his decision to send large numbers of troops to Vietnam in 1965. Another politician might have decided, in these circumstances, to reconsider the tax policies or the domestic policies or the decision to send troops to Vietnam so as not to strain the budget excessively nor to anger the Congress, which might wonder how he could engage in multiple endeavors that so stressed the federal budget. However, Johnson was committed to *each* of these policies. He wanted to save the world from Communism by decisively defeating the Vietcong, and he wanted to be the greatest reform president in American history.[105] Moreover, he knew that if he asked the Congress to raise taxes to pay for the war and his social

reforms, conservatives from both parties would demand, as their price, that he cut "nonessential" social spending, much as they had forced Franklin Roosevelt in World War II to terminate the WPA, CCC, and NYA.[106]

To extricate himself from this situation, Johnson engaged in activities that can only be called devious and manipulative. To minimize the strain on the federal budget and the size of the deficit, he sold huge amounts of American assets, including stockpiled metals such as aluminum and copper that the government had accumulated in case of war.[107] He made the true costs of Vietnam appear somewhat smaller by taking much of the personnel and equipment that had been devoted to defending Europe and transferring them to Vietnam. He constructed his military budget on the premise that the war would be over by June 1966—hardly a realistic scenario. By this means, he was able to give the impression that spending on Vietnam would be relatively small.[108] Although he enacted vast numbers of social programs, he often devoted little money to each one, so as to diminish their fiscal impact. For example, the much-publicized War on Poverty never received more than $2 billion in any given year.

These various tactics, in turn, angered political groups on whom Johnson depended. Conservatives of both parties, already angered by the numbers of social reforms that Johnson proposed, accused him of hiding the true costs of the war—a charge readily supported by antiwar factions, who resented the diversion of funds from social reforms. Social reformers wondered nervously if Johnson's Vietnam policy would curtail his domestic agenda; they also came to realize that, unlike previous wars, it was disproportionately fought by troops drawn from the African American and Latino communities.

When viewed in fiscal terms, the Great Society could aptly be renamed the Frugal Society. It is true: Johnson increased spending on education, training, employment, and social (nonmedical) programs more than threefold during his administration. But this increase was relatively modest considering that the federal government had hardly spent any resources on these programs when

Johnson came into office. So Johnson created scores of new programs that were poorly funded, making them even more vulnerable to the charge that they were ineffective. Moreover, Johnson increased military and related spending almost three times as much as spending on education, training, employment, and social programs—or by $63 billion as compared with $23.3 billion when measured in constant 1992 dollars. When we add entitlements like Social Security, Medicare, and Medicaid to his expenditures on education, training, employment, and social programs, Johnson's domestic programs accounted for only 28 percent of the federal budget, whereas military and related spending, as well as interest on the national debt, comprised almost 70 percent of the federal budget.

By early 1967, however, even the politically agile Johnson was running out of options. With changing circumstances, Johnson lost support across the political spectrum. Conservatives in Congress began to attack his credibility more assertively; they accused him of submitting deceptive budgets and suggested he should cut social spending. Equally troubling were public opinion polls suggesting that the widespread sympathy of middle- and working-class Americans for the plight of low-income Americans and African Americans that had existed in 1964 and 1965 had waned by 1968—resulting in white backlash.[109] Many of these white Americans believed Johnson had unfairly favored African Americans with an array of social programs that they believed disproportionately helped them. Moreover, many white working-class Americans were angered at the growth of liberal opposition to the Vietnam War—and often wanted Johnson to send even more troops to Vietnam. Some of them believed domestic reforms were absorbing resources that would have allowed the Johnson to push even harder in Vietnam.

Once African Americans had obtained civil rights legislation that decreased discrimination in the South, they sought reforms to address poverty, housing discrimination, education, and other problems in the North. Northern whites, who had often supported efforts to reduce discrimination in the South, were enraged when *they* became the

targets of protest. Indeed, Martin Luther King, Jr., observed that he had never seen more hatred than he experienced in open housing marches in white Chicago suburbs in 1967.[110] The Northern whites who applauded when the Department of Justice attacked de jure segregation (which stems from policies creating segregated schools) in the South did not realize that the de facto segregation (which stems from geographic segregation of races) in their school districts would soon become the focus of reform. Many of them opposed policies to desegregate Northern schools by the use of busing, viewed affirmative action with skepticism, and believed that the Warren Court had been too kind to criminal offenders. Scandals in the War on Poverty, which were seized on by Republicans and conservatives, also soured public support for domestic reforms.

Many whites responded negatively as well to the increasingly militant tactics of African Americans (and also of women, Latinos, and First Americans).[111] King, who remained an influential leader until his assassination in 1968, found it increasingly difficult to persuade a new breed of African American leaders that nonviolence represented an inviolable principle rather than a tactic. Stokely Carmichael, who coined the term *black power* during a civil rights march in 1966, personified the trend among many African Americans toward separatism, the development of African American economic institutions, and (even) violent protest.[112] This militance seemed to many white Americans to be reflected in the large number of urban riots and disturbances that occurred in Northern—and some Southern—cities between 1965 and 1968; 239 civil disturbances erupted, with 8,133 persons killed and 49,604 persons arrested.[113]

The uneasiness of white Americans was compounded by economic problems in the nation. When Johnson proclaimed the War on Poverty in 1964, it was widely assumed that greater domestic spending would speed economic growth. But the growth of inflation led many Americans to favor cuts in spending, as indicated by public opinion polls conducted in 1968.

Johnson's popularity with liberals and social reformers also began to wane. Although many liberals had remained silent on Vietnam in 1966 and even early 1967, the silence was decisively broken in August 1967, when *The New York Times* called the war a "bottomless pit" and urged Johnson to curtail the American commitment to it—and when Martin Luther King spoke out against the war.[114]

Moreover, some liberals even became disenchanted with Johnson's domestic policy, despite the torrent of reforms that were enacted. They noticed that many of the reforms were not well funded. Some were angered by periodic cuts in social spending that Johnson made to deflect conservatives' charges that he was fiscally irresponsible.

And then there was the unfolding debacle in Vietnam, where Johnson had engaged in a bombing campaign that was unprecedented in military history, against a small, largely agricultural nation, and had little to show for it except a weekly tally of returning body bags. Johnson had escalated the Vietnam conflict from a few military advisors and spies in 1964 to more than 540,000 troops in 1968. The resulting military defeat had a staggering cost in lives and resources. By the conclusion of American involvement in 1973, more than 55,000 Americans had been killed and 304,000 Americans had been injured. The U.S. Senate estimates that 1.4 million South Vietnamese were killed and wounded, another 850,000 enemy soldiers were killed, and 10.3 million refugees were created. Americans expended more than $135 billion on the war.[115] (See Insert 8.4.)

Johnson believed that a communist victory in South Vietnam would lead to others throughout Southeast Asia, and he assumed that the non-communist regimes in South Vietnam possessed relatively broad support despite their corruption, intransigent resistance to land reform, and domination by conservative elites. Johnson reasoned that the U.S. Air Force, with napalm, helicopters, and B-52 bombers, could prevail over poorly supplied and sparsely clad Asians, that air strikes would demoralize the North Vietnamese, and that the enemy would accept his promises to provide them with billions of dollars on the cessation of hostilities. But Johnson underestimated the resolve of the North Vietnamese, who were deeply committed to a long-term conflict that they had already waged for decades.[116]

The war had both indirect and direct effects on social policy. By focusing attention on foreign affairs, it created an atmosphere that was not conducive to the continuation of social reform. It alienated key supporters of social reforms who began to divert their energies from social advocacy to fighting the war, including many African Americans, liberals, young people, intellectuals, and clergy.[117] The increasingly militant demonstrations against the war

---

INSERT 8.4 Ethical Analysis of Key Issues and Policies: Balancing National Security and Domestic Needs

Any nation legitimately wants to protect itself from foreign intruders and to involve itself in foreign policy issues that are germane to its interests. Yet nations also possess domestic problems that require the expenditure of resources, not to mention leadership from elected officials.

- Analyze the ethical merit of the decision during the 1950s to commit about 68 percent of the nation's budget to military and military-related expenditures. Would it have been ethically principled, even when confronting a dictator like Stalin, to limit military spending to a smaller percentage of the nation's budget? Would fewer missiles and fewer troops in Europe have sufficed to protect the nation's security needs?

- Analyze how the Vietnam War affected the development of the Great Society. Was Martin Luther King correct when he opposed the war after several years of silence?

- How do you think the Iraq War during the administration of George W. Bush has influenced domestic policy in the contemporary period? What similarities or differences do you see in its domestic impact as compared with the Vietnam War?

- Should policy advocacy extend not only to domestic but to international issues?

antagonized some moderate whites who supported the war effort. The war also led to reductions in levels of funding for social programs.

Most of all, the war eroded Johnson's credibility. Many Americans remembered bitterly that Johnson had run in 1964 as a peace candidate against Goldwater. His deception in hiding the true costs of the war and his habit of overstating American military gains made many Americans distrust him.[118] Much as Franklin Roosevelt had squandered his landslide electoral victory of 1936 by attempting to pack the Supreme Court, Johnson lost his political momentum when he committed the nation to the war.[119]

Some liberals were also infuriated in 1968 when Johnson orchestrated support for a tax increase to pay for the war by promising conservatives that he would call for substantial cuts in social spending. He had long promised that the nation could have both "guns and butter," but he seemed now to acknowledge that Vietnam would lead to significant cuts in butter.

Caught in conflicting forces, Johnson tried to conciliate each side by making concessions. He consented to tax increases and cuts in social spending, as well as a continuing commitment to the war, to assuage conservatives. He continued to propose social reforms to keep the support of liberals—and generally chose to avoid coercive policies in the wake of the urban riots. Indeed, following the Detroit and Newark riots, he established, in 1967, the National Advisory Committee on Civil Disorders—often called the Kerner Commission after its chairperson, Otto Kerner—to investigate the causes of riots. As the political debate became increasingly polarized, however, his concessions to one side served to antagonize the other.

By the spring of 1968, Johnson's ratings in public opinion polls had sunk to such low levels that many pundits began to wonder if he could win reelection. His hand was forced by the New Hampshire primary, in which he was almost defeated by Eugene McCarthy, a relatively unknown senator running on an antiwar platform. Stung by this humiliation, Johnson withdrew from the presidential race, in the hope that he could orchestrate a peace settlement in Vietnam. In

November, when Richard Nixon defeated Vice President Hubert Humphrey, the Democratic candidate, the Great Society came to an official close. But actually the Great Society had ended in the rice paddies of Vietnam, long before the election results were tallied.

Johnson left the presidency a tormented man. His international policies had led to uncertain outcomes and a loss of popularity. In his last year in office, he toyed with initiating some new and massive reforms—such as a child health program—but he realized that they faced certain defeat. Almost all Great Society reforms had been enacted in two years, 1964 and 1965—a period that seemed light-years removed from the troubled final years of Johnson's presidency.

Yet Johnson, despite all of his failed decisions, *had* succeeded in enacting a remarkable array of domestic reforms that extended into many areas that had not been touched by the social reforms of the New Deal. Many of these policies still survive, such as civil rights, Medicare, Medicaid, Food Stamps, ESEA, and housing programs.

THE OPPRESSION OF VULNERABLE POPULATIONS IN THE 1960s

Having already discussed policy reforms that affect African Americans throughout this chapter, we now turn to the oppression of other vulnerable populations.

The civil rights struggles of African Americans captured the attention of the nation from 1955—when Rosa Parks refused to move to the back of the bus and triggered the bus boycott in Montgomery—through most of the 1960s. It was an epic struggle, with drama, violence, defeats, and victories. This struggle—and its key civil rights successes—motivated women, Latinos, gay men and lesbians, Asian Americans, and First Americans *also* to engage in policy advocacy. Each of these groups, in turn, developed reformist leaders and engaged in various forms of protest. Indeed, the momentum of their mobilizing carried protest well into the 1970s, before reform ebbed somewhat in the 1980s.

The Oppression of Women

Things were never the same once Rosie the Riveter entered the workforce. In World War II, millions of women went to work in production plants. They were supposed to return to their domestic roles when the war ended—and indeed 3.25 million women were forced, or persuaded, to leave industrial jobs after World War II. But the genie was out of the bottle. Women had tasted economic freedom, and a dramatic upturn in female employment occurred throughout the 1950s. By 1952, more women were employed than at the height of World War II, and the trend continued during the next four decades.[120] But women were not made to feel good about their work; indeed, the mass media and many theorists implied or stated that working women risked harming their children or destroying their femininity.[121]

Following World War II, an effort to secure an Equal Rights Amendment (ERA) to the Constitution assumed center stage among female activists. A host of distinguished women— Margaret Sanger, Pearl S. Buck, and Katharine Hepburn among them—supported the amendment and formed a coalition of organizations under the Women's Joint Legislative Committee. Advocates hoped the ERA would sweep aside many state laws that still limited the rights of women to own and sell property, to make contracts, to control bequests, and to exercise parental authority. But other female leaders opposed the amendment on the grounds that women *needed* special protections, such as protective labor legislation, which might be erased by the amendment. Its fate was sealed, however, when it passed the Senate but failed to obtain the necessary two-thirds majority.[122] Other women sought legislation to guarantee women equal pay for equal work in private employment; many legislators opposed it on the grounds that higher female wages might entice many women to abdicate their parenting role.

But women who sought new challenges discovered innumerable barriers in the early 1960s. Relatively few women obtained access to work in the building trades or to training in male-dominated professions like law, medicine, and business; they were usually limited to gender-segregated jobs in clerical, sales, unskilled manufacturing, teaching, nursing, and social work. Women were widely perceived as fragile—they were not even allowed to run long distances in track meets—and so "protective laws" kept them from arduous work. Other cultural factors also hindered them. Women were required to be absent from the labor force for extended periods—often at least until their children had reached high school—and could not easily reenter it; if they did, they could not easily match the career gains of male workers who had been working continuously. Women had to contend, as well, with opposition from their husbands and lack of sympathy from their children, who often had expectations that women should do the bulk of household chores. Moreover, because the nation had virtually no governmentally subsidized child care in the early 1960s, working women had to pay for day care from their own—usually low—paychecks.

As the 1960s began, some female activists hoped that President Kennedy would be sympathetic. At first, he was unresponsive. Under pressure, however, he appointed Esther Peterson as director of the Women's Bureau in the Department of Labor. Peterson mobilized a campaign for enactment of equal pay legislation, which had foundered after World War II. Congress enacted an Equal Pay Act in 1963, but this legislation left out large groups of women, including domestics and farm workers, and did not speak to discrimination that blocked women from certain kinds of jobs and promotions.[123] (Because many women were confined to a gender-segregated workplace, the subject of equal pay was moot.) Moreover, Kennedy established a Commission on the Status of Women in 1961 to review existing policies regarding employment, social insurance, tax, labor, and social services. In its report, the commission recommended against an Equal Rights

Amendment to the Constitution, on the grounds that women could bring suit under existing constitutional provisions such as the equal protection clause of the Fourteenth Amendment. The commission made many constructive suggestions; it advocated a reduction in gender-based pay and promotion discrimination in the civil service and recommended more high-level presidential appointees. (Kennedy had already issued an executive order in 1961 requiring private employers with federal contracts not to discriminate on the basis of race *or* gender.) It also recommended broadening women's access to education. However, the commission did not offer encouragement for women's entry into male-dominated fields; it did not attack the fundamental gender role structure of American society or the prevailing notion that women should have primary responsibility for child rearing; and it did not seek basic changes in Social Security, which discriminated against single women who were not dependents or widows.[124]

American women needed a theorist akin to Simone de Beauvoir, the French feminist who had so articulately analyzed the constraints placed on women in modern society. They found this theorist in Betty Friedan, whose classic book, *The Feminine Mystique*, was published in 1963.[125] Friedan dissected the malaise of the suburban woman who, "as she made the beds, shopped for groceries, matched slipcover material, ate peanut butter sandwiches with her children, chauffeured Cub Scouts and Brownies ... was afraid to ask even of herself—'Is this all?'"[126] Friedan contended that society had developed a mystique of feminine fulfillment, in which the American woman achieved a kind of happiness as housewife and mother that no women had ever obtained in prior eras. If she lacked this happiness, Friedan contended, she was taught to blame herself—that is, to look inward for neurotic tendencies, "penis envy," or other personal failings. Isolated in her suburban "concentration camp," the married woman had no chance to explore options or seek new challenges.[127] Friedan's book ended with a ringing plea for "a new life plan for women"—a society in which, emancipated from past myths, women would "see through the delusions of the

feminine mystique" to develop careers that would fully challenge them.[128]

Lyndon Johnson made a promising start when he appointed many more females to high-policy posts than had Kennedy, but Johnson was indifferent to the inclusion of a ban on gender-based discrimination in Title VII of the Civil Rights Act of 1964. A number of legislators opposed this provision on the grounds that it could threaten protective labor legislation for women, such as laws regulating the hours and conditions of women's work. Some powerful Southern legislators supported it for the wrong reasons. They hoped that the addition of the controversial provision would kill the entire Civil Rights Act, which they opposed. But 11 of the 12 female legislators in the House of Representatives spoke eloquently for the measure, by insisting that women deserved the same protections as the racial groups who were included in Title VII.[129] When the ban and the legislation were passed by the Senate, women had finally been included in major civil rights legislation, almost a century after their exclusion in the wake of the Civil War—but their inclusion did not stem from any militant support by the administration. Nor did the Equal Opportunities Commission, established to investigate discrimination in employment by Title VII, focus on gender-based discrimination; it was too preoccupied with racial discrimination. As Harrison notes, some of the EEOC commissioners and staff regarded the gender-discrimination provisions of the Civil Rights Act not as a legitimate protection but as something conservatives had placed in the legislation to obtain its defeat.[130]

Some advances were made through legal rulings. For example, in 1965, the Supreme Court ruled in *Griswold v. Connecticut* that a law that made the use of contraceptives a crime was illegal. However, the ruling left intact the ban on abortions in many states and did not speak to the absence of family-planning clinics in many jurisdictions. Other court rulings abolished certain residency requirements, midnight raids, and man-in-the-house rules that various states had devised to cut AFDC rolls.

Although these early policy successes represented important gains, they were token measures or inadequately implemented. Recognizing that women needed to develop political clout, Betty Friedan and other women formed the National Organization for Women (NOW) in 1966 to seek federal action on women's employment issues, such as tighter bans on sex discrimination by federal contractors, full deductibility of day care expenses, and more enforcement powers for the EEOC. Most significantly, NOW from the outset questioned the long-standing assumption that females should primarily be the child rearers and their husbands the breadwinners.[131]

NOW assertively sought to pressure Johnson to include women within the scope of his September 1965 executive order that required affirmative action programs to ensure equal opportunity for all races. By October of 1967, they had succeeded; this paved the way for affirmative action programs by local and state governments, federal contractors, and the federal government—and established the precedent that the term *sex* would appear whenever the phrase "race, creed, color, or national origin" appeared.[132] NOW also initiated another bid for an Equal Rights Amendment and secured widespread support for the measure from many candidates.

A development that was as important as these political developments was that women had begun to form consciousness-raising groups, where issues like sexual abuse, harassment on the job, rape, women's health, abortion, and job discrimination became topics of conversation rather than taboo subjects. These topics would become important policy issues over the next several decades, although the government response was uneven and often inadequate.

By the end of the Johnson administration, then, women had made important gains but, in retrospect, they were only token advances. Even though women had made huge gains in obtaining higher education, had received one-third of all the master's degrees granted in the United States by 1968, and represented 58 percent of the labor force, the economic position of white women relative to white men declined during the decades after World War II. Full-time female workers earned, on average, only 58.2 percent of the income of men in 1969, down from 63.3 percent in 1956.[133]

Critics of the feminist movement in the 1960s note that it often did not speak to the needs of African American or low-income women. African American women, who often had to work in order to survive, were less worried about the feminine mystique and more worried about the lack of economic opportunity and decent wages for themselves and for African American men. Another criticism was that, by their single-minded advocacy of women's right to a career, feminists made women who chose to emphasize child rearing feel guilty, much as working women in earlier periods felt guilty that they didn't prioritize child rearing.

The Oppression of Gay Men and Lesbians

The extent of prejudice against gay men and lesbians in the early 1950s is best revealed by a quote from Senator Kenneth Wherry (R., Neb.), who asserted that he wished to "harry every last pervert from the federal government services" on the grounds that "homosexuals in government are a moral and security issue … the lack of emotional stability which is found in most sex perverts, and the weakness of their moral fiber, makes them susceptible to the blandishments of foreign espionage agents."[134] This virulent prejudice must be placed in the context of long-standing harassment, incarceration, and discrimination against gay men and lesbians. Underlying this systematic homophobia was a combination of religious ideas, which equated homosexuality with sin; psychiatric and medical thought, which saw it as mental or physical pathology; and criminology, which was inclined to perceive homosexual behavior as criminal. (Sodomy and other homosexual acts were widely punishable as crimes.) In this social climate, many gay men and lesbians came to think of themselves as diseased.

World War II brought more attention to homosexuality, not only because the army made strenuous efforts to screen gay men and lesbians from service but also because so many escaped its net. For the first time, gay men and lesbians discovered that many others shared their sexual orientations—and same-gender associations were surprisingly common and open in barracks, dance halls, and combat zones.[135]

Soldiers formed gay communities in New York, San Francisco, Los Angeles, and other major cities following the war, and institutions such as gay and lesbian bars became widespread. Sexual behavior became more openly discussed in the conservative 1950s, as reflected by the widely read Kinsey report, which addressed taboo topics like masturbation.[136] But gay men and lesbians in the 1950s led a life constricted by societal laws and prejudices. Witch hunts against communists in government often included gay men and lesbians. Eisenhower, in an executive order aimed at dismissing loyalty risks from government, explicitly listed "sexual perversion" and proceeded to remove presumed homosexuals from government at the rate of 40 per month in the first 16 months after the order; job seekers who were judged to be homosexual by the interviewer were denied employment.[137] Moreover, 2,000 persons per year were removed from the military in the early 1950s—a number that rose by another 50 percent by the early 1960s. State and local governments screened their 12.5 million employees with similar zeal and also cited homosexuality as grounds for dismissal.[138]

Gay men and lesbians were also subject to arrests by local police and vice squads, who raided gay bars, restrooms, lesbian bars, and even personal residences. D'Emilio estimates that there were more than 1,000 arrests per year in the District of Columbia in the early 1950s.[139] Gay bashing by local gangs and petty criminals was also common.

The gay and lesbian community began to develop organizations and leadership in the 1950s, but these organizations lacked a mass membership and had little success in changing social policies. A major problem among gay men and lesbians was that they were reluctant to publicly reveal their sexual orientation for fear of reprisal from law authorities or recrimination from landlords or employers. Moreover, many gay men and lesbians had internalized homophobia.[140]

The emergence of a less oppressive social climate in the 1960s promoted the development of activism among gay men and lesbians. A succession of court rulings had gradually limited the ability of local and federal governments to censor or prohibit "obscene literature," and so publications by gay and lesbian writers and groups could circulate more freely. As with so many other policies, the Warren Court led the way; finally, in 1967, it ruled that "a book cannot be proscribed unless it is found to be *utterly* without redeeming social value" even though the book is "patently offensive." In the more permissive climate of the 1960s, mass-based magazines like *Playboy* were circulated—an unthinkable development in the 1950s. Howard Becker and other sociologists wrote on deviance from a relativistic perspective. Avoiding moral judgments about homosexual behavior, they urged an end to criminal penalties and exclusion from the armed forces. Lawyers began to develop suits against antisodomy statutes on the grounds that they violated personal liberty, and some local chapters of the American Civil Liberties Union (ACLU) became interested in pursuing discriminatory actions such as exclusion of gay men and lesbians from the civil service. Court decisions in a few states had legitimized the right of gay men and lesbians to assemble in local bars, and the possibility of further progress was suggested by movements in Europe that sought to decriminalize sex acts among consenting adults.[141] Some courageous clergy declared that the sexual orientations of gay men and lesbians were not immoral. And some city governments, such as the Civil Service Commission of New York City, began to relax the restrictions against the hiring of gay men and lesbians. Even mental health and health professionals began to reexamine traditional perspectives, and a committee established by the National Institute of Mental Health in 1967, though it refrained from declaring their orientation to be normal, urged tolerance of gay men and lesbians.[142]

By the late 1960s, just as the black power philosophy emerged in the civil rights movement, the accommodationist and gradualist perspectives of other out-groups had begun to be supplanted by more radical perspectives. Thus, in 1969, a pivotal development in New York City ignited the gay liberation movement. Some police officers and detectives raided the Stonewall Inn, a gay bar in Greenwich Village. When the officers arrested the bartender, the Stonewall's bouncer, and three drag queens, a riot broke out; it spread into the Village and continued through the next night. In the wake of the Stonewall riots, the gay and lesbian movements attracted a mass membership and developed a political agenda—to modify government policies at every level and to change the diagnostic categories of the American Psychiatric Association. Moreover, they made "coming out" a key organizing strategy; they hoped to persuade millions of gay men and lesbians to publicly announce their sexual orientations, despite possible reprisals.[143] Organizers' spirits were buoyed by early successes, such as the decision of the American Psychiatric Association in 1973 that gay men and lesbians would no longer be regarded as mentally ill. But their work had barely begun. Generations of prejudice hung heavy over a nation that was only starting to rethink traditional stereotypes.

The Oppression of Latinos

At the beginning of the 1960s, Latinos, like African Americans, still lived in their traditional rural areas—for example, on the farms and ranches of the Southwest and the farms of the upper Midwest—but had also formed rapidly growing communities in some urban areas—in particular, in the Southwest and in Midwestern cities like Chicago and Kansas City. In the 1950s, moreover, there was a huge influx of Puerto Ricans to East Coast cities, particularly New York City, where between 850,000 and 1.2 million Puerto Ricans resided by 1970.[144] They often came to the United States for economic reasons because they had been displaced by the expansion of large American sugar and coffee corporations and because factories and service industries in New York wanted and solicited cheap labor. As with prior immigrant groups, many Puerto Ricans hoped to return to their homeland after they had improved their economic condition—but, in the end, most remained. Moreover, a substantial population of Cubans settled

in the United States, particularly in South Florida, in the wake of the Cuban Revolution of 1959, which brought Fidel Castro to power.

The so-called Chicano movement signaled the beginning of militant organizing projects that centered on Mexican Americans and undocumented workers. That movement was led by a series of charismatic leaders, including Reies Lopez Tijerina, who sought to restore lost Spanish and Mexican land grants in New Mexico, and Corky Gonzales, who organized grassroots groups in Denver. It was César Chavez, however, who captured national attention when he developed the United Farm Workers Organizing Committee to empower Mexican agricultural laborers. Recall that the Wagner Act of 1936, which established federal protection for persons who sought to organize unions, did not apply to farmworkers. As a result, organizers could be summarily fired or intimidated if employers thought they were making trouble. In 1966, after building a cadre of leaders, Chavez organized a march on Sacramento, the capital of California, to dramatize the plight of farmworkers. This march was followed by a flurry of organizing activities—most memorably, by well-publicized national boycotts of crops like grapes and lettuce to pressure agribusiness to recognize farmworkers' right to organize. Simultaneously, Chavez pressured politicians in California to enact legislation that would provide agricultural laborers with the kinds of protections that the Wagner Act afforded other workers. The Latino community was active on many fronts: voter registration drives, pressure on the EEOC to assertively investigate job discrimination against Latinos, the development of the Mexican American Legal Defense and Education Fund (a Latino counterpart to the NAACP), pressure that led to an extension of the provisions of the Voting Rights Act of 1965 to Latinos, and the development of various coordinating councils to link the work of many advocacy groups.[145]

Puerto Ricans, because of their strong personal ties to their homeland, had more difficulty in organizing protests against poor working conditions and wages, as well as atrocious living conditions; their patterns of migration back and forth to Puerto

Rico undermined the cohesion of their communities in East Coast cities.[146] Moreover, unlike the farmworkers, who had a relatively identifiable enemy in agribusiness, and African Americans, who could attack Jim Crow laws, most Puerto Ricans were enmeshed in the constellation of factors that perpetuate urban poverty.

The Oppression of First Americans

First Americans had been placed on reservations during the 19th century following their eviction from their ancestral lands. These reservations were frequently assigned to one tribe; the government agreed to supply certain commodities or services (such as a school) in return for the tribe's agreement to cede its ancestral lands. The early reservation experience was difficult for First Americans; because the reservations were too small to allow them to hunt and be self-sufficient, they had to rely on financial assistance from government agents and missionary groups. As we discussed in Chapter 5, the federal government decided in 1887, soon after establishing the reservations, to break up tribes; the Dawes Act individualized First Americans' land holdings, made some of them American citizens, and provided them with a government school system, so as to socialize them to American ways. The chief instruments of this Americanizing strategy were the agents of the Bureau of Indian Affairs.[147] Congress conferred citizenship on all remaining First Americans in 1924.

But the Americanization strategy did not work because the First Americans held on to their indigenous culture. However, many First Americans lost their land to speculators and crooks, or else chose to lease it to others to farm; still living on or near reservations, they became dependent on government rations. The Indian agent and his staff were empowered by the Snyder Act in 1921 to help First Americans with a range of education, welfare, health, agricultural, and other functions and to provide technical assistance to First American policy makers and judges.

By the 1920s and 1930s, government policy had again reversed itself, to emphasize preservation of reservations and culture. Indeed, the Indian Reorganization Act of 1934 promoted the establishment of tribal organizations, economies, and government, as well as the purchase of additional lands for the reservations. This desire to help First Americans become self-sufficient stemmed partly from their economic desperation in the Great Depression. In the 1940s and 1950s, the pendulum swung again, as legislators and officials sought to diminish federal responsibilities by adopting an assimilationist strategy. Termination acts in the 1950s and early 1960s ended federal responsibility for various tribes, who had to turn to state governments for economic and other assistance.

In the 1960s and 1970s, the pendulum swung back again. The War on Poverty placed considerable emphasis on supporting the culture of First Americans, as well as their indigenous communities and tribal functions. Some of the reservations that had been terminated in the 1950s were restored to federal authority. Many Great Society programs channeled funds to the reservations for housing assistance, education, and economic development. The Bureau of Indian Affairs, which had often sought to force mainstream American customs on First Americans, became an advocate for First Americans "in the same manner as the Department of Agriculture is pro-farmer and the Department of Labor, pro-labor."[148] Both Presidents Johnson and Nixon strongly opposed the termination policy, sought to develop First American participation in their governance, and favored continuation of federal technical and economic assistance to tribes. Indeed, the Indian Self-Determination and Education Assistance Act, as well as other legislation in the 1970s, sought to give tribes the authority to decide whether to assume responsibility for administering federal programs of the Interior Department or the Department of Health, Education, and Welfare.

Nor were First Americans quiescent politically during the turbulence of the 1960s. Indigenous groups demanded compensation for lands that were taken from First Americans illegally, sought protections for minerals and timber on reservations, and challenged stereotypical portrayals of First Americans in films. Like African Americans and

Latinos, they dramatized their demands by direct action—for example, the occupation of Alcatraz, an abandoned federal prison on an island in San Francisco Bay.

As with other people of color, a significant number of First Americans moved to urban areas, where they often resided in deteriorated communities and in poverty. Caught between two cultures, and not inclined to assimilate to the extent that many other groups did, Native Americans often had difficulty establishing their personal and collective identities. When the colonists arrived in the 17th century, there were roughly 10 million Native Americans, but by 1970 their numbers had dwindled to some 827,000, though many of them had been absorbed into the general population.[149]

The Oppression of Asian Americans

Asian Americans in Hawaii and California made important gains in achieving their civil rights in the wake of World War II and in the 1950s. Disenfranchised before World War II, Asian plantation laborers were registered in a massive drive by the International Longshoremen's and Warehousemen's Union during the war and secured an act by the Hawaii legislature that was akin to the Wagner Act. Sugar workers were able to unionize in a multiracial union that included Filipino, Japanese, and Portuguese laborers. California's Japanese Americans were able to obtain from the Supreme Court a ruling that the California laws that prohibited a noncitizen alien from conveying his or her land to a citizen child were unconstitutional. The California Supreme Court ruled in 1948 that laws that prohibited people of different races from having sexual contact (antimiscegenation laws) were unconstitutional. In 1946, California voters decisively defeated an initiative that was placed on the ballot to reaffirm the alien land laws. In 1956, Japanese Americans placed on the ballot an initiative to overturn the alien land laws altogether and won. In 1952, the federal government finally terminated provisions of the 1790 naturalization law that refused citizenship to nonwhite individuals, partly because of lobbying by Japanese Americans.[150]

But immigration limitations on Asians continued, despite token concessions to various nationalities following World War II. The blatantly racist immigration policies of the United States, which gave larger annual quotas to European nations than to Asian nations, were finally reversed in the Immigration Act of 1965. This act abolished the national-origin quotas and allowed annual admissions of 170,000 immigrants from the Eastern Hemisphere and 120,000 from the Western Hemisphere, not including immediate family members. As Takaki notes, "the new law represented a sharp ideological departure from the traditional view of America as a homogeneous white society."[151] Indeed, a second wave of Asian immigrants during the next 30 years brought a massive increase in the Asian population; significant Japanese, Chinese, and Filipino populations were supplemented by Vietnamese, Korean, Asian Indian, Laotian, and Cambodian groups, as we will discuss in Chapter 11.

The Oppression of People of Color in the Urban Ghettoes

By the end of the 1960s, people of color in the United States had predominantly been segregated within urban ghettoes, but this pattern was to become even more marked over the next two decades. As Latinos and African Americans entered American cities, they tended to reside in segregated communities—often communities that had been abandoned by other ethnic groups as they fled to suburban areas. New York City provides an example; in 1970, whites comprised 63.3 percent of its population, whereas African Americans and Latinos, respectively, comprised 19.2 and 15.2 percent of its population. By 1990, the white population had declined to 41.3 percent, whereas the African American and Latino populations had, respectively, risen to 27.7 and 23.7 percent.[152] (The statistics for other major American cities were similar.)

Of course, Irish, Italian, Jewish, and other ethnic enclaves had traditionally existed in American cities, but their plight was enviable compared with that of people of color. Their upward mobility—that is, their ability to become wealthy so that they could eventually afford more expensive housing in better communities and the suburbs—was enhanced by the fact that they immigrated just as the United States was industrializing, so that they secured a position from the outset in the growing American economy—albeit a position that was poorly paid at first. By the time large numbers of Latinos and African Americans reached the cities in the 1950s, they found it difficult to penetrate an economic structure dominated by the whites who had preceded them. Moreover, white immigrants did not find themselves segregated by race in low-income communities that were encircled by vast middle-class suburbs, where most jobs were located. Denied education in rural areas before they left for the cities, African Americans and Latinos were probably less prepared to use education as the vehicle of upward mobility than were the Jews, Asian Americans, and white ethnic populations of prior eras. Moreover, inner-city schools often lacked staff who could relate to African American and Latino youth or lacked teaching skills—and segregated schools were often overcrowded, dilapidated, and lacked books and equipment prevalent in schools attended by white students.

In addition to these problems, the segregation of these communities into urban ghettoes was coupled with selective outmigration of those individuals who *were* upwardly mobile. As a result, those who remained behind not only lived in poverty but also often lacked the role models, indigenous businesses, vibrant churches, and community cohesiveness that white ethnic groups had enjoyed.

SOCIAL WORK IN THE 1960s

Social work emerged from the Great Depression with a determination to upgrade the profession by making a bachelor's degree mandatory for admission to graduate programs and by making all graduate programs last for two years. Casework remained the dominant methodology of the profession; macro practice occupied a decidedly secondary niche. Moreover, social workers in many states wanted to

establish state-enforced standards and tests to register or certify social workers; that is, they wanted to establish lists of certified social workers who could then receive priority over nontrained workers in filling government and agency positions. The profession was trying, in effect, to distinguish its members from the legions of untrained staff who worked in government and nongovernment agencies.[153] Some people wondered if the profession risked being too elitist by requiring extended graduate training, but advocates of the master's degree insisted that it was required to improve standards and to obtain competence in casework.

The National Council on Social Work Education was established in 1946 to launch a study of social work education that would clarify relationships between undergraduate and graduate education; it was renamed the Council on Social Work Education (CSWE) in 1952. The study concluded that graduate education was needed for professional practice and that undergraduate education provided only a preprofessional base. Though diminished in status, undergraduate education nevertheless continued; in 1951, 400 schools taught undergraduate courses in social work.[154] In 1955, seven separate social work associations were merged to form the National Association of Social Workers (NASW), with roughly 18,000 members; new members were required to have completed two years of graduate study.

An important question remained: To what extent would this profession be committed to social action and social justice, in the tradition of Jane Addams and the rank-and-file movement of the 1930s? Would casework, with its emphasis on individual counseling, draw into social work only those students with a narrow focus on individual remedies? And would it socialize students to view social action as extraneous to professional work? Developments in the 1950s did not augur well for those who wanted a social action perspective to be prominent in the profession. The macro side of the profession, such as community organization and administration, remained ill defined. Social policy offerings in schools of social work were uneven and often emphasized historical materials without also giving students the tools to engage in advocacy for the poor or other populations. A prominent set of educators infused casework with so much psychiatric content that it became irrelevant to those working-class and poor persons unable or unwilling to participate in extended intrapsychic explorations. Still, a movement to have a generalist curriculum began to give social work students breadth of content, rather than narrowly defined casework training.

The profession was influenced by the turbulence of the 1960s. Even in the late 1950s, an exhaustive study of social work education recommended that community organization and administration join casework and group work as fully recognized interventions in social work, even if policy was still relegated to largely theoretical, philosophical, and historical roles. The advocacy of the War on Poverty infused life into community organizing and other macro aspects of social work; many scores of students joined these branches in the growing numbers of schools that offered relevant study.[155] The NASW engaged in extensive lobbying and advocacy in the 1960s, in contrast to its lower profile in the 1950s.[156] Social work, which remained the dominant profession in many nongovernmental social agencies, also retained its foothold in public agencies in the 1960s; its members were much involved in mental health, child welfare, and public welfare agencies. Thus enriching its mission and buoyed by the expansion of the welfare state, social work seemed positioned to provide much of the staff for a range of agencies and functions while retaining a reformist mission.

But the profession was hardly free from controversy. Some people believed it to be too conservative. Protests by students in various schools of social work in the 1960s and by activists at national conferences called for social workers to be more assertive in challenging existing programs and policies.[157] Questions remained about the continuing—though somewhat diminished—dominance of casework in social work. A decision by the NASW in 1969 to give regular membership to holders of bachelor's degrees from those undergraduate programs that met CSWE criteria was controversial within the profession; its advocates insisted that it would give

NASW more political clout by vastly enlarging its membership, but its detractors insisted that it would lower standards and decrease the prestige—and thus the power—of the social work profession by diluting its membership.[158]

EVOLUTION OF THE RELUCTANT WELFARE STATE

Johnson possessed genuine sympathy for persons in need, yet he was no more disposed than Kennedy to expand income maintenance, public works, unemployment, or Social Security programs.[159] Fortuitous circumstances and his formidable legislative skills enabled him to enact a flood of social legislation. But critics contend that this highly ambitious man, who wanted to enact more programs than Franklin Roosevelt, became seduced by his legislative successes and equated quantity with quality.[160] So obsessed was he with enacting measures that he gave insufficient attention to their implementation. Moreover, because of Johnson's budgetary frugality, which stemmed from his dislike of big spenders and from his diversion of national resources to the Vietnam conflict, many of his programs received woefully inadequate funding.[161]

The Great Society represented a curious paradox; though it was a period of unprecedented social reform, the Great Society era was not marked by significant increases in social spending, when expressed as a percentage of total federal spending; this was partly because Johnson did not commit major funds to many of his initiatives, and programs like Medicare had not become fully established.[162] The economic circumstances of poor persons and people of color improved considerably, but these improvements probably stemmed primarily from the economic growth of the period. Johnson nonetheless vastly broadened the policy roles of the federal government—to include federal funding of medical, nutritional, preschool, educational, legal, civil rights, and gerontological programs. Roosevelt had established the foundations of the American welfare state;

Johnson dramatically expanded its scope in a remark-ably brief period.

Social reforms occurred at a dizzying pace in the 1960s but for reasons quite different from those in the New Deal era. In the 1960s, unlike the 1930s, reforms did not stem from the overall economic plight of the population; it was a period of economic growth in the United States. A com-bination of factors stimulated reform. One factor was that few new social programs had been estab-lished since the onset of World War II, owing to the conservative hold on Congress in the Truman administration, the conservatism of Eisenhower, the inability of Kennedy to obtain passage of his domestic measures, and the diversion of funds and presidential attention to the crises of the Cold War. We might say there was a pent-up demand for reform.

Furthermore, we can speculate that Kennedy reinstilled a sense of idealism in certain segments of the population, even if few reforms had been enacted by the time of his death. American public opinion was profoundly influenced, moreover, by the civil rights movement, which daily brought to the public gaze an unending series of atrocities in the South, as civil rights activists dramatically chal-lenged a range of discriminatory laws and practices.

Nor can we underestimate the efforts of Lyndon Johnson, who seized the moment to turn Kennedy's assassination into a series of legislative victories even in 1964. Moreover, Johnson's land-slide victory in 1964 gave the Democrats such com-manding majorities in both chambers of Congress that Johnson could use his formidable skills to fash-ion a torrent of legislative successes. The civil rights movement, the women's movement, people with disabilities, gay men and lesbians, and other activist groups kept pressure on legislators to maintain the pace of reform. And the riots in the cities were a constant and grim reminder that America had a large population of citizens whose economic and social plight had not been frontally addressed by civil rights legislation.

As might be expected in a nation that had cre-ated a sizable welfare state so late in its history, sub-stantial opposition to the rate of growth of federal social programs began to appear by 1966. There was a resurgence of racial animosity, dislike of big government, antipathy to the poor, and dislike of radicals and social reformers, which had been some-what muted from 1964 to 1966. The Vietnam War probably accelerated and intensified polarization between factions who favored and opposed social reforms because they also tended to take divergent positions on the war.

The Great Society was, then, a significant reform movement but, like the New Deal, it occurred in a nation that was reluctant to embrace a robust welfare state. As the nation headed toward the 1970s, reformers wondered if the set of pro-grams would endure or would be swept away in a new conservative era as had happened to the work programs of the New Deal. As with the provisions of the Social Security Act, time would show the surprising resilience of many Great Society pro-grams. By the same token, the size and nature of the American welfare state would prove highly controversial in the coming decades, with liberals and conservatives often at odds.

LINKING THE GREAT SOCIETY TO CONTEMPORARY SOCIETY

What We Can Learn from Policy Advocates of the Great Society

We have discussed the extraordinary policy advo-cacy of Martin Luther King as he persisted for almost two decades in enduring unimaginable hos-tility and danger from many white Americans. We can also get lessons on policy advocacy from César Estrada Chavez, who used policy advocacy tactics similar to those of Martin Luther King, but with a Latino population of Mexican heritage mostly located in California and in the Southwest in the 1960s (see Insert 8.5)—as well as social worker Whitney Young, who changed the Urban League into an instrument of social justice.

Both Martin Luther King and César Chavez were strong adherents of nonviolence in the

---

INSERT 8.5 Profiles in Leadership: César Estrada Chavez (1927–1993)

César Estrada Chavez—farm labor rights activist and leader of the United Farm Workers Union—is best remembered for his leadership role in the grape boycotts of California and his nonviolent approach to social and labor reform. Chavez was born in 1927, in the North Gila Valley of Arizona, 20 miles outside of Yuma. In the years following the Great Depression, his parents sold their farm to pay taxes. The Chavez family subsequently migrated to the Central Valley of California in search of agricultural work. As the family followed the harvest from one town to the next, keeping César and his four siblings in school became more and more challenging. And aside from the difficulty of keeping the children enrolled in school, there was a practical rationale for keeping extra hands in the fields. By the time César reached the seventh grade, he had been enrolled in at least 30 different schools. In 1946, after serving in the U.S. Navy for two years, César returned to the life of a migrant farm laborer. Two years later, he married Helen Fabela, and, in 1950, they moved to San Jose, California. There he had his first experience in the politics of farm labor reform and labor union organizing. In 1962, Chavez and his family moved to Delano, California, where he began organizing workers; since then, California's agriculture industry has not been the same.

Like many reformers who came before him, César Chavez faced intense, at times violent, opposition from those who favored maintaining the status quo—a situation in which a substantially large group of farm laborers was denied its civil rights and access to social justice. The opposition included many powerful and politically well-connected farmers and political leaders who believed that Chavez was promoting a communist revolution within the United States. Ironically, even a few of the communities to which César was trying to bring relief opposed his reform efforts. Several groups began forming counter-movements, such as *Mothers Against Chavez*, which was established in the hub of the famous grape strikes of 1965—Delano, California. Another counter-movement, the *Agricultural Workers Freedom-to-Work Association*, made up mostly of

Mexican Americans, was created with the help of several grape growers to thwart the grape strike, the boycott, the United Farm Workers, and César Chavez. But after many years of hard work and personal sacrifice, César Chavez, together with many who supported his reform movement, succeeded in bringing much-needed reform to perhaps the most backward, repressive, and certainly one of this country's last strongholds of cheap labor—the agriculture industry.

Part of Chavez's success can be directly attributed to the strength of his character and his deep moral convictions, which were based on selflessness, patience, concern for his community, discipline, and commitment to nonviolent activism. Undoubtedly, these personal attributes sustained César on his treks across California's San Joaquin Valley and provided strength and courage during his extensive fasts (hunger strikes). The other part has to do with the fact that César quickly learned that the most useful tool in effecting positive change was his willingness and ability to build and maintain coalitions and alliances with individuals and groups outside his own movement. The strength of the agriculture reform movement was also augmented by Chavez's ability to reach out to prominent politicians and Hollywood celebrities who supported the promotion of civil rights in farm labor. Because of the publicity that followed these figures, national and international scrutiny was drawn to the working conditions faced by migrant laborers. With the nation's attention focused on the abuses suffered by farm laborers, Chavez appealed to the American conscience by presenting the boycott of grapes as a moral issue.

The combination of his personal character and his strategic approach to social reform allowed Chavez and his followers to withstand the many assaults that were launched against their movement to bring social justice to farm laborers. Thus, César Estrada Chavez earned the right to be recognized as the individual responsible for bringing the benefits of organized labor to the last large segment of unorganized American workers and for providing the farm laborer a sense of dignity and pride.

---

movements that they created. Partly this was an ethical choice stemming from both men's abhorrence of violence. Partly, however, it was based on tactical considerations. Had Latinos or African Americans resorted to the deliberate use of violence—as did such dissident groups in the 1960s as the Symbionese

Liberation Army or (to a far lesser degree) the Black Panthers—they not only would have been ruthlessly suppressed, but would have alienated large portions of the white population whose support they desperately needed to obtain policy reforms in state and federal legislatures.

Both King and Chavez realized that African American and Latino populations were minority groups that lacked the political clout to obtain major policy reforms without considerable assistance from the general public and from key public officials. This dependence on others for support was magnified by the gross underrepresentation of both groups in public offices.

Both men realized that they could exponentially increase their power as compared to their adversaries in the South and in rural parts of California if they could take higher (moral) ground. If their adversaries often resorted to violence and flagrant violation of human rights, they would use nonviolent strategies. If their adversaries were portrayed in the mass media and television as attacking African Americans and Latinos, they were portrayed as demonstrating remarkable courage as they peaceably stood their ground even as dogs, fire hoses, and epithets were used against them.

Both men used the mass media to build support in the broader population by informing and inviting the media to their nonviolent demonstrations. Both men skillfully enlisted persons from the white community as volunteers or helpers in their movements, whether white students and liberals from the North who engaged in voter registration and freedom rides in the South or white Americans who boycotted grapes and lettuce to put pressure on the corporate growers who refused to let farmworkers develop a union.

Heroic as King and Chavez were, they point to tactical challenges confronting all policy advocates who seek social reforms for vulnerable populations. Many legislators are indifferent to the needs of vulnerable populations, whether because they identify with relatively affluent citizens or do not have sufficient numbers of members of specific vulnerable groups in their constituencies. Policy advocates need, then, to surmount this political opposition or indifference by framing their issues in moral or economic terms that appeal to a broader audience. Martin Luther King portrayed the needs of African Americans in moral terms, often invoking religious and moral principles—and appealing to the higher nature of persons. Cesar Chavez appealed not just to ethics, but to economics when often noting that Americans would literally not receive food commodities unless farmworkers were treated fairly and allowed to organize unions. We, too, must struggle with ways to frame issues so that we appeal to an audience broader than the relatively small group of persons who naturally resonate to the needs of underdogs.

The policy advocacy of Whitney Young demonstrates how social workers can assume influential roles in developing national policy. Not only was Whitney Young a dean of a school of social work, but he became an important advisor to President Lyndon Johnson (see Insert 8.6).

Moving from the School of Social Work at Atlanta University, Young became the leader of the National Urban League. His policy advocacy involved, moreover, organizational change as he converted the National Urban League from a staid, relatively conservative organization into a full-fledged participant in the civil rights movement—and a developer of major policy proposals such as the concept of a Domestic Marshall Plan.

Realizing that organizational change is an integral part of policy advocacy, Young focused on changing the policies and procedures of the National Urban League rather than focusing only on changes in public policy. If organizations do not speak to social justice issues or address deep-seated needs of their communities, they do not fulfill the mandate provided by the Code of Ethics of the National Association of Social Workers, which requires professionals to advance the ethical principle of social justice.

Policy advocates seeking organizational change—whether they are line staff, supervisors, executives, or members of a board of directors—engage in the same eight tasks depicted in the policy advocacy framework in Figure 2.1. They use ethical reasoning to detect flaws in existing services, use navigational skills to decide what aspects of agency services need to be changed, place issues or ideas on the agendas of key decision makers, analyze specific issues or social problems, develop proposals, seek their enactment, troubleshoot their implementation, and assess their effectiveness.

INSERT 8.6   Profiles in Leadership: Whitney Moore Young, Jr. (1921–1971)

Whitney Moore Young, Jr.—social worker and race relations expert—is best remembered for the role he played in drawing the once conservative National Urban League into the civil rights movement of the 1960s. Young, who was born in Lincoln Ridge, Kentucky, on July 31, 1921, was the second of three children born to Laura (Ray) Young and Whitney M. Young, Sr. His father was an African American leader in Kentucky and president of the Lincoln Institute. His mother was an educator and postmistress of Lincoln Ridge. After finishing high school Young attended Kentucky State College for Negroes and the University of Minnesota, earning his B.S. and M.S.W. degrees, respectively, in 1941 and 1947.

Young chose social work instead of medicine as a career following a poignant racial experience in the U.S. Army during World War II. He was placed in a segregated anti-aircraft unit with white officers—and forced to mediate between them and African American privates when he was promoted to sergeant after just three weeks. While at the University of Minnesota, Young became involved with the Minneapolis Urban League, where he did fieldwork. In 1947, he was appointed industrial relations secretary of the St. Paul Urban League and was successful at integrating the workforces of several firms in the area. In 1950, due to his success in St. Paul, Young was appointed the Omaha Urban League's executive director. His efforts in Omaha led to the hiring of several African American cab drivers, stenographers, telephone operators, and architects. In each case, it was the first time an African American had been hired to fill these positions. Meanwhile, Young also tried to open up the housing market to racial integration. As an instructor at Creighton University, Young developed administrative skills, which he used once he arrived at Atlanta University.

From 1954 to 1960, Young served as dean of the School of Social Work of Atlanta University. There, he worked to integrate the faculty and student body and introduce changes in the curriculum. Together with other African American professionals, Young organized the Atlanta Committee for Cooperative Action, which reported on the racial conditions in the city. Young received a fellowship from the General Education Board to Harvard University and was appointed executive director of the National Urban League.

Throughout the 1960s, under the leadership of Whitney Young, the National Urban League instituted numerous programs aimed at providing solutions to the critical social and economic problems faced by African Americans. The League's efforts included programs to assist African American veterans of the Vietnam War, to promote the development of African American leadership within local communities, and to improve the living conditions of residents of the inner city. In 1963, Young championed a Domestic Marshall Plan, which recommended spending $145 million over a 10-year period to eliminate this nation's racial ghettoes. The reform efforts of Whitney Young and the National Urban League attracted the attention and financial support of major corporations and important agencies, including the Ford, Rockefeller, Taconic, Alfred P. Sloan, and Field foundations.

By the middle of the 1960s, it was clear Young had succeeded in drawing the once conservative National Urban League into the civil rights movement. The League became involved in voter registration drives within the African American community and helped plan—and was present during—the March on Washington, DC, in 1963. Financially backed by the Taconic Foundation, Young organized the Council for United Civil Rights Leadership, which provided funds to the Student Nonviolent Coordinating Committee, to the Congress of Racial Equality, to the Southern Christian Leadership Conference, and to the National Association for the Advancement of Colored People.

Recognizing his outstanding leadership abilities, several U.S. presidents, including John F. Kennedy, Lyndon Johnson, and Richard Nixon, called on Young to advise them on civil rights matters. President Johnson, with whom he maintained a close relationship, allowed Young to contribute his ideas to the War on Poverty and made him an observer during the Vietnam War to examine the conditions faced by African American soldiers. Young was also instrumental in strengthening several civil rights laws during the Johnson years. His genuine commitment to the African American community and his work in expanding civil rights resulted in a $28 million federal grant to the National Urban League during the Nixon administration.

Whitney Moore Young, Jr., suffered a tragic and untimely death on March 11, 1971, in Lagos, Nigeria.

As also illustrated by Jane Addams more than 50 years earlier, Young demonstrated that social workers can be effective advocates for social justice no matter where they are employed or the focus of their work. They can join coalitions, lobby policy makers, assist candidates who favor social justice, run for office, take positions in government or reform-minded nongovernmental organizations, bring public attention to unmet needs, and empower clients.

What We Can Learn from the Persistence of Unmet Needs and Policy Issues during the Great Society

When Martin Luther King relocated his movement to Chicago in 1966 to focus upon poverty in Northern cities, he encountered extreme poverty. Inner-city African Americans often lived in squalid housing and unsafe neighborhoods. They attended understaffed and ill-equipped inner-city schools. They lived in extreme segregation. They had scant access to union jobs and were denied many other jobs due to racial discrimination in hiring practices. They were marginalized in the political process. They were not given job training. Substantial numbers of African American male youth were incarcerated for minor offenses—and then not given education, services, and job training to allow them to reenter society.

Considerable progress was made in the 1960s and 1970s in reducing the amount of poverty in the United States. Yet the number of persons living below official poverty lines increased in subsequent decades and included not only persons of color but single (mostly female) heads of households, youth, homeless persons, young graduates of foster care, white males with no more than high school education, elderly persons with chronic health conditions, and many immigrants.

It seemed that the nation was beginning a national dialogue about poverty in the wake of Hurricane Katrina in the fall of 2005 because of the televised images of stranded and impoverished African Americans on freeways, in the New Orleans

Superdome, and on the roofs of homes. But New Orleans was soon placed on the back pages of the media as time went by.

If we fast-forward to the presidential campaigns of Democratic and Republican candidates in 2007, only one of them (John Edwards) devoted significant time to this issue. As social workers, we need to work to keep this issue alive in an affluent nation that ought not tolerate poverty—and propose policies that might reduce poverty.

What We Can Learn from Failed Policy Strategies of the Great Society

The Vietnam War demonstrates that policy advocates don't have the luxury of focusing exclusively on domestic issues. Had the nation not plunged into this war, far greater resources would have been available for domestic policies. The attention of the president and the Congress would not have been diverted as much from important social policy issues. Moreover, hundreds of thousands of innocent Vietnamese civilians would not have been injured or killed.

The Iraq War has eerie similarities to the Vietnam War. It will have diverted trillions of dollars from other worthwhile policies by the time the injured veterans have received medical care over a period of decades. It, too, has diverted presidential and congressional time to prosecuting—and seeking an end—to the war. It has resulted in injuries and death to countless innocent Iraqi citizens. Rather than curtailing terrorism, it is likely that the American invasion and occupation of Iraq stimulated terrorism by giving Al-Qaeda a recruiting tool for Arab youth across the Middle East to "drive out the American imperialists."

The Great Society illustrates, too, that huge tax cuts can often constrict resources needed for domestic reforms. Had Johnson not enacted his tax cut, he might even have considered such sweeping reforms as national health insurance once the Democrats obtained huge congressional majorities in the election of 1964. Or he might have fully funded Food Stamps rather than merely beginning a pilot program. Or he might have fully funded his War on Poverty, including vastly larger training and job programs for low-income minority youth.

What We Can Learn from Promising Strategies of the Great Society

The Civil Rights Acts of 1964 and 1965 represented a giant leap forward for the United States after more than 350 years of trampling on the rights of African Americans. Not only were these acts highly successful policies with respect to African Americans, but they spawned scores of additional civil rights measures for many of the 13 vulnerable populations we have discussed in this book.

Civil rights legislation is part of the regulatory portion of the American welfare state because it establishes rules that guide conduct and that have the force of law. When working with clients in contemporary society, social workers need to understand what civil rights laws exist so that they can refer clients to enforcement authorities that monitor and police adherence to these laws.

What We Can Learn from the Great Society about the Structure of the American Welfare State

During the Great Society three major additions were made to the American welfare state that are still integral parts of it. First, we have just discussed civil rights legislation that contained key provisions with respect to persons of color and women—legislation that would be augmented in coming decades with civil rights legislation for women, disabled persons, GLBT persons, and other vulnerable populations. Some of this legislation would be enacted at the federal level of government, while other civil rights legislation would be enacted by specific states.

Second, myriad federal programs were enacted that were funded by the so-called *discretionary budget* and that were also called *categorical programs*. The

federal budget consists of two major portions. One of them funds so-called *entitlements* (such as Social Security, Medicare, and Medicaid) which are *automatically* funded to the level of claimed benefits in any specific year. In other words, *all* persons who seek retirement pensions from Social Security or health benefits from Medicare or Medicaid receive them in a specific year because no annual funding ceiling is placed upon them. By contrast, programs funded by the discretionary portion of the federal budget are funded to levels each year that Congress establishes for each nonentitlement program. Take the example of the Head Start program that was established in the Great Society. Congress decides to fund it at a specific level for a specific year, such as $300 million. Once Head Start's expenditures exceed this amount in that year, it cannot serve additional children—and may even have to cut the funding of some programs.

President Johnson secured the enactment of more than 150 programs funded by the discretionary budget. They were also called "categorical programs" because the legislation specified how the money was to be used—thus *not* allowing the states or local governments to use the funds for other purposes. In the case of the Head Start, for example, the legislation specified in some detail that children had to be of preschool age and listed the kinds of services the children would receive.

Third, President Johnson enacted two new "entitlements," namely, Medicare and Medicaid (Food Stamps later became an entitlement), to add to the entitlements enacted by President Franklin Roosevelt (Social Security pensions, unemployment insurance, ADC, AB, and OAA). Since they are automatically funded to the level of claimed benefits each year, entitlements have a privileged position in the federal budget process since they cannot be cut in annual budget fights as easily as programs funded by the discretionary budget.

To summarize, then, the Great Society established the modern American welfare state by greatly expanding it in three directions. We shall note in subsequent chapters how most of these programs remain in place, but many were changed to give states far more power in shaping their direction—and in 1996 AFDC was converted from an entitlement to a discretionary program called Temporary Assistance to Needy Families (TANF).

WHAT YOU CAN DO NOW

After reading Chapter 8, you are now equipped to:

- Analyze the chilling effect of the Cold War on domestic reforms.

- Discuss the origins of the civil rights movement in the 1950s in the South and in the nation.

- Analyze how John F. Kennedy bested Richard Nixon to become president in 1960—and describe those reforms he initiated before his assassination in 1963.

- Discuss why President Kennedy was relatively timid in seeking civil rights legislation while nonetheless giving the first presidential address on the subject.

- Analyze political and other differences between President Kennedy and President Lyndon Johnson.

- Discuss President Johnson's "policy gluttony" on tax, domestic, and international fronts.

- Analyze the civil rights achievements of President Johnson and the Congress in 1964 and 1965—as well as other landmark legislation that he achieved in health, education, poverty, welfare, Food Stamps, housing, and gerontology areas.

- Discuss why political support for President Johnson had eroded significantly by 1967—and why he chose not to run for the presidency in 1968—in the context of the war in Vietnam, deficits, and white backlash.

- Analyze the causes and nature of the oppression of women, gay men and lesbians, Latinos, First Americans, Asian Americans, and persons of color in urban ghettoes during the 1960s.

- Discuss developments in the social work profession in the 1960s.

- Analyze the impact of policy advocates such as Martin Luther King, César Chavez, and Whitney Young.

- Analyze what we can learn from the Great Society about persistent unmet needs, failed strategies, promising strategies, and the structure of the American welfare state.

ENDNOTES

1. Stephen Bailey, *Congress Makes a Law* (New York: Columbia University Press, 1950), pp. 220–234.

2. Mary Hinchey, "The Frustration of the New Deal Revival: 1944–1946." Unpublished dissertation (Columbia, MO: University of Missouri, 1965).

3. James Savage, *Balanced Budgets and American Politics* (Ithaca, NY: Cornell University Press, 1988), pp. 161–175.

4. See, for example, Barton Bernstein, "The Ambiguous Legacy: The Truman Administration and Civil Rights." In Barton Bernstein, ed., *Politics and Policies of the Truman Administration* (Chicago: Quadrangle Books, 1970), pp. 269–314.

5. Bernstein, "The Ambiguous Legacy," pp. 269–314.

6. Paul Nitze, *From Hiroshima to Glasnost: At the Center of Decision* (New York: Grove Weidenfeld, 1989).

7. Richard Davies, *Age of Asphalt: The Automobile, the Freeway, and the Condition of Metropolitan America* (Philadelphia: J. B. Lippincott, 1975).

8. Herbert Parmet, *Eisenhower and the American Crusades* (New York: Macmillan, 1972), pp. 570–572.

9. Stephen Ambrose, *Eisenhower, the President*, Vol. II (New York: Simon & Schuster, 1984), pp. 411–435.

10. William Leuchtenberg, *In the Shadow of FDR: From Harry Truman to Ronald Reagan* (Ithaca, NY:

Cornell University Press, 1983), pp. 78–84; Allen Matusow, *The Unraveling of America: A History of Liberalism in the 1960's* (New York: Harper & Row, 1984), pp. 15–17.

11. Charles Hulton, "The Legacy of Reaganomics." In John Palmer and Isabel Sawhill, eds., *The Legacy of Reaganomics* (Washington, DC: Urban Institute, 1984), p. 7.

12. Geoffrey Hodgson, *America in Our Time* (Garden City, NY: Doubleday, 1976), p. 51.

13. Ibid., pp. 54–64, 184–189.

14. Ibid., pp. 58–60.

15. Paul Taubman, *Income Distribution and Redistribution* (Reading, MA: Addison-Wesley, 1978), p. 15.

16. Winifred Bell, *Aid to Dependent Children* (New York: Columbia University Press, 1965), pp. 93–110; Frances Piven and Richard Cloward, *Regulating the Poor: The Functions of Public Welfare* (New York: Pantheon, 1971), pp. 123–177.

17. Gilbert Steiner, *State of Welfare* (Washington, DC: Brookings Institution, 1971), pp. 226–227.

18. Peter Gottschalk and Sheldon Danziger, "Macroeconomic Conditions, Income Transfers, and the Trend in Poverty." In D. Lee Bawden, ed., *The Social Contract Revisited: Aims and Outcomes of President Reagan's Social Welfare Policy* (Washington, DC: Urban Institute, 1984), p. 191.

19. William Chafe, *The American Woman: Her Changing Social, Economic, and Political Roles* (New York: Oxford University Press, 1972), pp. 174–195.

20. Bernard Bloom, *Community Mental Health* (Pacific Grove, CA: Brooks/Cole, 1977), pp. 11–20.

21. Peter Tyor and Leland Bell, *Caring for the Retarded in America: A History* (Westport, CT: Greenwood Press, 1984), pp. 123–145.

22. The number of persons with disabilities is discussed by Frank Bowe, *Rehabilitating America: Toward Independence for Disabled and Elderly People* (New York: Harper & Row, 1980), pp. 24–54.

23. Jonathan Katz, *Gay American History: Lesbians and Gay Men in the U.S.A.* (New York: Harper Colophon Books, 1976), pp. 432, 596.

24. Hodgson, *America in Our Time*, p. 45.

25. Theodore Sorenson, *Kennedy* (New York: Harper & Row, 1965); Arthur Schlesinger, Jr., *A Thousand Days: John F. Kennedy in the White House* (Boston: Houghton Mifflin, 1965); and William Manchester, *Portrait of a President* (Boston: Little, Brown, 1962).

26. Henry Fairlie, *The Kennedy Promise* (Garden City, NY: Doubleday, 1973); Victor Lasky, *J.F.K., the Man and the Myth* (New York: Macmillan, 1963); and Richard Walton, *Cold War and Counterrevolution: The Foreign Policy of John F. Kennedy* (New York: Viking Press, 1972).

27. Leuchtenberg, *In the Shadow of FDR*, pp. 76–84.

28. Ibid., p. 77; Matusow, *The Unraveling of America*, p. 14.

29. Henry Aaron, *Politics and the Professors* (Washington, DC: Brookings Institution, 1981), pp. 17–25; James Patterson, *America's Struggle against Poverty* (Cambridge, MA: Harvard University Press, 1981), pp. 115–125.

30. Aaron, *Politics and the Professors*, pp. 35–49, 220–225.

31. William Ryan, *Blaming the Victim* (New York: Pantheon, 1971), pp. 112–135.

32. Vincent Burke, *Nixon's Good Deed: Welfare Reform* (New York: Columbia University Press, 1974), p. 36; Hodgson, *America in Our Time*, pp. 82–98.

33. Tom Wicker, *JFK and LBJ: The Influence of Personality upon Politics* (New York: Morrow, 1968), pp. 85–87.

34. Ibid., pp. 90–92.

35. Leuchtenberg, *In the Shadow of FDR*, pp. 85–88.

36. Aaron, *Politics and the Professors*, p. 17.

37. Michael Harrington, *The Other America: Poverty in the United States* (New York: Macmillan, 1962).

38. Matusow, *The Unraveling of America*, pp. 60–96.

39. Juan Williams, *Eyes on the Prize: America's Civil Rights Years, 1954–1965* (New York: Viking, 1987), pp. 39–61.

40. Ibid., p. 41.

41. Ibid., pp. 39–61.

42. Matusow, *The Unraveling of America*, pp. 62–63.

43. Carl Brauer, *John F. Kennedy and the Second Reconstruction* (New York: Columbia University Press, 1977), pp. 16–17, 204.

44. Ibid., pp. 112–113.

45. Matusow, *The Unraveling of America*, p. 348.

46. Ibid., pp. 90–91; Brauer, *John F. Kennedy*, pp. 265–268.

47. Theodore Marmor, *The Politics of Medicare* (Chicago: Aldine Books, 1975), pp. 39–53.

48. Wicker, *JFK and LBJ*, pp. 132–146.

49. Hodgson, *America in Our Time*, pp. 247–248.

50. Matusow, *The Unraveling of America*, pp. 104–105; James Sundquist, *Politics and Policy: The Eisenhower, Kennedy, and Johnson Years* (Washington, DC: Brookings Institution, 1968), pp. 85–91.

51. Matusow, *The Unraveling of America*, p. 105.

52. Ibid., p. 100.

53. James Singer, "A Subminimum Wage—Jobs for Youths or a Break for Their Employers?" *National Journal* (January 24, 1981), pp. 146–148.

54. Sundquist, *Politics and Policy*, pp. 97–105.

55. Matusow, *The Unraveling of America*, pp. 100–102.

56. Bloom, *Community Mental Health*, pp. 19–25.

57. Steiner, *State of Welfare*, pp. 35–40.

58. David Halberstam, *The Best and the Brightest* (New York: Random House, 1972), pp. 154–301.

59. Robert Caro, *The Years of Lyndon Johnson* (New York: Knopf, 1982); Doris Kearns, *Lyndon Johnson and the American Dream* (New York: Harper & Row, 1976), pp. 19–96.

60. Kearns, *Lyndon Johnson*, pp. 103–106.

61. Ibid., p. 179; Wicker, *JFK and LBJ*, pp. 161–163.

62. Joseph Califano, *The Triumph and Tragedy of Lyndon Johnson: The White House Years* (New York: Simon & Schuster, 1991), pp. 106–121.

63. Wicker, *JFK and LBJ*, pp. 163–169; Kearns, *Lyndon Johnson*, pp. 170–176.

64. Kearns, *Lyndon Johnson*, pp. 190, 224–227; Wicker, *JFK and LBJ*, pp. 209–211.

65. Vaughn Bornet, *The Presidency of Lyndon B. Johnson* (Lawrence, KS: University of Kansas, 1983), pp. 134, 225, 333, 343; Patterson, *America's Struggle*, p. 141; and Wicker, *JFK and LBJ*, pp. 177–178.

66. Kearns, *Lyndon Johnson*, pp. 190, 224–227.

67. Wicker, *JFK and LBJ*, pp. 212–235.

68. Sundquist, *Politics and Policy*, pp. 259–271.

69. Matusow, *The Unraveling of America*, pp. 203–213.

70. Ibid., pp. 180–187.

71. Ambrose, *Eisenhower, the President*, Vol. II, p. 425.

72. Williams, *Eyes on the Prize*, pp. 23, 32.

73. Ibid., p. 23.

74. Paul Starr, *The Social Transformation of American Medicine* (New York: Basic Books, 1984), pp. 369–370.

75. Ibid., pp. 97–103, 373; Frank Thompson, *Health Policy and the Bureaucracy: Politics and Implementation* (Cambridge, MA: M.I.T. Press, 1981), pp. 180–185.

76. Nancy Eustis, Jay Greenberg, and Sharon Patten, *Long-Term Care for Older Persons: A Policy Perspective* (Pacific Grove, CA: Brooks/Cole, 1984), pp. 135–137.

77. Ibid., pp. 133–135.

78. Starr, *The Social Transformation*, pp. 375–378.

79. Many legislative proposals to develop innovative outreach and community projects have been considered. See Eustis, Greenberg, and Patten, *Long-Term Care*, pp. 189–192.

80. Rosemary Stevens, *Welfare Medicine in America: The Case of Medicaid* (New York: Free Press, 1974), pp. 51–71.

81. Ibid., p. 131.

82. Karen Davis and Cathy Schoen, *Health and the War on Poverty: A Ten-Year Appraisal* (Washington, DC: Brookings Institution, 1978), pp. 62–67; Thompson, *Health Policy*, pp. 148–153.

83. Davis and Schoen, *Health and the War on Poverty*, pp. 67–91; Dorothy Kupcha, "Medicaid: In or Out of the Mainstream?" *California Journal*, 10 (May 1979), pp. 181–183.

84. Donald Gelfand and Jody Olsen, *The Aging Network: Programs and Services* (New York: Springer, 1980), pp. 9–16.

85. William Lammers, *Public Policy and the Aging* (Washington, DC: Congressional Quarterly Press, 1983), pp. 180–183.

86. Sundquist, *Politics and Policy*, pp. 210–215.

87. Matusow, *The Unraveling of America*, pp. 223–226.

88. Aaron, *Politics and the Professors*, pp. 70–92.

89. Bornet, *The Presidency of Lyndon Johnson*, pp. 223–224.

90. Ibid., pp. 224–227.

91. Sundquist, *Politics and Policy*, pp. 134–150.

92. Daniel Moynihan, *Maximum Feasible Misunderstanding: Community Action in the War on Poverty* (New York: Free Press, 1969), pp. 79–100.

93. Matusow, *The Unraveling of America*, pp. 243–265.

94. Burke, *Nixon's Good Deed*, pp. 18, 23–24.

95. Matusow, *The Unraveling of America*, pp. 266–267.

96. Davis and Schoen, *Health and the War on Poverty*, pp. 133–134, 177–189.

97. Matusow, *The Unraveling of America*, p. 266.

98. Bruce Jansson, *The History and Politics of Selected Children's Programs and Related Legislation in the Context of Four Models of Political Behavior.* Doctoral dissertation (Chicago: University of Chicago, 1975), pp. 145–146, 160–161.

99. Steiner, *State of Welfare*, pp. 40–50.

100. Burke, *Nixon's Good Deed*, pp. 22–24, 35–41.

101. Califano, *The Triumph and Tragedy of Lyndon Johnson*, p. 149.

102. William Gibbons, *The U.S. Government and the Vietnam War: Executive and Legislative Roles and Relationships*, Part III (Princeton, NJ: Princeton University Press, 1990).

103. Michael Boll, *National Security Planning: Roosevelt through Reagan* (Lexington, KY: University of Kentucky Press, 1988).

104. See the oral histories by Walter Heller at the Lyndon Johnson Presidential Library.

105. Califano, *The Triumph and Tragedy of Lyndon Johnson*, pp. 106–121.

106. Ibid., pp. 94–97.

107. Ibid., pp. 97–98.

108. Ibid., p. 111.

109. Matusow, *The Unraveling of America*, pp. 204–206.

110. Ibid., p. 205.

111. Ibid., pp. 422–426; Hodgson, *America in Our Time*, pp. 368–383.

112. Matusow, *The Unraveling of America*, pp. 345–360.

113. William Leuchtenberg, *The Perils of Prosperity* (Chicago: University of Chicago Press, 1958), p. 173.

114. Califano, *The Triumph and Tragedy of Lyndon Johnson*, p. 248.

115. Gloria Emerson, *Winners and Losers* (New York: Random House, 1976), p. 357; Guenter Lewy, *America in Vietnam* (New York: Oxford University Press, 1978), p. 445; and Alan Millette, ed., *A Short History of the Vietnam Conflict* (Bloomington, IN: University of Indiana, 1978), p. 131.

116. Kearns, *Lyndon Johnson*, pp. 251–275; Wicker, *JFK and LBJ*, pp. 252–253.

117. Matusow, *The Unraveling of America*, pp. 376–394.

118. Kearns, *Lyndon Johnson*, pp. 302–304.

119. Leuchtenberg, *In the Shadow of FDR*, pp. 147–150.

120. Susan Faludi, *Backlash: The Undeclared War against American Women* (New York: Crown Publishers, 1991), p. 56.

121. Ibid., p. 57.

122. Cynthia Harrison, *On Account of Sex: The Politics of Women's Issues, 1945–1968* (Berkeley: University of California Press, 1988), pp. 3–23.

123. Ibid., pp. 89–105.

124. Ibid., pp. 139–156.

125. Betty Friedan, *The Feminine Mystique* (New York: W.W. Norton, 1963).

126. Ibid., p. 15.

127. Ibid., p. 282.

128. Ibid., pp. 338–378.

129. Harrison, *On Account of Sex*, pp. 176–180.

130. Ibid., pp. 187–191.

131. Ibid., p. 200.

132. Ibid., pp. 201–202.

133. Ibid., p. 171.

134. Jonathan Katz, *Gay American History*, p. 99.

135. John D'Emilio, *Sexual Politics, Sexual Communities: The Making of a Homosexual Minority in the United States, 1940–1970* (Chicago: University of Chicago Press, 1983).

136. Ibid., p. 35.

137. Ibid., p. 44.

138. Ibid., p. 46.

139. Ibid., p. 49.

140. Ibid., pp. 124–125.

141. Ibid., pp. 129–148.

142. Ibid., p. 217.

143. Ibid., p. 235.

144. James Jennings, "The Puerto Rican Community: Its Political Background." In F. Chris Garcia, ed., *Latinos and the Political System* (Notre Dame, IN: University of Notre Dame Press, 1988), p. 65.

145. Juan Gomez Quinones, *Chicano Politics* (Albuquerque, NM: University of New Mexico Press, 1990), pp. 101–153.

146. Jennings, "The Puerto Rican Community," p. 75.

147. Theodore Taylor, *The Bureau of Indian Affairs* (Boulder, CO: Westview Press, 1984), pp. 18–19.

148. Ibid., p. 25.

149. Ibid., p. 27.

150. Ronald Takaki, *Strangers from a Different Shore* (Boston: Little, Brown, 1989), pp. 406–420.

151. Ibid., p. 419.

152. Angelo Falcon, "Black and Latino Politics in New York City: Race and Ethnicity in a Changing Urban Context." In Garcia, ed., *Latinos and the Political System*, pp. 172–173.

153. Stanley Wenocur and Michael Reisch, *From Charity to Enterprise: The Development of American Social Work in a Market Economy* (Urbana, IL: University of Illinois Press, 1989), pp. 211–213.

154. Ibid., pp. 252–255.

155. Jack Rothman, "Macro Social Work in a Tightening Economy," *Social Work*, 24 (May 1980), pp. 274–282.

156. Leslie Leighninger, *Social Work: Search for Identity* (New York: Greenwood Press, 1987), p. 217.

157. Ibid., p. 217.

158. Ibid., pp. 214–215.

159. Burke, *Nixon's Good Deed*, pp. 20, 22–24, 36–39.

160. Lawrence O'Brien, *No Final Victories: A Life in Politics from John F. Kennedy to Watergate* (Garden City, NY: Doubleday, 1974), pp. 196–197.

161. Kearns, *Lyndon Johnson*, pp. 282–284.

162. Jack Meyer, "Budget Cuts in the Reagan Administration: A Question of Fairness." In D. Lee Bawden, ed., *The Social Contract Revisited: Aims and Outcomes of President Reagan's Social Welfare Policy* (Washington, DC: Urban Institute, 1984), p. 36.

9

The Paradoxical Era: 1968–1980

T A B L E 9.1 **Selected Orienting Events**

1968	Richard Nixon wins narrow presidential victory over Hubert Humphrey
1969	Nixon proposes Family Assistance Plan
1970	Family Planning and Population Research Act enacted; Occupational Safety and Health Act (OSHA) enacted
1971	National eligibility standards established for Food Stamps Program
1972	Local Fiscal Assistance Act establishes general revenue sharing; Social Security benefits indexed to rise with inflation; Supplementary Security Income (SSI) program established
1972	Nixon wins landslide victory over George McGovern
1973	Comprehensive Employment and Training Act (CETA) enacted; Food Stamps Program federalized and made mandatory; Rehabilitation Act passed
1973	Supreme Court issues *Roe v. Wade* decision, which legalizes abortion
1974	Juvenile Justice and Delinquency Prevention Act enacted; Title XX (social services) added to Social Security Act
1974	Nixon resigns presidency under threat of impeachment due to the Watergate scandal and is succeeded by Gerald Ford
1975	Education for All Handicapped Children Act passed; Earned Income Tax Credit (EITC) enacted for poor wage earners
1976	Jimmy Carter elected president
1977	Carter introduces welfare reform plan, which is later defeated
1978	Report of President's Commission on Mental Health issued

TABLE 9.1   (continued)

1979	Carter introduces unsuccessful national health insurance plan; Office of Education becomes the Department of Education when it is separated from the Department of Health, Education, and Welfare (HEW), which becomes the Department of Health and Human Services (DHHS)
1980	Adoption Assistance and Child Welfare Act enacted; Mental Health Systems Act passed

Presidents Richard Nixon (1969–1974), Gerald Ford (1974–1976), and Jimmy Carter (1977–1980) were relatively conservative presidents who had little outward interest in major social reforms. Yet social spending rose dramatically during this ostensibly conservative period. Indeed, few people realize that the first term of Nixon's presidency (1969–1972) ranks as a major period of social reform and was supplemented by some reforms in his remaining years in the presidency. Sar Levitan, a noted policy commentator, argues that "the greatest extensions of the modern welfare system were enacted under the conservative presidency of Richard Nixon with bipartisan congressional support, dwarfing in size and scope the initiatives of Lyndon Johnson's Great Society."[1] Although Levitan seems to forget that many of Nixon's reforms consisted of simply expanding programs he inherited from the Great Society, such as the Food Stamps Program, he correctly notes that many social reforms and considerable increases in social spending occurred during the Nixon years; Tom Wicker, a biographer of Nixon, concurs.[2] Nevertheless, Nixon was extremely conservative in much of his rhetoric and turned sharply to the right in 1972. With its conflicting tendencies, this was a transitional era between the reformist period of the Great Society and the conservative presidency of Ronald Reagan in the 1980s.

At the end of this chapter, we discuss what we can learn from the Paradoxical Era about policy advocacy, social policy, and the structure of the American welfare state in contemporary society.

RICHARD NIXON: POLITICAL OPPORTUNIST

Richard Nixon achieved early successes in House and Senate races in the late 1940s and early 1950s by alleging that his opponents had left-wing tendencies and by spearheading congressional investigations of Alger Hiss, a State Department official who was accused and ultimately convicted of spying for Russia. These tactics earned him the disdain of liberals, but they brought sufficient public support that Dwight Eisenhower chose Nixon as his running mate in his presidential campaigns of 1952 and 1956. Nixon obtained the Republican nomination for the presidency in 1960 but narrowly lost to John Kennedy. After losing a bid for a California Senate seat in 1962, Nixon retired from politics, only to resurface as the Republican presidential candidate in 1968 against Hubert Humphrey, whom he subsequently defeated by a thin margin.

Liberal critics of Nixon had long accused him of willingness to use red-baiting and other dubious tactics to secure power, but his opportunism also led him to support liberal domestic policies when he believed they would enhance his political career. These calculations sometimes led him to support moderate positions during the 1950s, when Republicans understood that frontal attacks on New Deal programs, such as Social Security, were unpopular.[3]

Nixon correctly perceived that a power vacuum existed in the Republican Party in the wake of the Democratic landslide victory over Goldwater in

---

I N S E R T 9.1   **Using the Web to Understand the Shaping of Policies during the Paradoxical Era of the 1970S**

Visit **academic.cengage.com/social_work/jansson** to view these links and a variety of study tools.

Go to **http://www.pbs.org/wgbh/amex/presidents/nf/resource/nixon/nixscript.html** What additional information does this material provide you about the mind-set and tactics of President Richard Nixon? Was he "conservative," "liberal," or "both"?

Go to **http://scriptorium.lib.duke.edu/wlm/covert/** and read "Covert Sex Discrimination against Women as Medical Patients," a speech given by Carol Downer in September 1972 to the American Psychological Association. What does this speech reveal about the subtle form of discrimination that women encountered in medical care?

Go to **http://scriptorium.lib.duke.edu/wlm/notes/** Read the article by Carol Hanish and Elizabeth Sutherland, "Women of the World Unite—We Have Nothing to Lose But Our Men." Identify an array of factors that feminists had to encounter from males as they sought to fashion a movement—including their husbands' prejudices. Read Shulamith Firestone's "The Women's Rights Movement in the U.S.: A New View" as well as other documents from the women's liberation movement. What new insights do they give you about the oppression of women in the United States?

1964. By assuming the role of mediator and statesman within the leaderless and demoralized party and by aggressively campaigning for Republicans of all persuasions in succeeding years, he successfully positioned himself for the presidential bid in 1968.[4] Nixon obtained the nomination for the presidency in 1968 because he convinced each segment of the Republican Party, including liberal, moderate, and conservative wings, that he represented them.[5]

His election campaign in 1968 did not suggest that he would soon initiate or support a series of domestic reforms. Sensing that the Democratic contender, Hubert Humphrey, was vulnerable among working- and middle-class voters because he was identified with the Vietnam conflict and with black power and other reform groups, Nixon avoided major social issues, promised peace with honor, and pledged he would be tough on the issue of crime. He appealed to Southerners by promising to terminate federal efforts to desegregate schools and by giving Senator Strom Thurmond, a conservative Southerner, a prominent role in selecting the law-and-order theme of his campaign. He chose Spiro Agnew as his vice president in an obvious effort to appeal to white backlash sentiment

and repeatedly attacked alleged social reform excesses of the Great Society.[6]

Nixon's conservative rhetoric in the campaign of 1968 was not a good predictor of his subsequent policy choices, particularly in the first three years of his presidency. His motivation for supporting various social reforms defies easy analysis because he was an enigmatic man, to whom Churchill's characterization of Russia ("a riddle wrapped in a mystery inside an enigma") might aptly apply. Wicker contends that Nixon was not devoid of sympathy for the poor because of his own experience of poverty during his childhood; however, Wicker also notes that Nixon's choices were dictated by political concerns, such as his desire to broaden the base of the Republican Party.[7] Indeed, other writers place considerable stock in the Disraeli thesis— that is, that Nixon's reading of English history inspired him to be an American conservative who, much like Disraeli, the English conservative prime minister of the 19th century, would support certain reforms to pull new working-class constituents into his political party.[8] Likewise, many theorists believe that he was persuaded by the arguments of Kevin Phillips, who maintained that the Republican Party could construct a new majority by attracting large numbers of working-class voters, Catholics, members of white ethnic groups, and residents of the Sunbelt.[9] Yet other commentators suggest that much of his behavior derived from a perverse pleasure in upstaging or surprising the Democrats.[10] Another intriguing theory is that Nixon supported social reform mainly to retain the support of liberals in both political parties for his foreign policies, including his Vietnam policy.[11] If this was indeed the case, it represented an interesting reversal from Franklin Roosevelt and Lyndon Johnson, both of whom had to *cut* social spending to placate conservative congressional foes. Nixon also knew that Democrats, who controlled both houses of Congress, would push him to support many liberal measures. Doubtless, Nixon was often driven by some combination of these motivations, but the bottom line was that he supported or agreed to an array of social reforms.

Nevertheless, Nixon's reform strategy rested on profound ambivalence, both ideological and political. Nixon was not instinctively a liberal, even if he was willing to espouse liberal causes for political reasons. He despised many liberal Republican senators, such as Charles Percy of Illinois. Many of his advisors, as well as broad sections of his party, were conservative and unlikely to support liberal policies. An inner circle of ambivalence thus existed in the White House in Nixon's first term and led to contradictory policies. By 1972, this ambivalence turned to outright opposition to many social policies and to a determination to cut social spending, even by impounding funds that Congress had already appropriated for specific programs.[12]

NIXON'S STRATEGY: FLOATING COALITIONS AND OUTBIDDING

Nixon both initiated social legislation and responded positively to congressional initiatives. When Nixon supported social reforms, he used a floating coalition and political outbidding. The *floating coalition strategy* depended on fashioning a coalition that included the support of some liberal Republicans, some moderate Republicans who were loyal to the president, and some Democratic liberals and moderates who placed their ideology before their party—that is, a bipartisan coalition of moderates and liberals to oppose conservatives, with the precise composition of the coalition varying from issue to issue.[13] In the *political outbidding strategy*, he endorsed social reforms that were initiated by Democrats but offered expansive amendments to them—or accepted them with little change—so that he could obtain partial credit for their passage.[14] It was a strange spectacle to many political observers; no Republican president since Theodore Roosevelt had sought to enact so many domestic reforms, much less to try to beat the Democrats at their own game.

Floating coalitions and outbidding represented bold strategies that could be successful only in a particular political environment. To employ this strategy, Nixon first had to want to expand the political base of the Republican Party and had to believe, as well, that blue-collar and white ethnic voters desired social reforms. Second, he had to believe that he could persuade members of his own party that the social reforms he developed were different from the Democratic reforms that they had opposed since the New Deal. Where Lyndon Johnson had sought programs that emphasized social and medical services, community participation of the poor, and expanded roles for the federal government, Nixon sought reforms that provided jobs and income, expanded the policy roles of local governments, and used private market mechanisms rather than direct government provision.[15] He believed that, by portraying his programs as "hard benefits" that were superior to the social services offered by Democrats, he could gain the support of many Republicans and also of blue-collar voters, local officials, and the business community (see Insert 9.2).

To underscore the distinctiveness of Republican reforms, Nixon unleashed scathing attacks on the innovations of the Great Society, which he depicted as undisciplined and ineffective programs that enriched bureaucrats and social workers.[16]

INSERT 9.2 Critical Analysis: Services versus Hard Benefits

Nixon framed social policy as a choice between social services and hard benefits. Was he correct?

1. Analyze the functions of *both* service and benefit programs in the welfare state.
2. What would society look like if either kind of program were largely eliminated?
3. Choosing any major social problem, discuss how those upon whom it has the greatest impact often need both social services and hard benefits.

Third, Nixon had to believe that increased domestic spending would not jeopardize the nation's economic growth by causing deficits or by drawing capital from investments. He believed that, following the Vietnam conflict, there would be economic surpluses sufficient to fund new programs, and he favored the use of increased social spending to bring about economic recovery during and after a sharp recession in 1970.[17] Finally, he needed to have a significant number of liberal advisors to provide him with reform ideas and to fend off conservative advisors who were beholden to the conservative wing of the Republican Party; nevertheless, in keeping with his policy ambivalence in his first term, he also appointed many conservative advisors.[18] He named the relatively liberal Robert Finch as his secretary of the Department of Health, Education, and Welfare and, when Finch suffered a nervous breakdown, replaced him with Elliot Richardson. He appointed Daniel Moynihan, a moderate Democrat who was critical of the Great Society but favored income, job, and other reforms, as the director of his Urban Affairs Council.

FROM STRATEGY TO POLICY

Reforms enacted during Nixon's first term (1969–1972) included the Supplementary Security Income (SSI) program; major revisions in the Food Stamps Program; indexing of the Social Security program; revenue sharing; the consolidation of social services in Title XX to the Social Security Act; addition of a family planning program to the Public Health Act; assorted health legislation; development of affirmative action policies; establishment of the Occupational Safety and Health Administration (OSHA); and policies that led to the desegregation of virtually all Southern schools. These policy enactments, which would have represented a remarkable achievement even for a Democratic president, were supplemented by two major proposals that were not enacted: a proposal to reform welfare programs (the Family Assistance Program, or FAP) and a proposal for national health insurance. In Nixon's second term (1973–1974), the Comprehensive Employment and Training Act (CETA), the Community Development Block Grant Program, the Rehabilitation Act of 1973, and the Child Abuse Prevention Act of 1973 were enacted.

Welfare Policy

Virtually no one was satisfied with the AFDC program. Liberals believed it limited assistance to families with single parents in many states and disliked its low eligibility levels and often paltry grants; conservatives believed it encouraged substantial numbers of women not to work and included too many working mothers who had retained their eligibility owing to the work incentive provisions of 1967.[19] Faced with this cross-fire from liberals and conservatives, Nixon had several options. He could have sought incremental and liberalizing reforms to increase the levels of benefits in low-benefit states, as suggested by a task force headed by Richard Nathan, or he could have favored incremental and conservative reforms, such as those suggested by economist Arthur Burns, to strengthen the work requirement and to create public service jobs.

At the urging of Daniel Moynihan, however, Nixon decided to seek a comprehensive reform of the nation's welfare system, partly because his advisors feared that the Democrats would preempt the issue by announcing their own reform measure from a commission that had been appointed by Johnson.[20] Moynihan convinced Nixon that his plan offered a lasting policy solution to a vexing problem because it focused on provision of income, work incentives, and public service jobs. At a critical juncture, Moynihan told Nixon that the new program would permit the termination of scores of social workers, whom Nixon detested and associated with Democratic reforms, and would extend benefits to many blue-collar and white ethnic voters, as intact families and working (but poor) persons were both eligible.[21]

Democrats and Republicans alike were astonished when President Nixon announced in August of 1969 that he wanted to revamp the nation's welfare programs by establishing a Family Assistance Plan (FAP) to replace the AFDC and AFDC-U programs with a program that would provide federal assistance to all families who fell beneath a federally prescribed minimum income. (Enacted in 1961, AFDC-U had given states the option to offer AFDC assistance to families with unemployed fathers, but fewer than half of the states had exercised this option.) FAP provided for all intact families a nationwide guaranteed income that was higher than prevailing welfare standards in many Southern states. It had even more generous work incentives than the 1967 provisions, proposed the creation of large numbers of public service jobs for welfare recipients, and contained a large day care program. In one policy stroke, then, FAP proposed to repeal the AFDC program and replace it with a national program. It did not constitute truly massive redistribution of resources to the poor, however; it would have provided only $4.5 billion in additional federal outlays.[22]

FAP soon became enmeshed in the same crossfire between liberals and conservatives that had plagued the AFDC program. Fearing its defeat by a combination of Republican and Democratic conservatives, Nixon stressed that FAP contained a strong work incentive and work requirement. The legislation breezed through the House because of the diligent help of Wilbur Mills, chair of the Ways and Means Committee; but it encountered opposition from conservative Republicans and Democrats in

the Senate Finance Committee, who succeeded in demonstrating that thousands of FAP recipients would lose eligibility for Medicaid, public housing, and Food Stamps as their welfare benefits and earnings catapulted them above the eligibility ceiling of these programs. Loss of these benefits would, they argued, severely jeopardize recipients' incentives to work.[23] Many liberal senators also attacked FAP because trade unions, which supported the minimum wage, objected to provisions that required federal authorities to pay only the prevailing wages in local jurisdictions. The National Welfare Rights Organization (NWRO), the grassroots protest movement of welfare recipients, contended that the national minimum benefit should be significantly increased and also objected to work requirements in the legislation. Most members of NWRO, who resided in Northern cities within high-benefit states, would have obtained little direct benefit from FAP, which emphasized improvement of benefits in low-benefit states in the South. NWRO leaders sought amendments to increase benefit levels, weaken the work requirement, expand day care provisions, and raise wage levels in public service jobs.[24]

Despite this sniping from both conservatives and liberals, FAP came surprisingly close to passage, thanks to numerous amendments that the administration introduced to appease both factions; however, it finally lost a decisive vote in the Senate in 1970. Reintroduced with minor changes in 1971, it was caught in an even more furious exchange between liberals and conservatives and was finally defeated in 1972.[25] FAP's demise was hastened by lack of constituency support; some key legislators noted that they did not receive a single supportive letter in 1971.

An important policy reform was nonetheless achieved. An obscure provision attached to the welfare reform measure in 1971 proposed to replace the adult welfare programs of Old Age Assistance, Aid to the Blind, and Aid to the Disabled with the Supplementary Security Income (SSI) program.[26] Although FAP was defeated, its SSI provision was enacted in 1972. SSI proposed to federalize these adult programs, just as FAP had proposed to federalize AFDC; but older persons and those with disabilities were not associated with the long tradition of controversy that had beset AFDC beneficiaries, who were variously accused of malingering, seeking welfare funds to have more kids, and leading immoral lives.

The federal government assumed responsibility for most of the welfare costs for these adult recipients under SSI. Because SSI was administered by the Social Security Administration and its local offices, elderly citizens no longer received their financial support from public welfare offices and so were spared the stigma visited upon welfare recipients. The legislation rescued older persons from the often punitive federal-state Old Age Assistance program, assisted hundreds of thousands of deinstitutionalized persons with mental disorders, and provided funds for many persons with physical disabilities, including Vietnam vets. Over the years, the SSI rolls expanded considerably—from 3.1 million persons in 1970 to 4.1 million persons in 1980.[27]

SSI nonetheless had serious flaws. Elderly persons and those with disabilities were allowed to keep their homes and could not have their estates attached, but they were not entitled to use Food Stamps. Grants were hardly munificent. Additionally, elderly persons who lived in states that did not supplement the federal minimum benefits received lower benefits than their peers in more generous states. The early federal guidelines that defined mental and physical disability were vague; Presidents Carter and Reagan instituted guidelines and procedures that discontinued grants to tens of thousands of persons with serious disabilities.[28]

Democrats had initiated and received political credit for the Food Stamps Program when it was enacted in 1964. They continued their leadership in this area when George McGovern, the liberal Democratic senator, held hearings during the late 1960s on issues of nutrition and hunger in the United States.[29] He contended that the Food Stamps program addressed the nutritional needs of only a small fraction of hungry Americans. Furthermore, conservatives had shown that the eligibility criteria for Food Stamps did not mesh with the FAP criteria. Nixon believed that he could solve the technical problems of Food Stamps and

regain the initiative from the Democrats by federalizing Food Stamps, establishing national eligibility standards, making participation in the program mandatory for all states, and developing a revised benefit schedule that would provide additional benefits to families with no earned income, as well as larger families. By securing these bold changes, Nixon transformed Food Stamps from a welfare program to a program used by large numbers of the working poor.[30] These liberal reforms were enacted in 1970 and 1973 and dramatically increased the size of the program—from 10.4 million enrollees in 1970 to 19.4 million enrollees in 1980.[31] A broad constituency of protest groups, liberals, agricultural interests, and conservative politicians from rural areas supported these reforms.

Social Security

Congress had periodically revised Social Security benefits upward to compensate for their erosion by inflation; this ritual was used by both Democrats and Republicans to garner support from elderly constituents. But members of both parties saw a need to index benefits—that is, to adjust benefits automatically and annually so as to compensate for the erosion in their value due to inflation. Nixon proposed a small benefit increase in Social Security and indexing in 1972. However, Wilbur Mills, a Democratic Congressman with presidential aspirations, realized that championing the needs of elderly voters would benefit Democrats in the 1972 elections and consequently proposed not only indexing but also a 20 percent increase in benefits![32] Such generous increases would normally have required major increases in payroll taxes. However, Mills refrained from proposing such tax increases, in part to avoid the ensuing political outcry but also because actuaries for the Social Security Administration, whose new economic models were based on overoptimistic assumptions, predicted that the trust fund would remain solvent even with massive increases in benefits. Nixon decided to support Mills's proposals, so as to obtain partial credit for them and to compensate for the defeat of FAP, which had deprived his administration of credit for a major social reform.[33]

Everyone realized that indexing would increase benefits, but virtually no one predicted that the onset of double-digit inflation in the 1970s would lead to extraordinary increases in Social Security benefits—or that the technical formulas used to compute benefit increases would allow these increases even to exceed rates of inflation.[34] The old system of incremental and periodic benefit increases had been replaced by an automatic system that led to rapid increases in benefits without associated increases in payroll taxes. Furthermore, an increase in the ratio of benefit receivers to employed workers also depleted the fund. Benefit outlays of the Social Security program increased from $68.2 billion in 1970 to $135 billion in 1980.[35]

As with FAP and SSI, competitive bidding between the two parties and Nixon's desire to expand the base of the Republican Party led a conservative president to support massive increases in social spending. Nixon's failure to increase payroll taxes, when coupled with a steady decline in the proportion of wage earners to retirees, ensured the emergence of a funding crisis for Social Security, which had to be addressed by subsequent presidents. However, largely as a result of the Social Security increases the percentage of elderly persons below the poverty line decreased from 29.5 to 15 percent between 1967 and 1979—and to less than 5 percent when the value of in-kind benefits, such as medical care, was included.

Revenue Sharing and Social Services

In response to Republican concerns that the New Deal and the Great Society had concentrated excessive power in the federal bureaucracy, Nixon developed the idea of revenue sharing. He proposed to give federal funds directly to local units of government, with few strings attached, so that local officials could decide how they wished to use them. Nixon also had more sinister motivations for this policy. He had become increasingly paranoid about the federal bureaucracy in his first three years of office and was convinced that federal bureaucrats, in liaison with sympathetic legislators and supportive (liberal) interest groups, had wrested

power from him. By giving funds directly to the local and state units of government, he hoped to bypass the federal bureaucracy and even, to some extent, the Congress, which no longer would be able to develop specific programs. (Congress would merely allocate funds that local governments could use, more or less, as they pleased.)[36]

The Local Fiscal Assistance Act of 1972 gave funds to local governments to use for their operating expenses. To supplement this general revenue sharing, Nixon also proposed special revenue sharing, in the form of six block grants to local governments to provide resources in broad areas such as housing and job training. This special revenue sharing would, Nixon argued, eventually replace many of the existing federal programs, which he portrayed as encumbered by excessive federal rules, guidelines, and regulations.[37] Why not, he asked, simultaneously terminate some existing programs and give local governments relatively unrestricted funds to spend on broad program areas? He had little success in obtaining special revenue sharing, however, because many members of Congress did not want to relinquish their control of federal programs and feared that some states would deny support to relatively powerless groups who benefited from existing federal programs. Nixon obtained passage of only two special revenue-sharing programs, the Comprehensive Employment and Training Act of 1973 (CETA) and the Community Development Block Grant portion of the Housing and Community Development Act of 1974 (CDBG).

General and special revenue sharing were suited to Nixon's political strategy, for they represented a brand of social reform that was different from traditional Democratic programs. Some of Lyndon Johnson's advisors, notably economist Walter Heller, had themselves urged passage of revenue sharing, but Johnson had demurred in favor of traditional categorical programs.[38] The policy field was thus open to Nixon, and he seized the opportunity to enact his version of reform. By so doing, Nixon hoped to gain the support of state and local officials, who liked revenue sharing because it augmented their funds. Between 1973 and 1980, the federal government paid roughly $6 billion a year in general revenue sharing to local governments, which substantially eased their fiscal problems during the 1970s.[39] Critics noted, however, that local authorities often did not use these resources to help disadvantaged citizens. In one city, CDBG funds were used to build a municipal golf course!

Job-training programs had proliferated in a disorderly fashion during the 1960s. Nixon proposed to consolidate them in the Comprehensive Employment and Training Act (CETA). The administrative mechanism devised for CETA vested considerable power in state and local organizations, known as prime sponsors, which issued contracts with public agencies and industry to provide jobs and job training. Under Title VI, CETA subsidized hundreds of thousands of public service jobs in both public and nonprofit agencies. These jobs were not means-tested; applicants had merely to demonstrate that they were unemployed. Incredibly, a Republican president had proposed and obtained enactment of a proposal that recalled the public works programs of the 1930s.[40]

As we discussed in Chapter 8, Congress gave states 75 percent matching funds in 1962 to provide social services to existing or potential recipients of AFDC. Some states seemed unaware of the legislation or used the money only for traditional services, such as home visits to AFDC recipients; but discerning policy analysts in various states, including California, Oregon, Pennsylvania, and Washington, realized that they could use these funds to develop a range of programs. Furthermore, when a federal administrator who prized expansiveness replaced a cost-conscious one, the use of the funds increased dramatically; some state officials were allowed to use the funds for drug, mental health, public education, and even highway construction programs.[41]

In 1972, the Nixon administration sought to place a ceiling on this runaway program. To protect the program and to counter HEW regulations that limited its services to persons currently receiving or applying for welfare, the Congress created Title XX of the Social Security Act, which allocated funds to states according to a prescribed formula for use—with broad latitude by each state—in programs to enhance individuals' ability to be self-supporting, family care or self-care, community-based care, and institutional care. The legislation was enacted in 1974.[42] States usually chose relatively traditional services, such as day care, that were provided by established agencies. To impose discipline on the program, a ceiling of $2.5 billion was established for annual expenditures—a figure that remained relatively constant in succeeding years. Title XX represented the first time that the federal government had officially committed itself to funding a variety of social services to persons who were usually near or under the poverty line. It also illustrated the reformist nature of Nixon's first term. Nixon, who despised services and social workers, did not veto legislation that covered services for existing and potential welfare recipients in a block grant.

Civil Rights

Nixon's strange mixture of conservative rhetoric and liberal deeds was nowhere more conspicuous than in civil rights. Nixon had won five Southern states in the presidential election of 1968 and hoped to increase his Southern gains in 1972, but he feared that George Wallace would again try to sweep the South by supporting racist policies. Thus, Nixon did not support desegregation of Southern schools in 1969 and 1970. He fired a liberal attorney in the Justice Department who favored cutting federal funds from segregated districts, and he supported a proposed constitutional amendment to prohibit busing. Nixon often used rhetoric that relied on code words—for example, "the silent majority of law-abiding citizens"—to appeal to racial animosities in the broader population.

Yet some commentators believe that Nixon's policies on racial issues constitute a strength of his administration.[43] When federal courts insisted that intentional segregation had to be terminated, Nixon finally relented and empowered George Shultz, his secretary of labor, to organize a series of Southern committees that succeeded in securing voluntary desegregation. When the number of African American students in segregated Southern schools was reduced from 68 percent in 1968 to 8 percent in 1972, the cycle of reform in the South that had begun with the Civil Rights Act of 1964 and the Voting Rights Act of 1965 was completed.[44] Nixon's successes in the South were not matched by similar efforts in the North, where he chose to oppose busing to combat the de facto segregation. However, federal courts issued rulings in the 1970s and 1980s that led to the massive use of busing in Northern cities to desegregate schools—a policy that proved to be exceedingly controversial. Indeed, extensive "white flight" to suburban areas and to private schools ensued in the next three decades; however, he chose not to use busing to combat de facto segregation.

Between 1971 and 1974, Congress and the administration enacted a variety of laws and administrative measures that prohibited gender-based discrimination in training programs and employment. HEW instituted legal action to force colleges to end discrimination against women, just as the Supreme Court struck down various local laws that discriminated against women. The Justice Department brought suit against such corporations as American Telephone and Telegraph (AT&T) and won large awards for women who had been denied promotions. Women made extraordinary gains in obtaining training and membership in the professions and business.[45] Nixon approved the Equal Employment Opportunity Act of 1972, which gave the Equal Employment Opportunity Commission the power to use court rulings to enforce its orders. His administration included women in affirmative action orders that were sent to federal contractors.[46]

Moreover, the Nixon administration developed the so-called Philadelphia plan, which required building contractors that obtained federal contracts to institute affirmative action—a policy stoutly opposed by trade unions. This plan was subsequently extended to all federal contractors, as well as to state and local employees such as local police and fire departments. (These policies led to extraordinary increases in the employment of people of color and women by public agencies.)[47]

The Rehabilitation Act of 1973 was a historic measure to accord persons with disabilities protections from discrimination (see Figure 9.1). Section 504 states that "no otherwise qualified handicapped individual … shall … be excluded from participating

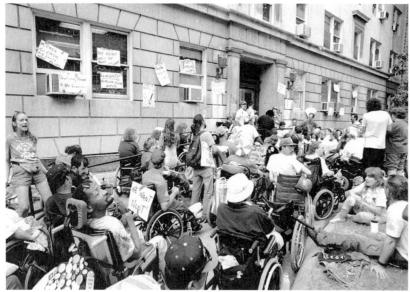

© AP Photo/Joe Marquette

F I G U R E 9.1 Championing the rights of physically challenged persons.

in, be denied the benefits of, or be subjected to discrimination under any program or activity receiving federal assistance." This legislation, as well as associated lawsuits, led to massive efforts to make buildings, public transportation, and jobs accessible to persons with disabilities.[48] Funds were appropriated to assist the mainstreaming of students with disabilities in public schools under the Education for All Handicapped Act of 1975.[49]

Health Policy and Other Legislation

Various health and family measures were enacted during Nixon's administration. Medicare was revised in 1973 to extend coverage to nonelderly persons with kidney disease. The Health Maintenance Act of 1973 provided seed money to promote the establishment of medical organizations funded by annual payments from enrollees rather than traditional fee-for-service payments.[50] The Family Planning and Population Research Act of 1970 had helped 4 million low-income women, including 1.3 million teenagers, obtain family-planning services by 1980.[51] The Juvenile Justice and Delinquency Act of 1974 provided resources to local juvenile diversion projects to help runaways and truants who had previously been stigmatized by court and juvenile detention services.[52] The Child Abuse Prevention Act of 1974 provided research funds to be disseminated to universities and pilot projects to develop effective interventions.[53]

The Occupational Safety and Health Act of 1970 (OSHA) was landmark legislation that propelled the federal government into oversight of safety standards in American industry, in an era when toxic chemicals and new technology demanded new protections. The Department of Labor was charged with devising standards and establishing local agencies to implement inspection.[54]

Finally, legislation enacted in 1975 established an Earned Income Tax Credit (EITC). Workers who earned less than $4,000 per year were given a tax credit (a payment) equivalent to 10 percent of their earnings. Though modest, it was the first legislation to use the tax system as a vehicle for giving resources to the poor.

Housing Legislation

The United States had developed public housing projects for poor and elderly persons since the 1930s, but it had not evolved a system for subsidizing the rents of tenants in housing owned by private landlords. This was a serious omission because it meant that low-income tenants *had* to live in public housing projects—often segregated by class and race—rather than having a range of housing choices that included living in mixed-income and integrated neighborhoods.

The Housing and Community Development Act of 1974 established the Section 8 housing program to pay up to 70 percent of the housing costs of tenants who rent from private landlords. It is administered by local public housing authorities. Eligibility is determined by household income of tenants—with most families having incomes not exceeding 30 percent of the median income for a specific geographic area.

Section 8 provided, then, vouchers to low-income families—and came to serve 1.8 million persons by 2004 with appropriations of roughly $17 billion. Even with these resources, only a small fraction of low-income persons are served by the program, which has long waiting lists in most jurisdictions.

NIXON'S SHIFT FROM REFORM TO CONSERVATISM

Social reform flourished in the first three years of Nixon's first term. Spending for poverty programs had increased by $27 billion in the Kennedy and Johnson administrations (in 1986 dollars), but it increased by $54 billion in the Nixon and Ford administrations.[55] When confronted with a deep recession, trade deficits, and inflation, Nixon even imposed wage and price controls in 1971.[56] But during this liberal period, Nixon's rhetoric remained staunchly conservative, even as he supported reform measures; he regularly lambasted programs of the Great Society, "big spenders," and liberalism and remained silent on the subjects of civil rights and race relations. He repeatedly attacked service programs staffed by social workers, child development specialists, psychologists, psychiatrists, and community activists. He believed that these programs were ineffective, coddled the poor, and represented a misguided Democratic approach to social reform. He sought major reductions in federal funding of neighborhood health centers, community action programs, and community mental health centers.[57] Head Start was saved from massive cuts only because of its extraordinary political popularity.

Nixon's antipathy to service programs was illustrated by his veto of child development legislation in 1971. The Head Start program had stimulated interest in expanding funding for preschool, day care, regional planning, and advocacy services for children, and some experts were convinced that many families were endangered by high divorce rates and women's increasing rates of employment. In that context, legislation was initiated in House and Senate committees to provide a variety of free or low-cost services to American families. It was the veto of this legislation that partly led Marian Wright Edelman to found the Children's Defense Fund in 1973.

It was uncertain whether Nixon would support this legislation. When his HEW secretary, Elliot Richardson, insisted in 1971 that the legislation be amended to make it more acceptable to the administration, some observers took this as a promising sign. But Nixon vetoed it, with conservative language that reflected the ideology of the right wing of the Republican Party. He charged that the legislation would destroy the institution of the family, which should be retained "in its rightful position as the keystone of our civilization [and] would commit the vast moral authority to [institutional] child rearing as against the family-centered approach." It was a devastating blow to reformers, who were unable to obtain similar legislation in succeeding years.[58]

A changing political climate shaped Nixon's decision by the summer of 1972—and even more obviously by the fall of 1973—to disavow new social legislation. It had been reasonable to assume in 1968, after the Great Society, that blue-collar and white ethnic Americans could be wooed by social initiatives like FAP, SSI, national health insurance, and the indexing of Social Security. Partly because of the conservative rhetoric of Nixon and Agnew, however, many white ethnic, blue-collar, and middle-class persons had become preoccupied with issues of crime, inflation, and government spending by 1972 and had become resentful of African Americans, who were, they believed, receiving unwarranted or disproportionate benefits from federal programs. The term *white backlash* has been used to characterize the resentments of these citizens.[59]

White Americans had also become alarmed by the tactics and language used by the various reform groups that had emerged in the late 1960s.[60] The new militancy of these groups stemmed in considerable measure from disillusionment with the Great Society. African Americans realized that the civil rights gains of the 1960s, which had largely addressed legal and overt discrimination in the South, had not slowed the segregation of African Americans into urban ghettoes or the expansion of an African American underclass, whose members had limited education and high unemployment and often depended on AFDC, Food Stamps, and other social programs. Leaders of vulnerable populations—African Americans, women, Latinos, First Americans, gay men and lesbians, and people with disabilities—spoke of their feelings of inferiority that stemmed from living in a society that overtly or covertly discriminated against them. African Americans urged one another to develop pride in their race and heritage; women advocated feminist education to develop solidarity; First Americans and Latinos organized protests against government officials, schools, and universities; leaders of the gay and lesbian communities urged their members to declare their sexual orientations publicly and pressured politicians and employers to end discriminatory practices; and people with disabilities demanded access to jobs, buildings, and public transportation. Efforts to mobilize these populations alienated many white Americans, who resented the separatism and the challenge to dominant policies that the new rhetoric implied. (See Insert 9.3.)

Nixon and Agnew realized that they could exploit this situation for their political benefit.[61] Why

---

I N S E R T 9.3   Critical Analysis: What Created White Backlash?

People in the working class or in the lower middle class ought, in theory, to support social programs. Possessing relatively meager resources and experiencing job insecurity, they or their family members sometimes use social programs such as Medicaid and Food Stamps, just as their parents use Medicare. Yet white backlash developed most acutely in this group, such as Catholic voters in the North and white blue-collar voters in the South. Its most celebrated representative was the fictional character Archie Bunker from the TV show *All in the Family*.

   Analyze why this group, whose ancestors had often been part of the Roosevelt coalition in the New Deal, became disenchanted with the American welfare state, often voted for presidential candidates such as George Wallace in the 1960s, Richard Nixon in the 1970s, and Ronald Reagan in the 1980s, and granted Newt Gingrich a Republican landslide in the 1994 congressional elections and George W. Bush in two elections.

1.   What, if anything, might reformers have done differently to retain the goodwill of this group?
2.   Is white backlash in evidence in contemporary society? Has it been present in recent debates about immigration policy?

---

not, they reasoned, condemn the rhetoric and tactics of reformist groups to turn working-class and middle-class persons against activists and reformers? Why not try to identify the Democratic Party with these groups—and themselves with "the silent majority of law-abiding citizens"? Their resolve was strengthened when public opinion polls indicated that crime and inflation were the issues of most concern to many Americans, who believed that civil rights, social spending, and social reform efforts had proceeded too rapidly. These sentiments were linked to the growing economic distress of *stagflation*, the combination of high unemployment and inflation.[62] Economic stagnation made some blue-collar Americans fear that African Americans, women, and others might take jobs from them, and inflation reduced the real income of many families and made credit hard to obtain as interest rates soared. Furthermore, many Americans believed that the only way to decrease the rate of inflation was to cut social spending.[63]

   Nixon was also quick to capitalize on developments within the Democratic Party. Following the 1968 election, Democrats made a concerted effort to increase participation by African Americans, women, and others in party councils at the expense of the power of incumbent politicians and power brokers, such as Mayor Richard Daley of Chicago. These reforms, however, boosted the political fortunes of Richard Nixon, who was able to argue that the Democratic Party had been taken over by special interests. When the party reforms allowed a particularly liberal senator—George McGovern—to obtain the Democratic nomination for the presidency in 1972, Nixon portrayed him as an extremist who was beholden to these interests.[64]

   Nixon's conservative policies were also promoted, of course, by Republican conservatives, who believed that they represented the mainstream of the party. At first, Nixon's conservative advisors, such as the economist Arthur Burns and Martin Anderson, had been outflanked by liberal advisors, such as Robert Finch, Daniel Moynihan, and Elliot Richardson; but there was a definite thinning in the ranks of liberal advisors as Nixon's first term progressed. Indeed, by 1972, conservative John Ehrlichman emerged as Nixon's leading advisor on domestic matters.[65]

   Soon after his reelection in 1972, Nixon began a personal war against liberals that was motivated by his political decision to move toward the right, to fight inflation with budget cuts, and to discipline federal civil servants, who, he had come to believe, colluded with special interests and liberal congressional aides to resist the implementation of conservative policies. Nixon manipulated the civil service system to place into office conservative persons of dubious merit, impounded funds that had already been appropriated by Congress for social programs, proposed significant decreases in the funds of most major programs, and demanded a drastic reduction of the federal workforce. Because many members of Congress and the federal bureaucracy were embittered by these tactics, an atmosphere of suspicion and polarization developed in the Capitol.[66] Huge battles over national priorities took place from 1971 onward as Nixon vetoed many budget recommendations of the Congress on the grounds they gave too much money to the nonentitlement portion of the domestic agenda.

Social spending increased markedly in the Nixon years, primarily due to a dramatic rise in spending on entitlements, which more than doubled between 1960 and 1975. (Indeed, total spending on entitlements actually exceeded total spending on military and related spending in 1974.) Moreover, military spending markedly declined as American involvement in Vietnam diminished and finally ended by early 1973. When spending on entitlements is aggregated with spending on education, training, employment, and social programs, the American welfare state consumed almost 45 percent of the federal budget as compared with less than 20 percent in 1960—a startling turnaround in fiscal terms.

Yet Nixon established conditions that would lead to a battle for resources during the late 1970s and the 1980s. By cutting the military only back to the levels that had preceded the Vietnam War in 1964 (when measured in constant dollars), he kept military spending at its Cold War levels even though many critics wondered why the United States needed such vast "overkill" of nuclear warheads. (The United States possessed more than 11,000 nuclear warheads in 1975 as compared with less than 4,000 in the Soviet Union.) Many persons wondered, as well, why the United States did not insist that European nations carry a greater burden of their own defense rather than relying so heavily on the United States for ground and air forces.

Nixon also waged war on a portion of the welfare state financed by so-called discretionary funding. If entitlements like Social Security, Medicare,

and Food Stamps are automatically funded by the federal government to the level of claimed benefits during a specific year, other domestic programs (such as education, training, employment, and social programs) are funded from the discretionary budget that Congress can control each year. Nixon repeatedly attacked these discretionary social programs as "ineffective" and "wasteful." He often failed to spend the funds that Congress had appropriated for them in a practice known as impoundment. By arguing that they belonged under the purview of local and state governments, he implied that the federal government's primary domestic obligation was to fund entitlements. Nixon's attack on these discretionary social and educational programs was unwarranted. Persons desperately needed additional education and training to secure jobs that paid an adequate wage as increasing numbers of unionized, well-paying jobs disappeared in the United States when many American corporations located their assembly lines abroad and as Japanese and European corporations competed more effectively with American corporations. If persons who possessed a high school education had been able to find high-paying unionized assembly-line jobs in prior decades, they increasingly became unemployed or cast into low-wage service jobs in restaurants, emerging fast-food chains, or in malls. Such cities as Flint and Detroit, Michigan, which had been relatively affluent, became blighted with boarded-up stores, vacant houses, and growing poverty. Other social problems became more serious in the 1970s, such as substance abuse, which took a tragic toll on millions of Americans who became addicted to cocaine. With nearly two times the amount of revenues as all state and local governments put together, the federal government possessed resources desperately needed to upgrade an array of social programs in addition to funding entitlements. A good case can be made, then, that federal discretionary spending should have been markedly increased in the 1970s rather than bitterly assaulted by the incumbent president.

Nixon's effectiveness in waging this war against liberalism was stymied, however, by the aftermath of a break-in at the Democratic campaign headquarters in the Watergate Office Building in 1972. Investigations by the Justice Department and by Congress, which focused at first on the burglars, soon implicated presidential aides, cabinet officials, and Nixon himself. The Congress was on the verge of impeachment proceedings when Nixon resigned from office in August of 1974. He was succeeded by Vice President Gerald Ford.

THE BRIEF REIGN OF
GERALD FORD

Ford was a political conservative who had spent years in the Congress criticizing programs of the Great Society. He was, moreover, an unimaginative man who was unable to initiate legislation even when urged by his advisors. As did Nixon, he became even more conservative as his term progressed. Nelson Rockefeller, his vice president, pressured Ford to endorse urban development reforms, to expand health care, and to support other policy reforms; but Rockefeller's power, as well as that of other liberal Republicans, was soon eclipsed in internal power struggles within the administration.[67] Ford's major policy became the presidential veto, which he used with remarkable frequency to stymie legislation and spending increases proposed by the Congress.

Because of Democratic majorities in both houses, Congress was able to override a number of vetoes and to increase funding for school lunches, education, and health care programs. Ford finally realized that increases in social spending were needed to counter the deep recession of 1975, though Congress had to override his veto to establish a public works program to help the unemployed. His term can best be characterized as a continuing stalemate between conservatives and liberals over the size of social spending.[68]

Little social legislation was enacted during Ford's tenure. The Education for All Handicapped Children Act, which was passed in 1975, provided federal subsidies to schools so that children with physical and mental disabilities could be mainstreamed into regular classes. Although it allowed many children with disabilities to escape special institutions, inadequate funding in succeeding years much diminished its effects.[69]

JIMMY CARTER: OUTSIDER
IN THE WHITE HOUSE

A journalist who had covered five prior presidential campaigns wrote that he had never experienced more pervasive suspicion of government among the electorate than in 1976.[70] Jimmy Carter, an astute Southern politician who had recently finished his term as governor of Georgia, decided in 1972 to mount a campaign to secure the Democratic nomination for the presidency in 1976. He was relatively unknown outside the South and had virtually no links to trade unions, powerful incumbent politicians, or other groups that usually helped Democratic aspirants, but his relative obscurity became an asset in the post-Watergate political climate of 1976. When he lambasted the federal bureaucracy, red tape, and undue centralization of authority in the nation, he did not seem hypocritical because he had not participated in their development.[71]

Carter's outsider status enabled him to develop a strategy to appeal to a cross-section of political opinion. His attacks on the political establishment appealed to some populist liberals. To obtain support from conservatives, he emphasized moral values, his religious convictions as a born-again Baptist, his Southern background, his dislike of big-spending liberals, and his support of major increases in defense spending. Moderates liked his cultivation of big business, his internationalism, and his emphasis on making the federal government less corrupt and more efficient. Most moderates and conservatives liked his antigovernment rhetoric. Carter told all groups that he was an efficient problem solver who would not succumb to politics-as-usual when making decisions.[72]

Carter obtained the Democratic nomination by developing grassroots organizations in primary states before other Democratic candidates did so. He also ran a clever race against Gerald Ford, who was tainted by his prior association with the discredited Nixon—and, in particular, by his decision to pardon Nixon and so exempt him from prosecution for Watergate. Ford's membership in the Washington establishment and the recession of 1975 were also liabilities. Carter won the election by a slim margin when he carried the South and key Midwestern states.

Even the most astute president would have found it difficult to govern in 1976, however. Congressional legislators insisted on full participation in the legislative process after Watergate and were eager to demonstrate their resentment of Carter's repeated criticisms of Congress. Many legislators had also developed specific programs that they wanted to enact after a string of vetoes by Nixon and Ford.[73] Carter encountered a bleak economic situation, as well. He inherited a massive deficit from Ford, high rates of inflation, and increasing levels of social spending. Inflation became a national crisis when Middle Eastern countries decided to stop shipments of oil to the United States, in reprisal for American assistance to Israel. When gasoline prices rose from 37 cents per gallon in 1970 to $1.60 in 1977, double-digit inflation became a reality.

Carter was ill equipped to contend with these harsh political and economic realities. As an aloof problem solver, he did not enjoy the give-and-take of the political process. He liked to tackle problems in the isolation of the White House.[74] His condescending attitude toward legislators infuriated them, as did his disinclination to consult them. Carter surrounded himself, moreover, with untested advisors from Georgia who did not communicate with legislators. Several years after the election, Tip O'Neill, the Democratic majority leader in the House, had not even met Hamilton Jordan, Carter's chief advisor. Carter failed to develop alliances with groups and legislators who would normally have assisted a Democratic president. Union leaders distrusted him because he opposed increases in the minimum wage; Catholics and Jews were antagonized by his flaunting of his Protestant fundamentalism; big-city mayors believed that he did not understand urban problems; and social reformers believed him to be indifferent to the needs of the poor.[75] Carter was

unable, moreover, to intelligently schedule his domestic measures. Disdaining partial or incremental approaches in favor of comprehensive solutions, Carter overwhelmed Congress with his rapid-fire delivery of comprehensive energy, welfare, government reorganization, and health measures.[76]

Carter's Domestic Legislation

Unlike Roosevelt, Truman, and Johnson, Carter was not much interested in domestic legislation. His priorities were reorganization of the federal bureaucracy, the Middle East, renegotiation of the Panama Canal Treaty, and energy policy. He did not like proposals that required major funding of social programs because he favored reductions in federal spending.[77] Critics contend, as well, that he was ill disposed to welfare recipients, alcoholics, and drug addicts, whom he believed to make fraudulent use of government programs.[78] He enacted relatively little social legislation because of his political style and intrinsic conservatism, as well as the difficult political and economic environment that he encountered.

Carter supported national health insurance in his campaign of 1976 but, once elected, he took no action on this measure until Senator Edward Kennedy, brother of the late president, accused him of reneging on his campaign promise. Fearing that this issue could be used against him if Kennedy opposed him for the presidential nomination in 1980, Carter belatedly introduced his own version of health insurance in 1979. Carter's proposal combined an insurance plan for employees, to be financed by payroll deductions, and a government-funded scheme for nonworkers.[79] Kennedy's scheme favored government controls, government financing, and government regulation of health care. Neither Carter's nor Kennedy's scheme was politically feasible in the climate of 1979, as double-digit inflation and large deficits made politicians unwilling to increase government spending.

In 1977, Carter introduced a comprehensive scheme for welfare reform, which, like Nixon's a few years earlier, became caught in a cross-fire between liberals and conservatives. Carter's scheme was imaginative and more ambitious than FAP. He proposed to consolidate AFDC, Food Stamps, and SSI so as to provide a national minimum income for families, individuals, and elderly persons. He envisioned a three-tiered benefit system, in which able-bodied but nonworking persons received the lowest benefits, persons who were exempted from work (persons with disabilities and women with preschool children) received middle-level benefits, and the working poor received the highest benefits (when added to their earned income). He also proposed the creation of 1.4 million public service jobs for recipients.[80]

Controversy was heated and wide-ranging; Joseph Califano, secretary of the Department of Health and Human Services from 1977 to 1979, described welfare reform as the Middle East of domestic politics.[81] Conservatives wanted to exempt only women with children under the age of 6 from the work requirement, whereas many liberals wanted to exempt women with children under the age of 14. Conservatives insisted that persons holding public service jobs receive prevailing wages, whereas liberals wanted them to be paid the federal minimum wage. Some defenders of Food Stamps and SSI objected to their merger into the larger welfare reform program. Legislators quibbled about the relative size of the minimum benefits for nonworking recipients and the monies to be spent on work incentives for the employed poor. Many conservatives feared that the extension of governmental benefits to working persons would pauperize them.[82]

Not surprisingly, then, welfare reform was defeated in the Senate in 1978. Califano concluded in 1981 that comprehensive reform of the American welfare system was probably not politically feasible; attention should focus instead on incremental improvements, as well as experiments to test controversial policies.[83] This pessimistic appraisal could be extended to national health insurance, which seemed as politically elusive as welfare reform.

Despite the existence of CETA, millions of Americans had suffered the trauma of unemployment during the 1970s, at least briefly; its toll on their physical and mental health was considerable. People of color and teenagers bore a particularly heavy burden; more than 30 percent of them

were unemployed in many areas. In 1974, Senator Hubert Humphrey and Congressman Augustus Hawkins introduced legislation to improve the situation by requiring the creation of federal public service jobs whenever the national unemployment rate exceeded 3 percent.[84] The legislation was strongly opposed by the Ford administration on the grounds that it was not feasible to create this many jobs, that federal jobs would draw persons away from the private sector, that the cost of the measure was prohibitive, and that public sector jobs would make many persons dependent on government.[85] Humphrey and Hawkins reintroduced their legislation in 1976, after Carter had been elected, hoping that strong support by the administration would facilitate its passage. Though he gave his support, Carter did not aggressively fight efforts by conservatives to amend the legislation. When finally enacted in 1978, the Full Employment and Balanced Growth Act was so diluted that it had become meaningless.[86]

Carter's conservatism curbed his support for various measures to help children. His legislation to provide comprehensive services to families headed by teenagers was enacted but was hardly funded because the administration did not decisively promote it.[87] He did not support expanded federal funding of child care because it would have required major new federal expenditures.[88] Carter vacillated on legislation to extend federal subsidies to local centers that helped battered women; strong opposition from conservatives, who insisted that social workers exaggerated the extent of the problem, defeated the legislation in 1980.[89]

Carter was nonetheless able to obtain passage of legislation that sought to rescue children from long-term stays in the foster care system, which provided inadequate care and shuffled children from one short-term placement to another. Although AFDC paid the costs of court-ordered foster care placements, the federal government had traditionally left the funding and planning of adoption and foster care services to local public and private agencies. Hundreds of thousands of children were served by this system; unless they were adopted or returned to their parental homes, children had no escape from it. Those most likely to remain in foster care were children of color, older children, and children with serious physical and mental disabilities. To encourage local child welfare agencies to pursue adoptions for these children, the Adoption Assistance and Child Welfare Act of 1980 provided federal subsidies to families that adopted children and required states to maintain status reports on all children in foster care so that they could be expeditiously placed for adoption or returned to their parental homes within specified time limits. In addition, the legislation expanded federal assistance to states for foster care.[90]

Carter was also able to expand Medicaid programs to screen and treat low-income children and to help pregnant women.[91] The federal government had required local authorities to screen low-income children under the 1965 Medicaid legislation, but compliance had been inadequate, and screened children were often not helped with treatment even when serious problems were found.

In the area of civil rights, Carter seemed more intent on consolidating existing laws than adding new protections because he wanted to retain the support of Southerners, who had been indispensable to his victory in 1976. He was sufficiently indifferent to issues of affirmative action that he supported a white plaintiff, Allan Bakke, who sued a public medical school of the University of California on the grounds that its admission policies gave preference to people of color with lesser qualifications. After Joseph Califano, the HEW secretary, persuaded the administration to oppose Bakke, the Justice Department provided testimony that eventually influenced the Supreme Court to uphold the principle of affirmative action while disallowing the use of numerical quotas.[92]

The rights of persons with disabilities were enhanced during the Carter administration, though only after extensive pressure from certain interest groups. The Architectural and Transportation Compliance Board, established in 1973, issued regulations in 1980 that required extensive modifications in federal buildings.[93]

Rosalynn Carter, the wife of the president, made mental health her major domestic issue and

assumed an important role in establishing a Presidential Commission on Mental Health. In 1978, this commission issued a four-volume report that analyzed many program, policy, and financing issues in the mental health system. The report cited the lack of insurance coverage for outpatient services, inadequate community services for persons with chronic and severe mental problems in community settings, and a lack of services for elderly and adolescent populations.[94] Its findings did not lead to major reforms, however, for the resulting legislation, the Mental Health Systems Act of 1980, did not provide centers with sufficient funds to implement the new services that it mandated.

A financing crisis in the Social Security program prompted an important policy debate in the administration. Califano believed that Social Security should provide a safety net for those elderly persons who were poor, but he proposed taxing the benefits of more affluent elderly persons so that proceeds from the tax could be used to bail out the trust fund. However, some of the founders of the Social Security program, such as Wilbur Cohen, believed that benefits should continue to bear a strong relationship to the amount of payroll taxes that persons had paid into the system—that affluent persons, having paid higher taxes, should receive higher benefits than other persons. Cohen feared that Califano's proposal would encourage the transformation of Social Security into a welfare rather than a universal program.[95] Califano lost this battle, but his recommendation was approved during Ronald Reagan's first term, when it became obvious that even the major increases in the payroll taxes that Carter had engineered were insufficient to preserve the solvency of the trust fund.[96]

The SSI program grew at a fantastic pace during the mid-1970s because thousands of persons with mental and physical disabilities were using it. Carter resolved to slow its rate of increase by restricting benefits to the level of wages that recipients had received before their disability and by allowing them to retain their Medicaid benefits. He also pressured administrative judges, who were hired by the government to decide whether persons were entitled to SSI, to make fewer favorable decisions. Although there had been abuse of the program, the new policy had its own dangers, for it deprived some persons with severe disabilities of the benefits they needed.[97]

The Department of Health, Education, and Welfare grew rapidly during the 1960s and 1970s, but staff morale plummeted following successive cuts in personnel and heavier workloads. The staff needed leadership from a president who would empathize with their problems, reduce pointless regulations, and troubleshoot logistical and other problems.[98] Carter was often as paranoid as Nixon about federal bureaucrats. Nonetheless, he placed Medicare and Medicaid under a single office known as the Health Care and Finance Administration, eliminated many unnecessary regulations, and established a department for tracking and assessing programs and policies and imposing budgetary controls. Finally, in a controversial move that was partly inspired by Carter's desire to repay the National Education Association for its assistance in the 1976 election, the Office of Education was separated from HEW, which was renamed the Department of Health and Human Services (DHHS).[99]

By 1978, Carter had decided to effect massive cuts in social programs as part of his desperate effort to stem double-digit inflation and to accommodate substantial increases in military spending. The budget cuts in the last two years of Carter's administration can be seen as the beginning of a long conservative assault on social spending, which extended through the presidency of Ronald Reagan.[100]

To the chagrin of feminists, Carter was militantly against abortion and supported a constitutional amendment to overrule the Supreme Court's 1973 *Roe v. Wade* decision, which had declared unconstitutional state laws that prohibited abortions during the first trimester. When a constitutional amendment proved to be politically impractical, Carter supported legislation to prohibit use of federal Medicaid funds for abortions.[101] The legislation, eventually enacted, allowed the use of Medicaid funds for abortions only in very narrowly defined circumstances; in practice, low-income women could obtain abortions with Medicaid funds only if their lives were endangered by childbirth or else within 72 hours of a rape or

incest.[102] As a result of this legislation, the number of federally financed abortions declined from 275,000 in 1976 to 1,250 in 1978, and most abortions for low-income women had to be financed by local government and charitable institutions, not just in the late 1970s but in the next two decades. Unlike more affluent women, some poor women were driven to illegal (and frequently dangerous) low-cost abortions or delivered unwanted children because of the difficulty of obtaining abortions from local institutions.[103]

Carter's Fall

Only two years after his election, Carter had the worst popularity rating of any president in recent American history at a comparable point in his term. It sank even further by 1979, in the wake of soaring oil prices, continuing stagflation, a Congress that wanted to assert its independence, and widespread public disenchantment with government.[104]

Carter was nonetheless able to obtain the Democratic nomination for the presidency in 1980, despite a vigorous challenge by Senator Edward Kennedy. But Carter faced another outsider, who used many of the same anti-establishment tactics that he himself had used in 1976. This time, however, Carter was the insider; the outsider was Ronald Reagan, his Republican opponent. Carter was dealt a final misfortune when he failed to free a group of hostages captured by a band of terrorists who overran the American embassy in Iran. Reagan defeated Carter easily in the 1980 election and began a new era of conservative policies that attacked the liberal reforms of the preceding 50 years.

THE HIDDEN SOCIAL SPENDING REVOLUTION OF THE 1970s

The policy changes that were made in the 1970s constitute a hidden social spending revolution in American social policy. Nondefense spending went from 8.1 percent of the gross national product in 1961 to 11.3 percent in 1971 and 15.6 percent in 1981. About two-thirds of this domestic budget consisted of social insurance and means-tested social programs. Total federal social spending rose from $67 billion in 1960 to $158 billion in 1970 (in 1980 dollars) and to $314 billion in 1980.[105] Many social programs grew tremendously in their total cost during the 1970s, as Table 9.2 illustrates.[106]

For the first time in American history, a relatively sophisticated safety net of social programs existed for persons who lacked resources, whether because they were old, unemployed, ill, or poor. Many persons used only a single program. A man who became unemployed during the recession of 1976 might use only unemployment benefits because he considered use of Food Stamps or Medicaid programs to be unnecessary or stigmatizing or because his net income made him ineligible for them. Other families used only the Food Stamps Program, and still others only received Medicaid. Other families qualified for Section 8 housing assistance. The wide range of cash transfer, in-kind, and services programs allowed families to select specific

programs that improved their quality of life at a specific point in time.[107]

Other consumers used combinations of programs. A single woman with several preschool or school-age children might receive AFDC, Food Stamps, and health services reimbursed by Medicaid and live in publicly subsidized housing. An elderly family might use Medicare, SSI, and Social Security benefits. A young adult who had received a kidney transplant could receive SSI as well as medical services from Medicare. An unemployed person could receive unemployment insurance, job training from CETA, Food Stamps, and Medicaid. The availability of combinations of programs was crucial to many individuals and families—especially to large families, whose members needed a range of services and resources.[108]

Many people used such programs as unemployment insurance, Food Stamps, and Medicaid for brief periods of unemployment, illness, or poverty; others needed assistance for longer periods. Of all the recipients of the nation's welfare programs, about 50 percent used them for less than three years; about 33 percent used them for three to seven years; and

T A B L E 9.2   Increases in Outlays for Specific Programs (in Billions of Constant Dollars) during the 1970s

	1970		1980	
	Federal	Total	Federal	Total
Food Stamps	2.0	2.0	10.0	10.0
SSI	—	4.1	7.0	8.6
Unemployment insurance	7.7	7.7	18.5	18.5
Medicaid	5.8	10.9	15.3	25.4
Medicare	15.2	15.2	38.3	38.3
AFDC	5.1	9.2	8.8	13.9
CETA and MDTA	2.4	2.4	3.6	3.6
Social Security[*]	68.2	68.2	134.8	134.8
Housing assistance	2.8	2.8	4.9	4.9
Total	109.2	122.5	241.4	258.0

* Expenditures include federal costs as well as spending from funds generated by payroll taxes.

about 12 percent used them for eight or more years.[109] Impoverished women with children were likely to use AFDC, Food Stamps, and Medicaid. Unemployed men tended to use unemployment insurance and Food Stamps. Elderly people used SSI, Social Security, Medicare, and Medicaid. Persons with disabilities used SSI and Social Security disability benefits. (The Social Security program had become far more than a pension program for elderly people by the 1970s because its benefits often subsidized surviving family members when a parent died and helped pay for the education of surviving children.)[110] The programs were not used only by low-income persons; indeed, roughly three of every four dollars of social welfare benefits (whether cash, in-kind benefits, or services) were delivered in programs that were not means-tested, such as Medicare, Social Security, and unemployment insurance.[111] Government loan programs for college students were greatly expanded in the 1970s and were used extensively by middle- and even upper-income families. Countless people found their quality of life improved by receipt of cash, in-kind benefits, or services from one or more of the social programs.

Evidence also suggests that extraordinary progress was made during the 1970s in reducing the incidence of poverty, as measured by the percentage of the population that fell under official poverty lines. By this measure, the poverty rate declined from 14.2 percent of the population in 1967 to 11.1 percent in 1979. When in-kind transfers, such as Food Stamps and Medicaid, are also included, the poverty rate declined to 6.4 percent in 1979—an extraordinary accomplishment. However, 15 percent of African Americans, 12 percent of Latinos, and 18 percent of female-headed households remained in poverty.[112]

The reduction in poverty during the 1970s was even more impressive than the gains made during the 1960s, which were facilitated by the Vietnam War and the economic activity that accompanied it. Expenditures for the military declined from 8 percent of the GNP in 1966 to 5.5 percent of the GNP in 1981.[113] Indeed, in contrast to the boom of the 1960s, the economy was plagued by stagflation in the 1970s. The striking successes in reducing poverty

in the 1970s can be attributed in considerable measure to expansion of cash and in-kind social programs. The average value of payments, benefits, and services to families and individuals was $1,252 in 1970 (in 1980 dollars), but it reached $1,896 in 1980.[114] Thus, progress in reducing poverty was made only because social programs were more comprehensive than during any other period in American history.

Of course, increases in spending on entitlements did not address the job-related income of Americans. Because the United States had dominated world markets through the 1960s, few people realized that vast numbers of unionized, industrial jobs were disappearing, whether through migration of American firms abroad in search of cheaper labor or from competition with European nations and Japan. In the 1970s, little attention was given to job-training programs, improvements in public education, and relocation of jobs to inner-city areas.

The progress in improving the economic status of Americans was accompanied by a revolution in human rights. Regulations and litigation by the Equal Employment Opportunity Commission (EEOC) were supplemented by many court rulings that bolstered the rights of people of color and women in job markets and in college admissions. The rights of persons with physical and mental disabilities were advanced by important court decisions, by legislation, and by government regulations. These measures significantly decreased the extent to which people with disabilities were warehoused in custodial institutions and increased their access to public facilities. Advocates for gay men and lesbians defeated local government attempts to deny them teaching positions.

WHY WAS THE SPENDING REVOLUTION HIDDEN?

In the 1980s, secure in the knowledge that one of their own—Ronald Reagan—was in the White House, conservatives attacked social spending and the welfare state. They focused their attacks on the New Deal and Great Society reforms, but they ought also to have attacked Richard Nixon and his presidential successors during the 1970s, who permitted startling increases in social spending that rivaled earlier periods of reform. Many factors combined to hide the extent of the 1970s reforms. Nixon's political rhetoric was often conservative, in contrast to Roosevelt's denunciation of "monied interests" and Johnson's expressions of sympathy for those in poverty. Each of the three presidents in the 1970s began his administration with relatively liberal emphases but ended his term as a determined conservative, which made him appear to focus on reductions rather than increases in social spending. Nixon was far more conservative in his second term than in his first, Ford more conservative in 1976 than in 1975, and Carter more conservative after 1978 than in his first two years.[115] Each president was forced to abandon reform measures by his Southern constituencies, high inflation and deficits, and public indifference to reform.

Moreover, the nature of the 1970s reforms tended to render them invisible. Whereas Democrats had typically sought new programs, some of Nixon's reforms—such as the indexing of Social Security, federalizing of Food Stamps, and SSI—were simply procedural and administrative changes in existing programs. Nixon's reforms often had a conservative appearance because they deemphasized the role of the federal government; both CETA and revenue sharing allocated funds to localities. Such appearances are deceiving, however, because CETA and revenue sharing were substantial additions to the American welfare state, as Ronald Reagan realized a few years later when he succeeded in virtually eliminating them. Nixon's reforms were also unobtrusive because they lacked a dramatic name like the New Deal.

Finally, where the New Deal and Great Society reforms resulted from the successful mobilizing of a liberal coalition of unions, intellectuals, Jews, blue-collar voters, racial groups, and other interest groups against conservatives, passage of reforms in the 1970s often resulted from a more complex and less dramatic political process, in which members of both parties sought partial credit for reforms.

THE OPPRESSION OF VULNERABLE POPULATIONS IN THE 1970s

Oppression of Women: The Women's Movement

Groups representing women, people of color, and gay men and lesbians made important changes in tactics and organization in the 1970s. The middle and late 1960s saw the emergence of relatively radical leadership who focused on nonviolent marches and demonstrations, building group pride, and recruiting mass membership. Among African Americans, the nonviolent precepts of Martin Luther King, Jr., were losing ground to the black power philosophy of Malcolm X and Stokely Carmichael.

In the mid-1970s, as this first wave of activists from vulnerable populations burned out, were intimidated by the FBI and other federal officials, or became discouraged by intragroup dissension between radicals and those more inclined to accept incremental changes, they were replaced by a second wave.[116] It had also become clear by the mid-1970s that each of the vulnerable populations faced dauntingly complicated problems in obtaining legislative and legal advances—problems that could not easily be addressed by direct action. They needed to work on a number of fronts simultaneously, to obtain expert legal advice, to surmount honest differences within their groups about how best to proceed, and to develop staying power as complex legal initiatives were processed and litigated. Indeed, within each movement, specialized groups that worked on specific issues supplemented the older general-purpose groups such as the National Association for the Advancement of Colored People and the National Organization for Women.

The women's movement illustrates this transformation of organizing in the 1970s. (See Figure 9.2.) Women found that they had to work on multiple fronts—to redress job discrimination, reform state laws on rape, develop funding for battered women's

© Bettmann/Corbis

FIGURE 9.2 The women's liberation movement.

shelters, seek resources for child care, obtain legislation allowing maternal (and paternal) leaves for pregnant women and for parents of newly born children, secure equal pay for comparable work, increase child support payments from divorced or absent fathers, increase training and assistance to "displaced homemakers," work for enactment of an Equal Rights Amendment, develop lawsuits to force promotions and hiring of women in the face of discrimination, contest court rulings that threatened affirmative action, and seek legislation to ban sexual harassment in the workplace. Specialized organizations formed to deal with each of these issues; they developed loose connections with each other and with the National Organization for Women.[117]

The women's movement also illustrates how different groups had to try to overcome dissent *within* their movement. African American women and other women of color sometimes contended that the leadership of the established groups was insensitive to their needs; thus, some African American women thought that more attention should be devoted to the needs of poor women and that radical feminists' attacks on the institution of marriage did not reflect the interest of the African American community in supporting African American males within their marriages.[118] Old controversies resurfaced, such as those between women who favored protectionist legislation and women who favored strict equality for women and men. Whereas protectionists wanted legislation that gave *women* maternity leaves, custody rights, alimony, and child support, other women wanted legislation that gave men and women complete equality under the law—that is, that gave men and women equal rights to child support, alimony, support payments, and leaves.[119] Heterosexual women and lesbians disagreed about how much emphasis the women's movement should place on fighting discrimination encountered by lesbians.

The Mobilization of New Sets of Vulnerable Populations

We discussed African Americans, Asian Americans, Latinos, First Americans, and women in Chapter 8, but the members of other vulnerable populations also developed leadership and organizations in the late 1960s. Many policies that affected older persons were developed in the 1960s and early 1970s, including Medicare, the Older Americans Act, Supplementary Security Income (SSI), and indexing of Social Security benefits.[120] A "gray lobby" was energized by rapid growth in the membership of the American Association of Retired Persons (AARP), the National Council of Senior Citizens (NCSC), the Gray Panthers, and many other groups.[121] Indeed, by the 1980s, AARP used its vast resources to mobilize support for those legislators who were sympathetic to programs that benefited older persons.

In the 1960s, automobile accidents and the Vietnam War led to substantial increases in the numbers of Americans with disabilities. Toward the end of the decade, a robust movement to assert the rights of people with disabilities developed. Various groups had long represented veterans with disabilities, persons with vision and hearing impairment, those with developmental disabilities, and people with specific diseases such as cerebral palsy. However, none of these groups focused on the civil rights of persons with disabilities, and each was dominated by providers of specific services.

Whereas long-standing programs such as the federal vocational rehabilitation program already provided services to persons with physical disabilities, the emerging interest in extending their rights was first reflected in the 1968 Architectural Barriers Act, which promoted the modification of federal facilities. Various local groups with an interest in civil rights, such as the Center for Independent Living in Berkeley, California, developed in the 1960s and early 1970s. Persons with disabilities came to be concerned about discrimination in the workplace and about the many physical impediments—such as the absence of ramps and elevators—that made their access to transportation and facilities problematic.

However, there was little networking among individuals with different disabilities until 1972, when President Nixon vetoed the Rehabilitation Act. In response, an array of persons demonstrated in support of the legislation at the annual conference of the President's Committee on Employment of the Handicapped. The disability movement took off after the enactment of the Rehabilitation Act of 1973, whose Section 504 prohibited discrimination against persons with disabilities. The American Coalition of Citizens with Disabilities (ACCD) sought to pressure the Nixon, Ford, and Carter administrations to put resources, legal advocacy, and commitment behind the civil rights provisions of the act.[122]

Americans had lagged behind Europeans in developing child care and children's allowances, but little pressure was placed on federal politicians prior to the mid 1960s, except by small professional organizations such as the Child Welfare League of America. A White House Conference on Children was held about every 10 years, but it tended to be a symbolic event. The establishment of the Head Start program in 1964 provided a dramatic breakthrough for children, even if it was poorly funded. President Nixon's veto of child development legislation in 1971 provided the impetus for the founding of the Children's Defense Fund in 1973 by Marian Wright Edelman—the most assertive advocate for children in Washington, DC, during the next two decades. Over the years, various coalitions of professional groups banded together to seek passage of measures such as the Adoption Assistance and Child Welfare Act of 1980. Child advocacy groups developed in local and state jurisdictions as well. Unlike groups with mass memberships, such as AARP, advocates for children had to depend on the goodwill and interest of other groups, such as the National Organization for Women, which often gave relatively little attention to the needs of children.[123]

The 1970s as a Revolution in Rights

Although civil rights are commonly associated with the pivotal Civil Rights Acts of 1964 and 1965, the rights revolution reached its zenith in the mid-1970s. Working with advocacy groups or within the Justice Department itself, attorneys who had received their training in the civil rights movement of the 1960s developed a vast quantity of litigation for the various out-groups. As one example, in *O'Connor v. Donaldson*, the Supreme Court ruled that individuals who are placed in mental institutions have a right to treatment and cannot simply be warehoused, as had often been done.

Other rulings extended protections to immigrants in detention camps, to gay men and lesbians, to persons with physical disabilities, to the indigent, to persons with developmental disabilities, to persons in jail, and to prisoners on death row. The federal courts required the Justice Department to enforce their orders outlawing segregated school systems in the South. The courts also required Northern schools to end de facto segregation, often by means of busing. Women won class action lawsuits against corporations such as AT&T, which were required to make back payments of huge sums of money to women who had been unfairly denied promotions or who had encountered wage discrimination. The Supreme Court's *Roe v. Wade* ruling disallowed state laws that prohibited abortion during the first trimester. The building trades, which had historically excluded people of color and women from apprenticeship programs and jobs, were the subject of Court judgments that forced them to train minorities and women. Litigation promoted by the Age Discrimination Act of 1967 and the Rehabilitation Act of 1973 required some employers to hire or retain elderly persons and persons with disabilities.[124] Advocates found a generally receptive response from the Supreme Court even after Earl Warren's retirement as chief justice in 1969 and his replacement by Warren Burger, who remained chief justice until 1986.

This explosion of litigation and rulings was supplemented by the growth of government regulatory bodies, such as the Equal Employment Opportunities Commission, whose budget rose from $3.25 million in 1966 to $111.4 million in 1979. Court rulings and regulatory pressure had a marked impact on the decisions of colleges, corporations, and public agencies such as fire and police departments. For example, the percentage of African American police officers in Atlanta increased from 10 to 29.9 percent between 1968 and 1975.[125]

The Beginnings of White Backlash

Each of the out-groups obtained policy successes in the 1970s and 1980s, but each also encountered a significant backlash from conservatives and movements that opposed social change. In the case of women, Phyllis Schlafly became an outspoken critic of the Equal Rights Amendment (ERA), as well as several other policy measures that feminists sought. Schlafly wanted to preserve traditional sex roles and was convinced that the ERA would force women to take jobs to provide half the family's income, end laws that gave mothers custody of children, and deprive them of the right to obtain alimony.[126] During the 1970s and 1980s, many conservatives shared her opposition to policies that feminists sought.

Republican legislators, hopeful of gaining votes from low- and moderate-income whites who believed they were losing jobs to people of color, mounted a vigorous attack on affirmative action as well as busing. Leaders of the building trades often chose to disregard federal regulations until forced to act by litigation or federal regulators.

Persons with disabilities encountered resistance from many colleges and some employers, who made little effort to make buildings accessible and jobs available to them. At one point, frustrated by this resistance, they orchestrated a sit-down strike in the office of the HEW secretary to force the drafting of regulations to implement the Rehabilitation Act of 1973.[127]

Gay men and lesbians encountered a backlash orchestrated by the New Right. Gay rights ordinances were repealed in 1977 and 1978 in Dade County, Florida, St. Paul, Minnesota, Wichita,

Kansas, and Eugene, Oregon. In the late 1970s, a California legislator mounted a campaign for a ballot initiative to prohibit gay men and lesbians from teaching in public schools. Harvey Milk, a gay member of the board of supervisors in San Francisco, was assassinated in 1978, along with the city's mayor, who supported gay and lesbian issues.[128]

THE EVOLUTION OF THE RELUCTANT WELFARE STATE

We have emphasized the hidden nature of social reforms in the 1970s, but we can also discern in this paradoxical era the harbingers of a more conservative time. Though Nixon often supported, and even initiated, social reforms, his rhetoric in public utterances, as well as during private conferences with advisors, reflected racism and anti-Semitism. Although he supported the Family Assistance Plan, he also led highly publicized efforts to attack welfare fraud. He sometimes supported policies for women and other groups, but he also endorsed FBI infiltration of dissident groups. His brooding presence symbolizes the contradictions of the 1970s; he balanced conservative rhetoric and support of social initiatives in his first term, only to swing decisively toward conservative policies in his second term. As we have noted, Presidents Ford and Carter were basically conservative in their domestic policies, even though they supported certain reforms. Full-fledged conservative movements against the supposed excesses of reform emerged in the form of a backlash against feminism, affirmative action, social spending, and taxes, so that advocates for women, gay men and lesbians, and people of color felt increasingly on the defensive.

With the end of the Vietnam War, major and ongoing reductions in military spending were expected. Sharp reductions *did* occur and were used to fund increases in social spending during the decade. By the mid-1970s, however, some Americans became convinced that the Soviet Union, which had dramatically increased the number and power of its missiles, threatened to overtake the American lead in military weapons. Angered by several arms control treaties, which they believed made undue concessions to the Russians, these Americans led a crusade to dramatically increase military spending—a plea that fell on the receptive ears of Ronald Reagan, who made increases in military spending a major pledge in his campaign of 1980.[129]

Historians sometimes err by characterizing historical eras as liberal *or* conservative. The decade of the 1970s was a peculiar mixture of both of these tendencies. Major policy reforms took place but in the context of a nation with an emerging conservative movement, which came to view even Richard Nixon as too liberal. Conservatives confidently awaited the 1980 presidential election, and they were not disappointed by the results.

LINKING THE PARADOXICAL ERA TO CONTEMPORARY SOCIETY

What We Can Learn from Policy Advocates of the Paradoxical Era

Policy advocates seldom seek policy changes without collaborating with existing advocacy groups. Examples of effective policy advocacy include the founding of the Children's Defense Fund by Marian Wright Edelman (see Insert 9.4) and mobilization of welfare recipients by George Wiley (see Insert 9.5). Policy advocacy groups that help specific vulnerable populations, whether they are based in a single national location (such as Washington, DC), a specific state or locality, or in many states, provide remarkable assistance to policy advocates. They collect data from recent research. They are knowledgeable about existing policies at local, state, and national levels. They are familiar with recent attempts to change existing policies. They have contacts with key public officials. They know about other advocacy groups whose interests and knowledge overlap

INSERT 9.4 Profiles in Policy Advocacy: Marian Wright Edelman (1939–)

Marian Wright Edelman—civil rights activist, lawyer, children's rights crusader, and organization founder—was born in Bennettsville, South Carolina, on June 6, 1939, the youngest of five children born to Maggie Leola (Bowen) Wright and Arthur Jerome Wright. A minister of the Shiloh Baptist Church and an adherent of Booker T. Washington's self-help philosophy, Marian's father was a major influence in her life and thought. He expected his children to get an education and devote themselves to the betterment of their community. Marian Wright Edelman successfully met both expectations and continues to work toward the betterment of her world even today.

In 1956, after graduating from Marlboro Training High School, Marian entered Spelman College in Atlanta, Georgia. Her outstanding scholarship won her a Charles Merrill study/travel grant for study abroad. During the first summer of her junior year, Marian studied French civilization at Sorbonne University. She spent the remainder of that academic year at the University of Geneva in Switzerland. For two months during her second semester abroad, Marian studied in the Soviet Union under a Lisle Fellowship. In 1959, the year of the first student protests in the South, she returned to Spelman for her senior year and became active in the civil rights movement. Before graduating in 1960, she would participate in one of the largest sit-ins at the Atlanta City Hall, and, along with 14 other students, be arrested for protesting the civil rights abuses occurring throughout the South. Her involvement in the civil rights movement made her aware of the fact that there was a scarcity of civil rights lawyers. Thus, Marian decided to sacrifice her aspirations for a career in foreign service and instead pursued a career as a civil rights attorney.

In 1960, after graduating as valedictorian of her Spelman class, Marian was admitted to Yale University Law School as a John Hay Whitney Fellow. In 1963, her last spring break of law school, Marian went to Mississippi and participated in the voter registration drives sponsored by the Student Nonviolent Coordinating Committee. Following her graduation from Yale and a year's training in New York, Marian went to Jackson, Mississippi, where she was one of the first two NAACP Legal Defense and Educational Fund interns. By the summer of 1964, she had opened a law office and was busy handling civil rights cases, most of which involved getting students out of jail. Because of her role as a leading supporter of the civil rights movement, Marian was often threatened by dogs and thrown into jail. Moreover, she was prohibited from entering a state courthouse to aid her clients until she took and passed the Mississippi bar. Marian Wright Edelman became the first African American woman to pass the bar in the state of Mississippi. In addition to the work she did at her own law office, Marian headed the NAACP Legal Defense and Education Fund in Mississippi from 1964 to 1968.

Marian's efforts to effect positive change in the South led her to realize that, to improve the civil rights situation in the South, she would have to begin working on reforming federal civil rights policy. In March of 1968, after receiving a Field Foundation grant to learn how to effect positive changes in the law for the benefit of the poor, Marian moved to Washington, DC, and launched the Washington Research Project. In July of 1968, Marian Wright married Peter Edelman, who was one of Robert Kennedy's legislative assistants working on the Senate's Subcommittee on Employment, Manpower, and Poverty. In 1971, the Edelmans left Washington and moved to Boston, where Marian became director of the Harvard University Center for Law and Education.

One of Marian Edelman's greatest achievements was the founding of the Children's Defense Fund (CDF) in 1973. The CDF is a nonprofit child advocacy organization based in Washington, DC. It was designed to provide systematic and long-term assistance to children and adolescents and to ensure that their needs are an important matter of public policy. Some of the children's issues the CDF has brought to the attention of the American public include teen pregnancy, the child care situation, child welfare and mental health, and family support systems.

The CDF, under Marian Edelman's leadership, has served as one of the most visibly active and successful organizations concerned with a broad range of children's and family issues. Today, the CDF's primary mission is to teach the American public about the needs children have and promote preventive intervention in children's lives before it is too late to rescue them from treatable diseases, dropping out of school, early pregnancies, and other problems children and adolescents face. The CDF is also a primary source of information for government officials and often lobbies Congress through continuing research and its authoritative reports.

with their group. A first task for policy advocates, then, is to use navigational skills to identify existing advocacy groups that are relevant to a specific issue, such as through Internet searches or other inquiries. Before they begin their work, they find out what is known. They discover, too, whether specific advocacy groups are interested in collaborating with them.

The Children's Defense Fund (CDF) is one of the preeminent advocacy groups in the United States—operating not only out of Washington, DC, but through various of its state chapters. Marian Wright Edelman is an assertive, knowledgeable, and experienced advocate with many policy victories throughout her career.

Edelman illustrates the importance of *persistence* in policy advocacy. While policy advocates sometimes achieve rapid victories in a specific legislative season, they often must engage in advocacy for specific issues for extended periods as they gradually develop supportive coalitions, educate lawmakers, and surmount opposition. In Edelman's case, for example, she was instrumental in securing federal subsidies for child care in 1990—but only after a 20-year struggle marked by many setbacks. That's why policy advocates often work with or support specific advocacy groups such as the CDF—because they possess the staying power to advance specific policy issues over relatively long periods of time.

In thinking about policy advocacy, an interesting question to consider is this one: can (or should) policy advocates involve their clients or consumers in their work? The National Welfare Rights Organization (NWRO) was possibly the most successful project that actually mobilized consumers (welfare recipients) to seek and obtain their benefits. The NWRO established a national office as well as local chapters in most of the nation's major cities. The prime mover in the establishment of NWRO was George Wiley. (See Insert 9.5.)

The national chapter of NWRO was a significant player in trying to fashion the content of the welfare reform plan initially proposed by Richard Nixon. Welfare recipients frequently effectively testified before Congressional committees as they deliberated about welfare rights legislation—even

if Congress was unable to agree on a final version. Welfare recipients in local NWRO chapters met with welfare administrators in specific cities and counties to seek streamlined eligibility procedures and insist that specific rights given to welfare recipients be honored.

It is interesting to speculate why an organization like NWRO was not established when AFDC was drastically reformed in 1996 and replaced with Temporary Assistance to Needy Families (TANF). Since TANF imposed a set of harsh policies on recipients, a watchdog organization of recipients might have prevented many abuses in specific cases by working to involve clients or consumers in policy advocacy. Such efforts would fulfill the goal of empowering clients—whether by joining delegations to the administrators of agencies or departments, testifying before legislative committees, writing letters to public officials, visiting public officials, or joining protests. Clients possess considerable legitimacy in the eyes of public officials because they have actually experienced the effects of specific policies, such as a homeless person for whom the lack of affordable housing is not an abstract concept.

What We Can Learn from the Persistence of Unmet Needs and Policy Issues during the Paradoxical Era

Many policy advocates hoped that some version of the Family Assistance Plan that was initially proposed by President Nixon would be approved by Congress. Some versions that were considered by Congress would have established nationwide benefit standards, provided truly significant child care assistance, and included significant resources for job training. All families whose income was less than a specific level, established nationally, would have been eligible.

Because Congress was unable to reach an agreement, the existing AFDC program continued in place for the next 25 years. Even though AFDC rolls

INSERT 9.5   Profiles in Leadership: George Alvin Wiley (1931–1973)

George Alvin Wiley, who is best remembered for creating the first national organization of welfare recipients, was born on February 26, 1931, in Bayonne, New Jersey, one of six children born to William Daniel Wiley and Olive (Thomas) Wiley. He spent most of his childhood in Warwick, Rhode Island, a small town just outside Providence.

Wiley, whose family was extremely religious, hardworking, and focused on achievement, was expected to work hard and contribute to the well-being of his family. He demonstrated exceptional abilities in high school, where he scored in the highly gifted range on IQ tests and earned a place in the Rhode Island Honor Society. It was during this time that Wiley became interested in science in general and chemistry in particular. During his senior year in high school, Wiley entered a statewide science fair and won a scholarship to Rhode Island State College, which in 1952 was renamed Rhode Island University.

In college, Wiley majored in organic chemistry. He maintained a strong academic performance, worked, and participated extensively in extracurricular activities. He was the first African American member of the fraternity to which he belonged. Wiley also became involved in activities that helped develop the leadership skills he would take with him throughout his career.

In 1953, Wiley graduated from Rhode Island University and began graduate studies at Cornell University. In 1957, he received his Ph.D. in organic chemistry and was awarded a grant to complete his postdoctoral work at the University of California, Los Angeles. Prior to leaving for California, Wiley served a brief tour of army duty in Virginia. While there, he became interested in civil rights and joined the local chapter of the National Association for the Advancement of Colored People (NAACP).

In 1960, following the completion of his postdoctoral work and a brief faculty appointment to UCLA's chemistry department, Wiley left California and moved to Syracuse, New York, where he joined the faculty of the chemistry department at Syracuse University. Shortly thereafter, he met Wretha Frances Whittle, a white graduate student whom he married in June of 1961. After the couple had two children, Wiley decided to settle down and devote his remaining years to research work in organic chemistry. But his plans would soon change.

Wiley, whose brief experience in Virginia's civil rights movement stayed forever in his mind, became active in efforts to eliminate racial discrimination in the educational setting. In the early 1960s, he wrote an open letter to Syracuse University's newspaper to protest the discrimination he knew existed within fraternities and sororities. Wiley was also instrumental in organizing the Syracuse chapter of the Congress of Racial Equality, or CORE, which he later chaired and led in a series of antidiscrimination demonstrations. CORE's chief objective was to expose segregation in the public school system and to protest discrimination against people of color in employment. CORE members also attempted a boycott of businesses in hopes of bringing reform to the urban renewal program. Due to the success of his organizing efforts in Syracuse, Wiley was offered the position of associate national director of CORE in November of 1964. Shortly after accepting the offer, Wiley arranged a sabbatical from Syracuse University and moved his family to New York.

Once in New York, Wiley found himself in charge of an administrative system in need of strong leadership and severe reorganization. Staff members who were suspicious of Wiley, and his intentions made his job even more difficult. By 1965, he had managed to solve CORE's administrative problems and to develop good rapport with the staff members, who later became Wiley's strongest allies.

But by the middle of the year, Wiley was once again faced with problems stemming from within CORE. These problems revolved around the need to reexamine CORE's commitment to racial integration and nonviolent activism. On one side of the debate, members who supported the black power philosophy argued, successfully, that CORE should abandon its interracial stance, reducing the power and presence of whites, and become an all African American organization. On the other side, Wiley and his supporters rejected the exclusion of whites, arguing that the minority status of African Americans made participation by whites essential to the success of CORE.

Disappointed and disheartened by the national board's decision to replace outgoing director James Farmer with Floyd McKissack instead of him, in January of 1966 Wiley resigned from CORE. A few months later, he formally resigned from Syracuse University and moved to Washington, DC, where he devoted the remainder of his life to crusading for the poor.

After a brief stint as national action coordinator of the Citizens Crusade Against Poverty, Wiley founded the Poverty/Rights Action Center, or P/RAC. On June 30, 1966, P/RAC, which served as a vehicle to organize the

(Continued)

welfare poor, led marches on the Ohio state capital to pressure the legislature to increase welfare benefits to the minimum level mandated by the state for health and decency. On that same day, inspired by Wiley's leadership and commitment to reform, welfare groups organized by P/RAC demonstrated in 25 other cities in a show of solidarity. The success of these crusades led to the creation of the National Welfare Rights Organization, or NWRO, in August of 1967.

Shortly after its creation, Wiley became the executive director of NWRO and continued his efforts to organize the poor. Under his leadership, the NWRO became an advocate for the poor in court, where it challenged welfare laws. The NWRO also appeared on behalf of the poor before congressional committees, again to promote welfare reform. The NWRO's efforts were augmented by the volunteered legal services of lawyers who shared the organization's convictions and supported the welfare reform movement. Many cases were argued and won before the Supreme Court, resulting in the expansion of the rights of those on welfare.

By 1970, the NWRO and the welfare rights movement faced intense public opposition. Marches and public demonstrations no longer proved effective tools in the crusade to reform welfare. Internal conflicts led to a great division within the NWRO and eventually destroyed it. On December 31, 1972, after a dispute with the board of directors, Wiley resigned from the organization he was instrumental in creating.

After leaving the NWRO, Wiley founded the Movement for Economic Justice, which had as its main objective organizing not only the welfare poor but all of the poor in America. His efforts were cut short by his sudden and tragic death on August 8, 1973.

---

did not greatly expand in the 1980s and 1990s (unlike the 1950s and 1960s), the program remained highly controversial, attracting the ire of such notable conservatives as President Ronald Reagan and Newt Gingrich. With the eventual agreement of President Bill Clinton, conservatives drastically changed AFDC when it was converted to TANF in 1996. Not only was it no longer an entitlement—leaving Congress with the ability even to stop funding it—but the legislation placed many restrictive measures on the states such as lifetime limits on the number of years specific recipients could receive TANF, requirements for teen mothers on TANF to live with their parents, and an insistence that recipients be put into jobs.

Welfare rolls roughly halved in the succeeding 11 years—making it seem that "the welfare problem" had disappeared. Considerable evidence suggests, however, that the basic problem—impoverished single (mostly female) heads of households—continues to exist. Although most single mothers are working, many women have not substantially improved their economic status—and often cannot afford quality child care, health care, and transportation costs. The stress of meeting their survival needs makes parenting more difficult since many of them must work multiple jobs even to stay near the poverty threshold.

What We Can Learn from Failed Policy Strategies of the Paradoxical Era

The "War on Drugs" was born during the administration of Richard Nixon when he launched an ambitious effort to close off the supply of heroin and cocaine by preventing opium and coca from entering the country from nations such as Mexico and Turkey—a campaign continued by Presidents Gerald Ford and Jimmy Carter. By declaring a war on drugs, Nixon hoped to draw Southern conservatives and Northern Catholics into the Republican Party. Battling drug abuse strongly appealed to these groups, particularly as many of them opposed the "drug culture" of the 1960s. From the 1970s onward, the United States has spent tens of billions of dollars on "interdiction" that sought to cut the supply of illegal drugs from other nations, despite limited progress and considerable evidence that robust drug treatment and preventive programs would be more cost-effective.

In fact, a war on drugs was launched far earlier in American history.[130] Use of opium, as well as cocaine, was widespread and legal in American history during the 19th century among all social classes. Not only were these drugs not banned, but they were imported in large quantities—for example, 24,000 pounds of opium were brought into

New England during the 1840s. Wanting to reap revenues on imported drugs, the U.S. Congress levied a tax on opium and morphine in 1890. (Made from opium, heroin was invented in 1895 by the Bayer Company of Germany, which prepared the substance by diluting morphine with acetyls. Cocaine was made from the leaves of the coca shrub.) The United States took its first steps against drugs by banning opium in 1905 and requiring labeling on patent medicines when it enacted the Pure Food and Drug Act in 1906.

In 1914 the United States enacted the Harrison Narcotics Act, which sought to curb cocaine and heroin use by requiring doctors and pharmacists who prescribed narcotics to register and pay a tax. Americans banned the importation of opium except for medical use in 1922—and the U.S. Treasury Department Narcotics Division banned all legal narcotics sales, a policy that forced addicts to buy drugs from illegal street dealers. The Heroin Act of 1925 made the manufacture and possession of heroin illegal.

Made from hemp, two other drugs achieved prominence in the United States: marijuana (a weaker version) and hashish (a stronger version). Less addictive than heroin and cocaine but also producing strong neurological effects, marijuana was first used in significant quantities in the United States during the 1920s. Its use, sale, and possession were banned by the United States in 1937, but it nonetheless evolved into a widely used substance by youth in the 1960s when large amounts were smuggled into the United States from Mexico. (In succeeding decades, it reached the United States from many other nations, including Canada—and was illegally grown in many locations in the United States as well.)

The criminalization of specific drugs did not stop their importation into the United States. Mafia and other criminal elements imported vast quantities of drugs that were distributed through a robust black market in the 1930s and following World War II. Attempting to block the spread of communism in Southeast Asia, the United States protected drug warlords in return for their support in the 1950s and 1960s. Many military personnel

became addicted to heroin in the Vietnam War, with as many as 750,000 persons addicted to heroin in the United States by 1970. Cocaine and heroin were imported in large quantities into the United States from Mexico, Colombia, Iran, Afghanistan, Pakistan, and other nations from 1970 onward.

Congress enacted the Controlled Substances Act in 1970, which established four schedules (categories) of drugs. Schedule 1 includes substances with a high potential for abuse and with no currently accepted medical use even when supervised by a physician (schedule 1 includes more than 80 named drugs including marijuana, cocaine, and heroin). Schedule 2 includes substances with a high potential for abuse but with currently accepted medical use (schedule 2 includes methadone, which is used to help alcoholics). Schedules 3 and 4 include substances with less or low potential for abuse and with currently accepted medical use (many prescribed drugs fall into this category).

A series of "designer drugs" have emerged in recent decades in the United States, including ecstasy and methamphetamines, which are illicitly manufactured in laboratories in homes and elsewhere—making it very difficult for drug enforcement personnel to find and arrest persons who make them. Some designer drugs have dangerous physiological and mental impacts on persons who use them.

As the United States declared war on cocaine, heroin, and marijuana, it was far more tolerant regarding tobacco and alcohol—both of which are potentially addictive drugs that are extremely harmful to many people. (Rescinded by President Franklin Roosevelt in 1933, the prohibition of alcohol has not been revived in the United States.) Both substances were protected from regulation by a vast network of growers, distributors, and retail outlets. Both substances are far more widely used than illicit drugs and cause more physical and mental harm to their victims when viewed cumulatively.

Like other nations, the United States has had to make difficult policy choices regarding drugs. Which of these potentially addictive substances should be declared illegal and which ones should be legalized? Should some of them, like marijuana, be legalized for narrow medical uses under the supervision of physicians, such as the use of marijuana to diminish pain among terminally ill persons or persons with chronic diseases? Should personal possession of small quantities of marijuana be treated as a felony or should a lesser misdemeanor penalty—or no penalty—be imposed? At what levels should the nation fund and provide substance abuse services to the users of these various drugs? What approaches should be used to help persons overcome specific kinds of addictions? To the extent that drugs are criminalized, how can the nation make enforcement equitable so that penalties do not disproportionately fall upon certain kinds of users, such as African Americans and Latinos? As we have already seen, the United States criminalized many drugs and focused its resources on an interdiction and enforcement approach—including penalties for the possession and sale of marijuana.

The stakes were extremely high for the nation when fashioning its drug policies. As many as 440,000 persons died each year from the effects of tobacco in 2007. More than 10 million adults and 3 million children and adolescents suffer from alcoholism and its many adverse medical effects, including damage to the brain and other organs. Alcoholics are often not productive workers, disproportionately engage in spousal and child abuse, and often harm themselves and others when they drive while intoxicated. Alcoholic pregnant women often cause their babies to have birth defects—as do pregnant women addicted to cocaine and heroin. Persons addicted to cocaine and heroin often suffer from heart and respiratory problems, strokes, and premature deaths as well as psychological trauma. Although the percentage of 18- to 25-year-old Americans reporting use of cocaine declined from roughly 10 percent in 1980 to less than 5 percent in 2002, large numbers of Americans are addicted to cocaine or heroin. (In 2004, 34.2 million Americans aged 12 and over reported having used cocaine and 7.8 million reported having used crack cocaine—a kind of cocaine that is injected rather than smoked—and 466,000 persons received treatment for cocaine at a specialty clinic in 2004.) Chronic tobacco smokers suffer from acute

respiratory distress, premature heart attacks, strokes, and many kinds of cancer. Americans spend more than $500 billion per year on addictions when health, law enforcement, and prison costs are combined.[131]

Addictions cause yet other serious problems. The majority of roughly 55,000 fatalities per year from automobile accidents in the United States are caused by drivers who are drunk or "high." Emergency rooms of the nation's hospitals are overwhelmed by visits from persons who are drunk or high—or who suffer from physical effects of addictions. Drug-related admissions to hospital emergency rooms have markedly increased, rising from less than 10,000 persons respectively for heroin and cocaine in 1982 to about 100,000 for heroin and 200,000 for cocaine in 2002. Illicit drugs also divert huge resources from traditional law enforcement to efforts to locate, arrest, and prosecute the users and sellers. They fill prisons with persons convicted of drug-related offenses—particularly African American and Latino inmates from 18 to 25 years of age. They lead not just to deaths and injuries by users, but to violence among persons and gangs competing to obtain and sell illicit drug.[132]

Confronted with addictions of this magnitude, Americans have evolved one-sided and inequitable policies. Following President Nixon's lead, they have devoted far more resources to decreasing the *supply* of illicit drugs than to reducing the *demand*. In President George W. Bush's 2003 budget, for example, about 53 percent of drug-related expenditures were allocated to enforcement as compared to only 29 percent for treatment and 18 percent for prevention. Enforcement has not markedly reduced the amount of drugs in the United States over the past two decades due to the nation's vast borders and seacoasts. Nor has the United States been successful in convincing the growers of drugs in many developing nations to curtail or end their production. Many low-income farmers in developing nations rely upon income from the sale of drugs to survive. Government officials and criminal elements often do not try to curtail the production of drugs in developing nations, since they also receive resources from their sale or from groups that purchase and export them. It is often difficult to locate and destroy crops of drug-producing plants in jungles and other remote locations. It is not surprising, then, that the price of illicit drugs in the United States has *decreased* in the past two decades—suggesting that their quantity has *increased* despite the huge resources spent on enforcement.[133]

While domestic drug enforcement has brought convictions of many large drug dealers, it has led to disproportionate prosecutions and incarceration of persons of color, particularly African Americans and Latinos between the ages of 18 and 25 *even though* the use of illicit drugs by these populations is not markedly higher than that by Caucasian youth. This inequitable result stems from enforcement strategies of local police and drug enforcement personnel. Persons of color disproportionately use "crack cocaine," which is sold in small and less expensive batches and is injected—often in "shooting galleries" where persons exchange needles. Congress chose to make criminal penalties for crack cocaine far higher than for its powder form—including five-year mandatory sentences for five grams, which is the same penalty as for 500 grams of the powder form. Crack is distributed by an army of street vendors who are vulnerable to arrest because of their sheer numbers and because they are on the streets. Wanting lots of arrests, police have gone after these suppliers, as well as users who get their injections in relatively public places.[134]

By contrast, drug enforcement officials have had less incentive to find more affluent users in suburban locations. These users get their cocaine from a smaller number of dealers who distribute and sell it in relatively private locations. They use their drugs not on the streets but in their offices, homes, or other locations. They are, moreover, disproportionately Caucasian individuals who can hire private attorneys as compared to low-income African American and Latino users who rely on public defenders. Not surprisingly, then, most persons who are arrested for possession of crack are low-income persons of color—and disproportionately end up in prison as compared to Caucasian users. Their use of infected needles to receive their drugs has meant, as well, that they are subject to getting HIV/AIDS and hepatitis—dangers less likely for affluent users.

Jailed with virtually no social or substance abuse services, job training, or educational services, many of these youth resume their use of drugs soon after leaving prison—only to be reincarcerated. Substantial numbers become homeless.

By focusing largely on enforcement activities, the United States has failed sufficiently to curtail *demand* for illicit drugs—whether by providing substance abuse treatment services or by funding prevention programs. Treatment services have been so underfunded that many people do not receive them at all or wait for months to get them. Yet research strongly indicates that drug treatment services are more cost-effective than enforcement as a way to curtail drug usage even when many persons must engage in numerous courses of treatment to finally surmount their addiction.[135] Nor have Americans adequately funded educational and community programs to prevent the use of drugs, such as by helping teenagers surmount peer culture that often pressures them to use illicit drugs.

The United States has also erred, many critics contend, in treating marijuana similarly to cocaine, heroin, and methamphetamine. While most research suggests that the latter three drugs produce serious health and psychological effects and are highly addictive, considerable research attributes lesser effects to marijuana and suggests that it is not as addictive. Americans should ask whether they wish to place youth in jails for extended periods for possessing relatively small amounts of marijuana, or if this punishment far exceeds the seriousness of the offense and stigmatizes youth as felons. Some critics contend, as well, that the federal government errs by prosecuting physicians who prescribe marijuana in states such as California where citizens or legislators have enacted medical marijuana laws that legalize the growing and prescribing of this drug for persons with terminal cancer and some chronic diseases.

Public officials have shown little inclination to rethink the War on Drugs. It allows Americans to blame foreign nations for their drug problem. It blames the victims rather than defining addiction as a disease that should be treated. It allows local politicians to claim credit for numerous arrests. It provides large numbers of persons for the nation's prison industry. It allows

Americans to assume that addicts are primarily persons of color when, in fact, substance abuse devastates the lives of persons in all ethnic groups and social classes.

How might the United States improve its efforts to curtail addictions? Some persons favor legalizing drugs as in the Netherlands, where they can be legally purchased in bars and pharmacies—a policy not likely to be adopted in the United States. More politically feasible midcourse corrections include the following proposals:

- greatly increasing resources for treating people addicted to illicit drugs

- reconsidering whether possession of small amounts of marijuana should be treated as a felony

- considerably increasing resources for preventive programs

- vastly increasing treatment and prevention programs for alcoholism and smoking

- drastically modifying enforcement strategies so that they do not treat persons of color more harshly than the mainstream population

- rescinding the term "war on drugs" and replacing it with a public health approach to addictions that provides treatment and prevention to at-risk populations wherever they reside

Social workers are ideally positioned to engage in policy advocacy for persons with serious addictions because they frequently see people saddled with these problems. They should demand greater funding for treatment programs—and also seek policies (now present in some states) to provide treatment in lieu of imprisonment. They should work to make American drug policy more equitable for persons of color. They should seek to reform marijuana laws so that youth do not spend years in prison for minor drug infractions.

What We Can Learn from Promising Strategies of the Paradoxical Era

The major accomplishment in the 1970s was the establishment of an array of entitlements that included

Supplementary Security Income, the Earned Income Tax Credit, a greatly expanded Food Stamps Program, and Social Security retirement benefits indexed to inflation. These entitlements markedly reduced rates of poverty in the United States in the 1970s—channeling billions of dollars of benefits to residents over extended periods.

The beneficiaries of these entitlements were not merely AFDC recipients, but an array of Americans, including elderly people on fixed incomes, persons with disabilities, and families in which the parents earned income near official poverty levels. The EITC demonstrated that tax policy could be used to decrease poverty without, moreover, stigmatizing persons by mandating visits to welfare offices.

Entitlements have merit, as well, for other reasons. They reduce stigma because persons are *entitled* to their benefits. They are more difficult for legislators to cut in the budget process because they are automatically funded to the level of claimed benefits in any given year.

What We Can Learn from the Paradoxical Era about the Structure of the American Welfare State

With the addition of these entitlements and the continuation of many of the programs established during the Johnson administration, Americans had evolved a relatively sophisticated welfare state even if had many gaps in it. Federal social spending increased from $158 billion to $314 billion in only ten years (in 1980 dollars). The greatest additions occurred in the entitlement programs that still remain a critical part of the American welfare state.

The American welfare state consisted by 1980, then, of a series of overlays, as well as linked programs. At the lowest level, the social welfare programs that had traditionally been operated by local governments existed, including public schools, general assistance welfare programs, child welfare programs, some prisons and correctional facilities, and police departments. Even these programs were often linked to state-level funding and policies, such as when states contributed to some or all of them. In turn, state-level social welfare programs existed, particularly in those states with strongly developed state roles in funding, overseeing, and establishing policies for educational and child welfare programs. Many states had relatively strong mental health responsibilities not only in funding and running state mental hospitals, but in funding and overseeing local mental health clinics. All states, moreover, ran programs linked to federal funding and oversight in welfare, Medicaid, the Section 8 public housing program, child welfare, and mental health areas were linked to federal-state programs during the New Deal and the Great Society eras. Added to these programs were strictly federal programs wherein the federal government took major responsibility for funding and administering Food Stamps, SSI, Medicare, and the EITC. As the legacy of the Great Society, moreover, federal agencies gave grants to local programs in public health, child welfare, mental health, and other areas.

In making referrals, engaging in case advocacy, and participating in policy advocacy, social workers needed to understand these overlays and linked programs in their particular states. In some states, such as California, counties assumed major roles in administering child welfare Medicaid and mental health services, whereas in states such as New York stronger state-level administration and oversight of these programs existed.

Chafing at the sheer numbers of programs in local areas directly funded by federal agencies, President Nixon, as well as many conservatives, had wanted to create many so-called "block grants" through which the federal government would give money to the states in such broad areas as mental health and let them use the funds (more or less) as they wished. They preferred this option to the extensive federal power that existed when the federal government designated precisely how its federal money would be used in so-called categorical programs such as Head Start and scores of other programs that gave states little leeway in designing the programs that they wanted.

It would be the legacy of the administration of Ronald Reagan in the 1980s to greatly increase the power and role of states in social welfare in a movement known as "devolution," which will be discussed in the next chapter.

WHAT YOU CAN DO NOW

After reading Chapter 9, you are now equipped to:

- Analyze why President Richard Nixon, who held conservative positions on many issues, also was determined to enact a variety of domestic reforms often in competition or liaison with leading Democrats.

- Describe how President Nixon, who was particularly reform-minded during his first term, used floating coalitions and outbidding to achieve many reforms.

- Analyze welfare, Social Security, SSI, revenue-sharing, block grant, CETA, civil rights, OSHA, housing, and social services reforms during President Nixon's first term.

- Discuss why President Nixon turned to the right in his second term and how he sought to transform the Republican Party from minority to majority status—and how this goal was undermined by his forced departure from the presidency in the wake of the Watergate scandal.

- Discuss why Presidents Gerald Ford and Jimmy Carter obtained relatively few social reforms during their terms, despite enactment of some mental health and child welfare reforms during the Carter presidency.

- Discuss how social spending markedly increased in the 1970s as Americans developed for the first time in their history a set of interlocking safety net programs.

- Analyze the oppression of women during this period, as well as the mobilization of disabled persons and senior citizens.

- Discuss how a "revolution of rights" took place in the 1970s, accompanied by considerable white backlash.

- Analyze what we can learn about policy advocacy from Marian Wright Edelman, as well as George Wiley.

- Discuss what we can learn from the paradoxical era of the 1970s about persistent needs, failed strategies, promising strategies, and the structure of the American welfare state

ENDNOTES

1. Sar Levitan and Clifford Johnson, *Beyond the Safety Net: Reviving the Promise of Opportunity in America* (Cambridge, MA: Ballinger, 1984), p. 2.

2. Tom Wicker, *One of Us: Richard Nixon and the American Dream* (New York: Random House, 1991), pp. 484–541.

3. James Reichley, *Conservatives in an Age of Change: The Nixon and Ford Administrations* (Washington, DC: Brookings Institution, 1981), pp. 48–52.

4. Jules Witcover, *The Resurrection of Richard Nixon* (New York: Putnam, 1970), pp. 104–225.

5. Ibid., pp. 57–58.

6. Ibid., pp. 361–379.

7. Tom Wicker, *One of Us*, pp. 410–413.

8. Elliot Richardson, "The Paradox." In Kenneth Thompson, ed., *The Nixon Presidency* (New York: University Press of America, 1987), p. 53ff.

9. Rowland Evans and Robert Novak, *Nixon in the White House* (New York: Random House, 1971), pp. 42–43, 108, 117–118, 211–214; William Leuchtenberg, *In the Shadow of FDR: From Harry Truman to Ronald Reagan* (Ithaca, NY: Cornell University Press, 1983), pp. 168–169; and Reichley, *Conservatives in an Age of Change*, pp. 58–70.

10. Hugh Graham, *The Civil Rights Era: Origins and Development of National Policy, 1960–1972* (New York: Oxford University Press, 1990), p. 322.

11. Leonard Garment, "Richard Nixon." In Thompson, ed., *The Nixon Presidency*, p. 99ff.

12. Richard Nathan, *The Plot That Failed: Nixon and the Administrative Presidency* (New York: John Wiley & Sons, 1975), pp. 37–56.

13. Reichley, *Conservatives in an Age of Change*, pp. 79–87.

14. Bruce Jansson, *The History and Politics of Selected Children's Programs and Related Legislation in the Context of Four Models of Political Behavior.* Doctoral dissertation (Chicago: University of Chicago, 1975), pp. 54–55.

15. Reichley, *Conservatives in an Age of Change*, pp. 56, 72, 154–156.

16. Sar Levitan and Robert Taggart, *The Promise of Greatness* (Cambridge, MA: Harvard University Press, 1976), pp. 24–28.

17. Reichley, *Conservatives in an Age of Change*, pp. 219–224.

18. Ibid., pp. 59–64, 68–72; Evans and Novak, *Nixon*, pp. 37–74.

19. Daniel Moynihan, *The Politics of a Guaranteed Income* (New York: Random House, 1973), pp. 352–396.

20. Ibid., pp. 192–226; Reichley, *Conservatives in an Age of Change*, pp. 138–142.

21. Vincent Burke, *Nixon's Good Deed: Welfare Reform* (New York: Columbia University Press, 1974), p. 67.

22. W. Joseph Heffernan, *Introduction to Social Welfare Policy* (Itasca, IL: Peacock, 1979), pp. 241–250.

23. Moynihan, *The Politics of a Guaranteed Income*, pp. 458–483.

24. Ibid., pp. 439–452.

25. Burke, *Nixon's Good Deed*, pp. 177–187.

26. Ibid., pp. 198–204.

27. Timothy Smeeding, "Is the Safety Net Still Intact?" In D. Lee Bawden, ed., *The Social Contract Revisited: Aims and Outcomes of President Reagan's Social Welfare Policy* (Washington, DC: Urban Institute, 1984), pp. 75, 78.

28. Linda Demkovitch, "Administration About-Face on Disability Could Be a Blessing in Disguise," *National Journal*, 16 (April 28, 1984), pp. 823–825; Donald Chambers, "Policy Weaknesses and Political Opportunities," *Social Service Review*, 1 (March 1985), pp. 1–17.

29. Nicholas Kotz, *Let Them Eat Promises* (Garden City, NY: Doubleday, 1971), pp. 206–213.

30. Levitan and Taggart, *The Promise of Greatness*, p. 67; Moynihan, *The Politics of a Guaranteed Income*, pp. 493–494.

31. Smeeding, "Is the Safety Net Still Intact?" p. 78.

32. Martha Derthick, *Policymaking for Social Security* (Washington, DC: Brookings Institution, 1979), pp. 345–368.

33. Ibid., pp. 358–362.

34. Craig Roberts, *The Supply-Side Revolution: An Insider's Account of Policy-Making in Washington* (Cambridge, MA: Harvard University Press, 1984), pp. 260–261.

35. Peter Gottschalk and Sheldon Danziger, "Macroeconomic Conditions, Income Transfers, and the Trend in Poverty." In Bawden, ed., *The Social Contract Revisited*, p. 191.

36. Nathan, *The Plot That Failed*, pp. 37–56.

37. Robert Magill, *Social Policy in American Society* (New York: Human Sciences Press, 1984), pp. 127–128; Reichley, *Conservatives in an Age of Change*, pp. 156–159.

38. Reichley, *Conservatives in an Age of Change*, p. 155.

39. George Hale and Marian Palley, *The Politics of Federal Grants* (Washington, DC: Congressional Quarterly Press, 1981), pp. 111–113.

40. Walter Williams, *Government by Agency: Lessons from the Social Program Grants-in-Aid Experience* (New York: Academic Press, 1980), pp. 42–43.

41. Martha Derthick, *Uncontrollable Spending for Social Services Grants* (Washington, DC: Brookings Institution, 1975), pp. 29–34.

42. Congressional Quarterly Service, Inc., *Congressional Quarterly Almanac*, Vol. XXIX (Washington, DC, 1973), p. 575.

43. Wicker, *One of Us*, pp. 484–507, 522–523; Graham, *The Civil Rights Era*, pp. 475–476.

44. Reichley, *Conservatives in an Age of Change*, pp. 188–189.

45. Levitan and Taggart, *The Promise of Greatness*, pp. 150–155; Nancy Woloch, *Women and the American Experience* (New York: Knopf, 1984), pp. 524–526.

46. Graham, *The Civil Rights Era*, pp. 393–449.

47. Ibid., pp. 322–345.

48. Frank Bowe, *Rehabilitating America: Toward Independence for Disabled and Elderly People* (New York: Harper & Row, 1980), pp. 59–91.

49. Joseph Califano, *Governing America* (New York: Simon & Schuster, 1981), pp. 314–315.

50. Paul Starr, *The Social Transformation of American Medicine* (New York: Basic Books, 1984), pp. 396–401, 402–403.

51. Gilbert Steiner, *The Futility of Family Policy* (Washington, DC: Brookings Institution, 1981), pp. 49–50.

52. Lela Costin, *Child Welfare: Policies and Practice* (New York: McGraw-Hill, 1979), p. 49.

53. Bruce Jansson, *Theory and Practice of Social Welfare Policy* (Belmont, CA: Wadsworth, 1984), p. 335.

54. Frank Thompson, *Health Policy and the Bureaucracy: Politics and Implementation* (Cambridge, MA: M.I.T. Press, 1981), pp. 217–251.

55. David Stockman, *The Triumph of Politics* (New York: Harper & Row, 1986), p. 410.

56. Reichley, *Conservatives in an Age of Change*, pp. 219–221.

57. For example, funding pressures on neighborhood health centers are discussed by Isabel Marcus, *Dollars for Reform* (Lexington, MA: D. C. Heath, 1981), pp. 89–115.

58. Jansson, *The History and Politics*, pp. 233–309; Gilbert Steiner, *The Children's Cause* (Washington, DC: Brookings Institution, 1976), pp. 90–117.

59. Geoffrey Hodgson, *America in Our Time* (Garden City, NY: Doubleday, 1976), pp. 412–428; Kevin Phillips, *The Emerging Republican Majority* (New Rochelle, NY: Arlington House, 1969), pp. 168–175, 182–184, 321–330.

60. Hodgson, *America in Our Time*, pp. 401–411.

61. Reichley, *Conservatives in an Age of Change*, pp. 54–55; Tom Wicker, "Introduction." In John Osborne, *The Nixon Watch* (New York: Liveright, 1970), pp. viii–x.

62. Hodgson, *America in Our Time*, pp. 425–428, 455.

63. Reichley, *Conservatives in an Age of Change*, pp. 208–209.

64. Hodgson, *America in Our Time*, p. 366.

65. Reichley, *Conservatives in an Age of Change*, pp. 232–233, 239–242.

66. Ibid., pp. 234–237, 242–247.

67. Ibid., pp. 307–311.

68. Ibid., pp. 322–325.

69. Bowe, *Rehabilitating America*, pp. 102–107, 130; Peter Tyor and Leland Bell, *Caring for the Retarded in America: A History* (Westport, CT: Greenwood, 1984), p. 150.

70. Haynes Johnson, *In the Absence of Power* (New York: Viking Press, 1980), p. 114.

71. Robert Shogan, *Promises to Keep: Carter's First Hundred Days* (New York: Thomas Crowell, 1977), pp. 22–28.

72. Ibid., pp. 28–48.

73. Johnson, *In the Absence of Power*, pp. 38–48.

74. Ibid., p. 295.

75. Ibid., pp. 101, 154–168.

76. Ibid., pp. 163–164; Shogan, *Promises to Keep*, p. 199.

77. Califano, *Governing America*, p. 334; Johnson, *In the Absence of Power*, p. 217.

78. Shogan, *Promises to Keep*, p. 189.

79. Califano, *Governing America*, pp. 96–117.

80. Heffernan, *Introduction to Social Welfare Policy*, pp. 259–266.

81. Califano, *Governing America*, p. 321.

82. Ibid., pp. 320–366.

83. Ibid., pp. 364–367.

84. Reichley, *Conservatives in an Age of Change*, pp. 397–399.

85. Ibid.

86. Congressional Quarterly Service, Inc., *Congressional Quarterly Almanac*, Vol. XXXIV (Washington, DC: Congressional Quarterly Service, Inc., 1978), pp. 272–279.

87. Steiner, *The Futility of Family Policy*, pp. 85–88.

88. Ibid., pp. 93–94.

89. Ibid., pp. 163–173.

90. Ibid., pp. 144–155.

91. Karen Davis and Cathy Schoen, *Health and the War on Poverty: A Ten-Year Appraisal* (Washington, DC: Brookings Institution, 1978), p. 86.

92. Califano, *Governing America*, pp. 231–243.

93. Ibid., pp. 258–262, 314–315; Timothy Clark, "Here's One Midnight Regulation That Slipped through Reagan's Net," *National Journal*, 13 (February 7, 1981), pp. 221–224.

94. U.S. President's Commission on Mental Health, *Report to the President* (Washington, DC: Government Printing Office, 1978).

95. Jansson, *Theory and Practice of Social Welfare Policy*, pp. 444–446.

96. Califano, *Governing America*, pp. 388–396.

97. Ibid., pp. 384–386.

98. Johnson, *In the Absence of Power*, pp. 49–81.

99. Ibid., p. 293.

100. Meyer, "Budget Cuts in the Reagan Administration." In Bawden, ed., *The Social Contract Revisited*, p. 36.

101. Califano, *Governing America*, p. 67; Johnson, *In the Absence of Power*, pp. 299–300.

102. Califano, *Governing America*, pp. 82–86.

103. Ibid.

104. Johnson, *In the Absence of Power*, pp. 277–317.

105. Meyer, "Budget Cuts in the Reagan Administration," p. 35; Gregory Mills and John Palmer, "The Federal Budget in Flux." In Gregory Mills and John Palmer, eds., *Federal Budget Policy in the 1980s* (Washington, DC: Urban Institute, 1984), p. 14; Stockman, *The Triumph of Politics*, p. 411.

106. Table 10.1 from Smeeding, "Is the Safety Net Still Intact?" p. 75.

107. Levitan and Taggart, *The Promise of Greatness*, pp. 70–74.

108. Ibid., pp. 72–73.

109. Blanche Bernstein, "Welfare Dependency." In Bawden, ed., *The Social Contract Revisited*, pp. 129–130.

110. Derthick, *Policymaking for Social Security*, pp. 254–270.

111. Meyer, "Budget Cuts in the Reagan Administration," p. 38.

112. Gottschalk and Danziger, "Macroeconomic Conditions," p. 191.

113. Mills and Palmer, "The Federal Budget in Flux," p. 14.

114. Gottschalk and Danziger, "Macroeconomic Conditions," pp. 188–189.

115. Evans and Novak, *Nixon*, pp. 227–228; Reichley, *Conservatives in an Age of Change*, p. 314; and Califano, *Governing America*, pp. 402–448.

116. Flora Davis, *Moving the Mountain: The Women's Movement in America since 1960* (New York: Simon & Schuster, 1991), pp. 137–138.

117. Ibid., pp. 137–154.

118. Ibid., pp. 362–367.

119. Ibid., pp. 305–307.

120. C. L. Estes, *The Aging Enterprise* (San Francisco: Jossey-Bass, 1979).

121. H. J. Pratt, *The Gray Lobby* (Chicago: University of Chicago Press, 1976).

122. Richard Scotch, *From Good Will to Civil Rights* (Philadelphia: Temple University Press, 1984), pp. 34–59, 82–120.

123. Susan Tolchin and Martin Tolchin, *Clout: Women's Power and Politics* (New York: Coward, McCann, and Geoghegan, 1974), p. 230.

124. Thomas Edsall, *Chain Reaction: The Impact of Race, Rights, and Taxes on American Politics* (New York: W. W. Norton, 1991), pp. 107–115.

125. Edsall, *Chain Reaction*, p. 117.

126. Donald Mathews and Jane Sherron De Hart, *Sex, Gender, and the Politics of ERA* (New York: Oxford University Press, 1990), pp. 154–165.

127. Scotch, *From Good Will*, pp. 111–120.

128. John D'Emilio, "Gay Politics and Community in San Francisco since World War II." In Martin Duberman, Martha Vicinus, and George Chauncey, *Hidden From History: Reclaiming the Gay and Lesbian Past* (New York: Meridian Books, 1990), pp. 468–473.

129. Michael Boll, *National Security Planning: Roosevelt through Reagan* (Lexington, KY: University of Kentucky Press, 1988), pp. 188–197.

130. For a chronology of drug policies, go to http://www.heroinaddiction.com/heroin_timeline.html.

131. Impacts of use of illicit drugs are discussed in an occasional paper of the Rand Corporation titled "How Goes the 'War on Drugs'?" (Santa Monica, CA: 2005), pp. 5–9.

132. Ibid., pp. 9–14.

133. Mathea Falco, "US Drug Policy: Addicted to Failure," *Foreign Policy*, no. 102 (Spring 1996), pp. 120–133.

134. Cathy Lisa Schneider, "Racism, Drug Policy, and AIDS," *Political Science Quarterly*, 111(1) (1998), pp. 427–446.

135. "How Goes the War on Drugs?" pp. 15–22.

10

The Conservative Counterrevolution in the Era of Reagan and Bush, Sr.

T A B L E 10.1   Selected Orienting Events

1978	Tax revolt initiated by the passage of Proposition 13 in California
1980	Ronald Reagan wins landslide victory over Jimmy Carter
1981	Omnibus Budget Reconciliation Act (OBRA) makes deep cuts in social programs and establishes seven block grants; Economic Recovery Tax Act of 1981 (ERTA) sharply reduces personal and corporate taxes; Presidential Task Force on Regulatory Relief established; Executive Order mandates review of regulations by the Office of Management and Budget
1981–1983	Nation's deepest recession since the 1930s
1982	Job Training Partnership Act (JTPA) enacted; Tax Equity and Fiscal Responsibility Act (TEFRA) raises corporate taxes and cuts social programs
1983	Diagnostic-related groups (DRGs) introduced by DHHS to finance Medicare's hospital fees; Social Security amendments increase retirement age, reduce some benefits, and subject pensions of some retirees to taxes
1984	Reagan wins landslide victory over Walter Mondale
1985	Balanced Budget and Emergency Deficit Control Act (Gramm-Rudman-Hollings Act) enacted
1986	Tax reform reduces highest tax rate and eliminates many deductions
1987	Enactment of Stewart B. McKinney Homeless Assistance Act
1988	Enactment of Family Support Act
1988	Election of George Bush
1990	Enactment of Americans with Disabilities Act and the Child Care and Development Block Grant program
1992	Los Angeles uprising in the wake of Rodney King verdict

Domestic federal spending had risen rapidly during the 1970s, largely due to entitlements. Even domestic discretionary spending had risen somewhat. If conservative themes had existed during the paradoxical decade of the 1970s, they had contended with liberal policy changes in federal spending and civil rights. Almost overnight, however, conservatives achieved supremacy as a former actor, Ronald Reagan, achieved a landslide victory in 1980 as well as Republican control of the U.S. Senate.

At the end of this chapter, we discuss what we can learn in contemporary society from the era of Presidents Reagan and George Bush, Sr. about policy advocacy, social policy, and the structure of the American welfare state.

THE ASCENDANCY OF CONSERVATISM

Conservatism was the political mainstream of the nation in the Gilded Age, the 1920s, and the 1950s, when localism, limited federal social welfare roles, and unfettered capitalism prevailed, but it gave way to liberal policies during the Great Depression and in the early 1960s.[1] The minority status of conservatives was illustrated by the landslide defeat in 1964 of Barry Goldwater by Lyndon Johnson, who accused Goldwater of attacking Social Security, TVA, and other legacies of the New Deal. When the Goldwater defeat was swiftly followed by Johnson's legislative successes in 1965 and 1966, it seemed as if conservatism had run its course in national politics.

Between 1966 and 1980, however, a number of developments led to a remarkable resurgence of conservatism that culminated in the election of Ronald Reagan. The standard of living of the American working and middle classes had improved markedly during the 1950s and 1960s, despite occasional recessions and sharp inflation in the early 1950s. Most people believed that government officials, armed with Keynesian economic theory, could continue this rosy scenario by adjusting government spending downward (to reduce inflation) or upward (to reduce unemployment). The American economy was widely perceived to be an expanding pie that would benefit all segments of the population.[2]

The simultaneous appearance of inflation and unemployment in the 1970s rudely upset this economic utopia. Many middle-class Americans found their earnings sharply eroded by inflation, which not only increased the cost of living but also pushed them into higher federal tax brackets.[3] Many local taxes were also rising to cover the higher costs of local and municipal services and to pay the local costs of federally mandated programs.

In California, Howard Jarvis campaigned successfully in 1978 for Proposition 13, which drastically reduced local property taxes. This victory was followed by grassroots tax revolts in many other states. Liberal legislators watched these local tax revolts with trepidation, for they realized that they could eventually stimulate protests against the federal tax system and the social programs it funded.[4] Social reform in the 1970s was also undermined by concern about federal deficits, which, according to conservatives, could be reduced only by sharp cuts in social spending.[5]

Conservatives' hopes were buoyed by the declining strength of the Democratic Party. Richard Nixon carried five Southern states in 1968, a Republican achievement that had not been matched since Reconstruction. The liberal flank of the Democratic Party began to weaken as blue-collar workers became increasingly uneasy about social reform and preoccupied with their own economic problems. White backlash led to widespread opposition to affirmative action and social programs, which were widely perceived to disproportionately benefit women, African Americans, and other people of color. Many Jewish voters opposed the use of quotas, because this policy had often been used to exclude them from admission to colleges and the professions.[6]

INSERT 10.1   Using the Web to Understand the Shaping of Policies during the Reagan and George Bush, SR., Presidencies

Visit **academic.cengage.com/social_work/jansson** to view these links and a variety of study tools.

Go to **http://www.pbs.org/wgbh/amex/ presidents/nf/resource/reagan/reaganscript .html** What additional information does this material provide you about the mind-set and tactics of President Ronald Reagan and his top officials?

Go to **http://ncd.gov** for a discussion of contemporary issues confronted by disabled persons. Click on recent proceedings of panels of the

National Council on Disability, such as the October 1, 2007, document titled "Issues in Creating Livable Communities for People with Disabilities."

Go to **http://fohn.net/history_of_aids/** for a history of AIDS from 1981 to 2005 in the United States.

Go to **http://en.wikipedia.org/wiki/Homelessness** and click on "History of Homelessness" for a discussion of this social issue in the United States.

Feminists and African American activists were increasingly viewed with suspicion in a nation that resisted affirmative action. Conservatives spoke of "big-spending liberals" as an anachronism in a society that experienced large deficits.[7] Trade unions, which had provided electoral and campaign support for the Democrats, were weakened as the economy shifted from manufacturing to service industries, as new jobs were increasingly located in the non-unionized South, and as many industries moved to foreign nations to reduce their labor costs. The ill-fated presidencies of Lyndon Johnson and Jimmy Carter, as well as the assassinations of John and Robert Kennedy, also weakened the Democratic Party.

Americans had lived through a long period of social reform, from 1960 through the 1970s. In prior eras, they had only tolerated social reforms for a limited time, and so it was not surprising that the pendulum swung toward conservatism. Conservatives found the public to be more receptive to their arguments that social programs had not solved poverty and other social problems and that social spending was incompatible with economic growth.

The exodus of persons and jobs to the Sun Belt throughout the 1950s, 1960s, and 1970s, in which nearly 40 million Americans left the Northeast and the Midwest, depleted traditional Democratic bastions and greatly increased the electoral strength of conservatives. When placed in this new environment—and removed from trade unions, big-city mayors, and incumbent liberal politicians—these voters, who tended to be relatively conservative and middle class, often became even more conservative. Throughout the country, moreover, there was a continuing shift of population to the suburbs. Suburban voters were far more conservative than urban voters because they had little stake in social programs for urban residents.[8]

The traditional strength of the Democratic Party was also undermined by the maturing of the large war-baby generation, born from 1946 to the late 1950s. These Americans had not lived through the Great Depression and, if they were Caucasian and lived in the suburbs, had grown up having little or no contact with people of color. They were often preoccupied with material wealth and with personal survival in labor markets crowded with young job seekers from their generation.[9]

Together, these various demographic and social trends placed the Democratic Party in jeopardy, particularly as Republicans developed marketing and campaign tactics to reach Sun Belt, suburban, service-oriented, and youthful citizens. There was no sudden erosion in the strength of the Democratic Party, particularly in local elections, but its power in senatorial and presidential elections had diminished significantly by the early 1980s.

The Republican Party skillfully used these various developments in the 1970s to wrest from the Democratic Party two specific groups of voters: Northern white Catholic voters and working-class and lower-middle-class Southern white voters. Knowing that many of these voters believed that the Great Society had disproportionately assisted people of color and that their rising taxes were caused by this expansion of the welfare state, Republican strategists sought, often successfully, to associate the Democrats with welfare programs, urban riots, high taxes, busing, and affirmative action—and to identify their own party with law-abiding citizens. Using advanced marketing techniques, they addressed literature to these two groups of voters and succeeded in persuading many of them to vote for Republican candidates in presidential races. When added to their traditional suburban and relatively affluent constituency, these new voters gave the Republicans a decided advantage, particularly in the presidential elections of 1968, 1972, 1980, 1984, and 1988.[10]

The Legitimization of Conservatism

Liberal reformers had dominated political dialogue from the New Deal through the presidency of Lyndon Johnson.[11] During the 1950s and early 1960s, a cadre of conservative thinkers, such as sociologist Robert Nisbet, had promulgated theories about the merits of limiting the federal government's policy roles and about the need to establish the family, neighborhoods, and local government as buffers between citizens and central government. Other theorists, such as Richard Weaver, had established Libertarian positions, which emphasized policies that maximized freedom by abolishing most government regulations and minimizing taxes. But conservative theorists of the 1950s were relatively isolated from the political process and even distrustful of the general public, who, they believed, were easily manipulated by liberals and the mass media.[12]

The defeat of Goldwater in 1964 made conservatives realize that they needed to participate in the political process if they were to gain power and that they had to use aggressive advertising and outreach

to convince the American public to elect conservative legislators.[13] As we have seen, Nixon and his allies used the term *silent majority* in 1968 to describe their belief that most Americans favored localism, elimination of government regulations, and reductions in social spending.

In a departure from the abstract conservative philosophy of the 1950s, a number of theorists began to analyze public policy and to offer recommendations that stemmed from their conservative ideology. Milton Friedman, the conservative economist from the University of Chicago who published *Capitalism and Freedom* in 1962, discussed a series of policies to radically reduce the regulatory power of government; he denounced public housing programs, licensing of professionals, traditional welfare programs, and a host of other liberal policies.[14] In 1964, Martin Anderson advanced a critique of existing urban renewal programs in *The Federal Bulldozer*, where he argued that private housing markets more effectively met consumer needs than government urban renewal and housing programs.[15] By the end of the 1960s, conservatives had established think tanks, including the American Enterprise Institute and the Heritage Foundation, to compete with such liberal organizations as the Brookings Institution and the Urban Institute. William Buckley initiated a national television show, *Firing Line*, which he used as a forum to present conservative views, and developed *The National Review*, a conservative journal that supplemented viewpoints in *The Public Interest, Commentary*, and other conservative publications.

The chastening effect of the Goldwater defeat also made conservatives more willing to participate in political campaigns. Some analysts, such as Kevin Phillips, developed theories about how conservatives could wrest political power from the Democrats by appealing to blue-collar, white ethnic, and Sun Belt voters. Although Presidents Nixon and Ford preferred to have businesspeople and attorneys in their administrations, conservative economists such as Alan Greenspan and William Simon received top positions. The respectability of conservative points of view was further enhanced by criticisms of the Democratic Party and Great

Society reforms by prominent intellectuals, such as Nathan Glazer and Daniel Moynihan, who pointedly attacked social programs, community action programs, affirmative action, and liberalism.[16]

The constituency of conservatism expanded considerably in the late 1970s, when it obtained a large grassroots following within fundamentalist religious groups, particularly the Southern Baptist Church. White parents, who had sent their children to segregated private schools to escape integrated public schools as well as curriculum they believed to represent secular humanism, were outraged that the Internal Revenue Service (IRS) did not grant tax exemptions to those schools, and they turned to the Republicans, who promised to help rescind the IRS ruling.[17] The New Religious-Political Right (NRPR) was formed as an umbrella group that contained many independent congregations, individual members, and groups like the Moral Majority. By 1980, it contained 90 constituent organizations—from the national Pro-Life Political Action Committee to the Interfaith Committee Against Blasphemy.[18] Jerry Falwell, an outspoken Baptist preacher, quickly became the leader of the Moral Majority, a grassroots pressure group that favored the abolition of abortion, censorship of literature to limit pornography, and policies to allow prayer in schools; the Moral Majority lent its support to many political conservatives who advocated sharp reductions in social spending. The various member groups of the NRPR engaged in educational programs, funded by tax-deductible contributions, in which millions of items of literature were distributed through the mails, at churches, and by personal contacts. Some groups also engaged in extensive political activities, including lobbying and contributions to political campaigns.[19]

Ronald Reagan as Catalyst

By the late 1970s, the political climate was ripe for the emergence of a conservative movement, and it found a catalyst in Ronald Reagan, a former movie actor turned politician. Reagan came from a family in Illinois that had suffered some poverty and turmoil because Reagan's father was an alcoholic; it seems likely that Reagan's dislike of welfare recipients and poor people stemmed in part from the trauma his family encountered as it sought to remain independent despite his father's erratic behavior.[20]

In the 1930s, Reagan was a devoted follower of Franklin Roosevelt. However, during his postwar acting career, he became convinced that government regulations had unfairly forced a movie company with which he was associated to divest its holdings in a chain of theaters. He increasingly resented the high taxes that he had to pay as his income from movies increased. His distrust of communists, which was to assume paranoid proportions in succeeding decades, increased as he observed the power of radicals in his union, the Screen Actors Guild. During the late 1940s, he devoted himself to his movie career, choosing roles that mirrored his personal philosophy—for example, Notre Dame football coach Knute Rockne, a self-made man who preached the virtues of hard work and morality. Reagan remained a Democrat until 1962, but he had gradually moved to the right during the 1950s, when he developed a national reputation as a public speaker for conservative audiences.[21]

Reagan idealized self-made men who achieved upward mobility through the traditional virtues of hard work, persistence, and risk taking. He realized that some Americans encountered hard times, but he was convinced that private philanthropy and the assistance of family and friends were usually sufficient remedies. Since he discounted the importance of racism and discrimination, he believed that, if they tried, African Americans, Latinos, and Native Americans could emulate the successes of white citizens.[22] The economy worked best, he believed, when government assumed virtually no role in its regulation and did not tax citizens beyond the minimal amount needed to fund defense spending and keep a police force. He regarded the 19th century as America's golden era, when individualism, localism, risk taking, and free enterprise dominated the nation. (See Insert 10.2.)

Reagan's political hero was Calvin Coolidge, who articulated a conservative philosophy and made deep and successive cuts in federal taxes during the 1920s.[23] Although Reagan admired Franklin Roosevelt's political skills and decisive leadership, he held Roosevelt responsible for the introduction of alien and destructive policies, including the development of the federal bureaucracy, federal regulations, handouts or doles to millions of Americans, and heavy federal taxes. In Reagan's view, Roosevelt had systematically destroyed the vision of the founding fathers and developed massive welfare and public works programs to gain a political constituency for the Democratic Party. Reagan was critical of liberal rulings of the Supreme Court in the 1950s and 1960s under Chief Justice Earl Warren; he believed that liberal justices had erred in limiting the powers of the police excessively. Reagan did not support federal civil rights legislation in the 1960s because he believed that states could protect the civil rights of their citizens.[24]

His political philosophy can be criticized on many counts. The nostalgic view of American history that eulogized generations of self-made men overlooked the systematic oppression of people of color and women. As his "frontier philosophy" accorded women primarily domestic functions, he did not appoint many women to policy positions during his terms as governor of California and as president.[25] He did not fully realize that many persons who led salutary lives often encountered hard times. Roosevelt's New Deal, far from consisting of a radical departure, provided a minimal set of subsistence

---

INSERT 10.2   Critical Analysis: Reagan's Romantic View of the 19th Century

Drawing on materials from Chapters 4 and 5 of this book, critique Reagan's romantic view of the 19th century, particularly his belief that the nation benefited from the federal government's lack of involvement in social policy.

In light of our knowledge of social problems in the 19th century, why would Reagan believe that it was the golden age of American history?

---

supports for such persons. Reagan's emphasis on self-sufficiency precluded him from understanding the plight of millions of working but poor Americans who could not support their families. He did not favor social welfare programs to aid poor persons because he regarded economic inequality as an incentive for the poor to improve their economic conditions.[26]

Other troubling characteristics of Reagan appeared even when he was governor, only to resurface during his presidency. Lou Cannon, a reporter who followed him over decades and interviewed him more than 40 times, believes that Reagan's childhood experiences with an alcoholic father led him to live largely in a fantasy world of movies, Western heroes, and war heroes that made him inattentive to details and unable to grasp the consequences of some of his decisions—for example, his irresponsible fiscal policies, which led to huge deficits.[27] He was too obsessed with the three themes of lowering taxes, increasing America's defenses, and cutting social spending to be interested in other issues.[28]

Reagan's Emergence as a National Hero

Those who shared Reagan's ideology were widely viewed as extremist in the 1960s, even by many Republicans; but Reagan began to shed the label of extremism by winning the 1966 and 1970 elections as governor of California, a state where liberals, trade unions, and people of color have considerable political power. Although his policies were decidedly conservative, Reagan often displayed political pragmatism. While criticizing intellectuals, he substantially increased the budget of the state university, as well as state assistance to public schools; while criticizing social spending, he permitted significant increases in the state's budget; while criticizing taxes, he increased the state's taxes by $1 billion; and while criticizing sexual permissiveness and abortion, he supported policies that allowed large state funding of abortions.

Even as governor, however, Reagan's pragmatic accommodations were accompanied by harsh and uncompromising attitudes toward people in poverty; for example, he slashed the budgets of selected public welfare, mental health, and child welfare programs. His open opposition to the federal Civil Rights Acts of 1964 and 1965 was matched by his indifference to civil rights as governor. Reagan also initiated a punitive workfare program that forced some recipients into low-paying and menial jobs. He appointed conservative "law and order" justices and continued the rhetoric that extolled conservative values.[29] Moreover, he exhibited a penchant for fiscal irresponsibility as governor by making such large tax cuts that he later had to increase taxes to reduce the budget deficit.[30]

Conservatives persuaded Reagan to run against Gerald Ford for the Republican nomination for the presidency in 1976, but his poor showing in the primaries suggested that he was still regarded as a political maverick. Unhappy with the politically moderate Ford, conservatives tried to persuade Reagan to start a new conservative party both during and after the 1976 race, but he refused because he realized that it would ruin his chances to enter the mainstream of the Republican Party.[31] He decided to pursue the presidency in 1980 in the aftermath of his defeat for the nomination in 1976, but, like Nixon before him, he realized that Republicans' traditional negative policies would not suffice to attract a broad range of voters.

Supply-Side Economics: A Positive Way to Be Negative

It was during this period of drift that Reagan and his aides chanced on a theory known as *supply-side economics*, which became a major theme of his candidacy.[32] Keynesian economics, which had dominated economic thinking in the United States since the late 1930s, emphasized the use of government spending and changes in interest rates to offset recessions and inflation. In recessions, spending was increased and interest rates were decreased; to combat inflation, these policies were reversed. Even Republican presidents Eisenhower, Nixon, and Ford had used its tenets to guide their economic policies. But Keynesian economics was increasingly

under attack by the mid-1970s because it seemed inadequate to solve stagflation. Milton Friedman added new doubts when he suggested that monetary policy—increases or decreases in the supply of money—could powerfully influence the economy. When the government increased the money supply too rapidly, he argued, the nation experienced rapid growth with ensuing inflation, whereas severe reductions in the supply of money often caused recessions.

In this welter of economic theories, economist Arthur Laffer, whose ideas were popularized by journalist Jude Wanniski, argued that Keynesian economists had neglected the importance of the supply of capital to economic growth because of their preoccupation with consumer demand, interest rates, and government spending. Laffer reasoned that economic growth requires steady increases in investment, but investment can occur only if sufficient amounts of capital are accumulated by wealthy persons and corporations and invested in job-creating businesses. However, affluent persons are unlikely to invest their excess money in such businesses, Laffer argued, if their money is subject to high marginal rates of taxation that reduce their profits from investments; in such circumstances, he contended, affluent persons buy expensive cars, antiques, and other luxuries rather than placing their funds in income-producing investments. No amount of consumer demand, Laffer concluded, can cause economic growth if a shortage of investment capital exists.[33] Some Republican politicians, including Congressman Jack Kemp, accepted the logic of supply-side economics and vigorously promoted tax reduction.

Quite apart from its technical merits, supply-side theory appealed to Reagan and his advisors on political grounds because it purported to offer a solution to stagflation by simultaneously addressing problems of inflation and unemployment.[34] Increases in pools of investment capital would, they argued, increase employment by creating jobs, whereas inflation would decrease as entrepreneurs invested in technology and new machinery that made workers more productive. Supply-side economics also provided a justification for major reductions in taxes, which are usually popular with conservatives and with many voters. But would not tax cuts exacerbate the nation's mounting deficits, which had approached $50 billion by the mid-1970s? Not so, countered the supply-siders, because increases in investments prompted by the lower tax rates would stimulate economic activity and hence produce an overall gain in government revenues, even with reductions in tax rates.[35]

Supply-side economics also provided a convenient way to appeal not only to the traditional Republican constituency but to blue-collar voters. Supply-side theorists were most interested in tax reductions for affluent persons, but it was relatively easy to also introduce some reductions for blue-collar and middle-class persons by proposing reductions in the appropriate federal tax brackets.[36] In short, Reagan hoped to achieve Nixon's dream of enlarging the base of the Republican Party, not by the development of social programs but by economic policy.[37]

Ronald Reagan was not alone in his advocacy of supply-side economics. By 1978, the concepts had obtained sufficient appeal that tax cut proposals nearly passed both houses of Congress with bipartisan support.[38] However, in 1980, Reagan was the only presidential contender in either party who strongly supported the theory; indeed, in the Republican primaries, George Bush attacked Reagan's policies as "voodoo economics."[39] Supply-side economics, then, provided a positive way to be negative. Reagan could demand tax cuts (a negative policy) to promote economic growth, reductions in both unemployment and inflation, reductions of the federal deficit, and increases in the income of Americans of all social classes (positive policies).

Since supply-side economists were convinced that economic growth would follow tax cuts, they did not believe that major cuts in government spending were required to curtail deficits. Reagan coupled supply-side economics, however, with his traditional demands that social spending be radically reduced and that many government regulations be rescinded. Reagan's demands for reductions in the role of the federal government might have been dismissed earlier in the decade as Republican negativism, but they

struck a sympathetic chord in the political climate of the late 1970s, when Americans were distrustful of federal bureaucrats and Congress.[40] Moreover, many white Americans were convinced their taxes rose during the 1970s because of increases in spending for social programs that they believed were used primarily by people of color.

The Campaign of 1980: Two Styles

Reagan won the nomination of the Republican Party in 1980, but Carter, the Democratic incumbent, enjoyed a substantial lead in polls in early September, scored heavily when he attacked Reagan as trigger-happy, and used his presidential access to the media to advantage.[41] The political climate of 1980 was very different from that of 1964, however, and Reagan was far more politically adept than Goldwater. His political success stemmed from his ability to adapt his political message to the mood of voters in 1980, with considerable aid from media and political consultants. Carter's response to the nation's economic ills was to cut social spending, but Reagan coupled this response with his supply-side vision of sweeping tax cuts. Carter projected an image of policy vacillation, but Reagan consistently presented his conservative philosophy and advocacy of rearmament. Reagan's rugged image appealed to those male voters who regarded Carter as soft. (Carter was more appealing to female voters, but not enough to offset Reagan's lead with male voters.) Carter's campaign promises to specific interest groups, such as the National Education Association, made him seem beholden to them, but Reagan claimed to be speaking for the entire nation. Carter emphasized the difficulties in righting the economy, but Reagan exuded an optimism reminiscent of Roosevelt's in 1932.

Reagan was aided by public opinion that strongly favored conservatism. After the trauma of Vietnam, Watergate, stagflation, and the Iran hostage crisis, many Americans wanted a respite with a president who could make the world seem simple, who could unite the nation behind patriotism and national pride, and who seemed to stand for moral values. Reagan appealed to many white Americans' distress at the pace of reform in the preceding two decades and their opposition to affirmative action, quotas, and busing. He made extraordinary promises that appealed to those Americans who sought easy answers to stagflation; he even predicted that he could cut taxes, increase defense spending, *and* balance the budget![42] He played on the racial and social fears of white voters by stressing opposition to busing, affirmative action, quotas, and welfare; indeed, he loved to recount the story of a "welfare queen" who had enriched herself through welfare fraud.[43] In the 1980 presidential election, Reagan won a landslide victory; he obtained a large majority of the male vote, carried the entire Southern and Western regions of the nation, and wrested large numbers of blue-collar votes from the Democratic Party.[44]

THE REAGAN POLICY BLITZKRIEG

In the conservative equivalent of Roosevelt's first 100 days in office, Reagan during his first eight months secured major budget cuts, tax cuts, the elimination of many regulations, reductions in the federal government's policy roles, and massive increases in military spending. A number of conditions allowed Reagan to move quickly and successfully on his conservative agenda. First of all, the Democrats were thoroughly demoralized by the size of Reagan's victory in 1980. They feared that it might presage a permanent shift of blue-collar and white ethnic populations to the Republican Party.[45] Thus intimidated by Reagan, the Democrats were also in disarray as they planned their political strategy. Some wanted their party to militantly oppose Reagan's policies and to reassert liberal principles; others feared that opposition would allow Reagan to accuse them of resisting the will of the people; still other Democrats hoped to obtain partial credit for conservative policies by offering budget and tax alternatives to Reagan's positions.[46]

Democrats also encountered serious practical and leadership problems. Having obtained numerical superiority in the Senate in 1980, Republicans possessed a crucial bastion in the Congress as long as they remained united. In the House, the Democratic Party maintained only a slim majority of 38 seats, which could be overcome if there were defections to the Republicans from conservative Southern Democrats, whose constituencies often favored Reagan's policies. The Democrats lacked effective leadership to develop their policy strategy because Tip O'Neill, the majority leader in the House, was widely perceived to lack skills in initiating policies and had awarded crucial committee and party positions to conservative Democrats following an internal party struggle in 1980.[47]

Reagan and his aides plotted a brilliant strategy to capitalize on the Democrats' weakness and the desperate economic situation. Their tactics included militance, centralization, surprise, preparedness, co-optation of conservative Southern Democrats, and preemption of federal revenues through tax cuts and increases in military spending. Let's see how these tactics played out in practice.

The term *militance* is usually applied to the strategy of radicals, but it usefully describes the risk-taking orientation of Reagan and his top advisors, who wanted drastic reductions in social programs and regulations.[48] Reagan knew that he could not instantly eradicate most of the welfare state because of political support for many social programs, but he hoped to reduce government spending from 23 percent to 19 percent of the GNP by 1984 and to hold government spending increases to 7 percent per year, which was far below the 16 percent increases in the last years of the Carter administration. Cuts in social spending were particularly needed because of projected massive increases in military spending, which Reagan wanted to increase by 160 percent over the defense budget during the next six years—rising from $142 billion in 1980 to $368 billion by 1986.

Reagan's inner circle of advisors quickly decided that they could be successful only if they created a climate in which virtually every program and governmental unit was asked to sacrifice for the common good and opposition to cuts in particular programs was viewed as sabotaging efforts to reduce deficits and restore economic growth.[49] They intimidated recalcitrant members of Congress with the prospect of opposition from Reagan in upcoming elections, particularly in those districts in the South and West where Reagan had run more strongly than incumbents. They even hoped to persuade some Southern Democrats to become Republicans in return for choice committee assignments and other political concessions.[50]

Although Reagan was committed to budget cuts, he was equally interested in tax cuts, both to spark economic growth and to reduce federal revenues that might otherwise be used to fund social programs.[51] In a sense, then, Reagan was using the tax cuts to force budget cuts. He calculated that, because tax cuts were politically popular, members of Congress would be pressured to enact them—and that the resulting decreases in revenues would *force* spending cuts unless the Congress wanted to take the blame for budget deficits.[52] Indeed, as David Stockman, the budget director, revealed to Senator Daniel Moynihan in 1985, Reagan had acknowledged in 1981 that he *wanted* a huge deficit to force Congress to cut costly social spending.[53]

Many Democrats were acutely aware of Reagan's strategy, but they encountered a political predicament. In the conservative political atmosphere of 1980, it would have been difficult to oppose *both* tax and budget cuts. Accordingly, many liberal Democrats decided to support budget cuts and oppose tax cuts. They regarded tax cuts as particularly pernicious, as they diminished revenues that were needed to fund social programs.[54] Democrats reasoned, then, that consenting to large budget cuts would make it clear that they were not obstructionists, and so they would then be free to oppose the tax cuts. Their strategy backfired, however, because they did not realize that the tax cuts were so popular with their colleagues and with the electorate that the Congress would enact them despite massive budget cuts.

Military spending, although it had increased in absolute terms during most of the 1970s, had de-creased from 49 percent of the federal budget in 1960 to 21 percent in 1980 as the size of the budget grew because of increased spending on entitlements. President Carter had initiated increases in military spending. However, Reagan sought increases that were unprecedented during peacetime. Indeed, his advisors wanted to expend $1.46 trillion on defense in the next five years—a sum so large that even the hawkish David Stockman believed it would make a massive federal deficit inevitable.[55] These incredible increases in defense spending, like the proposed tax cuts, were highly popular with an American public convinced that the United States needed to deal with the Soviet Union from a position of strength, though a number of legislators questioned its sheer size (see Insert 10.7). Realizing that Reagan would obtain major increases in defense spending, members of Congress recognized that cuts in social programs would be needed to restrain budget deficits. The issue of guns versus butter surfaced once again; this time, many Americans believed that guns should take precedence. Like the tax cuts, the increase in defense spending was a threat to social spending because it diminished resources that could be invested in social programs.

Reagan soon realized, however, that his budget cuts would be endangered if he attacked social programs with powerful constituencies, such as Social Security, Medicare, Head Start, SSI, disability payments for veterans, summer jobs programs, and school lunch programs. In addition to declaring these programs immune from cuts, Reagan cleverly argued that he was not cutting aggregate social spending in absolute terms but was merely cutting the rate of increase in social spending. He also announced that he would preserve a safety net of basic programs for Americans who were poor or ill, so that none of them would lose welfare protections.[56] These arguments, he hoped, would make him appear compassionate, even as he proposed massive cuts in many social programs.

Reagan's decision to focus on cutbacks in means-tested programs rather than so-called entitlement programs like Medicare and Social Security had profound—and   disastrous—consequences   for many Americans. Entitlements constituted 41 percent of the nation's spending in 1980; indeed, Social Security alone constituted almost 33 percent of the nation's domestic budget. To achieve his target of $50 billion in cuts, therefore, Reagan had to slash programs that specifically gave services and resources to poor persons.[57] Certainly, his argument that he was only slowing the rate of increase of aggregate social spending was technically correct; nevertheless, many specific programs that assisted poor persons were eliminated or severely slashed. For example, Reagan proposed decreasing the federal share of AFDC, even though the real value of AFDC benefits had eroded during the late 1970s. He called for massive cuts in Food Stamps and Medicaid, as well as in nutritional, mental health, and public health programs.[58]

Anticipating efforts by lobbyists and defenders of specific programs to mobilize opposition to his cuts, Reagan called on David Stockman and Edwin Meese to develop and implement a centralized strategy to push them through.[59] The youthful Stockman, formerly a conservative member of the House, had gained detailed knowledge of government programs and finance when he fashioned Republican alternatives to Carter's budgets in the late 1970s. Impressed by Stockman's knowledge, Reagan appointed him director of the Office of Management and Budget (OMB), the agency that develops the president's budget. Meese, a conservative attorney who had been Reagan's attorney general in California, was given the authority to manage domestic policy decisions within the White House and to control the flow of paper to Reagan. He was joined by James Baker, a clever negotiator who orchestrated policy compromises with Congress, and Michael Deaver, an expert in public relations.

Reagan and his advisors realized that their objective of securing cuts in social programs could not be accomplished if they gave the opposition time to organize, if they allowed recently appointed cabinet officials to advocate increased funds for their departments, or if they gave opponents of specific cuts the opportunity to join forces with opponents of other cuts. Stockman, Meese, and Baker quickly held a series of briefings with recently appointed cabinet officials, where they announced plans for major cuts in their departments' programs and urged them to be team players. Richard Schweiker, the newly appointed secretary of the Department of Health and Human Services, conceded to most of the proposed cuts in social programs, not only because of the pressure that was placed on him but also because he had converted to conservatism after a relatively liberal voting record as a senator.[60]

Stockman also met with many members of Congress to inform them of proposed cuts and seek their ideas for further cuts. He compiled in a large black book the growing list of proposed cuts, which quickly totaled $50 billion, a staggering and unprecedented sum. No one was allowed access to this book, which was stored in a safe in Stockman's office, but the repeated leaks of proposed cuts kept the opposition off guard and strengthened the impression that everyone would have to sacrifice. Reagan's team created a siege atmosphere, in which it seemed unpatriotic to oppose cuts in specific programs.[61]

The Democrats threatened to defeat Reagan's policies in the House, where they held a majority, but Reagan remedied this situation by cultivating the support of conservative Southern Democrats who favored his tax, military, and budget-cutting policies. These renegade Southern Democrats, who were called "boll weevils," repeatedly gave Reagan a majority of votes in the House. To gain their support, Reagan's team consulted with them and gave some of them, such as Phil Gramm of Texas, important roles as sponsors and designers of legislation. The boll weevils' threat of defection put House Democrats under even more pressure to capitulate to Reagan's policies, in the knowledge that they could be outvoted by the Reagan coalition of Republicans and boll weevils.[62]

The Triumph of Conservatism

Reagan's strategy led to three major victories for conservatives in 1981: Budget cuts were achieved

---

INSERT 10.3 Ethical Analysis of Key Issues and Policies: Should We Block-Grant All Federal Programs?

The concept of returning federal funds to the states has deep roots in American history. For example, President Andrew Jackson proposed such transfers when he ran a budget surplus. More recently, the liberal economist Walter Heller was a prime advocate of revenue sharing in the 1960s.

The federal government *could* transfer all of its tax revenues, save those used for military and international programs, to the states and localities. Were this to happen, what would be the consequences? As two examples, discuss the advisability of block granting Food Stamps, SSI, and Medicaid. Remember that, once programs *are* block granted when they were entitlements, Congress no longer has to fund them to the

level of claimed benefits. Moreover, relatively conservative states can impose particularly harsh eligibility and benefit policies. (We will ask in Chapter 11 whether shifting AFDC to a block grant program known as Temporary Assistance to Needy Families or TANF was ethically meritorious.)

Yet some transfers of funds are probably beneficial, because local and state governments do not possess the borrowing power, or the large income tax revenues, of the federal government. What kinds of programs could states and localities implement with little or no guidance from federal authorities—and which ones should federal authorities retain?

---

through passage of the Omnibus Budget Reconciliation Act (OBRA) in July, tax cuts were enacted in August, and increases in defense spending were made final in the fall.

It is difficult under ordinary conditions for a president to control the budgetary process because numerous congressional committees can override his budgetary suggestions. Without describing the complex budgetary maneuvering in detail, suffice it to say that David Stockman became the orchestrator of administration policy. To obtain enactment of OBRA, tax cuts, and increases in defense spending, he literally camped out in the Congress, arranged coalitions of Republicans and boll weevils, outmaneuvered liberal Democrats, and made extensive use of Reagan's popularity and the mass media.

OBRA made deep cuts in social programs and eliminated 57 social programs by folding them into seven block grants: social services; community services; alcohol, drug abuse, and mental health services; maternal and child health services; community development services; primary health services; and preventive health services.[63] By creating block grants and allocating limited funds to each of them, Reagan was able to cut social spending for those programs within the block grants. (See Insert

10.3 for critical questions about the extent to which the United State should resort to block grants.)

Reagan achieved another victory in August, when the largest tax cut since the end of World War II was enacted. It made substantial reductions in the taxes of individuals and even larger cuts in the taxes of many corporations. This legislation markedly increased economic inequality by granting larger tax cuts to affluent persons than to middle- and working-class Americans, at the same time that social programs for the poor were being decimated. In the end, the tax cuts gained the support not only of boll weevils and Republicans but also of many Democrats who had initially planned to contest them but who feared retaliation from voters.[64]

Reagan also succeeded in obtaining the huge increases in defense spending that he had so fervently sought. By so doing, Reagan had obtained the counterrevolution that he had espoused since the early 1950s—tax cuts, social spending reductions, and defense increases.

When characterizing Reagan's policy successes in 1981, it is important to reiterate that, though he cut the funding of many programs that help low-income persons, he chose not to cut big-ticket social programs with large middle-class constituencies, such as Medicare and Social Security. In subsequent years, he again chose to exclude these programs from his cuts. Indeed, one commentator calls Reagan the guns *and* butter president because aggregate social spending continued to rise along with defense spending.[65] He chose to make this strategic concession partly because his aides had calculated that Congress, including many Democrats, would not accede to his increased military spending if he also sought to cut these middle-class programs.

OBRA, Tax Reductions, and Deregulation

A host of conservative policies were included within the complex tangle of the OBRA legislation, which recommended budget cuts that totaled $40 billion for 1982 and an additional $50 billion by 1984. First, the legislation terminated some programs—for example, CETA, the public service program for unemployed workers. Second, deep cuts were made in many means-tested programs. The extent of the cuts in these programs for low-income persons was deeply disturbing to many liberals—and Reagan relentlessly sought to cut these programs further in succeeding years. All told, Reagan managed during his administration to cut AFDC by 17.4 percent; 400,000 persons were removed from the rolls. One million persons lost eligibility for Food Stamps; the program was cut by 14.3 percent. The social services block grant, which provided an array of services to poor people, was cut by 23.5 percent.[66] In the Department of Housing and Urban Development, funding for low- and moderate-income housing was reduced from $33.5 billion in 1981 to $14 billion in 1987—a cut of 57 percent.[67]

Third, OBRA enacted indirect methods of cutting expenditures. Believing that social programs should assist only truly needy persons, Reagan hoped to reduce the number of able-bodied persons who received welfare and other benefits.[68] To do so, he reduced eligibility for Food Stamps, state AFDC programs, and unemployment insurance. He also eliminated work incentive payments in the AFDC program so that many working women could no longer receive welfare benefits, even if they were beneath official poverty lines. AFDC rolls were cut dramatically by this policy, but it was ironic that an administration that wanted to encourage, even require, work for welfare recipients had provided a disincentive to work by forcing many women working in low-wage jobs to return to welfare rolls.[69]

The Economic Recovery Tax Act that passed the Congress in August of 1981 provided for 20 percent cuts in the income taxes of most Americans, spread over three years, and a major reduction in corporate taxes.[70] But these cuts were highly inequitable. Between 1981 and 1985, for example, the combined tax rates for the lowest one-fifth of the population went from 8.4 to 10.6 percent (or $137 in additional taxes per payer), whereas the tax rate of persons in the top one-fifth declined from 27.3 percent to 24 percent (or tax reductions of $2,531 per payer). What made these tax increases even more onerous on poor persons was that their *pretax* income declined during the decade because low-paid service jobs steadily replaced unionized industrial jobs.[71] The tax legislation also violated the principle of progressive taxation that liberals had traditionally championed; it gave larger tax breaks to rich people than to poor people. Further, the tax credits given in 1973 to low-income persons who earned less than $5,600 were not indexed; their value had been seriously eroded by the inflation of the 1970s.[72]

In 1981, Reagan issued an executive order that gave OMB the duty of reviewing government regulations and deleting those that were not demonstrated to be cost-effective, and a cabinet-level Task Force on Regulatory Relief, chaired by Vice President George Bush, was established. Between 1980 and 1984, the number of federal regulations was reduced from 90,000 to 76,000. To the consternation of some liberals, the administration drastically reduced regulations in the EEOC, OSHA, and many social programs; key civil rights matters and other provisions were deleted.[73] Reagan severely curtailed the effectiveness of OSHA, the EEOC, and the Department of Labor's Office of Contract Compliance Programs. He cut their staffs, delegated many monitoring functions to states, sought to enforce affirmative action only after proof of discrimination by employers had been obtained, and limited affirmative action monitoring to very large corporations. Reagan appointed officials who did not favor affirmative action to oversee its enforcement; for example, he chose Clarence Thomas to head the EEOC, and he appointed Clarence Pendleton to direct the Civil Rights Commission, where he used his power to fight the principle of affirmative action.[74]

Reagan's Loss of Momentum

It seemed in September of 1981 that the Reagan counterrevolution would continue unabated for years to come, but he did not achieve striking policy successes during the remainder of his first term. There were a number of reasons for this loss of momentum. First, the administration split into two factions.[75] One group, headed by David Stockman and James Baker, feared that the federal deficit would continue to grow uncontrollably unless taxes were increased, further cuts were made in social spending, and reductions were made in defense spending. Another group, which included supply-side economists, adamantly opposed tax increases, which they feared would jeopardize economic growth. They believed that the economic growth generated by the 1981 tax cuts would produce additional tax revenues to ease the federal deficit. Some of them were so confident in this prediction that they did not believe further deep cuts in social programs were needed.

Stockman had embraced tax reduction policies uneasily during the early and middle 1980s because he feared massive increases in the federal deficit. However, he advocated delaying or reducing tax cuts in the summer of 1981.[76] In interviews during the summer and fall of 1981, which were published in December of 1981, he admitted that top officials in the administration had tinkered with economic models so as to make it appear that federal deficits would not be exacerbated by the tax cuts, and he alleged that some officials in the administration had used supply-side theory as a convenient rationale for giving huge tax concessions to affluent persons

and corporations.[77] Supply-siders were also furious with Stockman and Baker for not protesting the tight-money policy of the Federal Reserve Board. This policy had been devised by its chairman to drive down the extraordinary inflation that plagued the nation, but supply-siders feared that it would create a recession and thereby discredit their approach. Some even believed that Stockman would welcome a recession so as to discredit them.[78]

Both sides in this titanic struggle within the administration were convinced of the rightness of their cause and attributed evil intentions to their opponents. To the delight of supply-siders, Reagan resisted pleas by Stockman and Baker to increase taxes. However, in the spring of 1982, when he finally assented to a large tax increase known as the Tax Equity and Fiscal Responsibility Act (TEFRA), which took away some of the massive tax concessions given to corporations in 1981, some supply-side officials left the administration.[79] Rumors circulated of dissension among Meese, Deaver, and Baker. Meanwhile, observers began to wonder whether anyone was in charge at the White House because Reagan appeared to lack understanding of policy issues.[80]

Another factor that slowed Reagan's momentum was a deep recession, which began in 1981 and extended into 1983. Unemployment rose to double-digit figures; its impact was greatest on people of color, teenagers, and women. The recession contributed to growing doubts about the administration's economic policies; it also increased the federal deficit because government tax revenues decreased as economic activity slackened.[81] By the end of fiscal year 1984, the cumulative deficits in the Reagan administration had surpassed the cumulative deficits of *all* preceding American presidents; indeed, some commentators feared that the United States would be reduced to the status of nations such as Mexico and Brazil, which found their economic growth impeded by the size of interest payments on their national debts.

With the recession came growing awareness of the plight of poor persons, who were hard hit by unemployment and the cuts in means-tested social programs. National media ran extended stories

INSERT 10.4   Ethical Analysis of Key Issues and Policies: When to Retreat and When to Resist?

Most of the budget cuts of 1981 focused on programs for poor people; so-called middle-class entitlements such as Medicare and Social Security were untouched. Northern Democrats, who represent the liberal wing of the party, faced a dilemma. Many Southern Democrats were defecting to the Republican budget and tax policies. The Reagan presidency seemed to be invincible; Democrats feared that they might be routed in upcoming elections if they obstructed his policies. Yet

those policies contradicted deeply held liberal values and violated the principle of social justice.

Should liberal Democrats have made a last stand in 1981 against the budget cuts? Should they have opposed *both* budget cuts and tax cuts, on the grounds that the latter *forced* the budget cuts by depleting the government's revenue? Is a principled stand sometimes effective in politics?

about increases in poverty rates across the nation, the growing inequality between rich and poor Americans, and pockets of unemployment in cities like Youngstown and Cleveland, Ohio, where steel and other basic industries had closed plants in response to foreign competition.[82] Congress was unhappy about the lack of equity in administration policies. Reagan had declared virtually all the entitlement programs off limits for cuts, but he proposed further cuts of means-tested programs for the poor. His tax policies had led to windfall gains for many corporations and affluent persons. The charge that Reagan lacked compassion seemed to be gathering strength in 1982 and 1983 because of the cumulative effects of his budget-cutting and tax policies, as well as his fiscal and monetary policy, which had contributed to the recession.[83]

Many members of Congress also believed they had been manipulated by the White House and by Stockman during budget and tax deliberations in 1981. Should the OMB director, they asked, personally orchestrate budget objectives and goals of the Congress? Some in Congress felt betrayed by the White House; although Stockman had implied in 1981 that the OBRA cuts would suffice, he proposed further deep cuts in late 1981 and in succeeding years. Was it fair for Reagan, some asked, to force the Congress to make cuts in social programs by reducing government revenues—both by slashing taxes and by dramatically increasing military spending? Moreover, Reagan's frequent use of television and radio to apply public pressure on Congress made members increasingly resentful.[84] (See Insert 10.4.)

Whereas many Democrats had capitulated to Reagan's blitzkrieg in 1981, they were more willing to resist Reagan's cuts during the remainder of his first term—especially now that, thanks to the recession, their constituents were more concerned about unemployment than about inflation. In addition, Reagan's ability to outvote Democrats with a coalition of boll weevils and Republicans was curtailed when the Democrats gained a number of House seats in congressional elections of 1982. Indeed, some liberal Republicans, known as "gypsy moths," sided with Democrats against many spending cuts. Though still in disarray, the Democrats held their ground against further cuts, in the hope that they could defeat Reagan in 1984.

Social Security, Job Training, and Medicare

Reagan's policy successes during the remainder of his first term were modest, though he was able to obtain additional cuts in social programs, to make major changes in the Social Security program and Medicare, and to create his own job-training legislation.

Stockman had hoped from the outset to include Social Security and Medicare in the budget cuts because they constituted a large portion of domestic spending. When he became further concerned about deficits, Stockman pushed the president to rescind the minimum Social Security benefit that was given to persons—such as elderly nuns—who had not paid into the trust fund during their working years. Stockman also sought to institute a penalty for those who sought early retirement benefits. A storm of political protest greeted these proposals when the president made them public. Democrats accused him of reneging on his pledge to exempt the Social Security program from budget cuts, and many Republicans dissociated themselves from policies that they believed could be politically disastrous. The proposals were defeated by a vote of 96 to 0 by the Senate in 1981.[85]

Reagan and most legislators realized, however, that changes had to be made in Social Security because benefit outlays continued to exceed revenues from payroll deductions despite the sharp increases in payroll taxes introduced by President Carter. To deflect controversy from himself, Reagan appointed a blue-ribbon task force, which recommended that the option to take Social Security benefits at age 62 be rescinded and that benefits be delayed until persons reached age 68. The commission also concluded that retired persons whose earnings exceeded $20,000, whether from work or investments, should pay taxes on a substantial portion of their Social Security benefits, with ensuing revenues to be returned to the trust fund. To decrease the size of reductions in general benefits, many politicians supported the taxation of affluent persons' benefits, a policy that partially offset the regressive nature of Social Security payroll taxes.[86] Some of these recommendations received bipartisan support and were enacted in 1983, including the taxing of some benefits received by affluent persons and the phasing upward of the retirement age to age 67 by the year 2027.

Reagan also encountered a funding emergency in Part A of the Medicare program, whose outlays for hospital bills had increased faster than payroll tax revenues. Federal Medicare expenditures had increased from $15.2 billion in 1970 to $38.3 billion in 1980 because of the aging of the population, the increasing use of technology, and the failure of government authorities to prevent doctors and hospitals from charging excessive fees and providing unnecessary treatments.[87] Reagan's advisors developed an indirect method of restraining Medicare costs. To place pressure on hospitals to discharge patients as soon as possible and to prevent them from charging excessive fees, Congress established national levels of payment for 467 specific diagnoses or diagnostic-related groups (DRGs). Thus, federal authorities paid hospitals an established fee for all patients who were admitted for appendectomies, no matter how long they remained in the hospital or whether they developed complications. The policy led to some decreases in health expenditures by 1986, but critics argued that this reimbursement approach created additional problems. Would not many hospitals try to discharge patients prematurely —or serve only those patients who were not likely to develop complications? Would not affluent persons purchase insurance to finance supplemental services so that, once again, public policy would create a two-tiered system of health care? The formula also seemed to favor the growing network of for-profit hospitals that primarily served those middle- and upper-class clientele who were least likely to experience medical complications.[88]

Federal authorities also wanted to contain the increasing costs of Medicaid, whose combined federal and state funding had increased from $10.9 billion in 1970 to $25.4 billion in 1980. They cut the federal share of Medicaid funding in the OBRA legislation and offered states incentives to reduce the growth rates of Medicaid. Finally, they encouraged states to offer Medicaid contracts only to those hospitals and clinics that offered low bids; as a result, Medicaid patients found that they could use even fewer providers than were previously available.[89]

The health care system was characterized in 1986 by increasing competition and turmoil. There had been some easing of the rate of price increases for medical care by the middle of the decade, but basic flaws in the American medical system, such as its excessive use of technology and absence of preventive care, still had not been addressed.[90] Critics lamented continuing inequities in medical care. Roughly 30 million Americans had no health insurance and were ineligible for the means-tested Medicaid program and the age-tested Medicare programs. Millions of Medicaid patients could obtain treatment only in inner-city clinics, partly because most physicians would not serve Medicaid patients for reasons of financial self-interest; they received considerably larger fees from other insurers.[91]

Federal authorities had not developed adequate policies to help elderly patients with chronic health problems. Medicare was intended to help elderly persons with acute conditions. Those with chronic conditions soon exhausted it (and their private insurance) and had to deplete their assets to obtain eligibility for the means-tested Medicaid program, which covered ongoing costs of convalescent homes, nursing homes, and home health care. Medicaid authorities had, in turn, developed confusing and poorly monitored federal and state policies to regulate nursing home care and to fund community-based care of frail and elderly persons. Medicare and Medicaid authorities, as well as private insurance companies, had commissioned a series of experiments in the 1980s to test various community-based methods of helping frail elderly persons, but no comprehensive national policy had been developed by the late 1980s.[92] Perhaps the most serious health problem of the 1980s was the emergence of acquired immunodeficiency syndrome (AIDS), which we will discuss in more detail later.[93]

Reagan was determined to terminate the CETA program because he believed its subsidy of tens of thousands of public service jobs in public and not-for-profit agencies interfered with private job markets. After slashing its funds, Reagan finally abolished it in favor of his own program, the Job Training Partnership Act (JTPA), enacted in 1982. The federal government gave funds with relatively few restrictions to states, which, in turn, funded local private industry councils (PICs). PICs, made up of business, agency, and government officials, awarded contracts to job placement agencies and to local industries, which received a fee for each person that they placed with private business. Critics contended, however, that the training and reimbursement policies of JTPA made it irrelevant to the needs of many low-income persons because placement agencies often were reimbursed only for successful placements. Moreover, the failure of JTPA to provide training and day care subsidies to placement agencies, businesses, or trainees made it impossible for many women and low-income persons to use the program.[94]

In 1981, Reagan had folded 57 categorical programs into seven block grants. In 1982, he proposed to reduce the federal role in social welfare much further by offering to undertake complete federal financing and administration of Medicaid if the states carried full costs and responsibility for AFDC, Food Stamps, and 43 other programs. To attract the support of governors, he offered to cede to states a limited proportion of federal gasoline and cigarette excise taxes. The proposed swap was defeated, however, for several reasons. Although Reagan claimed that he did not want to short-change the states, astute analysts computed that the scheme would lead them to suffer large net losses in revenue. As in the case of the OBRA block grants, Reagan could not resist the impulse to couple defederalization with budget cuts. Officials in industrialized states in the Midwest and New England, which had particularly high expenses for welfare, believed that defederalization would mainly benefit Sun Belt states, where oil and gas production, as well as high rates of economic growth, already provided sufficient resources to address social needs.[95] Many state officials were disinclined to support the scheme because they were still angry at the budgetary turmoil provoked by Reagan's earlier cuts. Reductions in federal funding for social programs had meant that local authorities had to assume additional expenses at the very time when popular tax revolts had led to sharp reductions in local taxes. Few federal legislators desired to carry defederalization further because they derived political support from federal programs.

Indeed, it can be argued that the Reagan years reduced both federal and state budgets to chaos. The huge deficits at the federal level meant that congressional officials devoted more time to the budgetary process than to other, more pressing domestic issues. Moreover, the deficits placed extraordinary pressure on programs for low-income persons, as we have noted. The budgets of many states rose sharply in the 1980s, as they sought to address problems of family dissolution, homelessness, AIDS, and drug and crack babies; they also faced costs due to immigration from abroad, increased costs of prisons, remarkable increases in Medicaid and AFDC costs, and a doubling of education spending—all during a decade when federal aid went from $110 billion in 1978, in inflation-adjusted dollars, to $88 billion in 1982 and only back up to $96 billion by 1990. Indeed, when AFDC and portions of the Medicaid program are not considered, federal aid to the states fell by one-third during the 1980s.[96] These escalating social costs, coupled with federal cuts, produced serious budget deficits in many local jurisdictions.

Moral Reforms

The Moral Majority had hoped that Reagan would take strong action to stop abortions, to attack pornography, to allow prayer in the public schools, and to provide tax concessions for tuition payments to private schools, but their confidence in him was premature. Reagan knew that these issues, like temperance in the 19th century and in the 1920s, were divisive. The demand for tax concessions for the tuition costs of private schools was widely viewed as public underwriting of educational segregation. Many women opposed a constitutional amendment to override the 1973 Supreme Court ruling that legalized abortion. Many persons in both parties opposed federal legislation or a constitutional amendment to allow prayer in schools, and civil libertarians stoutly resisted federal laws to outlaw pornography. Reagan feared that personal identification with these divisive issues would jeopardize his other budget-cutting, tax, and deregulatory legislation.[97] Accordingly, he voiced support for moral reforms but did not invest time or resources in them.

Meese became Reagan's emissary to leaders of the Moral Majority and tried to placate them. Disappointed by Reagan's inaction, the Moral Majority nevertheless had notable victories. The Congress continued to disallow use of Medicaid funds for abortion and to cut funds for family planning, which the Moral Majority believed fostered promiscuity. The Justice Department advocated the Moral Majority's position in court cases regarding pornography, school prayer, and other matters, though it received few favorable rulings. A Presidential Commission on Pornography requested national censorship of magazines like *Playboy* in 1986. The Supreme Court upheld a Georgia statute that declared acts of sodomy between consenting adults to be illegal.

The Moral Majority and its allies also developed expertise in targeting liberal legislators in election campaigns. Vast media, advertising, mailing, and door-to-door campaigns sought to portray liberal candidates as murderers (of fetuses), supporters of pornography, and atheists. By engaging in character assassination of liberal candidates, the Moral Majority and its allies allowed conservative candidates to take the high road and yet still reap the electoral benefits. These tactics contributed to the defeat of a number of liberal legislators in close races.[98]

However, the nation was hardly embracing the tenets of the Moral Majority. Courts often ruled against them in school prayer, pornography, and abortion cases. Their tactics in political campaigns sometimes caused a sympathy vote for liberal candidates. Many observers wondered whether a secular and urban society would truly accept the ideas of individuals who, like temperance crusaders in earlier periods, sought to impose their moral standards on others.[99]

STALEMATE

The Election of 1984

Reagan relished the opportunity to face Walter Mondale, the Democratic candidate in 1984, who not only had served as vice president to the unpopular Jimmy Carter but was identified with unions and liberalism. After some vacillation, Reagan's resolve to run again was strengthened by improvement in the nation's economy following the recession of 1983.[100]

The election in 1984 was a rerun of the 1980 campaign. Many major Democratic candidates ran in the presidential primaries. Mondale obtained early endorsements from trade unions, as well as from professional groups, but Senator Gary Hart made Mondale appear politically vulnerable by winning decisive victories in key primaries. These two candidates represented a deep split in the Democratic Party. Some Democrats, including civil rights groups, many trade unions, intellectuals, and some mayors, continued to embrace federal social welfare programs and civil rights. Mondale felt most at home with this group, but even here he had to contend with the African American civil rights activist Jesse Jackson, whose determined campaign mobilized unprecedented numbers of African American voters. Other Democrats, such as Hart, were neoliberals who disdained major increases in social spending but favored federal incentives to promote American industry's ability to compete with the Japanese.[101] Hart's support came mainly from young professionals who had little knowledge of social reform movements in either the Great Depression or the Great Society.[102]

Mondale finally won the Democratic nomination, but he did not overcome Reagan's lead in the polls. In a major victory for feminists, Mondale chose Geraldine Ferraro as the vice presidential candidate, but her family finances became a major campaign issue that slowed Mondale's momentum. Mondale tried to make the mounting budget deficit a campaign issue—he actually proposed major increases in federal taxes—but the issue was too abstract for most voters, who did not believe the deficits slowed economic growth and did not like his remedy of increased taxes. As front-runner, Reagan avoided substantive issues during most of the campaign and focused instead on his leadership and personal skills, as well as his success in restoring economic growth. As in 1980, he targeted white voters and used code words like *affirmative action* and *quotas* to mobilize them against the Democrats. By holding his own during his second televised debate with Mondale, he deflected the charge that he was too old to be president. He won another landslide victory, though the Democrats maintained their numbers in Congress.

Reagan's Second Term

Unlike Reagan's victory in 1980, when tax and budget reduction were his central themes, his reelection in 1984 did not constitute a mandate for specific policies. The American people, who stood to the left of Reagan in public opinion polls, liked him as a person, believed him to be a decisive leader, and favored his buildup of the military, but did not elect him to continue his assault on the welfare state.

The politics of his second term can best be described as a stalemate. As in his first term, Reagan used the specter of the federal deficit to increase pressure on the Congress to reduce social spending. Once again, he proposed massive increases in defense spending—in particular, for the Strategic Defense Initiative (SDI), a space-based, laser-guided antimissile system for which appropriate technology had not yet been developed. At an estimated cost of $1 trillion, spread over a decade, this program quickly became a priority of defense spending. However, congressional legislators balked at his proposals to cut domestic spending, and even made modest increases in some programs. Entitlements remained out of bounds for cuts, though Reagan tried to cut them indirectly by proposing major increases in consumer fees for services subsidized by Medicare.

In this stalemated atmosphere, an unlikely coalition in Congress enacted legislation to address the unprecedented federal deficits, which had continued to increase. The Balanced Budget and Emergency Deficit Control Act, commonly known as the Gramm-Rudman-Hollings Act, was enacted by Congress in 1985. Furious that Reagan proposed neither tax increases nor cuts in military spending to alleviate the deficit, members of Congress assented to a measure that required across-the-board cuts in domestic and military programs if specific planned reductions in the federal deficit did not occur that would eventually bring the budget into balance. But this measure could hardly be expected to eliminate the deficit, inasmuch as it implied that the basic problem was *spending*, rather than the combination of inadequate *revenues* (from taxes) and large military budgets. It was this combination of tax cuts and increases in military spending that had led to the budget deficits in 1981, but few politicians wanted to propose tax increases. A few legislators proposed sharp decreases in military spending, but most politicians were hesitant to cut the defense budget when it funded projects in their districts. Many commentators doubted that Congress would actually bring the budget into balance even with the enactment of Gramm-Rudman-Hollings.

When viewed in tandem, Reagan's military, budget, and tax policies placed extraordinary downward pressure on two kinds of social programs: means-tested entitlements (such as Food Stamps and SSI) and social programs funded by the discretionary budget. His military buildup exceeded the *combined* size of military spending for the Korean and Vietnam Wars as the United States hugely increased the size of its navy and air force, developed scores of new weapons, and launched a fleet of new submarines—at a time when the United States was not engaged in a shooting war. Reagan coupled these huge increases in military spending with large increases in interest payments on the massive debt that he had created when he cut taxes so deeply in 1981. (Reagan's cumulative deficits were larger than all deficits of all presidents in American history combined.) Reagan also decided to exempt "big-ticket" entitlements that were popular with the middle and upper classes from cuts, particularly Medicare and Social Security.

Having created these huge deficits, Reagan took almost no responsibility for resolving them. Each year, he submitted a "dead-on-arrival" budget that retained his military buildup and that rejected major increases in taxes. Various leaders in Congress, in turn, would often propose to redress the deficits by raising taxes, cutting military spending, or cutting Medicare or Social Security—but Reagan would not support these policies and other legislators would often oppose them as well. In this stalemated environment, Reagan's policies of 1981—tax cuts, huge military spending, and massive deficits—remained largely intact.

In this environment of budgetary scarcity, Reagan annually sought to cut deficits by slashing

funding for discretionary social programs even further than they had been cut in 1981—and he proposed further cuts in Food Stamps, Medicaid, and SSI. Only the determined opposition of congressional liberals prevented Reagan from achieving these cuts, but liberals could not increase funding for discretionary social programs or means-tested entitlements when such huge deficits existed. At a time when economic inequality was increasing in the United States as many persons with only high school diplomas lost job prospects as unionized jobs in steel manufacturing, automobile plants, and other basic industries relocated abroad, federal spending on education and vocational training remained stagnant. When economic inequality increased markedly in the 1980s, expenditures of the federal government for discretionary social programs declined in constant dollars and as a share of the gross domestic product.

Tax reform became a central issue in Reagan's second term and eclipsed deficit reduction in congressional deliberations. Finally enacted in 1986 after complicated political maneuvering, the resulting legislation simplified federal taxes by decreasing the number of tax brackets and loopholes, vastly increased corporate taxes, and took roughly 6 million low-wage earners from the tax rolls. But it also repudiated the liberal belief that the federal tax system should be progressive, by reducing the top tax bracket of affluent Americans to a modest 33 percent, which was not much higher than the rate paid by middle- and working-class Americans. Moreover, the tax reform did not generate considerably more revenues than the old tax system, and consequently the federal deficit was not reduced; federal revenues were still insufficient to fund social programs.[103]

Social reformers could nonetheless count several modest victories during Reagan's second term. The denial of SSI payments to persons with disabilities, which had often been arbitrary and unwarranted during Reagan's first term, was challenged by several court rulings, and benefits were restored in thousands of cases. The Department of Health and Human Services was forced to concede that many persons with mental disabilities such as schizophrenia could not work and required ongoing assistance from the federal government.[104] The Family Support Act of 1988 provided funds to the states for training projects and child care to help AFDC recipients enter the labor force, though many critics doubted if the program was sufficiently generous to make much difference. Perhaps most important, Congress managed to fend off Reagan's continuing demands for further cuts in many social programs, even if funding for programs that helped poor people had not recovered from cuts earlier in the decade.

PASSING THE TORCH: FROM REAGAN TO BUSH, SR.

It was, some commentators have argued, the last campaign of the Cold War when George Bush, who had been Reagan's vice president, battled Michael Dukakis for the presidency in 1988.[105] Both candidates believed that the party that could attract blue-collar and white voters to its side would win the election. It was the quintessential public relations campaign; both candidates were guided by advertising and marketing experts.

The candidates tried to depict themselves as tough on crime, as patriotic, and as believers in a strong defense. Bush sought to depict Dukakis as soft on crime; a television advertisement argued that, while governor of Massachusetts, Dukakis had unadvisedly released an African American prisoner called Willie Horton from jail. Bush accused Dukakis of being liberal; in the conservative 1980s, the opprobrium associated with liberalism was hardly less than the stigma of communism in the early 1950s! Dukakis, in turn, pledged that he would fight crime and drugs—and even rode, unconvincingly, in a tank to show that he would maintain a strong defense establishment. Social issues, such as poverty, homelessness, and AIDS, were hardly discussed during most of the campaign.

When it finally became clear that Bush was leading in the public opinion polls, Dukakis attempted to develop more traditional Democratic themes, such as social reform, but his newfound liberalism came too late to help him. Nor was the American public, which had been lulled into complacency by the Reagan administration, in a mood for fundamental changes in domestic or international arenas. George Bush was elected by an overwhelming majority, but the Democrats retained control of both chambers of Congress.

It was unclear when Bush took office how he would use his victory because, unlike Reagan in 1980, he had not developed a clear agenda. Once elected, he essentially continued the central themes of the Reagan administration—large military spending and resistance to tax increases. As former head of the Central Intelligence Agency and ambassador to China and to the United Nations, Bush was preoccupied with foreign policy for most of his term. He gave domestic issues extraordinarily scant attention, despite campaign pledges to be the education president, the environmental president, and the president who would wage a successful war on drugs. Even with the dissolution of the Soviet empire in the early 1990s, Bush was loath to markedly reduce funds for the American military establishment, which continued to absorb about $300 billion a year. Moreover, Bush was constrained by a campaign pledge not to raise new taxes. Although Bush was less fiercely opposed to social spending than his predecessor had been, and although he assented to increases in social spending far greater than had occurred in the Reagan years, he was largely passive on domestic matters and freely used his veto to stymie an array of measures proposed by Democrats.[106]

Caught in this fiscal bind, preoccupied with foreign affairs, and guided by a conservative ideology that was strongly enforced by John Sununu, his chief of staff until mid-1991, Bush offered few social initiatives that were backed up with funding. The Bush administration, which also had to contend with a Democratic Congress, was marked by the same curious combination of policies as the Reagan administration: on the one hand, deficits, massive defense budgets, and the absence of dramatic social reform initiatives; on the other, maintenance of almost all of the existing programs of the American welfare state.

SOCIAL POLICIES OF THE BUSH, SR., ADMINISTRATION

Social Spending and the Politics of the Budget

The fate of social policy in the Bush era was considerably shaped during the annual budget process, when Congress and the executive branch determined what fraction of the budget to allocate to defense and social spending. The same had been true during much of the Reagan administration. Recall that Reagan's strategy to markedly reduce federal social spending by massively increasing the federal deficit—that is, by lowering taxes and increasing defense spending—had been only partially successful; even though many programs for poor people found their funding decreased, overall social spending increased. Congressmen who favored retention of the American welfare state were, in effect, able to obtain their preferences in the heated budget negotiations of the period, while Reagan was able to retain his tax and military preferences.[107]

No less than Reagan, Bush was committed to the notion that the United States should maintain a worldwide military presence and large conventional and strategic forces. Like Reagan, he was committed to not raising taxes, as illustrated by his often-repeated pledge in 1988: "Read my lips, no new taxes." However, Bush was less able to counter increases in domestic spending than Reagan had been because the Democrats now controlled both houses of Congress and because Bush was less fervent in his opposition to federal programs. Thus, in the Bush era, the budget stalemate continued with its huge deficits, but social spending rose at a much higher rate than in the Reagan administration.[108]

Social reformers were hardly satisfied with these gains in social spending, however, particularly in the wake of developments in Eastern Europe and the Soviet Union. Granted concessions by Soviet leader Mikhail Gorbachev and thus emboldened to assert their rights, Eastern European states achieved greater independence from the Soviet Union. Moreover, the Soviet Union rapidly disintegrated; it was dissolved by a historic decision of the leaders of its many republics in 1991.

Some social reformers perceived this thawing of the Cold War as a remarkable, unprecedented opportunity to recast the federal budget. Why not, they argued, declare a "peace dividend" to transfer as much as $150 billion annually from the military budget to the domestic spending budget? Why not pull American troops from Europe and Asia, dramatically reduce American nuclear forces, and increasingly rely on multinational forces and the United Nations to keep the peace?[109]

The ensuing budgetary battle in 1990 rivaled the ferocity and duration of that in 1981, when Reagan had obtained tax cuts, spending reductions, and military increases at the inception of his presidency. Many legislators wanted to markedly decrease military spending and increase social spending, but the Bush administration was adamantly opposed to reductions in military spending. Legislators concerned about the budget deficit pushed to increase federal taxes, but Bush was under great pressure from conservatives to remain true to his 1988 pledge not to do so.

In a complex and extended set of negotiations, which culminated in the budget summit of 1990, Congress and the administration fashioned an uneasy compromise that gave something to everyone but avoided fundamental changes in the federal budget. Under pressure to reduce the deficit, Bush agreed to allow some new taxes. The ratio of military and domestic spending in the budget was preserved, but the overall budget was to be reduced incrementally in coming years by placing caps on aggregate social spending and military spending.[110] To prevent social reformers from raiding the military budget, the agreement stipulated that reductions in defense spending could *not* be used to increase social spending. In effect, the agreement was a standoff, intended to delay reconsideration of budget priorities until 1993—conveniently after the next presidential election. At that point, it was widely predicted, all hell would break loose, as the two parties battled to shape the new configuration of the federal budget. Would the military budget be severely cut? If so, would the savings be used for social programs or merely to reduce the vast deficit or even to fund new tax cuts?

Many social reformers were dismayed by the budget agreement of 1990. It made an immediate peace dividend impossible because it explicitly disallowed the use of defense cuts to fund social programs. It required legislators to take funds from existing social programs whenever they proposed new social programs. Moreover, soon after the budget agreement, in early 1991, the war with Iraq quieted (for the moment) discussion of a peace dividend.

Inheriting Reagan's huge deficits, George Bush faced a fiscal dilemma. If he failed to cut deficits during his first term, citizens might retaliate against him in the 1992 presidential election. If he cut entitlements such as Social Security or Medicare, Democrats would attack him as mean-minded. If he sought to raise taxes, he would be attacked by many Republicans.

Rather than leaving his options open, Bush made a strategic error at the Republican Convention in 1988 by saying, "Read my lips: No new taxes." (Unless he was willing to attack popular entitlements, Bush *had* to cut taxes to redress the soaring deficits.) Realizing that no serious progress could be made in reducing Reagan's deficits without raising taxes, Democratic congressional leaders cleverly insisted on new taxes as part of a budget deal in 1990. Fearing a government shutdown just as the nation was heading into a war with Saddam Hussein, the leader of Iraq who had invaded Kuwait during the summer of 1988, Bush broke his no-tax pledge by agreeing to substantial tax increases. With a Republican representative by the name of Newt Gingrich leading the charge against these new taxes, House Republicans rejected Bush's budget deal and attacked him for breaking his no-tax pledge—forcing him to accept a Democratic version that emphasized new taxes on affluent Americans and modest cuts in Medicare. (Large numbers of conservatives would later *not* vote for President Bush in the 1992 presidential elections, which was partly responsible for his defeat by opponent Bill Clinton.)

With military spending remaining high and with the budget still saddled with high interest payments to finance deficits inherited from Reagan, scant resources remained for discretionary spending for social, training, employment, and education programs. Indeed, the 1990 budget deal put severe caps on discretionary spending for years to come—caps that made it impossible for reformers to secure additional funds for an array of programs to help persons in low-income inner-city areas, homeless people, persons with persistent problems, children, and persons lacking skills to compete in job markets.

But it was clear that the budget settlement of 1990 was merely the first salvo in budget controversies that would extend through the 1990s and that would profoundly shape the course of the American welfare state. Nor were these budget debates likely to be amicable. Conservative Republicans, who had been bolstered and emboldened during the Reagan era, were so infuriated when Bush agreed to a modest tax increase in 1990 that they forced him to apologize for his decision in 1992 and to pledge never again to raise taxes. Having worshipped Reagan, they remained distrustful of Bush and pressured him to veto civil rights and other social reform measures and to resist efforts by liberals to raid the defense budget.[111] A strong coalition—between the Pentagon, the vast network of military contractors who existed in the districts of every federal politician, and politicians who retained a Cold War perspective—would likely resist major cuts in defense spending. And social reformers would find it difficult to enact new initiatives as long as the deficit remained and Americans continued to believe conservatives' claims that "you can't solve problems by throwing money at them" and "the federal government is the cause of the problem, not the solution."

Domestic Reforms

Few social reform initiatives were enacted from 1989 through 1992 because of budget deficits, the conservatism of Bush and his aides, and the president's preoccupation with international affairs. We will discuss some civil rights initiatives and child care legislation when we consider the experiences of out-groups in the era of Reagan and Bush.

In the areas of education, antidrug programs, and welfare, Bush expressed lofty goals but committed few resources and little presidential attention.[112] Bush's policy on substance abuse, for example, called for new funds to interdict drugs from abroad but failed to emphasize treatment or prevention programs. His education policy emphasized procedural reforms, such as the development of national tests and proposals to test voucher systems, but provided little direct assistance to local schools, which often labored under severe shortages of resources.

Bush seemed oblivious to many other domestic issues. His plan for reform of the national health system, unveiled in 1992, proposed the use of tax deductions and credits to help low-income persons purchase private health insurance, but the suggested levels of these tax concessions were far beneath the likely health needs of low- and moderate-income Americans. He took little interest in the homeless population and took few steps to address the housing needs of millions of low-income Americans who often could not obtain decent housing or had to pay 50 percent or more of their modest income for it.[113] Nor did Bush attend to the problem of poverty, despite the increasing economic inequality that had developed in the United States during the 1980s.

Events in Los Angeles reminded Americans of the hardships of inner-city life, despite the development of social programs following the urban unrest of the 1960s. In the spring of 1991, an African American by the name of Rodney King was viciously beaten by Los Angeles policemen. Unlike many other instances of police brutality, the incident was recorded on videotape by a bystander. Most Americans—and virtually all African Americans—saw the tape on national television; it depicted 80 seconds of merciless beating of King by a group of policemen. After King brought charges against the police officers, an extended trial took place in the spring of 1992. At the end of the trial, the all-white jury found the officers not guilty.

Most Americans were astonished, but African Americans in Los Angeles reacted with a fury that led to three days of burning and looting of business establishments. (Some Latinos also participated in the urban unrest.)

Caught by surprise, the Bush administration initially blamed the urban unrest on the Great Society social programs. When it became clear that this simplistic assertion was not widely accepted, the administration engaged in complex negotiations with the Congress to develop a program to provide various job-training, housing, recreation, and other programs for the inner cities—and for Los Angeles in particular—that would cost several billion dollars.

Critics of the emerging legislation suggested that it was grossly inadequate. Led by the mayors of many major cities, for example, about 150,000 people marched on Washington, DC, on May 17, 1992, to demand massive increases in federal aid to the cities, as well as health, housing, and job-training programs for inner-city residents. They argued that spending for the military increased by $579 billion during the 1980s, while federal funds to cities and states were cut by $78 billion.

As Bush's first term neared its end, the Los Angeles riots raised important questions about the reaction of white, suburban Americans, who constituted a majority of the nation's voters. Physically and culturally distant from inner-city residents, would they be happy with law-and-order strategies and symbolic remedies, particularly in light of long-standing efforts by politicians—and especially the Republican Party—to exploit white voters' antagonisms toward people of color? Or would they realize that, as the burning of some suburban shopping malls in the Los Angeles riots grimly suggested, their own well-being hinged on efforts to bring inner-city residents into the economic mainstream of American society? The early response of politicians of both parties was not encouraging, but some observers hoped that the events in Los Angeles, by dramatizing social distress in American cities, would invigorate a debate about national priorities in a period of reduced international tensions.

THE OPPRESSION OF VULNERABLE POPULATIONS IN THE ERA OF REAGAN AND BUSH, SR.

Many members of vulnerable populations were dismayed when Ronald Reagan became president in 1980 because they knew that the implementation of conservative policies would jeopardize the gains that they had made in the preceding two decades. After all, the twin leaders of the conservative movement, Ronald Reagan and Barry Goldwater, had both strongly opposed the enactment of the Civil Rights Acts of 1964 and 1965, on the grounds that states should be charged with such matters. Conservatives tended to reject programs that sought to equalize conditions between groups in the population—for example, between people of color and the white majority—on the grounds that they represented reverse discrimination.

Members of vulnerable populations feared, as well, that Reagan (and then Bush) would pack the Supreme Court, as well as lower federal courts, with appointees who would overrule many of the decisions of the Warren and Burger Courts, which had supported civil rights, affirmative action, the legalization of abortion, and desegregation. Conservatives tended to take a strict constructionist approach to constitutional interpretation; that is, rulings had to conform to the intentions of the framers of the Constitution. This doctrine was hardly promising for reformers, in that, as we noted in Chapter 3, the founders had legitimized slavery in the Constitution, and many contemporary social issues, such as abortion and affirmative action, had not emerged in colonial society. Moreover, enormous gains in employment opportunities for women and people of color had been obtained in the 1960s and 1970s through class action suits identifying patterns of discrimination. However, conservatives generally opposed the assertion of *group* rights and needs through class action suits; they were inclined to restrict legal recourse to instances when *individuals* could prove specific discriminatory

actions had been taken against themselves by persons who *intended* to harm them.[114]

Members of the various vulnerable populations realized, even before Reagan's election, that he would seek to diminish the size and roles of regulatory agencies such as the Equal Employment Opportunity Commission. By weakening these agencies, the Reagan administration could prevent effective implementation of civil rights and related statutes.

Members of vulnerable populations were also acutely aware that the conservative movement in the 1970s had bitterly opposed policies to extend their rights, including the Equal Rights Amendment, affirmative action, school desegregation, and local ordinances protecting gay men and lesbians from job discrimination.[115]

Nor were members of vulnerable populations and their advocates sanguine about the prospects for social programs to redress poverty, which provided assistance to many women, African Americans, Latinos, and First Americans. Conservative politicians had sought throughout the 1970s to identify programs like AFDC, Food Stamps, public housing, and public employment with people of color in an effort to capitalize on, and inflame, white citizens' resentments; it was widely expected that the Reagan administration would scale back these programs.

As if these fears were not enough, many members of vulnerable populations expected Reagan's tax and economic policies to harm low-income Americans. Supply-side economics, which was akin to the trickle-down economics of the 1920s, would give huge tax concessions to affluent persons without necessarily increasing the income of poorer citizens. Strategies to induce economic growth in the economy would not likely include bottom-up approaches such as investing in the nation's infrastructure and schools or in training programs for its workers.

Predictions Come True

The Reagan and Bush years constitute the largest redistribution of resources and rights *upward* in the nation's history. Though the welfare state remained intact—and specific programs within it grew considerably—from 1980 through 1992, the actual economic situation of poor persons worsened, owing to a deterioration of wages, *and* reductions in social benefits and services, *and* increases in Social Security taxes. Those near the bottom of the economic ladder became poorer not only in absolute dollars (adjusted for inflation) but also in comparison with the wealthiest Americans. Moreover, the rights won during the 1960s and 1970s, such as protections against job-related discrimination and the right to abortion, were put at risk by the appointment of conservative justices to the Supreme Court and to lower courts.[116] It is important to remember that spending cuts and upward redistribution would have been even greater had not many legislators opposed Reagan's and Bush's spending policies.

Many of the fears of members of vulnerable populations were realized during the Reagan period—particularly during his first term, when the Republicans controlled the Senate and often could muster a conservative majority in the House. Although Bush presented a more accommodating posture, his court appointments, as well as many of his policies, did not represent a fundamental departure from the politics of Reagan, despite conservatives' anger at Bush for consenting to tax increases and signing civil rights legislation.

The Oppression of Women

As Faludi notes, a curious paradox emerged in the 1980s: the women's liberation movement was widely blamed for depriving women of their femininity, their traditional rights to custody and alimony, and their special protections from hazardous work—in effect, for being too militant and thus jeopardizing traditional rights—yet women remained underpaid, denied access to many kinds of jobs, subject to a "glass ceiling," and greatly underrepresented in political offices.[117] Unlike other nations, moreover, the United States lacked a family leave program, and more than 99 percent of American employers did not provide child care. Family planning services for the poor remained poorly funded, and the *Roe v. Wade* decision legalizing

abortion seemed vulnerable to new court rulings. Attitudes toward women were cast into the public spotlight in 1991, when law professor Anita Hill alleged in Senate hearings that Supreme Court nominee Clarence Thomas had sexually harassed her while they both worked at the EEOC. The arrogance and insensitivity of the all-male group of senators conducting the hearings radicalized many women.[118]

Women encountered major political opposition in the 1980s from conservatives. Far from insisting that males should assume larger roles in parenting, some spokespersons for the New Right openly advocated turning the clock back to the 1950s with respect to employment of women, abortion rights, and women's rights. They fought the Equal Rights Amendment and even introduced the Family Protection Act in Congress in 1981, which sought to rescind federal laws that support equal education for boys and girls; prohibit what it called "intermingling of the sexes" in sports or other school-related activities; require schools to endorse marriage and motherhood as the proper career for girls; cut off federal funding to any school that uses textbooks in which women are shown in nontraditional roles; and prevent women who seek abortion counseling or a divorce from obtaining federally funded legal aid.[119]

The decade was characterized by considerable backsliding—for example, fewer women were appointed to the judiciary and to top policy positions. The Supreme Court narrowed women's rights in the 1989 *Webster v. Reproductive Health Services* decision, which allowed Missouri to make major new restrictions on abortion; the 1991 *Rust v. Sullivan* decision, which upheld regulations of the Reagan administration that prohibited federally funded clinics from counseling pregnant women about abortion; and also various rulings attacking affirmative action and quotas. The labor force became even more gender segregated. In 1986, women earned, on average, 64 cents to every dollar earned by male workers—the same ratio that had existed 31 years earlier, in 1955. The EEOC no longer vigorously litigated cases against large corporations that excluded women from entire job categories—for example, from high-paying commission sales jobs.

The crusade by the New Right against abortions illustrates the temper of the 1980s. Anti-abortion groups burned or bombed 77 family planning clinics between 1977 and 1989. By 1987, 85 percent of counties in the nation did not provide abortion services; as a result, many women had to travel across county or state boundaries to find such services. Medicaid funding had not been available for abortions since the mid-1970s, and only 12 states continued to fund abortions; consequently, women had to obtain funding from a small number of private agencies or from private insurance or personal funds. Muzzled by regulations, health providers that received federal funds could not even discuss reproductive alternatives with women—and sex education classes funded by the Adolescent Family Life Act withheld all information on abortion and birth control from students.[120]

The Democrats did not vigorously attack the Republicans' indifference to women's issues, even though many women felt alienated from the Republican Party. Intimidated by the conservatives, they often reflected the anti-female bias of the decade; even Michael Dukakis, the Democratic contender in 1988, chose to be silent on women's issues.[121]

In 1990, women's groups and their allies were able to obtain legislation that channeled some funding for child care programs to the states. A coalition of labor, senior citizens', and women's groups lobbied for a family leave bill, which would allow men and women paid leave from work before and after the birth of a child. They were able to move it through the Senate in 1991 but ultimately failed to surmount opposition by conservatives, who argued that it represented an unfair obligation for corporations, even though the policy had already been enacted in many industrialized nations.[122]

The Oppression of Poor People and Persons of Color

By 1992, a good deal of evidence, assembled by an array of authors and studies, showed that the economic position of the lowest quintile—the lowest one-fifth—of citizens had eroded considerably during the tenure of Presidents Reagan and Bush.[123] The data implicated three factors:

1. With the loss of American industrial and unionized jobs during the 1970s and 1980s, increasing numbers of workers found an erosion in the real value of their paychecks. Moreover, many companies cut their fringe benefits, such as health benefits, during these two decades—though many enterprises that employed people in the lowest quintile had never provided health benefits.

2. Poor individuals suffered economically as a result of the cuts in social benefits and services of the American welfare state. We have already discussed extensive cuts in AFDC, Food Stamps, and public housing programs. Poor persons also had to pay higher fees in Medicaid, Medicare, and other social programs.

3. Although some concessions were made in certain tax provisions—such as a tax credit extended by the federal government to some working but poor persons—the overall tax rates of poor and working persons increased, if payroll taxes for Social Security and Medicare are added to increases in the regular income tax.

The economic decline of the lowest quintile was matched by a decline of persons in the second-lowest quintile.[124] As the two lowest quintiles suffered these losses, many affluent Americans vastly increased their wealth; for example, the 400 richest Americans saw a tripling of their net worth in this period.[125] Viewed in this light, the Reagan and Bush years represented an economic counterrevolution. Some observers foresaw a transformation of the United States' economic structure to resemble that of some third-world nations, with vast disparities between rich and poor and a relatively small middle class—indeed, a society resembling that of the Gilded Age, which we discussed in Chapter 5.

Economic data do not fully describe the constricted quality of life in the inner-city neighborhoods where low-income African Americans, Latinos, and Native Americans live. These segregated populations have extraordinary rates of poverty, drug usage, poor health, poor educational attainment, unemployment, homicides, and gang violence. Large numbers of low-income males are killed in violent encounters or are incarcerated. And the rates of single-parent families in these inner-city populations have markedly increased over the last 25 years.

In the 1970s and 1980s, conservatives dominated policy discussions of urban poverty, which were very limited in scope.[126] However, as Peterson notes, a range of theories to explain the social and economic problems of these segregated populations now exists. Some observers contend that the welfare state has been inadequately developed and does not sufficiently help inner-city residents with economic, health, social service, educational, and job-training remedies. Conservatives argue that inner-city residents are to blame for the conditions in which they live, and implicate cultural factors that prompt behaviors such as teenage pregnancy. Conservatives maintain that welfare and other programs provide "perverse incentives," which discourage poor people from seeking work and self-improvement. Others argue that the loss of well-paying unionized industrial jobs in the past 20 years has deprived relatively unskilled persons of employment or consigned them to service jobs that pay only the minimum wage.[127]

The Reagan and Bush administrations, as well as presidential candidates in 1980, 1984, and 1988, displayed scant interest in these inner-city problems. Although the Los Angeles unrest of May 1992 suggested the need for sweeping social reforms to bring inner-city residents into the economic mainstream, the palliatives proposed by Congress and the Bush administration in the wake of the urban unrest provided little prospect of decisive action. And with huge federal deficits, as well as budget deficits in most states and major cities, funds to assist this population were not available—and would not be available, as long as the nation was disinclined either to raise its taxes or to dramatically cut its defense spending. Public opinion remained indifferent to inner-city residents, whose plight was largely invisible to the white suburban majority.

The Oppression of Immigrants

The enactment of the Immigration Act of 1965 and succeeding legislation—such as the 1975 Indochina Migration and Refugee Assistance Act and the 1980 Refugee Act—heralded a large influx of immigrants to the United States from Central America and Mexico and also from Asian nations such as Vietnam, China, Laos, Thailand, India, Cambodia, South Korea, and the Philippines. This immigration legislation revolutionized patterns of inflows of persons to the United States. National quotas were abolished, as were discriminatory Asian restrictions. Previously, only 120,000 visas had been reserved for Eastern Hemisphere nations from the overall ceiling of 270,000 established by 1980 legislation. Legislation in 1985 established three immigrant groups. First, immediate relatives of American citizens were exempt from the overall ceiling. Second, some immigrants entered under the overall ceiling of 270,000, though every foreign country was limited to 20,000 visas annually. Third, refugees were admitted annually in numbers to be determined annually by the president after consultation with the Congress. These new arrivals came to join relatives, to escape political persecution, or to seek better conditions. The Asian American population grew from 1 million in 1965 to 5 million in 1985; the number of Asians arriving in that 20-year period was almost four times as great as the Asian influx between 1849 and 1965.[128] Though immigrants settled disproportionately on the West Coast, large enclaves existed throughout the nation.

The immigrant population was so diverse that generalizations are difficult and fraught with inaccuracy. Some immigrants were highly educated professionals and persons with sophisticated technical skills. Others gravitated to businesses. Refugees from Vietnam, Central America, and the Caribbean, including boat people, came from a wide range of social backgrounds.

Even some entrants who possessed advanced skills found the adjustment problematic, not only because of language difficulties but also because of discrimination in employment and in society at large. About half of those Vietnamese refugees who reside in California were on public assistance in 1990.[129] Some refugees suffered from mental trauma due to harrowing experiences in refugee camps and war zones. As with immigrants in preceding eras, tensions often developed between first-generation immigrants and their children, who quickly learned English and the mores of the dominant culture.

Advocates for refugees from political persecution in countries like El Salvador fought a determined battle to stop their deportation, through the courts and through hearings of the Immigration Service; these refugees were offered sanctuary in churches and homes.

Congress had long wondered what to do with millions of undocumented workers who had come from Mexico and Central America to the United States. Agribusiness, tourism, factories, and other employers relied heavily on this low-wage labor force. Yet they were a fugitive population contributing taxes to Social Security and often paying income taxes, but with uncertain rights to social services, health care, and education. If they were assaulted or subject to other criminal actions, they could not call the police and seek legal recourse for fear of deportation. In many cases, employers paid them less than the minimum wage because they knew these workers feared to question authorities. Many immigrants worked in places where working conditions were unsafe, such as in meat packing plants in beef and poultry industries and in garment factories. Work safety standards were often not enforced by federal and state authorities.

The Immigration Reform and Control Act of 1986 was enacted in this context. It granted asylum to 3 million undocumented workers in the United States if they could prove they had lived in the country for at least four years. Able now to obtain visas and apply for citizenship, this group finally had legal status after years of contributing to the nation's economy.

Many legislators assumed that this legislation would slow the movement of persons across the Mexican border into the United States as well as from other nations. Had some of them realized that immigration into the United States would *accelerate* after the legislation was enacted, they might not have supported it. The number of undocumented immigrants had increased to roughly 12 million persons by 2008 as legislation to create amnesty for most of them in another piece of legislation stalled in the Congress (see Insert 10.5).

Many of these new immigrants worked under the same unsafe and unregulated conditions that had existed for many of their predecessors. It was inhumane, moreover, that families were often separated for long periods of time or forever. Many mothers, for example, traveled across borders to earn income to support their families, but left their children with relatives in Mexico and other nations—creating extraordinary family problems. When these children sometimes attempted to cross borders to find their mothers, they often were robbed or even died as they undertook the perilous journey to, and then across, the border.

Many immigrants from other nations died in transit, such as when crossing the desert in states such as California, Arizona, and New Mexico. Yet others were victimized by professional guides known as *coyotes* who charged them exorbitant amounts of money and often packed them into unsafe vehicles.

The Oppression of Gay Men and Lesbians

In the 1970s, gay men and lesbians had focused on winning civil rights, with some success. In the 1980s, however, they found themselves confronting the worst medical catastrophe of modern times, the AIDS epidemic. In the spring of 1982, researchers at the National Centers for Disease Control acknowledged the existence of an epidemic that had already killed 119 persons, but they did not know the cause of the disease and had not even assigned a name to it. However, they knew that it progressively destroyed the immune system and they had determined that it was concentrated in the gay male population. When the

---

I N S E R T 10.5 **Ethical Analysis of Key Issues and Policies: What Policies Should Americans Adopt for Undocumented Immigrants?**

Many Americans did not realize in 1986 that the world economy had already shifted toward globalization, a process in which labor and capital moved across national boundaries at an accelerating rate. Even a decade earlier, for example, automobile manufacturers such as Toyota were viewed as purveyors of cheap products that could not compete against American industry. (By 2008, Toyota had surpassed General Motors as the world's largest automobile company.) Spurred by the quest for jobs, as well as the desire to join family members, many persons crossed national boundaries even without following formal immigration procedures.

Americans would have to grapple with difficult issues in coming decades, including questions such as these:

- To what extent should "amnesty" be extended to persons who have crossed borders without following formal immigration procedures?

- To what extent should immigration be allowed for relatives of persons who crossed borders without following formal immigration procedures?

- To what extent is a "guest worker" program advisable, such as the so-called bracero program that existed from 1942 to 1964? Do guest worker programs inevitably lead to poor treatment of immigrants?

- Should strong sanctions exist—and be monitored —against employers of persons who crossed borders without following formal immigration procedures?

- Since the United States took much of the American Southwest from Mexico by force of arms in the Mexican American War (as discussed in Chapter 5), do immigrants from Mexico have a right to enter the United States even when not following formal immigration procedures?

- Is the contemporary "sanctuary movement," where churches shelter persons who would otherwise be deported, meritorious?

---

virus that caused the disease was finally identified in early 1984 (it was officially designated the human immunodeficiency virus, or HIV, in 1986), the horrific nature of the epidemic became clear. Transmitted by an exchange of fluids during sexual relations, the disease threatened to become a sort of biologic genocide visited on an unsuspecting population.

The gay community made unrelenting efforts to mobilize action against the epidemic. Edward Brandt, the assistant secretary for health, who asked in early 1984 for a modest outlay of $55 million on research to develop a blood test, a vaccine, and a cure, encountered indifference from the Reagan administration. The American Life Lobby, a conservative group, claimed that Brandt's plea to make AIDS a top priority of the Health Service was "an outrageous legitimization of a lifestyle repugnant to the vast majority of Americans."[130]

Researchers discovered by mid-1984 that the disease was also transmitted through blood transfusions, through intravenous drug use, by prostitutes, and by bisexuals to their spouses. The disease spread rapidly among African American and Latino addicts in the inner city who shared nonsterilized needles.

Americans are prone to cycles of interest in particular social problems. After a rash of news reports on the disease in 1983, coverage soon diminished, despite the mounting deaths. The Reagan administration requested only $51 million for 1985. At the same time, conservatives in Congress sought to require that health workers conducting blood tests for AIDS report positive results to public health departments. It was widely feared that this policy, which would compromise the confidentiality of the AIDS test, would lead to boycotts of the test because persons with AIDS encountered virulent prejudice and discrimination in housing, in the workplace, and also from insurance companies. Though congressional pressure pushed funding to $96 million in 1985, the Reagan administration sought to *reduce* the funding to $85.5 million in the ensuing year, despite a prediction by government researchers that the epidemic could kill up to 50,000 persons (or the same number of fatalities as occurred during the Vietnam War) within a few years.[131] The gay community developed a massive education and self-help campaign to provide assistance to people with AIDS and to promote safe sex, but they received scant assistance from the federal government. African American and Latino communities proved less able to develop self-help campaigns, partly because of prejudices against gay men in those cultures. Governmental authorities did not make it a priority to develop a determined preventive program in inner-city areas; this failure, which consigned thousands of persons to death, was a national disgrace.

With the revelation that movie star Rock Hudson had AIDS in mid-1985, and the publication of a report on the epidemic by Surgeon General C. Everett Koop in October of 1986, government action increased markedly. However, increases in funding were still sufficiently modest that gay men, lesbians, and their allies repeatedly demonstrated in Washington; a 1987 march attracted 600,000 people. Efforts to combat the disease continued to be hamstrung by prejudice: Many states failed to enact laws prohibiting discrimination against people with AIDS; there was widespread opposition to providing addicts with sterilized needles; many physicians decided not to treat persons who were HIV-positive; and conservatives continued to demand mandatory reporting of persons who tested HIV-positive. Nor did President Bush demonstrate active interest in the issue.

Moreover, the nation's disinclination to provide sex education and condoms to its youth had slowed effective preventive programs. Although the public schools of New York City decided in 1991 to distribute condoms to high school students, most other school districts were not as enlightened. Nor did Americans develop public service announcements, such as were widely used in European countries, to promote safe sex. Activists hoped that the announcement by basketball player Magic Johnson in late 1991 that he was HIV-positive might finally force a massive prevention program.

As the epidemic neared the end of its first decade in the United States, the death toll exceeded 138,000 persons, and the disease was making rapid advances in heterosexual populations, particularly among intravenous drug users. About 1 million persons were HIV-positive in May of 1992.

Though often preoccupied with AIDS, gay and lesbian activists also worked on many other fronts. They sought legislation in various states to outlaw job discrimination in the civil service, military, police and fire departments, and private markets; to outlaw housing discrimination; to allow same-gender couples to obtain access to Social Security and job-related fringe benefits; to obtain the right to adopt children; to obtain custody and visitation rights; and to overturn antisodomy laws in 26 states.[132]

The Oppression of People with Disabilities

Buoyed by the Rehabilitation Act of 1973, a robust movement of persons with disabilities evolved and mobilized behind an "independent living centers" movement. Wishing to shed traditional images of helplessness, some advocates favored the term *physically challenged* to describe persons with disabilities. A national network of local organizations received federal funding to provide an array of outreach, educational, and advocacy services, with the intent of freeing persons from dependence on medical institutions. When possible, these organizations helped secure government payments for nonworking persons with disabilities, whether under the means-tested SSI program or under Social Security disability insurance (SSDI) for persons disabled on the job. With the use of technology and advocacy, they also succeeded in increasing the employment of persons with chronic physical, developmental, and mental problems. Many public facilities were made accessible by way of ramps, elevators, and other aids, and vast progress was made in obtaining special programs to help persons with conditions like dyslexia in the educational system. Even with these improvements, many persons with chronic conditions remained mired in poverty or lacked access to the latest technology. Equally important, persons with chronic problems often needed personal assistants to help them with chores, transportation, and other matters, but government programs rarely provided these aides. Moreover, persons with chronic problems often encountered a dilemma: If they worked, their benefits would be taken from them, but the wages they could earn were so low that they needed their benefits to survive. Many persons with disabilities thus returned to their SSI or SSDI benefits rather than remaining in the workforce.

Advocates obtained enactment of the Americans with Disabilities Act of 1990, which barred discrimination in the workplace, housing, and public accommodations. (It provided far more detailed language than the Rehabilitation Act of 1973.) Though this legislation represented progress, activists feared that the government would confine itself to policing the rights of persons with disabilities, rather than funding an array of services—such as personal aides—that they needed to become full-fledged members of society.[133]

The Oppression of Children

The well-being of children depends on the economic and social condition of their parents, as well as on the kinds of health, educational, and social service programs that society provides them. In the 1980s, the scorecard was not impressive on either count. After declining in the 1960s and remaining stable in the 1970s, the rates of poverty among children and youth rose rapidly to around 25 percent in the early 1980s and then stabilized at those high levels for the rest of the decade. Whereas roughly 15 percent of white children were poor in 1989, about 44 percent of African American children and 36 percent of Latino children were poor. Falling earnings, low levels of AFDC and Food Stamps, and poor child support enforcement contributed to this high rate.

The poverty of growing numbers of children was linked, as well, to the growth in the percentage of families that had only a single head of household.

The term *feminization of poverty* was coined to describe the extent of poverty in female-headed households. Whereas only 23 percent of all poor families were headed by women in 1959, this figure had risen to 52 percent by 1989. About 51 percent of children in families headed by a woman were poor in 1989 compared with only 10 percent in two-parent families. Families headed by a woman tend to be poorer because they can draw on only a single source of wage income and because women tend to be segregated in lower-paying work.[134] According to Ozawa, increasing rates of teenage pregnancy and of divorce explain the growth in female-headed households.[135]

As well as poverty, American children faced an array of other problems, for which no adequate policies had been developed. Roughly 300,000 cocaine-addicted babies were born each year, and drug treatment and prevention programs had failed to reach many teenagers who used drugs. Between 1965 and 1988, the arrest rate for violent crimes by 18-year-old males more than doubled; rates were particularly high in the lower economic strata. Homicides accounted for almost half of all deaths among young males. As Kozol documents in his book *Savage Inequalities*, the schools of poor children were overcrowded, lacked instructional aids, and often had less competent teachers than more affluent districts.[136]

There were many indications that the child welfare system could not cope with the sheer number of children who were reported to be neglected or abused by their caregivers. In the wake of the Adoption Assistance and Child Welfare Act of 1980, which gave funds to the states to hire more child welfare staff and required them to develop a "permanency plan" for all children removed from their natural homes, the number of children in foster care was almost halved in five years. But the number zoomed upward by 29 percent, to about 360,000 children by 1991—and was predicted to exceed 500,000 children by the year 2000. (This threshold was reached as early as 1997.) Though staff were added in many jurisdictions, acute shortages developed because of a 147 percent increase in reports of abused and neglected children between 1979 and 1989, for an astonishing total of 2.4 million reported cases in 1989.[137]

Children's advocates nonetheless gained a number of incremental policy victories in the 1980s and seemed on the verge of some additional ones in 1992. By securing more funding for the Education for All Handicapped Children Act of 1975, millions of disabled children were mainstreamed into the regular public schools. The Medicaid program was amended to include a program that gave 1 million low-income children preventive checkups. Despite its inadequate funding and implementation, the Adoption Assistance and Child Welfare Act led to better foster care for many children, as well as higher rates of adoption and reunification with their natural families. In 1991, under pressure from children's advocates, Congress agreed in principle to expand the Head Start program to cover all eligible children in coming years. In the 1980s, incremental increases had been obtained in the Earned Income Tax Credit—a means-tested program that gave a tax rebate to qualify-ing families—and Congress agreed to raise the credit so that the benefit would rise another 70 percent by 1994. (A family earning less than $10,730 could claim a tax refund of almost $1,000 in 1990.)

With passage of the child care and development block grant in 1990, children's advocates finally obtained the first major, national child care program since World War II. It channeled funds through the states for child care services, administration, and staff training. Although the program was inadequately funded, it established a precedent that child care belonged within the purview of the federal government.

The AFDC program had been highly controversial since the mid-1960s, when many citizens became alarmed at its rate of growth. But the benefits of this program, which was designed to help destitute heads of households and their children, had eroded during the 1970s and 1980s to the point where the grants of the median state were only 45 percent of the official poverty line in 1990, or only $367 a month for a family of three. Even when supplemented by Food Stamps and Medicaid, these resources were insufficient to meet the basic needs

of many families. When the Family Support Act of 1988 was enacted, people hoped that its job training and child care funds would allow many women on AFDC to enter the labor market, but the act fell far short of its potential, owing to inadequate funding at federal and state levels and the harsh realities of labor markets; relatively unskilled female workers often could obtain only minimum-wage jobs that rendered them even poorer than they had been on AFDC.

Thus, incremental gains in some aspects of children's welfare during the decade were offset by the rapid growth of social problems—such as cocaine-addicted babies and huge increases in reported cases of child abuse and neglect—that existing programs could not adequately address. Children's advocates urged the United States to emulate programs in Europe and Canada, such as parental leave, expanded child care, and children's allowances.[138]

The Oppression of Aging Americans

Aging Americans appeared at first glance to have improved their condition in the 1970s and 1980s. Rates of poverty in this population had plummeted from 35 percent to 12.8 percent between 1959 and 1989. With the enactment of Medicare and the Older Americans Act in 1965 and the enactment of SSI and the indexing of Social Security in the early 1970s, older people obtained major new medical services, social services, and resources. Indeed, many commentators noted that a huge portion of the federal budget was devoted to older persons, including the 29.4 percent of the 1990 federal budget (or $341.4 billion) consumed by just two programs—Medicare and Social Security. Unlike poor Americans, elderly persons were largely spared the budget cuts of the 1980s because Reagan (and then Bush) feared antagonizing this politically powerful group.[139]

But elderly persons had many serious problems of their own. Because consumer fees associated with Medicare were so high and so many services were not covered, elderly persons paid roughly 50 percent of their own medical costs. Moreover, they paid upward of 50 percent of their costs for home

INSERT 10.6 Ethical Analysis of Key Issues and Policies: Pitting Groups against One Another

It is true: older Americans absorb a large share of the expenditures of the welfare state, partly on account of the high cost of their medical programs and long-term care programs. It is also true that children receive a small share of social spending in the United States.

Analyze the ethical merit of *cutting* expenditures on older people to divert funds to children. Some ethicists favor, for example, making a rule that no person over age 80 can receive extraordinary medical interventions. Others want older citizens to self-fund far larger portions of their health care expenses and other costs.

health care and long-term care because Medicare, with its focus on short-term, hospital-based care, offered scant coverage for those services. As a result, many older citizens experiencing catastrophic health conditions had to divest themselves of their savings to obtain medical funds from the means-tested Medicaid program.[140] Moreover, many older persons and their families were heavily burdened—financially and otherwise—by Alzheimer's Disease, which had become the fourth greatest killer of older persons by 1992. Day treatment and other services for persons with Alzheimer's Disease remained very limited.

As if these problems were not enough, older persons also had to contend with a strong movement in the 1980s that sought to cut social spending on their needs. Former Governor Richard Lamm of Colorado and others argued that much of the money spent on older Americans should be diverted to children because society would reap economic gains by making younger people more productive. Daniel Callahan, a prominent moral philosopher, advocated that the United States refuse heroic and expensive health remedies to all persons over the age of 80—for example, by disallowing stays in intensive care units—so as to permit these funds to be spent on younger people. Others argued that lobbyist groups representing older persons, such as the American Association of Retired Persons, possessed such power that older citizens were able unfairly to obtain a disproportionate share of the public purse. In an era of deficits in federal and state budgets, many legislators feared making home health care and long-term care more available because of its likely costs.[141] (See Insert 10.6.)

The Oppression of Homeless Persons

Many social problems of the 1980s and 1990s have an impact on individuals from several out-groups, as well as the general population. Consider homelessness. As the 1980s began, most Americans would likely have associated homelessness with relatively small areas of cities where alcoholic persons resided. (Such an area was often known as skid row.) A public opinion poll in 1991, however, found that 54 percent of Americans reported they saw homeless people in their communities or on their way to work—and the Urban Institute in 1987 estimated the homeless population of the United States at about 600,000 persons, including persons in shelters, using soup kitchens, and on the streets (see Figure 10.1). Homeless people are a diverse group. When examining the characteristics of homeless people in cities of more than 100,000 people, the Urban Institute concluded that about one-fifth of them had a history of mental hospitalization; about 15 percent were children; about 81 percent were male; about one-third had been patients in a detoxification, alcohol treatment, or drug treatment program; and about 29 percent of single men had served time in prison. These homeless people had an average monthly income of $135, or less than one-third of the federal poverty level, and half of them had not had a steady job in more than two years. Persons had been homeless for a median of 10 months.[142]

FIGURE 10.1 The resurgence of homelessness in the 1980s.

The response of federal and state governments to this problem in the Reagan and Bush era was half-hearted, at best. Most vexing to advocates for the homeless was the presidents' disinclination to publicly discuss the issue; even Democratic candidates in 1984 and 1988 were unwilling to demand ameliorative policies. Congress enacted the Stewart B. McKinney Homeless Assistance Act of 1987, but it focused its resources on construction costs for shelters and was burdened with bureaucratic delays in disbursing funds to states. States and localities devoted considerable funds to the problem by the late 1980s and were particularly effective in meeting the emergency needs of those homeless people who used their shelters. But most jurisdictions made little provision for outreach programs to homeless people who avoided organized services and shelters, transitional programs to help homeless people obtain housing and jobs, and programs to help prevent people from becoming homeless. Nor did most jurisdictions provide case management services to homeless persons, even in shelters. For want of leadership from federal or state authorities, voluntary agencies—including missions, churches, neighborhood coalitions, and social agencies—often took the lead in providing services.[143]

As Rossi notes, it is easy to ignore the simple fact that "the essential and defining symptom of homelessness is lack of access to conventional housing." The stocks of inexpensive housing were depleted in the 1980s by rising rents, conversion of many rental apartments to condominiums, and the continuing destruction of low-income housing (particularly buildings with apartments for single persons) for urban renewal.[144] As we have already noted, the Reagan administration virtually ended many programs of the Department of Housing and Urban Development. Furthermore, the policy of deinstitutionalizing patients from the nation's mental hospitals from the early 1960s onward, when coupled with stricter rules for involuntary commitments, placed hundreds of thousands of former mental patients on the streets without adequate services. And increasing numbers of individuals and families could not afford housing because of the loss

of industrialized, unionized employment in the United States during the 1980s.

The Erosion of Legal Rights

A prime objective of Ronald Reagan and George Bush was to transform the federal judiciary into an instrument of conservative ideology. They succeeded to an extent unrivaled in modern times. With the appointment of Justice Clarence Thomas in late 1991, the number of liberals on the Supreme Court had been reduced to two justices (Harry Blackmun and John Paul Stevens). Under the leadership of William Rehnquist, who succeeded Warren Burger in 1986, the Court seemed poised to stress conservative goals in the 1990–1991 session, when it overturned a number of precedents and contemplated "shattering the Warren and Burger legacies … in the areas of abortion, separation of church and state, affirmative action, and free speech."[145] Moreover, by 1992, Reagan and Bush had appointed more than half of the 828 federal appeals and court judges in the United States—judges who had usually been given "ideological litmus tests" to be certain that they would support conservative positions on controversial issues.[146]

It was too soon to tell precisely what directions the Supreme Court would take, but advocates for women and people of color feared a rollback in many policies that had been sanctioned by the Warren or Burger Court or by Congress. Advocates realized that they would need to secure new legislation to offset adverse rulings by the Court; thus, gay activists, chagrined that the Supreme Court in 1986 upheld a Georgia statute that declared sodomy illegal, responded by pressuring state legislatures to overturn similar statutes. Advocates for people with disabilities secured the enactment of the Americans with Disabilities Act in 1990, after the Court had declined to cover people with disabilities under existing civil rights statutes.

Another landmark in this campaign of resistance was the Civil Rights Act of 1991, enacted after two years of negotiations between the

Congress and the White House. This legislation was a response to a series of 10 rulings by the Supreme Court that called into question the principle of affirmative action and limited individuals' ability to seek remedies to bias in the workplace. In its decision in 1989 in *Wards Cove Packing Co. v. Atonio*, for example, the Court held that the burden of proof rested with an employee who alleged that a company's practices had an adverse impact on people of color, women, or other groups; she or he had to prove that the practices did not serve a legitimate business purpose. The antidiscrimination provisions of the Civil Rights Act of 1991 applied to both governmental and private places of employment and reaffirmed the ability of employees to bring "disparate impact lawsuits" under Title VII of the Civil Rights Act of 1964—that is, lawsuits alleging that specific hiring or promotion decisions adversely affected women, people of color, or other groups. The legislation also allowed workers to seek monetary damages in cases of alleged intentional discrimination.[147]

Thus, the ideological divergence between Congress and the Supreme Court suggested that the House and Senate would be revisiting issues during the next decades that they *thought* they had resolved, until the Court declared the relevant statutes unconstitutional. In effect, the rulings of the Supreme Court were setting a major portion of Congress's legislative agenda, which was frustrating and time-consuming for liberal and moderate lawmakers. This standoff was reminiscent of the New Deal era, when the intransigence of the conservative Court led Franklin Roosevelt to try to pack the Court with liberal justices. As a final example of the Court's uncompassionate rulings, note that in March of 1992, by a 7 to 2 vote, the Court found that federal judges cannot force states to improve their care of abused and neglected children under the 1980 Adoption Assistance and Child Welfare Act, on the grounds that the legislation did not specifically mention that persons can sue in federal court. Outraged children's advocates faced the task of amending the legislation in Congress.[148]

THE SOCIAL WORK PROFESSION

The profession of social work proved remarkably resilient during the decades after the Great Society, despite the conservative attack on the kinds of social programs that employed social workers. Schools of social work at the graduate level held their own during this period, as did undergraduate programs. Membership of the National Association of Social Workers (NASW) exceeded 100,000 persons by the mid-1980s, and roughly nine-tenths of them had a master's in social work; more than 200,000 persons in the workforce had either a bachelor's or master's degree in social work. About 40 percent of NASW members were employed in not-for-profit agencies, 45 percent in public agencies (mostly at state, county, or local levels), and the balance in for-profit agencies. Large numbers of social workers were employed in health, mental health, and child and family sectors. Though most social workers held direct service positions, many held administrative posts, and some worked in community-organizing and policy-making positions as well.

The profession had successes and failures in political battles to preserve its access to jobs. On the positive side, the profession succeeded in obtaining licensing in many states, which in turn, often led to the inclusion of social work in reimbursement by private insurance companies and Medicare. A number of public positions in agencies such as child welfare, however, were declassified in the 1970s and 1980s in particular jurisdictions; that is, certain local authorities ceased to specify a social work degree as a qualification for particular kinds of jobs. But a number of public agencies actively recruited trained social workers by the early 1990s in fields such as protective services for abused children, and many positions in the large not-for-profit sector required a social work degree or even a social work license. The inexorable expansion of some social problems and the rise to prominence of others—including AIDS, substance abuse, homelessness, and Alzheimer's Disease—created new openings for a field whose technologies could easily be adapted to an array of social needs.

Perhaps the most controversial issue in the field of social work during this period concerned the role of private practice in the profession. Although most social workers were salaried, many had private practices on the side and aspired to full-time private practice, for its monetary rewards and the autonomy it offered. Critics feared that these private practitioners could draw the profession away from its role as service provider to persons with limited financial means and as an advocate for relatively powerless groups.[149] Indeed, some private practitioners sought to avoid being called social workers; they preferred to be known, for example, as psychotherapists, though the term *clinical social worker* was also used.

It remained unclear precisely what effects the emergence of private practice would have on the profession. On the one hand, insofar as it represented a retreat from the precepts of social work, from agency practice, and from advocacy for groups with little power, private practice *was* a threat to the reformist mission of the profession. Private practice, however, did not seem to have fundamentally changed the field by the early 1990s; indeed, it seemed less of a threat to a broad-based mission for the field than psychiatric social work had been in the 1950s, when the profession seemed much more congruent with the conservatism of the era. Nor was it even clear that most persons who aspired to private practice rejected the mission of the profession; more than a few of them simply wished to avoid the stifling work requirements of some social agencies, particularly public ones, where workloads had often become excessive.[150]

Although we cannot use the positions of NASW as the only measure of sentiments within the profession, they suggest that social work had not veered to the right in the 1970s and 1980s. NASW in the 1980s, in its conferences, policy positions, and newsletter, frequently attacked the conservative positions of the Reagan and Bush administrations, assertively sought national health insurance and an array of social reforms, and actively participated in

coalitions with advocacy groups such as the Children's Defense Fund. In 1975, it established a political action arm, the Political Action Committee for Candidate Election (PACE), that backed candidates who supported social reforms. Official policies that NASW's delegate assembly adopted over a period of 20 years suggest that the field took an array of progressive, even radical, positions on subjects as diverse as AIDS, economic policy, long-term care, and the rights of children.[151] (Of course, NASW's positions do not necessarily reflect the positions of rank-and-file social workers.)

Nor does the work of social work theorists suggest that the profession veered to the right in the 1980s. Most theorists maintained an ecological perspective that required social workers to examine human functioning in a broad context, including environmental and policy issues. There was an emphasis on *diversity*—that is, making social work services relevant to a range of oppressed populations, including African Americans, Latinos, Native Americans, women, gay men and lesbians, and the poor. Macro practitioners often remained on the fringes in many schools, but they maintained a determined existence and were strongly represented in national conferences of the Council on Social Work Education.[152]

By the same token, social work could hardly be called a radical presence in a society with enormous unmet needs. *All* professions are influenced by conservatizing forces, such as funding from government and business elites, referrals from other professionals, and recruits who are predominantly white and from the middle and upper classes. As Wenocur and Reisch established when discussing its origins, social work is no exception—and Rothman makes a similar point about the profession in the contemporary period.[153] But social work remained *relatively* more reformist than other professions such as law, medicine, and business, whose professional associations did not usually take controversial positions on current issues.[154] Social work should not be placed on a pedestal, but neither should it be accused of forsaking its reformist heritage.

THE EVOLUTION OF THE RELUCTANT WELFARE STATE

The presidencies of Reagan and Bush constituted the first major era of conservatism since the 1950s. Their election required a shift in the votes of white Americans, particularly Northern white Catholics and Southern whites in lower and moderate income brackets. Skillfully using rhetoric that fanned the flames of racial animosities and social tensions, Reagan and Bush cultivated these white voters and secured their support in pivotal elections. They appealed, as well, to Americans who wanted political and social stability after such traumas of the 1960s and 1970s as Vietnam, Watergate, and stagflation.

Compared with many other nations, the United States developed a welfare state belatedly. Even after the spending increases of the 1960s and 1970s, U.S. governmental social spending, expressed as a percentage of the gross national product, fell short of that in other industrialized nations, and a host of serious social problems remained unresolved.

Just as programs established in the 1960s and 1970s began to address a variety of social needs, the Reagan administration decided to curb their funding. Reagan's conservative counterrevolution substantially reduced domestic spending, massively increased military spending, and drastically reduced the policy roles of the federal government. Conservatives' successes were held in check, however, by the many legislators and citizens who did not share their goals and by the Democratic control of the House of Representatives throughout the Reagan and Bush years and of the Senate from 1986 onward.

Some historians are likely to criticize Reagan's policies as self-serving and inequitable. Far from cutting all social programs, the administration cut primarily those used by low-income Americans. Tax cuts in 1981 enriched affluent individuals and corporations far more than other Americans; the tax reform of 1986 drastically reduced the tax rates of affluent Americans. The defense industry reaped unprecedented peacetime profits, even without considering the trillion-dollar SDI initiative. Affirmative action policies were attacked by the president, the Justice Department, and the director of the Civil Rights Commission. By increasing deficit spending, Reagan was asking future generations to fund his defense and tax reduction policies. Moreover, the administration hoped to foster conservative policies long after the 1980s by devising tax, deficit, and defense policies that would create a shortage of resources for social spending.

Crippled by international scandals in Iran and Nicaragua in late 1987, and reduced to lame-duck status, Reagan had lost political momentum by the midpoint of his second term. Democrats once again controlled both houses of Congress after the 1986 elections.

Although President George Bush was more responsive to some social problems than Reagan had been, and although his rhetoric was often more diplomatic, his policies were fundamentally the same. Partly because the Democrats had larger majorities in the House and Senate under Bush than under Reagan, Bush *had* to accept larger spending increases in many social programs.

By 1992, however, emerging political uncertainties suggested that conservative hegemony might one day end. Many Americans had descended from the middle class to lesser economic status, as unionized jobs were replaced (if at all) by lesser-paying service jobs. The easing of the Cold War made it harder for conservatives to rally their constituency by invoking the threat of communism. Members of the various out-groups had reasons for wanting more liberal administrations, as they fought adverse court rulings and program cuts.

Still, many persons wondered whether, given budget deficits and a decade of conservative rhetoric, the nation could find the resources and the will to attack entrenched social problems as it moved toward the 21st century. Lack of medical insurance, homelessness, AIDS, growing economic inequality, poor schools, poverty in the racial ghettoes of inner cities, family violence, the feminization of poverty, gang warfare—all of these problems cried out for solutions and creative programs, but burdened human services systems were inadequate to the task.

LINKING THE CONSERVATIVE COUNTERREVOLUTION TO CONTEMPORARY SOCIETY

What We Can Learn from Policy Advocates of the Conservative Counterrevolution

Former Congressman and social worker Ron Dellums illustrates how policy advocates must increasingly cross national boundaries in their work. With the remarkable rise of globalization during the past three decades, policy issues in the United States are often linked to social problems and institutions in other nations. (See Insert 10.7.) Like many social workers who run for public office, Dellums obtained credentials needed to run a credible campaign from his work *as* a social worker, rising from the line-worker position as a psychiatric social worker to administrative and planning positions. When he was ready to run for Congress, then, he was highly knowledgeable about many domestic social issues.

Almost from the outset of his congressional tenure, however, Dellums involved himself in international issues. He attacked the Vietnam War. He was appointed to the Armed Services Committee. He opposed what he viewed as unneeded weapons systems throughout his career, even when Democrats such as Jimmy Carter supported them. He lambasted President Reagan's military buildup as excessive. He monitored expenditures on overseas bases in the 1980s. He fought apartheid in South Africa prior to the freeing of Nelson Mandela from jail and got sanctions enacted against that nation. He finally became chair of the House Armed Services Committee in the early 1990s.

Dellums recognized that social programs funded by the discretionary budget are threatened by military spending in a way that entitlement programs are not. Since entitlements are automatically funded each year to the level of claimed benefits, they are relatively immune to cuts in annual budget deliberations. By contrast, domestic social programs compete with military spending because *both* sets of programs are funded by discretionary spending that Congress determines each year in its budget deliberations. Roughly *half* of the annual federal discretionary budget is still expended on military spending, so each new unneeded military expenditure cuts the pool of resources available for domestic discretionary programs.

Dellums's policy advocacy also illustrates how many policy advocates devote a considerable share of their work to *blocking* policy initiatives from conservatives. Had Dellums and a large corps of policy advocates *not* effectively resisted many policy initiatives from President Reagan and his allies, they would have obtained even deeper cuts in many social programs serving vulnerable populations—as well as greater erosion of their rights.

Dellums's successor from the same congressional district, social worker Barbara Lee, has continued his crusade against excessive military spending and strongly opposed the American invasion of Iraq even before the invasion took place in 2003.

What We Can Learn from the Persistence of Unmet Needs and Policy Issues during the Conservative Counterrevolution

While the United States has had a homeless population dating back to the 19th century when they were known as "vagabonds," it greatly grew in size during the presidency of Ronald Reagan for combined economic and policy reasons. Reagan's quest to cut SSI and Social Security disability payments to persons with mental issues greatly increased the number of persons who were cast onto the streets because they could not afford rents. Afflicted with mental, physical, and substance abuse problems, many Vietnam veterans became homeless persons—particularly as programs to help them from the Veterans' Administration were insufficiently funded. Increasing levels of poverty in the Reagan administration from cuts in means-tested entitlements such as AFDC also contributed to

I N S E R T   10.7   Profiles in Policy Advocacy: Ronald Vernie Dellums (1935–)

Ronald Vernie Dellums—social worker, politician, civil rights activist, and reformer—was born on November 24, 1935, in Oakland, California, to Vernie Dellums, a longshoreman, and Willa Dellums, a clerk-typist for the government. As a child growing up in a rough section of Oakland, Dellums dreamed of becoming a major-league pitcher, but he was discouraged by the prejudice of his high school coaches. In 1954, after failing to find work, Dellums enlisted in the United States Marine Corps, where he served for two years. Following his discharge, he used his GI Bill benefits and enrolled at Oakland City College, receiving an associate of arts degree in 1958. He went on to receive his B.A. degree from San Francisco State College (1960) and an M.S.W. degree from the University of California at Berkeley in 1962.

Throughout the 1960s, Dellums held various positions in many areas within public social services. He was a psychiatric social worker for the California Department of Mental Hygiene (1962–1964), program director for the Bayview Community Center in San Francisco (1964–1965), associate director and subsequently director of the Hunters Point Youth Opportunity Center (1965–1966), planning consultant for the Bay Area Social Planning Council (1966–1967), and director of the concentrated employment program of the San Francisco Economic Opportunity Council (1967–1968). Upon returning to the private sector, Dellums became a senior consultant for manpower programs at Social Dynamics, Inc.

In 1967, Dellums launched his political career with a run for the Berkeley City Council. While on the council, Dellums spoke out against what he saw as police brutality against students and minorities, and he assumed the role of liaison between the council and the students on the Berkeley campus. In the 1970 Democratic primary, Dellums, whose political aspirations had broadened during his brief stint on the city council, challenged the reelection of Jeffery Cohelan to the seat representing California's Seventh Congressional District, the Oakland-Berkeley area.

Throughout his campaign, Dellums resisted the pressure to conform to the more conventional approach to politics. He ran as a self-avowed reformist and radical, not afraid to take a solid position on hot issues such as the Vietnam War. His sincerity won him the support of a coalition of minorities, students, labor groups, and intellectuals. Dellums won the primary, taking 55 percent of the votes to Cohelan's 45 percent.

During the general election, his Republican challenger, John E. Healey, tried to establish a link between Dellums and the activities of the Black Panthers, or what he called the "lunatic left wing." Dellums also faced attacks by Vice President Spiro T. Agnew, who was campaigning on Healey's behalf. The vice president considered Dellums a "radical extremist," which was the exact image Ronald V. Dellums hoped to project. Despite his opponent's attempts to steal his victory, Dellums won the election by a margin of 57 to 41 percent. After winning, Dellums offered his sincerest appreciation to the man he credited with running his public relations campaign, Spiro T. Agnew.

Once in Washington, DC, Dellums concentrated most of his efforts on issues involving the military and civil rights. During his first year in Congress, he was appointed to serve on the Armed Services Committee, the first African American to sit on the committee. In 1971, at his request, Dellums was appointed to the committee that oversees the District of Columbia. He later became the committee's chairman, and he used his position to fight for and win minimized federal interference in district affairs.

Dellums quickly became an outspoken figure on Capitol Hill. In 1971, he introduced resolutions calling for an investigation into war crimes allegedly committed by the U.S. armed forces in Vietnam and raised questions concerning racism in the military. Though the Armed Services Committee ignored his pleas, he organized and conducted his own unofficial hearings, drawing significant national publicity to the concerns he was raising. That same year, Dellums helped organize, and spoke at, an antiwar rally on the steps of the Capitol, at which hundreds of protesters were arrested.

A staunch, yet responsible critic of defense spending, Ronald Dellums consistently opposed many new major weapons systems and the use of U.S. military force in other countries. Moreover, his criticism of military spending has been evenly dispensed to both Democratic and Republican officials. During the Carter administration, Dellums objected to the president's plans to develop the MX mobile missile, upgrade the Minuteman III missile, and develop the Trident II submarine-launched missile. During the Reagan era, Dellums denounced the president's pursuit of a massive defense buildup at the expense of domestic programs. From 1983 to 1989, Dellums, as chairman of the Military Installations and Facilities Subcommittee, monitored expenditures on overseas bases, making sure Reagan did not order them upgraded in preparation for a military exercise in the Third World. It was during the Reagan era that many in Congress began to recognize Dellums's leadership.

In June of 1986, Dellums's influence on Capitol Hill became especially visible. From the beginning of his tenure in Congress, he had called on the United States to severely punish the government of South Africa for its system of apartheid by imposing strict economic sanctions. So committed to the cause to end apartheid in Africa was Dellums that in 1984 he was among a group of demonstrators arrested outside the South African embassy in Washington, DC. For 15 years he spoke out, introduced legislation, and joined in public demonstrations against the inhumane treatment of people in Africa and around the world. In June of 1986, the House adopted Dellums's sanction bill, which barred virtually all trade with and investment in South Africa and suspended commercial air travel between the United States and South Africa.

With the exception of the 1992 emergency relief effort undertaken in Somalia, Dellums has opposed every U.S. military intervention abroad since arriving in Washington. He criticized Reagan for sending U.S. troops to invade Grenada (1983), Reagan's decision to station U.S. marines in Lebanon (1983), Bush's "Just Cause" invasion of Panama (1989), and the use of force to expel Iraqi troops from Kuwait (1991). In October of 1990, Dellums led 83 of his fellow representatives in signing a statement opposing military action in Iraq, and in December of that same year, he and 52 other legislators filed suit in federal court against President Bush, charging the president with acting militarily without congressional consultation or approval.

In January of 1993, the Democratic Caucus chose Dellums to succeed Les Aspin as chairman of the Armed Services Committee. During his tenure as chairman, Dellums continued to push for cuts in defense spending, which he justified by pointing to the end of the Cold War. In Dellums's view, reducing defense spending is not an end in itself but a means to convert the U.S. economy from warfare to welfare.

---

homelessness. The Reagan administration also slashed funding of federal Section 8 housing and other programs geared to producing affordable housing. Deep cuts in AFDC cast some single mothers and their children on the streets.

The shift from a skid-row based homeless population composed primarily of males with substance abuse problems to a much larger and broader population represented a long-term social problem as successive administrations failed to frontally address it—even to the present period. (We discuss homeless persons in more detail in Chapter 14.)

What We Can Learn from Failed Policy Strategies of the Conservative Counterrevolution

President Reagan and his allies subscribed to supply-side or "trickle-down" economic theory, which maintains that disproportionate tax cuts for wealthy persons will ultimately propel everyone toward greater prosperity. As compared with the 1960s and 1970s, however, economic inequality greatly increased in the 1980s—and the number of persons falling beneath federal poverty levels also increased. Subscribing to Reagan's economic philosophy, President George W. Bush, too, cut federal taxes by trillions of dollars with affluent persons also receiving disproportionate cuts. As in the 1980s, economic inequality increased, as did the numbers of persons under official poverty lines.

The argument that economic growth can *only* take place if affluent persons pay relatively low levels of taxes has been refuted by history. During the 1960s and 1990s, economic growth was relatively robust and affluent persons paid relatively high rates of taxes as compared to the 1980s. Conversely, during the first decade of the 21st century taxes, as well as economic growth, fell. Moreover, supply-side economic theory has been refuted by relatively high rates of economic growth in Europe, where tax rates on affluent persons have been far higher than in the United States. In the case of European societies, far fewer persons live in poverty than in the United States—and these nations possess far lower rates of economic inequality.

What We Can Learn from Promising Strategies of the Conservative Counterrevolution

Americans should not be able to have it both ways: using the labor of millions of undocumented immigrants while *also* denying them basic human rights. (Americans also benefit from the payroll and other taxes that these immigrants pay even as they receive only emergency health care.) When a bipartisan coalition enacted the Immigration Reform and Control Act of 1986, they cut through this American hypocrisy by granting amnesty to roughly 3 million immigrants who could prove that they had worked in the United States for four or more years.

Yet this legislation did not provide a lasting solution to this issue. By 2008, roughly 12 million additional immigrants resided in the United States who lacked official documents or who possessed only temporary visas. Once again, American corporations and employers used their labor—often contending that they could not locate American citizens to fill these positions. Once again, the United States denied these productive persons basic benefits and rights—often paying them at levels beneath the federal minimum wage, not enforcing work safety standards, subjecting them to police harassment, and dividing families by deporting parents of children.

To their credit, many federal legislators, as well as President George W. Bush, urgently sought to enact immigration legislation that would give some of these immigrants amnesty, while providing more rights and benefits to the remaining immigrants with temporary visas. But this legislation was stymied in 2007. Even so, it is likely that legislation with some of the features of the Immigration Reform and Control Act of 1986 will again be enacted to help the nation cope with its immigration issues.

What We Can Learn from the Conservative Counterrevolution about the Structure of the American Welfare State

A significant shift in the structure of the American welfare state took place in the 1980s with the enactment of block grants that gave states far greater policy roles in scores of programs that were placed in them. If states had become relatively weak participants in the American welfare state with the enactment of many federal entitlement programs, as well as categorical programs, states now became central players. States developed large bureaucracies to administer these programs even as much of their funding continued to come from the federal government.

Devolution of policy responsibilities was substantial in the 1980s—and supported not only by conservatives in Washington, DC, but by state officials from both parties who wanted to become more powerful partners in the American welfare state.

The lesson is clear to social workers, whether in their roles in case referrals, case advocacy, or policy advocacy. They cannot be effective in their work if they do not fully understand the operations of their state governments, including their central agencies and their Web sites. Indeed, state agencies, legislatures, and governors have become as important to the welfare state as their federal counterparts—and far more powerful than local governments.

WHAT YOU CAN DO NOW

After reading Chapter 10, you are now equipped to:

- Analyze why a powerful conservative movement grew in the wake of the defeat of Barry Goldwater in the presidential race of 1964 and through the 1970s.

- Discuss how Ronald Reagan won the presidency in 1980.

- Analyze President Reagan's core beliefs about taxation, limited government, anti-communism, and supply-side economics.

- Analyze how President Reagan secured a number of tax, spending cut, block grant, and military spending policies in 1981—and why leading Democrats proved unable to defeat them.

- Discuss how President Reagan markedly de-volved federal power to the states by folding 57 social programs into seven block grants.

- Discuss the reasons why President Reagan was far less successful in the remainder of his first term in obtaining major policy reforms—in-cluding opposition that developed to the huge budget deficits that his policies created.

- Analyze why a political stalemate developed in the wake of Reagan's defeat of Democrat Walter Mondale in the 1984 presidential elec-tion—and continued through the rest of his second term.

- Discuss why relatively few social policies were enacted during the presidency of George Bush, Sr., from 1989 through 1992.

- Analyze why the dissolution of the Soviet Union during President George Bush, Sr.'s presidency did not markedly reduce military spending.

- Discuss how the greatest *upward* redistribution of resources and rights took place during the presidencies of Ronald Reagan and George Bush, Sr.

- Analyze the oppression of women, persons of color and poor people, immigrants, gay men and lesbians, persons with HIV and AIDS, persons with disabilities, children, aging Americans, and homeless persons—despite notable reforms for immigrants and disabled persons.

- Analyze some tensions and issues that devel-oped in the social work profession.

- Discuss what we can learn about policy advo-cacy from social worker Ron Dellums.

- Analyze what we can learn from the conser-vative period extending from 1981 through 1992 about persistent needs, failed strategies, promising strategies, and the structure of the American welfare state.

ENDNOTES

1. George Nash, *The Conservative Intellectual Movement in America since 1945* (New York: Basic Books, 1976), pp. 253–295.

2. Geoffrey Hodgson, *America in Our Time* (Garden City, NY: Doubleday, 1976), pp. 473–478.

3. Craig Roberts, *The Supply-Side Revolution: An Insider's Account of Policy-Making in Washington* (Cambridge, MA: Harvard University Press, 1984), p. 18.

4. Robert Kuttner, *Revolt of the Haves: Tax Rebellions and Hard Times* (New York: Simon & Schuster, 1980), pp. 349–350.

5. James Reichley, *Conservatives in an Age of Change: The Nixon and Ford Administrations* (Washington, DC: Brookings Institution, 1981), pp. 387–390.

6. Pete Hamill, "The Revolt of the White Lower-Middle Class." In Louise Howe, ed., *The White Majority: Between Poverty and Affluence* (New York: Random House, 1970), pp. 10–22.

7. T. R. Reid, "Kennedy." In David Broder et al., eds., *The Pursuit of the Presidency, 1980* (Washington, DC: Berkeley Books, 1980), pp. 68, 77; Martin Schram, "Carter." In Broder, et al., eds., *The Pursuit*, p. 116.

8. Kevin Phillips, *Post-Conservative America: People, Politics, and Ideology in a Time of Crisis* (New York: Vintage Books, 1983), pp. 53–63.

9. Susan Littwin, *The Postponed Generation: Why America's Grown-Up Kids Are Growing Up Later* (New York: Morrow, 1986), pp. 18–25, 191–213.

10. William Leuchtenberg, *In the Shadow of FDR: From Harry Truman to Ronald Reagan* (Ithaca, NY: Cornell University Press, 1983), pp. 1–160.

11. Thomas Edsall, *Chain Reaction: The Impact of Race, Rights, and Taxes on American Politics* (New York: W. W. Norton, 1991), pp. ix–xiv, 1–7, 174.

12. Nash, *The Conservative Intellectual Movement*, pp. 36–56.

13. Ibid., pp. 291–295.

14. Milton Friedman, *Capitalism and Freedom* (Chicago: University of Chicago Press, 1962).

15. Martin Anderson, *The Federal Bulldozer: A Critical Analysis of Urban Renewal, 1949–1962* (Cambridge, MA: M.I.T. Press, 1964).

16. Peter Steinfels, *The Neoconservatives: The Men Who Are Changing America's Politics* (New York: Simon & Schuster, 1979), pp. 45–46, 108–160.

17. Edsall, *Chain Reaction*, p. 131.

18. Phillips, *Post-Conservative America*, pp. 180–192.

19. Samuel Hill and Dennis Owen, *The New Religious Political Right in America* (Nashville, TN: Abingdon, 1982), pp. 51–76.

20. Robert Dallek, *Ronald Reagan: The Politics of Symbolism* (Cambridge, MA: Harvard University Press, 1984), pp. 13–18.

21. Lou Cannon, *Reagan* (New York: Putnam, 1982), pp. 91–97.

22. Ibid., pp. 147–165.

23. Laurence Barrett, *Gambling with History: Reagan in the White House* (New York: Penguin Books, 1983), pp. 44–63; Rowland Evans and Robert Novak, *The Reagan Revolution* (New York: Dutton, 1981), pp. 91–95.

24. Dallek, *Ronald Reagan*, p. 34.

25. Barrett, *Gambling with History*, pp. 426–427.

26. See the views of a top aide, Martin Anderson, in *Welfare: The Political Economy of Welfare Reform in the United States* (Palo Alto, CA: Hoover Institution, 1978), pp. 87–132.

27. Lou Cannon, *President Reagan: The Role of a Lifetime* (New York: Simon & Schuster, 1991), pp. 206–231.

28. Haynes Johnson, *Sleepwalking through History: America in the Reagan Years* (New York: W. W. Norton, 1991), pp. 65–76.

29. Cannon, *Reagan*, pp. 176–184.

30. Johnson, *Sleepwalking through History*, p. 87.

31. Ibid., p. 197.

32. Evans and Novak, *The Reagan Revolution*, pp. 84–111.

33. Roberts, *The Supply-Side Revolution*, pp. 24–25.

34. Barrett, *Gambling with History*, p. 236.

35. Evans and Novak, *The Reagan Revolution*, pp. 95–96.

36. Roberts, *The Supply-Side Revolution*, pp. 12–13.

37. William Greider, "Republicans." In Broder et al., eds., *The Pursuit*, pp. 163, 168–169.

38. Roberts, *The Supply-Side Revolution*, pp. 69–88.

39. Cannon, *Reagan*, p. 325.

40. David Stockman, *The Triumph of Politics* (New York: Harper & Row, 1986), pp. 56–57.

41. Cannon, *Reagan*, pp. 273–278.

42. Johnson, *Sleepwalking through History*, p. 131.

43. Edsall, *Chain Reaction*, p. 206.

44. "Death of the Pony." In Broder et al., eds., *The Pursuit*, p. 341.

45. Richard Cohen, "They're Still a Majority," *National Journal*, 13 (January 31, 1981), pp. 189–191.

46. Ibid.

47. Barrett, *Gambling with History*, pp. 146–147.

48. Stockman, *The Triumph of Politics*, pp. 8–9, 11.

49. Timothy Clark, "Want to Know Where the Budget Ax Will Fall? Read Stockman's Big Black Book," *National Journal*, 13 (February 14, 1981), pp. 274–281.

50. "Party Switchers," *National Journal*, 13 (June 20, 1981), p. 1095.

51. Robert Samuelson, "Reagan's Bet," *National Journal*, 13 (February 21, 1981), pp. 301–307.

52. Evans and Novak, *The Reagan Revolution*, pp. 109–110.

53. Stephen Engelberg, "Moynihan Asserts Stockman Said Reagan Doubted Tax-Cut Theory," *The New York Times* (July 11, 1985), part A, p. 14.

54. Evans and Novak, *The Reagan Revolution*, pp. 109–110.

55. Stockman, *The Triumph of Politics*, pp. 269–298.

56. Ibid., p. 92; Barrett, *Gambling with History*, pp. 144–145.

57. Jack Meyer, "Budget Cuts in the Reagan Administration: A Question of Fairness." In D. Lee Bawden, ed., *The Social Contract Revisited* (Washington, DC: Urban Institute, 1984), pp. 33–68.

58. Clark, "Want to Know Where the Budget Ax Will Fall?" pp. 274–281.

59. Barrett, *Gambling with History*, pp. 94–106, 187–198.

60. Ibid., p. 71.

61. Clark, "Want to Know Where the Budget Ax Will Fall?" pp. 274–281.

62. Timothy Clark et al., "Congress Works a Minor Revolution—Making Cuts to Meet Its Budget Goals," *National Journal*, 13 (June 20, 1981), pp. 1114–1115.

63. Richard Cohen, "For Spending Cuts, Only the Beginning," *National Journal*, 13 (August 8, 1981), p. 1414.

64. Barrett, *Gambling with History*, pp. 164–170.

65. Cannon, *President Reagan*, p. 279.

66. Edsall, *Chain Reaction*, p. 192.

67. Johnson, *Sleepwalking through History*, p. 181.

68. Anderson, *Welfare*, pp. 43–58.

69. Blanche Bernstein, "Welfare Dependency." In Bawden, ed., *The Social Contract Revisited*, p. 138.

70. Robert Samuelson, "For the Economy, Unanswered Questions," *National Journal*, 13 (August 8, 1981), p. 1407.

71. Edsall, *Chain Reaction*, pp. 159–161.

72. W. Joseph Heffernan, *Introduction to Social Welfare Policy* (Itasca, IL: Peacock, 1979), pp. 179–180.

73. Murray Weidenbaum, "Regulatory Reform." In George Eads and Michael Fix, eds., *The Reagan Regulatory Strategy* (Washington, DC: Urban Institute, 1984), pp. 15–41.

74. Timothy Clark, "Affirmative Action May Fall Victim to Reagan's Regulatory Reform Drive," *National Journal*, 13 (August 11, 1981), pp. 1248–1252.

75. Roberts, *The Supply-Side Revolution*, pp. 226–245; Stockman, *The Triumph of Politics*, pp. 320–323.

76. Roberts, *The Supply-Side Revolution*, pp. 165–179.

77. William Greider, "The Education of David Stockman," *Atlantic Monthly*, 248 (December 1981), pp. 27–54.

78. Roberts, *The Supply-Side Revolution*, pp. 197–212.

79. Barrett, *Gambling with History*, p. 139.

80. Alexander Haig, *Caveat: Realism, Reagan, and Foreign Policy* (New York: Macmillan, 1984), pp. 303–316.

81. Charles Stone and Isabel Sawhill, *Economic Policy in the Reagan Years* (Washington, DC: Urban Institute, 1984), pp. 22–25.

82. "Reagan's Polarized America," *Newsweek* (April 5, 1982), pp. 20–28.

83. Barrett, *Gambling with History*, pp. 401–402.

84. Ibid., pp. 348–349.

85. Stockman, *The Triumph of Politics*, pp. 192–193.

86. Timothy Clark, "Social Security Ball in Your Court, Greenspan Panel Tells Reagan, O'Neill," *National Journal*, 14 (November 20, 1982), pp. 1889–1991.

87. Paul Starr, *The Social Transformation of American Medicine* (New York: Basic Books, 1984), pp. 383–388.

88. Linda Demkovitch, "Hospitals That Provide for the Poor Are Reeling from Uncompensated Costs," *National Journal*, 16 (November 24, 1984), pp. 2245–2249.

89. Ibid.

90. Joseph Califano, *America's Health Care Revolution: Who Lives? Who Dies? Who Pays?* (New York: Random House, 1986), pp. 11–36, 58–68.

91. Dorothy Kupcha, "Medicaid: In or Out of the Mainstream?" *California Journal*, 10 (May 1979), pp. 181–183.

92. Nancy Eustis, Jay Greenberg, and Sharon Patten, *Long-Term Care for Older Persons: A Policy Perspective* (Pacific Grove, CA: Brooks/Cole, 1984), pp. 1–7.

93. Marlene Cimons, "AIDS Shock Wave Due to Sweep U.S.," *Los Angeles Times* (December 7, 1986), pp. 1, 35.

94. Richard Corrigan, "Private Sector on the Spot as It Prepares to Take Over Job Training," *National Journal*, 15 (April 30, 1983), pp. 894–897.

95. Bruce Jansson, *Theory and Practice of Social Welfare Policy: Analysis, Processes, and Current Issues* (Belmont, CA: Wadsworth, 1984), pp. 133–134.

96. Neil Pierce, "The Myth of the Spendthrift States," *National Journal* (August 3, 1991), p. 1941.

97. Barrett, *Gambling with History*, p. 61.

98. Hill and Owen, *The New Religious Political Right*, pp. 72–76.

99. Peter Goldman and Tony Full, *The Quest for the Presidency, 1984* (New York: Bantam Books, 1985), pp. 35–36.

100. TRB, "Neoliberals, Paleoliberals," *New Republic* (April 9, 1984), pp. 6, 41.

101. Goldman and Full, *The Quest for the Presidency*, pp. 48–58.

102. Ibid., pp. 368–374.

103. Jeffrey Birnbaum and Alan Murray, *Showdown at Gucci Gulch* (New York: Vintage Books, 1988), pp. 284–291.

104. Donald Chambers, "Policy Weaknesses and Political Opportunities," *Social Service Review*, 59(1) (March 1985), pp. 1–17.

105. Sidney Blumenthal, *Pledging Allegiance: The Last Campaign of the Cold War* (New York: HarperCollins, 1990).

106. Burt Solomon, "Grading Bush," *National Journal* (July 8, 1991), pp. 1331–1335.

107. Cannon, *President Reagan*, p. 279.

108. See, for example, the series of articles on the peace dividend in *The New York Times* in 1991, such as its editorial on May 9, 1990, part A, p. 30.

109. Barbara Sinclair, "Governing Unheroically (and Sometimes Unappetizingly): Bush and the 101st Congress." In Colin Campbell and Bert Rockman, eds., *The Bush Presidency: First Assessments* (Chatham, NJ: Chatham House Publishers, 1991), pp. 174–181.

110. Ibid.

111. Bert Rockman, "Leadership Style of George Bush." In Campbell and Rockman, eds., *The Bush Presidency*, pp. 1–35.

112. Paul Quirk, "Domestic Policy: Divided Government and Cooperative Presidential Leadership." In Campbell and Rockman, eds., *The Bush Presidency*, pp. 69–91.

113. Solomon, "Grading Bush," p. 1335.

114. Edsall, *Chain Reaction*, p. 186.

115. Ibid., pp. 99–115.

116. Ibid., pp. 192–197, 215–255.

117. Susan Faludi, *Backlash: The Undeclared War against American Women* (New York: Crown Publishers, 1991), pp. 59–72.

118. Ibid., pp. xiii–xxiii.

119. Ibid., p. 236.

120. Ibid., pp. 412–421.

121. Ibid., pp. 273–275.

122. Richard Cohen, "Family Leave Fight Perplexes Advocates," *National Journal* (November 23, 1991), p. 2878.

123. See, for example, U.S. House Ways and Means Committee, *The 1990 Green Book* (Washington, DC: U.S. Government Printing Office, June 5, 1990), pp. 1106–1107; Kevin Phillips, *Rich and Poor: Wealth and the American Electorate in the Reagan Aftermath* (New York: Random House, 1990), pp. 8–25, 74–91; and Edsall, *Chain Reaction*, pp. 160–161.

124. Phillips, *Rich and Poor*, pp. 8–25, 74–91.

125. Ibid., p. 166.

126. William Wilson, "Cycles of Deprivation and the Underclass Debate," *Social Service Review*, 59 (December 1985), pp. 541–559.

127. Paul Peterson, "The Poverty Paradox." In Christopher Jencks and Paul Peterson, eds., *The Urban Underclass* (Washington, DC: Brookings Institution, 1990), pp. 9–16.

128. Ronald Takaki, *Strangers from a Different Shore* (Boston: Little, Brown, 1989), p. 420.

129. Sucheng Chen, *Asian Americans: An Interpretive History* (Boston: Twayne Publishers, 1991), p. 170.

130. Randy Shilts, *And the Band Played On* (New York: St. Martins Press, 1987), p. 456.

131. Ibid., p. 525.

132. *San Francisco Examiner* (June 5, 1989), p. 12.

133. Julie Kosterlitz, "Enablement," *National Journal* (August 31, 1991), p. 2093.

134. Children's Defense Fund, *State of America's Children* (Washington, DC, 1991), pp. 24–25.

135. Martha Ozawa, "Introduction: An Overview." In Martha Ozawa, ed., *Women's Life Cycle and Economic Security* (New York: Greenwood Press, 1989), pp. 2–8.

136. Jonathan Kozol, *Savage Inequalities: Children in America's Schools* (New York: Crown Publishers, 1991).

137. Children's Defense Fund, *State of America's Children*, p. 122.

138. Sheila Kamerman and Alfred Kahn, "Social Policy and Children in the United States and Europe." In John Palmer, Timothy Smeeding, and Barbara Torrey, eds., *The Vulnerable* (Washington, DC: Urban Institute Press, 1988), pp. 351–380.

139. Robert Binstock, "The Politics and Economics of Aging and Diversity." In Scott Bass, Elizabeth Kutza, and Fernando Torres-Gil, eds., *Diversity in Aging: Challenges Facing Planners and Policy Makers in the 1990s* (Glenview, IL: Scott, Foresman, 1990), pp. 73–77.

140. Jack Meyer and Marilyn Moon, "Health Care Spending on Children and the Elderly." In Palmer, Smeeding, and Torrey, eds., *The Vulnerable*, p. 180.

141. Binstock, "The Politics and Economics of Aging," pp. 77–82.

142. Martha Burt and Barbara Cohen, *America's Homeless: Numbers, Characteristics, and Programs That Serve Them* (Washington, DC: Urban Institute Press, 1989), pp. 2–4, 27–31.

143. Ibid., pp. 141–161.

144. Peter Rossi, *Down and Out in America: The Origins of Homelessness* (Chicago: University of Chicago Press, 1989), pp. 181–184.

145. Joan Biskupic, *The Supreme Court Yearbook, 1990–1991* (Washington, DC: Congressional Quarterly, Inc., 1992), p. 10.

146. W. John Moore, "Righting the Courts," *National Journal* (January 25, 1992), p. 200.

147. W. John Moore, "In Whose Court?" *National Journal* (October 5, 1991), p. 2397.

148. Linda Greenhouse, "Justices Bar Using Civil Rights Suits to Enforce U.S. Child Welfare Law," *New York Times* (March 26, 1992), part A, p. 15.

149. Harry Specht, "Social Work and the Popular Psychotherapies," *Social Service Review*, 64 (September 1990), pp. 345–357.

150. Amy Butler, "The Attractiveness of Private Practice," *Journal of Social Work Education* (Winter 1992), pp. 47–60.

151. *Social Work Speaks: NASW Policy Statements*, 2nd ed. (Silver Spring, MD: National Association of Social Workers, 1991).

152. Bruce Jansson, *Social Welfare Policy: From Theory to Practice* (Belmont, CA: Wadsworth, 1990), pp. 8–11.

153. Stanley Wenocur and Michael Reisch, *From Charity to Enterprise: The Development of American Social Work in a Market Economy* (Urbana, IL: University of Illinois Press, 1989), pp. 6–18; Gerald Rothman, *Philanthropists, Therapists, and Activists* (Cambridge, MA: Schenkman Publishing Co., 1985), pp. 155–161.

154. See the discussion of the American Medical Association throughout Paul Starr, *The Social Transformation of American Medicine* (New York: Basic Books, 1984).

11

Reluctance Illustrated: Policy Uncertainty during the Clinton Administration

TABLE 11.1   Selected Orienting Events

1992	Bill Clinton defeats George Bush and Ross Perot
1993	Clinton announces tax increases and spending cuts
1993	Clinton places Hillary Clinton in charge of a task force to develop a health care reform proposal
1993	Family and Medical Leave Act enacted
1993	Clinton signs the 1993 Omnibus Reconciliation Bill, which cuts the deficit, raises taxes, and increases the Earned Income Tax Credit
1993	Clinton presents ambitious plan to reform health care
1993	North American Free Trade Agreement enacted
1993	Federal policy on gays in the military is modified
1994	Congress enacts legislation that makes it a federal crime to intimidate abortion clinic workers and clients by force or threat of force
1994	Crime Bill enacted
1994	Some Republican leaders issue Contract with America
1994	Republicans obtain control of both houses of Congress
1995	Republican Newt Gingrich becomes Speaker of the House
1995	Congress enacts 1995 Omnibus Reconciliation Act, which seeks to eliminate the entitlement status of AFDC, Medicaid, and Food Stamps
1995	Clinton vetoes 1995 Omnibus Reconciliation Act, as well as specific appropriation bills
1996	Budget stalemate between Clinton and Congress continues
1996	Enactment of the Personal Responsibility and Work Opportunities Act

TABLE 11.1 **(continued)**

1997	Balanced Budget Act enacted with extension of caps on discretionary spending
1997	Impeachment of Bill Clinton
1998	Emergence of federal budget surpluses
1998	Resignation of Newt Gingrich announced
1998	Clinton foresees an extended period of budget surpluses

In its first three years, the presidency of Bill Clinton was characterized by more conflict than any administration since the second term of Richard Nixon. In his 1992 campaign, Clinton ran on a relatively liberal agenda that featured increased spending on a range of social programs, as well as health and welfare reform. Clinton was able to enact some social reforms in his first two years in office and to avoid deep cuts in many social programs, but he was placed on the defensive in 1995 after Republicans under the leadership of Newt Gingrich swept the 1994 congressional elections and gained control of both houses of Congress. Republicans proceeded to advance a conservative agenda based on cutting taxes, slashing social spending, ending entitlements, and devolving many federal policy roles to the states. A titanic confrontation ensued between the Democratic administration and the Republican Congress. The central issues were the size and priorities of the national budget in 1995 and the nation's commitment to entitlements such as AFDC and Medicaid. Yet Clinton made a remarkable comeback, winning reelection in 1996 and obtaining many small victories in his second term despite Republicans' control of both Houses of Congress.

Clinton's situation resembles that of another Democratic president, Harry Truman, who in 1947 and 1948 confronted a Republican congress determined to use its budget and taxing powers to impose its conservative agenda on the nation.

We call the Truman, Nixon, and Clinton presidencies periods of policy uncertainty, in which liberal, moderate, and conservative ideologies were pitted against one another in dramatic fashion. In the Clinton years, the shaping of annual budgets was the focus of conflict in 1993 through 1997, as well as in the final two years of his presidency.

At the end of this chapter, we discuss what we can learn in the contemporary period from the Clinton years about policy advocacy, social policy, and the structure of the American welfare state.

THE ASCENDANCY OF BILL CLINTON

Like Lyndon Johnson, Clinton was preoccupied with obtaining power; he sought it directly and he made connections for himself by participating in other people's campaigns. In his youth, he won class presidencies in high school and at Georgetown University. Using his contacts with Senator William Fulbright, he obtained a clerkship with the Senate Foreign Relations Committee while a college student and thus learned the inner workings of the Senate. By deft maneuvering he obtained a Rhodes Scholarship, which allowed him to study at Oxford University for two years before obtaining a law degree at Yale. Even before he returned to Arkansas in 1973, at the age of 27, he had participated in four major campaigns at state and federal levels, culminating in the ill-fated presidential campaign of George McGovern in 1972.

Throughout all of these experiences, Clinton developed thousands of contacts that he meticulously filed on index cards—contacts that he later cultivated and freely used to obtain funds, support, and advice for his own political races. Undeterred by a losing run for the House of Representatives from a rural part of Arkansas in 1974, he was elected attorney general in 1976 and governor in 1978; that victory made him the youngest governor in the United States in four decades. Aside from a single loss in 1980, he held the governorship for four terms; in 1991, during his fifth term, he decided to run for president. His political career was profoundly shaped by his wife, Hillary, who became his closest advisor in Arkansas and during his presidency.

The Search for the Real Bill Clinton

From the beginning of his career, Clinton has left many people uncertain where he really stood.[1] He supported liberal policies on some occasions and moderate or conservative policies on others. He frequently retreated from liberal positions, to the dismay of liberal supporters, only to subsequently return to them.[2] His inconsistency stemmed from several sources. As a Southern politician, he *had* to present a moderate or conservative profile to succeed in a rural state that had supported politicians such as Orval Faubus, the governor who defied federal school desegregation orders in the 1950s. Like many Southern politicians, including Jimmy Carter and ex-Senator Sam Nunn, Clinton feared that the Southern Democratic Party might not survive Southern Republicans' attempts to win over white voters by means of anti-tax, anti-spending, and conservative rhetoric.[3]

However, Clinton had strong social reform and populist convictions. As a child, Clinton had been repulsed by the racist policies of Orval Faubus, as well as the segregationist policies of the South. John Kennedy was his personal hero. Partly because he opposed the Vietnam War but also because he possessed liberal views, Clinton campaigned for George McGovern in 1972. As a populist or social reformer, Clinton sought reforms in the educational system of Arkansas, tried to lower utility rates, participated in a lawsuit against physicians who refused to serve Medicaid patients, and favored job training for welfare recipients. Although he did not support civil rights legislation in Arkansas, he appointed many African Americans and women to governmental posts. He favored major tax increases in Arkansas to fund road construction and improvements in public education.[4]

Intensely ambitious and determined to win elections in his Southern state, Clinton was a chameleon even before he became president. He viewed himself as a social reformer and felt most comfortable when championing social causes and attacking vested interests. However, when attacked by Southern opponents as a tax-and-spend Democrat, Clinton would backtrack if he believed his political base was jeopardized. He would repudiate former allies, such as organized labor or school teachers; seek tougher work requirements for welfare recipients; fail to seek civil rights legislation; or demand that the national Democratic Party become more moderate. Clinton's political style contributed to fears that he lacked deep convictions. From 1980 onward, he relied heavily on Dick Morris, a political consultant who placed extraordinary reliance on political polls. Under Morris's tutelage, Clinton shaped his rhetoric and positions almost daily in response to the most recent poll results. Morris preached that politicians should couple pragmatism with idealism, in a kind of permanent campaign.[5]

Observers began to wonder if Clinton possessed any core values. They worried that he was overly eager to be liked by everyone and unable to take strong, confrontational positions, even when pitted against arch conservatives. Some saw him as too academic, a policy wonk who mulled over endless options without reaching closure.

The Search for the New Democrat

Clinton's ill-defined views and Southern origins would have made his ascension to the presidency difficult in the 1960s, when Northern, liberal Democrats possessed considerable power in the national party. But by the early 1990s, these characteristics became assets rather than liabilities, for several reasons. With the extraordinary movement of people from the North to the Sun Belt from the 1950s through the 1980s, the electoral votes of the South and of California exceeded those of the Northern industrial states. The power of suburban voters had steadily increased since the 1960s, as well, to the point that a majority of voters in the 1992 presidential elections were suburbanites. Increasingly, Democratic leaders came to fear that, if they were to concede the South and Northern suburbs to Republicans, they might become a minority party for decades. Moreover, the ultraliberal McGovern's one-sided defeat in 1972 led many Democrats to worry that the party was positioning itself so far to the left that it would no longer appeal to the white ethnic voters who had been a bastion of Democratic support since the 1930s. This threat had become more ominous by the 1980s, when substantial numbers of Republicans replaced Democrats in Congress. In an equally disturbing trend, some Democratic officeholders, such as Phil Gramm of Texas, had switched parties.

In the wake of McGovern's defeat, Democrats like Ben Wattenberg sought to move the party back to the center; they feared that it had been captured by special interest groups such as feminists, civil rights groups, and organized labor. These Democrats were particularly opposed to affirmative action, liberal welfare programs, and the eclipse of the states' policy roles.[6] Clinton signaled his decision to identify with the moderate wing of the party in 1980 by strongly supporting Jimmy Carter, a fellow Southern governor, against Teddy Kennedy's bid for the presidential nomination.

In 1985, he helped found the Democratic Leadership Council (DLC), which sought to define a third way—that is, a political platform that fell between traditional liberal and conservative positions. Whereas traditional Democrats had favored redistribution of resources to the poor, civil rights legislation, affirmative action, and cuts in defense spending, the new Democrats emphasized a narrower range of economic reforms—job training, national standards in education, free trade,

and infrastructure improvements. Whereas traditional Democrats favored new spending on social programs *and* retention of existing spending, the new Democrats favored balanced budgets. Whereas traditional Democrats were opposed to free trade, partly because trade unions feared it might hurt their domestic markets, new Democrats (with some exceptions) liked it; they believed that free trade would eventually expand markets for American goods by forcing efficiencies in American industry and lowering other nations' trade barriers. Whereas traditional Democrats wanted large cuts in the military in the wake of the Cold War, new Democrats favored only selective cuts. New Democrats were determined, as well, to challenge conservatives' charges that Democrats were soft on welfare and crime. Whereas traditional Democrats had often championed higher welfare benefits, new Democrats emphasized work requirements and limits on benefits. They often favored stiffer penalties for various crimes such as drug dealing, as well as extension of the death penalty to new crimes. Whereas traditional Democrats discussed the obligations of citizens to help others, new Democrats emphasized the responsibilities of citizens—for example, to seek work, raise families, and help their communities.

Perhaps most important, the new Democrats emphasized the economic needs of the middle class rather than low-income groups or racial out-groups, partly because they attributed the Republicans' upsurge in the 1980s to the alienation of white voters who perceived the Democrats as beholden to feminists, civil rights activists, and gays. Believing that this alienation was partly due to the erosion of living standards for many working-class and middle-class Americans, new Democrats often advocated education, job training, and tax cuts that would help this group; thus, they placed less emphasis on programs to help poor inner-city residents and other out-groups.[7]

However, these new Democrats did not dominate the party in the early 1990s. Liberal Democrats maintained a strong presence in party councils, as did activists from an array of civil rights, feminist, and labor groups. Party chieftains in Congress, such

INSERT 11.1 Using the Web to Understand the Shaping of Policies during the Clinton Presidency

Visit **academic.cengage.com/social_work/jansson** to view these links and a variety of study tools.

Go to **http://en.wikipedia.org/wiki/Bill_Clinton** for an analysis of his presidency. View the various legislative enactments. In light of the context he encountered, how successful do you think he was in

as House Speaker Tom Foley and Senate Majority Leader George Mitchell, did not belong to the Democratic Leadership Council, even if they also feared the desertion of many white voters to the Republican cause.

Bill Clinton's ill-defined views positioned him perfectly to obtain the allegiance of the divided Democratic Party, if he could convince both factions that he favored their positions. He appealed to those Democrats who believed a Southern candidate was needed to avert further Republican inroads in the Sun Belt—and could point to his election as chair of the DLC in 1990 as proof that he could appeal to Democratic moderates and conservatives. Having campaigned for McGovern and sought various reforms in Arkansas, he often spoke like a traditional Democrat. Himself a Baptist, he often spoke in African American churches and gave Vernon Jordan, a prominent African American attorney, important roles in his campaign and presidency. His wife, Hillary Rodham Clinton, who had chaired the board of directors of the Children's Defense Fund, broadened his appeal to liberals.

As an outsider who had never been elected to federal office, Clinton could also attract widespread support from independents and those citizens who were deeply cynical about the federal government and about the Congress. Many good reasons existed

for cynicism. Americans had heard endless promises from politicians that budgets would be balanced since 1981, only to find mounting deficits. They had seen many news reports about government waste in both defense and domestic agencies. They knew that many elections were bought by politicians who could obtain huge contributions from special interests and wealthy people. Finally, the bitter wrangling between Republican presidents and the Democratic Congress during the Reagan and Bush years, punctuated by presidential vetoes, had fueled widespread frustration at government gridlock.

THE PRESIDENTIAL CAMPAIGN OF 1992

Most Democrats regarded George Bush as unbeatable in the fall of 1991, in the wake of Operation Desert Storm, a highly popular war against Iraq. Facing candidates with little name recognition or uncertain reputations, like Paul Tsongas, John Kerry, and Jerry Brown, Clinton relied on his superior campaign skills, his adeptness at using the mass media, his vast network of contacts, and his ability to raise money to easily win the Democratic nomination in July of 1992.

Clinton's road to the presidency was complicated by the third-party candidacy of Ross Perot, a maverick billionaire from Texas. Drawing on widespread cynicism about politicians and the government, Perot vowed to clean up Washington. Perot was vague about his likely policies, with one notable exception: He vowed to end the budget deficit soon after taking office, though he did not explain precisely how he would do so. By focusing on the budget deficit, Perot elevated that issue in the public's consciousness and stimulated other candidates to address it. Fearful that Perot would draw votes from them, both Bush and Clinton emphasized deficit reduction in their own campaigns; Clinton promised to halve the deficit within four years, from $237 billion to $118 billion.

Clinton fashioned a clever strategy in this complex environment. He maintained the allegiance of liberals by supporting the policy recommendations of Robert Reich, a professor Clinton knew from Oxford University and Yale Law School. Reich believed that the economy no longer revolved around nation-states, but had become globalized as corporations dispersed their operations in many nations in search of cheap labor (for unskilled jobs) or educated, technologically sophisticated labor (for skilled jobs). In this globalized economy, Reich contended, the American workforce was polarizing into two factions. Symbolic analysts, who had higher degrees and were adept at information age technologies, had expanding options in an array of highly paid professional, technical, and corporate positions. By contrast, with the sharp decline in well-paid, unionized industrial jobs since the 1960s, tens of millions of Americans worked in low-paid, unskilled jobs. These low-paid workers in clerical, sales, and fast-food jobs faced a bleak economic future: Reich predicted that corporations would continue to place their manufacturing operations in low-wage nations, such as Mexico and Thailand, and in consequence, the wages and economic security of unskilled American workers would deteriorate even further. Concluding that the nation could retain and develop better-paying jobs only if it invested in its human capital and its infrastructure, such as roads and telecommunications, Reich recommended large expenditures in education, job training, and public improvements.[8] In addition to these social investment expenditures, which required outlays over many years, Clinton also advocated immediate spending—so-called stimulus spending—on an array of public projects to invigorate the stagnant economy.

Clinton also promised to reform the health care system. He had long been concerned about the plight of Americans who lacked health coverage; as governor of Arkansas, he sought to develop public health, maternal health, and family-planning services in the state. In 1991, when Democrat Harrison Wofford ran a successful senatorial campaign in Pennsylvania on a health reform platform, Clinton became convinced that public opinion favored an overhaul of the American health system. To strengthen his liberal credentials, he advocated unpaid leaves to allow employees to care for babies or ailing relatives, and he vowed to overturn the ban on gay men and lesbians in the military. He solicited support from environmentalists by selecting as his vice president Senator Albert Gore, Jr., who had supported many environmental causes.

He cemented the support of liberal Democrats by promising to increase taxes on affluent Americans, who had, he argued, enriched themselves throughout the 1980s as a result of the Reagan administration's tax cuts.

Intent on capturing moderate and conservative votes and on securing the support of white ethnic voters, Clinton also used campaign language that the Democratic Leadership Council favored. Words like "responsibility," "community," and "opportunity" and glowing references to the middle class were scattered throughout his speeches. He promised to enact welfare reform that coupled strong work requirements with liberal subsidies for child care and job training. In a widely publicized statement, he criticized Sister Souljah, an African American rap singer, for militant language; that accusation brought a public confrontation with Jesse Jackson, the civil rights leader, who accused Clinton of currying the favor of white citizens. Clinton promised a significant tax cut for middle-class Americans, even though he had received confidential information that the federal deficit would be far higher than the Bush administration had publicly admitted. To neutralize Ross Perot, Clinton promised that he would support campaign reforms, consider some cuts in entitlements, and halve the nation's deficit during his term. Most important, Clinton understood that presidential races often hinge on the state of the economy.

To Clinton's astonishment, Bush failed to emphasize a strategy for reinvigorating the economy and thus alienated many of the working-class and middle-class voters who had defected to the Republican Party from the Democratic Party in the 1980s. Lacking a focus for his campaign in its early stages, Clinton's strategists successfully guided its later stages on the basis of a motto posted prominently in their campaign headquarters: "It's the economy, stupid."

Clinton won the election, but by the narrowest margin since 1968. He obtained only 43 percent of the popular vote, as compared with 38 percent for Bush and 19 percent for Perot. Clinton's support in California, industrial states of the Midwest, and New York State carried him to victory. Democrats controlled both houses of Congress. However, their margin in the Senate was insufficient to stop a Republican filibuster, and their majority in the House would be destroyed if only 30 conservative Democrats voted with the Republicans. Thus, in both the House and the Senate, Clinton would be vulnerable to a coalition of Southern (or border state) Democrats and Republicans if they viewed his policies as excessively liberal.

CLINTON'S GRIM OPTIONS

Even before his inauguration, Clinton knew that his first challenge would be to fashion a budget and an economic policy. Perot's single-minded focus upon the budget deficit during the campaign had forced the issue to center stage. Were Clinton *not* to devise policies to reduce the deficit markedly, he would be accused of abandoning his campaign promise to halve it within four years—and would face a rebellious Congress, where many newly elected legislators were determined to diminish it.

Clinton's dilemma was that he had proposed contradictory policies during the campaign: He had promised to halve the nation's deficit, but he had also promised to fund social investments and provide an immediate economic stimulus. Moreover, he had promised a tax cut for middle-class citizens and had downplayed the need for tax increases. To further complicate his deficit-reducing task, Clinton had rarely discussed spending cuts during the campaign; he had promised only to end subsidies to beekeepers and to consider modest premium increases for wealthy Medicare recipients.

With his advisors and cabinet named, Clinton came face to face with daunting economic realities that would further frustrate deficit reduction. While

he had learned in August that the Bush administration would soon issue a higher estimate of the budget deficit, he had not focused on these figures.

Eventually, Bush estimated the deficit for 1997 at $305 billion, or $68 billion higher than he had predicted in the summer. (Many Democrats, including Clinton, feared it would rise to $360 billion or more.) With soaring Medicare and Medicaid costs, deficits would again begin to rise after 1997, even if a strong anti-deficit program were implemented in the interim. These economic realities meant that Clinton had to seriously consider two options that were certain to attract political opposition: increasing taxes and cutting spending on existing programs.[9]

Obstacles to tax increases had been introduced by Reagan, who had developed wide support for tax cuts, and by Bush, who had been vilified for breaking his promise to the 1988 Republican convention: "Read my lips. No new taxes." Nor were spending cuts palatable to the liberal wing of the Democratic Party, which was anxious to enact a large agenda of social reforms after 12 years of Republican presidents.

Clinton also encountered another reality that would profoundly influence his economic strategy. During the campaign, he had emphasized spending increases as the primary means of stimulating the economy—a traditional Democratic method of restoring economic growth. Soon after he was elected, however, he met with Alan Greenspan, the Chair of the Federal Reserve Board. Greenspan contended that economic growth would hinge *not* on stimulus spending but on interest rates charged to borrowers, such as home buyers, consumers, and corporations. Were interest rates to rise, these borrowers would have to pay more for their loans and would thus be discouraged from expenditures and investments. The best route to economic growth, Greenspan asserted, was to *cut* the large deficit. If the deficit were lower, he argued, interest rates would fall because fewer investment funds would be diverted from the private sector to the purchase of government bonds. It became clear to Clinton, as well, that bond traders on Wall Street possessed extraordinary power over the economy, through their trading actions; they would sell and buy bonds at lower interest rates only if they believed that the government was pursuing anti-deficit policies—for example, by cutting social spending. Greenspan implied, moreover, that he and the Federal Reserve Board would cut the so-called prime rate, which powerfully influences interest rates of banks, but they would do so only if the Clinton administration developed a credible deficit reduction plan. (At various points subsequently, Clinton felt that Greenspan and Wall Street bond traders controlled his policies; he feared that they might increase interest rates if he failed to emphasize deficit reduction over spending increases.)[10]

Before tackling his budget dilemma, Clinton devoted the month of December to selecting his cabinet and his economic team. His choices signified that he wanted an array of perspectives in his administration. On the conservative side, he chose advisors likely to emphasize deficit reduction—Senator Lloyd Bentsen as Secretary of the Treasury, Wall Street banker Robert Rubin to head his economic team, and deficit hawks Representative Leon Panetta and Alice Rivlin to run the Office of Management and Budget. He named the relatively liberal Laura D'Andrea Tyson to chair the Council of Economic Advisors. He also gave key posts to other liberal advisors—Robert Reich as Secretary of Labor, Donna Shalala as Secretary of Health and Human Services, and Henry Cisneros as Secretary of Housing and Urban Development. The liberal emphasis of his first two years was accentuated, moreover, by his decision to grant his wife, Hillary, a large role in overseeing domestic policy and by his frequent consultations with campaign strategists James Carville, Paul Begala, Stan Greenberg, and Mandy Grunwald, who insisted that Clinton follow through on his campaign promises to increase social investments.

FROM SOCIAL INVESTMENT TO DEFICIT REDUCTION

Even before his inauguration, Clinton was drawn in different directions by an array of powerful forces and people. Strong pressure for deficit reduction came from Bentsen and Rubin, who were convinced by Greenspan's logic. Members of Congress from both parties—particularly those newly elected—believed they had been given a mandate by the people to push for deficit reduction. Clinton realized that he risked losing popular support if he did not take dramatic action against the deficit; he had promised to cut it in half within four years and it was rapidly expanding. He knew, as well, that the Republicans would make deficit reduction a central theme in their political strategy in 1993; they were eager to continue their attack on him as a tax-and-spend Democrat.

On the other hand, many people tried to convince Clinton not to abandon his campaign promises of social investments, health reform, and welfare reform. Liberal Democrats hadn't controlled the presidency for 12 years, and they had seen many social programs severely cut during this period. They urged Clinton to pursue social investments and stimulus spending, as did many interest groups, such as the Children's Defense Fund and the American Association of Retired Persons. The strongest advocates for social investments within the administration were campaign strategists like Carville, Begala, and Grunwald, sometimes joined by Reich, Tyson, and Hillary Clinton. Nor should we minimize Clinton's own social reform proclivities; he deeply believed that social investments were needed to help working Americans improve their economic options. In behind-the-scenes meetings during the first months of his administration, he frequently expressed reluctance to break his campaign promises.[11] With the Democrats in control of Congress, he had considerable political leverage to enact social reforms and to fund a liberal agenda.

Developing an Economic Package

Presidents who come into office for the first time inherit their predecessor's budget, even though they may modify it. Bush's budget emphasized cuts in social spending—including spending caps on many entitlement programs—and no new taxes and thus pressured Clinton to follow suit in his own economic plans.

 content merely to adopt Bush's budget, which did not reflect his interest in social investments, Clinton decided to develop his own economic package—a set of targets for spending, taxes, and deficit reduction that he wanted the Democratic Congress to incorporate in its Budget Resolution in the spring. (He planned to give the Congress his own detailed budget later in the spring to show how he would meet the targets that he proposed.) In the course of many meetings with his top advisors, Clinton made several key decisions. He decided to backtrack from his campaign promise to halve the deficit by 1996; instead, he proposed to reduce it only to $205 billion in 1997. Even to reach this figure, he would need new tax revenues, particularly if he wanted immediate stimulus spending of $30 billion and social investments of $230 billion over five years. So he decided to include a broad-based energy tax based on heat output (expressed in British thermal units, or BTUs), and he also proposed to make permanent a 2.5-cents-per-gallon addition to the federal gas tax that had been scheduled to expire in 1995. He announced major tax increases for wealthy Americans; the new top rate would be 36 percent for couples earning more than $140,000 and individuals earning more than $115,000. Altogether, his tax increases totaled $328 billion over five years. He combined these tax increases with spending cuts of $375 billion over five years; among other things, he proposed to eliminate 100,000 positions from the federal government, to slow the rate of increase in fees paid to providers under Medicare, to extend a Medicare premium increase that was due to expire, and to cut defense modestly. (Indeed, Clinton "blinked" with respect to military spending, deciding to make virtually no cuts in military spending partly because Bush had made his alleged evasion of the draft during the Vietnam War a campaign issue in 1992.)

In effect, Clinton forged a compromise between his liberal and his conservative advisors that included both spending increases and deficit reduction. The president's package delighted many deficit hawks, including Greenspan, who viewed it as a major advance toward diminishing the deficit in his first term. Newspapers hailed the economic package and applauded Clinton's embrace of deficit reduction. Liberals liked its social investment and stimulus spending. Even at this early point, however, some liberal advisors within the administration were chagrined by the fact that deficit reduction, not social spending, was dominating discussion of the budget. They also knew that Clinton, already bowing to economic advisors like Bentsen, had cut his proposed social investments in behind-the-scenes discussions before he announced his economic package on February 17. In his speeches, moreover, he emphasized deficit reduction rather than social investments.[12]

A Brief Digression: The Budget Process

To understand the fate of Clinton's social investments—and the continuing conflict between Republicans, Democrats, and the president—we must first comprehend the budget process, which dominated the nation's politics in 1993, 1995, and much of 1996. An examination of this process will give us important insights into the reasons why many social programs, such as child care, child welfare, and mental health services, are chronically underfunded.

The budget process begins when the president submits his proposed budget for the coming fiscal year, typically in February. He outlines how much money he wants to allocate to each program in the coming year, whether he wants new taxes, his estimate of the likely budget deficit, and his estimate of the likely effects of his budget on the budget deficit. Federal spending can be placed in two categories: entitlements and discretionary spending. Programs such as AFDC, Medicare, Medicaid, SSI, and Food Stamps are entitlements; the statutes that establish the programs lay out standards that recipients must meet, and the government automatically grants funds to pay the benefits of all recipients who meet those standards in a given year. Unlike entitlements, the funds for discretionary programs are determined annually by votes of the appropriations committees in each chamber. The Congress might decide in a given year, for example, to cut funding of a child nutrition program or to increase funding of a public health program.

In Clinton's budget proposal for the 1994 fiscal year (Figure 11.1), expenditures were divided among entitlements and mandatory spending (roughly 50 percent of the budget), discretionary spending (roughly 33 percent of the budget), and interest on the national debt (roughly one-sixth of the budget). Inspection of Figure 11.1 reveals that the discretionary spending in Clinton's budget includes approximately equal components of domestic and military spending. Only $68.1 billion (or about 4 percent of the entire federal budget) is devoted to the combined discretionary programs of the Department of Health and Human Services and the Department of Labor, which constitute (aside from entitlements) the heart of the American welfare state.[13]

Four facets of this federal budget are of particular interest to social workers:

1. *Funding of entitlements.* Cuts in expenditures on entitlements have a severe impact on social workers' clients, who often depend on Medicare, Medicaid, AFDC, SSI, and Food Stamps.

2. *Domestic discretionary spending.* This section of the budget, which accounts for only about 16 percent of the total, funds social programs related to mental health, child welfare, substance abuse, public health, AIDS treatment/prevention, homelessness, child care, and many other areas.

3. *Tax policy.* Tax cuts decrease the revenues needed to fund entitlements and domestic discretionary spending. Moreover, when taxes are cut excessively, budget deficits increase, and concern about budget deficits and the national debt often leads legislators to cut social programs.

4. *Military spending.* Military programs compete with domestic programs for discretionary funds. Indeed, more than one-half of discretionary funds is devoted to military spending.

After the president has submitted his budget, Congress takes center stage. After reviewing the president's budget, a Budget Committee of each chamber puts together a Budget Resolution, a document that establishes spending goals for each entitlement program; develops spending goals for discretionary spending in 13 areas, including domestic and military programs; outlines tax revenue targets for the coming fiscal year; and sets a target for the overall size of the budget deficit (or surplus). When the Budget Committees want to reduce the budget deficit, as was the case in 1993 and 1995, their Budget Resolutions mandate spending cuts or tax increases or some combination of both. (If a Budget Committee chooses to *reduce* taxes, as both Republicans in Congress and President Clinton proposed in 1995, its Budget Resolution must mandate even deeper spending cuts to reduce the budget deficit.)

Each chamber must vote on the Budget Resolution that its Budget Committee has

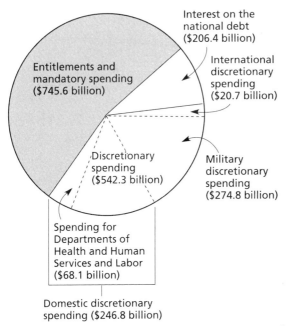

FIGURE 11.1 An overview of the president's proposed budget for fiscal year 1994.

SOURCE: President's budget. Office of Management and Budget, Appropriations Committee.

fashioned. Once approved, these two documents are sent to a conference committee that includes members from each chamber. That committee negotiates a compromise Budget Resolution, which must then be ratified by both chambers. The resulting Congressional Budget Resolution instructs the committees of Congress to develop legislation and appropriations bills that conform to its directives. Rather than telling Congress specifically how to reach the spending, tax, and budget reduction goals, the Budget Resolution merely instructs particular congressional committees to increase or decrease spending by stipulated amounts. It might want, say, $3 billion in cuts in Medicare over five years; Congressional committees then face the task of deciding how to achieve these savings by changing the Medicare statutes. The Budget Resolution in 1993 instructed the House Committee on Education and Labor, for example, to make changes in laws within its jurisdiction to allow increases in outlays of $118 million in the coming budget year and reductions in outlays in the succeeding three years totaling nearly $6 billion. To make laws conform to these directives, the House Committee on Education and Labor has to change eligibility and benefit levels of many programs in its jurisdiction, and the House Appropriations Committee, which recommends what funds will actually be spent in a given year, has to implement these funding guidelines in its spending recommendations. Similarly, the Budget Resolution instructs committees that deal with tax legislation to raise (or lower) tax revenues by specific amounts.

To meet the targets of the Budget Resolution, then, a vast system of tasks must be implemented by the Congress. It is useful to conceptualize this system as consisting of two parallel tracks. One track deals with entitlements and tax legislation. In this track, the spending goals of the Budget Resolution are met by changing those statutes that govern specific programs and tax policy. The House Ways and Means Committee and the Senate Finance Committee assume pivotal roles here because they process most tax legislation, as well as entitlements like Medicare, Medicaid, and AFDC. To obtain cuts in the Medicare program recommended by

the Budget Resolution, the House Ways and Means Committee might consider raising premiums for elderly persons using Part B (physician services), cutting coverage of certain services (such as mental health services), or lowering reimbursement fees for doctors and hospitals. The other track consists of legislative committees (such as the House Committee on Education and Labor) and appropriations committees (such as the House Appropriations Committee) that deal with domestic discretionary programs. As the House Ways and Means Committee is amending tax laws and entitlement statutes that govern programs such as Medicaid, other House committees are working to fashion spending (or appropriations) recommendations for programs such as Head Start that are funded by the discretionary budget.

Two kinds of recommendations emerge from the Congress. First, each chamber often bundles its entitlement and tax recommendations into a *reconciliation bill*, so called because its recommendations reconcile tax and entitlement policies with the spending and tax guidelines of the Budget Resolution.

Each chamber must vote on its reconciliation bill; a conference committee then develops a compromise version that must be ratified by each chamber. Second, to specify discretionary spending, each chamber develops 13 separate *appropriations bills*, including one that focuses on programs administered by the Department of Health and Human Services and the Department of Labor. These bills conform to guidelines in the Budget Resolution. As with each chamber's reconciliation bill, conference committees fashion compromise appropriations measures that must be ratified by each chamber.

By late summer or fall, attention shifts back to the president, who has to decide whether to sign or veto the congressional recommendations from both tracks. If he signs the reconciliation bills and the 13 appropriation bills, the budget is set for the coming year. If he vetoes any of these bills, the president and Congress must agree on a continuing resolution that temporarily funds federal programs.

With the continuing resolution in place, Congress attempts to fashion modifications of the vetoed bills that the president is willing to sign. (If Congress and the president cannot agree on a continuing resolution, some government programs may come to a temporary halt, as occurred during the turbulent budget impasse of 1995 and 1996.)

The Demise of the Stimulus Package

Recall that, in his economic package, Clinton proposed two kinds of new spending: an immediate economic stimulus to get the economy moving and social investments. House leaders introduced his $30 billion stimulus package in mid-February. (Only $16.3 billion was new spending; the rest consisted of business tax incentives and construction loans.) The stimulus spending was vulnerable on several counts. Because this spending was relatively small, it would not have a large economic effect even if enacted. Moreover, unlike the social investments, which were guided by Robert Reich's philosophy of making the nation competitive in a global economy, the stimulus package contained a lot of pork—that is, expenditures for various projects in the districts of important Democrats, such as road construction grants to particular cities. Conservatives were certain to attack it as inconsistent with deficit reduction.

Clinton moved to get immediate action on his stimulus package. The Republicans, urged forward by deficit hawks like Newt Gingrich and John Kasich, opposed it en masse and tried to portray the new president as a big spender. But the response of many House Democrats, particularly moderates and conservatives, was even more disconcerting. They wanted to cast their deficit reduction vote *before* casting their vote for stimulus spending so that they could tell their constituents that they prioritized spending cuts. Consequently, they insisted that the vote on the stimulus package be delayed until the Budget Resolution, which emphasized deficit reduction, was also ready for a vote in the House.

After heavy lobbying by Clinton, the House did pass the stimulus package. But it was then subjected to devastating opposition from moderate and conservative Democrats in the Senate.

Senators David Boren and John Breaux, who had been saying for weeks that Congress should make actual spending cuts before approving the stimulus package, wanted to spend only half of the stimulus package and to delay approval of the rest of it until Congress enacted those tax increases and spending cuts detailed in the House Budget Resolution. Strong-arm parliamentary tactics by Senator Robert Byrd, the Senate Majority Leader, angered Republican senators by making it impossible for them to amend the legislation. Realizing that they lacked the votes to stop it, Republicans decided to filibuster. When the Senate recessed and legislators returned to their districts to get constituents' feedback, Clinton received another bad piece of news; many voters told their representatives that *they* prioritized deficit reduction over stimulus spending. When Clinton offered to cut the stimulus bill by one-fourth, to only $12.2 billion, Republicans insisted that *all* spending in the legislation be deleted, except for a $4 billion provision to fund extensions of unemployment insurance. Unable to stop the filibuster otherwise, the Democrats conceded on April 21, and, in gutted form, the stimulus package was finally passed.[14]

Early Warning Signs

If stimulus spending was gutted, what happened to the social investments in Clinton's economic package?

They faced their first test when both chambers developed their Budget Resolutions. It seemed, at first glance, that Clinton won a decisive victory on March 19 when the House enacted Clinton's economic package in its Budget Resolution and thereby established the spending, tax, and deficit reduction targets that Clinton had recommended. The Senate followed suit with a similar Budget Resolution on March 25. Budget Resolutions merely establish targets, however: Clinton now needed Congress to make appropriations that would allocate funds toward his social investments.

Early warning signs suggested that Clinton's social investments would not emerge unscathed during the appropriations process. House Democratic leaders encountered substantial pressure from conservative and moderate members to cut spending further. To mollify them, the House added $63 billion in deficit reduction in its Budget Resolution by making additional cuts in social spending, mostly from appropriated programs rather than entitlements. With John Kasich leading, Republicans tried to outbid the Democrats; they proposed $429 billion in deficit reduction over five years without any of Clinton's tax increases—a strategy that would have required huge cuts in social spending. Acting virtually in unison, the Democrats repelled this Republican effort.

Conservative dislike of the spending and tax provisions was even stronger in the Senate. To put conservative and moderate Democrats on the spot, Republicans forced them to vote against many amendments that sought to delete specific spending and tax increases in the president's package. They realized that the legislation's energy tax—the so-called BTU tax—was particularly vulnerable, both because key Democrats came from energy-producing states like Oklahoma and because it could be portrayed as hurting the middle class, the very group Clinton and the new Democrats wanted to help. Moreover, were this tax defeated, the whole plan could be thrown into turmoil because it would lack the revenues to fund the social investments.

Throughout the debates in the House and the Senate, conservatives demanded that spending cuts far *exceed* tax increases; they wanted spending cuts, rather than tax increases, to bear the burden of deficit reduction. (Clinton had wanted roughly even amounts of tax increases and spending cuts.)

There was also considerable pressure to cut entitlements, which the president's economic plan left largely intact. An amendment to cap Medicare and Medicaid by Sam Nunn, a Southern Democrat, was narrowly defeated on the Senate floor.[15]

Because it processes tax and entitlement legislation, the Senate Finance Committee played a pivotal role in enacting the Senate's Budget Resolution—and this committee barely passed it, by an 11–9 vote. If even a single Democrat were

to defect to the Republican side later in the summer, when the Congress enacted its reconciliation bill, the committee would be deadlocked.

Once the House and Senate versions were speedily reconciled in the Conference Committee, the Congress enacted its Budget Resolution on April 1. In its final form, the Budget Resolution retained many social investments, even if they would be diminished from $200 billion to $140 billion by 1998. But the Budget Resolution also contained a provision—not widely understood even by many liberals—that would have momentous implications for social investments. The Congress was instructed to hold discretionary spending to an overall limit about $12 billion less than that included in a 1990 budget-cutting agreement between President Bush and the Congress. Moreover, the Budget Resolution capped discretionary spending at $539 billion in 1994 and permitted an increase only to $548 billion by 1998.

In the wake of huge cuts in discretionary programs for poor people in the Reagan and Bush years, this "hard freeze" meant that these programs would not even keep pace with inflation. Their prognosis was especially bleak because the discretionary budget included defense spending. If cuts in defense spending did not continue, even greater pressure would be placed on domestic programs. (Many legislators already were balking at the initial cuts in defense spending that Clinton had proposed; even though the Cold War had ended, they argued that cuts would imperil the nation's security.) This hard freeze also meant that Clinton's $140 billion in social investments would be imperiled in coming years. He could fund them *only* by cutting other discretionary domestic programs or by cutting defense spending. But such cuts in other domestic programs or defense would be strongly resisted by legislators; as a result, large increases in social investments were extremely unlikely. Nor would the outlook for social investments improve if Republicans were able to capture control of either chamber in the 1994 Congressional elections. Republicans might seek to cut taxes and thus force Congress to cut spending even further to reduce the deficit. Or they might seek major increases in defense spending, thereby forcing cuts in domestic spending.[16]

The Sacrifice of Social Investments

Enacting the Budget Resolution proved far easier than enacting specific tax, entitlement, and spending policies. The Budget Resolution merely set targets. Legislators now faced the task of approving specific tax and spending policies; this task, as they knew, required them to negotiate the conflicting objections of lobbyists and constituents to particular tax increases, cuts in entitlements, or cuts in spending. At the same time, in the deficit-cutting mood of 1993, legislators were aware that they would be heavily criticized for *not* cutting spending and entitlements. Deficit reduction was a top priority for large numbers of newly elected legislators in both parties, including many moderate and conservative Democrats who were members of groups such as the Conservative Democratic Forum and the House's Mainstream Forum, an organ of the DLC.[17]

The battle over the reconciliation bill, which contained Clinton's BTU tax and his cuts in Medicare, illustrated the extent that the Congress was in an anti-tax, anti-spending, and deficit reduction mode. Clinton soon realized that he would have to work furiously to get the tax measures through the House. Many legislators wanted to delete, or drastically modify, the energy tax and wanted larger cuts in entitlements. He was able to obtain a close victory in the House on his energy tax—over the opposition of 43 Democrats and virtually all Republicans—only by agreeing that he would accede to large cuts in the energy tax and larger cuts in entitlements when the legislation came to the Senate.

The Achilles tendon of the entire package was its huge energy tax. Were the BTU tax not to be passed, the entire package might unravel because the lost revenues would require huge new spending cuts or diminution of Clinton's social investments. The tax was bitterly opposed by an array of special interests, as well as by oil state senators under the leadership of Senator David Boren of Oklahoma.

(Republicans continued to demand that all tax increases be deleted from the legislation and that the spending cuts be far larger.) At Boren's insistence, the BTU tax was deleted; another battle was then fought over the size of the gasoline tax. (A small gas tax was eventually approved.) When the dust had settled, Democrats partly offset these lost revenues by increasing Medicare and Social Security taxes, cutting tax breaks that Clinton favored for low-income persons, and scaling back tax breaks to encourage business to locate in so-called inner-city empowerment zones. Even with these changes, the legislation only passed by a 50–49 margin; Vice President Gore cast the tie-breaking vote.

At a raucous conference committee meeting to reconcile the House and Senate versions, members of the Congressional Black Caucus threatened to vote with Republicans if tax breaks for low-income persons or empowerment zones were dropped, and conservatives and moderate Democrats threatened to oppose the legislation if certain energy taxes were restored. With more than 200 House and Senate members engaged in around-the-clock bargaining, a reconciliation bill was finally approved. The bill, which provided for $500 billion in new taxes over five years, included large tax increases on wealthy Americans and a gasoline tax, but the BTU tax that energy state legislators disliked was removed. In the prevailing anti-tax climate, many legislators feared rejection by their constituents in forthcoming elections if they voted for these tax increases. Clinton won with a tight 218–216 vote in the House. (The crucial vote was cast by a grim-faced female Democrat from Pennsylvania, who knew she would probably lose her next election as a result; her forecast proved to be accurate.) The Senate approved the revised reconciliation bill only by a 51–50 vote; Gore's tie-breaking vote was needed again.

Once again, Clinton seemed to have prevailed. Over a five-year period, he achieved over $500 billion in deficit reduction by combining $250 billion in new taxes with $179 billion in spending cuts. When viewed in the context of his campaign promises for social investments, however, the reconciliation bill seemed less impressive. As we have seen, the reconciliation bill contained a hard freeze on discretionary spending that would force an additional $56 billion in cuts over five years. Even by August, it was clear that Clinton's social investments would be savaged by the Congress in the coming year. As Jonathan Rauch noted, "Clinton will get some of his investment agenda, but only about half over all, and more like 20 cents on the dollar for education. The total for new investment in [the coming year] looks to come out under $10 billion. In a $6 trillion economy, hardly anyone will notice."[18]

As if these cuts in Clinton's domestic spending were not enough, the House leadership and the White House had to agree to *another* round of spending cuts in the fall of 1993, in appropriation bills that had already passed the Congress. (Cuts in appropriations that have already been enacted are called *rescissions*.) Debates over these additional cuts made clear that a bipartisan coalition of deficit hawks in the House would demand far more drastic deficit reduction in the future. Not content with Clinton's promise to reduce the federal workforce by 252,000 people over the next five years or to rely on the hard freeze on discretionary spending through 1998, they wanted an additional $103 billion in cuts over five years, much of it from premium increases on Medicare recipients—and they wanted these cuts to be applied to deficit reduction rather than to be used to fund new programs. Many deficit hawks also wanted a balanced budget amendment to the Constitution that would allow deficits in any particular year only if 60 percent of members of both chambers approved, except during wars. (They hoped this measure would take effect by 1999.) Additionally, they wanted a line-item veto to let the president cut appropriations already approved by Congress, subject to a vote by Congress on them. They reasoned that members of Congress would be more frugal if they realized that the president might veto wasteful spending and so force them to vote publicly to restore it.

The deficit hawks, led by Republicans like Newt Gingrich, were defeated in their efforts to seek large spending cuts, the balanced budget amendment, or a line-item veto in the fall of 1993.

However, they had publicized their intent to seek huge, additional spending cuts in the wake of the 1994 congressional elections if, as they correctly predicted, their numbers were swelled by voters who favored their cause. Indeed, they planned to attack Clinton as a tax-and-spend Democrat in those elections.[19]

THE SECOND YEAR: ANTI-CRIME LEGISLATION BUT NO HEALTH REFORM

The Fight for Health Reform

Long before the presidential campaign of 1992, Clinton realized that the American health care system had many flaws. Unlike most other industrialized nations, the United States had developed a health care system that revolved around employers and private insurance companies. Many employers paid, in part or in full, the monthly premiums on private health insurance policies for employees and their families. This system often worked well for those who were covered by it, but others lacked coverage because they were unemployed, because their employers chose not to offer health insurance, or because chronic or catastrophic conditions had exhausted their benefits. Moreover, individuals beginning a new job might be denied coverage if the employer's health insurance company determined that they had a preexisting health condition. The enactment of Medicare and Medicaid had provided government-funded benefits to citizens over age 65 (Medicare) and to low-income persons who lacked private health insurance and met income eligibility standards (Medicaid). Even with these programs, about 40 million Americans lacked private health insurance *or* access to Medicare and Medicaid in 1992.

In addition, the American health care system was extraordinarily costly; it absorbed about 15 percent of the GNP in 1992, as compared with less than 10 percent in other industrialized nations. Costs were increasing at such an extraordinary rate that some experts guessed they would reach 20 percent of the GNP soon after the turn of the century. Americans had constructed a health care system that provided physicians and hospitals with incentives to perform costly procedures and to provide expensive tests, in contrast to government-managed systems in Canada and most of Europe, where physicians' and hospitals' remuneration did not hinge on the volume of surgeries and procedures they provided. The use of private health insurance companies, with considerable marketing and administrative overheads, added huge costs—estimated at about 20 percent—to the American medical system, as compared with Canada and Europe. Nor should we forget Americans' insatiable appetite for costly technology and drugs, which was further stimulated by the endless stream of innovations from huge biotechnology and pharmaceutical firms. Another factor increasing the nation's health care costs was that tens of millions of poor and uninsured Americans, lacking access to primary care and preventive services, sought services only after their medical condition had become serious.

Nor would it prove easy to surmount political barriers to basic reforms in the American health care system. Many entrenched interests—including private health insurance companies, physicians, hospitals, and pharmaceutical companies—would resist reforms that curtailed their profits, revenues, or autonomy. Americans who already had coverage might resist any reforms that they feared would raise their health care costs or deplete their benefits. Moreover, those 40 million uninsured Americans—the people most needing health reforms—were not politically organized and often did not vote.

Aware of the complexity of the health system and the political barriers in his path, Clinton nonetheless chose to prioritize health reform, partly for moral reasons but also to enhance his political fortunes, in the way that educational reform had helped him in Arkansas. He decided in early 1993 to place Hillary Clinton in charge of health care reform, with the assistance of Ira Magaziner, a liberal aide.

Even in the spring and summer of 1993, controversy erupted within the administration about the scope of health reform. Advisors such as Lloyd Bentsen and Robert Rubin cautioned Clinton not to seek comprehensive reform; they feared it might increase federal expenditures at a time when the administration was under political pressure to diminish the budget deficit. While restructuring the health care system might eventually bring savings by reducing medical inflation, they warned that coverage of the 40 million uninsured Americans would require vast governmental outlays in the short term. Dismissing the warnings of Bill Clinton's economic advisors, Hillary Clinton and Magaziner chose universal coverage as the central goal. They were convinced that huge savings could be realized by using market forces to contain providers' fees and by using governmental power to force drug companies not to charge excessive prices. They realized, however, that health reform might mean large costs in the short run—even as much as $100 billion—to give uninsured Americans coverage. Indeed, they warned Clinton that health reform would require new taxes at the very time he was encountering increasing opposition to tax increases.[20]

Despite opposition from key advisors, Bill Clinton clearly agreed with Hillary Clinton and Magaziner that a major overhaul of American health care was required. He knew, however, that he could not get health legislation through the Congress in 1993 because he had to devote most of his energies to his economic package. He decided to establish a large task force, headed by Hillary Clinton and Magaziner, to define policy options. Partly as protection against special interests, such as physicians and hospitals, the task force met in secret. By early August, Clinton had made a pivotal choice: to establish universal coverage as the one principle for which he would risk losing the whole program; he was willing to negotiate other details of health reform.[21] He had decided by mid-August not to seek major new taxes to fund health care but to rely instead on a tax hike on cigarettes, cuts in existing programs such as Medicare and Medicaid, and savings from efficiencies resulting from government-enforced competition.[22]

Even before the task force began its work, Clinton had decided to rely on a market-driven system with private insurances rather than a governmental single-payer system similar to those used in Canada and Britain. In a single-payer system, the government pays the medical fees of citizens in a manner akin to the Medicare program; private insurance companies are unnecessary. As the single payer, the government has extraordinary power over the medical system, both through its purchasing decisions (it determines what procedures it will fund and at what cost) and its regulations (it can regulate providers and drug companies; it can even decide what fraction of physicians will be specialists or general practitioners). Clinton rejected the single-payer system for several reasons. He knew that entrenched medical interests, such as doctors, would strongly oppose it. He also knew that Republicans and conservatives would attack a single-payer system as "big government." Clinton also understood a simple economic fact: a single-payer system would require vast governmental resources at its outset; retention of the existing employer-funded benefits of the American system would demand far fewer tax revenues. When most citizens get their health benefits from employers, government has to fund benefits only for those citizens who are not covered by employers, such as unemployed people or older citizens. Were the United States to make the government the prime funder of benefits, hundreds of billions of dollars would have to be found to replace the expenditures currently borne by employers.

Clinton released his plan in September in a nationally televised address to a joint session of Congress. He hoped his proposal would appeal to both moderate and liberal factions. Its emphasis on market competition, employers' funding of benefits, and retention of private insurances made it consonant with the current health care system. Liberals liked its emphasis on universal coverage and requiring providers to give a basic package of benefits.

In searching for a market-driven alternative to a single-payer system, Clinton drew on the work of many American economists, including Alain Enthoven. Enthoven had urged for many years that the government enroll all Americans in health maintenance organizations (HMOs). If the costs,

quality, and scope of their plans were publicized, Enthoven reasoned, competition between HMOs would hold down health care costs. Clinton's plan would establish regional health organizations (or alliances) that would provide competing plans—including both HMOs and plans initiated by insurance companies and providers—among which consumers could choose. The major provisions of Clinton's plan were as follows:

1. Most employers would be required to fund health care for their employees, with some government subsidies to small employers.

2. The federal government would fund the purchase of private health insurance policies for unemployed people or part-time workers.

3. The government would establish the basic minimum coverage to be included in *all* health policies—including preventive services, drugs, and curative services.

4. Regional health care alliances would be developed to publicize competing health insurance policies so that consumers could select the plan that they wished—and change plans when they liked another plan better.

5. Private insurance companies would not be allowed to discontinue coverage for preexisting conditions.

6. The government would develop controls over the prices charged by pharmaceutical companies for existing and new drugs.

7. The government would provide every American with a health security card to be used when seeking services from health care plans.

8. Medicare and Medicaid would be retained, but their enrollees could join competing plans offered by regional health care alliances.

Clinton outlined these general principles in September, and presented actual legislation on October 27. Already, however, battle lines had begun to be drawn. Many people criticized the sheer complexity of Clinton's plan; his proposed legislation totaled 1,342 pages. Even top advisors in the administration could not grasp many of its technical features. Questions arose about the plan's cost. Could it be funded only by efficiencies and a cigarette tax when it proposed to cover 40 million uninsured Americans and to add five new entitlements? (The Clintons insisted that the plan would cut the deficit by $91 billion by the year 2000 because they believed competition would markedly reduce costs.) Would insured Americans have to pay higher fees to help finance the plan? Would small employers be able to afford their employees' health costs, even with government subsidies? What about doctors, hospitals, insurance companies, and drug companies? They had been entirely left out of planning. Would they oppose the legislation? Would the regional alliances' preference for HMOs reduce freedom of choice?[23]

The foes of Clinton's plan wasted no time. Within days, rumors circulated that many insured Americans would pay higher fees. Polls showed that many Americans feared they would pay more for health insurance under the plan. Small businesses feared they would face huge new costs. Many middle-class Americans believed the plan would primarily help lower-income persons. Nor were providers and Republicans cautious about opposing the plan. Almost immediately, private health insurance companies encouraged these fears by financing a television campaign that featured Harry and Louise, a fictional middle-class couple who discussed their concerns about the Clinton plan.

Neither liberals nor conservatives rallied to the plan. Many liberal Democrats favored a single-payer system akin to Canada's and supported a plan by Representative Jim McDermott. Conservatives proposed an array of plans that minimized government involvement in health care; some did not include requirements that all businesses cover their employees, and some encouraged consumers to put aside savings for their own health care expenses. In turn, moderates wanted a scaled-back version of Clinton's plan; some urged that universal coverage be delayed until after the turn of the century.

These political problems were accentuated by the logistical problems of enacting health care in the Congress, where it fell under the jurisdiction of several committees—three in the House and two

in the Senate. Adrift in this maze of committees, the Clinton plan lost momentum; different committees came to differing conclusions. As providers continued to run advertisements attacking the legislation, the reservations of many middle-class citizens remained. Sensing an election-year issue, Republicans branded the Clinton proposal as unworkable or as excessively costly.[24] It was painfully clear by August that no plan would command a majority of legislators in either chamber. It is easy to blame Clinton's plan for the failure of health reform, but it is not clear that *any* plan would have gained support from the Congress in 1994. In the extraordinarily complex U.S. health care system, too many groups—not least the private insurance companies—have a vested interest in the status quo. The American health care system polarizes Americans into insured people (who mostly get their insurance through their employers) and uninsured Americans (who tend to be relatively poor); insured people are fearful that their coverage will suffer, or their fees will rise, if uninsured Americans are brought into their system.

The defeat of his health care plan was a crushing blow to Clinton. He had gambled that it could be enacted just prior to the congressional elections of 1994; instead, its defeat made him look ineffectual and renewed the public's distaste for government gridlock. By portraying his plan as a bureaucratic, big-government scheme, Republicans persuaded many voters that Clinton was a traditional liberal and thus eroded Democrats' support in moderate and conservative districts.

Anti-Crime Legislation

The largest measure to be enacted in Clinton's first term was not health care or other social reforms but an anti-crime measure. Realizing that many Americans listed crime as the nation's most serious problem, Clinton was determined not to let Republicans monopolize the issue. He outlined the basic elements of a Democratic anti-crime plan in August of 1993: funds for 100,000 new police officers, new federal death penalties, and fewer appeals for death row inmates. By November of

1993, Senate Democrats had obtained the Senate's approval for a huge, $22.3 billion bill that also included funds for prison construction, a ban on some semiautomatic weapons, and programs to prevent violence against women. In April of 1994, the House approved a similar measure; the House version also included significant funds for social services to prevent crime, such as recreation programs. Responding to charges that death sentences were disproportionately levied on African American inmates, the House bill also included a controversial measure to allow defendants to challenge their death sentences as racially discriminatory, on the basis of sentencing statistics. After deleting this measure, a conference committee approved a $30.2 billion bill, an unprecedented involvement by the federal government in local law enforcement.

During deliberations on the conference report in the Senate, conservatives sought to portray the legislation as a monument to freewheeling Democratic spending; they were particularly offended by its generous funding of social services. In turn, Democrats charged that Republicans' opposition to the legislation was an effort to appease the powerful National Rifle Association, which opposed the ban on 19 assault-type weapons. When finally signed by the president in mid-September, the legislation provided $8.8 billion to hire 100,000 new officers, $7.9 billion to help states build new prisons and boot camps, and $6.9 billion for social programs, including $1.6 billion to fund the Violence Against Women Act, which provided federal penalties and programs to reduce domestic violence.

It is ironic that Clinton's major achievement in his first term proved not to be health care or social investments but a huge anti-crime bill that largely funded expansion of police forces and new prisons. In its size, this bill rivaled his new spending for social investments of 1993. Its expenditures for social programs barely survived an onslaught from conservatives, who viewed them as social reform through the back door—and conservatives vowed to rescind these social programs if they controlled Congress after the impending 1994 elections.[25]

BUILDING A REVOLUTION WITHIN THE COUNTERREVOLUTION

Ronald Reagan had fashioned a counterrevolution against Democratic liberalism in the 1980s, but many conservatives were deeply dissatisfied by the mid-1980s. Whereas Reagan had cut many discretionary programs, total spending continued to escalate rapidly, largely driven by increased expenditures for Social Security, Medicare, and Medicaid. Even if Reagan had shifted many federal programs into block grants, many others remained intact. It was Reagan's tax and defense policies that created the huge budget deficit, but conservatives came to view it as a product of big-spending liberalism and special interests. Had social spending been radically cut, they reasoned, the deficit would not have been created or sustained. As the deficit soared during the 1980s and early 1990s, their frustration with government spending rose.

Convinced in 1987 that Robert Bork, President Reagan's nominee for the Supreme Court, had been defeated by a coalition of feminist and civil rights groups, conservatives were determined not to let liberals shape future appointments. Many conservatives were still angry that President Bush accepted major tax increases as part of a deficit reduction package in 1990; they had long wanted social spending cuts, not tax increases, to bear the onus for deficit reduction. (Since the New Deal, many conservatives had believed that the welfare state would be curtailed only if the tax revenues that funded it were slashed.) The election of Bill Clinton in 1992 infuriated conservatives further; they regarded him as a political threat because he sought to co-opt conservative issues like reducing crime and cutting deficits. They feared that, left unchecked, Clinton might win back Democrats who had voted for Republicans in the Reagan era.[26]

Increasingly discontented, some conservative Republicans believed that they could complete Reagan's work only by capturing control of the Congress, and especially the elusive House of Representatives, which had been controlled by Democrats since 1955. (Republicans would be well positioned to get spending cuts if they controlled the House, which initiates budget and tax legislation.)

It fell to a politician by the unlikely name of Newt Gingrich to realize the conservatives' dreams. An army brat whose family lived on a succession of military bases, he had a great epiphany in 1958, when he visited Verdun, a battle site where 970,000 European troops had died in World War I. Determined to become a political leader who would prevent such cataclysms, he also decided that politics was like war, where brute power allows one side to prevail. Even by the mid-1970s, he wanted to become Speaker of the House, convinced that the Speaker was even more powerful than the president. After a brief stint as a college history teacher, Gingrich was finally elected to the House on his third attempt, in 1978.

Initially a liberal Republican, Gingrich converted to conservatism after attending a campaign school run by Paul Weyrich, often called the father of the New Right. In a strategy meeting with Weyrich and others in 1980, Gingrich plotted how Republicans could take control of the House by 1992. He emphasized the importance of framing issues to allow conservatives to take the moral high ground from Democrats, by contrasting the "conservative opportunity society" (portrayed as emphasizing lower taxes, protection of innocent people from crime, responsible fatherhood, and work) with the "liberal welfare state" (portrayed as emphasizing higher taxes, the rights of criminals, and welfare dependency). He placed extraordinary emphasis on *perceptions*; he argued that what actually happens is less crucial than how people perceive it. Conservatives could increase their power by manipulating and shaping popular perceptions to discredit liberals—a strategy that required frequent use of focus groups of voters to gauge what language and actions would allow conservatives to upstage liberals. He also emphasized tactics that featured surprise, manipulation, deception, and tactical ingenuity.[27]

Gingrich operated on two levels in the 1980s. He destabilized the House by waging a kind of guerilla warfare against its Democratic leadership; he performed this role with such relish that he was nicknamed Neutron. He also masterminded a national strategy for electing conservative Republicans when he became the chair of GOPAC, a private organization that funded Republican campaigns using resources from wealthy donors. Drawing on GOPAC funds, Gingrich targeted roughly 50 House districts; he carefully chose conservative constituencies, for which he could find candidates who met his conservative litmus test. He built a cadre of loyal supporters and trained them by means of tapes and seminars that provided tactical suggestions—for example, attacking Democrats as "traitors," "corrupt," and "sick." When elected, these conservatives acted cohesively in the Congress under his direction.

With a growing contingent in the House, Gingrich and his allies needed to get control of leadership positions in the Republican Party to supplant older Republicans like Bob Dole, the Senate Minority Leader, and Robert Michel, the House Minority Leader. These older leaders were unacceptable to Gingrich for several reasons. Having lived through World War II and its aftermath, they were not as critical of the welfare state as Gingrich; their generation had benefited from such government programs as the GI Bill, FHA housing, and Social Security. Used to serving in Congress as the minority party, they excelled at cutting deals with Democrats rather than adopting intransigent positions. Gingrich narrowly won the position of Minority Whip in 1989—and his close friend Dick Armey became chair of the House Republican Conference in late 1992. With Michel's retirement in late 1993, Gingrich became Minority Leader in early 1994.[28]

In addition to party leadership and GOPAC funds, conservatives supplemented their power with a "loosely knit group that included think tanks, foundations, columnists, direct-mail operations, talk-show hosts, and various self-appointed spokespeople."[29] Formed by Weyrich, the Heritage Foundation viewed itself as a public relations firm, providing conservative solutions to a range of issues. So-called pro-family research groups, which stressed traditional family roles and anti-welfare positions, included the Family Research Council, the Eagle Forum (headed by Phyllis Schlafly), and Concerned Women for America. Republicans possessed remarkable access to the mass media.

(See Insert 11.2.) Weyrich's National Empowerment Television distributed conservative ideology to 11 million cable subscribers; televangelists such as Pat Robertson coupled religious and political messages; and talk show hosts like Rush Limbaugh reached tens of millions of Americans on radio and television. Conservative opinions were regularly disseminated by columnists such as Robert Novak and by the editorial page of *The Wall Street Journal.* Wealthy individuals, such as beer magnate Joseph Coors and Richard Scaife of the Mellon family, as well as large foundations like the Bradley and Olin foundations, contributed tens of millions of dollars to think tanks, publications, research, and political campaigns. The conservative message was also outlined in best-selling books by authors such as Charles Murray and William Bennett. Pat Robertson's Christian Coalition, the successor to the Moral Majority, continued to organize huge mailings to voters in pivotal districts.

Conservatives were more adept than liberals at reaching the broader public and using their economic resources to promote their ideas. While conservatives often depicted the media as liberal, the major news shows were usually neutral in their coverage; liberals had virtually no mass audience outlets. Whereas the Brookings Institution and other relatively liberal think tanks operated in the same way as academic departments, conservative think tanks were intensely partisan; they disseminated research and opinions that conformed to conservative tenets. Whereas fundamentalist religious groups possessed large mailing lists and actively intervened in elections, relatively liberal religious groups lacked a massive grassroots capability.[30]

THE HOUSE REPUBLICANS TAKE CHARGE

This conservative network was adept at shaping the public's perceptions of the Clinton administration in negative ways in 1993 and 1994. Armey's Republican Conference fashioned health reform and welfare reform proposals that emphasized market forces and work requirements, which Republicans contrasted with Clinton's proposals. *The Wall Street Journal* and congressional Republicans publicized what they called the Whitewater scandal, which cen-

---

I N S E R T 11.2   Critical Analysis: The Causes of Births to Unwed Women

Conservatives have often argued that "illegitimacy" stems from the "perverse incentives" provided by the welfare system. In this perspective, unwed women, often in their teens, decide to have children to secure welfare benefits.

Analyze this contention by asking the following questions:

1. Under what circumstances *are* our actions shaped or determined by externally imposed rewards or punishments? So as to be specific, identify cases where your actions are (or are not) shaped by rewards and punishments. (To get started, you might begin with relatively trivial actions—for example, whether the speed at which you drive is determined by the danger of receiving tickets. Then proceed to major life decisions of various kinds.)
2. In the case of unwed teenage women, to what extent are their pregnancies shaped or caused by:

   a. calculation of likely welfare benefits
   b. role models, such as a mother who was unwed at the time her children were born
   c. rape or forced sex
   d. lack of knowledge of birth control or lack of availability of birth control devices
   e. a desire for meaning or companionship in life
   f. cultural factors—for example, the belief among people of all social classes that unwed pregnancies are a legitimate lifestyle choice

3. To what extent do teenage women become pregnant because they believe that they lack economic, educational, or career options?
4. In light of the preceding discussion, would you expect coercive policies, such as denying or cutting benefits, to markedly decrease rates of births to unwed women?

tered on allegations of financial improprieties by the Clintons in Arkansas. Talk show hosts circulated sexual misconduct allegations against Clinton. Not wanting Clinton to benefit in the 1994 elections, Republicans stymied his health reform and welfare legislation in 1994.

Even though Clinton had proposed a plan to reduce the federal deficit markedly in his first term, Republicans portrayed him as a big spender who did not care about the deficit. When Clinton raised taxes on affluent people, Republicans said that he waged "class warfare"; they neglected to mention that many of their policies would help affluent Americans. Nor were some Republicans hesitant to attack Hillary Clinton's policy roles as inappropriate for the first lady. Throughout 1994, the administration was aware that, historically, the party that sits in the White House has usually incurred some losses in off-year congressional elections, but it clearly was not expecting the bombshell that hit Washington on November 8, 1994.

In the lead-up to the November 1994 congressional elections, Republicans issued a policy document that outlined their goals for the coming session of the Congress were they to gain majorities in each chamber. (See Box 11.1.)

The Republican gains in November were truly devastating for the Democrats. Not only did the Republicans gain majority status in both houses of Congress, thereby ending 40 years of Democratic control of at least one house, but they also gained a majority of the nation's governorships and control of 17 more state legislative chambers. (Not a single incumbent Republican governor or federal legislator was defeated.) A large majority of these Republican winners, especially in the House, were young and extremely conservative; they wanted to dismantle the remnants of the Great Society, which they felt had caused America's moral decline. (Gingrich now possessed a cadre of nearly 80 conservatives in the House, as well as many Republican moderates, who were dedicated to slashing government domestic spending.) Long a minority party in the South, Republicans emerged as its major party in national elections.[31]

Interpreting the election results as a repudiation of President Clinton and the Democratic party, Republicans vowed to enact a series of policies that were described in the Contract with America, a document created during the campaign by House Republican members and candidates.[32] The basic tenets of the contract were articulated in February of 1994: individual liberty, economic opportunity, limited government, personal responsibility, and security at home and abroad. When they released the completed contract on September 27, 1994, House Republican members and candidates promised that, if they controlled the House, they would enact its 10 provisions in 100 days (Box 11.1).

With the contract as its guiding framework, House Republicans took the offensive in the spring of 1995, when they dominated policy discourse in the United States. Clinton was relegated to a background role, as the House Republicans fulfilled their promise of enacting most items of the contract within 100 days. (Some provisions were not enacted by the Senate, however.)

THE BUDGET CONFRONTATION OF 1995

In 1995, the major political event was a titanic budget confrontation between Democrats and Republicans and between the White House and the Congress. Republicans could accomplish their goal of shrinking the federal government only by shaping the federal budget through Budget Resolutions, a reconciliation bill, and 13 appropriation bills. Like Reagan in 1981, Gingrich wanted to use the budget process to implement his conservative agenda; he hoped to force huge spending cuts and the return of many federally funded programs to the states at the same time as he was enacting large tax cuts and significant increases in defense spending. More militant than Reagan, Gingrich wanted to terminate three entitlement programs (Food Stamps, Medicaid, and AFDC) by converting them to block grants to the states. This elimination of

---

B O X 11.1   **Provisions of the Contract with America**

---

1. Balancing the budget and tax limitation:

    - a constitutional amendment requiring that Congress submit a balanced budget each year;

    - a requirement that tax increases could be enacted only if a three-fifths majority of Congress voted for them—a policy that would usually put the burden of balancing the budget on spending cuts rather than tax increases;

    - a legislative line-item veto to restore fiscal responsibility.

2. Strengthening national defense:

    - legislation requiring that no U.S. troops be placed under UN command;

    - restoration of funding for essential parts of national security.

3. Tax cuts to strengthen families and to benefit middle-class people:

    - a $500-per-child tax credit for families with annual incomes up to $200,000;

    - repeal of the marriage tax penalty, which causes many married couples to pay higher taxes than are levied on two single people;

    - creation of American Dream Savings Accounts to allow individuals to contribute up to $2,000 a year to a tax-free account for retirement income, the purchase of a first home, education expenses, or medical costs.

4. Aid to senior citizens:

    - an increase in the Social Security earnings limit—which currently forces seniors out of the workforce—from $11,160 to $30,000 over five years.

5. Welfare reform:

    - denial of welfare to mothers under age 18

    - denial of higher payments to mothers who give birth to additional children while on welfare;

    - a strict two-years-and-out provision for recipients;

    - more stringent work requirements, to promote individual responsibility;

    - a cap on spending for AFDC, SSI, and public housing programs;

    - consolidation of nutrition programs such as Food Stamps, the Women's, Infants', and Children's (WIC) program, and the school lunch program into a block grant to states;

    - permission for states to opt out of the current AFDC program by converting their share of AFDC payments into fixed annual block grants.

6. Reform of unfunded mandates and incentives to business:

    - termination or reform of unfunded mandates, in which the federal government requires state and local governments to implement specific policies without providing the resources for them to do so;

    - a cut in the capital gains tax to stimulate investment.

7. Strengthening the family:

    - more stringent child support enforcement;

    - larger tax incentives for adoption;

    - stronger child pornography laws;

    - tax credit for people who care for an elderly parent or grandparent.

8. Legal reforms to curb litigation:

    - loser-pays laws;

    - reasonable limits on punitive damage awards;

    - reform of product liability laws.

9. Anti-crime legislation:

    - stronger truth-in-sentencing laws;

    - effective death penalty provisions;

    - elimination of social spending included in the 1994 Crime Bill and use of these resources to fund prison construction and additional police officers;

    - easier deportation of illegal aliens convicted of felonies.

10. Term limits:

    - limits on the years that federal politicians can serve—for example, six 2-year terms for House members and two 6-year terms for senators.

entitlements was a massive assault on the American welfare state; it attacked the fundamental concept that the federal government ought to avert starvation and dire suffering—an obligation first articulated by Franklin Roosevelt six decades earlier. Gingrich planned to use confrontational tactics; even in April of 1995, he predicted that the government might have to shut down when the president and the Congress reached an impasse over the budget.

Gingrich needed a dramatic goal that would galvanize Americans and Republicans to support cuts in spending. Early in the debate, House members decided not merely to seek a constitutional amendment requiring a balanced budget but also to commit Congress to balancing the budget within seven years. Adopting a specific time frame forced Clinton and the Democrats onto the defensive; in 1993, after all, they had merely sought to *decrease* the annual deficits. When Senate Republicans supported the proposal to balance the budget in seven years, the stage was set for Budget Resolutions to accomplish this target.

In demanding that the budget be balanced by the year 2002, House Republicans took a calculated political gamble. They would have to cut more than $1.5 trillion from the budget, even without considering the large tax cuts and considerable increases in defense spending that they wanted. They could reach their goal only by focusing on entitlements, particularly Medicare, Medicaid, Food Stamps, and Social Security, which constituted the bulk of the domestic budget, as illustrated in Figure 11.1. (Analysts estimated that health costs would cause government spending *just* on entitlements to rise above the federal government's total revenues in just over 25 years.) Republicans knew that these entitlements had strong support from the public, as well as from powerful interest groups—support so strong that even Reagan had demurred from seeking major cuts in them. They hoped that public support for deficit reduction would allow them to cut some entitlements and to terminate others by passing them to the states in block grants. Even in November, Gingrich had admitted that all entitlements except Social Security would be put on the table for trimming. Because discretionary spending had already been cut extensively during the Reagan and Bush years, as well as by Clinton's deficit reduction plan of 1993, further cuts would not provide the bulk of the funds needed to bring a balanced budget.[33]

After the House GOP announced its plans to balance the budget in seven years, the congressional Democrats complained that the goal could be reached only by a mean-spirited slashing of America's social programs for the poor as well as for the middle class. The Democrats also charged the GOP with attempting to fund tax cuts for the rich by slashing social programs. They demanded that the House leadership reveal exactly how they would balance the budget in seven years. Aware that the public supported balancing the budget in general terms, the Democrats instead attempted to focus on the pain that would occur when *specific* cuts were made in programs widely used by Americans, such as Medicare.

Toward a Budget Resolution

The House Republicans originally intended to reveal their budget proposals in January of 1995 but decided to wait until the president had presented his own budget in February. They were certain that he would not seek significant cuts in discretionary spending because he had threatened to veto Republican attempts to cut his domestic service corps and the social spending included in the Crime Bill of 1994. They also knew that Clinton would not propose defense cuts; under Republican pressure on issues of military readiness, he had already promised the Department of Defense $25 billion in additional funds over six years. Thus, certain that the president would not make deep cuts in spending, the House Republicans waited for him to present his budget so that they could reply that he was not serious about deficit reduction. If he *did* propose deep spending cuts, they could simply incorporate them into *their* spending cuts—and also make the president take the political heat for proposing them.

Clinton refused to walk into this budget trap. The president's budget neither dramatically reduced the deficit nor changed the level of spending for most government programs. Instead, the president offered something for everyone in his budget: a tax cut, in the form of a $500 per child tax credit; $25 billion in defense increases; and $81 billion in deficit reduction. Realizing that Republicans would have to cut entitlements to reach their balanced budget goals, the administration wanted to force them to show their hand, making them pay the political price. Clinton was also aware that any spending cuts that he proposed would make the Republicans' task easier. According to Joseph White, a budget expert at the Brookings Institution, "It would have been politically idiotic for the Administration to propose more spending cuts. The Republicans just would have turned around and used them to pay for their tax cuts."[34] Clinton's strategy paid off handsomely. When Republicans subsequently promised an array of cuts in social programs, Clinton attacked them. For example, he paid a number of visits to school cafeterias, where he declared that Republicans' cuts in subsidized school lunches would harm children.[35]

As was to be expected, the Republicans attacked the administration for its apparent lack of leadership and charged that it was not serious about reducing the deficit. Republican leaders also accused the president of failing to control the growth of entitlement spending and refusing to make any hard budget-cutting choices. House Republicans could stall no longer and finally presented their Budget Resolution for balancing the budget by the year 2002 on May 10. Over the next seven years, it proposed a large tax cut of $353 billion and huge cuts in entitlement and discretionary spending that totaled nearly $1 trillion. More than half of these savings came from cuts in projected spending for Medicare and Medicaid. Medicare would be cut by $288 billion over seven years (reducing its growth rate from 10 percent a year to an average of 5.4 percent a year), and Medicaid would be cut by $187 billion by converting it into a block grant (reducing its growth rate from 10 percent to 4 percent a year). The House Budget Resolution also targeted other entitlements—such as the Earned Income Tax Credit for the working poor (EITC), welfare programs, federal pensions, veterans benefits, farm subsidies, and student loans—for a total saving of $219 billion over seven years. Discretionary spending, except that for defense, did not escape the budget knife; the House Budget Resolution called for $192 billion in savings over seven years from non-military discretionary programs. The Republicans also wanted increased spending for the military.

The Senate presented its Budget Resolution in May. The major difference between the House and Senate plans was in the area of tax cuts. Whereas the House plan contained $340 billion in tax cuts, the Senate plan allowed tax cuts of up to $170 billion over seven years on condition that a deficit reduction plan was enacted and the Congressional Budget Office confirmed that the plan would balance the budget by 2002. Like the House version, the Senate Budget Resolution also made sharp cutbacks in projected spending for Medicare, Medicaid, and other entitlement programs, as well as discretionary programs.

When faced with these Republican budget-cutting plans, the administration complained that Republicans sought to balance the budget on the backs of the poor—that programs for the poor were cut but affluent people received large tax breaks. Congressional Democrats were even more critical of the plan; they highlighted the hardship that older Americans would face as a result of cuts in Medicare. Public opinion polls suggested that Democrats were gaining ground on Republicans and revealed widespread hesitation about the Republicans' plans to cut popular social programs.

Just as the Democrats' counteroffensive seemed to be working, Clinton dropped a bombshell on his party on June 13, by presenting his own plan to balance the budget in 10 years—a mere three years longer than the Republicans' plan. The president's plan contained $105 billion in tax cuts for the middle class, as well as significant cuts in Medicare and Medicaid; it sought savings of $128 billion from the Medicare program and capped Medicaid's per capita spending for savings of $54 billion. (Medicaid retained entitlement status, however.) Clinton's proposal also called for savings of $38 billion from poverty programs, such as AFDC, the EITC, and benefits for immigrants, but increased spending for nutritional programs such as WIC and Food Stamps.

Clinton proposed cuts averaging 20 percent in domestic discretionary programs, for savings of $197 billion; he exempted programs that he favored, such as education, national service, health research, and crime control.[36] By developing his own deadline to balance the budget, Clinton hoped to prevent Republicans from monopolizing the balanced-budget theme. By selecting 10 years rather than 7, he intended to emphasize the differences in priorities between his proposal and the Republicans'—including far lower cuts in Medicare, his decision not to rescind entitlement status for Medicaid and AFDC, and his opposition to huge tax cuts for affluent Americans.

The president's about-face infuriated congressional Democrats, whom he did not consult in drawing up his plan. After they had invested extraordinary time in battling the Republicans' spending and tax cuts, they felt the president had left them high and dry. Democratic leaders such as Senate Minority Leader Tom Daschle and House Minority Leader Richard Gephardt criticized even the scaled-back Medicare cuts that Clinton proposed. Many Democrats believed that Clinton's switch betrayed his lack of core values, as well as his determination to fashion a political strategy for the 1996 presidential elections without concern for the priorities of congressional Democrats.

Why did Clinton make this abrupt shift? With the guidance of his old pollster and advisor, Dick Morris, Clinton decided to take a decisively different strategy in the 1996 elections. He had been relatively liberal in his campaign of 1992, when he had promised social investments, and during his first two years, when he sought funding for these investments and pursued health reform. With advice from Morris, he became convinced that he could not win in 1996 if he did not distance himself from his liberal record and from liberal Democrats in Congress. Morris urged him to resort to triangulation, a strategy in which he would stand at the apex of a triangle above the other two corners—liberal Democrats and conservative Republicans. He should, Morris advised, alternately make concessions to, and flout, *both* groups in a complex, changing strategy that would present

him to voters as a centrist who wanted to fashion compromises. Morris wanted Clinton to prevent Republicans from preempting such themes as balancing the budget or cutting taxes. Clinton should periodically give ground by acceding to some conservative demands, while nonetheless seeking centrist positions that would make conservatives seem extremist.

Yet he should not be too strident in his opposition to conservatives, for fear of seeming too liberal—a perception that would frighten white centrist voters into the Republican camp or toward a third-party candidate. By shedding his liberal past, Clinton could run his campaign of 1996 as a centrist, with a focus on middle-class issues like education and the environment; social programs for the poor would be deemphasized.[37]

This strategy carried both political and ethical risks for Clinton, however. While Clinton could not win the 1996 election with liberal support alone, triangulation might alienate many liberal allies, much as they had become disenchanted with Lyndon Johnson in his second term and with Jimmy Carter when he ran in 1980. This zigzag strategy might confirm his reputation as someone who lacked core values, in the same way that Richard Nixon's opportunism had led people to distrust him. This strategy required Clinton to abandon poor people at the very time that their programs were under the most determined assault since 1981. Would he fight to retain entitlement status for AFDC, Food Stamps, and Medicaid in the face of the Republicans' congressional onslaught? Would he accede to further large cuts in domestic discretionary spending when it had already been savaged for a decade and a half? Would he accede to significant increases in defense spending, which he knew would further erode domestic spending?

Toward a Reconciliation Bill

The Republicans quickly dismissed Clinton's 10-year plan to balance the budget as inadequate. Once House and Senate negotiations had produced a Budget Resolution, Republicans worked over the summer to fashion a reconciliation bill and appropriations bills that would meet spending and budget targets. Welfare provisions and health care entitlements dominated policy discussion.[38]

Welfare Reform.   Clinton had promised "to end welfare as we know it" in his 1992 campaign, supporting two-year time limits for recipients to leave AFDC rolls as well as tougher work requirements.

While not discussing details of possible legislation, he promised to enact a welfare reform plan during his first term. The administration moved toward developing its welfare reform plan in 1993, giving key roles to such liberal welfare experts as David Ellwood and Mary Joe Bane in the Department of Health and Human Services. A series of factors delayed the development of a welfare plan, however.[39] It was removed from Clinton's agenda in 1993 because Clinton did not want to propose a costly new program when he and the Congress were trying to cut the deficit. It was further delayed when Clinton assembled a huge and unwieldy planning task force that only slowly developed a plan. Finally released in the spring of 1994, the plan sought to remove only one-third of AFDC recipients from the rolls in an initial phase to save money on its relatively spartan training and day care components. (With deficit reduction in gear and with freezes on discretionary spending, Clinton aides found it difficult to find money for welfare reform.) Congressional action on the plan was further delayed by considerable opposition to the two-year time limit by House liberals—and by the preoccupation by the Congress and administration with health reform in 1994.

These various delays in getting an administration plan before the Congress proved to be calamitous because the welfare reform issue would come before a Republican rather than a Democratic Congress after the Republicans' victory in November of 1994.[40] Although even Republican conservatives such as Gingrich had not proposed to remove AFDC as an entitlement in 1993, they were gradually radicalized on the issue by the writings of Charles Murray, who insisted that *any* welfare benefits made recipients disinclined to seek work. (He advocated ending

AFDC entirely.) Searching for campaign issues to distinguish themselves from the Democrats in 1994, Republicans moved toward a more conservative version of welfare reform than Clinton's in their Contract with America, proposing to place a cap on spending for AFDC, to deny welfare to minor mothers, to deny higher payments to mothers giving birth to additional children while on welfare rolls, and to give states the ability to opt out of AFDC by converting their share of AFDC payments into fixed annual block grants. Once Republicans controlled both chambers of Congress in the wake of the 1994 election, they resolved by early 1995 to end the AFDC entitlement by converting the program into a mere block grant that would not even increase with inflation for five years. Indeed, Democrats were on the defensive during 1995 and 1996 as they responded to many Republican versions of welfare reform and as Clinton vetoed two versions before he finally signed welfare reform legislation in August of 1996.

House Republicans issued their version of welfare reform in March of 1995. It sought to remove AFDC and Food Stamps from entitlement status by transforming them into block grants while removing most federal regulations over them. It allowed states to contribute whatever sums they wished to their own welfare programs; states need not even increase their funding if the numbers of destitute persons rose. At the same time as they were giving states more authority over Food Stamps, child welfare programs, and child nutrition programs like school lunches, they imposed an array of restrictions on state-initiated programs for single mothers. Recipients would be required to work within two years of receiving welfare benefits and could not receive benefits for more than five years. Moreover, states could not use federal block grant funds to provide welfare for children born within 10 months of when a family first received welfare benefits or for children born out of wedlock to a mother under age 18. While retaining SSI as a federal program, the legislators decided to exclude alcoholism or drug addiction as qualifying conditions and chose to disqualify many children with behavioral disorders. Responding to a surge in

---

I N S E R T 11.3 **Ethical Analysis of Key Issues and Policies: Clinton's Dilemma**

Clinton knew that he had received only 43 percent of the popular vote in 1992. He did not yet know if a popular third-party candidate—such as retired General Colin Powell, a much-admired African American with centrist views—might enter the race in 1996. Believing that he could not win with liberal support alone, he had to compete for moderate white voters in the North and the South.

Assume that marketing analyses provided by Morris suggested that these moderate voters wanted a balanced budget, but also wanted somewhat more compassionate policies than Republicans like Gingrich. Yet they remained suspicious of AFDC recipients, whom they believed largely to be cheaters.

Also assume the polls showed that moderate voters remained opposed to Medicare and Medicaid cuts and generally supported the Democrats' opposition to the Republicans' harsh seven-year strategy for balancing the budget.

Discuss alternative strategies that Clinton could take under these circumstances—and their ethical implications. Be certain to consider the liberals' nightmare: If moderate white voters rejected Clinton, he might be replaced by a Republican contender in 1996 *and* Republicans might still control both houses of Congress (with Gingrich continuing to occupy the powerful Speaker's position). Should such pragmatic considerations be included in your ethical reasoning?

---

anti-immigrant sentiment in the nation, the House declared that most legal immigrants who were not citizens could not receive benefits from a range of federal programs.

The legislators hoped to save about $62.1 billion over five years. In one bill, the legislators hoped to reduce drastically the power of the federal government, which would merely fund block grants; tens of millions of Americans would then be at the mercy of policies enacted by specific states. States would set their own eligibility requirements and benefit levels and would be able to transfer up to 30 percent of specific block grants to other programs. They could decide whether they wanted to supplement the block grants with their own funds. Whereas federal regulations had generally sought to protect the rights of AFDC recipients in the New Deal and subsequent eras, these new federal regulations *prohibited* relatively generous policies, even by those states who wished to pursue them.

Liberals were shocked by this legislation. As the history of AFDC amply suggested, many states had used the policy leeway given to them in the program to enact welfare benefits that were extraordinarily low. After the House passed this legislation, President Clinton immediately dismissed it as being "weak on work and tough on children" because it contained little or no funding for education, job training, and job placement, themes that he had

outlined during his 1992 presidential campaign. He opposed the Republicans' plan to deny benefits to children whose mothers were under 18 or were already on welfare. Later in the week, a top administration aide warned that Clinton would veto the House welfare legislation unless it was changed by the Senate.

Many congressional Democrats joined the President in criticizing the Republican measure. They emphasized that the measure would harm children—especially children whose teenage mothers were severed from rolls or children born to mothers who were already on the rolls. Above all, Democrats objected to ending AFDC as a federal entitlement that guaranteed federal funding for all single mothers meeting states' eligibility standards. (Under the Republicans' legislation, a specific state could decide *not* to fund benefits for some impoverished single mothers if the funds allocated for welfare in the state's budget had been exhausted.) Many Democrats feared that some states, faced with limited budgets, would prioritize other projects such as highway maintenance. They also feared that states would embark on a race to reduce their benefits, so as to preempt an influx of welfare recipients from states with lower benefits. They accused the Republicans of stripping minimal financial support from millions of children, under the guise of granting states greater flexibility in using federal funds. Democrats feared that, with block grants capped at current levels for five years, many states would be unable or unwilling to handle increases in the number of needy people. They also charged that the Republicans' welfare cuts were intended to finance cuts in the capital gains tax, which would help wealthy people. (Democrats failed to pass a provision that would have required any savings from welfare reform to be reserved for deficit reduction.)

Lacking a Democratic majority in the House, the administration hoped for extensive changes in the bill by the Senate, which tends to be more moderate. Indeed, the legislation immediately sparked controversy in the Senate. No Republican senator questioned the idea of ending the 60-year-old entitlement status of AFDC, but moderate Republicans in the Senate disagreed with the most controversial items in the House bill; they did not want to deny benefits to unwed teenage mothers and children born to welfare recipients. Conservative senators like Phil Gramm threatened to withhold their support from the welfare plan unless these items were included. Moderate Republicans also wanted to be sure that states would maintain their current level of welfare spending and that recipients who were required to work would have access to child care.[41]

Finally, on September 19, the Senate approved a welfare reform bill that was supported even by Democratic senators and the White House, who concluded that it was the best bill they could get. While it retained the general direction of the House version, the Senate bill softened some of the more drastic provisions. It sought to protect destitute people by requiring states to spend at least 80 percent of their expenditures in 1993–1994; where the House bill had allowed states to exempt 10 percent of recipients from the five-year limit on benefits, the Senate bill raised that limit to 15 percent. It sought to give relatively liberal states more latitude, such as the option of not denying assistance to children born to families already receiving welfare benefits or to children born to mothers under age 18. Unlike the House version, which gave states a lump-sum payment for child welfare, the Senate

version retained child welfare programs as separate programs with continuing federal oversight—and kept child nutrition programs under federal control.

As often occurs in policy debates, Democratic senators had to decide, on balance, whether changes in the details of legislation were sufficient to warrant its support. Many Democrats in the Senate reluctantly voted for the welfare reform plan because they feared that otherwise the House plan would prevail. (The bill passed overwhelmingly, by an 87–12 vote.) Minority leader Tom Daschle commented that the Senate's welfare plan was "the best bill that we are going to get under the circumstances." However, Daschle and other Democratic leaders also cautioned that, if the welfare plan that emerged from the House-Senate conference committee was closer to the House plan, they would vote against it and urge Clinton to veto it. Clinton, in turn, implied he would veto welfare legislation if it was not similar to the Senate's version; he warned that "if the Congress gives in to extremist pressure and walks away from this bipartisan American common ground, they will kill welfare reform."[42]

Many liberals disagreed with those senators who voted for the Senate version and were furious that Clinton had supported it. The National Association of Social Workers enlisted 1,000 social workers as sponsors of a full-page ad in *The New York Times* that demanded either congressional action to kill the bill or a presidential veto. Nor were they happy with the compromise version of welfare reform produced by House and Senate negotiators on November 13 because it retained many House provisions. It provided far fewer funds than the Senate version for jobs and child care and cut far more deeply into SSI cash benefits for disabled children, Food Stamp benefits, and social services for legal immigrants.

At this juncture, liberals knew that their only hope was a presidential veto. The president's press secretary said that Clinton was likely to veto the measure, whether it was part of the reconciliation bill or freestanding legislation. (Republicans *also* planned to introduce it as a freestanding welfare bill. We will discuss the ultimate fate of this legislation subsequently.)

Medicare and Medicaid. The Republicans' Budget Resolution called for savings of $270 billion from Medicare and $182 billion from Medicaid but did not detail precisely how they would be made. Democrats demanded public hearings so that options could be openly discussed. In extended discussions behind closed doors, Republicans considered a range of options for cutting Medicare—for example, raising premiums for Part B (the monthly payment elderly people make to help defray physician costs); excluding certain services; raising deductibles (the amount patients pay *before* receiving Medicare reimbursements, such as $100 for surgeries); making wealthy elderly people pay higher premiums or other charges; and lowering the reimbursable fees of providers. Many Republicans wanted to require older people to use health maintenance organizations (HMOs), rather than fee-for-service providers, on the grounds that they provide less expensive services. Still others wanted to encourage seniors to develop their own "medical savings accounts" so that they could even opt out of the Medicare program.

Realizing that the Republicans' proposals might excite political opposition, Gingrich orchestrated elaborate negotiations between providers so that he could sweeten the deal for each interest group. He granted the American Association of Retired Persons (AARP) their wish that the elderly pay only slightly higher premiums for Part B and that they not face additional deductibles for lab tests or home health care. Instead, affluent beneficiaries were charged more for Part B. Republicans decided not to *compel* seniors to use HMOs—a policy that private insurance companies opposed—but instead to encourage the use of HMOs by providing Medicare beneficiaries with a range of options: for example, joining an HMO; establishing a personal medical savings account coupled with a high-deductible insurance policy; or using a network of providers. The legislation granted the AMA many provisions for its doctors; they were allowed to charge 15 percent more than Medicare-approved

costs in certain circumstances, for example, and doctors and hospitals were allowed to form their own organizations to compete with HMOs. Republicans decided to cut levels of reimbursement to hospitals, doctors, and nursing homes and to establish uniform fees for home health services.

Democrats criticized the Medicare proposal—in particular, the small increases in premiums that seniors would pay for Part B. However, Medicare emerged relatively unscathed as compared with Medicaid, the health care program for low-income individuals. Recognizing the limited political clout of poor people, Republicans decided to transform the federal-state entitlement program into a sharply reduced block grant, with a cap on the federal government's contribution. (See Insert 11.4.) (Federal payments would be reduced from 50 percent of Medicaid costs to 40 percent under the new formula.) States would be given extraordinary latitude in designing their programs; the federal government would only require coverage of children and pregnant women falling beneath specific income guidelines.

As in the case of AFDC and nutritional programs, many critics wondered whether states would choose to fund medical care for poor people at reasonable levels, in an era of budgetary constraints. Even at current levels of Medicaid funding, beneficiaries had to endure extended waits for care of uncertain quality in antiquated facilities. What could they expect when federal reimbursement was diminished? In states where the numbers of poor persons increased, would coverage expand to meet the needs? As with welfare benefits, would some states diminish their health coverage to prevent immigration from states with lower coverage? Middle-class families failed to realize that nursing home coverage for their elderly parents might be imperiled by Medicaid cuts. Many older people relied on means-tested Medicaid nursing home benefits once they had exhausted their Medicare coverage and their personal savings.

Taxes. Clinton had achieved a remarkable policy victory in 1993 when he greatly increased the numbers of working-class Americans who received

---

I N S E R T 11.4   Critical Analysis: Why Keep Entitlements?

In their quest to shrink the federal government, conservatives sought to end entitlement status for AFDC, Food Stamps, and Medicaid in 1995. Discuss the rationale for entitlements and the possible dangers of block grants by asking what forces or political factors might lead many states *not* to fund programs for poor people.

When discussing possible dangers, consider some economic realities in a federal system of government. Take your state as an example and assume that its legislators and governor are determined to be particularly generous to recipients of welfare, Food Stamps, and Medicaid once these programs have been block-granted. Also assume that such generosity requires a substantial increase in state taxes.

Might the following adverse consequences ensue—and, if they did, would your state's voters and politicians soon decide to emulate less generous states after all?

1. Facing higher taxes, some corporate leaders threaten to relocate to lower-tax states. If they carry out their threat, the tax revenues needed to fund the state's programs will be depleted.

2. Low-income citizens from less generous states relocate to your state and, as a result, the cost of your state's welfare programs increases.

3. Legislators in your state *fear* an exodus of corporations and an influx of poor individuals, even if these circumstances don't occur, and thus oppose generous programs. (Remember that *perceptions* often are more important in politics than actual events.)

4. A recession in your state is accompanied *both* by a decline in tax revenues *and* by a rise in welfare costs.

5. Local counties and cities are asked to bear some of the costs of your state's generous welfare, nutritional, and medical programs, but jurisdictions with large numbers of poor people, such as urban areas, are unable or unwilling to fund these programs.

Discuss whether entitlement status alleviates these problems. Also discuss whether advocates for poor people are more or less able to obtain relatively generous policies at the national or state levels of government.

---

annual tax rebates (or credits). In a society where the disparity between the upper quintile and the lower three quintiles was rapidly increasing, this policy (the Earned Income Tax Credit or EITC) seemed a sensible approach to reducing inequality. Many Republicans viewed the EITC not as a tax benefit but as a welfare program; they believed it wrong to compel middle-income taxpayers to subsidize people who made somewhat less than themselves. The tax credits were cut by roughly one-fifth by restricting eligibility, freezing the maximum credit, and eliminating the credit for taxpayers without children.

Republicans proposed huge tax cuts, totaling $245 billion. More than half of these cuts consisted of a $500-per-child tax credit for families with adjusted gross incomes of up to $110,000 per year.

On its face, this tax credit also seemed sensible because it reduced taxes on families. Some Democrats contended, however, that the cuts in the EITC for low-income families—as well as some cuts

in AFDC and Medicaid—would not have been needed if Republicans had not proposed this tax credit or if they had limited it to less affluent families.

Nor were many Democrats happy with some other tax cuts in the reconciliation bill. Republicans wanted to expand individual retirement accounts (IRAs) so as to benefit relatively wealthy taxpayers. They favored cutting capital gains taxes by nearly one-third—a concession that would also favor wealthy families and corporations. They even proposed increasing the amount of estates not subject to inheritance taxes from $500,000 to $650,000, on the grounds that this provision had not kept up with inflation. Republicans notably failed to consider this factor in their deliberations on AFDC, whose real benefits had halved since 1970 because of inflation.

Discretionary Spending: Social Programs and Military Spending.   As Republicans fashioned their reconciliation bill, with its tax and entitlement provisions, they forged ahead on 13 separate appropriations bills that had to meet their spending targets in the Budget Resolution—in particular, $10 billion in cuts below the 1994 levels for nondefense discretionary spending. As George Hager reported in July, "Republicans [in the appropriations committees] went straight at long-held Democratic priorities, slashing housing, environmental regulation, summer jobs and—in a seemingly personal twist of the knife—killing off two of President Clinton's most cherished projects: the National Service initiative and the Goals 2000 education reform program."[43] In their early decisions, House Republicans made cuts even exceeding targets in the Budget Resolution. Democrats attacked some of the cuts; for example, they charged that Republicans waged a "midnight massacre" on children's programs such as Head Start and Healthy Start. Speaking through his Chief of Staff, Leon Panetta, Clinton vowed to veto the appropriations bill for the Department of Health and Human Services unless it was improved, but the House retained most of the cuts in the legislation that they enacted in early August. Some of the cuts were subsequently reduced, at least modestly, in the Senate.

At the same time that Congress was making huge cuts in social spending, it was adding to military spending. In early August, for example, the Senate added $6 billion to Clinton's $243 billion Pentagon budget. The Republicans approved funding for more jet fighters and warships than the administration had requested, on the grounds that they were needed to repel countries such as North Korea and Libya. In the fall, huge sums were added to procure heavy bombers.

CLINTON'S ZIGZAG COURSE IN LATE 1995 AND 1996

The Republicans and the Clinton administration engaged in a peculiar dance in November and December. (See Figure 11.2.) To force the president to sign the reconciliation bill, Republicans refused to increase the national debt limit. Without such an agreement, the government could no longer borrow funds to pay its ongoing expenses, and many government agencies would be forced to shut down temporarily until a continuing resolution was enacted. Aware that Clinton had already retreated on many previous occasions, Republicans assumed that, if they incorporated their draconian funding cuts and their tax cuts in the reconciliation bill, Clinton would meekly accept their policies and allow them to win the day. His startling proposal in June to erase the deficit in 10 years seemed to have been a capitulation to the Republicans. Would he not, when pushed to the wall, agree to their seven-year timetable?

When the government did shut down, in November and again in late December, for a total of 43 days, people wondered where Clinton would draw his line in the sand. Would he demand that all entitlements be retained, even though he had already implied that he would agree to place AFDC in a block grant? Would he demand that Republicans' tax increases be rescinded so that further cuts in discretionary spending could be avoided?

He chose neither of those paths. Instead, he continued his zigzag course. In November, to secure Republican support for a continuing resolution to end the government shutdown, Clinton agreed to a seven-year deadline for balancing the budget. However, he also insisted that the agreement include a vaguely worded promise of adequate funding for the environment and medical programs. He remained noncommittal about other facets of the reconciliation bill, such as its provisions on welfare and Food Stamps. However, he demonstrated that he would not accede to Republicans' demands on January 9, 1996, when he vetoed a welfare reform bill that Congress had enacted outside of the rubric of the reconciliation bill.

Clinton became less inclined to compromise when polls showed that Newt Gingrich's popularity had plummeted in late 1995 and early 1996, whereas Clinton's had risen markedly. Although many Americans supported the idea of scaling back federal spending and authority, they often

© AP Photo/Wilfredo Lee

F I G U R E 11.2 Contending leaders meet the press during the budget negotiations.

became apprehensive when faced with cuts in specific programs. Realizing that environmental, education, and health programs were particularly popular, Clinton adeptly focused on them in his budget negotiations with the Republicans in November and December; he contended that Republicans' policies would wreak havoc in these areas. Many voters, moreover, blamed Republicans for the partial government shutdown.[44] In addition, Democrats continued to charge that Republicans' deep tax cuts would enrich affluent Americans and would be funded by cuts in social programs used by less affluent people. Clinton's resolve was further strengthened in early 1996, when a bitter primary battle between Republican presidential candidates revealed a split in the party between so-called fiscal conservatives (such as Steve Forbes, who emphasized balancing the budget and downsizing the federal government) and social conservatives (such as Pat Buchanan, who sought to end legalized abortion).[45]

Curiously, a staunch conservative, Pat Buchanan, stimulated renewed interest in the economic fate of American workers. Although he trailed far behind frontrunner Bob Dole in most of the primaries, he found that many white blue-collar voters resonated to his populist message. Buchanan called for government regulation of corporations to prevent them from moving production to low-wage nations and firing vast numbers of American workers. To protect American workers from foreign competition, he also wanted to rescind such treaties as the North American Free Trade Agreement, which was fashioned in 1993, with bipartisan support, to cut tariffs between Mexico, the United States, and Canada. Aware that the outcome of the 1996 election might hinge on the votes of fearful or displaced workers, leaders of both parties began to bid for those votes in March. Republicans like House Majority Leader Dick Armey evolved a nine-point agenda that included tax cuts for working families, cuts in the capital gains tax, and reductions in regulations to stimulate business, as well as tax concessions to corporations that would agree not to increase short-term profits by means of mass layoffs. In turn, Democrats like House Minority Leader Dick Gephardt sought tax cuts and considered tax incentives to discourage layoffs.[46]

The budgetary stalemate remained unresolved in March of 1996. Accusing Congress of evading its responsibilities, Clinton avoided yet another partial government shutdown by signing a continuing resolution on March 15—the 10th resolution in the current fiscal year. (Senate Democrats supported this $160 billion measure only after Republicans included additional environmental funds.) Five of 13 appropriation bills had not yet been approved; Clinton pledged to veto any bills that cut health care, education, or environmental programs excessively.

Meanwhile, Republicans used the continuing resolutions to effect severe cuts in social programs by only including partial funding for them; for example, they cut the Substance Abuse and Mental Health Services Administration by $400 million. Nor had the Republicans and the president reached agreement on measures in the reconciliation bill; each side was likely to seek a mandate for its position in the November 1996 elections. In late February, the Clinton administration indicated increased support for AFDC, Food Stamps, and child welfare when Donna Shalala criticized a compromise proposal put forth by the National Governors Association (NGA). Shalala rejected the AFDC block grant unless it included safeguards such as the requirement that states give support to children whose mothers exceeded the proposed five-year time limit on benefits. She also rejected the conversion of Food Stamps, foster care, and adoption programs to block grants. (Some liberals wanted Shalala—and Clinton—to go even further: to reject even the concept of a block grant for AFDC. They contended that eliminating the entitlement status of AFDC would violate a fundamental responsibility of the federal government for impoverished children.) Finally, she rejected the NGA's proposal that states should have complete control

of Medicaid; she insisted on the need for federal regulation of nursing home care, the quality of services, and coverage of adolescents.[47]

On April 24, Congress and the White House finally agreed on a budget for the 1995–1996 fiscal year that covered discretionary spending. Republicans got $23 billion in cuts below the preceding year's level, though Clinton got $5 billion added for education, job training, and the environment. Left unresolved, and certain to be the subject of intense political conflict in an election year, were the fate of entitlements and the amount of tax cuts. Republicans planned to present Clinton with huge tax cuts and conservative policies on AFDC and Medicaid, hoping to force him to make politically damaging vetoes that would help Bob Dole, his all-but-certain opponent in the 1996 elections. (In May of 1996, Dole, the Republican Senate Majority Leader, resigned from his Senate seat to run against Bill Clinton in the 1996 presidential race.)

As the nation headed into the summer, Republicans were convinced they could use the welfare issue to their advantage in the forthcoming presidential elections. They aired commercials blaming Clinton for vetoing welfare reform measures, saying he had broken his 1992 campaign promise to "end welfare as we know it." When presented with another Republican version of welfare reform in August that was similar to prior versions but that retained Medicaid as an entitlement rather than a block grant, Clinton signed it over the vehement opposition of some cabinet members and data generated by top civil servants that it would cast millions of children into poverty when their families lost access to safety net programs (see Insert 12.4). Although Clinton removed the issue of welfare reform from the presidential campaign of 1996 by signing the legislation, he ended the AFDC entitlement while providing scant resources for extended child care and job training.

The Personal Responsibility and Work Opportunities Act of 1996 consisted of nine titles or sets of provisions that covered welfare, SSI, eligibility of immigrants for public benefits, child care, child nutrition, and Food Stamps. Its welfare provisions replaced AFDC with the Temporary Assistance for Needy Families Block Grant (TANF) to be funded until the year 2002 roughly at the annual level of federal expenditures for AFDC in the year preceding the enactment of TANF. (After 2002, the Congress could fund TANF at any level that it desired.)[48] With the AFDC entitlement gone, the federal government would not have to fund welfare benefits to the level of claimed benefits each year, so many liberals feared that a conservative Congress might slash federal involvement considerably or entirely in the years after 2002, leaving the major responsibility for welfare to the states. This scenario was ominous because many policy analysts believed the states would commence a "race to the bottom" where they would lower benefits to prevent recipients from other states (with lower benefits) from migrating to states with higher benefits.[49] (States with costly social programs also might fear that they would have to raise taxes to pay for them—a policy that could lead citizens and corporations to relocate in states with lower taxes.)

TANF stipulated that the states must ensure that adult recipients participate in work or work-related activities after receiving two years of cumulative benefits, with 25 percent of the single-parent family caseload participating by 1997 and 50 percent by 2002. (Seventy-five percent of two-parent families would be required to participate by 1997.) It stated that recipients could receive cash assistance for a maximum of five years over a lifetime with limited exceptions for no more than 20 percent of caseloads. It prohibited the use of federal funds for minor parents under 18 not participating in school activities or living in an adult-supervised setting.

While imposing these regulations on the states, the legislation gave them remarkable latitude in other areas, unlike the defunct AFDC program. They could eliminate cash aid entirely if they chose, replacing it with any combination of cash and in-kind benefits; deny assistance to teen parents or other kinds of recipients; establish even more severe time limits; provide benefits to new residents at the same level as the state from which they emigrated for up to one year; or deny aid to persons convicted of a drug felony after August of 1996 unless they participated in a rehabilitation program. Nor did the legislation require uniform statewide standards. The legislation gave local welfare workers enormous discretion in deciding whom to cut off the rolls as recipients faced time limits and as they tried to comply with work requirements—discretion that had been greatly reduced in the AFDC program by legislation and court rulings. TANF families were no longer automatically eligible for Medicaid, even though persons meeting the old AFDC income standards could often receive it based on income. Food Stamp benefits were reduced by changing the eligibility formula, such as not allowing families to deduct more than 50 percent of their rent or housing costs from their income to determine the amount of stamps they could receive. Furthermore, the maximum Food Stamp benefit level was reduced by 3 percent—and severe restrictions were placed on benefits of childless able-bodied individuals. The legislation contained, as well, an array of other extraneous restrictive measures involving Medicaid, Food Stamps, children, and immigrants. (We discuss measures involving children and immigrants subsequently.)

Clinton did not *have* to sign welfare reform legislation in light of his substantial lead in the polls over Republican opponent Bob Dole in August of 1999. He might, for example, have insisted on more ample training, child care, and education funds—or upon procedural safeguards for former recipients by requiring states to provide them with ongoing assistance if their wages and assistance from other programs did not raise them above poverty lines. He could have insisted that the federal entitlement be retained even if welfare was substantially reformed so that future Congresses could not severely cut welfare funding beneath claimed benefits. He could have insisted that single mothers with children be included in a broader program of training and education for all workers, male and female, who lacked credentials and skills to obtain jobs that paid sufficient wages to bring them above poverty lines.[50]

Pitted against Dole in the presidential contest, Clinton won a landslide victory in November of

1996, but he again faced a Republican Congress during his second term because Democrats made only minor inroads in the House and the Senate.

CLINTON'S SECOND TERM

While the budget legislation of 1996 had established the goal of balancing the federal budget by 2002, it had not stated how this goal would be achieved. The Balanced Budget Act of 1997 provided the answers: huge cuts in Medicare and Medicaid, as well as severe caps on discretionary spending. It made the most sweeping changes in the Medicare Program since its inception 32 years previously. The legislation envisioned that most elderly recipients would eventually obtain Medicare health care from managed care organizations in a cost-saving move. While elderly Medicare patients had possessed considerable latitude in selecting physicians, just as their physicians had possessed autonomy in selecting those treatments and medications that they wished to offer or prescribe, many health economists regarded these traditional arrangements as wasteful. They feared that patients often demanded and received treatments that were not necessary or that were excessively expensive. Why not, many legislators demanded, place Medicare patients in managed care organizations where central administrators would scrutinize (and veto in some instances) treatment decisions and where patients would obtain care only from those physicians and hospitals that agreed to discounted rates? While Medicare had long offered an HMO option to Medicare enrollees, the 1997 legislation now required other managed care options, including provider-sponsored organizations (where hospitals or physicians developed plans) and preferred provider organizations (where insurance companies or providers developed plans whose enrollees had to obtain treatment from a roster of physicians and hospitals that agreed to charge discounted fees and to secure central approval for treatments).

Fearing that home health care that provided Medicare-funded services to seniors in their homes was becoming excessively costly, the legislation slashed home health fees by 15 percent. Cuts were made, as well, in Medicaid by deleting higher federal Medicaid subsidies to hospitals serving large numbers of poor or uninsured persons—a blow to many teaching hospitals that served these persons disproportionately. The legislation also allowed governors to place Medicaid recipients in managed care organizations without having to secure permission (or waivers) from federal authorities.[51]

The 1997 budget deal also resorted to harsh cuts in discretionary spending, establishing caps on it that were so severe that it could not even keep up with inflation through 2002—a policy that boded ill for federal spending on social services, education, training, and employment for the next six years. Future federal funding of these domestic programs was rendered even bleaker because the president and Congress supported substantial increases in military spending in coming years, which is also funded by the discretionary budget. Whereas Congress prevented direct competition between domestic and military components of the discretionary budget before 2000 by earmarking what share would go to domestic and military programs, it allowed them to compete with one another from the year 2000 onward when increases in military spending might further erode resources for the domestic agenda. (Even in the mid and late 1990s, many critics wondered if the military needed huge budgets in a post-Cold War era when the United States primarily had to deal with regional conflicts such as those in Somalia, Bosnia, and Kosovo.)[52]

With scant resources available to him in the discretionary budget, Clinton cleverly obtained major educational reforms in 1997 by securing enactment of several tax expenditures (or tax concessions) that together provided $35 billion in benefits. (Unlike social programs funded by discretionary spending, tax expenditures do not have to compete with other programs in annual budget battles since citizens automatically obtain their benefits through the tax code.) He enacted HOPE scholarships, which were tax credits (or rebates) of up to $1,500 for the first two years of postsecondary education for students whose parents possessed adjusted gross income of less than $50,000 for a single parent or $100,000 for two parents. He established a Lifetime Learning Credit for students in the last two years of college or in graduate school, allowing them to claim credits up to $1,000 per year assuming their parents met income eligibility standards similar to the HOPE scholarships. He established education savings accounts to be formed by annual contributions (not to exceed $500) of parents whose principal and interest could be withdrawn tax free to finance a portion of their children's postsecondary education.[53] (He also signed the Adoption and Safe Families Act in 1997, as will be discussed subsequently.)

However, the relatively amicable atmosphere of 1997 soon dissipated in 1998 and led to polarized, stalemated politics during 1998 and 1999. Much of 1998, as well as early 1999, was consumed by a sexual scandal involving the president and Monica Lewinsky, a woman that Clinton met when she was a student intern assigned to the White House. After falsely denying he had had an affair to a grand jury, a judge, and the public, Clinton belatedly admitted it. Contending that Clinton had committed perjury, Republican leaders made the affair the centerpiece of their quest to defeat Democrats in the 1998 congressional elections. Partly because the public had tired of the issue, this tactic backfired when the public delivered a crushing defeat to Republicans in elections that reduced their hold on the House to a razor-thin majority and brought the sudden resignation of Gingrich from the House Speakership after Republican legislators, blaming him for this failed tactic, said they would no longer support him. Collaboration between Clinton and Republicans was further diminished by the decision of House Republicans to impeach Clinton, by approving a resolution in late 1998 asking the Senate to hold a trial to determine whether he would be removed from office. The matter was dismissed when the Senate failed to secure a two-thirds vote for removal of the president in early 1999.

Neither Republican leadership nor Clinton was inclined to collaborate under these circumstances, even though major issues, such as the future of Medicare and Social Security, gun control, and patient rights hung in the balance, as well as policies about the spending of an emerging budget surplus.

Federal legislation on guns had first emerged in the so-called Brady bill in Clinton's first term, which established a waiting period and criminal check for purchasers of handguns. Although subsequent federal legislation also banned certain kinds of assault weapons, these modest measures did not prevent the proliferation of guns in the United States, whether handguns, rifles, or assault weapons. Gun control reemerged into the national spotlight after 1996 in the wake of mass slayings in schools, churches, and places of employment, culminating in the massacre of 12 students and a teacher in Columbine High School in Littleton, Colorado, in April of 1999. Clinton and Democrats took the initiative in seeking bans on gun sales on the Internet and at gun shows, expanded federal criminal background checks of purchasers of guns, increases in the minimum age for purchasing firearms from 18 to 21, bans of high-capacity ammunition clips, and installation of mandatory lock devices on guns. When the Republican Party belatedly agreed to ban the sale of guns at gun shows, Clinton attacked their proposal as inadequate. No new legislation had been enacted by mid-2000.

Social Security entered the spotlight in 1998 as data were widely publicized that the Trust Fund would be depleted around 2032 as the ratio of employed workers to retirees diminished with the anticipated retirement of millions of baby boomers who were born between the end of World War II and 1960. If many Republicans and conservatives wanted to partially or completely privatize Social Security by allowing citizens to manage their own federal retirement funds, most liberals staunchly opposed this policy on the grounds that some citizens might make ill-advised investment choices that rendered themselves impoverished in their retirement years or that privatization would eventually lead many middle- and upper-class persons to diminish their support for Social Security itself by demanding that they be exempted from having to pay payroll taxes to allow themselves to manage their own funds. (Under this scenario, they contended, Social Security would become a poor persons' or voluntary program.) Considerable controversy arose, as well, about the advisability of raising the early retirement age from 62 to 65 and the normal retirement age to 70 in the next century as a cost-saving measure. (The normal retirement age was already scheduled to rise from 65 to 67 in 2020.)[54]

Nor could Congress and the president reach an agreement on ways to preserve the solvency of Medicare, which might prove unable to fund hospital benefits as early as 2012 due to the growing elderly population.[55] A bipartisan Medicare Commission failed to reach agreement on central issues, even as its co-chairpersons supported giving senior citizens and disabled persons vouchers to purchase health care in the private sector. After liberals objected to this strategy on the grounds that it would undermine Medicare by privatizing it, Clinton then seized the initiative by proposing to expand Medicare to cover prescription drugs. Contending that senior citizens' health care was often compromised when they could not afford increasingly expensive and sophisticated medications, Clinton also proposed to help senior citizens obtain price concessions from drug companies through volume purchases.

Republicans rejected Clinton's proposals, so no reforms of Medicare were enacted in 1999. The Congress stalemated, as well, on the issue of patient rights in managed care systems. If only a small fraction of Americans were enrolled in managed care systems at the start of the 1990s, most Americans received their health care through them by the end of the decade partly because employers, wishing to cut the cost of the health insurance fringe benefit, required employees to select managed care policies. Flagrant abuses often existed in these systems, which were often for-profit organizations.

Central administrators sometimes issued so-called gag orders to physicians, instructing them not to tell patients about certain procedures, medications, or tests even when they were medically advisable. Sometimes central administrators denied needed treatments to patients—or developed such lengthy reviews of physician requests that patients

died before they could secure advisable treatments. Patients were often denied access to specialists by screening physicians even when they needed their care—or were not even told that specialists existed. Managed care systems often required enrollees to sign statements they would not sue for malpractice, while also not establishing patient appeal procedures. (Some denials of treatment were, of course, meritorious when ill-advised procedures were suggested by physicians or demanded by patients.)[56]

Nor were these abuses limited to the treatment of physical conditions, as mental health services were often provided by managed care systems as well. Many social workers in managed care organizations complained that they were excessively circumscribed by central managers and staff in providing necessary treatments. Indeed, the National Association of Social Workers supported a federal class action suit (*Hostein v. Green Spring*) against nine managed care behavioral health companies that served 115 million people in 1999 on the grounds that they reduced rates paid to care providers "to reap higher profits."[57]

During Clinton's second term, two important policy victories occurred in the mental health and health fields despite stalemated congressional politics. Partly due to the leadership of Tipper Gore, the wife of Vice President Al Gore, federal legislation was enacted in 1996 that required private health insurance companies not to discriminate against mental health problems in their plans. Using the simplistic argument that coverage of these problems would trigger excessive use of counseling services, health insurance companies had provided no or scant coverage for mental problems for decades—a deficit that was compounded by meager coverage of these problems by Medicare and Medicaid.

While public attention focused on cuts in Medicare and Medicaid, an important enhancement occurred in 1997 when Clinton secured enactment of a children's health program to give grants of $20 billion to the states to provide health insurance to uninsured children. (States could use the funds to expand their Medicaid programs to include children, or they could establish special plans for them. This health program was plagued, however, by poor implementation as many states failed to enroll eligible children.)

A signal failure of the Clinton administration was its failure to enact sweeping campaign finance legislation.[58] While caps were placed on individuals' and corporate contributions made directly to candidates, no caps existed on so-called "soft money" that was given to political parties. Political parties, in turn, often used these funds for mailings and mass media spots that highlighted specific issues during campaigns that were clearly intended to assist specific candidates, thus providing them with publicity identical to mailings and spots financed by their own funds. Parties sometimes poured millions of dollars into specific campaigns at the behest of special interests. Various techniques were used, as well, to get around caps on contributions to individuals, allowing George W. Bush, for example, to amass $50 million months before the first primary in the presidential contest of 2000. Although the House enacted campaign finance legislation several times, it was filibustered to death by Republican senators, thus defeating legislation developed by Senators John McCain and Russell Feingold to place some limits on campaign contributions. The American system of financing campaigns biases social policy toward preferences of corporations and wealthy individuals, whose combined contributions far exceed contributions of unions, teachers, and the AARP. That the United States had failed by 2000 to develop comprehensive health insurance, for example, was partly due to decades of campaign contributions by physicians, managed care corporations, and pharmaceutical companies.

Nearly 45 million Americans were medically uninsured in 1999, including at least 10 million children. Millions of elderly citizens with chronic medical conditions had to bankrupt themselves to obtain eligibility for Medicaid. In fact, domestic discretionary spending *declined* from the late 1970s through 2000 as a percentage of GDP, as will be discussed more fully in Chapter 13.

In the midst of this budget scarcity, a glimmer of hope finally emerged in early 1998 when

Clinton predicted a $219 billion *surplus* over five years as he announced a balanced budget on February 2. It seemed too good to be true after 17 years of megadeficits, particularly when he predicted that surpluses would rise from $10 billion to $258 billion between 1999 and 2008—and the Congressional Budget Office doubled its estimate of the likely surplus within the next months to $1.6 trillion over the next decade.

What would normally be good news triggered new rounds of political conflict in the polarized and stalemated atmosphere of the late 1990s. Realizing that Republicans would insist that the surplus be used to fund massive tax cuts, Clinton's budget in early 1998 sought to use the imminent surplus to fund modest spending increases in domestic programs while using the remaining funds to "save" Social Security even if he provided few specifics. Republicans immediately demanded tax cuts and large cuts in domestic discretionary programs, but they capitulated in late 1998 by accepting Clinton's modest spending increases for child care and education in return for a small tax cut.

The budget battle of 1998 was a mere skirmish, however, as compared with the budget battle of 1999, which both parties viewed as a prelude to the elections of 2000 when both the presidency and Congress would be up for grabs. Now the budget surpluses were estimated by the administration to run $117 billion in the coming fiscal year—and $4.47 *trillion* over the next 15 years. Clinton developed a clever proposal for putting Republicans on the defensive by *both* "saving" Social Security and Medicare *and* reducing the nearly $7 trillion national debt that had largely accumulated after President Reagan's large tax cuts of 1981. He proposed to place surplus monies from the budget in the Social Security Trust Fund, which, in turn, would receive IOUs from the Treasury Department when it lent these funds to it so that it could pay off the federal debt by retiring the bonds issued to fund it. (Retirement of the national debt would have positive economic consequences, Clinton contended, such as reducing interest rates as the federal government preempted less private capital to fund its debt.) When it was unable to completely fund Social Security pensions in 2014 when payroll taxes were no longer sufficient, the Trust Fund would redeem these IOUs by obtaining monies from the Treasury Department—a policy that would allow it to remain solvent to 2050. (Its existing IOUs, obtained by using its surpluses to help fund general government expenses in the 1970s, 1980s, and 1990s, sufficed to the year 2032, but the new IOUs would keep the Trust Fund solvent until 2050.[59])

Clinton's double-barreled strategy of coupling the rescue of Social Security with reducing the federal debt allowed him to attack Republican demands for a tax cut of nearly $1 trillion spread over several years. He attacked these tax cuts on the grounds that they would *both* undermine Social Security *and* increase the national debt.

Republicans attacked Clinton's proposal as a budgeting gimmick that would deplete surplus resources so as to disallow a large tax cut. Clinton's plan could be attacked, as well, from a liberal perspective. Although reducing the national debt made good economic sense, the diversion of trillions of dollars to this effort over a period of years meant that domestic discretionary spending would continue to be shortchanged. Subject to caps and freezes during the Reagan, Bush, and Clinton administrations, domestic discretionary spending had actually declined from more than 4 percent of GDP in the late 1970s to less than 2.5 percent by 2000— and budget experts expected it to decline to roughly 2 percent by 2004. Federal spending on education, training, employment, and social programs, moreover, had declined from roughly 1.75 percent of GDP to less than 1 percent of GDP from the late 1970s to 2000.[60] Why not use more of these surplus funds for discretionary spending—or even for augmenting such means-tested programs as Food Stamps and the EITC? Or why not use some of the funds to allow some cuts in the taxes of persons in the lowest two economic quintiles?

Undeterred, Republicans proposed huge tax cuts as well as a "lock-box" proposal to disallow the use of any Social Security revenues for the funding of costs of the general government. They proposed massive cuts in discretionary domestic spending, wanting to reduce it by 18 percent by 2001 and by nearly 30 percent by 2009. (Clinton was not generous to domestic discretionary spending, either, but his proposed cuts were less than half the size of the Republicans' cuts.)

As the president and the Republican Congress staked out opposing positions, it became obvious that the two parties would battle over how to spend budget surpluses for years to come. If the president pledged to veto any large tax cuts as well as excessive cuts in domestic discretionary programs, Republicans vowed to fight for their tax and spending cuts.

THE OPPRESSION OF VULNERABLE POPULATIONS

The Oppression of Women

Women's reproductive rights were under attack by conservatives during the Clinton era. Although Congress enacted a measure that made the use or threat of force against workers or clients of abortion clinics a federal crime, women found it difficult to exercise reproductive choice when confronted with pickets at clinics or when forced to travel 50 miles, on average, to find a clinic that would perform abortions.[61] The so-called morning-after pill, a simple means of abortion that was commonly used in Europe, was not widely available in the United States, partly because pharmaceutical companies feared boycotts of their other products by abortion foes.[62] The medical profession itself retreated from providing abortion services; most hospitals did not offer the procedure, and most medical students were not even taught how to perform it.[63] Conservative members of Congress, having succeeded in blocking the use of federal funds for abortions, attached riders to legislation to restrict abortion further.

They hoped to make late-term abortions illegal, even when the mother's life was endangered. By attaching a rider to a defense authorization bill that President Clinton felt he had to sign, they secured the prohibition of abortions in military hospitals. Opponents of abortion relentlessly attached amendments to many pieces of legislation, including the Hyde amendment (named after Representative Henry Hyde), which was annually attached to appropriations for DHHS and the Department of Labor and that prohibited federal funding of abortions except in the case of rape or incest or if a woman's life was in jeopardy. (It was later expanded to preclude use of Medicaid funds to pay for managed care health plans that covered abortions.) They attached an amendment beginning in 1995 that banned federal employees' health plans from financing abortions. But proponents of choice also won some victories. Because it did not exempt women whose health or lives would otherwise be in jeopardy, Clinton vetoed a ban on "partial birth" abortions—abortions in the third trimester when a living fetus is partially delivered before it is killed. Opponents of choice failed to bar aid to international family planning groups that promote or perform abortions.

On the economic front, women had made substantial gains in some areas during the 1990s. Large numbers of women continued to gain admission to professional schools in law, business, and medicine.

With the help of federally funded training programs, some women had entered nontraditional fields such as the trades. These gains were offset, however, by a continuing and extraordinary gap between the median wages of men and women. Moreover, many professional women continued to encounter the so-called glass ceiling; they were not promoted to higher positions even when their job performance excelled. Republicans' policies—in particular, their challenges to AFDC and the earned-income tax credit—threatened the economic standing of the many women who were single heads of families in low-wage jobs. Moreover, feminists feared that women's economic progress would lose its momentum if Republicans succeeded in terminating affirmative action and set-asides that reserved federal job-training slots and contracts for women.

Most European nations have funded absences from work for parents after the birth of a child or the death of a family member. In the United States, however, corporations and many conservatives have staunchly resisted such policies. Social reformers gained a limited victory with the enactment of the Family and Medical Leave Act of 1993, which required employers to give all but their top employees up to 12 weeks of leave to take care of a new baby or an ill family member. However, the legislation excluded individuals who had not worked for an employer for at least 12 months and excluded businesses with fewer than 50 employees. Although workers were guaranteed leaves, employers were not required to pay them during those periods. Thus, low-income workers were not easily able to take advantage of this new policy.[64]

We have already discussed the mixed record of the Personal Responsibility and Work Opportunities Act of 1996 during the three years after its enactment. (We discuss the outcomes of this legislation more fully in the next chapter.) Clinton was able to obtain some modifications of the 1996 welfare reform legislation in succeeding years, such as getting a $3 billion fund enacted to help states put long-term recipients into the workforce; clarifying that recipients placed in public employment programs had to be paid at least the minimum wage; providing Medicaid benefits for disabled children who lost SSI benefits; and restoring some Food Stamp benefits in 1997. States experienced, moreover, a remarkable fiscal windfall in the wake of welfare reform. Recall that the federal government agreed in 1996 to fund TANF at levels (for each state) equaling federal payments for AFDC benefits in the year preceding implementation of TANF. Because the rolls dropped markedly in most states, they possessed millions of dollars of excess resources that could be used to assist welfare populations, whether in their benefits or in programs to help them leave the rolls. (No one had anticipated the sheer size of this windfall.) Unfortunately, many states did not spend their windfall—or failed to develop innovative programs to help welfare recipients enter the economic and social mainstream.

The Oppression of Persons of Color and the Attack on Affirmative Action

During Clinton's first term, policies to help persons of color came under increasing political attack. In California, Governor Pete Wilson, who was contemplating a run for the presidency, pledged to end affirmative action policies in the state. At his initiative, affirmative action was rescinded in the University of California system; he also supported a proposition on the California ballot in 1996 to end affirmative action throughout state government. Since their introduction, affirmative action policies had allowed many persons of color and

FIGURE 11.3 Welfare recipients try to enter the economic mainstream.

© AP Photo/Lynsey Addario

women to obtain jobs, education, and government contracts, even if beneficiaries sometimes came from middle-class, rather than poor, families. However, the perception that white claimants were being denied positions and opportunities prompted massive public resentment. Many civil rights advocates feared the erosion of job and college gains by persons of color if the government abandoned affirmative action altogether. Others feared that fundamental changes in the nation's economy—in particular, the growing importance of higher education and technical skills—would imperil the employment opportunities of African Americans and Latinos.

At the same time, influential books by conservative intellectuals disparaged government policies to provide special assistance to persons of color. As we saw in Chapter 5, *The Bell Curve*, by Richard Herrnstein and Charles Murray, asserted that African Americans are genetically predisposed to low intelligence.[65] While many social scientists criticized the methodology and data used by Herrnstein and Murray, the book became a best-seller, and some readers came to believe that the authors had proved their assertion by using advanced social science statistics and methodology. In *The End of Racism*, Dinesh D'Souza alleged that "cultural dysfunctionality," not racism, is the main reason that African Americans lag behind the rest of the population economically.[66] Contending that affirmative action, as well as programs such as AFDC, institutionalized a culture of dependency among African Americans, D'Souza suggested that "race-neutral" policies, including the abandonment of affirmative action, would promote entrepreneurialism and the work ethic among African Americans. Though these two books implicated different causes, they came to the same conclusion: African Americans' economic status and educational performance derived from personal characteristics, whether their intelligence or their character, rather than from institutionalized racism or other social obstacles.

From a social policy perspective, both books provided simplistic analyses of complex phenomena. If African Americans are genetically or culturally inferior, why has a large African American middle (and upper) class developed in the decades after the 1960s—that is, since the enactment of civil rights laws and opportunity-creating social programs, the mass migration of African Americans from rural to urban areas, and the use of affirmative action? Might not the low economic status of many African Americans be, in large part, a consequence of their segregation in rural Southern areas until relatively recently? Even if there has been a decline in the overt racism that was endemic until the early 1960s, do other, more subtle forms of racism persist, as reflected in a pervasive bias by employers and gatekeepers of large institutions against African American candidates? And might these prejudices flourish if government pressure and protections were to be removed? Finally, if African Americans are characterized by permanent intellectual deficits, why do numerous pilot projects, as well as research on well-established job training, Head Start, and educational programs, suggest that government intervention *can* improve the educational and economic standing of African Americans?

Perhaps most disturbing, *The Bell Curve* and *The End of Racism* lead us toward fatalistic outlook on social policy. If impoverished African Americans possess characterological and intellectual deficits that are relatively intractable, government (or society) can play little role in helping them. However, to be fatalistic about African Americans, while believing that government policies can help other persons better their lot, is a form of racism. If we are pessimistic about the efficacy of social policies in helping African Americans, should we not also be pessimistic about policies intended to help white citizens better their condition? Why should we pay for schools, nursery schools, and other amenities in white, suburban areas?

The debate over affirmative action intensified with the passage of Proposition 209 in California in 1997, which forbade public universities from displaying *any* preference for persons of color in their admissions processes. (The proposition won by a landslide vote.) Because the social class of test takers correlates with their scores on the Student Achievement Test (SAT) and because fewer persons of color have taken and passed advanced placement tests in specific subjects, opponents of Proposition 209 predicted a marked decline in enrollments in California's public universities by persons of color—a prediction that proved correct when freshman minority enrollment halved in 1998 and when minority enrollment plummeted in public professional schools and in graduate programs. By decreasing a population that was allready underrepresented in the ranks of college graduates and the professions, this proposition was viewed by many as arresting those gains that had been painstakingly made toward increasing rates of higher education among persons of color. In the words of Jerome Karabel, a leading authority on affirmative action, Proposition 209 was "the biggest negative redistribution of educational opportunity in the history of the country."[67] Opponents of affirmative action sought passage of similar propositions in other states and initiated lawsuits against many affirmative action programs on the grounds that they violated the due process clause of the Fourteenth Amendment.

Despite its immediate negative outcomes, Proposition 209 forced policy makers to give more attention to enhanced educational programs for persons of color in secondary schools—emphases that ought to have accompanied affirmative action from the outset. Indeed, the state legislature authorized $38.5 million to expand the pool of eligible minority students by enriching the curriculum and providing special tutoring to African American, Latino, Native American, Asian American, and other minority students in the public secondary schools.[68] Some community colleges developed special enriched programs for minority students so that they could move into public universities once they had completed two years of coursework.

A healthy debate commenced, as well, about the admissions criteria of universities. MALDEF (the Mexican American Legal Defense Fund) sued California's public universities on the grounds that it was unfair to emphasize scores on advanced placement tests in the admissions process when few advanced placement tests were even offered in schools attended by most Latino students. Feminist groups brought suit against the College Board Testing Service on grounds that females tended to have lower scores on the Student Achievement Test than men, alleging that subtle biases existed in the tests or the testing procedures.

Another debate swirled around affirmative action: What should be the relative emphasis accorded social class versus membership in a specific minority group? Although a disproportionate number of Latino applicants come from the lowest two economic quintiles, for example, some are children of middle- and upper-class parents just as some Caucasian applicants come from low-income families in impoverished areas such as Appalachian communities. Should priority be given to applicants from low-income backgrounds regardless of their ethnicity or gender?

One thing was certain: If Americans failed to develop policies that distributed academic credentials and jobs more fairly among different groups in the population, the nation, itself, would ultimately be the loser. It would forfeit the contributions of millions of women and persons of color to decisions and jobs in myriad settings—and accentuate America's need to import skilled labor from abroad in a technological age. It would increase inequality in income and status between individuals of different ethnic and gender groups, exacerbating alienation and violating the ethical principle of social justice. It would dampen economic growth by diminishing the wealth and productivity of significant portions of the population.

The issue of affirmative action was closely linked, as well, to the broader issue of school vouchers, which had been implemented in cities such as Chicago and Cleveland, as well as in the state of Minnesota. Pointing to troubled public school systems, proponents of vouchers—citing the ethical principle of autonomy—contended that low-income parents ought to be able to send their children to private schools if they wished. Why not, they contended, publicly subsidize vouchers to enable parents to purchase educational services wherever they wished? Opponents countered that public funding of church-related schools, such as parochial schools, violated the Constitutional separation of church and state. (Children were required to attend prayer and religious sessions in parochial and most other sectarian schools.) They contended, as well, that taxpayers were unwilling to fund vouchers at levels that allowed low-income parents a full range of choice, usually forcing them to select low-tuition parochial schools if they could even gain admission to them because of fierce competition for limited slots. Why not, opponents asked, use the voucher funds to improve existing public schools? Several court rulings declared vouchers to be unconstitutional by mid-2000.

The Oppression of Immigrants

As we discussed in Chapter 6, anti-immigrant sentiment has often grown more strident during periods of economic uncertainty. This pattern continued in the 1990s, when corporate downsizing and globalization brought economic insecurity and anxiety to many American homes. In 1994, California voters passed Proposition 187, which declared illegal aliens ineligible for medical, social, and educational services. Though its implementation was halted pending the outcome of court challenges and appeals, this law nonetheless triggered a national debate about immigration.

The immigrant population can be divided into three groups: "legal immigrants" with visas or other documents from federal immigration officials, so-called undocumented or illegal immigrants, and immigrants with uncertain legal status who fall between these two categories. Large numbers of legal immigrants have resided in the United States for years or even decades, dutifully paying Social Security payroll taxes, Medicare payroll taxes, federal taxes, and state and local taxes.

Whether because they retire, develop disabilities, or have low income, immigrants often need benefits from social programs like SSI, Medicaid, and Food Stamps—programs that they have helped fund through their taxes. Betraying their prejudice even against legal immigrants, the Republican majority placed an array of restrictive policies in the Personal Responsibility and Work Opportunities Act of 1996, including giving states the option of terminating legal immigrants from Medicaid and exempting legal immigrants who had worked for less than 10 years in the United States from eligibility for SSI and Food Stamps.

California's Proposition 187, enacted in 1994, banned illegal immigrants from participating in any state-funded programs and Medicaid, as well as use of public schools by their children. (It passed by a landslide vote despite determined opposition by many liberals and Latinos.) Republicans took a particularly hard stand on immigration in 1996 because they perceived the issue to be a wedge issue that could entice moderate and conservative Democrats to vote for the Republican ticket in forthcoming elections, enacting legislation that greatly increased the size of the border patrol and that made it more difficult for illegal immigrants to obtain legal status. (Some favored federal legislation to ban illegal immigrants from using federal programs.) Opponents of harsh policies toward undocumented immigrants insisted that they made extraordinary economic contributions to the United States, often filling positions in agriculture, restaurants, hotels, and elsewhere that American citizens did not want while often paying payroll and income taxes. They contended, as well, that denying undocumented workers access to medical programs was not only ethically misguided, but it could cause epidemics of diseases like tuberculosis and AIDS that could affect the broader population. Denial of education to the children of undocumented workers would force them to roam the streets, possibly increasing gang and criminal activity.

A 1996 immigration law required immigrants with uncertain legal status to return to their countries of origin to apply for permanent U.S. visas while also not allowing them to return to the United States in the interim. Many of these immigrants, moreover, were subject to denials of Food Stamps, SSI, and Medicaid that had been placed on legal immigrants in the 1996 welfare reform legislation.

The hostile national mood toward these three kinds of immigrants began receding by 1997, however, for several reasons.[69] Most importantly, the huge Spanish-speaking population in the United States was angered by immigrant bashing as many of them had been immigrants or were sympathetic with them. (Republicans lost a landslide gubernatorial election in California in 1998 partly because they had authored Proposition 187—and presidential candidate Bob Dole lost Florida to Bill Clinton in the presidential election of 1996 partly because he had supported anti-immigrant legislation.)[70] The booming economy diminished prejudice against immigrants among those citizens who had been fearful they would take their jobs. Aware that immigration no longer was suitable as a wedge to divide the Democratic Party, Republicans backed off the issue.

As the hostile mood abated, some restrictive policies were modified. Proposition 187 was never implemented because of legal injunctions and adverse court rulings. Beating a hasty retreat, the Congress restored SSI and Medicaid in 1997 for legal immigrants who had been in the United States since August of 1996, while restoring Food Stamp benefits in 1998. (It also allowed immigrants whose legal status was unclear to be permanently eligible for SSI and Medicaid in 1997.) Moreover, Congress gave special considerations to refugees from repressive regimes in Cuba, Haiti, Guatemala, El Salvador, and Nicaragua—and immigration officials doubled the number of visas granted to immigrants with computer, engineering, or other special skills needed by American corporations.

The Oppression of Children

Knowing that Hillary Clinton was a former board member of the Children's Defense Fund, children's advocates hoped for major legislation to further their goals during Clinton's first term. Some marginal gains were made; for example, a nationwide immunization program for children was initiated, and Congress approved $1 billion for demonstration programs in local jurisdictions to strengthen troubled families. However, major policy changes proposed by the Republican-controlled Congress—including the elimination of entitlement status for AFDC, the block-granting of Food Stamps, and revision of Medicaid policies to end the phased inclusion of children over age 12—threatened to cast even larger numbers of children into poverty.

The drawbacks of indiscriminate block-granting are well illustrated by child welfare. In

1996, 21 states were under court supervision for failing to properly care for children in child protective services and in foster care. Social workers, who have often been blamed for failing to detect child abuse or neglect, typically carried caseloads exceeding 50 cases, although the Child Welfare League of America, a respected private organization, recommended no more than 15. Many states, straining to meet the budgetary demands of education, Medicaid, and prisons, failed sufficiently to augment federal subsidies with their own resources. Yet Republicans insisted that the $4 billion in federal subsidies for child welfare be given as block grants to the states, which could administer them with few restrictions.[71] They tried to include block granting of child welfare in welfare reform legislation of 1996, but they were defeated by a bipartisan coalition.

When they enacted the Personal Responsibility and Work Opportunities Act of 1996, most legislators focused not on the well-being of children but on methods of reducing the welfare rolls as rapidly as possible. Few of them even wondered if the earnings of former recipients would be sufficient to reduce rates of childhood poverty or whether reduced income of some formal recipients (as compared with their prior income plus in-kind benefits) would increase rates of child abuse and neglect or whether rates of families' homelessness would increase. Some early findings offered grounds for caution in the fall of 1999. A study of census data by the Center on Budget and Policy Priorities showed that, although "the average earnings and overall incomes of low-income female-headed families rose substantially between 1993 and 1995 as the economy expanded … the average incomes of the poorest 20 percent of female-headed families with children fell from 1995 to 1997 despite economic growth, as welfare system changes took effect on a large scale. …"[72]

The welfare reform legislation restricted eligibility to SSI for children with behavioral disorders even though Congress agreed in 1997 to continue Medicaid benefits to children that lost their SSI eligibility. (It also disqualified adults whose primary disability is substance abuse or alcoholism.) It decreased funding for meals of children in family day care homes, as well as cut reimbursements for summer food programs—and eliminated start-up and expansion funding of the School Breakfast Program.

The welfare reform legislation eliminated the *guarantee* of child care for welfare recipients trying to move into employment that existed under AFDC, leaving it to individual states to determine whether and for how long former recipients received subsidized child care.[73] It did, however, consolidate federal child care programs under the existing Child Care and Development Block Grant and increase funding through a new child care block grant. It also allowed states to transfer up to 30 percent of their TANF block grant funds to the Child Care and Development Block Grant and the Title XX Social Services Block Grant.

Clinton signed, as well, the Adoption and Safe Families Act that was designed to hasten adoptions of children in foster care. Whereas the Adoption Assistance and Child Welfare Act of 1980 had aimed to reduce the number of children in foster care by imposing regulations on the states and expanding child welfare services, it had emphasized protection of the rights of natural families, strongly affirming reunification with natural families whenever possible. In the ensuing two decades, however, sentiment slowly shifted toward emphasizing *whatever* disposition would protect the children's well-being and safety—including adoptions instead of reunification in instances when clear patterns of child abuse had existed in the natural family. (Disillusionment with the possibility of reunification for many children was reinforced, moreover, by the growing numbers of children in foster care, totaling roughly 500,000 in 1997, with many of them in foster care for more than two years.) The Adoption and Safe Families Act sought to double the number of adoptions of children in foster care from 27,000 children in 1996 to 54,000 in the near future by stating that reunification need not even be attempted if a child was subjected to "aggravated circumstances" like serious physical abuse or if parents had killed or assaulted another child; offering $4,000 to each state for every adoption that exceeded

its previous annual total; requiring states to terminate parental rights and to begin adoption proceedings once a child had been in foster care for 15 of the preceding 22 months; and stipulating that children were entitled to judicial hearings within 12 months of entering foster care rather than 18 months in existing law.[74] Even the Family Preservation Program, which was created by the 1993 budget reconciliation law to provide impetus to family reunification, was mandated to promote adoptions as well as reunification and was renamed the Promoting Safe and Stable Families Program.

The Oppression of Gay Men and Lesbians

A policy controversy during Clinton's first months in office illustrated the continuing discrimination against gay men and lesbians. Clinton had made a campaign promise to end the military's homophobic policies, under which candidates known to be gay men or lesbians were denied admission and military personnel who came out as gay or lesbian or were determined to have engaged in homosexual acts were dismissed. (About 14,000 people had been dismissed under these rules between 1983 and 1993; roughly 25 percent were women.) Most military leaders opposed any change in policy on the grounds that gay and lesbian personnel undermined unit cohesion by alienating their heterosexual peers. However, a U.S. District Court judge had ordered the Navy to reinstate Keith Meinhold, who had been discharged after identifying himself as a gay man on national television. Caught between military leaders and conservatives on the one hand, and gay and lesbian activists on the other, Clinton fashioned an initial compromise in which the existing policy would remain in place for six months, pending consultation with military leaders, but all actions against gay men and lesbians would be suspended, unless they had been charged with homosexual conduct.

Unwilling to await the president's resolution, Democratic Senator Sam Nunn held extended hearings on the issue. Nunn advanced a "don't ask and don't tell" approach, under which military leaders would be prevented from questioning recruits or personnel about their sexual orientation but could still dismiss personnel who identified themselves as gay men or lesbians, engaged in homosexual acts, or sought to marry a person of the same gender. This compromise enraged many gay men and lesbians because sexual orientation remained sufficient cause for dismissal, regardless of the individual's job-related proficiency. When the president accepted a "don't ask, don't tell" approach, Senator Sam Nunn pushed for legislation that contained even more restrictive language—for example, the declaration that those who "demonstrate a propensity or intent to engage in homosexual acts would create an unacceptable risk" to military standards. Placed in a military authorization bill, Clinton's compromise with Nunn's tougher wording was finally codified into law as part of a military authorization bill in November of 1993.[75] Data suggested in 1999 that the "don't ask, don't tell" policy had had virtually no effect in reducing the number of dismissals of gays and lesbians from the military.

The gay community continued to be plagued by the AIDS epidemic. Although combinations of medications had allowed many infected persons to live, many medical uncertainties remained. Some HIV-positive persons could not tolerate the medications or found their side effects to be unacceptable.

As the panic about the epidemic abated, many persons stopped practicing safe sex and rates of infection, after having dropped for several years, began to rise again. The epidemic began to spread to minority communities to the extent that the Board of Supervisors in Los Angeles County declared a state of medical emergency in late 1999, calling for an all-out campaign of HIV education and outreach to arrest its spread, particularly in low-income areas.

RELUCTANCE ILLUSTRATED

In the first two years of his presidency, Clinton sought relatively liberal policies, including social

investments, health reform, and many smaller measures. A combination of forces frustrated his attempts at reform. A resurgent Republican minority in both chambers was able to align with moderate and conservative Democrats who balked at the president's proposals. Outside of Congress, large numbers of Americans, cynical about government, did not want major social initiatives; they were more interested in putting an end to gridlock, implementing campaign reforms, and achieving a balanced budget. Nor had the electorate given Clinton a mandate; he barely won the election, receiving only 43 percent of the popular vote. Finally, Clinton and his advisors made many errors of their own during the first two years; in particular, the health reform proposal that they developed was far too complex to win broad support.

The third year of the Clinton presidency might even be called the Newt Gingrich era, inasmuch as Republicans' victory in the 1994 elections left them in control of both chambers of Congress and allowed Gingrich to set the legislative agenda. Resorting to a zigzagging retreat by June, Clinton acceded to most of the Republicans' budget demands as the year proceeded. This third year strongly resembled the politics of 1981, when Ronald Reagan had orchestrated huge cuts in domestic spending—except that the cuts in 1995 were orchestrated not by the president but by a congressional leader.

Clinton's zigzagging strategy proved politically successful in slowing the momentum of conservatives, particularly as they overreached to land a knockout blow to their retreating opponent. Underestimating the tenacity of Clinton, Republicans assumed they could force him to accept their tax and spending cuts in late 1995 by shutting the government down, only to discover that most citizens blamed them for the loss of government services. If Clinton had been widely viewed as inept and excessively liberal in 1994, leaders such as Gingrich were widely viewed in 1996 as too far to the right and unwilling to compromise. The result was a landslide victory of Clinton over Dole in the 1996 election, even though both Houses of Congress remained in Republican hands.

Clinton's second term was devoid of many large social policy accomplishments because the two parties, as well as the president and the Congress, were stalemated and polarized. Domestic discretionary spending remained frozen by caps that were made even more severe by the 1997 budget deal. Military spending again began to rise after falling somewhat in earlier years of the Clinton administration. As in prior years of the Clinton administration, attention focused in 1997 on obtaining a balanced budget by 2002—a focus that inhibited domestic reforms save for a major initiative to provide health insurance to children and various tax entitlements for education.

From the vantage point of social policy, Clinton's presidency was significantly a defensive one with a sprinkling of new and modestly small initiatives. He managed to limit many of the tax and spending cuts that Republicans sought in budget deals of 1993, 1995, 1996, 1997, and 1998. He was able, as well, to end the megadeficits that the nation had inherited from the Reagan and Bush years, thus removing a major constraint to renewed social spending. He defeated conservatives' efforts to end affirmative action at the federal level and to limit choice by pregnant women. He cleverly thwarted Republicans' resurgence in the wake of the taking of control of both Houses of Congress in 1994, not only winning a significant victory for himself in 1996 but helping to cut Republicans' majorities in the House and Senate in 1998. He greatly expanded the Earned Income Tax Credit by raising its eligibility level and subsidies—making it into the largest federal antipoverty program. He expanded Head Start—and secured enactment of a major program to extend health insurance to poor children not eligible for Medicaid.

However, Clinton also contributed to liberals' malaise. While his zigzagging maneuvers kept Republicans off balance from 1995 onward, they also prioritized political expediency over principles on numerous occasions. Essentially a centrist president who could veer to the right on occasion to preempt conservatives' themes on crime, welfare, military spending, and spending cuts, Clinton failed sufficiently to articulate a progressive vision. He further jeopardized progressive legislation through his ill-advised personal behavior in his second term, which provided conservatives with ammunition to attack Clinton and his policies.

From a liberal perspective, then, Clinton had a mixed record. He often warded off conservatives and adroitly got important reforms enacted, but his domestic accomplishments were relatively modest. Domestic discretionary spending actually declined as a percentage of GDP during his tenure—although he got social programs funded by tax expenditures significantly increased, such as the Earned Income Tax Credit and the Hope scholarship funds for college. He assented to caps and freezes on domestic discretionary spending in budget deals of 1993 and 1997. He signed welfare legislation in 1996 even knowing that conservative states would implement it punitively. Developed in 1999, his plan to use trillions of dollars of the impending surplus to reduce the national debt ignored myriad domestic programs that needed new resources.

No administration illustrates the battle for resources faced by liberals more dramatically than the Clinton administration. Entire legislative sessions in 1993, 1995, 1996, and 1997 were devoted to budget deals that were (except for 1997) sharply contested.

Bill Clinton came into office facing huge deficits bequeathed to him by the Reagan and Bush administrations. With little money in the till and with the focus on diminishing deficits, Clinton could not develop a robust domestic agenda. Budget deals of 1993 and 1997 froze and capped domestic discretionary spending, meaning that Clinton could fund his small domestic initiatives like Americorps (a kind of domestic Peace Corps) and various educational initiatives only by cutting other domestic programs. The Congress scuttled his stimulus spending and social investment proposals in 1993 on the grounds that deficit reduction should be prioritized. His proposal for national health insurance was defeated in 1994 partly because opponents contended the nation could not afford it during a period of high deficits.

Clinton deserves credit for securing some initiatives from 1993 through 1999 in this austere fiscal environment. He sometimes resorted to tax expenditures, funding most of his education initiatives "off budget" through the tax code, as well as huge increases in the EITC in 1993. His congressional allies placed preventive social programs in the crime legislation in a kind of back-door method of funding social programs. He increased the minimum wage and frequently issued federal regulations—strategies not requiring federal expenditures. He secured small child care and job-training additions to welfare reform legislation.

Clinton also deserves credit for defeating or diminishing some Republican cuts in social spending, as well as the downsizing of several proposed Republican tax cuts in years such as 1993 and 1997. (Tax cuts often force spending cuts to pay for them.) He was aided by many moderate and liberal legislators, as well as by effective advocacy groups such as the Center on Budget and Policy Priorities. Clinton was able, as well, to reduce the extent to which some tax cuts showered their benefits disproportionately upon affluent Americans, such as with various education tax expenditures that he obtained in 1998.

Clinton also deserves some credit for ending the nation's annual budget deficits—even positioning the nation for trillions of dollars of surpluses that could have been applied to shoring up the Social Security and Medicare trust funds. Had this occurred, Americans in succeeding decades would have encountered a less severe budget crunch that posed less of a threat to domestic discretionary spending.

It was clear in the 1990s that the United States was a deeply divided nation. If liberals mostly liked Clinton, conservatives detested him and even voted in the House to impeach him. As the presidential election of 2000 neared, everyone wondered if the stalemate of the 1990s would continue into the new millennium.

LINKING UNCERTAINTY DURING THE 1990s TO CONTEMPORARY SOCIETY

What We Can Learn from Policy Advocates of the 1990s

Most attention has been given in policy advocacy to proposing, amending, or blocking specific legislative proposals. The presidency of Bill Clinton graphically illustrates the importance of the budget process in federal, state, and local jurisdictions. We may get meritorious legislation enacted, but without adequate funding it won't achieve its goals. Social worker Barbara Ann Mikulski exemplifies a policy advocate who sought out a key position on the Appropriations Committee of the U.S. Senate when she was elected to it in the late 1980s. (See Insert 11.5.)

As we have seen in this chapter, budget politics can be relatively complex because of jargon, budgeting procedures, and budget data. Such national budget advocacy groups as the Center on Budget and Policy Priorities help us to understand specific budget issues—and similar budget advocacy groups exist in most state capitols.

What We Can Learn from the Persistence of Unmet Needs and Policy Issues during the 1990s

The lack of resources for discretionary social spending was a key issue in the 1990s as the Clinton administration struggled to cut the nation's budget deficits while also fending off some huge tax cuts proposed by Republicans.

The United States will face relatively harsh budgetary realities in coming decades in what could even be a "perfect storm" of fiscal shortages as revealed by an imbalance between *revenues* and *expenditures*. Revenues are primarily provided at the national level by the federal income tax on

---

I N S E R T   11.5 Profiles in Leadership: Barbara Ann Mikulski, United States Representative (1977–1987) and United States Senator (1987–Present)

Barbara Ann Mikulski—social worker, social activist, crusader for women's rights, and politician—has been described as earthy, flamboyant, feisty, and outspoken. She describes herself as a "progressive populist" and "a cross between Eleanor Roosevelt and Harry Truman," and said she was going to Washington, DC, "to raise hell." Indeed, Mikulski's political career has been devoted to promoting reform, despite the challenges this type of leadership inevitably faces.

Mikulski was born in Baltimore, MD, on July 20, 1936, to William and Christine Eleanor (Kutz) Mikulski. She grew up in Highlandtown, one of Baltimore's ethnic and working-class neighborhoods, where her parents ran a grocery store. There, she attended Sacred Heart of Jesus elementary school and the Institute of Notre Dame High School. When she wasn't in school, Mikulski worked in the family's store alongside her mother and father.

In 1958, Mikulski received a B.A. in social work from Mount Saint Agnes College (now a part of Loyola University). After graduation, she began working as a caseworker for several agencies in Baltimore, including the Associated Catholic Charities, the Department of Social Services, and the York Family Agency. Meanwhile, she took evening courses at the University of Maryland toward a master's degree in social work, which she received in 1965. Armed with her new degree, Mikulski took a job teaching at VISTA training center and worked for REASON (Responding to the Elderly's Ability and Sickness Otherwise Neglected), Narcotics Anonymous, and other community projects.

Shortly after launching her career in social work, Mikulski became aware of her political consciousness. Her one-on-one work with people led her to realize that, in many cases, institutions were the cause of many of her clients' problems. She became increasingly involved in the civil rights movement and fought for residential desegregation in Baltimore while working in the Kennedy and Johnson campaigns. At age 27, she shocked her parents, who believed children should live at home until they were married, by moving into her own apartment in an integrated area of Baltimore. Her parents, who were aware of her involvement in the civil rights movement, often brought it to Mikulski's attention that there were people in her old neighborhood who needed her help as much as anyone else. Moreover, the people who lived in her old neighborhood often felt as though African Americans were

"getting everything" as a result of civil rights legislation. In a 1970 interview in *America*, Mikulski responded to those charges by saying, "…I know that black programs were token efforts… The result was that the two groups [African Americans and the Polish Americans living in her old neighborhood] were turned against each other instead of the system."

By the end of 1968, Mikulski had experienced the two incidents that were the catalysts of her full transformation from social worker to social activist: the assassinations of Robert F. Kennedy and Martin Luther King, Jr. These tragic events not only left her angry and confused but also inspired her to undergo a complete change of her life. At first, she sought answers through more study at Mount Saint Agnes College in 1969 and in the field of urban affairs at Baltimore Community College from 1970 to 1971. She also continued her social work at various agencies in Baltimore. But after all her searching, Mikulski finally determined that political activism was the solution.

Moving back to her old neighborhood, she helped found the Southeast Baltimore Organization, a coalition of Polish, Italian, African American, and Lumbee Indian groups. Mikulski's first major achievement came when, under her leadership, the organization successfully campaigned to stop the construction of a proposed freeway that would have necessitated tearing down 400 homes of retired and elderly persons in the neighborhood. Shortly thereafter, the organization started a neighborhood restoration project and persuaded the city to develop a park in their community.

Inspired by her success in the organization, by 1971 Mikulski was ready to take her political ambitions to the next level. With the help of her parents, who distributed flyers with the weekly grocery specials saying, "Please vote for our daughter," Mikulski's image as a liberal reformer, and her door-to-door campaign, she won a seat on the Baltimore City Council. During her tenure on the council, she was instrumental in introducing legislation to create the Commission on Aging and Retirement Education (CARE), which had as its main purpose the reduction of bus fares for the elderly and the establishment of a commission to study the impact of rape on its victims.

Councilwoman Mikulski's political style and message quickly gained national attention. In 1976, two years after losing her first congressional election to Charles Mathias, Jr., Barbara Mikulski, who had won reelection in 1975 to the Baltimore City Council, was elected to represent Maryland's 3rd Congressional District. Once in Congress, she quickly became the first woman appointed to the powerful Interstate and Foreign Commerce Committee and the Merchant Marine and Fisheries Committee, whose actions were extremely important to the Baltimore port. Congresswoman Mikulski consistently supported Democratic pro-consumer legislation, including strict regulation of the energy industry and price controls. Never losing sight of her social work background, Mikulski was one of many who passionately opposed Ronald Reagan's cutbacks in social spending. In 1983, she told *Working Woman* that "If the government truly wants to nourish the family, it must give the family what it needs," including decent jobs, access to education, and access to health care. Her relentless attacks against Reagan's social spending cuts led many in Congress to conclude that perhaps she really had gone to Washington, DC, to raise hell.

Mikulski was reelected to the House of Representatives four times in succession before being elected to the Senate in 1986. As a U.S. Senator, Mikulski has sat on the Appropriations Committee, the Labor and Human Resources Committee, and the Small Business Committee. She has also chaired the Appropriations Subcommittee on VA, HUD, and Independent Agencies. Even before she was elected to the Senate, she demonstrated her interest in budget issues when she assumed a leadership role in the U.S. House of Representatives in attacking proposed cuts in social spending by President Ronald Reagan.

---

individuals and corporations, but the United States had the lowest tax rates of any industrialized nation as it entered the 21st century—tax rates that were lowered yet further during the presidency of George W. Bush as he succeeded in getting Congress to enact trillions of dollars of new tax cuts.

On the expenditure side of the federal budget, the following factors will greatly increase the cost of the federal government in coming decades:

- The aging of the baby boomers (persons born between 1946 and 1964) will vastly increase federal spending on Social Security pensions, Medicare, Medicaid, and Supplementary Security Income (SSI) as the number of persons over age 65 increases from 12.4% in 2000 to 19.6% in 2030. In turn, baby boomers' Social Security pensions and their health costs (funded primarily by Medicare and Medicaid) will vastly rise.

- Funds required to finance the nation's debt will rise dramatically to the extent that budget deficits accumulated in the presidency of George W. Bush continue into the future.

- Increased funding will be needed for pensions of retired federal workers.

- The cost of Medicaid for nonelderly persons— which already has surpassed Medicare in size—

will continue to rise dramatically if the cost of health care continues to outpace inflation.

- The cost of military spending will remain high if the United States continues to be the preeminent military power in the world—and it will continue to compete head-to-head with domestic discretionary spending since it is funded from the discretionary portion of the federal budget.

- The cost of health care for veterans of the wars in Vietnam, Afghanistan, and Iraq will increase.

- The cost of environmental damage from global warming will become increasingly apparent, as will the cost of converting from a petroleum-based economy to an economy that produces far less carbon dioxide.

States, too, will face major budget shortfalls in coming decades. They must fund the pensions of government workers. They have to fund states' share of Medicaid costs, which currently amount to more than 25 percent of the budgets of many states. They must fund the growing cost of prisons and correctional programs. If they wish to equalize expenditures on schools used by low-income students, states must dramatically increase expenditures on public education.

In both federal and state legislatures, budget politics will often erupt into conflict between conservatives and liberals. As during the presidency of Bill Clinton, conservatives will often insist that taxes be cut or not raised—and they will often support tax cuts, particularly for relatively affluent persons and corporations. They will often seek cuts in spending on social programs while favoring increases in spending on the military and correctional programs. Liberals will be more likely to take divergent positions on these tax and spending issues from conservatives—seeking tax increases on relatively affluent persons while favoring greater spending on many social programs.

If they seek to advance the ethical principle of social justice, policy advocates won't have the luxury of standing on the sidelines in these conflicts over taxes and spending.

What We Can Learn from Failed Policy Strategies of the 1990s

It is true that welfare rolls declined by 50 percent (or more) in many states in the decade following the enactment of the Personal Responsibility and Work Opportunities Act of 1996. Welfare reform was a dramatic success if "success" is measured by the size of welfare rolls. It is also true that some women not only entered the workforce far faster than would have been the case without welfare reform—and some of them climbed the economic ladder so that they and their families were no longer below or near official poverty lines.

For most single heads of household, however, welfare reform was not a success because they remained under or near official poverty lines. Many of them worked two or even three jobs, leaving them physically and mentally exhausted as they also parented their children. Moreover, roughly half of women on welfare rolls remained on those rolls because of personal disabilities (such as depression, anxiety, or schizophrenia) or because one or more of their children had physical or mental disabilities.

No panaceas exist, but the nation might have at least provided free and quality child care to single heads of household, continuing medical coverage, and subsidized transportation. In addition to providing these amenities, the nation could have greatly increased the availability of free education so that single heads of household could not only have completed high school, but enrolled in community and four-year colleges.

Still afflicted with a poorhouse mentality, many public officials from both political parties continue to view single heads of household as victimized by defects of character rather than persons who need amenities that more affluent persons take for granted.

What We Can Learn from Promising Strategies of the 1990s

Several policy initiatives of President Bill Clinton demonstrated that government can and should help working persons of moderate means. He greatly increased tax benefits and eligibility for the Earned Income Tax Credit (EITC), which gives a tax rebate to families with working parents of moderate income. He enacted HOPE scholarships so that parents with less than $50,000 for a single parent or $100,000 for two parents could also get tax rebates up to $1,500 for the first two years of postsecondary education, Lifetime Learning Credits for students in college or graduate school that would provide up to $1,000 per year of education with income eligibility similar to HOPE scholarships, and education savings accounts in which parents could set aside up to $500 per year that could be withdrawn tax-free when their children were in college.

Both the EITC and the HOPE scholarships illustrate that policies that help persons to thrive in the economy should be a strong part of the American welfare state. Although people often require assistance with their immediate health and welfare needs, they also need policies that provide them with employment-related skills (the HOPE scholarships) and policies that help them improve their economic well-being in job markets (the EITC). It is not difficult to identify other policies that should be considered or amplified, such as loan and grant programs to help citizens purchase houses, start small businesses, and obtain job training.

The ethical principle of social justice, which often focuses on desperately poor people, ought also to include families with moderate means that cannot afford basic amenities like education or health care.

What We Can Learn from the 1990s about the Structure of the American Welfare State

Our discussion of HOPE scholarships and the EITC illustrates the "hidden" side of the American welfare state—tax credits, deductions, deferrals, and exemptions. All told, this hidden side represents more than $600 billion (as of 2008) in government spending each year, since they cost the government precisely what they would cost the government if they were appropriated resources (rather than tax concessions) for programs like Head Start.

In making referrals, then, social workers should be adept at informing their clients about these hidden resources, which many clients do not use because they do not know about them or understand how to use them. In the case of the EITC—now the largest federal antipoverty program for nonelderly persons—as many as 50 percent of eligible families eligible *fail* to apply for its considerable benefits.

WHAT YOU CAN DO NOW

After reading this chapter, you are now equipped to do the following:

- Critically analyze the mind-set of Bill Clinton based on his background, political context, and values, including his policy of triangulation.

- Analyze why Clinton lost his quest for expanded "social investments" while increasingly focusing on deficit reduction during his presidency.

- Analyze why he failed to secure national health insurance in 1994.

- Discuss why conservatives won a landslide victory in the congressional elections of 1994, and describe their policy goals.

- Analyze how President Clinton outmaneuvered Republicans in 1995 and 1996, leading to his one-sided victory against Senator Bob Dole in 1996.

- Critically analyze President Clinton's decision to support enactment of the Personal Responsibility and Work Opportunities Act of 1996.

- Analyze President Clinton's creation of a budget surplus in 1998—and describe how he planned to use it to buttress Social Security and Medicare trust funds.

- Critically analyze the relative successes and failures of Clinton's presidency with respect to social policy.

ENDNOTES

1. David Maraniss, *First in His Class: A Biography of Bill Clinton* (New York: Simon and Schuster, 1995).

2. Ibid., pp. 72, 348, 366, 415.

3. Richard Cohen, "Democratic Leadership Council Sees Party Void and Is Ready to Fill It," *National Journal* (February 1, 1986), 267–270.

4. Maraniss, *First in His Class,* pp. 72, 239, 360, 453.

5. Ibid., p. 407ff.

6. Ben Wattenberg, *Values Matter Most* (New York: Free Press, 1995).

7. Cohen, "Democratic Leadership Council."

8. Robert Reich, *The Work of Nations: Preparing Ourselves for Twenty-First Century Capitalism* (New York: Knopf, 1991).

9. *1993 Congressional Quarterly Almanac*, pp. 82–84.

10. Bob Woodward, *The Agenda: Inside the Clinton White House* (New York: Simon and Schuster, 1994), p. 88ff.

11. Ibid., pp. 113–118, 135–138.

12. Ibid., pp. 43, 95, 108, 139–141.

13. Figure 11.1 uses budget data from the *1993 Congressional Quarterly Almanac*, p. 538.

14. Elizabeth Drew, *On the Edge: The Clinton Presidency* (New York: Simon and Schuster, 1994), pp. 119–123.

15. Graeme Browning, "The Old Shell Game?" *National Journal* (March 27, 1993), pp. 746–748; *1993 Congressional Quarterly Almanac*, p. 105.

16. Jonathan Rauch, "Stage Two," *National Journal* (August 7, 1993), pp. 1962–1966.

17. Viveca Novak, "After the Boll Weevils," *National Journal* (June 26, 1993), pp. 1630–1664.

18. Rauch, "Stage Two," p. 1964.

19. Richard Cohen, "On the Edge," *National Journal* (December 4, 1993), pp. 2888–2892.

20. Woodward, *The Agenda*, pp. 146, 164–168.

21. Drew, *On the Edge*, p. 285ff.

22. Woodward, *The Agenda*, p. 315.

23. Drew, *On the Edge*, pp. 300–310.

24. For an extended discussion of health reform, see *1994 Congressional Quarterly Almanac*, pp. 319–357.

25. For discussion of the crime bill, see *1994 Congressional Quarterly Almanac*, pp. 273–293.

26. Jason DeParle, "Sheila Burke Is the Militant Feminist Commie Peacenik Who's Telling Bob Dole What to Think," *New York Times Magazine* (November 12, 1995), pp. 32–38, 90, 100–105.

27. Howard Fineman, "The Warrior," *Newsweek* (January 9, 1995), pp. 28–34; Connie Bruck, "The Politics of Perception," *New Yorker* (October 9, 1995), pp. 50–76.

28. Bruck, "The Politics of Perception."

29. DeParle, "Sheila Burke."

30. Ibid.

31. Don Balz and Ronald Brownstein, *Storming the Gates: Protest Politics and the Republican Revival* (Boston: Little, Brown), pp. 240–245.

32. Ed Gillespie and Bob Schellhas, eds., *Contract with America* (New York: Random House, 1994).

33. Jeff Shear, "The Big Fix," *National Journal* (March 25, 1995), pp. 734–735.

34. Jeff Shear, "Hey, What's Happened to the Budget?" *National Journal* (February 11, 1995), p. 357.

35. Burt Solomon, "As Republicans Sock, Sock, Sock, for Clinton Opportunities Knock," *National Journal* (March 18, 1995), pp. 700–701.

36. George Hager, "Clinton Shifts Tactics, Projects Erasing Deficit in Ten Years," *Congressional Quarterly Weekly* (June 17, 1995), pp. 1715–1720.

37. Jane Mayer, "Lonely Guy," *New Yorker* (October 30, 1995), pp. 58–62.

38. George Hager and Alissa Rubin, "Last-Minute Maneuvers Forge a Conference Agreement," *Congressional Quarterly Weekly* (June 24, 1995), p. 1814.

39. David Ellwood, "Welfare Reform as I Knew It," *American Prospect* 26 (May-June 1996), pp. 26–27.

40. Ibid.

41. George Hager and David Cloud, "Clinton and Congress: Speeding toward Collision over Budget," *Congressional Quarterly Weekly* (September 2, 1995), p. 2643.

42. George Hager, "GOP Ready to Take Debt Limit to the Brink and Beyond," *Congressional Quarterly Weekly* (September 23, 1995), pp. 2908–2911.

43. George Hager, "Furor over First Spending Bills Promises a Stormy Summer," *Congressional Quarterly Weekly* (July 15, 1995), p. 2041.

44. George Hager, "A Battered GOP Calls Workers Back to the Job," *Congressional Quarterly Weekly* (January 6, 1996), pp. 53–57.

45. Burt Solomon, "Christian Soldiers," *National Journal* (February 24, 1996), pp. 410–415.

46. Jackie Koszczuk, "With Humor and Firm Hand, Armey Rules the House," *Congressional Quarterly Weekly* (March 2, 1996), pp. 523–529.

47. Jeffrey Katz, "Shalala: Governors' Proposals Give States Too Much Power," *Congressional Quarterly Weekly* (March 2, 1996), pp. 558–560.

48. For discussion of details of the legislation, see Jennifer Wolch and Heidi Sommer, *Los Angeles in an Era of Welfare Reform: Implications for Poor People and Community Well-Being* (Los Angeles: Inter-University Consortium on Homelessness and Poverty, 1997), pp. 1–7.

49. Paul Peterson, "Budget Deficits and the Race to the Bottom." In Sheila Kamerman and Alfred Kahn, eds., *Whither American Social Policy* (New York: Columbia University Press, 1996), pp. 43–63.

50. For an ethical critique of Clinton's decision to sign welfare reform, see Peter Edelman, "The Worst Thing Bill Clinton Has Done," *Atlantic Monthly* (March 1997), pp. 43–50.

51. For discussion of the 1997 reforms of Medicare and Medicaid, see *The 1997 Congressional Quarterly Almanac* (Washington, DC: Congressional Quarterly Service, 1998), pp. 2-41–2-56.

52. Lawrence Korb, "An Overstuffed Military," *Foreign Affairs,* 74 (November and December 1995), pp. 26–27.

53. For discussion of his educational reforms, see the *1997 Congressional Quarterly Almanac* (Washington, DC: Congressional Quarterly Service, 1998), pp. 9-14–9-18, 2-65–2-69.

54. For discussion of Social Security politics, see Richard Cohen and David Baumann, "No Done Deal on the Hill," *National Journal* (January 1, 1999), pp. 24–26.

55. See "Congress Seeking Way to Bail Out Medicare," *Congressional Quarterly Outlook* (May 1, 1999), pp. 25–26.

56. See *1998 Congressional Quarterly Almanac* (Washington, DC: Congressional Quarterly Service, 1999), pp. 14-10–14-12.

57. John O'Neill, "Managed Care Lawsuit Going Forward," *NASW News* (September 1999), pp. 1, 10.

58. For discussion of gun control politics, see the *Congressional Quarterly Weekly* (May 15, 1999), pp. 532–533.

59. John Broder, "Clinton Offers His Budget, and the Battle Begins," *The New York Times* (February 2, 1999), p. A16.

60. Data on discretionary spending is found in *U.S. Budget, FY 2000, Historical Tables,* Table 8.3 (Washington, DC: Government Printing Office, 1999).

61. B. R. Gottlieb, "Sounding Board: Abortion 1995," *New England Journal of Medicine* (February 23, 1995), p. 532.

62. Ibid., p. 533; Jan Hoffman, "The Morning-After Pill," *New York Times Magazine* (January 10, 1993), pp. 12–14, 30.

63. Barbara Gottlieb, "Abortion, 1995," *New England Journal of Medicine* (February 23, 1995), pp. 532–533.

64. For provisions of the family leave law, see *1993 Congressional Quarterly Almanac,* p. 390.

65. Richard Herrnstein and Charles Murray, *The Bell Curve: Intelligence and Class Structure in American Life* (New York: Free Press, 1994). For a critique of Murray's work, see the essay review by Leon Kamin, "Behind the Curve," *Scientific American* (February 1995), pp. 99–103.

66. Dinesh D'Souza, *The End of Racism* (New York: Free Press, 1995). For further explication of D'Souza's views, see the extended interview of D'Souza by Nicholas Lemann, "The End of Racism?" *American Heritage* (February/March 1996), pp. 93–105.

67. James Traub, "The Class of Prop. 209," *New York Times Magazine* (May 2, 1999), pp. 44–51, 76–79.

68. Ibid.

69. See Dan Carney, "GOP Casts a Kinder Eye on 'Huddled Masses,'" *Congressional Quarterly Weekly* (May 15, 1999), pp. 1127–1129.

70. Ibid.

71. Ibid.

72. For analysis of various states' child welfare programs, as well as the controversy about block-granting federal child welfare assistance, see Rochelle Stanfield, "Kids on the Block," *National Journal* (February 3, 1996), pp. 247–251; Robert Pear, "Many States Fail to Meet Mandates on Child Welfare," *The New York Times* (March 17, 1996), pp. 1, 14.

73. Robert Greenstein, Wendell Primus, and Michelle Bazie, *The Initial Impacts of Welfare Reform on the Economic Well-Being of Single-Mother Families with Children* (Washington, DC: Center on Budget and Policy Priorities, 1999), executive summary, p. 1.

74. Wolch and Sommer, *Los Angeles in an Era of Welfare Reform,* p. 5.

75. For an extended discussion of the issue, see *1993 Congressional Quarterly Almanac,* pp. 454–462.

12

Bush's Quest for Realignment

Everything was up for grabs as President Bill Clinton neared the end of his second term. The nation was polarized between the two major parties in the presidential elections of 1992 and 1996, with both parties hoping to achieve a solid majority by capturing moderate or swing voters. Many social policies hung in the balance, as well as what would happen to the huge budget surpluses that had finally replaced the large deficits of the 1980s and 1990s. Would the Democrats, who had finally won the presidency in 1992 after 12 years of Republican control, hold onto the presidency and perhaps gain control in one or more Houses of Congress? Or would Republicans regain the presidency and keep their control over the Congress? Would either party break the nation's deadlock by gaining a decisive advantage? What consequences would electoral outcomes have for vulnerable populations as well as other citizens?

At the end of this chapter, we discuss whether the terms *vulnerable populations* and *out-groups* still describe the 13 groups that we have examined while tracing the evolution of the American welfare state.

BUSH'S AMBITIOUS GOAL

The Democrats seemed to be in the ascendancy in the mid-1960s: Save for brief periods, they had controlled both houses of Congress since the New Deal as well as the presidency with the exception of Eisenhower's two terms. By the 1970s and 1980s, many Republican strategists hungered for "realignment" to achieve for the Republicans what Franklin Roosevelt had brought the Democrats: control of Congress and the Presidency, as well as the Supreme Court for three decades. Their hopes depended on getting Southern voters and many blue-collar voters to shift from the Democratic to the Republican Party. They made some progress in the 1970s under President Nixon and huge progress in the 1980s under President Reagan when they regained control of the presidency and controlled the Senate for six years. They regained control of the House, as well as the Senate, in the congressional elections of 1994. With the selection of Clarence

Thomas, William Rehnquist, and Anthony Scalia, moreover, Republicans obtained a conservative cadre in the Supreme Court that was able to obtain many conservative rulings by teaming with moderate jurists.

Many Republicans were not satisfied with their progress, however, as Bill Clinton neared the end of his two terms in 1999. Democrats had not only won the presidency in the Clinton years, but had fought Republicans to a standstill in the Congress while securing the appointment of a liberal jurist, Ruth Bader Ginsburg, to the Supreme Court.

Federal spending had continued to increase in the 1980s and 1990s; affirmative action was still in effect in many places; women still had the right to obtain abortions; many safety net programs (including Food Stamps, the Earned Income Tax Credit, and Medicaid) held their ground and were not devolved to the states; and huge federal entitlement programs like Social Security, Medicare, and Medicaid grew at a remarkable pace. Smaller than the welfare states of many other nations when measured as a percentage of GDP, the American welfare state had nonetheless grown substantially since the late 1960s.[1]

Karl Rove, a Republican political consultant in Texas, had dreamed of realignment from the 1970s onward. Working with other Republicans, he had helped transform Texas from a Democratic to a Republican state over a period of decades. Often working for George Walker Bush, Sr., as a political consultant, he had become well acquainted with the Bush family over a period of decades—and had viewed the eldest son, George W. Bush, as a likely candidate for the presidency as early as the 1970s. Even then, Rove fancied himself as filling the same role for Bush as Mark Hanna had for President William McKinley in 1896 when he not only helped him get elected, but ushered in a three-decade period of Republican control of national politics. Little did Rove realize in the 1970s that he would have this chance in the year 2000 when he became Bush's chief political consultant—a position he retained in succeeding years as well. A master of hardball politics that included tactics of questionable morality and the raising of huge

---

INSERT 12.1   Using the Web to Understand the Shaping of Policies during the Bush Presidency

---

Visit **academic.cengage.com/social_work/jansson** to view these links and a variety of study tools.

Go to **http://en.wikipedia.org/wiki/No_Child_ Left_Behind** Examine claims made in favor of the act and claims made in criticism of it. On balance, do you think it is meritorious or not?

Go to **http://cato.org/pubs/briefs/bp62.pdf** for a critical analysis of government funding of faith-based charities. Then find an analysis of such funding by doing a Web search on "faith-based charity." On balance, do you support or oppose this policy?

---

sums of money, Rove would inject his perspectives into Bush's presidential campaigns and the running of the White House.[2]

The younger Bush had grown up in a privileged home in West Texas, where his father had become an affluent oilman in Midland, Texas. In a frontier town and a state with few social programs and with a conservative ethos, Bush came to believe that voluntary organizations, church-related charities, and rugged individualism could solve or avert most social ills. Bush was socialized to conservatism from an early age. His father ran on the conservative ethos of Barry Goldwater in his race for the Senate in 1964, even opposing civil rights legislation and the enactment of Medicare. He avidly read Goldwater's book *Conscience of a Conservative* when his father gave it to him in high school.[3] If Bush was socialized to conservatism from an early age, he also learned from his father that conservative Republicans risked political defeat if they were too conservative. His father attributed Goldwater's landslide defeat in 1964, for example, to his hard-right views, contending that Republicans would be unsuccessful if they were not "responsible conservatives."[4]

Bush was convinced that the decade of the 1960s had corrupted American values. He believed it had ushered in the drug culture, far-left political ideology, a runaway welfare state, and secularism. He was shocked when William Sloan Coffin, a liberal chaplain at Yale University, told him that his father deserved a recent defeat in a political race against a liberal protagonist because "... your father lost to a better man."[5] Bush's views about the 1960s

were diametrically opposed to liberals' views. If Bush perceived the decade in negative terms, liberals viewed the protests, social movements, and policy reforms of the era as an overdue response to major social problems such as poverty and discrimination against African Americans. (Many of them also condemned some excesses of the decade, including tactics of the radical left Weathermen that included bombings and bank robberies.)

Bush followed in his father's footsteps when he went to an elite private school in New England, graduated from Yale, became a Navy pilot in the National Guard, and returned to Midland in 1977 to seek his fortune in oil drilling. Unlike his father, Bush was not highly successful. If his father had been a highly successful athlete, student, war hero, and oilman, Bush had little success on any of these fronts. He was an alcoholic during portions of the 1970s and early 1980s—only quitting "cold turkey" in 1986 when he realized it was holding him back.[6] (He had converted to Christian fundamentalism in 1985 under the influence of evangelist Billy Graham.)

Bush was influenced in the 1980s and 1990s by the writings of three intellectuals who had recently converted to conservatism from liberal views; Marvin Olasky, David Horowitz, and Myron Magnet. Olasky, who had converted from Judaism and liberal ideology to Christian fundamentalism, contended that the welfare reforms of the 1960s had blunted the work ethic of low-income Americans. Much like Reagan, he wanted to return the United States to the values and policies of the late 19th century, when churches and church-related organizations had dominated social welfare. He believed that volunteers, not social work professionals, should be the primary purveyors of assistance to needy persons, often using spiritual guidance as part of their interventions.[7] David Horowitz and Myron Magnet shared similar views, though they acknowledged more than Olasky that the work of nongovernmental agencies had to be supplemented with residual governmental programs when the private sector lacked sufficient resources to meet the needs of deserving citizens, as illustrated by programs to avert malnutrition.[8]

Often using poor grammar and uninterested in books, Bush was viewed by many observers as lacking the intellect to emulate his father's success. Bush was widely underestimated, however. Unlike his patrician father, he loved the rough-and-tumble of political races. He participated in his father's political campaigns of 1964, 1966, 1970, 1988, and 1992. He ran unsuccessfully for Congress in 1978. He helped a conservative win a Senate seat in 1972 in Florida. He was tutored in political tactics by Lee Atwater, a well-known Republican political consultant who often used unsavory tactics in his campaigns, when he worked with him in his father's presidential race in 1988. He had a gregarious personality that allowed him to communicate successfully with persons of all social classes.

Bush had all of the key attributes needed to be a successful candidate by the mid-1980s. He had become a savvy political tactician from his participation in many campaigns; indeed, Mary Matalin, a top Republican strategist, called him a fully formed "political campaign terrorist" who is "not as hamhanded as the typical (political) terrorist" but "more of a stiletto as opposed to an ax murderer."[9] He had access to large sums of money through his family's connections with corporate and affluent elites, as well as high name recognition stemming from his father's and grandfather's high-profile positions in the public sector. He was highly motivated to succeed in politics. Often compared disparagingly to his father, he wanted to prove his own merit. Having converted to fundamentalist Christianity, he believed God intended him to restore traditional values. Viewing liberal reforms and liberal eras, such

as the 1960s, negatively, he wanted to move the nation in conservative directions. With formidable political skills, he was confident that he could ultimately win higher office.

Bush was also an admirer of Ronald Reagan's ideas. He accepted Reagan's supply-side economic strategy of giving investors, corporations, and affluent persons large tax cuts in order to stimulate job-creating investments—a policy derisively called "trickle-down economics" by many liberals. He agreed with Reagan's strategy to deplete resources that might otherwise be used to fund government programs and liberal reforms by creating large government deficits. He agreed with Reagan's huge increases in military spending. Like Reagan, he was convinced that Republicans could become the major American political party, relegating Democrats to a minority status.

Bush lacked a key attribute of many successful political candidates, however: a track record of his own. His dabbling in oil exploration in Midland in the 1970s and 1980s had been relatively unsuccessful. He had avoided service in Vietnam by using his father's connections to get into the Air National Guard. He was defeated in his only run for political office. Partly to demonstrate that he could be a successful businessman, Bush became a part owner and executive officer of the Texas Rangers, a baseball team based in Dallas in 1989. He considered running for the governorship of Texas in 1990, but was dissuaded by his mother on the grounds that the race might be seen as a referendum on his father's performance as president.

With his father's defeat by Bill Clinton in 1992, Bush decided to seek the governorship of Texas as a stepping-stone to the presidency when polls indicated that Ann Richards, the incumbent liberal governor, was viewed as too liberal by many moderate and conservative Texas voters. With Rove as his primary consultant, Bush fashioned a clever campaign against Richards in 1994 that emphasized four issues: greater local control of schools, trying many juvenile offenders as adults, reducing welfare rolls, and limiting damage awards in liability suits. As was true in many campaigns where Rove was a political consultant, the Bush campaign used negative tactics, such as insinuating that Richards had close connections with homosexuals and lesbians and that she would confiscate guns in a state where most citizens opposed gun control.[10]

After defeating Richards, Bush became governor in a state where the governor had little power not only because the legislature met only every second year, but because other state officials, such as the lieutenant governor, had powers usually given to a governor. Bush revealed considerable tactical skills as governor. He demonstrated an ability to work with Democrats when necessary; for example, he persuaded Bob Bullock, a powerful Democrat in the Texas legislature, to cooperate with him so that he could achieve legislative successes in a legislature controlled by Democrats. He enacted legislation in his first term that included bills stiffening testing standards in education, trying many juveniles in adult courts, and strengthening the work requirement for welfare recipients.

Cautioned by his father not to run for the presidency until he had won a second term as governor, Bush won a landslide victory in 1998. Focusing on getting himself ready for a run for the White House in 2000, he persuaded the legislature to enact a large tax cut in his second term—just the kind of policy likely to coalesce conservatives around him in his run for the presidency.

Bush was now positioned to become the Republican front-runner in the presidential race in 2000 that would almost certainly pit him against Vice President Al Gore. He already appeared to be a Republican version of Bill Clinton. Just as Clinton appealed to Democratic liberals, Bush had strong support from Republican conservatives because of his Southern credentials, his strong support of tax cuts, and his Christian fundamentalism. If Clinton appealed to Democratic centrists, Bush had considerable support among Republican moderates and independents because of his brand of compassionate conservatism that included educational reforms. If Clinton filled a leadership vacuum in the Democratic Party in 1992 stemming from Democrats' inability to win the presidency since the late 1970s, Bush came to the fore in the wake of the demise of Newt Gingrich, the far-right

Republican who had been tactically bested by Clinton.

Bush sensed that his timing was correct. His promise to restore traditional values had great appeal in the wake of Clinton's scandals. Because of his close association with Clinton, Gore was harmed by these scandals, as well as the widespread perception that he was excessively aloof. Bush was highly motivated, as well. He wanted to avenge his father's defeat by Clinton in 1992. He wanted to restore traditional and religious values to the United States, downsize the federal government, rebuild the military, and transfer many programs from the federal government to the states. He wanted to achieve the realignment that Reagan had begun by ushering in a Republican era that might last for decades.

After decisively beating Senator John McCain in the Republican primaries partly by initiating rumors that McCain, a Vietnam war hero, was insensitive to veterans and possessed mental problems stemming from his long incarceration by the communists in North Vietnam, Bush faced off against Gore, who had easily defeated Senator Bill Bradley in the Democratic primaries, as well as Ralph Nader from the Green Party. (See Insert 12.2.)

THE PRESIDENTIAL CAMPAIGN OF 2000

Bush cemented support from conservatives by pledging a huge tax cut of $1.3 trillion spread over 10 years. Realizing that Democrats were vulnerable with respect to values, Bush portrayed himself as a family man who could unite the nation. When asked about his prior use of drugs and alcohol, he attributed them to "youthful indiscretion." He appealed to moderates by arguing he was a compassionate conservative who would support some increases in federal aid to education and a limited prescription drugs plan for Medicare recipients even as he promised to cut taxes substantially and to privatize Social Security by allowing workers to invest some of their payroll tax funds in the stock

---

INSERT 12.2 Ethical Analysis of Key Issues and Policies: When Should We Support Third-Party Candidates?

Ralph Nader, a longtime consumer advocate, had impeccable reformist credentials when he accepted the presidential nomination of the Green Party in 2000 to run against the nominees of the Republican and Democratic Parties. He took positions to the left of both "establishment candidates," championing living-wage legislation, cuts in military spending, efforts to end slave labor in developing nations, cuts in military spending, and expanded environmental programs.

Liberals faced a dilemma, however. If they voted for Nader in states that were closely contested by Gore and Bush, they risked inadvertently giving Bush a victory he would not otherwise have had. Indeed, we now know that Gore would almost certainly have been president had Nader not run, because Gore would have gotten Florida's electoral votes had he received only a fraction of Nader's 90,000 votes in Florida.

Should liberals vote for a third-party candidate even if their votes might tip an election toward a conservative candidate? Do third-party candidates, even when they lose, change the policies and programs of establishment parties? In this case, did Nader's presidential run in 2000 change policies of the Democratic Party? Did it matter that Bush became president rather than Gore—or was Nader correct in contending that Bush and Gore were indistinguishable?

---

market. He appealed to Christian fundamentalists by supporting school prayer, promising government assistance to faith-based organizations that helped addicts, welfare mothers, and ex-prisoners, and opposing partial-birth abortions. He promised to initiate a voucher program for the public schools that would allow some low-income persons to transfer to church-related or other private schools. He pledged to commit a substantial portion of the multi-trillion-dollar surplus that was projected for the next decade to the Social Security and Medicare Trust Funds, as well as reducing the federal debt.[11]

Through most of the campaign, Gore presented positions that were only modestly different from Bush's.[12] He supported greater increases in aid to education, a larger prescription drug program for Medicare recipients, and a much smaller tax cut of $250 billion. (He also favored Clinton's plan to use projected surpluses to reduce the national debt and to infuse new resources into the Social Security and Medicare Trust Funds.) Nor did the candidates differ much on foreign policy, with Bush promising to be less interventionist than Gore abroad and even promising smaller increases in military spending.

Bush was far ahead in the polls during August, but the polls narrowed by mid-September. It became clear by early October that the election would be a cliff-hanger that could be determined by three states: Florida, Pennsylvania, and Michigan. Gore was plagued by Nader, who campaigned as a militant progressive who wanted to cut military spending, establish national health insurance, and prioritize environmental reforms. Nader contended that little difference existed between Gore and Bush, both of whom he characterized as captive to corporate and monied interests.[13] Since most of Nader's voters would otherwise have voted Democratic, he threatened to give Bush the presidency if he took sufficient votes from Gore to give Bush even a single victory he would not otherwise have received.

No one anticipated the election drama that followed the November election. The mass media initially called the election for Gore only to declare Bush as the next president later in the evening. Then the media reversed itself by early morning as it became clear that Bush's edge in Florida was so close that a recount was inevitable. A seven-week drama unfolded that involved courts, public opinion, and tactical moves by both candidates. Democrats demanded recounts in areas where black voters contended that election officials had harassed them and where Jewish voters said they had mistakenly voted for both candidates, for Bush, or for the anti-Semitic Pat Buchanan, because of a confusing "butterfly" ballot. Democrats alleged that many votes had been improperly discarded by election officials due to "hanging chads" and "dimples" when voters failed to punch outdated manual ballots forcefully.[14]

When Democrats demanded recounts primarily in Miami and Dade County, Republicans argued that existing results should be honored. When automatic recounts whittled Bush's advantage to merely 327 votes in Florida, the Bush campaign tried to delay further vote recounts until mid-December when each state was required to certify its electors to the electoral college. They intimidated local election officials by staging demonstrations against them with staff sent from Washington, DC. To convey yet further the legitimacy of his "victory," Bush's campaign asked Katherine Harris, Florida's Secretary of State, to "certify" Bush's victory.

Bush had a strategic advantage during this period of uncertainty. Because he had been the last of the two candidates to be called the victor, because some media outlets had already called him the 43rd American president, and because he had a razor-thin majority, he could more easily act as if he *was* the victor even though Gore had won the nation's popular vote by a significant margin. (If he ultimately won in Florida, Bush would prevail in the electoral college even though he had lost the popular vote.) Bush had another advantage: His brother, Jeb, was Florida's governor and controlled the state's electoral apparatus and Republican legislature. Not only did Jeb get Florida's Secretary of State to certify his brother's "victory," but he frequently stated or implied that the legislature would select the electors if the voting process remained confused. (Each state had to choose its electors by mid-December.)

With Rove at his side, Bush repeatedly outmaneuvered Gore. As the ordeal proceeded, Bush repeatedly claimed that he was the rightful victor, even appointing a transition team and beginning to name some cabinet officials—unlike Gore, who never contended he was the victor because he led in the national popular vote.

Both sides appealed to the courts to vindicate their positions. When a local judge decided that recounts should stop, Democrats appealed to the Florida Supreme Court, which ordered a recount of votes in each of Florida's counties—or a far larger area than the Democrats had requested. Bush, in turn, asked the U.S. Supreme Court to overrule Florida's Supreme Court. When the U.S. Supreme Court invalidated the Florida Supreme Court's decision by a 5-4 vote, Gore's only hope was further litigation in Florida. When he chose not to take further action, Bush became the next president.

TWO AMERICAS

The nation was narrowly divided. Gore received 48.4 percent of the popular vote against 47.9 percent for Bush. Most remaining votes went to Ralph Nader, including 90,000 votes in Florida that would have given Gore an easy victory had most of these voters cast their votes for Gore rather than Nader. Many congressional races were narrowly contested. When the tight elections of 1996, 1998, and 2000 are viewed in tandem, the United States had not had such a narrowly divided electorate since the 1880s.[15]

Republicans and Democrats had markedly different constituencies. If 80 percent of the religious right voted for Bush, 61 percent of people with no religion voted for Gore. If Jews mostly voted for Gore, most white Protestants voted for Bush. (Catholics gave Bush a narrow margin.) If African Americans and Hispanics voted overwhelmingly for Gore, affluent white voters and blue-collar voters favored Bush. If most women voted for Gore, most men voted for Bush. If Republicans dominated rural areas across the nation, as well as recently established suburban areas, voters in the 23 largest metropolitan areas voted decisively for Gore. If Bush won most of the nonindustrial Midwestern and Western states, Gore won California, New York, Pennsylvania, New Jersey, and Michigan. If upper-middle-class and upper-class Americans mostly voted Republican, persons earning less than $12,000 voted overwhelmingly for Gore. (A majority of blue-collar voters chose Bush.)[16]

These "two Americas" differed markedly in their values and policy preferences. If Bush's followers tended to be religious, Gore's followers were more secular. In contrast to Gore's supporters, Bush's followers tended to be pro-life, against gun control, and opposed to many environmental regulations. Bush's rural and suburban voters often believed that liberal Democrats sought to impose big-city views on them. If Bush's supporters favored diminishing the size of the federal government, Gore's were more likely to view it favorably.[17]

The narrow margins between the presidential candidates existed, as well, between congressional candidates. The Senate was evenly split between the two parties, though the vice president could cast a tie-breaking vote if necessary. Republicans had a margin of only five votes in the House of Representatives.

So-called independent or swing voters occupied an uneasy niche between relatively conservative and liberal Americans. These voters, who would likely determine which candidate would be victorious in 2000, included "soccer moms"—suburban mothers who wanted expansion of social programs such as child care but favored fiscal conservatism. Political candidates of both parties conducted endless focus groups of these swing voters to gauge which issues were important to them since their votes could determine the outcome of the election in suburbs where a majority of American voters now resided.

BUSH'S DOMESTIC POLICIES

Even though Bush had received fewer votes than Gore, he acted as if he had a mandate to cut taxes substantially not just to appease conservatives but to deplete resources that Democrats would otherwise use during the coming decade to propose domestic reforms. He delighted conservatives by taking a page out of Reagan's book, now proposing a $1.7 trillion tax cut—or virtually all surplus funds that would be left over in the next 10 years once Congress had funded an array of farm subsidies,

tax cuts, and other programs to which it was already committed—and he also used $2 trillion in surpluses to buttress the Social Security and Medicare Trust Funds. If Bush argued that the tax cut would stimulate a lagging economy, many economists argued that it would have little stimulatory effect because most of its benefits went to affluent Americans who would not (like poorer Americans) immediately spend their new resources on consumer goods. Almost 40 percent of the tax cut's benefits went to the wealthiest 1 percent.

Conservatives were delighted by Bush's tax cut. It rewarded Republicans' corporate and affluent campaign contributors by slashing corporate income taxes and the taxes of affluent Americans—and pleased conservatives who wanted to downsize the federal government. Bush's tax cut was enacted, but Democrats and Republicans were able to decrease it to $1.35 trillion. Bush invested far more political resources in his tax cut than he did in other domestic measures in the first three years of his presidency; indeed, David Frum, Bush's former speechwriter and strong supporter, viewed the tax cut as Bush's greatest—and last—domestic achievement.[18]

Many Democrats argued in vain against the tax cut. It would, they feared, plunge the United States back into deficits if economists' 10-year projections about economic growth (and therefore tax revenues) were excessively optimistic. It would increase economic inequality yet further, exacerbating a trend that had begun in the 1970s. No new federal resources would be available for schools, social services, prescription drug benefits under Medicare, or programs to give health insurance to uninsured persons. To their chagrin, sufficient numbers of moderate and conservative Democrats supported the tax cut to allow it to be enacted.[19]

Determined not to let Democrats seize the initiative, Bush also initiated education, faith-based, and prescription drug proposals, as well as proposals to privatize Social Security and a budget for the coming year that sought deep cuts in many programs used by low-income Americans.

Bush's ability to secure enactment of his domestic agenda was severely harmed, however, when Senator Jim Jeffords (D., NH) announced he was leaving the Republican Party to become an independent in May 2001. Senator Jeffords, a moderate Republican, had mostly voted with Democrats on domestic issues, so his defection not only gave the Democrats a one-person majority in the Senate, but a valuable ally. His defection was even more ominous for Bush because other moderate Republican senators might also defect, such as Lincoln Chafee (R., R.I.) and Olympia Snow (R., Me.). These senators wanted greater funding of education and environmental reforms—and were less favorable than other Republicans to privatization of Social Security. When teamed with Democrats, they could block Bush's initiatives—or demand substantial changes in them. Democrats now had greater control of the Senate's agenda because, as the majority party in the Senate, they took over the chairing of the Senate's committees.

The federal government had given resources to public schools with high concentrations of low-income students since 1965, but critics contended that students' educational performance had not significantly improved. Why not, Bush asked, develop federal tests for students in these public schools so that students in schools that did not improve their scores could be given vouchers to attend other schools of their choosing, including parochial or other religious-based schools? Critics from the liberal and moderate wings of both parties criticized his proposal. How can education improve, they asked, if the federal government doesn't increase its spending on education to allow the reduction of student-to-teacher ratios when many inner-city schools had classes with as many as 40 students in them—or when they had dilapidated schools? Would the use of standardized tests to measure the performance of schools merely lead teachers to "teach to the tests" rather than striving to enhance critical thinking? Minus funds to educate new teachers and incentives to entice them to teach in middle-income schools, would not inner-city schools suffer from lower-quality teachers than suburban areas? Did not schools need funds for social and public health programs to help truants and troubled children and to avert sexually transmitted

diseases? After substantial pressure from Republican moderates, Bush, to his credit, increased the funds devoted to education by several billion dollars.[20]

Many persons criticized Bush's school voucher proposal. Would vouchers that paid parents only $1,500 be sufficient to entice private schools to accept low-income students—and would these funds merely reduce funds available for public schools by taking money away from current budgets of public schools? Would affluent parents who were already sending their children to private schools get a kind of rebate on their private school tuition by using publicly funded vouchers themselves? Many critics feared that vouchers violated the Constitution's separation of church and state, since they would provide public funds to religious schools. In parochial schools, the largest system of church-sponsored schools in the United States, all students are required to attend religious instruction and to view religious symbols, such as crucifixes, that are prominently displayed. Critics wondered, as well, if private schools could be held accountable to the same standards that Bush proposed for public schools: Would they agree to test their students using the same instruments as public schools?[21]

Critics had similar fears about Bush's proposal to fund social services offered by churches and religious organizations, which he called "faith-based programs." The federal government, as well as state and local governments, had long funded social services sponsored by religious organizations provided they created separate and secular not-for-profit organizations that stripped religious content and symbols from their services and facilities. Indeed, Catholic, Lutheran, Baptist, and Jewish charitable organizations had provided outstanding services to citizens for decades that were heavily subsidized by public authorities. Even with these stipulations, however, some critics wondered if sufficient data were available to determine whether Catholic Charities—the largest private provider of social welfare services in the United States—had truly insulated its agencies from Catholic doctrine, such as with respect to clients who want abortions—a procedure that is forbidden by the Catholic faith—or homosexuals, whose preferences and lifestyles are opposed by Catholic doctrine.[22] Bush proposed, by contrast, that public funds could go to religious organizations even if they did not attempt to create social welfare agencies that were distinct from themselves.[23]

Critics wondered what standards would be used to assess the effectiveness of publicly funded faith-based programs. Might not religious organizations use some of their funds to pay a portion of the clergies' salaries? Would some use funds for faith healing even when persons needed traditional medical services? Would public funds be commingled with other church revenues, making it difficult to discern whether they were used for social services or for religious purposes? Could faith-based programs compromise clients' self-determination if clients were proselytized in the course of treatment, particularly if other secular services did not exist in the area or had long waiting lists? Would untrained persons in church-based charities harm some persons with serious mental and health conditions because they lacked sufficient knowledge about treating them? Do direct public subsidies of churches violate the separation of church and state enshrined in the Constitution? Should the federal government support organizations with hiring practices that discriminate against people on the basis of their religion or, in the case of agnostics and atheists, their nonreligion?[24] Critics also feared that Bush wished to use grants to faith-based groups to cement and increase support for Republicans among fundamentalist religious groups.

Bush found none of these criticisms to be convincing. Do not many persons with social problems benefit, he asked, from spiritual guidance and, in some cases, conversion? (His own recovery from alcoholism had been linked to his conversion to Christian fundamentalism.) Do not religious beliefs provide persons with the strength to surmount problems like substance abuse, mental illness, and marital conflict? Don't church-sponsored charities need public resources to allow them to reach many needy persons?

Bush created a White House Office of Faith-Based and Community Initiatives in 2001—and supported legislation in the House of Representatives to allow federal funding of these programs.

With opponents threatening lawsuits to test the constitutionality of faith-based programs and with even some fundamentalist Christians opposing them, the legislation stalled in Congress and was never enacted during his presidency. Undeterred, Bush made grants to faith-based groups subsequently in his administration by using the executive power of the presidency. (It was widely anticipated in 2008 that litigation testing the constitutionality of these grants would soon reach the Supreme Court.)

Leaders of both political parties realized that their political fortunes depended on support from senior citizens—a rapidly growing group as baby boomers (persons born between 1946 and 1964) neared retirement. Many seniors were angry that Medicare failed to fund enrollees' prescription drugs even though many seniors required expensive drugs to maintain their health. This omission became even more harmful to seniors in ensuing decades due to the development of numerous effective—and expensive—medications for chronic diseases that often cost seniors more than $2,500 annually. (Those seniors who relied on Social Security checks for survival, most of whom received less than $12,000 annually, could not afford supplemental private insurance to cover some of their drug expenses.)

Proposals advanced by Republicans and Democrats differed significantly. Democrats wanted Medicare to administer the prescription drug benefit because they believed volume purchases and price regulation would cut the cost of the medications. Republicans wanted to rely on market competition by letting private companies administer the drug benefit because they believed market competition between competing plans would drive prices downward. Democrats wanted to cover a larger portion of the cost of medications, amounting to $800 billion or more over 10 years, but Republicans proposed lower coverage costing $400 billion. Locked in ideological conflict and with different versions, no version made it through the deadlocked Congress in 2001 or 2002.[25]

The two parties locked horns, as well, over Social Security. Many Republicans favored a partial privatizing of Social Security that would allow workers to start "individual investment accounts" (IAAs) with a portion of their payroll taxes. These workers would invest their funds in the stock market rather than contributing them to Social Security's Trust Fund. The conservatives' logic seemed compelling because the stock market had historically yielded higher returns than the government bonds, where surplus funds in the Trust Fund have been invested. It appealed, as well, to Americans' individualism by allowing persons to maintain personal accounts rather than commingling all of their payroll taxes in the Trust Fund for the benefit of current retirees.[26]

Many Democrats feared, however, that some workers' investments could turn sour. Did not stocks often decline during economic downturns, such as during the huge stock market decline during the first two years of the Bush administration? Would some workers select risky investments and later require welfare payments to survive during their retirement years? Would the Republicans' proposal enrich Wall Street firms who would handle workers' investments? Would privatization further imperil the long-term solvency of the Trust Fund by diverting some payroll taxes from it to IAAs, particularly since the monies to fund them would have to come from the Trust Fund since Bush had proposed few additional sources of public funding?

In the case of vouchers for public schools, privatization of Social Security, and use of private insurance companies to administer Medicare's drug benefit, the Bush administration possessed a kind of private market fundamentalism.[27] They assumed that private markets work more efficiently than government programs and give consumers more choices. Critics of this view charged that Bush did not realize that private markets are often inefficient, as is illustrated by companies that go bankrupt, excessive salaries paid to top executives, resources wasted on marketing and advertising, and even fraud as was illustrated in the case of corporate scandals during the Bush administration. Government programs have their problems, these critics admitted, but why view private markets as a panacea?

The two parties differed, as well, with regard to the future of welfare reform that had been initiated when Clinton signed the Personal Responsibility and Work Opportunity Reconciliation Act in 1996 that provided welfare grants known as Temporary Assistance for Needy Families (TANF). The legislation required that welfare reform be reauthorized in 2002 when Congress would decide whether to change it or keep it relatively intact. While states were given the power to shape their welfare programs, they were also bound by numerous federal regulations such as a five-year limits for most welfare recipients and penalties if they failed to reduce welfare rolls.

If the success of welfare reform is measured by the reduction in rolls, it was a resounding success. To everyone's surprise, runaway economic growth in welfare reform's aftermath, as well as unanticipated growth in relatively unskilled jobs in clerical, sales, health care, and other areas, occurred in the wake of welfare reform. This economic growth, when coupled with a shift in the culture of local welfare offices that emphasized work, led to a roughly 50 percent reduction in welfare rolls by 2002. Critics conceded that many women benefited from working rather than remaining on welfare—and that some women found jobs that paid wages sufficient to elevate them above poverty levels.[28]

Yet welfare reform also led to problems. Most women who left welfare became mired in low-wage jobs with few or no fringe benefits such as health insurance. These women remained impoverished. Because welfare reform ceded many policy decisions to the states, moreover, former recipients fared poorly in states with relatively punitive policies. In contrast to more generous states, some of them found their child care and Medicaid benefits to be terminated soon after they left the rolls, leaving them sometimes poorer than when they had received welfare.

Focusing on reducing the rolls, many welfare offices provided recipients with scant assistance in upgrading their employment after they received their initial jobs. Welfare workers often viewed themselves exclusively as enforcers of work not only for existing recipients but for persons applying for welfare. They were not encouraged by supervisors to give recipients assistance in finding training programs, attending college, upgrading their work from dead-end to higher-level jobs, or finding a career.[29] Many recipients discovered that states did not count study in community colleges as "work," so they could not upgrade their skills while receiving welfare. Not surprisingly, then, many recipients got dead-end jobs initially—and did not advance beyond them as time progressed.

When welfare reform was enacted, few persons asked how recipients' children would fare as their mothers entered the workforce. A mixed picture emerged. Some research suggests that children of working mothers are not harmed. Other researchers find evidence that children who are placed in day care from an early age are more aggressive than other children—and a small but significant number become very aggressive. Still other experts believe that the quality of children's child care is pivotal: If children are put in centers, for example, with a high ratio of children to staff, they are more likely to be harmed than children in quality programs.[30] In fact, we still do not know definitively how children have fared in this huge welfare reform experiment. Some critics of welfare reform believed that its heavy emphasis on work put into doubt the legitimacy of the choice by some women to prioritize caring for young children rather than seeking full-time employment.

Critics of welfare reform cite, as well, the paucity of social services for those recipients who remained on the rolls. Considerable data suggest that women who left the rolls earliest had fewer mental and substance abuse problems than women who remained on the rolls. Many long-term users of welfare suffer from clinical depression, and many are alcoholic or chronic users of drugs. Yet few states funded sufficient services for recipients to enable them to enter the economic mainstream.[31]

Different approaches emerged for reforming TANF when it was scheduled to be reauthorized in 2002. If conservatives wanted to cut back federal funding for social services and exempt even fewer women from the five-year limits, liberals wanted to maintain or increase the federal funding while exempting more women from these limits. Some liberals also wanted to provide resources to allow states to place more emphasis on upgrading recipients' job skills or in helping them obtain high school diplomas or college degrees. The National Association of Social Workers wanted to upgrade and stabilize the workforce employed by welfare agencies since few line or supervising workers even possessed bachelor's degrees in the social sciences, much less in social work. Nor did they often possess skills to work with former recipients as they coped with low wages and child care issues, as well as helping them gain access to safety net programs such as Medicaid and Food Stamps. (Many former recipients failed to receive benefits from these programs even when they were eligible for them.) Due to partisan bickering, reauthorization of TANF by Congress did not occur until spring, when relatively few changes were made in the legislation.

SEPTEMBER 11, 2001

Bush's popularity sagged in the polls by midsummer 2001—and it began to appear that Bush, like his father, would be a one-term president. Democrats had realistic prospects of increasing their one-vote majority in the Senate and possibly regaining control of the House in congressional elections in November 2002 as voters became more concerned about the declining economy.

Everything changed when two hijacked commercial jet planes slammed into, and toppled, the Twin Towers of the World Trade Center in New York City on the morning of September 11, 2001; another crashed into the Pentagon, and yet another crashed in a Pennsylvania field after passengers thwarted hijackers who wanted to hit either the White House or the Capitol Building. The nation was stunned by the magnitude of casualties as well as the graphic images of the disaster portrayed on the mass media.

The nation learned within days that the culprit was a terrorist organization based in Afghanistan, known as Al-Qaeda, that was led by Osama bin

FIGURE 12.1   The World Trade Center under attack on September 11, 2001.

Laden. American intelligence services had known about Al-Qaeda for years. They knew it had orchestrated a prior bombing of the Twin Towers, an American destroyer at anchor in the Middle East, and American embassies in Kenya and Tanzania. Indeed, a diligent FBI agent who ironically was killed in the Twin Towers on September 11 had predicted an Al-Qaeda assault on the Twin Towers but had not been able to get the attention of higher American officials.[32]

Bin Laden glorified ancient Muslim religious traditions and the theocracy that existed during and after the life of Mohammed in the 6th and 7th centuries AD, where church leaders dictated the policies and moral rules of a paternalistic society. He believed that the spread of Western capitalism, secular culture, sexual mores, and feminism into the Middle East had undermined these traditional values and theocracies and led to the rise of leaders who were controlled by Western nations, were not observant Muslims, and who tolerated the infusion of Western customs into their nations. He was particularly angered by the ongoing presence of American troops in Saudi Arabia after America's war with Iraq in 1991. Convinced that diplomatic and peaceful remedies were not possible, bin Laden plotted guerilla warfare against Arab leaders and industrialized nations.[33]

Evicted from several Middle Eastern nations because he plotted against their leaders, bin Laden withdrew to Afghanistan, where a dictatorial Muslim theocracy known as the Taliban gave him sanctuary. From this remote bastion, bin Laden recruited and trained a large force of terrorists who were schooled in bombing, assassinations, and attacks on infrastructure. Bin Laden developed an unknown number of "sleeper cells" in Western nations composed of terrorists who would follow his instructions. One group of Al-Qaeda terrorists moved to Germany, where they enrolled in technical programs. Some of them relocated to the United States around 2000. Led by those who received pilot training in American schools, these terrorists orchestrated the terrorist attacks of September 11.[34]

Bush declared a war on global terrorism in the immediate aftermath of September 11. He said that this war would be the focus of his administration. He persuaded Congress to enact a war resolution that gave him the authority to use military force not only to defeat the Taliban, but to attack terrorist forces anywhere in the world as well as nations that harbored them. He issued an ultimatum to the Taliban to turn over bin Laden or face invasion. He assembled a broad coalition of nations to participate in possible military action at a time when world opinion was overwhelmingly supportive of the United States. When they refused, he ordered a massive bombing campaign in Afghanistan that was quickly followed by the introduction of ground troops. In liaison with forces of some other nations, the United States quickly defeated the Taliban and installed a new regime, but the elusive bin Laden apparently escaped—possibly due to miscues by American military leaders who failed to seal the border between Afghanistan and Pakistan.

GRIDLOCK

With bin Laden on the run, it seemed in the late spring of 2002 that the nation was returning to normalcy, although many citizens feared a renewal of terrorism on the home front. Their fears were intensified when an unknown person or group sent anthrax-dusted letters to several political leaders— causing the temporary shutdown of a Senate office building, the closure of some post office facilities, and several deaths. Many persons wondered if terrorists would use biological, chemical, and radiological weapons of mass destruction in coming years by gaining entry through poorly guarded ports and borders.

The nation took many domestic measures to diminish the risk of further terrorist attacks. Security precautions were increased at the nation's airports. The Congress enacted the Patriot Act in October 2001, which gave law enforcement agencies expanded powers of surveillance over communications within and outside the United States, gave the government significant power to fight the financing of terror through money-laundering operations, and gave the attorney general broad power to detain individuals suspected of terrorist connections. While Bush urged citizens not to discriminate against Muslims in the United States and said that hate crimes would not be tolerated, many persons feared that the Justice Department deprived many Muslims of their rights by incarcerating them without formal charges and denying them access to legal counsel. When they learned that many persons of Middle Eastern descent were placed in prisons or other facilities for extended periods, with no charges levied against them and without even being allowed to consult an attorney, critics of the Patriot Act contended that it gave the government excessive authority. Immigration procedures were tightened, particularly against persons of Middle Eastern backgrounds.

Realizing that the nation needed to coordinate the work of the FBI, the Immigration and Naturalization Service, the Federal Emergency Management Agency, and other programs to provide an effective defense against domestic terrorism, Democrats proposed the creation of a Homeland Security Agency, only to meet concerted opposition from Republicans who called the proposal a liberal big-government scheme.

Bush's education proposal, called No Child Left Behind, was finally enacted in January 2002 when Senator Ted Kennedy, deciding that half a loaf was better than none, rallied many Democrats to support the legislation. The revised bill increased federal subsidies to schools by about $11 billion but did not establish vouchers. It required states to develop or use existing standardized tests to measure the proficiency of students in reading and math—and then to monitor schools to see if their students' scores improved. If they did *not* improve, states had to put the schools on notice and eventually close them if students' test scores continued to show no improvement. Critics feared that the legislation would lead teachers to "teach to tests" rather than enhancing students' critical thinking skills and that failing schools would not receive sufficient technical and financial assistance to improve their programs. The noted, as well, that charter schools (private schools established with significant assistance from local public school districts under legislation enacted during the Clinton administration} were *not* covered by the No Child Left Behind legislation and often were not monitored by local or state public school authorities, giving them leeway *not* given to public schools. (Congressional supporters of education were disappointed to learn in the 2003 and 2004 budgets that Bush had requested many billions of dollars less than had been authorized by Congress in 2002.) Faith-based, prescription drug, and Social Security legislation stalled in Congress

The economy continued to deteriorate in 2002 as it became clear that the nation was mired in an economic downturn in the continuing aftermath of the "dot com bubble" of the middle and late 1990s—a bubble partly created by investment bankers who gave inflated accounts of the prospects of firms from which they received business in order to boost their stock prices artificially. Trillions of dollars of assets were lost as the stock market collapsed. For the first time since the Great Depression, some economists feared the specter of deflation as corporations cut prices of their products to sell them in the face of declining demand.

The stock market's collapse and the declining economic activity posed a growing fiscal challenge to many states, who found their revenues rapidly declining. If state governments had primarily focused on education, law enforcement, prisons, mental hospitals, and highways in the 1970s, they now carried a much larger burden in the wake of the devolution of many federal programs to them, such as the block grants established by the Reagan administration. Confronted with declining revenues as well as mounting counterterrorism expenses, many states slashed spending on social and educational programs.[35] (Unlike the federal government, which can issue treasury bonds to fund operating deficits, most state governments are required to run balanced budgets and solve budget shortfalls by cutting spending or raising taxes.) The pleas of some liberals to revive revenue sharing, where the federal government contributes some of its tax revenues to states—a policy that had been terminated by President Reagan—found little support from the Bush administration.

President Bush was embarrassed, as well, by corporate scandals. Corporations such as Enron, WorldCom, and Global Crossing had used fraudulent accounting to overstate their profits in a bid to keep their stock prices high in the late 1990s. When the companies entered bankruptcy proceedings, the extent of the fraud became clear. As Bush staunched criticism by changing the SEC's leadership and approving accounting reforms, many persons wondered if the corporate scandals of 2001 and 2002 were merely the tip of the iceberg. They also wondered if legislation enacted by Congress, which placed more responsibility on corporate directors and established stiff penalties for accounting irregularities, would bring genuine reforms.

A positive outcome of the corporate scandals was the enactment of campaign finance legislation. Both parties had received tens of millions of dollars of corporate contributions, as well as contributions from affluent individuals. While some of these funds went directly to candidates where prior legislation had established some upper limits, unregulated "soft money" went to the political parties themselves. In so-called issue ads, such as ones that opposed gun control, the parties could indirectly promote Republican or Democratic candidates without mentioning their names. Democrats received much of their funds from unions, and Republicans got vast amounts of corporate support.

With both parties fearing that campaign finance reforms would curtail their resources, legislation went nowhere for years. With the sponsorship of Senators Russ Feingold (D.,Wisc.) and John McCain (R., Ariz.), the campaign finance reforms finally got traction when Republicans, in the wake of the corporate scandals, realized they could not put it off any longer.[36] It remained to be seen if the reforms would make lasting changes. The reforms outlawed soft money but doubled the limit on contributions from individuals to candidates, capping them at $2,000. Both parties, but particularly the Republicans, solicited a growing army of affluent persons to give their parties the upper limit. By mid-2003, Bush operatives boasted that they would raise $100 million for Bush by 2004—doubling the record amount he had raised in 2000. While experts debated the precise effects of campaign contributions on politicians, there can be no doubt that money gave access to powerful interests as compared with advocacy groups representing poor people.

BUSH SHIFTS THE AGENDA ABROAD

In the middle of 2002, as in the summer of 2001, the Democrats' political fortunes seemed bright. With Bush's popularity declining amid a struggling economy and Congressional gridlock—and with fears about terrorism abating after the defeat of the Taliban—they hoped they would increase their majority in the Senate and acquire a majority in the House in the congressional elections of 2002. (The parties of the incumbent president usually lose seats in midterm elections.) If the events of September 11 had shattered their hopes in 2001, President Bush was their nemesis in 2002 when he abruptly shifted the agenda from domestic matters to terrorism and war. He suddenly proposed war with Iraq unless that nation immediately disclosed the whereabouts of biological, radiological,

and nuclear weapons of mass destruction that UN inspectors had discovered in the 1990s before being evicted from the country. (Inspectors had been allowed to enter Iraq as part of the surrender terms imposed on Iraq by the UN after the end of the war with the coalition forces led by the United States in the early 1990s.)

No apparent information or events caused Bush to focus on Iraq in August of 2002. Iraq had used weapons of mass destruction in the past, both against Iranians in the 1980s and against the Kurdish Iraqis in the wake of Desert Storm. UN inspectors had discovered some weapons of mass destruction, as well as plants to make them, in the 1990s but most experts believed they had been successful in finding them even though Saddam Hussein ousted them from his nation in the late 1990s. Iraq remained a weakened nation due to severe trade sanctions imposed by the UN after Desert Storm —sanctions so severe that many children starved because Iraq lacked sufficient food. The United States and Britain were allowed by the UN to conduct aerial surveillance of considerable portions of Iraq's territory so it could not resume the killing of Kurds and other tribal groups. Iraq could not export oil, its major asset, except to secure funds for food, drugs, and other survival needs. Iraq's economy was considerably smaller than Idaho's in 2000. Nor had any evidence surfaced that Hussein was linked to Al-Qaeda or had any role in the terrorist events of September 11. (Indeed, bin Laden had disliked Hussein and urged his overthrow because he viewed Hussein as a secular rather than a Muslim leader.) In short, Iraq did not appear to be an imminent threat to the United States in August of 2002.

Two journalists, who wrote a definitive account of the relationship between Karl Rove and Bush, conjecture that Bush brought up Iraq for political reasons.[37] With the congressional elections of 2002 looming and with Republicans' prospects declining, he wanted to rally the nation around himself and his party by creating a threat to the United States even when none existed. Bush wanted, as well, to punish Hussein for commissioning thugs to assassinate his father in the early 1990s even though they did not succeed. He wanted to finish the job his father had started in Desert Storm: not just to keep Hussein from invading other nations but to remove him from office.

Whatever his reasons, Bush now heeded those advisors who had wanted the United States to invade Iraq long before Bush was elected president, including then-Chairman of the Defense Policy Board Richard Perle, Deputy Secretary of Defense Paul Wolfowitz, and Vice President Dick Cheney. These men had urged Bill Clinton to launch an invasion on the grounds that Hussein represented an imminent threat to the United States They had urged Bush to invade Iraq immediately after September 11th even though no links between Hussein and Al-Qaeda had been established instead of or along with Afghanistan.[38] They pressured Bush to invade Iraq after the defeat of the Taliban.

Not only did Bush issue an ultimatum to Hussein, but he shifted American foreign policy to allow "preemptive strikes" when the United States suspected another nation was funding or preparing terrorist strikes against it or was preparing terrorists or giving them weapons of mass destruction. He argued that the United States could suffer catastrophic damage if it waited until terrorist acts had actually occurred. The new policy, issued by the White House in September 2002, said:

> While the United States will constantly strive to enlist the support of the international community, we will not hesitate to act alone, if necessary, to exercise our right of self defense by acting preemptively against such terrorists …

Critics wondered if the doctrine of preemptive strikes, which had never been propounded by an American president, might threaten the international order. Might not other nations, too, contend they could also initiate action against any nation they *suspected* might harm them rather than waiting for the other nation to take aggressive action, as had been the custom in the past? Koffi Annan, Secretary General of the UN, feared even after the Iraq War was over that the concept of preemptive strikes

threatened international order. Other critics feared that the United States policy would encourage some smaller nations, such as North Korea, to develop weapons of mass destruction to forestall American attacks.

Secretary of State Colin Powell convinced Bush not to act precipitously or unilaterally for fear that other nations, and particularly Middle Eastern nations, would view the United States as the aggressor. Reluctantly agreeing with Powell, Bush persuaded the Security Council to issue an ultimatum to Hussein: Allow UN inspectors to renew their inspections, disclose to the UN what had happened to weapons of mass destruction that Iraq had possessed, and show the inspectors any current weapons or plants to manufacture them. Hussein readmitted the inspectors, who could locate no weapons of mass destruction in months of exhaustive searches of Iraq. But Hussein was vague with respect to whether and how he had destroyed weapons of mass destruction that the UN had located in the 1990s.

Even before Bush changed his foreign policy, he had swung from opposition to support of the establishment of a Homeland Security Agency when he issued his version of it in June 2002. He insisted, however, that its workforce not be allowed to unionize—a policy that led many Democrats to oppose its establishment until this proviso was removed from the legislation.

Bush had decisively shifted the agenda from the economy and domestic issues to Iraq. He barnstormed the United States in the months preceding the November election, pledging to remove Hussein's weapons of mass destruction if Hussein did not remove them. He implied that Democrats were soft on terrorism because they held up the enactment of the Homeland Security Agency. Bush's and Republicans' ratings in the polls moved upward, especially among women, some elderly persons, and some blue-collar persons—the swing voters that could tip the balance between the two parties.

Bush's shift in the national agenda from domestic issues and the economy to Iraq and the establishment of the Homeland Security Agency paid huge political dividends in the 2002 congressional elections. If Democrats had even hoped to control both Houses of Congress, Republicans took back control of the Senate and widened their majority in the House. Bush was in a commanding position to launch his bid for reelection in 2004.

THE WAR WITH IRAQ

After the election, the United States moved rapidly toward an invasion of Iraq. Bush asked Congress for a resolution to give him the power to initiate hostilities with Iraq if it failed to disclose sufficient information about weapons of mass destruction. Even though UN inspectors could not find weapons of mass destruction, Bush insisted that Hussein's refusal to make a full accounting of his weapons meant that he possessed them. He alleged in his State of the Union address in January 2003 that British intelligence had discovered that Iraq had sought to obtain uranium from Niger, an African nation. Both he and Powell contended links existed between Hussein and Al-Qaeda, but neither of them produced definitive proof.

Deciding to bypass the UN's Security Council after the French, Germans, and Russians refused to support a UN resolution to sanction an American-led invasion, Bush took matters into his own hands by issuing an ultimatum to Hussein to give a full accounting of biological, radiological, and chemical materials or face an invasion.

Criticism of Bush's decisions escalated not only in the United States, but around the world. Large anti-war demonstrations took place at home and abroad. Critics contended that the Bush administration had not revealed convincing evidence that Hussein possessed weapons of mass destruction. Why not, they asked, give the UN inspectors more time to find the weapons of mass destruction? Would not a war with Iraq drain resources from America's domestic programs? Could it enmesh the United States in a lengthy and dangerous occupation of Iraq? Was it wise for the United States to proceed unilaterally (only Britain among large in-

dustrial nations agreed to cooperate with the United States) rather than, as in Desert Storm, with an international coalition?

Pivotal testimony by Colin Powell before the United Nations alleged that an African nation was exporting to Iraq materials needed to process uranium. It was revealed in subsequent years that this intelligence was false and that the administration had ignored warnings about the unreliable source of this information. Moreover, it was also revealed in 2007 that top intelligence officers had warned the United States that an American invasion of Iraq could assist Al-Qaeda in recruiting thousands of additional terrorists because American occupation of any Arab nation could be portrayed by them as offensive to Arab culture and imperialistic. Yet other intelligence experts warned the administration that the toppling of Hussein could instigate a civil war in Iraq between Sunni, Shiite, and Kurdish tribal factions. Were these warnings to come true—and many critics of the invasion believed by 2007 that they had come to pass—the American invasion might worsen the situation in Iraq and the Middle East as well as cause large numbers of deaths of American troops and Iraqi citizens.

The United States commenced a bombing campaign against Iraq in the spring of 2003 that was soon followed by a full-scale invasion. To their surprise, the Americans met little resistance as they moved across Iraq toward Baghdad—nor were weapons of mass destruction used against them or discovered. Bush declared a victory on May 1 on a navy carrier off the coast of Southern California.

The occupation of Iraq proved far more difficult than the Pentagon had foreseen. (The United States insisted that it take the primary role in reconstructing Iraq rather than ceding this function to the UN.) Looters pillaged power stations, water stations, government facilities, hospitals, museums, schools, and universities. Persons settled old scores by killing unknown numbers of Iraqis. Persons and groups disliking the American occupation launched guerrilla warfare that took a weekly toll on American forces in the summer of 2003, leading some critics to wonder if the United States was headed toward a Vietnam-style quagmire. Different factions within Iraq quarreled with one another as the United States found it difficult to establish a new regime. Iraq had been ruled by dictatorial and monarchical forms of government for centuries, and it remained to be seen if democratic regimes could emerge or if American troops and those of other nations would have to continue the occupation for an extended period. The nation required huge expenditures on infrastructure and social programs—and some experts believed the United States would have to keep about 150,000 troops in Iraq indefinitely at a cost of roughly $4 billion per month. It was unclear in the spring of 2004 when and how the United States would establish a new Iraqi government. Critics contended that United States officials had greatly underestimated the unrest that would occur in Iraq, as well as the number of troops needed to maintain order.

Controversy about the war did not abate even after the American invasion of Iraq had been completed and an occupation had begun. Critics had contended as early as 2003 that Bush and Powell had made pre-war allegations about Iraq's possession of weapons of mass destruction that were not accurate. Angry that the United States had proceeded without UN concurrence, most European nations refused to participate in the reconstruction of Iraq unless the UN was given a leading role—and only Great Britain contributed substantial troops—even though Bush frequently boasted that the United States had enlisted a broad coalition of nations to occupy Iraq. (By 2008, even most British troops had been withdrawn from Iraq.)

AMERICAN SOCIAL WELFARE
POLICY ABROAD

The wars in Afghanistan and Iraq raise broader issues about America's role in developing nations. Can a wealthy nation, with a reluctant welfare state at home, respond constructively to poverty and disease outside of its borders?

Critics wondered if the United States would commit itself to the long-term reconstruction of Afghanistan and Iraq in the wake of hostilities. They charged that the United States as well as other industrialized nations had reneged on resources that they had pledged for Afghanistan's reconstruction. Would it commit the forces and resources to these nations for years to come? Or would the United States quickly abandon these nations—or merely install puppet regimes?

Critics also wondered if the United States would address some of the basic discontent in the Arab world that allowed bin Laden and other terrorist leaders to recruit large numbers of young Muslims to their organizations in the first place. Many Arabs believed, for example, that Americans had favored Israel over the Palestinians since the establishment of the state of Israel in the late 1940s. They pointed to American involvement in the overthrow of a popular leader in Iran in the 1950s and his replacement with a leader beholden to the United States. Partly because of widespread negative perceptions of the United States in the Middle East, critics of the American invasion of Iraq wondered if it might actually provide a recruiting tool for Al-Qaeda, who could enlist Arab youth by pointing to the ongoing presence of American troops in Iraq.

Nor had the United States been generous to developing nations, allocating far less of its federal budget to foreign aid than many other industrialized nations. (The United States gives only 0.10 percent of its GDP to developing nations, while Denmark gives 1.06 percent, Britain gives 0.32 percent, and Japan gives 0.28 percent.)[39] World poverty is staggering in its dimensions: If 1.2 billion people (or 23 percent of the global population) around the world live on less than a dollar a day, 2.8 billion survive on less than $2 a day.[40] In the absence of strong public health institutions, diseases like malaria, typhoid fever, and AIDS devastated the health of citizens in developing nations. Nor could these nations afford expensive medications and diagnostic equipment widely used in industrial nations. (See Insert 12.3.)

The UN established goals in its Millennium Declaration of 2000 to halve poverty and hunger rates by 2015 and to reduce child mortality by two-thirds. Data indicate, however, that 54 nations have become poorer since 1990, hunger has increased in

INSERT 12.3   Ethical Analysis of Key Issues and Policies: Should We Be Concerned about Low Levels of American Foreign Aid?

International issues are not typically placed under the rubric of social welfare policy in the United States. To what extent do affluent industrial nations like the United States have an ethical obligation to provide resources to address poverty and disease in developing nations? What first-order ethical principles are at stake? What consequences could the United States encounter if it (and other industrialized nations) gave virtually no resources to developing nations?

21 nations, and child mortality has risen in 14 nations. Furthermore, the UN's Human Development Index, which includes economic, health, and education measures, fell in 21 nations during the 1990s as compared with only four nations during the 1980s.[41]

To Bush's credit, he became the first president to commit major resources ($10 billion initially in new funds followed by promises of $30 billion in 2007) toward combating the AIDS epidemic in Africa, where as many as 40 percent of citizens in some nations were HIV positive or had AIDS. Even greater resources were needed, however, not just in Africa, but in India, China, Russia, Eastern Europe, and other Asian nations where this disease was rapidly spreading. Even in 2007, more than one case of AIDS emerged for every new case that was treated in the world.

Nor had the United States always been sensitive to the needs of developing nations in trade negotiations under the aegis of the World Trade Organization (WTO). Many Americans had naively assumed that movement toward free trade would help all nations to improve their economic condition. While free trade often did increase the flow of goods between nations, it also had some negative repercussions.[42] Developing nations possessed less efficient businesses and agriculture than industrialized nations, such as small farms that lacked modern machinery, preventing them from competing with businesses and agribusinesses in industrialized nations. Peasant producers of corn in Mexico, for example, could not compete with corn from huge American agribusinesses, forcing them to leave their farms for urban areas in Mexico or to cross into the United States. For many of these farmers, the opening of their markets to American producers would mean financial disaster.

Nor did the United States always play by the rules. After insisting on free trade in agriculture with many nations, for example, Congress enacted $400 billion of federal agricultural subsidies in 2002 that gave American agribusiness an unfair advantage over farmers in developing nations. Not receiving these subsidies, it was impossible for them to compete with American produce that was heavily subsidized by the American government. The United States and other industrialized nations often retained trade barriers against developing nations, such as against their food products and apparel.

A major transformation of the world's economy, called globalization, accelerated in the 1990s and into the first decade of the 21st century. Defined as the free movement of capital and labor across national boundaries, globalization had both positive and negative consequences. As American corporations relocated plants in developing nations to take advantage of lower wages and fewer government regulations, they provided employment to citizens in these nations and brought low-priced goods to American consumers. The corporations often paid inadequate wages, however, and created unsafe working conditions as well as environmental hazards. American trade unionists argued, moreover, that corporations eliminated many domestic factories to reap profits from lower wages in developing nations. Globalization also placed pressure, some persons believed, on industrialized nations to reduce the size of their welfare states, since they sometimes lowered their taxes to stop corporations from relocating in developing nations that imposed few taxes on them and their personnel.[43]

The American-controlled World Bank and the International Monetary Fund (IMF), which gave loans to developing nations, funded many good projects but often imposed requirements on developing nations that exacerbated their social and economic problems. They often required draconian cuts in their budgets to curtail their deficits—cuts that often hurt their ability to provide needed social, health, and educational services. Sometimes, too, they urged nations to proceed directly to capitalism rather than viewing the process of transition as more gradual in nature.[44]

A robust international protest movement had developed by 2000 that targeted the economic policies of industrialized nations, as well as policies of the World Bank and the IMF. Protesters demanded the inclusion of wage and working condition stipulations in free trade agreements, as well as radical changes in policies of the World Bank and the IMF. They also demanded that industrialized nations forgive some of the debt that developing nations had incurred from loans they had received from their governments and banks. They insisted that developing nations not be told they had to cut domestic spending severely as a condition of getting loans and grants.

Developing nations need huge investments in their educational, infrastructure, health, and agricultural systems if they are to increase their economic growth by using the sophisticated technologies that industrialized nations possess. (Industrialized nations reached their current economic condition only because their governments invested heavily in these areas during the last century.) Since developing nations lack resources to fund these investments—and many of them were burdened with huge interest payments on their national debt—the funds must mostly come from industrialized nations. While Bush deserves credit for promising to raise American foreign aid from 0.10 percent of GDP to 0.15 percent by 2006, many other European nations have pledged to expand their foreign aid far more rapidly from a base much higher than that of the United States.[45]

Environmental issues had become increasingly important as degradation of the oceans, atmosphere, and rivers became increasingly evident. Initially dismissed by many people as conjectural, evidence mounted that the world was warming in a trend that could jeopardize the climates of many areas. A section of the Antarctic Ice Cap, the size of Rhode Island, broke free in 1999 in a development that could presage rising oceans that would ultimately endanger many coastal cities in the United States and abroad. To the disappointment of many environmentalists, Bush decided not to sign the Kyoto Agreement, in which many nations pledged to reduce carbon dioxide emissions to slow global warming. (Congress failed to ratify it during the Clinton administration but *did* ratify it in the Bush administration, only to have Bush not sign it.) Environmentalists charged the Bush administration with loosening clean air standards and other regulations. Bush also supported drilling for oil in Alaska, loosening logging restrictions in national forests, allowing higher levels of permissible arsenic levels in drinking water, easing deadlines for raising pollution standards for automobiles, and granting snowmobile access to Yellowstone National Park. Only in 2007 did Bush acknowledge that global warming might actually be in progress—partly because some fundamentalist members of his conservative coalition had come to the conclusion that it was occurring and that Christian principles mandated wise stewardship of the earth's natural resources.

A host of international economic, social, and environmental issues had arisen by the new millennium, then, that had profound importance to the United States. In a world where labor and capital migrated between nations, where nations shared the seas and atmosphere, and where telecommunications had shrunk the globe, no nation could wisely isolate itself from global issues. Epidemics like AIDS and SARS, an influenza-like illness that began in China and spread to Canada and other nations in 2003, illustrated that microbes pass easily between nations through global travel and commerce. Nor could Americans concerned about social justice turn a blind eye to the increasing gap between affluent and impoverished nations. Nor could Americans be impervious to dangers posed by globalization to workers and residents in developing nations as well as the United States.

LOOKING AHEAD TO THE PRESIDENTIAL ELECTION OF 2004

The presidential race was under way by July of 2003. Nine Democratic contenders vied for the Democratic nomination after Al Gore had withdrawn from the race, including former Vermont Governor Howard Dean; Senators and ex-Senators John Kerry, John Edwards, Joe Lieberman, and Carol Moseley; black activist Al Sharpton; and Representatives Dick Gephardt and Dennis Kucinich.

Democrats faced a difficult dilemma: Should they position themselves toward the liberal side of their party to present a clear alternative to Republicans, or should they follow Clinton's centrist model?[46] Many critics of the Democratic Party, such as Howard Dean, believed that it had suffered losses in the 2000 and 2002 elections because it had failed to offer a liberal alternative to Republicans in both domestic and foreign policy. (Dean had opposed the war with Iraq.) These critics believed that Bill Clinton had led the party too far to the center—and even to the right with respect to such issues as welfare reform. Without an energized base of relatively liberal voters, these critics believed Democrats would again succumb to the Republicans. Democratic centrists such as Lieberman believed, by contrast, that Democratic candidates' only chance in major elections was to run toward the center by emphasizing moderate positions on many issues, by strongly supporting Bush's foreign policy, and by continuing to take hard lines on crime.

Kerry soon took the lead by winning pivotal victories in the primaries—and clinched the Democratic nomination by early March of 2004.

Bush, in turn, was determined not t decisions that he believed had cost his f tion in 1992. Intent on keeping his c ﹍ervative constituency happy, he would not raise taxes as his father had done in 1990. Unlike his father, who had assumed that his victory over Iraq ensured his reelection, he would continue to advance domestic policies that would make voters see him as a compassionate conservative.

BUSH'S DOMESTIC AGENDA IN 2003 AND 2004

Even before the United States had invaded Iraq in the spring of 2003, Bush returned to his domestic agenda. Using the argument that it would stimulate the economy, he proposed an additional $700 billion multiyear tax cut in early 2003. The centerpiece of the tax legislation was a reduction in the tax on stock dividends, a change that favored affluent Americans who owned stocks. With Democrats and moderate Republicans leading the way, the Senate pared the proposed cuts to $350 billion and included some revenue-sharing funds for the states—with the conference committee approving a final version amounting to $400 billion.

Liberal critics of this second tax cut made similar criticisms to it as they had made to Bush's first tax cut. They argued that it was inequitable, with most of its benefits going to the top 10 percent of the nation's most affluent persons. They argued it would not stimulate the economy since most of its benefits went to affluent Americans, even though a child tax credit was affixed to it. (Remarkably, the legislation did not provide this child tax credit to the poorest families that paid no income tax.) They argued it would exacerbate huge deficits. To their consternation, Bush's tax cut passed when a small number of conservative Democrats voted for it.

Partly because the Congress and president had cut taxes so severely, Congress lacked resources to fund an expansive prescription drug measure that Democrats had supported in preceding years. With Senator Bill Frist, the Senate Majority

Leader, leading the way, the Senate developed a prescription drug measure for Medicare recipients estimated to cost $400 billion over 10 years—but one that had such limited eligibility that many seniors would still have to pay a large portion of their drug costs. The measure received bipartisan support because Senator Ted Kennedy, again deciding that half a loaf was better than none, supported it. But the House and Senate versions of the legislation were markedly different, with the House insisting that private insurance companies implement the drug benefit in contrast to the Senate, which wanted to give consumers greater choice. A drug benefit was finally enacted in November 2003 when a conference committee reached a compromise solution that allowed many private drug plans to compete for seniors' business rather than having Medicare itself administer the benefit—and by leaving a significant number of seniors to purchase their own drug benefits. The final Medicare drug prescription legislation was so complex than many critics wondered if most senior citizens would even understand it.

Bush proposed a nationwide pilot project for school vouchers in July 2003. Why not, he argued, give students in failing schools (such as those where students failed to improve their reading and math scores on standardized tests under the No Child Left Behind legislation) a $750 voucher so that they could attend private schools of their choice? Opponents immediately criticized the initiative. Not only would this policy undermine public schools, they said, but the amount was grossly insufficient for tuition even in inexpensive parochial schools. While the fate of the legislation was uncertain, Bush hoped that he could eventually expand it into a massive program if Congress let him get his foot in the door.

Bush's tax, international, domestic, and counterterrorism policies had radically changed America's national priorities from those that he had inherited from Clinton. He cut taxes by almost $1.7 trillion spread over 10 years. He increased military spending annually from $250 billion to $400 billion—or an increase of more than $1 trillion spread over 10 years. He devoted $70 billion

annually to counterterrorism—or at least $700 billion over 10 years. In other words, $3.4 *trillion* was taken from the federal budget in the coming decade that might otherwise have been used for domestic programs.

Any president would have had to increase counterterrorism spending after the 2001 terrorist attacks, of course. But Bush followed Reagan's precedent by supplementing huge increases in federal spending for military and related programs with massive cuts in revenues—in a double whammy that radically depleted resources for social welfare and other programs for the foreseeable future. These policies also resulted in huge increases in the federal debt since they led to annual federal deficits of $400 billion for years to come—deficits that would further deplete funds for domestic programs by markedly increasing annual interest payments on the federal debt. While the government's tax revenues will increase in coming years with economic growth, the Congressional Budget Office estimates that these megadeficits will occur even after these increases in tax revenues. The deficits, many economists contended, might slow economic growth by drawing private capital from job-producing investments to financing the national debt.

Nor would the fiscal shortfall be confined to the first decade of the 21st century due to the impending retirement and aging of the 76 million persons born between 1946 and 1964—the so-called boomer generation. If 12 percent of the population was age 65 or older in 2002, federal authorities estimated that 18 percent would be elderly in 2025 and 21 percent in 2050.[47] Seniors' medical costs had already risen rapidly in the 1990s with the advent of new drugs, diagnostic tests, joint and organ transplants, and surgeries—and were slated to rise much higher in coming decades. Seniors were expected, as well, to live longer—meaning even more of them would need extended and expensive medical help for chronic diseases such as congestive heart failure.

The combined costs of Social Security, Medicare, and Medicaid could rise, then, from 41 percent of the budget in 2000 to 66 percent of

GDP in 2030—displacing other programs in the current federal budget.[48] The nation will not have the luxury, however, of cutting spending for other people because the boomers' needs will compete with the 75 million members of Generation X (born between 1965 and 1985) and the projected 75 million members of Generation Y (born between 1986 and 2006).[49] Members of Generations X and Y will require large increases for social services, education, and health programs, not to mention greater investments in the nation's infrastructure.

Many liberals, as well as some conservatives, feared that the nation was heading for a grim scenario. The federal budget would be depleted if it had to cover a robust counterterrorism and military budget, increasing amounts for interest payments on the national debt, the boomers' rising costs, and rising costs for Generations X and Y. Political realities suggest that two kinds of programs could be markedly cut because their constituencies are relatively weak politically. First, programs funded by the federal discretionary portion of the budget might be slashed since block grant programs, housing subsidies, roads, airports, the environment, the federal park service, public health, mental health, child welfare, and education programs—currently about 15 percent of the federal budget—are relatively small.[50] Second, means-tested entitlements for the poor are vulnerable because poor people are relatively powerless; included in this group are the Earned Income Tax Credit, Food Stamps, and Supplementary Security Income (SSI).

The nation could, of course, raise its federal taxes above the traditional level of roughly 20 percent of GDP to finance the needs of boomers and succeeding generations. Proposals to increase federal taxes above this level will inspire a firestorm of protest from conservatives, who had pledged themselves to cut taxes on repeated occasions. It is likely that pitched battles will take place between liberals and conservatives. If many liberals will demand increases in taxes, as well as cuts in military spending to avert deficits and prevent cuts in many domestic programs, many conservatives will oppose tax increases, support high military spending, and demand large cuts in domestic programs.

Battles over priorities also are likely to occur in the states. Total state tax revenues have equaled about 10 percent of GDP since the late 1960s—or roughly half the size of federal tax revenues. States' budgets are vulnerable, however, during recessions, as was illustrated during the Bush administration when states' revenues declined so precipitously that they had to slash spending or increase taxes to balance their budgets. Like the federal government, many states face long-term budget problems as they try to finance markedly increasing prison populations; counterterrorism budgets; repairs of roads, bridges, and airports; and secondary and higher education. States' costs will increase even further as the federal government devolves policies and programs to them to solve *its* budget crunch. Even now the Bush administration wants to block-grant Medicaid—a policy that could make states pay a greater share of this expensive program whose costs will rise even further as it finances nursing home costs of many seniors.

Social workers will not have the luxury of ignoring these fiscal battles because most of them work for programs funded by local, state, and federal governments. Their jobs will be on the line, as will the needs of their clients.

OUTCOME OF THE 2004 ELECTIONS

Republicans won a narrow victory in the elections of 2004. Relying heavily on the argument that he could best safeguard the nation from terrorism, President Bush persuaded many independent and moderate voters to vote for him, while retaining the allegiance of persons with relatively strong religious affiliations. Enough citizens were sufficiently worried about national security against terrorism that Bush easily defeated John Kerry.

Republicans retained, moreover, their strong majority in the House, while gaining a narrow majority in the Senate. This margin of victory was not sufficient, however, for President Bush to enact many policies that he favored—leading to a policy stalemate in 2005 and 2006. He was unable to get his Social Security or Medicare reforms enacted to make them attuned to his free-market ideology, such as converting Social Security to a system of private investment accounts or enacting a system of medical savings accounts to allow persons to self-finance their health care costs rather than relying on Medicare.

Unable to convince Congress to enact legislation to allow the federal government to give funds to faith-based organizations, he used his presidential power to distribute considerable resources to them—hoping that opponents would not secure court rulings that ordered him to end this practice on the grounds that it violated the separation of church and state.

RETURNING TO IRAQ

The American occupation of Iraq, which Bush had believed would be relatively brief and effortless, turned into a nightmare in 2005 and thereafter, even though Saddam Hussein was captured in December 2003 and executed in December 2006. Critics believe that the administration made a bad situation even worse by disbanding Hussein's army when no alternative force existed for keeping order—and by deploying too few American troops. By insisting that government officials from Hussein's era be removed from government posts, moreover, the United States contributed to the erosion of government capabilities. The United States moved too slowly to develop competent Iraqi military forces and police so that the full onus of keeping peace fell on American and (to a lesser extent) British forces. In focusing on military occupation, moreover, the United States failed to invest sufficiently in the reconstruction of Iraq so that residents of the nation often lacked such basic requirements as electricity, sanitation, and health care. A considerable portion of funds that Americans devoted to reconstruction were depleted by corruption from American and Iraqi contractors and officials. Even in 2008, many Iraqi citizens lacked rudimentary services that they had possessed before the American invasion. These key mistakes, critics believed, were made by the American Secretary of Defense Donald Rumsfeld, who was finally replaced by Robert Gates in 2007.

The United States tried, as well, to facilitate the development of an Iraqi government that, its leaders hoped, would eventually take over most of the military and police actions in Iraq against militant forces, as well as attend to the basic needs of the nation's residents. After a long process of writing a constitution, elections were held with a large majority of the Iraqi population voting into place a national legislature with a majority of Shiite politicians in December 2005.

The national government soon proved to be relatively ineffective. It was riddled with corruption. It could not decide how to divide the nation's oil revenues among its Kurdish, Shiite, and Sunni peoples or areas. It could not restrain the Shiite and Sunni militias from warring on one another. It could not build competent military and police forces.

If violence before 2005 had mostly consisted of remnant forces of Hussein and local Al-Qaeda forces fighting American troops, it shifted toward tribal warfare after a particular prominent Shiite shrine was virtually destroyed by Sunni or Al-Qaeda militants in February 2006. A number of Sunni and Shiite militias had already emerged that were independent of the Iraqi government or that had infiltrated *its* military and police forces—often securing armaments from them. They engaged in escalating conflict against one another—to the point that many experts believed a full-blown civil war had emerged. (Even if the Bush administration was reluctant to admit it, experts such as Colin Powell believed a civil war was under way in mid-2007.)

Some critics wondered, too, if the American invasion of Iraq had excessively diverted American attention from Afghanistan. While the United States had quickly defeated the Taliban in 2001, it had diverted forces from that nation to Iraq in succeeding years—making a return to power by forces sympathetic with the Taliban more likely. Western nations had reneged, moreover, on economic and technical assistance that they had promised to the new government in Afghanistan, leading to widespread popular disenchantment with that government by Afghan citizens. (Resistance to the Afghan government by the Taliban had markedly increased by 2008, along with popular discontent.)

A major debate was under way in the United States by late 2006 that soon became central to the emerging presidential contest of 2008. Should the United States withdraw its forces rapidly to cut its losses and to avoid serving as a lightning rod for the recruiting of militant Al-Qaeda and other forces—as major Democratic leaders such as Nancy Pelosi believed? Or should the United States retain its forces in the nation or even increase them—as President Bush and many Republican leaders contended as they even supported a "surge" of American forces in the spring and summer of 2007?

SUPREME COURT SURPRISES
AND UNCERTAINTIES

The Supreme Court had assumed a pivotal role in social welfare policy during the 20th century. If it was a relatively conservative court in the century's first four decades, it became a relatively liberal court in the next three decades under the leadership of Chief Justice Earl Warren. It then entered a relatively conservative phase in the last three decades of the 20th century under the leadership of Chief Justice William Rehnquist when it favored states' rights, pull-backs from rulings that limited the powers of police, and elimination of quotas by universities. Many liberals feared that the Supreme Court might soon end affirmative action programs and rescind the right to abortion granted in the *Roe v. Wade* decision.

Even this relatively conservative court was deeply divided, however. Justices Antonin Scalia, Clarence Thomas, and William Rehnquist called themselves strict constructionists who took conservative positions on most rulings, though some liberal

critics contended that ideology—not a strict reading of the Constitution—shaped many of their positions. Justices Ruth Bader Ginsburg and John Paul Stevens usually took liberal positions, sometimes joined by David Souter. A moderate faction, including Justices Sandra Day O'Connor, Anthony Kennedy, and Stephen Breyer, were less predictable, often voting with or against the conservative or liberal judges. (O'Connor was particularly pivotal, often helping the liberal jurists to gain narrow victories in key decisions on abortion, affirmative action, and workers' rights.) The Court was so divided that many key decisions were made by a 5 to 4 vote. If even a single liberal or moderate justice retired and was replaced by a conservative Bush nominee, liberals feared virtually all decisions would be conservative ones.

To the surprise of court experts, the Supreme Court made several rulings in 2003 that were relatively liberal in nature. The two rulings that received the most attention involved affirmative action and gay rights. In the case of *The University of California Regents vs. Bakke*, Allen Bakke, the plaintiff, contended he had not been admitted to medical school due to a quota system that selected persons less qualified than himself. While the Court ruled in Bakke's favor in 1978 by declaring rigid quotas to be unconstitutional, it also maintained that race could be used as one of several factors in the admission process. In the ensuing decades, many conservatives hoped the Court would reverse itself by declaring *any* use of race to be unconstitutional. They found their chance when two Caucasian applicants, respectively to the University of Michigan's undergraduate program and law school, sued the university on grounds that it had used unfair admission procedures. If the undergraduate program used a point-based system that automatically gave minorities one-fifth of the points needed for admission, the law school used a less structured system that made race one of a number of factors to be considered to obtain a diverse student body. Both programs insisted that students in higher education receive an inferior education if they are not exposed to different perspectives—and the law school demonstrated that the minority representation in its student body would drop to only 4 percent if it admitted students only on the basis of grades and test scores.[51]

The Supreme Court struck down the undergraduate admission procedures by a 6 to 3 vote on grounds that it made race "a decisive factor for virtually every minimally qualified … minority applicant." But it upheld the law school's procedures by a 5 to 4 vote. Speaking for the majority, O'Connor maintained that race should have an important role in admissions since professions "must be inclusive of talented and qualified individuals of every race and ethnicity, so that all members of our heterogeneous society may participate in the educational institutions that provide the training and education to succeed in America."[52]

The Supreme Court struck down an anti-sodomy law in Texas in 2003 by a 6-3 vote. When police entered the apartment of Tyron Garner and John Lawrence and witnessed them performing a homosexual act, they arrested them and ultimately fined them $200. Even though the Supreme Court had upheld states' anti-sodomy laws in a ruling in 1986, it struck down the Texas law. While only 13 states still had anti-sodomy laws, the ruling had huge ramifications for homosexuals and lesbians, who now did not suffer the indignity of laws that questioned the legality of their sexual behavior. As Justice Kennedy wrote in the majority opinion, gays are "entitled to respect for their private lives."[53]

These relatively liberal rulings, while providing solace to many liberals, hardly eased their fears about the future Supreme Court if conservative appointments were made in coming years during the Bush administration should any of the Court's liberals, or Sandra Day O'Connor who had been a pivotal swing vote who often sided with the Court's liberals, retire.

THE BOTCHED RESPONSE TO HURRICANE KATRINA

A hurricane hit New Orleans and the Gulf Coast in August 2005 that was probably the most destructive natural disaster in the nation's history. It provided a key test of the American welfare state: Could it, or could it not, provide a humane response to this catastrophe—and particularly to the low-income African Americans who were most harmed by it?

A series of hurricanes had repeatedly struck the United States throughout its history, but they were particularly numerous in the 1960s and 1970s when Hurricanes Carla, Betsy, Camilla, and Agnes occurred. Nor had New Orleans been immune from them: Hurricane Betsy flooded one-half of New Orleans, for example, in 1965. Upset that relief work in these hurricanes' wake had been inadequate partly because it was spread between 100 federal agencies, state governors pressured President Jimmy Carter to establish the Federal Emergency Management Agency (FEMA) in 1979 to coordinate federal disaster relief. But FEMA was relatively ineffectual under Presidents Ronald Reagan and George Bush, Sr., since both presidents filled its top positions with political cronies who had scant expertise in natural disasters.

If FEMA's inadequacies were masked in the 1980s because the nation had few major natural disasters, it was subjected to widespread criticism when it failed to provide timely assistance to Floridians in the wake of Hurricane Andrew in 1992. A geographically small but exceedingly savage storm, Andrew, mercifully sidestepped Miami but destroyed vast portions of such cities as Florida City and Homestead—destroying or damaging 125,000 homes. When little assistance was forthcoming, irate citizens flooded the White House with phone calls—and FEMA's bumbling response may even have contributed to the electoral defeat of George Bush, Sr., in 1992, when Republicans lost Florida to Bill Clinton.

Determined not to face a similar situation, President Clinton selected the first FEMA director: James Lee Witt, an administrator who had substantial experience dealing with natural disasters. He not only energized FEMA but launched Project Impact to help an initial group of seven cities and eventually 250 cities prepare for natural disasters. (Tragically, New Orleans chose not to participate in Project Impact when it might have developed programs that could have softened the impact of major hurricanes for its residents.) FEMA performed admirably in the wakes of the Northridge Earthquake in Los Angeles and the flooding of the lower Mississippi with Hurricane Floyd during the Clinton administration.

But the context swung in a more negative direction with the election of George W. Bush in 2000. Like his father, he appointed political cronies to FEMA's top positions, such as his campaign director Joe Albaugh—who quickly enacted deep cuts in its budget and terminated Project Impact. FEMA was further marginalized in the wake of the destruction of the World Trade Center on September 11, 2001, when it was placed in a subordinate position in the Home Security Agency (HSA), which emphasized counterterrorism over natural disasters. When Albaugh left for the private sector, he was replaced by Michael Brown, another director with no disaster experience who had been in the horse-breeding business. Even more marginalized by the HSA and with an incompetent director, many of FEMA's staff best staff left the agency.

New Orleans and the Gulf Coast had experienced many hurricanes during the past two centuries—but New Orleans was particularly vulnerable to extreme damage due to its unusual topography. Not only was much of the city gradually sinking, but substantial communities had been constructed from the 1950s onward in land that had formerly been swamps that were as much as nine feet below sea level—including the lower Ninth Ward. The city relied on a system of levees and canals to keep it from filling up with water like a bowl if even a single major levee breached. FEMA helped to organize a planning exercise in 2004 to simulate what would happen if a category 5 hurricane (with winds as high as 170 mph) struck southern Louisiana. With technical modeling approaches developed by scientists at Louisiana State University (LSU), participants from parish (county), city, state, and federal agencies, as well as elected officials, received the grim news: A powerful hurricane (which they called "PAM") would flood large portions of New Orleans and surrounding areas, destroy vast amounts of housing, demolish thousands of businesses, and require massive

evacuations of citizens before the hurricane struck. Not only should residents take measures to strengthen their homes and office buildings, the experts urged, but the Army Corps of Engineers should proceed at once to fortify some levees. (Worried residents had reported for years to public officials that they saw water flowing from sections of some levees—but the Army Corps had taken no action.) Experts also urged all levels of government, under FEMA's direction, to pre-position water and food at key points in the community, develop evacuation plans, and develop mobile "interoperable" communication systems so that public agencies from every level of government could easily communicate with one another if existing phone and communication systems were disrupted by a hurricane. An elaborate plan was constructed in which *each* agency promised to take specific steps if a catastrophic hurricane headed toward New Orleans.

Even before this planning exercise, moreover, the Home Security Agency and FEMA had developed protocols for major natural disasters. They established federal coordinators that would link transportation, firefighting, public health, and medical officials. They developed a National Incident Management System that authorized federal officials to intervene even before "catastrophic disasters" rather than waiting for state and local governments to request their assistance through normal protocols to prevent suffering and save lives.

But Exercise PAM was soon forgotten as its funding was slashed, and no one was charged with making sure that its recommendations were implemented.

Residents of New Orleans at first believed they had dodged a bullet when they learned that Hurricane Katrina had shifted from a category 5 status (with winds exceeding 170 mph) to a category 4 status (with winds around 130 mph or less) *and* when they learned that the storm's center had veered just to the east of their city when it made landfall at 6:10 a.m. on August 29, 2005. They soon discovered in the early hours of August 30 that the water surge from Katrina had begun to flood portions of New Orleans when three levees breached. Many public officials remained incredulous, including Senator David Vitter (R-LA), who said, "I don't want to alarm everybody that ... New Orleans is filling up like a bowl. That's just not happening." By 10 p.m. on August 30, about 80 percent of New Orleans was under water as sandbagging of the broken levees failed.

The damage from Hurricane Katrina, when coupled with the flooding, caused more devastation than any other hurricane in recorded American history. Tens of thousands of houses were flooded. Entire communities were destroyed. Hundreds of thousands of residents fled New Orleans even before the storm made landfall. Thousands of businesses no longer existed. Hurricanes had been a fact of life in the Gulf Coast for centuries, but Hurricane Katrina was on an order of magnitude unprecedented during the past century.

The human devastation was monumental. Responding to voluntary and mandatory evacuation orders issued by Mayor Ray Nagin and Governor Kathleen Blanco in the days preceding landfall as the hurricane moved toward New Orleans, most of the city's population headed for an array of cities and towns that included Baton Rouge. Most of them would face months, even years, of uncertainty about whether to return to New Orleans or to abandon it with their housing and communities often destroyed, as well as their places of work. Many of them would experience physical and mental health problems caused by their trauma.

While most of New Orleans' population had fled, about 15,000 persons remained stranded in New Orleans—often the most vulnerable African Americans in New Orleans who had been disproportionately located to "lower ground" in the decades preceding Hurricane Katrina. They did *not* flee for reasons linked to their poverty and race. They found it harder to escape due to lack of cars—and public officials had failed to make buses and other kinds of public transportation available to them. Many of them possessed serious health problems. Many of them did not have televisions or radios and were therefore not apprised of the imminent danger. Many lacked the resources to stay in motels or hotels outside of New Orleans—and lacked

relatives or friends who could accommodate them in outlying areas. Many of them were not inclined to believe public officials—having received poor treatment from them for decades.

The failure of government officials to respond humanely to these stranded persons of color was televised to the nation and the world for days following Katrina. Viewers saw them begging for water for days after the disaster from freeways and rooftops. They saw them living in scandalous conditions without food, water, or operating restrooms at the Superdome. They saw President Bush remaining at his ranch for two days after the catastrophe—and then praising Michael Brown of FEMA for his "excellent work." They heard that Brown did not even know in Katrina's immediate aftermath that more than 10,000 stranded persons resided in the Superdome.

THE FAILURE OF A FREE-MARKET RECONSTRUCTION OF NEW ORLEANS AND THE GULF COAST

Everyone wondered, Could government officials who had been so inept in responding to this disaster develop effective plans for reconstructing New Orleans and the Gulf Coast? The flurry of action by Congress in September 2005 in the hurricane's immediate wake seemed promising as Congress allocated funds to various safety net programs and expanded eligibility. But would federal, state, and local governments rebuild New Orleans and the Gulf Coast expeditiously? This hurricane opened the policy agenda of the Congress and presidency, then, to issues of intractable or severe poverty. Reeling from criticism of him and his administration for inaction in Katrina's wake, President George W. Bush promised in mid-September "one the largest reconstruction efforts the nation has ever seen." Democratic leaders, in turn, wanted to offer their own proposals for rebuilding New Orleans. Precedents existed, such as the San

Francisco earthquake and subsequent fire that had killed 3,000 people and destroyed 28,000 buildings in 1906 or the hurricane that had hit Galveston, Texas, in 1900, in which 10,000 people were killed (or 25 percent of its residents) and 8,000 buildings destroyed. In each case, the government had played a central role in instilling confidence in ordinary citizens and investors by taking actions such as the following:

1. Ensuring public safety by constructing a seawall and raising the grade of the entire city by 1 to 15 feet (Galveston) or having the federal government guarantee a bond issue equal to 10 percent of total damages to help San Francisco repair its infrastructure and housing

2. Allocating and spending large sums of money from all levels of government to give employment to the homeless and jobless, to rebuild public buildings, and to make interest-free loans available to local governments and businesses

3. Putting nonpartisan experts in charge of reconstruction to avert charges of corruption

4. Pressuring insurers to pay claims rather than seeking not to pay them on grounds they were not liable for damage from natural disasters

5. Establishing the confidence of private investors to bring businesses and development into the area expeditiously

These same steps were essential to the reconstruction of New Orleans. Why would businesses and residents return if they were not assured that the Army Corps of Engineers and other government agencies would quickly develop and implement an effective plan to bolster the city's levees to protect it from future category 5 hurricanes? Unless pressured by the government, why would the companies that insured the structures in New Orleans make good on claims that would cut deeply into their profits—instead of claiming that most of the damage had been done by water (often excluded in insurance policies) rather than from wind (usually included in them)? How could the city of New Orleans and the State of Louisiana invest sufficient

resources in the area if they did not have long-term grants and zero-interest loans from the federal government? Why would citizens and businesses trust the reconstruction effort if it was not placed under the direction of nonpartisan experts with no conflicts of interests—and who insisted on competitive bids from contractors rather than doling out the funds to corporations with insider connections to the Bush administration?

Reconstruction of New Orleans and the Gulf Coast required, as well, a regional planning process to orchestrate it. Housing on higher ground had to be developed for those residents whose lower-ground neighborhoods could not be made safe from future hurricanes—so a regional authority needed to superintend its construction in areas within and outside New Orleans. The return of businesses, residents, and public services had to be planned to occur in tandem since many residents would not return if the area lacked grocery stores and other businesses, as well as adequate infrastructure, public transportation, utilities, and adequate police and fire protection. If reconstruction did not proceed at a relatively rapid rate, many former residents would never return to New Orleans since they would establish roots in other locations. If regional environmental remedies were not put in place, such as the eradication of canals dug by large oil companies in fragile wetlands, the erosion of offshore islands, which buffered the area from water surges of hurricanes, would continue.

Low-income residents particularly needed assistance from government. They needed tens of thousands of units of newly constructed affordable housing. They needed immediate jobs in clearing the rubble from the city. They needed public transportation. They needed free health care.

Unfortunately, none of these requirements were sufficiently met by the Bush administration in the two years following Hurricane Katrina, partly because of its private market ideology. Why not, top officials decided, give residents and businesses tax incentives and grants so that private markets could reconstruct New Orleans? Why not route government grants to clear rubble through local and state agencies—as well as to huge national contracting firms like Halliburton with inside connections to the Bush administration? Why not allow the Army Corps of Engineers to proceed at a relatively leisurely pace in reconstructing levees—while not even deciding which areas could and could not be protected from future hurricanes?

The resulting reconstruction was haphazard and slow, leaving many citizens and businesses afraid to return to New Orleans. Only about half of its residents had returned by the fall of 2007—and most businesses had not resumed operations. Since no one knew which areas would be made safe from future hurricanes—which required a huge 25-foot levee rather than the existing levees that often were only 10 feet high—persons and businesses did not know where they could safely return. While the Bush administration had committed $110 billion in the fall of 2006 to the reconstruction of New Orleans, it had spent only a fraction of these resources a year later.

The toll of this inept reconstruction, however, was most heavy on low-income African Americans. Citizens of the lower Ninth Ward were put in a state of limbo—with officials variously saying it would be reconstructed or that it would remain unsafe from future hurricanes. The federal government failed to build large amounts of affordable housing or public housing in New Orleans—and failed to rehabilitate many units of public housing. It even sold or rented many of these units to relatively affluent people. It failed sufficiently to subsidize the ruined public system of health care, which meant that poor residents often lacked access to health care.

Remarkably, as well, the government did not hire indigenous low-income persons to clear rubble or reconstruct the city. Rather, Instead, they encouraged construction companies to rely on as many 100,000 immigrants (primarily from Mexico) for labor. These immigrants were ruthlessly exploited. They often worked in toxic environments because the Bush administration relaxed protections normally offered by the Occupational Safety and Health Administration (OSHA). Many received meager pay because Louisiana was one of

few states not to enact a minimum wage law. They lived in motels with as many as 10 persons in a room. Many of them were not even paid because the Department of Labor failed to monitor and enforce federal work requirements.

The future of New Orleans remained in doubt in early 2008. With substantial political and financing backing, casinos were quickly restored—and developers had begun construction on many high-priced hotels to house tourists. Affluent homeowners on high ground benefited from a robust real estate market. But working-class and poor people remained largely on the fringes or outside of the city as huge parts of it remained only partly occupied. Billions of dollars of fraudulent expenditures had been uncovered—and many insurance companies denied reimbursement to many customers. FEMA officials were often insensitive to local citizens—not even investigating the charge until fall 2007 that many occupants of thousands of trailers were sickened by formaldehyde gas from materials used to construct them. Many critics charged that the administration favored the reconstruction of Mississippi because most of its public officials were Republican—as compared to Louisiana where many of the public officials were Democratic.

We do not know how a president and administration not so imbued with a free-market approach would have reconstructed New Orleans and the Gulf Coast. We can usefully return to President Franklin Roosevelt's Tennessee Valley Authority more than 50 years earlier when a different administration used a full range of government powers to reconstruct an area of the United States that had been ravaged by floods and poverty.

Had not many policy advocates and advocacy groups sought policies that would help vulnerable populations in Katrina's wake, even more persons would have failed to secure needed help. These included the Rebuilding Louisiana Coalition, which was formed by social worker Russell Henderson, who teaches social policy and community organization at Dillard University in New Orleans, as well as the Baton Rouge Crisis Intervention Center, Common Ground, the Grassroots Legal Network, the Hispanic Apostolate, Catholic Charities, the Archdiocese of New Orleans, the Family Service of Greater New Orleans, Hope House, INCITE (Women of Color Against Violence), the Latino Health Outreach Project, the Loyola Poverty Law Clinic, the Mary Queen Vietnam Catholic Church, the Mississippi Workers Center for Human Rights, the NAACP (in Lafayette, LA), the NAACP Gulf Coast Office, the New Orleans Worker Justice Coalition, the People's Hurricane Relief Fund and Oversight Coalition, the People's Institute for Survival and Beyond, the Southern Poverty Law Center (in Montgomery, AL), Safe Streets/Strong Communities, the Student Hurricane Network, and the Youth Empowerment Project—to name just a few of them. Policy advocates also included specific trade unions, local politicians, faculty at many New Orleans and Louisiana colleges and universities, and many private citizens—not to mention local, state, and federal public officials. These policy advocates sought to place issues, problems, and solutions on policy agendas in the city council, the mayor's office, specific planning groups in parishes and in the city, as well as state and federal agencies and legislatures. (See Insert 12.4.)

INSERT 12.4   Critical Analysis: Racism or Incompetence in Responding to Katrina?

To what extent do you think racist attitudes contributed to the slowness of the response to the needs of low-income African Americans in New Orleans—as well as the botched reconstruction of New Orleans? Would areas with mostly Caucasian and relatively affluent populations have fared better if subjected to this catastrophe? Or were the deficiencies in responding to residents' needs due primarily to incompetence—or difficulties caused by the magnitude of devastation wrought by Katrina?

THE HIGH STAKES FOR THE CONGRESSIONAL ELECTIONS OF 2006

The party that possesses a majority in specific chambers of the Congress has extraordinary power. It selects the chairpersons of each of the congressional committees and its subcommittees. It prevails on many votes within committees. It prevails on many votes on the House and Senate floors. It can control the scheduling of votes by controlling the chairpersonship and the votes in the House Rules Committee.

If this *same* party controls *both* the Senate and the House *and* the presidency, it truly has extraordinary power. The president can often secure most of his policy agenda through a Congress that is generally acquiescent when his party controls both chambers.

The Republican Party had this extraordinary power from 2001 through 2006 because it controlled both houses of Congress and the presidency of George W. Bush—with the minor exception of a brief interlude from May 2001 through 2002 when the Democrats had a majority in the Senate when Senator Jim Jeffords from Vermont left the Republican Party to become an independent—but this interlude ended in the congressional election of 2002 when Republicans regained their Senate majority and widened their majority in the House.

This extraordinary Republican power often meant that:

- Only Republicans could place items on the policy agenda in the Congress. If Democrats tried to initiate policy proposals in specific committees, they usually found that their proposals were not scheduled for hearings or even discussed.

- Only Republicans could get legislation assigned to committees in the House, since the Rules Committee acts as a scheduler.

- Republican committees in the House could send bills to the House floor under "closed rules" that allowed virtually no debate or discussion.

- Republicans could stop investigations of many congressional activities because they controlled the chairs and the membership of oversight committees.

- The Republican president could mostly get his way with a Congress controlled by his own party.

Had the Democrats controlled even a single chamber *or* the presidency, as they did during the presidency of Bill Clinton, they could at least have placed issues on the policy agendas of the committees of that chamber—or been able to use the presidential "bully pulpit" to get public support for some of their policies.

While Republicans had remarkable power from 2001 to 2006, it is important to remember that *moderate* Republicans often voted differently from *conservative* Republicans on many issues—and often joined ranks with many Democrats. These moderate Republicans included, for example, Senator Olympia Snowe of Maine, Senator Lincoln Chafee of Rhode Island, and Senator John McCain of Arizona, who, along with independent Jim Jefferds of Vermont, often averted spending cuts and other policies favored by conservative Republicans. Operating at the fringes of the Republican Party, however, Republican moderates in the Senate and the House often had scant influence on policies favored by the conservative mainstream of the Republican Party.

Since only a small number of Republican moderates were elected to Congress in 2000, 2002, and 2004, Republican conservatives had the power to downsize many programs. They opposed Democrats' efforts to increase the eligibility levels for federal funding of foster care, for example, so that most of its costs had to be borne by local and state governments—often leading to short funding that led to excessive caseloads for child welfare workers. They cut the Medicaid program and tried to disentitle it. They opposed increases in the minimum wage, so that it remained at its lowest level in real dollars since 1969. They proposed replacing Medicare and Medicaid with medical savings accounts, but set such low levels for these accounts that they would not cover the medical costs of many seniors and low-income persons. They made such huge cuts in taxes and increases in military spending that the nation developed huge deficits as opposed to the budget surpluses that had existed at the end of Bill Clinton's presidency.

It is true that the Democratic Party and its officeholders had their own faults. They, too, could be guilty of corruption. They, too, could get the United States into ill-advised military actions abroad, as well as a bloated military budget. Yet clear differences existed between the two parties on social legislation, with the Democrats favoring governmental regulations and programs to a greater extent than Republicans.

As the congressional elections of 2006 loomed, it became clear that this could be a so-called transformational election in which one party's dominance might be challenged.[54] Transformational elections don't occur very often; the last one had been in 1994 when Republicans took control of both chambers of Congress, as well as many governorships and state legislatures. To make the elections of 2006 transformational, Democrats would have to capture at least one chamber of Congress and reduce the size of the Republican majority in the other chamber. Even better for them would be to take control of both chambers. And better still would be to regain the presidency in 2008. Were Democrats to regain control of the House, they would need to have a net gain of at least 15 seats in the 435 elections for House seats—and they would need a net gain of six seats to take control of the Senate in the 33 elections for Senate seats. (Only one-third of senators come up for election during each congressional election since they serve staggered terms of 6 years as compared to 2 years for members of the House.)

Nobody knows precisely why transformational elections take place, but they are probably triggered by shifts in public opinion. When Republicans took control of the Congress in 1994, they were helped by scandals in the Clinton administration, Clinton's failure to get his national health insurance legislation enacted, dislike of Hillary Clinton, disenchantment with large federal deficits, and disenchantment with long-term Democratic control of one or both chambers of Congress.

Transformational elections are also triggered by high voter turnout by one party, particularly among their base of loyal supporters. Republicans were able to turn out their conservative base in extraordinary numbers in 1994—centering upon evangelical and conservative persons in the South, Midwest, and mountain states. It was, to say the least, a political massacre—not a *single* incumbent Republican governor or legislator was defeated in 1994, and many incumbent Democrats were defeated—as Republicans gained solid majorities in both chambers of the Congress and in many state legislatures.

Many Republicans feared that the Democrats would return the favor in the congressional elections of 2006. Even in the spring, Bush's job approval rating had fallen to 31 percent. By August, public approval of Congress had fallen below 30 percent. Polls in October showed that Bush's ratings had only improved slightly. Moreover, only 40 percent of voters believed the United States had "done the right thing" in taking military action against Iraq—and only 38 percent of the public believed the Republican Party "comes closer to sharing your moral values" as compared to 47 percent for the Democrats. Remarkably, only 46 percent of persons approved of the way President Bush had handled the campaign against terrorism despite his efforts to publicize his counterterrorist initiatives—down from almost 90 percent soon after the destruction of the Twin Towers in New York City in 2001. A solid majority of the public believed, moreover, that the Bush administration had lied to get the public to support the invasion of Iraq, such as alleging links between Saddam Hussein and Al-Qaeda that were later found not to exist. A majority of the public believed that the Iraq War made the United States even more vulnerable to terrorist attack by stimulating the growth of terrorist organizations in the Middle East.

The Republicans were bedeviled, as well, by corruption. Jack Abramoff, a high-powered lobbyist,

was indicted on multiple counts for laundering money and offering illegal kickbacks to politicians in return for helping such clients as offshore corporations and Indian casinos. Abramoff, in turn, was linked to Tom DeLay, the House majority leader—who resigned as he was indicted by Texas authorities for illegal donations of corporate money to Texas political campaigns. Bob Ney, a Republican congressman from Ohio, resigned when he became a focus for influence peddling. Even though some Democrats were likely, too, to be indicted, Abramoff had links with far more Republicans— even frequently meeting with Karl Rove, President Bush's chief political advisor.

Added to these discontents was a scandal involving Representative Mark Foley (R., Fla.) that broke in September. Foley resigned from office when e-mails were discovered and made public that contained sexual advances on male House pages. As the public perceived a cover-up of this scandal by Republican House leaders—or at least a failure to take action when informed of the congressman's behavior—public opinion turned against both the Republican Congress and the Republican leadership. This scandal was harmful to Republicans in yet another way: It soured on the GOP many conservative voters who strongly believed in family values and who disliked homosexuality. Republicans feared low voter turnout among the very group of evangelical and conservative voters that had powered them into control of Congress and the presidency during the prior decade.

The Republicans' problems with public opinion and their conservative base energized, moreover, many Democrats who saw the prospect of substantial gains in the 2006 elections after years of bad news at the polls. Not only could they be expected to turn out in record numbers, but they gave substantial sums of money to Democratic candidates.

All elections—save for the presidential election —are local, involving opposing candidates in congressional districts or in states. Using poll data and other information, political experts characterized these local elections in August as falling into seven categories: safe Republican, Republican favored, Republican leaning, no clear favorite, Democrat favored, Democrat leaning, and safe Democrat.[55] (In so-called safe seats, an upset was almost impossible, but in all the other races, upsets were deemed possible, especially in "leaning" districts but even in some "favored" districts.) These experts contended that a sufficient number of election districts or states existed where Democrats had a significant chance of winning that the party could potentially regain the House majority that it had lost in 1994—and that Democrats might even regain the control of the Senate that they had lost in 2002.

As the nation moved from August to early October, experts raised the number of districts that were toss-ups or that leaned toward Democrats. Even between August and October, the trend favored Democrats with as many as eight additional GOP House seats estimated by experts to be "at risk" of a Democratic victory. If 40 Republican seats had been "in play" in the House in August, as many as 48 districts were now estimated to be in play.[56]

The ultimate results would depend upon the campaign strategies of candidates in multiple districts and states. Candidates from both political parties would try to get their liberal or conservative bases to turn out in large numbers—and then to supplement them with moderate voters, whether from the ranks of the opposing party or from independent voters.

Democrats who had typically focused on urban voters in so-called blue states where they had prevailed in the congressional elections of 2004, such as California and New York, realized that they would have to convince rural and suburban voters in red states that had voted strongly for President Bush in 2000 and 2004 to switch their votes to the Democratic Party. In the Senate, for example, Democrats had a chance to unseat six Republican incumbent senators in Arizona, Missouri, Montana, Ohio, Tennessee, and Virginia—but they would need considerable votes from relatively conservative rural voters to achieve this result. Claire McCaskill, the Democratic contender for the Senate seat in Missouri against incumbent Republican Senator Jim Talent, crisscrossed the state talking with rural voters.[57]

To get votes from relatively conservative rural persons, McCaskill chose to assert her own religious faith as well as her family values. While Democrats as a group are less likely to attend church once a week or more as compared to Republicans, many of them *are* religious—or share the religious values of Christians, Jews, Muslims, and others. Why not, McCaskill decided, publicize her own religious background? McCaskill also criticized the administration's prosecution of the Iraq War not just because of her personal convictions, but because she knew that the war had become unpopular with many rural voters, whose communities had borne a disproportionate share of fatalities and injuries in American military forces.

Democrats discovered, as well, that rural voters often resonated to environmental and social issues that they experienced in their own communities.[58] Roughly 9 percent of the nation's 600,000 homeless persons live in small towns—and often are homeless due to plant closures, economically distressed farms, and rising housing costs. Citizens in rural areas experience relatively high rates of suicide, mental illness, family violence, and substance abuse—issues where Democrats and moderate Republicans are more likely than conservatives to favor public spending and programs. Many citizens in rural areas realize that their communities need affordable housing that can only be constructed with federal subsidies. Many women in rural areas favor choice when women have unwanted pregnancies. By talking about these issues in rural areas, candidates such as McCaskill hoped to convert sections of red states into Democratic areas, as had already happened in a number of Rocky Mountain states stretching from Montana down to New Mexico in the 2004 congressional elections.

The challenge of securing victories in close races would be magnified by the formidable resources and campaign expertise of the Republican Party. Unlike the Democratic Party, Republicans had developed a huge nationwide database on voters that contained extraordinary details about them—

details they used to target campaign literature to specific subgroups. Their database included, for example, information about which voters owned snowmobiles, so they targeted campaign literature to such persons in Michigan that asserted that the Democratic incumbent senator from Michigan, social worker Debbie Stabenow, had supported environmental regulations that limited access of snowmobile users to certain areas—an attack meant to help her Republican opponent, Detroit sheriff Mike Bouchard, gain their votes. With extraordinary corporate contributions, as well as contributions from relatively affluent persons, the GOP usually had a significant lead over Democrats in the resources it could spend on pivotal elections. Jim Webb, the opponent against the incumbent Republican senator from Virginia, had only $424,000 in cash on hand in July, for example, as compared to 15 times that amount for incumbent Senator George Allen.

Another pivotal battle pitted incumbent Senator Rick Santorum (R., Pennsylvania) against his opponent, Democrat Bill Casey, Jr., who was the state treasurer. This election had extraordinary symbolic importance because Santorum had become a pivotal leader among Republican conservatives in the Senate and the nation, often championing anti-gay legislation and banning of morning-after birth control pills, and strongly supporting President Bush's foreign policy.

Policy advocates' involvement in electoral contests was particularly essential in political races that experts viewed as up for grabs. Many of these races might be settled by a mere percentage point or less of the popular vote. Those candidates with the most volunteers, the most house-to-house contacts, the most effective campaign literature, the most resources, and the most sophisticated use of the Internet would prevail in close elections. Social workers' involvement in tight elections might even make the difference in some of them.

While Democratic candidates often led in the polls leading up to the 2006 elections, they faced a formidable GOP machine adept at turning out votes on election day. Republicans had a national strategy for getting nearly every Republican to vote through phone calls and home visits. In the so-called 72-Hour Project in Ohio, for example, volunteers worked phone banks on October 7, when they contacted 100,000 potential Republican voters and knocked on the doors of 50,000 voters. Not to be outdone, Democratic volunteers also completed 100,000 calls. Voters' opinions about candidates would be important, but so, too, would these practical organizing efforts.[59]

The Democrats won a resounding victory in 2006 congressional elections—in considerable measure because more than 60 percent of Americans believed that the American invasion of Iraq had been a mistake. Not only did Democrats McCaskill, Stebanow, Casey, and Webb win, but so did many others—resulting in a substantial Democratic majority in the House and a one-vote majority in the Senate. Their victories paved the way for substantial changes in social policies in the federal government.

SECURING SOME INITIAL SOCIAL REFORMS AND OVERSIGHT

With only a one-vote majority in the Senate, Democrats looked to the leadership of Nancy Pelosi (the new House majority leader) to demonstrate that they could point the nation in new directions. Pelosi and Democratic leaders had a full reform agenda, including increasing the minimum wage; increasing funding for No Child Left Behind; increasing funding for S/CHIP to provide health insurance to most children from low-income families; increasing funding for veterans' health care; eliminating funding for Cold War-era weapons; increasing funding for sex education and family planning; obtaining an Employment Non-Discrimination Act to ban workplace discrimination against persons on the basis of sexual orientation; increasing child care subsidies; and expanding eligibility for Food Stamps. Pelosi promised legislation,

INSERT 12.5   Critical Analysis: How Important Is Electoral Advocacy?

Does the 2006 election illustrate the importance of electoral advocacy? To address this question, ask how policy outcomes would have differed had Republicans, instead, kept their majorities in both houses of Congress in 2006. How might social workers engage in electoral advocacy?

as well, that would curtail lobbyists' contributions to political campaigns. (See Insert 12.5.)

Contending that the Republican-dominated Congress had rarely held hearings about activities of the Bush administration during its first six years, Democratic leaders immediately launched investigations of the Iraq War, the reconstruction of New Orleans and the Gulf Coast, the health care provided to returning veterans, and many other issues. They discovered billions of dollars of fraudulent expenditures in Iraq and New Orleans, as well as poor health care for returning veterans. These hearings were chaired by public officials such as Henry Waxman, the chair of the House Government Reform Committee.

The Democrats' legislative ambitions were partly realized when they quickly enacted a substantial increase in the minimum wage. Bush vetoed, however, increases in eligibility levels for S/CHIP. Their plans were also blocked by the huge budget deficits caused by the Iraq War and by Bush, who was intent on clamping down on new spending to offset the charge that he had created more national debt than any preceding president in American history. Democrats, too, found themselves diverted to unsuccessful efforts to enact legislation to require pull-out of American troops from Iraq by a specified timetable. President Bush vetoed such legislation even though many Republicans supported it in 2007—and Democrats lacked sufficient votes to secure the two-thirds majority required for Congress to override this veto.

MORE CRITICAL QUESTIONS ABOUT THE INVASION OF IRAQ AND BUSH'S TACTICS IN THE WAR ON TERRORISM

With Democrats chairing committees such as the House Armed Services Committee, as well as the House and Senate Appropriations Committees that funded military costs for the Iraq War, Democrats intended to pressure the Bush administration to change military and foreign policy directions. A series of revelations over a period of years had undermined public confidence in the American invasion of Iraq, including information that Saddam Hussein had not possessed weapons of mass destruction and that administration officials had ignored key information from American intelligence agencies that would otherwise have led them to this conclusion. They ignored, as well, intelligence reports that warned that Americans would likely ignite a civil war in Iraq between Shiite, Sunni, and Kurdish tribes if they invaded Iraq.

The United States faced a quandary in the fall of 2007, however. If the nation suddenly withdrew from Iraq, it risked inviting a bloodbath in Iraq because the newly installed Iraqi government had not developed sufficient military and police forces to keep order—and was itself dominated by Shiites and so-called Shiite militias that were dedicated to attacking Sunnis and had even infiltrated the nation's military forces and used its weapons to advance this civil war. Yet many critics believed the continued presence of American troops in Iraq had helped Al-Qaeda and other militia groups in Iraq and elsewhere to recruit Iraqi youth and entice them to engage in suicide bombing missions against American forces.

With some Democrats wanting rapid and complete withdrawal and others wanting a slower withdrawal with retention of some American forces in Iraq for an indefinite period to support, train, and advise military forces of the Iraqi government, Democrats enacted a war funding bill without attaching any timetable for withdrawal—and a nonbinding resolution asking Bush to withdraw forces—which he vetoed in the summer of 2007. With public support for the war continuing to erode in the fall of 2007, with growing numbers of Republicans deserting President Bush as they anticipated the elections of 2008, and public opinion polls showing a large majority of the public believed the American invasion had been a mistake, a phased withdrawal seemed possible by the spring of 2008.

Like the Vietnam War four decades earlier, the Iraq War raised troubling questions about the foreign policy of the United States. The war in Iraq had inflicted death and injury on more than 1 million residents of both countries—with little evidence that it had advanced the interests of the United States. As it had done in the Vietnam War, the United States had squandered several trillion dollars when the ongoing medical costs of military personnel were added to the cost of military conflict. Both wars had diverted attention of public officials from domestic and global social and economic issues for long periods of time. They had divided the nation along partisan lines, making bipartisan solutions to important problems more difficult to achieve. In both cases, an incumbent president and his top aides had manipulated the nation into war, often by presenting to the public false or misleading information.

President Bush's war on terrorism also raised troubling questions. Even Colin Powell said in 2007 that the military prison in Guantanamo, Cuba, ought to have been closed "yesterday" because of documented torture and abuse of alleged terrorists who had been deprived of due process. (Similar atrocities, in violation of the Geneva Accords, had taken place in American-supervised prisons in Iraq, as well as detention centers maintained by the Central Intelligence Agency in many European nations.) In addition, the examination of telephone and e-mail communications of many American citizens without court approval by the American Justice Department was widely criticized by civil libertarians in 2006 and subsequently.

THE SUPREME COURT MOVES TO THE RIGHT

If the United States Supreme Court had been narrowly divided between liberal and conservative jurists prior to 2007—with Sandra Day O'Connor often swinging many decisions in a liberal direction with regard to abortion, affirmative action, and many other issues—it had developed a solid majority of five conservative jurists by early 2007. Conservative jurists John Roberts and Samuel Alito respectively replaced Chief Justice William Rehnquist (who died) and O'Connor (who retired) so that, when joined with Justices Antonin Scalia, Clarence Thomas, and Anthony Kennedy, a five-judge conservative majority evolved. (Justices who usually voted in more liberal ways included Justices Ruth Bader Ginsburg, John Paul Stevens, David Souter, and Stephen Breyer—and liberals feared their ranks would further thin if Ginsburg, 73 years of age, and Stevens, 86 years of age, were to retire and if their replacements were to be appointed by a Republican president and Congress.)

Liberals were dismayed by a string of rulings in 2006 and 2007. When considering litigation against the Seattle School District and the Jefferson County Board of Education in Kentucky for using race as one factor in assigning children to schools, the Court ruled that the district and the county had violated the equal protection clause of the Fourteenth Amendment on the grounds that some white students were denied entry to schools that the school districts wished to integrate or keep integrated. (The districts wanted, instead, to replace them with African American students.) The ruling made it unclear whether, and under what circumstances, school districts can seek integrated schools.[60]

In another ruling, the Court ruled that the federal Partial-Birth Abortion Ban Act was constitutional—upholding for the first time in history an abortion restriction that did not contain an exception for the health of a woman. Would the Court proceed, some feminists wondered, to overturn *Roe v. Wade*—and would the ruling embolden abortion opponents to obtain legislation in different states that might, for example, mandate the use of ultrasound of a fetus as part of the abortion-counseling process?[61]

Advocates of gun control feared, as well, that the Supreme Court might follow the lead of a U.S. appeals court that had decided in the spring of 2007 that a ban against ownership of pistols and rifles by the District of Columbia violated the Second Amendment's protection of the right of individuals to keep and bear arms. An array of other rulings appeared to favor corporations over workers or persons who alleged work discrimination.

The swing of the Court in a conservative direction made the outcome of the 2008 presidential and congressional elections even more crucial. Were Republicans to prevail, even more conservative jurists might further buttress the conservative majority that had prevailed in many rulings in 2006 and 2007.

MOVING TOWARD THE PIVOTAL 2008 ELECTIONS

Most experts agreed that voters' perceptions of the course of the Iraq War would likely determine the outcome of the 2008 elections. It seemed in the fall of 2007 that the Democrats were more in tune with adverse public opinion about the Iraq War than Republicans. For the first time in American history, a woman and an African American had a real chance to become president (see Figure 12.2). Democratic candidates Hillary Clinton, the former First Lady and now U.S. senator from New York, and Barack Obama, a U.S. senator from Illinois, were the frontrunners in polls and fund-raising in the fall of 2007—although many other former and current public officials had also declared their candidacy, such as former Senator John Edwards, Governor Bill Richardson, and Representative Dennis Kucinich. The Democrats faced a large number of Republican candidates with Mitt Romney, the former governor of Massachusetts, Rudy Giuliani, the former mayor of New York, John McCain, the senator from Arizona, and Mike Huckabee, the former governor of Arkansas being the probable front-runners.

The nation faced a pivotal election in 2008. Did it prefer the relatively liberal ideology and policy positions of the Democrats, as well as their greater inclination to withdraw from Iraq, or the more conservative ideology and policy positions of the Republicans? Would the rapid decline of popularity of President Bush since the congressional elections of 2006 harm the Republican candidate who was nominated by his party in 2008?

Commentators such as economist Paul Krugman boldly predicted that the United States was moving in a progressive or liberal direction, citing public opinion polls averse to the Iraq War and favoring reforms such as national health insurance and rejection of privatization of Medicare and Social Security.[62] Columnist David Brooks, a conservative Republican, lamented the GOP's swing to the far right, as reflected in positions of many of its candidates for their party's presidential nomination

FIGURE 12.2 Hillary Clinton and Barack Obama make history for women and African Americans.

in 2008. If many of the Democratic candidates espoused an array of domestic reforms, for example, the Republican candidates mostly attacked government and supported privatization of Social Security, Medicare, and schools.[63]

ARE THE TERMS *OUT-GROUP* AND *VULNERABLE POPULATION* STILL APPROPRIATE?

I invented the term *out-group* in the early 1980s to describe an array of populations in American history discussed in preceding chapters—and have mostly replaced it with the term *vulnerable population* in this edition because it is more widely used in current literature.[64] *Either* term is still tragically accurate, however, when describing *any* of the 13 vulnerable populations discussed in this book, including women, persons of color, gays and lesbians, persons with mental and physical disabilities, the elderly, children, and poor persons in contemporary society—just as they accurately describe them in the various historical eras discussed in this text.

It is true that leaders and members of these vulnerable populations achieved signal successes by using various *empowerment* strategies. They developed social movements such as the African American civil rights movement, the feminist movement, and the gay rights movement. They contested negative policies in the courts.[65] They developed voting constituencies that elected public officials sympathetic to their needs. They developed coalitions with other groups. They lobbied legislatures. They designed self-help projects to allow members of their groups to start businesses, get educated, and improve neighborhoods. They used churches, synagogues, and mosques to provide supportive networks. They surmounted stigmatization by identifying and developing cultures that affirmed the dignity of their groups, such as black pride, gay awareness, and feminist ideology.

These activities brought notable successes in courts, legislatures, and communities, not to mention modifying some of the prejudices in the broader community. One need only compare present practices with the lynching of African Americans in the South, the routine firing of homosexuals from the civil service and other places of employment in the 1950s, the near exclusion of women from the medical and other professions from 1920 through the 1960s, and rampant discrimination against disabled persons prior to the 1960s.

Yet members of vulnerable populations still confront major obstacles to equality and to opportunities—suggesting, unfortunately, that the terms *vulnerable populations* and *out-groups* are still accurate. As we have already discussed, the United States Supreme Court has become a major threat to the rights of some vulnerable populations in 2007 with rulings that attack the ability of schools to integrate their facilities, freedom of choice for women, and workers' rights to safe working conditions.

The Continuing Oppression of Women

Women and their children bear the brunt of America's poverty. The United States needs a policy geared toward helping female single heads of household to enter the social and economic mainstream. We have discussed in this chapter how the Personal Responsibility and Work Opportunities Act of 1996 reduced welfare rolls by 50 percent in its first six years of implementation, but how it failed to upgrade the long-term earning capacity of many female heads of household by emphasizing brief job placement services rather than extended training and education. Because women with a high school education or less often cannot earn substantially more than poverty-level wages or have strong promotion prospects, they need not only to upgrade their job-related skills but to complete high school and obtain two-year or four-year college degrees. (Significant research suggested that so-called certificates, such as in cosmetology, have limited value in job markets unlike community college and college degrees.)[66] States and the federal government should therefore have invested billions of dollars annually in helping welfare recipients and former recipients—as well as impoverished single heads of household generally—to obtain these degrees, even if such training and education meant that women's entry into the labor force would be delayed or periodically interrupted. Single heads of household need career and training plans that can, over a period of time, enhance their earnings prospects as they alternate work, training, and education.

Indeed, it makes sense not to treat poorly educated female heads of household as a separate group since *any* worker, female or male, who lacks sufficient education or training is likely to be poverty-stricken. (Male workers with no more than high school education also face bleak economic prospects.) Why not create a national program geared toward helping all workers with high school educations or less? Community colleges, which now exist in virtually every geographic area, could be charged with developing and implementing workers' career plans. Enrolled persons could get child care, medical care, and transportation subsidies while receiving training and related work experiences.

Many women fail to receive any, or sufficient, child care subsidies, requiring them to use such a large portion of their wages for child care that they fall under official poverty standards. While the enactment of the Temporary Assistance for Needy Families Program (TANF) included child care subsidies, funding remained flat for many years. In 2008 many Democrats hoped to get an increase of $6 billion for these subsidies over the next five years.

With attention focused on younger women, less attention is devoted to the economic and social problems of older women—who will constitute a significant majority of the baby boom population in coming decades. Due to high divorce rates, many female retirees are single and must rely on their own savings, assets, and pensions. They usually have lower savings than men, not only because they had to interrupt their work careers to have children, but because they worked in lower-paying occupations. Since far fewer women than men get pensions from their former employers, they must rely on relatively low Social Security benefits. Since many of them do not own houses, they are vulnerable to rising rents. Women in their 80s and 90s often develop chronic health problems that are not covered by Medicare, forcing them to spend down to receive Medicaid. Nor are married women immune from these economic and social problems during retirement. As women typically outlive their husbands, widows often find their finances depleted by the medical costs used by their deceased partners or by other costs that the couple incurred before his death.[67] Because women live, on average, into their mid-80s, they must often exhaust their savings—forcing them onto SSI and Medicaid as they deplete their assets.

A considerable majority of baby boomers will be elderly women in coming decades. The nation has not even begun to prepare for this massive demographic shift. A large labor force of trained and well-paid home health aides will be needed, not to mention geriatric nurses, doctors, and social workers. Community-based networks of support services, respite services for caregivers, and day services need to be developed following innovative models already in operation in specific locations.

Civil rights legislation helped many women get training, education, and economic positions that would have been unthinkable decades earlier. Women still struggle, however, with myriad issues that defy easy solution. Violence against women remains at high levels in their homes with uneven protection of them by the police as well as inadequate prosecutions of violent offenders. Predatory sexual behaviors plague many women in colleges, workplaces, and elsewhere. Many women continue to report extensive on-the-job sexual harassment in both blue-collar and white-collar jobs. Female workers with children often suffer job discrimination from employers and supervisors who believe they are less reliable than childless workers—leading to dismissals or denial of promotions.

Revisions of existing civil rights statutes in many states, as well as of Title VII of the Civil Rights Act of 1964, the Americans with Disabilities Act (ADA), and the Family Medical Leave Act (FMLA), are needed to protect the rights of women more fully. The FMLA should be revised so that it actually funds leaves for parents and caregivers.

Many young women, as well as men, often receive inadequate sex education in schools that focuses only on abstinence even though extensive research shows that abstinence-only sex education is less effective than sex education that presents a range of options.[68] Existing sex education programs that are funded by the federal government should be required to discuss contraception. School districts should be funded and mandated to provide contraceptives to students as is already the case for many innovative districts—and is widespread in European nations.

The Continuing Oppression of Immigrants

When Congress enacted the Immigration Reform and Control Act of 1986, many persons believed that the nation had resolved immigration issues for the foreseeable future. Surely, they reasoned, the granting of amnesty to 3 million undocumented immigrants, as well as the establishment of sanctions against employers who hired them in the future, would stabilize the movement of persons into the United States who lacked green cards or other visas. To the contrary, as many as 12 million undocumented immigrants resided in the United States by 2007, principally from Mexico and Central America, but also from Asia, Russia, and some European nations. A diaspora of Latino immigrants had fanned across the nation, holding jobs in virtually every community in the United States in construction, ranching, mining, restaurant, hotel, manufacturing, hospital, home health, and other positions.

The nation expends vast resources on law enforcement activities. Border agents catch more than 1 million Mexicans a year and escort them back across the border in so-called "voluntary departure." Another 200,000 per year are officially deported under "formal removals"—with more than 40 percent of this group possessing criminal records. In addition, large numbers of border patrol agents and members of the National Guard have been deployed to the border; other border control measures include construction of fences, installation of surveillance devices, and use of airplanes.

A cumbersome system of admitting immigrants was in place in 2007 that frustrated everyone. Employers who wanted skilled workers because they could not find American citizens for specific jobs had to demonstrate that they were not discriminating against American citizens. They had to advertise these positions and require either a master's degree or a bachelor's degree with five years of experience to claim they needed "skilled" workers—and then hope that the workers they hired could obtain green cards (or permanent residency visas)—and then citizenship under the annual quotas on the number of immigrants from each country of origin. Since only a limited number of green cards are issued, other workers had to secure temporary worker visas under the H-1B program. These workers are required to work for specific employers for up to six years, at which time they must leave the United States. Many companies *must* use this kind of visa because they cannot get green cards for many job applicants—and even H-1B visas are greatly oversubscribed, requiring Immigration Services to use a lottery to fill positions. Applications are often lost or delayed in a bureaucratic labyrinth.[69]

A robust movement developed in the United States for new immigration legislation to give these immigrants basic rights and services—and to do away with cumbersome bureaucratic procedures. It orchestrated massive demonstrations in large American cities and in Washington, DC, in 2006 urging the enactment of federal immigration legislation—more than 2 million demonstrators in more than 120 cities called by an alliance of churches, unions, regional grassroots groups, and national policy organizations. Only entitled to emergency medical services, immigrants often lack police protection as well as access to an array of federal and state safety net programs, mental health services, subsidized child care, Head Start, and many other programs. They are often reluctant even to use educational and emergency health services for fear that they will be reported to, and deported by, the Department of Immigration and Naturalization Service (INS). Advocates for immigrants contended that immigrants deserved these rights and services in return not only for their labor and their payment of payroll and other taxes, but to preserve their fundamental human rights.

The cumbersome bureaucratic procedures, as well as the mismatch between demand for visas and green cards and their supply, gave many immigrants an incentive to enter the United States illegally and to use forged documents. It also gave employers who could not find American workers the incentive not to check immigrants' credentials carefully—and to knowingly hire undocumented workers.

Bipartisan immigration legislation co-authored by Senators Ted Kennedy and John McCain and endorsed by President Bush emerged in the spring of 2007. It would have given a considerable share of the 12 million undocumented immigrant residents amnesty—and established a large guest worker program. Immigrants would no longer have had to go through the Department of Labor and Immigration Services, but could apply on their own for work visas under a merit-based point system that would have awarded points for work experience, education, English skills, being in a high-demand occupation, and family ties. Only persons with relatively high scores would have gained admission.

This legislation ran into cross-fire from conservatives and liberals. Many employers feared that the large mismatch between supply of visas and demand for them would remain, so that employers would have to hire whoever won this lottery rather than picking the employees they wanted as they had done under the existing system. Many conservatives viewed immigrants not as residents who deserved civil rights and access to social programs, but as criminals who ought to be caught and deported—all 12

million of them. Many of them doubted that 400 miles of additional border fencing and other surveillance measures would stem the flow of undocumented immigrants to the United States—and they feared that amnesty for many families would only further increase the inflow of the family members and friends that immigrants had left behind in their native country.

Liberals wanted more weight to be given to family ties and less to the other factors. Often wanting immediate amnesty for undocumented persons who had worked in the United States for a specified period, they objected to requirements that these residents had to identify themselves to authorities *and* pay a fine of $5,000 only to get less than full legal status and the right to stay and apply for a permanent "Z visa" that would only be issued once the amplified border surveillance measures had been put in place.[70]

While Democrats overwhelmingly supported the legislation, opposition from Republicans ultimately defeated the legislation. Many Democrats vowed to secure immigration reforms if they won the presidency and majorities in Congress in 2008.

The Continuing Oppression of Racial and Ethnic Vulnerable Populations

In the case of ethnic and racial out-groups, intermarriage has somewhat blurred distinctions between white, African American, Latino, Native American, and Asian populations. A leading analyst of this trend, Richard Rodriguez, argues, "all things brown in time." He disputes the concept that Latinos are a racial group, noting "there are many cultures in Latin America" as well as physical characteristics such as skin color. He notes the emergence of new terms, such as "Blexicans" to describe persons of Latino and African American descent and "Hinjews" for persons of East Indian and Jewish descent. He predicts the U.S. Census will soon not even use racial categories as more and more people find them to be inapplicable.

Rodriguez's argument may be ahead of its time, however, because many people still describe themselves as belonging to a specific racial group, live in areas and attend schools dominated by it, are perceived by others as coming from it, and experience discrimination in employment and other places based on it.

The harsh realities of race are clear in Justice Ruth Bader Ginsburg's dissent to the Supreme Court decision that struck down the point system that gave 20 points to every minority person who applied to the University of Michigan's undergraduate program. She wrote:

> In the wake of a system of racial caste only recently ended … large disparities endure. Unemployment, poverty and access to health care vary by race. Neighborhoods and schools remain racially divided. African American and Hispanic children are all too often educated in poverty-stricken and under-performing institutions. Adult African Americans and Hispanics generally earn less than whites with equivalent levels of education … Bias both conscious and unconscious, reflecting traditional and unexamined habits of thought, keeps up barriers that must come down if equal opportunity and nondiscrimination are ever genuinely to become this country's law and practice.[71]

Ginsburg's comments suggest that the terms *outgroup* and *vulnerable population* are not outmoded. On virtually every indicator of well-being, African Americans, Latinos, and Native Americans lag behind the general population. Her comments apply, as well, to many other groups for whom these terms remain appropriate.

Latinos have made major gains in the United States with the creation of large middle class and affluent class. The Latino population leaped by 58 percent from 1990 to 2007, numbering 35.3 million persons as compared to a growth of the African American population by only 16 percent. Today, Latinos are the largest minority group in 23 states including Midwestern states such as Iowa and Nebraska.[72] The U.S. Census Bureau predicts that 20 percent of the U.S. population will be persons of Latino descent by 2020. The rapid growth of the Latino population has created a kind of role reversal with respect to African Americans. Together, African Americans and Latinos constitute roughly 25 percent of the nation's population and these groups could, if they worked together, secure major reforms in local, state, and federal jurisdictions. Indeed, major advocacy groups, such as the Mexican American Legal Defense and Education Fund, the NAACP, and the National Council of La Raza, have collaborated on getting more accurate census counts. But friction exists between these two vulnerable populations—friction that could grow as the Latino population surges ahead of the African American population. If African American advocacy groups have traditionally emphasized civil rights, the Latino groups want more emphasis placed on upgrading schools and economic issues. Advocacy groups representing the two populations have bickered, as well, about the distribution of federal resources to African American and Latino communities, representation in the federal civil service, and immigration issues. Fearing that African Americans have been displaced from jobs by the inflow of immigrants from Mexico and Central America, African American advocates have been less favorable to the granting of amnesty to new groups of immigrants. Whether African Americans and Latinos get policy reforms will depend in considerable measure on whether they can surmount intergroup competition by working collaboratively.[73]

Persons of color, as well as low-income persons of all ethnic and racial backgrounds, are particularly vulnerable to inadequate schools. Not only are their schools often staffed by poorer teachers and administrators, but often possess substandard equipment and facilities. To the extent that students are segregated in schools by social class, students encounter additional obstacles. Many of them lack adequate nutrition—and must get jobs to make ends meet. Still others lack mentoring and tutoring from parents who themselves dropped out of school.

Most people believed that enactme No Child Left Behind Act in 2001 public schools on notice by making them demonstrate that annual scores on reading and math tests improved for poor and minority students, as well as special education students—or face fiscal penalties or even closure. It also established the goal of every child reading and doing math on grade level by 2014. Students in grades 3 through 8 must be tested annually while high school students need be tested only once—and schools must show that each demographic group (low-income, minority, and special education students) is on course to perform at grade level by 2014.

Critics contended, however, that the legislation was poorly funded and that schools that failed to show improvements were given inadequate assistance to improve themselves. When some schools were closed, students had to scramble even to find new schools. With performance measures limited to math and reading scores, other measures of success were not counted, including high school graduation rates, test scores in other subjects, participation in advanced placement courses, and college preparatory curriculums. They noted, as well, that some schools were penalized or closed when only a specific group within them failed to improve performance rather than most of their students.[74] It remained to be seen if congressional legislators could fashion a bipartisan bill to reauthorize the legislation in 2008 that would address critics' complaints.

Even more controversial were so-called charter schools that were established in 1997 legislation by Congress with the concurrence of President Clinton—and that had evolved into a major movement by 2007 in most major cities. Because they were discouraged by the performance of many public schools, legislators wanted to establish competing private schools that would be freed of labor and curriculum constraints and regulations that confronted public schools. Parents, in turn, could select charter schools over public ones if they believed them to be secure. The legislation also required local school districts to give funds and facilities to these charter schools at levels equivalent to existing public schools. Each charter school, in turn, developed a board of directors that oversaw the hiring of ^ aff and the development of curriculum.

The record of charter schools was, at best, mixed. Some were clearly outstanding—and gave low-income and minority students better educational opportunities than competing public schools. Others were no better, or even worse, than existing public schools. Unlike public schools, moreover, charter schools were often not accountable for improving the reading and math performance of students under the No Child Left Behind Act. Worse yet, they absorbed resources and facilities often needed by existing public schools.

The Continuing Oppression of Populations That Are Physically or Mentally Challenged

Despite the successes of many persons who are covered by the Americans with Disabilities Act, many others live in institutional settings or cannot find employment because they lack the kinds of occupational and social services needed to mainstream them. The poverty rates of the disabled population exceed even the rates of some racial minority groups—and they often are unemployed at rates two times that of the general population. Some benefit from workplace accommodations that enable them to be productive employees, but many disabled persons are unemployed or not offered special accommodations to which they are entitled under federal law. Many of them cannot find affordable housing that has also been reconstructed to meet their special needs, such as specially designed kitchens, bathrooms, and wheelchair ramps. Many of them lack personal assistance with daily chores or help with transportation—assistance that can be crucial to getting and keep jobs or remaining at home. In short, the landmark Americans with Disabilities Act, enacted in 1990, has given physically and mentally challenged persons rights, but not sufficient nonmedical assistance.[75]

Great progress was made in treating persons with HIV in the 1990s with the development of a cocktail of drugs that slowed the development of AIDS and helped many persons with AIDS survive longer or even have normal life expectancies. Yet many persons with AIDS were thrown into poverty by their medical costs, side effects of drugs, and mental trauma. AIDS advocates were disheartened by Congress's decision to rewrite the Ryan White Care Act in December 2006 to decrease assistance for support programs like meals and legal aid—and to allow five new cities to join the program without providing additional funding so that services provided to cities such as New York and San Francisco were deeply cut—even as the Republican Congress capped its funding at $2.1 billion over the last several years. These cuts were devastating because 40,000 *additional* persons get HIV each year as women and persons of color have become the majority of new cases—and as more AIDS patients live longer and require prescription drugs that can cost thousands of dollars per month.[76]

Under these circumstances, administrators using Ryan White funds increasingly must choose to fund only medicines rather than provide support, food, transportation, and housing services. As the drug and medical payer of last resort, the program must often fund them because many state Medicaid programs do not.

Mentally challenged persons also encounter serious problems. The overall impact of mental illness in industrialized nations is staggering, with the World Health Organization estimating that mental illness and suicide account for more than 15 percent of the total mortality and disability burden—more than all kinds of cancer combined. The United States spends about $130 billion per year on mental health treatment including federal prescription coverage—with about 58 percent of this amount devoted to the 12 million Americans with schizophrenia, bipolar disorder, and major depression.[77]

Also staggering are the sheer numbers of these 12 million Americans who are homeless or in prison—about 25 percent of prison inmates and 33 percent of homeless persons.

Slots in supervised group homes and shared apartments are difficult to find. Absent other options, local authorities place 284,000 persons with mental conditions in prisons each year, where they seldom receive mental health services.[78] The nation's community mental health centers are insufficiently funded and staffed to handle the estimated 44 million Americans suffering from mental disorders.[79] Funding by the states for mental services has declined by 30 percent since the mid-1950s when adjusted for inflation and population growth. In Virginia, for example, 10,000 persons were recently on waiting lists for public mental health, substance abuse, or mental retardation services.

Inadequacies of mental health services partly stem from the chaotic system that the United States has evolved. State Medicaid budgets fund more than half of the treatment for persons with serious mental illness, but these resources are grossly inadequate. The federal government bans the use of Medicaid funds for mental health institutions, leading to a severe shortage of beds for those who need institutionalized services to diagnose and stabilize their conditions. In many cases, local police dump persons with psychotic conditions in emergency rooms, shelters, and jails. Private health insurance companies have sharply divergent policies on funding mental health services for persons with severe conditions—as advocates have failed to secure passage of federal legislation that requires insurance companies to fund mental health services on a par with treatment for physical conditions.

Incidents of violence in the nation's secondary schools, as well as universities, have highlighted the inadequacy of mental health services in these settings in a curious mixture of over- and undertreatment. Critics contend that local school districts often err when they routinely test students for mental problems—and when they encourage parents to medicate children at ever younger ages for depression, attention disorder, and hyperactivity. (Some parents have successfully filed suits against school districts alleging invasion of their children's privacy.)

Yet incidents of mass violence, such as at Columbine High School in Colorado and, more recently, at Virginia Tech where scores of students were massacred by a lone gunman, strongly suggest that teachers and peers often fail to heed warning signs from specific students—and then fail to get them into effective treatment programs or remove them from schools altogether. High rates of suicide in the adolescent population also suggest that diagnostic and treatment services are insufficient.

Yet progress has also been made. Primary care physicians today are far more likely than in the past to diagnose conditions such as depression among youth and adults, as well as psychosis. Suicide rates among adolescent boys dropped significantly from the early 1990s to the present. The federal government provided $9.7 million for 14 state anti-suicide programs. Short-term patient care episodes in United States mental health organizations increased markedly from 1980 to the present. In 2003 a total of 2.75 million persons received federal disability payments for mental problems.[80]

Nagging questions won't go away, however. When do mental health practitioners overdiagnose and overmedicate patients? When *are* students' privacy rights violated if all of them are given mental health screening tests? Do medications, such as recent ones developed for schizophrenia, produce worse side effects than older ones and at much greater cost? Are seemingly positive effects of medications "real" or produced by patients' beliefs that the drugs help them?

Another nagging question involves when it is acceptable for authorities to *require* specific persons to be institutionalized or to use outpatient services. If many patient advocates fear the use of excessive authority that deprives persons of the civil liberties and privacy, others contend that such persons as Seung-Hui Cho, the student at Virginia Tech who murdered students and faculty members at the University in early 2007, might *not* have been so destructive had a Virginia Court only asked him to get outpatient care in 2005. Legislation enacted in the 1960s and 1970s in many states put strong restraints on mental health personnel who wished to commit specific patients involuntarily, yet some states like New York have recently adopted forced-treatment laws—resulting in lower incidences of suicides, homelessness, hospital stays, and attacks on others, as well as greater use of prescribed drugs.[81] These kinds of questions strongly suggest that mental health services must increasingly rely on evidence-based research to determine what works best and for whom.

The nation's policies and programs for persons with substance abuse have been sorely flawed despite the prevalence of alcoholism and drug abuse in the United States. In the more than three decades since President Richard Nixon declared a war on drugs in 1971, the number of persons using them has actually increased annually to include 2.1 million trying marijuana, 872,000 experimenting with cocaine, 108,000 trying heroin, and 2.5 million trying nonmedical use of prescription drugs—with 20 million Americans currently using illicit drugs. About 30,000 persons suffered drug-induced deaths in 2005—and another 20,000 died from use of alcohol.[82]

Experts differ regarding whether the nation is moving in a more positive direction in this respect, since trends vary for each of these kinds of drugs. If some studies cite declining use of illicit drugs by high school students, others argue that marked increases are occurring in overuse of prescription drugs. If some cite closures of many methamphetamine labs and greater seizures of cocaine, others contend that the smuggling of illicit drugs from abroad has not abated.

Even if many experts believe that treatment is more cost-effective than interdiction at borders and placing persons in jail for using illicit drugs, funding of substance abuse clinics remains inadequate. Long waits often exist in clinics that treat persons with substance abuse problems even though promising advances in drug treatment have evolved.

The Continuing Oppression of Aging Americans

Although poverty has markedly decreased among persons over 65 due to the indexing of Social Security benefits for inflation in recent decades, about 50 percent of older persons retire with inadequate savings or assets. Relying mostly on their Social Security checks and Medicare, they face an uncertain economic future. Many seniors lack dental insurance just when they most need expensive dental procedures. If they cannot afford Medi-Gap private insurance, which covers medical care excluded from Medicare such as for chronic health conditions, they have to go through the demeaning process of "spending down" to deplete their assets so that they can qualify for the means-tested Medicaid program—meaning they have no resources for trips and cannot leave money to their children when they die. When transferring to Medicaid, however, they must often change physicians, hospitals, and health plans because large numbers of health care facilities and doctors do not serve Medicaid patients—a shift that is very disruptive to many seniors.

Age discrimination in places of employment is rampant, with many companies terminating older workers just as they are on the verge of qualifying for pensions, to replace them with lower-wage younger employees or with part-time employees who receive no health care coverage or other benefits.

Frail elderly persons often find it difficult to get services to help them remain at home. Medicare funds home health services only after specific episodes of hospitalization and only for relatively short periods. Medicaid funds home health care, but at such low levels that only untrained persons, often lacking even high school degrees, will provide the services. While many of these persons are highly dedicated and provide excellent care, most lack training—and a small minority can maltreat seniors and take their possessions. The burden of care for most seniors falls to their female children, relatives, and friends, who constitute a vast unpaid workforce that frequently suffers stress, health problems, and mental problems because of the enormity of their burdens.[83]

Those elderly persons who are institutionalized often face uncertain prospects. While nursing home standards have improved, they remain inadequate in many jurisdictions not only with respect to medical care, but with respect to social work and recreational services.

The Continuing Oppression of Poor People

In what has become a classic discussion of institutionalized inequality in the United States, author Barbara Ehrenreich in her book *Nickeled and Dimed* analyzed the lives of waitresses, persons working in Wal-Mart, and persons working on crews that clean houses.[84] Living paycheck to paycheck in low-wage jobs, these women eked out a bare existence. Many of them worked at as many as three jobs to make ends meet. If they had families, they could not count on receiving quality child care. Rarely receiving health insurance while encountering unsafe or stressful working conditions, they often delayed seeking health care even when they had serious health problems. Over 50 percent of persons who qualify for Food Stamps do not use them, often because they are unaware that they are eligible since the federal government only sporadically advertises the program. Similarly, only a fraction of eligible families use the Earned Income Tax Credit and S/CHIP medical insurance for children in low-income families, leaving about 9 million children uninsured in 2007.

Anti-poverty advocacy groups could not win even inflation-adjusted increases in many safety net programs during the Bush administration—though the Democratic Congress obtained increases in the minimum wage in 2007. The average benefit of the Food Stamps Program, for example, was only $1 per meal per person, which is an insufficient amount to meet the nutritional needs of low-income recipients.

The growing gap between rich and poor persons is a troublesome trend in the United States. If inequality markedly diminished from World War II to the late 1960s, it markedly increased in ensuing decades to the present despite a slight decline during the economic boom of the 1990s. Between 2000 and 2004, 5.3 million additional persons fell into poverty—leaving 37 million people (or 1 in 8 Americans) below the federal poverty line of $20,000 annual income for a family of four. About 25 million Americans sought assistance from food banks in 2006—about 20 percent more than in 1997. (See Insert 12.6.)

The Continuing Oppression of the LGBT Population

Gays and lesbians still encounter virulent prejudice, as is illustrated by Justice Scalia's scathing

---

I N S E R T   12.6   Critical Analysis: Should We Be Concerned about Relative Poverty?

Poverty is usually discussed in terms of persons' ability to afford bare essentials, such as food and housing. Indeed, the nation's official poverty standard is geared to the value of a "market basket" of specific goods that are needed for bare survival. Persons who use this approach count the number of persons who fall beneath official poverty standards.

Alternatively, poverty can be measured in *relative* rather than market-basket terms. Persons who use this approach measure the degree of resource discrepancy between, say, persons living in the bottom 20 percent and persons in the top 20 percent of the economic order.

Assume that the U.S. *did* largely eradicate market-basket poverty. Would it matter if relative poverty kept climbing until it reached levels that existed in the Gilded Age at the end of the 19th century? What specific kinds of negative or positive consequences would persons at the bottom of the economic order experience, as well as persons at the top of the economic order?

---

denunciation of the Supreme Court's decision to invalidate Texas's anti-sodomy law. He said the Court's majority had "largely signed onto the so-called homosexual agenda." He contended that most Americans do not want homosexuals "as partners in their business, as scoutmasters for their children, as teachers in their children's schools, or as boarders in their homes." He viewed the decision as a precursor to laws that would legitimate gay marriage—and that would undermine laws barring bigamy, incest, and prostitution.[85] Shortly after the Supreme Court's decision, some persons vowed to get a constitutional amendment enacted that would limit "marriage" to heterosexual couples.

Many of gays' and lesbians' battles are waged in state and local jurisdictions. No jurisdiction recognizes gay marriages, although Vermont accepts "civil unions" that are essentially marriages but with a different name. Massachusetts soon followed suit, but 37 states and the federal government have adopted "Defense of Marriage acts" that assert that gay marriages in one state are invalid in others. By not having their partnerships legitimated, gay and lesbian partners cannot legally share property or insurance. When one partner receives health insurance from an employer, the other partner cannot be covered under his or her policy. Unlike married heterosexual couples, one partner is not legally entitled to Social Security benefits accrued by the other partner. Nor can they legally share retirement benefits under many retirement plans. With their

unions not legitimated, they do not have access to legal proceedings used by heterosexual couples to determine who gets what in the wake of dissolution of their partnerships.

While state legislation to allow civil unions or even marriage are praiseworthy, they do not allow partners to quality for marriage benefits under *federal* law, such as Social Security and the tax code. (Federal law affects married couples in more than 1,000 ways.) Minus federal legislation that protects gay marriage, then, parity between heterosexual marriage and marriages between members of the GLBT population will not occur.

When the Supreme Court struck down a Texas law in 2003 that made homosexual acts illegal, it seemed that same-sex unions might get legal sanction in many states. Instead, the nation became polarized around this issue. Angered by the Supreme Court's decision, conservatives vowed to seek a constitutional amendment that would limit marriage to heterosexual unions. The Catholic Church repeated its position that marriages between persons of the same sex run counter to God's wishes—and urged parishioners to oppose same-sex civil unions or marriages. Public opinion polls suggested that the public was divided, but a small majority of Democrats and a large majority of Republicans opposed legal recognition of same-sex unions.

Some progress has been made with respect to employers offering benefits to gay and lesbian partners. Realizing that they are often excellent employees, many employers now provide benefits to partners of gay and lesbian employees. Only one *Fortune* 500 company offered them in 1992, but 197 offer such benefits today. Yet the nation needs an employment nondiscrimination act that prohibits workplace discrimination against LGBT persons.

While most states permit *single* gay and lesbian persons to adopt children, only 11 states permit same-sex partners to adopt children jointly even though considerable research suggests that children raised by gay or lesbian parents are not more likely to be gay than children raised by heterosexual parents. Research also suggests they are developmentally as well adjusted or better adjusted than children raised by heterosexual parents.[86] Florida is the most restrictive state, not allowing adoptions by single or partnered gay and lesbian persons.[87] National civil rights legislation should be developed to protect gay and lesbian rights to adopt children.

Gays and lesbians in the military continue to experience an ambiguous position under the "don't ask, don't tell" policy established in the Clinton administration. Numerous gays and lesbians have been discharged from the military for disclosing their sexual orientation even when they have superior records of service. Indeed, some men who were hired to participate in counterterrorist projects by the federal government because they are fluent in Arabic were fired once it was discovered that they were gay. The "don't ask, don't tell" policy should be rescinded in favor of policy that accords to the LGBT population full rights in the military.

The nation also needs national legislation that bans hate crimes against all members of vulnerable populations, including the LGBT population. While such legislation passed the House in 2005, it was deleted from a larger anti-crime bill in 2006.

The Continuing Oppression of Persons with Criminal Records

The United States has a prison population of roughly 1.4 million persons—up from 200,000 persons in the nation's state and federal prisons in 1970

on any given day. Another 700,000 persons are imprisoned in local jails for a grand total of 2.1 million prisoners—or four times the average per capita rate in prior decades. These increases stem partly from tougher enforcement of drug laws, as well as more severe sentencing, such as the "three strikes" policy in California that gives life sentences to offenders who have committed three crimes *even* if the crimes are not violent. It costs the United States about $26,650 per year to keep a person in prison.[88]

The United States incarcerates more people and at a higher rate than any other nation in the world—2.3 million persons in 2005, or 491 sentenced inmates per 100,000 U.S. residents, up from 411 a decade earlier.[89] Even though homicides have decreased in the last decade, incarceration continues to rise due to policies such as "three strikes," mandatory minimum sentences, and reduced options for parole. Moreover, 53 percent of all state and federal prisoners are incarcerated for nonviolent crimes such as drug usage and petty theft.

Even though they comprise only 27.4 percent of the United States population, African Americans and Latinos constitute 60 percent of all state and federal prisoners. The incarceration rates for African Americans and Latinos are respectively 6.6 and 2.5 times the rate for white males.

As we discussed in Chapter 9, many persons of color and significant numbers of women who are convicted of drug offenses go to jail, where they often receive little or no help for their addictions. Indeed, many persons placed in prisons for nonviolent offenses should be diverted to social service programs that address their needs and help them to improve their economic condition.

High recidivism rates exist among incarcerated adults. Not only do about one-fourth of them possess serious mental illness, but many have substance abuse problems. Prisons socialize many of them, particularly younger offenders, to crime, because they fail to provide inmates with mental health and substance abuse services, much less remedial education and job training services.

Nor does the nation provide aftercare for most persons who have been released from jail. Often given a small amount of cash and placed on a bus to a nearby destination, most released prisoners are not only desperately poor, but often lack even a place to stay. Their record of imprisonment, which must often be listed on job applications, often precludes them from receiving employment. Many former inmates depend on general assistance from local counties and cities to meet their survival needs—the harshest welfare program in the United States.

The more than 3 million children with an imprisoned parent—or the more than 10 million children who have had a parent in jail at some time during their youth—are forgotten victims of incarceration. A variety of community groups have reached out to this population, giving them mentoring and advocacy services, including Big Brothers Big Sisters of America as well as some faith-based groups. Realizing they may undercut the role of the imprisoned parent, these groups often try to foster prison visits with parents. But most children with imprisoned parents do not receive this assistance.

After the Supreme Court reinstated capital punishment in 1976, annual executions rose to a high of 98 persons in 1999—and death sentences imposed on prisoners rose to 317 in 1996. Yet the introduction of DNA tests in criminal cases in the 1990s and afterward indicated that many persons had been wrongly convicted, with one advocacy group finding 200 erroneous convictions. With such evidence before him, Governor George Ryan of Illinois commuted the sentences of 171 persons in his state in 2003, John Kerry, the Democratic presidential contender in 2004, urged the abolition of death penalties on moral grounds, and New Jersey abolished them in 2007.[90]

It is unclear whether the United States, which alone among Western industrialized nations uses death penalties, will move toward ending them, particularly in light of the widespread, but probably false, idea that the threat of capital punishment deters homicides. Indeed, a recent poll found that 67 percent of persons continue to favor capital punishment as compared with 80 percent who approved of it in a poll taken in 1994.

The Impact of the Lack of National Health Insurance on Vulnerable Populations

The failure of the United States to give health insurance to all of its citizens has harmed members of many vulnerable populations because they disproportionately are members of the roughly 45 million Americans who lack it. Female workers are far more likely than male workers *not* to receive health insurance from their employers—or to have insufficient coverage. Women who leave welfare rolls are often eligible for Medicaid only for a specific period, but are not covered when it expires. Because women live about six years longer, on average, than men, they are far more likely to have chronic diseases, such as congestive heart failure, osteoporosis, arthritis, diabetes, and chronic obstructive pulmonary disease, that are poorly covered by Medicare—forcing them to spend down their assets to get access to Medicaid.

Persons of color, particularly Latinos, disproportionately do not have private health insurance. Latinos with chronic health conditions such as diabetes often do not receive early diagnostic and preventive care because they often use emergency rooms as their major access to health care.

Because levels of income and education are excellent predictors of health and longevity, low-income persons particularly need preventive care and health education. Not wanting to endure long waits in public clinics, they often wait until they have a serious condition before seeking care in emergency rooms. Here, too, they often endure long waits, with many patients leaving the lines in frustration. Because many emergency rooms are poorly linked to outpatient clinics, low-income persons often don't get linked to physicians and support workers who can provide continuous care.

Persons with mental and physical disabilities who lack health insurance must devote much time to finding who will pay for their medical and support services. We have discussed how persons with HIV and AIDS must negotiate systems that will pay for some of their medical and drug needs, but not supportive services. Many immigrants qualify for only obstetric and emergency services, leaving them without preventive care even as they engage in work that exposes them to toxic chemicals and harsh working conditions.

The 85 percent of Americans who *do* receive private health insurance from their employers also encounter difficulties in using health care. In a health system that pays doctors and health plans for services rendered, patients are often overmedicated and given surgery when they do not need it. Because health personnel are often *not* reimbursed for preventive services, including time spent by health personnel in educating patients about their health needs, many Americans are not educated about how to prevent heart disease, cancer, and other diseases—or even how to manage them once they get them.

Americans spend about 16 percent of the GDP on health care as compared to less than 10 percent for European nations—yet their morbidity and mortality outcomes are considerably worse. Not only do Europeans have better access to health care since all of them are insured, but they have more primary care physicians and clinics as compared to an American health system that features specialists. At the time this book went to press, it remained to be seen if Democrats would be more successful than prior presidents in obtaining universal health insurance if they prevailed in the 2008 elections.

Revisiting the Terms *Out-group* and *Vulnerable Population*

Even our brief discussion suggests that the terms *vulnerable population* and *out-group* describe many stigmatized groups in American society even though progress has occurred for some or many members of specific out-groups during the last 40 years. We will know that the term is outmoded for a specific population when its members perceive themselves to be part of the social and economic mainstream of society.

The United States has gone through specific stages. Small gains were achieved in the decades and centuries prior to the 1960s due to the determined work of advocates and group empowerment strategies that we have discussed in prior chapters. Civil rights legislation was enacted principally in the 1960s and 1970s, although some important measures were enacted more recently. From the 1970s onward, reformers worked to prevent the erosion of these civil rights by conservative presidents and jurists.

We now realize that vulnerable populations require far more than formal rights. Single heads of household need child care, subsidized transportation, and free health care, not to mention job training and education subsidies. Disabled persons need home health aides, affordable and disability-friendly housing, and special accommodations at work. Persons of color need innovative schools, outreach public health programs, subsidized transportation to suburban places of employment, and access to job training. These amenities cost money, so they need to be prioritized in budgets of local, state, and federal governments. Vulnerable populations' fate is inextricably linked to the health of the American welfare state, as well as to their own tenacity in overcoming odds in an inegalitarian society.

RELUCTANCE ILLUSTRATED IN THE BUSH ADMINISTRATION

Greatly underestimated by liberals and Democrats, President George W. Bush developed a multifaceted plan to downsize the federal government, to shift programs to the private sector, to devolve more policies to the states, and to make the federal courts more conservative. Taken in tandem, his policies increased inequality in the United States by coupling large tax cuts for affluent Americans with substantial cuts in programs used by poor people. Under the rubric of compassionate conservatism, Bush also supported some reforms in the nation's schools and Medicare.

He markedly altered the nation's priorities in the wake of September 11. In his defense, he mobilized the nation against serious threats to its security. *Any* president would have had to recommend increases in counterterrorist spending, and possibly military spending, in the wake of the terrorist events of September 11, 2001. Bush linked these policies, however, to huge tax cuts and deficits, thus skewing national priorities away from domestic programs. He also masterminded a strategy to get the Congress to approve an American invasion of Iraq, including disseminating untrue information about Iraq's possession of weapons of mass destruction. It is doubtful that Al Gore, had he been elected president, would have made such deep tax cuts at the very time the nation's spending rose precipitously for national security—or that he would have invaded Iraq. The war not only required hundreds of millions of dollars, but distracted attention from an array of needed domestic reforms as well as humane policies for developing nations.

Bush was unable to get some reforms enacted that he favored due to the coalition between Democrats and moderate Republicans in the Senate prior to 2006—and then because Democrats possessed a majority in both the House and the Senate from 2006 through 2008. He did not get a voucher program enacted for schools. He failed to get a large faith-based initiative enacted. He found it difficult to devolve new programs to the states, as illustrated by Congress's reluctance to enact his proposal to turn Head Start back to the states and to make Medicaid a block grant program. He failed to secure the enactment of private retirement accounts that would supplant Social Security.

Bush *did* succeed in making the Supreme Court considerably more conservative in its makeup and rulings when he persuaded the United States Senate to approve John Roberts and Samuel Alioto to its membership.

To Bush's credit, he markedly increased federal spending for education and included important tax concessions in his tax legislation for some low-income Americans. He also vastly increased American funding of programs to prevent HIV/ AIDS and to help its victims in Africa and other developing nations.

Bush's domestic accomplishments were very minimal considering that he occupied the White House for eight years. He will be most remembered for his controversial foreign policy decisions. His conservative coalition was fraying in 2008. It remained to be seen if liberals, who had made a major comeback in the elections of 2006, would reemerge into a position of political and policy prominence in the coming decade.

WHAT YOU CAN DO NOW

After reading this chapter, you are now equipped to do the following:

- Analyze the ideology and policy preferences of President George W. Bush in the context of his upbringing and personal history.

- Understand the critical importance of elections on national social policies by comparing the policy choices of the Republican Congress from 2001 through 2006 to those of the Democratic Congress from 2007 through 2008.

- Critically examine the foreign and military policy choices of the Bush administration—and make some comparisons between the Iraq War and the Vietnam War.

- Critically evaluate free-market strategies for Social Security, Medicare, and educational policy.

- Critically evaluate the national response to Hurricane Katrina and the rebuilding of New Orleans and the Gulf Coast.

- Analyze the impact of the Iraq War on American domestic policy.

- Critically analyze whether the terms *vulnerable population* and *out-group* are still relevant in contemporary America with respect to the 13 groups discussed in this text.

ENDNOTES

1. Bruce S. Jansson, *The Sixteen-Trillion-Dollar Mistake: How the U.S. Bungled Its National Priorities from the New Deal to the Present* (New York: Columbia University Press, 2001), pp. 350–354.

2. For an analysis of Rove's influence in the Bush campaigns and White House, see James Moore and Wayne Slater, *Bush's Brain: How Karl Rove Made George W. Bush Presidential* (Hoboken, NJ: John Wiley & Sons, 2003).

3. Elizabeth Mitchell, *W: Revenge of the Bush Dynasty* (New York: Hyperion, 2000), pp. 64–67.

4. Biographies of George W. Bush include Elizabeth Mitchell, *W: Revenge of the Bush Dynasty* (New York: Hyperion, 2000) and Bill Minutaglio, *First Son: George W. Bush and the Bush Family Dynasty* (New York: Times Books, 1999).

5. Mitchell, *W*, p. 87.

6. Ibid., pp. 203–206.

7. See Marvin Olasky, *Tragedy of American Compassion* (Lanham, MD: Regenery Gateway, 1992).

8. Minutaglio, *First Son*, pp. 290–291.

9. Ibid., p. 260.

10. Moore and Slater, *Bush's Brain*, pp. 187–210.

11. See Roger Simon, *Divided We Stand: How Al Gore Beat George Bush and Lost the Presidency* (New York: Crown Publishers, 2001).

12. Ralph Nader, *Crashing the Party* (New York: Thomas Dunne Books, 2002), pp. 242–247.

13. Ibid.

14. Simon, *Divided We Stand*, pp. 251–269.

15. Michael Barone, "The 49 Percent Nation," *National Journal* (2001), 1710–1716.

16. Ibid.

17. Ibid.

18. David Frum, *The Right Man* (New York: Random House, 2003), p. 52.

19. For discussion of the tax cut, see James Barnes, David Baumann, and Richard Cohen, "Surplus Politics," *National Journal* (March 3, 2001), pp. 624–627.

20. For discussion of the education legislation, see Siobhan Gorman, "The Makings of a Deal," *National Journal* (March 31, 2001), pp. 630–631.

21. Ibid.

22. Charles Degeneffe, "What Is Catholic about Catholic Charities?" *Social Work,* 48 (July, 2003), pp. 374–383.

23. See Martin Davis, "Faith, Hope, and Uncertainty," *National Journal* (April 28, 2001), pp. 1228–1238.

24. Ibid.

25. John Inglehart, "Medicare and Prescription Drugs," *New England Journal of Medicine,* 344 (March 29, 2001), pp. 1010–1015.

26. See Tish Durkin, "The Scene," *National Journal* (May 5, 2001), pp. 1287–1288.

27. Joseph Stiglitz applies this term to the Bush administration in "Terrorism: There's No Future in It," *Los Angeles Times* (July 31, 2003), pp. B17.

28. Mark Murray, Marilyn Serafini, and Megan Twohey, "Untested Safety Net," *National Journal* (March 10, 2001), pp. 684–687.

29. Marcia Meyers, "How Welfare Offices Undermine Welfare Reform," *American Prospect* (2000), pp. 40–45.

30. Carolee Howes, Deborah Phillips, and Marcy Whitebock, "Thresholds of Quality, Implications to the Social Development of Children in Center-Based Care," *Child Development,* 43 (April 1992), pp. 449–460.

31. Michelle Derr, Sarah Douglas, and La Donna Pavetti, "Providing Mental Health Services to TANF Recipients," *Mathematica Policy Research* (August 2001).

32. John Cooley, *Unholy Wars: Afghanistan, America, and International Terrorism* (London: Pluto Press, 2002), pp. 198–200.

33. Peter Bergen, *Holy War, Inc.* (New York: Simon & Schuster, 2002), pp. 44–65.

34. Ibid., pp. 146–170.

35. For a discussion of state finances, see Louis Uchitelle, "Red Ink Beginning to Hurt Economic Recovery," *The New York Times* (July 28, 2003), pp. A1, A10.

36. For discussion of the campaign finance legislation, see the 2001 *Congressional Quarterly Almanac* (Washington, DC: Congressional Research Service, 2001), pp. 6–3 to 6–7.

37. Moore and Slater, *Bush's Brain,* pp. 308–318.

38. Bob Woodward, *Bush at War* (New York: Simon & Schuster, 2002), pp. 49, 60–61, 83–85, 88.

39. Bruce Stokes, "Monterey Morass?" *National Journal* (March 16, 2002), pp. 790.

40. Joseph Stiglitz, *Globalization and Its Discontents* (New York: W. W. Norton, 2002), p. 25.

41. Jeff Madrick, "Economic Scene," *The New York Times* (August 7, 2003), p. C2.

42. Ibid., pp. 59–67.

43. Dani Rodrik, "Sense and Nonsense in the Globalization Debate," *Foreign Policy,* 107 (1997), pp. 19–36.

44. Stiglitz, *Globalization and Its Discontents,* pp. 23–52.

45. Madrick, "Economic Scene," p. C2.

46. See Adam Nagourney, "Centrist Democrats Warn Party Not to Present Itself as 'Far Left,'" *The New York Times* (July 29, 2003), pp. A1, A18.

47. U.S. Congressional Budget Office, "The Looming Budgetary Impact of Society's Aging," July 3, 2002, p. 3.

48. This estimate was made by economist Eugene Steuerle of the Urban Institute. See Michael Weinstein, "No Comfort in New Solvency Figures," *The New York Times* (April 1, 1999), p. A22.

49. For discussion of Generations X and Y, see N. Howe and S. William, *Millennials Rising: The Next Great Generation* (New York: Vintage Books, 2000).

50. See Bruce Jansson, Sarah-Jane Dodd, and Susan Smith, "Empowering Domestic Discretionary Spending in Federal Budget Allocations," *Social Policy Journal,* 1 (2002), pp. 5–18.

51. *Grutter v. Bollinger et al.*: see http://caselaw.lp. findlaw.com/scripts/getcase.pl?court=us&vol=000 &invol=02-241.

52. Ibid.

53. Trent Gegax et al., "The War over Gay Marriage," *Newsweek* (July 7, 2003), pp. 38–45.

54. Bob Benenson, "Blue State Special," *Congressional Quarterly Weekly,* August 14, 2006, pp. 2224–2241.

55. Ibid., p. 2226.

56. Adam Nagourney, "In House Races, More G.O.P. Seats Are Seen at Risk," *The New York Times* (October 7, 2006), p. 1.

57. Ronald Brownstein, "Democrats Aim at the Red," *Los Angeles Times* (October 11, 2006), pp. 1, 22.

58. Randal Archibold, "Far from Big City, Hidden Toll of Homelessness," *The New York Times* (October 11, 2006), pp. 1, 25.

59. Robin Toner, "Democrats Have an Intensity, but GOP Has Its Machine," *The New York Times* (October 15, 2006), pp. 1, 25.

60. Neil Munro, "Equal but Diverse," *National Journal* (October 14, 2006), pp. 54–55.

61. Bara Vaida, "Abortion Wars Return," *National Journal* (May 26, 2007), pp. 28–32.

62. Paul Krugman, *The Conscience of a Liberal* (New York: W. W. Norton, 2007).

63. David Brooks, "The Hamiltonian Ground," *The New York Times* (October 12, 2007), opinion page.

64. I first used the term in *The Theory and Practice of Social Welfare Policy: Analysis, Processes, and Current Issues* (Belmont, CA: Wadsworth Publishing Co., 1984), pp. 12–18.

65. Charles Hurst, "Social Inequality and Social Movements" in Hurst, *Social Inequality,* 6th ed. (Boston: Allyn & Bacon, 2007), pp. 295–330.

66. Norton Grubb, *Learning to Work: The Case for Reintegrating Job Training and Education* (New York: Russell Sage, 1996).

67. N. Dailey, *When Baby Boom Women Retire* (Westport, CT: Praeger, 1998).

68. Jodie Levin-Epstein, "Reproductive Roulette," *American Prospect* (Fall 2001), pp. 19–20.

69. Lisa Caruso, "Behind Closed Doors," *National Journal* (June 9, 2007), p. 60.

70. Clive Brook, "Still Baffled by Immigration," *National Journal* (May 26, 2007), pp. 16–17.

71. Justice Ginsburg, dissenting in *Grotz v. Bollinger* (02-516), Supreme Court of the United States, No. 02-516, June 23, 2003 (see *The New York Times,* "The Supreme Court: Excerpts from Justices' Opinions in the Michigan Affirmative Action Cases," June 24, 2003, p. E1).

72. Megan Twohey, "Role Reversal Jolts Blacks, Hispanics," *National Journal* (April 14, 2001), p. 1122.

73. Ibid.

74. Diana Jean Schemo, "Crucial Lawmaker Outlines Changes to Education Law," *The New York Times* (July 31, 2007), p. A12.

75. See Julie Kosterlitz, "Enablement," *National Journal* (August 31, 1991), pp. 2092–3006.

76. Erik Eckholm, "H.I.V. Patients Anxious as Support Programs Are Cut Back," *The New York Times* (August 1, 2007), p. A11.

77. Randy Barrett, *National Journal* (January 20, 2007), p. 35.

78. Julie Kosterlitz, *National Journal* (August 31, 1991), pp. 2092–3006.

79. See Marilyn Weber Serafini, "Through the Cracks," *National Journal* (April 20, 2002), pp. 1124–1131.

80. Neil Munro, "Nature or Nurture," *National Journal* (May 20, 2006), pp. 31–32.

81. Randy Barrett and Neil Munro, "Paved with Good Intentions," *National Journal* (April 28, 2007), pp. 60–62.

82. Paul Singer, "Getting High on Whatever," *National Journal* (January 20, 2007), pp. 32–33.

83. P. Fox, N. Max, and P. Arnsberger, "Estimating the Costs of Caring for People with Alzheimer's Disease in California, 2000–2040," *Policy,* 22 (2001), pp. 88–97 Barbara Stucki, *Who Will Pα Long-term Care Needs?* (Wash Council of Life Insurance, 19

84. Barbara Ehrenreich, *Nickel-anα Dimed* (New York: Metropolitan Books, 2001).

85. See Gegax et al., "The War over Gay Marriage," pp. 38–45.

86. Judith Stacey and Timothy Biblarz, "How Does the Sexual Orientation of Parents Matter?" *American Sociological Review,* 66 (2001), pp. 161–83.

87. Ibid.

88. Carl Cannon, "Stepchildren of Justice," *National Journal* (February 18, 2006), pp. 28–34.

89. *Human Rights News* at http://hrw.org/english/docs/ 2006/12/01/usdom14728.htm.

90. Carl Cannon, "Death and Innocence," *National Journal* (April 28, 2007), pp. 36–40.

13

Why Has the American Welfare State Been Reluctant—And What Can We Do about It?

In this chapter we will explore the following questions:

- Is the American welfare state ethically flawed as it now exists?

- To the extent that the American welfare state possesses characteristics that are *both* ethically troublesome and meritorious, how did the two-sided context of social policy in the United States contribute to this seemingly contradictory result?

- Do contemporary social workers possess ethical responsibilities similar to those of Americans in prior historical eras?

- What lessons can we learn from policy advocates who have preceded us?

At the end of this chapter, we will discuss what you can do in contemporary society to make the American welfare state more humane—following in the footsteps of thousands of policy advocates who have preceded you during the more than the 200 years that it took the American welfare state to evolve to its present condition. In the next chapter, we discuss how your knowledge of the evolution of the American welfare state advances social work practice in contemporary society through policy-sensitive practice, policy-related practice, and policy advocacy.

DECIDING WHETHER THE CONTEMPORARY WELFARE STATE IS MORALLY FLAWED

An excellent case can be made that the contemporary American welfare state is morally flawed—and also has many morally redeeming features. This ethically ambiguous nature of the American welfare state suggests that we—just like citizens of prior eras—have to decide what is right and what is wrong, as indicated by circle 1 of Figure 2.1. We will begin by discussing ethical flaws in the contemporary welfare state and then proceed to some of its ethically redeeming features later in this chapter.

MANIFESTATIONS OF RELUCTANCE

As summarized in Box 13.1, we can identify eight manifestations of reluctance that distinguish the American welfare state from that of most European nations.[1]

1. Even when domestic expenditures of local, state, and federal authorities are aggregated,

Americans devote (and have devoted at least since World War II) a relatively smaller share of their GDP to domestic spending than many other industrialized nations. As can be seen in Figure 13.1, American and Japanese outlays averaged considerably less than 35 percent of their GDPs from 1981 through 1997 as compared with average spending far in excess of 40 percent for Canada and Germany and in excess of 50 percent for France and Italy during these same years.[2] (Even the United Kingdom, whose domestic budgets were slashed during the conservative rule of Margaret Thatcher, spent a considerably larger share of GDP than the United States.)

2. Most nations provide a combination of universal programs, which deliver services or benefits to people regardless of their income, and means-tested programs, which can be used only by people who fall beneath specific levels of income. Whereas many European nations offer a range of universal programs, the United States places more emphasis upon means-tested programs. Only elderly Americans benefit from anything resembling universal health care, through the Medicare program —and even this program fails to cover long-term care and many specific services. Unlike most European nations, the United States does not provide a children's allowance to families—and restricts

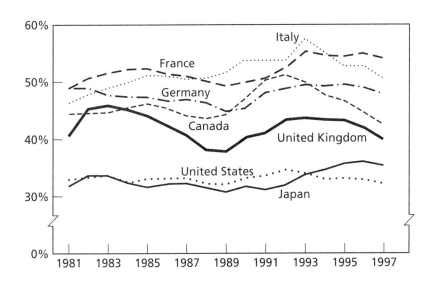

FIGURE 13.1 Total government outlays as a percentage of GDP.

publicly funded child care to persons who meet specific income tests. In some European nations, housing programs, vacation subsidies, and even educational sabbaticals are not means-tested.[3]

3. Whereas European welfare programs are relatively stable, their American counterparts are subject to considerable volatility or uncertainty. New Deal public works programs, the National Youth Administration, many programs of the War on Poverty, and various housing programs have been terminated. Fluctuations in program funding are endemic: Various New Deal programs underwent drastic cuts, the funding of many Great Society programs was cut in the late 1960s, and mental health centers and a variety of means-tested programs for the poor suffered deep cuts during the administrations of Richard Nixon and Ronald Reagan. Liberal reformers have often found their legislative successes attacked in subsequent conservative periods, such as the 1920s, the 1950s, the 1980s, and the 1990s.

Although actual spending on many social programs has not diminished, the same is not true for others; for example, many programs that helped low-income people were slashed during the 1980s. Even when cuts were not made, *threats* to reduce domestic spending have often forced American reformers to devote considerable effort to maintaining existing funding. Flux has occurred in European nations, as well—for example, many had conservative regimes of their own during the 1980s—but the volatility of their programs has been less marked.[4]

The fragility of the American welfare state was dramatically illustrated in the wake of the 1994 congressional elections, when the new Republican majority, under the leadership of House Speaker Newt Gingrich, proposed to end AFDC as an entitlement program, to terminate numerous federal programs, and to markedly reduce federal tax revenues. It was illustrated during the administration of George W he attempted to privatize Social ...icare—and to convert Medicaid ...program. If European conserva- ...of their welfare states and often

propose cuts in specific programs, they lack the assertiveness of their American counterparts, whose rhetoric, writings, and actions often attack the welfare state itself.

4. Many American consumers pay relatively large shares of their personal income for social, medical, and educational services—a trend that increased sharply in the 1980s and 1990s—and local and federal governments have increased fees and payment shares for many public programs. Elderly persons, for example, pay a large share of medical costs under Medicare in the form of various fees associated with the program, and many must deplete their savings altogether when they develop chronic or catastrophic health problems. Mothers continue to fund a large share of day care costs because of inadequate public funding or stringent eligibility conditions. We are not suggesting that consumers ought not to shoulder some share of the cost of the services they use, but Americans risk placing a sizable burden on many low-income, moderate-income, and middle-income residents.

In a sense, Americans are gamblers against fate. Paying relatively low taxes when compared with Europeans, Americans must resort to personal savings, accumulation of assets, and fringe benefits (such as corporate pension funds) to self-fund major personal expenses. The many Americans who cannot save sufficient sums *and* who experience personal adversity—for example, a major health problem—must use means-tested programs such as SSI or Medicaid, but only after they have divested themselves of personal resources sufficiently to qualify. By contrast, Americans who *can* save money, who *do* qualify for liberal private pensions, and who are *not* beset by major social problems win the personal gamble; low U.S. taxes allow them to accumulate enormous personal resources.

5. In comparison with European nations, the United States has subjected single heads of household (usually women) and their families to extraordinarily harsh policies. It was not until the mid-1930s that a federal program was created to

---

B O X   13.1   **Some Characteristics of the American Response to Social Needs**

1. Low spending on social programs as a percentage of the GNP throughout the 20th century
2. Emphasis on means-tested programs rather than universal programs
3. Policy volatility: rapid changes in social policies within and between different eras
4. Significant out-of-pocket costs by consumers and citizens for an array of social needs
5. Restrictive welfare programs, particularly for families with single (usually female) heads
6. Concentration of social problems and unmet needs in vulnerable populations
7. Heavy reliance on tax expenditures to address social welfare needs
8. Regional variations that expose some residents to particularly harsh policies

---

help them, and even this modest program had become engulfed in controversy by the early 1960s. In succeeding decades, it has been constantly attacked by conservatives; its modest benefits have been markedly eroded, and stringent restrictions on its beneficiaries have been proposed. The enactment of the Personal Responsibility and Work Opportunities Act of 1996 not only removed the welfare entitlement that had been embedded in the AFDC program but established even more stringent policies to force millions of persons off welfare rolls without providing them guarantees of health care, child care, transportation assistance, and housing assistance if their wages were insufficient to bring them above official poverty levels. (Nor did this legislation give them sufficient training, education, and social service assistance to improve their long-term earning potential, thus consigning relatively unskilled and poorly educated women to low-paying jobs.) As a corollary to this point, children in the United States are treated more harshly than are children in many European nations, partly because so many of them reside in families with single heads and partly because the United States has not developed universal health care, universal child care, and children's allowances. Single heads of household in European nations endure hardships of their own, but they and their children have access to universal health care, free child care, efficient and cheap public transportation,

well-funded vocational and training programs, and efficient job search agencies.[5]

6. In this text, we have identified 13 vulnerable populations, including racial, sociological, dependent, low-income, and socially stigmatized groups. Of course, all industrialized nations possess vulnerable populations or out-groups—that is, populations that suffer inequalities and discrimination. For various reasons, however, specific groups in the United States often confront even greater hardships than do their counterparts abroad. Take the case of low-income populations in the United States, as compared with the lowest quintile in many European nations. Contrast a walking tour of the great cities of Europe, such as Paris, Florence, Copenhagen, or Munich, with a walking tour of New York City, Los Angeles, Cleveland, or St. Louis. Cities on both continents include low-income areas, but the devastation found in American cities has not been seen in their European counterparts since the aftermath of World War II. Older Americans, while usually above the poverty line, encounter insecurities not known to the European elderly, such as fears of medical bankruptcy. Vast numbers of American children live with poor nutrition, poor health care, and physical danger from crime. We have already discussed the feminization of poverty in the United States; European nations subsidize child care and offer more munificent payments to single mothers.[6]

No single reason exists for the deprivation of vulnerable populations in the United States. One factor is the gaps and meager benefits of the American welfare state, as illustrated by the absence of a national health care system, inadequate child care, and lack of a children's allowance. The American tax system does not redistribute income from the upper quintiles to the lower quintiles; Americans of all social classes pay roughly equal tax rates when all sources, including sales and property taxes as well as Social Security payroll taxes, are included—and when we include tax loopholes and tax deductions used primarily by relatively affluent Americans. We must look, as well, to historical factors, such as the prolonged exclusion of many African Americans, Latinos, and Native Americans from the industrial order and their subsequent attempts to play economic catch-up, with little assistance from white management and unions. Prejudice and racism, present in all nations, has assumed a larger role in the United States than in Europe, partly because of the United States' larger populations of color, who have experienced rampant discrimination. With weaker trade unions than European societies possess, the wages of many low- and moderate-income American workers lag behind those of working-class Europeans.

Nor can we ignore the effects of poverty and inequality upon vulnerable populations themselves. Social scientists such as William Julius Wilson have argued compellingly that people who live under onerous conditions, such as inner-city populations, sometimes develop destructive behaviors that contribute to their plight, including gang membership, violence, and substance abuse, even if these behaviors may be attributed in part to the harsh social and economic environments in which they live.[7]

Even this cursory discussion suggests that a concentration of social problems in specific vulnerable populations in the United States is linked to interlocking circumstances that do not affect their counterparts as strongly in Europe, save for many low-income immigrants who are often marginalized in nations such as Great Britain and France.

7. Unlike other industrialized nations, the United States delivers an extraordinary amount of its social welfare benefits through the tax code rather than through programs funded directly from government budgets. These benefits are delivered through "tax expenditures," which are exemptions, deductions, and credits in the tax code, as well as deferred taxes that allow citizens to pay less than their normal tax. *Exemptions* allow citizens not to pay taxes on some of their income. *Deductions* allow citizens to reduce their taxable income by deducting from it some or all of certain kinds of expenditures, such as mortgage interest payments, payments into pensions, and health care costs. Corporations deduct from their taxable income such expenses as the cost of their employees' health insurance premiums and corporate pensions. *Tax credits*, which give citizens or corporations tax rebates, include the Earned Income Tax Credit (EITC) and tax credits for certain corporate job training programs. *Deferred taxes* allow citizens to postpone taxes on income that is placed in private pension funds. The fiscal magnitude of specific tax expenditures is determined by calculating the extent to which they reduce tax revenues.

The United States is unique in the extent to which it uses the tax code to fund social welfare. Tax expenditures currently account for one-third of all social welfare expenditures in the United States, as compared with less than one-tenth in other industrialized nations. When tax expenditures are added to budget expenditures, aggregate U.S. social welfare spending falls in the mid-range of these nations (when the cost of tax expenditures is added to direct funding of social welfare).[8]

Some tax expenditures help low-income people, such as the EITC, which has become the largest anti-poverty program for nonelderly persons in the United States. Many others, however, disproportionately help middle- and upper-income Americans. For example, low-income renters do not benefit from deductions from mortgage interest payments that deliver huge benefits to homeowners. Many low-wage workers, whose

---

INSERT 13.1 **Using the Web to Gain Perspective on the American Welfare State**

Visit **academic.cengage.com/social_work/jansson** to view these links and a variety of study tools.

To place the American welfare state in its historic and comparative context, visit the following websites.

Go to **http://www.oecd.org** to learn about the Organization for Economic Cooperation and Development, an international organization with 30 member nations. The site is a good source of information on economic and social issues in these countries, with much data on social welfare indicators and policies as well as analyses of social conditions. You can access comparative data or view data by country.

Go to **http://www.un.org** for information on the United Nations, which currently has 191 member nations. The UN website is a

good source for comparative data on social indicators. It also includes a database listing that may provide links to organizations involved in advocacy efforts, including humanitarian relief agencies and international NGOs.

Go to **http://www.census.gov** to view data from the U.S. Census Bureau. Within the Population Division, the Census Bureau operates an International Programs Center that provides demographic and socioeconomic statistics on 227 countries, "independent states," or "areas" of the world. The site offers both historical data going back as far as 1950 and projections to 2050.

To find websites for individual nations, go to **http://www.psr.keele.ac.uk/official.htm**

INSERT 13.2 **Critical Analysis: Does the United States Lag behind Canada and Sweden?**

Andrew Jackson, the Director of Research for the Canadian Council on Social Development, contends that the United States lags behind Canada and Sweden on "social performance."[9] Do you agree after examining his data? Later in this chapter we discuss some factors that help us better understand why the United States possesses a reluctant welfare state.

Canada Beats USA—But Loses Gold to Sweden

By Andrew Jackson, Director of Research, Canadian Council on Social Development, March 8, 2002

As we've all heard *ad nauseam*, Canada lags behind the USA in terms of productivity. But how are we doing when it comes to our social performance? In the afterglow of our gold-medal victories over our neighbours to the south, it seems timely to present a scorecard.

The bottom line? Canada beats the U.S. hands down on most social indicators, but we still fall well short of the Swedes. So there's reason for pride, but not for complacency.

Our 25-indicator scorecard looks at income and poverty; jobs; employment security; social supports for

families; health; crime; education; and civic participation.

In terms of average income, it's no surprise that we lag behind the U.S. Adjusted for purchasing power, the average Canadian family has 21% less income than the average American.

But our income is much more equally distributed. Using a common definition of poverty (having less than half the income of the average family), one in ten Canadians are poor compared to one in six Americans and just one in sixteen Swedes. One in six Canadian kids is poor, compared to almost one in four American children.

When it comes to jobs, the U.S. wins in terms of low unemployment, but there is little difference between the three countries in the proportion of people who have jobs. The U.S. does worse than Canada, however, when it comes to the quality of jobs, and here we both compare badly to the Swedes.

A common definition for being "low paid" is being paid one-third less than the national average. If we use this definition to compare the workforces of the three countries, 21% of Canadian workers are low paid, compared to 25% in the U.S. and just 5% in

(Continued)

Twenty-Five Key Indicators of Social Development

Legend: ▨ Gold ▨ Silver ▨ Bronze

	Canada	US	Sweden
INCOME AND POVERTY			
1. Income per person (%US)	79.0%	100.0%	70.2%
2. Poverty rate	10.3%	17.0%	6.4%
3. Child poverty rate	15.5%	22.4%	2.6%
JOBS			
4. Employment rate	71.1%	74.1%	74.2%
5. Unemployment rate	6.8%	4.0%	5.9%
6. Working long hours	22.0%	26.0%	17.0%
7. Low-paid jobs	20.9%	24.5%	5.3%
8. Earnings gap	3.7	4.6	2.2
EMPLOYMENT SECURITY			
9. UI benefits as % earnings	28.0%	14.0%	29.0%
10. Job supports (%GDP)	0.5%	0.2%	1.8%
11. Unionization rate	36.0%	18.0%	89.0%
SOCIAL SUPPORTS			
12. Health care (public share)	69.6%	44.7%	83.8%
13. Tertiary education (public share)	60.0%	51.0%	91.0%
14. Private social spending	4.5%	8.6%	3.0%
HEALTH			
15. Life expectancy (men)	75.3	72.5	75.9
16. Life expectancy (women)	81.3	79.2	81.3
17. Infant mortality/100,000	5.5	7.2	3.5
CRIME			
18. Homicides per 100,000	1.8	5.5	NA
19. Assault/threat per 100,000	4.0	5.7	4.2
20. Prisoners per 100,000	118	546	71
EDUCATION			
21. Adults/postsecondary ed.	38.8%	34.9%	28.0%
22. High literacy (% Adults)	25.1%	19.0%	35.5%
23. Low literacy (% Adults)	42.9%	49.6%	25.1%
24. Grade 12 math score	519	461	552
CIVIC PARTICIPATION			
25. Voter Turnout	56.2%	49.1%	83.2%

Sweden. More Americans than Canadians and Swedes work in jobs with very long hours. And Americans are much less likely to be in a union, to have access to unemployment insurance, and to qualify for government-paid retraining programs.

One of the biggest differences is in terms of social supports, where Canada again stands between the U.S. and Sweden. American families have to pay much more out of their own pockets for health care and education, which wipes out a lot of the benefits of those vaunted lower taxes.

Governments pick up 70% of the cost of health care and 60% of the cost of higher education in Canada, compared to 45% and 51% in the U.S. Overall, American families spend 9% of GDP on social protection—everything from health care to pensions—out of their own pockets, compared to only 4% in Canada and 3% in Sweden.

Greater income equality and more citizenship entitlement programs make Canada and Sweden clear winners over the U.S. when it comes to health outcomes, crime rates, and educational attainment. And we get to enjoy it longer—Canadians live more than two years longer than Americans: 75 years compared to 72 years for men, and 81 years compared to 79 years for women.

We in Canada are much, much less likely to be victims of violent crime than Americans. The murder rate in the U.S. is a staggering three times higher. And, for every 100,000 people, the U.S. has 546 prisoners, compared to 118 in Canada and just 71 in Sweden.

Based on the results of the International Adult Literacy Survey, 50% of Americans have low literacy skills, compared to 43% of Canadians and just 25% of Swedes. At the other end of the skills scale, 39% of Canadian adults have completed postsecondary education, compared to 35% of Americans and 28% of Swedes.

Final Medal Standings			
	US	Sweden	Canada
GOLD	2	20	4
SILVER	3	2	19
BRONZE	20	2	2

Finally, Canadians are more likely to be politically involved than Americans, though both of us compare badly to the Swedes: 56% of Canadians vote in parliamentary elections, compared to 49% of Americans and 83% of Swedes.

Beating the U.S. for the silver medal is something to be proud of, but we should be aiming to wrestle that gold away from the Swedes. Perhaps it's time to put some of our national pride to work to better our social performance.

Notes and Sources

Unless otherwise indicated, data are from the OECD Social Indicators Database.

1. GDP per capita at purchasing power parity for 2001 (OECD estimate.)
2. Poverty defined as less than half the median income of an equivalent household.
3. Definition of poverty as in 2. Source: UNICEF. Child Poverty in Rich Nations. 2000.
4. Proportion of population age 15–64 in employment. OECD Employment Outlook. 2001.
5. Source as in 4.
6. Men working more than 45 hours per week. OECD Employment Outlook. 1998.
7. Low pay is employed in a full-time job and earning less than 2/3 the median hourly wage.
8. Ratio of the top to bottom 10% (top of 9th decile to top of 1st decile of earners).
9. Earnings replacement rate: average by family type and unemployment duration.
10. Public spending on training and labor adjustment (excluding income support) as % GDP.
11. OECD Employment Outlook. 1998.
12. Public share of total health care expenditures.
13. Public share of tertiary education sector revenues. Education at a Glance. OECD.
14. Private social spending (health, pensions, disability insurance, etc.) as % GDP.
15. and 16. Life expectancy at birth.
18. Rate per 100,000 population. Statistics Canada Daily. December 18, 2001.
19. Victimization rate as reported by persons per 100,000.
21. Percentage of adults with postsecondary qualifications (not including CEGEPs).
22. and 23. Data from International Adult Literacy Survey.
24. Data from Third International Math and Science Survey.
25 Voting in parliamentary elections, 1995–1999.

employers often do not provide health insurance or pensions, do not benefit from tax code provisions that allow corporations to deduct their contributions to employees' health and pension plans. Moreover, low-income persons often do not benefit from tax policies that let relatively affluent persons defer taxes on their annual payments into their individual retirement accounts (IRAs)—or that provide tax exemption of payments to retirees from Roth retirement accounts.

Even when citizens of different social classes take deductions, they receive strikingly different benefits according to their income levels. A person with a top marginal tax rate of 39 percent gains $3,900 from a $10,000 deduction, as compared with only $1,500 for a person with a top marginal rate of 15 percent.

The sheer size of tax expenditures, which flow disproportionately to affluent persons, is revealed by comparing them with expenditures from the federal budget for social programs. From 1975 through 2004, for example, they cost only slightly less in aggregate than the nation's combined expenditures for Social Security, Medicare, and Medicaid from 1965 through 2004.[10]

As we will discuss later in this chapter, many conservatives hope to replace portions or all of certain existing social programs with tax expenditures that would help affluent people more than low- and moderate-income people. They have put forth proposals that would replace Medicare with medical savings accounts and Social Security with individual retirement accounts that would give citizens who used them substantial tax deductions, exemptions, or deferrals for income placed in them. As we have discussed, affluent people would disproportionately benefit from these proposals—and most low-income persons would not be able to use them.

8. Variations in social programs across geographic areas exist in all nations, but they are particularly prominent in the United States. Because the American federal government cedes many policies to states and localities, they shape their own welfare, health, and other policies. (Devolution in the 1980s and 1990s accentuated such localism.) States and localities vary greatly in their economic resources as well as in their political propensity to fund social programs. With regard to welfare programs like TANF, for example, some states fund particularly low grants and implement particularly severe time limits, whereas other states are more generous. Similarly, school districts in affluent suburban areas are more likely to offer enriched curricula than schools in inner-city areas. Medicaid benefits vary greatly between different states.

OTHER MORAL FLAWS OF THE AMERICAN WELFARE STATE

We have discussed the reluctance of the American welfare state in relatively broad terms. We can also assess its moral rectitude by asking whether it addresses key important social problems that afflict vulnerable populations as well as the entire society. We list eight problems as illustrative examples of ethical flaws in the contemporary American welfare state—and refer you to websites that examine them in more detail.

Poverty

The American poverty rate was 12.67 percent in 2006—or almost one percentage point higher than in 2001. See "Poverty Remains Higher," Center on Budget and Policy Priorities, September 1, 2006, at http://www.cbpp.org/8-29-06pov.htm.

Homelessness

About 744,000 people are homeless on any given night—and between 2.5 million and 3.5 million people experience homelessness over the course of a year. See "A Snapshot of Homelessness," National Alliance to End Homelessness. Go to http://www.endhomelessness.org/section/tools/tenyearplan/snapshot.

Persons Lacking Medical Insurance

The number of Americans who lack health insurance rose to 47 million in 2006—or 15.8 percent of the population. Included in this number are 8.7 million children—or 11.7 percent of all children. See "Number and Percentage of Americans Who

Are Uninsured Climbs Again," Center on Budget and Policy Priorities, August 31, 2007. See http://www.cbpp.org/8-28-07pov.pdf.

Youth Who "Graduate" from Foster Care

About 20,000 of the nation's 500,000 foster children "graduate" from foster care each year at age 18—only to encounter a difficult transition into life in the community. About 30 percent of America's homeless people were once in foster care. See "Graduation for Foster Children—An Uncertain Future," Annie E. Casey Foundation, 2007, at http://www.jimcaseyyouth.org/docs/grad_for_foster_children.pdf.

Assistance to Persons Who Are in Jail or Who Have Returned to the Community

Seventy percent of the 650,000 people released annually from state and federal prisons will commit new crimes within three years. The vast majority of them receive no reentry help before they leave prison. See Gary Fields, "Congress Prepares to Tackle Prisoner Recidivism," *The Wall Street Journal* (January 14, 2005), p. 1.

Low Wages

About one in five people (or 41 million) fall into a "hardship gap" where their earnings when combined with work benefits (such as health insurance and child care), together with assistance from programs such as Food Stamps and the Earned Income Tax Credit, do *not* meet their basic needs. See "Bridging the Gaps," Center for Economic and Policy Research and Center for Social Policy, October 10, 2007, at http://www.bridgingthegaps.org/publications/nationalreport.pdf.

Feminization of Poverty

If the poverty rate for all women 18 years and older was 12.7 percent in 2004, the poverty rate for women in households with no spouse present was 24.8 percent. Many of these female heads of household hold two or more jobs and still cannot reach, or barely reach, poverty levels. See ftp://ftp.hrsa.gov/mchb/whusa_06/w06pc.pdf.

Legal Status of Immigrants

More than 55 million immigrants have settled in the United States since its founding, yet every wave of immigrants has encountered hostility. The roughly 12 million undocumented immigrants in the United States are no exception. American corporations, food growers and processors, contractors, restaurants, and hotels eagerly use their work, yet Americans grant them few rights. Congress has repeatedly failed to enact legislation to clarify their rights, most recently in 2007. See "The Rights of Immigrants—ACLU Position Paper" at http://www.aclu.org/immigrants/gen/11713pub20000908.htm/.

CONTEXTUAL CAUSES OF RELUCTANCE

A range of theorists have implicated various cultural, political, and institutional causes of the reluctance of the American welfare state. Many of them identify a single primary cause. For example, Skocpol emphasizes political factors that shape policy choices—ideas of policy elites, organizational features of the U.S. state structure, and interest group pressures; Hartz emphasizes cultural variables; Shalev emphasizes the power of working-class organizations such as trade unions; Edsall emphasizes the manipulation of race by political elites; and Berkowitz and McQuaid emphasize the role of corporate capitalists.[11]

It would be simpler, of course, if the reluctance of the American welfare state could be explained by a single cause. Preceding chapters in this text suggest, however, that many factors, singly and together, have contributed to the reluctance of the American welfare state. Were we to push for a single explanation, we would not only risk ignoring the effects of other causes, but we would also fail to examine how the interactions of various factors shape the American welfare state.

Our discussion of the evolution of the American welfare state confirms the importance, singly and in tandem, of the constraining contextual forces that we discussed in Chapter 2. These include cultural, economic, institutional, and social factors; the chronological sequence of events; and legal and political factors, as discussed next.

Cultural Factors

Americans have developed a multifaceted mythology to justify their failure to develop a relatively generous welfare state. It includes a set of interrelated beliefs: that social programs do more harm than good, that social problems can be easily solved, that problems can be avoided by creating equal opportunity, and that laissez-faire policies can suffice to solve social problems. We call these interrelated beliefs a mythology because their validity remains unproven.

Problems and Panaceas.   Americans' optimistic faith in simple solutions has impeded deeper analysis of the causes and persistence of social problems throughout the nation's history. Poverty is linked to structural causes, such as recessions, low wages in certain sectors of the economy, disabling mental and physical conditions, low levels of skills and education, and discrimination.

Simple solutions did not eliminate or mitigate poverty in the 19th century, when bread lines formed during recessions or when immigrants found themselves at the mercy of employers who paid low wages. The government regulations of the Progressive Era did little to help destitute immigrant workers in the nation's cities. The Social Security program did not eradicate poverty among elderly persons, even though many of its framers were convinced that it would. Successive welfare reforms of the 1960s did not reduce the welfare rolls. The War on Poverty had minimal impact on the incidence of poverty in the United States. The Reagan administration's cuts in social spending and punitive welfare policies did not substantially reduce the size of welfare rolls.

Naive optimism that single programs can solve major social problems has fostered cynicism about the effectiveness of existing social programs. Time and time again, Americans have launched social programs with extravagant fanfare. When the programs failed to eliminate the problems, critics demanded their discontinuation, only to begin another cycle of hope and disillusionment. Americans have seldom realized that simple solutions rarely suffice to remedy complex problems or that the success of single programs is even less likely when they are poorly funded or implemented. The mental institutions of the mid-19th century became custodial institutions because they were poorly funded in subsequent decades. Regulations involving housing and public health were often rendered ineffective in the Progressive Era because they were not monitored. The War on Poverty never received more than $2 billion in any given year. The welfare reforms of the late 1990s were not accompanied with extensive funds for training and education.

Networks of mutually reinforcing programs are needed to address social problems. The problem of the feminization of poverty in the contemporary period could be reduced, for example, by a cluster of programs—a children's allowance, tax rebates and exemptions, enforcement of support payments from absentee fathers, and tax incentives to encourage employers to hire women who are single heads of household—but none of these remedies, by itself, would make a significant impact on the problem. It is also difficult for social programs to succeed in the absence of fundamental reforms designed to improve the economic and social status of disadvantaged persons. Individuals can benefit from services, job training, and improved education; but these positive benefits can be negated if people remain in blighted neighborhoods, suffer unemployment, or experience grinding poverty.

The Misleading Analogy of the Fair Footrace. Jefferson hoped that Americans could avoid the perils of a class-structured society if all residents were granted access to the land and to education. A combination of circumstances—the abundance of frontier lands, the remarkable speed of industrialization, the prosperity of many Americans, economic growth, and success stories of immigrants who achieved wealth—encouraged the perpetuation of Jefferson's dream and the corollary notion that an expansive welfare state was not needed in a society that had created ample opportunities for its citizens to become wealthy.

As our discussion in preceding chapters has indicated, many residents had an unfair advantage. For example, contrast the descendants of an Irish immigrant family that came to this country in the 1850s and the descendants of African American slaves. The Irish immigrant family lived in appalling conditions in Philadelphia and encountered considerable prejudice, but many members of the first two generations worked in industrial plants and attended public school. By the third generation (roughly 1940), various descendants had purchased homes, obtained jobs from Irish ward bosses, and completed high school. In the fourth generation, many family members no longer lived in Irish communities but in the suburbs, and a number of them attended colleges and entered professions.

The African American family, once emancipated from slavery, lived in grinding poverty in the rural South of the postbellum years. Public education was not available to its members, who lived in shanty homes near the fields they tended as sharecroppers and field hands. For three generations, family members eked out a subsistence existence. Although some members sporadically attended segregated schools, successive generations perceived little utility in education, because rural African Americans could not enter occupations where literacy was needed. Family members learned to live in their segregated conditions and saw little hope of improving their economic status. When a family migrated north to Chicago in the 1950s, it lived in a vast segregated African American community, in a city that was dominated by white politicians, white trade unions, and businesses owned by white entrepreneurs. Unlike the descendants of the Irish immigrants, who by 1960 had wealth, education, and desirable positions in the economic order in the North, most members of the African American family were illiterate and unskilled and faced the task of catching up in a society dominated by whites. They were subject to racial discrimination; they lacked the support of political machines; they found it hard to get industrial jobs; and the resources of African American churches in Northern cities had been overwhelmed by the enormous number of new arrivals from the South. Urban African Americans did not fare well in Northern schools, which were generally overcrowded and staffed by white teachers.

Beliefs about Markets and Government. American beliefs about markets and government have retarded the development of the welfare state. Many Americans have idealized private markets by suggesting that they worked best when left to themselves; this belief is perhaps best illustrated by economic theories in the Gilded Age, but it has flourished more recently with the advocacy of conservative economists such as Milton Friedman.

These theories—which were accepted in the United States more widely than in Europe—promoted opposition to factory regulations, taxes, redistribution of resources from affluent to less affluent persons, public works, and national economic planning. The welfare state itself has been viewed as interfering with private markets because it diverts economic resources to nonmarket endeavors, such as income maintenance programs.[12]

Ample evidence exists, however, that unregulated markets are not necessarily in the best public interest. Entrepreneurs have often victimized workers, consumers, and investors. Although many economic theorists have believed that implementation of their theories would end recessions, no one has yet succeeded. People of color and women have disproportionately borne the burden of economic suffering. Unregulated private markets do not br' an equitable distribution of wealth. If the pr' created by capitalism are to be addressed, government regulations, social programs, taxes on affluent persons, and economic planning are needed.

Beliefs about Equality.   Prejudice against poor persons, which has fostered punitive strategies and benign neglect, has been supplemented by theories that extol the merits of economic inequality. Many European aristocrats and American leaders in the 18th century contended that the leadership of social elites would prevent the rise of demagogues, who, they feared, could capitalize on the ignorance, emotions, and licentiousness of the common people.

When Benjamin Franklin wrote that "what the rich expend, the laboring poor receive in payment for their labour," he was arguing that affluence of an upper class is needed to support and sustain poor persons.[13] Many American politicians in the 20th century, including Calvin Coolidge and Ronald Reagan, argued that the nation had to increase economic inequality so that an affluent class would have the resources to make investments that would ultimately benefit poor persons.

These prejudices and economic theories, which have deterred the development of generous social programs and other policies to decrease economic inequality, have been less influential in Europe because they have been more effectively challenged by leaders of working-class organizations and political parties. European socialists and radicals countered that affluent persons were themselves social parasites who used their resources to victimize the working class and to maintain extravagant lifestyles. American liberals, spared the need to articulate more progressive positions by the absence of a powerful radical movement, have often advocated policies surprisingly similar to those of conservatives. Thus, Franklin Roosevelt supported relatively meager unemployment benefits and regressive Social Security taxes; Kennedy and Johnson enacted tax cuts that markedly increased economic
. . . . many liberals have supported mas-
. . . . . . hilitary spending at the expense of

. . . . ve tended to emphasize equality
. . . . ather than equality of status or

wealth. It is important, of course, to have equality in education so that citizens of different social classes and races have access to similar educational opportunities. But status and wealth are also important because they reflect the degree of equality between members of different social classes. Partly because European nations have had powerful socialist or labor parties, they are more likely to consider equality of status and wealth—a propensity that

T A B L E 13.1   **Total Tax Receipts as a Percentage of GDP in 28 Nations**

Denmark	51.6%
Sweden	51.0
Finland	47.3
Czech Republic	47.3
Belgium	46.6
Netherlands	45.9
Luxembourg	45.0
France	44.1
Poland	43.2
Austria	42.8
Greece	42.5
Italy	41.7
Norway	41.2
Hungary	41.0
Germany	39.3
Ireland	37.5
New Zealand	37.0
Canada	36.1
Spain	35.8
United Kingdom	34.1
Switzerland	33.9
Portugal	33.0
Iceland	30.9
Australia	29.9
Japan	27.8
UNITED STATES	27.6
Turkey	22.2
Mexico	18.8

leads them, in turn, to want to use the powers of government to redistribute resources from affluent to less affluent persons.

Economic Factors

Low Levels of Taxation. Low levels of taxation contribute to the reluctant welfare state by depriving social programs of funding. Already meager by comparison with those of many European nations, federal tax revenues have been depleted from 1950 onward by large military expenditures. An overview of the evolution of American taxes suggests that U.S. history has been an extended Boston Tea Party; taxes have been perceived as alien even when imposed by the American government.

Americans first developed a federal income tax during the Civil War but abruptly canceled it when the war was over. Although various reformers wanted an ongoing federal income tax, the Supreme Court declared an income tax law to be unconstitutional in 1894, setting the stage for enactment of the Sixteenth Amendment to the Constitution in 1913. However, the federal income tax did not assume significant proportions until World War II, when it was finally levied on most people. In subsequent decades up to the present, Americans collected far greater federal taxes than prior to World War II—but still far less per capita than European nations or Canada. (See Table 13.1.)

The relatively low levels of American taxes have placed significant downward pressure on budget allocations for social programs. Prior to the Reagan and Bush eras, most Americans opposed large budget deficits. Given their chronic reluctance to increase taxes, the budget could only be balanced

F I G U R E 13.2 President George W. Bush declaring an end to combat in the Iraq War on an aircraft carrier off San Diego, May 1, 2003.

by restraining expenditure. In this context, the nation's firm commitment to large military expenditures meant that social spending had to be kept in check. This tension between guns and butter was most dramatic during the Vietnam War but existed throughout the Cold War as well.

Military Spending. From 1950 onward, scarce federal revenues have been depleted by military spending. Though Britain and France have had significant armed forces, their military budgets, as a percentage of GNP, have been much smaller than U.S. defense spending. Throughout the Cold War, West Germany and Japan spent far smaller amounts than the United States.

Since 1950, the U.S. military budget has absorbed roughly $300 billion per year in constant 1992 dollars, for a staggering total of some $12.6 trillion. President Reagan increased military spending at a rate that was unprecedented during peacetime. He hoped to add another trillion dollars to military spending with his Strategic Defense Initiative, but Congress balked when its costs became evident. Bill Clinton made some cuts in military spending, but they were undramatic. While the United States was expending these huge resources on defense, European nations and Japan were devoting their revenues instead to productive investments and social programs. (See Figure 13.2.)

Institutional Factors

Jurisdictional Confusion. The American welfare state has been characterized by jurisdictional confusion, particularly from the New Deal onward. Unlike most welfare states in Europe, where national social programs that were funded by central governments developed decades or centuries ago, the American welfare state evolved from the bottom upward—that is, from local governments (in the colonial period and the early 19th century) to state governments (from the mid-19th century to the New Deal) to the federal government (from the New Deal onward). These different levels of government each contribute resources, programs,

and policies to the American welfare state. They are joined, moreover, by extensive involvement of the not-for-profit and for-profit sectors.

If conservatives tend to favor extensive use of the private sector, free markets, local government, and state government, liberals generally want large federal entitlements to remain intact. At an operational level, the sharing of policy responsibilities by all of these sectors and levels of government not only brings confusion to social policy, but can lead to extensive buck-passing as each sector and level of government seeks to shift programmatic responsibility for vulnerable populations to the others. Complex negotiations about the appropriate roles of state and federal governments have stymied several social reforms, including welfare reforms, national health insurance, and national child care policies.

Social Factors

Racism and Prejudice. European societies are more homogeneous than the United States because, until recently, they have not experienced waves of immigration. They possess far fewer persons of color as a proportion of their populations than the United States with its combined populations of African Americans, Asian Americans, Latinos, and Native Americans.

Attitudes to ethnic and racial vulnerable populations have certainly contributed to the relatively slow growth of the American welfare state. Because of the persistence of racism and prejudice, Americans have been inclined to believe that unemployment, crime, and other social ills were concentrated within ethnic and racial populations rather than distributed throughout the population. Consequently, they have felt little need to develop comprehensive welfare institutions. At various times, Irish Americans, Italian Americans, Russian Jews, African Americans, Asian Americans, and Latinos have each served as the scapegoat for the nation's social ills.

Considerable prejudice has slowed policy reforms, moreover, for each of the 13 vulnerable populations that we identified in Chapter 2 and then discussed in the context of specific historical eras. Sexism hindered the development of family planning, day care, and affirmative action programs; prejudice against mental patients slowed the growth of expenditures for a range of community services, such as halfway houses; homophobia delayed a social response to discrimination against gay men and lesbians and to the AIDS epidemic; and ageism delayed the development of humanitarian community-based alternatives to nursing homes, as well as the funding of policies for chronic medical conditions.

White Americans' resentments against the beneficiaries of social programs have few parallels in European nations. Whereas some middle- and upper-class Europeans have criticized people who use social programs, until recently these criticisms have lacked a *racial* dimension because most Europeans are white. Moreover, because European social programs are relatively universal, the welfare state is regarded as belonging to the entire nation rather than to specific subgroups.

The Sequence of Events

The Late Development of the American Welfare State.   When discussing the history of the American welfare state, a central fact is apparent: It emerged relatively recently, during the New Deal era (Figure 13.3). (As we argued in Chapter 5, Civil War pensions did not breach the American tradition of not vesting the federal government with social policy functions.) In many European nations, by contrast, an array of generous national programs—such as health insurance, old age pensions, housing programs, and unemployment benefits—were already well established by the 1930s.

After World War II, moreover, most European governments presided over a vast expansion of social spending, such as the Beveridge plan in Great Britain, whereas in the United States, social spending actually fell below New Deal levels in the 1940s, 1950s, and early 1960s. Most of the major programs of the U.S. welfare state were not enacted until the 1960s and 1970s.

This late development of the American welfare state contributed to its reluctance in several ways. Traditionally opposed to a significant social welfare role for the federal government, Americans would not support a generous welfare state until they learned that social programs could benefit a wide range of people. As we see, this learning process began relatively late in the nation's history.

The late development of the American welfare state also helps to explain the intensity of conservative opposition to it. From the conservatives' perspective, the welfare state is an intruder on a society that emphasized localism and state policies, as well as private philanthropy. By contrast, European conservatives, accustomed to monarchies, centralized government, and centralized social policies, viewed their emerging welfare states in the 20th century as a continuation of governmental activities that had long been present.

The Military State Precedes the Welfare State.   We have already discussed how military spending diverted funds from social spending from 1950 onward, but the timing of the military state's inception is also important. When the American welfare state finally emerged in its contemporary form in the 1960s, it had to compete with a military state already established by the large Cold War increases in military spending of the 1950s. The military state already absorbed nearly three-fourths of

New Deal | Great Society

1776   1876   1900   1930   197

F I G U R E 13.3 Recency of the American welfare state.

the federal budget in the 1960s, so it had first claim on the bulk of federal resources.

While conservatives depict the Great Society as an era of runaway social spending, funding for social programs was relatively limited, partly because of prior budgetary commitments to military programs and the Vietnam War. Even after the Great Society programs were established, military and social programs competed for the limited discretionary component of the federal budget--that is, the annual appropriations of Congress. In eras of financial stringency, this component is vulnerable to cutbacks, unlike the entitlements, whose benefits are automatically funded each year. In this way, military spending continued to place strong downward pressure on a range of social programs into the present. Imagine if the welfare state had preceded the military state, and military programs had to fight for funds that had already been largely committed to social programs!

Legal Factors

As we have noted in previous chapters, the Constitution slowed the growth of social programs in the United States by not explicitly defining social policy roles for the federal government. Coupled with a political philosophy that extolled local and state governments while criticizing the federal government, this constitutional silence enabled generations of politicians to stifle a federal welfare state until the New Deal. Even after the New Deal, conservative politicians tended to regard the federal welfare state as an intruder with no legal standing, and they attempted to return policy roles to local and state governments.

We have discussed, as well, the conflict between relatively liberal and conservative judges in the nation's various courts, including most prominently the U.S. Supreme Court. Even when Congress enacts laws to protect the rights of members of specific vulnerable populations, for example, these statutes are subject to judicial interpretation and even judicial overruling—even though the right of the federal government to develop, fund, [and] implement social programs was finally established [in] the mid-1930s.

Political Factors

Whatever the contribution of contextual forces, the reluctance of the American welfare state has also depended on political processes, as expressed in the policy decisions of local, state, and federal legislators.

Absence of a Powerful Radical Tradition.   The working class has the most to gain from the development of pension, welfare, work inspection, factory regulation, and other social programs because its members are most subject to economic uncertainty, poverty, and exploitation by employers. Welfare states are therefore likely to grow most rapidly in those nations where the working class is organized to demand the enactment of social programs and regulations and where radical ideology, such as socialism, promotes class struggle and the expansion of the welfare state. Indeed, radical ideology served two functions in European societies. First, it emphasized the need to develop programs and policies that would assist the working class. Second, it emphasized common or collective needs of the whole society—for example, public health measures and old age pensions. Both functions enhanced the expansion of the welfare state.

Although many conservatives in Europe supported the expansion of the welfare state, the primary impetus generally came from leftist parties. Socialist and labor parties were remarkably effective in national elections in the late 1940s, 1950s, and 1960s. These class-based parties had large constituencies, often held power, *and* possessed an ideology—in particular, socialism, which was supportive of large welfare states.

At first glance, the U.S. Democratic Party would seem analogous to these European leftist parties: It represented a significant segment of less affluent people, held significant power in the decades after World War II, and subscribed to a relatively liberal ideology. This American party was different from its European counterparts in several ways, however. Not least, it included a major wing that was decidedly conservative—the Southern Democrats, whose threats to vote Republican often forced concessions from Democratic leaders in Congress. Moreover, Democratic ideology was not as leftist as that of many European parties, which openly endorsed socialist ideas. Whereas the political base of the European leftist parties was the trade union movement, which militantly favored the expansion of the welfare state, American unions, with important exceptions, focused on measures relating to their own legal, collective bargaining powers. American unions became progressively weaker, moreover in the four decades following 1965 as their membership plummeted.

The Democratic leaders also had to contend with the Republican leaders, who were more strongly opposed to social reforms than were their counterparts in Europe. Whereas Republican leaders liked to tar Democrats as tax-and-spend reformers, many European conservatives, used to centuries of large central governments, supported social reforms; for example, Benjamin Disraeli, the 19th-century English conservative, believed that the affluent classes bore a responsibility to advance the welfare of the nation and of the lower classes.

Nor did the Democratic leaders pursue policies that enabled the nation to munificently fund social programs. They often supported large tax cuts; for example, the huge tax cut of 1964 depleted government revenues just as Lyndon Johnson was initiating the Great Society. And they supported large military expenditures during the Cold War, often without even pondering their implications for the domestic budget.

Americans have not lacked for social protest or radical movements. Utopian theorists favored the development of communal villages in the 19th century; legions of radical workers engaged in strikes and organizing in the 19th and 20th centuries; and radical organizations (such as the Industrial Workers of the World, the Socialist Party, and the Communist Party) were active in the Progressive and New Deal eras. As compared with European societies, however, working-class protest and radical ideologies were weak.[14]

In the absence of a strong working-class movement, advocacy organizations for vulnerable populations provided considerable impetus for reform. Encountering widespread discrimination, the various vulnerable populations often focused their political efforts toward gaining *rights* for their members. Civil rights activists in the 1950s and early 1960s sought to erase Jim Crow laws; Latinos sought collective bargaining powers for field workers; Asian Americans fought to eradicate laws that limited their rights to own land earlier in the century; and feminists sought to eradicate discrimination against themselves in education, employment, and medical settings. We do not mean to criticize the emphasis on civil rights, because each of the out-groups experienced profound prejudice and discriminatory policies; but this focus, however necessary, may have detracted from efforts to obtain national health insurance, child care, more munificent job training programs, and other social programs.

The development of working-class power in the United States was complicated by the successive waves of immigration and by the internal migration to Northern cities. Immigrant groups spoke different languages and established their own communities and political organizations. Conflict sometimes erupted as their members competed for jobs and local political offices.[15]

Another complicating factor is that many American workers did not identify strongly with their social class. In a nation that has strongly favored upward mobility, many Americans wanted to join the middle class, in contrast to European traditions of working-class solidarity. In the colonial period, indentured servants and immigrants aspired to purchase land or to start new businesses. In the 19th century, many working-class persons aspired to obtain gold, land, or wealth through hard work and luck. More recently, many blue-collar workers have aspired to (and gained) the trappings of suburban life, complete with two cars and home ownership. Seeking upward mobility, American workers have seldom pursued governmental progra~ vance the interests of the workin;

In the absence of a powerful radical tradition in the United States, political compromises have been fashioned between moderate and conservative politicians. When Franklin Roosevelt and John Kennedy wrote their tax and social legislation, they were unconcerned about the views of radicals; rather, they were afraid that a coalition of Republicans and conservative Democrats would scuttle their domestic legislation. Had radicals also been part of the negotiating process, major legislation might have been more redistributive, made fewer concessions to the rights of states, and been broader in scope.

In the absence of class-based politics, interest groups have assumed far more importance in the United States than in Europe. Unfortunately for citizens seeking relief from social problems, the most powerful interest groups tend to represent corporations and conservatives, whose needs have been disproportionately represented in the negotiating process.[16]

Nonvoters.   Voting rates in the United States have long been lower than in European nations. Significantly, nonvoters are predominantly from low-income groups—the very persons whose interests would be served by social programs. This group is so large that it could aptly be called the party of nonvoters. Social scientists differ in their explanations of the size of this group: Some emphasize procedural barriers to registration and voting, which have been slightly eased by recent policy enactments; others believe that low-income Americans are even more cynical about American politics than are middle-class Americans. Believing the deck is stacked against them and that private interests, corporations, and affluent Americans dominate politics, many decide that their votes count for nothing.[17]

The   Power   of   American   Conservatives.   American conservatives have fought social reforms because such reforms required increases in taxation, enlarged the federal government, interfered with local prerogatives, equalized economic and social conditions, or ran counter to the economic interests of corporations. Conservative defense of the status quo ' its golden era in the United States in the 19th

century, but its proponents possessed extraordinary power even during the liberal reform periods of the Progressive, New Deal, and Great Society eras because they could meld the power of the Republican Party with that of conservative Southern Democrats. We have discussed the extraordinary power of conservatives during the presidencies of Ronald Reagan, George Bush, Sr., Bill Clinton, and George W. Bush, when they slashed spending on many domestic programs and obtained significant tax cuts that depleted resources for the domestic agenda.

American conservatism provided a more devastating resistance to the development of social reforms than did European conservatism. European conservatives had helped construct the strong monarchies and central governments of European nations from the 16th through the 19th centuries because they wished to facilitate national economic planning; preserve their own prerogatives; place controls and regulations on industrialists and bankers, whom they sometimes regarded as rivals; or advance their paternalistic traditions in helping the downtrodden. Even when conservatives supported a central government to quell social uprisings, they enhanced its power and hence its ability to finance and administer social programs. By contrast, American conservatives obtained their ideology not from the traditions of the landed aristocracy but from theorists like John Locke. Whereas European aristocrats often used government to perpetuate their paternal status, American conservatives wanted to obliterate government, except as it specifically helped corporations, facilitated economic growth, and served national defense.

In Europe, there was often tension between the aristocracy and industrialists. American industrialists, however, had no serious competitors in local and national governments in the Gilded Age. Taxes, tariffs, and subsidies were devised to advance their interests. Their power was gradually diminished in the 20th century as unions, reformers, and people at the grassroots demanded various regulations, but corporate lobbying efforts and campaign contributions have made them powerful political forces.

Corporations have not always opposed the expansion of the welfare state, but organizations like

FIGURE 13.4 "Right to lifers" seek to outlaw abortions in the 1980s.

In the contemporary era, the efforts of the Christian Coalition and kindred groups have focused on lifestyle issues, such as restricting the rights of gay men and lesbians, limiting women's access to abortions, allowing prayer in public schools, fighting programs to give sex education and condoms to youth, and opposing efforts to prevent the spread of AIDS through distribution of sterilized needles. Each of these projects, in turn, has required out-groups to develop protracted and difficult countercampaigns. In European societies, where such moral clashes are less common, reformers can pay more attention to advancing their agenda.

A Rigged System. Powerful interest groups and well-heeled contributors have exercised extraordinary influence over American elected officials, to the detriment of social reform. Despite recent efforts to limit their influence, wealthy people and corporations continue to shape policies by taking advantage of numerous loopholes in campaign funding legislation. Our discussion of the Gilded Age in Chapter 5, a time when corporate interests often dominated American policy making, suggests that these contemporary phenomena have deep historical roots.

the U.S. Chamber of Commerce and the National Association of Manufacturers have consistently fought proposals that would significantly increase government welfare expenditures or subvert their corporate interests.

Moral Crusades. Although the term *crusades* may seem melodramatic, it describes the fervor of many temperance, anti-drug, anti-obscenity, anti-gay, anti-crime, and anti-abortion projects (see Figure 13.4). Throughout American history, determined reformers have expended enormous effort in trying to eradicate immoral behavior, whether by prohibiting it or by engaging in public education. These crusades have diverted attention from other kinds of social reforms and have often exacerbated discrimination against persons whose personal lifestyle choices were publicly condemned.[18]

RELUCTANCE AS THE OUTCOME OF NUMEROUS FACTORS

Even a cursory examination of social policy history suggests that no single factor suffices to explain the reluctance of the American welfare state. We have uniquely identified a wide array of factors and suggested that together they have promoted a relatively reluctant American welfare state. (See Insert 13.3.)

When it finally emerged, the American welfare state was structured so as to deter widespread support. The eligibility of many means-tested programs was established at such low levels in the United States that white, blue-collar workers, who provided strong support for the expansion of European

---

INSERT 13.3   Critical Analysis: A Comparison of Americans and Europeans Approaching Retirement

As Americans enter their 50s, they must engage in a series of financial maneuvers if they want to secure sufficient resources to protect themselves from economic bankruptcy in their retirement years. They can expect to encounter health problems as they grow older, and a significant fraction of them will experience chronic—long-term—health conditions that require them to obtain costly medical services for a protracted period. A significant number will have to enter a nursing home or receive long-term services in their homes—for example, from visiting nurses.

Many factors make Americans nervous as they face retirement. Because of corporate downsizing, increasing numbers of employees in their 50s are losing their jobs, and some may find that they deplete their personal resources even before they reach their 60s. As companies increasingly curtail or eliminate pensions, aging Americans face further drains on their personal resources. Some know that Medicare covers treatment only for *acute*—short-term—medical conditions, and that they themselves will be required to pay for medical care that extends beyond specific surgeries or other brief treatments. Some are anxious that even the Social Security and Medicare entitlements will not survive the uncertainties of the American political process. Might conservatives succeed in eliminating or further curtailing them? If retirees want to purchase medical security by entering retirement villages or homes, such as Leisure Village in Southern California, they need to have sufficient assets to pay the roughly $200,000 entrance fee *and* the roughly $2,000 monthly fees.

Contrast these aging Americans with their counterparts in Scandinavia, who know that they will enter their senior years with national health insurance that requires them to pay virtually nothing for short- *or* long-term care. Scandinavians know that government-funded retirement facilities charge minimal entrance fees and minimal monthly fees, even for relatively affluent people. Because their pensions are more munificent than American Social Security pensions, they have sufficient funds for recreation.

What are some implications of these two situations? Is the American gamble worth it, psychologically and financially? Do American policies create a class of persons who enter their senior years with extraordinary life options and another class of people with very restricted options—as contrasted with a Scandinavian system where most people exceed a threshold of security?

---

welfare states, found social programs irrelevant to their needs; indeed, they were inclined to believe that such programs were primarily used by people of color. Fewer universal programs existed in the United States. Funding and policy responsibilities were so dispersed that it was difficult for reformers to know where to apply pressure. Moreover, support for social reform was scattered among a large number of vulnerable populations, whereas in Europe it was sustained by class-based, mass political parties such as the Labor, Socialist, and Communist parties.

To illustrate how different factors interact, we can look at the Republicans' surprising successes from the early 1970s through 2004 in attacking the scope of the American welfare state. We can begin with the relatively conservative stance of many American workers, who have rarely sought far-reaching social reforms, even if labor organizations were relatively liberal in the decades following the New Deal. In the 1970s, 1980s, and 1990s, a second antireform factor was white backlash, itself a euphemism for racism; large numbers of white ethnic voters defected from the Democratic Party to the Republican Party during this period. A third factor was the Republican tenet that doing good causes harm; accepting this premise, many ethnic voters came to believe that the generosity of American welfare programs had *caused* a precipitous rise in welfare rolls and the economic plight of African Americans. Finally, congressional action in the 1980s, 1990s, and during the presidency of George W. Bush was profoundly constrained by powerful moral crusades of the Christian right, which gave Republicans additional grassroots and campaign support. When discussing the recent attacks on the American welfare state, then, we need to link *at least* four factors: the absence of radical pressure from working-class Americans, racism, the belief that welfare programs do harm, and moral crusades.

LOOKING AT THE BRIGHT SIDE: REDEEMING MORAL FEATURES OF THE AMERICAN WELFARE STATE

Americans *have* lagged behind many industrialized nations in developing their welfare states, but we ought not to overstate the extent of the lag. Whereas European nations possessed various smaller programs, the major burst of social reform occurred in the immediate aftermath of World War II. That was when Great Britain, for example, enacted the Beveridge plan, including national health insurance, national social services, and other economic reforms. Canada followed suit, as did many other European nations.

In short, despite pressure from relatively radical parties, many European nations were relatively insensitive to the needs of many of their constituents until relatively recently. And their reforms were not immune from rollbacks, such as Margaret Thatcher's sweeping cuts in Britain's social programs in the 1980s or cuts made in Canadian social programs in the 1990s.

In discussing obstacles to social reforms in the United States, then, we should not imply that obstacles did not exist in other nations. Nor should we overstate the size of their welfare states prior to the end of World War II.

Asserting the Ethical Case for the American Welfare State

Whereas many conservatives correctly argue that social problems persist despite the existence of the American welfare state, they fail to consider that many problems would be even worse if Americans had not developed social policies.

Assume, for example, that Medicaid had not been enacted in the mid-1960s. Without Medicaid, the health care needs of low-income populations, already seriously underserved by public clinics, would have reached catastrophic proportions because local and state governments lacked the resources to address them. Older people who had exhausted their Medicare benefits would have been unable to rely on the Medicaid program; thus, hundreds of thousands of them would have been forced into nursing homes even worse than those they encountered in the 1970s and succeeding decades. Persons with AIDS, often financially devastated by the expense of medical procedures, would have received no services unless physicians and hospitals had donated them.

Indeed, we can proceed through each of the major enactments of the 1960s and succeeding decades and render a similar prognosis. Assume, for example, that SSI and Food Stamps did not exist. Would not this erasure of social enactments have led to a homeless population many times its size from 1980 to the present? Without these programs, what would have happened to economic inequality in the United States, which is already far greater than in European nations, Canada, and Japan? As just one example of the positive effects of social policy, the Democrats were able to pass legislation to increase the federal minimum wage after they gained control of Congress in 2006. As indicated in Figure 13.5, when the policy is phased in by 2009 raising the minimum wage from $5.15 to $7.25 per hour, the income for a family of four (consisting of wages from 2,000 hours of work annually plus benefits from EITC and Food Stamps) will go from 89 percent to 105 percent of the estimated poverty level.

Some conservatives would retort, "But would not the reductions in government spending allow further tax reductions and thus increase the funds available for investment and consumption? And would not greater investment and consumption fuel higher rates of economic growth, which would ultimately help low-income populations to find work?" The historical record provides little evidence that economic growth follows reductions in

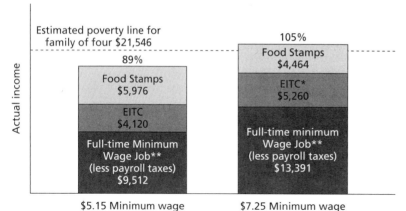

*Includes additional child tax credit of $334.
**Assumes 2,000 hours of work per year.

FIGURE 13.5 Increasing the minimum wage will help lift working families out of poverty.

social spending. Affluent people use excess cash in many ways; they may make such nonproductive expenditures as luxury cars, second homes, and expensive vacations, or invest their funds abroad rather than in the United States. Moreover, expenditures on social programs themselves produce positive economic effects. Programs such as Medicare and Medicaid have funded hundreds of thousands of jobs and, by increasing the resources of their beneficiaries, vastly increased consumption not only by the beneficiaries themselves but also by relatives who might otherwise have had to fund the beneficiaries' medical services.

We ought not to concede, moreover, that *all* problems have become more severe in recent decades. Considerable progress has been made, for example, in addressing poverty among elderly persons; challenges to the civil rights of vulnerable populations; unemployment and lack of services for persons with disabilities; malnutrition; the health needs of certain groups in the population, such as persons with kidney failure; the preschool needs of low-income children; and psychological conditions such as depression. Many persons of color markedly improved their economic and social situation in the decades following the 1960s; leading to significant growth in numbers of middle-class and upper-middle-class African Americans and Latinos, partly as a result of affirmative action and civil rights laws prohibiting job-related discrimination. Children in Head Start classes often show educational gains years after their enrollment.

Nor should we ignore the short-term humanitarian function of social programs. Even when they do not solve social problems, they provide resources and support to people who are experiencing unemployment, catastrophic health conditions, or mental trauma, for example.

In many cases, problems that were seldom recognized in prior eras have been publicized and addressed by new policies. Rape, child abuse, Alzheimer's Disease, spousal abuse, reading and learning disorders, discrimination against gay men and lesbians, and the needs of people with disabilities have existed throughout American history but have come to be widely recognized as important problems only recently. Victims of rape, for example, have often been subjected to punitive treatment, such as imputations of blame by judges and doctors. Children with developmental disabilities were routinely placed in institutions in the 1950s, in contrast to efforts to mainstream them in schools, communities, and employment in the 1990s. Children with reading difficulties were routinely discontinued from school in the 1950s, whereas they often receive special services in the 1990s.

Persons with Alzheimer's Disease in the 1950s were rarely diagnosed and seldom received day treatment and other services.

Government policies both emanated from heightened public awareness of these problems *and* contributed to the public's knowledge of them, as individuals saw the benefits of social programs to themselves, their relatives, or their friends. Moreover, the existence of social programs has often raised public expectations about the rights and needs of specific groups in the population. Whereas Americans in 1950 commonly assumed, for example, that paraplegics would be bedridden and institutionalized, many Americans in the 1990s were aware of these individuals' rights and capabilities, such as access to mechanized wheelchairs, independent living arrangements, occupational therapy, and employment.

We can reasonably argue that the nation would have suffered harm in the absence of reforms enacted in the Progressive Era, the New Deal, and the Great Society, expansions of civil rights and entitlements in the 1970s, or specific reforms of the 1980s and 1990s such as the child care and development block grant of 1990. We can hardly imagine what the United States would be like were it to return to social policies that prevailed at the beginning of the 20th century. American life has been profoundly changed by policy initiatives of various types.

When the welfare state is defined broadly so as to include these many kinds of people-helping policies, its scope becomes clear; it assists every member of the population at many points during their lives. Affluent people take *their* welfare state for granted; they seldom recognize its effects on their lives or question the efficacy of those benefits that they receive. Unfortunately, the programs and tax benefits that persons of lesser means receive are often attacked and cut, as occurred during the Reagan years and in the wake of the Republicans' 1994 election victories.

Of course, people in the latter portion of the 19th century *did* survive without most of these kinds of policies. Unlike Marvin Olasky, who contends that the latter portion of the 19th century was

an idyllic, nearly utopian, period agree that people in this period w inequality, economic insecurity, ep working conditions, food poisoning, ...ous-ing conditions, rampant discrimination against persons of color and women, and many other social problems.[19]

Not Blaming the Welfare State for Things It Cannot Do

Some critics of the American welfare state rely upon a false premise to conclude that the American welfare state—or some specific program within it—is ineffective. How can it be effective, they ask, if it fails to *solve* a specific social problem? In fact, many social problems defy "solution" because they are so complex. When viewed from the vantage point of history, many social problems display a remarkable persistence partly due to the difficulty of eradicating the factors that cause them: for example, social and economic inequalities (which foster alienation, desperation, and stress); lack of economic opportunities for unskilled people (which breeds unemployment, substance abuse, and crime); genetic factors (which promote certain diseases, particularly when coupled with poor diet and substance abuse); viruses (which bring new ailments such as AIDS, even as old ones persist); biology (which is responsible for degenerative diseases and new diseases like AIDS); corporate greed (which causes unsafe working conditions, pollution, and low wages); discrimination (which works to exclude specific populations from opportunities and jobs); family pathology (which underlies family violence and the problem of runaway youth); and individual pathology (which is associated with mental illness, suicide, and substance abuse). These various factors interact with one another, often in complex fashion, to cause specific problems. Substance abuse, such as alcoholism, often stems from the combined interaction of biology, corporate advertising, family pathology, individual pathology, and lack of economic opportunities. Social programs can provide much-needed assistance and even promote certain changes in cultural attitudes, but, even if they are well-conceived and well-funded, they often cannot eradicate major social problems.

Many social problems come from capitalism itself. Left to its own devices, capitalism does not necessarily provide economic equality or a living wage. As Kevin Phillips has superbly documented, economic inequality increased markedly during the 1980s, in a trend that has continued in ensuing years.[20]

Nor can social programs magically change the behaviors of individuals, families, and communities. Considerable research suggests that students' achievement in schools hinges in considerable measure upon their families. Children who are not exposed to a varied and large vocabulary in their interactions with caregivers or parents are less likely to be successful in school than other children. Persons who smoke or use harmful drugs, who eat unhealthful foods, and who fail to exercise are less likely to be healthy than persons with better habits.

Nor are social programs likely to solve some problems when they exist in an inegalitarian society with a huge impoverished population. Those who face bleak economic prospects in the first decades of the new millennium include single (mostly female) heads of household and their children; former factory workers forced into unemployment or low-wage service jobs; impoverished inner-city populations of persons of color; persons working at or near the minimum wage; isolated and impoverished rural populations; and older persons who lack pensions or who confront chronic medical conditions.

We cannot say with precision how many people will develop *additional* social problems because of the desperation and alienation provoked by their bleak economic conditions. Despite the remarkable persistence and resilience of people in these groups, considerable evidence suggests that their economic status contributes to their problems.

Unemployment greatly increases such problems as substance abuse, family violence, and mental illness. The vast majority of children in foster care come from low-income families, partly because economic desperation contributes to neglect as well as family violence. Dire economic circumstances partly explain why American prison cells are disproportionately inhabited by persons of color, who also experience high rates of substance abuse and deaths from homicide.

Our discussion suggests that social policies cannot be expected to miraculously solve major social problems. When conservatives contend that the American welfare state has failed because it has not solved problems like poverty and homelessness, they are arguing from a false premise; in the real world, social policies do not eradicate social problems even though they can help many persons surmount them.

To better understand some of its redeeming moral features, let's summarize a partial list of social policies—which we will call a Policy Scoreboard—that are now part of the American welfare state thanks to the work of many policy advocates. (I exclude social policies that have been terminated, and I include some policies not discussed in this text to convey the sheer number and range of social policies in the United States *even* when many policies are not included in this Policy Scoreboard.)

Key Mental Health Reforms

- Community Mental Health Centers Act of 1963
- Coverage of mental health benefits by Medicare and Medicaid—and requirements by many states that private medical insurance plans must, if they cover mental health benefits, do so in a way that is equivalent to insurance coverage for physical ailments

Key Health Reforms

- Health Maintenance Organization Act of 1973
- Enactment of Medicare and Medicaid
- Federal funding of medications for persons with HIV and AIDS under Medicaid
- Federal funding of many outpatient services in low-income areas through disproportionate share funding of Medicaid
- Enactment of S/CHIP to provide health insurance to children not covered by private insurance

- Pharmaceutical benefit added to Medicare in 2003 in Medicare Prescription Drug, Improvement, and Modernization Act

- Establishment of Veterans Administration

Key Safety Net Reforms

- Unemployment insurance (enacted in 1935, with many modifications during recessions)

- Enactment of entitlements such as Supplementary Security Insurance (SSI), Food Stamps, and the Earned Income Tax Credit (EITC)

- Temporary Assistance to Needy Families (TANF)

- Enactment of Section 8 housing vouchers (the Housing Choice Voucher Program)

Key Civil Rights Reforms

- Civil Rights Acts of 1964 and 1965, as well as many additional policies such as the Equal Employment Opportunity Commission (EEOC)

- Pregnancy Discrimination Act of 1978, which amended Title VII of the Civil Rights Act of 1964 to prohibit workplace discrimination on the basis of pregnancy

- Age Discrimination Act of 1975

- Fair Housing Act of 1968

- Americans with Disabilities Act of 1990

- Protection of the rights of many vulnerable populations by civil rights laws in specific states, including protections of the LGBT population from job discrimination

Key Child and Family Reforms

- Title XX of the Social Security Act for social services

- Child Care and Development Block Grant of 1990

- Child care tax credit

- Special Supplemental Nutrition Program for Women, Infants, and Children (better known as the WIC Program)

- Head Start Program

- Provision of federal assistance to child welfare agencies through Title V of the Social Security Act, the Adoption Assistance and Child Welfare Act of 1980, the Family Support and Preservation Act of 1993 as extended by the Promoting Safe and Stable Families Act

- Federal subsidies for child care in the Child Development and Family Block Grant

- The Child and Dependent Care Tax Credit

- The Family and Medical Leave Act

Key Regulatory Reforms

- Myriad housing, sanitation, and public health standards in local communities and states

- Establishment of the Occupational Safety and Health Administration (OSHA) to regulate work safety conditions

Key Education Reforms

- The Elementary and Secondary Education Act of 1965

- The Mainstreaming of Children with Disabilities Act

- The No Child Left Behind Act

- Federal legislation establishing charter schools in 1997

Key Workplace Reforms

- Fair Labor Standards Act of 1938 establishing a federal minimum wage

Key Block Grants

- Nine block grants, created or amended in 1981, that gave funds to states, as well as broad latitude for programs in the following areas: (1) community services; (2) alcohol, drug abuse, and mental health services; (3) primary care; (4) social services; (5) maternal and child health; (6) preventive health and health services; (7) education; (8) low-income energy assistance; (9) community development

Policies Germane to Globalization

- North American Free Trade Agreement of 1994 (NAFTA)
- International Monetary Fund created after World War II
- World Bank created after World War II
- World Trade Organization established in 1995

Key Housing Reforms

- Department of Housing and Urban Development (HUD) established in 1965
- Low-Income Housing Tax Credits in 1986
- Section 8 Housing Vouchers established by the Housing and Community Development Act of 1974
- Public housing program established by the Wagner-Steagall Housing Act of 1937
- An array of federal housing subsidies developed during the 1960s and 1970s to promote the construction of affordable housing units

Key Organizational Changes

- Federal Department of Health and Human Services (HHS) established in 1976 to replace the Department of Health, Education, and Welfare (HEW)
- Federal Office of Education separated from HEW to create the Department of Education in 1976

Key Policies for Specific Populations

- Older Americans Act of 1965
- Indian Child Welfare Act of 1978
- Ryan White HIV/AIDS Program of 1990
- Social Security pensions (with many subsequent amendments that gave benefits to widows and to children of deceased enrollees in Social Security)

Key Immigration Policies

- 1965 amendments to the Immigration and Nationality Act (created in 1952) repeal the national origins quota system
- Immigration Reform and Control Act of 1986 grants amnesty and creates sanctions on employers
- Refugee Act of 1980

Key Job Training Reforms

- Work Force Investment Act of 1998

Key Drug Policies

- Food and Drug Administration established in 1906
- Controlled Substances Act of 1970

Key Tax Expenditures

- Earned Income Tax Credit of 1975
- Deductions for home mortgages
- Deductions for health expenditures
- Deductions and delays in taxes on income set aside in specific private retirement accounts such as Individual Retirement Accounts (IRAs)

Key Family Planning Reforms

- Family Planning and Population Research Act of 1970

Note: Email names of additional policies for an expanded list in the next edition to jansson@usc .edu (use subject heading New Policies).

CRITIQUING CONSERVATIVES' CASE AGAINST THE AMERICAN WELFARE STATE

Let's analyze some likely effects of six policies often supported by conservatives: reducing social spending, delegating most policy functions to state and local governments, privatizing social services, relying more heavily on private philanthropy, instituting deterrent policies for welfare recipients, and rewarding personal responsibility.

Reducing Social Spending

Some social programs *do* waste resources on unnecessary administrative staff—and some consumers make fraudulent use of programs' benefits. But the preponderant share of programs' costs go to benefits (in the case of benefit programs like Food Stamps) or to salaries (in the case of service programs like mental health and child welfare programs). While some adjustments and economies can be made, large spending cuts in social programs are usually achievable only by making deep cuts in benefits or in staff. Fraud rarely consumes a large share of social programs' costs.

Demands for cuts in program costs, then, often rest on an unrealistic assumption that huge savings can be achieved without sacrificing quality of services or the amounts of benefits. In the absence of major waste or fraud, this quest for huge savings often leads to poorer services and more meager benefits.

Nor does indiscriminate cost cutting address the *real* problems in human services, such as turf boundaries. Take the case of child welfare programs. Many critics contend that, to help families that neglect or abuse their children, it is not enough to rely on occasional visits from a child welfare worker. Rather, child welfare staff need to engage schools, courts, child guidance agencies, case managers, substance abuse agencies, and job training agencies in a collaborative effort. Slashing the budgets of child welfare agencies hardly promotes such collaboration—and may even impede it by forcing overworked social workers to focus on crisis management.

Cuts seem most feasible in medical programs, such as Medicare and Medicaid, whose costs have escalated extremely rapidly; the United States expends greater resources on medical care than other nations do. However, cost cutters encounter formidable obstacles even when seeking to scale back the budgets of these programs. Their high costs partly stem from inefficiencies in the medical system as a whole—such as high fees charged by doctors and hospitals, the emphasis on curative rather than preventive services, and extraordinary use of costly medical procedures even in the last months of life. Large cuts in Medicaid and Medicare would not address these broader causes of the rise in medical spending and would often subject elderly and poor patients to less effective services. If their fees were dramatically cut, physicians and hospitals would increasingly refuse to serve Medicaid and Medicare beneficiaries, who would thus be forced into public hospitals and clinics, which are already underfunded by counties and municipalities. Overall spending for medical care in the United States must be reduced, but that calls for reform of the American medical system, rather than large cuts in publicly funded programs. Policy makers seeking to cut medical costs must remember that roughly 47 million Americans lack health insurance *or* access to Medicare and Medicaid. How can public funding of medical services be cut when so many people are currently not covered by public or private programs?

Cuts in specific programs sometimes cause increases in the costs of *other* programs. Thus, confronted with cuts in their Medicaid and Medicare reimbursements, providers raise fees on their other patients. Likewise, if we cut prenatal programs or programs that provide food to young children and their mothers, we may find that costs of medical programs increase correspondingly.

Delegating Policy Responsibilities to State and Local Government

Some policy functions can usefully be delegated to local and state governments, which already assume major responsibility for public education and the correctional system. They share responsibility for many social programs with federal authorities; under the block grant programs enacted by the Nixon and Reagan administrations, federal authorities provide money to states for programs and impose relatively few stipulations on their administration. In the 1990s, even in programs where federal authorities have traditionally exercised strong policy roles, such as Medicaid, the federal government increasingly issued waivers that granted permission to states to devise their own programs. Democrats, too, have sometimes supported conservatives' quest to devolve policies to the states, as illustrated by President Bill Clinton's support of TANF in 1996, which gave states even more responsibility for funding and administering welfare programs than had existed under the AFDC program.

Conservatives often want to carry delegation of policy roles to far greater levels, as reflected by President George W. Bush's desire to block-grant Medicaid. They sometimes imply that it will save vast sums of money or that it will strikingly improve the quality of programs. Whereas state and local governments can sometimes achieve economies by deleting federal regulations, they often discover that most program costs are absorbed by benefits and salaries. Delegation, in short, often brings scant savings *unless* state and local governments cut the size of programs inherited from the federal government. Indeed, facing budget difficulties of their own and lacking the large revenues of the federal income tax, state and local governments often do cut benefits or services when granted exclusive responsibility for funding social service programs. The dangers of delegation are particularly marked when federal authorities fail to impose minimum standards, such as requirements that states provide certain basic services in their Medicaid programs or give certain protections to TANF clients.

We should remember that the federal government took on funding and oversight roles in the Great Depression and the Great Society because states and localities lacked the resources for social programs. Unlike the federal government, states and localities often want to keep taxes at low levels to stop corporations from fleeing to locations with lower tax rates. Given their reluctance to increase taxes and the considerable costs of prisons and educational programs, states are unlikely to fund programs for relatively powerless populations such as single mothers unless federal requirements force them to do so.

Privatizing Social Services

Many conservatives want to place the administration of social services in the hands of for-profit corporations. Some for-profit corporations provide exemplary administration of social programs and even cut costs by management techniques drawn from private industry. Yet privatization carries dangers of its own. Unlike public and not-for-profit agencies, for-profit corporations divert funds as profits to owners and stockholders—profits that add costs to social programs. To maximize profits, corporations sometimes achieve efficiencies by cutting services to clients, hiring untrained staff, and providing no fringe benefits to staff. Alternatively, they may exclude people with serious problems from their services—whether by discriminating against them or by locating their services in relatively affluent areas.

Of course, some not-for-profit agencies provide inferior services—and many for-profit agencies and corporations *do* provide quality services. Whenever the government contracts with nongovernmental agencies, it needs to establish clear standards that are carefully monitored.

Seeking Nongovernmental Substitutes for Publicly Funded Programs

Conservatives often suggest that private philanthropy, volunteers, and communities can serve as substitutes for government-funded social programs. These nongovernmental entities already intertwine with governmental programs extensively—far more than in many European nations. Not-for-profit agencies usually receive more than half of their budgets from the government. Volunteers work for not-for-profit agencies, as well as some public ones. Private philanthropy augments public funding in many social agencies.

Useful as supplements to publicly funded services, these nongovernmental entities cannot easily become substitutes for them. Private philanthropy funds a network of not-for-profit agencies that provides valuable services to many Americans, but the extent of these services is a mere fraction of those provided by publicly subsidized programs. By the late 1980s, many not-for-profit agencies found themselves unable to sustain their budgets from existing donations and, moreover, faced cuts in their federal subsidies. In response, they turned toward fee-based programs and thus curtailed their services to impoverished clients, at the very time that the federal government was making cuts in programs serving the poor.[21] A large share of philanthropic dollars goes, moreover, to the so-called respectable charities—including universities, hospitals, private schools, and cultural activities—rather than to agencies that serve stigmatized populations, such as persons who are homeless or mentally ill.

Volunteers play a vital role in the human services system, but they cannot substitute for paid staff. Lacking training, many volunteers cannot help clients with complex problems. Some volunteers serve for relatively brief periods; they may burn out, as many agencies helping people with AIDS have discovered. Moreover, since the 1970s, the pool of available volunteers has shrunk as more women have entered the workforce.

When public authorities rely on volunteers excessively, they risk exploiting them. Consider the lack of public services for older Americans with chronic problems. Many women, unable to find adequate home health care for their parents and relatives, take on the caregiving role themselves, even though they already have jobs and heavy parenting responsibilities. Viewed from a feminist perspective, politicians who refuse to provide public funding for home health care are extorting unpaid labor from these women.

Skilled social workers often use informal networks to help specific clients or to enhance community support for a specific project, such as a halfway house. They cannot easily be substitutes for publicly funded services, however, because many individuals are not linked to informal networks, do not want community members to know about their problems, or are enmeshed in destructive networks.

We have discussed, too, why it is not realistic to depend on faith-based organizations to provide a large share of services currently provided by public agencies and not-for-profit agencies that are registered as 501(c)(3) agencies with the federal Internal Revenue Service. Such agencies are often sponsored by religious organizations, such as the Catholic Church, but agree to offer services funded by government in separate facilities from the ones housed in their churches, agree not to display religious symbols, and agree not to proselytize their clients. Public grants to faith-based organizations *not* registered as 501(c)(3) organizations risk breaching constitutional separation of church and state if they seek to proselytize clients who come to them for services. Nor do many faith-based service organizations possess the facilities or staff sufficient to provide the volume of services needed by homeless persons and other at-risk populations.

Our discussion ought not suggest that volunteers, informal networks, faith-based organizations, and communities cannot assume important roles in the human services; but it would be wrong to suppose that they could massively substitute for public programs.

Using Deterrence

Deterrent policies—whether 19th-century workhouses or conservatives' efforts to place severe time limits on TANF benefits in 1996—sometimes diminish the expenses of social programs by frightening existing or potential users from seeking their benefits or by abbreviating their use. Penalties and investigations probably prevent fraudulent use of services by some people, much as audits by the Internal Revenue Service induce some people not to cheat on their taxes.

Deterrence often does not cut the costs of programs markedly, however, because it does not address the basic causes of social problems. Take the case of "three strikes" legislation in many states that imposed life imprisonment on persons with three convictions. This deterrent policy swelled prison populations at enormous cost while catching in its net many persons who had committed minor crimes.

In some cases, deterrent policies may even *raise* the costs of social programs, as Michael Kingsley recently argued. If the Internal Revenue Service simply distributed cash directly to people falling under poverty standards, public authorities would not need to fund the vast bureaucracy that currently investigates TANF clients. (Kingsley also pointed out that middle-class recipients of social benefits, such as tax deductions for mortgage payments, are not subjected to frequent investigations or caps on their benefits.)[22]

Paradoxically, deterrence sometimes *increases* the incentive to cheat. Assume that you are a single mother with three children and that TANF benefits are cut in half. Also assume that you can find only work that pays the minimum wage. Unable even to survive on these benefits, your economic incentive not to report certain income or to hide assets would increase as benefits were cut.

When seeking deterrent policies, conservatives risk overstating the extent to which people's decisions are influenced by rational considerations. For example, there are many reasons why teenagers become pregnant. Some young women are raped. Some become pregnant in the hope of cementing a relationship with a boyfriend. Some become pregnant for lack of information about birth control. Others want a child to make their lives more fulfilling. In light of these complex motivations, many social scientists doubt that deterrent policies, such as refusing or severely limiting public benefits to teenage mothers, will reduce out-of-wedlock birthrates—and they point to data from New Jersey, where these birthrates *increased* when deterrent policies were imposed.[23]

Finally, deterrent policies sometimes violate ethical principles. If individuals have become dependent on public programs because well-paying work is not available to them, punitive policies punish them for circumstances that they cannot control. If public benefits are denied to unwed teenagers who have children, those children will often experience malnutrition and other harmful outcomes.

Relying on Personal Responsibility

Conservatives often argue that the American welfare state has created a culture of dependency, within which people are accustomed to public subsidies when they encounter misfortune or to light sentences when they commit crimes. They want Americans to develop instead a culture of personal responsibility, which prizes personal efforts to be self-sufficient and to help others who experience social problems. If people are not self-sufficient or develop certain problems, conservatives often contend, they should shoulder the consequences, such as poverty or incarceration.[24]

No one would argue that citizens should not try to remain self-sufficient; but the ideology of personal responsibility often assumes that personal character is the primary reason people do, or do not, develop social problems. Even when they act responsibly, however, many people develop social problems.

Many homeless people, for example, are unable to pay the rent because they became unemployed when their employer downsized or because they work in low-wage jobs. People with high school educations occupy a precarious position in the service-oriented economy of the 1990s; although they can usually obtain work, they often receive wages that place them under poverty standards. Carried to an extreme, the ideology of personal responsibility blames victims of social circumstances for their plight, much as Americans in the 19th century assumed that poverty stemmed from poor character or laziness.

In some cases, public policies *should* reward responsible behaviors; for example, it is reasonable for nonsmokers to have lower health insurance premiums. People who commit destructive acts—for example, those who drive while drunk—should suffer penalties, such as prison sentences or suspension of their licenses. When carried too far, however, the idea of personal responsibility can unduly penalize people for conditions that they cannot readily control. People with substance abuse problems often have physiological and mental addictions that they cannot easily overcome even if they confront extraordinary penalties. If addiction is a disease, is it fair to penalize addicts excessively?

CONTEXTUAL FACTORS THAT HAVE PROMOTED ENACTMENT OF SOCIAL REFORMS

Let's discuss some of the factors that we identified in Chapter 2 as facilitating, rather than constraining, the enactment of social reforms in the United States.

1. *Cultural factors* include the way Americans perceived the importance and causes of specific social problems, the extent to which they believed that those in need were responsible for the problems, and the degree to which they thought that society had an obligation to assist those in need by providing ameliorative programs. We discussed how perceptions of various subgroups within the population, such as women and racial groups, have shaped social policies.

Cultural factors that have created *opportunities* for policy advocates include:

- Sympathizing with persons who are perceived to be victims of circumstance—and therefore to be "deserving" of assistance from the welfare state--such as children and older persons.

- Resenting persons and interests that unfairly victimize specific populations— therefore creating support for regulations and civil rights.

- Favoring provision of policies and programs that enhance opportunities for specific populations, such as preschool education and job training programs. Americans place extraordinary emphasis on providing *opportunities* to people. Thanks to extraordinary funding of junior colleges and four-year colleges, about one-half of American youth seek schooling beyond high school, as compared with lower numbers of youth in some European nations. (Budget cuts in the past few decades have put increasing pressure on American colleges, however.) Some critics of expansive postsecondary education contend that many American youth would be better served by vocational education and job training that outfitted them for specific positions in the job market. Those critics underestimate, however, the considerable benefits of postsecondary education, which has expanded job opportunities for millions of American youth. In a world where unskilled positions are increasingly scarce, widespread participation in postsecondary education must be regarded as a remarkable American innovation. Other opportunity-enhancing policies include Head Start, job training programs, literacy projects, and some tax incentives and grants to small businesses—though we should remember that some European nations fund some of these policies more munificently than the United States. (France, for example, subsidizes universal preschool programs—as do Scandinavian nations.)

- Favoring programs and policies that reflect rights conferred by the Constitution and statutes such as due process, civil rights, the ability of the federal government to regulate interstate commerce, and the right of the federal government to advance the "general welfare."

- Believing that all people should have their minimal survival needs met so that persons do not starve, go entirely without medical care, or have no shelter.

- Developing a powerful liberal ideology that favored the enactment of an array of social programs, regulations, and civil rights, particularly in the 20th and 21st centuries—thus becoming a driving force for many policy advocates and presidents such as Theodore Roosevelt, Woodrow Wilson, Franklin Roosevelt, and Lyndon Johnson.

- Creating a liberal coalition in the 1930s by President Franklin Roosevelt, often allied with the Democratic Party, that obtained enactment of a wide range of policies in succeeding decades up to the present—including persons of color, women, Jews, intellectuals, environmental groups, civil rights groups, and low-income persons. This coalition also included a large majority of white working-class and Catholic voters until the 1980s, when some of them switched their allegiance to Republican candidates.

2. *Economic factors* include the extent to which the government possessed resources, such as tax revenues, to fund social programs; the extent to which corporations provided social benefits to employees; and the budgetary priorities of governments. Economic factors that provide *opportunities* for policy advocates include the following:

- The sheer size of national economic resources in the United States, creating a large reservoir of national income that can fund social programs.

- The existence of *entitlements* that are less susceptible to cuts because they are automatically funded each year to the level of claimed benefits rather than having to compete for funding with other programs in the general budget—such as Medicare, Medicaid, Social Security, Supplementary Security Income (SSI), and unemployment insurance.

- The relatively high rate of economic growth in the United States in specific eras that created opportunities for many people.

- The American proclivity to use the tax code to help many low- and moderate-income persons obtain assets and gain income, such as tax deductions for interest payments on mortgages—and the Earned Income Tax Credit (EITC) for low-income families.

- The existence of a vast frontier in the colonial period and the 19th century that created opportunities for many people, including immigrants, to acquire land.

- The willingness of Americans to allow many immigrants to come to the United States.

3. *Institutional factors* include the extent to which governments possessed administrative capabilities to develop and implement social programs and the balance between federal, state, and local jurisdictions in social policy. Institutional factors that have provided *opportunities* to policy advocates include the following:

- The sheer number of entities that can contribute to policy solutions, including federal, state, and local governments, as well as the public and private sectors—providing policy advocates with many points of access. Nor should we ignore the salutary benefits of nongovernmental organizations (NGOs). In nations such as Denmark, a tradition of not-for-profit organizations hardly exists. For most Danes, the publicly funded welfare state is the only source of assistance for their social needs. By contrast, Americans have emphasized the not-for-profit sector from the origins of the republic. An exponential increase in sectarian agencies in the 19th century and the early 20th century was followed by the development of nonsectarian agencies, including previously sectarian agencies that shed their religious origins. For example, many hospitals still possess the names given to them by their sectarian founders, such as Cedars Sinai Hospital, a Jewish hospital, but they have essentially become nonsectarian agencies that serve clients or patients regardless of their religion or ethnicity.

  While we ought not to exaggerate their contributions, nongovernmental agencies have provided many benefits; they have, in effect, become partners with the public welfare state. By administering public programs under contract or grants with government, they have provided a network of facilities that allows outreach into every American community. To Americans who feel stigmatized when they use public programs, they provide an acceptable alternative. Less restricted by public regulations and civil service requirements, not-for-profit agencies have often pioneered innovative services. Millions of Americans have enriched their lives by volunteering in not-for-profit agencies— opportunities that would not exist if the nation relied exclusively on public services.

The viability of the not-for-profit sector has been threatened during the past two decades, however, by the reluctance of the American welfare state. As public funding of an array of programs has been reduced, not-for-profit agencies have increasingly lost their public contracts and grants. In turn, cuts in public programs have increased competition for the resources of philanthropic agencies and donors, so that hard-pressed not-for-profits have found it difficult to offset cuts in public funds from other nongovernmental sources. The result, some critics argue, has been increasing reliance by not-for-profits on the fees and memberships of clients—a reliance that has made them increasingly inaccessible to low-income persons, who lack the resources to pay these charges.

The American welfare state also places greater reliance on for-profit agencies, both as freestanding entities that fund themselves from fees or memberships and as partners of public programs that receive government contracts and grants, as well as reimbursements from public programs such as Medicare. Policy analysts do not agree about the relative merits of for-profit agencies and the extent to which their role should expand. For-profit agencies dominate the nursing home industry, own a significant share of American hospitals and child care centers, own a significant share of American psychiatric hospitals and substance abuse programs, and have even entered such areas as prison administration. Deriding the inefficiencies of public programs such as schools, some people want the role of for-profit agencies to be vastly increased through the use of vouchers that allow people to select services from competing (and frequently for-profit) agencies.

It is beyond our scope to analyze the relative merits of for-profit agencies in detail. Some provide innovative, high-quality services; others try to increase their profits by making excessive cuts in their programs, as illustrated by poor-quality nursing homes. Some critics see them as profit-maximizing entities that actually *increase* the costs of services by diverting resources to advertising and to owners' profits, and point out that they often locate their facilities only in areas where fee-paying clients exist, such as suburban communities. Many defenders of for-profits contend, however, that market competition forces them to provide services that are responsive to consumers' needs— and some argue that it is virtually impossible to distinguish between the services of for-profits and not-for-profits, which themselves try to maximize their income from fees and from efficiencies.

Curiously, the reluctance of the American welfare state may increase the role of for-profits, which can raise capital from private sources—for example, from issuance of stock and from investors' funds —whereas not-for-profits must rely on increasingly scarce donors and public contracts to accumulate resources. In some cases, funding cuts in the public sector also increase the role of for-profits by enabling them to purchase failing not-for-profit hospitals and other agencies.

- The diminishing of corruption, patronage, and nepotism in American government institutions in the 20th and 21st centuries as compared with 19th-century and early 20th-century practices, even though considerable corruption still exists, as illustrated by the sentencing of powerful lobbyist Jack Abramhoff for conspiracy to bribe public officials in 2005.

4. *Social factors* include wars, migrations of populations, demographic changes, industrialization, global economic competition, and urbanization—that is, changes in the social environment that created public support for policy reforms. Social factors that have created public awareness and *opportunities* are:

- The powerful role of the Great Depression in fostering social and political pressure for enactment of an array of social reforms.

- Discrimination created by racism, xenophobia, ageism, sexism, prejudice against disabled persons, homophobia, and other kinds of prejudice.

- Social problems created by industrialization, such as unemployment, low wages, and unsafe working conditions.

- Social problems created by urbanization, such as unsafe housing, poor sanitation, and lack of open spaces.

- Social problems created by capitalism, such as economic inequality and discrimination against domestic workers as corporations have moved plants abroad.

5. The *sequencing of events* describes the effects of the *timing* of important developments in the evolution of the U.S. welfare state. Sequencing events that provided *opportunities* to policy advocates include the following:

- Policy reforms in specific eras (such as the Progressive, New Deal, and Great Society eras) have facilitated reforms in succeeding eras by setting precedents that expanded the horizons of many Americans in succeeding

eras to include social reforms they might otherwise have considered to be not feasible.

6. *Legal factors* have assumed major significance in the development of the American welfare state because of the role of federal and state constitutions, as well as court decisions, in shaping public policies. Legal factors that have provided *opportunities* for policy advocates include the following:

- Court rulings that have supported the ability of state and federal governments to develop regulations, civil rights legislation, and social programs, particularly from the late 1930s onward. The emphasis on *individual rights* in the U.S. Constitution has prompted members of vulnerable populations to invest enormous energy in obtaining legal guarantees of their rights, with notable successes. People with disabilities provide an excellent example. Though Germany often provides better services to individuals with disabilities, it has not developed as much legislation as the United States that accords them protections against discrimination in employment, housing, and transportation.

- The emergence of public interest legal advocacy groups that have brought many successful class action suits on behalf of vulnerable populations.

7. *Political factors* include power resources and tactics of specific interest groups, legislators, presidents and other chief executives, and professional groups. Political factors that have provided *opportunities* for policy advocates include the following:

- Development of large unions in the late 1930s and succeeding decades that have financed relatively liberal political candidates and supported relatively liberal legislation.

- Some relatively liberal presidents, including Franklin Roosevelt, Lyndon Johnson, and Bill Clinton.

- The relatively liberal nature of the modern Democratic Party, particularly its Northern wing from the 1930s onward.

- The ability of social programs to attract additional support for themselves from their beneficiaries, such as elderly persons supporting Medicare and Social Security— and their ability to generate support from providers, such as support for Medicare from hospitals and physicians.

- Advocacy groups that have sought social policy reforms and have generated widespread support for specific causes such as civil rights, women's rights, and rights for LGBT persons.

WHERE DO WE STAND?

We have discussed both moral failings and moral successes of the American welfare state in contemporary society. We have placed both of these aspects in the societal context that produced them. We have enumerated an array of contextual factors that have discouraged or constrained social reforms and others that have provided opportunities.

Where does our study of the evolution of the American welfare state, then, leave us in contemporary society? It demonstrates that our relationship to the American welfare state is strikingly similar to those of policy advocates of prior eras. While we benefit from many social reforms that have been enacted in prior eras in contemporary society, we also confront an array of moral defects in the American welfare state—just as they did. We, too, use ethical reasoning to distinguish right from wrong. While we can have honest differences among ourselves as to the ethical merit of specific policies, we will often concur that many social policies are ethically flawed.

Just as they did, we confront both constraining and facilitating contextual factors. We, too, have to select those policy reforms that we wish to prioritize. We, too, have to navigate the American welfare state to decide where we will focus our policy

advocacy by selecting the level of government, the not-for-profit or for-profit sector, a specific agency or a network of agencies, and a specific policy sector—or some combination of these factors.

Like policy advocates of prior eras, we, too, have to place issues on decision makers' agendas, analyze problems, develop proposals, enact policy reforms, secure effective implementation of policies, and assess implemented policies to see if they are effective.

Our discussion in this chapter suggests that the policy advocacy framework in Figure 2.1 is just as relevant to contemporary Americans as it was to policy advocates in prior eras.

STANDING ON THE SHOULDERS OF POLICY ADVOCATES

Curiously, conservatives are more adept than liberals at identifying their historical roots; they boast of their affinity with many of the ideas of the founding fathers, for example. Indeed, some conservatives equate their ideology with patriotism itself, with the obvious implication that reformers possess alien ideas.

For all its faults and omissions, however, social reform in the United States has a rich and vibrant tradition that is just as integral to the nation's history as conservatism. Jane Addams exhorted Americans to define patriotism in the context of cooperative or sharing values rather than militaristic or competitive values and to find the meaning of their society from the altruism that was so evident in immigrant communities and among women. Reform ideas can sometimes be found in unlikely places. For example, Jefferson and many of the founding fathers were afraid that undue differences in wealth might cause social turmoil and demoralize persons in the lower economic strata. Dwight Eisenhower, who committed his life to a career in the military, warned of "the conjunction of an immense military establishment and a large arms industry" and urged Americans to "guard against the acquisition of unwarranted influence by the military-industrial complex."[25]

Reformers should not forget that conservative eras have been followed by liberal periods since the inception of the republic. It is worth remembering that abolitionists, progressives, New Dealers, and liberal reformers of the 1960s had their formative experiences not during reform periods but during the conservative eras that preceded them. Many reformers had despaired that their nation would again experience reform and had become accustomed to hearing rhetoric to the effect that conservative trends would dominate the nation for decades. Conservatives in the Gilded Age, the 1920s, the 1950s, the 1990s, and the present era had confidently predicted that the nation would experience unending prosperity and that its citizens would gratefully pay homage to corporate and conservative officials by choosing them to lead the nation. In each case, however, the nation had soon embarked on social reform, whether because citizens had tired of the narcissism and materialism of conservative eras; because of catastrophic events such as the Great Depression; because of popular anger against the exploitation of women, children, workers, or African Americans; or because of the failures of conservative policy prescriptions such as trickle-down economics, limited government, and unregulated markets.

In our analysis, we have emphasized the materialistic and individualistic characteristics of American culture, but these qualities coexist with altruism and other moral principles. Some social scientists contend that Americans have both private and public tendencies. Whereas materialism and personal goals prevail during conservative periods, altruism and concern about societal needs prevail during liberal periods. This insight into American culture, which is confirmed historically by the rhythm of conservative and reform periods, suggests that reformers can successfully appeal to those aspects of American culture that emphasize assistance to innocent victims, assurance of equal rights, and provision of resources to needy people.[26] (See Figure 13.6.)

Reformers should realize, too, that social reform is possible even during conservative periods. Fine

FIGURE 13.6 Young women demonstrating against child labor during the Progressive Era.

and Chambers, respectively, note that reformers obtained some successes even during the Gilded Age and the 1920s.[27] Partly because many Americans remembered how New Deal programs saved them from the hardships of the Great Depression, President Eisenhower did not attack those social programs that had survived World War II, and he even made substantial additions to the Social Security Act. We have noted that, in the 1970s, conservative presidents consented to increases in social spending that equaled those of the 1960s.

Although President Reagan made devastating cuts in means-tested programs, his major cuts occurred during the first year of his presidency. Indeed, public opinion polls suggest that he did not markedly change American policy preferences on domestic matters during his presidency and that most Americans favored retention (or even expansion) of existing federal social programs.[28] Reagan felt compelled to agree that he would preserve safety net programs from cuts. When he tried to frontally attack Social Security and Medicare, he suffered stinging defeats during both his first and second terms. Indeed, David Stockman, who favored sweeping cuts in social spending, noted remorsefully in 1986 that the Reagan revolution had failed.[29] Democratic candidates at local, state, and congressional levels bucked the national Republican trends not only in the 1980s but also in the 1920s and the 1950s.

Both Eisenhower and Reagan had to contend with powerful Democratic contingents in both chambers of Congress—and in state and local governments—that resisted cuts in social spending. Many pundits argued that the Republicans' electoral triumph in 1994 when they captured control of both Houses of Congress presaged on extended Republican domination of national politics. Instead, Democrats made major electoral gains in 1996 and 1998—and threatened to retake control of the House in 2000, 2002, and 2004, finally succeeding with majorities in both the House of Representatives and the Senate in 2006, where one of their first acts was to increase the minimum wage.

Reformers in conservative eras such as the 1950s and 1980s, as well as during the presidencies of George Bush, Sr., and George W. Bush, Jr., succeeded in blocking many measures that would have markedly curtailed or eliminated important social programs. They prevented conservatives from block-granting Medicaid, privatizing Social Security and Medicare, and ending affirmative action. Blocking such measures is as essential to policy advocacy as initiating new social reforms.

Reformers should also note the rich traditions of resistance within the many groups that have experienced discrimination in the United States. The emphasis in the late 1960s and the 1970s on the rights of women, African Americans, gay men and lesbians, Latinos, Asian Americans, and Native Americans had the salutary effect of making these groups more aware of historical reformers and of the possibility of political redress for grievances. A reform heritage has arisen to challenge conservative mythology; the formerly obscure names of distant and courageous persons have been brought to light, along with infamous events and persecutions. Discovery of older reform traditions has stimulated many Americans to become involved in social reform today.

During the nation's history, reformers have often benefited from the pragmatism of the American people, who tend to place problem solving above ideology. Conservatives can preach free-market and limited-government ideology, but Americans are unlikely to follow their dictates if they believe that assertive interventions are needed to redress pressing problems. Theodore Roosevelt, Franklin Roosevelt, John Kennedy, and Lyndon Johnson adeptly contrasted their activist, interventionist policies with the passivity of conservative politicians. Even some white, male, blue-collar voters who turned away from the Democratic Party in the 1980s may come to realize that, in an era of economic globalization and extreme job insecurity, they can benefit from social policies such as vocational training. A poll conducted by *The New York Times* found that 63 percent of Americans who had been hard hit by layoffs believed the government "should step in to do something about layoffs and loss of jobs" as compared with only 42 percent of those still untouched by layoffs.[30]

As in preceding eras, a central challenge to reformers in the early part of the 21st century is to make expansion of the welfare state an issue of concern to many of the groups who are becoming increasingly influential in the nation's politics. Elderly voters have medical and social welfare needs that are poorly addressed by existing policies. Workers in the service sector, including clerical and sales personnel, receive limited fringe benefits and are increasingly being supplanted by temporary workers. Women have trouble finding and paying for quality child care, often receive low wages, and face discriminatory hiring and promotion policies. Latino voters in Southwestern states contend with problems of poverty, poor education, and substance abuse. African Americans have high unemployment rates and would benefit from a variety of educational and social welfare benefits. Many young people realize that their economic prospects are bleaker than those of their parents.

Reformers may despair at the difficulties of establishing coalitions of the disparate groups that have the most to gain from expansion of the welfare state, but coalitions of reform-oriented groups have occurred at numerous points in the nation's history. We noted in Chapter 6 that immigrant, middle-class, and working-class voters supported progressive politicians. Franklin Roosevelt fashioned a coalition of blue-collar workers, people of color, intellectuals, Jews, and ethnic populations that maintained considerable cohesion during the three decades following the New Deal. Although this liberal coalition frayed during the 1970s and 1980s, it can be restored if the separate hardships of different groups lead their members to believe that reform-oriented candidates are again needed. But reformers will need to be skillful in forging coalitions in a society riven by racism and economic rivalry. They need to construct proposals that address the needs of diverse groups and to develop broad-based support for social reforms.

By understanding American social welfare history, social reformers can gain a greater sense of their importance and can also take courage from the endurance of their predecessors. However, analysis of this history should also prompt expanded definitions of reform. More than the liberal reformers of past eras, today's reformers need to broaden their concerns to include tax policies, economic planning, budget priorities, and military spending, all of which have important consequences for social welfare policy. Traditionally, social welfare policy has focused on income maintenance or public welfare, child welfare, mental health, and housing. Although these policies are vitally important, social reformers must broaden their activities as well.

In coming decades, social reformers need to emphasize the positive roles of social programs in helping the nation cope with the globalized economy. Large segments of society will be left behind as the importance of technological skills increases. Changing careers many times in their lives, Americans will need continuing access to education; they will need medical programs that are not provided by particular employers; and they will need income supports during their transitions between jobs. In short, they will need an array of social programs to help them cope with economic and career uncertainties.

Moreover, reformers should advocate policies to reduce economic inequality. The wealth of the highest quintile exceeds 10 times that of the lowest quintile. This extraordinary difference offends the principle of social justice and contributes to the economic suffering of persons in the lowest economic strata. Despite its importance, this issue has been missing from the agendas of most reformers in preceding eras.

Finally, social reformers should not be timid about making explicit reference to the values that justify their proposals. When Harry Hopkins told critics of his New Deal programs that relieving hunger was not debatable, he affirmed the principles of beneficence, social justice, and equality.

TOWARD POLICY PRACTICE AND POLICY ADVOCACY

Social reformers in American history rarely achieved their successes without investing time and effort—and without developing specific policy-changing skills. No matter how meritorious they may be, policy proposals fail if their proponents do not gain the support of decision makers, whether in legislatures, organizations, or communities. Reformers like Dorothea Dix, Jane Addams, Eleanor Roosevelt, Harry Hopkins, César Chavez, Martin Luther King, and Marian Wright Edelman were actively involved in the political process for decades.

Some professionals take a dim view of politics; they regard those involved in politics as opportunistic, power-hungry, or wedded to special interests. It is difficult to imagine a world where politics does not exist, however, because political processes provide the means for addressing the many value-laden issues in policy making.

The political playing field often is not level, as social policy history repeatedly demonstrates. Advocates for corporations possess greater resources to hire lobbyists and engage in public relations campaigns than do advocates for stigmatized populations. The organized electorate readily throws its support behind some issues, such as tax cuts, while proposals to fund a guaranteed income or a children's allowance, for example, often attract less support. Far from curing or improving politics, social reformers who withdraw from the political process simply strengthen its inequities.

People who prize social justice, fairness, and beneficence need to develop organizational, community, and legislative skills in policy practice and policy advocacy. I define *policy practice* as efforts to change policies in legislative, agency, and community settings, whether by establishing new policies, improving existing ones, or defeating the policy initiatives of other people. People who are skilled in policy practice increase the odds that *their* policy preferences will be advanced. I define *policy advocacy* as policy practice that aims to help powerless groups, such as women, children, poor people, persons of color, gay men and lesbians, and people with disabilities, to improve their resources and opportunities.[31] This text has provided many examples of policy practice and policy advocacy. *Each* of the many profiles in leadership included at the ends of Chapters 3 through 11 demonstrates how determined, principled, persistent, and skilled individuals have been able to change policies, even in the face of adversity.

Let's contrast some approaches to securing policy changes that are illustrated by historical events.

Participating in Social Movements

Welfare recipients in the early 1960s were treated unfairly by many welfare offices across the nation. African Americans were often denied benefits in Southern states, in defiance of federal regulations that prohibited racial discrimination in the administration of AFDC. Even in Northern welfare offices, they often endured long waits, slow processing of claims, underpayments of benefits, and derogatory treatment by staff. Sparked by George Wiley, a national welfare rights movement was initiated in the early 1960s. With the help of community workers hired by settlement houses and other agencies, local chapters of welfare recipients were organized, not only to pressure local offices to be more responsive but to initiate lawsuits to force compliance with federal regulations. Wiley headed the National Welfare Rights Organization, which sought to raise federal standards for benefits.

Establishing Advocacy Organizations

Having participated in the civil rights movement, as well as anti-poverty programs to help children in Mississippi, Marian Wright Edelman formed the Children's Defense Fund in 1973. Securing grants from foundations and private donors, she developed research and lobbying capabilities that she used to document a variety of problems encountered by the nation's children—in particular, inadequacies in the implementation of programs such as the Adoption Assistance and Child Welfare Act of 1980. She lobbied assertively for many pieces of legislation and played a key role in the enactment of the child care and development block grant of 1990, which provided the first major federal subsidies for child care in peacetime.

Seeking Social Reforms from within the Government

Wilbur Cohen's long career in the federal government, where he held various appointments in the executive branch in the Roosevelt, Truman, and

Johnson administrations, illustrates the tactics of officials who work inside bureaucracies. He favored what he called a salami approach to social reform; that is, he sought incremental slices that, when finally put together, represented major changes. Using this approach, he was able to gradually transform Social Security from merely an old age pension to a family assistance program that provides benefits (and financial aid for college education) to surviving members of families who have lost a parent.

He also helped to secure benefits from Social Security for persons with permanent disabilities. As an advocate for Social Security from inside government, he cultivated personal relationships with an extraordinary number of politicians from both parties and sought to construct policies that would help them gain the support of their constituents.[32]

Educating the Public as a Prelude to Social Reforms

Dorothea Dix was one of the most remarkable figures in American social policy history. Overhearing a conversation in 1841 about the treatment of "prisoners and lunatics" in East Cambridge, Massachusetts, she decided to visit the facility. Shocked by the conditions, she visited every jail and almshouse in Massachusetts and accumulated statistics and details that she presented in a "Memorial" to the state legislature. She included many personal cases; for example, she reported that, in the almshouse at Danvers, she saw

> a young woman exhibiting a condition of neglect and misery blotting out the faintest idea of comfort …there she stood, clinging to, or beating upon, the bars of her caged apartment … the unwashed frame invested with fragments of unclean garments; the air so extremely offensive … that it was not possible to remain beyond a few moments … irritation of the body, produced by utter filth and exposure, incited her to the horrid process of tearing off her skin by inches, her face, neck, and person were thus disfigured to hideousness.[33]

Her first Memorial had an enormous impact and prompted angry denunciations of her as a liar and sensationalist. Community leaders rallied to her side as they confirmed her findings, and a rising tide of public indignation forced the hand of the state's legislators, who funded space for 200 persons in the mental asylum in Worcester. She followed the same course in about 20 other states. In one three-year period, she traveled 10,000 miles by horseback, carriage, and steamboat and visited 300 county jails and 500 almshouses. She not only presented Memorials but also got to know legislators; she had influential people bring them to her room or alcove in the state capitol, where she talked to 15 or 20 at a time. Realizing that many states lacked revenues to fund mental institutions, she often had to persuade legislators to enact taxes as well. In 1854, she persuaded both chambers of Congress to enact legislation that would grant the proceeds from land sales to the states for the construction of mental institutions, only to have President Pierce veto the legislation.

Electing Reform-Oriented Candidates to Office

Realizing that its tax-exempt status as a not-for-profit organization could be threatened by direct participation in partisan politics, the National Association of Social Workers (NASW) formed PACE in 1975. Funded by contributions from NASW's membership and keeping its accounts separate from NASW, PACE asks political candidates in state and federal elections to respond to a questionnaire that probes their positions on social issues. Candidates who are approved by PACE receive contributions for their campaigns.

Many reformers have taken positions in the campaigns of specific candidates or have worked in local campaign offices on tasks such as media relations, outreach to voters, or fund-raising. Beginning with Jane Addams's work in helping to form the Progressive Party in 1912, many social reformers have worked for political parties at the national or state level. Some social workers have sought elective office; for example, Democrat Ron Dellums was regularly reelected to the House of Representatives from the Eighth District in Berkeley, California—an area now represented by his successor, Barbara Lee, also a social worker. Dellums went on to become the mayor of Oakland, California. Five other members of Congress are social workers, including two U.S. senators, Barbara Mikulski of Maryland and Debbie Stabenow of Michigan.

Influencing Policy from Organizational Settings

Often working with advocacy groups and professional associations, social workers have sought to influence the policies of legislative bodies from their positions in specific agencies. The situation for rape victims was bleak in the early 1970s, when they were commonly assumed to have incited attacks by their clothing or demeanor. Hospital staff often treated them with contempt in emergency rooms and failed even to collect evidence in a manner that could be used by the district attorney.

Rules of evidence in court often allowed the accused offender to place the woman on trial; for example, his attorney could question her about her prior sexual liaisons. Nor did rape victims receive monetary compensation from the state, even though other crime victims were often remunerated for injuries and lost time from work. Concerned that Los Angeles County failed to provide humane services for victims of rape, Gail Abarbanel, a social worker who directs the social work department at Santa Monica Hospital, developed a coalition that proceeded to pressure hospitals, the police department, and the district attorney to put in place new policies for treating rape victims and prosecuting offenders.

Whistleblowing

The progressive reformer Homer Folks illustrates how some reformers have sought policy reforms in the agencies and institutions that implement social policies. He was astonished to find, in the early 20th century, that mental institutions in New York State were riddled with corruption and hired staff on the basis of personal friendships. Working from outside the institutions, he mobilized pressure to force the state governor to implement a variety of reforms.

In some cases, social workers have obtained changes of agency policies while holding positions within them. Many of these reforms occur in low-conflict and undramatic fashion—for example, when a staff member alerts his or her supervisor to a dysfunctional policy or inadequate implementation of a meritorious policy. Staff sometimes believe that serious wrongdoing occurs in their agencies but find that they cannot challenge the unethical practices through ordinary channels for fear that they will lose their jobs. In these rare cases—and only after considerable contemplation—social workers can divulge their concerns to outside agencies or professional organizations.

MOVING BEYOND HISTORY TO POLICY ADVOCACY IN CONTEMPORARY SOCIETY

While social welfare history has great merit independent of social work practice in contemporary society, it also prepares us to become better social workers in our own professional practice.

Acquiring Policy Advocacy Skills

No matter how policy advocates attempt to reform specific social policies—or to create policies where none exist—they need to engage *skillfully* in policy-changing work if they wish to increase the probability that they will succeed. Just as in clinical, administrative, and community work, social workers need to *learn* how to be skillful policy advocate practitioners—following the examples of the policy advocates we have identified in specific historical eras, such as Dorothea Dix, Eleanor Roosevelt,

Wilbur Cohen, César Chavez, Whitney Young, Ron Dellums, and Barbara Mikulski.

Social welfare history provides an introduction to policy advocacy by developing our ethical reasoning and navigational skills, as well as our ability to diagnose context. It exposes us to the work of policy advocates from the colonial period to the present. It helps us to understand how policy advocates must place issues on policy agendas, analyze social problems, develop policy proposals, implement policies, and assess policies.

Unlike policy advocates in specific historical eras, contemporary social workers can draw upon an emerging body of professional literature that discusses policy practice and policy advocacy as interventions—literature that has emerged only recently. A variety of texts on policy advocacy now exist, including my text that is now in its fifth edition (*Becoming an Effective Policy Advocate*, 5th edition, Wadsworth Publishing Company, 2008). Growing numbers of departments and schools of social work are providing semester-long courses in policy advocacy, requiring students to engage in it during their field placements, and asking students to attend statewide lobbying days in their state capitols. Many students engage in policy advocacy projects.

Social workers should seek ways to engage in policy advocacy during their professional education in departments and schools of social work—even if their schools or departments do not offer semester-long courses in policy advocacy. (To see examples of policy advocacy projects of social work students around the nation, go to the website of an important national social work organization, Influencing State Policy, at http://www .statepolicy.org.) You should ask yourself whether during your professional education you can use your *ethical reasoning skills*—already sharpened by your study of social welfare history—to identify a flaw or omission in existing social policies, whether in specific agencies, communities, counties, or states, or at the federal level—or in some combination of these locations.

You should seek to develop your *navigational skills* to enable you to decide what specific policies, and in what location, need to be reformed. (You will often have several options since social policies relevant to specific social problems often exist in many locations.) Navigational skills are needed, as well, to identify existing advocacy groups, public officials, religious institutions, concerned citizens, or professional organizations that are (or might become) interested in policy advocacy with respect to the issue or problem that you have selected. In many cases, you will discover that policy advocacy work is *already* under way—or that you can persuade others to initiate it when you inform them why you believe an existing policy is ethically flawed.

You should seek to develop your *context-reading skills* so that you can discover contextual factors that both facilitate and impede specific policy reforms. Your knowledge of the context may lead you to favor certain policy reforms while dropping others as you decide what is feasible to enact in light of the context that you encounter.

You should seek to develop your *agenda-setting skills* so that the policy reform that you seek can be placed on the agendas of decision makers in whatever location you have chosen for your policy advocacy work. You should develop your *problem-analyzing skills, proposal-writing skills,* and *policy-enacting skills* as you move toward actually developing and enacting policy proposals.

You should develop *troubleshooting or implementing skills* as you realize that many meritorious enacted policies are inadequately implemented after they are enacted. You should develop *policy-assessing skills* to enhance your ability to gain evidence about the effectiveness of those policies that are enacted.

LEAVING A BETTER WELFARE STATE FOR FUTURE GENERATIONS

Our challenge is to use our knowledge of social welfare history to help us become policy advocates in contemporary society. As we understand how policy advocates have made the American welfare state more humane over a period of several centuries, we realize that we can stand on their shoulders to continue their work by making policy practice and policy advocacy integral to our professional role. By participating in the shaping of contemporary policies, we join reforming pioneers of the past, adding our strands to a tapestry that is beautiful to behold but never finished.

WHAT YOU CAN DO NOW

After reading this chapter, you are now equipped to do the following:

- Identify how the American welfare state is "reluctant" in comparison with many European welfare states—and place the American welfare state in a historical and comparative context.

- Discuss ethical shortcomings of the American welfare state with respect to eight social problems in contemporary society.

- Identify specific cultural, economic, institutional, social, sequential, and political factors that contributed to the reluctance of the American welfare state.

- Identify an array of reforms that have positive ethical merit in specific policy sectors and with respect to specific vulnerable populations.

- Give examples of specific cultural, economic, institutional, social, sequential, and political factors that contributed to the enactment of meritorious social policies.

- Critique widely used arguments that suggest that the United States does not need a welfare state—or that it can rely on deterrence, volunteers, and other panaceas.

- Assert the case for a welfare state, while admitting the limitations of public policy to solve major social problems.

- Identify ways that we can use our knowledge of social welfare history to promote policy advocacy in contemporary society so that we stand on the shoulders of policy advocates from prior eras.

ENDNOTES

1. The term *reluctant welfare state* was coined by Harold Wilensky and Charles Lebeaux in *Industrial Society and Social Welfare* (New York: Free Press, 1965), pp. xii–xxv.

2. OECD Information Management and Publication Service. 1981 through 1997. *OECD in Figures.*

3. Mary Walsh, "Germany's Reckoning," *Los Angeles Times* (February 25, 1996), p. D1.

4. Ibid.; Joel Blau, "Why the United States Is Not Sweden," *Journal of Progressive Human Services,* 4 (1993), pp. 1–16.

5. Patricia Evans, "Targeting Single Mothers for Employment: Comparisons from the United States, Britain and Canada," *Social Service Review,* 55 (September 1992), pp. 378–398.

6. Ibid.

7. William Julius Wilson, "Studying Inner City Dislocations: The Challenge of Public Policy Research," *American Sociological Review,* 56 (February 1991), pp. 1–4.

8. Bruce Jansson, *The Sixteen-Trillion-Dollar Mistake: How the United States Bungled Its National Priorities from the New Deal to the Present* (New York: Columbia University Press, 2001), pp. 373–381; and Jacob S. Hacker, *The Divided Welfare State* (New York: Cambridge University Press, 2002).

9. "Canada Beats USA—But Loses Gold to Sweden" from http://www.ccsd.ca/pubs/2002/olympic/indicators.htm. (Accessed November 15, 2007.)

10. Jansson, *The Sixteen-Trillion-Dollar Mistake,* p. 355.

11. Theda Skocpol, *Social Policy in the United States: Future Possibilities in Historical Perspective* (Princeton, NJ: Princeton University Press, 1995), pp. 11–36, 78–86; Louis Hartz, *The Liberal Tradition in America* (New York: Harcourt, Brace, 1955); Michael Shalev, "The Social Democratic Model and Beyond: Two Generations of Comparative Research on the Welfare State," *Comparative Social Research,* 6 (1983), pp. 315–351; Thomas Edsall, *Chain Reaction: The Impact of Race, Rights, and Taxes on American Politics* (New York: W. W. Norton, 1991); and Edward Berkowitz and Kim McQuaid, *Creating the Welfare State: The Political Economy of Twentieth-Century Reform* (New York: Praeger, 1980).

12. For the classic statement of this position, see Milton Friedman, *Capitalism and Freedom* (Chicago: University of Chicago Press, 1962).

13. Quoted in Axinn and Levin, *Social Welfare,* p. 30.

14. Hartz, *The Liberal Tradition,* pp. 134–136, 266–270.

15. Lizabeth Cohen, *Making a New Deal: Industrial Workers in Chicago, 1919–1939* (New York: Cambridge University Press, 1990), pp. 53–98.

16. Geoffrey Hodgson, *America in Our Time* (Garden City, NY: Doubleday, 1976), pp. 247, 484–490.

17. Frances Fox Piven and Richard Cloward, *Why Americans Don't Vote* (New York: Pantheon Books, 1988).

18. No one better captures the fervor of moral crusades than Paul Boyer, *Urban Masses and Moral Order in America, 1820–1920* (Cambridge, MA: Harvard University Press, 1978).

19. Marvin Olasky, *The Tragedy of American Compassion* (Lanham, MD: Regnery Gateway, 1992).

20. Kevin Phillips, *The Politics of Rich and Poor: Wealth and the American Electorate in the Reagan Aftermath* (New York: Harper Perennial, 1990).

21. Lester Salamon, "The Marketization of Welfare: Changing Nonprofit and For-Profit Roles in the American Welfare State," *Social Service Review* (March 1993), pp. 16–39.

22. Michael Kingsley, "The Ultimate Block Grant," *New Yorker* (May 29, 1995), pp. 36–40.

23. *The New York Times* (October 22, 1995), pp. xiii, 11.

24. Olasky, *The Tragedy of American Compassion,* pp. 35–42.

25. Chester Pach and Elmo Richardson, *The Presidency of Dwight D. Eisenhower* (Lawrence, KS: University of Kansas Press, 1991), pp. 229–230.

26. Herbert McClosky and John Zaller, *The American Ethos: Public Attitudes toward Capitalism and Democracy* (Cambridge, MA: Harvard University Press, 1984), pp. 162, 291–292; Arthur M. Schlesinger, *The Cycles of History* (Boston: Houghton Mifflin, 1986), pp. 23–48.

27. Clarke Chambers, *Seedtime of Reform: American Social Service and Social Action, 1918–1933* (Minneapolis, MN: University of Minnesota Press, 1963), pp. 29–58, 153–182; Sidney Fine, *Laissez-Faire and the General Welfare State: A Study of Conflict in America, 1865–1901* (Ann Arbor: University of Michigan Press, 1956), pp. 259–369.

28. Everett Ladd, "The Reagan Phenomenon and Public Attitudes toward Government." In Lester Salamon and Michael Lund, eds., *The Reagan Presidency and the Governing of America* (Washington, DC: Urban Institute, 1985), pp. 221–249.

29. David Stockman, *The Triumph of Politics: Why the Reagan Revolution Failed* (New York: Harper & Row, 1986), pp. 376–411.

30. Rick Bragg, "Big Holes Where the Dignity Used to Be," *The New York Times* (March 5, 1996), p. A8.

31. Bruce Jansson, *Becoming an Effective Policy Advocate: From Policy Practice to Social Justice* (Pacific Grove, CA: Wadsworth, 1999), pp. 10–13.

32. Edward Berkowitz, *Mr. Social Security: The Life of Wilbur Cohen* (Lawrence, KS: University of Kansas Press, 1995).

33. Francis Tiffany, *Life of Dorothea Lynde Dix* (Boston: Houghton Mifflin, 1891), pp. 78–79.

14

Using Knowledge of the Evolution of the American Welfare State to Improve Your Professional Practice

We have analyzed the evolution of the American welfare state over the course of more than 200 years. We now ask how this knowledge can help professionals improve their practice in contemporary society. We argue that ethical professionals engage in policy-sensitive and policy-related practice—and we discuss how knowledge of the evolution of the American welfare state helps professionals engage in each of these kinds of practice.

We will then discuss how social welfare history helps us to engage in policy advocacy, and we will explain how to develop *social policy background statements* that are useful to launching social policy advocacy projects in contemporary society. Using homelessness as our topic, we give an example of a policy background statement—and invite readers to develop statements of their own to get started on policy advocacy in a specific geographic area, state, or across the nation.

---

* This chapter is co-authored with Clinical Associate Professor Ralph Fertig, J.D., A.M.

THE MORAL IMPERATIVE TO HELP CONSUMERS AND CLIENTS ON MULTIPLE LEVELS

Professionals of all kinds are required by codes of ethics to place the needs of their clients first. They are morally obligated to select interventions, diagnostic tests, and treatments that will most enhance their clients' well-being. When credible research suggests that specific interventions are likely to help specific clients, professionals should use them—while relying on their best professional judgment when such research does not exist.

The evolution of the American welfare state strongly suggests, however, that clients' well-being extends beyond the scope of specific encounters with professionals, whether physicians, lawyers, or social workers. Specific bouts of therapy would not, for example, have addressed the full range of needs and wishes of persons cast into poorhouses because they were unemployed in the 19th century, whether due to recessions, physical or mental challenges, or discrimination. Specific encounters with professionals would similarly have not addressed the major needs of freed slaves, low-wage industrial workers in the 1880s, unemployed persons in the Great Depression, or African American soldiers returning from World War II to Jim Crow laws and

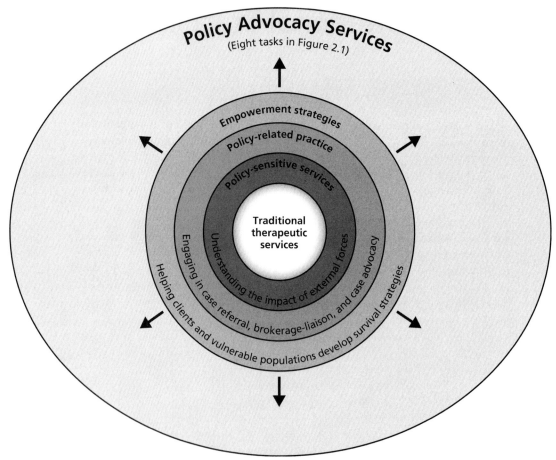

FIGURE 14.1 Engaging history to advance contemporary social work practice.

segregation in the American South or to segregated communities in Northern cities. Subjected to sexism in workplaces, schools, homes, and professions, women often needed more than counseling to address a full range of issues confronting them.

Professionals need to use *policy-sensitive* and *policy-related* practice, as well as *empowerment strategies*, that move beyond traditional therapeutic, medical, and legal services to give services that address a full range of the needs of their clients. They are morally obligated, as well, to engage in *policy advocacy* practice when they believe that existing social policies contribute to their clients' problems or needs.

POLICY-SENSITIVE PRACTICE

All professionals should engage in their work with the knowledge that their clients' well-being often extends beyond the scope of the traditional services that they provide. A woman who cannot afford an adequate diet for her children due to the cost of day care, transportation, and housing will often find her health—or the health of members of her family—to be compromised by this reality, *no matter how skillfully her physician, attorney, or social worker helps her with the traditional services they often provide.* The doctor, lawyer, or social worker who fails to refer her to the Food Stamps Program—or to other income-enhancing programs like the Women's, Infant, and Children's Program (WIC) or the Earned Income Tax Credit (EITC)—is not sufficiently improving her well-being by addressing an array of her, and her family members', needs.

Our analysis of the evolution of the American welfare state gives abundant examples of the impact of economic, housing, civil rights, environmental, and other external forces on the lives of members of vulnerable populations. Through most of the nation's history, a range of public safety net programs did not even exist, so persons and families were thrown back on their own resources, as well as the resources of their networks and communities. Imagine hardships experienced by settlers on the frontier who had to devote several years to getting their first crops planted and harvested when virtually no safety net programs existed—or immigrants who arrived with no resources; the victims of recessions and depressions; and women who were widowed with no inheritance or employment prospects under the same circumstances. It was precisely because voters and public officials recognized that persons' well-being was compromised by the absence of a minimum threshold of resources and services that the American welfare state gradually evolved from a primitive toward a more advanced one—even if this evolution required more than 200 years even to yield the very imperfect American welfare state of contemporary society.

Policy-sensitive practice also requires professionals to recognize the importance of rights and entitlements to people. Through most of American history, they hardly existed for members of the 13 vulnerable populations identified in this book. Imagine the impact on members of some of these groups when they were subject to random and systematic racism not just from neighbors and other residents, but from government officials, social agencies, churches, public transportation, hotels, restaurants, bankers, real estate agents, and landlords—with virtually no protections codified in law and virtually no government bodies charged with monitoring and protecting their rights. Persons who are subjected to unfair treatment suffer not just short-term problems such as restrictions on their employment, resources, recreation, ability to vote or hold public office, and movement around the countryside, but assaults to their mental and physical health, not to mention their sense of personhood. Many civil rights laws and regulations have been developed only relatively recently in American history, including the Civil Rights Acts of 1964 and 1965, immigration legislation in 1966, and the Americans with Disabilities Act of 1990. Professionals need to be aware of the importance of rights and entitlements as they serve specific persons to see if they are being denied specific rights and entitlements. They also need to know that many members of vulnerable populations are *still* denied basic rights or find that their rights are not being monitored or enforced—or are unaware that they even possess specific rights or entitlements under existing laws and regulations.

By the same token, professionals in contemporary society should be sensitized by their knowledge of the evolution of the American welfare state to specific gaps and omissions in its current social policies. As we learn from studying the evolution of the American welfare state, social policies evolve through a political process that often brings unfortunate compromises that impede their fairness or effectiveness. Professionals who work in relatively conservative states should recognize that many programs that have been devolved from the federal government to their states will be more poorly funded than ones in more liberal states—and will be administered with more punitive guidelines. Means-tested programs often possess unacceptably low eligibility levels—and their benefits are often inadequate. The culture of poor laws and poorhouses still exists in the United States, as reflected by punitive policies of TANF that were set in place in 1996 and remain mostly in force. Funding levels for many programs can be suddenly cut—or entire programs eliminated. Certain kinds of persons are not allowed to get benefits under some programs, such as (until recently) single parents for the EITC program.

Americans possess a reluctant welfare state that often creates problems for residents or even exacerbates them. Awareness of the reluctance of the American welfare state helps professionals better understand their clients' predicaments—and requires them to be creative in helping clients deal with the imperfect social policies that they confront.

Social welfare history teaches us not only that many policies are deficient, but that they are poorly monitored or implemented. We saw in post-Katrina New Orleans, for example, how the Department of Labor failed to monitor the extent to which corporations actually paid immigrant laborers. The Equal Employment Opportunity Commission (EEOC) sometimes fails to monitor or enforce job discrimination against women, such as when they become pregnant or give birth. Child welfare programs in specific jurisdictions have been so poorly implemented from the 1980s to the present that federal courts have ordered that many of them be placed under state management or other agencies—partly because the low funding given to them has required social workers to handle unmanageable caseloads.

POLICY-RELATED PRACTICE

If knowledge of the evolution of the American welfare state sensitizes us to the impact of policies on the lives of clients and consumers, it also demonstrates that professionals must ethically use *case referral*, *brokerage-liaison*, and *case advocacy* services for specific clients and for specific groups of clients within their practice.

Case Referrals

Professionals who engage in case referrals are intermediaries between clients and the American welfare state to see that persons receive those benefits and services for which they are eligible. Minus referrals from professionals to specific programs, many persons do not benefit from programs to which they are entitled (such as the EITC) or for which they are eligible (such as the Head Start Program). If professionals were truly effective referrers of clients, the participation rates in the EITC, Food Stamps Program, unemployment insurance, and other entitlements would be far higher than it is because more people would know about them and not be intimidated from applying to them—but we can hope that current participation rates are higher than they would have been without considerable efforts by professionals who *do* engage in case referrals.

Knowledge of the evolution of the American welfare state greatly increases professionals' ability to refer clients to relevant programs and services since professionals need to understand the structure and components of the American welfare state. They need to understand which programs are administered by federal, state, and local jurisdictions—or a combination of them. They need to be conversant with many of the social policies presented in the Policy Scoreboard in the preceding chapter. They need to be conversant with administrative guidelines from public agencies charged with implementing specific programs. They need to know the difference between entitlements and programs funded by discretionary spending, since clients *automatically* qualify for the former programs if they meet their requirements but must often stand in queues for the latter programs since their funding is limited—or even be denied service when annual funding runs out. They need to be familiar with programs in health, mental health, child welfare, gerontology, and other policy sectors—as well as case management and other services that attempt to link programs in different sectors.

We have seen in prior eras the pivotal role that social workers have played in referring persons to programs that could help them. They helped women get mothers' pensions in the Progressive Era, referred them to the WPA, CCC, and PWA during the Great Depression, and got welfare recipients into service programs in the 1960s—and they refer homeless persons to affordable housing and job programs in the contemporary period.

Knowledge of the evolution of the American welfare state also makes professionals aware that they face many challenges when engaging in case referrals. Due to widespread antipathy to welfare in the United States as well as prejudice against single female heads of household, for example, persons who genuinely need help are often reluctant to claim it. Imbued with prejudice or possessing a poor law mentality, eligibility staff and others sometimes intimidate applicants. Assuming government won't help them in a society possessing only a reluctant welfare state, many persons are ignorant about their entitlements and services. With an underfunded welfare state, many discretionary programs have such limited resources that only a fraction of persons get the services they need, such as substance abuse counseling.

Case referral is, then, a full-fledged professional intervention that goes far beyond merely telling clients to go to specific agencies or fill out specific applications. To provide effective case referrals, professionals must educate clients, support them, accompany them, monitor whether they are actually receiving services or benefits, use power resources, develop strategy, demonstrate persistence, troubleshoot why services or benefits were not received, and assess whether clients received effective services. As this list suggests, many of the tasks enumerated in Figure 2.1 *also* apply to the case referral role.

Brokerage and Liaison Services

While case referrals occur on an individual basis, many clients need *service and benefit systems* or *networks* that routinely give them an array of needed services. Brokerage and liaison services describe efforts by professionals to build partnerships between social agencies for specific kinds of clients. We have learned from our study of the evolution of the American welfare state that current services are often highly fragmented into mental health, health, child welfare, income assistance, education, housing, and other areas—with huge bureaucracies, funding, and policies grouped into these specific areas. As a consequence, clients or consumers find it difficult to access programs that speak to their total situation. Staff who work in these sectors often diagnose problems differently from one another, do not interact with one another, and even possess stereotypes about the staff in other sectors.

Many examples of brokerage and liaison services exist in the American welfare state. Even in the 1880s, the Charity Organization Society sought to link agencies to offset fragmentation. Various pilot projects have evolved in the last four decades to integrate or link services of different agencies, such as projects to develop helping networks for youth who graduate from foster care at age 18 and who experience high rates of homelessness, poverty, drug abuse, and mental illness. In such projects, staff use interagency agreements, joint funding, case meetings, contracts, and case management services to link agencies that provide mental health, job training, health, and housing services for these youth.

As with case referral services, professionals are ethically obliged to provide brokerage and liaison services because clients' well-being depends on them.

Case Advocacy

Professionals must ethically engage in case advocacy when they believe that specific persons or groups are not receiving services, benefits, and rights to which they are entitled. Knowledge of the evolution of the American welfare state helps us realize that persons have often not received services, benefits, or rights to which they are entitled, including African Americans who applied for welfare in the American South prior to enactment of federal civil rights legislation and promulgation of client rights by federal welfare officials; Asian Americans denied their freedom when they were incarcerated involuntarily in concentration camps with no evidence presented that they colluded with Japan during World War II; and women excluded from the CCC during the Great Depression. Persons do not receive services, benefits, and rights for various reasons, such as the following:

- prejudice of staff and government officials, such as sexism, racism, homophobia, and xenophobia

- actions by police that violate constitutional rights of persons

- favoritism, or giving some persons preferential treatment in providing services or benefits when limited funding exists

- inaccurate understanding or application of regulations by the staff who deliver benefits and services

- lack of standards in laws and regulations that protect the rights of specific groups—or presence of unconstitutional provisions in existing laws and regulations

Case advocacy resembles policy advocacy except that it focuses on getting benefits, services, and rights for individuals or groups under *existing* laws and regulations. Specific professionals can

themselves provide case advocacy to clients *or* use their case referral skills to route them to attorneys, advocacy groups, public officials, and others who provide case advocacy.

As with case referrals, professionals engage in many tasks that often resemble ones discussed in Figure 2.1. They use power resources by accompanying clients to the offices of specific agencies as their advocates with eligibility screeners and other personnel; writing letters on their behalf; and appealing to supervisors or top managers when they believe specific persons have been denied services or resources unfairly. They can appeal to specific public officials, such as elected officials, to get benefits or services for specific clients when programs are funded by government. They can empower clients to make these appeals themselves in person or in writing.

Professionals who are not themselves attorneys can sometimes help specific persons locate legal resources that may ultimately lead to *litigation* to get specific benefits or services—or to secure specific rights. As an example, some 12,000 to 16,000 homeless people regularly cluster in an area of downtown Los Angeles known as Skid Row. A number of social agencies provide social services and some housing. Still, there is not enough temporary shelter (in missions and shelters provided by social agencies), transitional (single-room-occupancy hotels and programs designed to help selected homeless people get through a crisis), or long-term assisted housing to meet the needs of all. The result is that thousands of the homeless sleep on the streets of Skid Row. A lucky few huddle in cardboard boxes, under a highway bridge, or in dumpsters. Their 24-hour presence affects the businesses and residents of the area. They constitute a subsociety, a magnet for other homeless people, many of whom have been released from prison or hospitals, and for social work agencies that serve them.

But the real estate that they sometimes occupy is alongside a burgeoning commercial and high-rent residential area. Developers want to clear the seamy sights of homeless people from the neighborhood and claim their sites for luxury high-rise residences.

Elected officials are often influenced by wealthy contributors to their campaigns, and are tempted by the prospect of private developments that would generate more taxes to provide increased services for everyone.

So complaints about the homeless blocking the sidewalks, creating a sanitary problem on the public way, or intimidating shoppers and office workers in nearby buildings, together with concerns about their drawing dope dealers and prostitutes to Skid Row, led the Los Angeles City Council to pass an ordinance (L.A. Cal. Mun. Code § 41.18(d) 2005), used by the police to clear the homeless away, tear down their cardboard shelters, and arrest those who slept on the streets.

Social workers led the protest and linked the homeless to ACLU lawyers. Two persons who were convicted and sentenced for violating the ordinance, along with four others who were threatened with arrest, prosecution, incarceration, and conviction for violating it, sought an injunction against the ordinance and the arrests. Under a federal civil rights statute (42 USC 1983), alleging that enforcement of the municipal code violated their constitutional rights, they filed suit in the U. S. District Court for the Central District of California (*Edware Jones v. City of Los Angeles*).

Though they lost at the trial court level, they appealed. On April 14, 2006, the Ninth Circuit reversed and remanded the case (*444 F.3d 1118*), ruling that because there was substantial and undisputed evidence that the number of homeless persons in the city far exceeded the number of available shelter beds at all times, the city encroached on the rights of the homeless by criminalizing the unavoidable act of sitting, lying, or sleeping at night on public sidewalks while being involuntarily homeless. The court found that the Eighth Amendment (which bars cruel and unusual punishment) prohibits the state from punishing an involuntary act or condition if it is the unavoidable consequence of one's status or being, here a consequence of being human and without shelter in the city.

Professionals can also direct clients to administrative tribunals or courts when they believe they have been denied benefits or services to which they are entitled. Once rights are established and programs are authorized (as seen in the examples above), programs have to be established to implement them. Generally, the enabling legislation delegates responsibility for administering such programs to a new or ongoing public agency, authorizing it to develop rules and procedures for carrying out its work. A first draft of such regulations is submitted for a period of public review, and comments are invited. Social workers frequently offer input to the proposed rules and procedures, which are considered by the agency and may be integrated into the final regulations. Once they are adopted, their implementation typically provides for an administrative tribunal to allow appeal, review, and possible modification of any actions taken with regard to any individual or group. Such tribunals are run by neutral administrative judges who can order the agency to change its practices or pay compensation when people have been denied benefits unfairly.

Social workers may advise their clients that they can appeal changes in their benefits from most federal and state programs such as Social Security, disability, or unemployment compensation. They can be linked with a lawyer (who in most cases will be paid a statutory fee, one set by law that will not cost the client anything). They can seek administrative review of discrimination in their jobs due to race, gender, religion, national origin, age (if 40 or older), or disability, drawing upon lawyers provided (without cost to the client) by the Equal Employment Opportunity Commission or the state's Fair Employment and Housing Commission. They can appeal denial of proper compensation for overtime hours, and the denial or constriction of countless benefits established in law.

As an example of an administrative tribunal, Judge Ralph Fertig (co-author of this chapter) was an administrative judge with the EEOC and was able to order the hiring of a qualified man, represented by a social worker, who had applied in vain to be a mail carrier. The Postal Service had repeatedly passed him over because he wore a large turban and insisted on his right, as a Sikh, to wear it on the job while delivering mail. Judge Fertig found the Postal Service had violated the law against religious discrimination. He was given the job and back pay to the time when he was first denied a position, and because the government appealed his ruling to the federal court, he got more. His order was upheld, the Postal Service had to pay him full salary for the years his case was tied up in appeal, and the Postal Service was enjoined to never deny any work benefits to anyone because he wore a turban.

Such rulings take place in administrative tribunals, but getting to that point can intimidate or confuse clients. Often, the details of a client's claim are lost in the bureaucratic procedures of the agencies and overloaded intake workers through which one must begin the process. But social workers can go with their clients to the administrative agencies to ensure that their entreaties are properly understood, filed, and moved on to the administrative tribunal.

Social workers may also work with lawyers in preparation for and at the hearing held by the administrative judge and be witnesses on their behalf. All administrative tribunals recognize the right of social workers to fully represent their clients as advocates in place of lawyers, as in the case above. Furthermore, it is in the interaction between the intended beneficiaries of social programs, those who manage and distribute those benefits, and lawyers that social workers can discern needs and help transmute them into rights by changing the system, its policies, procedures, and regulations. Sometimes that means going to court for injunctive relief (as in *Jones v. City of LA*, above); sometimes that means seeking new laws (as in *SB 2*, below); and sometimes it means serving as an advocate for clients, one at a time, before an administrative tribunal.

Empowerment Strategies

Professionals sometimes help clients or groups to develop survival and coping strategies. Were it not for such empowerment capabilities, members of many vulnerable populations would have succumbed to poverty, discrimination, and other adversities at many points during the evolution of the American welfare state when virtually no services, benefits, or rights existed. Women had, for example, few rights, were mostly excluded from many professions, and

rarely could be elected to public office—and suffered the indignity of hearing Laurence Sommers, the former president of Harvard University, recently proclaim that they were genetically unable to excel in math and science. By developing advocacy groups and links with public interest attorneys, many class action suits, as well as suits by individual women, women obtained marked changes in corporate policies regarding the hiring and promotion of women, as well as policies to decrease sexual harassment in workplaces, schools, and other settings. Irish Americans, Jewish Americans, and Asian Americans often developed mutual assistance strategies for surviving in a land where they often encountered prejudice.

Professionals can use empowerment strategies to help individuals and groups in at least two ways. They can help them develop strategies for mutual assistance, whether food banks, recreation programs, or giving loans and economic resources to one another. Such mutual assistance can involve churches that they attend, such as Baptist Churches in the African American community or the Catholic Church in the Latino community. Or professionals can use empowerment strategies to help individuals or groups engage in policy advocacy, such as by helping them to develop and participate in campaigns to develop specific kinds of legislation. We have recently witnessed, for example, hundreds of thousands of Latinos demonstrating for immigration reform in liaison with advocacy groups such as Esperanza USA (a large Latino faith-based community development organization) and the Mexican American Legal and Education Fund (MALDEF).

POLICY ADVOCACY

We have discussed policy advocacy throughout this book in our models of leadership, describing how professionals and others have used it to secure policy reforms for entire groups of persons—and we have linked it to the policy advocacy framework in Figure 2.1. We made the case, as stated in the NASW Code of Ethics, that policy advocacy is ethically required of social workers when they believe that existing policies harm specific persons or populations.

Policy advocates can seek policy changes in many settings. They can seek policy changes in specific agencies to improve services for their clients, such as initiating a new program, changing eligibility requirements, adding evening or weekend hours, and changing the agency mission to include new social issues or problems. They can seek changes in the administrative regulations of a specific program funded by government. They can seek legislation from local, state, and federal legislatures.

A policy advocacy project recently initiated by Professor Ralph Fertig to stimulate the building of affordable housing for homeless persons in various communities of Los Angeles County and elsewhere in California illustrates how social work students can engage in policy advocacy. He discovered that the goal of increasing the availability of affordable housing was sabotaged by the spirit of NIMBY ("Not In My Back Yard") that dominated local politics. Believing that the construction of affordable housing in their areas would harm their property values, bring crime and drug usage to their communities, and burden their communities with persons with mental illness, residents often opposed new projects—appealing to local zoning and planning officials to reject specific affordable housing projects or to deny the construction of new projects altogether.

Students in USC's graduate social welfare policy classes met with State Senator Gil Cedillo, whose district includes Skid Row. Cedillo introduced SB 1322, which would require every city or county in California to identify sites, in the housing element of its general plan, where emergency homeless shelters and residential service providers would be allowed to locate without the ability of the local governing body to change the plan once it was adopted. With these anti-NIMBY provisions, the bill established "housing by right." The sites identified in the plan would be available for emergency shelters and assisted transitional and long-term housing within the planning period, sufficient to shelter families and individuals in need of such service. Localities are free to finance the

housing, regulate developers to set aside a pr tion of new housing for low-income rentals, p haps in exchange for density bonuses or othe incentives, or fashion their own solutions. But they are mandated to do something to plan for and enable the housing of homeless residents.

Some students went to Sacramento, the capital of California, to lobby state senators; other students visited the legislators in their local offices. The bill passed the California Senate and the State Assembly, only to be vetoed by Governor Arnold Schwarzenegger in 2006. So Cedillo reintroduced the legislation in 2007 as SB2, and it was passed by both chambers and signed by the governor in fall 2007. Now USC students will fan out in 2008 to social agencies in the cities of Los Angeles and Orange Counties in organizing efforts to ensure its implementation at the local level. Where they run into resistance, they will turn to lawyers to seek injunctions, ordering local communities to comply with the provisions of the new law. By changing existing regulations, laws, and budgets, social workers can affect the lives of many clients and consumers. SB2, when implemented, may provide affordable housing for thousands of persons that they might not otherwise have possessed.

Practicing professionals must surmount some obstacles to engage in policy advocacy. They must convince agency administrators that the agency cannot address a full range of its clients' needs without engaging in policy advocacy. They must educate those administrators who falsely believe that policy advocacy violates regulations that govern public or private agencies by showing them that policy advocacy need not be *partisan* in nature— but geared toward seeking improved social policies that will help clients. (Voter registration and distribution of fact sheets about key issues or propositions that will be on an upcoming ballot also do not violate these regulations—nor does advocacy for a specific policy proposal such as SB2.) They must find time to engage in policy advocacy, even asking administrators for some release time.

Most professionals that engage in policy advocacy link themselves to an existing advocacy group or project or to a local or state chapter of a

ion such as the National
Vorkers. They may volunteer
oin delegations, find clients
ons, testify before legislative
petitions, organizing letter-
writing campaigns, hold press conferences, and provide data relevant to securing policy reforms. If
needed, several agencies and advocacy groups can
form coalitions to engage in policy advocacy. They
can pool their membership lists to organize letter-
writing campaigns and other projects.

WRITING A POLICY ADVOCACY BACKGROUND DOCUMENT

As a precursor to a policy advocacy project, it is
useful to develop a policy advocacy background
document that orients *contemporary* stakeholders to
a specific social problem or issue so that they can
better address it. The document can cover the following aspects of the issue:

- Describe how the specific issue or problem has
  evolved during the last several decades, including how widespread it is, whom it affects
  directly and indirectly, and where it geographically exists, along with trends in its size and
  composition through time.

- Summarize definitions of the issue or problem
  that have been dominant or prevalent during its
  evolution.

- Identify a *policy trail* so that contemporary
  stakeholders understand what prior efforts have
  been made to address it—at different levels of
  government and in the private and public sectors—and in different locations such as in several states or urban areas.

- Identify how public officials and residents have
  viewed the social policy or issue, as well as their
  prior attempts to address or resolve it—including
  ideological, partisan, and other cleavages that
  have surfaced as the policy trail has evolved.

- Explore important research conducted on prior
  policies to see how researchers have provided
  clues about how to develop policy reforms in
  the future.

- Identify policy proposals that have been *rejected*
  in the policy trail and describe why they were
  not approved—and discuss promising policy
  options that are currently in the air, describing
  their likely political feasibility.

- Identify a promising policy option that might
  currently be considered in terms of its merit in
  addressing the social problem or issue, as well as
  its possible political feasibility and its likely cost.

A policy advocacy background document is
highly useful because it grounds current issues and
policy options in the realities of prior events. It
doesn't tell us what to do, but it provides a foundation for moving forward.

Policy advocacy background documents can
lead us in different directions, depending on their
findings. Perhaps we will decide in one case that
incremental reforms are needed to address a specific
issue or problem because more ambitious ones have
been defeated or unsuccessful in the past. For example, a review of recent national health insurance
proposals in the United States, which have been
defeated on multiple occasions, most recently in
1994, led Democrats to focus on such incremental
reforms as increasing the size of the S/CHIP program for children. Yet some recent developments,
including growing awareness by corporate leaders
of the huge expenses they incur for their employees' health insurance as compared to European and
Japanese corporations that do not have these costs,
may augur well for more ambitious health insurance reforms in coming years—as might the election of a president committed to national health
insurance in 2008 or succeeding years.

Perhaps a policy advocacy background document on a different issue will lead us toward ambitious reforms if we find that a social problem has
become more widespread and if we find promising
signs in the existing policy trail that public officials are
willing to "think big" rather than contenting themselves with incremental reforms.

Professor Ralph Fertig has written a policy advocacy background document with respect to the social problem of homelessness. This document, which is included below, led to the passage of SB2 by the State of California, which we have just discussed.

A SAMPLE DOCUMENT ON HOMELESSNESS

A Policy Advocacy Background Document: Moving from the Recent Past to a Promising Policy Reform with Respect to Homelessness

Give me your tired, your poor,

Your huddled masses yearning to breathe free,

The wretched refuse of your teeming shore.

Send these, the homeless, tempest-tost, to me.

These words, by Emma Lazarus, engraved on the pedestal of the Statue of Liberty National Monument, affirm the historic promise of America. But today, homeless people are abandoned by an affluent society that has closed the golden door, wants them out of sight, and "not in my backyard."

Women flee domestic violence, often with their children, seeking shelter, a niche under the stairs of a hallway in a distant building, a plot of ground under a bridge, a piece of sidewalk in an anonymous part of town.

Veterans, many suffering with posttraumatic stress disorder (PTSD), wander through alleys, sleeping in dumpsters or on the streets.

Families, evicted because they could not pay the escalating rent and still buy the food and medicine that kept them alive, hover in front of a charitable shelter that has fewer beds than the people in line.

Teenagers, "emancipated" from foster care, seek bonds like families long lost on the asphalt of an uncaring metropolis.

Working men and women, with uncertain paychecks at minimum wage, unable to raise the security deposit and one month's advance on the rent, sleep in their cars or surf on friends' couches.

Persons suffering with severe and persistent mental illness, thrust out from institutional care with a promise of community resources that never came, wander in an abyss of neglect.

People dependent on drugs or alcohol, many of them seeking to numb the pain of homelessness, are forced into the maelstrom of pushing, use, and addiction on the streets.

Adolescents, breaking away from sexual abuse or ejected from their homes because of their sexual orientation, cluster on dissolute corners that invite their exploitation.

Patients discharged from hospitals are unceremoniously dumped on the streets of Skid Row.

Persons are released from jails and prisons with no funds or resources to come in from the cold, often wet, always unforgiving outdoors.

Migrant workers seeking jobs; middle-aged men and women, too young to receive Social Security and Medicare, too old to be hired; disabled and disconnected denizens; abandoned or widowed spouses—all add to the vanquished people of our nation's byways.

These are the poor and huddled masses, the wretched refuse, homeless, tempest-tossed of the world, once embraced by our nation.

The mission, indeed the very profession of social work, emerged from service to persons like these, the vulnerable populations, isolated in the shadows of an affluent society that becomes ever more distant.

A Recent History of Homelessness. The roots of social work lie in the settlement house movement that reached out to the teeming shores, working with people overcrowded in squalid tenements, crude shacks, and special neighborhoods, set aside in many American cities, where their derelict denizens were tolerated and served. These areas were often called "Skid Row" after that section in Seattle where, alongside men who slept on the street or in bordering flophouses, logs slid down a chute, skidding into an inlet to be floated to nearby mills. Although there were periods such as the Great Depression when large numbers of "hoboes" rode the rails and camped on the outskirts of towns seeking work, the visible homeless of most American cities throughout the 20th century have been contained in their skid rows.

One recent study of New York City found that:

> While homelessness is certainly not a new phenomenon in the United States and in New York City, where it dates back to at least the colonial era, there is no question that modern homelessness is a unique historical occurrence. Indeed, one must go back to the Great Depression to find another period when homelessness was such a routine, persistent, visible feature of urban life. From the end of World War II until the late 1970s it was a rare sight, outside of familiar "skid row" precincts like the Bowery, to see New Yorkers sleeping in the streets and other public spaces, or to witness tens of thousands of children and their families cycling each year through emergency shelters and welfare hotels.[1]

The first sign of modern homelessness in New York City was the appearance of thousands of homeless men sleeping in parks, on sidewalks, in transportation terminals, and in other public spaces in the late 1970s. Although historically the city had seen pockets of street homelessness in the Bowery and other "skid row" districts, the sight of homeless adults—many of them men living with mental illness—bedding down on streets became more commonplace throughout the city by the end of the 1970s.[2] At the same time, deaths and injuries among the street homeless also became commonplace. According to city officials, incidents of hypothermia and cold-related deaths and injuries among the homeless were "routine" in the early years of modern homelessness.[3]

Roots of Homelessness. New York City later addressed its problems of homelessness with policies that guaranteed shelter (see below). However, throughout most of the rest of our nation, homelessness has burgeoned, chiefly as a result of three major developments: (1) increasing poverty; (2) decreasing stock of affordable housing; and (3) evictions of the mentally ill from caregiving institutions.

1. *Poverty:* The one transcendent characteristic of homelessness, joined to all the other factors summarized above, is poverty. Eroding job opportunities, stagnant and declining wages, and cuts in the value and availability of public assistance all led to increases in poverty throughout America. In 1996, the welfare system was overhauled, shrinking the number of people receiving benefits such as TANF by 50 percent between 1996 and 2000.[4] By 2004, 37 million people, 12.7 percent of the population of the United States, lived below the poverty line.[5]

A recent survey in Los Angeles found that 11 percent of the homeless are employed, either full- or part-time, and that the top five reasons for unemployment of the others were as follows: 25 percent were disabled; 22 percent had no permanent address; 20 percent needed clothing; 20 percent required job training; and 10 percent had health problems.[6]

2. *Loss of dwelling units:* At the same time, the stock of affordable housing and the availability of housing assistance programs were slashed. Between 1973 and 1993, 2.2 million low-rent units disappeared from the market, destroyed, abandoned, their rents escalated beyond affordability, or converted into condominiums. While the supply of affordable units fell dramatically, public aid for the increasing numbers of those in need plummeted. In the period from 1980 to 2003, federal support for low-income housing fell by 49 percent.[7] At the same time, rents in most cities have soared, forcing many people into overcrowded and substandard housing, making them pay 50 percent or more of their income for rent, putting them at daily risk of ecoming homeless, and casting millions on streets throughout America.[8] In the year 2000,

22.5 percent of renter households in Los Angeles paid more than half of their income for housing. The hourly wage required to pay an average rent in that city in 2003 was $32, about four times the minimum wage.[9]

Countless millions of others are on the brink of homelessness. 45.8 million Americans have no health insurance.[10] A serious illness or disability depletes whatever savings there might have been, and competes with rent payments, often leading to eviction, setting people, their furniture, and their possessions on the street.

3. *Deinstitutionalization*: In the 1950s and 1960s, the asylums established to care for the mentally disabled emptied out. The number of persons living in mental institutions dropped from over 1 million to less than 100,000.[11] With a promise of care back in their home environments, the Community Mental Health Act of 1963 spurred the release of long-term psychiatric patients from state hospitals. Squeezed into single-room-occupancy hotels (SROs), many sought the promised community health centers for treatment and follow-up. But the community resources were never adequately funded, and this population soon found itself living on the sidewalks or in dumpsters with no sustainable support system.[12]

A Matter of Policies. By the early 1980s, the homeless, no longer just sequestered on skid rows, spread into a phenomenon of mass homelessness, associated with structural factors like those of the Great Depression, and bearing the dimensions of a social problem not merely attributable to individual failings.

Stoner (2002)[13] explains how the combination of high unemployment and inflation in the late 1970s led to the erosion of the Democratic Party coalition that had prevailed since the Great Depression and to the emergence of the anti-government Reagan revolution that contributed to an increase in poverty and a decline in the availability of affordable housing. From 1981 to 1988, all funds for federally subsidized housing were cut by 69 percent. The number of low-income housing starts, including public housing, Section 8 construction and rehabilitation, and Section 202 housing for the elderly, dropped from 183,000 units in 1980 to 28,000 by 1985.

Simultaneous cutbacks in social programs such as Aid to Families with Dependent Children (AFDC) and Social Security Disability Insurance (SSDI) frequently determined whether a poor family, a mentally ill person, or an otherwise disabled person could pay rent. By 1989, the United States Conference of Mayors issued a survey of homelessness in 27 cities concluding that none of the survey cities expected to meet the housing needs of low-income households (Fantasia and Isserman, 1994).

As increasingly visible masses of people became homeless, social welfare responses to the problem retreated to earlier distinctions between the "deserving" and "undeserving" poor. Emergency shelters and soup kitchens, under the auspices of local charities and religious institutions, proliferated in lieu of more expansive federal entitlement programs. Before long a new system of homeless assistance services characterized by emergency responses emerged, with more limited approaches to the provision of transitional and long-term housing.

A complex combination of poverty, lack of affordable housing, and personal vulnerability explains contemporary homelessness. Approximately one-half of the people who experience homelessness over the course of a year are single adults. Another half who are homeless during the course of one year live in family units. Most people in homeless families and single adults report a mismatch in service availability and service need. They report that their major needs are for help finding affordable housing, and financial help to pay for housing. In contrast, the help they most frequently receive is for clothing, transportation, and assistance in obtaining public benefits (National Alliance to End Hunger and Homelessness, 2002). Whether single or in families, today's homeless persons are severely marginalized to emergency homeless services that are beneath a safety net that proffers a minimum sense of decency. They are the extreme faces of poverty at the beginning of the 21st century. The National Coalition for the Homeless views the "unfinished business of the civil rights movement as poverty, homelessness, and the growing use of the prison system to oppress people experiencing poverty and homelessness" (National Coalition for the Homeless, 2002).

Actually, a study by "Poverty Matters" documents that the provision of permanent supportive housing would cost less than leaving the homeless on the streets. One night in a unit of supportive housing costs $30. In contrast, one night in a shelter costs $37; in jail, it is $64; in prison, $85; in a mental hospital, $607; and in a general hospital, $1,474. A core of homeless persons runs the circuit of placement in shelters, incarceration in jails or prisons, and hospitalization, at many times the cost of permanent housing.

Social Work and the Homeless Today.   Today, many social workers are insulated from the homeless *as a group* (in any of their manifestations) by agencies that proscribe access and regulate services. Most social welfare institutions that reach the poor do so one by one, determining eligibility and meting out services according to arcane rules, and managing cases through a labyrinth of multi-tiered procedures, as though each individual or family is without a home due to some personal disjuncture and must learn to negotiate the opportunities doled out by a limiting and ever more limited source of private and public funds.

But as we seek relief for the client seated before us, social workers also look for patterns, to determine if the continuing stream of persons who are homeless may be due, at least in some measure, to a *social problem* caused by social, economic, and political forces that are governed by policies of those in power and their institutions. The patterns and pervasiveness of our homeless people reveal the mutable social policies that help cause homelessness in America. To discover them, we shall look at (1) the distribution and (2) the extent of those who inhabit our nighttime streets.

1. *The distribution of homelessness:* Although they come from all ethnicities, the homeless are overwhelmingly poor and disproportionately people of color. Indeed, one prominent study found 49 percent of the homeless to be African American; another 13 percent Latino; only 35 percent Caucasian, 2 percent Native American, and 1 percent Asian.[14] Workers at the Los Angeles Community Action Network have described the homeless as those experiencing "Jim Crow, 21st century style."

The statement may be no exaggeration. In its review of *employment* practices regulated by Title VII of the Civil Rights Act of 1964, the Supreme Court, in *Griggs v. Duke Power,*[15] found (and the Congress later ratified its interpretation) that a practice, neutral on its face, which causes a disparate impact on people of different races violates laws against job discrimination. Although the ruling is limited to bias in the *workplace*, and there is not yet a counterpart protection in federal law for the *living-place*, the analysis may apply to policies that render a widely disparate impact of homelessness on people of color.

With the globalization of cheap labor, wages are driven down in the United States, and even working people face homelessness. In the median state, a minimum-wage worker would have to work 89 hours each week to afford a two-bedroom apartment at 30 percent of income.[16] Countless agricultural, casual, and other service workers labor at rates well below the minimum wage. Twenty-five percent of those on the streets of Los Angeles were homeless due to their loss of a job.[17]

Factors beyond the influence of the individual: wage levels, international trade agreements, welfare benefits, housing stock, condominium conversions, rents, zoning, land use, planning, clearance and development, health care and benefits regulated, subsidized, taxed, or circumscribed by public policies, many of which enrich some at the expense of others, any one of which may determine whether you sleep on silk or on the sidewalks.

Families, women, and children: Families with children[18] are one of the fastest-growing segments, now constituting 33 percent of those without homes. A recent study found that 37 percent of these families had their welfare benefits cut within the last year.[19] Children under the age of 18 accounted for 39 percent of the homeless population and 42 percent of those children are under the age of 5,[20] while single women comprise upward of 17 percent.[21] Approxima-tely half of all women and children experiencing homelessness have fled domestic violence.[22] Eleven percent of the homeless in Los Angeles were on the streets because of a conflict with a family member.[23] Laws against such abuse are not supported with sufficient resources for those they seek to protect.

Veterans: Forty percent of homeless men have served in the armed forces.[24] Many joined the service to escape poverty. They returned with the wounds of war, often with post-traumatic stress disorder or traumatic brain injury, the signature disability of the war in Iraq, now rejected by the affluent society for which they risked everything. One count in 1994 found that on any night in that year, some 271,000 veterans were homeless.[25] That number has only increased since then. Few of the opportunities provided in the "GI Bill of Rights" that subsidized the education, housing, and health benefits of those who came back from World War II are available to those returning from less popular fronts since then.

Persons with mental illness: Some 22 percent of single homeless adults have some form of severe and persistent mental illness.[26] One study indicated that only 5 to 7 percent of this population requires institutionalization; most can live in the community with supportive housing.[27]

Addiction disorders: Although most people who are addicted to alcohol and drugs never become homeless, the loss of single-room-occupancy housing has put increased numbers of those who are both poor and addicted on the streets. There is considerable disagreement over how many of the homeless are addicted; most studies that produced high rates grossly over representedlong-term shelter users and single men and used lifetime rather than current measures of addiction. Although a recent count in Los Angeles placed it at 21 percent,[28] the prevalence is likely somewhere between 30 percent[29] and 65 percent.[30] Policies on alternative treatment abound and are the subject of research, inquiry, controversy, and requests for adequate funding.

Other populations on the streets: At least 25 percent of those teenagers who are "emancipated" from foster care graduate into homelessness.[31] Patients discharged from hospitals, persons released from jails and prisons with no place to go, persons who have used up their TANF benefits, people in their 50s who are too young for Social Security but frequently too old to secure employment, and runaway and "throwaway" youths (many rejected by families because of their sexual orientation) add to the ranks of the homeless. Policies are needed to plan and provide care for each of these populations.

2. *Counting the homeless*: The measurement of homelessness is inexact and varied, according to differing definitions of the term. Federal law states that one is homeless who "lacks a fixed, regular, and adequate night-time residence; and... has a primary night-time residency that is: (A) a supervised publicly or privately operated shelter designed to provide temporary living accommodations... (B) an institution that provides a temporary residence for individuals intended to be institutionalized, or (C) a public or private place not designed for, or

ordinarily used as, a regular sleeping accommodation for human beings."[32] But the education subtitle of the McKinney-Vento Act includes a more comprehensive definition for the "homeless child and youth who lack a fixed, regular, and adequate night-time residence" that includes those who share "the housing of other persons due to loss of housing, economic hardship, or a similar reason; are living in motels, hotels, trailer parks, or camping grounds due to lack of alternative adequate accommodations; are living in emergency or transitional shelters; are abandoned in hospitals; or are awaiting foster care placement." It also includes "children and youth who have a primary night-time residence that is a private or public place not designed for or ordinarily used as a regular sleeping accommodation for human beings."[33] The Department of Housing and Urban Development interprets McKinney Vento to include only those who are on the streets, in shelters, or within a week of imminent eviction with no place to which to go.

Of 82,291 homeless in Los Angeles County, only 12 percent were sheltered in emergency shelters or transitional housing, while 88 percent were unsheltered (living on the streets, in a vehicle, encampment, or other place not normally used for human habitation).[34]

Point-in-time studies do not accurately identify those who are intermittently homeless, while some of those without homes are not in places that researchers can easily find. One national study of formerly homeless people found that 59.3 percent lived in vehicles and 24.6 percent lived in makeshift housing such as tents, boxes, caves, or boxcars.[35] The best approximation is from a study by the National Law Center on Homelessness and Poverty, conducted in 2004, in which it joined its findings with those of the Urban Institute and the National Survey of Homeless Assistance Providers.[36] It found that approximately 10 percent of those living in poverty, 3.5 million people (1.35 million of whom are children), are likely to experience homelessness in given year throughout America. A national survey of service providers of the actual magnitude of homelessness left out all those unknown who did not utilize such services, and is therefore likely an understatement. Their numbers, however, increased from 1987 to 1997; the number of shelter beds doubled in nine communities and four states, while it tripled in another two communities and two states.[37]

The differing definitions, often the basis for allocation of limited resources, contributes to the labyrinth that must be navigated by those seeking services. Confusion and conflict in standards feed the likelihood of failure in securing benefits.

Social Workers, Public Policies, and the Homeless.   The homeless people in each of the groups discussed above are squarely in the target populations of those served by social workers. Some critics note that their homelessness represents a failure of our social welfare system. It is, at least, an admission of the failure of our safety net, intended to protect all people in America from the extreme manifestations of poverty. The reduction of affordable housing, the wage level for workers, the cutback on public assistance programs, the lack of shelters for those in temporary need of housing for those with long-term problems, and the barriers of "Not In My Backyard" ordinances to block the siting of affordable housing in many communities are all set forth in public policies, laws, and rules passed by elected bodies and enforced by government units at state and local levels. Social workers cannot address the problems of their clients suffering from poverty, ill health, domestic violence, mental illness, addiction, foster care, and relationships between children and families, for example, without recognizing that they may be either without a home of their own or one paycheck, one medical emergency, or one conflict removed from the streets. To serve clients, the social worker must understand the policies that oppress and render them homeless, must seek alternatives, and must enter the realm of policy. It was in confronting and developing new policies that New York City dealt with its homeless population.

Ending Homelessness through Litigation or Legislation. In New York City, through the 1970s, a rudimentary system of emergency shelters was almost always filled to capacity, particularly in the winter. Thousands were exposed to tuberculosis and other contagious diseases in squalid, overcrowded "big rooms" while thousands more turned to the streets.

In 1979, Robert Hayes, a lawyer and co-founder of Coalition for the Homeless, brought a class action lawsuit on behalf of Robert Callahan, a homeless alcoholic, and all homeless men in New York City. He cited Article XVII of the State Constitution, which declares that "the aid, care and support of the needy are public concerns and shall be provided by the state and by such of its subdivisions…." for the proposition that a constitutional right to shelter existed in New York State. In 1981, *Callahan v. Carey* was settled as a consent decree in which the city and state agreed to provide shelter and board to all homeless men who met the need standard for welfare or who were homeless "by reason of physical, mental, or social dysfunction." The decree established a right to shelter for all homeless men in New York City, while also detailing minimum health and safety standards which the city and state must maintain in shelters. The right to decent shelter was later extended to women and to homeless families. Vast sums have been provided by New York City and State to house its homeless ever since then. Litigation has had various successes in selected jurisdictions throughout the country since then. What is needed is a constitutional or statutory right which must then be interpreted by a court, or as a result of a consent decree (as in New York, an agreement negotiated by the parties and sanctioned by the court), to compel local or state government to provide quarters for the housing of the homeless.

While a right to housing has not yet been established in California, campaigns are currently under way to secure that commitment. However, the voters in that state addressed the needs of their mentally ill population, including those who are homeless, and they passed Proposition 209 to tax those earning over $1 million per year to provide comprehensive community services, including housing, for them. Hundreds of millions of dollars are now available annually to house the mentally ill of California.

Thus, through litigation in New York or legislation (through the popular initiative) in California, policies may remedy at least the first stage of homelessness. Advocates for the homeless now gird for solutions beyond mere shelter and advocate permanent supportive housing.

One approach for decreasing homelessness is to increase the stock of available, affordable housing. Yet "Not In My Backyard" (NIMBY) organizations and local ordinances block housing for those in need. Not only do many communities not want housing to be constructed in their areas for persons with marginal income, but they don't want stigmatized populations like homeless persons, persons with addictions, or persons with mental problems to reside in their jurisdictions.

What is needed is state legislation that requires "fair share zoning" and "housing by right." Such legislation would mandate all cities and counties throughout California to survey and develop plans to house their homeless, overriding local NIMBY ordinances while leaving the manner of providing the housing to local jurisdictions, which could rely on public funds or regulate private development to include housing for the poor and very poor populations as a percentage of new construction, offer density bonuses to developers, or implement other land use incentives. But by requiring *every* jurisdiction in a state to bear its fair share, those previously homeless would be integrated into the fabric of mainstream communities. If such legislation became law, advocates in the private sector might be able to sue for implementation through the courts.

We have already discussed how a Policy Advocacy Background Document like this one led Assemblyman Gil Cedillo to sponsor SB2 in the California legislature and how this legislation was enacted by the legislature and signed by the governor in 2007. Similar documents can serve as a foundation for other policy advocacy projects on countless other issues in any state or local jurisdiction—or in the broader nation when policy advocates seek changes in federal policies and regulations.

WHAT YOU CAN DO NOW

After reading Chapter 14, you are now equipped to do the following:

- Discuss how social welfare history helps us develop multiple strategies for helping consumers of social services.

- Analyze how social welfare history helps us understand the need for policy-sensitive practice.

- Discuss how social welfare history helps us understand the need for such kinds of policy-related practice as case referrals, brokerage-liaison services, and case advocacy.

- Analyze how social welfare history demonstrates that members of vulnerable populations have often resorted to empowerment strategies to cope with adverse realities and policies that they have confronted—and helps us understand how social workers can sometimes help them with these strategies.

- Analyze how social welfare history introduces us to the work of many policy advocates past and present, as illustrated by the way policy advocates help develop constructive policies for the homeless population.

- Write a policy advocacy background document as a catalyst for policy advocacy in contemporary society.

ENDNOTES

1. Coalition for the Homeless, "History of Modern Homelessness in New York City," *Securing the Right to Shelter for Homeless New Yorkers,* March, 2003.

2. Ibid.

3. Ibid.

4. Office of Public Affairs, Urban Institute, "A Decade of Welfare Reform: Facts and Figures," June 2006 (http://www.urbaninstitute.org/UploadedPDF/90080_welfarereform.pdf).

5. U.S. Bureau of the Census, 2005.

6. Los Angeles Housing Services Agency, 2005 Homeless Census, Los Angeles.

7. National Low Income Housing Coalition Inter-University Consortium against Homelessness, "Talking Sense about Homelessness in Los Angeles." University of Southern California, November 26, 2006.

8. National Law Center on Homelessness and Poverty, 2004.

9. Inter-University Consortium against Homelessness, "Talking Sense about Homelessness in Los Angeles." University of Southern California, November 26, 2006.

10. U.S. Bureau of the Census, 2005.

11. Inter-University Consortium against Homelessness, "Talking Sense about Homelessness in Los Angeles." University of Southern California, November 26, 2006.

12. Wikipedia article on Homelessness.

13. Madeleine R. Stoner, "History of Homelessness in the United States" in John M. Herrick and Paul H. Stuart, eds., *The Encyclopedia of Social Welfare in North America* (Thousand Oaks, CA: Sage Publications, 2002).

14. U.S. Conference of Mayors, survey of 27 cities, 2004.

15. 401 U.S. 424, 1971. Although largely overruled by the court in *Atonio v. Wards Cove*, 490 US 642, 1989, the U.S. Congress revived and codified *Griggs* as the federal standard (signed by the president) in its 1991 amendments to Title VII of the Civil Rights Act of 1964, 42 USC 2000(e) et seq.

16. National Low-Income Housing Coalition, 2001.

17. Los Angeles Housing Services Agency, 2005 Homeless Census, Los Angeles.

18. U.S. Conference of Mayors, 2005.

19. Institute for Children and Poverty, 2001.

20. National Law Center on Homelessness and Poverty, 2004.

21. U.S. Conference of Mayors, 2005.

22. National Coalition against Domestic Violence, 2001.

23. Los Angeles Housing Services Agency, 2005 Homeless Census, Los Angeles.

24. Robert Rosenheck et al., "Homeless Veterans." In *Homelessness in America*, Oryx Press, 1966.

25. National Coalition for Homeless Veterans, 1994.

26. U.S. Conference of Mayors, 2005.

27. Federal Task Force on Homelessness and Severe Mental Illness, 1992.

28. Los Angeles Housing Services Agency, 2005 Homeless Census, Los Angeles County.

29. U.S. Conference of Mayors, 2005.

30. Paul Koegel et al., "The Causes of Homelessness." In *Homelessness in America*, Oryx Press, 1996.

31. Susan Kellam, "Unholy Freedom: Background on Adolescents and Foster Care," *Comment for Kids,* February 26, 1999.

32. Stewart B. McKinney Act, 42 USC 11301 et seq., 1994.

33. McKinney-Vento Act sec. 725(2); p 42 USC 11435 (2).

34. Los Angeles Housing Services Agency, 2005 Homeless Census, Los Angeles.

35. Link et al., 1995.

36. National Law Center on Homelessness and Poverty, 2004.

37. National Coalition for the Homeless, 1997.

Name Index

Subject Index

TO THE OWNER OF THIS BOOK:

I hope that you have found *The Reluctant Welfare State,* Sixth Edition, useful. So that this book can be improved in a future edition, would you take the time to complete this sheet and return it? Thank you.

School and address:_____

Department:_____

Instructor's name:_____

1. What I like most about this book is:_____

_____

_____

2. What I like least about this book is:_____

_____

_____

3. My general reaction to this book is:_____

_____

_____

4. The name of the course in which I used this book is:_____

_____

5. Were all of the chapters of the book assigned for you to read?_____

    If not, which ones weren't?_____

6. In the space below, or on a separate sheet of paper, please write specific suggestions for improving this book and anything else you'd care to share about your experience in using this book._____

_____

_____

_____

BROOKS/COLE
CENGAGE Learning

BUSINESS REPLY MAIL
FIRST-CLASS MAIL   PERMIT NO. 102   MONTEREY CA

POSTAGE WILL BE PAID BY ADDRESSEE

Attn: Seth Dobrin, Social Work

BrooksCole/Cengage Learning

10 Davis Drive

Belmont, CA 94002

OPTIONAL:

Your name: _____   Date: _____

May we quote you, either in promotion for *The Reluctant Welfare State,* Sixth Edition, or in future publishing ventures?

Yes: _____   No:_____

Sincerely yours,

Bruce S. Jansson